# Master Index
## and
## Correlations

PEARSON

Scott Foresman

**Editorial Offices:** Glenview, Illinois • Parsippany, New Jersey • New York, New York
**Sales Offices:** Boston, Massachusetts • Duluth, Georgia • Glenview, Illinois
Coppell, Texas • Sacramento, California • Mesa, Arizona

ISBN: 0-382-36774-X

4  5  6  7  8  9  10  V039  13  12  11  10  09  08  07  06

# Contents

*The Master Index and Correlation is a compilation of all music selections in Silver Burdett* MAKING MUSIC *©2005, Grades K–8.*

*Many teachers may wish to supplement and enrich their programs by using material from other grade levels. This series-wide resource makes it easy for teachers to plan and customize curriculum.*

*For your convenience, each listing in the Master Index and Correlation provides grade level and page number, and where appropriate, compact disc and track numbers.*

## MUSIC LITERATURE

### SONGS AND SPEECH PIECES INDEX . . . . . . . **4**

### PRONUNCIATION PRACTICE INDEX . . . . . . . **28**

### LISTENING INDEX . . . . . . . . . . . . . . . . . **35**
Listening Selections by Title. . . . . . . . . . . . 35
Listening Selections by Composer . . . . . . . 55
Montages. . . . . . . . . . . . . . . . . . . . . . . . . . . 74
Recorded Assessments . . . . . . . . . . . . . . . . 78
Recorded Dances . . . . . . . . . . . . . . . . . . . . 83
Recorded Interviews . . . . . . . . . . . . . . . . . . 85
Recorded Poems and Stories . . . . . . . . . . . 86
Sound Bank Instruments . . . . . . . . . . . . . . . 87

### BUILDING SKILLS THROUGH MUSIC . . . . . . **89**
Art . . . . . . . . . . . . . . . . . . . . . . . . . . . . . . . . . 89
Dance . . . . . . . . . . . . . . . . . . . . . . . . . . . . . . 89
Health Education . . . . . . . . . . . . . . . . . . . . . 89
Language Arts . . . . . . . . . . . . . . . . . . . . . . . 89
Math . . . . . . . . . . . . . . . . . . . . . . . . . . . . . . . 91
Physical Education . . . . . . . . . . . . . . . . . . . 92
Reading . . . . . . . . . . . . . . . . . . . . . . . . . . . . 92
Related Arts . . . . . . . . . . . . . . . . . . . . . . . . . 93
Science . . . . . . . . . . . . . . . . . . . . . . . . . . . . . 93
Social Studies. . . . . . . . . . . . . . . . . . . . . . . . 93
Technology . . . . . . . . . . . . . . . . . . . . . . . . . . 95
Theater . . . . . . . . . . . . . . . . . . . . . . . . . . . . . 95
Writing. . . . . . . . . . . . . . . . . . . . . . . . . . . . . 95

### CLASSIFIED INDEX . . . . . . . . . . . . . . . . . **97**
Analyzing. . . . . . . . . . . . . . . . . . . . . . . . . . . 97
Arranging . . . . . . . . . . . . . . . . . . . . . . . . . . . 97
Assessment . . . . . . . . . . . . . . . . . . . . . . . . . 97
Audience Etiquette . . . . . . . . . . . . . . . . . . . 98
Broadway, Theater, and Film . . . . . . . . . . . 99
Careers . . . . . . . . . . . . . . . . . . . . . . . . . . . . 99
Character Education . . . . . . . . . . . . . . . . . .100
Choral Singing . . . . . . . . . . . . . . . . . . . . . .101

Community Involvement . . . . . . . . . . . . . . .103
Composing . . . . . . . . . . . . . . . . . . . . . . . . .103
Creating. . . . . . . . . . . . . . . . . . . . . . . . . . . .103
Cultural Connections. . . . . . . . . . . . . . . . . .104
Curriculum, Across the . . . . . . . . . . . . . . . .107
Ensembles, Performing in . . . . . . . . . . . . .116
Expression . . . . . . . . . . . . . . . . . . . . . . . . .116
Folk, Traditional, and Regional Selections . . .121
Form . . . . . . . . . . . . . . . . . . . . . . . . . . . . . .135
Genre/Style . . . . . . . . . . . . . . . . . . . . . . . .141
Holiday, Seasonal, and Special Occasions. . .156
Improvising . . . . . . . . . . . . . . . . . . . . . . . . .160
Instruments, Identifying . . . . . . . . . . . . . . .160
Instruments, Making . . . . . . . . . . . . . . . . . .160
Listening . . . . . . . . . . . . . . . . . . . . . . . . . . .160
Literature . . . . . . . . . . . . . . . . . . . . . . . . . .163
Meeting Individual Needs. . . . . . . . . . . . . .166
Melody . . . . . . . . . . . . . . . . . . . . . . . . . . . .169
Movement . . . . . . . . . . . . . . . . . . . . . . . . . .174
Moving . . . . . . . . . . . . . . . . . . . . . . . . . . . .178
Music Makers . . . . . . . . . . . . . . . . . . . . . . .180
Musical Periods. . . . . . . . . . . . . . . . . . . . . .183
Music Reading Practice . . . . . . . . . . . . . . .186
Music Theory and Fundamentals . . . . . . . .187
Non-English Language Selections. . . . . . . .188
Notating. . . . . . . . . . . . . . . . . . . . . . . . . . . .190
Orff Accompaniments. . . . . . . . . . . . . . . . .190
Pentatonic Songs . . . . . . . . . . . . . . . . . . . .190
Performing. . . . . . . . . . . . . . . . . . . . . . . . . .193
Playing . . . . . . . . . . . . . . . . . . . . . . . . . . . .193
Playing Instruments. . . . . . . . . . . . . . . . . . .193
Program Ideas . . . . . . . . . . . . . . . . . . . . . .201
Pronunciation Practice, Recorded. . . . . . . .201
Reading . . . . . . . . . . . . . . . . . . . . . . . . . . . .203
Recorded Lessons. . . . . . . . . . . . . . . . . . . .203
Related Arts . . . . . . . . . . . . . . . . . . . . . . . . .203
Rhythm . . . . . . . . . . . . . . . . . . . . . . . . . . . .206

School to Home Connection . . . . . . . . . .214
Signing . . . . . . . . . . . . . . . . . . . . . . . .215
Singing . . . . . . . . . . . . . . . . . . . . . . . .215
Skills Reinforcement . . . . . . . . . . . . . . .216
Speech Pieces . . . . . . . . . . . . . . . . . . .225
Spotlight On . . . . . . . . . . . . . . . . . . . .225
Teacher to Teacher . . . . . . . . . . . . . . . .230
Technology/Media . . . . . . . . . . . . . . . .236
Texture/Harmony. . . . . . . . . . . . . . . . .247
Timbre. . . . . . . . . . . . . . . . . . . . . . . . .253
Vocal Development . . . . . . . . . . . . . . . .262

**PITCH AND RHYTHM INDEX. . . . . . . . . 264**
Pitch Index. . . . . . . . . . . . . . . . . . . . . .264
Rhythm Index. . . . . . . . . . . . . . . . . . . .291

**THEMATIC INDEX . . . . . . . . . . . . . . 301**
Adventures. . . . . . . . . . . . . . . . . . . . . .301
Alphabet . . . . . . . . . . . . . . . . . . . . . . .301
Animals . . . . . . . . . . . . . . . . . . . . . . . .301
Calendars. . . . . . . . . . . . . . . . . . . . . . .304
Change and Adaptation. . . . . . . . . . . . .304
Character Traits . . . . . . . . . . . . . . . . . .304
Citizenship . . . . . . . . . . . . . . . . . . . . . .309
Climates. . . . . . . . . . . . . . . . . . . . . . . .310
Colors . . . . . . . . . . . . . . . . . . . . . . . . .310
Counting and Computation . . . . . . . . . .310
Days of the Week . . . . . . . . . . . . . . . . .310
Diversity (Alike and Different). . . . . . . . .310
Dragons, Giants, and Monsters . . . . . . . .310
Earth, The . . . . . . . . . . . . . . . . . . . . . .310
Ecology and Natural Resources . . . . . . . .310
Environments. . . . . . . . . . . . . . . . . . . .311
Families . . . . . . . . . . . . . . . . . . . . . . . .312
Favorite Things. . . . . . . . . . . . . . . . . . .313
Following Directions . . . . . . . . . . . . . . .313
Food . . . . . . . . . . . . . . . . . . . . . . . . . .314
Force and Motion . . . . . . . . . . . . . . . . .314
Freedom, Justice, and Peace . . . . . . . . .315
Friendship . . . . . . . . . . . . . . . . . . . . . .316
Games and Play . . . . . . . . . . . . . . . . . .317
Greetings and Goodbyes . . . . . . . . . . . .318
Habitats and Homes . . . . . . . . . . . . . . .318
Healthy Living . . . . . . . . . . . . . . . . . . .318
Heat and Light . . . . . . . . . . . . . . . . . . .318
Heroes and Leaders . . . . . . . . . . . . . . .318
Hopes and Dreams. . . . . . . . . . . . . . . .319
Humor. . . . . . . . . . . . . . . . . . . . . . . . .320
Imagination and Fantasy . . . . . . . . . . . .321
Map and Globe. . . . . . . . . . . . . . . . . . .323
Measurement . . . . . . . . . . . . . . . . . . . .323

Money . . . . . . . . . . . . . . . . . . . . . . . . .323
Months . . . . . . . . . . . . . . . . . . . . . . . .323
Music Making, About . . . . . . . . . . . . . .323
Neighborhoods . . . . . . . . . . . . . . . . . .325
Night and Day . . . . . . . . . . . . . . . . . . .325
Parades . . . . . . . . . . . . . . . . . . . . . . . .326
Parts of the Body . . . . . . . . . . . . . . . . .326
Past and Present. . . . . . . . . . . . . . . . . .326
Patterns . . . . . . . . . . . . . . . . . . . . . . . .326
Places We Live . . . . . . . . . . . . . . . . . . .326
Plants and Trees . . . . . . . . . . . . . . . . . .329
Playing With Words. . . . . . . . . . . . . . . .329
Problem Solving . . . . . . . . . . . . . . . . . .330
Reading Is Fun . . . . . . . . . . . . . . . . . . .330
Safety . . . . . . . . . . . . . . . . . . . . . . . . .330
School. . . . . . . . . . . . . . . . . . . . . . . . .330
Seasons . . . . . . . . . . . . . . . . . . . . . . . .330
Self-Esteem . . . . . . . . . . . . . . . . . . . . .331
Senses . . . . . . . . . . . . . . . . . . . . . . . . .332
Shapes . . . . . . . . . . . . . . . . . . . . . . . .332
Social Studies . . . . . . . . . . . . . . . . . . . .332
Sounds Around Us . . . . . . . . . . . . . . . .333
Space . . . . . . . . . . . . . . . . . . . . . . . . .334
Sports . . . . . . . . . . . . . . . . . . . . . . . . .335
Teamwork . . . . . . . . . . . . . . . . . . . . . .335
Time . . . . . . . . . . . . . . . . . . . . . . . . . .335
Toys . . . . . . . . . . . . . . . . . . . . . . . . . .335
Travel and Transportation . . . . . . . . . . .335
Water in Our World. . . . . . . . . . . . . . . .336
Weather. . . . . . . . . . . . . . . . . . . . . . . .336
Work . . . . . . . . . . . . . . . . . . . . . . . . . .337
World Community, The. . . . . . . . . . . . . .338
Zoos . . . . . . . . . . . . . . . . . . . . . . . . . .340

# TEACHER SUPPORT RESOURCES

**BRIDGES TO ASIA** (Primary And Intermediate) **341**
**STEP INTO MUSIC** (Pre-kindergarten) **. . . . . 344**

# TECHNOLOGY RESOURCES

**MIDI SONG FILES** (Grades 1-8) **. . . . . . . . 346**
**MUSIC READING PRACTICE** (Grades 1-8) **. . 348**
**MUSIC MAGIC VIDEO LIBRARY** (Grades 1-8) **352**

# CORRELATIONS

**SCOTT FORESMAN ART** © 2005 **. . . . . . .358**
**SCOTT FORESMAN READING** © 2000 **. . . .387**

# Songs and Speech Pieces

*This section contains all the songs and speech pieces that are designated for students' performance in Silver Burdett* MAKING MUSIC. *The abbreviation following a song title describes the recording format of the song or speech piece.*

St. Voc. = Stereo Vocal
St. Perf. Tr. = Stereo Performance Track
St. Voc./Dance Perf. Tr. = Stereo Vocal and Dance Performance Track
T.A.P. = Teach-A-Part

| Title | Gr. | Pg. | CD Track |
|---|---|---|---|
| A la puerta del cielo (At the Gate of Heaven) (St. Voc.) | 5 | 60 | 3-29 |
| A la puerta del cielo (At the Gate of Heaven) (St. Perf. Tr.) | 5 | 60 | 3-31 |
| A la rurru niño (Hush, My Little Baby) (St. Voc.) | K | 180 | 6-33 |
| A la rurru niño (Hush, My Little Baby) (St. Perf. Tr.) | K | 180 | 6-35 |
| A Ram Sam Sam (St. Voc.) | 3 | 208 | 7-24 |
| A Ram Sam Sam (St. Perf. Tr.) | 3 | 208 | 7-25 |
| A-Tisket, A-Tasket (St. Voc.) | 2 | 238 | 8-24 |
| A-Tisket, A-Tasket (St. Perf. Tr.) | 2 | 238 | 8-25 |
| ABC Blues (St. Voc.) | K | 281 | 9-39 |
| ABC Blues (St. Perf. Tr.) | K | 281 | 9-40 |
| ABC Rock (St. Voc.) | 1 | 262 | 8-27 |
| ABC Rock (St. Perf. Tr.) | 1 | 262 | 8-28 |
| Abiyoyo (St. Voc.) | 2 | 108 | 4-25 |
| Abiyoyo (St. Perf. Tr.) | 2 | 108 | 4-26 |
| Abraham, Martin, and John (St. Voc.) | 6 | 466 | 22-3 |
| Abraham, Martin, and John (St. Perf. Tr.) | 6 | 466 | 22-4 |
| Achshav (Awake! Awake!) (St. Voc.) | 2 | 64 | 3-1 |
| Achshav (Awake! Awake!) (St. Perf. Tr.) | 2 | 64 | 3-3 |
| Ackabacka, Soda Cracker (speech piece) (St. Voc.) | 1 | 303 | 9-38 |
| Adana ya gidelim (Let's Go to Adana) (St. Voc./Dance Perf. Tr.) | 2 | 142 | 5-32 |
| Adana ya gidelim (Let's Go to Adana) (St. Perf. Tr.) | 2 | 142 | 5-34 |
| Addams Family, The (St. Voc.) | 5 | 456 | 19-22 |
| Addams Family, The (St. Perf. Tr.) | 5 | 456 | 19-23 |
| Adelita (Spanish) (St. Voc.) | 5 | 50 | 3-4 |
| Adelita (English) (St. Voc.) | 5 | 50 | 3-5 |
| Adelita (St. Perf. Tr.) | 5 | 50 | 3-6 |
| Adiós, amigos (Goodbye, My Friends) (St. Voc.) | 6 | 57 | 4-1 |
| Adiós, amigos (Goodbye, My Friends) (St. Perf. Tr.) | 6 | 57 | 4-3 |
| African Noel (St. Voc.) | 1 | 427 | 13-41 |
| African Noel (St. Perf. Tr.) | 1 | 427 | 13-42 |
| Aguinaldo (Spanish) (St. Voc.) | 3 | 402 | 14-20 |
| Aguinaldo (English) (St. Voc.) | 3 | 402 | 14-21 |
| Aguinaldo (St. Perf. Tr.) | 3 | 402 | 14-22 |
| Ah, eu entrei na roda (I Came to Try This Game) (St. Voc./Dance Perf. Tr.) | 3 | 308 | 10-40 |
| Ah, eu entrei na roda (I Came to Try This Game) (St. Perf. Tr.) | 3 | 308 | 10-42 |
| Ah! Les jolis papillons (Ah! The Pretty Butterflies) (St. Voc.) | 1 | 362 | 11-21 |
| Ah! Les jolis papillons (Ah! The Pretty Butterflies) (St. Perf. Tr.) | 1 | 362 | 11-23 |
| Ah, My Merry Dunaii (Ai Dunaiĭ moy) (St. Voc.) | 4 | 293 | 12-15 |
| Ah, Poor Bird (St. Voc.) | 4 | 196 | 8-36 |
| Ah, Poor Bird (St. Perf. Tr.) | 4 | 196 | 8-37 |
| Ah! The Pretty Butterflies (Ah! les jolis papillons) (St. Voc.) | 1 | 362 | 11-22 |
| Ah ya Zane (Zane from Abedeen) (St. Voc.) | 5 | 297 | 13-26 |
| Ah ya Zane (Zane from Abedeen) (St. Perf. Tr.) | 5 | 297 | 13-28 |
| Ahora voy a cantarles (Now Hear the Song) (St. Voc.) | 3 | 56 | 2-31 |
| Ahora voy a cantarles (Now Hear the Song) (St. Perf. Tr.) | 3 | 56 | 2-33 |
| Ai Dunaiĭ moy (Ah, My Merry Dunaii) (St. Voc.) | 4 | 293 | 12-14 |
| Ai Dunaiĭ moy (Ah, My Merry Dunaii) (St. Perf. Tr.) | 4 | 293 | 12-16 |
| Aiken Drum (St. Voc.) | 1 | 398 | 12-33 |
| Aiken Drum (St. Perf. Tr.) | 1 | 398 | 12-34 |
| Ain't Gonna Let Nobody Turn Me 'Round (St. Voc.) | 6 | 85 | 5-26 |
| Ain't Gonna Let Nobody Turn Me 'Round (St. Perf. Tr.) | 6 | 85 | 5-27 |
| Ain't Gonna Let Nobody Turn Me 'Round (St. Voc.) | 8 | F-16 | 10-27 |
| Ain't Gonna Let Nobody Turn Me 'Round (St. Perf. Tr.) | 8 | F-16 | 10-28 |
| Al ánimo (Spanish) (St. Voc.) | 3 | 322 | 11-19 |
| Al ánimo (English) (St. Voc.) | 3 | 322 | 11-20 |
| Al ánimo (St. Perf. Tr.) | 3 | 322 | 11-21 |
| Al citrón (St. Voc.) | 3 | 320 | 11-16 |
| Al citrón (St. Perf. Tr.) | 3 | 320 | 11-17 |
| Al quebrar la piñata (Piñata Song) (St. Voc.) | 4 | 432 | 18-15 |
| Al quebrar la piñata (Piñata Song) (St. Perf. Tr.) | 4 | 432 | 18-17 |
| Al tambor (The Drum Song) (St. Voc.) | 3 | 270 | 9-16 |
| Al tambor (The Drum Song) (St. Perf. Tr.) | 3 | 270 | 9-18 |
| Al yadee (St. Voc.) | 6 | 308 | 15-32 |
| Al yadee (St. Perf. Tr.) | 6 | 308 | 15-33 |
| Ala Da'lona (Arabic) (St. Voc.) | 4 | 136 | 6-18 |
| Ala Da'lona (English) (St. Voc.) | 4 | 136 | 6-19 |
| Ala Da'lona (St. Perf. Tr.) | 4 | 136 | 6-20 |
| Alabama Gal (St. Voc.) | 3 | 106 | 4-9 |
| Alabama Gal (St. Perf. Tr.) | 3 | 106 | 4-10 |
| Alexander's Ragtime Band (St. Voc.) | 6 | 136 | 8-1 |
| Alexander's Ragtime Band (St. Perf. Tr.) | 6 | 136 | 8-2 |
| Alison's Camel (St. Voc.) | K | 289 | 10-11 |
| Alison's Camel (St. Perf. Tr.) | K | 289 | 10-12 |
| All Around the Buttercup (St. Voc.) | 2 | 170 | 6-26 |
| All Around the Buttercup (St. Perf. Tr.) | 2 | 170 | 6-27 |
| All for One (St. Voc.) | 7 | E-8 | 9-21 |
| All for One (St. Perf. Tr.) | 7 | E-8 | 9-22 |
| All My Little Ducklings (Alle meine Entchen) (St. Voc.) | 1 | 98 | 3-25 |
| All Night, All Day (St. Voc.) | 4 | 180 | 8-13 |
| All Night, All Day (St. Perf. Tr.) | 4 | 180 | 8-14 |
| All the Way Around the World (St. Voc.) | 2 | 258 | 9-19 |
| All the Way Around the World (St. Perf. Tr.) | 2 | 258 | 9-20 |
| All Through the Night (T.A.P.) | 5 | 105 | 5-28 |
| Allá en la fuente (There at the Spring) (St. Voc.) | 2 | 92 | 3-48 |
| Allá en la fuente (There at the Spring) (St. Perf. Tr.) | 2 | 92 | 3-50 |
| Alle meine Entchen (All My Little Ducklings) (St. Voc.) | 1 | 98 | 3-24 |

| Title | Gr. | Pg. | CD Track |
|---|---|---|---|
| Alle meine Entchen (All My Little Ducklings) (St. Perf. Tr.) | 1 | 98 | 3-26 |
| Alleluia (St. Voc.) | 6 | 133 | 7-30 |
| Alleluia (St. Perf. Tr.) | 6 | 133 | 7-31 |
| Alleluia, Amen (St. Voc.) | 7 | A-12 | 1-9 |
| Alleluia, Amen (St. Perf. Tr.) | 7 | A-12 | 1-10 |
| Alligator, The (Se va el caimán) (St. Voc.) | 5 | 306 | 14-11 |
| Alligator Pie (speech piece) (St. Voc.) | 3 | 13 | 1-10 |
| Alligator Pie (speech piece) (St. Perf. Tr.) | 3 | 13 | 1-11 |
| Almost Day (St. Voc.) | 3 | 397 | 14-10 |
| Almost Day (St. Perf. Tr.) | 3 | 397 | 14-11 |
| Alphabet Song, The (St. Voc.) | K | 280 | 9-37 |
| Alphabet Song, The (St. Perf. Tr.) | K | 280 | 9-38 |
| Alumot (Sheaves of Grain) (St. Voc.) | 6 | 306 | 15-26 |
| Alumot (Sheaves of Grain) (St. Perf. Tr.) | 6 | 306 | 15-28 |
| Ama-Lama (St. Voc.) | 5 | 142 | 7-15 |
| Ama-Lama (St. Perf. Tr.) | 5 | 142 | 7-16 |
| Amarillo Armadillo (St. Voc.) | 2 | 82 | 3-33 |
| Amarillo Armadillo (St. Perf. Tr.) | 2 | 82 | 3-34 |
| Amasee (St. Voc.) | 1 | 172 | 5-31 |
| Amasee (St. Perf. Tr.) | 1 | 172 | 5-32 |
| Amazing Grace (St. Voc.) | 4 | 160 | 7-18 |
| Amazing Grace (St. Perf. Tr.) | 4 | 160 | 7-19 |
| Ambos a dos (Go Two by Two) (St. Voc.) | 3 | 20 | 1-31 |
| Ambos a dos (Go Two by Two) (St. Perf. Tr.) | 3 | 20 | 1-33 |
| Amefuri (Japanese Rain Song) (St. Voc.) | 1 | 144 | 4-43 |
| Amefuri (Japanese Rain Song) (St. Perf. Tr.) | 1 | 144 | 4-45 |
| America (St. Voc.) | 1 | 446 | 14-27 |
| America (St. Perf. Tr.) | 1 | 446 | 14-28 |
| America (St. Voc.) | 2 | 403 | 15-11 |
| America (St. Perf. Tr.) | 2 | 403 | 15-12 |
| America (St. Voc.) | 3 | 412 | 15-4 |
| America (St. Perf. Tr.) | 3 | 412 | 15-5 |
| America (written by N. Diamond) (St. Voc.) | 4 | 206 | 9-1 |
| America (written by N. Diamond) (St. Perf. Tr.) | 4 | 206 | 9-2 |
| America (St. Voc.) | 4 | 440 | 19-5 |
| America (St. Perf. Tr.) | 4 | 440 | 19-6 |
| America (St. Voc.) | 5 | 486 | 21-15 |
| America (St. Perf. Tr.) | 5 | 486 | 21-16 |
| America (St. Voc.) | 6 | 484 | 23-1 |
| America (St. Perf. Tr.) | 6 | 484 | 23-2 |
| America (St. Voc.) | 7 | I-2 | 13-1 |
| America (St. Perf. Tr.) | 7 | I-2 | 13-2 |
| America (St. Voc.) | 8 | I-2 | 13-1 |
| America (St. Perf. Tr.) | 8 | I-2 | 13-2 |
| America (St. Voc.) | K | 326 | 11-34 |
| America (St. Perf. Tr.) | K | 326 | 11-35 |
| America, I Hear You Singing (St. Voc.) | 2 | 402 | 15-9 |
| America, I Hear You Singing (St. Perf. Tr.) | 2 | 402 | 15-10 |
| America, the Beautiful (St. Voc.) | 3 | 413 | 15-6 |
| America, the Beautiful (St. Perf. Tr.) | 3 | 413 | 15-7 |
| America, the Beautiful (St. Voc.) | 4 | 158 | 7-15 |
| America, the Beautiful (St. Perf. Tr.) | 4 | 158 | 7-16 |
| America, the Beautiful (St. Voc.) | 5 | 76 | 4-19 |
| America, the Beautiful (St. Perf. Tr.) | 5 | 76 | 4-20 |
| America, the Beautiful (St. Voc.) | 6 | 485 | 23-4 |
| America, the Beautiful (St. Perf. Tr.) | 6 | 485 | 23-5 |
| America, the Beautiful (St. Voc.) | 7 | I-4 | 13-3 |
| America, the Beautiful (St. Perf. Tr.) | 7 | I-4 | 13-4 |
| America, the Beautiful (St. Voc.) | 8 | I-4 | 13-3 |
| America, the Beautiful (St. Perf. Tr.) | 8 | I-4 | 13-4 |
| America, the Beautiful/Let Freedom Ring (St. Voc.) | 5 | 77 | 4-22 |
| America, the Free (St. Voc.) | 4 | 210 | 9-3 |
| America, the Free (St. Perf. Tr.) | 4 | 210 | 9-4 |
| Andy Pandy (St. Voc.) | K | 46 | 2-22 |
| Andy Pandy (St. Perf. Tr.) | K | 46 | 2-23 |
| Angels on the Midnight Clear (St. Voc.) | 6 | 423 | 20-20 |
| Angels on the Midnight Clear (St. Perf. Tr.) | 6 | 423 | 20-21 |
| Ants Go Marching, The (St. Voc.) | 1 | 250 | 8-1 |
| Ants Go Marching, The (St. Perf. Tr.) | 1 | 250 | 8-2 |
| Apple Tree (St. Voc.) | 1 | 230 | 7-23 |
| Apple Tree (St. Perf. Tr.) | 1 | 230 | 7-24 |
| Apples and Bananas (St. Voc.) | 1 | 391 | 12-21 |
| Apples and Bananas (St. Perf. Tr.) | 1 | 391 | 12-22 |
| Apples, Peaches, Pears, and Plums (speech piece) (St. Voc.) | 1 | 17 | 1-27 |
| Apples, Peaches, Pears, and Plums (speech piece) (St. Perf. Tr.) | 1 | 17 | 1-28 |
| Are You Sleeping? (Frère Jacques) (St. Voc.) | 2 | 125 | 5-2 |
| Arirang (Korean) (St. Voc.) | 5 | 25 | 2-6 |
| Arirang (English) (St. Voc.) | 5 | 25 | 2-7 |
| Arirang (St. Perf. Tr.) | 5 | 25 | 2-8 |
| Artsa alinu (Come to the Land) (St. Voc.) | 3 | 285 | 10-1 |
| Artsa alinu (Come to the Land) (St. Perf. Tr.) | 3 | 285 | 10-3 |
| Asadoya (Okinawan) (St. Voc.) | 6 | 303 | 15-17 |
| Asadoya (English) (St. Voc.) | 6 | 303 | 15-18 |
| Asadoya (St. Perf. Tr.) | 6 | 303 | 15-19 |
| Ash Grove, The (St. Voc.) | 5 | 114 | 6-6 |
| Ash Grove, The (St. Perf. Tr.) | 5 | 114 | 6-7 |
| Así es mi tierra (This Is My Land) (St. Voc.) | 6 | 172 | 9-30 |
| Así es mi tierra (This Is My Land) (St. Perf. Tr.) | 6 | 172 | 9-32 |
| At the Gate of Heaven (A la puerta del cielo) (St. Voc.) | 5 | 60 | 3-30 |
| At the Hop (St. Voc.) | 4 | 168 | 7-27 |
| At the Hop (St. Perf. Tr.) | 4 | 168 | 7-28 |
| At the Same Time (St. Voc.) | 6 | 115 | 7-1 |
| At the Same Time (St. Perf. Tr.) | 6 | 115 | 7-2 |
| Au clair de la lune (In the Moonlight) (St. Voc.) | 3 | 18 | 1-26 |
| Au clair de la lune (In the Moonlight) (St. Perf. Tr.) | 3 | 18 | 1-28 |
| Autumn Canon (St. Voc.) | 5 | 148 | 7-25 |
| Autumn Canon (St. Perf. Tr.) | 5 | 148 | 7-26 |
| Awake! Awake! (Achshav) (St. Voc.) | 2 | 64 | 3-2 |
| Away to America (St. Voc.) | 5 | 57 | 3-23 |
| ¡Ay, Jalisco no te rajes! (Oh, Jalisco!) (T.A.P.) | 7 | I-6 | 13-5 |
| ¡Ay, Jalisco no te rajes! (Oh, Jalisco!) (St. Perf. Tr.) | 7 | I-6 | 13-7 |
| Ayelivi (Ewe) (St. Voc.) | 2 | 70 | 3-9 |
| Ayelivi (English) (St. Voc.) | 2 | 70 | 3-10 |
| Ayelivi (St. Perf. Tr.) | 2 | 70 | 3-11 |
| Ayliluli, num tsipor (Ayliluli, Sleep My Bird) (St. Voc.) | 1 | 204 | 6-36 |
| Ayliluli, Sleep, My Bird (Ayliluli, num tsipor) (St. Voc.) | 1 | 204 | 6-37 |
| Ayliluli, num tsipor (St. Perf. Tr.) | 1 | 204 | 6-38 |
| B-A, Bay (St. Voc.) | 1 | 220 | 7-11 |
| B-A, Bay (St. Perf. Tr.) | 1 | 220 | 7-12 |
| Baby Beluga (St. Voc.) | K | 272 | 9-28 |
| Baby Beluga (St. Perf. Tr.) | K | 272 | 9-29 |
| Baby Chicks (Los pollitos) (St. Voc.) | K | 166 | 6-13 |
| Back of the Bus (St. Voc.) | 3 | 410 | 15-1 |
| Back of the Bus (St. Perf. Tr.) | 3 | 410 | 15-2 |
| Bam, chi, chi, bam (St. Voc.) | K | 109 | 4-13 |
| Bam, chi, chi, bam (St. Perf. Tr.) | K | 109 | 4-14 |
| Bamboo Flute (Xiao) (St. Voc.) | 4 | 314 | 13-25 |
| Banana (St. Voc.) | 2 | 114 | 4-32 |
| Banana (St. Perf. Tr.) | 2 | 114 | 4-33 |
| Banana Splits (St. Voc.) | 1 | 320 | 10-11 |

| Title | Gr. | Pg. | CD Track |
|---|---|---|---|
| Banana Splits (St. Perf. Tr.) | 1 | 320 | 10-12 |
| Bananas and Cream (speech piece) (St. Voc.) | 3 | 210 | 7-26 |
| Bananas and Cream (speech piece) (St. Perf. Tr.) | 3 | 210 | 7-27 |
| Banjo Sam (St. Voc.) | 2 | 314 | 11-22 |
| Banjo Sam (St. Perf. Tr.) | 2 | 314 | 11-23 |
| Bantama kra kro (Akan) (St. Voc.) | 5 | 308 | 14-14 |
| Bantama kra kro (English) (St. Voc.) | 5 | 308 | 14-15 |
| Bantama kra kro (St. Perf. Tr.) | 5 | 308 | 14-16 |
| Banuwa (St. Voc.) | 6 | 294 | 15-1 |
| Banuwa (St. Perf. Tr.) | 6 | 294 | 15-2 |
| Barb'ry Allen (St. Voc.) | 6 | 44 | 3-8 |
| Bard of Armagh, The (St. Voc.) | 4 | 296 | 12-24 |
| Bard of Armagh, The (St. Perf. Tr.) | 4 | 296 | 12-25 |
| Basin Street Blues (St. Voc.) | 5 | 354 | 16-14 |
| Basin Street Blues (St. Perf. Tr.) | 5 | 354 | 16-15 |
| Bát kim thang (Setting Up the Golden Ladder) (St. Voc.) | 6 | 13 | 1-13 |
| Bát kim thang (Setting Up the Golden Ladder) (St. Perf. Tr.) | 6 | 13 | 1-15 |
| Battle Cry of Freedom (St. Voc.) | 5 | 272 | 12-31 |
| Battle Cry of Freedom (St. Perf. Tr.) | 5 | 272 | 12-32 |
| Battle Hymn of the Republic (St. Voc.) | 5 | 274 | 12-33 |
| Battle Hymn of the Republic (St. Perf. Tr.) | 5 | 274 | 12-34 |
| Beach Rap (speech piece) (St. Voc.) | 1 | 354 | 11-9 |
| Beach Rap (speech piece) (St. Perf. Tr.) | 1 | 354 | 11-10 |
| Bear Dance (vocables) (St. Voc.) | 7 | I-10 | 13-11 |
| Bear Dance (St. Voc.) | K | 127 | 5-1 |
| Bear Dance (St. Perf. Tr.) | K | 127 | 5-2 |
| Bee, Bee, Bumblebee (speech piece) (St. Voc.) | 1 | 50 | 2-23 |
| Bee, Bee, Bumblebee (speech piece) (St. Perf. Tr.) | 1 | 50 | 2-24 |
| Beloved Island Home (La borinqueña) (T.A.P.) | 8 | D-19 | 8-27 |
| Bereleh (Little Snail) (St. Voc.) | K | 151 | 5-34 |
| Bereleh (Little Snail) (St. Perf. Tr.) | K | 151 | 5-36 |
| Beriozka (The Birch Tree) (St. Voc.) | 4 | 294 | 12-19 |
| Beriozka (The Birch Tree) (St. Perf. Tr.) | 4 | 294 | 12-21 |
| Beyond Borders (St. Voc.) | 5 | 292 | 13-18 |
| Beyond Borders (St. Perf. Tr.) | 5 | 292 | 13-19 |
| Big Beautiful Planet (St. Voc.) | 3 | 326 | 11-23 |
| Big Beautiful Planet (St. Perf. Tr.) | 3 | 326 | 11-24 |
| Big Old Storm a-Comin' (St. Voc.) | K | 257 | 9-4 |
| Big Old Storm a-Comin' (St. Perf. Tr.) | K | 257 | 9-5 |
| Big Ranch, The (El rancho grande) (St. Voc.) | 4 | 215 | 9-7 |
| Big Ranch, The (El rancho grande) (St. Voc.) | 8 | I-22 | 13-25 |
| Big Rock Candy Mountain (St. Voc.) | 4 | 330 | 14-10 |
| Big Rock Candy Mountain (St. Perf. Tr.) | 4 | 330 | 14-11 |
| Bingo (St. Voc.) | 1 | 170 | 5-29 |
| Bingo (St. Perf. Tr.) | 1 | 170 | 5-30 |
| Birch Tree, The (Beriozka) (St. Voc.) | 4 | 294 | 12-20 |
| Bird Song (Sarika keo) (St. Voc.) | 3 | 275 | 9-27 |
| Birds in Granny's Garden (Ptashky u babusi sadochku) (St. Voc.) | 1 | 192 | 6-25 |
| Birthday (St. Voc.) | 6 | 90 | 6-1 |
| Birthday (St. Perf. Tr.) | 6 | 90 | 6-2 |
| Biting Wind (Osamu kosamu) (St. Voc.) | 4 | 96 | 5-3 |
| Black Snake (St. Voc.) | 3 | 53 | 2-21 |
| Black Snake (St. Perf. Tr.) | 3 | 53 | 2-22 |
| Bling Blang (St. Voc.) | 3 | 240 | 8-6 |
| Bling Blang (St. Perf. Tr.) | 3 | 240 | 8-7 |
| Blow the Wind Southerly (St. Voc.) | 5 | 178 | 9-8 |
| Blow the Wind Southerly (St. Perf. Tr.) | 5 | 178 | 9-9 |
| Blow, Ye Winds (St. Voc./Dance Perf. Tr.) | 4 | 255 | 10-25 |
| Blow, Ye Winds (St. Perf. Tr.) | 4 | 255 | 10-26 |
| Blowin' in the Wind (St. Voc.) | 5 | 382 | 17-19 |
| Blowin' in the Wind (St. Perf. Tr.) | 5 | 382 | 17-20 |
| Blue Mountain Lake (St. Voc.) | 6 | 205 | 11-4 |
| Blue Mountain Lake (St. Perf. Tr.) | 6 | 205 | 11-5 |
| Blue Skies (St. Voc.) | 6 | 88 | 5-31 |
| Blue Skies (St. Perf. Tr.) | 6 | 88 | 5-32 |
| Bluebells (Doraji) (St. Voc.) | 4 | 174 | 7-37 |
| Bluebird, Bluebird (St. Voc.) | K | 105 | 4-5 |
| Bluebird, Bluebird (St. Perf. Tr.) | K | 105 | 4-6 |
| Bluebonnets of Texas (St. Voc.) | 3 | 332 | 11-34 |
| Bluebonnets of Texas (St. Perf. Tr.) | 3 | 332 | 11-35 |
| Blues with a Feeling (St. Voc.) | 8 | I-6 | 13-5 |
| Blues with a Feeling (St. Perf. Tr.) | 8 | I-6 | 13-6 |
| Bo-bo-skee, Watten-tatten (speech piece) (St. Voc.) | 1 | 259 | 8-21 |
| Bo-bo-skee, Watten-tatten (speech piece) (St. Perf. Tr.) | 1 | 259 | 8-22 |
| Bob-a-Needle (St. Voc.) | 2 | 232 | 8-19 |
| Bob-a-Needle (St. Perf. Tr.) | 2 | 232 | 8-20 |
| Bogando a la luz del sol (Rowing Toward the Sunlight) (St. Voc.) | 4 | 306 | 13-7 |
| Bogando a la luz del sol (Rowing Toward the Sunlight) (St. Perf. Tr.) | 4 | 306 | 13-9 |
| Boil Them Cabbage Down (St. Voc.) | 6 | 370 | 19-1 |
| Boil Them Cabbage Down (St. Perf. Tr.) | 6 | 370 | 19-2 |
| Bonavist' Harbour (St. Voc./Dance Perf. Tr.) | 3 | 294 | 10-16 |
| Bonavist' Harbour (St. Perf. Tr.) | 3 | 294 | 10-17 |
| Bonga (St. Voc.) | K | 78 | 3-13 |
| Bonga (St. Perf. Tr.) | K | 78 | 3-14 |
| Bonjour, mes amis (Hello, My Friends) (St. Voc.) | 1 | 316 | 10-6 |
| Bonjour, mes amis (Hello, My Friends) (St. Perf. Tr.) | 1 | 316 | 10-8 |
| Boogie Chant and Dance (speech piece) (St. Voc.) | 2 | 78 | 3-22 |
| Boogie Chant and Dance (speech piece) (St. Perf. Tr.) | 2 | 78 | 3-23 |
| Book of Love (St. Voc.) | 8 | G-27 | 12-9 |
| Book of Love (St. Perf. Tr.) | 8 | G-27 | 12-10 |
| Bounce High, Bounce Low (St. Voc.) | 1 | 152 | 4-58 |
| Bounce High, Bounce Low (St. Perf. Tr.) | 1 | 152 | 4-59 |
| Bouncing Balls (Pai pi qiu) (St. Voc.) | 1 | 324 | 10-20 |
| Bound for South Australia (St. Voc.) | 5 | 22 | 2-1 |
| Bound for South Australia (St. Perf. Tr.) | 5 | 22 | 2-2 |
| Boysie (St. Voc.) | 2 | 195 | 7-25 |
| Boysie (St. Perf. Tr.) | 2 | 195 | 7-26 |
| Brand New Day, A (St. Voc.) | 6 | 7 | 1-3 |
| Brand New Day, A "Everybody Rejoice" (St. Perf. Tr.) | 6 | 7 | 1-4 |
| Bridges (St. Voc.) | 6 | 86 | 5-28 |
| Bridges (St. Perf. Tr.) | 6 | 86 | 5-29 |
| Brush Your Teeth (St. Voc.) | 1 | 284 | 9-12 |
| Brush Your Teeth (St. Perf. Tr.) | 1 | 284 | 9-13 |
| Buenos días (Good Morning!) (St. Voc.) | 1 | 13 | 1-19 |
| Buenos días (Good Morning!) (St. Perf. Tr.) | 1 | 13 | 1-21 |
| Bundle-Buggy Boogie Woogie (speech piece) (St. Voc.) | 4 | 120 | 5-37 |
| Bundle-Buggy Boogie Woogie (speech piece) (St. Perf. Tr.) | 4 | 120 | 5-38 |
| Bury Me Not on the Lone Prairie (St. Voc.) | 6 | 19 | 2-1 |
| Bury Me Not on the Lone Prairie (St. Perf. Tr.) | 6 | 19 | 2-2 |
| Bus, The (St. Voc.) | K | 82 | 3-20 |
| Bus, The (St. Perf. Tr.) | K | 82 | 3-21 |
| Busy Buzzy Bee (St. Voc.) | K | 77 | 3-11 |
| Busy Buzzy Bee (St. Perf. Tr.) | K | 77 | 3-12 |
| But the Cat Came Back (St. Voc.) | 2 | 190 | 7-16 |
| But the Cat Came Back (St. Perf. Tr.) | 2 | 190 | 7-17 |
| Butterfly, The (La mariposa) (St. Voc.) | 6 | 58 | 4-9 |
| By the Waters of Babylon (St. Voc.) | 6 | 311 | 16-1 |

| Title | Gr. | Pg. | CD Track |
|---|---|---|---|
| By the Waters of Babylon (St. Perf. Tr.) | 6 | 311 | 16-2 |
| Bye Bye, Love (St. Voc.) | 8 | F-9 | 10-19 |
| Bye Bye, Love (St. Perf. Tr.) | 8 | F-9 | 10-20 |
| Caballito blanco (Little White Pony) (St. Voc.) | 2 | 193 | 7-18 |
| Caballito blanco (Little White Pony) (St. Perf. Tr.) | 2 | 193 | 7-20 |
| Cake! Cake! Cake! (Uga uga uga) (St. Voc.) | K | 305 | 10-32 |
| California (St. Voc.) | 5 | 52 | 3-9 |
| California (St. Perf. Tr.) | 5 | 52 | 3-10 |
| California Dreamin' (St. Voc.) | 8 | G-31 | 12-13 |
| California Dreamin' (St. Perf. Tr.) | 8 | G-31 | 12-14 |
| California, Here I Come (St. Voc.) | 4 | 287 | 12-7 |
| California, Here I Come (St. Perf. Tr.) | 4 | 287 | 12-8 |
| Camptown Races (St. Voc.) | 5 | 270 | 12-29 |
| Camptown Races (St. Perf. Tr.) | 5 | 270 | 12-30 |
| Can You Canoe? (speech piece) (St. Voc.) | 4 | 170 | 7-29 |
| Can You Canoe? (speech piece) (St. Perf. Tr.) | 4 | 170 | 7-30 |
| Canción de cuna (Cradle Song) (St. Voc.) | 4 | 144 | 6-31 |
| Canción de cuna (Cradle Song) (St. Perf. Tr.) | 4 | 144 | 6-33 |
| Canción Mixteca (Mixteca Song) (St. Voc.) | 5 | 326 | 15-11 |
| Canción Mixteca (Mixteca Song) (St. Perf. Tr.) | 5 | 326 | 15-13 |
| Candle Burning Bright (Ég a gyerta) (St. Voc.) | K | 96 | 3-51 |
| Candles Burning Bright (Las velitas) (St. Voc.) | 5 | 147 | 7-19 |
| Canoe Song (St. Voc.) | 4 | 76 | 4-17 |
| Canoe Song (St. Perf. Tr.) | 4 | 76 | 4-18 |
| Cantando mentiras (Singing Tall Tales) (St. Voc.) | 4 | 146 | 6-38 |
| Cantando mentiras (Singing Tall Tales) (St. Perf. Tr.) | 4 | 146 | 6-40 |
| Cantaré, cantarás (I Will Sing, You Will Sing) (St. Voc.) | 6 | 413 | 20-11 |
| Cantaré, cantarás (I Will Sing, You Will Sing) (St. Perf. Tr.) | 6 | 413 | 20-13 |
| Canto del agua (Song of the Water) (St. Voc.) | 8 | I-10 | 13-7 |
| Canto del agua (Song of the Water) (St. Perf. Tr.) | 8 | I-10 | 13-9 |
| Caroling, Caroling (St. Voc.) | 6 | 458 | 21-22 |
| Caroling, Caroling (St. Perf. Tr.) | 6 | 458 | 21-23 |
| Cattle Call (St. Voc.) | 5 | 344 | 16-3 |
| Cattle Call (St. Perf. Tr.) | 5 | 344 | 16-4 |
| Celebrate! (St. Voc.) | 1 | 406 | 13-5 |
| Celebrate! (St. Perf. Tr.) | 1 | 406 | 13-6 |
| Cement Mixer (St. Voc.) | 4 | 102 | 5-14 |
| Cement Mixer (St. Perf. Tr.) | 4 | 102 | 5-15 |
| Certainly, Lord (St. Voc.) | 7 | I-13 | 13-12 |
| Certainly, Lord (St. Perf. Tr.) | 7 | I-13 | 13-13 |
| Cha yang wu (Rice Planting Song) (St. Voc.) | 1 | 90 | 3-5 |
| Cha yang wu (Rice Planting Song) (St. Perf. Tr.) | 1 | 90 | 3-7 |
| Chag Purim (Purim Song) (St. Voc.) | 1 | 438 | 14-14 |
| Chag Purim (Purim Song) (St. Perf. Tr.) | 1 | 438 | 14-16 |
| Chairs to Mend (St. Voc.) | 4 | 149 | 7-1 |
| Chairs to Mend (St. Perf. Tr.) | 4 | 149 | 7-2 |
| Chang (Elephant) (St. Voc.) | 1 | 156 | 5-1 |
| Chang (St. Perf. Tr.) | 1 | 156 | 5-3 |
| Chanukah, Chanukah (Joyous Chanukah) (St. Voc.) | 1 | 420 | 13-23 |
| Chanukah, Chanukah (Joyous Chanukah) (St. Perf. Tr.) | 1 | 420 | 13-25 |
| Chanukah Games (St. Voc.) | 3 | 389 | 13-24 |
| Chanukah Games (St. Perf. Tr.) | 3 | 389 | 13-25 |
| Chanukah Is Here! (St. Voc.) | 2 | 382 | 14-15 |
| Chanukah Is Here! (St. Perf. Tr.) | 2 | 382 | 14-16 |
| Chanukiyah li yesh (I Have a Chanukah Menorah) (St. Voc.) | 1 | 421 | 13-27 |
| Chanukiyah li yesh (I Have a Chanukah Menorah) (St. Perf. Tr.) | 1 | 421 | 13-29 |
| Chapel of Love (St. Voc.) | 7 | G-27 | 12-18 |
| Chapel of Love (St. Perf. Tr.) | 7 | G-27 | 12-19 |
| Charlie over the Water (St. Voc.) | 1 | 68 | 2-43 |
| Charlie over the Water (St. Perf. Tr.) | 1 | 68 | 2-44 |
| Chawe chidyo chem'chero (St. Voc.) | 2 | 297 | 11-2 |
| Chawe chidyo chem'chero (St. Perf. Tr.) | 2 | 297 | 11-3 |
| Che che koolay (St. Voc./Dance Perf. Tr.) | 2 | 266 | 9-32 |
| Che che koolay (St. Perf. Tr.) | 2 | 266 | 9-33 |
| Cheki, morena (Shake It!) (St. Voc.) | 2 | 180 | 7-1 |
| Cheki, morena (Shake It!) (St. Perf. Tr.) | 2 | 180 | 7-3 |
| Cheki, morena (Shake It!) (St. Voc.) | 7 | I-16 | 13-14 |
| Cheki, morena (Shake It!) (St. Perf. Tr.) | 7 | I-16 | 13-16 |
| Chiapanecas (The Girl from Chiapas) (St. Voc.) | 5 | 92 | 5-7 |
| Chiapanecas (The Girl from Chiapas) (St. Perf. Tr.) | 5 | 92 | 5-9 |
| Chicka Hanka (St. Voc.) | 2 | 211 | 8-1 |
| Chicka Hanka (St. Perf. Tr.) | 2 | 211 | 8-2 |
| Chicka Hanka (St. Voc.) | 8 | F-15 | 10-25 |
| Chicka Hanka (St. Perf. Tr.) | 8 | F-15 | 10-26 |
| Chicken on the Fence Post (St. Voc.) | 3 | 92 | 3-25 |
| Chicken on the Fence Post (St. Perf. Tr.) | 3 | 92 | 3-26 |
| Children, Go Where I Send Thee (St. Voc.) | 3 | 392 | 14-1 |
| Children, Go Where I Send Thee (St. Perf. Tr.) | 3 | 392 | 14-2 |
| Chippewa Lullaby (St. Voc.) | K | 181 | 6-37 |
| Chippewa Lullaby (St. Perf. Tr.) | K | 181 | 6-38 |
| Chirimbolo Game, The (El juego chirimbolo) (St. Voc.) | 2 | 54 | 2-28 |
| Cho'i hát bôi (The Theater Game) (St. Voc.) | 5 | 318 | 14-32 |
| Cho'i hát bôi (The Theater Game) (St. Perf. Tr.) | 5 | 318 | 14-34 |
| Chocolate (El chocolate ) (St. Voc.) | 1 | 380 | 12-8 |
| Choo Choo Ch'Boogie (St. Voc.) | 5 | 44 | 2-38 |
| Choo Choo Ch'Boogie (St. Perf. Tr.) | 5 | 44 | 2-39 |
| Chrismus a Come (St. Voc.) | 3 | 396 | 14-8 |
| Chrismus a Come (St. Perf. Tr.) | 3 | 396 | 14-9 |
| Christmas, Don't Be Late (The Chipmunk Song) (St. Voc.) | 2 | 386 | 14-27 |
| Christmas, Don't Be Late (The Chipmunk Song) (St. Perf. Tr.) | 2 | 386 | 14-28 |
| Christmas Season, The (Las Navidades) (St. Voc.) | 5 | 472 | 20-22 |
| Chuhwuht (St. Voc.) | 2 | 356 | 13-12 |
| Chuhwuht (St. Perf. Tr.) | 2 | 356 | 13-13 |
| Cielito lindo (Spanish) (St. Voc.) | 4 | 270 | 11-10 |
| Cielito lindo (English) (St. Voc.) | 4 | 270 | 11-11 |
| Cielito lindo (St. Perf. Tr.) | 4 | 270 | 11-12 |
| Cielito lindo (Spanish) (St. Voc.) | 7 | I-20 | 13-18 |
| Cielito lindo (English) (St. Voc.) | 7 | I-20 | 13-19 |
| Cielito lindo (St. Perf. Tr.) | 7 | I-20 | 13-20 |
| Cindy (St. Voc./Dance Perf. Tr.) | 4 | 384 | 16-22 |
| Cindy (St. Perf. Tr.) | 4 | 384 | 16-23 |
| Ciranda (A Ring of Roses) (St. Voc.) | 2 | 272 | 10-1 |
| Ciranda (A Ring of Roses) (St. Perf. Tr.) | 2 | 272 | 10-3 |
| Circle 'Round the Moon (from Reflections of Youth) (St. Voc.) | 4 | 403 | 17-13 |
| Circle 'Round the Moon (from Reflections of Youth) (St. Perf. Tr.) | 4 | 403 | 17-14 |
| Circle 'Round the Zero (St. Voc.) | K | 293 | 10-15 |
| Circle 'Round the Zero (St. Perf. Tr.) | K | 293 | 10-16 |
| Cirmos cica (Naughty Tabby Cat) (St. Voc.) | 1 | 130 | 4-19 |
| Cirmos cica (Naughty Tabby Cat) (St. Perf. Tr.) | 1 | 130 | 4-21 |
| City of Juaja, The (La ciudad de Juaja) (St. Voc.) | 5 | 58 | 3-25 |
| Clap, Wiggle and Stomp (St. Voc.) | K | 34 | 2-5 |
| Clap, Wiggle and Stomp (St. Perf. Tr.) | K | 34 | 2-6 |
| Clementine (St. Voc.) | 4 | 341 | 15-1 |
| Clementine (St. Perf. Tr.) | 4 | 341 | 15-2 |
| Close Your Eyes (Fais dodo) (St. Voc.) | K | 158 | 5-50 |
| Clouds (St. Voc.) | K | 254 | 9-1 |
| Clouds (St. Perf. Tr.) | K | 254 | 9-2 |

| Title | Gr. | Pg. | CD Track |
|---|---|---|---|
| Clouds of Gray (St. Voc.) | 2 | 56 | 2-32 |
| Clouds of Gray (St. Perf. Tr.) | 2 | 56 | 2-33 |
| Cobbler, The (El zapatero) (St. Voc.) | 1 | 298 | 9-30 |
| Cobbler, Cobbler (speech piece) (St. Voc.) | 1 | 299 | 9-33 |
| Coffee Grows on White Oak Trees (St. Voc.) | 3 | 168 | 6-8 |
| Coffee Grows on White Oak Trees (St. Perf. Tr.) | 3 | 168 | 6-9 |
| Cold December (El desembre congelat) (St. Voc.) | 5 | 473 | 20-26 |
| Colorado Trail (St. Voc.) | 5 | 276 | 12-36 |
| Colorado Trail (St. Perf. Tr.) | 5 | 276 | 12-37 |
| Come and Go With Me to That Land (St. Voc.) | 5 | 390 | 18-5 |
| Come and Go With Me to That Land (St. Perf. Tr.) | 5 | 390 | 18-6 |
| Come, Firefly (Hotaru Koi) (St. Voc.) | 1 | 356 | 11-14 |
| Come Running, You Shepherds (O Laufet, ihr Hirten) (St. Voc.) | 2 | 384 | 14-22 |
| Come to the Land (Artsa alinu) (St. Voc.) | 3 | 285 | 10-2 |
| Come, Ye Thankful People, Come (T.A.P.) | 5 | 459 | 19-25 |
| Come, Ye Thankful People, Come (St. Perf. Tr.) | 5 | 459 | 19-26 |
| Computer, The (St. Voc.) | 4 | 199 | 8-42 |
| Computer, The (St. Perf. Tr.) | 4 | 199 | 8-43 |
| Con el vito (Spanish) (St. Voc.) | 7 | G-15 | 12-5 |
| Con el vito (English) (St. Voc.) | 7 | G-15 | 12-6 |
| Con el vito (St. Perf. Tr.) | 7 | G-15 | 12-7 |
| Connemara Lullaby (St. Voc.) | 5 | 232 | 11-21 |
| Connemara Lullaby (St. Perf. Tr.) | 5 | 232 | 11-22 |
| Continents, The (speech piece) (St. Voc.) | 4 | 357 | 15-20 |
| Continents, The (speech piece) (St. Perf. Tr.) | 4 | 357 | 15-21 |
| Cookie (St. Voc.) | 2 | 172 | 6-31 |
| Cookie (St. Perf. Tr.) | 2 | 172 | 6-32 |
| Corn Grinding Song (St. Voc.) | K | 67 | 2-53 |
| Corn Grinding Song (St. Perf. Tr.) | K | 67 | 2-54 |
| Cornfields, The (Los maizales) (St. Voc.) | 1 | 296 | 9-25 |
| Corrido de Kansas (Kansas Corrido) (St. Voc.) | 4 | 274 | 11-17 |
| Corrido de Kansas (Kansas Corrido) (St. Perf. Tr.) | 4 | 274 | 11-19 |
| Corta la caña (Head for the Canefields) (St. Voc.) | 6 | 364 | 18-14 |
| Corta la caña (Head for the Canefields) (St. Perf. Tr.) | 6 | 364 | 18-16 |
| Costume Capers (St. Voc.) | 1 | 412 | 13-11 |
| Costume Capers (St. Perf. Tr.) | 1 | 412 | 13-12 |
| Cotton-Eye Joe (St. Voc.) | 4 | 288 | 12-9 |
| Cotton-Eye Joe (St. Perf. Tr.) | 4 | 288 | 12-10 |
| Counting Song (St. Voc.) | 1 | 253 | 8-9 |
| Counting Song (St. Perf. Tr.) | 1 | 253 | 8-10 |
| Counting-Out Rhyme (speech piece) (St. Voc.) | 1 | 357 | 11-17 |
| Counting-Out Rhyme (speech piece) (St. Perf. Tr.) | 1 | 357 | 11-18 |
| Cow's Woc Backward (St. Voc.) | 1 | 390 | 12-19 |
| Cow's Woc Backward (St. Perf. Tr.) | 1 | 390 | 12-20 |
| Cowboys' Christmas Ball (St. Voc.) | 6 | 239 | 12-15 |
| Cowboys' Christmas Ball (St. Perf. Tr.) | 6 | 239 | 12-16 |
| Cowherd and the Weaving Maid, The (Niu lang zhi nü) (St. Voc.) | 4 | 335 | 14-16 |
| Cowpoke, The (El payo) (St. Voc.) | 6 | 145 | 8-9 |
| Cradle Song (Canción de cuna) (St. Voc.) | 4 | 144 | 6-32 |
| Crawfish! (St. Voc.) | 2 | 86 | 3-41 |
| Crawfish! (St. Perf. Tr.) | 2 | 86 | 3-42 |
| Crescent Moon (Yüe liang wan wan) (St. Voc.) | 5 | 314 | 14-24 |
| Crocodile, The (St. Voc.) | 2 | 362 | 13-19 |
| Crocodile, The (St. Perf. Tr.) | 2 | 362 | 13-20 |
| Cuando pa' Chile me voy (Leavin' for Chile) (St. Voc.) | 6 | 376 | 19-11 |
| Cuando pa' Chile me voy (Leavin' for Chile) (St. Perf. Tr.) | 6 | 376 | 19-13 |
| Cuckoo, Cuckoo (St. Voc.) | 1 | 110 | 3-45 |
| Cuculí (St. Voc.) | K | 238 | 8-23 |
| Cuculí (St. Perf. Tr.) | K | 238 | 8-24 |
| Cumberland Gap (St. Voc.) | 4 | 138 | 6-22 |
| Cumberland Gap (St. Perf. Tr.) | 4 | 138 | 6-23 |
| Cycle Song of Life "The River Song" (St. Voc.) | 4 | 370 | 16-6 |
| Cycle Song of Life "The River Song" (St. Perf. Tr.) | 4 | 370 | 16-7 |
| Da pacem, Domine (Grant Us Peace) (St. Voc.) | 5 | 62 | 3-38 |
| Da pacem, Domine (Grant Us Peace) (St. Perf. Tr.) | 5 | 62 | 3-40 |
| Dance for the Nations (St. Voc.) | 6 | 122 | 7-15 |
| Dance for the Nations (St. Perf. Tr.) | 6 | 122 | 7-16 |
| Dancin' in the Street (St. Voc.) | 5 | 361 | 16-21 |
| Dancin' in the Street (St. Perf. Tr.) | 5 | 361 | 16-22 |
| Dancing (Tancovacka) (St. Voc.) | 4 | 230 | 9-40 |
| Day - O! (Banana Boat Loader's Song) (St. Voc.) | 5 | 18 | 1-28 |
| Day - O! (Banana Boat Loader's Song) (St. Perf. Tr.) | 5 | 18 | 1-29 |
| Dayenu (It Would Have Been Enough) (St. Voc.) | 4 | 439 | 19-1 |
| Dayenu (It Would Have Been Enough) (St. Perf. Tr.) | 4 | 439 | 19-3 |
| De colores (Spanish) (St. Voc.) | 5 | 90 | 5-1 |
| De colores (English) (St. Voc.) | 5 | 90 | 5-2 |
| De colores (St. Perf. Tr.) | 5 | 90 | 5-3 |
| De colores (Spanish) (St. Voc.) | 8 | I-14 | 13-13 |
| De colores (English) (St. Voc.) | 8 | I-14 | 13-14 |
| De colores (St. Perf. Tr.) | 8 | I-14 | 13-15 |
| Dearest Child (Niño querido) (St. Voc.) | 1 | 308 | 9-42 |
| Deau-deau, ti pitit maman (Sleep, My Little One) (St. Voc.) | 2 | 306 | 11-13 |
| Deau-deau, ti pitit maman (Sleep, My Little One) (St. Perf. Tr.) | 2 | 306 | 11-15 |
| Debajo el botón (Under the Button) (St. Voc.) | 1 | 210 | 6-43 |
| Debajo el botón (Under the Button) (St. Perf. Tr.) | 1 | 210 | 6-45 |
| Deck the Hall (St. Voc.) | 5 | 474 | 20-29 |
| Deck the Hall (St. Perf. Tr.) | 5 | 474 | 20-30 |
| Deep in the Heart of Texas (St. Voc.) | 4 | 22 | 1-33 |
| Deep in the Heart of Texas (St. Perf. Tr.) | 4 | 22 | 1-34 |
| Deep in the Heart of Texas (St. Voc.) | 8 | I-18 | 13-18 |
| Deep in the Heart of Texas (St. Perf. Tr.) | 8 | I-18 | 13-19 |
| Der sad to katte (Two Cats) (St. Voc.) | 2 | 300 | 11-5 |
| Der sad to katte (Two Cats) (St. Perf. Tr.) | 2 | 300 | 11-7 |
| Deux cocodries (Two Crocodiles) (St. Voc.) | 2 | 364 | 13-21 |
| Deux cocodries (Two Crocodiles) (St. Perf. Tr.) | 2 | 364 | 13-23 |
| Dewdrops (Hej pada pada) (St. Voc.) | 3 | 78 | 3-7 |
| Different Beat, A (St. Voc.) | 1 | 6 | 1-8 |
| Different Beat, A (St. Perf. Tr.) | 1 | 6 | 1-9 |
| Dinah (St. Voc.) | 2 | 120 | 4-39 |
| Dinah (St. Perf. Tr.) | 2 | 120 | 4-40 |
| Ding, Dong, Diggidiggidong (St. Voc.) | 3 | 14 | 1-15 |
| Ding, Dong, Diggidiggidong (St. Perf. Tr.) | 3 | 14 | 1-16 |
| Ding Dong! Merrily on High (St. Voc.) | 6 | 427 | 20-22 |
| Ding Dong! Merrily on High (St. Perf. Tr.) | 6 | 427 | 20-23 |
| Dinner Music (St. Voc.) | K | 70 | 3-1 |
| Dinner Music (St. Perf. Tr.) | K | 70 | 3-2 |
| Dinosaur Dance, The (St. Voc.) | 2 | 168 | 6-24 |
| Dinosaur Dance, The (St. Perf. Tr.) | 2 | 168 | 6-25 |
| Diou shou juan'er (Hide the Scarf) (St. Voc.) | 2 | 277 | 10-12 |
| Diou shou juan'er (Hide the Scarf) (St. Perf. Tr.) | 2 | 277 | 10-14 |
| Do, Lord (St. Voc.) | 3 | 164 | 6-1 |
| Do, Lord (St. Perf. Tr.) | 3 | 164 | 6-2 |
| Do, Re, Mi, Fa (St. Voc.) | 6 | 80 | 5-8 |
| Do, Re, Mi, Fa (St. Perf. Tr.) | 6 | 80 | 5-9 |
| Do Wah Diddy Diddy (St. Voc.) | 4 | 203 | 8-47 |
| Do Wah Diddy Diddy (St. Perf. Tr.) | 4 | 203 | 8-48 |
| Do Wah Diddy Diddy (St. Voc.) | 7 | F-21 | 11-6 |
| Do Wah Diddy Diddy (St. Perf. Tr.) | 7 | F-21 | 11-7 |

| Title | Gr. | Pg. | CD Track |
|---|---|---|---|
| Doctor Knickerbocker (speech piece) (St. Voc.) | 1 | 302 | 9-36 |
| Doctor Knickerbocker (speech piece) (St. Perf. Tr.) | 1 | 302 | 9-37 |
| Dok djampa (Jasmine Flower) (St. Voc.) | 8 | I-20 | 13-20 |
| Dok djampa (Jasmine Flower) (St. Perf. Tr.) | 8 | I-20 | 13-22 |
| Don Alfonso (Spanish) (St. Voc./Dance Perf. Tr.) | 5 | 177 | 9-2 |
| Don Alfonso (English) (St. Voc.) | 5 | 177 | 9-3 |
| Don Alfonso (St. Perf. Tr.) | 5 | 177 | 9-4 |
| Don Gato (Spanish) (St. Voc.) | 3 | 352 | 12-8 |
| Don Gato (English) (St. Voc.) | 3 | 352 | 12-9 |
| Don Gato (St. Perf. Tr.) | 3 | 352 | 12-10 |
| Don't Be Cruel (St. Voc.) | 6 | 255 | 13-13 |
| Don't Be Cruel (St. Perf. Tr.) | 6 | 255 | 13-14 |
| Don't Cry for Me, Argentina (St. Voc.) | 6 | 74 | 4-37 |
| Don't Dump Trash (St. Voc.) | 2 | 318 | 11-26 |
| Don't Dump Trash (St. Perf. Tr.) | 2 | 318 | 11-27 |
| Don't Let the Wind (St. Voc.) | 3 | 180 | 6-22 |
| Don't Let the Wind (St. Perf. Tr.) | 3 | 180 | 6-23 |
| Don't Let Your Watch Run Down (St. Voc.) | 3 | 166 | 6-3 |
| Don't Let Your Watch Run Down (St. Perf. Tr.) | 3 | 166 | 6-4 |
| Don't Want to Know You (Nie chcę cię znáć) (St. Voc.) | 3 | 314 | 11-4 |
| Don't You Hear the Lambs? (St. Voc.) | 5 | 97 | 5-19 |
| Don't You Hear the Lambs? (St. Perf. Tr.) | 5 | 97 | 5-20 |
| Dona nobis pacem (Grant Us Peace) (St. Voc.) | 6 | 125 | 7-17 |
| Dona nobis pacem (Grant Us Peace) (St. Perf. Tr.) | 6 | 125 | 7-18 |
| ¿Dónde lo escondí? (Where Did I Hide It?) (St. Voc.) | K | 209 | 7-21 |
| ¿Dónde lo escondí? (St. Perf. Tr.) | K | 209 | 7-23 |
| Doong gul ge ('Round and Around We Go) (St. Voc.) | 3 | 134 | 4-49 |
| Doong gul ge ('Round and Around We Go) (St. Perf. Tr.) | 3 | 134 | 4-51 |
| Doraji (Bluebells) (St. Voc.) | 4 | 174 | 7-36 |
| Doraji (Bluebells) (St. Perf. Tr.) | 4 | 174 | 7-38 |
| Dove That Flew Away, The (La paloma se fué ) (St. Voc.) | 6 | 51 | 3-23 |
| Down by the Bay (St. Voc.) | 1 | 18 | 1-29 |
| Down by the Bay (St. Perf. Tr.) | 1 | 18 | 1-30 |
| Down by the Riverside (St. Voc.) | 5 | 256 | 12-10 |
| Down by the Riverside (St. Perf. Tr.) | 5 | 256 | 12-11 |
| Down by the Riverside (T.A.P.) | 8 | G-8 | 11-21 |
| Down by the Riverside (St. Perf. Tr.) | 8 | G-8 | 11-22 |
| Down, Down, Baby (St. Voc.) | 2 | 32 | 1-41 |
| Down, Down, Baby (St. Perf. Tr.) | 2 | 32 | 1-42 |
| Down in the Meadow (St. Voc.) | K | 147 | 5-29 |
| Down in the Meadow (St. Perf. Tr.) | K | 147 | 5-30 |
| Down in the Valley (St. Voc.) | 6 | 375 | 19-9 |
| Down in the Valley (St. Perf. Tr.) | 6 | 375 | 19-10 |
| Down the Listening Lane (St. Voc.) | K | 192 | 7-3 |
| Down the Listening Lane (St. Perf. Tr.) | K | 192 | 7-4 |
| Down the Ohio (St. Voc.) | 2 | 60 | 2-42 |
| Down the Ohio (St. Perf. Tr.) | 2 | 60 | 2-43 |
| Downtown (St. Voc.) | 6 | 258 | 13-18 |
| Downtown (St. Perf. Tr.) | 6 | 258 | 13-19 |
| Draw Me a Bucket of Water (St. Voc./Dance Perf. Tr.) | 3 | 124 | 4-31 |
| Draw Me a Bucket of Water (St. Perf. Tr.) | 3 | 124 | 4-32 |
| Dreydl (S'vivon) (St. Voc.) | 6 | 452 | 21-16 |
| Drill, Ye Tarriers (St. Voc./Dance Perf. Tr.) | 5 | 54 | 3-16 |
| Drill, Ye Tarriers (St. Perf. Tr.) | 5 | 54 | 3-17 |
| Drum, The (El tambor) (St. Voc.) | 2 | 274 | 10-8 |
| Drum Song, The (Al tambor) (St. Voc.) | 3 | 270 | 9-17 |
| Dry Bones (St. Voc.) | 4 | 162 | 7-21 |
| Dry Bones (St. Perf. Tr.) | 4 | 162 | 7-22 |
| Dry Bones Come Skipping (St. Voc.) | 4 | 218 | 9-15 |
| Dry Bones Come Skipping (St. Perf. Tr.) | 4 | 218 | 9-16 |
| Duck Dance (St. Voc.) | 2 | 249 | 9-9 |
| Duck Dance (St. Perf. Tr.) | 2 | 249 | 9-10 |
| Duérmete, mi niño (Go to Sleep, My Baby) (St. Voc.) | 1 | 292 | 9-19 |
| Duérmete, mi niño (Go to Sleep, My Baby) (St. Perf. Tr.) | 1 | 292 | 9-21 |
| Dundai (Hebrew) (St. Voc.) | 5 | 106 | 5-34 |
| Dundai (English) (St. Voc.) | 5 | 106 | 5-35 |
| Dundai (St. Perf. Tr.) | 5 | 106 | 5-36 |
| Each of Us Is a Flower (St. Voc.) | 3 | 154 | 5-28 |
| Each of Us Is a Flower (St. Perf. Tr.) | 3 | 154 | 5-29 |
| Earth Is My Mother, The (St. Voc.) | 1 | 340 | 10-35 |
| Earth Is My Mother, The (St. Perf. Tr.) | 1 | 340 | 10-36 |
| Earth Is Our Mother, The (Traditional) (St. Voc.) | 4 | 358 | 15-22 |
| Earth Is Our Mother, The (Traditional) (St. Perf. Tr.) | 4 | 358 | 15-23 |
| Earth Is Our Mother, The (Contemporary) (St. Voc.) | 4 | 358 | 15-24 |
| Earth Is Our Mother, The (Contemporary) (St. Perf. Tr.) | 4 | 358 | 15-25 |
| Earth Is Our Mother, The (Traditional) (St. Voc.) | 8 | F-25 | 11-6 |
| Earth Is Our Mother, The (Traditional) (St. Perf. Tr.) | 8 | F-25 | 11-7 |
| Earth Is Our Mother, The (Contemporary) (St. Voc.) | 8 | F-25 | 11-8 |
| Earth Is Our Mother, The (Contemporary) (St. Perf. Tr.) | 8 | F-25 | 11-9 |
| Ee jer ha ba go (The Hungry Dog) (St. Voc.) | K | 133 | 5-10 |
| Ee jer ha ba go (The Hungry Dog) (St. Perf. Tr.) | K | 133 | 5-12 |
| Eensy Weensy Spider (St. Voc.) | K | 187 | 6-46 |
| Eensy Weensy Spider (St. Perf. Tr.) | K | 187 | 6-47 |
| Ég a gyertya (Candle Burning Bright) (St. Voc.) | K | 96 | 3-50 |
| Ég a gyertya (Candle Burning Bright) (St. Perf. Tr.) | K | 96 | 3-52 |
| Ego sum pauper (Nothing Do I Own) (St. Voc.) | 5 | 158 | 8-7 |
| Ego sum pauper (Nothing Do I Own) (St. Perf. Tr.) | 5 | 158 | 8-9 |
| Eh, cumpari! (Hey, Buddy!) (St. Voc.) | 4 | 68 | 3-37 |
| Eh, cumpari! (Hey, Buddy!) (St. Perf. Tr.) | 4 | 68 | 3-39 |
| Eight Little Candles (Ocho kandelikas) (St. Voc.) | 4 | 429 | 18-9 |
| Ein Männlein steht im Walde (A Little Man in the Woods) (St. Voc.) | 2 | 90 | 3-43 |
| Ein Männlein steht im Walde (A Little Man in the Woods) (St. Perf. Tr.) | 2 | 90 | 3-45 |
| Einini (St. Voc.) | 4 | 391 | 17-1 |
| Einini (St. Perf. Tr.) | 4 | 391 | 17-2 |
| El barquito (The Tiny Boat) (St. Voc.) | 3 | 358 | 12-15 |
| El barquito (The Tiny Boat) (St. Perf. Tr.) | 3 | 358 | 12-17 |
| El borrego (The Lamb) (St. Voc.) | 4 | 242 | 10-12 |
| El borrego (The Lamb) (St. Perf. Tr.) | 4 | 242 | 10-14 |
| El burrito enfermo (The Sick Little Donkey) (St. Voc.) | K | 271 | 9-23 |
| El burrito enfermo (The Sick Little Donkey) (St. Perf. Tr.) | K | 271 | 9-25 |
| El caracol (The Snail's Dance) (St. Voc.) | K | 130 | 5-6 |
| El caracol (The Snail's Dance) (St. Perf. Tr.) | K | 130 | 5-8 |
| El carite (The Kingfish) (St. Voc.) | 5 | 305 | 14-6 |
| El carite (The Kingfish) (St. Perf. Tr.) | 5 | 305 | 14-8 |
| El carnavalito humahuaqueño (The Little Humahuacan Carnival) (St. Voc.) | 6 | 482 | 22-21 |
| El carnavalito humahuaqueño (The Little Humahuacan Carnival) (St. Perf. Tr.) | 6 | 482 | 22-23 |
| El chocolate (chocolate) (St. Voc.) | 1 | 380 | 12-7 |
| El chocolate (chocolate) (St. Perf. Tr.) | 1 | 380 | 12-9 |
| El condor pasa (Spanish) (St. Voc.) | 6 | 46 | 3-16 |
| El condor pasa (English) (St. Voc.) | 6 | 46 | 3-17 |
| El condor pasa (St. Perf. Tr.) | 6 | 46 | 3-18 |
| El coquí (The Little Frog) (St. Voc.) | 2 | 292 | 10-36 |
| El coquí (The Little Frog) (St. Perf. Tr.) | 2 | 292 | 10-38 |
| El desembre congelat (Cold December) (St. Voc.) | 5 | 473 | 20-25 |
| El desembre congelat (Cold December) (St. Perf. Tr.) | 5 | 473 | 20-27 |
| El día de mamita (Mommy's Day) (St. Voc.) | K | 325 | 11-29 |
| El día de mamita (Mommy's Day) (St. Perf. Tr.) | K | 325 | 11-31 |
| El florón (The Flower) (St. Voc.) | 2 | 246 | 9-1 |

**Songs and Speech Pieces**

| Title | Gr. | Pg. | CD Track |
|---|---|---|---|
| El florón (The Flower) (St. Perf. Tr.) | 2 | 246 | 9-3 |
| El gallo pinto (The Painted Rooster) (St. Voc.) | 3 | 86 | 3-18 |
| El gallo pinto (The Painted Rooster) (St. Perf. Tr.) | 3 | 86 | 3-20 |
| El juego chirimbolo (The Chirimbolo Game) (St. Voc.) | 2 | 54 | 2-27 |
| El juego chirimbolo (The Chirimbolo Game) (St. Perf. Tr.) | 2 | 54 | 2-29 |
| El mes de abril (The Month of April) (St. Voc.) | 3 | 328 | 11-25 |
| El mes de abril (The Month of April) (St. Perf. Tr.) | 3 | 328 | 11-27 |
| El payo (The Cowpoke) (St. Voc.) | 6 | 145 | 8-8 |
| El payo (The Cowpoke) (St. Perf. Tr.) | 6 | 145 | 8-10 |
| El rabel (The Violin) (St. Voc.) | 3 | 362 | 12-20 |
| El rabel (The Violin) (St. Perf. Tr.) | 3 | 362 | 12-22 |
| El rancho grande (The Big Ranch) (St. Voc.) | 4 | 215 | 9-6 |
| El rancho grande (The Big Ranch) (St. Perf. Tr.) | 4 | 215 | 9-8 |
| El rancho grande (The Big Ranch) (St. Voc.) | 8 | I-22 | 13-24 |
| El rancho grande (The Big Ranch) (St. Perf. Tr.) | 8 | I-22 | 13-26 |
| El sapito (The Little Toad) (St. Voc.) | 3 | 336 | 11-37 |
| El sapito (The Little Toad) (St. Perf. Tr.) | 3 | 336 | 11-39 |
| El tambor (The Drum) (St. Voc.) | 2 | 274 | 10-7 |
| El tambor (The Drum) (St. Perf. Tr.) | 2 | 274 | 10-9 |
| El tren (The Train) (St. Voc.) | 2 | 260 | 9-21 |
| El tren (The Train) (St. Perf. Tr.) | 2 | 260 | 9-23 |
| El zapatero (The Cobbler) (St. Voc.) | 1 | 298 | 9-29 |
| El zapatero (The Cobbler) (St. Perf. Tr.) | 1 | 298 | 9-31 |
| Elegua (Spanish) (T.A.P.) | 7 | D-8 | 8-19 |
| Elegua (English) (T.A.P.) | 7 | D-8 | 8-20 |
| Elegua (St. Perf. Tr.) | 7 | D-8 | 8-21 |
| Elephant (Chang) (St. Voc.) | 1 | 156 | 5-2 |
| Elephant, An (Un elefante) (St. Voc.) | 2 | 160 | 6-13 |
| Éliza Kongo (French) (St. Voc.) | 5 | 14 | 1-23 |
| Éliza Kongo (English) (St. Voc.) | 5 | 14 | 1-24 |
| Éliza Kongo (St. Perf. Tr.) | 5 | 14 | 1-25 |
| En nuestra Tierra tan linda (On Our Beautiful Planet Earth) (St. Voc.) | 2 | 335 | 12-9 |
| En nuestra Tierra tan linda (On Our Beautiful Planet Earth) (St. Perf. Tr.) | 2 | 335 | 12-10 |
| Erdö, erdö de magos (In the Silent Forest) (St. Voc.) | 3 | 182 | 6-27 |
| Erdö, erdö de magos (In the Silent Forest) (St. Perf. Tr.) | 3 | 182 | 6-29 |
| Eres tú (Touch the Wind) (St. Voc.) | 6 | 473 | 22-10 |
| Eres tú (St. Perf. Tr.) | 6 | 473 | 22-12 |
| Erie Canal (St. Voc./Dance Perf. Tr.) | 5 | 262 | 12-18 |
| Erie Canal (St. Perf. Tr.) | 5 | 262 | 12-19 |
| Ev'ry Kind of Music (St. Voc.) | 2 | 226 | 8-14 |
| Ev'ry Kind of Music (St. Perf. Tr.) | 2 | 226 | 8-15 |
| Ev'ry Time I Feel the Spirit (St. Voc.) | 5 | 242 | 11-34 |
| Ev'ry Time I Feel the Spirit (St. Perf. Tr.) | 5 | 242 | 11-35 |
| Ev'rybody Loves Saturday Night (St. Voc.) | 7 | I-24 | 13-22 |
| Ev'rybody Loves Saturday Night (St. Perf. Tr.) | 7 | I-24 | 13-23 |
| Every Morning When I Wake Up (St. Voc.) | 2 | 320 | 11-28 |
| Every Morning When I Wake Up (St. Perf. Tr.) | 2 | 320 | 11-29 |
| Every Night When the Sun Goes In (St. Voc.) | 8 | I-28 | 14-1 |
| Every Night When the Sun Goes In (St. Perf. Tr.) | 8 | I-28 | 14-2 |
| Everybody Loves Saturday Night (St. Voc.) | 6 | 296 | 15-4 |
| Everybody Loves Saturday Night (St. Perf. Tr.) | 6 | 296 | 15-5 |
| Everybody Says (St. Voc.) | 1 | 288 | 9-15 |
| Everybody Says (St. Perf. Tr.) | 1 | 288 | 9-16 |
| Ezekiel Saw the Wheel (St. Voc.) | 6 | 379 | 19-16 |
| Ezekiel Saw the Wheel (St. Perf. Tr.) | 6 | 379 | 19-17 |
| Fais do do (Go to Sleep) (St. Voc.) | 6 | 403 | 20-1 |
| Fais do do (Go to Sleep) (St. Perf. Tr.) | 6 | 403 | 20-3 |
| Fais dodo (Close Your Eyes) (St. Voc.) | K | 158 | 5-49 |
| Fais dodo (Close Your Eyes) (St. Perf. Tr.) | K | 158 | 5-51 |
| Faith of the Heart (St. Voc.) | 8 | G-3 | 11-18 |
| Faith of the Heart (St. Perf. Tr.) | 8 | G-3 | 11-19 |
| Falling Rain (St. Voc.) | 2 | 328 | 12-1 |
| Falling Rain (St. Perf. Tr.) | 2 | 328 | 12-2 |
| Families (St. Voc.) | 1 | 282 | 9-10 |
| Families (St. Perf. Tr.) | 1 | 282 | 9-11 |
| Family Tree (St. Voc.) | 3 | 72 | 2-53 |
| Family Tree (St. Perf. Tr.) | 3 | 72 | 2-54 |
| Farewell (Haere) | 2 | 285 | 10-28 |
| Farewell to Tarwathie (St. Voc.) | 6 | 43 | 3-1 |
| Farewell to Tarwathie (St. Perf. Tr.) | 6 | 43 | 3-2 |
| Farewell to the Warriors (St. Voc.) | 4 | 284 | 12-3 |
| Farewell to the Warriors (St. Perf. Tr.) | 4 | 284 | 12-4 |
| Farmer in the Dell, The (St. Voc.) | K | 232 | 8-13 |
| Farmer in the Dell, The (St. Perf. Tr.) | K | 232 | 8-14 |
| Farmer's Dairy Key, The (St. Voc.) | 2 | 182 | 7-6 |
| Farmer's Dairy Key, The (St. Perf. Tr.) | 2 | 182 | 7-7 |
| Feliz Navidad (Merry Christmas) (St. Voc.) | 7 | I-28 | 13-24 |
| Feliz Navidad (Merry Christmas) (St. Perf. Tr.) | 7 | I-28 | 13-25 |
| Feng yang hua gu (Feng Yang Song) (St. Voc.) | 4 | 313 | 13-20 |
| Feng yang hua gu (Feng Yang Song) (St. Perf. Tr.) | 4 | 313 | 13-22 |
| Feng Yang Song (Feng yang hua gu) (St. Voc.) | 4 | 313 | 13-21 |
| Fiddler on the Roof (from Fiddler on the Roof) (St. Voc.) | 7 | E-5 | 9-19 |
| Fiddler on the Roof (from Fiddler on the Roof) (St. Perf. Tr.) | 7 | E-5 | 9-20 |
| Fifty Nifty United States (St. Voc.) | 5 | 251 | 12-8 |
| Fifty Nifty United States (St. Perf. Tr.) | 5 | 251 | 12-9 |
| Five Little Chickadees (St. Voc.) | K | 179 | 6-31 |
| Five Little Chickadees (St. Perf. Tr.) | K | 179 | 6-32 |
| Five Little Snowmen (St. Voc.) | K | 313 | 11-9 |
| Five Little Snowmen (St. Perf. Tr.) | K | 313 | 11-10 |
| Flat Foot Floogee, The (St. Voc.) | 3 | 160 | 5-34 |
| Flat Foot Floogee, The (St. Perf. Tr.) | 3 | 160 | 5-35 |
| Flip, Flop and Fly (St. Voc.) | 7 | I-32 | 13-27 |
| Flip, Flop and Fly (St. Perf. Tr.) | 7 | I-32 | 13-28 |
| Flower, The (El florón) (St. Voc.) | 2 | 246 | 9-2 |
| Fly and the Bumblebee, The (Fiddle-De-Dee) (St. Voc.) | 1 | 384 | 12-14 |
| Fly and the Bumblebee, The (Fiddle-De-Dee) (St. Perf. Tr.) | 1 | 384 | 12-15 |
| Fly By, Fly By (Perná, perná, i melissa) (St. Voc.) | K | 264 | 9-14 |
| Follow the Drinkin' Gourd (St. Voc.) | 4 | 266 | 11-5 |
| Follow the Drinkin' Gourd (St. Perf. Tr.) | 4 | 266 | 11-6 |
| For Children Safe and Strong (St. Voc.) | 5 | 484 | 21-12 |
| For Children Safe and Strong (St. Perf. Tr.) | 5 | 484 | 21-13 |
| For the Beauty of the Earth (St. Voc.) | 4 | 356 | 15-18 |
| For the Beauty of the Earth (St. Perf. Tr.) | 4 | 356 | 15-19 |
| Four in a Boat (St. Voc.) | 2 | 46 | 2-13 |
| Four in a Boat (St. Perf. Tr.) | 2 | 46 | 2-14 |
| Four Strong Winds (from Song to a Seagull) (St. Voc.) | 6 | 170 | 9-28 |
| Four Strong Winds (from Song to a Seagull) (St. Perf. Tr.) | 6 | 170 | 9-29 |
| Four White Horses (St. Voc.) | 3 | 304 | 10-34 |
| Four White Horses (St. Perf. Tr.) | 3 | 304 | 10-35 |
| Free at Last (St. Voc.) | 2 | 396 | 14-40 |
| Free at Last (St. Perf. Tr.) | 2 | 396 | 14-41 |
| Free at Last (St. Voc.) | 6 | 468 | 22-5 |
| Free at Last (St. Perf. Tr.) | 6 | 468 | 22-6 |
| Freedom Is Coming (St. Voc.) | 5 | 415 | 18-25 |
| Freedom Is Coming (St. Perf. Tr.) | 5 | 415 | 18-26 |
| Freight Train (St. Voc.) | 1 | 46 | 2-15 |
| Freight Train (St. Perf. Tr.) | 1 | 46 | 2-16 |
| Frère Jacques (Are You Sleeping?) (St. Voc.) | 2 | 125 | 5-1 |

| Title | Gr. | Pg. | CD Track |
|---|---|---|---|
| Frère Jacques (Are You Sleeping?) (St. Perf. Tr.) | 2 | 125 | 5-3 |
| Friend of Mine (St. Voc.) | 1 | 310 | 9-46 |
| Friend of Mine (St. Perf. Tr.) | 1 | 310 | 9-47 |
| Friends Today (St. Voc.) | 7 | D-12 | 8-29 |
| Friends Today (St. Perf. Tr.) | 7 | D-12 | 8-30 |
| Frog in the Millpond (St. Voc.) | 2 | 44 | 2-8 |
| Frog in the Millpond (St. Perf. Tr.) | 2 | 44 | 2-9 |
| Frog Music (St. Voc.) | 4 | 200 | 8-45 |
| Frog Music (St. Perf. Tr.) | 4 | 200 | 8-46 |
| Frog Song, The (Kaeru no uta) (St. Voc.) | K | 183 | 6-41 |
| Frogs (Shu ha mo) (St. Voc.) | 3 | 276 | 9-31 |
| From Sea to Shining Sea (St. Voc.) | 2 | 342 | 12-19 |
| From Sea to Shining Sea (St. Perf. Tr.) | 2 | 342 | 12-20 |
| Fruit (Perot) (St. Voc.) | 2 | 378 | 14-10 |
| Funwa alafia (Welcome, My Friends) (St. Voc.) | 5 | 32 | 2-19 |
| Funwa alafia (Welcome, My Friends) (St. Perf. Tr.) | 5 | 32 | 2-21 |
| Fuzzy Caterpillar (St. Voc.) | K | 102 | 4-2 |
| Fuzzy Caterpillar (St. Perf. Tr.) | K | 102 | 4-3 |
| Gakavik (The Partridge) (St. Voc.) | 4 | 14 | 1-17 |
| Gakavik (The Partridge) (St. Perf. Tr.) | 4 | 14 | 1-19 |
| Garden Lullaby (Hwa yuan li-de young wa wa) (St. Voc.) | 3 | 102 | 4-2 |
| Gaudeamus igitur (Hail to Youth and Hail to Love) (St. Voc.) | 8 | C-20 | 6-2 |
| Gaudeamus igitur (Hail to Youth and Hail to Love) (St. Perf. Tr.) | 8 | C-20 | 6-4 |
| Geef jij mij die schoen (Pass This Shoe) (St. Voc.) | 1 | 126 | 4-12 |
| Geef jij mij die schoen (Pass This Shoe) (St. Perf. Tr.) | 1 | 126 | 4-14 |
| Get on Board (St. Voc.) | K | 89 | 3-33 |
| Get on Board (St. Perf. Tr.) | K | 89 | 3-34 |
| Get on Your Feet (St. Voc.) | 5 | 6 | 1-4 |
| Get on Your Feet (St. Perf. Tr.) | 5 | 6 | 1-5 |
| Gift to Share, A (The Gift to Be Me) (St. Voc.) | 6 | 393 | 19-24 |
| Gift to Share, A (The Gift to Be Me) (St. Perf. Tr.) | 6 | 393 | 19-25 |
| Girl from Chiapas, The (Chiapancecas) (St. Voc.) | 5 | 92 | 5-8 |
| Give a Little Love (St. Voc.) | 6 | 140 | 8-5 |
| Give a Little Love (St. Perf. Tr.) | 6 | 140 | 8-6 |
| Give My Regards to Broadway (from ) (St. Voc.) | 6 | 39 | 2-34 |
| Give My Regards to Broadway (from ) (St. Perf. Tr.) | 6 | 39 | 2-35 |
| Glad to Have a Friend Like You (St. Voc.) | 2 | 228 | 8-16 |
| Glad to Have a Friend Like You (St. Perf. Tr.) | 2 | 228 | 8-17 |
| Glendy Burke, The (St. Voc.) | 4 | 262 | 11-1 |
| Glendy Burke, The (St. Perf. Tr.) | 4 | 262 | 11-2 |
| Gloria, Gloria (St. Voc.) | 6 | 459 | 21-24 |
| Gloria, Gloria (St. Perf. Tr.) | 6 | 459 | 21-25 |
| Glory, Glory, Hallelujah (St. Voc.) | 6 | 52 | 3-27 |
| Glory, Glory, Hallelujah (St. Perf. Tr.) | 6 | 52 | 3-28 |
| Go Around the Cat's Eye (O ma washi) (St. Voc.) | K | 13 | 1-17 |
| Go Around the Corn, Sally (St. Voc.) | 2 | 12 | 1-8 |
| Go Around the Corn, Sally (St. Perf. Tr.) | 2 | 12 | 1-9 |
| Go Down, Moses (St. Voc.) | 5 | 190 | 9-26 |
| Go Down, Moses (St. Perf. Tr.) | 5 | 190 | 9-27 |
| Go, My Son (St. Voc.) | 6 | 188 | 10-24 |
| Go, My Son (St. Perf. Tr.) | 6 | 188 | 10-25 |
| Go to Sleep (Fais do do) (St. Voc.) | 6 | 403 | 20-2 |
| Go to Sleep, My Baby (Duérmete, mi niño) (St. Voc.) | 1 | 292 | 9-20 |
| Go Two by Two (Ambos a dos) (St. Voc.) | 3 | 20 | 1-32 |
| Go With the Music and Sing (St. Voc.) | 3 | 376 | 13-9 |
| Go With the Music and Sing (St. Perf. Tr.) | 3 | 376 | 13-10 |
| God Bless America (St. Voc.) | 5 | 4 | 1-2 |
| God Bless America (St. Perf. Tr.) | 5 | 4 | 1-3 |
| God Bless the Child (St. Voc.) | 7 | B-27 | 4-5 |

| Title | Gr. | Pg. | CD Track |
|---|---|---|---|
| God Bless the Child (St. Perf. Tr.) | 7 | B-27 | 4-6 |
| God Bless the Grass (St. Voc.) | 8 | F-13 | 10-22 |
| God Bless the Grass (St. Voc.) | 8 | F-13 | 10-23 |
| God Bless the U.S.A. (T.A.P.) | 8 | G-37 | 12-15 |
| God Bless the U.S.A. (St. Perf. Tr.) | 8 | G-37 | 12-16 |
| Goin' Down the Road Feelin' Bad (St. Voc.) | 5 | 282 | 13-8 |
| Goin' Down the Road Feelin' Bad (St. Perf. Tr.) | 5 | 282 | 13-9 |
| Goin' Down the Road Feelin' Bad (St. Voc.) | 7 | F-13 | 10-30 |
| Goin' Down the Road Feelin' Bad (St. Perf. Tr.) | 7 | F-13 | 10-31 |
| Goin' to Boston (St. Voc.) | 6 | 433 | 20-24 |
| Goin' to Boston (St. Perf. Tr.) | 6 | 433 | 20-25 |
| Goin' to the Fair (St. Voc.) | K | 156 | 5-45 |
| Goin' to the Fair (St. Perf. Tr.) | K | 156 | 5-46 |
| Going on a Picnic (St. Voc.) | K | 190 | 7-1 |
| Going on a Picnic (St. Perf. Tr.) | K | 190 | 7-2 |
| Going 'Round (Hashewie) (St. Voc.) | 4 | 63 | 3-22 |
| Going to the Zoo (St. Voc.) | K | 216 | 7-36 |
| Going to the Zoo (St. Perf. Tr.) | K | 216 | 7-37 |
| Going upon the Mountain (St. Voc.) | 6 | 105 | 6-21 |
| Going upon the Mountain (St. Perf. Tr.) | 6 | 105 | 6-22 |
| Golden Ring Around Susan Girl (St. Voc.) | 3 | 16 | 1-23 |
| Golden Ring Around Susan Girl (St. Perf. Tr.) | 3 | 16 | 1-24 |
| Gonna Build a Mountain (from Stop the World-I Want to Get Off) (St. Voc.) | 6 | 21 | 2-6 |
| Gonna Build a Mountain (from Stop the World-I Want to Get Offb) (St. Perf. Tr.) | 6 | 21 | 2-7 |
| Gonna Have a Good Time (St. Voc.) | 2 | 4 | 1-1 |
| Gonna Have a Good Time (St. Perf. Tr.) | 2 | 4 | 1-2 |
| Gonna Ride Up in the Chariot (St. Voc.) | 4 | 20 | 1-28 |
| Gonna Ride Up in the Chariot (St. Perf. Tr.) | 4 | 20 | 1-29 |
| Good King Wenceslas (St. Voc.) | 6 | 460 | 21-27 |
| Good King Wenceslas (St. Perf. Tr.) | 6 | 460 | 21-28 |
| Good Mornin', Blues (St. Voc.) | 2 | 52 | 2-24 |
| Good Mornin', Blues (St. Perf. Tr.) | 2 | 52 | 2-25 |
| Good Mornin', Blues (St. Voc.) | 5 | 224 | 11-7 |
| Good Mornin', Blues (St. Perf. Tr.) | 5 | 224 | 11-8 |
| Good Morning! (Buenos días) (St. Voc.) | 1 | 13 | 1-20 |
| Good Morning (St. Voc.) | 3 | 192 | 7-1 |
| Good Morning (St. Perf. Tr.) | 3 | 192 | 7-2 |
| Good Old Happy Song, A (St. Voc.) | K | 201 | 7-12 |
| Good Old Happy Song, A (St. Perf. Tr.) | K | 201 | 7-13 |
| Goodbye, Julie (St. Voc.) | 1 | 334 | 10-29 |
| Goodbye, Julie (St. Perf. Tr.) | 1 | 334 | 10-30 |
| Goodbye, Julie (St. Voc.) | 8 | E-2 | 9-8 |
| Goodbye, Julie (St. Perf. Tr.) | 8 | E-2 | 9-9 |
| Goodbye, My Friends (Adiós, amigos) (St. Voc.) | 6 | 57 | 4-2 |
| Gospel Train, The (St. Voc.) | 6 | 398 | 19-26 |
| Gospel Train, The (St. Perf. Tr.) | 6 | 398 | 19-27 |
| Grant Us Peace (Da pacem, domine) (St. Voc.) | 5 | 62 | 3-39 |
| Grass Game (St. Voc.) | 1 | 371 | 11-43 |
| Grass Game (St. Perf. Tr.) | 1 | 371 | 11-44 |
| Great Big House (St. Voc.) | 2 | 204 | 7-42 |
| Great Big House (St. Perf. Tr.) | 2 | 204 | 7-43 |
| Great Big Stars (St. Voc.) | 1 | 60 | 2-35 |
| Great Big Stars (St. Perf. Tr.) | 1 | 60 | 2-36 |
| Great Day (St. Voc.) | 3 | 58 | 2-35 |
| Great Day (St. Perf. Tr.) | 3 | 58 | 2-36 |
| Green Corn Song (St. Voc.) | 5 | 462 | 20-5 |
| Green Corn Song (St. Perf. Tr.) | 5 | 462 | 20-6 |
| Green, Green Grass of Home (St. Voc.) | 6 | 248 | 13-7 |
| Green, Green Grass of Home (St. Perf. Tr.) | 6 | 248 | 13-8 |

| Title | Gr. | Pg. | CD Track |
|---|---|---|---|
| Green, Green, Rocky (St. Voc.) | 1 | 321 | 10-13 |
| Green, Green, Rocky (St. Perf. Tr.) | 1 | 321 | 10-14 |
| Greenland Whale Fishery, The (St. Voc.) | 5 | 230 | 11-16 |
| Greenland Whale Fishery, The (St. Perf. Tr.) | 5 | 230 | 11-17 |
| Greensleeves (St. Voc.) | 6 | 49 | 3-20 |
| Greensleeves (St. Perf. Tr.) | 6 | 49 | 3-21 |
| Greetings (speech piece) (St. Voc.) | 3 | 316 | 11-9 |
| Greetings (speech piece) (St. Perf. Tr.) | 3 | 316 | 11-10 |
| Grizzly Bear (St. Voc.) | K | 33 | 2-3 |
| Grizzly Bear (St. Perf. Tr.) | K | 33 | 2-4 |
| Groundhog Blues, The (St. Voc.) | 3 | 122 | 4-29 |
| Groundhog Blues, The (St. Perf. Tr.) | 3 | 122 | 4-30 |
| Guantanamera (Spanish) (St. Voc.) | 8 | I-32 | 14-4 |
| Guantanamera (English) (St. Voc.) | 8 | I-32 | 14-5 |
| Guantanamera (St. Perf. Tr.) | 8 | I-32 | 14-6 |
| Gypsy in the Moonlight (St. Voc.) | 3 | 12 | 1-8 |
| Gypsy in the Moonlight (St. Perf. Tr.) | 3 | 12 | 1-9 |
| Ha'kyo jong (School Bell Sounding) (St. Voc.) | 2 | 135 | 5-22 |
| Ha'kyo jong (School Bell Sounding) (St. Perf. Tr.) | 2 | 135 | 5-24 |
| Habari Gani (St. Voc.) | 3 | 404 | 14-24 |
| Habari Gani (St. Perf. Tr.) | 3 | 404 | 14-25 |
| Habemos llegado (We Have Arrived) (St. Voc.) | 6 | 174 | 10-1 |
| Habemos llegado (We Have Arrived) (St. Perf. Tr.) | 6 | 174 | 10-3 |
| Had to Get Up This Mornin' Soon (St. Voc.) | 3 | 114 | 4-20 |
| Had to Get Up This Mornin' Soon (St. Perf. Tr.) | 3 | 114 | 4-21 |
| Haere (Farewell) (St. Voc.) | 2 | 285 | 10-27 |
| Haere (Farewell) (St. Perf. Tr.) | 2 | 285 | 10-29 |
| Hail to Youth and Hail to Love (Gaudeamus Igitur) (St. Voc.) | 8 | C-20 | 6-3 |
| Haliwa-Saponi Canoe Song (St. Voc.) | 5 | 302 | 14-3 |
| Haliwa-Saponi Canoe Song (St. Perf. Tr.) | 5 | 302 | 14-4 |
| Halloween Is a Very Unusual Night (St. Voc.) | 3 | 382 | 13-18 |
| Halloween Is a Very Unusual Night (St. Perf. Tr.) | 3 | 382 | 13-19 |
| Halloween Song (St. Voc.) | K | 309 | 11-3 |
| Halloween Song (St. Perf. Tr.) | K | 309 | 11-4 |
| Hama chi dori (Plovers) (St. Voc.) | 3 | 330 | 11-30 |
| Hama chi dori (Plovers) (St. Perf. Tr.) | 3 | 330 | 11-32 |
| Hambone (St. Voc.) | 1 | 202 | 6-34 |
| Hambone (St. Perf. Tr.) | 1 | 202 | 6-35 |
| Hambone (St. Voc.) | 7 | D-3 | 8-16 |
| Hambone (St. Perf. Tr.) | 7 | D-3 | 8-17 |
| Hand in Hand-A Song for Peace (Shir l'shalom) (St. Voc.) | 4 | 419 | 17-24 |
| Hanuka, Hanuka (Ladino) (St. Voc.) | 3 | 390 | 13-26 |
| Hanuka, Hanuka (English) (St. Voc.) | 3 | 390 | 13-27 |
| Hanuka, Hanuka (St. Perf. Tr.) | 3 | 390 | 13-28 |
| Hanuka, Hanuka (Ladino) (St. Voc.) | 8 | I-36 | 14-9 |
| Hanuka, Hanuka (English) (St. Voc.) | 8 | I-36 | 14-10 |
| Hanuka, Hanuka (St. Perf. Tr.) | 8 | I-36 | 14-11 |
| Happy Birthday (Mubärak) (St. Voc.) | 3 | 282 | 9-41 |
| Happy Birthday to You (St. Voc.) | K | 305 | 10-29 |
| Happy Birthday to You (St. Perf. Tr.) | K | 305 | 10-30 |
| Happy Days Are Here Again (St. Voc.) | 5 | 284 | 13-11 |
| Happy Days Are Here Again (St. Perf. Tr.) | 5 | 284 | 13-12 |
| Happy Feet (St. Voc.) | 2 | 252 | 9-15 |
| Happy Feet (St. Perf. Tr.) | 2 | 252 | 9-16 |
| Happy Wanderer, The (St. Voc.) | 4 | 89 | 4-32 |
| Happy Wanderer, The (St. Perf. Tr.) | 4 | 89 | 4-33 |
| Harambee (St. Voc.) | 4 | 434 | 18-20 |
| Harambee (St. Perf. Tr.) | 4 | 434 | 18-21 |
| Harrison Town (St. Voc.) | 6 | 97 | 6-9 |
| Harrison Town (St. Perf. Tr.) | 6 | 97 | 6-10 |
| Haru ga kita (Springtime Has Come) (St. Voc.) | 2 | 401 | 15-5 |
| Haru ga kita (Springtime Has Come) (St. Perf. Tr.) | 2 | 401 | 15-7 |
| Hashewie (Going 'Round) (St. Voc.) | 4 | 63 | 3-21 |
| Hashewie (Going 'Round) (St. Perf. Tr.) | 4 | 63 | 3-23 |
| Hashkediya (Tu b'Shvat Is Here) (St. Voc.) | 3 | 206 | 7-17 |
| Hashkediya (Tu b'Shvat Is Here) (St. Perf. Tr.) | 3 | 206 | 7-19 |
| Hato popo (Pigeons) (St. Voc.) | 1 | 186 | 6-13 |
| Hato popo (St. Perf. Tr.) | 1 | 186 | 6-15 |
| Haul Away, Joe (St. Voc.) | 4 | 13 | 1-15 |
| Haul Away, Joe (St. Perf. Tr.) | 4 | 13 | 1-16 |
| Hava nagila (St. Voc./Dance Perf. Tr.) | 6 | 153 | 8-23 |
| Hava nagila (St. Perf. Tr.) | 6 | 153 | 8-24 |
| Hava nashira (Sing and Be Joyful) (St. Voc.) | 6 | 82 | 5-16 |
| He's Got the Whole World in His Hands (St. Voc.) | 3 | 230 | 7-56 |
| He's Got the Whole World in His Hands (St. Perf. Tr.) | 3 | 230 | 7-57 |
| He's Got the Whole World in His Hands (St. Voc.) | 7 | I-36 | 13-29 |
| He's Got the Whole World in His Hands (St. Perf. Tr.) | 7 | I-36 | 13-30 |
| Head for the Canefields (Corta la caña) (St. Voc.) | 6 | 364 | 18-15 |
| Head, Shoulders, Baby (St. Voc.) | 1 | 82 | 2-67 |
| Head, Shoulders, Baby (St. Perf. Tr.) | 1 | 82 | 2-68 |
| Hear the Rooster Crowing (Kum bachur atzel) (St. Voc.) | 3 | 138 | 5-2 |
| Heave-Ho/Going, Going, Gone/The Snow (speech piece) (St. Voc.) | 4 | 182 | 8-15 |
| Heave-Ho/Going, Going, Gone/The Snow (speech piece) (St. Perf. Tr.) | 4 | 182 | 8-16 |
| Heigh-Ho (from Snow White and the Seven Dwarfs) (St. Voc.) | 2 | 7 | 1-3 |
| Heigh-Ho (from Snow White and the Seven Dwarfs) (St. Perf. Tr.) | 2 | 7 | 1-4 |
| Hej pada pada (Dewdrops) (St. Voc.) | 3 | 78 | 3-6 |
| Hej pada pada (Dewdrops) (St. Perf. Tr.) | 3 | 78 | 3-8 |
| Hello! (St. Voc.) | 2 | 262 | 9-25 |
| Hello! (St. Perf. Tr.) | 2 | 262 | 9-26 |
| Hello, My Friends (Bonjour, mes amis) (St. Voc.) | 1 | 316 | 10-7 |
| Hello Song, The (Sawatdee tuh jah) (St. Voc.) | 2 | 265 | 9-29 |
| Hello, There! (St. Voc.) | K | 6 | 1-6 |
| Hello, There! (St. Perf. Tr.) | K | 6 | 1-7 |
| Hello to All the Children of the World (St. Voc.) | 3 | 4 | 1-1 |
| Hello to All the Children of the World (St. Perf. Tr.) | 3 | 4 | 1-2 |
| Here Comes Valerie (St. Voc.) | 1 | 32 | 1-51 |
| Here Comes Valerie (St. Perf. Tr.) | 1 | 32 | 1-52 |
| Here I Go! (St. Voc.) | K | 73 | 3-4 |
| Here I Go! (St. Perf. Tr.) | K | 73 | 3-5 |
| Heri za kwanzaa (Happy Kwanzaa) (St. Voc.) | 5 | 476 | 20-32 |
| Heri za kwanzaa (Happy Kwanzaa) (St. Perf. Tr.) | 5 | 476 | 20-33 |
| Hevenu shalom aleichem (We Come to Greet You In Peace) (St. Voc.) | 3 | 378 | 13-11 |
| Hevenu shalom aleichem (We Come to Greet You in Peace) (St. Perf. Tr.) | 3 | 378 | 13-13 |
| Hey, Buddy! (Eh, cumpari!) (St. Voc.) | 4 | 68 | 3-38 |
| Hey, Diddle, Diddle (St. Voc.) | K | 246 | 8-33 |
| Hey, Diddle, Diddle (St. Perf. Tr.) | K | 247 | 8-34 |
| Hey, Hey, Look at Me (St. Voc.) | 1 | 70 | 2-49 |
| Hey, Hey, Look at Me (St. Perf. Tr.) | 1 | 70 | 2-50 |
| Hey, Ho! Nobody Home (St. Voc.) | 6 | 28 | 2-22 |
| Hey, Ho! Nobody Home (St. Perf. Tr.) | 6 | 28 | 2-23 |
| Hey, m'tswala (St. Voc.) | 4 | 79 | 4-19 |
| Hey, m'tswala (St. Perf. Tr.) | 4 | 79 | 4-20 |
| Heyoo! Heyoo! (¡Jeu! ¡Jeu!) (St. Voc.) | 1 | 216 | 7-7 |

| Title | Gr. | Pg. | CD Track |
|---|---|---|---|
| Hi Heidi Ho (St. Voc.) | 1 | 394 | 12-23 |
| Hi Heidi Ho (St. Perf. Tr.) | 1 | 394 | 12-24 |
| Hi-Dee-Roon (St. Voc.) | K | 10 | 1-10 |
| Hi-Dee-Roon (St. Perf. Tr.) | K | 10 | 1-11 |
| Hickory, Dickory, Dock (so-la-so-mi Version) (St. Voc.) | 1 | 226 | 7-16 |
| Hickory, Dickory, Dock (so-la-so-mi Version) (St. Perf. Tr.) | 1 | 226 | 7-17 |
| Hide the Scarf (Leak kanseng) (St. Voc.) | 1 | 156 | 5-6 |
| Hide the Scarf (Diou shou juan'er) (St. Voc.) | 2 | 277 | 10-13 |
| Higglety, Pigglety, Pop! (St. Voc.) | K | 22 | 1-31 |
| Higglety, Pigglety, Pop! (St. Perf. Tr.) | K | 22 | 1-32 |
| Himmel und Erde (Music Alone Shall Live) (St. Voc.) | 5 | 94 | 5-11 |
| Himmel und Erde (Music Alone Shall Live) (St. Perf. Tr.) | 5 | 94 | 5-13 |
| Hine mah tov (St. Voc.) | 5 | 431 | 19-6 |
| Hine mah tov (St. Perf. Tr.) | 5 | 431 | 19-7 |
| Hit Me with a Hot Note and Watch Me Bounce (St. Voc.) | 6 | 112 | 6-29 |
| Hit Me with a Hot Note and Watch Me Bounce (St. Perf. Tr.) | 6 | 112 | 6-30 |
| Hitotsu toya (Temple Bells) (St. Voc.) | 5 | 478 | 21-1 |
| Hitotsu toya (Temple Bells) (St. Perf. Tr.) | 5 | 478 | 21-3 |
| Hokey Pokey (St. Voc.) | K | 296 | 10-19 |
| Hokey Pokey (St. Perf. Tr.) | K | 296 | 10-20 |
| Home from School (Hui jia qü) (St. Voc.) | 2 | 158 | 6-6 |
| Home on the Range (St. Voc.) | 5 | 69 | 4-11 |
| Home on the Range (St. Perf. Tr.) | 5 | 69 | 4-12 |
| Home on the Range/Live in the City (St. Voc.) | 5 | 71 | 4-15 |
| Home on the Range/Live in the City (St. Perf. Tr.) | 5 | 71 | 4-16 |
| Honeybee Song, The (St. Voc.) | 1 | 358 | 11-19 |
| Honeybee Song, The (St. Perf. Tr.) | 1 | 358 | 11-20 |
| Hop Up, My Ladies (St. Voc.) | 3 | 142 | 5-11 |
| Hop Up, My Ladies (St. Perf. Tr.) | 3 | 142 | 5-12 |
| Hosanna, Me Build a House (St. Voc.) | 5 | 132 | 6-26 |
| Hosanna, Me Build a House (St. Perf. Tr.) | 5 | 132 | 6-27 |
| Hosisipa (St. Voc.) | 3 | 70 | 2-48 |
| Hosisipa (St. Perf. Tr.) | 3 | 70 | 2-49 |
| Hot Cross Buns (Version 1) (St. Voc.) | 3 | 218 | 7-38 |
| Hot Cross Buns (Version 1) (St. Perf. Tr.) | 3 | 218 | 7-39 |
| Hot Cross Buns (Version 2) (St. Voc.) | 3 | 221 | 7-43 |
| Hot Cross Buns (Version 2) (St. Perf. Tr.) | 3 | 221 | 7-44 |
| Hotaru koi (Come, Firefly) (St. Voc.) | 1 | 356 | 11-13 |
| Hotaru koi (Come, Firefly) (St. Perf. Tr.) | 1 | 356 | 11-15 |
| Hound Dog (St. Voc.) | 5 | 212 | 10-27 |
| Hound Dog (St. Perf. Tr.) | 5 | 212 | 10-28 |
| Hours, The (Las horas) (St. Voc.) | 1 | 246 | 7-46 |
| How Can I Keep from Singing? (St. Voc.) | 4 | 261 | 10-33 |
| How Can I Keep from Singing? (St. Perf. Tr.) | 4 | 261 | 10-34 |
| How Do You Doo-tee? (speech piece) (St. Voc.) | 4 | 186 | 8-24 |
| How Many Miles to Babylon? (St. Voc.) | 2 | 128 | 5-10 |
| How Many Miles to Babylon? (St. Perf. Tr.) | 2 | 128 | 5-11 |
| How Much Wood Could a Woodchuck Chuck (speech piece) (St. Voc.) | 3 | 120 | 4-27 |
| How Much Wood Could a Woodchuck Chuck (speech piece) (St. Perf. Tr.) | 3 | 120 | 4-28 |
| Hui jia qü (Home from School) (St. Voc.) | 2 | 158 | 6-5 |
| Hui jia qü (Home from School) (St. Perf. Tr.) | 2 | 158 | 6-7 |
| Hungry Dog, The (Ee jer ha ba go) (St. Voc.) | K | 133 | 5-11 |
| Hush, Hush (St. Voc.) | 3 | 162 | 5-36 |
| Hush, Hush (St. Perf. Tr.) | 3 | 162 | 5-37 |
| Hush, My Little Baby (A la rurru niño) (St. Voc.) | K | 180 | 6-34 |
| Hush Up the Baby (St. Voc.) | K | 222 | 7-42 |
| Hush Up the Baby (St. Perf. Tr.) | K | 222 | 7-43 |
| Hwa yuan li-de young wa wa (Garden Lullaby) (St. Voc.) | 3 | 102 | 4-1 |
| Hwa yuan li-de young wa wa (Garden Lullaby) | 3 | 102 | 4-3 |
| I Am But a Small Voice (T.A.P.) (St. Perf. Tr.) | 6 | 446 | 21-7 |
| I Am But a Small Voice (St. Perf. Tr.) | 6 | 446 | 21-8 |
| I Believe I Can Fly (St. Voc.) | 5 | 170 | 8-26 |
| I Believe I Can Fly (St. Perf. Tr.) | 5 | 170 | 8-27 |
| I Bought Me a Cat (St. Voc.) | 2 | 308 | 11-17 |
| I Bought Me a Cat (St. Perf. Tr.) | 2 | 308 | 11-18 |
| I Came to Try This Game (Ah, eu entrei na roda) (St. Voc.) | 3 | 308 | 10-41 |
| I Can't Spell Hippopotamus (St. Voc.) | 1 | 266 | 8-30 |
| I Can't Spell Hippopotamus (St. Perf. Tr.) | 1 | 266 | 8-31 |
| I Don't Care If the Rain Comes Down (St. Voc.) | 3 | 24 | 1-37 |
| I Don't Care If the Rain Comes Down (St. Perf. Tr.) | 3 | 24 | 1-38 |
| I Don't Want Silver (No quiero plata) (St. Voc.) | 1 | 424 | 13-36 |
| I Dream a World (St. Voc.) | 8 | G-40 | 12-17 |
| I Dream a World (St. Perf. Tr.) | 8 | G-40 | 12-18 |
| I Fed My Horse (St. Voc.) | 2 | 94 | 4-1 |
| I Fed My Horse (St. Perf. Tr.) | 2 | 94 | 4-2 |
| I Got a Letter This Morning (St. Voc.) | K | 68 | 2-56 |
| I Got a Letter This Morning (St. Perf. Tr.) | K | 68 | 2-57 |
| I Got Rhythm (St. Voc.) | 6 | 101 | 6-16 |
| I Got Rhythm (St. Perf. Tr.) | 6 | 101 | 6-17 |
| I Got Shoes (St. Voc.) | 2 | 242 | 8-30 |
| I Got Shoes (St. Perf. Tr.) | 2 | 242 | 8-31 |
| I Have a Chanukah Menorah (Chanukiyah li yesh) (St. Voc.) | 1 | 421 | 13-28 |
| I Have a Dog (St. Voc.) | K | 262 | 9-10 |
| I Have a Dog (St. Perf. Tr.) | K | 262 | 9-11 |
| I Have Three Sheep (Tengo, Tengo, Tengo) (St. Voc.) | 4 | 228 | 9-36 |
| I Know an Old Lady (St. Voc.) | 1 | 388 | 12-17 |
| I Know an Old Lady (St. Perf. Tr.) | 1 | 388 | 12-18 |
| I Love Peanuts (hip-hop style) (St. Voc.) | 1 | 162 | 5-22 |
| I Love Peanuts (hip-hop style) (St. Perf. Tr.) | 1 | 162 | 5-23 |
| I Love Peanuts (St. Voc.) | 7 | E-20 | 10-4 |
| I Love Peanuts (St. Perf. Tr.) | 7 | E-20 | 10-5 |
| I Love Soccer! (¡Viva el fútbol!) (St. Voc.) | 1 | 96 | 3-20 |
| I Love the Mountains (St. Voc.) | 5 | 34 | 2-26 |
| I Love the Mountains (St. Perf. Tr.) | 5 | 34 | 2-27 |
| I Saw Three Ships (St. Voc.) | 1 | 426 | 13-39 |
| I Saw Three Ships (St. Perf. Tr.) | 1 | 426 | 13-40 |
| I See the Moon (St. Voc.) | 2 | 58 | 2-37 |
| I See the Moon (St. Perf. Tr.) | 2 | 58 | 2-38 |
| I See with My Hands (St. Voc.) | 2 | 148 | 5-47 |
| I See with My Hands (St. Perf. Tr.) | 2 | 148 | 5-48 |
| I Shall Sing (St. Voc.) | 8 | I-38 | 14-13 |
| I Shall Sing (St. Perf. Tr.) | 8 | I-38 | 14-14 |
| I Vow to You, My Country (St. Voc.) | 5 | 418 | 18-27 |
| I Vow to You, My Country (St. Perf. Tr.) | 5 | 418 | 18-28 |
| I Walk in Beauty (St. Voc.) | 4 | 282 | 12-1 |
| I Walk in Beauty (St. Perf. Tr.) | 4 | 282 | 12-2 |
| I Walk the Unfrequented Road (St. Voc.) | 6 | 79 | 5-6 |
| I Walk the Unfrequented Road (St. Perf. Tr.) | 6 | 79 | 5-7 |
| I Will Sing, You Will Sing (Cantaré, cantarás) (St. Voc.) | 6 | 413 | 20-12 |
| I Wish I Knew How It Would Feel to Be Free (St. Voc.) | 6 | 470 | 22-8 |
| I Wish I Knew How It Would Feel to Be Free (St. Perf. Tr.) | 6 | 470 | 22-9 |
| I Wonder Where Maria's Gone (St. Voc./Dance Perf. Tr.) | 3 | 318 | 11-13 |

| Title | Gr. | Pg. | CD Track |
|---|---|---|---|
| I Wonder Where Maria's Gone (St. Perf. Tr.) | 3 | 318 | 11-14 |
| I'd Like to Teach the World to Sing (St. Voc.) | 3 | 198 | 7-9 |
| I'd Like to Teach the World to Sing (St. Perf. Tr.) | 3 | 198 | 7-10 |
| I'll Fly Away (St. Voc.) | 8 | I-42 | 14-16 |
| I'll Fly Away (St. Perf. Tr.) | 8 | I-42 | 14-17 |
| I'm a Believer (St. Voc.) | 7 | G-33 | 12-23 |
| I'm a Believer (St. Perf. Tr.) | 7 | G-33 | 12-24 |
| I'm a Dreydl (St. Voc.) | K | 315 | 11-14 |
| I'm a Dreydl (St. Perf. Tr.) | K | 315 | 11-15 |
| I'm a Very Fine Turkey (St. Voc.) | K | 310 | 11-5 |
| I'm a Very Fine Turkey (St. Perf. Tr.) | K | 310 | 11-6 |
| I'm Curious (St. Voc.) | K | 276 | 9-31 |
| I'm Curious (St. Perf. Tr.) | K | 276 | 9-32 |
| I'm Flying Home (St. Voc.) | 2 | 286 | 10-31 |
| I'm Flying Home (St. Perf. Tr.) | 2 | 286 | 10-32 |
| I'm Going to the Moon (Me voy para la luna) (St. Voc.) | 1 | 397 | 12-30 |
| I'm Gonna Sing (St. Voc.) | 4 | 33 | 2-7 |
| I'm Gonna Sing (St. Perf. Tr.) | 4 | 33 | 2-8 |
| I'm in the Mood (St. Voc.) | K | 86 | 3-31 |
| I'm in the Mood (St. Perf. Tr.) | K | 86 | 3-32 |
| I'm on My Way (St. Voc.) | 3 | 76 | 3-1 |
| I'm on My Way (St. Perf. Tr.) | 3 | 76 | 3-2 |
| I'm on My Way (St. Voc.) | 7 | A-15 | 1-11 |
| I'm on My Way (St. Perf. Tr.) | 7 | A-15 | 1-12 |
| I'm Tall, I'm Small (St. Voc.) | K | 18 | 1-26 |
| I'm Tall, I'm Small (St. Perf. Tr.) | K | 18 | 1-27 |
| I'm Thankful (St. Voc.) | 1 | 414 | 13-16 |
| I'm Thankful (St. Perf. Tr.) | 1 | 414 | 13-17 |
| I've Been Everywhere (St. Voc.) | 6 | 226 | 11-38 |
| I've Been Everywhere (St. Perf. Tr.) | 6 | 226 | 11-39 |
| I've Been Working on the Railroad (St. Voc.) | 3 | 242 | 8-9 |
| I've Been Working on the Railroad (St. Perf. Tr.) | 3 | 242 | 8-10 |
| Ichi-gatsu tsuitachi (A New Year's Greeting) (St. Voc.) | 3 | 406 | 14-26 |
| Ichi-gatsu tsuitachi (A New Year's Greeting) (St. Perf. Tr.) | 3 | 406 | 14-28 |
| Ichi-gatsu tsuitachi (A New Year's Greeting) (St. Voc.) | 7 | I-40 | 13-31 |
| Ichi-gatsu tsuitachi (A New Year's Greeting) (St. Perf. Tr.) | 7 | I-40 | 13-33 |
| Ida Red (St. Voc.) | 3 | 30 | 1-48 |
| Ida Red (St. Perf. Tr.) | 3 | 30 | 1-49 |
| If a Tiger Calls (St. Voc.) | 3 | 354 | 12-12 |
| If a Tiger Calls (St. Perf. Tr.) | 3 | 354 | 12-13 |
| If I Had a Hammer (St. Voc.) | 5 | 287 | 13-13 |
| If I Had a Hammer (St. Perf. Tr.) | 5 | 287 | 13-14 |
| If You Give Me Pastries (Si me dan pasteles) (St. Voc.) | 1 | 432 | 14-2 |
| If You're Happy (St. Voc.) | K | 94 | 3-47 |
| If You're Happy (St. Perf. Tr.) | K | 94 | 3-48 |
| Ikhanda, maslombe (My Head and My Shoulders) (St. Voc.) | K | 14 | 1-20 |
| Ikhanda, maslombe (St. Perf. Tr.) | K | 14 | 1-22 |
| Imbabura (Spanish) (St. Voc.) | 5 | 203 | 10-12 |
| Imbabura (English) (St. Voc.) | 5 | 203 | 10-13 |
| Imbabura (St. Perf. Tr.) | 5 | 203 | 10-14 |
| In Spain, the Children Sing (Los niños en España cantan) (St. Voc.) | 4 | 197 | 8-39 |
| In the Moonlight (Au clair de la lune) (St. Voc.) | 3 | 18 | 1-27 |
| In the Pumpkin Patch (St. Voc.) | 3 | 380 | 13-16 |
| In the Pumpkin Patch (St. Perf. Tr.) | 3 | 380 | 13-17 |
| In the Silent Forest (Erdö, erdö de magos) (St. Voc.) | 3 | 182 | 6-28 |
| Inkpataya (Traditional) (St. Voc.) | 3 | 254 | 8-26 |
| Inkpataya (Traditional) (St. Perf. Tr.) | 3 | 254 | 8-27 |
| Inkpataya (Contemporary) (St. Voc.) | 3 | 254 | 8-28 |
| Inkpataya (Contemporary) (St. Perf. Tr.) | 3 | 254 | 8-29 |
| Ise oluwa (St. Voc.) | 2 | 102 | 4-17 |
| Ise oluwa (St. Perf. Tr.) | 2 | 102 | 4-18 |
| Ise oluwa (St. Voc.) | 6 | 230 | 12-3 |
| Ise oluwa (St. Perf. Tr.) | 6 | 230 | 12-4 |
| It Don't Mean a Thing (If It Ain't Got That Swing) (St. Voc.) | 5 | 336 | 15-23 |
| It Don't Mean a Thing (If It Ain't Got That Swing) (St. Perf. Tr.) | 5 | 336 | 15-24 |
| It Would Have Been Enough (Dayenu) (St. Voc.) | 4 | 439 | 19-2 |
| It's a Beautiful Day (St. Voc.) | 3 | 338 | 11-41 |
| It's a Beautiful Day (St. Perf. Tr.) | 3 | 338 | 11-42 |
| It's a Celebration! (St. Voc.) | 2 | 372 | 13-30 |
| It's a Celebration! (St. Perf. Tr.) | 2 | 372 | 13-31 |
| It's a Small World (St. Voc.) | 3 | 268 | 9-14 |
| It's a Small World (St. Perf. Tr.) | 3 | 268 | 9-15 |
| It's Raining! (¡Que llueva!) (St. Voc.) | K | 81 | 3-16 |
| It's Santa-Again! (St. Voc.) | 2 | 385 | 14-25 |
| It's Santa-Again! (St. Perf. Tr.) | 2 | 385 | 14-26 |
| It's Time (St. Voc.) | 6 | 274 | 14-10 |
| It's Time (St. Perf. Tr.) | 6 | 274 | 14-11 |
| Ja-Da (St. Voc.) | 2 | 188 | 7-13 |
| Ja-Da (St. Perf. Tr.) | 2 | 188 | 7-14 |
| Ja-Da (St. Voc.) | 7 | G-20 | 12-13 |
| Ja-Da (St. Perf. Tr.) | 7 | G-20 | 12-14 |
| Jambalaya (On the Bayou) (St. Voc.) | 6 | 244 | 13-1 |
| Jambalaya (On the Bayou) (St. Perf. Tr.) | 6 | 244 | 13-2 |
| Jambalaya (On the Bayou) (St. Voc.) | 8 | I-46 | 14-19 |
| Jambalaya (On the Bayou) (St. Perf. Tr.) | 8 | I-46 | 14-20 |
| James Brown (St. Voc.) | K | 206 | 7-19 |
| James Brown (St. Perf. Tr.) | K | 206 | 7-20 |
| Jan ken pon (Japanese) (St. Voc.) | 3 | 302 | 10-30 |
| Jan ken pon (English) (St. Voc.) | 3 | 302 | 10-31 |
| Jan ken pon (St. Perf. Tr.) | 3 | 302 | 10-32 |
| Japanese Rain Song (Amefuri) (St. Voc.) | 1 | 144 | 4-44 |
| Jasmine Flower (Dok djampa) (St. Voc.) | 8 | I-20 | 13-21 |
| Jasmine Flowers (St. Voc.) | 5 | 316 | 14-27 |
| Jasmine Flowers (St. Perf. Tr.) | 5 | 316 | 14-28 |
| Jelly in a Dish (speech piece) (St. Voc.) | 2 | 83 | 3-38 |
| Jelly in a Dish (speech piece) (St. Perf. Tr.) | 2 | 83 | 3-39 |
| ¡Jeu! ¡Jeu! (Heyoo! Heyoo!) (St. Voc.) | 1 | 216 | 7-6 |
| ¡Jeu! ¡Jeu! (St. Perf. Tr.) | 1 | 216 | 7-8 |
| Jig Along Home (St. Voc.) | 2 | 366 | 13-25 |
| Jig Along Home (St. Perf. Tr.) | 2 | 366 | 13-26 |
| Jim Along, Josie (St. Voc.) | K | 39 | 2-10 |
| Jim Along, Josie (St. Perf. Tr.) | K | 39 | 2-11 |
| Jingle Bells (St. Voc.) | 2 | 388 | 14-30 |
| Jingle Bells (St. Perf. Tr.) | 2 | 388 | 14-31 |
| Jinny Go 'Round (St. Voc.) | K | 228 | 8-6 |
| Jinny Go 'Round (St. Perf. Tr.) | K | 228 | 8-7 |
| Jo'ashila (Walking Together) (St. Voc.) | 5 | 108 | 5-43 |
| Jo'ashila (Walking Together) (St. Perf. Tr.) | 5 | 108 | 5-44 |
| Joe Turner Blues (St. Voc./Dance Perf. Tr.) | 4 | 56 | 3-14 |
| Joe Turner Blues (St. Perf. Tr.) | 4 | 56 | 3-15 |
| John Kanaka (St. Voc.) | 3 | 60 | 2-37 |
| John Kanaka (St. Perf. Tr.) | 3 | 60 | 2-38 |
| John Lollypop-Seller (Juan pirulero) (St. Voc.) | K | 215 | 7-31 |
| Johnny Appleseed (St. Voc.) | 4 | 345 | 15-7 |
| Johnny Appleseed (St. Perf. Tr.) | 4 | 345 | 15-8 |
| Johnny Caught a Flea (St. Voc.) | 1 | 227 | 7-18 |
| Johnny Caught a Flea (St. Perf. Tr.) | 1 | 227 | 7-19 |
| Johnny Has Gone for a Soldier (St. Voc.) | 5 | 188 | 9-21 |

| Title | Gr. | Pg. | CD Track |
|---|---|---|---|
| Johnny Has Gone for a Soldier (St. Perf. Tr.) | 5 | 188 | 9-22 |
| Johnny Mister Brown (St. Voc.) | K | 37 | 2-8 |
| Johnny Mister Brown (St. Perf. Tr.) | K | 37 | 2-9 |
| Jolly Old St. Nicholas (St. Voc.) | K | 316 | 11-16 |
| Jolly Old St. Nicholas (St. Perf. Tr.) | K | 316 | 11-17 |
| Joshua Fought the Battle of Jericho (St. Voc.) | 5 | 101 | 5-25 |
| Joshua Fought the Battle of Jericho (St. Voc.) | 8 | E-18 | 9-20 |
| Joy of Kwanzaa, The (St. Voc.) | 6 | 462 | 22-1 |
| Joy of Kwanzaa, The (St. Perf. Tr.) | 6 | 462 | 22-2 |
| Joy to the World (St. Voc.) | 3 | 22 | 1-35 |
| Joy to the World (St. Perf. Tr.) | 3 | 22 | 1-36 |
| Joyous Chanukah (Chanukah, Chanukah) (St. Voc.) | 1 | 420 | 13-24 |
| Juan pirulero (John Lollypop-Seller) (St. Voc.) | K | 215 | 7-30 |
| Juan pirulero (John Lollypop-Seller) (St. Perf. Tr.) | K | 215 | 7-32 |
| Juanito (Little Johnny) (St. Voc.) | K | 300 | 10-23 |
| Juanito (Little Johnny) (St. Perf. Tr.) | K | 300 | 10-25 |
| Juba (St. Voc.) | K | 13 | 1-13 |
| Juba (St. Perf. Tr.) | K | 13 | 1-14 |
| Jump That Jody (St. Voc.) | K | 212 | 7-27 |
| Jump That Jody (St. Perf. Tr.) | K | 212 | 7-28 |
| Juniper Tree, The (St. Voc.) | 3 | 131 | 4-40 |
| Juniper Tree, The (St. Perf. Tr.) | 3 | 131 | 4-41 |
| Just a Snap-Happy Blues (St. Voc.) | 6 | 388 | 19-22 |
| Just a Snap-Happy Blues (St. Perf. Tr.) | 6 | 388 | 19-23 |
| Just from the Kitchen (St. Voc.) | K | 55 | 2-31 |
| Just from the Kitchen (St. Perf. Tr.) | K | 55 | 2-32 |
| Kaeru no uta (The Frog Song) (St. Voc.) | K | 183 | 6-40 |
| Kaeru no uta (The Frog Song) (St. Perf. Tr.) | K | 183 | 6-42 |
| Kangaroo Song, The (St. Voc.) | K | 44 | 2-18 |
| Kangaroo Song, The (St. Perf. Tr.) | K | 44 | 2-19 |
| Kansas Corrido (Corrido de Kansas) (St. Voc.) | 4 | 274 | 11-18 |
| Kapulu kane (Puili Game Song) (St. Voc.) | 2 | 270 | 9-37 |
| Kapulu kane (Puili Game Song) (St. Perf. Tr.) | 2 | 270 | 9-38 |
| Karangatia ra (St. Voc.) | 3 | 272 | 9-20 |
| Karangatia ra (St. Perf. Tr.) | 3 | 272 | 9-21 |
| Karangatia ra (St. Voc.) | 8 | F-23 | 11-3 |
| Karangatia ra (St. Perf. Tr.) | 8 | F-23 | 11-4 |
| Kébé Mama (My Dear Mama) (St. Voc.) | 1 | 442 | 14-22 |
| Kébé Mama (My Dear Mama) (St. Perf. Tr.) | 1 | 442 | 14-24 |
| Keel Row, The (St. Voc.) | 4 | 240 | 10-10 |
| Keel Row, The (St. Perf. Tr.) | 4 | 240 | 10-11 |
| Keep Your Eyes on the Prize (St. Voc.) | 3 | 408 | 14-31 |
| Keep Your Eyes on the Prize (St. Perf. Tr.) | 3 | 408 | 14-32 |
| Keep Your Eyes on the Prize (St. Voc.) | 8 | E-16 | 9-17 |
| Keep Your Eyes on the Prize (St. Perf. Tr.) | 8 | E-16 | 9-18 |
| Kelo aba w'ye (St. Voc.) | 6 | 290 | 14-20 |
| Key to the Highway (St. Voc.) | 6 | 243 | 12-22 |
| Key to the Highway (St. Perf. Tr.) | 6 | 243 | 12-23 |
| Key to the Highway (St. Voc.) | 8 | F-29 | 11-12 |
| Key to the Highway (St. Perf. Tr.) | 8 | F-29 | 11-13 |
| Khorovod (Round Dance) (St. Voc./Dance Perf. Tr.) | 1 | 374 | 12-1 |
| Khorovod (Round Dance) (St. Perf. Tr.) | 1 | 374 | 12-2 |
| Kibungo (Portuguese) (St. Voc.) | 2 | 354 | 13-2 |
| Kibungo (English) (St. Voc.) | 2 | 354 | 13-3 |
| Kibungo (St. Perf. Tr.) | 2 | 354 | 13-4 |
| Kid Like Me, A (St. Voc.) | 2 | 394 | 14-38 |
| Kid Like Me, A (St. Perf. Tr.) | 2 | 394 | 14-39 |
| Kingfish, The (El carite) (St. Voc.) | 5 | 305 | 14-7 |
| Kings from the East, The (Los reyes de Oriente) (St. Voc.) | 5 | 480 | 21-6 |
| Kings from the East, The (Los reyes de Oriente) (St. Voc.) | 8 | I-58 | 15-11 |
| Kingston Market (St. Voc.) | 3 | 90 | 3-23 |
| Kingston Market (St. Perf. Tr.) | 3 | 90 | 3-24 |
| Knock No More (St. Voc.) | 3 | 386 | 13-22 |
| Knock No More (St. Perf. Tr.) | 3 | 386 | 13-23 |
| Knock the Cymbals (St. Voc.) | 1 | 176 | 5-37 |
| Knock the Cymbals (St. Perf. Tr.) | 1 | 176 | 5-38 |
| Kokoleoko (St. Voc.) | 5 | 33 | 2-23 |
| Kokoleoko (St. Perf. Tr.) | 5 | 33 | 2-24 |
| Kookaburra (St. Voc.) | 4 | 186 | 8-19 |
| Kookaburra (St. Perf. Tr.) | 4 | 186 | 8-20 |
| Koriko! (St. Voc.) | K | 154 | 5-41 |
| Koriko! (St. Perf. Tr.) | K | 154 | 5-42 |
| Kou ri lengay (The Strength of the Lion) (St. Voc.) | 2 | 217 | 8-7 |
| Kou ri lengay (The Strength of the Lion) (St. Perf. Tr.) | 2 | 217 | 8-8 |
| Kou ri lengay (The Strength of the Lion) (St. Voc.) | 7 | E-2 | 9-16 |
| Kou ri lengay (The Strength of the Lion) (St. Perf. Tr.) | 7 | E-2 | 9-17 |
| Kum ba yah (T.A.P.) | 5 | 244 | 11-36 |
| Kum ba yah (St. Perf. Tr.) | 5 | 244 | 11-37 |
| Kum bachur atzel (Hear the Rooster Crowing) (St. Voc.) | 3 | 138 | 5-1 |
| Kum bachur atzel (Hear the Rooster Crowing) (St. Perf. Tr.) | 3 | 138 | 5-3 |
| Kuma san (Little Bear) (St. Voc.) | K | 40 | 2-12 |
| Kuma san (Little Bear) (St. Perf. Tr.) | K | 40 | 2-14 |
| Kunolounkwa (St. Voc.) | K | 110 | 4-16 |
| Kunolounkwa (St. Perf. Tr.) | K | 110 | 4-17 |
| Kwa-nu-te (St. Voc.) | 3 | 214 | 7-31 |
| Kwa-nu-te (St. Perf. Tr.) | 3 | 214 | 7-32 |
| Kwanzaa Carol, A (St. Voc.) | 2 | 392 | 14-36 |
| Kwanzaa Carol, A (St. Perf. Tr.) | 2 | 392 | 14-37 |
| Kyrie (St. Voc.) | 6 | 206 | 11-11 |
| Kyrie (St. Perf. Tr.) | 6 | 206 | 11-12 |
| L'inverno è passato (Winter Is Over) (St. Voc.) | 2 | 400 | 15-1 |
| L'inverno è passato (Winter Is Over) (St. Perf. Tr.) | 2 | 400 | 15-3 |
| La bamba (Spanish) (St. Voc.) | 5 | 128 | 6-20 |
| La bamba (English) (St. Voc.) | 5 | 128 | 6-21 |
| La bamba (St. Perf. Tr.) | 5 | 128 | 6-22 |
| La borinqueña (Beloved Island Home) (T.A.P.) | 8 | D-19 | 8-26 |
| La borinqueña (Beloved Island Home) (St. Perf. Tr.) | 8 | D-19 | 8-28 |
| La calle ancha (The Wide Street) (St. Voc.) | 3 | 297 | 10-23 |
| La calle ancha (The Wide Street) (St. Perf. Tr.) | 3 | 297 | 10-25 |
| La ciudad de Juaja (The City of Juaja) (St. Voc.) | 5 | 58 | 3-24 |
| La ciudad de Juaja (The City of Juaja) (St. Perf. Tr.) | 5 | 58 | 3-26 |
| La copa de la vida (The Cup of Life) (St. Voc.) | 4 | 414 | 17-20 |
| La copa de la vida (The Cup of Life) (St. Perf. Tr.) | 4 | 414 | 17-21 |
| La golondrina (The Swallow) (St. Voc.) | 8 | I-50 | 15-1 |
| La golondrina (The Swallow) (St. Perf. Tr.) | 8 | I-50 | 15-3 |
| La Jesusita (Spanish) (St. Voc.) | 5 | 322 | 15-5 |
| La Jesusita (English) (St. Voc.) | 5 | 322 | 15-6 |
| La Jesusita (St. Perf. Tr.) | 5 | 322 | 15-7 |
| La mar estaba serena (The Sea Is Calm) (St. Voc.) | 2 | 345 | 12-21 |
| La mar estaba serena (The Sea Is Calm) (St. Perf. Tr.) | 2 | 345 | 12-23 |
| La mariposa (The Butterfly) (St. Voc.) | 6 | 58 | 4-8 |
| La mariposa (The Butterfly) (St. Perf. Tr.) | 6 | 58 | 4-10 |
| La paloma blanca (The White Dove) (St. Voc.) | 3 | 252 | 8-22 |
| La paloma blanca (The White Dove) (St. Perf. Tr.) | 3 | 252 | 8-24 |
| La paloma se fué (The Dove That Flew Away) (St. Voc.) | 6 | 51 | 3-22 |
| La paloma se fué (The Dove That Flew Away) (St. Perf. Tr.) | 6 | 51 | 3-24 |
| La piñata (The Piñata) (St. Voc.) | 3 | 399 | 14-12 |
| La piñata (The Piñata) (St. Perf. Tr.) | 3 | 399 | 14-14 |
| La pulga de San José (St. Voc.) | 3 | 40 | 2-7 |

| Title | Gr. | Pg. | CD Track |
|---|---|---|---|
| La pulga de San José (St. Perf. Tr.) | 3 | 40 | 2-8 |
| La raspa (Spanish) (St. Voc./Dance Perf. Tr.) | 4 | 302 | 13-1 |
| La raspa (English) (St. Voc.) | 4 | 302 | 13-2 |
| La raspa (St. Perf. Tr.) | 4 | 302 | 13-3 |
| La Tarara (Spanish) (St. Voc.) | 4 | 176 | 8-1 |
| La Tarara (English) (St. Voc.) | 4 | 176 | 8-2 |
| La Tarara (St. Perf. Tr.) | 4 | 176 | 8-3 |
| La tormenta tropical (The Tropical Storm) (St. Voc.) | 2 | 116 | 4-34 |
| La tormenta tropical (The Tropical Storm) (St. Perf. Tr.) | 2 | 116 | 4-36 |
| La víbora (The Serpent) (St. Voc.) | 1 | 322 | 10-15 |
| La víbora (The Serpent) (St. Perf. Tr.) | 1 | 322 | 10-17 |
| Lady, Lady (St. Voc.) | 1 | 62 | 2-37 |
| Lady, Lady (St. Perf. Tr.) | 1 | 62 | 2-38 |
| Lahk gei mohlee (St. Voc.) | 5 | 317 | 14-29 |
| Lahk gei mohlee (St. Perf. Tr.) | 5 | 317 | 14-30 |
| Lamb, The (El borrego) (St. Voc.) | 4 | 242 | 10-13 |
| Land of a Thousand Dances (St. Voc.) | 5 | 330 | 15-16 |
| Land of a Thousand Dances (St. Perf. Tr.) | 5 | 330 | 15-17 |
| Laredo (Spanish) (St. Voc.) | 5 | 10 | 1-9 |
| Laredo (English) (St. Voc.) | 5 | 10 | 1-10 |
| Laredo (St. Perf. Tr.) | 5 | 10 | 1-11 |
| Las estaciones (The Seasons) (St. Voc.) | 1 | 29 | 1-40 |
| Las estaciones (The Seasons) (St. Perf. Tr.) | 1 | 29 | 1-42 |
| Las estrellitas del cielo (Stars of the Heavens) (St. Voc.) | 5 | 175 | 8-29 |
| Las estrellitas del cielo (Stars of the Heavens) (St. Perf. Tr.) | 5 | 175 | 8-31 |
| Las horas (The Hours) (St. Voc.) | 1 | 246 | 7-45 |
| Las horas (The Hours) (St. Perf. Tr.) | 1 | 246 | 7-47 |
| Las mañanitas (Spanish) (St. Voc.) | 6 | 481 | 22-16 |
| Las mañanitas (English) (St. Voc.) | 6 | 481 | 22-17 |
| Las mañanitas (St. Perf. Tr.) | 6 | 481 | 22-18 |
| Las Navidades (The Christmas Season) (St. Voc.) | 5 | 472 | 20-21 |
| Las Navidades (The Christmas Season) (St. Perf. Tr.) | 5 | 472 | 20-23 |
| Las velitas (Candles Burning Bright) (St. Voc.) | 5 | 147 | 7-18 |
| Las velitas (Candles Burning Bright) (St. Perf. Tr.) | 5 | 147 | 7-20 |
| Leak kanseng (Hide the Scarf) (St. Voc.) | 1 | 156 | 5-5 |
| Leak kanseng (St. Perf. Tr.) | 1 | 156 | 5-7 |
| Lean on Me (T.A.P.) | 6 | 14 | 1-20 |
| Lean on Me (St. Perf. Tr.) | 6 | 14 | 1-21 |
| Lean on Me (T.A.P.) | 7 | E-22 | 10-6 |
| Lean on Me (St. Perf. Tr.) | 7 | E-22 | 10-7 |
| Leatherwing Bat (St. Voc.) | 2 | 303 | 11-9 |
| Leatherwing Bat (St. Perf. Tr.) | 2 | 303 | 11-10 |
| Leaves (St. Voc.) | 1 | 28 | 1-38 |
| Leaves (St. Perf. Tr.) | 1 | 28 | 1-39 |
| Leavin' for Chile (Cuando pa' Chile me voy) (St. Voc.) | 6 | 376 | 19-12 |
| Leila (St. Voc./Dance Perf. Tr.) | 1 | 258 | 8-18 |
| Leila (St. Perf. Tr.) | 1 | 258 | 8-19 |
| Lemonade (St. Voc.) | 1 | 190 | 6-22 |
| Lemonade (St. Perf. Tr.) | 1 | 190 | 6-23 |
| Les petites marionettes (The Little Marionettes) (St. Voc.) | K | 237 | 8-18 |
| Les petites marionettes (The Little Marionettes) (St. Perf. Tr.) | K | 237 | 8-20 |
| Let Freedom Ring (St. Voc.) | 5 | 77 | 4-21 |
| Let Freedom Ring and America, the Beautiful/ Let Freedom Ring (St. Perf. Tr.) | 5 | 77 | 4-23 |
| Let It Snow! Let It Snow! Let It Snow! (St. Voc.) | 4 | 426 | 18-5 |
| Let It Snow! Let It Snow! Let It Snow! (St. Perf. Tr.) | 4 | 426 | 18-6 |
| Let Music Surround You (St. Voc.) | 4 | 236 | 10-6 |
| Let Music Surround You (St. Perf. Tr.) | 4 | 236 | 10-7 |
| Let the Music Begin! (St. Voc.) | 1 | 2 | 1-1 |
| Let the Music Begin! (St. Perf. Tr.) | 1 | 2 | 1-2 |
| Let Us Sing Together (St. Voc.) | 6 | 156 | 8-28 |
| Let Us Sing Together (St. Perf. Tr.) | 6 | 156 | 8-29 |
| Let's Celebrate (St. Voc.) | 3 | 374 | 13-7 |
| Let's Celebrate (St. Perf. Tr.) | 3 | 374 | 13-8 |
| Let's Get Ready (St. Voc.) | K | 312 | 11-7 |
| Let's Get Ready (St. Perf. Tr.) | K | 312 | 11-8 |
| Let's Get the Rhythm of the Band (St. Voc.) | 3 | 84 | 3-16 |
| Let's Get the Rhythm of the Band (St. Perf. Tr.) | 3 | 84 | 3-17 |
| Let's Get the Rhythm of the Band (St. Voc.) | 7 | E-29 | 10-10 |
| Let's Get the Rhythm of the Band (St. Perf. Tr.) | 7 | E-29 | 10-11 |
| Let's Go Fly a Kite (from Mary Poppins) (St. Voc.) | 2 | 327 | 11-36 |
| Let's Go Fly a Kite (from Mary Poppins) (St. Perf. Tr.) | 2 | 327 | 11-37 |
| Let's Go to Adana (Adana ya gidelim) (St. Voc.) | 2 | 142 | 5-33 |
| Let's Go to the Party (Vamos a la fiesta) (St. Voc.) | 2 | 374 | 14-2 |
| Let's Go to the Sea (Vamos a la mar) (St. Voc.) | 3 | 226 | 7-50 |
| Let's Make a Circle (Vamos a hacer la ronda) (St. Voc.) | K | 124 | 4-40 |
| Let's Pretend (St. Voc.) | K | 227 | 8-4 |
| Let's Pretend (St. Perf. Tr.) | K | 227 | 8-5 |
| Let's Sing! (Vamos a cantar) (St. Voc.) | K | 278 | 9-34 |
| Li'l Liza Jane (St. Voc.) | 3 | 140 | 5-6 |
| Li'l Liza Jane (St. Perf. Tr.) | 3 | 140 | 5-7 |
| Lift Ev'ry Voice and Sing (St. Voc.) | 5 | 482 | 21-10 |
| Lift Ev'ry Voice and Sing (St. Perf. Tr.) | 5 | 482 | 21-11 |
| Lift Ev'ry Voice and Sing (St. Voc.) | 8 | I-54 | 15-6 |
| Lift Ev'ry Voice and Sing (St. Perf. Tr.) | 8 | I-54 | 15-7 |
| Light, The (Ner li) (St. Voc.) | 2 | 383 | 14-18 |
| Light Up the World With a Song (St. Voc.) | 8 | G-25 | 12-7 |
| Light Up the World With a Song (St. Perf. Tr.) | 8 | G-25 | 12-8 |
| Like a Bird (St. Voc.) | 6 | 167 | 9-21 |
| Like a Bird (St. Perf. Tr.) | 6 | 167 | 9-22 |
| Limbo Like Me (St. Voc.) | 4 | 18 | 1-25 |
| Limbo Like Me (St. Perf. Tr.) | 4 | 18 | 1-26 |
| Linstead Market (St. Voc.) | 5 | 241 | 11-32 |
| Linstead Market (St. Perf. Tr.) | 5 | 241 | 11-33 |
| Lion Sleeps Tonight, The (Wimoweh, Mbube) (St. Voc.) | 4 | 131 | 6-4 |
| Lion Sleeps Tonight, The (Wimoweh, Mbube) (St. Perf. Tr.) | 4 | 131 | 6-5 |
| Lion Sleeps Tonight, The (Wimoweh, Mbube) (St. Voc.) | 8 | I-56 | 15-8 |
| Lion Sleeps Tonight, The (Wimoweh, Mbube) (St. Perf. Tr.) | 8 | I-56 | 15-9 |
| Lions (St. Voc.) | 1 | 238 | 7-32 |
| Lions (St. Perf. Tr.) | 1 | 238 | 7-33 |
| Listen to the Water (St. Voc.) | 2 | 294 | 10-40 |
| Listen to the Water (St. Perf. Tr.) | 2 | 294 | 10-41 |
| Little and Lots (St. Voc.) | K | 323 | 11-25 |
| Little and Lots (St. Perf. Tr.) | K | 323 | 11-26 |
| Little Bear (Kuma san) (St. Voc.) | K | 40 | 2-13 |
| Little Bird, A (Un pajarito) (St. Voc.) | 2 | 16 | 1-21 |
| Little Black Bug (St. Voc.) | 1 | 214 | 7-1 |
| Little Black Bug (St. Perf. Tr.) | 1 | 214 | 7-2 |
| Little Butterfly (Mariposita) (St. Voc.) | 2 | 156 | 6-2 |
| Little Darlin' (St. Voc.) | 7 | F-30 | 11-17 |
| Little Darlin' (St. Perf. Tr.) | 7 | F-30 | 11-18 |
| Little David (St. Voc.) | 1 | 232 | 7-28 |
| Little David (St. Perf. Tr.) | 1 | 232 | 7-29 |
| Little David, Play on Your Harp (St. Voc.) | 4 | 394 | 17-4 |
| Little David, Play on Your Harp (St. Perf. Tr.) | 4 | 394 | 17-5 |
| Little Fish, The (Los pececitos) (St. Voc.) | 1 | 178 | 5-43 |
| Little Frog, The (El coquí) (St. Voc.) | 2 | 292 | 10-37 |

| Title | Gr. | Pg. | CD Track |
|---|---|---|---|
| Little Green Frog, The (St. Voc.) | 1 | 24 | 1-35 |
| Little Green Frog, The (St. Perf. Tr.) | 1 | 24 | 1-36 |
| Little Humahuacan Carnival, The (El carnavalito humahuaqueña) (St. Voc.) | 6 | 482 | 22-22 |
| Little Johnny (Juanito) (St. Voc.) | K | 300 | 10-24 |
| Little Johnny Brown (St. Voc.) | 3 | 313 | 11-1 |
| Little Johnny Brown (St. Perf. Tr.) | 3 | 313 | 11-2 |
| Little Man in the Woods, A (Ein Männlein steht im Walde) (St. Voc.) | 2 | 90 | 3-44 |
| Little Marionettes, The (Les petites marionettes) (St. Voc.) | K | 237 | 8-19 |
| Little Mouse, The (St. Voc.) | 1 | 350 | 11-7 |
| Little Mouse, The (St. Perf. Tr.) | 1 | 350 | 11-8 |
| Little Red Caboose (St. Voc.) | K | 229 | 8-8 |
| Little Red Caboose (St. Perf. Tr.) | K | 229 | 8-9 |
| Little Red Wagon (St. Voc.) | K | 152 | 5-38 |
| Little Red Wagon (St. Perf. Tr.) | K | 152 | 5-39 |
| Little Shell (St. Voc.) | 1 | 355 | 11-11 |
| Little Shell (St. Perf. Tr.) | 1 | 355 | 11-12 |
| Little Shop of Horrors (St. Voc.) | 4 | 422 | 18-1 |
| Little Shop of Horrors (St. Perf. Tr.) | 4 | 422 | 18-2 |
| Little Snail (Bereleh) (St. Voc.) | K | 151 | 5-35 |
| Little Spider (St. Voc.) | K | 93 | 3-44 |
| Little Spider (St. Perf. Tr.) | K | 93 | 3-45 |
| Little Toad, The (El sapito) (St. Voc.) | 3 | 336 | 11-38 |
| Little Trains (Los trencitos) (St. Voc.) | K | 24 | 1-35 |
| Little White Pony (Caballito blanco) (St. Voc.) | 2 | 193 | 7-19 |
| Live in the City (St. Voc.) | 5 | 71 | 4-13 |
| Live in the City (St. Perf. Tr.) | 5 | 71 | 4-14 |
| Lo yisa (Vine and Fig Tree) (St. Voc.) | 6 | 130 | 7-23 |
| Lo yisa (St. Perf. Tr.) | 6 | 130 | 7-25 |
| Loch Lomond (St. Voc.) | 5 | 140 | 7-13 |
| Loch Lomond (St. Perf. Tr.) | 5 | 140 | 7-14 |
| Loco-Motion, The (St. Voc.) | 3 | 64 | 2-40 |
| Loco-Motion, The (St. Perf. Tr.) | 3 | 64 | 2-41 |
| Locomoto-vation (St. Voc.) | K | 61 | 2-43 |
| Locomoto-vation (St. Perf. Tr.) | K | 61 | 2-44 |
| Loigratong (Thai) (St. Voc.) | 6 | 451 | 21-11 |
| Loigratong (English) (St. Voc.) | 6 | 451 | 21-12 |
| Loigratong (St. Perf. Tr.) | 6 | 451 | 21-13 |
| London Bridge (St. Voc.) | K | 244 | 8-29 |
| London Bridge (St. Perf. Tr.) | K | 244 | 8-30 |
| Lone Star Trail (St. Voc.) | 2 | 21 | 1-26 |
| Lone Star Trail (St. Perf. Tr.) | 2 | 21 | 1-27 |
| Long Way Home, A (St. Voc.) | 1 | 382 | 12-11 |
| Long Way Home, A (St. Perf. Tr.) | 1 | 382 | 12-12 |
| Looby Loo (St. Voc.) | K | 210 | 7-25 |
| Looby Loo (St. Perf. Tr.) | K | 210 | 7-26 |
| Look! Look! The Sun Woke Up! (St. Voc.) | 1 | 368 | 11-38 |
| Look! Look! The Sun Woke Up! (St. Perf. Tr.) | 1 | 368 | 11-39 |
| Look Out Below! (St. Voc.) | 2 | 370 | 13-28 |
| Look Out Below! (St. Perf. Tr.) | 2 | 370 | 13-29 |
| Look Out for Mother Earth (St. Voc.) | 3 | 341 | 11-43 |
| Look Out for Mother Earth (St. Perf. Tr.) | 3 | 341 | 11-44 |
| Los días de la semana (The Days of the Week) (St. Voc.) | 1 | 268 | 8-32 |
| Los días de la semana (The Days of the Week) (St. Perf. Tr.) | 1 | 268 | 8-33 |
| Los maizales (The Cornfields) (St. Voc.) | 1 | 296 | 9-24 |
| Los maizales (The Cornfields) (St. Perf. Tr.) | 1 | 296 | 9-26 |
| Los niños en España cantan (In Spain, the Children Sing) (St. Voc.) | 4 | 197 | 8-38 |
| Los niños en España cantan (In Spain, the Children Sing) (St. Perf. Tr.) | 4 | 197 | 8-40 |
| Los pececitos (The Little Fish) (St. Voc.) | 1 | 178 | 5-42 |
| Los pececitos (The Little Fish) (St. Perf. Tr.) | 1 | 178 | 5-44 |
| Los pollitos (Baby Chicks) (St. Voc.) | K | 166 | 6-12 |
| Los pollitos (Baby Chicks) (St. Perf. Tr.) | K | 166 | 6-14 |
| Los reyes de Oriente (The Kings from the East) (St. Voc.) | 5 | 480 | 21-5 |
| Los reyes de Oriente (The Kings from the East) (St. Perf. Tr.) | 5 | 480 | 21-7 |
| Los reyes de Oriente (The Kings from the East) (St. Voc.) | 8 | I-58 | 15-10 |
| Los reyes de Oriente (The Kings from the East) (St. Perf. Tr.) | 8 | I-58 | 15-12 |
| Los trencitos (Little Trains) (St. Voc.) | K | 24 | 1-34 |
| Los trencitos (Little Trains) (St. Perf. Tr.) | K | 24 | 1-36 |
| Lost My Gold Ring (St. Voc.) | 6 | 158 | 9-1 |
| Lost My Gold Ring (St. Perf. Tr.) | 6 | 158 | 9-2 |
| Lots of Worms (St. Voc.) | 2 | 310 | 11-19 |
| Lots of Worms (St. Perf. Tr.) | 2 | 310 | 11-20 |
| Love Can Build a Bridge (St. Voc.) | 4 | 324 | 14-3 |
| Love Can Build a Bridge (St. Perf. Tr.) | 4 | 324 | 14-4 |
| Love in Any Language (St. Voc.) | 6 | 476 | 22-14 |
| Love in Any Language (St. Perf. Tr.) | 6 | 476 | 22-15 |
| Love Is on Our Side (St. Voc.) | 5 | 324 | 15-9 |
| Love Is on Our Side (St. Perf. Tr.) | 5 | 324 | 15-10 |
| Love Somebody (St. Voc.) | 3 | 94 | 3-31 |
| Love Somebody (St. Perf. Tr.) | 3 | 94 | 3-32 |
| Love Will Guide Us (St. Voc.) | 4 | 328 | 14-8 |
| Love Will Guide Us (St. Perf. Tr.) | 4 | 328 | 14-9 |
| Lovely Hala Trees (Nani wale na hala) (St. Voc.) | 3 | 260 | 9-2 |
| Lucy Locket (St. Voc.) | 2 | 27 | 1-32 |
| Lullaby and Dance (St. Voc.) | 4 | 387 | 16-26 |
| Lullaby and Dance (St. Perf. Tr.) | 4 | 387 | 16-27 |
| Luna lunera (Moon, Moonlight) (speech piece) (St. Voc.) | K | 90 | 3-36 |
| Luna lunera (Moon, Moonlight) (speech piece) (St. Perf. Tr.) | K | 90 | 3-38 |
| Má Teodora (Spanish) (St. Voc.) | 6 | 301 | 15-12 |
| Má Teodora (English) (St. Voc.) | 6 | 301 | 15-13 |
| Má Teodora (St. Perf. Tr.) | 6 | 301 | 15-14 |
| Magnolia (Spanish) (St. Voc.) | 6 | 16 | 1-22 |
| Magnolia (English) (St. Voc.) | 6 | 16 | 1-23 |
| Magnolia (St. Perf. Tr.) | 6 | 16 | 1-24 |
| Make New Friends (St. Voc.) | 3 | 36 | 2-1 |
| Make New Friends (a cappella version) (St. Voc.) | 3 | 36 | 2-2 |
| Make New Friends (St. Perf. Tr.) | 3 | 36 | 2-3 |
| Making Valentines (St. Voc.) | 1 | 437 | 14-10 |
| Making Valentines (St. Perf. Tr.) | 1 | 437 | 14-11 |
| Mama, Buy Me a Chiney Doll (St. Voc.) | K | 120 | 4-33 |
| Mama, Buy Me a Chiney Doll (St. Perf. Tr.) | K | 120 | 4-34 |
| Mama Don't 'Low (St. Voc./Dance Perf. Tr.) | 6 | 358 | 18-6 |
| Mama Don't 'Low (St. Perf. Tr.) | 6 | 358 | 18-7 |
| Man of Constant Sorrow (St. Voc.) | 7 | F-28 | 11-14 |
| Man of Constant Sorrow (St. Perf. Tr.) | 7 | F-28 | 11-15 |
| Mañana (Tomorrow) (St. Voc.) | 7 | E-14 | 9-26 |
| Mañana (Tomorrow) (St. Perf. Tr.) | 7 | E-14 | 9-28 |
| Mango Walk (St. Voc.) | 5 | 200 | 10-9 |
| Mango Walk (St. Perf. Tr.) | 5 | 200 | 10-10 |
| Marines' Hymn, The (St. Voc.) | 8 | C-39 | 7-9 |
| Marines' Hymn, The (St. Perf. Tr.) | 8 | C-39 | 7-10 |
| Mariposita (Little Butterfly) (St. Voc.) | 2 | 156 | 6-1 |
| Mariposita (Little Butterfly) (St. Perf. Tr.) | 2 | 156 | 6-3 |

**Songs and Speech Pieces**

| Title | Gr. | Pg. | CD Track |
|---|---|---|---|
| Martin Luther King (St. Voc.) | 1 | 434 | 14-6 |
| Martin Luther King (St. Perf. Tr.) | 1 | 434 | 14-7 |
| Mary Ann (St. Voc./Dance Perf. Tr.) | 6 | 180 | 10-10 |
| Mary Ann (St. Perf. Tr.) | 6 | 180 | 10-11 |
| Mary Ann (St. Voc.) | K | 253 | 8-40 |
| Mary Ann (St. Perf. Tr.) | K | 253 | 8-41 |
| Mary Came a-Running (St. Voc.) | K | 294 | 10-17 |
| Mary Came a-Running (St. Perf. Tr.) | K | 294 | 10-18 |
| Mary Wore Her Red Dress (St. Voc.) | K | 74 | 3-6 |
| Mary Wore Her Red Dress (St. Perf. Tr.) | K | 74 | 3-7 |
| Mashed Potatoes (St. Voc.) | 1 | 20 | 1-32 |
| Mashed Potatoes (St. Perf. Tr.) | 1 | 20 | 1-33 |
| May the Sun Shine Forever (Pust' 'vsegda budet sonse) (St. Voc.) | 3 | 278 | 9-35 |
| Mbombera (St. Voc.) | K | 24 | 1-38 |
| Mbombera (St. Perf. Tr.) | K | 24 | 1-39 |
| Me voy para la luna (I'm Going to the Moon) (St. Voc.) | 1 | 397 | 12-29 |
| Me voy para la luna (I'm Going to the Moon) (St. Perf. Tr.) | 1 | 397 | 12-30 |
| Meng Jian Nu (Mandarin) (St. Voc.) | 5 | 194 | 10-1 |
| Meng Jian Nu (English) (St. Voc.) | 5 | 194 | 10-2 |
| Meng Jian Nu (St. Perf. Tr.) | 5 | 194 | 10-3 |
| Merry Modal Christmas, A (French and English version) (St. Voc.) | 4 | 411 | 17-15 |
| Merry Modal Christmas, A (English only version) (St. Voc.) | 4 | 411 | 17-16 |
| Merry Modal Christmas, A (St. Perf. Tr.) | 4 | 411 | 17-17 |
| Merry-Go-Round (St. Voc.) | K | 290 | 10-13 |
| Merry-Go-Round (St. Perf. Tr.) | K | 290 | 10-14 |
| Mi chacra (My Farm) (St. Voc.) | 1 | 364 | 11-28 |
| Mi chacra (My Farm) (St. Perf. Tr.) | 1 | 364 | 11-30 |
| Mi cuerpo hace música (There's Music Inside Me) (St. Voc.) | K | 106 | 4-8 |
| Mi cuerpo hace música (St. Perf. Tr.) | K | 106 | 4-10 |
| Michael Finnigan (St. Voc.) | 3 | 153 | 5-25 |
| Michael Finnigan (St. Perf. Tr.) | 3 | 153 | 5-26 |
| Michael Finnigan/This Old Man (Partner Songs) (St. Voc.) | 3 | 153 | 5-27 |
| Michael, Row the Boat Ashore (St. Voc.) | 2 | 18 | 1-24 |
| Michael, Row the Boat Ashore (St. Perf. Tr.) | 2 | 18 | 1-25 |
| Midnight Special, The (St. Voc.) | 7 | F-23 | 11-8 |
| Midnight Special, The (St. Perf. Tr.) | 7 | F-23 | 11-9 |
| Minka (Ukrainian) (St. Voc./Dance Perf. Tr.) | 4 | 222 | 9-21 |
| Minka (English) (St. Voc.) | 4 | 222 | 9-22 |
| Minka (St. Perf. Tr.) | 4 | 222 | 9-23 |
| Miss Mary Mack (St. Voc.) | 2 | 42 | 2-4 |
| Miss Mary Mack (St. Perf. Tr.) | 2 | 42 | 2-5 |
| Miss Susie Anna Sue (St. Voc.) | K | 242 | 8-27 |
| Miss Susie Anna Sue (St. Perf. Tr.) | K | 242 | 8-28 |
| Mississippi River Chant (speech piece) (St. Voc.) | 2 | 132 | 5-20 |
| Mississippi River Chant (speech piece) (St. Perf. Tr.) | 2 | 132 | 5-21 |
| Missy-La, Massa-La (St. Voc.) | 4 | 188 | 8-25 |
| Missy-La, Massa-La (St. Perf. Tr.) | 4 | 188 | 8-26 |
| Mister Rabbit (St. Voc.) | K | 128 | 5-4 |
| Mister Rabbit (St. Perf. Tr.) | K | 128 | 5-5 |
| Mister Ram Goat-O (St. Voc.) | 3 | 54 | 2-26 |
| Mister Ram Goat-O (St. Perf. Tr.) | 3 | 54 | 2-27 |
| Mister Snow Rap (speech piece) (St. Voc.) | 2 | 391 | 14-34 |
| Mister Snow Rap (speech piece) (St. Perf. Tr.) | 2 | 391 | 14-35 |
| Mixteca Song (Canción Mixteca) (St. Voc.) | 5 | 326 | 15-12 |
| Mommy's Day (El día de mamita) (St. Voc.) | K | 325 | 11-30 |
| Mon Hides the Cloth (Mon son pha) (speech piece) (St. Voc.) | K | 91 | 3-41 |
| Mon papa (My Papa) (St. Voc.) | 2 | 280 | 10-17 |
| Mon papa (My Papa) (St. Perf. Tr.) | 2 | 280 | 10-19 |
| Mon son pha (Mon Hides the Cloth) (speech piece) (St. Voc.) | K | 91 | 3-40 |
| Mon son pha (speech piece) (St. Perf. Tr.) | K | 91 | 3-42 |
| Month of April, The (El mes de abril) (St. Voc.) | 3 | 328 | 11-26 |
| Moon, The (Tsuki) (St. Voc.) | 4 | 25 | 1-37 |
| Moon, Moonlight (Luna lunera) (speech piece) (St. Voc.) | K | 90 | 3-37 |
| Moonlight Lullaby (Yü guang guang) (St. Voc.) | 6 | 60 | 4-16 |
| Morning Comes Early (St. Voc./Dance Perf. Tr.) | 5 | 13 | 1-17 |
| Morning Comes Early (St. Perf. Tr.) | 5 | 13 | 1-18 |
| Morning Has Broken (St. Voc.) | 5 | 29 | 2-16 |
| Morning Has Broken (St. Perf. Tr.) | 5 | 29 | 2-17 |
| Morning Is Come (St. Voc.) | 3 | 128 | 4-35 |
| Morning Is Come (St. Perf. Tr.) | 3 | 128 | 4-36 |
| Mos mos (St. Voc.) | 1 | 130 | 4-26 |
| Mr. Tambourine Man (St. Voc.) | 6 | 150 | 8-21 |
| Mr. Tambourine Man (St. Perf. Tr.) | 6 | 150 | 8-22 |
| Mübaräk (Happy Birthday) (St. Voc./Dance Perf. Tr.) | 3 | 282 | 9-40 |
| Mübaräk (Happy Birthday) (St. Perf. Tr.) | 3 | 282 | 9-42 |
| Mud (St. Voc.) | 3 | 32 | 1-53 |
| Mud (St. Perf. Tr.) | 3 | 32 | 1-54 |
| Music Alone Shall Live (Himmel und Erde) (St. Voc.) | 5 | 94 | 5-12 |
| Music's in Me, The (St. Voc.) | 2 | 40 | 2-2 |
| Music's in Me, The (St. Perf. Tr.) | 2 | 40 | 2-3 |
| Must Be Santa (St. Voc.) | K | 318 | 11-19 |
| Must Be Santa (St. Perf. Tr.) | K | 318 | 11-20 |
| My Bonnie Lies Over the Ocean (St. Voc.) | 4 | 338 | 14-20 |
| My Bonnie Lies Over the Ocean (St. Perf. Tr.) | 4 | 338 | 14-21 |
| My Dear Companion (St. Voc.) | 6 | 23 | 2-11 |
| My Dear Companion (St. Perf. Tr.) | 6 | 23 | 2-12 |
| My Dear Mama (Kébé mama) (St. Voc.) | 1 | 442 | 14-23 |
| My Dreydl (St. Voc.) | K | 314 | 11-11 |
| My Dreydl (St. Perf. Tr.) | K | 314 | 11-12 |
| My Farm (Mi chacra) (St. Voc.) | 1 | 364 | 11-29 |
| My Father's House (St. Voc.) | 2 | 25 | 1-29 |
| My Father's House (St. Perf. Tr.) | 2 | 25 | 1-30 |
| My Foot's in My Stirrup (St. Voc.) | 2 | 234 | 8-21 |
| My Foot's in My Stirrup (St. Perf. Tr.) | 2 | 234 | 8-22 |
| My Head and My Shoulders (Ikhanda, maslombe) (St. Voc.) | K | 14 | 1-21 |
| My Home's Across the Blue Ridge Mountains (St. Voc.) | 4 | 84 | 4-29 |
| My Home's Across the Blue Ridge Mountains (St. Perf. Tr.) | 4 | 84 | 4-30 |
| My Home's Across the Blue Ridge Mountains (St. Voc.) | 7 | F-6 | 10-22 |
| My Home's Across the Blue Ridge Mountains (St. Perf. Tr.) | 7 | F-6 | 10-23 |
| My Mama's Calling Me (St. Voc.) | 1 | 261 | 8-25 |
| My Mama's Calling Me (St. Perf. Tr.) | 1 | 261 | 8-26 |
| My Papa (Mon papa) (St. Voc.) | 2 | 280 | 10-18 |
| My Pony, Macaroni (St. Voc.) | 1 | 158 | 5-10 |
| My Pony, Macaroni (St. Perf. Tr.) | 1 | 158 | 5-11 |
| My Valentine (St. Voc.) | K | 323 | 11-27 |
| My Valentine (St. Perf. Tr.) | K | 323 | 11-28 |
| Name Game, The (speech piece) (St. Voc.) | 1 | 315 | 10-3 |
| Name Game, The (speech piece) (St. Perf. Tr.) | 1 | 315 | 10-4 |
| Name, Name, What's Your Name? (speech piece) (St. Voc.) | 3 | 10 | 1-6 |

| Title | Gr. | Pg. | CD Track |
|---|---|---|---|
| Name, Name, What's Your Name? (speech piece) (St. Perf. Tr.) | 3 | 10 | 1-7 |
| Nampaya omame (There Come Our Mothers) (St. Voc.) | 1 | 138 | 4-35 |
| Nampaya omame (There Come Our Mothers) (St. Perf. Tr.) | 1 | 138 | 4-37 |
| Nampaya omame (There Come Our Mothers) (St. Voc.) | 7 | D-10 | 8-25 |
| Nampaya omame (There Come Our Mothers) (St. Perf. Tr.) | 7 | D-10 | 8-27 |
| Nana Kru (St. Voc.) | 6 | 282 | 14-13 |
| Nana Kru (St. Perf. Tr.) | 6 | 282 | 14-14 |
| Nana, Thread Needle (St. Voc.) | 1 | 38 | 2-1 |
| Nana, Thread Needle (St. Perf. Tr.) | 1 | 38 | 2-2 |
| Nani wale na hala (Lovely Hala Trees) | 3 | 260 | 9-1 |
| Nani wale na hala (Lovely Hala Trees) (St. Perf. Tr.) (St. Voc./Dance Perf. Tr.) | 3 | 260 | 9-3 |
| Nanny Goat (St. Voc.) | K | 161 | 6-1 |
| Nanny Goat (St. Perf. Tr.) | K | 161 | 6-2 |
| Naranja dulce (Sweet Orange) (St. Voc.) | 2 | 96 | 4-3 |
| Naranja dulce (Sweet Orange) (St. Perf. Tr.) | 2 | 96 | 4-5 |
| Naughty Tabby Cat (Cirmos cica) (St. Voc.) | 1 | 130 | 4-20 |
| Ner li (The Light) (St. Voc.) | 2 | 383 | 14-17 |
| Ner li (The Light) (St. Perf. Tr.) | 2 | 383 | 14-19 |
| Never Smile at a Crocodile (from Peter Pan) (St. Voc.) | 3 | 100 | 3-40 |
| Never Smile at a Crocodile (from Peter Pan) (St. Perf. Tr.) | 3 | 100 | 3-41 |
| New Hungarian Folk Song (St. Voc.) | 6 | 196 | 10-35 |
| New Hungarian Folk Song (St. Perf. Tr.) | 6 | 196 | 10-36 |
| New Way to Walk, A (St. Voc.) | K | 117 | 4-28 |
| New Way to Walk, A (St. Perf. Tr.) | K | 117 | 4-29 |
| New Year's Greeting, A (Ichi-gatsu tsuitachi) (St. Voc.) | 3 | 406 | 14-27 |
| New Year's Greeting, A (Ichi-gatsu tsuitachi) (St. Voc.) | 7 | I-40 | 13-32 |
| Nie chcę cię znác (Don't Want to Know You) (St. Voc.) | 3 | 314 | 11-3 |
| Nie chcę cię znác (Don't Want to Know You) (St. Perf. Tr.) | 3 | 314 | 11-5 |
| Niño querido (Dearest Child) (St. Voc.) | 1 | 308 | 9-41 |
| Niño querido (Dearest Child) (St. Perf. Tr.) | 1 | 308 | 9-43 |
| Niu lang zhi nü (The Cowherd and the Weaving Maid) (St. Voc.) | 4 | 335 | 14-15 |
| Niu lang zhi nü (The Cowherd and the Weaving Maid) (St. Perf. Tr.) | 4 | 335 | 14-17 |
| No quiero plata (I Don't Want Silver) (St. Voc.) | 1 | 424 | 13-35 |
| No quiero plata (I Don't Want Silver) (St. Perf. Tr.) | 1 | 424 | 13-37 |
| Noah's Shanty (St. Voc.) | 1 | 344 | 11-1 |
| Noah's Shanty (St. Perf. Tr.) | 1 | 344 | 11-2 |
| Nothing Do I Own (Ego sum pauper) (St. Voc.) | 5 | 158 | 8-8 |
| Now Hear the Song (Ahora voy a cantarles) (St. Voc.) | 3 | 56 | 2-32 |
| Now Let Me Fly (St. Voc.) | 3 | 178 | 6-20 |
| Now Let Me Fly (St. Perf. Tr.) | 3 | 178 | 6-21 |
| Now That's Tap (speech piece) (St. Voc.) | 6 | 320 | 16-11 |
| Now That's Tap (speech piece) (St. Perf. Tr.) | 6 | 320 | 16-12 |
| Now's the Time (St. Voc.) | 5 | 445 | 19-16 |
| Now's the Time (St. Perf. Tr.) | 5 | 445 | 19-17 |
| Nu wahtan (Waking Song) (St. Voc.) | 1 | 279 | 9-6 |
| Nu wahtan (Waking Song) (St. Perf. Tr.) | 1 | 279 | 9-8 |
| Number One, Touch Your Tongue (speech piece) (St. Voc.) | K | 204 | 7-15 |
| Number One, Touch Your Tongue (speech piece) (St. Perf. Tr.) | K | 204 | 7-16 |
| Nursery Song (Yang wa wa) (St. Voc.) | K | 162 | 6-4 |
| O, Chanukah (Oy, Hanuka) (St. Voc.) | 5 | 464 | 20-8 |
| O, Chanukah (Oy, Hanuka) (St. Voc.) | 7 | I-44 | 14-2 |
| O, Desayo (St. Voc.) | 5 | 411 | 18-22 |
| O, Desayo (St. Perf. Tr.) | 5 | 411 | 18-23 |
| O hal'lwe (St. Voc.) | 3 | 256 | 8-32 |
| O hal'lwe (St. Perf. Tr.) | 3 | 256 | 8-33 |
| O laufet, ihr Hirten (Come Running, You Shepherds) (St. Voc.) | 2 | 384 | 14-21 |
| O laufet, ihr Hirten (Come Running, You Shepherds) (St. Perf. Tr.) | 2 | 384 | 14-23 |
| O lê lê O Bahía (O Le O La) (St. Voc.) | 6 | 165 | 9-14 |
| O lê lê O Bahía (O Le O La) (St. Perf. Tr.) | 6 | 165 | 9-16 |
| O Le O La (O lê lê O Bahía) (St. Voc.) | 6 | 165 | 9-15 |
| O ma washi (Go Around the Cat's Eye) (St. Voc.) | K | 13 | 1-16 |
| O ma washi (Go Around the Cat's Eye) (St. Perf. Tr.) | K | 13 | 1-18 |
| O Music (St. Voc.) | 5 | 162 | 8-15 |
| O Music (St. Perf. Tr.) | 5 | 162 | 8-16 |
| O pião entrou (The Top Joined the Circle) (St. Voc.) | 2 | 355 | 13-6 |
| O pião entrou (The Top Joined the Circle) (St. Perf. Tr.) | 2 | 355 | 13-8 |
| Ochimbo (St. Voc.) | 4 | 134 | 6-11 |
| Ochimbo (St. Perf. Tr.) | 4 | 134 | 6-12 |
| Ocho kandelikas (Eight Little Candles) (St. Voc.) | 4 | 429 | 18-8 |
| Ocho kandelikas (Eight Little Candles) (St. Perf. Tr.) | 4 | 429 | 18-10 |
| Ode to Joy (German) (St. Voc.) | 4 | 152 | 7-7 |
| Ode to Joy (English) (St. Voc.) | 4 | 152 | 7-8 |
| Ode to Joy (St. Perf. Tr.) | 4 | 152 | 7-9 |
| Oh, Danny Boy (St. Voc.) | 4 | 48 | 2-30 |
| Oh, Danny Boy (St. Perf. Tr.) | 4 | 48 | 2-31 |
| Oh, Freedom (St. Voc.) | 5 | 392 | 18-7 |
| Oh, Freedom (St. Perf. Tr.) | 5 | 392 | 18-8 |
| Oh, Freedom (St. Voc.) | 7 | G-30 | 12-20 |
| Oh, Freedom (St. Perf. Tr.) | 7 | G-30 | 12-21 |
| Oh, How Lovely Is the Evening (St. Voc.) | 4 | 217 | 9-10 |
| Oh, How Lovely Is the Evening (St. Perf. Tr.) | 4 | 217 | 9-11 |
| Oh, Jalisco! (¡Ay, Jalisco no te Rajes!) (T.A.P.) | 7 | I-6 | 13-6 |
| Oh, Susanna (St. Voc.) | 4 | 264 | 11-3 |
| Oh, Susanna (St. Perf. Tr.) | 4 | 264 | 11-4 |
| Oh, Watch the Stars (St. Voc.) | 2 | 144 | 5-38 |
| Oh, Watch the Stars (St. Perf. Tr.) | 2 | 144 | 5-39 |
| Oh, Watch the Stars (St. Voc.) | 5 | 216 | 10-29 |
| Oh, Watch the Stars (St. Perf. Tr.) | 5 | 216 | 10-30 |
| Oh, What a Day! (St. Voc.) | K | 302 | 10-27 |
| Oh, What a Day! (St. Perf. Tr.) | K | 302 | 10-28 |
| Oh, Won't You Sit Down (St. Voc.) | 3 | 28 | 1-43 |
| Oh, Won't You Sit Down (St. Perf. Tr.) | 3 | 28 | 1-44 |
| Oklahoma (St. Voc.) | 5 | 36 | 2-29 |
| Oklahoma (St. Perf. Tr.) | 5 | 36 | 2-30 |
| Old Abram Brown (St. Voc.) | 5 | 222 | 10-38 |
| Old Abram Brown (St. Perf. Tr.) | 5 | 222 | 10-39 |
| Old Blue (St. Voc.) | K | 122 | 4-35 |
| Old Blue (St. Perf. Tr.) | K | 122 | 4-36 |
| Old Brass Wagon (St. Voc.) | 2 | 122 | 4-44 |
| Old Brass Wagon (St. Perf. Tr.) | 2 | 122 | 4-45 |
| Old Chisholm Trail, The (St. Voc.) | 6 | 237 | 12-12 |
| Old Chisholm Trail, The (St. Perf. Tr.) | 6 | 237 | 12-13 |
| Old Dan Tucker (St. Voc.) | 3 | 96 | 3-36 |
| Old Dan Tucker (St. Perf. Tr.) | 3 | 96 | 3-37 |
| Old House, Tear It Down! (St. Voc.) | 4 | 178 | 8-8 |
| Old House, Tear It Down! (St. Perf. Tr.) | 4 | 178 | 8-9 |
| Old Man Mosie (St. Voc.) | 3 | 108 | 4-15 |
| Old Man Mosie (St. Perf. Tr.) | 3 | 108 | 4-16 |
| Old Texas (St. Voc.) | 3 | 77 | 3-3 |
| Old Texas (St. Perf. Tr.) | 3 | 77 | 3-4 |
| Oliver Jump (speech piece) (St. Voc.) | K | 205 | 7-17 |
| Oliver Jump (speech piece) (St. Perf. Tr.) | K | 205 | 7-18 |

Songs and Speech Pieces

| Title | Gr. | Pg. | CD Track |
|---|---|---|---|
| Oliver Twist (St. Voc.) | K | 138 | 5-18 |
| Oliver Twist (St. Perf. Tr.) | K | 138 | 5-19 |
| On a Log, Mister Frog (St. Voc.) | K | 148 | 5-31 |
| On a Log, Mister Frog (St. Perf. Tr.) | K | 148 | 5-32 |
| On My Way (St. Voc.) | 6 | 313 | 16-4 |
| On My Way (St. Perf. Tr.) | 6 | 313 | 16-5 |
| One Family (St. Voc.) | 7 | G-17 | 12-11 |
| One Family (St. Perf. Tr.) | 7 | G-17 | 12-12 |
| One Green Jelly Bean (St. Voc.) | K | 287 | 10-7 |
| One Green Jelly Bean (St. Perf. Tr.) | K | 287 | 10-8 |
| One Moment in Time (St. Voc.) | 6 | 352 | 18-2 |
| One Moment in Time (St. Perf. Tr.) | 6 | 352 | 18-3 |
| One Morning in May (St. Voc.) | 6 | 121 | 7-8 |
| One Morning in May (St. Perf. Tr.) | 6 | 121 | 7-9 |
| One Morning Soon (St. Voc.) | 3 | 68 | 2-43 |
| One Morning Soon (St. Perf. Tr.) | 3 | 68 | 2-44 |
| One Small Step (St. Voc.) | 5 | 126 | 6-18 |
| One Small Step (St. Perf. Tr.) | 5 | 126 | 6-19 |
| One, Two, and Three (Uno, dos, y tres) (St. Voc.) | 5 | 427 | 19-2 |
| One, Two, Three (Un, deux, trois) (St. Voc.) | 2 | 198 | 7-32 |
| Orange Blossom Special (St. Voc.) | 5 | 266 | 12-24 |
| Orange Blossom Special (St. Perf. Tr.) | 5 | 266 | 12-25 |
| Orange Blossom Special (St. Voc.) | 8 | E-6 | 9-11 |
| Orange Blossom Special (St. Perf. Tr.) | 8 | E-6 | 9-12 |
| Osamu kosamu (Biting Wind) (St. Voc.) | 4 | 96 | 5-2 |
| Osamu kosamu (Biting Wind) (St. Perf. Tr.) | 4 | 96 | 5-4 |
| Over in the Meadow (St. Voc.) | 1 | 346 | 11-4 |
| Over in the Meadow (St. Perf. Tr.) | 1 | 346 | 11-5 |
| Over My Head (St. Voc.) | 4 | 118 | 5-35 |
| Over My Head (St. Perf. Tr.) | 4 | 118 | 5-36 |
| Over My Head (St. Voc.) | 7 | G-9 | 11-23 |
| Over My Head (St. Perf. Tr.) | 7 | G-9 | 11-24 |
| Over the Rainbow (from The Wizard of Oz) (St. Voc.) | 4 | 140 | 6-27 |
| Over the Rainbow (from The Wizard of Oz) (St. Perf. Tr.) | 4 | 140 | 6-28 |
| Over the River and Through the Wood (St. Voc.) | 3 | 384 | 13-20 |
| Over the River and Through the Wood (St. Perf. Tr.) | 3 | 384 | 13-21 |
| Over There (St. Voc.) | 5 | 279 | 13-3 |
| Over There (St. Perf. Tr.) | 5 | 279 | 13-4 |
| Owl and The Pumpkin, The (St. Voc.) | 2 | 377 | 14-7 |
| Owl and The Pumpkin, The (St. Perf. Tr.) | 2 | 377 | 14-8 |
| Oy, Hanuka (O, Chanukah) (St. Voc.) | 5 | 464 | 20-7 |
| Oy, Hanuka (O, Chanukah) (St. Perf. Tr.) | 5 | 464 | 20-9 |
| Oy, Hanuka (O, Chanukah) (St. Voc.) | 7 | I-44 | 14-1 |
| Oy, Hanuka (O, Chanukah) (St. Perf. Tr.) | 7 | I-44 | 14-3 |
| Oye (Listen) (St. Voc.) | 6 | 336 | 17-5 |
| Oye (Listen) (St. Perf. Tr.) | 6 | 336 | 17-6 |
| Pai pi qiu (Bouncing Balls ) (St. Voc.) | 1 | 324 | 10-19 |
| Pai pi qiu (Bouncing Balls ) (St. Perf. Tr.) | 1 | 324 | 10-21 |
| Painted Rooster, The (El gallo pinto) (St. Voc.) | 3 | 86 | 3-19 |
| Painting Song: A Dribble and a Dot (St. Voc.) | K | 175 | 6-26 |
| Painting Song: A Dribble and a Dot (St. Perf. Tr.) | K | 175 | 6-27 |
| Panamam tombé (St. Voc.) | 7 | D-18 | 9-2 |
| Panamam tombé (St. Perf. Tr.) | 7 | D-18 | 9-3 |
| Parade Came Marching, The (St. Voc.) | 1 | 166 | 5-26 |
| Parade Came Marching, The (St. Perf. Tr.) | 1 | 166 | 5-27 |
| Partridge, The (Gakavik) (St. Voc.) | 4 | 14 | 1-18 |
| Party Tonight! (St. Voc.) | 2 | 152 | 5-50 |
| Party Tonight! (St. Perf. Tr.) | 2 | 152 | 5-51 |
| Pass This Shoe (Geef jij mij die schoen) (St. Voc.) | 1 | 126 | 4-13 |
| Pastures of Plenty (St. Voc.) | 4 | 280 | 11-25 |
| Pastures of Plenty (St. Perf. Tr.) | 4 | 280 | 11-26 |
| Pat Works on the Railway (St. Voc.) | 5 | 182 | 9-15 |
| Pat Works on the Railway (St. Perf. Tr.) | 5 | 182 | 9-16 |
| Paths of Victory (St. Voc.) | 6 | 195 | 10-30 |
| Paths of Victory (St. Perf. Tr.) | 6 | 195 | 10-31 |
| Pavo, pavo (The Turkey Game) (St. Voc.) | 1 | 416 | 13-18 |
| Pavo, pavo (The Turkey Game) (St. Perf. Tr.) | 1 | 416 | 13-20 |
| Paw-Paw Patch (St. Voc.) | 4 | 93 | 4-36 |
| Paw-Paw Patch (St. Perf. Tr.) | 4 | 93 | 4-37 |
| Pay Me My Money Down (St. Voc.) | 4 | 38 | 2-18 |
| Pay Me My Money Down (St. Perf. Tr.) | 4 | 38 | 2-19 |
| Pay Me My Money Down (St. Voc.) | 7 | I-46 | 14-5 |
| Pay Me My Money Down (St. Perf. Tr.) | 7 | I-46 | 14-6 |
| Peace Like a River (St. Voc.) | 3 | 246 | 8-13 |
| Peace Like a River (St. Perf. Tr.) | 3 | 246 | 8-14 |
| Peace Like a River (T.A.P.) | 6 | 190 | 10-26 |
| Peace Like a River (St. Perf. Tr.) | 6 | 190 | 10-27 |
| Peace Round (St. Voc.) | 4 | 348 | 15-10 |
| Peace Round (St. Perf. Tr.) | 4 | 348 | 15-11 |
| Peanut Butter (St. Voc.) | 1 | 173 | 5-33 |
| Peanut Butter (St. Perf. Tr.) | 1 | 173 | 5-34 |
| Pease Porridge Hot (St. Voc.) | 1 | 134 | 4-30 |
| Pease Porridge Hot (St. Perf. Tr.) | 1 | 134 | 4-31 |
| Peppermint Twist (St. Voc.) | 3 | 46 | 2-15 |
| Peppermint Twist (St. Perf. Tr.) | 3 | 46 | 2-16 |
| Perná, perná, i mélissá (Fly By, Fly By) (St. Voc.) | K | 264 | 9-13 |
| Perná, perná, i mélissá (Fly By! Fly By!) (St. Perf. Tr.) | K | 264 | 9-15 |
| Perot (Fruit) (St. Voc.) | 2 | 378 | 14-9 |
| Perot (Fruit) (St. Perf. Tr.) | 2 | 378 | 14-11 |
| Phoebe (St. Voc.) | 1 | 30 | 1-45 |
| Phoebe (St. Perf. Tr.) | 1 | 30 | 1-46 |
| Pigeons (Hato popo) (St. Voc.) | 1 | 186 | 6-14 |
| Pin Pon (Spanish) (St. Voc.) | 1 | 146 | 4-48 |
| Pin Pon (English) (St. Voc.) | 1 | 146 | 4-49 |
| Pin Pon (St. Perf. Tr.) | 1 | 146 | 4-50 |
| Piñata, The (La piñata) (St. Voc.) | 3 | 399 | 14-13 |
| Piñata Song (Al quebrar la piñata) (St. Voc.) | 4 | 432 | 18-16 |
| Piñon, pirulín (Spanish) (St. Voc.) | 2 | 174 | 6-33 |
| Piñon, pirulín (English) (St. Voc.) | 2 | 174 | 6-34 |
| Piñon, pirulín (St. Perf. Tr.) | 2 | 174 | 6-35 |
| Pizza, Pizza, Daddy-o (St. Voc.) | 2 | 28 | 1-36 |
| Pizza, Pizza, Daddy-o (St. Perf. Tr.) | 2 | 28 | 1-37 |
| Planets Chant, The (speech piece) (St. Voc.) | 4 | 377 | 16-16 |
| Planets Chant, The (speech piece) (St. Perf. Tr.) | 4 | 377 | 16-17 |
| Plant Four Seeds (St. Voc.) | 2 | 130 | 5-17 |
| Plant Four Seeds (St. Perf. Tr.) | 2 | 130 | 5-18 |
| Play a Simple Melody (St. Voc.) | 5 | 72 | 4-17 |
| Play a Simple Melody (St. Perf. Tr.) | 5 | 72 | 4-18 |
| Plovers (Hama chi dori) (St. Voc.) | 3 | 330 | 11-31 |
| Poco, Le' Me 'Lone (St. Voc.) | 3 | 300 | 10-28 |
| Poco, Le' Me 'Lone (St. Perf. Tr.) | 3 | 300 | 10-29 |
| Pollerita (Spanish) (St. Voc.) | 5 | 151 | 7-30 |
| Pollerita (English) (St. Voc.) | 5 | 151 | 7-31 |
| Pollerita (St. Perf. Tr.) | 5 | 151 | 7-32 |
| Polly Wee (The Frog Song) (St. Voc.) | K | 119 | 4-31 |
| Polly Wee (The Frog Song) (St. Perf. Tr.) | K | 119 | 4-32 |
| Pon, pon, pon (Tap, Tap, Tap) (St. Voc.) | K | 50 | 2-27 |
| Pon, pon, pon (St. Perf. Tr.) | K | 50 | 2-29 |
| Popcorn Popping (St. Voc.) | 1 | 440 | 14-19 |
| Popcorn Popping (St. Perf. Tr.) | 1 | 440 | 14-20 |

Songs and Speech Pieces

| Title | Gr. | Pg. | CD Track |
|---|---|---|---|
| Pottery Dance (St. Voc.) | 1 | 370 | 11-41 |
| Pottery Dance (St. Perf. Tr.) | 1 | 370 | 11-42 |
| Pretty Saro (St. Voc.) | 3 | 216 | 7-33 |
| Pretty Saro (St. Perf. Tr.) | 3 | 216 | 7-34 |
| Pretty Trappings (St. Voc.) | Pre K | | |
| Promised Land, The (St. Voc.) | 5 | 258 | 12-12 |
| Promised Land, The (St. Perf. Tr.) | 5 | 258 | 12-13 |
| Proud (St. Voc.) | 7 | G-3 | 11-20 |
| Proud (St. Perf. Tr.) | 7 | G-3 | 11-21 |
| Ptashky u babusi sadochku (Birds in Granny's Garden) (St. Voc.) | 1 | 192 | 6-24 |
| Ptashky u babusi sadochku (St. Perf. Tr.) | 1 | 192 | 6-26 |
| Puff, the Magic Dragon (St. Voc.) | 2 | 350 | 12-28 |
| Puff, the Magic Dragon (St. Perf. Tr.) | 2 | 350 | 12-29 |
| Pull the Canoe (To'ia mai te waka) (St. Voc.) | 1 | 77 | 2-56 |
| Pumpkin, Pumpkin (St. Voc.) | 1 | 413 | 13-13 |
| Pumpkin, Pumpkin (St. Perf. Tr.) | 1 | 413 | 13-14 |
| Purim Song (Chag purim) (St. Voc.) | 1 | 438 | 14-15 |
| Purple People Eater, The (St. Voc.) | 6 | 448 | 21-9 |
| Purple People Eater, The (St. Perf. Tr.) | 6 | 448 | 21-10 |
| Pust' 'vsegda budet sonse (May the Sun Shine Forever) (St. Voc./Dance Perf. Tr.) | 3 | 278 | 9-34 |
| Pust' 'vsegda budet sonse (May the Sun Shine Forever) (St. Perf. Tr.) | 3 | 278 | 9-36 |
| Put a Little Love in Your Heart (St. Voc.) | 4 | 6 | 1-3 |
| Put a Little Love in Your Heart (St. Perf. Tr.) | 4 | 6 | 1-4 |
| Put Your Finger in the Air (St. Voc.) | K | 114 | 4-25 |
| Put Your Finger in the Air (St. Perf. Tr.) | K | 114 | 4-26 |
| Put Your Hand in My Hand (St. Voc.) | 1 | 332 | 10-26 |
| Put Your Hand in My Hand (St. Perf. Tr.) | 1 | 332 | 10-27 |
| Quâ câu gió bay (The Wind on the Bridge) (St. Voc.) | 5 | 460 | 20-1 |
| Quâ câu gió bay (The Wind on the Bridge) (St. Perf. Tr.) | 5 | 460 | 20-3 |
| ¡Qué bonita bandera! (What a Beautiful Banner!) (St. Voc.) | 5 | 294 | 13-20 |
| ¡Qué bonita bandera! (What a Beautiful Banner!) (St. Perf. Tr.) | 5 | 294 | 13-22 |
| ¡Qué gusto! (What Pleasure) (St. Voc.) | 3 | 132 | 4-45 |
| ¡Qué gusto! (What Pleasure) (St. Perf. Tr.) | 3 | 132 | 4-47 |
| ¡Qué llueva! (It's Raining!) (St. Voc.) | K | 81 | 3-15 |
| ¡Qué llueva! (It's Raining!) (St. Perf. Tr.) | K | 81 | 3-17 |
| Rabbit (Usagi) (St. Voc.) | 1 | 396 | 12-26 |
| Rabbit Footprints (St. Voc.) | 2 | 304 | 11-11 |
| Rabbit Footprints (St. Perf. Tr.) | 2 | 304 | 11-12 |
| Raccoon Dance Song (St. Voc.) | 1 | 260 | 8-23 |
| Raccoon Dance Song (St. Perf. Tr.) | 1 | 260 | 8-24 |
| Race You Down the Mountain (St. Voc.) | 1 | 127 | 4-16 |
| Race You Down the Mountain (St. Perf. Tr.) | 1 | 127 | 4-17 |
| Rags (St. Voc.) | 1 | 290 | 9-17 |
| Rags (St. Perf. Tr.) | 1 | 290 | 9-18 |
| Ragtime Cowboy Joe (St. Voc.) | 2 | 250 | 9-12 |
| Ragtime Cowboy Joe (St. Perf. Tr.) | 2 | 250 | 9-13 |
| Ragupati Ragava Raja Ram (St. Voc.) | 5 | 321 | 15-2 |
| Ragupati Ragava Raja Ram (St. Perf. Tr.) | 5 | 321 | 15-3 |
| Railroad Corral (St. Voc.) | 3 | 174 | 6-17 |
| Railroad Corral (St. Perf. Tr.) | 3 | 174 | 6-18 |
| Rain, Rain (St. Voc.) | 1 | 54 | 2-27 |
| Rain, Rain (St. Perf. Tr.) | 1 | 54 | 2-28 |
| Rain Sings a Song, The (St. Voc.) | 1 | 102 | 3-31 |
| Rain Sings a Song, The (St. Perf. Tr.) | 1 | 102 | 3-32 |
| Rainbow, The (St. Voc.) | 2 | 332 | 12-6 |
| Rainbow, The (St. Perf. Tr.) | 2 | 332 | 12-7 |
| Red River Valley (St. Voc.) | 6 | 11 | 1-6 |
| Red River Valley (St. Perf. Tr.) | 6 | 11 | 1-7 |
| Rhythm Is Gonna Get You, The (St. Voc.) | 6 | 348 | 17-19 |
| Rhythm Is Gonna Get You, The (St. Perf. Tr.) | 6 | 348 | 17-20 |
| Rice Planting Song (Cha yang wu) (St. Voc.) | 1 | 90 | 3-6 |
| Riddle Ree (speech piece) (St. Voc.) | 2 | 34 | 1-43 |
| Riddle Ree (speech piece) (St. Perf. Tr.) | 2 | 34 | 1-44 |
| Riendo el río corre (Run, Run, River) (St. Voc.) | 6 | 263 | 13-24 |
| Riendo el río corre (St. Perf. Tr.) | 6 | 263 | 13-26 |
| Rig-a-Jig-Jig (St. Voc.) | K | 99 | 3-55 |
| Rig-a-Jig-Jig (St. Perf. Tr.) | K | 99 | 3-56 |
| Ring of Roses, A (Ciranda) (St. Voc.) | 2 | 272 | 10-2 |
| Rinsho, rinsho (Japanese) (St. Voc.) | K | 285 | 10-3 |
| Rinsho, rinsho (English) (St. Voc.) | K | 285 | 10-4 |
| Rinsho, rinsho (St. Perf. Tr.) | K | 285 | 10-5 |
| Rio Grande (St. Voc.) | 4 | 256 | 10-28 |
| Rio Grande (St. Perf. Tr.) | 4 | 256 | 10-29 |
| Río, río (River, River) (St. Voc.) | 5 | 370 | 17-7 |
| Río, río (River, River) (St. Perf. Tr.) | 5 | 370 | 17-9 |
| Riqui rán (Spanish) (St. Voc.) | 1 | 48 | 2-18 |
| Riqui rán (English) (St. Voc.) | 1 | 48 | 2-19 |
| Riqui rán (St. Perf. Tr.) | 1 | 48 | 2-20 |
| Riqui rán (Spanish) (St. Voc.) | 4 | 66 | 3-33 |
| Riqui rán (English) (St. Voc.) | 4 | 66 | 3-34 |
| Riqui rán (St. Perf. Tr.) | 4 | 66 | 3-35 |
| Rise and Shine (St. Voc.) | 1 | 122 | 4-9 |
| Rise and Shine (St. Perf. Tr.) | 1 | 122 | 4-10 |
| Rise and Shine (St. Voc.) | 4 | 98 | 5-7 |
| Rise and Shine (St. Perf. Tr.) | 4 | 98 | 5-8 |
| Rise Up, Shepherd, and Follow (St. Voc.) | 5 | 471 | 20-19 |
| Rise Up, Shepherd, and Follow (St. Perf. Tr.) | 5 | 471 | 20-20 |
| Ríu ríu chíu (St. Voc.) | 5 | 435 | 19-9 |
| Ríu ríu chíu (St. Perf. Tr.) | 5 | 435 | 19-10 |
| River (St. Voc.) | 4 | 58 | 3-18 |
| River (St. Perf. Tr.) | 4 | 58 | 3-19 |
| River, River (Río, Río) (St. Voc.) | 5 | 370 | 17-8 |
| Rock and Roll Is Here to Stay (St. Voc.) | 6 | 36 | 2-32 |
| Rock and Roll Is Here to Stay (St. Perf. Tr.) | 6 | 36 | 2-33 |
| Rock Around the Clock (St. Voc.) | 7 | B-18 | 3-3 |
| Rock Around the Clock (St. Perf. Tr.) | 7 | B-18 | 3-4 |
| Rock Island Line (St. Voc.) | 4 | 54 | 3-9 |
| Rock Island Line (St. Perf. Tr.) | 4 | 54 | 3-10 |
| Rockin' Around the Christmas Tree (St. Voc./Dance Perf. Tr.) | 5 | 466 | 20-11 |
| Rockin' Around the Christmas Tree (St. Perf. Tr.) | 5 | 466 | 20-12 |
| Rockin' Robin (St. Voc.) | 3 | 368 | 13-1 |
| Rockin' Robin (St. Perf. Tr.) | 3 | 368 | 13-2 |
| Rocky Mountain (St. Voc.) | 2 | 98 | 4-7 |
| Rocky Mountain (St. Perf. Tr.) | 2 | 98 | 4-8 |
| Rocky Top (St. Voc.) | 5 | 348 | 16-6 |
| Rocky Top (St. Perf. Tr.) | 5 | 348 | 16-7 |
| Roll On, Columbia (St. Voc.) | 5 | 116 | 6-8 |
| Roll On, Columbia (St. Perf. Tr.) | 5 | 116 | 6-9 |
| Roll Over (St. Voc.) | K | 288 | 10-9 |
| Roll Over (St. Perf. Tr.) | K | 288 | 10-10 |
| Rondo for Lunch, A (speech piece) (St. Voc.) | 3 | 212 | 7-29 |
| Rondo for Lunch, A (speech piece) (St. Perf. Tr.) | 3 | 212 | 7-30 |
| Rosie, Darling Rosie (St. Voc.) | 2 | 214 | 8-5 |
| Rosie, Darling Rosie (St. Perf. Tr.) | 2 | 214 | 8-6 |
| 'Round and Around We Go (Doong gul ge) (St. Voc.) | 3 | 134 | 4-50 |
| 'Round and 'Round (St. Voc.) | 1 | 148 | 4-53 |
| 'Round and 'Round (St. Perf. Tr.) | 1 | 148 | 4-54 |

| Title | Gr. | Pg. | CD Track |
|---|---|---|---|
| 'Round the Bay of Mexico (St. Voc.) | 4 | 258 | 10-31 |
| 'Round the Bay of Mexico (St. Perf. Tr.) | 4 | 258 | 10-32 |
| Route 66 (St. Voc.) | 4 | 276 | 11-21 |
| Route 66 (St. Perf. Tr.) | 4 | 276 | 11-22 |
| Rowing Toward the Sunlight (Bogando a la luz del sol) (St. Voc.) | 4 | 306 | 13-8 |
| Rudolph, the Red-Nosed Reindeer (St. Voc.) | 1 | 428 | 13-44 |
| Rudolph, the Red-Nosed Reindeer (St. Perf. Tr.) | 1 | 428 | 13-45 |
| Run, Molly, Run (St. Voc.) | 1 | 8 | 1-11 |
| Run, Molly, Run (St. Perf. Tr.) | 1 | 8 | 1-12 |
| Run! Run! Hide! (St. Voc.) | 6 | 340 | 17-11 |
| Run! Run! Hide! (St. Perf. Tr.) | 6 | 340 | 17-12 |
| Run, Run, River (Riendo el río corre) (St. Voc.) | 6 | 263 | 13-25 |
| S'vivon (Dreydl) (St. Voc.) | 6 | 452 | 21-15 |
| S'vivon (Dreydl) (St. Perf. Tr.) | 6 | 452 | 21-17 |
| Sail Away (St. Voc.) | 5 | 404 | 18-20 |
| Sail Away (St. Perf. Tr.) | 5 | 404 | 18-21 |
| Sailboat in the Sky (Korean) (St. Voc.) | 4 | 374 | 16-11 |
| Sailboat in the Sky (English) (St. Voc.) | 4 | 374 | 16-12 |
| Sailboat in the Sky (St. Perf. Tr.) | 4 | 374 | 16-13 |
| Sailing Down My Golden River (St. Voc.) | 4 | 332 | 14-12 |
| Sailing Down My Golden River (St. Perf. Tr.) | 4 | 332 | 14-13 |
| Sailing to the Sea (St. Voc.) | 1 | 338 | 10-32 |
| Sailing to the Sea (St. Perf. Tr.) | 1 | 338 | 10-33 |
| Sakura (Japanese) (St. Voc.) | 4 | 308 | 13-13 |
| Sakura (English) (St. Voc.) | 4 | 308 | 13-14 |
| Sakura (St. Perf. Tr.) | 4 | 308 | 13-15 |
| Sambalele (Portuguese) (St. Voc.) | 4 | 397 | 17-8 |
| Sambalele (English) (St. Voc.) | 4 | 397 | 17-9 |
| Sambalele (St. Perf. Tr.) | 4 | 397 | 17-10 |
| Same Train (St. Voc.) | 2 | 164 | 6-20 |
| Same Train (St. Perf. Tr.) | 2 | 164 | 6-21 |
| San Antonio Rose (St. Voc.) | 5 | 134 | 6-28 |
| San Antonio Rose (St. Perf. Tr.) | 5 | 134 | 6-29 |
| Sansaw akroma (St. Voc.) | 3 | 286 | 10-7 |
| Sansaw akroma (St. Perf. Tr.) | 3 | 286 | 10-8 |
| Santa Clara (Tagalog) (St. Voc.) | 4 | 172 | 7-32 |
| Santa Clara (English) (St. Voc.) | 4 | 172 | 7-33 |
| Santa Clara (St. Perf. Tr.) | 4 | 172 | 7-34 |
| Sarika keo (Bird Song) (St. Voc.) | 3 | 275 | 9-26 |
| Sarika keo (Bird Song) (St. Perf. Tr.) | 3 | 275 | 9-28 |
| Saw, Saw, Lumberjack (Serra, serra, serrador) (St. Voc.) | 1 | 112 | 3-51 |
| Sawatdee tuh jah (The Hello Song) (St. Voc.) | 2 | 265 | 9-28 |
| Sawatdee tuh jah (The Hello Song) (St. Perf. Tr.) | 2 | 265 | 9-30 |
| Scarborough Fair (St. Voc.) | 6 | 95 | 6-4 |
| Scarborough Fair (St. Perf. Tr.) | 6 | 95 | 6-5 |
| Scattin' A-Round Variations on Row3 (St. Voc.) | 6 | 160 | 9-10 |
| Scattin' A-Round Variations on Row3 (St. Perf. Tr.) | 6 | 160 | 9-11 |
| School Bell Sounding (Ha'kyo jong) (St. Voc.) | 2 | 135 | 5-23 |
| Scotland the Brave (St. Voc.) | 5 | 138 | 7-6 |
| Scotland the Brave (St. Perf. Tr.) | 5 | 138 | 7-7 |
| Scrub Brush Shuffle, The (St. Voc.) | 1 | 118 | 3-55 |
| Scrub Brush Shuffle, The (St. Perf. Tr.) | 1 | 118 | 3-56 |
| Scrub-a-dub (St. Voc.) | 1 | 306 | 9-39 |
| Scrub-a-dub (St. Perf. Tr.) | 1 | 306 | 9-40 |
| Se va el caimán (The Alligator) (St. Voc.) | 5 | 306 | 14-10 |
| Se va el caimán (The Alligator) (St. Perf. Tr.) | 5 | 306 | 14-12 |
| Sea Is Calm, The (La mar estaba serena) (St. Voc.) | 2 | 345 | 12-22 |
| Sea Shell (St. Voc.) | 2 | 100 | 4-12 |
| Sea Shell (St. Perf. Tr.) | 2 | 100 | 4-13 |
| Seagull, Seagull, Sit on the Shore (St. Voc.) | 4 | 383 | 16-20 |
| Seagull, Seagull, Sit on the Shore (St. Perf. Tr.) | 4 | 383 | 16-21 |
| Seasons, The (Las estaciones) (St. Voc.) | 1 | 29 | 1-41 |
| Seasons (St. Voc.) | K | 4 | 1-4 |
| Seasons (St. Perf. Tr.) | K | 4 | 1-5 |
| Seasons of Love (from Rent) (St. Voc.) | 8 | A-22 | 1-18 |
| Seasons of Love (from Rent) (St. Perf. Tr.) | 8 | A-22 | 1-19 |
| See and Touch (St. Voc.) | K | 172 | 6-22 |
| See and Touch (St. Perf. Tr.) | K | 172 | 6-23 |
| See the Children Playin' (St. Voc.) | 4 | 107 | 5-22 |
| See the Children Playin' (St. Perf. Tr.) | 4 | 107 | 5-23 |
| See-Saw Sacradown (St. Voc.) | 2 | 208 | 7-49 |
| See-Saw Sacradown (St. Perf. Tr.) | 2 | 208 | 7-50 |
| Serpent, The (La víbora) (St. Voc.) | 1 | 322 | 10-16 |
| Serra, serra, serrador (Saw, Saw, Lumberjack) (St. Voc.) | 1 | 112 | 3-50 |
| Serra, serra, serrador (Saw, Saw, Lumberjack) (St. Perf. Tr.) | 1 | 112 | 3-52 |
| Setting Up the Golden Ladder (Bát kim thang) (St. Voc.) | 6 | 13 | 1-14 |
| Sh'ney dubim (Two Bears) (St. Voc.) | K | 268 | 9-19 |
| Sh'ney dubim (Two Bears) (St. Perf. Tr.) | K | 268 | 9-21 |
| Shady Grove (St. Voc.) | 5 | 260 | 12-15 |
| Shady Grove (St. Perf. Tr.) | 5 | 260 | 12-16 |
| Shake It! (Cheki, morena) (St. Voc.) | 2 | 180 | 7-2 |
| Shake It! (Cheki, morena) (St. Voc.) | 7 | I-16 | 13-15 |
| Shake the Papaya Down (St. Voc.) | 4 | 378 | 16-18 |
| Shake the Papaya Down (St. Perf. Tr.) | 4 | 378 | 16-19 |
| Shake Them 'Simmons Down (St. Voc.) | 2 | 244 | 8-32 |
| Shake Them 'Simmons Down (St. Perf. Tr.) | 2 | 244 | 8-33 |
| Shalom aleichem (St. Voc.) | 6 | 409 | 20-7 |
| Shalom aleichem (St. Perf. Tr.) | 6 | 409 | 20-8 |
| Shanghai Chicken (St. Voc.) | 1 | 140 | 4-41 |
| Shanghai Chicken (St. Perf. Tr.) | 1 | 140 | 4-42 |
| Sharing (St. Voc.) | K | 198 | 7-10 |
| Sharing (St. Perf. Tr.) | K | 198 | 7-11 |
| She'll Be Comin' 'Round the Mountain (St. Voc.) | 2 | 358 | 13-15 |
| She'll Be Comin' 'Round the Mountain (St. Perf. Tr.) | 2 | 358 | 13-16 |
| Sheaves of Grain (Alumot) (St. Voc.) | 6 | 306 | 15-27 |
| Shenandoah (St. Voc.) | 5 | 264 | 12-21 |
| Shenandoah (St. Perf. Tr.) | 5 | 264 | 12-22 |
| Shine, Shine, Shine (St. Voc.) | 1 | 42 | 2-13 |
| Shine, Shine, Shine (St. Perf. Tr.) | 1 | 42 | 2-14 |
| Ship that Never Returned, The (St. Voc.) | 5 | 402 | 18-17 |
| Ship that Never Returned, The (St. Perf. Tr.) | 5 | 402 | 18-18 |
| Shir l'shalom (Hand in Hand-A Song for Peace) (St. Voc.) | 4 | 419 | 17-23 |
| Shir l'shalom (Hand in Hand-A Song for Peace) (St. Perf. Tr.) | 4 | 419 | 17-25 |
| Shoo, Fly (St. Voc.) | 2 | 200 | 7-38 |
| Shoo, Fly (St. Perf. Tr.) | 2 | 200 | 7-39 |
| Shoo, Turkey (St. Voc.) | 1 | 104 | 3-33 |
| Shoo, Turkey (St. Perf. Tr.) | 1 | 104 | 3-34 |
| Shortnin' Bread (St. Voc.) | 1 | 57 | 2-33 |
| Shortnin' Bread (St. Perf. Tr.) | 1 | 57 | 2-34 |
| Shortnin' Bread (St. Voc.) | 7 | F-27 | 11-12 |
| Shortnin' Bread (St. Perf. Tr.) | 7 | F-27 | 11-13 |
| Shri Ram, jai Ram (St. Voc.) | 4 | 311 | 13-17 |
| Shri Ram, jai Ram (St. Perf. Tr.) | 4 | 311 | 13-18 |
| Shu ha mo (Frogs) (St. Voc.) | 3 | 276 | 9-30 |
| Shu ha mo (Frogs) (St. Perf. Tr.) | 3 | 276 | 9-32 |
| Si me dan pasteles (If You Give Me Pastries) (St. Voc.) | 1 | 432 | 14-1 |
| Si me dan pasteles (If You Give Me Pastries) (St. Perf. Tr.) | 1 | 432 | 14-3 |
| Si si si (St. Voc.) | 7 | G-13 | 12-1 |

| Title | Gr. | Pg. | CD Track |
|---|---|---|---|
| Si si si (St. Perf. Tr.) | 7 | G-13 | 12-2 |
| Sick Little Donkey, The (El burrito enfermo) (St. Voc.) | K | 271 | 9-24 |
| Sierra Morena (Spanish) (St. Voc.) | 3 | 296 | 10-19 |
| Sierra Morena (English) (St. Voc.) | 3 | 296 | 10-20 |
| Sierra Morena (St. Perf. Tr.) | 3 | 296 | 10-21 |
| Silent Night (St. Voc.) | 3 | 394 | 14-4 |
| Silent Night (St. Perf. Tr.) | 3 | 394 | 14-5 |
| Silent Night (Stille Nacht) (St. Voc.) | 7 | I-54 | 14-8 |
| Silent Night (Stille Nacht) (St. Perf. Tr.) | 7 | I-54 | 14-9 |
| Silly Street (St. Voc.) | K | 224 | 8-1 |
| Silly Street (St. Perf. Tr.) | K | 224 | 8-2 |
| Silver Moon Boat (Xiao yin chuan) (St. Voc.) | 2 | 14 | 1-14 |
| Simple Gifts (St. Voc.) | 5 | 184 | 9-17 |
| Simple Gifts (St. Perf. Tr.) | 5 | 184 | 9-18 |
| Simple Gifts (St. Voc.) | 8 | A-17 | 1-10 |
| Simple Gifts (St. Perf. Tr.) | 8 | A-17 | 1-11 |
| Sing a Little Song (St. Voc.) | K | 30 | 2-1 |
| Sing a Little Song (St. Perf. Tr.) | K | 30 | 2-2 |
| Sing a Rainbow (St. Voc.) | 2 | 166 | 6-22 |
| Sing a Rainbow (St. Perf. Tr.) | 2 | 166 | 6-23 |
| Sing a Song of Peace (T.A.P.) | 6 | 66 | 4-26 |
| Sing a Song of Peace (St. Perf. Tr.) | 6 | 66 | 4-27 |
| Sing About Martin (St. Voc.) | K | 321 | 11-23 |
| Sing About Martin (St. Perf. Tr.) | K | 321 | 11-24 |
| Sing, America, Sing! (St. Voc.) | 3 | 238 | 8-4 |
| Sing, America, Sing! (St. Perf. Tr.) | 3 | 238 | 8-5 |
| Sing and Be Joyful (Hava Nashira) (St. Voc.) | 6 | 82 | 5-17 |
| Sing Me a Story (St. Voc.) | 2 | 346 | 12-25 |
| Sing Me a Story (St. Perf. Tr.) | 2 | 346 | 12-26 |
| Sing, Sing, Sing! (St. Voc.) | 5 | 340 | 15-26 |
| Sing, Sing, Sing! (St. Perf. Tr.) | 5 | 340 | 15-27 |
| Sing! Speak! Whisper! Shout! (St. Voc.) | 1 | 36 | 1-57 |
| Sing! Speak! Whisper! Shout! (St. Perf. Tr.) | 1 | 36 | 1-58 |
| Sing Your Story (St. Voc.) | 3 | 350 | 12-6 |
| Sing Your Story (St. Perf. Tr.) | 3 | 350 | 12-7 |
| Singin' in the Rain (St. Voc.) | 4 | 360 | 15-26 |
| Singin' in the Rain (St. Perf. Tr.) | 4 | 360 | 15-27 |
| Singin' in the Tub (St. Voc.) | K | 220 | 7-40 |
| Singin' in the Tub (St. Perf. Tr.) | K | 220 | 7-41 |
| Singing Tall Tales (Cantando mentiras) (St. Voc.) | 4 | 146 | 6-39 |
| Six Little Ducks (St. Voc.) | K | 234 | 8-16 |
| Six Little Ducks (St. Perf. Tr.) | K | 234 | 8-17 |
| Six-Inch Boots in a Nine-Inch Puddle (St. Voc.) | 1 | 366 | 11-32 |
| Six-Inch Boots in a Nine-Inch Puddle (St. Perf. Tr.) | 1 | 366 | 11-33 |
| Siyahamba (Zulu) (St. Voc.) | 6 | 212 | 11-20 |
| Siyahamba (English) (St. Voc.) | 6 | 212 | 11-21 |
| Siyahamba (St. Perf. Tr.) | 6 | 212 | 11-22 |
| Skin and Bones (St. Voc.) | 2 | 376 | 14-5 |
| Skin and Bones (St. Perf. Tr.) | 2 | 376 | 14-6 |
| Skip to My Lou (St. Voc.) | K | 58 | 2-41 |
| Skip to My Lou (St. Perf. Tr.) | K | 58 | 2-42 |
| Skye Boat Song (St. Voc.) | 6 | 372 | 19-5 |
| Skye Boat Song (St. Perf. Tr.) | 6 | 372 | 19-6 |
| Sleep, Baby, Sleep (St. Voc.) | 2 | 197 | 7-27 |
| Sleep, Baby, Sleep (St. Perf. Tr.) | 2 | 197 | 7-28 |
| Sleep, Dearest Child (Still, Still, Still) (St. Voc.) | 5 | 468 | 20-15 |
| Sleep, My Little One (Deau-deau, ti pitit maman) (St. Voc.) | 2 | 306 | 11-14 |
| Sleep, Sleep, Baby (Thula, thula, ngoana) (St. Voc.) | 4 | 227 | 9-28 |
| Small Job, A (St. Voc.) | 3 | 224 | 7-47 |
| Small Job, A (St. Perf. Tr.) | 3 | 224 | 7-48 |

| Title | Gr. | Pg. | CD Track |
|---|---|---|---|
| Snail, Snail (St. Voc.) | 1 | 190 | 6-17 |
| Snail, Snail (St. Perf. Tr.) | 1 | 190 | 6-18 |
| Snail's Dance, The (El caracol) (St. Voc.) | K | 130 | 5-7 |
| Snowflakes (St. Voc.) | 1 | 422 | 13-32 |
| Snowflakes (St. Perf. Tr.) | 1 | 422 | 13-33 |
| Softly, Softly (T'hola, t'hola) (St. Voc.) | 4 | 132 | 6-8 |
| Sol, solecito (Sun, Little Sun) (St. Voc.) | 1 | 367 | 11-34 |
| Sol, solecito (Sun, Little Sun) (St. Perf. Tr.) | 1 | 367 | 11-36 |
| Soldier, Soldier (St. Voc.) | 4 | 11 | 1-7 |
| Soldier, Soldier (St. Perf. Tr.) | 4 | 11 | 1-8 |
| Somebody Waiting (St. Voc.) | 2 | 283 | 10-23 |
| Somebody Waiting (St. Perf. Tr.) | 2 | 283 | 10-24 |
| Somebody's Knockin' at Your Door (St. Voc.) | 4 | 53 | 3-3 |
| Someday Very Soon (St. Voc.) | 1 | 376 | 12-5 |
| Someday Very Soon (St. Perf. Tr.) | 1 | 376 | 12-6 |
| Something Told the Wild Geese (St. Voc.) | 7 | G-39 | 12-25 |
| Something Told the Wild Geese (St. Perf. Tr.) | 7 | G-39 | 12-26 |
| Sometimes I Feel Like a Motherless Child (St. Voc.) | 6 | 241 | 12-17 |
| Sometimes I Feel Like a Motherless Child (St. Perf. Tr.) | 6 | 241 | 12-18 |
| Somewhere Out There (from An American Tail) (St. Voc.) | 5 | 368 | 17-4 |
| Somewhere Out There (from An American Tail) (St. Perf. Tr.) | 5 | 368 | 17-5 |
| Somos el barco (We Are the Boat) (St. Voc.) | 4 | 352 | 15-13 |
| Somos el barco (We Are the Boat) (St. Perf. Tr.) | 4 | 352 | 15-14 |
| Son macaron (St. Voc.) | 4 | 109 | 5-27 |
| Son macaron (St. Perf. Tr.) | 4 | 109 | 5-28 |
| Sonando (Spanish) (St. Voc./Dance Perf. Tr.) | 4 | 34 | 2-9 |
| Sonando (English) (St. Voc.) | 4 | 34 | 2-10 |
| Sonando (St. Perf. Tr.) | 4 | 34 | 2-11 |
| Song of One, A (St. Voc.) | 3 | 344 | 12-3 |
| Song of One, A (St. Perf. Tr.) | 3 | 344 | 12-4 |
| Song of the Eagle (St. Voc.) | 2 | 248 | 9-6 |
| Song of the Eagle (St. Perf. Tr.) | 2 | 248 | 9-7 |
| Song of the Fishes (St. Voc.) | 3 | 244 | 8-11 |
| Song of the Fishes (St. Perf. Tr.) | 3 | 244 | 8-12 |
| Song of the Water (Canto del agua) (St. Voc.) | 8 | I-10 | 13-8 |
| Song That's Just for You, A (St. Voc.) | 2 | 126 | 5-8 |
| Song That's Just for You, A (St. Perf. Tr.) | 2 | 126 | 5-9 |
| Sorida (St. Voc.) | 1 | 314 | 10-1 |
| Sorida (St. Perf. Tr.) | 1 | 314 | 10-2 |
| Sourwood Mountain (St. Voc.) | 4 | 65 | 3-28 |
| Sourwood Mountain (St. Perf. Tr.) | 4 | 65 | 3-29 |
| Spaceworms (St. Voc.) | 1 | 400 | 13-1 |
| Spaceworms (St. Perf. Tr.) | 1 | 400 | 13-2 |
| Spring Has Sprung! (St. Voc.) | K | 142 | 5-24 |
| Spring Has Sprung! (St. Perf. Tr.) | K | 142 | 5-25 |
| Springtime Has Come (Haru ga kita) (St. Voc.) | 2 | 401 | 15-6 |
| St. Louis Blues (St. Voc.) | 5 | 352 | 16-11 |
| St. Louis Blues (St. Perf. Tr.) | 5 | 352 | 16-12 |
| St. Patrick Was a Gentleman (St. Voc.) | 3 | 290 | 10-11 |
| St. Patrick Was a Gentleman (St. Perf. Tr.) | 3 | 290 | 10-12 |
| Stand By Me (St. Voc.) | 5 | 46 | 3-1 |
| Stand By Me (St. Perf. Tr.) | 5 | 46 | 3-2 |
| Stand By Me (St. Voc.) | 8 | E-25 | 9-24 |
| Stand By Me (St. Perf. Tr.) | 8 | E-25 | 9-25 |
| Star Festival (Tanabata-sama) (St. Voc.) | 2 | 336 | 12-13 |
| Star Light, Star Bright (St. Voc.) | 1 | 108 | 3-36 |
| Star Light, Star Bright (St. Perf. Tr.) | 1 | 108 | 3-37 |
| Star-Spangled Banner, The (St. Voc.) | 3 | 415 | 15-12 |

| Title | Gr. | Pg. | CD Track |
|---|---|---|---|
| Star-Spangled Banner, The (St. Perf. Tr.) | 3 | 415 | 15-13 |
| Star-Spangled Banner, The (St. Voc.) | 4 | 441 | 19-7 |
| Star-Spangled Banner, The (St. Perf. Tr.) | 4 | 441 | 19-8 |
| Star-Spangled Banner, The (St. Voc.) | 5 | 488 | 21-17 |
| Star-Spangled Banner, The (St. Perf. Tr.) | 5 | 488 | 21-18 |
| Star-Spangled Banner, The (St. Voc.) | 6 | 486 | 23-6 |
| Star-Spangled Banner, The (St. Perf. Tr.) | 6 | 486 | 23-7 |
| Star-Spangled Banner, The (St. Voc.) | 7 | I-56 | 14-12 |
| Star-Spangled Banner, The (St. Perf. Tr.) | 7 | I-56 | 14-13 |
| Star-Spangled Banner, The (St. Voc.) | 8 | I-62 | 15-16 |
| Star-Spangled Banner, The (St. Perf. Tr.) | 8 | I-62 | 15-17 |
| Starlight, Star Bright (St. Voc.) | 4 | 373 | 16-9 |
| Starlight, Star Bright (St. Perf. Tr.) | 4 | 373 | 16-10 |
| Stars of the Heavens (Las estrellitas del cielo) (St. Voc.) | 5 | 175 | 8-30 |
| Stately House, The (Wir hatten gebauet) (St. Voc.) | 8 | C-21 | 6-11 |
| Step in Time (from Mary Poppins) (St. Voc.) | 2 | 74 | 3-19 |
| Step in Time (from Mary Poppins) (St. Perf. Tr.) | 2 | 74 | 3-20 |
| Still, Still, Still (Sleep, Dearest Child) (St. Voc.) | 5 | 468 | 20-14 |
| Still, Still, Still (St. Perf. Tr.) | 5 | 468 | 20-16 |
| Stille Nacht (Silent Night) (St. Voc.) | 7 | I-54 | 14-7 |
| Storm Dance (speech piece) (St. Voc.) | K | 145 | 5-26 |
| Storm Dance (speech piece) (St. Perf. Tr.) | K | 145 | 5-27 |
| Straighten Up and Fly Right (St. Voc.) | 4 | 128 | 6-2 |
| Straighten Up and Fly Right (St. Perf. Tr.) | 4 | 128 | 6-3 |
| Streets of Laredo (St. Voc.) | 4 | 272 | 11-14 |
| Streets of Laredo (St. Perf. Tr.) | 4 | 272 | 11-15 |
| Strike Up the Band (St. Voc.) | 6 | 135 | 7-36 |
| Strike Up the Band (St. Perf. Tr.) | 6 | 135 | 7-37 |
| Sugar "Shuga" Bee (St. Voc.) | K | 64 | 2-50 |
| Sugar "Shuga" Bee (St. Perf. Tr.) | K | 64 | 2-51 |
| Summertime (St. Perf. Tr.) | 6 | 250 | 13-11 |
| Sun Gonna Shine (St. Voc.) | 6 | 242 | 12-19 |
| Sun Gonna Shine (St. Perf. Tr.) | 6 | 242 | 12-20 |
| Sun, Little Sun (Sol, solecito) (St. Voc.) | 1 | 367 | 11-35 |
| Supercalifragilisticexpialidocious (from Mary Poppins) (St. Voc.) | 3 | 7 | 1-3 |
| Supercalifragilisticexpialidocious (from Mary Poppins) (St. Perf. Tr.) | 3 | 7 | 1-4 |
| Surfin' U.S.A. (St. Voc.) | 6 | 260 | 13-21 |
| Surfin' U.S.A. (St. Perf. Tr.) | 6 | 260 | 13-22 |
| Surfin' U.S.A. (St. Voc.) | 7 | I-58 | 14-14 |
| Surfin' U.S.A. (St. Perf. Tr.) | 7 | I-58 | 14-15 |
| Swallow, The (La golondrina) (St. Voc.) | 8 | I-50 | 15-2 |
| Swanee (St. Voc.) | 6 | 118 | 7-3 |
| Swanee (St. Perf. Tr.) | 6 | 118 | 7-4 |
| Sweet Betsy from Pike (St. Voc.) | 4 | 244 | 10-16 |
| Sweet Betsy from Pike (St. Perf. Tr.) | 4 | 244 | 10-17 |
| Sweet Orange (Naranja dulce) (St. Voc.) | 2 | 96 | 4-4 |
| Sweet Potatoes (St. Voc.) | 3 | 228 | 7-53 |
| Sweet Potatoes (St. Perf. Tr.) | 3 | 228 | 7-54 |
| Swing Low, Sweet Chariot (St. Voc.) | 7 | C-41 | 8-3 |
| T'hola, t'hola (Softly, Softly) (St. Voc.) | 4 | 132 | 6-7 |
| T'hola, t'hola (Softly, Softly) (St. Perf. Tr.) | 4 | 132 | 6-9 |
| Table Manners (speech piece) (St. Voc.) | 3 | 190 | 6-41 |
| Table Manners (speech piece) (St. Perf. Tr.) | 3 | 190 | 6-42 |
| Take a Chance on Me (St. Voc.) | 8 | G-15 | 12-1 |
| Take a Chance on Me (St. Perf. Tr.) | 8 | G-15 | 12-2 |
| Take Me Out to the Ball Game (St. Voc.) | 3 | 263 | 9-6 |
| Take Me Out to the Ball Game (St. Perf. Tr.) | 3 | 263 | 9-7 |
| Take Time in Life (St. Voc.) | 6 | 292 | 14-22 |
| Take Time in Life (St. Perf. Tr.) | 6 | 292 | 14-23 |

| Title | Gr. | Pg. | CD Track |
|---|---|---|---|
| Take Your Feet Out 'the Sand (St. Voc.) | K | 231 | 8-11 |
| Take Your Feet Out 'the Sand (St. Perf. Tr.) | K | 231 | 8-12 |
| Tall Cedar Tree (St. Voc.) | 2 | 322 | 11-30 |
| Tall Cedar Tree (St. Perf. Tr.) | 2 | 322 | 11-31 |
| Tanabata-sama (Star Festival) (St. Voc.) | 2 | 336 | 12-12 |
| Tanabata-sama (Star Festival) (St. Perf. Tr.) | 2 | 336 | 12-14 |
| Tancovačka (Dancing) (St. Voc./Dance Perf. Tr.) | 4 | 230 | 9-39 |
| Tancovačka (Dancing) (St. Perf. Tr.) | 4 | 230 | 9-41 |
| Tap It! Rap It! (speech piece) (St. Voc.) | K | 194 | 7-6 |
| Tap It! Rap It! (speech piece) (St. Perf. Tr.) | K | 194 | 7-7 |
| Tap, Tap, Tap (Pon, pon, pon) (St. Voc.) | K | 50 | 2-28 |
| Teach Me to Swing (St. Voc.) | 5 | 84 | 4-28 |
| Teach Me to Swing (St. Perf. Tr.) | 5 | 84 | 4-29 |
| Temple Bells (Hitotsu toya) (St. Voc.) | 5 | 478 | 21-2 |
| Tender Shepherd (St. Voc.) | 3 | 116 | 4-22 |
| Tender Shepherd (St. Perf. Tr.) | 3 | 116 | 4-23 |
| Tengo, Tengo, Tengo (I Have Three Sheep) (St. Voc.) | 4 | 228 | 9-35 |
| Tengo, Tengo, Tengo (I Have Three Sheep) (St. Perf. Tr.) | 4 | 228 | 9-37 |
| Texas Cowboy (St. Voc.) | 3 | 250 | 8-19 |
| Texas Cowboy (St. Perf. Tr.) | 3 | 250 | 8-20 |
| Thanksgiving Is Near (St. Voc.) | 2 | 380 | 14-13 |
| Thanksgiving Is Near (St. Perf. Tr.) | 2 | 380 | 14-14 |
| That's What's New with Me! (St. Voc.) | K | 2 | 1-1 |
| That's What's New with Me! (St. Perf. Tr.) | K | 2 | 1-2 |
| Theater Game, The (Cho'i hát bôi) (St. Voc.) | 5 | 318 | 14-33 |
| Theme from New York, New York (St. Voc./Dance Perf. Tr.) | 4 | 250 | 10-22 |
| Theme from New York, New York (St. Perf. Tr.) | 4 | 250 | 10-23 |
| There at the Spring (Allá en la fuente) (St. Voc.) | 2 | 92 | 3-49 |
| There Come Our Mothers (Nampaya omame) (St. Voc.) | 1 | 138 | 4-36 |
| There Come Our Mothers (Nampaya omame) (St. Voc.) | 7 | D-10 | 8-26 |
| There Is Love Somewhere (St. Voc.) | 6 | 318 | 16-7 |
| There Is Love Somewhere (St. Perf. Tr.) | 6 | 318 | 16-8 |
| There Was an Old Man (speech piece) (St. Voc.) | 3 | 191 | 6-43 |
| There Was an Old Man (speech piece) (St. Perf. Tr.) | 3 | 191 | 6-44 |
| There's a Place (St. Voc.) | 5 | 210 | 10-25 |
| There's a Place (St. Perf. Tr.) | 5 | 210 | 10-26 |
| There's Music in Me (Mi cuerpo hace música) (St. Voc.) | K | 106 | 4-9 |
| This Is My Land (Así es mi tierra) (St. Voc.) | 6 | 172 | 9-31 |
| This Is My Song (St. Voc.) | 6 | 77 | 5-1 |
| This Is My Song (St. Perf. Tr.) | 6 | 77 | 5-2 |
| This Land Is Your Land (refrain) (St. Voc.) | 1 | 276 | 9-1 |
| This Land Is Your Land (refrain) (St. Perf. Tr.) | 1 | 276 | 9-2 |
| This Land Is Your Land (St. Voc.) | 5 | 118 | 6-10 |
| This Land Is Your Land (St. Perf. Tr.) | 5 | 118 | 6-11 |
| This Land Is Your Land (St. Voc.) | 7 | I-66 | 14-16 |
| This Land Is Your Land (St. Perf. Tr.) | 7 | I-66 | 14-17 |
| This Little Light of Mine (St. Voc.) | 6 | 232 | 12-6 |
| This Little Light of Mine (St. Perf. Tr.) | 6 | 232 | 12-7 |
| This Old Man (St. Voc.) | 3 | 152 | 5-23 |
| This Old Man (St. Perf. Tr.) | 3 | 152 | 5-24 |
| This Pretty Planet (St. Voc.) | 4 | 355 | 15-16 |
| This Pretty Planet (St. Perf. Tr.) | 4 | 355 | 15-17 |
| This Train (St. Voc.) | 5 | 27 | 2-10 |
| This Train (St. Perf. Tr.) | 5 | 27 | 2-11 |
| This World (from The Me Nobody Knows) (St. Voc.) | 5 | 168 | 8-24 |
| This World (from The Me Nobody Knows) (St. Perf. Tr.) | 5 | 168 | 8-25 |
| Those Magic Changes (St. Voc.) | 8 | E-30 | 10-6 |
| Those Magic Changes (St. Perf. Tr.) | 8 | E-30 | 10-7 |
| Three Little Birds (St. Voc.) | 4 | 321 | 14-1 |

| Title | Gr. | Pg. | CD Track |
|---|---|---|---|
| Three Little Birds (St. Perf. Tr.) | 4 | 321 | 14-2 |
| Three Little Birds (St. Voc.) | 8 | F-7 | 10-16 |
| Three Little Birds (St. Perf. Tr.) | 8 | F-7 | 10-17 |
| Three Little Pigs (St. Voc.) | K | 21 | 1-28 |
| Three Little Pigs (St. Perf. Tr.) | K | 21 | 1-29 |
| Thula, thula, ngoana (Sleep, Sleep, Baby) (St. Voc.) | 4 | 227 | 9-27 |
| Thula, thula, ngoana (Sleep, Sleep, Baby) (St. Perf. Tr.) | 4 | 227 | 9-29 |
| Tic, tac (Tick, Tock) (St. Voc.) | 1 | 252 | 8-5 |
| Tic, tac (St. Perf. Tr.) | 1 | 252 | 8-7 |
| Tick, Tock (Tic, tac) (St. Voc.) | 1 | 252 | 8-6 |
| Tideo (St. Voc.) | 2 | 80 | 3-26 |
| Tideo (St. Perf. Tr.) | 2 | 80 | 3-27 |
| Tie Me Kangaroo Down, Sport (St. Voc.) | 4 | 37 | 2-15 |
| Tie Me Kangaroo Down, Sport (St. Perf. Tr.) | 4 | 37 | 2-16 |
| Time to Move (St. Voc.) | 1 | 244 | 7-42 |
| Time to Move (St. Perf. Tr.) | 1 | 244 | 7-43 |
| Time to Sing (St. Voc.) | 2 | 8 | 1-5 |
| Time to Sing (St. Perf. Tr.) | 2 | 8 | 1-6 |
| Tina singu (Zulu) (St. Voc.) | 4 | 300 | 12-30 |
| Tina singu (English) (St. Voc.) | 4 | 300 | 12-31 |
| Tina singu (St. Perf. Tr.) | 4 | 300 | 12-32 |
| Tiny Boat, The (El barquito) (St. Voc.) | 3 | 358 | 12-16 |
| To'ia mai te waka (Pull the Canoe) (St. Voc.) | 1 | 77 | 2-55 |
| To'ia mai te waka (Pull the Canoe) (St. Perf. Tr.) | 1 | 77 | 2-57 |
| Today Is Your Birthday (St. Voc.) | 1 | 410 | 13-9 |
| Today Is Your Birthday (St. Perf. Tr.) | 1 | 410 | 13-10 |
| Together in Unity (St. Voc.) | K | 320 | 11-21 |
| Together in Unity (St. Perf. Tr.) | K | 320 | 11-22 |
| Tom Dooley (St. Voc.) | 6 | 374 | 19-7 |
| Tom Dooley (St. Perf. Tr.) | 6 | 374 | 19-8 |
| Tomorrow (Mañana) (St. Voc.) | 7 | E-14 | 9-27 |
| Toodala (St. Voc.) | 1 | 326 | 10-23 |
| Toodala (St. Perf. Tr.) | 1 | 326 | 10-24 |
| Top Joined the Circle, The (O pião entrou) (St. Voc.) | 2 | 355 | 13-7 |
| Touch the Wind (Eres tú) (St. Voc.) | 6 | 473 | 22-11 |
| Train, The (El tren) (St. Voc.) | 2 | 260 | 9-22 |
| Train Is A-Comin' (St. Voc.) | 3 | 48 | 2-17 |
| Train Is A-Comin' (St. Perf. Tr.) | 3 | 48 | 2-18 |
| Tree in the Wood, The (St. Voc.) | 2 | 360 | 13-17 |
| Tree in the Wood, The (St. Perf. Tr.) | 2 | 360 | 13-18 |
| Tropical Storm, The (La tormenta tropical) (St. Voc.) | 2 | 116 | 4-35 |
| Trouble Is a Mountain (St. Voc.) | 2 | 202 | 7-40 |
| Trouble Is a Mountain (St. Perf. Tr.) | 2 | 202 | 7-41 |
| Tsuki (The Moon) (St. Voc.) | 4 | 25 | 1-36 |
| Tsuki (The Moon) (St. Perf. Tr.) | 4 | 25 | 1-38 |
| Tu b'Shvat Is Here (Hashkediya) (St. Voc.) | 3 | 206 | 7-18 |
| Tumba (St. Voc./Dance Perf. Tr.) | 5 | 161 | 8-12 |
| Tumba (St. Perf. Tr.) | 5 | 161 | 8-13 |
| Turkey Game, The (Pavo, pavo) (St. Voc.) | 1 | 416 | 13-19 |
| Turn the Beat Around (St. Voc.) | 4 | 2 | 1-1 |
| Turn the Beat Around (St. Perf. Tr.) | 4 | 2 | 1-2 |
| Turn the Glasses Over (St. Voc.) | 3 | 204 | 7-12 |
| Turn the Glasses Over (St. Perf. Tr.) | 3 | 204 | 7-13 |
| Turn the World Around (St. Voc.) | 4 | 114 | 5-32 |
| Turn the World Around (St. Perf. Tr.) | 4 | 114 | 5-33 |
| Turn, Turn, Turn (To Everything There Is a Season) (St. Voc.) | 5 | 378 | 17-15 |
| Turn, Turn, Turn (To Everything There Is a Season) (St. Perf. Tr.) | 5 | 378 | 17-16 |
| Tuxedo Junction (St. Voc.) | 8 | G-21 | 12-4 |
| Tuxedo Junction (St. Perf. Tr.) | 8 | G-21 | 12-5 |
| Twelve Days of Christmas, The (St. Voc.) | 4 | 430 | 18-12 |
| Twelve Days of Christmas, The (St. Perf. Tr.) | 4 | 430 | 18-13 |
| Twelve Gates to the City (St. Voc.) | 5 | 280 | 13-5 |
| Twelve Gates to the City (St. Perf. Tr.) | 5 | 280 | 13-6 |
| Twist with a Burger, Jitter with a Bug (speech piece) (St. Voc.) | 1 | 132 | 4-28 |
| Twist with a Burger, Jitter with a Bug (speech piece) (St. Perf. Tr.) | 1 | 132 | 4-29 |
| Two Bears (Sh'ney dubim) (St. Voc.) | K | 268 | 9-20 |
| Two Cats (Der sad to katte) "Der sad to katte" (St. Voc.) | 2 | 300 | 11-6 |
| Two Crocodiles (Deux cocodries) (St. Voc.) | 2 | 364 | 13-22 |
| Two Little Sausages (speech piece) (St. Voc.) | 2 | 79 | 3-24 |
| Two Little Sausages (speech piece) (St. Perf. Tr.) | 2 | 79 | 3-25 |
| Tzena, tzena (St. Voc./Dance Perf. Tr.) | 5 | 298 | 13-30 |
| Tzena, tzena (St. Perf. Tr.) | 5 | 298 | 13-31 |
| Tzena, tzena (Round) (St. Voc.) | 5 | 298 | 13-32 |
| Tzena, tzena (Round) (St. Perf. Tr.) | 5 | 298 | 13-33 |
| Uga uga uga (Cake! Cake! Cake!) (St. Voc.) | K | 305 | 10-31 |
| Uga uga uga (St. Perf. Tr.) | K | 305 | 10-33 |
| Ujima (St. Voc.) | 1 | 430 | 13-46 |
| Ujima (St. Perf. Tr.) | 1 | 430 | 13-47 |
| 'Ūlili E (St. Voc.) | 5 | 441 | 19-13 |
| 'Ūlili E (St. Perf. Tr.) | 5 | 441 | 19-14 |
| Un, deux, trois (One, Two, Three) (St. Voc.) | 2 | 198 | 7-31 |
| Un, deux, trois (One, Two, Three) (St. Perf. Tr.) | 2 | 198 | 7-33 |
| Un elefante (An Elephant) (St. Voc.) | 2 | 160 | 6-12 |
| Un elefante (An Elephant) (St. Perf. Tr.) | 2 | 160 | 6-14 |
| Un pajarito (A Little Bird) (St. Voc.) | 2 | 16 | 1-20 |
| Un pajarito (A Little Bird) (St. Perf. Tr.) | 2 | 16 | 1-22 |
| Under the Button (Debajo el botón) (St. Voc.) | 1 | 210 | 6-44 |
| Under the Same Sun (St. Voc.) | 6 | 440 | 21-2 |
| Under the Same Sun (St. Perf. Tr.) | 6 | 440 | 21-3 |
| Under the Sea (St. Voc.) | 5 | 372 | 17-12 |
| Under the Sea (St. Perf. Tr.) | 5 | 372 | 17-13 |
| United Nations on the March, The (St. Voc.) | 6 | 443 | 21-4 |
| United Nations on the March, The (St. Perf. Tr.) | 6 | 443 | 21-5 |
| Uno, dos, y tres (One, Two, and Three) (St. Voc.) | 5 | 427 | 19-1 |
| Uno, dos, y tres (One, Two, and Three) (St. Perf. Tr.) | 5 | 427 | 19-3 |
| Usagi (Rabbit) (St. Voc.) | 1 | 396 | 12-25 |
| Usagi (St. Perf. Tr.) | 1 | 396 | 12-27 |
| Valentines (St. Voc.) | 2 | 398 | 14-42 |
| Valentines (St. Perf. Tr.) | 2 | 398 | 14-43 |
| Vamos a cantar (Let's Sing) (St. Voc.) | K | 278 | 9-33 |
| Vamos a cantar (St. Perf. Tr.) | K | 278 | 9-35 |
| Vamos a hacer la ronda (Let's Make a Circle) (St. Voc.) | K | 124 | 4-39 |
| Vamos a hacer la ronda (Let's Make a Circle) (St. Perf. Tr.) | K | 124 | 4-41 |
| Vamos a la fiesta (Let's Go to the Party) (St. Voc.) | 2 | 374 | 14-1 |
| Vamos a la fiesta (Let's Go to the Party) (St. Perf. Tr.) | 2 | 374 | 14-3 |
| Vamos a la mar (Let's Go to the Sea) (St. Voc.) | 3 | 226 | 7-49 |
| Vamos a la mar (Let's Go to the Sea) (St. Perf. Tr.) | 3 | 226 | 7-51 |
| Vem kan segla? (Who Can Sail?) (St. Voc.) | 6 | 417 | 20-16 |
| Vem kan segla? (Who Can Sail?) (St. Perf. Tr.) | 6 | 417 | 20-18 |
| Vil du? (Will You?) (St. Voc.) | 1 | 92 | 3-15 |
| Vil du? (Will You?) (St. Perf. Tr.) | 1 | 92 | 3-17 |
| Vine and Fig Tree (Lo yisa ) (St. Voc.) | 6 | 130 | 7-24 |
| Violin, The (El rabel) (St. Voc.) | 3 | 362 | 12-21 |
| ¡Viva el fútbol! (I Love Soccer!) (St. Voc.) | 1 | 96 | 3-19 |
| ¡Viva el fútbol! (I Love Soccer!) (St. Perf. Tr.) | 1 | 96 | 3-21 |
| Viva Jujuy (Spanish) (St. Voc.) | 5 | 228 | 11-11 |
| Viva Jujuy (English) (St. Voc.) | 5 | 228 | 11-12 |
| Viva Jujuy (St. Perf. Tr.) | 5 | 228 | 11-13 |

| Title | Gr. | Pg. | CD Track |
|---|---|---|---|
| Vive l'amour (St. Voc.) | 6 | 176 | 10-6 |
| Vive l'amour (St. Perf. Tr.) | 6 | 176 | 10-7 |
| Voice Choice (St. Voc.) | K | 27 | 1-42 |
| Voice Choice (St. Perf. Tr.) | K | 27 | 1-43 |
| Voices of Pride, The (St. Voc.) | 5 | 86 | 4-30 |
| Voices of Pride, The (St. Perf. Tr.) | 5 | 86 | 4-31 |
| Wabash Cannon Ball (St. Voc.) | 5 | 136 | 7-1 |
| Wabash Cannon Ball (St. Perf. Tr.) | 5 | 136 | 7-2 |
| Wade in the Water (St. Voc.) | 4 | 268 | 11-7 |
| Wade in the Water (St. Perf. Tr.) | 4 | 268 | 11-8 |
| Wade in the Water (St. Voc.) | 8 | I-64 | 15-18 |
| Wade in the Water (St. Perf. Tr.) | 8 | I-64 | 15-19 |
| Wai bamba (St. Voc.) | 6 | 26 | 2-19 |
| Wai bamba (St. Perf. Tr.) | 6 | 26 | 2-20 |
| Wai bamba (St. Voc.) | 8 | G-13 | 11-26 |
| Wai bamba (St. Perf. Tr.) | 8 | G-13 | 11-27 |
| Waitin' for the Light to Shine (from Big River) (St. Voc.) | 4 | 26 | 1-43 |
| Waitin' for the Light to Shine (from Big River) (St. Perf. Tr.) | 4 | 26 | 1-44 |
| Waiting for the Traffic Light (St. Voc.) | 2 | 107 | 4-23 |
| Waiting for the Traffic Light (St. Perf. Tr.) | 2 | 107 | 4-24 |
| Wake Me, Shake Me (St. Voc.) | 1 | 278 | 9-4 |
| Wake Me, Shake Me (St. Perf. Tr.) | 1 | 278 | 9-5 |
| Waking Song (Nu wahtan) (St. Voc.) | 1 | 279 | 9-7 |
| Walk in Jerusalem (St. Voc.) | 4 | 100 | 5-12 |
| Walk in Jerusalem (St. Perf. Tr.) | 4 | 100 | 5-13 |
| Walk in the Room (St. Voc.) | 1 | 12 | 1-15 |
| Walk in the Room (St. Perf. Tr.) | 1 | 12 | 1-16 |
| Walk Together, Children (St. Voc.) | 3 | 146 | 5-17 |
| Walk Together, Children (St. Perf. Tr.) | 3 | 146 | 5-18 |
| Waltzing with Bears (St. Voc.) | 3 | 170 | 6-14 |
| Waltzing with Bears (St. Perf. Tr.) | 3 | 170 | 6-15 |
| Was kommt dort von der Höh'? (What Comes There O'er the Hill?) (St. Voc.) | 8 | C-21 | 6-6 |
| Was kommt dort von der Höh'? (What Comes There O'er the Hill?) (St. Perf. Tr.) | 8 | C-21 | 6-8 |
| Water Come a Me Eye (St. Voc.) | 6 | 300 | 15-10 |
| Water Come a Me Eye (St. Perf. Tr.) | 6 | 300 | 15-11 |
| Water Is Wide, The (St. Voc.) | 6 | 228 | 12-1 |
| Water Is Wide, The (St. Perf. Tr.) | 6 | 228 | 12-2 |
| Way Down in the Schoolyard (St. Voc.) | 2 | 50 | 2-21 |
| Way Down in the Schoolyard (St. Perf. Tr.) | 2 | 50 | 2-22 |
| We Are Dear Little Birdies (St. Voc.) | K | 176 | 6-28 |
| We Are Dear Little Birdies (St. Perf. Tr.) | K | 176 | 6-29 |
| We Come to Greet You in Peace (Hevenu shalom aleichem) (St. Voc.) | 3 | 378 | 13-12 |
| We Go Together (from Grease) (St. Voc.) | 4 | 44 | 2-27 |
| We Go Together (from Grease) (St. Perf. Tr.) | 4 | 44 | 2-28 |
| We Have a Goat (Yesh lanu taish) (St. Voc.) | 1 | 182 | 6-2 |
| We Have Arrived (Habemos llegado) (St. Voc.) | 6 | 174 | 10-2 |
| We Shall Not Be Moved (St. Voc.) | 4 | 437 | 18-22 |
| We Shall Not Be Moved (St. Perf. Tr.) | 4 | 437 | 18-23 |
| We Shall Overcome (St. Voc.) | 4 | 326 | 14-5 |
| We Shall Overcome (St. Perf. Tr.) | 4 | 326 | 14-6 |
| We Wish You a Merry Christmas (St. Voc.) | 3 | 395 | 14-6 |
| We Wish You a Merry Christmas (St. Perf. Tr.) | 3 | 395 | 14-7 |
| We're All Gonna Shine Tonight (St. Voc.) | 2 | 240 | 8-27 |
| We're All Gonna Shine Tonight (St. Perf. Tr.) | 2 | 240 | 8-28 |
| We're Making Popcorn (speech piece) (St. Voc.) | 1 | 86 | 3-1 |
| We're Making Popcorn (speech piece) (St. Perf. Tr.) | 1 | 86 | 3-2 |
| We've Got Lots in Common (Charlotte's Web) (St. Voc.) | 3 | 366 | 12-25 |
| We've Got Lots in Common (Charlotte's Web) (St. Perf. Tr.) | 3 | 366 | 12-26 |
| Weevily Wheat (St. Voc.) | 4 | 105 | 5-17 |
| Weevily Wheat (St. Perf. Tr.) | 4 | 105 | 5-18 |
| Welcome, My Friends (Funwa alafia) (St. Voc.) | 5 | 32 | 2-20 |
| What a Beautiful Banner! (¡Qué bonita bandera!) (St. Voc.) | 5 | 294 | 13-21 |
| What a Wonderful World (St. Voc.) | 6 | 62 | 4-20 |
| What a Wonderful World (St. Perf. Tr.) | 6 | 62 | 4-21 |
| What Comes There O'er the Hill? (Was kommt dort von der Höh'?) (St. Voc.) | 8 | C-21 | 6-7 |
| What Do Animals Need? (St. Voc.) | 2 | 288 | 10-34 |
| What Do Animals Need? (St. Perf. Tr.) | 2 | 288 | 10-35 |
| What Pleasure (¡Qué gusto!) (St. Voc.) | 3 | 132 | 4-46 |
| What Will You Be on Halloween? (St. Voc.) | K | 308 | 11-1 |
| What Will You Be on Halloween? (St. Perf. Tr.) | K | 308 | 11-2 |
| Wheel of the Water, The (St. Voc.) | 4 | 362 | 16-1 |
| Wheel of the Water, The (St. Perf. Tr.) | 4 | 362 | 16-2 |
| When Johnny Comes Marching Home (T.A.P.) | 5 | 180 | 9-13 |
| When Johnny Comes Marching Home (St. Perf. Tr.) | 5 | 180 | 9-14 |
| When the Saints Go Marching In (St. Voc.) | 2 | 178 | 6-41 |
| When the Saints Go Marching In (St. Perf. Tr.) | 2 | 178 | 6-42 |
| When the Train Comes Along (St. Voc.) | 1 | 300 | 9-34 |
| When the Train Comes Along (St. Perf. Tr.) | 1 | 300 | 9-35 |
| Where Did I Hide It? (¿Dónde lo escondí?) (St. Voc.) | K | 209 | 7-22 |
| White Dove, The (La paloma blanca) (St. Voc.) | 3 | 252 | 8-23 |
| Who Can Sail? (Vem kan segla?) (St. Voc.) | 6 | 417 | 20-17 |
| Who Has Seen the Wind? (St. Voc.) | 2 | 324 | 11-33 |
| Who Has Seen the Wind? (St. Perf. Tr.) | 2 | 324 | 11-34 |
| Who Has the Penny? (St. Voc.) | K | 42 | 2-16 |
| Who Has the Penny? (St. Perf. Tr.) | K | 42 | 2-17 |
| Wichita Hand Game Song 1 (St. Voc.) | 3 | 306 | 10-36 |
| Wichita Hand Game Song 1 (St. Perf. Tr.) | 3 | 306 | 10-37 |
| Wichita Hand Game Song 2 (St. Voc.) | 3 | 306 | 10-38 |
| Wichita Hand Game Song 2 (St. Perf. Tr.) | 3 | 306 | 10-39 |
| Wide Street, The (La calle ancha) (St. Voc.) | 3 | 297 | 10-24 |
| Will You? (Vil du?) (St. Voc.) | 1 | 92 | 3-16 |
| Willoughby, Wallaby, Woo (St. Voc.) | K | 282 | 10-1 |
| Willoughby, Wallaby, Woo (St. Perf. Tr.) | K | 282 | 10-2 |
| Willowbee (St. Voc.) | 1 | 222 | 7-13 |
| Willowbee (St. Perf. Tr.) | 1 | 222 | 7-14 |
| Wind Blew East, The (St. Voc.) | 1 | 64 | 2-40 |
| Wind Blew East, The (St. Perf. Tr.) | 1 | 64 | 2-41 |
| Wind on the Bridge, The (Quâ câu gió bay) (St. Voc.) | 5 | 460 | 20-2 |
| Wind Up the Apple Tree (St. Voc.) | 1 | 184 | 6-8 |
| Wind Up the Apple Tree (St. Perf. Tr.) | 1 | 184 | 6-9 |
| Wings of a Dove (St. Voc.) | 4 | 318 | 13-35 |
| Wings of a Dove (St. Perf. Tr.) | 4 | 318 | 13-36 |
| Winter (St. Voc.) | 8 | G-11 | 11-24 |
| Winter (St. Perf. Tr.) | 8 | G-11 | 11-25 |
| Winter Fantasy (St. Voc.) | 4 | 424 | 18-3 |
| Winter Fantasy (St. Perf. Tr.) | 4 | 424 | 18-4 |
| Winter Is Over (L'inverno è passato) (St. Voc.) | 2 | 400 | 15-2 |
| Winter Song (St. Voc.) | 6 | 455 | 21-19 |
| Winter Song (St. Perf. Tr.) | 6 | 455 | 21-20 |
| Winter Wonderland (St. Voc.) | 5 | 454 | 19-19 |
| Winter Wonderland (St. Perf. Tr.) | 5 | 454 | 19-20 |
| Wir hatten gebauet (The Stately House) (St. Voc.) | 8 | C-21 | 6-10 |
| Wir hatten gebauet (The Stately House) (St. Perf. Tr.) | 8 | C-21 | 6-12 |

| Title | Gr. | Pg. | CD Track |
|---|---|---|---|
| Woke Up This Morning (St. Voc.) | 5 | 288 | 13-16 |
| Woke Up This Morning (St. Perf. Tr.) | 5 | 288 | 13-17 |
| Woodland Chorus (St. Voc.) | K | 250 | 8-38 |
| Woodland Chorus (St. Perf. Tr.) | K | 250 | 8-39 |
| Wooly Bully (St. Voc.) | 3 | 373 | 13-5 |
| Wooly Bully (St. Perf. Tr.) | 3 | 373 | 13-6 |
| World of Difference, A (St. Voc.) | 5 | 386 | 18-2 |
| World of Difference, A (St. Perf. Tr.) | 5 | 386 | 18-3 |
| World We Love, The (St. Voc.) | 3 | 342 | 12-1 |
| World We Love, The (St. Perf. Tr.) | 3 | 342 | 12-2 |
| Worried Man Blues (St. Voc.) | 6 | 371 | 19-3 |
| Worried Man Blues (St. Perf. Tr.) | 6 | 371 | 19-4 |
| Xiao (Bamboo Flute) (St. Voc.) | 4 | 314 | 13-24 |
| Xiao (Bamboo Flute) (St. Perf. Tr.) | 4 | 314 | 13-26 |
| Xiao yin chuan (Silver Moon Boat) (St. Voc.) | 2 | 14 | 1-13 |
| Xiao yin chuan (Silver Moon Boat) (St. Perf. Tr.) | 2 | 14 | 1-15 |
| Yakety Yak (St. Voc.) | 5 | 205 | 10-17 |
| Yakety Yak (St. Perf. Tr.) | 5 | 205 | 10-18 |
| Yang wa wa (Nursery Song) (St. Voc.) | K | 162 | 6-3 |
| Yang wa wa (Nursery Song) (St. Perf. Tr.) | K | 162 | 6-5 |
| Yankee Doodle (St. Voc.) | 2 | 405 | 15-13 |
| Yankee Doodle (St. Perf. Tr.) | 2 | 405 | 15-14 |
| Yankee Doodle (St. Voc./Dance Perf. Tr.) | 3 | 414 | 15-9 |
| Yankee Doodle (St. Perf. Tr.) | 3 | 414 | 15-10 |
| Ye jaliya da (St. Voc.) | 5 | 67 | 4-7 |
| Ye jaliya da (St. Perf. Tr.) | 5 | 67 | 4-8 |
| Yellow Rose of Texas, The (T.A.P.) | 7 | I-70 | 14-18 |
| Yellow Rose of Texas, The (St. Perf. Tr.) | 7 | I-70 | 14-19 |
| Yesh lanu taish (We Have a Goat) (St. Voc.) | 1 | 182 | 6-1 |
| Yesh lanu taish (We Have a Goat) (St. Perf. Tr.) | 1 | 182 | 6-3 |
| Yibane amenu (Hebrew) (St. Voc.) | 4 | 316 | 13-29 |
| Yibane amenu (English) (St. Voc.) | 4 | 316 | 13-30 |

| Title | Gr. | Pg. | CD Track |
|---|---|---|---|
| Yibane amenu (St. Perf. Tr.) | 4 | 316 | 13-31 |
| Yo-shi nai (St. Voc.) | 6 | 286 | 14-17 |
| Yo-shi nai (St. Perf. Tr.) | 6 | 286 | 14-18 |
| Yonder Come Day (T.A.P.) | 8 | I-68 | 15-20 |
| You Are My Sunshine (St. Voc.) | 6 | 246 | 13-4 |
| You Are My Sunshine (St. Perf. Tr.) | 6 | 246 | 13-5 |
| You Were on My Mind (St. Voc.) | 7 | G-23 | 12-15 |
| You Were on My Mind (St. Perf. Tr.) | 7 | G-23 | 12-16 |
| You're a Grand Old Flag (St. Voc.) | 3 | 264 | 9-8 |
| You're a Grand Old Flag (St. Perf. Tr.) | 3 | 264 | 9-9 |
| You've Got a Friend (St. Voc.) | 5 | 366 | 17-2 |
| You've Got a Friend (St. Perf. Tr.) | 5 | 366 | 17-3 |
| Your Friends Shall Be the Tall Wind (St. Voc.) | 6 | 201 | 11-1 |
| Your Friends Shall Be the Tall Wind (St. Perf. Tr.) | 6 | 201 | 11-2 |
| Your Life Is Now (St. Voc.) | 6 | 4 | 1-1 |
| Your Life Is Now (St. Perf. Tr.) | 6 | 4 | 1-2 |
| Yü guang guang (Moonlight Lullaby) (St. Voc.) | 6 | 60 | 4-15 |
| Yü guang guang (Moonlight Lullaby) (St. Perf. Tr.) | 6 | 60 | 4-17 |
| Yüe liang wan wan (Crescent Moon) (St. Voc.) | 5 | 314 | 14-23 |
| Yüe liang wan wan (Cresent Moon) (St. Perf. Tr.) | 5 | 314 | 14-25 |
| Zane from Abedeen (Ah ya Zane) (St. Voc.) | 5 | 297 | 13-27 |
| Zip-a-Dee-Doo-Dah (St. Voc.) | 2 | 330 | 12-4 |
| Zip-a-Dee-Doo-Dah (St. Perf. Tr.) | 2 | 330 | 12-5 |
| Zudio (St. Voc.) | 2 | 269 | 9-35 |
| Zudio (St. Perf. Tr.) | 2 | 269 | 9-36 |
| Zum gali gali (Hebrew) (St. Voc.) | 5 | 401 | 18-13 |
| Zum gali gali (English) (St. Voc.) | 5 | 401 | 18-14 |
| Zum gali gali (St. Perf. Tr.) | 5 | 401 | 18-15 |
| Zumba, zumba (Spanish) (St. Voc.) | 3 | 400 | 14-16 |
| Zumba, zumba (English) (St. Voc.) | 3 | 400 | 14-17 |
| Zumba, zumba (St. Perf. Tr.) | 3 | 400 | 14-18 |
| Zuni Sunrise Call (St. Voc.) | 5 | 396 | 18-10 |

# Pronunciation Practice Index

This section provides an alphabetical listing of songs that have recorded Pronunciation Practice tracks in Silver Burdett MAKING MUSIC. The listing indicates where the song is found in the Teacher Edition, as well as the page numbers where the printed pronunciation practice guide can be found in both the Teacher Edition and the Resource Book.

| Title | Grade | SE/TE Lesson Page | CD Pron. Prac. Track | TE Pron. Prac. Page | Resource Book Page |
|---|---|---|---|---|---|
| A la puerta del cielo | 5 | 60 | 3-32 | 524 | A-8 |
| A la rurru niño | K | 180 | 6-36 | 345 | A-24 |
| Achshav | 2 | 64 | 3-4 | 428 | A-5 |
| Adana ya gidelim | 2 | 142 | 5-35 | 433 | A-14 |
| Adelita (melody) | 5 | 50 | 3-7 | 523 | A-6 |
| Adelita (harmony) | 5 | 50 | 3-8 | 523 | A-6 |
| Adiós, amigos | 6 | 57 | 4-4 | 524 | A-8 |
| Aguinaldo | 3 | 402 | 14-23 | 465 | A-46 |
| Ah, eu entrei na roda | 3 | 308 | 10-43 | 455 | A-27 |
| Ah! Les jolis papillons | 1 | 362 | 11-24 | 493 | A-46 |
| Ah ya Zane | 5 | 297 | 13-29 | 532 | A-26 |
| Ahora voy a cantarles | 3 | 56 | 2-34 | 443 | A-6 |
| Ai Dunaii moy | 4 | 293 | 12-17 | 486 | A-29 |
| Al ánimo | 3 | 322 | 11-22 | 457 | A-31 |
| Al citrón | 3 | 320 | 11-18 | 457 | A-30 |
| Al quebrar la piñata | 4 | 432 | 18-18 | 498 | A-51 |
| Al tambor | 3 | 270 | 9-19 | 449 | A-16 |
| Ala Da'lona | 4 | 136 | 6-21 | 479 | A-12 |
| Allá en la fuente | 2 | 92 | 3-51 | 430 | A-7 |
| Alle meine Entchen | 1 | 98 | 3-27 | 476 | A-10 |
| Alumot | 6 | 306 | 15-29 | 535 | A-25 |
| Ambos a dos | 3 | 20 | 1-34 | 441 | A-3 |
| Amefuri | 1 | 144 | 4-46 | 481 | A-17 |
| Arirang | 5 | 25 | 2-9 | 522 | A-5 |
| Artsa alinu | 3 | 285 | 10-4 | 453 | A-22 |
| Asadoya | 6 | 303 | 15-20 | 534 | A-24 |
| Así es mi tierra (melody) | 6 | 172 | 9-33 | 529 | A-16 |
| Así es mi tierra (harmony) | 6 | 172 | 9-34 | 529 | A-16 |
| Au clair de la lune | 3 | 18 | 1-29 | 441 | A-2 |
| ¡Ay, Jalisco no te rajes! (melody) | 7 | I-6 | 13-8 | J-6 | L-3 |
| ¡Ay, Jalisco no te rajes! (harmony) | 7 | I-6 | 13-9 | J-6 | L-3 |
| Ayelivi | 2 | 70 | 3-12 | 429 | A-5 |
| Ayliluli, num tsipor | 1 | 204 | 6-39 | 485 | A-27 |
| Bantama kra kro (melody) | 5 | 308 | 14-17 | 536 | A-34 |
| Bantama kra kro (harmony) | 5 | 308 | 14-18 | 536 | A-34 |
| Banuwa | 6 | 294 | 15-3 | 533 | A-22 |
| Bát kim thang | 6 | 13 | 1-16 | 521 | A-2 |
| Bereleh | K | 151 | 5-37 | 342 | A-19 |
| Beriozka | 4 | 294 | 12-22 | 486 | A-30 |
| Bogando a la luz del sol (melody) | 4 | 306 | 13-10 | 488 | A-33 |
| Bogando a la luz del sol (countermelody) | 4 | 306 | 13-11 | 488 | A-33 |
| Bonjour, mes amis | 1 | 316 | 10-9 | 491 | A-39 |
| Buenos días | 1 | 13 | 1-22 | 473 | A-2 |
| Caballito blanco | 2 | 193 | 7-21 | 437 | A-20 |
| Canción de cuna | 4 | 144 | 6-34 | 479 | A-13 |
| Canción Mixteca (melody) | 5 | 326 | 15-14 | 539 | A-40 |
| Canción Mixteca (harmony) | 5 | 326 | 15-15 | 539 | A-40 |
| Cantando mentiras | 4 | 146 | 6-41 | 479 | A-14 |

| Title | Grade | SE/TE Lesson Page | CD Pron. Prac. Track | TE Pron. Prac. Page | Resource Book Page |
|---|---|---|---|---|---|
| Cantaré, cantarás (melody) | 6 | 413 | 20-14 | 542 | A-35 |
| Cantaré, cantarás (harmony) | 6 | 413 | 20-15 | 542 | A-35 |
| Canto del agua (melody) | 8 | I-10 | 13-10 | J-7 | L-3 |
| Canto del agua (harmony) | 8 | I-10 | 13-11 | J-7 | L-3 |
| Cha yang wu | 1 | 90 | 3-8 | 475 | A-7 |
| Chag Purim | 1 | 438 | 14-17 | 499 | A-58 |
| Chang | 1 | 156 | 5-4 | 482 | A-20 |
| Chanukah, Chanukah | 1 | 420 | 13-26 | 497 | A-54 |
| Chanukiyah li yesh | 1 | 421 | 13-30 | 497 | A-55 |
| Chawe chidyo chem'chero | 2 | 297 | 11-4 | 444 | A-34 |
| Cheki, morena | 2 | 180 | 7-4 | 436 | A-19 |
| Cheki, morena | 7 | I-16 | 13-17 | J-7 | L-4 |
| Chiapanecas | 5 | 92 | 5-10 | 526 | A-11 |
| Cho'i hát bội | 5 | 318 | 14-35 | 537 | A-37 |
| Chuhwuht | 2 | 356 | 13-14 | 448 | A-42 |
| Cielito lindo | 4 | 270 | 11-13 | 484 | A-26 |
| Cielito lindo | 7 | I-20 | 13-21 | J-8 | L-5 |
| Ciranda | 2 | 272 | 10-4 | 440 | A-28 |
| Cirmos cica | 1 | 130 | 4-22 | 478 | A-13 |
| Con el vito (melody) | 7 | G-15 | 12-8 | J-5 | L-6 |
| Con el vito (harmony) | 7 | G-15 | 12-9 | J-5 | L-6 |
| Corrido de Kansas | 4 | 274 | 11-20 | 485 | A-27 |
| Corta la caña | 6 | 364 | 18-17 | 536 | A-27 |
| Counting Song | 1 | 253 | 8-11 | 488 | A-33 |
| Cuando pa' Chile me voy (melody) | 6 | 376 | 19-14 | 537 | A-28 |
| Cuando pa' Chile me voy (harmony) | 6 | 376 | 19-15 | 537 | A-28 |
| Da pacem, Domine | 5 | 62 | 3-41 | 525 | A-9 |
| Dayenu | 4 | 439 | 19-4 | 499 | A-52 |
| De colores (melody) | 5 | 90 | 5-4 | 525 | A-10 |
| De colores (harmony) | 5 | 90 | 5-5 | 525 | A-10 |
| De colores (melody) | 8 | I-14 | 13-16 | J-8 | L-5 |
| De colores (harmony) | 8 | I-14 | 13-17 | J-8 | L-5 |
| Deau-deau, ti pitit maman | 2 | 306 | 11-16 | 445 | A-36 |
| Debajo el botón | 1 | 210 | 6-46 | 486 | A-28 |
| Der sad to katte | 2 | 300 | 11-8 | 444 | A-35 |
| Deux cocodries | 2 | 364 | 13-24 | 448 | A-43 |
| Diou shou juan'er | 2 | 277 | 10-15 | 441 | A-30 |
| Dok djampa | 8 | I-20 | 13-23 | J-8 | L-6 |
| Don Alfonso (melody) | 5 | 177 | 9-5 | 530 | A-20 |
| Don Alfonso (harmony) | 5 | 177 | 9-6 | 530 | A-20 |
| Don Gato | 3 | 352 | 12-11 | 459 | A-35 |
| Dona nobis pacem | 6 | 125 | 7-19 | 526 | A-11 |
| ¿Dónde lo escondí? | K | 209 | 7-24 | 346 | A-26 |
| Doong gul ge | 3 | 134 | 4-52 | 445 | A-9 |
| Doraji | 4 | 174 | 7-39 | 481 | A-17 |
| Duck Dance | 2 | 249 | 9-11 | 439 | A-23 |
| Duérmete, mi niño | 1 | 292 | 9-22 | 489 | A-35 |
| Dundai | 5 | 106 | 5-37 | 527 | A-14 |
| Ee jer ha ba go | K | 133 | 5-13 | 341 | A-18 |
| Ég a gyertya | K | 96 | 3-53 | 337 | A-11 |
| Ego sum pauper | 5 | 158 | 8-10 | 529 | A-19 |
| Eh, cumpari! | 4 | 68 | 3-40 | 476 | A-8 |
| Ein Männlein steht im Walde | 2 | 90 | 3-46 | 429 | A-6 |
| Einini | 4 | 391 | 17-3 | 492 | A-40 |
| El barquito | 3 | 358 | 12-18 | 461 | A-38 |
| El borrego | 4 | 242 | 10-15 | 484 | A-25 |
| El burrito enfermo | K | 271 | 9-26 | 349 | A-30 |
| El caracol | K | 130 | 5-9 | 341 | A-17 |

| Title | Grade | SE/TE Lesson Page | CD Pron. Prac. Track | TE Pron. Prac. Page | Resource Book Page |
|---|---|---|---|---|---|
| El carite | 5 | 305 | 14-9 | 534 | A-30 |
| El carnavalito humahuaqueño | 6 | 482 | 22-24 | 547 | A-46 |
| El chocolate | 1 | 380 | 12-10 | 495 | A-50 |
| El cóndor pasa | 6 | 46 | 3-19 | 523 | A-6 |
| El coquí | 2 | 292 | 10-39 | 443 | A-33 |
| El desembre congelat | 5 | 473 | 20-28 | 546 | A-53 |
| El día de mamita | K | 325 | 11-32 | 355 | A-42 |
| El florón | 2 | 246 | 9-4 | 438 | A-22 |
| El gallo pinto | 3 | 86 | 3-21 | 444 | A-7 |
| El juego chirimbolo | 2 | 54 | 2-30 | 428 | A-4 |
| El mes de abril | 3 | 328 | 11-28 | 458 | A-32 |
| El payo | 6 | 145 | 8-11 | 527 | A-12 |
| El rabel | 3 | 362 | 12-23 | 461 | A-39 |
| El rancho grande | 4 | 215 | 9-9 | 482 | A-20 |
| El rancho grande | 8 | I-22 | 13-27 | J-9 | L-7 |
| El sapito | 3 | 336 | 11-40 | 458 | A-34 |
| El tambor | 2 | 274 | 10-10 | 441 | A-29 |
| El tren | 2 | 260 | 9-24 | 439 | A-24 |
| El zapatero | 1 | 298 | 9-32 | 490 | A-37 |
| Elegua | 7 | D-8 | 8-22 | J-3 | L-7 |
| Éliza Kongo | 5 | 14 | 1-26 | 522 | A-4 |
| En nuestra Tierra tan linda | 2 | 335 | 12-11 | 445 | A-37 |
| Erdö, erdö de magos | 3 | 182 | 6-30 | 446 | A-11 |
| Eres tú | 6 | 473 | 22-13 | 545 | A-42 |
| Fais do do (vocal Part 1) | 6 | 403 | 20-4 | 539 | A-31 |
| Fais do do (vocal Part 2) | 6 | 403 | 20-5 | 539 | A-31 |
| Fais do do (vocal Part 3) | 6 | 403 | 20-6 | 539 | A-31 |
| Fais dodo | K | 158 | 5-52 | 343 | A-21 |
| Farewell to the Warriors | 4 | 284 | 12-5 | 485 | A-28 |
| Feliz Navidad | 7 | I-28 | 13-26 | J-9 | L-8 |
| Feng yang hua gu | 4 | 313 | 13-23 | 489 | A-35 |
| Frère Jacques | 2 | 125 | 5-4 | 432 | A-12 |
| Funwa alafia | 5 | 32 | 2-22 | 522 | A-5 |
| Gakavik | 4 | 14 | 1-20 | 473 | A-2 |
| Gaudeamus Igitur | 8 | C-20 | 6-5 | J-3 | L-8 |
| Geef jij mij die schoen | 1 | 126 | 4-15 | 478 | A-12 |
| Gloria, Gloria | 6 | 459 | 21-26 | 545 | A-41 |
| Greetings | 3 | 316 | 11-11 | 456 | A-29 |
| Guantanamera | 8 | I-32 | 14-7 | J-10 | L-9 |
| Ha'kyo jong | 2 | 135 | 5-25 | 433 | A-13 |
| Habemos llegado (melody) | 6 | 174 | 10-4 | 530 | A-17 |
| Habemos llegado (harmony) | 6 | 174 | 10-5 | 530 | A-17 |
| Haere | 2 | 285 | 10-30 | 443 | A-32 |
| Hama chi dori | 3 | 330 | 11-33 | 458 | A-33 |
| Hanuka, Hanuka | 3 | 390 | 13-29 | 462 | A-41 |
| Hanuka, Hanuka | 8 | I-36 | 14-12 | J-11 | L-11 |
| Haru ga kita | 2 | 401 | 15-8 | 451 | A-49 |
| Hashewie | 4 | 63 | 3-24 | 474 | A-5 |
| Hashkediya | 3 | 206 | 7-20 | 447 | A-12 |
| Hato popo | 1 | 186 | 6-16 | 484 | A-24 |
| Hava nagila | 6 | 153 | 8-25 | 528 | A-14 |
| Hava nashira | 6 | 82 | 5-18 | 526 | A-11 |
| Hej pada pada | 3 | 78 | 3-9 | 443 | A-7 |
| Hevenu shalom aleichem | 3 | 378 | 13-14 | 462 | A-40 |
| Hey, m'tswala | 4 | 79 | 4-21 | 477 | A-9 |
| Himmel und Erde | 5 | 94 | 5-14 | 527 | A-13 |
| Hine mah tov | 5 | 431 | 19-8 | 541 | A-46 |
| Hitotsu toya | 5 | 478 | 21-4 | 547 | A-55 |

| Title | Grade | SE/TE Lesson Page | CD Pron. Prac. Track | TE Pron. Prac. Page | Resource Book Page |
|---|---|---|---|---|---|
| Hotaru koi | 1 | 356 | 11-16 | 493 | A-45 |
| Hui jia qü | 2 | 158 | 6-8 | 434 | A-15 |
| Hwa yuan li-de young wa wa | 3 | 102 | 4-4 | 444 | A-8 |
| Ichi-gatsu tsuitachi | 3 | 406 | 14-29 | 465 | A-48 |
| Ichi-gatsu tsuitachi | 7 | I-40 | 13-34 | J-9 | L-9 |
| Ikhanda, maslombe | K | 14 | 1-23 | 333 | A-3 |
| Imbabura | 5 | 203 | 10-15 | 531 | A-22 |
| Inkpataya | 3 | 254 | 8-30 | 448 | A-15 |
| Ise oluwa | 2 | 102 | 4-19 | 431 | A-9 |
| Ise oluwa | 6 | 230 | 12-5 | 531 | A-19 |
| Jan ken pon | 3 | 302 | 10-33 | 455 | A-26 |
| ¡Jeu! ¡Jeu! | 1 | 216 | 7-9 | 486 | A-29 |
| Jo'ashila | 5 | 108 | 5-45 | 527 | A-15 |
| Juan pirulero | K | 215 | 7-33 | 346 | A-26 |
| Juanito | K | 300 | 10-26 | 353 | A-37 |
| Kaeru no uta | K | 183 | 6-43 | 345 | A-25 |
| Kapulu kane | 2 | 270 | 9-39 | 440 | A-27 |
| Karangatia ra | 3 | 272 | 9-22 | 450 | A-17 |
| Karangatia ra | 8 | F-23 | 11-5 | J-6 | L-13 |
| Kébé Mama | 1 | 442 | 14-25 | 499 | A-59 |
| Kibungo | 2 | 354 | 13-5 | 447 | A-40 |
| Koriko! | K | 154 | 5-43 | 342 | A-20 |
| Kou ri lengay | 2 | 217 | 8-9 | 438 | A-21 |
| Kum bachur atzel | 3 | 138 | 5-4 | 446 | A-10 |
| Kuma san | K | 40 | 2-15 | 334 | A-6 |
| Kunolounkwa | K | 110 | 4-18 | 339 | A-13 |
| L'inverno è passato | 2 | 400 | 15-4 | 450 | A-48 |
| La bamba | 5 | 128 | 6-23 | 528 | A-16 |
| La borinqueña | 8 | D-19 | 8-29 | J-5 | L-14 |
| La calle ancha | 3 | 297 | 10-26 | 454 | A-25 |
| La ciudad de Juaja | 5 | 58 | 3-27 | 523 | A-7 |
| La copa de la vida | 4 | 414 | 17-22 | 495 | A-45 |
| La golondrina (melody) | 8 | I-50 | 15-4 | J-12 | L-15 |
| La golondrina (harmony) | 8 | I-50 | 15-5 | J-12 | L-15 |
| La Jesusita | 5 | 322 | 15-8 | 538 | A-39 |
| La mar estaba serena | 2 | 345 | 12-24 | 446 | A-40 |
| La marche des rois | 4 | 411 | 17-19 | 494 | A-43 |
| La mariposa | 6 | 58 | 4-11 | 525 | A-9 |
| La paloma blanca | 3 | 252 | 8-25 | 448 | A-14 |
| La paloma se fué (melody) | 6 | 51 | 3-25 | 524 | A-7 |
| La paloma se fué (harmony) | 6 | 51 | 3-26 | 524 | A-7 |
| La piñata | 3 | 399 | 14-15 | 463 | A-43 |
| La pulga de San José | 3 | 40 | 2-9 | 442 | A-4 |
| La raspa | 4 | 302 | 13-4 | 487 | A-32 |
| La Tarara | 4 | 176 | 8-4 | 481 | A-18 |
| La tormenta tropical | 2 | 116 | 4-37 | 431 | A-10 |
| La víbora | 1 | 322 | 10-18 | 492 | A-42 |
| Lahk gei mohlee | 5 | 317 | 14-31 | 537 | A-36 |
| Laredo (melody) | 5 | 10 | 1-12 | 521 | A-2 |
| Laredo (harmony) | 5 | 10 | 1-13 | 521 | A-2 |
| Las estaciones | 1 | 29 | 1-43 | 473 | A-3 |
| Las estrellitas del cielo | 5 | 175 | 8-32 | 529 | A-19 |
| Las horas | 1 | 246 | 7-48 | 487 | A-30 |
| Las mañanitas (melody) | 6 | 481 | 22-19 | 546 | A-45 |
| Las mañanitas (harmony) | 6 | 481 | 22-20 | 546 | A-45 |
| Las Navidades | 5 | 472 | 20-24 | 545 | A-52 |
| Las velitas | 5 | 147 | 7-21 | 528 | A-17 |
| Leak kanseng | 1 | 156 | 5-8 | 483 | A-21 |

Pronunciation Practice

| Title | Grade | SE/TE Lesson Page | CD Pron. Prac. Track | TE Pron. Prac. Page | Resource Book Page |
|---|---|---|---|---|---|
| Les petites marionettes | K | 237 | 8-21 | 347 | A-27 |
| Lo yisa | 6 | 130 | 7-26 | 526 | A-12 |
| Loigratong | 6 | 451 | 21-14 | 544 | A-39 |
| Los maizales | 1 | 296 | 9-27 | 490 | A-36 |
| Los niños en España cantan | 4 | 197 | 8-41 | 482 | A-19 |
| Los pececitos | 1 | 178 | 5-45 | 483 | A-22 |
| Los pollitos | K | 166 | 6-15 | 344 | A-23 |
| Los reyes de Oriente (melody) | 5 | 480 | 21-8 | 547 | A-56 |
| Los reyes de Oriente (harmony) | 5 | 480 | 21-9 | 547 | A-56 |
| Los reyes de Oriente (melody) | 8 | I-58 | 15-13 | J-13 | L-16 |
| Los reyes de Oriente (harmony) | 8 | I-58 | 15-14 | J-13 | L-16 |
| Los trencitos | K | 24 | 1-37 | 333 | A-4 |
| Luna lunera | K | 90 | 3-39 | 336 | A-9 |
| Má Teodora (melody) | 6 | 301 | 15-15 | 533 | A-23 |
| Má Teodora (harmony) | 6 | 301 | 15-16 | 533 | A-23 |
| Magnolia | 6 | 16 | 1-25 | 521 | A-3 |
| Mañana | 7 | E-14 | 9-29 | J-5 | L-10 |
| Mariposita | 2 | 156 | 6-4 | 434 | A-14 |
| Mbombera | K | 24 | 1-40 | 334 | A-5 |
| Me voy para la luna | 1 | 397 | 12-32 | 496 | A-52 |
| Meng Jian Nu | 5 | 194 | 10-4 | 530 | A-21 |
| Mi chacra | 1 | 364 | 11-31 | 494 | A-47 |
| Mi cuerpo hace música | K | 106 | 4-11 | 338 | A-12 |
| Minka | 4 | 222 | 9-24 | 482 | A-21 |
| Mon papa | 2 | 280 | 10-20 | 442 | A-31 |
| Mon son pha | K | 91 | 3-43 | 337 | A-10 |
| Múbärak | 3 | 282 | 9-43 | 453 | A-21 |
| Nampaya omame | 1 | 138 | 4-38 | 479 | A-14 |
| Nampaya omame | 7 | D-10 | 8-28 | J-3 | L-11 |
| Nani wale na hala | 3 | 260 | 9-4 | 449 | A-15 |
| Naranja dulce | 2 | 96 | 4-6 | 430 | A-8 |
| Ner li | 2 | 383 | 14-20 | 449 | A-46 |
| Nie chcę cię znác | 3 | 314 | 11-6 | 456 | A-28 |
| Niño querido | 1 | 308 | 9-44 | 490 | A-38 |
| Niu lang zhi nü | 4 | 335 | 14-18 | 491 | A-38 |
| No quiero plata | 1 | 424 | 13-38 | 498 | A-56 |
| Nu wahtan | 1 | 279 | 9-9 | 489 | A-34 |
| O, Desayo | 5 | 411 | 18-24 | 541 | A-44 |
| O laufet, ihr Hirten | 2 | 384 | 14-24 | 450 | A-47 |
| O lê lê O Bahía | 6 | 165 | 9-17 | 528 | A-15 |
| O ma washi | K | 13 | 1-19 | 333 | A-2 |
| O pião entrou | 2 | 355 | 13-9 | 447 | A-41 |
| Ocho kandelikas | 4 | 429 | 18-11 | 497 | A-49 |
| Ode to Joy | 4 | 152 | 7-10 | 480 | A-15 |
| Ōsamu kosamu (Part 1) | 4 | 96 | 5-5 | 477 | A-10 |
| Ōsamu kosamu (Part 2) | 4 | 96 | 5-6 | 477 | A-10 |
| Oy, Hanuka | 5 | 464 | 20-10 | 544 | A-50 |
| Oy, Hanuka | 7 | I-44 | 14-4 | J-10 | L-13 |
| Oye | 6 | 336 | 17-7 | 535 | A-26 |
| Pai pi qiu | 1 | 324 | 10-22 | 492 | A-44 |
| Pat-a-pan | 4 | 411 | 17-18 | 494 | A-43 |
| Pavo, pavo | 1 | 416 | 13-21 | 496 | A-53 |
| Perná, perná, i mélissá | K | 264 | 9-16 | 348 | A-28 |
| Perot | 2 | 378 | 14-12 | 449 | A-45 |
| Pin Pon | 1 | 146 | 4-51 | 482 | A-18 |
| Piñon, pirulín | 2 | 174 | 6-36 | 436 | A-18 |
| Pollerita | 5 | 151 | 7-33 | 529 | A-18 |
| Pon, pon, pon | K | 50 | 2-30 | 335 | A-7 |

Pronunciation Practice

| Title | Grade | SE/TE Lesson Page | CD Pron. Prac. Track | TE Pron. Prac. Page | Resource Book Page |
|---|---|---|---|---|---|
| Ptashky u babusi sadochku | 1 | 192 | 6-27 | 484 | A-25 |
| Pust' 'vsegda budet sonse | 3 | 278 | 9-37 | 452 | A-20 |
| Quâ câu gió bay | 5 | 460 | 20-4 | 543 | A-49 |
| ¡Qué bonita bandera! (melody) | 5 | 294 | 13-23 | 532 | A-24 |
| ¡Qué bonita bandera! (harmony) | 5 | 294 | 13-24 | 532 | A-24 |
| ¡Qué gusto! | 3 | 132 | 4-48 | 444 | A-8 |
| ¡Qué llueva! | K | 81 | 3-18 | 336 | A-8 |
| Ragupati Ragava Raja Ram | 5 | 321 | 15-4 | 538 | A-38 |
| Riendo el río corre | 6 | 263 | 13-27 | 532 | A-20 |
| Rinsho, rinsho | K | 285 | 10-6 | 352 | A-36 |
| Río, río (melody) | 5 | 370 | 17-10 | 540 | A-42 |
| Río, río (harmony) | 5 | 370 | 17-11 | 540 | A-42 |
| Riqui rán | 1 | 48 | 2-21 | 474 | A-5 |
| Riqui rán | 4 | 66 | 3-36 | 475 | A-6 |
| Ríu ríu chíu | 5 | 435 | 19-11 | 541 | A-46 |
| S'vivon | 6 | 452 | 21-18 | 544 | A-40 |
| Sailboat in the Sky | 4 | 374 | 16-14 | 492 | A-39 |
| Sakura | 4 | 308 | 13-16 | 488 | A-34 |
| Sambalele | 4 | 397 | 17-11 | 493 | A-41 |
| Sansaw akroma | 3 | 286 | 10-9 | 454 | A-23 |
| Santa Clara | 4 | 172 | 7-35 | 480 | A-16 |
| Sarika keo | 3 | 275 | 9-29 | 451 | A-18 |
| Sawatdee tuh jah | 2 | 265 | 9-31 | 440 | A-26 |
| Se va el caimán | 5 | 306 | 14-13 | 534 | A-31 |
| Serra, serra, serrador | 1 | 112 | 3-53 | 477 | A-11 |
| Sh'ney dubim | K | 268 | 9-22 | 348 | A-29 |
| Shalom aleichem (melody) | 6 | 409 | 20-9 | 541 | A-34 |
| Shalom aleichem (harmony) | 6 | 409 | 20-10 | 541 | A-34 |
| Shir l'shalom | 4 | 419 | 17-26 | 496 | A-46 |
| Shu ha mo | 3 | 276 | 9-33 | 452 | A-19 |
| Si me dan pasteles | 1 | 432 | 14-4 | 498 | A-57 |
| Sierra Morena | 3 | 296 | 10-22 | 454 | A-24 |
| Siyahamba (melody) | 6 | 212 | 11-23 | 531 | A-18 |
| Siyahamba (harmony) | 6 | 212 | 11-24 | 531 | A-18 |
| Sol, solecito | 1 | 367 | 11-37 | 495 | A-49 |
| Somos el barco | 4 | 352 | 15-15 | 491 | A-39 |
| Sonando | 4 | 34 | 2-12 | 474 | A-4 |
| Song of the Eagle | 2 | 248 | 9-8 | 438 | A-22 |
| Still, Still, Still | 5 | 468 | 20-17 | 544 | A-51 |
| Stille Nacht (melody) | 7 | I-54 | 14-10 | J-11 | L-14 |
| Stille Nacht (harmony) | 7 | I-54 | 14-11 | J-11 | L-14 |
| T'hola, t'hola | 4 | 132 | 6-10 | 478 | A-11 |
| Tanabata-sama | 2 | 336 | 12-15 | 446 | A-39 |
| Tancovačka | 4 | 230 | 9-42 | 483 | A-24 |
| Tengo, tengo, tengo | 4 | 228 | 9-38 | 483 | A-23 |
| Thula, thula, ngoana | 4 | 227 | 9-30 | 483 | A-22 |
| Tic, tac | 1 | 252 | 8-8 | 488 | A-32 |
| Tina singu | 4 | 300 | 12-33 | 487 | A-31 |
| To'ia mai te waka | 1 | 77 | 2-58 | 474 | A-6 |
| Tsuki | 4 | 25 | 1-39 | 473 | A-3 |
| Tzena, tzena (Hebrew verse) | 5 | 298 | 13-34 | 533 | A-27 |
| Tzena, tzena (Arabic verse) | 5 | 298 | 13-35 | 533 | A-27 |
| Uga uga uga | K | 305 | 10-34 | 355 | A-41 |
| 'Ūlili E | 5 | 441 | 19-15 | 542 | A-47 |
| Un, deux, trois | 2 | 198 | 7-34 | 437 | A-21 |
| Un elefante | 2 | 160 | 6-15 | 435 | A-16 |
| Un pajarito | 2 | 16 | 1-23 | 427 | A-3 |
| Uno, dos, y tres (Part 1) | 5 | 427 | 19-4 | 541 | A-44 |

| Title | Grade | SE/TE Lesson Page | CD Pron. Prac. Track | TE Pron. Prac. Page | Resource Book Page |
|---|---|---|---|---|---|
| Uno, dos, y tres (Part 2) | 5 | 427 | 19-5 | 541 | A-44 |
| Usagi | 1 | 396 | 12-28 | 495 | A-51 |
| Vamos a cantar | K | 278 | 9-36 | 350 | A-32 |
| Vamos a hacer la ronda | K | 124 | 4-42 | 339 | A-14 |
| Vamos a la fiesta | 2 | 374 | 14-4 | 449 | A-44 |
| Vamos a la mar | 3 | 226 | 7-52 | 447 | A-13 |
| Vem kan segla? | 6 | 417 | 20-19 | 543 | A-36 |
| Vil du? | 1 | 92 | 3-18 | 475 | A-8 |
| ¡Viva el fútbol! | 1 | 96 | 3-22 | 476 | A-9 |
| Viva Jujuy | 5 | 228 | 11-14 | 531 | A-23 |
| Was kommt dort von der Höh'? | 8 | C-21 | 6-9 | J-3 | L-17 |
| Wir hatten gebauet | 8 | C-21 | 6-13 | J-4 | L-19 |
| Xiao | 4 | 314 | 13-27 | 490 | A-36 |
| Xiao yin chuan | 2 | 14 | 1-16 | 427 | A-2 |
| Yang wa wa | K | 162 | 6-6 | 343 | A-22 |
| Ye jaliya da | 5 | 67 | 4-9 | 525 | A-9 |
| Yesh lanu taish | 1 | 182 | 6-4 | 483 | A-23 |
| Yibane amenu | 4 | 316 | 13-32 | 490 | A-37 |
| Yü guang guang | 6 | 60 | 4-18 | 525 | A-10 |
| Yüe Liang wan wan | 5 | 314 | 14-26 | 536 | A-35 |
| Zum gali gali | 5 | 401 | 18-16 | 540 | A-43 |
| Zumba, zumba | 3 | 400 | 14-19 | 464 | A-45 |

# Listening Index

## Listening Selections by Title

*This section presents an alphabetical listing by title of all listening selections found in Silver Burdett Making Music.*

| Title | Composer | Gr. | Pg. | CD Track |
|---|---|---|---|---|
| 12 Variations in C "Ah, vous dirai-je, Maman" (excerpt) | Wolfgang Amadeus Mozart | 3 | 19 | 1-30 |
| 1812 Overture (excerpt) | Piotr Ilyich Tchaikovsky | 4 | 293 | 12-18 |
| 3 + 2 | Donald Knaack | 2 | 316 | 11-25 |
| 5 Stücke im Volkston No. 1 "Mit Humor" | Robert Schumann | 3 | 39 | 2-5 |
| A mi querido Austin | Eva Ybarra | 8 | B-24 | 3-10 |
| A-You're Adorable | Kaye/Lippman/Wise | 1 | 263 | 8-29 |
| A-Cling, A-Cling (excerpt) | Traditional Caribbean | 4 | 190 | 8-30 |
| A-Tisket, A-Tasket | Traditional American Folk | 2 | 239 | 8-26 |
| ABACA Dabble | Bryan Louiselle | 4 | 184 | 8-17 |
| Abbots Bromley Horn Dance (excerpt) | Traditional English Folk | 7 | C-24 | 7-5 |
| Academic Festival Overture (excerpt) | Johannes Brahms | 8 | C-20 | 6-1 |
| Acadian Songs "Walking Song" | Virgil Thomson | 4 | 347 | 15-9 |
| Add-On Machine, The | Eric Chappelle | K | 298 | 10-22 |
| Adzogbo-Ovitse (excerpt) | Traditional African | 8 | D-13 | 8-17 |
| Aerial Boundaries | Michael Hedges | 8 | F-20 | 10-30 |
| Africa | David Paich and Jeff Porcaro | 7 | B-6 | 2-5 |
| African Suite "Mbira" | William Kanengiser | K | 61 | 2-45 |
| After You've Gone | H. Creamer/T. Layton | 2 | 189 | 7-15 |
| Ahi! Amours (excerpt) | Canon de Bethune | 8 | C-4 | 4-30 |
| Aida (Grand March) "Gloria all'Egitto" | Giuseppe Verdi | 8 | C-24 | 6-16 |
| Ain't That Love | Ray Charles | 5 | 20 | 1-30 |
| Ajaja (excerpt) | Babatunde Olatunji | 8 | B-3 | 2-1 |
| Akua Tuta (excerpt) | Vallant/McKenzie/Poirier | 7 | D-24 | 9-8 |
| Alasdair mhic cholla ghasda | Traditional Celtic | 8 | B-44 | 4-15 |
| All in One (excerpt) | Eric Chappelle | 1 | 13 | 1-23 |
| All Through the Night | Traditional Welsh; Arranged: Joseph Haydn | 5 | 104 | 5-27 |
| Alle Psallite Cum Luya (Alle, Praise with, luia) (excerpt) | Anonymous | 7 | C-5 | 5-27 |
| Allegretto | Gunild Keetman | 2 | 131 | 5-19 |
| Allons danser, Colinda | Traditional American Folk | K | 219 | 7-38 |
| Altered Landscapes: Part One (excerpt) | Guy Klusevcek | 8 | E-21 | 9-22 |
| Amahl and the Night Visitors "This Is My Box" | Gian Carlo Menotti | 1 | 433 | 14-5 |
| Amazing Grace | Traditional American; Words: John Newton | 5 | 259 | 12-14 |
| Amazing Grace (excerpt) | Traditional American; Words: John Newton | 4 | 161 | 7-20 |
| America | Traditional American; Words: Samuel Francis Smith | 7 | A-22 | 1-14 |
| America (from West Side Story) | Leonard Bernstein | 8 | C-45 | 7-15 |
| America, the Beautiful | Samuel Ward/Katharine Lee Bates | 3 | 413 | 15-8 |
| America, the Beautiful (gospel) | Music: Samuel Ward; Words: Katharine Lee Bates | 6 | 485 | 23-3 |
| American Salute | Morton Gould | 5 | 275 | 12-35 |
| Amores hallarás | Victor M. Salgado | 5 | 153 | 7-35 |
| Angry Anymore | Ani DiFranco | 8 | F-32 | 11-16 |
| Appalachian Spring "Variations on Simple Gifts" | Aaron Copland | 5 | 185 | 9-19 |
| April Joy | Pat Metheny | 8 | A-18 | 1-13 |
| Apu Min'Tan | Vollant/McKenzie | 8 | D-21 | 8-31 |
| Arirang (excerpt) | Traditional Korean | 2 | 137 | 5-29 |
| Arkansas Traveler/Angeline the Baker | Traditional American Folk | K | 115 | 4-27 |
| Arrival of the Queen of Sheba, The (Solomon) | George Frideric Handel | 2 | 348 | 12-27 |
| At the Hop | Singer/Medora/White | 4 | 166 | 7-26 |
| Avaz-e dashti (excerpt) | Traditional Persian | 8 | B-42 | 4-10 |
| Awa ewe iwoyi (excerpt) | Ebenezer Obey | 8 | D-9 | 8-16 |
| Awakening | Osel Tutu | 7 | D-14 | 8-31 |
| Awakening (excerpt) | Osei Tutu | 3 | 289 | 10-10 |

Listening Index

| Title | Composer | Gr. | Pg. | CD Track |
|---|---|---|---|---|
| Aweigh, Santy Ano (excerpt) | Hellerman/Gilbert/Seeger/Hays | 1 | 339 | 10-34 |
| Ayer (Yesterday) | Juanito Marquez | 6 | 266 | 14-1 |
| B. B.'s Blues (excerpt) | Branford Marsalis | 4 | 70 | 4-1 |
| Baa, Baa, Black Sheep | Traditional English; Arranged: Mayo/Compton | K | 102 | 4-4 |
| Baby Elephant Walk | Henry Mancini | 2 | 163 | 6-19 |
| Bachianas Bra5sileiras No. 5 "Aria" | Heitor Villa-Lobos | 8 | C-37 | 7-4 |
| Badenma (Friendship) | Alpha Yaya Diallo | 8 | B-28 | 3-15 |
| Bai, bai, bai, bai | Traditional Russian | 2 | 197 | 7-29 |
| Bairagi (excerpt) | Ravi Shankar | 8 | A-19 | 1-16 |
| Bambodansarna (excerpt) | Olav Johansson | 8 | B-20 | 3-1 |
| Bamboula | Louis Moreau Gottschalk | 3 | 229 | 7-55 |
| Banuwa (excerpt) | Traditional Liberian | 8 | B-4 | 2-5 |
| Bate-papo | Traditional Brazilian | 4 | 401 | 17-12 |
| Battle of Jericho, The | Traditional African American | 6 | 234 | 12-8 |
| Battle of New Orleans, The | Jimmie Driftwood | 6 | 105 | 6-23 |
| Bawa (excerpt) | Traditional African; Arranged: Sowah Mensah | 7 | D-32 | 9-15 |
| Be Still, My Child (excerpt) | Joseph Shabalala | 1 | 39 | 2-4 |
| Bear Dance | Traditional Native American; Southern Ute People of Colorado | 7 | C-5 | 5-30 |
| Bear Dance Song | Traditional Native American (Southern Ute) | K | 127 | 5-3 |
| Beat of My Heart, The | Burke/Spina | 4 | 9 | 1-6 |
| Beat of the Tango, The | David Eddleman | K | 106 | 4-12 |
| Beautiful | Carole King | 3 | 67 | 2-42 |
| Bee, The (L'Abeille) (excerpt) | Franz Schubert; Arranged: J. Mohler | 4 | 70 | 4-2 |
| Beggar's Opera, The "Constant Billy" | John Gay | 7 | C-24 | 7-6 |
| Believer (excerpt) | Brian Transeau | 7 | A-2 | 1-1 |
| Bembe de Plena (excerpt) | Traditional Puerto Rican | 8 | D-18 | 8-25 |
| Bethena Waltz (excerpt) | Scott Joplin | 6 | 157 | 8-33 |
| Big Country, The | Jerome Moross | 2 | 236 | 8-23 |
| Billy the Kid "Celebration" (excerpt) | Aaron Copland | 3 | 251 | 8-21 |
| Bird | Linda Hirschhorn | 1 | 39 | 2-3 |
| Bird call-Cuckoo | | 1 | 110 | 3-44 |
| Bird call-Loon | | 1 | 110 | 3-42 |
| Bird call-Mockingbird | | 1 | 110 | 3-43 |
| Bird call-Phoebe | | 1 | 31 | 1-50 |
| Birdland (excerpt) | Joe Zawinul | 5 | 155 | 8-2 |
| Birds in the Forest (excerpt) | Yi Jianquan | 4 | 315 | 13-28 |
| Black Suits Comin' (Nod Ya Head) (excerpt) | Will Smith | 7 | A-5 | 1-6 |
| Block Party (excerpt) | Smith/Kelley/Robinson/Rambert/Iverson/Ralf | 7 | B-13 | 2-19 |
| Blower's Daughter, The (excerpt) | Damien Rice | 8 | B-13 | 2-38 |
| Blowin' in the Wind | Bob Dylan | 5 | 384 | 17-21 |
| Blue Danube, The (excerpt) | Johann Strauss, Jr. | 6 | 192 | 10-29 |
| Blue Eyes Crying in the Rain | Fred Rose | 7 | B-28 | 4-9 |
| "Body" Song, The | Brenda Russell | 6 | 438 | 21-1 |
| Bomba te traigo yo (excerpt) | Jose Gonzales | 8 | B-3 | 2-2 |
| Bombay Dreams (excerpt) | Music: A.R. Rahman; Words: Don Black | 8 | B-35 | 3-31 |
| Bombé/Ruht wohl, ruht wohl, ihr heiligen Gebeine | Johann Sebastian Bach; Arranged: Pierre Akendengué | 8 | B-39 | 4-3 |
| Bon jour! | Papillion | 1 | 3 | 1-3b |
| Boogie Down | Leroy Brown/Lawrence Smith | 8 | G-29 | 12-11 |
| Boogie-Woogie | Pine Top Smith | 6 | 93 | 6-3 |
| Boogie-Woogie (excerpt) | Pine Top Smith | 1 | 256 | 8-14 |
| Bonaparte's Retreat | Traditional American | 4 | 385 | 16-25 |
| Boston Ball Game 1967 | Jack Bruce/Pete Brown | 8 | F-32 | 11-17 |
| Both Sides Now | Joni Mitchell | 5 | 385 | 18-1 |
| Brace Yourself | Howie Day | 8 | A-19 | 1-15 |
| Brandenburg Concerto No. 2 "Allegro Assai," Movement 3 | Johann Sebastian Bach | 7 | C-8 | 6-1 |
| Brandenburg Concerto No. 4 "Allegro" (excerpt) | Johann Sebastian Bach | 5 | 111 | 6-2 |
| Brass Rap | Deanna Swoboda | 3 | 189 | 6-40 |
| Breaks, The | J.B. Moore, Robert Ford, Kurtis Blow, Russell Simmons, Larry Smith | 7 | B-12 | 2-17 |

| Title | Composer | Gr. | Pg. | CD Track |
|---|---|---|---|---|
| Breathe | Eric Chappelle | 1 | 404 | 13-3 |
| Brisad del Zulia (excerpt) | Traditional Calypso | 4 | 19 | 1-27 |
| Brolga (The Brolga Bird) (excerpt) | Traditional Australian | 6 | 271 | 14-8 |
| Brolga One | Traditional Australian | 4 | 37 | 2-17 |
| Bumper Harvest Celebration | Lu Zaiyi/Xu Caoming | 4 | 337 | 14-19 |
| Bye Bye, Love | Felice Bryant/Boudleaux Bryant | 5 | 357 | 16-17 |
| Bye Bye, Love (excerpt) | Felice Bryant/Boudleaux Bryant | 8 | A-15 | 1-8 |
| C-Jam Blues | Duke Ellington | 8 | C-43 | 7-13 |
| Cafe Europa | Eric Mouquett/Michel Sanchez | 7 | B-43 | 5-12 |
| California Counterpoint: The Twittering Machine (excerpt) | Cindy McTee | 8 | C-47 | 8-4 |
| Camino de piedra | Wilson Lopez | 5 | 152 | 7-34 |
| (Can't Live Without Your) Love and Affection | Nelson/Nelson/Tanner | 7 | B-23 | 3-7 |
| Can't Take My Joy (excerpt) | Michele Shocked | 7 | B-40 | 5-7 |
| Candy Man, Salty Dog | Traditional American Folk | K | 27 | 1-44 |
| Canon for Violin and Cello | Jean Sibelius | 6 | 126 | 7-20 |
| Canon No. 110 in G | Franz Joseph Haydn | 6 | 133 | 7-35 |
| Cantata No. 140 "Wachet auf, ruft uns die Stimme," Movement 4 (as performed by American Bach Soloists) | Johann Sebastian Bach | 7 | C-9 | 6-2 |
| Cantata No. 140 "Wachet auf, ruft uns die Stimme," Movement 4 (as performed by The Swingle Singers) (excerpt) | Johann Sebastian Bach | 7 | C-10 | 6-4 |
| Canzon in Echo Duodecimi Toni a 10 | Giovanni Gabrieli | 8 | C-7 | 5-4 |
| Canzoni et Sonate "Canzoni prima a 5" | Giovanni Gabrieli | 4 | 193 | 8-33 |
| Capoeira na vila (excerpt) | Traditional Brazilian | 8 | D-25 | 9-3 |
| Caprice Basque (excerpt) | Pablo de Sarasate | 1 | 256 | 8-17 |
| Caprice No. 1 in E Major (excerpt) | Nicolló Paganini | 7 | C-22 | 7-1 |
| Caravan (excerpt) | Juan Tizol | 7 | B-31 | 4-14 |
| Caribbean Leaps | Eric Chappelle | K | 149 | 5-33 |
| Carmina Burana "Chramer, gip die Varwe mir" | Carl Orff | K | 63 | 2-49 |
| Carnaval "Valse Noble" Un poco maestoso | Robert Schumann | 3 | 202 | 7-11 |
| Carnaval Llanero | Traditional Venezuelan; Arranged: Rafael Angel Aparicio | 4 | 307 | 13-12 |
| Carnival of the Animals "Aquarium" | Camille Saint-Saëns | 5 | 376 | 17-14 |
| Carnival of the Animals "Aviary" (excerpt) | Camille Saint-Saëns | 4 | 70 | 4-5 |
| Carnival of the Animals "Fossils" (excerpt) | Camille Saint-Saëns | 1 | 237 | 7-31 |
| Carnival of the Animals "Fossils" (excerpt) | Camille Saint-Saëns | 4 | 220 | 9-20 |
| Carnival of the Animals "The Aviary" | Camille Saint-Saëns | K | 45 | 2-20 |
| Carnival of the Animals "The Elephant" | Camille Saint-Saëns | K | 45 | 2-21 |
| Carnival of the Animals "The Royal March of the Lion" (excerpt) | Camille Saint-Saëns | 3 | 357 | 12-14 |
| Carol of the Bells (excerpt) | Mykola Leontovych | 8 | G-10 | 11-23 |
| Carolina Sunday Waltz (excerpt) | Adrian Legg | 7 | F-9 | 10-27 |
| Carrament News (excerpt) | Traditional French | 8 | B-22 | 3-7 |
| Carry On | Crosby/Stills/Nash/Young | 7 | B-2 | 2-1 |
| Carry On Wayward Son (excerpt) | Kerry Livgren | 7 | B-20 | 3-5 |
| Catalana "Andante" | Andrés Segovia | K | 134 | 5-14 |
| Cattle Call | Tex Owens | 5 | 347 | 16-5 |
| Cauyaqa Nauwa? (Where's My Drum?) | Pamyua | 8 | D-20 | 8-30 |
| Cedar Swamp | Traditional American Folk | 5 | 261 | 12-17 |
| Changed My Name | Adapted/Arranged: Linda Twine | 6 | 338 | 17-9 |
| Chansons madecasses "Nahandove" (excerpt) | Maurice Ravel | 4 | 32 | 2-5 |
| Charukeshi (excerpt) | Ravi Shankar | 4 | 311 | 13-19 |
| Checkerboard (excerpt) | Eric Chappelle | 1 | 7 | 1-10 |
| Cherokee Morning Song (excerpt) | Traditional Native American (Cherokee) | 8 | B-19 | 2-55 |
| (Chi Chi Chi) Cha Cha Cha (excerpt) | Marco Rizo/Kevin Morgan | 6 | 334 | 17-3 |
| Chica chica boom chic | Warren/Gordon | 2 | 112 | 4-31 |
| Chigamba (excerpt) | Traditional from Zimbabwe | 6 | 27 | 2-21 |
| Children's Corner "Jimbo's Lullaby" (excerpt) | Claude Debussy | 1 | 271 | 8-34 |
| Children's Corner Suite "Doctor Gradus ad Parnassum" | Claude Debussy | 8 | C-27 | 6-18 |
| Children's Corner Suite No. 4 "Snowflakes Are Dancing" | Claude Debussy | 5 | 239 | 11-31 |
| Children's Garden, The | Eric Tingstad/Nancy Rumbel | K | 267 | 9-18 |
| China Gates | John Adams | 7 | C-45 | 8-6 |

Listening Index

| Title | Composer | Gr. | Pg. | CD Track |
|---|---|---|---|---|
| Choo Choo Boogaloo (excerpt) | Leib Ostrow | 1 | 127 | 4-18 |
| Choo-Choo Joubert | Joseph Joubert | 3 | 51 | 2-20 |
| Chorale Prelude for Organ "Wachet auf, ruft uns die Stimme" | Johann Sebastian Bach | 7 | C-9 | 6-3 |
| Circle of Life, The (from The Lion King) | Music: Elton John; Words: Tim Rice | 3 | 367 | 12-27 |
| Circle of Life, The (from The Lion King) | Music: Elton John; Words: Tim Rice | 6 | 316 | 16-6 |
| Circlesong 7 | Bobby McFerrin | 4 | 80 | 4-22 |
| Circlesong Five (excerpt) | Bobby McFerrin | 1 | 239 | 7-34 |
| Clair de lune | Claude Debussy | K | 165 | 6-7 |
| Close Encounters of the Third Kind (excerpt) | John Williams | 4 | 235 | 10-5 |
| Close Encounters of the Third Kind (excerpt) | John Williams | 8 | B-34 | 3-28 |
| Cold and Frosty Morning | Traditional English; Arranged: Mary Ellen Junda/Dana Mayo | 2 | 139 | 5-30 |
| College Hornpipe | Traditional American | 4 | 95 | 5-1 |
| Colorado Trail | Traditional Cowboy Song | 5 | 277 | 13-1 |
| Colours of the World | Jing-Ran Zhu/Qui-Hong Her | 6 | 271 | 14-7 |
| Come Out and Play (excerpt) | Brian Holland | 5 | 238 | 11-30 |
| Coming Home from the Sea-I (from The Perfect Storm) (excerpt) | James Horner | 6 | 345 | 17-14 |
| Coming Home from the Sea-II (from The Perfect Storm) (excerpt) | James Horner | 6 | 345 | 17-15 |
| Common Ground (excerpt) | Ivan Lins | 3 | 379 | 13-15 |
| Concert for Piano and Orchestra (excerpt) | John Cage | 6 | 209 | 11-17 |
| Concerto for Flute and Harp in C Major, Movement 2 (excerpt) | Wolfgang Amadeus Mozart | 8 | C-10 | 5-9 |
| Concerto for French Horn in E-flat Major No. 4, Movement 3 | Wolfgang Amadeus Mozart | 8 | C-11 | 5-10 |
| Concerto for Marimba and String Orchestra "Saudação" | Ney Rosauro | 2 | 119 | 4-38 |
| Concerto for Orchestra "Presentation of Pairs" | Béla Bartók | 4 | 72 | 4-12 |
| Concerto for Trumpet and Orchestra in E-flat Major "Rondo: Allegro molto" (excerpt) | Johann Nepomuk Hummel | 1 | 256 | 8-13 |
| Concerto for Two Trumpets in C Major "Allegro," Movement 1 (excerpt) | Antonio Vivaldi | 4 | 71 | 4-7 |
| Concerto for Two Trumpets in C Major "Allegro," Movement 1 (excerpt) | Antonio Vivaldi | 4 | 75 | 4-16 |
| Concerto for Viola and Orchestra, Movement 3 (excerpt) | Béla Bartók | 7 | C-35 | 7-22 |
| Concerto in D Major for Flute and Orchestra "Allegro," III | Wolfgang Amadeus Mozart | K | 123 | 4-38 |
| Concerto in E-flat for Horn and Orchestra "Rondo," Movement 3 (excerpt) | Wolfgang Amadeus Mozart | 4 | 71 | 4-8 |
| Concerto No. 1 for Horn and Orchestra "Rondo (Allegro)" | Wolfgang Amadeus Mozart | 5 | 145 | 7-17 |
| Concierto de Aranjuez "Allegro con spirito," Movement 1 (excerpt) | Joaquín Rodrigo | 6 | 199 | 10-41 |
| Concierto Madrigal for Two Guitars and Orchestra "Caccía a la española" (excerpt) | Joaquín Rodrigo | 5 | 176 | 9-1 |
| Concierto Madrigal for Two Guitars and Orchestra "Fanfarre" | Joaquín Rodrigo | 2 | 150 | 5-49 |
| Conga Kings Grand Finale (excerpt) | Camero/Hidalgo/Valdes | 5 | 156 | 8-5 |
| Contigo otra vez | Abarahm Quintanilla III and Luigi Giraldo, Performered by Jennifer Pena | 7 | B-32 | 4-17 |
| Cookie Crew, The | David Eddleman | K | 196 | 7-9 |
| Copycat | Steven Traugh | K | 9 | 1-9 |
| Corn Grinding Song | Traditional Native American | K | 67 | 2-55 |
| Cotton Boll Rag | Charles Hunter | 5 | 333 | 15-18 |
| Country Blues | Muddy Waters | 5 | 225 | 11-9 |
| Country Dance | Charles Dibdin | 3 | 211 | 7-28 |
| Country Gardens | Percy Grainger | 1 | 440 | 14-18 |
| Cow Barn Cha Cha (excerpt) | Kim Bejot | 8 | D-33 | 9-7 |
| Cowboys' Christmas Ball (excerpt) | Traditional Cowboy Song; Original Words: Larry Chittenden | 6 | 238 | 12-14 |
| Cradle Song | Béla Bartók | K | 97 | 3-54 |
| Crazy Blues | P. Bradford | 7 | B-8 | 2-10 |
| Crouching Tiger, Hidden Dragon | Tan Dun | 8 | A-11 | 1-4 |
| Crowley's Reel | Traditional Irish | 4 | 297 | 12-27 |

| Title | Composer | Gr. | Pg. | CD Track |
|---|---|---|---|---|
| Crowley's/Jackson's | Traditional Irish; Arranged: Eileen Ivers/Doyle | 4 | 298 | 12-28 |
| Crowley's/Jackson's | Traditional Irish; Arranged: Eileen Ivers/Doyle | 8 | B-7 | 2-12 |
| Crunchy, Crunchy, Crunchy (excerpt) (performance piece) | Walt Hampton | 8 | D-14 | 8-19 |
| Da pacem, Domine | Melchior Franck | 5 | 62 | 4-4 |
| Dance at the Gym (from West Side Story) (excerpt) | Leonard Bernstein/Stephen Sondheim | 5 | 9 | 1-7 |
| Dance Suite "Waltz" | Leonard Bernstein | K | 145 | 5-28 |
| Dances from Terpsichore "Bransle de la Torche" | Michael Praetorius | 3 | 63 | 2-39 |
| Dances of Galanta (excerpt) | Z. Kodály | 7 | C-34 | 7-15 |
| Dancin' in the Street | Gaye/Hunter/Stevenson | 5 | 360 | 16-20 |
| Dancing in the Street | Gaye/Stevenson/Hunter | 2 | 254 | 9-17 |
| Dancing Queen (excerpt) | Andersson/Anderson/Ulvaeus | 8 | G-19 | 12-3 |
| Dancing Tree, The | Tom T. Hall | K | 203 | 7-14 |
| Danse macabre | Camille Saint-Saëns | 5 | 457 | 19-24 |
| Danses Populaires Francaises "Branle Double, Branle Simple" (excerpt) | Thoinot Arbeau | 7 | C-25 | 7-7 |
| Danza (Dance) | Anonymous | 7 | C-7 | 5-32 |
| Danzas Puertorriqueñas "Vano empeño" | Juan Morel Campos | 7 | E-13 | 9-25 |
| Daphne of the Dunes (excerpt) | Harry Partch | 8 | D-29 | 9-5 |
| Das Jahr "Mai" | Fanny Mendelssohn-Hensel | 8 | C-18 | 5-20 |
| Day - O! (excerpt) | Traditional Jamaican | 5 | 21 | 1-31 |
| Daybreak Vision | R. Carlos Nakai | 5 | 398 | 18-11 |
| Deck the Hall | Traditional Welsh | 5 | 475 | 20-31 |
| Den III. Ende VI. Ronde & Quatre Branles | Tylman Susato | 7 | C-7 | 5-33 |
| Den III. Ende VI. Ronde & Quatre Branles | Tylman Susato | 8 | C-7 | 5-3 |
| Dharpa (Tree) | Yunupingu/Kellaway | 8 | B-38 | 4-2 |
| Diamonds and Rust (excerpt) | Joan Baez | 7 | A-4 | 1-5 |
| Die Forelle (The Trout) (excerpt) | Franz Schubert | 7 | C-20 | 6-20 |
| Die Walküre (The Ride of the Valkyries) "The Valkyries" (excerpt) | Richard Wagner | 8 | C-23 | 6-15 |
| Die Zauberflöte (The Magic Flute) "Pa-pa-pa-pa-pa-pa-pagena" | Wolfgang Amadeus Mozart | 8 | C-13 | 5-13 |
| Dinéh Round Dance (excerpt) | Traditional Native American | 6 | 186 | 10-22 |
| Ding, Dong, Diggidiggidong | Carl Orff/Gunild Keetman | 3 | 15 | 1-22 |
| Dippermouth Blues | King Oliver | 7 | B-14 | 2-21 |
| Disco Worm | Bryan Louiselle | 2 | 312 | 11-21 |
| Divertimento for Orchestra "Samba" | Leonard Bernstein | 5 | 9 | 1-8 |
| DJ Beat | Rick Bassett | 7 | B-13 | 2-18 |
| Do-Re-Mi (from The Sound of Music) | Music: Richard Rodgers; Words: Oscar Hammerstein II | 5 | 38 | 2-31 |
| Doing the Penguin | Tony Geiss | K | 35 | 2-7 |
| Domna, pos vos ay chausida (Lady, for You) | Anonymous | 8 | C-6 | 5-1 |
| Don Giovanni (Give Me Your Hand) "Lá ci darem la mano" | Wolfgang Amadeus Mozart | 8 | C-13 | 5-12 |
| Don Manolito "Viva Madrid, que sí, que sí..." | Pablo Sorozábal | 7 | G-14 | 12-4 |
| Don't Get Around Much Anymore (excerpt) | Duke Ellington | 1 | 33 | 1-56 |
| Don't Look Down | Wendy Waldman/Lindsey Buckingham | 6 | 249 | 13-9 |
| Don't You Hear the Lambs? | Traditional American | 5 | 99 | 5-24 |
| Doraji (excerpt) | Traditional Korean | 4 | 175 | 7-40 |
| Down in the Valley | Traditional American Folk; Arranged: Buddy Skipper | 7 | A-23 | 1-15 |
| Dreydl Song, The | Traditional Hebrew | 3 | 391 | 13-30 |
| Drift (excerpt) | Qiu Xia He | 8 | B-42 | 4-11 |
| Dúlamán | Traditional Irish | 4 | 299 | 12-29 |
| Dusty Miller | Traditional American | 4 | 291 | 12-13 |
| Dusty Rag | May Aufderheide | K | 165 | 6-8 |
| Dziban (excerpt) | Trey Gunn | 7 | F-18 | 11-4 |
| Eccosaise in E-flat Major | Ludwig van Beethoven | 1 | 223 | 7-15 |
| Eine kleine Nachtmusik (A Little Night Music) (excerpt) | Wolfgang Amadeus Mozart | 4 | 41 | 2-21 |
| Eine kleine Nachtmusik "Minuet" | Wolfgang Amadeus Mozart | 4 | 111 | 5-30 |
| Ekombi (excerpt) | Sowah Mensah | 8 | B-31 | 3-25 |
| El amor brujo "Danza ritual del fuego" | Manuel de Falla; Arranged: Ian Krouse | 8 | F-20 | 10-29 |

Listening Index

| Title | Composer | Gr. | Pg. | CD Track |
|---|---|---|---|---|
| El cóndor pasa (excerpt) | Robles/Milchberg/Simon; Arranged: DJ Sammy | 7 | A-2 | 1-2 |
| El dulcerito llego (The Sweets Vendor Is Here) | Hernandez/Alvarez | K | 124 | 4-43 |
| El mariachi (excerpt) | Traditional Mexican | 4 | 303 | 13-6 |
| El nuevo caiman (excerpt) | Ernesto "Fruko" Estrada | 8 | B-17 | 2-52 |
| El Salón México (excerpt) | Aaron Copland | 6 | 199 | 10-40 |
| El siquisirí | Traditional Mexican | 4 | 273 | 11-16 |
| El tilingo lingo | Traditional Mexican | 2 | 176 | 6-40 |
| Elegguá | Traditional Cuban | 8 | D-13 | 8-18 |
| Elias (excerpt) | Music: Dispatch; Words: Pete Heimbold | 7 | B-21 | 3-6 |
| Elite Syncopations | Scott Joplin | 6 | 159 | 9-9 |
| En prière | Gabriel Fauré; Arranged: Gilbert/Shames | K | 158 | 5-47 |
| Ennanga, Movement III (excerpt) | William Grant Still | 3 | 127 | 4-34 |
| Entertainer, The | Scott Joplin | 2 | 76 | 3-21 |
| Eriskummainen kantele | Kurki-Suonio | 5 | 199 | 10-8 |
| Erlkönig (The Erlking) (excerpt) | Franz Schubert | K | 165 | 6-11 |
| Estancia "Danza del trigo" | Alberto Ginastera | 5 | 229 | 11-15 |
| Eternal Flame | Hoffs/Steinberg/Kelly | 7 | B-6 | 2-6 |
| Etude Fantasy for Piano No. 3 "Fifths to Thirds" | John Corigliano | 8 | C-46 | 8-3 |
| Étude in E major | Frédéric Chopin | K | 241 | 8-26 |
| Ev'ry Time I Feel the Spirit | Traditional African American | 3 | 248 | 8-16 |
| Ev'ry Time I Feel the Spirit (excerpt) | Traditional African American Spiritual; Arranged: William Dawson | 7 | C-40 | 8-1 |
| Ev'rybody Ought to Know | Traditional African American | 1 | 435 | 14-8 |
| Evening Chaconne (performance piece) | Konnie Saliba | 6 | 202 | 11-3 |
| Evening Samba | Mickey Hart | 6 | 297 | 15-8 |
| Every Morning | Keb' Mo' | 7 | B-8 | 2-9 |
| Every Night When the Sun Goes Down (excerpt) | Traditional American; Arranged: Sylvia Fricker | 8 | I-29 | 14-3 |
| Everyday People | Sylvester Stewart | 5 | 389 | 18-4 |
| Everyday People | Sly Stone | 7 | G-16 | 12-10 |
| Everything Grows | Raffi/D. Pike | K | 267 | 9-17 |
| Everything Is Everything | Lauryn Hill/Johari Newton | 7 | B-29 | 4-11 |
| Face of Love, The (excerpt) | Eddie Vedder | 8 | B-15 | 2-49 |
| Faerie Stories (excerpt) | P. Morrison | 8 | B-5 | 2-7 |
| Fanfare for Freedom | Morton Gould | 6 | 139 | 8-4 |
| Fanfare for the Common Man | Aaron Copland | 7 | C-43 | 8-5 |
| Fantasia on Greensleeves | Ralph Vaughan Williams | 5 | 235 | 11-26 |
| Fantasy for Chanukah | David Eddleman | 1 | 421 | 13-31 |
| Farmer in the Dell | Traditional English Folk | K | 233 | 8-15 |
| Fascinatin' Rhythm (as performed by Ella Fitzgerald) | Music: George Gershwin; Words: Ira Gershwin | 7 | E-11 | 9-24 |
| Fascinatin' Rhythm (as performed by Frances Veri) | Music: George Gershwin; Words: Ira Gershwin | 7 | E-11 | 9-23 |
| Fatou yo (I Am Fatou) | Ismael Tidiane Touré/Sixu Tidiane Touré | K | 154 | 5-44 |
| Feliz Navidad | Jose Feliciano | 4 | 433 | 18-19 |
| Fiesta "Tarantella" | Horatio Salinas; Arranged: Scott Tennant | K | 134 | 5-17 |
| Fingerprints (excerpt) | Chick Corea | 7 | B-42 | 5-10 |
| Finlandia (excerpt) | Jean Sibelius | 6 | 78 | 5-3 |
| Fire Brigade Water the Road (excerpt) | Vasco de Freitas | 7 | D-22 | 9-5 |
| Firebird, The "Finale" | Igor Stravinsky | 8 | C-30 | 6-24 |
| Firebird, The "Infernal Dance" | Igor Stravinsky | 5 | 173 | 8-28 |
| Fish Food | Gideon Freudmann | 2 | 212 | 8-4 |
| Flat Foot Floogee, The | Gillard/Stewart/Green | 3 | 158 | 5-33 |
| Flight of the Bumblebee | Nikolai Rimsky-Korsakov (from Tsar Sultan) | 1 | 385 | 12-16 |
| Flight of the Bumblebee | Nikolai Rimsky-Korsakov | 3 | 188 | 6-37 |
| Flight of the Bumblebee | Nikolai Rimsky-Korsakav (from Tsar Sultan) | K | 76 | 3-10 |
| Flight of the Ibis (excerpt) | Richard Cooke | 8 | D-16 | 8-21 |
| Flip, Flop and Fly | Charles Calhoun/Lou Willie Turner | 7 | F-15 | 11-2 |
| Flop-Eared Mule | Traditional American | 3 | 99 | 3-39 |
| Florida Suite "Everglades" (excerpt) | Chip Davis | 1 | 413 | 13-15 |
| Flowing Bowl, The (excerpt) | Seamas Egan | 8 | B-29 | 3-16 |
| Flying Home | Benny Goodman/Lionel Hampton | 7 | B-15 | 2-22 |
| Fontane di Roma (Fountains of Rome) "La fontana di Trevi al meriggio" | Ottorino Respighi | 2 | 93 | 3-52 |

Listening Index

| Title | Composer | Gr. | Pg. | CD Track |
|---|---|---|---|---|
| Footloose | Kenny Loggins/Dean Pitchford | 7 | B-11 | 2-16 |
| For Children (Sz 42), Volume II No. 33 "Allegro non troppo" | Béla Bartók | 2 | 49 | 2-20 |
| Forever, for Now (excerpt) | Harry Connick, Jr./Richard McLean | 7 | B-16 | 3-1 |
| Forked Deer/Fisher's Hornpipe | Traditional American | 4 | 343 | 15-4 |
| Four Scottish Dances "Allegretto" | Malcolm Arnold | 6 | 43 | 3-6 |
| Four Seasons, Concerto No. 2, The "Summer," Movement 3 | Antonio Vivaldi | 6 | 102 | 6-18 |
| Four Seasons, The "Spring" (excerpt) | Antonio Vivaldi | 1 | 29 | 1-44 |
| Four Seasons, The "Spring," Movement 1 | Antonio Vivaldi | 4 | 371 | 16-8 |
| Four Seasons, The "Winter," Movement 2 | Antonio Vivaldi | 3 | 113 | 4-18 |
| Fourth of July, The | Morton Gould | 5 | 489 | 21-19 |
| Free Music #1 | Percy Grainger | 2 | 212 | 8-3 |
| French Suite No. 5 "Gigue" (excerpt) | Johann Sebastian Bach | 4 | 232 | 10-1 |
| Frère Jacques | Traditional; Arranged: Buryl Red | 3 | 113 | 4-17 |
| Frostiana (from Stopping by Woods on a Snowy Evening) | Randall Thompson | 6 | 40 | 2-37 |
| Frosty, the Snowman | Steve Nelson/Jack Rollins | 2 | 391 | 14-33 |
| Gahu (excerpt) | Traditional from Benin | 7 | D-27 | 9-10 |
| Galbi (excerpt) | Aharon Amram | 1 | 183 | 6-7 |
| Galliard battaglia | Samuel Scheidt | 6 | 362 | 18-11 |
| Galliard Battaglia (excerpt) | Samuel Scheidt | 8 | C-14 | 5-15 |
| Game of the Mechanical Nightingale "The Nightingale" (excerpt) | Igor Stravinsky | 8 | C-33 | 6-28 |
| Gamelan angklung (excerpt) | Traditional Indonesian | 6 | 384 | 19-19 |
| Gapu | Traditional Australian; Arranged: G. Yunupingu | 8 | B-38 | 4-1 |
| Garden of the Earth | Traditional Russian | 5 | 399 | 18-12 |
| Gavotte | François-Joseph Gossec | 3 | 88 | 3-22 |
| Gazebo Dances "Tarantella" | John Corigliano | 8 | C-46 | 8-1 |
| George and Gracie (excerpt) | Arranged: Paul Winter/Roger Payne | 1 | 69 | 2-48 |
| Get on Board | Traditional African American | K | 89 | 3-35 |
| Get on Your Feet | De Faria/Casas/Ostwald | 5 | 8 | 1-6 |
| Ghel moma (excerpt) | S. Moutaftshiev | 4 | 31 | 2-1 |
| Gidden riddum (excerpt) | Emile Borde | 6 | 299 | 15-9 |
| Give Me Your Tired, Your Poor | Irving Berlin/Emma Lazarus | 5 | 166 | 8-23 |
| Give Us Hope | Jim Papoulis | 6 | 337 | 17-8 |
| Gloria in excelsis | Antonio Vivaldi | 6 | 210 | 11-19 |
| Glory, Glory, Hallelujah (Gospel) | Traditional Gospel Song | 6 | 54 | 3-29 |
| Glory, Glory, Hallelujah (Gospel) | Traditional Gospel Song | 8 | B-14 | 2-43 |
| Glory Hallelujah Grand March | W.K. Batchelder | 8 | C-38 | 7-7 |
| Go Down, Moses | Traditional African American | 7 | G-10 | 11-25 |
| Go, Tell It on the Mountain | Traditional African American | 3 | 393 | 14-3 |
| God Bless the Child (as performed by Billie Holiday) | Billie Holiday/Arthur Herzog Jr. | 7 | B-26 | 4-3 |
| God Bless the Child (as performed by Blood, Sweat & Tears) (excerpt) | Billie Holiday/Arthur Herzog Jr. | 7 | B-26 | 4-4 |
| Goin' Down the Road Feelin' Bad | Adapted/Arranged: Woody Guthrie/Lee Hays | 5 | 283 | 13-10 |
| Golden Ring Around the Susan Girl | Traditional American Folk | 3 | 17 | 1-25 |
| Goldilocks and the Three Bears | Attributed to Karen Carter | K | 49 | 2-24 |
| Gonna Move | Paul Pena | 7 | F-12 | 10-29 |
| Good Golly, Miss Molly | Robert Blackwell/John Marascalco | 8 | E-10 | 9-14 |
| Good King Wenceslas | Traditional carol | 4 | 431 | 18-14 |
| Good King Wenceslas | Traditional carol | 6 | 461 | 21-29 |
| Good Morning, Aztlán (excerpt) | David Hidalgo/Louie Pérez | 7 | B-7 | 2-8 |
| Good Vibrations | Brian Wilson | 8 | E-28 | 10-2 |
| Goodbye, Ev'rybody "Farewell Shout" | Traditional American | 7 | D-2 | 8-15 |
| Grand Canyon Suite "Cloudburst" | Ferde Grofé | K | 260 | 9-9 |
| Grand Canyon Suite "On the Trail" (excerpt) | Ferde Grofé | 3 | 77 | 3-5 |
| Great Pretender, The | Buck Ram | 5 | 358 | 16-18 |
| Groundhog Jig, The | Ned Ginsburg | 1 | 436 | 14-9 |
| Guaguancó pá las tumbadoras (excerpt) | Ray Santos | 7 | D-9 | 8-23 |
| Guantanamera (excerpt) | Jose Fernandez Diaz | 8 | I-33 | 14-8 |
| Guide Right | John Philip Sousa | 1 | 447 | 14-29 |
| Gymnopedie No. 1 | Erik Satie | K | 175 | 6-24 |

| Title | Composers | Gr. | Pg. | CD Track |
|---|---|---|---|---|
| Haliwa-Saponi Canoe Song | Traditional Native American; Transcribed: J. Bryan Burton | 5 | 303 | 14-5 |
| Halley Came to Jackson | Mary Chapin Carpenter | 2 | 341 | 12-18 |
| Hänsel und Gretel "Ein Männlein steht im Walde" | Engelbert Humperdinck | 2 | 91 | 3-47 |
| Happy Mariachi Band (Mariachi alegre) | Traditional Mexican | 1 | 210 | 6-48 |
| Hard Day Blues | Muddy Waters | 7 | B-9 | 2-11 |
| Hard Times (excerpt) | Len "Boogsie" Sharpe | 1 | 196 | 6-29 |
| Hard Way | T. Bone Walker | 7 | E-33 | 10-14 |
| Harukoma "Spring Horse Dance" (excerpt) | Hiro Fujikake | 1 | 145 | 4-47 |
| Háry János Suite "Intermezzo," Movement 5 (excerpt) | Zoltán Kodály | 7 | C-34 | 7-16 |
| Havanaise for Violin and Orchestra (excerpt) | Camille Saint-Saëns | 5 | 217 | 10-34 |
| Have a Little Faith in Me | John Hiatt | 8 | A-18 | 1-12 |
| He's Got the Whole World in His Hands (excerpt) | Traditional African American | 3 | 249 | 8-17 |
| Heads Carolina, Tails California | Tim Nichols/Mark T. Sanders | 7 | B-25 | 3-10 |
| Hermit Songs "The Monk and His Cat" | Samuel Barber | 7 | C-21 | 6-22 |
| Hey, Diddle, Diddle | Traditional Nursery Rhyme | K | 247 | 8-35 |
| Highway to Kilkenny (excerpt) | Keith Lockhart; Arranged: Patrick Hollenbeck | 6 | 43 | 3-7 |
| Hindewhu (whistle) solo (excerpt) | Traditional African | 6 | 269 | 14-4 |
| Hippopotamus Song, The | Michael Flanders/Donald Swann | 3 | 33 | 1-55 |
| Honiesuckle, The | Anthony Holborne | 5 | 504 | 21-20 |
| Hotter Than That | Lil Hardin Armstrong | 6 | 65 | 4-25 |
| How Can I Keep from Singing? (excerpt) | Traditional Celtic | 4 | 261 | 10-35 |
| How High the Moon (excerpt) | Lewis Morgan/Nancy Hamilton | 5 | 341 | 15-28 |
| Howjidoo | Woody Guthrie | 1 | 315 | 10-5 |
| Huagu ge "Flower Drum Song" (excerpt) | Folk Song from China; Arranged: Han Kuo-Huang | 8 | D-27 | 9-4 |
| Humpty Dumpty | Traditional English | K | 23 | 1-33 |
| Hungarian Dance No. 19 | Johannes Brahms | 4 | 171 | 7-31 |
| Hungarian Dance No. 3 in F Major | Johannes Brahms | 1 | 208 | 6-42 |
| Hungarian Dance No. 6 | Johannes Brahms | 4 | 50 | 2-33 |
| Hungarian Rhapsody No. 2 in C- sharp Minor No. S.244 (excerpt) | Franz Liszt | 7 | E-17 | 10-2 |
| Hunt, The | Mickey Hart | 6 | 363 | 18-12 |
| Hush, Little Baby | Traditional American; Arranged: Tim Ries | K | 222 | 7-44 |
| Hush, Little Baby | Traditional American; Arranged: Bobby McFerrin | K | 222 | 7-45 |
| I Am a Man of Constant Sorrow | Traditional American Folk | 7 | F-29 | 11-16 |
| I Can't Get Started (excerpt) | Vernon Duke/Ira Gershwin | 7 | B-26 | 4-2 |
| I Don't Want to Feel Like That (excerpt) | Teresa Radigan/Donald Schlitz, Jr. | 4 | 31 | 2-3 |
| I Get Out | Ziggy Marley | 8 | F-6 | 10-15 |
| I Know You Mardi Gras (excerpt) | Eddie Bo | 8 | B-17 | 2-53 |
| I Love Peanuts (swing style) | Roslyn Burrough | 1 | 163a | 5-25 |
| I Shall Sing | Van Morrison | 8 | I-41 | 14-15 |
| I Walk the Line | Johnny Cash | 7 | B-28 | 4-7 |
| I Will Survive (excerpt) | D. Fekaris/F. Perren | 7 | B-10 | 2-14 |
| I Wish I Knew How It Would Feel to Be Free (excerpt) | Billy Taylor | 6 | 470 | 22-7 |
| I'll Fly Away | Alfred Brumley | 8 | I-43 | 14-18 |
| I'm a Believer | Neil Diamond | 7 | G-32 | 12-22 |
| I'm a Yankee Doodle Dandy (excerpt) | George M. Cohan | 5 | 278 | 13-2 |
| I'm Gonna Sing a Silly Song | David Eddleman | K | 225 | 8-3 |
| I've Been Everywhere | Geoff Mack | 6 | 224 | 11-37 |
| If I Had a Hammer | Pete Seeger | 3 | 241 | 8-8 |
| If These Walls Could Speak | Jimmy Webb | 7 | B-41 | 5-9 |
| If You Asked Me To | Diane Warren | 8 | G-5 | 11-20 |
| If You Can Walk | Linda Hirschhorn | 1 | 19 | 1-31 |
| If You Look (excerpt) | Will Ackerman/Chuck Greenburg | 7 | B-5 | 2-3 |
| Il trovatore "Anvil Chorus" (excerpt) | Guiseppi Verdi | 6 | 25 | 2-16 |
| Illusions | Edward Pearsall | 6 | 347 | 17-18 |
| Imbube (Wimoweh) (excerpt) | Traditional South African; Arranged: G. Beggs, S.R./T. Khemese/M. Mnguni | 8 | B-30 | 3-19 |
| In My Own Little Corner (from Cinderella) Spanish | Richard Rodgers/Oscar Hammerstein | 3 | 9 | 1-5 |
| In the Mood | Garland Joseph | 6 | 110 | 6-28 |
| In the Still of the Night | Fred Parris | 4 | 47 | 2-29 |

Listening Index

| Title | Composers | Gr. | Pg. | CD Track |
|---|---|---|---|---|
| Intertribal Song (excerpt) | Traditional Native American (Blackfoot) | 8 | B-18 | 2-54 |
| Into the Faddisphere | Jon Faddis | K | 21 | 1-30 |
| Invention No. 5 in E-flat | Johann Sebastian Bach | 5 | 59 | 3-28 |
| Ionisation | Edgar Varèse | 6 | 357 | 18-5 |
| Irish Tune from County Derry | Traditional Irish; Arranged: Percy Grainger | 4 | 49 | 2-32 |
| Istanbul Coffee House (Kafe neio) (excerpt) | Daghan Baydur/Richard Thomas | 8 | B-34 | 3-30 |
| It Don't Mean a Thing (If It Ain't Got That Swing) (as performed by Ella Fitzgerald) (excerpt) | Music: Duke Ellington; Words: Irving Mills | 5 | 338 | 15-25 |
| It Don't Mean a Thing (If It Ain't Got That Swing) (as performed by Mel Tormé) (excerpt) | Music: Duke Ellington; Words: Irving Mills | 6 | 386 | 19-21 |
| It Won't Be Wrong | R. McGuinn/Gerst | 7 | F-17 | 11-3 |
| It's Time | Lebo M./Van Tongeren/Rifkin | 6 | 319 | 16-9 |
| Itsy Bitsy Spider, The | Traditional American | K | 187 | 6-48 |
| Ja-Da | Bob Carleton | 2 | 187 | 7-12 |
| Jamaican Rumba | Arthur Benjamin | 5 | 201 | 10-11 |
| Jambalaya | Hank Williams | 6 | 245 | 13-3 |
| Janitzio (excerpt) | Silvestre Revueltas | 5 | 91 | 5-6 |
| Jarabe tapatio | Alfonso A. Partichela | 7 | I-7 | 13-10 |
| Jazz in the Box (excerpt) | Doyle Dykes | 8 | F-11 | 10-21 |
| Je m'endors | Traditional American; Arranged: Michael Doucet | K | 219 | 7-39 |
| Jelly Roll, The | Rene/Rene/Johnson | 7 | B-36 | 5-1 |
| Jesu, Joy of Man's Desiring | Johann Sebastian Bach | 6 | 87 | 5-30 |
| Jo'ashila (Walking Together) | Traditional Native American | 6 | 286 | 14-19 |
| John B. Sails, The | Traditional Jamaican | K | 11 | 1-12 |
| John Henry (excerpt) | Traditional American | 8 | C-34 | 7-1 |
| John Wayne's Teeth (excerpt) | Eaglebear Singers/Sherman Alexie | 8 | B-37 | 3-36 |
| Jolie Blonde | Traditional American | 4 | 389 | 16-28 |
| Jonah | Traditional African American | 6 | 235 | 12-10 |
| Joy | Michele Shocked | 7 | B-40 | 5-6 |
| Joy to the World | Isaac Watts/Lowell Mason | 7 | A-27 | 1-18 |
| Juba | Traditional African American | K | 13 | 1-15 |
| Jug Band Music | Geoff Muldaur | 6 | 361 | 18-9 |
| Julie-O | Mark Summer | 5 | 311 | 14-20 |
| Jump for Joy | Joanie Bartels | K | 213 | 7-29 |
| Jump for Joy (excerpt) | Austin Lyons | 7 | D-20 | 9-4 |
| Jump in the Line (excerpt) | Belafonte/DeLeon/Oller/Samuel | 4 | 117 | 5-34 |
| Jungle Beat | Edward Pearsall | 6 | 347 | 17-17 |
| Kansas City Stomp | Jelly Roll Morton | 2 | 251 | 9-14 |
| Karangatia ra | Traditional from New Zealand | 3 | 272 | 9-23 |
| Kargyraa-Style Song | Traditional Tuvan | 8 | B-40 | 4-5 |
| Katura (excerpt) | Mujuru/Maraire | 7 | D-27 | 9-11 |
| Kayagum pyongch'ang-sae t'aryug (excerpt) | Traditional Korean | 3 | 137 | 4-53 |
| Kayagum pyongch'ang-sae t'aryug (excerpt) | Traditional Korean | 8 | B-13 | 2-37 |
| Kazak (excerpt) | Traditional Ukrainian | 1 | 193 | 6-28 |
| Kebjar teruna (excerpt) | Traditional Indonesian | 6 | 385 | 19-20 |
| Keep a Cool Head | Desmond Dekker | 7 | B-34 | 4-19 |
| Kerry Dance, The | J. L. Molloy | 5 | 28 | 2-15 |
| Key to the Highway | Bill Broonzy/Charles Segar | 6 | 243 | 12-21 |
| Key to the Highway (excerpt) | Big Bill Broonzy/Charles Segar | 8 | F-28 | 11-11 |
| Ki mua | Opetaia Foa'i | 8 | B-27 | 3-14 |
| Kitchen Stomp (from Stomp Out Loud) | Cast members of "Stomp" | 4 | 122 | 5-39 |
| Klezmer Dances "Freilachs" | Traditional Eastern European; Arranged: Chelyapov/Charnofsky | K | 314 | 11-13 |
| Knozz-Moe-King (excerpt) | Wynton Marsalis | 4 | 75 | 4-14 |
| Kokopelli Wandering Song | Traditional Native American | 5 | 110 | 6-1 |
| Kpanlogo for 2 (excerpt) | Sowah Mensah | 6 | 296 | 15-6 |
| Kui.Kyon.pan (The Praise to Tara) (excerpt) | Traditional Tibetan | 6 | 25 | 2-17 |
| Kunolounkwa (contemporary) | Traditional Native American Oneida Lullaby; Adapted: Joanne Shenandoah | K | 110 | 4-19 |
| Kunolounkwa (Shenandoah) | Joanne Shenandoah | K | 110 | 4-20 |
| Kyrie "Missa Luba" | Traditional American; Arranged: Guido Haazen | 7 | G-13 | 12-3 |

| Title | Composer | Gr. | Pg. | CD Track |
|---|---|---|---|---|
| L'arc en ciel | Sharon Arms Doucet | 2 | 333 | 12-8 |
| L'Arlésienne Suite No. 2 "Farandole" | Georges Bizet | 6 | 68 | 4-28 |
| L'Enfant et les sortiléges "Love for Two Cats" | Maurice Ravel | K | 101 | 4-1 |
| L'union (excerpt) | Louis Moreau Gottschalk | 6 | 487 | 23-8 |
| La bamba (as performed by Ritchie Valens) | Traditional Mexican; Arranged: Ritchie Valens | 5 | 130 | 6-24 |
| La bamba (excerpt) | Traditional Mexican | 5 | 131 | 6-25 |
| La boutique fantasque "Can Can" | Ottorino Respighi | 1 | 147 | 4-52 |
| La mer "Dialogue du vent et de mer" | Claude Debussy | 8 | C-27 | 6-19 |
| La mer "Jeux de vagues" (excerpt) | Claude Debussy | 7 | C-39 | 7-28 |
| La Peri "Fanfare" | Paul Dukas | 4 | 71 | 4-11 |
| La Rosa | Ramón Montoya | K | 134 | 5-15 |
| La tierche estampie real (excerpt) | Anonymous | 8 | C-6 | 5-2 |
| Las copetonas | Jorge Lerma; Arranged: Steve Carrillo | 7 | B-33 | 4-18 |
| Las mañanitas | Traditional Mexican; English Words: Lupe Allegria | K | 325 | 11-33 |
| Last Thing on My Mind, The | Tom Paxton | 7 | F-7 | 10-24 |
| Lazy John | Jean Ritchie | 4 | 11 | 1-14 |
| Le cou cou (The Cuckoo) | Louis-Claude Daquin | 3 | 329 | 11-29 |
| Le Hoogie Boogie | Traditional American | K | 296 | 10-21 |
| Le jig Français | Reed/Doucet; Arranged: Doucet | K | 64 | 2-52 |
| Le Sacre de Printemps (The Rite of Spring) "Dance of the Youths and Maidens" (excerpt) | Igor Stravinsky | 8 | C-30 | 6-25 |
| Le tombeau de Couperin "Prelude" (orchestral version) | Maurice Ravel | 8 | C-28 | 6-21 |
| Le tombeau de Couperin "Prelude" (piano version) | Maurice Ravel | 8 | C-28 | 6-20 |
| Les Patineurs (The Skaters) | Emile Waldteufel | 2 | 387 | 14-29 |
| Les pêcheurs des perles (In the Depths of the Temple) "Au fond du temple saint" (excerpt) | George Bizet | 7 | C-30 | 7-11 |
| Les Rêves de Columbine (Under the Stars) "Sous les étoiles" (1907) | Amy Beach | 2 | 338 | 12-16 |
| Let It Snow! Let It Snow! Let It Snow! | Cahn/Styne | 4 | 427 | 18-7 |
| Let the Children Play | Carlos Santana/Jackie Patillo | 7 | B-30 | 4-12 |
| Let's Dance (excerpt) | Baldridge/Stone/Bonine | 1 | 256 | 8-16 |
| Let's Face the Music | Irving Berlin | 7 | B-14 | 2-20 |
| Let's Twist Again | David Appell/Kal Mann | 6 | 257 | 13-16 |
| Lian xi qu (étude) | Traditional Chinese | 4 | 157 | 7-14 |
| Liberty/Chicken Reel (excerpt) | Traditional American | 2 | 38 | 2-1 |
| Lieutenant Kijé "Troika" | Sergei Prokofiev | 6 | 457 | 21-21 |
| Lifetime | Musze/Matthewman/David | 7 | B-39 | 5-5 |
| Light up the World | Joanne Shenandoah | 2 | 197 | 7-30 |
| Limbo Rock | William Stranger/Jon Sheldon | 3 | 298 | 10-27 |
| Lincolnshire Posy "Lord Melbourne" | Percy Grainger | 4 | 74 | 4-13 |
| Linus and Lucy | Vincent Guaraldi; Arranged: Muriel Anderson | 8 | A-29 | 1-20 |
| Lion (excerpt) | Eto | 6 | 303 | 15-21 |
| Lion Sleeps Tonight, The | Weiss/Peretti/Creatore | 4 | 132 | 6-6 |
| Lion Sleeps Tonight, The (Mbube) | Music: Solomon Linda; Words: Peretti/Creatore/Weiss | 8 | E-8 | 9-13 |
| Little Birdie | Vince Guaraldi | 4 | 75 | 4-15 |
| Little David, Play on Your Harp | Traditional African American | 4 | 395 | 17-6 |
| "Little" Fugue in G Minor (brass) | Johann Sebastian Bach | 6 | 129 | 7-22 |
| "Little" Fugue in G Minor (organ) | Johann Sebastian Bach | 6 | 129 | 7-21 |
| Little Pearls, The | Traditional Mexican | K | 215 | 7-35 |
| Little Red Caboose | Traditional African American | K | 229 | 8-10 |
| Little Red Hen, The (story) | Judith Thomas | 1 | 255 | 8-12 |
| Little Shepherd, The (excerpt) | Claude Debussy | 1 | 256 | 8-15 |
| Little Train of the Caipira, The | Heitor Villa-Lobos | K | 25 | 1-41 |
| Llactamanta | Traditional Edcuadorian | 6 | 382 | 19-18 |
| Lluvia-I (The Rain) (excerpt) | Franco de Vita | 6 | 332 | 17-1 |
| Lluvia-II (The Rain) | Franco de Vita | 6 | 332 | 17-2 |
| Lo, How a Rose E'er Blooming (excerpt) | Michael Praetorius | 6 | 210 | 11-18 |
| Loco bossa nova | Tito Puente | 2 | 247 | 9-5 |
| Lohengrin "Prelude to Act III" | Richard Wagner | 8 | C-22 | 6-14 |
| Loose Tooth Blues | Sandor Slomovitz | 1 | 285 | 9-14 |
| Lorca (excerpt) | Nova Menco | 1 | 49 | 2-22 |

Listening Index

| Title | Composer | Gr. | Pg. | CD Track |
|---|---|---|---|---|
| Lord of the Dance Medley (excerpt) | Ron Hardiman | 6 | 326 | 16-14 |
| Los machetes | Traditional Mexican; Arranged: Rubén Fuentes | 8 | I-22 | 13-28 |
| Los pollitos | Traditional Mexican | K | 166 | 6-16 |
| Lost River | Mickey Hart | 6 | 283 | 14-15 |
| Love for Three Oranges "March" | Sergei Prokofiev | K | 117 | 4-30 |
| Love You Forever (excerpt) | Lord Nelson | 8 | B-23 | 3-8 |
| Lua afe (2000) (excerpt) | Opetaia Foa'i | 8 | B-27 | 3-13 |
| Lullaby | Johannes Brahms | 3 | 188 | 6-38 |
| Lullaby for Strings (excerpt) | George Gershwin | 1 | 293 | 9-23 |
| Luna hermosa (Beautiful Moon) | Traditional Venezuelan | 8 | I-13 | 13-12 |
| Lyric Pieces No. 1 "Butterfly" | Edvard Grieg; Arranged: Gordon Langford | 1 | 363 | 11-27 |
| Lyric Pieces No. 4 "Little Bird" | Edvard Grieg; Arranged: Gordon Langford | 1 | 347 | 11-6 |
| Lyric Suite "Allegretto gioviale," Movement 1 | Alban Berg | 6 | 169 | 9-26 |
| Lyric Suite No. 6 "Wedding Day at Troldhaugen" | Edvard Grieg | 6 | 9 | 1-5 |
| M.T.A. (excerpt) | Steiner/Hawes | 5 | 403 | 18-19 |
| Ma Vlast (My Fatherland) "The Moldau" | Bedrich Smetana | 7 | C-33 | 7-14 |
| MacAllistrum's March-Mairseail Alasdroim | Traditional Irish | 4 | 297 | 12-26 |
| Mack the Knife | Music: Kurt Weill; Words: Burt Brecht | 7 | B-26 | 4-1 |
| Mad, Sad, Glad ... A Suite in Three Mood-ments | Bryan Louiselle | K | 248 | 8-37 |
| Magic Flute, The "Der Hölle Rache (The Revenge Aria)" | Wolfgang Amadeus Mozart | K | 49 | 2-25 |
| Magic Flute, The "In diesen heil'gen Hallen (In These Bright Halls)" | Wolfgang Amadeus Mozart | K | 49 | 2-26 |
| Magic Flute, The "Queen of the Night Aria" (excerpt) | Wolfgang Amadeus Mozart | 7 | C-31 | 7-13 |
| Magnificent Seven, The (from The Magnificent Seven) (excerpt) | Elmer Bernstein | 3 | 144 | 5-16 |
| Magnificent Tree, The | Hooverphonic | 7 | E-31 | 10-13 |
| Maha ganapathim (excerpt) | Muthuswami Dikshtar | 6 | 305 | 15-23 |
| Mahk jchi | Ulali | 7 | D-25 | 9-9 |
| Mai varamba | Oliver Mtakudzi | 8 | B-39 | 4-4 |
| Main Titles (from Edward Scissorhands) | Danny Elfman | 8 | A-10 | 1-3 |
| Maitreem (excerpt) | Banzi/Banzi/Krishnar | 8 | B-42 | 4-12 |
| Makam sehnaz (excerpt) | Traditional Turkish | 2 | 142 | 5-37 |
| Make Your Own Kind of Music | Barry Mann/Cynthia Weil | 8 | G-30 | 12-12 |
| Malagueña (excerpt) | Ernesto Lecuona | 5 | 154 | 8-1 |
| Malê Debalê (excerpt) | E. Pachecho/P.C. Pinheiro | 8 | B-16 | 2-50 |
| Mambo UK (excerpt) | Jesús Alemeñy | 7 | D-9 | 8-24 |
| Manteca | Gillespie/Fuller/Pozo | 7 | B-3 | 2-2 |
| Marche Militaire No. 1 | Franz Schubert | 6 | 17 | 1-26 |
| Marines' Hymn, The | Traditional American | 8 | C-39 | 7-8 |
| Mars Suite "Orbital View," Movement 1 | Michael McNabb | 4 | 199 | 8-44 |
| Máru-bihág (excerpt) | Traditional Indian | 6 | 304 | 15-22 |
| Marvelous Toy, The | Tom Paxton | 1 | 383 | 12-13 |
| Masquerade Suite "Galop" (excerpt) | Aram Khachaturian | 4 | 16 | 1-24 |
| Mass "Responsory: Alleluia" | Leonard Bernstein | 6 | 217 | 11-25 |
| Mass for the 21st Century "Alleluia" (excerpt) | Carman Moore | 3 | 163 | 5-38 |
| Mazurka No. 3 (excerpt) | Frédéric Chopin | 3 | 317 | 11-12 |
| Mea haarit | Traditional Cambodian | 3 | 274 | 9-25 |
| Memories of the Seashore (excerpt) | Keiko Abe | 3 | 150 | 5-21 |
| Men's Fancy Dance (excerpt) | Irvin Waskewitch | 7 | D-24 | 9-7 |
| Mensu | Kwame Twusasi-Fofie | 8 | D-6 | 8-14 |
| Messiah "Behold, I Tell You a Mystery" | George Frideric Handel | 8 | C-8 | 5-6 |
| Messiah "Hallelujah!" | George Frideric Handel | 8 | C-8 | 5-5 |
| Messiah "The Trumpet Shall Sound" | George Frideric Handel | 8 | C-8 | 5-7 |
| Mexican Hat Dance | Traditional Mexican | K | 215 | 7-34 |
| Mi humilde corazon | Nicandro Mier | 7 | B-32 | 4-16 |
| Mi tierra (My Homeland) | Estefano | 6 | 365 | 18-18 |
| Mido Mountain (excerpt) | Traditional Chinese | 8 | B-42 | 4-9 |
| Mill Pond, The | Traditional Irish Jig | 8 | B-8 | 2-17 |
| Miniature Odyssey, A | Timothy Polashek | 8 | E-29 | 10-4 |
| Minstrels | Claude Debussy | K | 175 | 6-25 |
| Moment So Close, A (excerpt) | Béla Fleck | 8 | B-40 | 4-6 |

| Title | Composer | Gr. | Pg. | CD Track |
|---|---|---|---|---|
| Mongolian Long Song | Traditional Mongolian | 8 | B-14 | 2-44 |
| Moon Mirrored in the Pool, The (excerpt) | Hua Yanjun | 6 | 103 | 6-19 |
| Moravian Dance "Kalamajka" | Leos Janácek | 3 | 79 | 3-10 |
| More It Snows, The | A.A. Milne/H. Fraser Simpson | K | 259 | 9-8 |
| Mother Goose Bounce, The | Gary Lapow | K | 247 | 8-36 |
| Mr. Bojangles (excerpt 1) (excerpt) | Jerry Jeff Walker | 7 | F-7 | 10-25 |
| Mr. Bojangles (excerpt 2) (excerpt) | Jerry Jeff Walker | 7 | F-7 | 10-26 |
| Mr. Tambourine Man | Bob Dylan | 6 | 148 | 8-20 |
| Musette (excerpt) | Johann Sebastian Bach | 3 | 39 | 2-6 |
| Musical Offering No. 11 "Canon a 4" | Johann Sebastian Bach | 3 | 193 | 7-3 |
| Musical Sleigh Ride, A "Divertimento in F" | Leopold Mozart | 5 | 455 | 19-21 |
| Mwen boyko samba | Traditional Dominican | 4 | 319 | 13-37 |
| My Father's House (Gospel Style) | Traditional African American | 2 | 25 | 1-31 |
| My Girl Josephine (excerpt) | Fats Domino/Dave Bartholomew | 8 | E-21 | 9-21 |
| Na rechenki | Traditional Russian | 1 | 375 | 12-4 |
| Nanafushi | Tetsuro Naito | 7 | D-16 | 9-1 |
| Nangapè | Yaya Diallo | 2 | 103 | 4-20 |
| Native Stepson | Sonny Landreth | 7 | F-26 | 11-10 |
| Nele's Dances, No. 17 | Thomas Koppel | 6 | 503 | 23-9 |
| Nele's Dances, No. 18 | Thomas Koppel | 6 | 503 | 23-10 |
| New England Triptych "Chester" | William Schuman | 6 | 83 | 5-25 |
| New Horizons in Music Appreciation-Beethoven's Fifth Symphony, Movement 1 (excerpt) | Professor Peter Schickele | 6 | 98 | 6-15 |
| New San Antonio Rose | Bob Wills | 5 | 135 | 6-30 |
| New York State of Mind (excerpt) | Billy Joel | 7 | E-19 | 10-3 |
| Night in Tunisia, A (excerpt) | Paparelli/Gillespie | 4 | 35 | 2-14 |
| Nights in the Gardens of Spain "En el generalife" (excerpt) | Manuel de Falla | 2 | 144 | 5-40 |
| Noah's Zoo in the Big, Big Rain | David Eddleman | K | 274 | 9-30 |
| Nobody Knows the Trouble I've Seen (excerpt) | Traditional African American | 3 | 249 | 8-18 |
| Northfield | Music: Jeremiah Ingalls; Words: Isaac Watts | 6 | 25 | 2-15 |
| Now's the Time | Charlie Parker | 5 | 451 | 19-18 |
| Nutcracker Suite, The "Arabian Dance" (excerpt) | Piotr Ilyich Tchaikovsky | 7 | C-26 | 7-8 |
| Nutcracker Suite, The "Chinese Dance" | Piotr Ilyich Tchaikovsky | K | 105 | 4-7 |
| Nutcracker Suite, The "Chinese Dance" (excerpt) | Piotr Ilyich Tchaikovsky | 7 | C-26 | 7-9 |
| Nutcracker Suite, The "Trepak" | Piotr Ilyich Tchaikovsky | 3 | 280 | 9-39 |
| Nutcracker Suite, The "Trepak" | Piotr Ilyich Tchaikovsky | 6 | 207 | 11-16 |
| Nutcracker Suite, The "Waltz of the Flowers" | Piotr Ilyich Tchaikovsky | 6 | 325 | 16-13 |
| Nyamphemphe (excerpt) | Marube Jagome/Marks Mankwane | 8 | B-3 | 2-3 |
| Nyoka (excerpt) (performance piece) | Walt Hampton | 7 | D-32 | 9-14 |
| O Christmas Tree (excerpt) | Traditional carol | 6 | 24 | 2-13 |
| O ignis spiritus Paracliti (O Holy Fire that Soothes the Spirit) (excerpt) | Hildegard von Bingen | 7 | C-4 | 5-26 |
| O tocius Asie gloria (Oh, Glory of All Asia) (excerpt) | Anonymous | 8 | C-4 | 4-31 |
| O'Sullivan's March | Traditional Irish | 5 | 157 | 8-6 |
| Obokete (excerpt) | Sowah Mensah | 6 | 291 | 14-21 |
| Oh, Freedom and Come and Go with Me | Traditional African American | 5 | 394 | 18-9 |
| Old American Songs "The Boatman's Dance" | Aaron Copland | 4 | 61 | 3-20 |
| Old Chisholm Trail, The (excerpt) | Traditional American; Arranged: Charlie Daniels | 6 | 236 | 12-11 |
| Old King Cole | Traditional English | K | 245 | 8-31 |
| Old King Cole | Traditional English | K | 245 | 8-32 |
| Olympic Spirit | John Williams | 6 | 350 | 18-1 |
| Ombrose e care selve | Luca Marenzio | 8 | C-5 | 4-32 |
| Omo (excerpt) | Traditional African | 1 | 443 | 14-26 |
| On Christmas Morning | Raffi | K | 316 | 11-18 |
| On Fire Suite (excerpt) | Smith/Picard | 8 | B-36 | 3-33 |
| On Green Dolphin Street | Kaper/Washington | 4 | 126 | 6-1 |
| On Parade | John Philip Sousa | K | 327 | 11-37 |
| On the Mall | Edwin Franko Goldman | 5 | 2 | 1-1 |
| One Fine Day | Edward Pearsall | 6 | 347 | 17-16 |
| One Fine Mama (excerpt) | Ryan/Sackman/Thomas | 8 | B-41 | 4-8 |
| Onomatapoeia Study No. 2 | Timothy Polashek | 7 | E-31 | 10-12 |

| Title | Composer | Gr. | Pg. | CD Track |
|---|---|---|---|---|
| Open the Kingdom (excerpt) | Glass/Byrne | 6 | 31 | 2-24 |
| Orange Blossom Special | Ervin T. Rouse | 1 | 47 | 2-17 |
| Orange Blossom Special | Ervin T. Rouse | 5 | 268 | 12-26 |
| Orchestral Suite No. 2 in B Minor "Minuet" | Johann Sebastian Bach | 6 | 192 | 10-28 |
| Orchestral Suite No. 3 "Air in D," Movement 2 (excerpt) | Johann Sebastian Bach | 4 | 23 | 1-35 |
| Orfferondo (performance piece) | Mary Shamrock | 4 | 194 | 8-35 |
| Over the Rainbow (as performed by Judy Garland) | Harburg/Arlen | 4 | 143 | 6-29 |
| Over the Rainbow (as performed by Aretha Franklin) | Harburg/Arlen | 4 | 143 | 6-30 |
| Overture to Candide | Leonard Bernstein | 6 | 218 | 11-26 |
| Overture to Candide (excerpt) | Leonard Bernstein | 6 | 219 | 11-27 |
| Overture/All That Jazz (from Chicago) (excerpt) | Danny Elfman | 7 | A-23 | 1-16 |
| Oya "Primitive Fire" | Babatunde Olatunji | 5 | 67 | 4-10 |
| Oye como va (excerpt) | Tito Puente | 2 | 255 | 9-18 |
| Oye mi canto (Hear My Voice) | Estefan/Casas/Ostwald | 6 | 114 | 6-34 |
| Ozark Mountain Jubilee | Murrah/Anders | 4 | 86 | 4-31 |
| P'tit galop pour Mamou (excerpt) | Traditional American; Arranged: Michael Doucet | 1 | 317 | 10-10 |
| Pacific 231 | Arthur Honegger | 2 | 286 | 10-33 |
| Partita in A Minor "Sarabande" | Johann Sebastian Bach | 3 | 185 | 6-35 |
| Partita in E Major "Gigue" | Johann Sebastian Bach | 4 | 113 | 5-31 |
| Partita in E Major No. BWV 1006 "Gavotte en Rondeau," Movement 3 | Johann Sebastian Bach | 4 | 124 | 5-41 |
| Pasodoble | Traditional Puerto Rican | 7 | F-11 | 10-28 |
| Patalon | Traditional Indonesian | 5 | 319 | 14-36 |
| Pavane et Gaillarde | Thoinot Arbeau | 2 | 279 | 10-16 |
| Pay Me (excerpt) | Traditional African American Shanty | 7 | F-5 | 10-21 |
| Pay Me My Money Down (excerpt) | Traditional African American | 4 | 39 | 2-20 |
| Peak Moments (excerpt) | Jeff Hellmer | 8 | E-4 | 9-10 |
| Peer Gynt Suite No. 1 "Morning" (excerpt) | Edvard Grieg | 1 | 369 | 11-40 |
| Peñas (excerpt) | Traditional; Arranged: Carlos Arguedas/Julio Arguedas | 2 | 54 | 2-31 |
| Pennsylvania 6-5000 | Sigman/Gray | 5 | 342 | 16-1 |
| Penny Lane | John Lennon/Paul McCartney | 6 | 257 | 13-17 |
| Peshte longuita (excerpt) | Traditional Incan | 1 | 217 | 7-10 |
| Phleng pradall | Traditional Cambodian | 1 | 157 | 5-9 |
| Piano Concerto in A Minor, Movement 1 (excerpt) | Edvard Grieg | 8 | E-11 | 9-16 |
| Piano Concerto in E-flat Major No. 5 "Emperor," Movement 3, Rondo: Allegro | Ludwig van Beethoven | 7 | C-18 | 6-17 |
| Piano Sonata No. 8 in C Minor "Rondo: Allegro" | Ludwig van Beethoven | 4 | 185 | 8-18 |
| Piano Trio in G Minor "Allegro," Movement 1 (excerpt) | Clara Schumann | 8 | C-19 | 5-22 |
| Piano Trio No. 2 in E-flat Major "Scherzo" (excerpt) | Franz Schubert | 4 | 192 | 8-31 |
| Picadillo | Tito Puente | 3 | 361 | 12-19 |
| Pick-a-Rib | Goodman/Hampton | 3 | 151 | 5-22 |
| Picking Red Chestnuts | Traditional Chinese | 5 | 310 | 14-19 |
| Pictures at an Exhibition "Ballet of the Unhatched Chicks" | Modest Mussorgsky | K | 167 | 6-17 |
| Pictures at an Exhibition "The Great Gate of Kiev" | Modest Mussorgsky | 6 | 154 | 8-27 |
| Pictures at an Exhibition "The Great Gate of Kiev (orchestra)" (excerpt) | Modest Mussorgsky; Arranged: Maurice Ravel | 8 | A-12 | 1-6 |
| Pictures at an Exhibition "The Great Gate of Kiev (piano)" (excerpt) | Modest Mussorgsky | 8 | A-12 | 1-5 |
| Pictures at an Exhibition "The Great Gate of Kiev (synthesizer)" (excerpt) | Modest Mussorgsky; Arranged: Isao Tomita | 8 | A-14 | 1-7 |
| Pictures at an Exhibition "The Hut of Baba Yaga" (excerpt) | Modest Mussorgsky | 4 | 103 | 5-16 |
| Piki mai (excerpt) | Traditional from New Zealand | 1 | 79 | 2-59 |
| PIZZ Ah! (excerpt) | Eric Chappelle | 1 | 105 | 3-35 |
| Planets, The "Jupiter" | Gustav Holst | 5 | 424 | 18-29 |
| Planets, The "Jupiter" (excerpt) | Gustav Holst | 1 | 405 | 13-4 |
| Planets, The "Mars, the Bringer of War" (excerpt) | Gustav Holst | 4 | 377 | 16-15 |
| Planxty Madame Maxwell | Turlough O'Carolan | K | 134 | 5-16 |
| Plenty o' Nuttin' (excerpt) | George Gershwin; Arranged: Clay Jenkins | 7 | B-45 | 5-13 |
| Plow that Broke the Plains, The "Cattle" | Virgil Thomson | 3 | 177 | 6-19 |
| Popcorn | Hot Butter | 8 | E-27 | 10-1 |
| Powwow Song (excerpt) | Traditional Native American | 4 | 32 | 2-4 |

Listening Index

| Title | Composer | Gr. | Pg. | CD Track |
|---|---|---|---|---|
| Prayer, The (excerpt) | Foster/Sager | 7 | A-10 | 1-8 |
| Prelude in A Major | Frédéric Chopin | 4 | 234 | 10-4 |
| Prelude in E Minor No. 4 | Frédéric Chopin | 3 | 27 | 1-42 |
| Prelude No. 16 in B-flat Minor | Frederic Chopin | 7 | C-22 | 7-2 |
| Prelude in G-sharp Minor No. 12 | Sergei Rachmaninoff | 7 | E-4 | 9-18 |
| Prelude to the Afternoon of a Faun (excerpt) | Claude Debussy | 5 | 113 | 6-5 |
| Pride and Joy | Stevie Ray Vaughan | 7 | B-9 | 2-12 |
| Primitive Fire "Oya" | Babatunde Olatunji | 2 | 69 | 3-8 |
| Prince of Denmark's March (excerpt) | Jeremiah Clarke | 6 | 55 | 3-30 |
| Princess Hundred Flowers, The "Falling in the Trap" (excerpt) | Anonymous | 8 | C-25 | 6-17 |
| Pulcinella Suite "Minuetto" (excerpt) | Igor Stravinsky | 8 | C-15 | 5-16 |
| Pulcinella Suite "Serenata" (excerpt) | Igor Stravinsky | 4 | 70 | 4-3 |
| Pulcinella Suite "Serenata" (excerpt) | Igor Stravinsky | 8 | C-32 | 6-26 |
| Pulcinella Suite "Vivo (Duetto)" (excerpt) | Igor Stravinsky | 4 | 71 | 4-9 |
| Puppy Love | Sandor Slomovits | K | 262 | 9-12 |
| Pupu hinu hinu (Shiny Shell Lullaby) (excerpt) | Nona Beamer | 1 | 109 | 3-41 |
| Put a Little Love in Your Heart | Holiday/Myers/De Shannon | 4 | 8 | 1-5 |
| Putting Baby to Bed (excerpt) | Merrill Jenson | 1 | 63 | 2-39 |
| Qiugaviit | Traditional Inuit (adapted) | 3 | 259 | 8-35 |
| Quartet "Allegro molto" | Jean Françaix | 4 | 70 | 4-6 |
| Quartetto buffo di gatti "Comic Quartet for Cats" | Gioachino Rossini | 1 | 131 | 4-27 |
| Queen's Suite, The "Sunset and the Mocking Bird" | Duke Ellington | 8 | E-10 | 9-15 |
| Quiet City (excerpt) | Jim Beard | 8 | E-29 | 10-3 |
| Quintet for Piano and Strings in A Major ("Trout"), Movement 3, Scherzo (excerpt) | Franz Schubert | 1 | 179 | 5-46 |
| Quintet for Piano and Strings in E-flat Major, Movement 1 (excerpt) | Robert Schumann | 8 | C-19 | 5-23 |
| Radio City Christmas Spectacular Jingle | Nancy Coyne/Steve Karmen; Arranged: Bryan Louiselle | 8 | A-5 | 1-2 |
| Rag puria kalyan-gat in tintal (excerpt) | Traditional Indian | 4 | 192 | 8-32 |
| Ragtime Annie | Traditional American | 2 | 122 | 4-48 |
| Railroad Bill | Traditional American | 8 | F-14 | 10-24 |
| Rain, Rain, Beautiful Rain (excerpt) | Joseph Shabalala | 4 | 32 | 2-6 |
| Rain Song, The | Sharon Burch | 2 | 323 | 11-32 |
| Rainbow in the Sky | Ziggy Marley | 7 | B-35 | 4-20 |
| Raindrop Prelude (excerpt) | Frédéric Chopin | 3 | 26 | 1-41 |
| Raindrops (excerpt) | Liam Teague | 7 | D-23 | 9-6 |
| Rainy Day Blues | Eric Herbst | 2 | 328 | 12-3 |
| Rap Intro (excerpt) | Traditional Native American | 8 | B-32 | 3-26 |
| Red Poppy, The "Russian Sailors' Dance" | Reinhold Glière | 4 | 224 | 9-26 |
| Reggae Is Now | Ziggy Marley | 6 | 143 | 8-7 |
| Requiem "Pie Jesu" (as performed by David Horton/Debra Hayes) | Andrew Lloyd Webber | 6 | 178 | 10-8 |
| Requiem "Pie Jesu" (as performed by Charlotte Church) (excerpt) | Andrew Lloyd Webber | 6 | 178 | 10-9 |
| Reservation Blues (excerpt) | Jim Boyd/Sherman Alexie | 8 | B-37 | 3-35 |
| Retounen (excerpt) | King Posse | 8 | B-17 | 2-51 |
| Return to Misty Mountain | Richard Cooke | 7 | D-28 | 9-12 |
| Reuben's Train | Traditional American; Arranged: Doc Watson | 1 | 335 | 10-31 |
| Reverie (1890) (excerpt) | Claude Debussy | 1 | 6 | 1-6 |
| Rhapsody in Blue | George Gershwin | K | 75 | 3-9 |
| Rhapsody in Blue (excerpt) | George Gershwin | 7 | C-42 | 8-4 |
| Rice Bowl (excerpt) | Asiabeat | 8 | B-30 | 3-20 |
| Rigoletto (Beautiful Daughter of Love) "Bella figlia dell'amore" | Guiseppi Verdi | 7 | C-29 | 7-10 |
| Río de la miel (River of Honey) (excerpt) | Francisco Sánchez Gómez | 5 | 296 | 13-25 |
| Rippa Medley, The "Block-Block, One Leg Up, Let the Beat Go, Uh-Oh" (excerpt) | Junk Yard Band | 8 | D-32 | 9-6 |
| Rise Up, Shepherd, and Follow | Traditional African American | 5 | 470 | 20-18 |
| Rising of the Mourning Sun (excerpt) | Lyle Workman | 7 | F-19 | 11-5 |
| Ríu ríu chíu | Sixteenth Century Carol from Spain | 5 | 439 | 19-12 |
| River Suite, The "Finale" | Virgil Thomson | 5 | 121 | 6-13 |
| Riverdance Suite (excerpt) | Bill Whelan; Arranged: Patrick Hollenbeck | 2 | 141 | 5-31 |
| Rock Around the Clock | J. DeKnight/M. Friedman | 5 | 356 | 16-16 |
| Rock It (excerpt) | Hancock/Laswell/Beinhorn | 7 | B-11 | 2-15 |

| Title | Composer | Gr. | Pg. | CD Track |
|---|---|---|---|---|
| Rock 'n' Roll Doctor (excerpt) | George/Martin/Kibbee/Lowell | 7 | B-38 | 5-2 |
| Rocky Point Holiday | Ron Nelson | 6 | 331 | 16-19 |
| Roddy McCaulay | Traditional Irish; Adapted/Arranged: The Clancy Brothers | 3 | 292 | 10-15 |
| Rodeo "Buckaroo Holiday" (excerpt) | Aaron Copland | 2 | 23 | 1-28 |
| Rodeo "Hoedown" | Aaron Copland | 5 | 312 | 14-22 |
| Rodeo "Hoedown" | Aaron Copland | 8 | B-45 | 4-16 |
| Rodeo "Hoedown" (excerpt) | Aaron Copland | 1 | 6 | 1-4 |
| Rodeo "Saturday Night Waltz" (excerpt) | Aaron Copland | 4 | 342 | 15-3 |
| Rods and Cones | Matt Goldman | 7 | D-5 | 8-18 |
| Roll Over Vaughan Williams | Richard Thompson | 8 | F-22 | 11-1 |
| Rose (excerpt) | James Horner | 8 | B-34 | 3-29 |
| Round Dance | Traditional Native American | 3 | 257 | 8-34 |
| Round Dance (excerpt) | Traditional Native American | 6 | 445 | 21-6 |
| Route 66 | Bobby Troup | 4 | 279 | 11-23 |
| Route 66 | Bobby Troup | 4 | 279 | 11-24 |
| Rumblin' On | Traditional American | 2 | 315 | 11-24 |
| Rundadinella (performance piece) | Carl Orff | 8 | I-60 | 15-15 |
| Rwakanembe (excerpt) | Anonymous | 8 | C-14 | 5-14 |
| Sabhyatâ (Civilization) | Mohammed Bellal/Jyoti Mahtani | 8 | B-43 | 4-13 |
| Sai da frente | Traditional Brazilan | 8 | D-24 | 9-1 |
| Salt Peanuts (excerpt) | Dizzy Gillespie | 1 | 163a | 5-21 |
| Saltarello detto Trivella (excerpt) | Orazio Vecchi | 7 | C-6 | 5-31 |
| Saludo de Matanzas (excerpt) | Traditional Cuban | 5 | 17 | 1-27 |
| Salute to Sunnyland Slim | Chuck Goering | 8 | E-33 | 10-8 |
| Samanfo, begye nsa nom | Traditional African | 8 | D-6 | 8-15 |
| Same, The (excerpt) | Youssou N'Dour/Habib Faye | 6 | 268 | 14-3 |
| San Miguel Jolonicapan (excerpt) | Traditional Guatemalan | 8 | D-16 | 8-20 |
| Sanjo (excerpt) | Hi-za Yoo | 4 | 175 | 7-41 |
| Saqian da dhol (excerpt) | Saqi | 8 | B-22 | 3-5 |
| Scaramouche "Brasiliera" | Darius Milhaud | 8 | C-29 | 6-23 |
| Scenes from Childhood (Kinderszenen) "Reverie (Träumerei)" (excerpt) | Robert Schumann | 1 | 6 | 1-5 |
| Scherzo for Wind Quintet | Eugene Bozza | 1 | 329 | 10-25 |
| Scott Joplin's New Rag | Scott Joplin | 5 | 335 | 15-21 |
| Scuttle Buttin' | Stevie Ray Vaughan | 8 | F-26 | 11-10 |
| Search for the Hero (excerpt) | Pickering/Heard | 7 | G-5 | 11-22 |
| Sekar jepun (excerpt) | Traditional Balinese | 1 | 196 | 6-30 |
| Semper Fidelis | John Philip Sousa | K | 327 | 11-36 |
| Sensemaya (excerpt) | Silvestre Revueltas | 8 | C-15 | 5-17 |
| Serenade No. 5 | Franz Joseph Haydn | 4 | 90 | 4-34 |
| Serenade for Strings in C "Finale" (excerpt) | Piotr Ilyich Tchaikovsky | 6 | 363 | 18-13 |
| Seven Tunes Heard in China "Guessing Song" | Bright Sheng | 7 | C-45 | 8-8 |
| Sevilla | Isaac Albéniz | 8 | F-22 | 11-2 |
| Sextet for Winds and Piano, Movement 1 (excerpt) | Francis Poulenc | 8 | C-29 | 6-22 |
| Shadow Dancer | Eric Tingstad/Nancy Rumbel | K | 253 | 8-42 |
| Shake Your Brain | Red Grammer | 1 | 250 | 8-3 |
| Sha Sha Sha (performance piece) | Edward Pearsall | 6 | 328 | 16-18 |
| Shashee | Steven Springer | K | 109 | 4-15 |
| Shchedryk (Carol of the Bells) | Traditional Ukrainian | 6 | 103 | 6-20 |
| She Is Like the Swallow | Traditional Irish | 8 | B-12 | 2-34 |
| She'll Be Coming 'Round the Mountain When She Comes | Traditional American | 4 | 333 | 14-14 |
| Shed a Little Light | James Taylor | 8 | E-17 | 9-19 |
| Shed a Little Light (excerpt) | James Taylor | 3 | 409 | 14-33 |
| Shenandoah | Traditional River Shanty; Arranged: James Erb | 2 | 62 | 2-46 |
| Shenandoah | Traditional River Shanty | 5 | 265 | 12-23 |
| Shepherds Hey | Percy Grainger | 1 | 209 | 6-43 |
| Shika no Tone (excerpt) | Traditional Japanese | 5 | 112 | 6-3 |
| Shoveling | Michael Mark/Tom Chapin | 1 | 423 | 13-34 |
| Shumba (Lion) (excerpt) | Thomas Mapfumo | 8 | B-12 | 2-33 |

| Title | Composer | Gr. | Pg. | CD Track |
|---|---|---|---|---|
| Si tú no estás (If You're Not Here) | Franco de Vita | 6 | 267 | 14-2 |
| Sigit "Alash" (excerpt) | Traditional Russian | 4 | 31 | 2-2 |
| Sikelela (excerpt) | Traditional South African | 1 | 139 | 4-40 |
| Silver Apples of the Moon (excerpt) | Morton Subotnick | 1 | 12 | 1-18 |
| Silver Swan, The | Orlando Gibbons | 8 | C-5 | 4-33 |
| Simple Gifts | Traditional American | 8 | A-17 | 1-9 |
| Simple Song, A (from Mass) | Leonard Bernstein | 8 | C-45 | 7-16 |
| Simple Symphony "Playful Pizzicato" (excerpt) | Benjamin Britten | 1 | 205 | 6-41 |
| Sindhi-Bhairavi (excerpt) | Traditional Indian | 5 | 320 | 15-1 |
| Sinfonia Antarctica "Epilogue" (excerpt) | Ralph Vaughan Williams | 2 | 326 | 11-35 |
| Sing We and Chant It (excerpt) | Thomas Morley | 8 | C-5 | 4-34 |
| Sister Rosa (excerpt) | The Neville Brothers | 3 | 411 | 15-3 |
| Six Dances from La Danserie "La Mourisque" | Tylman Susato | 1 | 407b | 13-7 |
| Six Metamorphoses After Ovid "Bacchus" (excerpt) | Benjamin Britten | 7 | C-13 | 6-11 |
| Skippy (excerpt) | Eric Chappelle | 1 | 245b | 7-44 |
| Slavonic Dance No. 1 (excerpt) | Antonin Dvorak | 4 | 227 | 9-34 |
| Slavonic Dance No. 1 No. 1 "Presto" (excerpt) | Antonin Dvorák | 1 | 6 | 1-7 |
| Sleigh Ride | Leroy Anderson | 2 | 390 | 14-32 |
| Slow Hora/Freylekhs (excerpt) | Hankus Netsky | 8 | B-25 | 3-11 |
| Soldier's Joy | Traditional Appalachian | 8 | B-29 | 3-17 |
| Soldier's Tale, The "Waltz" | Igor Stravinsky | K | 237 | 8-22 |
| Solo Flight (excerpt) | Susie Hansen | 5 | 312 | 14-21 |
| Solsbury Hill (excerpt) | Peter Gabriel | 8 | E-29 | 10-5 |
| Somebody (excerpt) | Winsford deVine | 4 | 41 | 2-22 |
| Sometimes I Feel Like a Motherless Child | Traditional African American | 5 | 193 | 9-33 |
| Somewhere (from West Side Story) | Leonard Bernstein/Stephen Sondheim | 8 | C-44 | 7-14 |
| Somewhere Out There (from An American Tail) | Horner/Mann/Weil | 5 | 369 | 17-6 |
| Sonata for Clarinet and Piano "Allegro animato," Movement 2 | Camille Saint-Saëns | 7 | C-12 | 6-9 |
| Sonata for Violin and Piano "Allegro" | John Corigliano | 8 | C-46 | 8-2 |
| Sonata in A Major "Allegretto poco mosso," Movement 4 (excerpt) | César Franck | 5 | 159 | 8-11 |
| Sonata in A Minor "Allegro" (excerpt) | C. P. E. Bach | 7 | C-12 | 6-8 |
| Sonata in C Major for Recorder and Basso Continuo No. 7 "Gavotte" | George Frideric Handel | K | 75 | 3-8 |
| Sonata in F Major for Violin and Piano No. 5 "Spring," Movement 3, Scherzo | Ludwig van Beethoven | 7 | C-19 | 6-19 |
| Sonata in F Minor for Bassoon "Vivace" (excerpt) | Georg Philipp Telemann | 4 | 70 | 4-4 |
| Sonata in G Minor No. 1, Movement 2 (excerpt) | George Frederic Handel | 7 | C-12 | 6-7 |
| Sonata No. 11 "Turkish Rondo" | Wolfgang Amadeus Mozart | K | 165 | 6-9 |
| Sonata No. 14 in C-sharp Minor No. 2 "Moonlight," Movement 1 | Ludwig van Beethoven | 7 | C-19 | 6-18 |
| Sonata Seconda | Dario Castello | 3 | 431 | 15-14 |
| Sonatina for Bassoon and Piano "Allegro con moto," Movement 1 | Alexander Tansman | 7 | C-13 | 6-10 |
| Song for Bells, A (excerpt) | Daniel Pinkham | 1 | 427 | 13-43 |
| Song for George | Eric Johnson | 8 | F-8 | 10-18 |
| Song of the Nightingale "The Nightingale" (excerpt) | Igor Stravinsky | 8 | C-32 | 6-27 |
| Songs from Letters "So Like Your Father" (excerpt) | Libby Larsen | 7 | C-21 | 6-23 |
| Sorta Fairytale, A | Tori Amos | 7 | A-5 | 1-7 |
| Soulville | Turner/Levy/Glover/Washington | 5 | 363 | 16-23 |
| Soulville | Turner/Levy/Glover/Washington | 7 | B-17 | 3-2 |
| Soundings "Fanfare" | Cindy McTee | 8 | C-47 | 8-5 |
| Sounds of the Circus | Buryl Red | K | 241 | 8-25 |
| Souvenirs L'Amerique (Yankee Doodle) | Henri Vieuxtemps; Arranged: James Richards | 2 | 405 | 15-15 |
| Spider's Web | Charlotte Diamond | K | 93 | 3-46 |
| Spinning Song | Felix Mendelssohn | K | 165 | 6-10 |
| Spring Walk "Du xuân" (excerpt) | Traditional Vietnamese; Arranged: Khac Chí | 1 | 441 | 14-21 |
| St. Louis Blues | W.C. Handy | 5 | 353 | 16-13 |
| St. Louis Blues (excerpt) | W. C. Handy | 4 | 57 | 3-17 |

| Title | Composer | Gr. | Pg. | CD Track |
|-------|----------|-----|-----|----------|
| Stalia, Stalia | Traditional Grecian | 8 | B-21 | 3-3 |
| Stand By Me | King/Leiber/Stoller | 5 | 49 | 3-3 |
| Stand By Me | King/Leiber/Stoller | 8 | E-24 | 9-23 |
| Standin' in the Need of Prayer | Traditional African American | 5 | 103 | 5-26 |
| Stars and Stripes Forever, The | John Philip Sousa | 1 | 167 | 5-28 |
| Stars and Stripes Forever, The | John Philip Sousa | 4 | 159 | 7-17 |
| Stick Together | John McCutcheon/Si Kahn | 2 | 231 | 8-18 |
| Storm, The (excerpt) | Jay Richards | 1 | 55 | 2-32 |
| Strike Up The Band Medley (Strike Up The Band, Mardi Gras March, Listen To That Dixie Band) (excerpt) | Music: Gerswin/Webster/Fain/Cobb; Arranged: Gentil | 6 | 25 | 2-18 |
| String Quartet in D Major No. 5 "The Lark," Movement 1 (excerpt) | Franz Joseph Haydn | 7 | C-15 | 6-14 |
| String Quartet No. 4 "Allegretto pizzicato," Movement 4 | Béla Bartók | 4 | 90 | 4-35 |
| String Quartet No. 5 "Andante," Movement 4 (excerpt) | Béla Bartók | 3 | 113 | 4-19 |
| Study War No More (excerpt) | Traditional African American Spiritual | 7 | C-40 | 8-2 |
| Sube (excerpt) | Eddie Palmieri | 7 | B-31 | 4-15 |
| Suite Española No. 3 "Sevilla" (excerpt) | I. Albéniz | 7 | C-23 | 7-4 |
| Suite for Wind Quintet, Movement 1 (excerpt) | Ruth Crawford Seeger | 8 | C-34 | 7-2 |
| Suite No. 2 in F "March," Movement 1 | Gustav Holst | 6 | 139 | 8-3 |
| Suite No. 2 in F No. 2 "Fantasia on the Dargason," Movement 4 (excerpt) | Gustav Holst | 7 | C-36 | 7-23 |
| Suite No. 3 in C Major for Unaccompanied Cello "Bourrée 1" | Johann Sebastian Bach | 3 | 38 | 2-4 |
| Suite No. 4 in E-flat Major for Cello No. 1010 "Gigue (Dance)" (excerpt) | Johann Sebastian Bach | 7 | C-11 | 6-5 |
| Sumer Is Icumen In (excerpt) | Traditional English | 5 | 35 | 2-28 |
| Summertime | George Gershwin | 6 | 252 | 13-12 |
| Sun Gonna Shine | Traditional American | 7 | F-14 | 11-1 |
| Suo gan (excerpt) | Edward Flower | 1 | 309 | 9-45 |
| Surfin' Safari | Mike Love/Brian Wilson | 6 | 261 | 13-23 |
| Suzuki (excerpt) | Burnt Friedman | 7 | A-2 | 1-3 |
| Sweet Georgia Brown (excerpt) | Bernie/Casey/Pinkard | 4 | 71 | 4-10 |
| Swing Low, Sweet Chariot (excerpt) | Traditional African American | 6 | 234 | 12-9 |
| Symphony in G No. 88, Movement 4 (excerpt) | Franz Joseph Haydn | 2 | 84 | 3-40 |
| Symphony No. 1, Movement 3 (excerpt) | Gustav Mahler | 4 | 237 | 10-8 |
| Symphony No. 1 in D Major "Gavotte" | Philharmonia Virtuosi/Richard Kapp | 2 | 338 | 12-17 |
| Symphony No. 3 in E-flat Major "Allegro con brio," Movement 1 (excerpt) | Ludwig van Beethoven | 8 | C-17 | 5-18 |
| Symphony No. 3 in E-flat Major "Marcia funebre," Movement 2 (excerpt) | Ludwig van Beethoven | 8 | C-17 | 5-19 |
| Symphony No. 4, Movement 4 (excerpt) | Piotr Ilyich Tchaikovsky | 4 | 295 | 12-23 |
| Symphony No. 4 in F Minor Movement 4, Finale: Allegro con fuoco (excerpt) | Piotr Ilyich Tchaikovsky | 1 | 175 | 5-35 |
| Symphony No. 40 in G Minor "Molto allegro," Movement 1 (excerpt) | Wolfgang Amadeus Mozart | 8 | B-30 | 3-18 |
| Symphony No. 40 in G Minor, Movement 1 | Wolfgang Amadeus Mozart | 8 | C-12 | 5-11 |
| Symphony No. 47 in G Major "Menuet" | Franz Joseph Haydn | 7 | C-14 | 6-13 |
| Symphony No. 5 in C Minor, Movement 1 | Ludwig van Beethoven | 7 | C-16 | 6-15 |
| Symphony No. 5 in C Minor, Movement 1 (excerpt) | Ludwig van Beethoven | 6 | 98 | 6-14 |
| Symphony No. 5 in C Minor, Movement 4 (excerpt) | Ludwig van Beethoven | 7 | C-18 | 6-16 |
| Symphony No. 6 "The Storm," Movement 4 | Ludwig van Beethoven | 4 | 365 | 16-3 |
| Symphony No. 7, Movement 2 (excerpt) | Ludwig van Beethoven | 1 | 97 | 3-23 |
| Symphony No. 9 from "The New World", Movement 1 | Antonin Dvorák | 5 | 55 | 3-22 |
| Symphony No. 9 in D Minor "Ode to Joy," Movement 4 (excerpt) | Ludwig van Beethoven | 4 | 151 | 7-6 |
| Symphony No. 94 in G Major ("Surprise") Andante (excerpt) | Franz Joseph Haydn | 1 | 86 | 3-3 |
| Symphony No. 94 in G Major ("Surprise") Andante (excerpt) | Franz Joseph Haydn | 7 | C-14 | 6-12 |
| Syrinx | Claude Debussy | 5 | 113 | 6-4 |
| Tabla solo (excerpt) | Ustad Mohammed Omar/Zakir Hussein | 8 | B-32 | 3-27 |
| Tahi (excerpt) | Moana and the Moahunters | 8 | B-14 | 2-45 |
| Taiwan Suite "Lantern Festival" | Ma Shui-Long | 3 | 104 | 4-8 |

| Title | Composer | Gr. | Pg. | CD Track |
|-------|----------|-----|-----|----------|
| Take Five (excerpt) | Paul Desmond | 5 | 220 | 10-37 |
| Take Five (excerpt) | Paul Desmond | 7 | B-15 | 2-23 |
| Take Me There | Metheny/Mays | 7 | F-26 | 11-11 |
| Take the "A" Train | Billy Strayhorn | 8 | C-42 | 7-12 |
| Talaque talaque o romance da María | Pestana/Jorginho do Pandeiro | 8 | D-24 | 9-2 |
| Tamaiti hunahia (excerpt) | Traditional Tahitian; Arranged: Pierrot Faraire | 6 | 24 | 2-14 |
| Tarakihi (The Locust) | Traditional from New Zealand | 3 | 273 | 9-24 |
| Te dejo Madrid | Shakira/Mitchell/Noriega | 7 | B-30 | 4-13 |
| Tears of a Clown | Robinson/Crosby/Wonder | 7 | B-39 | 5-4 |
| Tema de maimara (excerpt) | Traditional Peruvian | 1 | 297 | 9-28 |
| Ten Easy Pieces "Bear Dance" | Béla Bartók | 3 | 172 | 6-16 |
| Tennessee River | Randy Owen | 5 | 349 | 16-8 |
| Terian gulabi buliyan (excerpt) | A. S. Kang | 8 | B-26 | 3-12 |
| That'll Be the Day | Allison/Petty/Holly | 6 | 256 | 13-15 |
| That's the Way | Greg Clark/Scott Leonard | 4 | 193 | 8-34 |
| That's the Way It Is (excerpt) | Martin/Lundin/Carlsson | 7 | B-23 | 3-8 |
| Theme and Variations for Percussion | William Kraft | 5 | 65 | 4-5 |
| Themes (from The 7th Guest) (excerpt) | George Alistair Sanger | 8 | A-3 | 1-1 |
| Think (excerpt) | Paul Robb | 6 | 367 | 18-20 |
| This Is Your Night | Berman/Berman/Cremers; Arranged: Vasquez, Jr. | 6 | 368 | 18-21 |
| This Is Your Night (Dance Mix) (excerpt) | Berman/Berman/Cremers | 6 | 369 | 18-22 |
| This Land Is Your Land | Woody Guthrie | 5 | 120 | 6-12 |
| This Little Light of Mine | Traditional African American; Arranged: Linda Twine/Joseph Joubert | 2 | 241 | 8-29 |
| Three Nocturnes for Piano Trio "Andante quieto" (excerpt) | Ernest Bloch | 1 | 25 | 1-37 |
| Thunder and Lightning Polka | Johann Strauss | 4 | 213 | 9-5 |
| Thunderer, The | John Philip Sousa | 5 | 79 | 4-24 |
| Tihore Mai (excerpt) | Hirini Melbourne | 8 | B-12 | 2-35 |
| Times They Are A-Changin', The | Bob Dylan | 5 | 384 | 17-22 |
| Toccata and Fugue in D Minor (excerpt) | Johann Sebastian Bach | 7 | E-25 | 10-8 |
| Toccata and Fugue in D Minor (excerpt) | Johann Sebastian Bach | 7 | E-25 | 10-9 |
| Toccata and Tango (excerpt) | David Hanson | 2 | 154 | 5-52 |
| Toccata for Percussion, Movement 3 | Carlos Chávez | 4 | 155 | 7-11 |
| Toccata in D Minor | Johann Sebastian Bach | 4 | 233 | 10-2 |
| Toei khong (excerpt) | Traditional Asian | 8 | B-21 | 3-4 |
| Tommy Peoples (excerpt) | Tommy Peoples | 8 | B-20 | 3-2 |
| Tosca (I Live for Art) "Vissi d'arte" (excerpt) | Giacomo Puccini | 7 | C-31 | 7-12 |
| Toy Symphony, Movement 4 | Leopold Mozart | 1 | 111 | 3-49 |
| Transcendental Etude No. 3 in G-sharp Minor "La Campanella" (excerpt) | Franz Liszt | 7 | C-23 | 7-3 |
| Trash Can Stomp (from Stomp Out Loud) | Cast members of "Stomp" | 6 | 328 | 16-17 |
| Traveling Shoes | Traditional African American | 3 | 248 | 8-15 |
| Treaties (excerpt) | Jim Boyd/Sherman Alexie | 8 | B-36 | 3-34 |
| Tumba | Kidjo/Brown | 7 | D-14 | 8-32 |
| Tutti Frutti | Penniman/Lubin/La Bostrie | 7 | B-29 | 4-10 |
| Twist and Shout | Medley/Russell | 4 | 238 | 10-9 |
| Twist, The | Henry Ballard | 5 | 359 | 16-19 |
| Twist, The | Henry Ballard | 7 | B-10 | 2-13 |
| Two Dances for Three Xylophones "Hornpipe and Jig" (excerpt) | Margaret Murray | 8 | D-17 | 8-22 |
| Two Heads Are Better Than One | Joanie Bartels/Chris Rhyne | 1 | 333 | 10-28 |
| Two-Part Invention in A Major (harpsichord) | Johann Sebastian Bach | 5 | 236 | 11-27 |
| Two-Part Invention in A Major (piano) | Johann Sebastian Bach | 5 | 237 | 11-28 |
| Two-Part Invention in A Major (synthesizer) | Johann Sebastian Bach | 5 | 237 | 11-29 |
| Tzlil Zugim | Traditional Israeli | 3 | 139 | 5-5 |
| Udu Pot (excerpt) | Gavin Bates | 8 | D-4 | 8-13 |
| Ue ue | Traditional Bora Bora | 8 | D-2 | 8-12 |
| Ujan mas (excerpt) | Traditional Indonesian | 2 | 105 | 4-22 |
| Uma história de Ifá | Ytthmar Tropicália/Rey Zulu | 6 | 362 | 18-10 |
| Uma história de Ifá (excerpt) | Ytthmar Tropicália/Rey Zulu | 3 | 311 | 10-45 |
| Variations on "America" | Charles Ives | 6 | 162 | 9-13 |

| Title | Composer | Gr. | Pg. | CD Track |
|---|---|---|---|---|
| Variations on "The Carnival of Venice" (excerpt) | Jean-Baptiste Arban | 6 | 161 | 9-12 |
| Vaya Puente | Tito Puente | 2 | 181 | 7-5 |
| Violin Concerto in E Minor, Movement 1 (excerpt) | Felix Mendelssohn | 8 | C-18 | 5-21 |
| Viva Jujuy | Traditional Argentinian | 8 | B-22 | 3-6 |
| Viva la musica | Michael Praetorius | 5 | 95 | 5-18 |
| Vocalise | Sergei Rachmaninoff | K | 123 | 4-37 |
| Voiles (Sails) (excerpt) | Claude Debussy | 7 | C-39 | 7-27 |
| Vonjeo (excerpt) | Rajery | 8 | B-12 | 2-36 |
| Vulani ringi ring | Sophie Mcgina | 1 | 139 | 4-39 |
| Waitin' for a Train | Jimmie Rodgers | 7 | B-24 | 3-9 |
| Walkin' Blues | Robert Johnson | 5 | 227 | 11-10 |
| Walkin' to New Orleans | Domino/Bartholomew/Guidry | 3 | 371 | 13-3 |
| Waltz in D-flat ("Minute" Waltz) | Frédéric Chopin | 4 | 234 | 10-3 |
| Washington Post, The (march) | John Philip Sousa | 1 | 175 | 5-36 |
| Washington Post, The (march) | John Philip Sousa | 8 | C-40 | 7-11 |
| Watchers of the Canyon | Burning Sky | 6 | 270 | 14-6 |
| Water Music "Allegro Maestoso" | George Frideric Handel | 3 | 189 | 6-39 |
| Water Music "Hornpipe" (excerpt) | George Frideric Handel | 8 | C-9 | 5-8 |
| Watermelon Man (excerpt) | Herbie Hancock | 1 | 12 | 1-17 |
| Watermelon Man (excerpt) | Herbie Hancock | 6 | 270 | 14-5 |
| Way Down Yonder in the Brickyard | Traditional African American | 2 | 51 | 2-23 |
| We Shall Overcome | Traditional African American | 5 | 485 | 21-14 |
| Wedding Qawwali (excerpt) | Music: A.R. Rahman; Words: Don Black | 8 | B-35 | 3-32 |
| Welcome to Our World | Lebo M. | 6 | 272 | 14-9 |
| Well-Tempered Clavier, Book 1, The "Prelude and Fugue in C Minor" | Johann Sebastian Bach | 7 | E-16 | 10-1 |
| Well-Tempered Clavier, The "Be-Bop Bach: Prelude No. 2" (excerpt) | Johann Sebastian Bach | 7 | C-11 | 6-6 |
| What a Wonderful World (as performed by Eva Cassidy) | George D. Weiss/Robert Thiele | 6 | 64 | 4-23 |
| What a Wonderful World (as performed by Joey Ramone) | George D. Weiss/Robert Thiele | 6 | 64 | 4-24 |
| What a Wonderful World (as performed by Louis Armstrong) | George D. Weiss/Robert Thiele | 6 | 63 | 4-22 |
| What Could I Do | Thomas A. Dorsey | 5 | 281 | 13-7 |
| What Kind of Land? (excerpt) | Bernice Johnson Reagon | 4 | 327 | 14-7 |
| What's Going On? | Cleveland/Gaye/Benson | 7 | B-38 | 5-3 |
| When a Man's a Long Way from Home | Traditional African American | 2 | 53 | 2-26 |
| When Johnny Comes Marching Home | Patrick S. Gilmore; Arranged: Roy Harris | 5 | 88 | 4-32 |
| When the Saints Go Marching In | Traditional African American | 2 | 179 | 6-43 |
| Where Have All the Flowers Gone? | Pete Seeger | 5 | 287 | 13-15 |
| Whirlwind | Joe Green | 3 | 149 | 5-19 |
| Who Can Sail? | Traditional Scandinavian | 5 | 30 | 2-18 |
| Who Will Buy? (from Oliver) (excerpt) | Lionel Bart | 1 | 16 | 1-26 |
| Why Walk When You Can Fly? | Mary Chapin Carpenter | 7 | B-28 | 4-8 |
| Widmung No. 1 (Dedication) | Robert Schumann | 7 | C-20 | 6-21 |
| Wild Bull (excerpt) | Morton Subotnick | 6 | 366 | 18-19 |
| Wild Horseman, The | Robert Schumann | 1 | 159 | 5-12 |
| Wilder Reiter "The Wild Rider" | Robert Schumann | 8 | D-17 | 8-23 |
| Wildlife (excerpt) | Traditional African | 1 | 345 | 11-3 |
| Wings (excerpt) | Joan Tower | 7 | C-45 | 8-7 |
| Winter Birds Flying over the Water (excerpt) | Traditional Chinese | 1 | 91 | 3-14 |
| Wioste Olowan Inkpa Ta-Ya | Traditional Native American | 3 | 255 | 8-31 |
| Wipe Out | Berryhill/Connolly/Fuller/Wilson | 5 | 155 | 8-3 |
| Wipe Out | Berryhill/Connolly/Fuller/Wilson | 7 | F-33 | 11-19 |
| Woodlands | Nancy Rumble | K | 254 | 9-3 |
| Wooly Bully | Domingo Samudio | 3 | 372 | 13-4 |
| Work It Out (Blow Your Horn Dub Mix) (excerpt) | Beyonce Knowles; Arranged: Victor Calderone | 7 | A-3 | 1-4 |
| Would? | Jerry Cantrell | 8 | F-30 | 11-14 |
| Wu long (Dragon Dance) | Traditional Chinese | 4 | 156 | 7-12 |
| Wu long (Dragon Dance) | Traditional Chinese | 4 | 156 | 7-13 |
| X-Beats (excerpt) | Micky Mann | 7 | B-5 | 2-4 |
| Xochipilli "An Imagined Aztec Music" (excerpt) | Carlos Chavez | 8 | C-37 | 7-6 |
| Yakety Yak | Jerry Leiber/Mike Stoller | 5 | 204 | 10-16 |

Listening Index

| Title | Composer | Gr. | Pg. | CD Track |
|---|---|---|---|---|
| Yamaji (excerpt) | Kozo Masuda | 3 | 407 | 14-30 |
| Yankee Doodle Boy, The (from Little Johnny Jones) (excerpt) | George M. Cohan | 3 | 265 | 9-12 |
| Yaudachi (excerpt) | Traditional Japanese | 5 | 156 | 8-4 |
| Yellow Cake Review, The "Farewell to Stromness" | Peter Maxwell Davies | K | 61 | 2-46 |
| Yellow Rose of Texas, The | Charles H. Brown | 7 | I-73 | 14-20 |
| Yemaya | Marytha Paffrath | 8 | G-24 | 12-6 |
| Yemeni baglamis telli basina (excerpt) | Traditional Turkish; Arranged: Farabi | 6 | 309 | 15-36 |
| Yertle the Turtle | Red Hot Chili Peppers | 2 | 368 | 13-27 |
| Yo Lé Lé (Fulani Groove) (excerpt) | Traditional West African | 5 | 33 | 2-25 |
| You Are My Sunshine | Jimmie Davis/Charles Mitchell | 6 | 247 | 13-6 |
| You Are My Sunshine (excerpt) | Jimmy Davis/Charlie Mitchell | 7 | B-7 | 2-7 |
| You Sang to Me | Anthony/Rooney | 6 | 335 | 17-4 |
| You Were on My Mind | Sylvia Fricker | 7 | G-25 | 12-17 |
| You're a Grand Old Flag | George M. Cohan | 1 | 276 | 9-3 |
| You've Got a Friend | Carole King | 5 | 364 | 17-1 |
| Yours Forever (from The Perfect Storm) | Mellencamp/Green/Horner | 6 | 344 | 17-13 |
| Zoila | Traditional Puerto Rican; Additional Words: Emanual Dufrasnel; Arranged: Emanuel Dufrasnel | 8 | D-18 | 8-24 |
| Zulu Lullaby | Soweto String Quartet | K | 158 | 5-48 |
| Zydeco Dancing | Frishberg/Ostrow/Seifert | 1 | 21 | 1-34 |

Listening Index

# Listening Selections by Composer

*This section presents an alphabetical listing by title of all listening selections found in Silver Burdett Making Music.*

| Composer | Title | Gr. | Pg. | CD Track |
|---|---|---|---|---|
| Abe, Keiko | Memories of the Seashore (excerpt) | 3 | 150 | 5-21 |
| Adams, John | China Gates | 7 | C-45 | 8-6 |
| Albéniz, I. | Suite Española No. 3 $Sevilla$ (excerpt) | 7 | C-23 | 7-4 |
| Albéniz, Isaac | Sevilla | 8 | F-22 | 11-2 |
| Alemeñy, Jesús | Mambo UK (excerpt) | 7 | D-9 | 8-24 |
| Allison/Petty/Holly | That'll Be the Day | 6 | 256 | 13-15 |
| Amos, Tori | Sorta Fairytale, A | 7 | A-5 | 1-7 |
| Amram, Aharon | Galbi (excerpt) | 1 | 183 | 6-7 |
| Anderson, Leroy | Sleigh Ride | 2 | 390 | 14-32 |
| Andersson/Anderson/Ulvaeus | Dancing Queen (excerpt) | 8 | G-19 | 12-3 |
| Anonymous | Alle Psallite Cum Luya (Alle, Praise with, luia) (excerpt) | 7 | C-5 | 5-27 |
| Anonymous | Danza (Dance) | 7 | C-7 | 5-32 |
| Anonymous | Domna, pos vos ay chausida (Lady, for You) | 8 | C-6 | 5-1 |
| Anonymous | La tierche estampie real (excerpt) | 8 | C-6 | 5-2 |
| Anonymous | O tocius Asie gloria (Oh, Glory of All Asia) (excerpt) | 8 | C-4 | 4-31 |
| Anonymous | Princess Hundred Flowers, The "Falling in the Trap" (excerpt) | 8 | C-25 | 6-17 |
| Anonymous | Rwakanembe (excerpt) | 8 | C-14 | 5-14 |
| Anthony/Rooney | You Sang to Me | 6 | 335 | 17-4 |
| Appell/Mann | Let's Twist Again | 6 | 257 | 13-16 |
| Arban | Variations on "The Carnival of Venice" (excerpt) | 6 | 161 | 9-12 |
| Arbeau, Thoinot | Danses Populaires Francaises "Branle Double, Branle Simple" (excerpt) | 7 | C-25 | 7-7 |
| Arbeau, Thoinot | Pavane et Gaillarde | 2 | 279 | 10-16 |
| Armstrong, Lil Hardin | Hotter Than That | 6 | 65 | 4-25 |
| Arnold, Malcolm | Four Scottish Dances "Allegretto" | 6 | 43 | 3-6 |
| Asiabeat | Rice Bowl (excerpt) | 8 | B-30 | 3-20 |
| Aufderheide, May | Dusty Rag | K | 165 | 6-8 |
| Bach, C. P. E. | Sonata in A Minor "Allegro" (excerpt) | 7 | C-12 | 6-8 |
| Bach, Johann Sebastian | Brandenburg Concerto No. 2 "Allegro Assai," Movement 3 | 7 | C-8 | 6-1 |
| Bach, Johann Sebastian | Brandenburg Concerto No. 4 "Allegro" (excerpt) | 5 | 111 | 6-2 |
| Bach, Johann Sebastian | Cantata No. 140 "Wachet auf, ruft uns die Stimme," Movement 4 (as performed by American Bach Soloists) | 7 | C-9 | 6-2 |
| Bach, Johann Sebastian | Cantata No. 140 "Wachet auf, ruft uns die Stimme," Movement 4 (as performed by The Swingle Singers) (excerpt) | 7 | C-10 | 6-4 |
| Bach, Johann Sebastian | Chorale Prelude for Organ "Wachet auf, ruft uns die Stimme" | 7 | C-9 | 6-3 |
| Bach, Johann Sebastian | French Suite No. 5 "Gigue" (excerpt) | 4 | 232 | 10-1 |
| Bach, Johann Sebastian | Invention No. 5 in E-flat | 5 | 59 | 3-28 |
| Bach, Johann Sebastian | Jesu, Joy of Man's Desiring | 6 | 87 | 5-30 |
| Bach, Johann Sebastian | "Little" Fugue in G Minor (brass) | 6 | 129 | 7-22 |
| Bach, Johann Sebastian | "Little" Fugue in G Minor (organ) | 6 | 129 | 7-21 |
| Bach, Johann Sebastian | Musette (excerpt) | 3 | 39 | 2-6 |
| Bach, Johann Sebastian | Musical Offering No. 11 "Canon a 4" | 3 | 193 | 7-3 |
| Bach, Johann Sebastian | Orchestral Suite No. 2 in B Minor "Minuet" | 6 | 192 | 10-28 |
| Bach, Johann Sebastian | Orchestral Suite No. 3 "Air in D," Movement 2 (excerpt) | 4 | 23 | 1-35 |
| Bach, Johann Sebastian | Partita in A Minor "Sarabande" | 3 | 185 | 6-35 |
| Bach, Johann Sebastian | Partita in E Major "Gigue" | 4 | 113 | 5-31 |
| Bach, Johann Sebastian | Partita in E Major No. BWV 1006 "Gavotte en Rondeau," Movement 3 | 4 | 124 | 5-41 |
| Bach, Johann Sebastian | Suite No. 3 in C Major for Unaccompanied Cello "Bourrée 1" | 3 | 38 | 2-4 |
| Bach, Johann Sebastian | Suite No. 4 in E-flat Major for Cello No. 1010 "Gigue (Dance)" (excerpt) | 7 | C-11 | 6-5 |
| Bach, Johann Sebastian | Toccata and Fugue in D Minor (excerpt) | 7 | E-25 | 10-8 |
| Bach, Johann Sebastian | Toccata and Fugue in D Minor (excerpt) | 7 | E-25 | 10-9 |
| Bach, Johann Sebastian | Toccata in D Minor | 4 | 233 | 10-2 |
| Bach, Johann Sebastian | Two-Part Invention in A Major (harpsichord) | 5 | 236 | 11-27 |
| Bach, Johann Sebastian | Two-Part Invention in A Major (piano) | 5 | 237 | 11-28 |
| Bach, Johann Sebastian | Two-Part Invention in A Major (synthesizer) | 5 | 237 | 11-29 |
| Bach, Johann Sebastian | Well-Tempered Clavier, Book 1, The "Prelude and Fugue in C Minor" | 7 | E-16 | 10-1 |

| Composer | Title | Gr. | Pg. | CD Track |
|----------|-------|-----|-----|----------|
| Bach, Johann Sebastian | Well-Tempered Clavier, The "Be-Bop Bach: Prelude No. 2 " (excerpt) | 7 | C-11 | 6-6 |
| Bach, Johann Sebastian; Arr: Akendengué | Bombé/Ruht wohl, ruht wohl, ihr heiligen Gebeine | 8 | B-39 | 4-3 |
| Baez, Joan | Diamonds and Rust (excerpt) | 7 | A-4 | 1-5 |
| Baldridge/Stone/Bonine | Let's Dance (excerpt) | 1 | 256 | 8-16 |
| Ballard, Henry | Twist, The | 5 | 359 | 16-19 |
| Ballard, Henry | Twist, The | 7 | B-10 | 2-13 |
| Ballard, Henry | Twist, The | 8 | B-42 | 4-12 |
| Banzi/Banzi/Krishnar | Maitreem (excerpt) | 7 | C-21 | 6-22 |
| Barber, Samuel | Hermit Songs "The Monk and His Cat" | 7 | C-21 | 6-22 |
| Bart, Lionel | Who Will Buy? (from Oliver) (excerpt) | 1 | 16 | 1-26 |
| Bartels, Joanie | Jump for Joy | K | 213 | 7-29 |
| Bartels/Rhyne | Two Heads Are Better Than One | 1 | 333 | 10-28 |
| Bartók, Béla | Concerto for Orchestra "Presentation of Pairs" | 4 | 72 | 4-12 |
| Bartók, Béla | Concerto for Viola and Orchestra, Movement 3 (excerpt) | 7 | C-35 | 7-22 |
| Bartók, Béla | Cradle Song | K | 97 | 3-54 |
| Bartók, Béla | For Children (Sz 42), Volume II No. 33 "Allegro non troppo" | 2 | 49 | 2-20 |
| Bartók, Béla | String Quartet No. 4 "Allegretto pizzicato," Movement 4 | 4 | 90 | 4-35 |
| Bartók, Béla | String Quartet No. 5 "Andante," Movement 4 (excerpt) | 3 | 113 | 4-19 |
| Bartók, Béla | Ten Easy Pieces "Bear Dance" | 3 | 172 | 6-16 |
| Bassett, Rick | DJ Beat | 7 | B-13 | 2-18 |
| Batchelder, W.K. | Glory Hallelujah Grand March | 8 | C-38 | 7-7 |
| Bates, Gavin | Udu Pot (excerpt) | 8 | D-4 | 8-13 |
| Baydur, Daghan/Thomas, Richard | Istanbul Coffee House (Kafe neio) (excerpt) | 8 | B-34 | 3-30 |
| Beach, Amy | Les Rêves de Columbine (Under the Stars) "Sous les étoiles" (1907) | 2 | 338 | 12-16 |
| Beamer, Nona | Pupu hinu hinu "Shiny Shell Lullaby" (excerpt) | 1 | 109 | 3-41 |
| Beard, Jim | Quiet City (excerpt) | 8 | E-29 | 10-3 |
| Beethoven, Ludwig van | Eccosaise in E-flat Major | 1 | 223 | 7-15 |
| Beethoven, Ludwig van | Piano Concerto in E-flat Major No. 5 "Emperor," Movement 3, Rondo: Allegro | 7 | C-18 | 6-17 |
| Beethoven, Ludwig van | Piano Sonata No. 8 in C Minor "Rondo: Allegro" | 4 | 185 | 8-18 |
| Beethoven, Ludwig van | Sonata in F Major for Violin and Piano No. 5 "Spring," Movement 3, Scherzo | 7 | C-19 | 6-19 |
| Beethoven, Ludwig van | Sonata No. 14 in C-sharp Minor  No. 2 "Moonlight," Movement 1 | 7 | C-19 | 6-18 |
| Beethoven, Ludwig van | Symphony No. 3 in E-flat Major "Allegro con brio," Movement 1 (excerpt) | 8 | C-17 | 5-18 |
| Beethoven, Ludwig van | Symphony No. 3 in E-flat Major "Marcia funebre," Movement 2 (excerpt) | 8 | C-17 | 5-19 |
| Beethoven, Ludwig van | Symphony No. 5 in C Minor, Movement 1 | 7 | C-16 | 6-15 |
| Beethoven, Ludwig van | Symphony No. 5 in C Minor, Movement 1 (excerpt) | 6 | 98 | 6-14 |
| Beethoven, Ludwig van | Symphony No. 5 in C Minor, Movement 4 (excerpt) | 7 | C-18 | 6-16 |
| Beethoven, Ludwig van | Symphony No. 6 "The Storm," Movement 4 | 4 | 365 | 16-3 |
| Beethoven, Ludwig van | Symphony No. 7, Movement 2 (excerpt) | 1 | 97 | 3-23 |
| Beethoven, Ludwig van | Symphony No. 9 in D Minor "Ode to Joy," Movement 4 (excerpt) | 4 | 151 | 7-6 |
| Bejot, Kim | Cow Barn Cha Cha (excerpt) | 8 | D-33 | 9-7 |
| Belafonte/Freedman | Jump in the Line (excerpt) | 4 | 117 | 5-34 |
| Bellal, Mohammed/Mahtani, Jyoti | Sabhyatâ (Civilization) | 8 | B-43 | 4-13 |
| Benjamin, Arthur | Jamaican Rumba | 5 | 201 | 10-11 |
| Berg, Alban | Lyric Suite "Allegretto gioviale," Movement 1 | 6 | 169 | 9-26 |
| Berlin, Irving | Let's Face the Music | 7 | B-14 | 2-20 |
| Berlin/Lazarus | Give Me Your Tired, Your Poor | 5 | 166 | 8-23 |
| Berman/Berman/Cremers | This Is Your Night (Dance Mix) (excerpt) | 6 | 369 | 18-22 |
| Berman/Berman/Cremers; Arr: Vasquez, Jr. | This Is Your Night | 6 | 368 | 18-21 |
| Bernie/Casey/Pinkard | Sweet Georgia Brown (excerpt) | 4 | 71 | 4-10 |
| Bernstein, Elmer | Magnificent Seven, The (from The Magnificent Seven) (excerpt) | 3 | 144 | 5-16 |
| Bernstein, Leonard | Dance Suite "Waltz" | K | 145 | 5-28 |
| Bernstein, Leonard | Divertimento for Orchestra "Samba" | 5 | 9 | 1-8 |
| Bernstein, Leonard | Mass "Responsory: Alleluia" | 6 | 217 | 11-25 |
| Bernstein, Leonard | Overture to Candide | 6 | 218 | 11-26 |
| Bernstein, Leonard | Overture to Candide (excerpt) | 6 | 219 | 11-27 |
| Bernstein, Leonard | Simple Song, A (from Mass) | 8 | C-45 | 7-16 |
| Bernstein, Leonard/Sondheim, Stephen | America (from West Side Story) | 8 | C-45 | 7-15 |
| Bernstein, Leonard/Sondheim, Stephen | Somewhere (from West Side Story) | 8 | C-44 | 7-14 |
| Bernstein/Sondheim | Dance at the Gym (from West Side Story) (excerpt) | 5 | 9 | 1-7 |

| Composer | Title | Gr. | Pg. | CD Track |
|---|---|---|---|---|
| Berryhill/Connolly/Fuller/Wilson | Wipe Out | 5 | 155 | 8-3 |
| Berryhill/Connolly/Fuller/Wilson | Wipe Out | 7 | F-33 | 11-19 |
| Bizet, George | Les pêcheurs des perles (In the Depths of the Temple) "Au fond du temple saint" (excerpt) | 7 | C-30 | 7-11 |
| Bizet, Georges | L'Arlésienne Suite No. 2 "Farandole" | 6 | 68 | 4-28 |
| Blackwell, Robert/Marascalco, John | Good Golly, Miss Molly | 8 | E-10 | 9-14 |
| Bloch, Ernest | Three Nocturnes for Piano Trio "Andante quieto" (excerpt) | 1 | 25 | 1-37 |
| Bo, Eddie | I Know You Mardi Gras (excerpt) | 8 | B-17 | 2-53 |
| Borde, Emile | Gidden riddum (excerpt) | 6 | 299 | 15-9 |
| Boyd, Jim/Alexie, Sherman | Reservation Blues (excerpt) | 8 | B-37 | 3-35 |
| Boyd, Jim/Alexie, Sherman | Treaties (excerpt) | 8 | B-36 | 3-34 |
| Bozza, Eugene | Scherzo for Wind Quintet | 1 | 329 | 10-25 |
| Bradford, P. | Crazy Blues | 7 | B-8 | 2-10 |
| Brahms, Johannes | Academic Festival Overture (excerpt) | 8 | C-20 | 6-1 |
| Brahms, Johannes | Hungarian Dance No. 19 | 4 | 171 | 7-31 |
| Brahms, Johannes | Hungarian Dance No. 3 in F Major | 1 | 208 | 6-41 |
| Brahms, Johannes | Hungarian Dance No. 6 | 4 | 50 | 2-33 |
| Brahms, Johannes | Lullaby | 3 | 188 | 6-38 |
| Britten, Benjamin | Simple Symphony "Playful Pizzicato" (excerpt) | 1 | 205 | 6-40 |
| Britten, Benjamin | Six Metamorphoses After Ovid "Bacchus" (excerpt) | 7 | C-13 | 6-11 |
| Broonzy, Big Bill/Segar, Charles | Key to the Highway (excerpt) | 8 | F-28 | 11-11 |
| Broonzy/Segar | Key to the Highway | 6 | 243 | 12-21 |
| Brown, Charles H. | Yellow Rose of Texas, The | 7 | I-73 | 14-20 |
| Brown, Leroy/Smith, Lawrence | Boogie Down | 8 | G-29 | 12-11 |
| Bruce, Jack/Brown, Pete | Boston Ball Game 1967 | 8 | F-32 | 11-17 |
| Brumley, Alfred | I'll Fly Away | 8 | I-43 | 14-18 |
| Bryant, Felice /Bryant, Boudleaux | Bye Bye, Love (excerpt) | 8 | A-15 | 1-8 |
| Bryant/Bryant | Bye Bye, Love | 5 | 357 | 16-17 |
| Burch, Sharon | Rain Song, The | 2 | 323 | 11-32 |
| Burke/Spina | Beat of My Heart, The | 4 | 9 | 1-6 |
| Burning Sky | Watchers of the Canyon | 6 | 270 | 14-6 |
| Burrough, Roslyn | I Love Peanuts (swing style) | 1 | 163a | 5-25 |
| Cage, John | Concert for Piano and Orchestra (excerpt) | 6 | 209 | 11-17 |
| Cahn/Styne | Let It Snow! Let It Snow! Let It Snow! | 4 | 427 | 18-7 |
| Calhoun, Charles/Turner, Lou Willie | Flip, Flop and Fly | 7 | F-15 | 11-2 |
| Camero/Hidalgo/Valdes | Conga Kings Grand Finale (excerpt) | 5 | 156 | 8-5 |
| Campos, Juan Morel | Danzas Puertorriqueñas "Vano empeño" | 7 | E-13 | 9-25 |
| Cantrell, Jerry | Would? | 8 | F-30 | 11-14 |
| Carleton, Bob | Ja-Da | 2 | 187 | 7-12 |
| Carpenter, Mary Chapin | Halley Came to Jackson | 2 | 341 | 12-18 |
| Carpenter, Mary Chapin | Why Walk When You Can Fly? | 7 | B-28 | 4-8 |
| Cash, Johnny | I Walk the Line | 7 | B-28 | 4-7 |
| Cast members of "Stomp" | Kitchen Stomp (from Stomp Out Loud) | 4 | 122 | 5-39 |
| Cast members of "Stomp" | Trash Can Stomp (from Stomp Out Loud) | 6 | 328 | 16-17 |
| Castello, Dario | Sonata Seconda | 3 | 431 | 15-14 |
| Chappelle, Eric | Add-On Machine, The | K | 298 | 10-22 |
| Chappelle, Eric | All in One (excerpt) | 1 | 13 | 1-23 |
| Chappelle, Eric | Breathe | 1 | 404 | 13-3 |
| Chappelle, Eric | Caribbean Leaps | K | 149 | 5-33 |
| Chappelle, Eric | Checkerboard (excerpt) | 1 | 7 | 1-10 |
| Chappelle, Eric | PIZZ Ah! (excerpt) | 1 | 105 | 3-35 |
| Chappelle, Eric | Skippy (excerpt) | 1 | 245b | 7-44 |
| Charles, Ray | Ain't That Love | 5 | 20 | 1-30 |
| Chávez, Carlos | Toccata for Percussion, Movement 3 | 4 | 155 | 7-11 |
| Chavez, Carlos | Xochipilli "An Imagined Aztec Music" (excerpt) | 8 | C-37 | 7-6 |
| Chopin, Frédéric | Étude in E major | K | 241 | 8-26 |
| Chopin, Frédéric | Mazurka No. 3 (excerpt) | 3 | 317 | 11-12 |
| Chopin, Frédéric | Prelude in A Major | 4 | 234 | 10-4 |
| Chopin, Frédéric | Prelude in E Minor No. 4 | 3 | 27 | 1-42 |
| Chopin, Frédéric | Prelude No. 16 in B-flat Minor | 7 | C-22 | 7-2 |
| Chopin, Frédéric | Raindrop Prelude (excerpt) | 3 | 26 | 1-41 |

| Composer | Title | Gr. | Pg. | CD Track |
|---|---|---|---|---|
| Chopin, Frédéric | Waltz in D-flat ("Minute" Waltz) | 4 | 234 | 10-3 |
| Clark/Leonard | That's the Way | 4 | 193 | 8-34 |
| Clarke, Jeremiah | Prince of Denmark's March (excerpt) | 6 | 55 | 3-30 |
| Cleveland/Gaye/Benson | What's Going On? | 7 | B-38 | 5-3 |
| Cohan, George M. | I'm a Yankee Doodle Dandy (excerpt) | 5 | 278 | 13-2 |
| Cohan, George M. | Yankee Doodle Boy, The (from Little Johnny Jones) (excerpt) | 3 | 265 | 9-12 |
| Cohan, George M. | You're a Grand Old Flag | 1 | 276 | 9-3 |
| Connick Jr., Harry/McLean, Richard | Forever, for Now (excerpt) | 7 | B-16 | 3-1 |
| Cooke, Richard | Flight of the Ibis (excerpt) | 8 | D-16 | 8-21 |
| Cooke, Richard | Return to Misty Mountain | 7 | D-28 | 9-12 |
| Copland, Aaron | Appalachian Spring "Variations on Simple Gifts" | 5 | 185 | 9-19 |
| Copland, Aaron | Billy the Kid "Celebration" (excerpt) | 3 | 251 | 8-21 |
| Copland, Aaron | El Salón México (excerpt) | 6 | 199 | 10-40 |
| Copland, Aaron | Fanfare for the Common Man | 7 | C-43 | 8-5 |
| Copland, Aaron | Old American Songs "The Boatman's Dance" | 4 | 61 | 3-20 |
| Copland, Aaron | Rodeo "Buckaroo Holiday" (excerpt) | 2 | 23 | 1-28 |
| Copland, Aaron | Rodeo "Hoedown" | 5 | 312 | 14-22 |
| Copland, Aaron | Rodeo "Hoedown" | 8 | B-45 | 4-16 |
| Copland, Aaron | Rodeo "Hoedown" (excerpt) | 1 | 6 | 1-4 |
| Copland, Aaron | Rodeo "Saturday Night Waltz" (excerpt) | 4 | 342 | 15-3 |
| Corea, Chick | Fingerprints (excerpt) | 7 | B-42 | 5-10 |
| Corigliano, John | Etude Fantasy for Piano No. 3 "Fifths to Thirds" | 8 | C-46 | 8-3 |
| Corigliano, John | Gazebo Dances "Tarantella" | 8 | C-46 | 8-1 |
| Corigliano, John | Sonata for Violin and Piano "Allegro" | 8 | C-46 | 8-2 |
| Coyne, Nancy/Karmen, Steve; Arr: Louiselle | Radio City Christmas Spectacular Jingle | 8 | A-5 | 1-2 |
| Creamer/Layton | After You've Gone | 2 | 189 | 7-15 |
| Crosby/Stills/Nash/Young | Carry On | 7 | B-2 | 2-1 |
| D. Fekaris/F. Perren | I Will Survive (excerpt) | 7 | B-10 | 2-14 |
| Daquin, Louis-Claude | Le cou cou (The Cuckoo) | 3 | 329 | 11-29 |
| Davies, Peter Maxwell | Yellow Cake Review, The "Farewell to Stromness" | K | 61 | 2-46 |
| Davis, Chip | Florida Suite "Everglades" (excerpt) | 1 | 413 | 13-15 |
| Davis/Mitchell | You Are My Sunshine | 6 | 247 | 13-6 |
| Day, Howie | Brace Yourself | 8 | A-19 | 1-15 |
| de Bethune, Canon | Ahi! Amours (excerpt) | 8 | C-4 | 4-30 |
| de Falla, Manuel | Nights in the Gardens of Spain "En el generalife" (excerpt) | 2 | 144 | 5-40 |
| de Falla, Manuel; Arr: Krouse | El amor brujo "Danza ritual del fuego" | 8 | F-20 | 10-29 |
| De Faria/Casas/Ostwald | Get on Your Feet | 5 | 8 | 1-6 |
| de Sarasate, Pablo | Caprice Basque (excerpt) | 1 | 256 | 8-17 |
| Debussy, Claude | Children's Corner "Jimbo's Lullaby" (excerpt) | 1 | 271 | 8-34 |
| Debussy, Claude | Children's Corner Suite "Doctor Gradus ad Parnassum" | 8 | C-27 | 6-18 |
| Debussy, Claude | Children's Corner Suite No. 4 "Snowflakes Are Dancing" | 5 | 239 | 11-31 |
| Debussy, Claude | Clair de lune | K | 165 | 6-7 |
| Debussy, Claude | La mer "Dialogue du vent et de mer" | 8 | C-27 | 6-19 |
| Debussy, Claude | La mer "Jeux de vagues" (excerpt) | 7 | C-39 | 7-28 |
| Debussy, Claude | Little Shepherd, The (excerpt) | 1 | 256 | 8-15 |
| Debussy, Claude | Minstrels | K | 175 | 6-25 |
| Debussy, Claude | Prelude to the Afternoon of a Faun (excerpt) | 5 | 113 | 6-5 |
| Debussy, Claude | Reverie (1890) (excerpt) | 1 | 6 | 1-6 |
| Debussy, Claude | Syrinx | 5 | 113 | 6-4 |
| Debussy, Claude | Voiles (Sails) (excerpt) | 7 | C-39 | 7-27 |
| Dekker, Desmond | Keep a Cool Head | 7 | B-34 | 4-19 |
| DeKnight/Friedman | Rock Around the Clock | 5 | 356 | 16-16 |
| Desmond, Paul | Take Five (excerpt) | 5 | 220 | 10-37 |
| Desmond, Paul | Take Five (excerpt) | 7 | B-15 | 2-23 |
| deVine, Winsford | Somebody (excerpt) | 4 | 41 | 2-22 |
| Diallo, Alpha Yaya | Badenma (Friendship) | 8 | B-28 | 3-15 |
| Diallo, Yaya | Nangapè | 2 | 103 | 4-20 |
| Diamond, Charlotte | Spider's Web | K | 93 | 3-46 |

| Composer | Title | Gr. | Pg. | CD Track |
|---|---|---|---|---|
| Diamond, Neil | I'm a Believer | 7 | G-32 | 12-22 |
| Diaz, Jose Fernandez | Guantanamera (excerpt) | 8 | I-33 | 14-8 |
| Dibdin, Charles | Country Dance | 3 | 211 | 7-28 |
| DiFranco, Ani | Angry Anymore | 8 | F-32 | 11-16 |
| Dikshtar, Muthuswami | Maha ganapathim (excerpt) | 6 | 305 | 15-23 |
| Dispatch/Heimbold | Elias (excerpt) | 7 | B-21 | 3-6 |
| Domino, Fats/Bartholomew, Dave | My Girl Josephine (excerpt) | 8 | E-21 | 9-21 |
| Domino/Bartholomew/Guidry | Walkin' to New Orleans | 3 | 371 | 13-3 |
| Dorsey, Thomas A. | What Could I Do | 5 | 281 | 13-7 |
| Doucet, Sharon Arms | L'arc en ciel | 2 | 333 | 12-8 |
| Driftwood | Battle of New Orleans, The | 6 | 105 | 6-23 |
| Dukas, Paul | La Peri "Fanfare" | 4 | 71 | 4-11 |
| Duke, Vernon/Gershwin, Ira | I Can't Get Started (excerpt) | 7 | B-26 | 4-2 |
| Dun, Tan | Crouching Tiger, Hidden Dragon | 8 | A-11 | 1-4 |
| Dvorak, Antonin | Slavonic Dance No. 1 (excerpt) | 4 | 227 | 9-34 |
| Dvorák, Antonin | Slavonic Dance No. 1 No. 1 "Presto" (excerpt) | 1 | 6 | 1-7 |
| Dvorák, Antonin | Symphony No. 9 from "The New World", Movement 1 | 5 | 55 | 3-22 |
| Dykes, Doyle | Jazz in the Box (excerpt) | 8 | F-11 | 10-21 |
| Dylan, Bob | Blowin' in the Wind | 5 | 384 | 17-21 |
| Dylan, Bob | Mr. Tambourine Man | 6 | 148 | 8-20 |
| Dylan, Bob | Times They Are A-Changin', The | 5 | 384 | 17-22 |
| Eddleman, David | Beat of the Tango, The | K | 106 | 4-12 |
| Eddleman, David | Cookie Crew, The | K | 196 | 7-9 |
| Eddleman, David | Fantasy for Chanukah | 1 | 421 | 13-31 |
| Eddleman, David | I'm Gonna Sing a Silly Song | K | 225 | 8-3 |
| Eddleman, David | Noah's Zoo in the Big, Big Rain | K | 274 | 9-30 |
| Egan, Seamas | Flowing Bowl, The (excerpt) | 8 | B-29 | 3-16 |
| Elfman, Danny | Main Titles (from Edward Scissorhands) | 8 | A-10 | 1-3 |
| Elfman, Danny | Overture/All That Jazz (from Chicago) (excerpt) | 7 | A-23 | 1-16 |
| Ellington, Duke | C-Jam Blues | 8 | C-43 | 7-13 |
| Ellington, Duke | Don't Get Around Much Anymore (excerpt) | 1 | 33 | 1-56 |
| Ellington, Duke | It Don't Mean a Thing (If It Ain't Got That Swing) (as performed by Mel Tormé) (excerpt) | 6 | 386 | 19-21 |
| Ellington, Duke | Queen's Suite, The "Sunset and the Mocking Bird" | 8 | E-10 | 9-15 |
| Ellington/Mills | It Don't Mean a Thing (If It Ain't Got That Swing) (as performed by Ella Fitzgerald) (excerpt) | 5 | 338 | 15-25 |
| Estefan/Casas/Ostwald | Oye mi canto (Hear My Voice) | 6 | 114 | 6-34 |
| Estefano | Mi tierra (My Homeland) | 6 | 365 | 18-18 |
| Estrada, Ernesto "Fruko" | El nuevo caiman (excerpt) | 8 | B-17 | 2-52 |
| Eto | Lion (excerpt) | 6 | 303 | 15-21 |
| Faddis, Jon | Into the Faddisphere | K | 21 | 1-30 |
| Fauré, Gabriel; Arranged: Gilbert/Shames | En prière | K | 158 | 5-47 |
| Feliciano, Jose | Feliz Navidad | 4 | 433 | 18-19 |
| Flanders/Swann | Hippopotamus Song, The | 3 | 33 | 1-55 |
| Fleck, Béla | Moment So Close, A (excerpt) | 8 | B-40 | 4-6 |
| Flower, Edward | Suo gan (excerpt) | 1 | 309 | 9-45 |
| Foa'i, Opetaia | Ki mua | 8 | B-27 | 3-14 |
| Foa'i, Opetaia | Lua afe (2000) (excerpt) | 8 | B-27 | 3-13 |
| Foster/Sager | Prayer, The (excerpt) | 7 | A-10 | 1-8 |
| Françaix, Jean | Quartet "Allegro molto" | 4 | 70 | 4-6 |
| Franck, César | Sonata in A Major "Allegretto poco mosso," Movement 4 (excerpt) | 5 | 159 | 8-11 |
| Franck, Melchior | Da pacem, Domine | 5 | 62 | 4-4 |
| Freudmann, Gideon | Fish Food | 2 | 212 | 8-4 |
| Fricker, Sylvia | You Were on My Mind | 7 | G-25 | 12-17 |
| Friedman, Burnt | Suzuki (excerpt) | 7 | A-2 | 1-3 |
| Frishberg/Ostrow/Seifert | Zydeco Dancing | 1 | 21 | 1-34 |
| Fujikake, Hiro | Harukoma "Spring Horse Dance" (excerpt) | 1 | 145 | 4-47 |
| Gabriel, Peter | Solsbury Hill (excerpt) | 8 | E-29 | 10-5 |
| Gabrieli, Giovanni | Canzon in Echo Duodecimi Toni a 10 | 8 | C-7 | 5-4 |
| Gabrieli, Giovanni | Canzoni et Sonate "Canzoni prima a 5" | 4 | 193 | 8-33 |

Listening Index

| Composer | Title | Gr. | Pg. | CD Track |
|---|---|---|---|---|
| Gay, John | Beggar's Opera, The "Constant Billy" | 7 | C-24 | 7-6 |
| Gaye/Hunter/Stevenson | Dancin' in the Street | 5 | 360 | 16-20 |
| Gaye/Stevenson/Hunter | Dancing in the Street | 2 | 254 | 9-17 |
| Geiss, Tony | Doing the Penguin | K | 35 | 2-7 |
| George/Martin/Kibbee/Lowell | Rock 'n' Roll Doctor (excerpt) | 7 | B-38 | 5-2 |
| Gershwin, George | Lullaby for Strings (excerpt) | 1 | 293 | 9-23 |
| Gershwin, George | Rhapsody in Blue | K | 75 | 3-9 |
| Gershwin, George | Rhapsody in Blue (excerpt) | 7 | C-42 | 8-4 |
| Gershwin, George | Summertime | 6 | 252 | 13-12 |
| Gershwin, George; Arr: Jenkins | Plenty o' Nuttin' (excerpt) | 7 | B-45 | 5-13 |
| Gershwin, George/Gershwin, Ira | Fascinatin' Rhythm (as performed by Ella Fitzgerald) | 7 | E-11 | 9-24 |
| Gershwin, George/Gershwin, Ira | Fascinatin' Rhythm (as performed by Frances Veri) | 7 | E-11 | 9-23 |
| Gerswin/Webster/Fain/Cobb; Arr: Gentil | Strike Up The Band Medley (Strike Up The Band, Mardi Gras March, Listen To That Dixie Band) (excerpt) | 6 | 25 | 2-18 |
| Gibbons, Orlando | Silver Swan, The | 8 | C-5 | 4-33 |
| Gillard/Stewart/Green | Flat Foot Floogee, The | 3 | 158 | 5-33 |
| Gillespie, Dizzy | Salt Peanuts (excerpt) | 1 | 163a | 5-21 |
| Gillespie/Fuller/Pozo | Manteca | 7 | B-3 | 2-2 |
| Gilmore, Patrick S.; Arr: Harris | When Johnny Comes Marching Home | 5 | 88 | 4-32 |
| Ginastera, Alberto | Estancia "Danza del trigo" | 5 | 229 | 11-15 |
| Ginsburg, Ned | Groundhog Jig, The | 1 | 436 | 14-9 |
| Glass/Byrne | Open the Kingdom (excerpt) | 6 | 31 | 2-24 |
| Glière, Reinhold | Red Poppy, The "Russian Sailors' Dance" | 4 | 224 | 9-26 |
| Goering, Chuck | Salute to Sunnyland Slim | 8 | E-33 | 10-8 |
| Goldman, Edwin Franko | On the Mall | 5 | 2 | 1-1 |
| Goldman, Matt | Rods and Cones | 7 | D-5 | 8-18 |
| Gómez, Francisco Sánchez | Río de la miel (River of Honey) (excerpt) | 5 | 296 | 13-25 |
| Gonzales, Jose | Bomba te traigo yo (excerpt) | 8 | B-3 | 2-2 |
| Goodman, Benny/Hampton, Lionel | Flying Home | 7 | B-15 | 2-22 |
| Goodman/Hampton | Pick-a-Rib | 3 | 151 | 5-22 |
| Gossec, François-Joseph | Gavotte | 3 | 88 | 3-22 |
| Gottschalk, Louis Moreau | Bamboula | 3 | 229 | 7-55 |
| Gottschalk, Louis Moreau | L'union (excerpt) | 6 | 487 | 23-8 |
| Gould, Morton | American Salute | 5 | 275 | 12-35 |
| Gould, Morton | Fanfare for Freedom | 6 | 139 | 8-4 |
| Gould, Morton | Fourth of July, The | 5 | 489 | 21-19 |
| Grainger, Percy | Country Gardens | 1 | 440 | 14-18 |
| Grainger, Percy | Free Music #1 | 2 | 212 | 8-3 |
| Grainger, Percy | Lincolnshire Posy "Lord Melbourne" | 4 | 74 | 4-13 |
| Grainger, Percy | Shepherds Hey | 1 | 209 | 6-43 |
| Grammer, Red | Shake Your Brain | 1 | 250 | 8-3 |
| Green, Joe | Whirlwind | 3 | 149 | 5-19 |
| Grieg, Edvard | Lyric Suite No. 6 "Wedding Day at Troldhaugen" | 6 | 9 | 1-5 |
| Grieg, Edvard | Peer Gynt Suite No. 1 "Morning" (excerpt) | 1 | 369 | 11-40 |
| Grieg, Edvard | Piano Concerto in A Minor, Movement 1 (excerpt) | 8 | E-11 | 9-16 |
| Grieg, Edvard; Arr: Langford | Lyric Pieces No. 1 "Butterfly" | 1 | 363 | 11-27 |
| Grieg, Edvard; Arr: Langford | Lyric Pieces No. 4 "Little Bird" | 1 | 347 | 11-6 |
| Grofé, Ferde | Grand Canyon Suite "Cloudburst" | K | 260 | 9-9 |
| Grofé, Ferde | Grand Canyon Suite "On the Trail" (excerpt) | 3 | 77 | 3-5 |
| Guaraldi, Vince | Little Birdie | 4 | 75 | 4-15 |
| Guaraldi, Vincent; Arr: Anderson | Linus and Lucy | 8 | A-29 | 1-20 |
| Gunn, Trey | Dziban (excerpt) | 7 | F-18 | 11-4 |
| Guthrie, Woody | Howjidoo | 1 | 315 | 10-5 |
| Guthrie, Woody | This Land Is Your Land | 5 | 120 | 6-12 |
| Guthrie/Hays | Goin' Down the Road Feelin' Bad | 5 | 283 | 13-10 |
| Hall, Tom T. | Dancing Tree, The | K | 203 | 7-14 |
| Hamilton/Lewis | How High the Moon (excerpt) | 5 | 341 | 15-28 |
| Hampton, Walt | Crunchy, Crunchy, Crunchy (excerpt) (performance piece) | 8 | D-14 | 8-19 |
| Hampton, Walt | Nyoka (excerpt) (performance piece) | 7 | D-32 | 9-14 |
| Hancock, Herbie | Watermelon Man (excerpt) | 1 | 12 | 1-17 |
| Hancock, Herbie | Watermelon Man (excerpt) | 6 | 270 | 14-5 |

Listening Index

| Composer | Title | Gr. | Pg. | CD Track |
|---|---|---|---|---|
| Hancock/Laswell/Beinhorn | Rock It (excerpt) | 7 | B-11 | 2-15 |
| Handel, George Frideric | Arrival of the Queen of Sheba, The (Solomon) | 2 | 348 | 12-27 |
| Handel, George Frideric | Messiah "Behold, I Tell You a Mystery" | 8 | C-8 | 5-6 |
| Handel, George Frideric | Messiah "Hallelujah!" | 8 | C-8 | 5-5 |
| Handel, George Frideric | Messiah "The Trumpet Shall Sound" | 8 | C-8 | 5-7 |
| Handel, George Frideric | Sonata in C Major for Recorder and Basso Continuo No. 7 "Gavotte" | K | 75 | 3-8 |
| Handel, George Frideric | Sonata in G Minor No. 1, Movement 2 (excerpt) | 7 | C-12 | 6-7 |
| Handel, George Frideric | Water Music "Allegro Maestoso" | 3 | 189 | 6-39 |
| Handel, George Frideric | Water Music "Hornpipe" (excerpt) | 8 | C-9 | 5-8 |
| Handy, W.C. | St. Louis Blues | 5 | 353 | 16-13 |
| Handy, W. C. | St. Louis Blues (excerpt) | 4 | 57 | 3-17 |
| Hansen, Susie | Solo Flight (excerpt) | 5 | 312 | 14-21 |
| Hanson, David | Toccata and Tango (excerpt) | 2 | 154 | 5-52 |
| Harburg/Arlen | Over the Rainbow (as performed by Aretha Franklin) | 4 | 143 | 6-30 |
| Harburg/Arlen | Over the Rainbow (as performed by Judy Garland) | 4 | 143 | 6-29 |
| Hardiman, Ron | Lord of the Dance Medley (excerpt) | 6 | 326 | 16-14 |
| Hart, Mickey | Evening Samba | 6 | 297 | 15-8 |
| Hart, Mickey | Hunt, The | 6 | 363 | 18-12 |
| Hart, Mickey | Lost River | 6 | 283 | 14-15 |
| Haydn, Franz Joseph | Canon No. 110 in G | 6 | 133 | 7-35 |
| Haydn, Franz Joseph | Serenade No. 5 | 4 | 90 | 4-34 |
| Haydn, Franz Joseph | String Quartet in D Major No. 5 "The Lark," Movement 1 (excerpt) | 7 | C-15 | 6-14 |
| Haydn, Franz Joseph | Symphony in G No. 88, Movement 4 (excerpt) | 2 | 84 | 3-40 |
| Haydn, Franz Joseph | Symphony No. 47 in G Major "Menuet" | 7 | C-14 | 6-13 |
| Haydn, Franz Joseph | Symphony No. 94 in G Major, ("Surprise") Andante (excerpt) | 1 | 86 | 3-3 |
| Haydn, Franz Joseph | Symphony No. 94 in G Major, ("Surprise") Andante (excerpt) | 7 | C-14 | 6-12 |
| Hedges, Michael | Aerial Boundaries | 8 | F-20 | 10-30 |
| Hellerman/Gilbert/Seeger/Hays | Aweigh, Santy Ano (excerpt) | 1 | 339 | 10-34 |
| Hellmer, Jeff | Peak Moments (excerpt) | 8 | E-4 | 9-10 |
| Herbst, Eric | Rainy Day Blues | 2 | 328 | 12-3 |
| Hernandez/Alvarez | El dulcerito llego (The Sweets Vendor Is Here) | K | 124 | 4-43 |
| Hiatt, John | Have a Little Faith in Me | 8 | A-18 | 1-12 |
| Hidalgo, David/Pérez, Louie | Good Morning, Aztlán (excerpt) | 7 | B-7 | 2-8 |
| Hill, Lauryn/Newton, Johari | Everything Is Everything | 7 | B-29 | 4-11 |
| Hirschhorn, Linda | Bird | 1 | 39 | 2-3 |
| Hirschhorn, Linda | If You Can Walk | 1 | 19 | 1-31 |
| Hoffs/Steinberg/Kelly | Eternal Flame | 7 | B-6 | 2-6 |
| Holborne, Anthony | Honiesuckle, The | 5 | 504 | 21-20 |
| Holiday, Billie/Herzog Jr., Arthur | God Bless the Child (as performed by Billie Holiday) | 7 | B-26 | 4-3 |
| Holiday, Billie/Herzog Jr., Arthur | God Bless the Child (as performed by Blood, Sweat & Tears) (excerpt) | 7 | B-26 | 4-4 |
| Holiday/Myers/DeShannon | Put a Little Love in Your Heart | 4 | 8 | 1-5 |
| Holland, Brian | Come Out and Play (excerpt) | 5 | 238 | 11-30 |
| Holst, Gustav | Planets, The "Jupiter" | 5 | 424 | 18-29 |
| Holst, Gustav | Planets, The "Jupiter" (excerpt) | 1 | 405 | 13-4 |
| Holst, Gustav | Planets, The "Mars, the Bringer of War" (excerpt) | 4 | 377 | 16-15 |
| Holst, Gustav | Suite No. 2 in F "March," Movement 1 | 6 | 139 | 8-3 |
| Holst, Gustav | Suite No. 2 in F No. 2 "Fantasia on the Dargason," Movement 4 (excerpt) | 7 | C-36 | 7-23 |
| Honegger, Arthur | Pacific 231 | 2 | 286 | 10-33 |
| Hooverphonic | Magnificent Tree, The | 7 | E-31 | 10-13 |
| Horner, James | Coming Home from the Sea-I (from The Perfect Storm) (excerpt) | 6 | 345 | 17-14 |
| Horner, James | Coming Home from the Sea-II (from The Perfect Storm) (excerpt) | 6 | 345 | 17-15 |
| Horner, James | Rose (excerpt) | 8 | B-34 | 3-29 |
| Horner/Mann/Weil | Somewhere Out There (from An American Tail) | 5 | 369 | 17-6 |
| Hot Butter | Popcorn | 8 | E-27 | 10-1 |
| Hua Yanjun | Moon Mirrored in the Pool, The (excerpt) | 6 | 103 | 6-19 |
| Hummel, Johann Nepomuk | Concerto for Trumpet and Orchestra in E-flat Major "Rondo: Allegro molto" (excerpt) | 1 | 256 | 8-13 |
| Humperdinck, Engelbert | Hänsel und Gretel "Ein Männlein steht im Walde" | 2 | 91 | 3-47 |
| Hunter, Charles | Cotton Boll Rag | 5 | 333 | 15-18 |
| Ingalls, Jeremiah | Northfield | 6 | 25 | 2-15 |

| Composer | Title | Gr. | Pg. | CD Track |
|---|---|---|---|---|
| Ismael Tidiane Touré/Sixu Tidiane Touré | Fatou yo (I Am Fatou) | K | 154 | 5-44 |
| Ives, Charles | Variations on "America" | 6 | 162 | 9-13 |
| Jagome, Marube /Mankwane, Marks | Nyamphemphe (excerpt) | 8 | B-3 | 2-3 |
| Janácek, Leos | Moravian Dance No. 2 "Kalamajka" | 3 | 79 | 3-10 |
| Jelly Roll Morton | Kansas City Stomp | 2 | 251 | 9-14 |
| Jenson, Merrill | Putting Baby to Bed (excerpt) | 1 | 63 | 2-39 |
| Jimmy Davis/Charlie Mitchell | You Are My Sunshine (excerpt) | 7 | B-7 | 2-7 |
| Jing-Ran Zhu/Qui-Hong Her | Colours of the World | 6 | 271 | 14-7 |
| Joel, Billy | New York State of Mind (excerpt) | 7 | E-19 | 10-3 |
| Johansson, Olav | Bambodansarna (excerpt) | 8 | B-20 | 3-1 |
| John, Elton/Rice, John | Circle of Life, The (from The Lion King) | 3 | 367 | 12-27 |
| Johnson, Eric | Song for George | 8 | F-8 | 10-18 |
| Johnson, Robert | Walkin' Blues | 5 | 227 | 11-10 |
| Joplin, Scott | Bethena Waltz (excerpt) | 6 | 157 | 8-33 |
| Joplin, Scott | Elite Syncopations | 6 | 159 | 9-9 |
| Joplin, Scott | Entertainer, The | 2 | 76 | 3-21 |
| Joplin, Scott | Scott Joplin's New Rag | 5 | 335 | 15-21 |
| Joseph, Garland | In the Mood | 6 | 110 | 6-28 |
| Joubert, Joseph | Choo-Choo Joubert | 3 | 51 | 2-20 |
| Junk Yard Band | Rippa Medley, The "Block-Block, One Leg Up, Let the Beat Go, Uh-Oh" (excerpt) | 8 | D-32 | 9-6 |
| Kahn, Nusrat Fateh Ali | Allah Hoo Allah Hoo (excerpt) | 8 | B-13 | 2-37 |
| Kanengiser, William | African Suite "Mbira" | K | 61 | 2-45 |
| Kang, A. S. | Terian gulabi buliyan (excerpt) | 8 | B-26 | 3-12 |
| Kaper/Washington | On Green Dolphin Street | 4 | 126 | 6-1 |
| Kapp, Richard | Symphony No. 1 in D Major "Gavotte" | 2 | 338 | 12-17 |
| Kaye/Lippman/Wise | A-You're Adorable | 1 | 263 | 8-29 |
| Keb' Mo' | Every Morning | 7 | B-8 | 2-9 |
| Keetman, Gunild | Allegretto | 2 | 131 | 5-19 |
| Khachaturian, Aram | Masquerade Suite "Galop" (excerpt) | 4 | 16 | 1-24 |
| Kidjo/Brown | Tumba | 7 | D-14 | 8-32 |
| King, Carole | Beautiful | 3 | 67 | 2-42 |
| King, Carole | You've Got a Friend | 5 | 364 | 17-1 |
| King/Leiber/Stoller | Stand By Me | 5 | 49 | 3-3 |
| King/Leiber/Stoller | Stand By Me | 8 | E-24 | 9-23 |
| Klusevcek, Guy | Altered Landscapes: Part One (excerpt) | 8 | E-21 | 9-22 |
| Knaack, Donald | 3 + 2 | 2 | 316 | 11-25 |
| Knowles, Beyoncé; Arr: Calderone | Work It Out (Blow Your Horn Dub Mix) (excerpt) | 7 | A-3 | 1-4 |
| Kodály, Z. | Dances of Galanta (excerpt) | 7 | C-34 | 7-15 |
| Koppel, Thomas | Nele's Dances, No. 17 | 6 | 503 | 23-9 |
| Koppel, Thomas | Nele's Dances, No. 18 | 6 | 503 | 23-10 |
| Kozo Masuda | Yamaji (excerpt) | 3 | 407 | 14-30 |
| Kraft, William | Theme and Variations for Percussion | 5 | 65 | 4-5 |
| Kurki-Suonio | Eriskummainen kantele | 5 | 199 | 10-8 |
| Landreth, Sonny | Native Stepson | 7 | F-26 | 11-10 |
| Lapow, Gary | Mother Goose Bounce, The | K | 247 | 8-36 |
| Larsen, Libby | Songs from Letters "So Like Your Father" (excerpt) | 7 | C-21 | 6-23 |
| Lebo M/Tongeren/Rifkin | It's Time | 6 | 319 | 16-9 |
| Lecuona, Ernesto | Malagueña (excerpt) | 5 | 154 | 8-1 |
| Legg, Adrian | Carolina Sunday Waltz (excerpt) | 7 | F-9 | 10-27 |
| Leiber/Stoller | Yakety Yak | 5 | 204 | 10-16 |
| Lennon/McCartney | Penny Lane | 6 | 257 | 13-17 |
| Leontovych, Mykola | Carol of the Bells (excerpt) | 8 | G-10 | 11-23 |
| Lhamo, Yungchen | Gi pai pa yul chola (excerpt) | 8 | B-40 | 4-7 |
| Lins, Ivan | Common Ground (excerpt) | 3 | 379 | 13-15 |
| Liszt, Franz | Hungarian Rhapsody No. 2 in C- sharp Minor No. S.244 (excerpt) | 7 | E-17 | 10-2 |
| Liszt, Franz | Transcendental Etude No. 3 in G-sharp Minor "La Campanella" (excerpt) | 7 | C-23 | 7-3 |
| Livgren, Kerry | Carry On Wayward Son (excerpt) | 7 | B-20 | 3-5 |
| Lockhart, Keith; Arr: Hollenbaeck | Highway to Kilkenny (excerpt) | 6 | 43 | 3-7 |
| Loggins, Kenny/Pitchford, Dean | Footloose | 7 | B-11 | 2-16 |

| Composer | Title | Gr. | Pg. | CD Track |
|---|---|---|---|---|
| Lopez, Wilson | Camino de piedra | 5 | 152 | 7-34 |
| Louiselle, Bryan | ABACA Dabble | 4 | 184 | 8-17 |
| Louiselle, Bryan | Disco Worm | 2 | 312 | 11-21 |
| Louiselle, Bryan | Mad, Sad, Glad... A Suite in Three Mood-ments | K | 248 | 8-37 |
| Love/Wilson | Surfin' Safari | 6 | 261 | 13-23 |
| Lu Zaiyi/Xu Caoming | Bumper Harvest Celebration | 4 | 337 | 14-19 |
| Lyons, Austin | Jump for Joy (excerpt) | 7 | D-20 | 9-4 |
| M, Lebo | Welcome to Our World | 6 | 272 | 14-9 |
| Ma Shui-Long | Taiwan Suite "Lantern Festival" | 3 | 104 | 4-8 |
| Mack, Geoff | I've Been Everywhere | 6 | 224 | 11-37 |
| Mahler, Gustav | Symphony No. 1, Movement 3 (excerpt) | 4 | 237 | 10-8 |
| Mancini, Henry | Baby Elephant Walk | 2 | 163 | 6-19 |
| Mann, Barry/Weil, Cynthia | Make Your Own Kind of Music | 8 | G-30 | 12-12 |
| Mann, Micky | X-Beats (excerpt) | 7 | B-5 | 2-4 |
| Mapfumo, Thomas | Shumba (Lion) (excerpt) | 8 | B-12 | 2-33 |
| Marenzio, Luca | Ombrose e care selve | 8 | C-5 | 4-32 |
| Mark/Chapin | Shoveling | 1 | 423 | 13-34 |
| Marley, Ziggy | I Get Out | 8 | F-6 | 10-15 |
| Marley, Ziggy | Rainbow in the Sky | 7 | B-35 | 4-20 |
| Marley, Ziggy | Reggae Is Now | 6 | 143 | 8-7 |
| Marquez, Juanito | Ayer (Yesterday) | 6 | 266 | 14-1 |
| Marsalis, Branford | B. B.'s Blues (excerpt) | 4 | 70 | 4-1 |
| Marsalis, Wynton | Knozz-Moe-King (excerpt) | 4 | 75 | 4-14 |
| Martin/Lundin/Carlsson | That's the Way It Is (excerpt) | 7 | B-23 | 3-8 |
| McCutcheon/Kahn | Stick Together | 2 | 231 | 8-18 |
| McFerrin, Bobby | Circlesong 7 | 4 | 80 | 4-22 |
| McFerrin, Bobby | Circlesong Five (excerpt) | 1 | 239 | 7-34 |
| Mcgina, Sophie | Vulani ringi ring | 1 | 139 | 4-39 |
| McGuinn/Gerst | It Won't Be Wrong | 7 | F-17 | 11-3 |
| McNabb, Michael | Mars Suite "Orbital View," Movement 1 | 4 | 199 | 8-44 |
| McTee, Cindy | California Counterpoint: The Twittering Machine (excerpt) | 8 | C-47 | 8-4 |
| McTee, Cindy | Soundings "Fanfare" | 8 | C-47 | 8-5 |
| Medley/Russell | Twist and Shout | 4 | 238 | 10-9 |
| Melbourne, Hirini | Tihore Mai (excerpt) | 8 | B-12 | 2-35 |
| Mellencamp/Green/Horner | Yours Forever (from The Perfect Storm) | 6 | 344 | 17-13 |
| Mendelssohn, Felix | Spinning Song | K | 165 | 6-10 |
| Mendelssohn, Felix | Violin Concerto in E Minor, Movement 1 (excerpt) | 8 | C-18 | 5-21 |
| Mendelssohn-Hensel, Fanny | Das Jahr "Mai" | 8 | C-18 | 5-20 |
| Menotti, Gian Carlo | Amahl and the Night Visitors "This Is My Box" | 1 | 433 | 14-5 |
| Mensah, Sowah | Ekombi (excerpt) | 8 | B-31 | 3-25 |
| Mensah, Sowah | Kpanlogo for 2 (excerpt) | 6 | 296 | 15-6 |
| Mensah, Sowah | Obokete (excerpt) | 6 | 291 | 14-21 |
| Messager, Andre | Solo de concours (excerpt) | 8 | A-19 | 1-14 |
| Metheny, Pat | April Joy | 8 | A-18 | 1-13 |
| Metheny/Mays | Take Me There | 7 | F-26 | 11-11 |
| Mier, Nicandro | Mi humilde corazon | 7 | B-32 | 4-16 |
| Milhaud, Darius | Scaramouche "Brasiliera" | 8 | C-29 | 6-23 |
| Milne/Simpson | More It Snows, The | K | 259 | 9-8 |
| Mitchell, Joni | Both Sides Now | 5 | 385 | 18-1 |
| Moana and the Moahunters | Tahi (excerpt) | 8 | B-14 | 2-45 |
| Molloy/Arr: McNamara | Kerry Dance, The | 5 | 28 | 2-15 |
| Montoya, Ramón | La Rosa | K | 134 | 5-15 |
| Moore, Carman | Mass for the 21st Century "Alleluia" (excerpt) | 3 | 163 | 5-38 |
| Moore/Ford/Blow/Simmons/Smith | Breaks, The | 7 | B-12 | 2-17 |
| Morley, Thomas | Sing We and Chant It (excerpt) | 8 | C-5 | 4-34 |
| Moross, Jerome | Big Country, The | 2 | 236 | 8-23 |
| Morrison, P. | Faerie Stories (excerpt) | 8 | B-5 | 2-7 |
| Morrison, Van | I Shall Sing | 8 | I-41 | 14-15 |
| Mouquett/Sanchez | Cafe Europa | 7 | B-43 | 5-12 |
| Moutaftshiev, S. | Ghel moma (excerpt) | 4 | 31 | 2-1 |
| Mozart, Leopold | Musical Sleigh Ride, A "Divertimento in F" | 5 | 455 | 19-21 |

Listening Index

| Composer | Title | Gr. | Pg. | CD Track |
|---|---|---|---|---|
| Mozart, Leopold | Toy Symphony, Movement 4 | 1 | 111 | 3-49 |
| Mozart, Wolfgang Amadeus | 12 Variations in C "Ah, vous dirai-je, Maman" (excerpt) | 3 | 19 | 1-30 |
| Mozart, Wolfgang Amadeus | Concerto for Flute and Harp in C Major, Movement 2 (excerpt) | 8 | C-10 | 5-9 |
| Mozart, Wolfgang Amadeus | Concerto for French Horn in E-flat Major No. 4, Movement 3 | 8 | C-11 | 5-10 |
| Mozart, Wolfgang Amadeus | Concerto in D Major for Flute and Orchestra "Allegro," III | K | 123 | 4-38 |
| Mozart, Wolfgang Amadeus | Concerto in E-flat for Horn and Orchestra "Rondo," Movement 3 (excerpt) | 4 | 71 | 4-8 |
| Mozart, Wolfgang Amadeus | Concerto No. 1 for Horn and Orchestra "Rondo (Allegro)" | 5 | 145 | 7-17 |
| Mozart, Wolfgang Amadeus | Die Zauberflöte (The Magic Flute) "Pa-pa-pa-pa-pa-pa-pagena" | 8 | C-13 | 5-13 |
| Mozart, Wolfgang Amadeus | Don Giovanni (Give Me Your Hand) "Lá ci darem la mano" | 8 | C-13 | 5-12 |
| Mozart, Wolfgang Amadeus | Eine kleine Nachtmusik (A Little Night Music) (excerpt) | 4 | 41 | 2-21 |
| Mozart, Wolfgang Amadeus | Eine kleine Nachtmusik "Minuet" | 4 | 111 | 5-30 |
| Mozart, Wolfgang Amadeus | Magic Flute, The "Der Hölle Rache (The Revenge Aria)" | K | 49 | 2-25 |
| Mozart, Wolfgang Amadeus | Magic Flute, The "In diesen heil'gen Hallen (In These Bright Halls)" | K | 49 | 2-26 |
| Mozart, Wolfgang Amadeus | Magic Flute, The "Queen of the Night Aria" (excerpt) | 7 | C-31 | 7-13 |
| Mozart, Wolfgang Amadeus | Sonata No. 11 "Turkish Rondo" | K | 165 | 6-9 |
| Mozart, Wolfgang Amadeus | Symphony No. 40 in G Minor "Molto allegro," Movement 1 (excerpt) | 8 | B-30 | 3-18 |
| Mozart, Wolfgang Amadeus | Symphony No. 40 in G Minor, Movement 1 | 8 | C-12 | 5-11 |
| Mtukudzi, Oliver | Mai varamba | 8 | B-39 | 4-4 |
| Mujuru/Maraire | Katura (excerpt) | 7 | D-27 | 9-11 |
| Muldaur, Geoff | Jug Band Music | 6 | 361 | 18-9 |
| Murrah/Anders | Ozark Mountain Jubilee | 4 | 86 | 4-31 |
| Murray, Margaret | Two Dances for Three Xylophones "Hornpipe and Jig" (excerpt) | 8 | D-17 | 8-22 |
| Mussorgsky, Modest | Pictures at an Exhibition "Ballet of the Unhatched Chicks" | K | 167 | 6-17 |
| Mussorgsky, Modest | Pictures at an Exhibition "The Great Gate of Kiev" | 6 | 154 | 8-27 |
| Mussorgsky, Modest | Pictures at an Exhibition "The Great Gate of Kiev (piano)" (excerpt) | 8 | A-12 | 1-5 |
| Mussorgsky, Modest | Pictures at an Exhibition "The Hut of Baba Yaga" (excerpt) | 4 | 103 | 5-16 |
| Mussorgsky, Modest; Arr: Kodály | Háry János Suite "Intermezzo," Movement 5 (excerpt) | 7 | C-34 | 7-16 |
| Mussorgsky, Modest; Arr: Ravel | Pictures at an Exhibition "The Great Gate of Kiev (orchestra)" (excerpt) | 8 | A-12 | 1-6 |
| Mussorgsky, Modest; Arr: Tomita | Pictures at an Exhibition "The Great Gate of Kiev (synthesizer)" (excerpt) | 8 | A-14 | 1-7 |
| Musze/Matthewman/David | Lifetime | 7 | B-39 | 5-5 |
| N'Dour/Faye | Same, The (excerpt) | 6 | 268 | 14-3 |
| Naito, Tetsuro | Nanafushi | 7 | D-16 | 9-1 |
| Nakai, R. Carlos | Daybreak Vision | 5 | 398 | 18-11 |
| Nelson, Lord | Love You Forever (excerpt) | 8 | B-23 | 3-8 |
| Nelson, Ron | Rocky Point Holiday | 6 | 331 | 16-19 |
| Nelson/Nelson/Tanner | (Can't Live Without Your) Love and Affection | 7 | B-23 | 3-7 |
| Nelson/Rollins | Frosty, the Snowman | 2 | 391 | 14-33 |
| Netsky, Hankus | Slow Hora/Freylekhs (excerpt) | 8 | B-25 | 3-11 |
| Neville Brothers, The | Sister Rosa (excerpt) | 3 | 411 | 15-3 |
| Nichols, Tim/Sanders, Mark T. | Heads Carolina, Tails California | 7 | B-25 | 3-10 |
| Nova Menco | Lorca (excerpt) | 1 | 49 | 2-22 |
| O'Carolan, Turlough | Planxty Madame Maxwell | K | 134 | 5-16 |
| Obey, Ebenezer | Awa ewe iwoyi (excerpt) | 8 | D-9 | 8-16 |
| Olatunji, Babatunde | Ajaja (excerpt) | 8 | B-3 | 2-1 |
| Olatunji, Babatunde | Oya "Primitive Fire" | 5 | 67 | 4-10 |
| Olatunji, Babatunde | Primitive Fire "Oya" | 2 | 69 | 3-8 |
| Oliver, King | Dippermouth Blues | 7 | B-14 | 2-21 |
| Omar, Ustad Mohammed /Hussein, Zakir | Tabla solo (excerpt) | 8 | B-32 | 3-27 |
| Orff, Carl | Carmina Burana "Chramer, gip die Varwe mir" | K | 63 | 2-49 |
| Orff, Carl | Rundadinella (performance piece) | 8 | I-60 | 15-15 |
| Orff/Keetman | Ding, Dong, Diggidiggidong | 3 | 15 | 1-22 |
| Ostrow, Leib | Choo Choo Boogaloo (excerpt) | 1 | 127 | 4-18 |
| Owen, Randy | Tennessee River | 5 | 349 | 16-8 |
| Owens, Tex | Cattle Call | 5 | 347 | 16-5 |
| Pachecho/Pinheiro | Malê Debalê (excerpt) | 8 | B-16 | 2-50 |
| Paffrath, Marytha | Yemaya | 8 | G-24 | 12-6 |
| Paganini, Nicolló | Caprice No. 1 in E Major (excerpt) | 7 | C-22 | 7-1 |
| Paich, David/Porcaro, Jeff | Africa | 7 | B-6 | 2-5 |
| Palmieri, Eddie | Billie | 8 | B-23 | 3-9 |
| Palmieri, Eddie | Sube (excerpt) | 7 | B-31 | 4-15 |

Listening Index

| Composer | Title | Gr. | Pg. | CD Track |
|---|---|---|---|---|
| Pamyua | Cauyaqa Nauwa? (Where's My Drum?) | 8 | D-20 | 8-30 |
| Paparelli/Gillespie | Night in Tunisia, A (excerpt) | 4 | 35 | 2-14 |
| Papillion | Bon jour! | 1 | 3b | 1-3 |
| Papoulis, Jim | Give Us Hope | 6 | 337 | 17-8 |
| Parker, Charlie | Now's the Time | 5 | 451 | 19-18 |
| Parris, Fred | In the Still of the Night | 4 | 47 | 2-29 |
| Partch, Harry | Daphne of the Dunes (excerpt) | 8 | D-29 | 9-5 |
| Partichela, Alfonso A. | Jarabe tapatio | 7 | I-7 | 13-10 |
| Paxton, Tom | Last Thing on My Mind, The | 7 | F-7 | 10-24 |
| Paxton, Tom | Marvelous Toy, The | 1 | 383 | 12-13 |
| Pearsall, Edward | Illusions | 6 | 347 | 17-18 |
| Pearsall, Edward | Jungle Beat | 6 | 347 | 17-17 |
| Pearsall, Edward | One Fine Day | 6 | 347 | 17-16 |
| Pearsall, Edward | Sha Sha Sha (performance piece) | 6 | 328 | 16-18 |
| Pena, Paul | Gonna Move | 7 | F-12 | 10-29 |
| Penniman/Lubin/La Bostrie | Tutti Frutti | 7 | B-29 | 4-10 |
| Peoples, Tommy | Tommy Peoples (excerpt) | 8 | B-20 | 3-2 |
| Pestana/do Pandeiro | Talaque talaque o romance da María | 8 | D-24 | 9-2 |
| Pickering/Heard | Search for the Hero (excerpt) | 7 | G-5 | 11-22 |
| Pine Top Smith | Boogie-Woogie | 6 | 93 | 6-3 |
| Pine Top Smith | Boogie-Woogie (excerpt) | 1 | 256 | 8-14 |
| Pinkham, Daniel | Song for Bells, A (excerpt) | 1 | 427 | 13-43 |
| Polashek, Timothy | Miniature Odyssey, A | 8 | E-29 | 10-4 |
| Polashek, Timothy | Onomatapoeia Study No. 2 | 7 | E-31 | 10-12 |
| Posse, King | Retounen (excerpt) | 8 | B-17 | 2-51 |
| Poulenc, Francis | Sextet for Winds and Piano, Movement 1 (excerpt) | 8 | C-29 | 6-22 |
| Praetorius, Michael | Dances from Terpsichore "Bransle de la Torche" | 3 | 63 | 2-39 |
| Praetorius, Michael | Lo, How a Rose E'er Blooming (excerpt) | 6 | 210 | 11-18 |
| Praetorius, Michael | Viva la musica | 5 | 95 | 5-18 |
| Prokofiev, Sergei | Lieutenant Kijé "Troika" | 6 | 457 | 21-21 |
| Prokofiev, Sergei | Love for Three Oranges "March" | K | 117 | 4-30 |
| Puccini, Giacomo | Tosca (I Live for Art) "Vissi d'arte" (excerpt) | 7 | C-31 | 7-12 |
| Puente, Tito | Loco bossa nova | 2 | 247 | 9-5 |
| Puente, Tito | Oye como va (excerpt) | 2 | 255 | 9-18 |
| Puente, Tito | Picadillo | 3 | 361 | 12-19 |
| Puente, Tito | Vaya Puente | 2 | 181 | 7-5 |
| Qiu Xia He | Drift (excerpt) | 8 | B-42 | 4-11 |
| Quintanilla/Giraldo | Contigo otra vez | 7 | B-32 | 4-17 |
| Rachmaninoff, Sergei | Prelude in G-sharp Minor No. 12 | 7 | E-4 | 9-18 |
| Rachmaninoff, Sergei | Vocalise | K | 123 | 4-37 |
| Radigan/Schlitz | I Don't Want to Feel Like That (excerpt) | 4 | 31 | 2-3 |
| Raffi | On Christmas Morning | K | 316 | 11-18 |
| Raffi/D. Pike | Everything Grows | K | 267 | 9-17 |
| Rahman, A.R./Black, Don | Bombay Dreams (excerpt) | 8 | B-35 | 3-31 |
| Rahman, A. R. /Black, Don | Wedding Qawwali (excerpt) | 8 | B-35 | 3-32 |
| Rajery | Vonjeo (excerpt) | 8 | B-12 | 2-36 |
| Ram, Buck | Great Pretender, The | 5 | 358 | 16-18 |
| Ravel, Maurice | Chansons madecasses "Nahandove" (excerpt) | 4 | 32 | 2-5 |
| Ravel, Maurice | L'Enfant et les sortiléges "Love for Two Cats" | K | 101 | 4-1 |
| Ravel, Maurice | Le tombeau de Couperin "Prelude" (orchestral version) | 8 | C-28 | 6-21 |
| Ravel, Maurice | Le tombeau de Couperin "Prelude" (piano version) | 8 | C-28 | 6-20 |
| Reagon, Bernice Johnson | What Kind of Land? (excerpt) | 4 | 327 | 14-7 |
| Red, Buryl | Sounds of the Circus | K | 241 | 8-25 |
| Red Hot Chili Peppers | Yertle the Turtle | 2 | 368 | 13-27 |
| Reed/Doucet; Arr: Doucet | Le jig Français | K | 64 | 2-52 |
| Rene/Rene/Johnson | Jelly Roll, The | 7 | B-36 | 5-1 |
| Respighi, Ottorino | Fontane di Roma (Fountains of Rome) "La fontana di Trevi al meriggio" | 2 | 93 | 3-52 |
| Respighi, Ottorino | La boutique fantasque "Can Can" | 1 | 147 | 4-52 |
| Revueltas, Silvestre | Janitzio (excerpt) | 5 | 91 | 5-6 |
| Revueltas, Silvestre | Sensemaya (excerpt) | 8 | C-15 | 5-17 |

**Listening Index: Listening Selections by Composer** 65

Listening Index

| Composer | Title | Gr. | Pg. | CD Track |
|---|---|---|---|---|
| Rice, Damien | Blower's Daughter, The (excerpt) | 8 | B-13 | 2-38 |
| Rice/John | Circle of Life, The (from The Lion King) | 6 | 316 | 16-6 |
| Richards, Jay | Storm, The (excerpt) | 1 | 55 | 2-32 |
| Rimsky-Korsakav, Nikolai | Flight of the Bumblebee (from Tsar Sultan) | K | 76 | 3-10 |
| Rimsky-Korsakov, Nikolai | Flight of the Bumblebee (from Tsar Sultan) | 1 | 385 | 12-16 |
| Rimsky-Korsakov, Nikolai | Flight of the Bumblebee | 3 | 188 | 6-37 |
| Ritchie, Jean | Lazy John | 4 | 11 | 1-14 |
| Rizo and Morgan | (Chi Chi Chi) Cha Cha Cha (excerpt) | 6 | 334 | 17-3 |
| Robb, Paul | Think (excerpt) | 6 | 367 | 18-20 |
| Robinson/Crosby/Wonder | Tears of a Clown | 7 | B-39 | 5-4 |
| Robles/Milchberg/Simon; Arr: DJ Sammy | El cóndor pasa (excerpt) | 7 | A-2 | 1-2 |
| Rodgers, Jimmie | Waitin' for a Train | 7 | B-24 | 3-9 |
| Rodgers/Hammerstein | Do-Re-Mi (from The Sound of Music) | 5 | 38 | 2-31 |
| Rodgers/Hammerstein | In My Own Little Corner (from Cinderella) Spanish | 3 | 9 | 1-5 |
| Rodrigo, Joaquín | Concierto de Aranjuez "Allegro con spirito," Movement 1 (excerpt) | 6 | 199 | 10-41 |
| Rodrigo, Joaquín | Concierto Madrigal for Two Guitars and Orchestra "Caccía a la española" (excerpt) | 5 | 176 | 9-1 |
| Rodrigo, Joaquín | Concierto Madrigal for Two Guitars and Orchestra "Fanfarre" | 2 | 150 | 5-49 |
| Rosauro, Ney | Concerto for Marimba and String Orchestra "Saudação" | 2 | 119 | 4-38 |
| Rose, Fred | Blue Eyes Crying in the Rain | 7 | B-28 | 4-9 |
| Rossini, Gioachino | Quartetto buffo di gatti "Comic Quartet for Cats" | 1 | 131 | 4-27 |
| Rouse, Ervin T. | Orange Blossom Special | 1 | 47 | 2-17 |
| Rouse, Ervin T. | Orange Blossom Special | 5 | 268 | 12-26 |
| Rumble, Nancy | Woodlands | K | 254 | 9-3 |
| Russell, Brenda | "Body" Song, The | 6 | 438 | 21-1 |
| Ryan/Sackman/Thomas | One Fine Mama (excerpt) | 8 | B-41 | 4-8 |
| Saint-Saëns, Camille | Carnival of the Animals "Aquarium" | 5 | 376 | 17-14 |
| Saint-Saëns, Camille | Carnival of the Animals "Aviary" (excerpt) | 4 | 70 | 4-5 |
| Saint-Saëns, Camille | Carnival of the Animals "Fossils" (excerpt) | 1 | 237 | 7-31 |
| Saint-Saëns, Camille | Carnival of the Animals "Fossils" (excerpt) | 4 | 220 | 9-20 |
| Saint-Saëns, Camille | Carnival of the Animals "The Aviary" | K | 45 | 2-20 |
| Saint-Saëns, Camille | Carnival of the Animals "The Elephant" | K | 45 | 2-21 |
| Saint-Saëns, Camille | Carnival of the Animals "The Royal March of the Lion" (excerpt) | 3 | 357 | 12-14 |
| Saint-Saëns, Camille | Danse macabre | 5 | 457 | 19-24 |
| Saint-Saëns, Camille | Havanaise for Violin and Orchestra (excerpt) | 5 | 217 | 10-34 |
| Saint-Saëns, Camille | Sonata for Clarinet and Piano "Allegro animato," Movement 2 | 7 | C-12 | 6-9 |
| Salgado, Victor M. | Amores hallarás | 5 | 153 | 7-35 |
| Salgado, Victor M. | Baila caporal (excerpt) | 8 | B-22 | 3-6 |
| Saliba, Konnie | Evening Chaconne (performance piece) | 6 | 202 | 11-3 |
| Salinas, Horatio; Arr: Tennant | Fiesta "Tarantella" | K | 134 | 5-17 |
| Samudio, Domingo | Wooly Bully | 3 | 372 | 13-4 |
| Sanger, George Alistair | Themes (from The 7th Guest) (excerpt) | 8 | A-3 | 1-1 |
| Santana, Carlos/Patillo, Jackie | Let the Children Play | 7 | B-30 | 4-12 |
| Santos, Ray | Guaguancó pá las tumbadoras (excerpt) | 7 | D-9 | 8-23 |
| Saqi | Saqian da dhol (excerpt) | 8 | B-22 | 3-5 |
| Satie, Erik | Gymnopedie No. 1 | K | 175 | 6-24 |
| Scheidt, Samuel | Galliard battaglia | 6 | 362 | 18-11 |
| Scheidt, Samuel | Galliard Battaglia (excerpt) | 8 | C-14 | 5-15 |
| Schickele, Peter | New Horizons in Music Appreciation-Beethoven's Fifth Symphony, Movement 1 (excerpt) | 6 | 98 | 6-15 |
| Schubert, Franz | Die Forelle (The Trout) (excerpt) | 7 | C-20 | 6-20 |
| Schubert, Franz | Erlkönig (The Erlking) (excerpt) | K | 165 | 6-11 |
| Schubert, Franz | Marche Militaire No. 1 | 6 | 17 | 1-26 |
| Schubert, Franz | Piano Trio No. 2 in E-flat Major "Scherzo" (excerpt) | 4 | 192 | 8-31 |
| Schubert, Franz | Quintet for Piano and Strings in A Major ("Trout"), Movement 3, Scherzo (excerpt) | 1 | 179 | 5-46 |
| Schubert, Franz; Arr: Mohler | Bee, The (L'Abeille) (excerpt) | 4 | 70 | 4-2 |
| Schuman, William | New England Triptych "Chester" | 6 | 83 | 5-25 |
| Schumann, Clara | Piano Trio in G Minor "Allegro," Movement 1 (excerpt) | 8 | C-19 | 5-22 |
| Schumann, Robert | 5 Stücke im Volkston No. 1 "Mit Humor" | 3 | 39 | 2-5 |
| Schumann, Robert | Carnaval "Valse Noble" Un poco maestoso | 3 | 202 | 7-11 |
| Schumann, Robert | Quintet for Piano and Strings in E-flat Major, Movement 1 (excerpt) | 8 | C-19 | 5-23 |

Listening Index

| Composer | Title | Gr. | Pg. | CD Track |
|---|---|---|---|---|
| Schumann, Robert | Scenes from Childhood (Kinderszenen) "Reverie (Träumerei)" (excerpt) | 1 | 6 | 1-5 |
| Schumann, Robert | Widmung No. 1 (Dedication) | 7 | C-20 | 6-21 |
| Schumann, Robert | Wild Horseman, The | 1 | 159 | 5-12 |
| Schumann, Robert | Wilder Reiter "The Wild Rider" | 8 | D-17 | 8-23 |
| Seeger, Pete | If I Had a Hammer | 3 | 241 | 8-8 |
| Seeger, Pete | Where Have All the Flowers Gone? | 5 | 287 | 13-15 |
| Seeger, Ruth Crawford | Suite for Wind Quintet, Movement 1 (excerpt) | 8 | C-34 | 7-2 |
| Segovia, Andrés | Catalana "Andante" | K | 134 | 5-14 |
| Shabalala, Joseph | Be Still, My Child (excerpt) | 1 | 39 | 2-4 |
| Shabalala, Joseph | Rain, Rain, Beautiful Rain (excerpt) | 4 | 32 | 2-6 |
| Shakira/Mitchell/Noriega | Te dejo Madrid | 7 | B-30 | 4-13 |
| Shamrock, Mary | Orfferondo (performance piece) | 4 | 194 | 8-35 |
| Shankar, Ravi | Bairagi (excerpt) | 8 | A-19 | 1-16 |
| Shankar, Ravi | Charukeshi (excerpt) | 4 | 311 | 13-19 |
| Sharpe, Len "Boogsie" | Hard Times (excerpt) | 1 | 196 | 6-29 |
| Shenandoah, Joanne | Kunolounkwa (Shenandoah) | K | 110 | 4-20 |
| Shenandoah, Joanne | Light up the World | 2 | 197 | 7-30 |
| Sheng, Bright | Seven Tunes Heard in China "Guessing Song" | 7 | C-45 | 8-8 |
| Shocked, Michele | Can't Take My Joy (excerpt) | 7 | B-40 | 5-7 |
| Shocked, Michele | Joy | 7 | B-40 | 5-6 |
| Sibelius, Jean | Canon for Violin and Cello | 6 | 126 | 7-20 |
| Sibelius, Jean | Finlandia (excerpt) | 6 | 78 | 5-3 |
| Sigman/Gray | Pennsylvania 6-5000 | 5 | 342 | 16-1 |
| Singer/Medora/White | At the Hop | 4 | 166 | 7-26 |
| Singers, Eaglebear/Sherman, Alexie | John Wayne's Teeth (excerpt) | 8 | B-37 | 3-36 |
| Sixteenth Century Carol from Spain | Ríu ríu chíu | 5 | 439 | 19-12 |
| Skipper, Buddy | Down in the Valley | 7 | A-23 | 1-15 |
| Slomovits, Sandor | Puppy Love | K | 262 | 9-12 |
| Slomovitz, Sandor | Loose Tooth Blues | 1 | 285 | 9-14 |
| Smetana, Bedrich | Ma Vlast (My Fatherland) "The Moldau" | 7 | C-33 | 7-14 |
| Smith, Will | Black Suits Comin' (Nod Ya Head) (excerpt) | 7 | A-5 | 1-6 |
| Smith/Kelley/Robinson/Rambert/Iverson/Ralf | Block Party (excerpt) | 7 | B-13 | 2-19 |
| Smith/Picard | On Fire Suite (excerpt) | 8 | B-36 | 3-33 |
| Solomon/Peretti/Creatore/Weiss | Lion Sleeps Tonight, The (Mbube) | 8 | E-8 | 9-13 |
| Sorozábal, Pablo | Don Manolito-Ensalada madrileña "Viva Madrid, que sí, que sí..." | 7 | G-14 | 12-4 |
| Sousa, John Philip | Guide Right | 1 | 447 | 14-29 |
| Sousa, John Philip | On Parade | K | 327 | 11-37 |
| Sousa, John Philip | Semper Fidelis | K | 327 | 11-36 |
| Sousa, John Philip | Stars and Stripes Forever, The | 1 | 167 | 5-28 |
| Sousa, John Philip | Stars and Stripes Forever, The | 4 | 159 | 7-17 |
| Sousa, John Philip | Thunderer, The | 5 | 79 | 4-24 |
| Sousa, John Philip | Washington Post, The (march) | 1 | 175 | 5-36 |
| Sousa, John Philip | Washington Post, The (march) | 8 | C-40 | 7-11 |
| Soweto String Quartet | Zulu Lullaby | K | 158 | 5-48 |
| Springer, Steven | Shashee | K | 109 | 4-15 |
| Steiner/Hawes | M.T.A. (excerpt) | 5 | 403 | 18-19 |
| Stewart, Sylvester | Everyday People | 5 | 389 | 18-4 |
| Still, William Grant | Ennanga, Movement III (excerpt) | 3 | 127 | 4-34 |
| Stone, Sly | Everyday People | 7 | G-16 | 12-10 |
| Stranger/Sheldon | Limbo Rock | 3 | 298 | 10-27 |
| Strauss, Johann | Thunder and Lightning Polka | 4 | 213 | 9-5 |
| Strauss Jr., Johann | Blue Danube, The (excerpt) | 6 | 192 | 10-29 |
| Stravinsky, Igor | Firebird, The "Finale" | 8 | C-30 | 6-24 |
| Stravinsky, Igor | Firebird, The "Infernal Dance" | 5 | 173 | 8-28 |
| Stravinsky, Igor | Game of the Mechanical Nightingale "The Nightingale" (excerpt) | 8 | C-33 | 6-28 |
| Stravinsky, Igor | Le Sacre de Printemps (The Rite of Spring) "Dance of the Youths and Maidens" (excerpt) | 8 | C-30 | 6-25 |
| Stravinsky, Igor | Pulcinella Suite "Minuetto" (excerpt) | 8 | C-15 | 5-16 |
| Stravinsky, Igor | Pulcinella Suite "Serenata" (excerpt) | 4 | 70 | 4-3 |
| Stravinsky, Igor | Pulcinella Suite "Serenata" (excerpt) | 8 | C-32 | 6-26 |
| Stravinsky, Igor | Pulcinella Suite "Vivo (Duetto)" (excerpt) | 4 | 71 | 4-9 |

Listening Index

| Composer | Title | Gr. | Pg. | CD Track |
|---|---|---|---|---|
| Stravinsky, Igor | Soldier's Tale, The "Waltz" | K | 237 | 8-22 |
| Stravinsky, Igor | Song of the Nightingale "The Nightingale" (excerpt) | 8 | C-32 | 6-27 |
| Strayhorn, Billy | Take the "A" Train | 8 | C-42 | 7-12 |
| Subotnick, Morton | Silver Apples of the Moon (excerpt) | 1 | 12 | 1-18 |
| Subotnick, Morton | Wild Bull (excerpt) | 6 | 366 | 18-19 |
| Summer, Mark | Julie-O | 5 | 311 | 14-20 |
| Susato, Tylman | Den III. Ende VI. Ronde & Quatre Branles | 7 | C-7 | 5-33 |
| Susato, Tylman | Den III. Ende VI. Ronde & Quatre Branles | 8 | C-7 | 5-3 |
| Susato, Tylman | Six Dances from La Danserie "La Mourisque" | 1 | 407b | 13-7 |
| Swoboda, Deanna | Brass Rap | 3 | 189 | 6-40 |
| Tansman, Alexander | Sonatina for Bassoon and Piano "Allegro con moto," Movement 1 | 7 | C-13 | 6-10 |
| Taylor, Billy | I Wish I Knew How It Would Feel to Be Free (excerpt) | 6 | 470 | 22-7 |
| Taylor, James | Shed a Little Light | 8 | E-17 | 9-19 |
| Taylor, James | Shed a Little Light (excerpt) | 3 | 409 | 14-33 |
| Tchaikovsky, Piotr Ilyich | 1812 Overture (excerpt) | 4 | 293 | 12-18 |
| Tchaikovsky, Piotr Ilyich | Nutcracker Suite, The "Arabian Dance" (excerpt) | 7 | C-26 | 7-8 |
| Tchaikovsky, Piotr Ilyich | Nutcracker Suite, The "Chinese Dance" | K | 105 | 4-7 |
| Tchaikovsky, Piotr Ilyich | Nutcracker Suite, The "Chinese Dance" (excerpt) | 7 | C-26 | 7-9 |
| Tchaikovsky, Piotr Ilyich | Nutcracker Suite, The "Trepak" | 3 | 280 | 9-39 |
| Tchaikovsky, Piotr Ilyich | Nutcracker Suite, The "Trepak" | 6 | 207 | 11-16 |
| Tchaikovsky, Piotr Ilyich | Nutcracker Suite, The "Waltz of the Flowers" | 6 | 325 | 16-13 |
| Tchaikovsky, Piotr Ilyich | Serenade for Strings in C "Finale" (excerpt) | 6 | 363 | 18-13 |
| Tchaikovsky, Piotr Ilyich | Symphony No. 4, Movement 4 (excerpt) | 4 | 295 | 12-23 |
| Tchaikovsky, Piotr Ilyich | Symphony No. 4 in F Minor, Movement 4, Finale: Allegro con fuoco (excerpt) | 1 | 175 | 5-35 |
| Teague, Liam | Raindrops (excerpt) | 7 | D-23 | 9-6 |
| Telemann, Georg Philipp | Sonata in F Minor for Bassoon "Vivace" (excerpt) | 4 | 70 | 4-4 |
| Thomas, Judith | Little Red Hen, The (story) | 1 | 255 | 8-12 |
| Thompson, Randall | Frostiana (from Stopping by Woods on a Snowy Evening) | 6 | 40 | 2-37 |
| Thompson, Richard | Roll Over Vaughan Williams | 8 | F-22 | 11-1 |
| Thomson, Virgil | Acadian Songs "Walking Song" | 4 | 347 | 15-9 |
| Thomson, Virgil | Plow that Broke the Plains, The "Cattle" | 3 | 177 | 6-19 |
| Thomson, Virgil | River Suite, The "Finale" | 5 | 121 | 6-13 |
| Tingstad/Rumbel | Children's Garden, The | K | 267 | 9-18 |
| Tingstad/Rumbel | Shadow Dancer | K | 253 | 8-42 |
| Tizol, Juan | Caravan (excerpt) | 7 | B-31 | 4-14 |
| Tower, Joan | Wings (excerpt) | 7 | C-45 | 8-7 |
| Traditional | Wioste Olowan Inkpa Ta-Ya | 3 | 255 | 8-31 |
| | Changed My Name; Adapted/Arr: Twine | 6 | 338 | 17-9 |
| African | Adzogbo-Ovitse (excerpt) | 8 | D-13 | 8-17 |
| | Banuwa (excerpt) | 8 | B-4 | 2-5 |
| | Hindewhu (whistle) solo (excerpt) | 6 | 269 | 14-4 |
| | Omo (excerpt) | 1 | 443 | 14-26 |
| | Samanfo, begye nsa nom | 8 | D-6 | 8-15 |
| | Wildlife (excerpt) | 1 | 345 | 11-3 |
| African American | Battle of Jericho, The | 6 | 234 | 12-8 |
| | Ev'ry Time I Feel the Spirit | 3 | 248 | 8-16 |
| | Ev'rybody Ought to Know | 1 | 435 | 14-8 |
| | Get on Board | K | 89 | 3-35 |
| | Glory, Glory, Hallelujah | 8 | B-14 | 2-43 |
| | Go Down, Moses | 7 | G-10 | 11-25 |
| | Go, Tell It on the Mountain | 3 | 393 | 14-3 |
| | He's Got the Whole World in His Hands (excerpt) | 3 | 249 | 8-17 |
| | Jonah | 6 | 235 | 12-10 |
| | Juba | K | 13 | 1-15 |
| | Little David, Play on Your Harp | 4 | 395 | 17-6 |
| | Little Red Caboose | K | 229 | 8-10 |
| | My Father's House (Gospel Style) | 2 | 25 | 1-31 |
| | Nobody Knows the Trouble I've Seen (excerpt) | 3 | 249 | 8-18 |
| | Oh, Freedom and Come and Go with Me | 5 | 394 | 18-9 |
| | Pay Me My Money Down (excerpt) | 4 | 39 | 2-20 |

| Composer | Title | Gr. | Pg. | CD Track |
|---|---|---|---|---|
| | Rise Up, Shepherd, and Follow | 5 | 470 | 20-18 |
| | Sometimes I Feel Like a Motherless Child | 5 | 193 | 9-33 |
| | Standin' in the Need of Prayer | 5 | 103 | 5-26 |
| | Swing Low, Sweet Chariot (excerpt) | 6 | 234 | 12-9 |
| | Traveling Shoes | 3 | 248 | 8-15 |
| | Way Down Yonder in the Brickyard | 2 | 51 | 2-23 |
| | We Shall Overcome | 5 | 485 | 21-14 |
| | When a Man's a Long Way from Home | 2 | 53 | 2-26 |
| | When the Saints Go Marching In | 2 | 179 | 6-43 |
| | Ev'ry Time I Feel the Spirit (excerpt); Arr: Dawson | 7 | C-40 | 8-1 |
| | This Little Light of Mine; Arr: Twine/Joubert | 2 | 241 | 8-29 |
| | Pay Me (excerpt) | 7 | F-5 | 10-21 |
| | Study War No More (excerpt) | 7 | C-40 | 8-2 |
| African | Bawa (excerpt); Arr: Mensah | 7 | D-32 | 9-15 |
| American | A-Tisket, A-Tasket | 2 | 239 | 8-26 |
| | Allons danser, Colinda | K | 219 | 7-38 |
| | Amazing Grace; Words: Newton | 5 | 259 | 12-14 |
| | Amazing Grace (excerpt); Words: Newton | 4 | 161 | 7-20 |
| | America; Words: Smith | 7 | A-22 | 1-14 |
| | Arkansas Traveler/Angeline the Baker | K | 115 | 4-27 |
| | Bonaparte's Retreat | 4 | 385 | 16-25 |
| | Candy Man, Salty Dog | K | 27 | 1-44 |
| | Cedar Swamp | 5 | 261 | 12-17 |
| | College Hornpipe | 4 | 95 | 5-1 |
| | Don't You Hear the Lambs? | 5 | 99 | 5-24 |
| | Down in the Valley; Arr: Louiselle | 7 | A-23 | 1-15 |
| | Dusty Miller | 4 | 291 | 12-13 |
| | Every Night When the Sun Goes Down (excerpt); Arr: Fricker | 8 | I-29 | 14-3 |
| | Flop-Eared Mule | 3 | 99 | 3-39 |
| | Forked Deer/Fisher's Hornpipe | 4 | 343 | 15-4 |
| | Golden Ring Around the Susan Girl | 3 | 17 | 1-25 |
| | Goldilocks and the Three Bears | K | 49 | 2-24 |
| | Goodbye, Ev'rybody "Farewell Shout" | 7 | D-2 | 8-15 |
| | Hush, Little Baby; Arr: McFerrin | K | 222 | 7-45 |
| | Hush, Little Baby; Arr: Ries | K | 222 | 7-44 |
| | I Am a Man of Constant Sorrow | 7 | F-29 | 11-16 |
| | Itsy Bitsy Spider, The | K | 187 | 6-48 |
| | Je m'endors; Arr: Doucet | K | 219 | 7-39 |
| | John Henry (excerpt) | 8 | C-34 | 7-1 |
| | Jolie Blonde | 4 | 389 | 16-28 |
| | Kyrie "Missa Luba"; Arr: Haazen | 7 | G-13 | 12-3 |
| | Le Hoogie Boogie | K | 296 | 10-21 |
| | Liberty/Chicken Reel (excerpt) | 2 | 38 | 2-1 |
| | Marines' Hymn, The | 8 | C-39 | 7-8 |
| | Old Chisholm Trail, The (excerpt); Arr: Daniels | 6 | 236 | 12-11 |
| | P'tit galop pour Mamou (excerpt); Arr: Doucet | 1 | 317 | 10-10 |
| | Ragtime Annie | 2 | 122 | 4-48 |
| | Railroad Bill | 8 | F-14 | 10-24 |
| | Reuben's Train; Arr: Watson | 1 | 335 | 10-31 |
| | Rumblin' On | 2 | 315 | 11-24 |
| | She'll Be Coming 'Round the Mountain When She Comes | 4 | 333 | 14-14 |
| | Shenandoah; Arr: Erb (River Shanty) | 2 | 62 | 2-46 |
| | Simple Gifts | 8 | A-17 | 1-9 |
| | Sun Gonna Shine | 7 | F-14 | 11-1 |
| Appalachian | Soldier's Joy | 8 | B-29 | 3-17 |
| Argentina | Viva Jujuy | 8 | B-22 | 3-6 |
| Asian | Toei khong (excerpt) | 8 | B-21 | 3-4 |
| Australian | Brolga (The Brolga Bird) (excerpt) | 6 | 271 | 14-8 |
| | Brolga One | 4 | 37 | 2-17 |
| | Gapu; Arr: Yunupingu | 8 | B-38 | 4-1 |
| Balinese | Sekar jepun (excerpt) | 1 | 196 | 6-30 |

Listening Index: Listening Selections by Composer **69**

Listening Index

| Composer | Title | Gr. | Pg. | CD Track |
|----------|-------|-----|-----|----------|
| Benin | Gahu (excerpt) | 7 | D-27 | 9-10 |
| Bora Bora | Ue ue | 8 | D-2 | 8-12 |
| Brazilian | Sai da frente | 8 | D-24 | 9-1 |
| | Bate-papo | 4 | 401 | 17-12 |
| | Capoeira na vila (excerpt) | 8 | D-25 | 9-3 |
| Calypso | Brisad del Zulia (excerpt) | 4 | 19 | 1-27 |
| Cambodian | Mea haarit | 3 | 274 | 9-25 |
| | Phleng pradall | 1 | 157 | 5-9 |
| Caribbean | A-Cling, A-Cling (excerpt) | 4 | 190 | 8-30 |
| carol | Good King Wenceslas | 4 | 431 | 18-14 |
| | Good King Wenceslas | 6 | 461 | 21-29 |
| | O Christmas Tree (excerpt) | 6 | 24 | 2-13 |
| Celtic | Alasdair mhic cholla ghasda | 8 | B-44 | 4-15 |
| | How Can I Keep from Singing? (excerpt) | 4 | 261 | 10-35 |
| Chinese | Lian xi qu (étude) | 4 | 157 | 7-14 |
| | Mido Mountain (excerpt) | 8 | B-42 | 4-9 |
| | Picking Red Chestnuts | 5 | 310 | 14-19 |
| | Winter Birds Flying over the Water (excerpt) | 1 | 91 | 3-14 |
| | Wu long (Dragon Dance) | 4 | 156 | 7-12 |
| | Wu long (Dragon Dance) | 4 | 156 | 7-13 |
| | Huagu ge "Flower Drum song" (excerpt); Arr: Han Kuo-Huang | 8 | D-27 | 9-4 |
| Cowboy Song | Colorado Trail | 5 | 277 | 13-1 |
| | Cowboys' Christmas Ball (excerpt) | 6 | 238 | 12-14 |
| Cuban | Elegguá | 8 | D-13 | 8-18 |
| | Saludo de Matanzas (excerpt) | 5 | 17 | 1-27 |
| Dominican | Mwen boyko samba | 4 | 319 | 13-37 |
| Eastern European | Klezmer Dances "Freilachs"; Arr: Chelyapov/Charnofsky | K | 314 | 11-13 |
| Ecuadorian | Llactamanta | 6 | 382 | 19-18 |
| | Peñas (excerpt); Arr: Arguedas/Arguedas | 2 | 54 | 2-31 |
| English | Humpty Dumpty | K | 23 | 1-33 |
| | Old King Cole | K | 245 | 8-31 |
| | Old King Cole | K | 245 | 8-32 |
| | Sumer Is Icumen In (excerpt) | 5 | 35 | 2-28 |
| | Cold and Frosty Morning; Arr: Junda/Mayo | 2 | 139 | 5-30 |
| | Baa, Baa, Black Sheep; Arr: Mayo/Compton | K | 102 | 4-4 |
| English Folk | Abbots Bromley Horn Dance (excerpt) | 7 | C-24 | 7-5 |
| | Farmer in the Dell | K | 233 | 8-15 |
| French | Carrament News (excerpt) | 8 | B-22 | 3-7 |
| | Frère Jacques | 3 | 113 | 4-17 |
| Gospel Song | Glory, Glory, Hallelujah (Gospel) | 6 | 54 | 3-29 |
| Grecian | Stalia, Stalia | 8 | B-21 | 3-3 |
| Guatemalan | San Miguel Jolonicapan (excerpt) | 8 | D-16 | 8-20 |
| Hebrew | Dreydl Song, The | 3 | 391 | 13-30 |
| Incan | Peshte longuita (excerpt) | 1 | 217 | 7-10 |
| Indian | Máru-bihág (excerpt) | 6 | 304 | 15-22 |
| | Rag puria kalyan-gat in tintal (excerpt) | 4 | 192 | 8-32 |
| | Sindhi-Bhairavi (excerpt) | 5 | 320 | 15-1 |
| Indonesian | Gamelan angklung (excerpt) | 6 | 384 | 19-19 |
| | Kebjar teruna (excerpt) | 6 | 385 | 19-20 |
| | Patalon | 5 | 319 | 14-36 |
| | Ujan mas (excerpt) | 2 | 105 | 4-22 |
| Inuit (adapted) | Qiugaviit | 3 | 259 | 8-35 |
| Irish | Crowley's Reel | 4 | 297 | 12-27 |
| | Crowley's/Jackson's; Arr: Ivers/Doyle | 4 | 298 | 12-28 |
| | Crowley's/Jackson's; Arr: Ivers/Doyle | 8 | B-7 | 2-12 |
| | Dúlamán | 4 | 299 | 12-29 |
| | Geese in the Bog, The (excerpt) | 8 | B-9 | 2-21 |
| | Irish Tune from County Derry; Arr: Grainger | 4 | 49 | 2-32 |
| | MacAllistrum's March-Mairseail Alasdroim | 4 | 297 | 12-26 |
| | Mill Pond, The (excerpt) | 8 | B-8 | 2-17 |
| | O'Sullivan's March | 5 | 157 | 8-6 |

| Composer | Title | Gr. | Pg. | CD Track |
|---|---|---|---|---|
| (*Traditional Irish* continued) | Roddy McCaulay | 3 | 292 | 10-15 |
| | She Is Like the Swallow | 8 | B-12 | 2-34 |
| Israeli | Tzlil Zugim | 3 | 139 | 5-5 |
| Jamaican | Day - O! (excerpt) | 5 | 21 | 1-31 |
| | John B. Sails, The | K | 11 | 1-12 |
| Japanese | Shika no Tone (excerpt) | 5 | 112 | 6-3 |
| | Yaudachi (excerpt) | 5 | 156 | 8-4 |
| Korean | Arirang (excerpt) | 2 | 137 | 5-29 |
| | Doraji (excerpt) | 4 | 175 | 7-40 |
| | Kayagum pyongch'ang-sae t'aryug (excerpt) | 3 | 137 | 4-53 |
| | Kayagum pyongch'ang-sae t'aryug (excerpt) | 8 | B-13 | 2-37 |
| Mexican | El mariachi (excerpt) | 4 | 303 | 13-6 |
| | El siquisirí | 4 | 273 | 11-16 |
| | El tilingo lingo | 2 | 176 | 6-40 |
| | Happy Mariachi Band (Mariachi alegre) | 1 | 211 | 6-47 |
| | La bamba (as performed by Ritchie Valens); Arr: Valens | 5 | 130 | 6-24 |
| | La bamba (excerpt) | 5 | 131 | 6-25 |
| | Las manañitas | K | 325 | 11-33 |
| | Little Pearls, The | K | 215 | 7-35 |
| | Los pollitos | K | 166 | 6-16 |
| | Mexican Hat Dance | K | 215 | 7-34 |
| | Los machetes; Arr: Fuentes | 8 | I-22 | 13-28 |
| Mongolian | Mongolian Long Song | 8 | B-14 | 2-44 |
| Native American | Bear Dance | 7 | C-5 | 5-30 |
| | Corn Grinding Song | K | 67 | 2-55 |
| | Dinéh Round Dance (excerpt) | 6 | 186 | 10-22 |
| | Jo'ashila (Walking Together) | 6 | 286 | 14-19 |
| | Kokopelli Wandering Song | 5 | 110 | 6-1 |
| | Powwow Song (excerpt) | 4 | 32 | 2-4 |
| | Rap Intro (excerpt) | 8 | B-32 | 3-26 |
| | Round Dance | 3 | 257 | 8-34 |
| | Round Dance (excerpt) | 6 | 445 | 21-6 |
| | Kunolounkwa (contemporary); Adapted: Shenandoah | K | 110 | 4-19 |
| (Blackfoot) | Intertribal Song (excerpt) | 8 | B-18 | 2-54 |
| (Cherokee) | Cherokee Morning Song (excerpt) | 8 | B-19 | 2-55 |
| (Southern Ute) | Bear Dance Song | K | 127 | 5-3 |
| | Haliwa-Saponi Canoe Song; Transcribed: Burton | 5 | 303 | 14-5 |
| New Zealand | Karangatia ra | 3 | 272 | 9-23 |
| | Piki mai (excerpt) | 1 | 79 | 2-59 |
| | Tarakihi (The Locust) | 3 | 273 | 9-24 |
| nursery rhyme | Hey, Diddle, Diddle | K | 247 | 8-35 |
| Persian | Avaz-e dashti (excerpt) | 8 | B-42 | 4-10 |
| Peruvian | Tema de maimara (excerpt) | 1 | 297 | 9-28 |
| Puerto Rican | Bembe de Plena (excerpt) | 8 | D-18 | 8-25 |
| | Pasodoble | 7 | F-11 | 10-28 |
| | Zoila; Arr: Dufrasnel | 8 | D-18 | 8-24 |
| river shanty | Shenandoah | 5 | 265 | 12-23 |
| Russian | Bai, bai, bai, bai | 2 | 197 | 7-29 |
| | Garden of the Earth | 5 | 399 | 18-12 |
| | Na rechenki | 1 | 375 | 12-4 |
| | Sigit "Alash" (excerpt) | 4 | 31 | 2-2 |
| Scandinavian | Who Can Sail? | 5 | 30 | 2-18 |
| South African | Sikelela (excerpt) | 1 | 139 | 4-40 |
| South African | Imbube (Wimoweh) (excerpt); Arr: Beggs/Khemese/Mnguni | 8 | B-30 | 3-19 |
| Tahitian | Tamaiti hunahia (excerpt); Arr: Faraire | 6 | 24 | 2-14 |
| Tibetan | Kui.Kyon.pan (The Praise to Tara) (excerpt) | 6 | 25 | 2-17 |
| Turkish | Makam sehnaz (excerpt) | 2 | 142 | 5-37 |
| | Yemeni baglamis telli basina (excerpt); Arr: Farabi | 6 | 309 | 15-36 |
| Tuvan | Kargyraa-Style Song | 8 | B-40 | 4-5 |
| Ukrainian | Kazak (excerpt) | 1 | 193 | 6-28 |
| Ukrainian | Shchedryk (Carol of the Bells) | 6 | 103 | 6-20 |

Listening Index

| Composer | Title | Gr. | Pg. | CD Track |
|---|---|---|---|---|
| Venezuelan | Luna hermosa (Beautiful Moon) | 8 | I-13 | 13-12 |
| | Carnaval Llanero; Arr: Aparicio | 4 | 307 | 13-12 |
| Vietnamese | Spring Walk "Du xuân" (excerpt); Arr: Khac Chí | 1 | 441 | 14-21 |
| Welsh | Deck the Hall | 5 | 475 | 20-31 |
| | All Through the Night; Arr: Haydn | 5 | 104 | 5-27 |
| West African | Yo Lé Lé (Fulani Groove) (excerpt) | 5 | 33 | 2-25 |
| Zimbabwe | Chigamba (excerpt) | 6 | 27 | 2-21 |
| Transeau, Brian | Believer (excerpt) | 7 | A-2 | 1-1 |
| Traugh, Steven | Copycat | K | 9 | 1-9 |
| Tropicália/Zulu | Uma história de Ifá | 6 | 362 | 18-10 |
| Tropicália/Zulu | Uma história de Ifá (excerpt) | 3 | 311 | 10-45 |
| Troup, Bobby | Route 66 | 4 | 279 | 11-23 |
| Troup, Bobby | Route 66 | 4 | 279 | 11-24 |
| Turner/Levy/Glover/Washington | Soulville | 5 | 363 | 16-23 |
| Turner/Levy/Glover/Washington | Soulville | 7 | B-17 | 3-2 |
| Tutu, Osei | Awakening (excerpt) | 3 | 289 | 10-10 |
| Tutu, Osel | Awakening | 7 | D-14 | 8-31 |
| Twusasi-Fofie, Kwame | Mensu | 8 | D-6 | 8-14 |
| Ulali | Mahk jchi | 7 | D-25 | 9-9 |
| Vallant/McKenzie/Poirier | Akua Tuta (excerpt) | 7 | D-24 | 9-8 |
| Varèse, Edgar | Ionisation | 6 | 357 | 18-5 |
| Vargas, Gaspar/Fuentes, Rubén; Arr: Carrillo | Las copetonas | 7 | B-33 | 4-18 |
| Vasco, de Freitas | Fire Brigade Water the Road (excerpt) | 7 | D-22 | 9-5 |
| Vaughan, Stevie Ray | Pride and Joy | 7 | B-9 | 2-12 |
| Vaughan, Stevie Ray | Scuttle Buttin' | 8 | F-26 | 11-10 |
| Vaughan Williams, Ralph | Fantasia on Greensleeves | 5 | 235 | 11-26 |
| Vaughan Williams, Ralph | Sinfonia Antarctica "Epilogue" (excerpt) | 2 | 326 | 11-35 |
| Vecchi, Orazio | Saltarello detto Trivella (excerpt) | 7 | C-6 | 5-31 |
| Vedder, Eddie | Face of Love, The (excerpt) | 8 | B-15 | 2-49 |
| Verdi, Giuseppe | Aida (Grand March) "Gloria all'Egitto" | 8 | C-24 | 6-16 |
| Verdi, Guiseppi | Il trovatore "Anvil Chorus" (excerpt) | 6 | 25 | 2-16 |
| Verdi, Guiseppi | Rigoletto (Beautiful Daughter of Love) "Bella figlia dell'amore" | 7 | C-29 | 7-10 |
| Vieuxtemps, Henri; Arr: Richards | Souvenirs L'Amerique (Yankee Doodle) | 2 | 405 | 15-15 |
| Villa-Lobos, Heitor | Bachianas Brasileiras No. 5 "Aria" | 8 | C-37 | 7-4 |
| Villa-Lobos, Heitor | Little Train of the Caipira, The | K | 25 | 1-41 |
| Vita, Franco de | Lluvia-I (The Rain) (excerpt) | 6 | 332 | 17-1 |
| Vita, Franco de | Lluvia-II (The Rain) | 6 | 332 | 17-2 |
| Vita, Franco de | Si tú no estás (If You're Not Here) | 6 | 267 | 14-2 |
| Vivaldi, Antonio | Concerto for Two Trumpets in C Major "Allegro," Movement 1 (excerpt) | 4 | 71 | 4-7 |
| Vivaldi, Antonio | Concerto for Two Trumpets in C Major "Allegro," Movement 1 (excerpt) | 4 | 75 | 4-16 |
| Vivaldi, Antonio | Four Seasons, Concerto No. 2, The "Summer," Movement 3 | 6 | 102 | 6-18 |
| Vivaldi, Antonio | Four Seasons, The "Spring" (excerpt) | 1 | 29 | 1-44 |
| Vivaldi, Antonio | Four Seasons, The "Spring," Movement 1 | 4 | 371 | 16-8 |
| Vivaldi, Antonio | Four Seasons, The "Winter," Movement 2 | 3 | 113 | 4-18 |
| Vivaldi, Antonio | Gloria in excelsis | 6 | 210 | 11-19 |
| Vollant/McKenzie | Apu Min'Tan | 8 | D-21 | 8-31 |
| von Bingen, Hildegard | O ignis spiritus Paracliti (O Holy Fire that Soothes the Spirit) (excerpt) | 7 | C-4 | 5-26 |
| Wagner, Richard | Die Walküre (The Ride of the Valkyries) "The Valkyries" (excerpt) | 8 | C-23 | 6-15 |
| Wagner, Richard | Lohengrin "Prelude to Act III" | 8 | C-22 | 6-14 |
| Waldman/Buckingham | Don't Look Down | 6 | 249 | 13-9 |
| Waldteufel, Emile | Les Patineurs (The Skaters) | 2 | 387 | 14-29 |
| Walker, Jerry Jeff | Mr. Bojangles (excerpt 1) (excerpt) | 7 | F-7 | 10-25 |
| Walker, Jerry Jeff | Mr. Bojangles (excerpt 2) (excerpt) | 7 | F-7 | 10-26 |
| Walker, T. Bone | Hard Way | 7 | E-33 | 10-14 |
| Ward/Bates | America, the Beautiful | 3 | 413 | 15-8 |
| Ward/Bates | America, the Beautiful (gospel) | 6 | 485 | 23-3 |
| Warren, Diane | If You Asked Me To | 8 | G-5 | 11-20 |
| Warren/Gordon | Chica chica boom chic | 2 | 112 | 4-31 |
| Waskewitch, Irvin | Men's Fancy Dance (excerpt) | 7 | D-24 | 9-7 |

| Composer | Title | Gr. | Pg. | CD Track |
|---|---|---|---|---|
| Waters, Muddy | Country Blues | 5 | 225 | 11-9 |
| Waters, Muddy | Hard Day Blues | 7 | B-9 | 2-11 |
| Watts, Isaac/Mason, Lowell | Joy to the World | 7 | A-27 | 1-18 |
| Webb, Jimmy | If These Walls Could Speak | 7 | B-41 | 5-9 |
| Webber, Andrew Lloyd | Requiem "Pie Jesu" (as performed by Charlotte Church) (excerpt) | 6 | 178 | 10-9 |
| Webber, Andrew Lloyd | Requiem "Pie Jesu" (as performed by David Horton/Debra Hayes) | 6 | 178 | 10-8 |
| Weill/Brecht/Blitzstein | Mack the Knife | 7 | B-26 | 4-1 |
| Weiss/Peretti/Creatore | Lion Sleeps Tonight, The | 4 | 132 | 6-6 |
| Weiss/Thiele | What a Wonderful World (as performed by Eva Cassidy) | 6 | 64 | 4-23 |
| Weiss/Thiele | What a Wonderful World (as performed by Joey Ramone) | 6 | 64 | 4-24 |
| Weiss/Thiele | What a Wonderful World (as performed by Louis Armstrong) | 6 | 63 | 4-22 |
| Whelan; Arr: Hollenbaeck | Riverdance Suite (excerpt) | 2 | 141 | 5-31 |
| Will Ackerman/Chuck Greenburg | If You Look (excerpt) | 7 | B-5 | 2-3 |
| Williams, Hank | Jambalaya | 6 | 245 | 13-3 |
| Williams, John | Close Encounters of the Third Kind (excerpt) | 4 | 235 | 10-5 |
| Williams, John | Close Encounters of the Third Kind (excerpt) | 8 | B-34 | 3-28 |
| Williams, John | Olympic Spirit | 6 | 350 | 18-1 |
| Wills, Bob | New San Antonio Rose | 5 | 135 | 6-30 |
| Wilson, Brian | Good Vibrations | 8 | E-28 | 10-2 |
| Winter/Payne; Arr: Winter | George and Gracie (excerpt) | 1 | 69 | 2-48 |
| Workman, Lyle | Rising of the Mourning Sun (excerpt) | 7 | F-19 | 11-5 |
| Ybarra, Eva | A mi querido Austin | 8 | B-24 | 3-10 |
| Yi Jianquan | Birds in the Forest (excerpt) | 4 | 315 | 13-28 |
| Yoo, Hi-za | Sanjo (excerpt) | 4 | 175 | 7-41 |
| Yunupingu/Kellaway | Dharpa (Tree) | 8 | B-38 | 4-2 |
| Zawinul, Joe | Birdland (excerpt) | 5 | 155 | 8-2 |

# Montages

*This section is an alphabetical listing of recorded montages found in Silver Burdett* MAKING MUSIC.

| Title | Description | Gr. | Pg. | CD Track |
|---|---|---|---|---|
| American Band Montage | | 3 | 82 | 3-15 |
| American Music Styles | Marching Band<br>Native American<br>Bluegrass<br>Jazz<br>Mariachi<br>Musical Theater | 2 | 224 | 8-13 |
| Bird Calls, Bird Songs | Black-capped chickadee<br>White-throated sparrow | K | 178 | 6-30 |
| Chant Montage | Recitation of Verses of the Qu'ranRecitation of Verses of the Qu'ran (excerpt)<br>Hannya-ShingyoHannya-Shingyo (excerpt) | 7 | C-5 | 5-28<br>5-29 |
| Chinese Instruments Montage | Erhu<br>Sheng<br>Zheng | 2 | 276 | 10-11 |
| Dig-a Dum Variations | Vale do javariVale do javari (excerpt)<br>KarawKaraw (excerpt)<br>Ijexá, Filhos de GandhiIjexá, Filhos de Gandhi (excerpt)<br>Wo ba wo ba shueWo ba wo ba shue (excerpt) | 8 | B-31 | 3-21<br>3-22<br>3-23<br>3-24 |
| Drums from Around the World | | 6 | 277 | 14-12 |
| Drums of the Iroquois and Sioux | | 6 | 285 | 14-16 |
| Fifteen Hungarian Peasant Songs | Fifteen Hungarian Peasant Songs No. 7<br>Fifteen Hungarian Peasant Songs No. 9, Allegro<br>Fifteen Hungarian Peasant Songs Songs No. 10, Allegro<br>Fifteen Hungarian Peasant Songs No. 13, Allegro<br>Fifteen Hungarian Peasant Songs No. 14, Allegro | 7 | C-35 | 7-17<br>7-18<br>7-19<br>7-20<br>7-21 |
| Flute Montage | Shakuhachi flute<br>Panpipes<br>Sao<br>Western flute | 3 | 184 | 6-34 |
| Gamelan Instruments | Kendang<br>Gong<br>Gangsa<br>Kempli | 2 | 104 | 4-21 |
| Is the Sound High or Low? | A bird chirping<br>A garbage truck being emptied<br>A cow mooing<br>A fire engine siren<br>A bicycle bell<br>Dogs barking<br>A cat meowing<br>A tea kettle whistling | K | 17 | 1-24 |

| Title | Description | Gr. | Pg. | CD Track |
|-------|-------------|-----|-----|----------|
| Junk Music Montage | Drum sticks playing tin cans of various sizes; Chains rattling; Paper being crumpled; Paper tearing; Playing on a cookie tin lid; Water glasses filled to varying levels of water being played with a spoon; Sounds of hand jive (body percussion); Large piece of thin sheet metal being struck and shaken (thunder); 55-gallon oil drum being played; Object being scraped over steel grating; Pan lids being struck; Rice being shaken in a cardboard container; Keys jangling; Popcorn seeds being shaken in a plastic bottle; Spaghetti being shaken in a pan | 1 | 73 | 2-54 |
| Keyboard Instrument Montage | Piano<br>Clavichord<br>Harpsichord | 5 | 197 | 10-6 |
| Louds and Softs of the Seasons, The | A loud wind with thunder<br>Children whispering<br>Children squealing with joy<br>The soft gurgling of a stream<br>An adult humming<br>Fireworks | K | 4 | 1-3 |
| Machine Music | An airplane<br>A washing machine<br>The wheels of a train<br>A jack hammer<br>A vacuum cleaner<br>A garbage truck | K | 82 | 3-19 |
| Montage of African Instruments | Dundun<br>Mbira<br>Axatse | 5 | 66 | 4-6 |
| Montage of Historical Styles | Symphony No. 5 in C Minor, Movement 1 (excerpt)<br>Ev'ry Time I Feel the Spirit (excerpt)<br>O ignis spiritus Paracliti (O Holy Fire that Soothes the Spirit) (excerpt)<br>La campanella No. 3 (excerpt)<br>Brandenburg Concerto No. 2, Movement 3, Allegro Assai (excerpt)<br>Seven Tunes Heard in China (excerpt)<br>Rigoletto "Bella figlia dell'amore" (excerpt)<br>Suite No. 2 in F "Fantasia on the Dargason" (excerpt) | 7 | C-3 | 5-18<br>5-19<br>5-20<br><br>5-21<br>5-22<br><br>5-23<br>5-24<br>5-25 |
| One Frog, Two Frogs, Three Frogs…Sing! | Three frog calls | K | 182 | 6-39 |
| Ostinatos Around the World | Sabhyatâ (excerpt)<br>Banuwa (excerpt)<br>Over and Under a Theme of Mark Isham's (excerpt) | 8 | B-4 | 2-4<br>2-5<br>2-6 |
| Percussion Montage | Shekere<br>Djembe<br>Tabla<br>Taiko drums<br>Snare drums<br>Guiro, claves, maracas, then all three together<br>Timpani | 1 | 115 | 3-54 |
| Pipes Around the World | Didgeridoo<br>Panpipe<br>Shakuhachi<br>Native American flute<br>Recorder<br>Kudu Horn | 4 | 458 | 19-9 |

| Title | Description | Gr. | Pg. | CD Track |
|---|---|---|---|---|
| Planet Drone | Bairagi (excerpt)<br>Khöömei (excerpt)<br>Eanáir (excerpt)<br>Gapu (excerpt) | 8 | B-10 | 2-25<br>2-26<br>2-27<br>2-28 |
| Plucked String Montage | Sitar<br>Banjo<br>Harp<br>Guitar<br>Lute<br>Ud | 5 | 198 | 10-7 |
| Samples of Historical Styles | Soundings "Fanfare" (excerpt)<br>Messiah "Hallelujah!" (excerpt)<br>Bachianas brasileiras No. 5 "Aria" (excerpt)<br>O tocius Asie gloria (excerpt)<br>Piano Trio in G Minor "Allegro" (excerpt)<br>Le tombeau de Couperin "Prélude" (excerpt)<br>Concerto for French Horn in E-flat No. 4, Movement 3 (excerpt)<br>C-Jam Blues (excerpt)<br>Ombrose e care selve (excerpt) | 8 | C-3 | 4-21<br>4-22<br>4-23<br>4-24<br>4-25<br>4-26<br>4-27<br><br>4-28<br>4-29 |
| Shepherd's Hey Sampler | Shepherd's Hey, No. 1 (piano)<br>Shepherd's Hey, No. 2 (orchestra)<br>Shepherd's Hey, No. 3 (band) | 7 | C-37 | 7-24<br>7-25<br>7-26 |
| Singing Scales | Vaka atua (excerpt)<br>The Face of Love (excerpt)<br>Neend Koyi (excerpt)<br>Mayingo (excerpt) | 8 | B-11 | 2-29<br>2-30<br>2-31<br>2-32 |
| Sound Waves Montage | Piccolo<br>Bassoon<br>Violin<br>Cello<br>String bass | 6 | 354 | 18-4 |
| String Instrument Montage | Koto<br>Lute<br>Sitar<br>Rebab | 4 | 110 | 5-29 |
| Vocal Olympics | Round Dance (excerpt)<br>Cô hang xóm (excerpt)<br>Kargyraa-Style Song (excerpt) | 8 | B-15 | 2-46<br>2-47<br>2-48 |
| Vocal Ornamentations | Hai wedi (excerpt)<br>Byala stala (excerpt)<br>Siuil á ruin (excerpt)<br>Akita kusakari uta (excerpt) | 8 | B-13 | 2-39<br>2-40<br>2-41<br>2-42 |
| Vocal Styles Around the World | Corn grinding song (Navajo)<br>As-shuu dekei-oo (Tuvan Throat Singers)<br>Siúil a ruin (Celtic voices)<br>Mi tierra (Cuban)<br>Stand Still (Gospel & Blues) | 6 | 61 | 4-19 |
| Vocal Timbres Around the World | Grace (Bobby McFerrin)<br>Every Morning (Gospel; Keb' Mo')<br>Leró pa' Cico Mangual (South American; Paracumbé)<br>Crying My Heart Out Over You (Ricky Skaggs) | 6 | 170 | 9-27 |
| Whale of a Tale, A | Whale sounds | K | 272 | 9-27 |

| Title | Description | Gr. | Pg. | CD Track |
|---|---|---|---|---|
| World Instruments Families | Geese in the Bog, The (excerpt)<br>Chang on Jew's Harp (excerpt)<br>Toei Khong (excerpt)<br>Inongo (excerpt) | 8 | B-9 | 2-21<br>2-22<br>2-23<br>2-24 |
| World Music Montage | Western symphony orchestra<br>German oompah band<br>Korean kayagum<br>African drummers | 3 | 266 | 9-13 |
| World of Drums Montage | East Indian tabla drums<br>Timpani<br>Japanese taiko drums<br>Drum set<br>West African djembe | 2 | 66 | 3-6 |
| World Percussion Sounds | Rain (excerpt)<br>Wandenza (excerpt)<br>Quality of Seven, A (excerpt)<br>Rhythms of the Cook Islands (excerpt) | 8 | B-6 | 2-8<br>2-9<br>2-10<br>2-11 |
| World String Sounds | Crowley's/Jackson's (excerpt)<br>Puente de los Alunados (excerpt)<br>Bebiendo al alba (excerpt)<br>Drift (excerpt)<br>Duniya (excerpt) | 8 | B-7 | 2-12<br>2-13<br>2-14<br>2-15<br>2-16 |
| World Winds | Mill Pond, The (excerpt)<br>Through My Eyes (excerpt)<br>Tema de maimara (excerpt)<br>Gimpel the Fool (excerpt) | 8 | B-8 | 2-17<br>2-18<br>2-19<br>2-20 |
| Zither Montage | Hammered dulcimer<br>Koto<br>Dan tranh | 5 | 196 | 10-5 |

Listening Index

# Recorded Assessments

*In this section, you will find a grade-order listing of the What Do You Hear?*
*assessments used in Silver Burdett* MAKING MUSIC.

| Subject | Ex. | Title | Gr. | Pg. | CD Track |
|---|---|---|---|---|---|
| What Do You Hear? 1<br>Expression: Loud and Soft | 1<br>2<br>3<br>4 | Stars and Stripes Forever, The (excerpt)<br>Nocturnes "Nuages" (excerpt)<br>Red Pony, The "Circus Music" (excerpt)<br>Firebird Suite "Berceuse" (excerpt) | K | 28 | 1-45<br>1-46<br>1-47<br>1-48 |
| What Do You Hear? 2A<br>Melody: High Voice? Low Voice? | 1<br>2<br>3<br>4 | Giant, The (from Jack and the Beanstalk)<br>Three Little Piggies, The (from The Three Little Pigs)<br>Gingerbread Man, The (from The Three Little Pigs)<br>Wolf, The (from The Three Little Pigs) | K | 56 | 2-33<br>2-34<br>2-35<br>2-36 |
| What Do You Hear? 2B<br>Timbre: Sing, Speak, Shout, Whisper | 1<br>2<br>3<br>4 | Down by the Bay<br>Shake-'n'-Bake a Jelly<br>Sounds of the Circus<br>Louds and Softs of the Seasons | K | 56 | 2-37<br>2-38<br>2-39<br>2-40 |
| What Do You Hear? 3A<br>Expression: Fast and Slow | 1<br>2<br>3<br>4 | Preludes for Piano, No. 2 (excerpt)<br>Pulcinella Suite "Tarantella" (excerpt)<br>Pictures at an Exhibition "Great Gate of Kiev"<br>Minuet in G Major (excerpt) | K | 84 | 3-23<br>3-24<br><br>3-26 |
| What Do You Hear? 3B<br>Timbre: Nature Sounds/Machine Sounds | 1<br>2<br>3<br>4 | Rain Sounds<br>Machine Music "Garbage Truck"<br>Los trencitos (Little Trains)<br>Bird Calls, Bird Songs "Black-Capped Chickadee" | K | 84 | 3-27<br>3-28<br>3-29<br>3-30 |
| What Do You Hear? 4<br>Melody: Upward-Downward | 1<br>2<br>3<br>4 | Cello Arpeggio<br>Trumpet Arpeggio<br>Flute Arpeggio<br>Bassoon Arpeggio | K | 112 | 4-21<br>4-22<br>4-23<br>4-24 |
| What Do You Hear? 5<br>Rhythm: Long and Short | 1<br>2<br>3<br>4 | Midsummer Night's Dream, A "Nocturne" (excerpt)<br>Six Ings "Scooting" (excerpt)<br>Water Music Suite "Bourrée" (excerpt)<br>L'Arlésienne Suite No. 1 "Adagietto" (excerpt) | K | 140 | 5-20<br>5-21<br>5-22<br>5-23 |
| What Do You Hear? 6<br>Form: Same and Different Parts | 1<br>2<br>3<br>4 | Let's Make a Circle (Vamos a hacer la ronda)<br>Rig-a-Jig-Jig<br>Bear Dance<br>Goin' to the Fair | K | 168 | 6-18<br>6-19<br>6-20<br>6-21 |
| What Do You Hear? 1A<br>Rhythm: Beat/No beat | 1<br>2<br>3<br>4 | Guide Right (excerpt)<br>Silver Apples of the Moon (excerpt)<br>Trois Visages de Liège, "L'Aire et L'Eau" (excerpt)<br>Different Beat, A (excerpt) | 1 | 40 | 2-5<br>2-6<br>2-7<br>2-8 |
| What Do You Hear? 1B<br>Melody: High sounds/Low sounds | 1<br>2<br>3<br><br>4 | Lyric Pieces "Butterfly" No. 1 (excerpt)<br>Siegfried "Forest Murmurs" (excerpt)<br>Háry János Suite "The Battle and Defeat of Napoleon"<br>  (excerpt)<br>Symphony No. 6 "Pathetique," Movement 4 (excerpt) | 1 | 40 | 2-9<br>2-10<br>2-11<br><br>2-12 |
| What Do You Hear? 2A<br>Expression: Tempo Changes | 1<br>2<br>3 | Minka (excerpt)<br>Freight Train (excerpt)<br>Peer Gynt Suite No. 1 "In the Hall of the Mountain King"<br>  (excerpt) | 1 | 80 | 2-60<br>2-61<br>2-62 |
| What Do You Hear? 2B<br>Form: Same and different parts | 1<br>2<br>3<br>4 | Down by the Bay (excerpt)<br>Earth Is My Mother, The (excerpt)<br>Shoo Turkey (excerpt)<br>My Mama's Calling Me (excerpt) | 1 | 80 | 2-63<br>2-64<br>2-65<br>2-66 |

Listening Index

| Subject | Ex. | Title | Gr. | Pg. | CD Track |
|---|---|---|---|---|---|
| What Do You Hear? 3A<br>Rhythm | 1<br>2<br>3<br>4 | Rhythm Pattern 1<br>Rhythm Pattern 2<br>Rhythm Pattern 3<br>Rhythm Pattern 4 | 1 | 120 | 4-1<br>4-2<br>4-3<br>4-4 |
| What Do You Hear? 3B<br>Timbre: Drums, rattles, scrapers | 1<br>2<br>3<br>4 | African Talking Drum<br>Mexican Animal-Shape Rattle<br>Guiro<br>Sandblocks | 1 | 120 | 4-5<br>4-6<br>4-7<br>4-8 |
| What Do You Hear? 4A<br>Rhythm | 1<br>2<br>3<br>4 | Rhythm Pattern 1<br>Rhythm Pattern 2<br>Rhythm Pattern 3<br>Rhythm Pattern 4 | 1 | 160 | 5-13<br>5-14<br>5-15<br>5-16 |
| What Do You Hear? 4B<br>Melody: Melody patterns | 1<br>2<br>3<br>4 | Melody Pattern 1<br>Melody Pattern 2<br>Melody Pattern 3<br>Melody Pattern 4 | 1 | 160 | 5-17<br>5-18<br>5-19<br>5-20 |
| What Do You Hear? 5<br>Expression: Dynamics changes | 1<br>2<br>3 | Peer Gynt Suite No. 1 "Morning" (excerpt)<br>Moldau, The (Vltava) (excerpt)<br>Planets, The "Jupiter" (excerpt) | 1 | 200 | 6-31<br>6-32<br>6-33 |
| What Do You Hear? 6A<br>Form | 1<br>2<br>3 | Goodbye, Julie (excerpt)<br>Run, Molly, Run (excerpt)<br>Nampaya omame (There Come Our Mothers) (excerpt) | 1 | 240 | 7-35<br>7-36<br>7-37 |
| What Do You Hear? 6B<br>Timbre: Woods and Metals | 1<br>2<br>3<br>4 | Cymbals<br>Glockenspiel<br>Tone Block<br>Xylophone | 1 | 240 | 7-38<br>7-39<br>7-40<br>7-41 |
| What Do You Hear? 1<br>Dynamics | 1<br>2<br>3<br>4 | Rodeo "Buckaroo Holiday"<br>Naranja dulce (Sweet Orange) (excerpt)<br>Allegretto (excerpt)<br>Ja-Da (excerpt) | 2 | 36 | 1-45<br>1-46<br>1-47<br>1-48 |
| What Do You Hear? 2<br>Expression: Tempo and Dynamics | 1<br>2<br><br>3<br>4<br>5<br>6 | Bob-a-Needle (excerpt)<br>Les Rêves de Columbine (1907) "Sous les étoiles (Under the Stars)," Movement 4 (excerpt)<br>Mariposita (Little Butterfly) (excerpt)<br>Carmina Burana "O Fortuna" (excerpt)<br>Achshav (Awake! Awake!) (excerpt)<br>Bachianas Brasilieras, No. 2 "The Little Train of the Caipira" (excerpt) | 2 | 72 | 3-13<br>3-14<br><br>3-15<br>3-16<br>3-17<br>3-18 |
| What Do You Hear? 3<br>Rhythm Patterns | 1<br>2<br>3<br>4 | Rhythm Pattern 1<br>Rhythm Pattern 2<br>Rhythm Pattern 3<br>Rhythm Pattern 4 | 2 | 110 | 4-27<br>4-28<br>4-29<br>4-30 |
| What Do You Hear? 4A<br>Form: Same and Different Phrases | 1<br>2<br><br>3 | Michael, Row the Boat Ashore (excerpt)<br>Ein Männlein steht im Walde (A Little Man in the Woods) (excerpt)<br>Rocky Mountain (excerpt) | 2 | 146 | 5-41<br>5-42<br><br>5-43 |
| What Do You Hear? 4B<br>Timbre: String Instruments | 1<br>2<br>3 | Yangqin<br>Violin<br>Classical Guitar | 2 | 146 | 5-44<br>5-45<br>5-46 |
| What Do You Hear? 5<br>Timbre: Brass and Woodwinds | 1<br>2<br>3<br>4 | Saxophone<br>Trombone<br>Trumpet<br>Clarinet | 2 | 184 | 7-8<br>7-9<br>7-10<br>7-11 |

| Subject | Ex. | Title | Gr. | Pg. | CD Track |
|---------|-----|-------|-----|-----|----------|
| What Do You Hear? 6 AB and ABA Form | 1 | It's a Celebration! (excerpt) | 2 | 220 | 8-10 |
| | 2 | Boysie (excerpt) | | | 8-11 |
| | 3 | Shoo, Fly (excerpt) | | | 8-12 |
| What Do You Hear? 1 Melody | 1 | I Don't Care If the Rain Comes Down (excerpt) | 3 | 42 | 2-10 |
| | 2 | Old Dan Tucker (excerpt) | | | 2-11 |
| | 3 | Doong gul ge ('Round and Around We Go) (excerpt) | | | 2-12 |
| | 4 | Take Me Out to the Ball Game (excerpt) | | | 2-13 |
| | 5 | Hashkediya (excerpt) | | | 2-14 |
| What Do You Hear? 2 Tempo | 1 | Nutcracker Suite, The "Trepak" (excerpt) | 3 | 80 | 3-11 |
| | 2 | Ida Red (excerpt) | | | 3-12 |
| | 3 | Waltzing with Bears (excerpt) | | | 3-13 |
| | 4 | Choo-Choo Joubert (excerpt) | | | 3-14 |
| What Do You Hear? 3 Timbre | 1 | Viola | 3 | 118 | 4-24 |
| | 2 | String bass | | | 4-25 |
| | 3 | Violin | | | 4-26 |
| What Do You Hear? 4 Timbre | 1 | Xylophone | 3 | 156 | 5-30 |
| | 2 | Marimba | | | 5-31 |
| | 3 | Vibraphone | | | 5-32 |
| What Do You Hear? 5A Timbre | 1 | Flute (western) | 3 | 194 | 7-4 |
| | 2 | Shakuhachi | | | 7-5 |
| | 3 | Tuba | | | 7-6 |
| What Do You Hear? 5B Rhythm | 1 | World We Love, The (excerpt) | 3 | 194 | 7-7 |
| | 2 | St. Patrick Was a Gentleman (excerpt) | | | 7-8 |
| What Do You Hear? 6 Expression | 1 | I Got Shoes (excerpt) | 3 | 232 | 8-1 |
| | 2 | Fanfare for the Common Man (excerpt) | | | 8-2 |
| | 3 | Peer Gynt Suite No. 1 "Morning" (excerpt) | | | 8-3 |
| What Do You Hear? 1 Timbre | 1 | Rain, Rain Beautiful Rain (excerpt) | 4 | 42 | 2-23 |
| | 2 | I Don't Want to Feel Like That (excerpt) | | | 2-24 |
| | 3 | Chansons madecasses "Nahandove" (excerpt) | | | 2-25 |
| | 4 | Sigit "Alash" (excerpt) | | | 2-26 |
| What Do You Hear? 2 | 1 | Quartet for Oboe, Clarinet, Flute, and Bassoon "Allegro molto" (excerpt) | 4 | 82 | 4-23 |
| Timbre | 2 | La Péri "Fanfare" (excerpt) | | | 4-24 |
| | 3 | Pulcinella Suite "Serenata" (excerpt) | | | 4-25 |
| | 4 | Concerto in E-flat for Horn and Orchestra "Rondo" (excerpt) | | | 4-26 |
| | 5 | Sonata in F Minor for Bassoon "Vivace" (excerpt) | | | 4-27 |
| | 6 | Sweet Georgia Brown (excerpt) | | | 4-28 |
| What Do You Hear? 3 Timbre | 1 | Sakura (excerpt) | 4 | 124 | 5-40 |
| | 3 | Charukeshi (excerpt) | | | 5-42 |
| What Do You Hear? 4 Rhythm | 1 | Rhythm Patterns | 4 | 164 | 7-23 |
| | 2 | Rhythm Patterns | | | 7-24 |
| | 3 | Rhythm Patterns | | | 7-25 |
| What Do You Hear? 5 Timbre | 1 | Rag puria kalyan - gat in tintal (excerpt) | 4 | 204 | 8-49 |
| | 2 | That's the Way (excerpt) | | | 8-50 |
| | 3 | Piano Trio No. 2 in E-flat Major "Scherzo" (excerpt) | | | 8-51 |
| | 4 | Canzoni et Sonate "Canzoni prima a 5" (excerpt) | | | 8-52 |
| What Do You Hear? 6 Timbre | 1 | Toccata in D Minor (excerpt) | 4 | 246 | 10-18 |
| | 2 | Close Encounters of the Third Kind (excerpt) | | | 10-19 |
| | 3 | Waltz in D-flat ("Minute" Waltz) (excerpt) | | | 10-20 |
| | 4 | French Suite No. 5 "Gigue" (excerpt) | | | 10-21 |

Listening Index

| Subject | Ex. | Title | Gr. | Pg. | CD Track |
|---|---|---|---|---|---|
| What Do You Hear? 1A<br>Timbre | 1<br>2<br>3 | Kerry Dance, The (excerpt)<br>Freedom Is Coming (excerpt)<br>Kum ba yah (excerpt) | 5 | 40 | 2-34<br>2-35<br>2-36 |
| What Do You Hear? 1B<br>Form | 1 | Ise Oluwa | 5 | 40 | 2-37 |
| What Do You Hear? 2<br>Rhythm | 1<br>2<br>3 | Cattle Call (excerpt)<br>Himmel und Erde (excerpt)<br>Cindy (excerpt) | 5 | 80 | 4-25<br>4-26<br>4-27 |
| What Do You Hear? 3<br>Expression | 1<br>2<br>3<br>4 | Stars and Stripes Forever, The (excerpt)<br>Stars and Stripes Forever, The (excerpt)<br>Stars and Stripes Forever, The (excerpt)<br>Stars and Stripes Forever, The (excerpt) | 5 | 123 | 6-14<br>6-15<br>6-16<br>6-17 |
| What Do You Hear? 4<br>Melody | 1<br>2<br>3<br>4<br>5 | Pollerita (excerpt)<br>Pollerita (excerpt)<br>Pollerita (excerpt)<br>Pollerita (excerpt)<br>Pollerita (excerpt) | 5 | 164 | 8-17<br>8-18<br>8-19<br>8-20<br>8-21 |
| What Do You Hear? 5A<br>Rhythm | 1<br>2<br>3 | When the Saints Go Marching In (excerpt)<br>Give My Regards to Broadway (excerpt)<br>When Johnny Comes Marching Home (excerpt) | 5 | 206 | 10-19<br>10-20<br>10-21 |
| What Do You Hear? 5B<br>Timbre | 1<br>2<br>3 | String Instrumental (plucked) (excerpt)<br>String Instrumental (bowed) (excerpt)<br>String Instrumental (struck) (excerpt) | 5 | 206 | 10-22<br>10-23<br>10-24 |
| What Do You Hear? 6A<br>Melody | 1<br>2<br>3<br>4 | Vive l'amour (excerpt)<br>Drill, Ye Tarriers (excerpt)<br>Hava nagila (excerpt)<br>Orange Blossom Special (excerpt) | 5 | 246 | 12-1<br>12-2<br>12-3<br>12-4 |
| What Do You Hear? 6B<br>Timbre | 1<br>2<br>3 | Keyboard Instrumental/piano (excerpt)<br>Keyboard Instrumental/harpsichord (excerpt)<br>Keyboard Instrumental/synthesizer (excerpt) | 5 | 246 | 12-5<br>12-6<br>12-7 |
| What Do You Hear? 1A<br>Vocal Timbre | 1<br>2<br>3<br>4<br>5<br>6 | Strike Up The Band Medley (excerpt)<br>Tamaiti hunahia (excerpt)<br>Northfield (excerpt)<br>O Christmas Tree (excerpt)<br>Kui.Kyon.pan (excerpt)<br>Il trovatore "Anvil Chorus" (excerpt) | 6 | 32 | 2-25<br>2-26<br>2-27<br>2-28<br>2-29<br>2-30 |
| What Do You Hear? 1B<br>Form | 1 | Lean on Me (excerpt) (St. Voc.) | 6 | 33 | 2-31 |
| What Do You Hear? 2A<br>Texture | 1<br>2<br>3<br>4<br>5<br>6 | L'Arlésienne Suite No. 2 "Farandole," (Theme 1)<br>L'Arlésienne Suite No. 2 "Farandole," (Theme 2)<br>L'Arlésienne Suite No. 2 "Farandole"<br>L'Arlésienne Suite No. 2 "Farandole"<br>L'Arlésienne Suite No. 2 "Farandole"<br>L'Arlésienne Suite No. 2 "Farandole" | 6 | 70 | 4-29<br>4-30<br>4-31<br>4-32<br>4-33<br>4-34 |
| What Do You Hear? 2B<br>Vocal Timbre | 1<br>2 | What a Wonderful World (excerpt)<br>What a Wonderful World (as performed by Louis Armstrong) (excerpt) | 6 | 71 | 4-3<br>4-36 |
| What Do You Hear? 3<br>Timbre | 1<br>2<br>3<br>4 | Symphony No. 5 in C Minor, Movement 1 (excerpt)<br>Moon Mirrored in the Pool, The (excerpt)<br>Shchedryk (Carol of the Bells) (excerpt)<br>Four Seasons, Concerto No. 2, The "Summer, La tempesta," Movement 3 (excerpt) | 6 | 109 | 6-24<br>6-25<br>6-26<br>6-27 |

| Subject | Ex. | Title | Gr. | Pg. | CD Track |
|---|---|---|---|---|---|
| What Do You Hear? 4A<br>Form | 1 | Dance for the Nations (excerpt) (St. Voc.) | 6 | 146 | 8-12 |
| | 2 | Canon for Violin and Cello (excerpt) | | | 8-13 |
| | 3 | Barb'ry Allen (excerpt) (St. Voc.) | | | 8-14 |
| | 4 | "Little" Organ Fugue in G Minor (organ) (excerpt) | | | 8-15 |
| What Do You Hear? 4B<br>Timbre | 1 | Suite No. 2 in F "March," Movement 1 (excerpt) | 6 | 147 | 8-16 |
| | 2 | Stars and Stripes Forever, The (excerpt) | | | 8-17 |
| | 3 | Alexander's Ragtime Band (excerpt) (St. Perf. Tr.) | | | 8-18 |
| | 4 | Kerenski (excerpt) (St. Perf. Tr.) | | | 8-19 |
| What Do You Hear? 5A<br>Style | 1 | Crying My Heart Out Over You (excerpt) | 6 | 184 | 10-13 |
| | 2 | Every Morning (excerpt) | | | 10-14 |
| | 3 | Grace (excerpt) | | | 10-15 |
| | 4 | Leró pa' Cico Mangual (Homage to Cico Mangual) (excerpt) | | | 10-16 |
| What Do You Hear? 5B<br>Form | 1 | Variations on "The Carnival of Venice" 1 (excerpt) | 6 | 185 | 10-17 |
| | 2 | Variations on "The Carnival of Venice" 2 (excerpt) | | | 10-18 |
| | 3 | Variations on "The Carnival of Venice" 3 (excerpt) | | | 10-19 |
| | 4 | Variations on "The Carnival of Venice" 4 (excerpt) | | | 10-20 |
| | 5 | Variations on "The Carnival of Venice" 5 (excerpt) | | | 10-21 |
| What Do You Hear? 6A<br>Form | 1 | Skye Boat Song (excerpt) (St. Voc.) | 6 | 220 | 11-28 |
| | 2 | Kyrie (excerpt) (St. Voc.) | | | 11-29 |
| | 3 | Vive l'amour (excerpt) (St. Voc.) | | | 11-30 |
| | 4 | Concert for Piano and Orchestra (excerpt) | | | 11-31 |
| | 5 | Your Friends Shall Be the Tall Wind (excerpt) (St. Voc.) | | | 11-32 |
| What Do You Hear? 6B<br>Timbre | 1 | Gloria in excelsis (excerpt) | 6 | 221 | 11-33 |
| | 2 | Lo, How a Rose E'er Blooming (excerpt) | | | 11-34 |
| | 3 | Siyahamba (excerpt) (St. Voc.) | | | 11-35 |
| | 4 | America, the Beautiful (excerpt) | | | 11-36 |
| What Do You Hear? 1<br>American Pop | 1 | You Are My Sunshine (excerpt) | 7 | B-47 | 5-14 |
| | 2 | Twist, The (excerpt) | | | 5-15 |
| | 3 | Sube (excerpt) | | | 5-16 |
| | 4 | Tears of a Clown (excerpt) | | | 5-17 |
| What Do You Hear? 2<br>History | 1 | Symphony No. 94 in G Major, Andante ("Surprise") (excerpt) | 7 | C-47 | 8-9 |
| | 2 | Rhapsody in Blue (excerpt) | | | 8-10 |
| | 3 | Shepherd's Hey, No. 3 (band) (excerpt) | | | 8-11 |
| | 4 | Den III. Ende VI. Ronde & Quatre Branles (excerpt) | | | 8-12 |
| | 5 | Brandenburg Concerto No. 2, Movement 3, Allegro Assai (excerpt) | | | 8-13 |
| | 6 | Nutcracker Suite, The "Arabian Dance" (excerpt) | | | 8-14 |
| What Do You Hear? 1<br>World Pop | 1 | Shumba (Lion) (excerpt) | 8 | B-47 | 4-17 |
| | 2 | El nuevo caiman (excerpt) | | | 4-18 |
| | 3 | Faerie Stories (excerpt) | | | 4-19 |
| | 4 | Stalia, Stalia | | | 4-20 |
| What Do You Hear? 2<br>History | 1 | Water Music "Hornpipe" (excerpt) | 8 | C-49 | 8-6 |
| | 2 | La mer "Dialogue du vent et de la mer" (excerpt) | | | 8-7 |
| | 3 | Bachianas brasileiras No. 5 "Aria " (excerpt) | | | 8-8 |
| | 4 | Sing We and Chant It | | | 8-9 |
| | 5 | C-Jam Blues (excerpt) | | | 8-10 |
| | 6 | Quintet for Piano and Strings in E-flat Major, Movement 1 (excerpt) | | | 8-11 |

# Recorded Dances

*This section lists alphabetically the titles of those dances in Silver Burdett Making Music that have recorded dance performance tracks and practice tempo tracks.*

| Title | Gr. | Pg. | Performance Track CD | Practice Tempo CD |
|---|---|---|---|---|
| Achshav | 2 | 64 | 3-5 | |
| Adana ya gidelim (Let's Go to Adana) | 2 | 142 | 5-32 | 5-36 |
| Ah, eu entrei na roda (I Came to Try This Game) | 3 | 308 | 10-40 | 10-44 |
| Al yadee | 6 | 308 | 15-34 | 15-35 |
| Ala Da'lona | 5 | 301 | 14-1 | 14-2 |
| Alabama Gal | 3 | 106 | 4-14 | |
| Ali Pasha) | 5 | 218 | 10-35 | 10-36 |
| Alumot | 6 | 306 | 15-30 | 15-31 |
| Artsa alinu (Come to the Land) | 3 | 285 | 10-5 | 10-6 |
| Así es mi tierra (This Is My Land) | 6 | 172 | 9-35 | 9-36 |
| Blow, Ye Winds | 4 | 255 | 10-25 | 10-27 |
| Bonavist' Harbour | 3 | 294 | 10-16 | 10-18 |
| Che che koolay | 2 | 266 | 9-32 | 9-34 |
| Chicken Dance, The | 4 | 51 | 3-1 | 3-2 |
| Chicken on the Fence Post | 3 | 92 | 3-30 | |
| Cindy | 4 | 384 | 16-22 | 16-24 |
| Ciranda (A Ring of Roses) | 2 | 272 | 10-5 | 10-6 |
| Coffee Grows on White Oak Trees | 3 | 168 | 6-13 | |
| Cotton-Eye Joe | 4 | 290 | 12-11 | 12-12 |
| Dham dhamak dham samelu (excerpt) | 6 | 305 | 15-24 | 15-25 |
| Don Alfonso (Spanish) | 5 | 177 | 9-2 | 9-7 |
| Down the Ohio | 2 | 60 | 2-44 | 2-45 |
| Draw Me a Bucket of Water | 3 | 124 | 4-31 | 4-33 |
| Drill, Ye Tarriers | 5 | 54 | 3-16 | 3-21 |
| Erie Canal | 5 | 262 | 12-18 | 12-20 |
| First Night Quadrille | 4 | 343 | 15-5 | 15-6 |
| Four in a Boat | 2 | 46 | 2-18 | 2-19 |
| Four Potatoes Medley | 6 | 205 | 11-9 | 11-10 |
| Great Big House | 2 | 204 | 7-47 | 7-48 |
| Hava nagila | 6 | 153 | 8-23 | 8-26 |
| Hit Me with a Hot Note and Watch Me Bounce | 6 | 112 | 6-31 | 6-32 |
| How Many Miles to Babylon? | 2 | 128 | 5-15 | 5-16 |
| I Don't Care If the Rain Comes Down | 3 | 24 | 1-39 | 1-40 |
| I Love a Rainy Night | 5 | 350 | 16-9 | 16-10 |
| I Wonder Where Maria's Gone | 3 | 318 | 11-13 | 11-15 |
| Jin-go-lo-ba | 4 | 134 | 6-16 | 6-17 |
| Joe Turner Blues | 4 | 56 | 3-14 | 3-16 |
| Kalvelis | 2 | 42 | 2-6 | 2-7 |
| Kerenski | 6 | 78 | 5-4 | 5-5 |
| Khorovod (Round Dance) | 1 | 374 | 12-1 | 12-3 |
| Kpanlogo for 2 | 6 | 296 | 15-7 | |
| La raspa (Spanish) | 4 | 302 | 13-1 | 13-5 |
| Leila | 1 | 258 | 8-18 | 8-20 |
| Les saluts (excerpt) | 1 | 363 | 11-25 | 11-26 |
| Mama Don't 'Low | 6 | 358 | 18-6 | 18-8 |
| Mary Ann | 6 | 180 | 10-10 | 10-12 |
| Minka (Ukrainian) | 4 | 222 | 9-21 | 9-25 |
| Morning Comes Early | 5 | 13 | 1-17 | 1-22 |
| Mübärak (Happy Birthday) | 3 | 282 | 9-40 | 9-44 |
| My Bonnie Lies Over the Ocean | 4 | 338 | 14-22 | 14-23 |
| Nani wale na hala (Lovely Hala Trees) | 3 | 260 | 9-1 | 9-5 |
| Nie chcę cię znác (Don't Want to Know You) | 3 | 314 | 11-7 | 11-8 |
| North Carolina Breakdown | 5 | 334 | 15-19 | 15-20 |
| O pião entrou (The Top Joined the Circle) | 2 | 355 | 13-10 | 13-11 |
| Old Brass Wagon | 2 | 122 | 4-46 | 4-47 |

Listening Index

| Title | Gr. | Pg. | Performance Track CD | Practice Tempo CD |
|---|---|---|---|---|
| Old Dan Tucker | 3 | 96 | 3-38 | |
| Orange Blossom Special | 5 | 269 | 12-27 | 12-28 |
| Paddy Whack | 6 | 327 | 16-16 | 16-17 |
| Patty Cake Polka | 2 | 281 | 10-21 | 10-22 |
| Paw-Paw Patch | 4 | 93 | 4-43 | 4-44 |
| Pennsylvania 6-5000 | 5 | 342 | 16-2 | |
| Pust' 'vsegda budet sonse (May the Sun Shine Forever) | 3 | 278 | 9-34 | 9-38 |
| Red River Valley (Dance Perf. Tr.) | 6 | 11 | 1-11 | 1-12 |
| Rockin' Around the Christmas Tree | 5 | 466 | 20-11 | 20-13 |
| Scott Joplin's New Rag | 5 | 335 | 15-22 | |
| Scottish Medley | 5 | 139 | 7-11 | 7-12 |
| Sellenger's Round | 6 | 44 | 3-14 | 3-15 |
| Shake Them 'Simmons Down | 2 | 244 | 8-34 | 8-35 |
| Somebody Waiting | 2 | 283 | 10-25 | 10-26 |
| Sonando (Spanish) | 4 | 34 | 2-9 | 2-13 |
| St. Patrick Was a Gentleman | 3 | 290 | 10-13 | 10-14 |
| Tancovačka (Dancing) | 4 | 230 | 9-39 | 9-46 |
| Theme from New York, New York | 4 | 250 | 10-22 | 10-24 |
| Tideo | 2 | 80 | 3-31 | 3-32 |
| Tumba | 5 | 161 | 8-12 | 8-14 |
| Tzena, tzena | 5 | 298 | 13-30 | 13-36 |
| Valentine Dance | 1 | 437 | 14-12 | 14-13 |
| Ve' David y'fey enayiam | 4 | 317 | 13-33 | 13-34 |
| Yankee Doodle | 3 | 414 | 15-9 | 15-11 |
| Yesh lanu taish | 1 | 182 | 6-5 | 6-6 |
| You're a Grand Old Flag | 3 | 264 | 9-10 | 9-11 |

Listening Index

# Recorded Interviews

*This section provides an alphabetical listing of recorded interviews with professional musicians.*

| Title | Gr. | Pg. | CD Track |
|---|---|---|---|
| Bassett, Rick (Part 1) | 3 | 222 | 7-45 |
| Bassett, Rick (Part 2) | 3 | 223 | 7-46 |
| Burke, Liam | 2 | 11 | 1-7 |
| Burrough, Roslyn | 1 | 163b | 5-24 |
| Burton, J. Bryan | 4 | 285 | 12-6 |
| Callaway, Ann Hampton | 6 | 113 | 6-33 |
| Chávez, Carlos | 8 | C-37 | 7-5 |
| Clark, Petula | 6 | 259 | 13-20 |
| Copland, Aaron | 5 | 187 | 9-20 |
| Crawley, Brian | 6 | 312 | 16-3 |
| Glennie, Evelyn | 3 | 149 | 5-20 |
| Hogan, Moses | 4 | 395 | 17-7 |
| Joubert, Joseph | 3 | 50 | 2-19 |
| Louiselle, Bryan | 1 | 251 | 8-4 |
| Luker, Rebecca | 5 | 38 | 2-32 |
| Moore, Carman | 3 | 163 | 5-39 |
| Naranjo, Valerie Dee | 6 | 186 | 10-23 |
| Rafter, Michael | 6 | 113 | 6-33 |
| Rashad, Phylicia | 7 | A-27 | 1-17 |
| Red, Buryl | 7 | A-21 | 1-13 |
| Ritchie, Jean | 4 | 349 | 15-12 |
| Rodgers, Richard | 5 | 39 | 2-33 |
| Sanchez, David "Dakota" | 6 | 319 | 16-10 |
| Schuman, William | 6 | 83 | 5-24 |
| Seeger, Pete | 5 | 380 | 17-17 |
| Seeger, Pete | 8 | C-35 | 7-3 |
| Stravinsky, Igor | 2 | 264 | 9-27 |
| Stravinsky, Igor | 8 | C-33 | 6-29 |
| Swoboda, Deanna | 3 | 188 | 6-36 |
| Tesori, Jeanine | 8 | A-20 | 1-17 |
| Tesori, Jeanine | 6 | 312 | 16-3 |
| Twine, Linda | 6 | 339 | 17-10 |

# Recorded Poems and Stories

*This section lists alphabetically the titles of recorded poems and stories found in Silver Burdett Making Music. For additional poems and stories, see pp. 000-000 in the Classified Index.*

| Title | Gr. | Pg. | CD Track |
|---|---|---|---|
| Bubble Trouble (poem) | K | 184 | 6-44 |
| Bubbles (poem) | K | 185 | 6-45 |
| Cacophony (poem) | K | 83 | 3-22 |
| Chawe chidyo chem'chero "The Story of the Kudu" (story) | 2 | 296 | 11-1 |
| Children Learn What They Live (poem) | 5 | 381 | 17-18 |
| De Beat (poem) | 2 | 67 | 3-7 |
| Dragon Smoke (poem) | K | 258 | 9-6 |
| End, The (poem) | 1 | 409 | 13-8 |
| First Snowflake (poem) | K | 259 | 9-7 |
| Galoshes (poem) | K | 63 | 2-48 |
| Happiness (poem) | K | 62 | 2-47 |
| Harriet Tubman (poem) | 4 | 269 | 11-9 |
| It Is Fun to Sing (poem) | 1 | 64 | 2-42 |
| Kibungo, Beast of the Forest (story) | 2 | 352 | 13-1 |
| Louder than a Clap of Thunder (poem) | 1 | 87 | 3-4 |
| Mammoth (poem) | 1 | 235 | 7-30 |
| Manhattan Lullaby (poem) | K | 193 | 7-5 |
| Mmmmmm mmmmmmm (poem) | K | 71 | 3-3 |
| New Colossus, The (poem) | 5 | 166 | 8-22 |
| Nruab hnub thiab hmo ntuj (Why Is There Day and Night?) (story) | 4 | 366 | 16-4 |
| Paper (poem) | K | 195 | 7-8 |
| Rabbit Dance, The (story) | 3 | 334 | 11-36 |
| Sea Wolf, The (poem) | 4 | 257 | 10-30 |
| Shake-'n'-Bake a Jelly (poem) | K | 95 | 3-49 |
| Song of the Night, The (poem) | 3 | 346 | 12-5 |
| Song of the Train (poem) | K | 153 | 5-40 |
| Stopping by Woods on a Snowy Evening (poem) | 6 | 40 | 2-36 |
| Toaster Time (poem) | K | 17 | 1-25 |
| Why Is There Day and Night? (Nruab hnub thiab hmo ntuj) (story) | 4 | 366 | 16-5 |
| Wind Song (poem) | K | 7 | 1-8 |
| Windshield Wipers (poem) | 1 | 11 | 1-13 |
| Yellow Butter (poem) | 1 | 124 | 4-11 |
| Zomo the Rabbit "A Trickster Tale from West Africa" (story) | 3 | 364 | 12-24 |

Listening Index

# Sound Bank Instruments

*This section contains an alphabetical listing of the instruments found in the Sound Bank recordings in Silver Burdett Making Music.*

| Title | Grade | Pg. | CD Track | Title | Grade | Pg. | CD Track |
|---|---|---|---|---|---|---|---|
| Accordion | 6 | 512 | 23-11 | Dulcimer | 4 | 467 | 19-18 |
| Arpa | 5 | 514 | 21-21 | Dulcimer | 5 | 515 | 21-28 |
| Autoharp | 1 | 469 | 14-36 | Dulcimer (mountain) | 2 | 421 | 15-23 |
| Autoharp | 2 | 420 | 15-16 | Dundun | 2 | 421 | 15-24 |
| Axatse | 5 | 514 | 21-22 | Dundun | 5 | 515 | 21-29 |
| Bagpipe | 4 | 466 | 19-10 | Dundun Drums | 4 | 467 | 19-19 |
| Balalaika | 4 | 466 | 19-11 | Erhu | 2 | 421 | 15-25 |
| Bandura | 6 | 512 | 23-12 | Erhu | 4 | 467 | 19-20 |
| Banjo | 2 | 420 | 15-17 | Erhu | 5 | 515 | 21-30 |
| Bass Guitar | 6 | 512 | 23-13 | Erhu | 6 | 514 | 23-24 |
| Bassoon | 4 | 466 | 19-12 | Finger cymbals | K | 329 | 11-46 |
| Bassoon | 6 | 512 | 23-14 | Flute | 1 | 471 | 14-51 |
| Bodhrán | 5 | 514 | 21-23 | Flute | 2 | 421 | 15-26 |
| Bodhrán | 6 | 512 | 23-15 | Flute | 3 | 435 | 15-19 |
| Bombo | 1 | 470 | 14-41 | Flute | 4 | 468 | 19-21 |
| Bongo Drums | 5 | 514 | 21-24 | Flute | 5 | 515 | 21-31 |
| Caja | 3 | 434 | 15-15 | Flute | 6 | 514 | 23-25 |
| Castanets | K | 329 | 11-48 | Flute (Native American) | 3 | 435 | 15-20 |
| Cello | 2 | 420 | 15-18 | French Horn | 3 | 435 | 15-21 |
| Cello | 3 | 434 | 15-16 | French Horn | 4 | 468 | 19-22 |
| Cello | 4 | 466 | 19-13 | French Horn | 6 | 515 | 23-26 |
| Cello | 6 | 513 | 23-16 | Gankogui | 6 | 515 | 23-27 |
| Ch'ajch'as | 1 | 468 | 14-30 | Glockenspiel | 4 | 468 | 19-23 |
| Charango | 1 | 469 | 14-37 | Guiro | 1 | 468 | 14-33 |
| Clarinet | 1 | 471 | 14-47 | Guiro | K | 328 | 11-43 |
| Clarinet | 2 | 420 | 15-19 | Guitar | 2 | 422 | 15-27 |
| Clarinet | 3 | 434 | 15-17 | Guitar | 3 | 435 | 15-22 |
| Clarinet | 4 | 466 | 19-14 | Guitar | 4 | 468 | 19-24 |
| Clarinet | 5 | 514 | 21-25 | Guitar | 5 | 515 | 21-32 |
| Clarinet | 6 | 513 | 23-17 | Guitar (Electric) | 6 | 515 | 23-28 |
| Classical guitar | K | 330 | 11-55 | Guitarrón | 3 | 435 | 15-23 |
| Claves | 1 | 468 | 14-35 | Guitarrón | 5 | 516 | 21-33 |
| Claves | K | 328 | 11-40 | Hammered Dulcimer | 2 | 422 | 15-28 |
| Conga | 2 | 420 | 15-20 | Hand Bells | 5 | 516 | 21-34 |
| Conga | 3 | 434 | 15-18 | Hand drum | K | 329 | 11-50 |
| Conga | 4 | 467 | 19-15 | Harp | 5 | 516 | 21-36 |
| Conga | 6 | 513 | 23-18 | Harpsichord | 3 | 436 | 15-24 |
| Conga Drum | 5 | 514 | 21-26 | Harpsichord | 4 | 468 | 19-25 |
| Cowbell | K | 329 | 11-47 | Harpsichord | 5 | 516 | 21-35 |
| Cymbals | 1 | 468 | 14-34 | Harpsichord | K | 330 | 11-53 |
| Cymbals | 2 | 421 | 15-21 | Irish harp | 3 | 436 | 15-25 |
| Darabukah | 4 | 467 | 19-16 | Jarana | 3 | 436 | 15-26 |
| Didgeridoo | 4 | 467 | 19-17 | Jarana | 5 | 516 | 21-37 |
| Didgeridoo | 6 | 513 | 23-19 | Jingle bells | K | 329 | 11-45 |
| Djembe | 1 | 470 | 14-45 | Kendang | 6 | 515 | 23-29 |
| Djembe | 6 | 513 | 23-20 | Khong wong | 1 | 469 | 14-39 |
| Dombak | 6 | 514 | 23-22 | Koto | 2 | 422 | 15-29 |
| Donno | 6 | 514 | 23-21 | Koto | 3 | 436 | 15-27 |
| Doumbek | 5 | 515 | 21-27 | Koto | 4 | 468 | 19-26 |
| Drum Set | 2 | 421 | 15-22 | Koto | 5 | 516 | 21-38 |
| Drum Set | 6 | 514 | 23-23 | Koto | 6 | 515 | 23-30 |

Listening Index

| Title | Grade | Pg. | CD Track | Title | Grade | Pg. | CD Track |
|---|---|---|---|---|---|---|---|
| Kpanlogo | 6 | 516 | 23-31 | Synthesizer | 6 | 518 | 23-41 |
| Lute | 4 | 469 | 19-27 | Tabla | 1 | 470 | 14-42 |
| Maracas | 1 | 468 | 14-32 | Tabla | 2 | 424 | 15-38 |
| Maracas | 2 | 422 | 15-30 | Tabla | 6 | 518 | 23-42 |
| Maracas | 4 | 469 | 19-28 | Taiko | 5 | 518 | 21-48 |
| Maracas | K | 329 | 11-44 | Taiko drum | 1 | 470 | 14-46 |
| Marimba | 3 | 436 | 15-28 | Tamboura | 6 | 518 | 23-43 |
| Marimba | 4 | 469 | 19-29 | Tambourine | 2 | 424 | 15-39 |
| Mbira | 5 | 517 | 21-39 | Tambourine | K | 329 | 11-51 |
| Mbira | 6 | 516 | 23-32 | Timbales | 4 | 470 | 19-38 |
| Mridangam | 6 | 516 | 23-33 | Timpani | 1 | 470 | 14-43 |
| Musical Bow | 2 | 422 | 15-31 | Timpani | 2 | 424 | 15-40 |
| Native American Flute | 2 | 423 | 15-32 | Timpani | 3 | 438 | 15-37 |
| Native American Flute | 4 | 469 | 19-30 | Timpani | 4 | 470 | 19-39 |
| Oboe | 4 | 469 | 19-31 | Timpani | 5 | 518 | 21-49 |
| Odaiko Drum | 6 | 516 | 23-34 | Timpani | 6 | 518 | 23-44 |
| Organ | 4 | 469 | 19-32 | Tom-tom | K | 329 | 11-52 |
| Panpipes | 3 | 436 | 15-29 | Tone block | K | 328 | 11-38 |
| Piano | 3 | 437 | 15-30 | Triangle | K | 329 | 11-49 |
| Piano | 5 | 517 | 21-40 | Trombone | 1 | 471 | 14-49 |
| Piano | K | 330 | 11-54 | Trombone | 2 | 424 | 15-41 |
| Pipa | 2 | 423 | 15-33 | Trombone | 3 | 438 | 15-38 |
| Pujador | 3 | 437 | 15-31 | Trombone | 4 | 471 | 19-40 |
| Rain stick | K | 328 | 11-41 | Trombone | 5 | 519 | 21-50 |
| Ranat | 1 | 469 | 14-40 | Trombone | 6 | 518 | 23-45 |
| Recorder | 6 | 516 | 23-35 | Trumpet | 1 | 471 | 14-50 |
| Repicador | 3 | 437 | 15-32 | Trumpet | 2 | 424 | 15-42 |
| Requinto | 3 | 437 | 15-33 | Trumpet | 3 | 438 | 15-39 |
| Requinto | 5 | 517 | 21-41 | Trumpet | 4 | 471 | 19-41 |
| Sandblocks | K | 328 | 11-42 | Trumpet | 5 | 519 | 21-51 |
| Saxophone | 4 | 469 | 19-33 | Trumpet | 6 | 519 | 23-46 |
| Saxophone | 5 | 517 | 21-42 | Tuba | 2 | 425 | 15-43 |
| Saxophone | 6 | 517 | 23-36 | Tuba | 3 | 439 | 15-40 |
| Shakuhachi | 2 | 423 | 15-34 | Tuba | 4 | 471 | 19-42 |
| Shakuhachi | 3 | 437 | 15-34 | Tuba | 5 | 519 | 21-52 |
| Shakuhachi | 5 | 517 | 21-43 | Tuba | 6 | 519 | 23-47 |
| Shekere | 1 | 468 | 14-31 | Vibraphone | 3 | 439 | 15-41 |
| Shekere | 6 | 517 | 23-37 | Vihuela | 4 | 471 | 19-43 |
| Sheng | 2 | 423 | 15-35 | Vihuela | 5 | 519 | 21-53 |
| Sitar | 4 | 470 | 19-34 | Viola | 2 | 425 | 15-44 |
| Sitar | 5 | 518 | 21-44 | Viola | 3 | 439 | 15-42 |
| Snare Drum | 1 | 470 | 14-44 | Viola | 4 | 471 | 19-44 |
| Snare Drum | 3 | 438 | 15-35 | Violin | 1 | 469 | 14-38 |
| Snare Drum | 4 | 470 | 19-35 | Violin | 2 | 425 | 15-45 |
| Snare Drum | 5 | 518 | 21-45 | Violin | 3 | 439 | 15-43 |
| Snare Drum | 6 | 517 | 23-38 | Violin | 4 | 471 | 19-45 |
| Steel Drums | 4 | 470 | 19-36 | Violin | 5 | 519 | 21-54 |
| Steel Drums | 5 | 518 | 21-46 | Violin | 6 | 519 | 23-48 |
| Steel Drums | 6 | 517 | 23-39 | Woodblock | K | 328 | 11-39 |
| String Bass | 2 | 423 | 15-36 | Xylophone | 3 | 439 | 15-44 |
| String Bass | 3 | 438 | 15-36 | Xylophone | 5 | 519 | 21-55 |
| String Bass | 4 | 470 | 19-37 | Xylophone | 6 | 519 | 23-49 |
| String Bass | 6 | 517 | 23-40 | Yangqin | 2 | 425 | 15-46 |
| Synthesizer | 2 | 424 | 15-37 | Zampoña | 1 | 471 | 14-48 |
| Synthesizer | 5 | 518 | 21-47 | Zheng | 2 | 425 | 15-47 |

# Building Skills Through Music

**ART** *See also Related Arts.*
*1812 Overture* Gr. 4, 292
Autumn Canon Gr. 5, 148
*Brandenburg Concerto No. 2,*
    *Movement 3 Allegro Assai*
    Gr. 7, C-8
Cantaré, cantarás Gr. 6, 412
Cookie Crew, The Gr. K, 196
Court Ball at the Palais du Louvre (De
Médicis) Gr. 2, 278
Da pacem, Domine Gr. 5, 62
Dinah Gr. 2, 120
El chocolate Gr. 1, 378
Families Gr. 1, 280
Flip, Flop and Fly Gr. 7, E-32
Follow the Drinkin' Gourd Gr. 4, 266
Freedom Is Coming Gr. 5, 414
Girl with a Guitar (Vermeer) Gr. 4, 177
Goin' to the Fair Gr. K, 156
Good Morning Gr. 3, 192
Heri za Kwanzaa Gr. 5, 476
Hey, Ho! Nobody Home Gr. 6, 28
Hui jia qü Gr. 2, 158
I Was Walking in a Circle Gr. 3, 320
If You Find a Little Feather Gr. 1, 186
Ja-Da Gr. 7, G-20
Joe Turner Blues Gr. 4, 56
Kébé Mama Gr. 1, 442
*Lion Sleeps Tonight, The* Gr. 8, E-8
Listen to the Water Gr. 2, 294
Little Shop of Horrors Gr. 4, 422
Look! Look! The Sun Woke Up!
    Gr. 1, 368
Mi chacra Gr. 1, 364
Nanny Goat Gr. K, 160
Napping House, The Gr. 1, 198
New Way to Walk, A Gr. K, 116
Over the River and Through the Wood
    Gr. 3, 384
Oy, Hanuka Gr. 5, 464
Percussion Fun Rondo Gr. 7, I-50
Pin Pon Gr. 1, 146
Plant Four Seeds Gr. 2, 130
Purple People Eater, The Gr. 6, 448
Ríu ríu chíu Gr. 5, 434
Shady Grove Gr. 5, 260
She'll Be Comin' 'Round the Mountain
    Gr. 2, 358
Song That's Just for You, A Gr. 2, 126
Sorida Gr. 1, 312
Ten Little Ostinato Pieces Gr. 7, I-62
Texas Cowboy Gr. 3, 250
Tree in the Wood, The Gr. 2, 360
Twelve Gates to the City Gr. 5, 280
Winter Song Gr. 6, 454
Zuni Sunrise Call Gr. 5, 396

**DANCE**
Abbots Bromley Horn Dance
    Gr. 7, C-24
Alumot Gr. 6, 306
Cheki, morena Gr. 7, I-16
Over My Head Gr. 7, G-8
Rockin' Around the Christmas Tree
    Gr. 5, 466
Surfin' U.S.A. Gr. 7, F-32
Uno, dos, y tres Gr. 5, 426
*Ve'David Y'Fey Enayiam* Gr. 4, 316
Wai bamba Gr. 8, G-12

**HEALTH EDUCATION**
*Academic Festival Overture*, Op. 80
    Gr. 8, C-20
Alleluia, Amen Gr. 7, A-12
*Angry Anymore* Gr. 8, F-32
*Batucada* Parade Ensemble
    Gr. 8, D-22
Blues with a Feeling Gr. 8, I-6
*Children's Corner, "Jimbo's Lullaby"*
    Gr. 1, 270
Fais do do Gr. 6, 402
I'll Fly Away Gr. 8, I-42
Ikhanda, maslombe Gr. K, 14
*Keep a Cool Head* Gr. 7, B-34
Lean on Me Gr. 7, E-22
Mmmmmm mmmmmmm Gr. K, 70
Mood Music Gr. 8, A-6
Mother, Mother, I Am Sick Gr. K, 120
Music Therapist/Teacher Gr. 8, A-26
*Nruab hnub thiab hmo ntuj*
    Gr. 4, 366
Peter, Peter, Sugar Eater Gr. 1, 284
*Queen's Suite, The, "Sunset and the*
    *Mocking Bird"* Gr. 8, E-10
Thanksgiving Is Near Gr. 2, 380
Three Little Birds Gr. 4, 320
What's Happening to my Voice?
    Gr. 8, G-6
Yellow Butter Gr. 1, 124
You Were on My Mind Gr. 7, G-22
Your changing voice Gr. 7, G-6

**LANGUAGE ARTS**
A la puerta del cielo Gr. 5, 60
A-Tisket, A-Tasket Gr. 2, 238
Addams Family, The Gr. 5, 456
Ain't Gonna Let Nobody Turn Me
    'Round Gr. 6, 84
America Gr. 3, 412
America Gr. 4, 440
America Gr. 5, 486
America Gr. 7, I-2
America Gr. 8, I-2
America, the Beautiful Gr. 4, 158
Arirang Gr. 5, 25
Artsa alinu Gr. 3, 284

Avocational musicians Gr. 8, A-30
Away to America Gr. 5, 57
Ayliluli, num tsipor Gr. 1, 204
Bam, chi, chi, bam Gr. K, 108
Bananas and Cream Gr. 1, 49
Bling Blang Gr. 3, 240
Blow the Wind Southerly Gr. 5, 178
Bluebird, Bluebird Gr. K, 104
Bonga Gr. K, 78
Bridges Gr. 6, 86
Bubble Trouble Gr. K, 184
Bury Me Not on the Lone Prairie
    Gr. 6, 18
Bye Bye, Love Gr. 8, F-8
Cafe Europa Gr. 7, B-42
California Dreamin' Gr. 8, G-30
*(Can't Live Without Your) Love and*
    *Affection* Gr. 7, B-22
Canción Mixteca Gr. 5, 326
*Caprice No. 1 in E Major* Gr. 7, C-22
*Carnaval Calypso Ensemble*
    Gr. 7, D-20
*Catalana, "Andante"* Gr. K, 134
Cattle Call Gr. 5, 344
Chawe chidyo chem'chero Gr. 2, 296
Chickens, The Gr. 3, 92
Chippewa Lullaby Gr. K, 180
Chuhwuht Gr. 2, 356
Cinderella Dressed in Green
    Gr. K, 136
*Clair de lune* Gr. K, 164
Colorado Trail Gr. 5, 276
Come and Go with Me to That Land
    Gr. 5, 390
Come, Ye Thankful People, Come
    Gr. 5, 458
*Concerto for Orchestra,*
    *"Presentation of Pairs"* Gr. 4, 72
*Copycat* Gr. K, 9
Cow's Woc Backward Gr. 1, 390
*Crunchy, Crunchy, Crunchy*
    Gr. 8, D-14
Dayenu Gr. 4, 438
Deep in the Heart of Texas Gr. 8, E-22
Different Beat, A Gr. 1, 4
Diou shou juan'er Gr. 2, 276
Do Wah Diddy Diddy Gr. 7, F-20
Don't You Hear the Lambs? Gr. 5, 96
Dona nobis pacem Gr. 6, 124
Doong gul ge Gr. 3, 134
Down by the Riverside Gr. 5, 256
Down, Down, Baby Gr. 2, 32
*Drift* Gr. 8, B-42
Dundai Gr. 5, 106
*Dusty Rag* Gr. K, 164
Eensy Weensy Spider Gr. K, 186
El barquito Gr. 3, 358
El rancho grande Gr. 4, 214

Building Skills Through Music

El Salón México Gr. 6, 198
Estampie Gr. 8, I-26
Ev'rybody Loves Saturday Night Gr. 7, I-24
*Every Morning* Gr. 7, B-8
Extremes Gr. 4, 402
Falling Rain Gr. 2, 328
Farmer's Dairy Key, The Gr. 2, 182
*Fiesta, "Tarantella"* Gr. K, 134
*Fingerprints* Gr. 7, B-42
Flip, Flop and Fly Gr. 7, I-32
*Four Seasons, Concerto No. 2, The, "Summer," Movement 3, "La Tempesta"* Gr. 6, 102
Freight Train Gr. 1, 44
From Sea to Shining Sea Gr. 2, 342
*Gamelan angklung* Gr. 6, 384
Get on Your Feet Gr. 5, 6
Give a Little Love Gr. 6, 140
*Gloria In Excelsis* Gr. 6, 210
Gonna Ride Up in the Chariot Gr. 4, 20
Great Day Gr. 3, 58
Haliwa-Saponi Canoe Song Gr. 5, 302
Happy Feet Gr. 2, 252
Haul Away, Joe Gr. 4, 12
Hava nagila Gr. 6, 152
Heigh-Ho Gr. 2, 6
Hevenu shalom aleichem Gr. 3, 378
Hi Heidi Ho Gr. 1, 392
Hickory, Dickory, Dare (speech piece) Gr. K, 20
Hickory, Dickory, Dock (so-la-so-mi Version) Gr. 1, 224
Higglety, Pigglety, Pop! Gr. K, 22
Hitotsu toya Gr. 5, 478
Home on the Range Gr. 5, 68
Hop Up, My Ladies Gr. 3, 142
Hound Dog Gr. 5, 212
How Can I Keep from Singing? Gr. 4, 260
*Hungarian Dance No. 19* Gr. 4, 170
I Don't Care If the Rain Comes Down Gr. 3, 24
I Got Shoes Gr. 2, 242
I Love the Mountains Gr. 5, 34
If I Had a Hammer Gr. 5, 286
Imbabura Gr. 5, 202
Inkpataya Gr. 3, 254
*Ionisation* Gr. 6, 354
Isley Brothers, The Gr. 4, 238
It Don't Mean a Thing (If It Ain't Got That Swing) Gr. 5, 336
Jack and Jill Gr. K, 46
Jack, Be Nimble Gr. K, 96
*Jazz in the Box* Gr. 8, F-10
*Jelly Roll, The* Gr. 7, B-36
Jig Along Home Gr. 2, 366
Jingle Writing Gr. 8, A-4
Jo'ashila Gr. 5, 108
Joshua Fought the Battle of Jericho Gr. 8, E-18
Juniper Tree, The Gr. 3, 130

Kayagum pyongch'ang-sae t'aryug Gr. 8, B-13
Kingston Market Gr. 3, 90
*Kokopelli Wandering Song* Gr. 5, 110
Kookaburra Gr. 4, 186
Kum bachur atzel Gr. 3, 138
La ciudad de Juaja Gr. 5, 58
La mar estaba serena Gr. 2, 344
*La Rosa* Gr. K, 134
Lap Time Gr. K, 100
Laredo Gr. 5, 10
Lean on Me Gr. 6, 14
Lemonade Gr. 1, 188
Like a Bird Gr. 6, 166
*Lion* Gr. 6, 302
Locomoto-vation Gr. K, 60
Looking for the Mother Birds Gr. 3, 330
Los reyes de Oriente Gr. 5, 480
Lots of Worms Gr. 2, 310
Love Somebody Gr. 3, 94
Lullaby and Dance Gr. 4, 386
*Lyric Suite, "Allegretto gioviale," Movement 1* Gr. 6, 168
Mary Ann Gr. 6, 180
*Mass, "Responsory Alleluia"* Gr. 6, 216
Merry Modal Christmas, A Gr. 4, 410
Midnight Special, The Gr. 7, F-22
Modern Dragon, A Gr. 3, 242
Mother Sent Me to the Store Gr. K, 136
Mozart, Wolfgang Amadeus Gr. 4, 110
Mud Gr. 3, 32
My Bonnie Lies Over the Ocean Gr. 4, 338
My Fathers' House Gr. 2, 24
Name, Name, What's Your Name? (speech piece) Gr. 3, 10
New Hungarian Folk Song Gr. 6, 196
Nie chcę cię znać Gr. 3, 314
Night Will Never Stay, The Gr. 3, 182
*O ignis spiritus Paracliti* Gr. 7, C-4
O Laufet, ihr Hirten Gr. 2, 384
Ochimbo Gr. 4, 134
Oh, Freedom Gr. 5, 392
Oh, Freedom Gr. 7, G-30
Oh, Won't You Sit Down Gr. 3, 28
One Morning in May Gr. 6, 120
*Open the Kingdom* Gr. 6, 30
Orange Blossom Special Gr. 5, 266
Over in the Meadow Gr. 1, 346
Over the Rainbow Gr. 4, 140
Oy, Hanuka Gr. 7, I-44
Oye Gr. 6, 336
Parade Came Marching, The Gr. 1, 165
Party Tonight! Gr. 2, 152
Paths of Victory Gr. 6, 194
Peace Like a River Gr. 3, 246
Peace Like a River Gr. 6, 190
Pick 'n' Mix Zoo Gr. K, 138

*Pictures at an Exhibition, "The Great Gate of Kiev"* Gr. 8, A-12
*Planxty Madame Maxwell* Gr. K, 134
Play a Simple Melody Gr. 5, 72
Pon, pon, pon Gr. K, 50
Pretty Saro Gr. 3, 216
Producer Gr. 8, A-24
Pumpkin Poem Gr. 3, 380
Pust' 'vsegda budet sonse Gr. 3, 278
Put a Little Love in Your Heart Gr. 4, 6
Put Your Hand in My Hand Gr. 1, 330
Rags Gr. 1, 290
Ragtime Cowboy Joe Gr. 2, 250
Rainbow, The Gr. 2, 332
*Requiem, "Pie Jesu"* Gr. 6, 176
Riendo el río corre Gr. 6, 262
*Rig-a-Jig-Jig* Gr. K, 98
*Rigoletto, "Bella figlia dell'amore"* Gr. 7, C-28
*Rise Up, Shepherd, and Follow* Gr. 5, 470
*Rock Around the Clock* Gr. 5, 356
Rocky Top Gr. 5, 348
*Rose, (from the Motion Picture Titanic)* Gr. 8, B-34
Rosie, Darling Rosie Gr. 2, 214
'Round and 'Round Gr. 1, 148
Run, Molly, Run Gr. 1, 8
*Salute to Sunnyland Slim* Gr. 8, E-32
*Samanfo, begye nsa nom* Gr. 8, D-6
*Scherzo for Wind Quintet, Op. 48* Gr. 1, 328
Scotland the Brave Gr. 5, 138
Scrub Brush Shuffle, The Gr. 1, 118
Sea Wolf, The Gr. 4, 254
Seagull, Seagull, Sit on the Shore Gr. 4, 382
See the Children Playin' Gr. 4, 106
See-Saw Sacradown Gr. 2, 208
Serra, serra, serrador Gr. 1, 112
Shenandoah Gr. 5, 264
Shoo, Turkey Gr. 1, 104
Shri Ram, jai Ram Gr. 4, 310
Si me pongo yo a cantar Gr. 3, 132
Sing a Rainbow Gr. 2, 166
Sing! Speak! Whisper! Shout! Gr. 1, 36
Siyahamba Gr. 6, 212
Skye Boat Song Gr. 6, 370
Somebody's Knockin' at Your Door Gr. 4, 52
*Sonata in G Minor, Op. 1, No. 1, Movement 2* Gr. 7, C-12
Song of Greatness, A Gr. 3, 334
*Spain* Gr. 7, B-42
St. Louis Blues Gr. 5, 352
Still, Still, Still Gr. 5, 468
*String Quartet No. 5, Movement 4: Andante* Gr. 3, 110
Summertime Gr. 6, 250
Supercalifragilisticexpialidocious Gr. 3, 6
Surfin' U.S.A. Gr. 7, E-27

Building Skills Through Music

*Symphony No. 5 in C Minor, Movement 1* Gr. 6, 98
Table Manners (speech piece) Gr. 3, 190
Take a Chance on Me Gr. 8, G-14
Tall Cedar Tree Gr. 2, 322
*Tamaiti hunahia* Gr. 6, 24
Tanabata-sama Gr. 2, 336
Tender Shepherd (Count Your Sheep) Gr. 3, 116
*That's the Way It Is* Gr. 7, B-22
*Theme and Variations for Percussion* Gr. 5, 64
There is Joy Gr. 3, 258
*Toccata for Percussion, Movement 3* Gr. 4, 154
Tom Dooley Gr. 6, 374
Trouble Is a Mountain Gr. 2, 202
Turn the World Around Gr. 4, 114
Turn, Turn, Turn (To Everything There Is a Season) Gr. 5, 378
Tzena, tzena Gr. 5, 298
'Ūlili E Gr. 5, 440
Un, deux, trois Gr. 2, 198
Un elefante Gr. 2, 160
Un pajarito Gr. 2, 16
Valentines Gr. 2, 398
*Ve'David Y'Fey Enayiam* Gr. 4, 316
Walk Together, Children Gr. 3, 146
Water Come a Me Eye Gr. 6, 298
Water Is Wide, The Gr. 6, 228
We Shall Overcome Gr. 4, 326
We're Making Popcorn (speech piece) Gr. 1, 84
What a Wonderful World Gr. 6, 62
When Johnny Comes Marching Home Gr. 5, 180
Where's Your Drum? Ensemble Gr. 8, D-20
Who Has Seen the Wind? Gr. 2, 324
Who Has the Penny? Gr. K, 42
Willowbee Gr. 1, 222
Winter Gr. 8, G-10
Winter Fantasy Gr. 4, 424
Written in March Gr. 4, 354
Xiao yin chuan Gr. 2, 14
Yankee Doodle Gr. 3, 414
Yesh lanu taish Gr. 1, 180
Yüe liang wan wan Gr. 5, 314
Zip-a-Dee-Doo-Dah Gr. 2, 330

## MATH

A Ram Sam Sam Gr. 3, 208
ABC Rock Gr. 1, 262
Achshav Gr. 2, 64
Ah, eu entrei na roda Gr. 3, 308
Ah, Jolis Papillons Gr. 1, 360
Ala Da'lona Gr. 4, 136
All Through the Night Gr. 5, 104
Ants Go Marching, The Gr. 1, 248
*Baa-Baa Black Sheep* Gr. K, 102
Back of the Bus Gr. 3, 410
Banana Splits Gr. 1, 318

Bantama kra kro Gr. 5, 308
Bereleh Gr. K, 150
Bingo Gr. 1, 168
Blue Mountain Lake Gr. 6, 204
Blue Skies Gr. 6, 88
Book of Love Gr. 8, G-26
Busy Buzzy Bee Gr. K, 176
Caballito blanco Gr. 2, 192
Canción de cuna Gr. 4, 144
Certainly, Lord Gr. 7, I-12
Cha yang wu Gr. 1, 88
Chanukah Games Gr. 3, 388
Chanukah Is Here! Gr. 2, 382
Chapel of Love Gr. 7, G-26
Che che koolay Gr. 2, 266
Cielito lindo Gr. 7, I-20
Computer-generated fractal image Gr. 4, 198
Counting-Out Rhyme Gr. 1, 356
Cuckoo, Cuckoo Gr. 1, 110
Dance for the Nations Gr. 6, 122
Debajo 'el botón Gr. 1, 210
Digital revolution, The Gr. 7, B-44
Ding, Dong, Diggidiggidong Gr. 3, 14
Do, Re, Mi, Fa Gr. 6, 80
Don Gato Gr. 3, 352
*Dr Gradus ad Parnassum* Gr. 8, C-26
Drill, Ye Tarriers Gr. 5, 54
Each of Us Is a Flower Gr. 3, 154
Earth Is Our Mother, The Gr. 8, F-24
Einini Gr. 4, 390
El payo Gr. 6, 144
El tambor Gr. 2, 274
En nuestra Tierra tan linda Gr. 2, 334
Erie Canal Gr. 5, 262
Every Morning When I Wake Up Gr. 2, 320
Every Night When the Sun Goes In Gr. 8, I-28
Feng yang hua gu Gr. 4, 312
Fiddler on the Roof Gr. 7, E-4
Five Little Chickadees Gr. K, 178
Flight of the Bumblebee Gr. 3, 186
Four in a Boat Gr. 2, 46
Frère Jacques Gr. 2, 124
Frog in the Millpond Gr. 2, 44
Gakavik Gr. 4, 14
Get on Board Gr. K, 88
Goldilocks and the Three Bears Gr. K, 48
*Halley Came to Jackson* Gr. 2, 340
Hashewie Gr. 4, 62
*Heads Carolina, Tails California* Gr. 7, B-24
Hello! Gr. 2, 262
Hey, Hey, Look at Me Gr. 1, 70
Hickory, Dickory, Dock Gr. 1, 350
Hot Cross Buns (Version 1) Gr. 3, 218
*Hungarian Dance No. 3 in F Major* Gr. 1, 206
Hwa yuan li-de young wa wa Gr. 3, 102
I Got a Letter This Morning Gr. K, 68

I Love Peanuts Gr. 7, E-20
I Saw Three Ships Gr. 1, 426
I'm Flying Home Gr. 2, 286
Ichi-gatsu tsuitachi Gr. 7, I-40
Ida Red Gr. 3, 30
Ise oluwa Gr. 2, 102
It's a Beautiful Day Gr. 3, 338
Jan ken pon Gr. 3, 302
Jim Along, Josie Gr. K, 38
John Kanaka Gr. 3, 60
Just from the Kitchen Gr. K, 54
Kaeru no uta Gr. K, 183
Kangaroo Song, The Gr. K, 44
Karangatia ra Gr. 3, 272
Keel Row, The Gr. 4, 240
Keep Your Eyes on the Prize Gr. 8, E-16
Keys Gr. K, 188
Kpanlogo Highlife Ensemble Gr. 7, D-12
Kuma san Gr. K, 40
Kwa-nu-te Gr. 3, 214
La piñata Gr. 3, 398
La víbora Gr. 1, 322
Las horas Gr. 1, 246
Le jig Français Gr. K, 64
Lion and the Mouse, The Gr. 1, 238
Little Spider Gr. K, 92
Long Way Home, A Gr. 1, 382
Lucy Locket Gr. 2, 26
Make a Music Video! Gr. 7, A-28
Mama Don't 'Low Gr. 6, 358
Man of Constant Sorrow Gr. 7, F-28
Mi cuerpo hace música Gr. K, 106
Michael Finnigan Gr. 3, 152
Michael, Row the Boat Ashore Gr. 2, 18
Movie Sound Effects Gr. 8, A-8
Music delivery Gr. 7, A-30
Nampaya omame Gr. 1, 136
Noah's Shanty Gr. 1, 342
Nyoka Gr. 7, D-32
O lê lê O Bahía Gr. 6, 164
O ma washi Gr. K, 12
Old Blue Gr. K, 122
Pai pi qiu Gr. 1, 324
Pastures of Plenty Gr. 4, 280
Pay Me My Money Down Gr. 7, F-4
Peace Round Gr. 4, 348
Phoebe Gr. 1, 30
*Piano Trio No. 2 in E-flat Major, Op. 100, Scherzo* Gr. 4, 192
Pizza, Pizza, Daddy-o Gr. 2, 28
*Planet Drone* Gr. 8, B-10
Polly Wee Gr. K, 118
Ptashky u babusi sadochku Gr. 1, 192
Red River Valley Gr. 6, 10
Rhythm Is Gonna Get You, The Gr. 6, 348
River Gr. 4, 58
Rock Island Line Gr. 4, 54
'Round the Bay of Mexico Gr. 4, 258
S'vivon Gr. 6, 452

**Building Skills Through Music**

Santa Clara Gr. 4, 172
Scarborough Fair Gr. 6, 94
*Scherzo for Wind Quintet, Op. 48*
Gr. 1, 328
Scrub-a-dub Gr. 1, 304
Seasons Gr. K, 4
Shake Them 'Simmons Down
Gr. 2, 244
*Shekere* Gr. 1, 115
Shortnin' Bread Gr. 1, 56
Shortnin' Bread Gr. 7, F-26
Shu ha mo Gr. 3, 276
Sing a Song of Peace Gr. 6, 66
Six-Inch Boots in a Nine-Inch Puddle
Gr. 1, 366
Small Job, A Gr. 3, 224
Somebody Waiting Gr. 2, 282
Something Told the Wild Geese
Gr. 7, G-38
Son macaron Gr. 4, 108
*Sonata for Violin and Piano, Allegro*
Gr. 8, C-46
St. Patrick Was a Gentleman
Gr. 3, 290
*String Quartet No. 5, Movement 4:*
*Andante* Gr. 3, 110
*Symphony No. 40 in G Minor, K.*
*550, Movement 1* Gr. 8, B-30
*Symphony No. 5 in C Minor, Op. 67,*
*Movement 1* Gr. 7, C-16
This Old Man Gr. 3, 152
Thula, thula, ngoana Gr. 4, 226
Tic, tac Gr. 1, 252
Time to Sing Gr. 2, 8
Twelve Days of Christmas, The
Gr. 4, 430
Vamos a hacer la ronda Gr. K, 124
*Waitin' for a Train* Gr. 7, B-24
Walk in Jerusalem Gr. 4, 100
Way Down in the Schoolyard Gr. 2, 50
Weevily Wheat Gr. 4, 104
Windshield Wipers Gr. 1, 10
Wood Works Ensemble Gr. 8, D-28
Zudio Gr. 2, 268
Zum gali gali Gr. 5, 400

## PHYSICAL EDUCATION

Agbekor Ensemble Gr. 8, D-10
America, the Beautiful Gr. 8, I-4
Bounce High, Bounce Low Gr. 1, 150
Cindy Gr. 4, 384
Clap, Wiggle, and Stomp Gr. K, 34
*Copycat* Gr. K, 9
Deep in the Heart of Texas Gr. 8, I-18
Doumbek or Hand Drum Exercises
Gr. 7, D-30
Éliza Kongo Gr. 5, 14
Faerie Stories Gr. 8, B-2
God Bless the Grass Gr. 8, F-12
Hand Clap Ensemble Gr. 7, D-2
Hine mah tov Gr. 5, 430
Karangatia ra Gr. 8, F-22
La paloma blanca Gr. 3, 252

Let's Get the Rhythm of the Band
Gr. 7, E-28
Little David, Play on Your Harp
Gr. 4, 394
Little Johnny Brown Gr. 3, 312
Locomoto-vation Gr. K, 60
Love Will Guide Us Gr. 4, 328
New Way to Walk, A Gr. K, 116
Old Brass Wagon Gr. 2, 122
Sambalele Gr. 4, 396
*Sing We and Chant It* Gr. 8, C-4
Stand By Me Gr. 5, 46
*Stand By Me* Gr. 8, E-24
Surfin' U.S.A. Gr. 7, F-32
This Land is Your Land Gr. 7, F-24
Three Little Birds Gr. 8, F-6
Twist with a Burger, Jitter with a Bug
(speech piece) Gr. 1, 132
¡Viva el fútbol! Gr. 1, 94
Wai bamba Gr. 8, G-12
Waiting for the Traffic Light Gr. 2, 106

## READING

12-Bar Blues Rock Gr. 8, F-30
Ain't Gonna Let Nobody Turn Me
'Round Gr. 8, F-16
Alleluia Gr. 6, 132
America Gr. 1, 446
America Gr. 6, 484
America, the Beautiful Gr. 7, I-4
Amoco Renegades Gr. 4, 38
At the Same Time Gr. 6, 114
*Awakening* Gr. 3, 286
Ayelivi Gr. 2, 70
*Backstage with Jeanine Tesori*
Gr. 8, A-20
Barb'ry Allen Gr. 6, 44
Boogie Chant and Dance (speech
piece) Gr. 2, 78
Bound for South Australia Gr. 5, 22
But the Cat Came Back Gr. 2, 190
California Gr. 5, 52
*Carry On Wayward Son* Gr. 7, B-18
Chicka Hanka Gr. 8, F-14
Corn Grinding Song Gr. K, 66
Cowboys' Christmas Ball Gr. 6, 236
Crawfish! Gr. 2, 86
De colores Gr. 5, 90
De colores Gr. 8, I-14
Dok djampa Gr. 8, I-20
Don't Let the Wind Gr. 3, 180
El carnavalito humahuaqueño
Gr. 6, 482
El gallo pinto Gr. 3, 86
Elegua Gr. 7, D-6
*Evening Chaconne* Gr. 6, 202
Faith of the Heart Gr. 8, G-2
Goin' Down the Road Feelin' Bad
Gr. 7, F-12
Goin' to Boston Gr. 6, 432
Good King Wenceslas Gr. 6, 458
Gotta Find a Footprint Gr. 4, 218
Guantanamera Gr. 8, I-32

Ha'kyo jong Gr. 2, 134
Happiness Gr. K, 62
I Am But a Small Voice Gr. 6, 444
I Dream a World Gr. 8, G-40
I Vow to You, My Country Gr. 5, 418
I Wish I Knew How It Would Feel to Be
Free Gr. 6, 466
I Wonder Where Maria's Gone
Gr. 3, 318
I'm on My Way Gr. 3, 76
In the Morning Gr. 1, 216
Johnny Mister Brown Gr. K, 36
Joy of Kwanzaa, The Gr. 6, 462
Joy to the World Gr. 3, 20
*Key to the Highway* Gr. 8, F-28
Kunolounkwa Gr. K, 110
La bamba Gr. 5, 128
La golondrina Gr. 8, I-50
La tormenta tropical Gr. 2, 116
Lady, Lady Gr. 1, 62
Las Navidades Gr. 5, 472
Light Up the World with a Song
Gr. 8, G-24
Limbo Like Me Gr. 4, 18
Lion Sleeps Tonight, The Gr. 8, I-56
Los pececitos Gr. 1, 178
Lost My Gold Ring Gr. 6, 158
Love in Any Language Gr. 6, 472
Mashed Potatoes (speech piece)
Gr. 1, 20
Moon's the North Wind's Cooky, The
Gr. 4, 374
Musical classification of instruments
Gr. 6, 362
My Dear Companion Gr. 6, 22
Niño querido Gr. 1, 308
Now That's Tap (speech piece)
Gr. 6, 320
Oh, Danny Boy Gr. 4, 48
Old Texas Gr. 3, 76
Panamam tombé Gr. 7, D-18
Poem Gr. 3, 162
Pollerita Gr. 5, 151
Quiet Night Gr. 4, 334
Railroad Corral Gr. 3, 174
Shanghai Chicken Gr. 1, 140
*Songs from Letters, "So Like Your*
*Father"* Gr. 7, C-20
Sourwood Mountain Gr. 4, 64
Spaceworms Gr. 1, 400
Storm Dance Gr. K, 144
This Is My Song Gr. 6, 76
This Land Is Your Land Gr. 5, 118
Those Magic Changes Gr. 8, E-30
Train Is A-Comin' Gr. 3, 48
Tree House Gr. 3, 206
Viva Jujuy Gr. 5, 228
Wade in the Water Gr. 8, I-64
When the Saints Go Marching In
Gr. 2, 178
Wind Song (poem) Gr. K, 6

**RELATED ARTS** *See also Art.*
*Believer* Gr. 7, A-2
*Firebird, The, "Finale"* Gr. 8, C-30
God Bless the Child Gr. 7, B-26
Instrument Maker Gr. 8, A-28
*Let's Face the Music* Gr. 7, B-14

**SCIENCE**
A-Cling, A-Cling Gr. 4, 188
Ackabacka, Soda Cracker Gr. 1, 302
Aiken Drum Gr. 1, 398
All Around the Buttercup Gr. 2, 170
Alle meine Entchen Gr. 1, 98
*Altered Landscapes: Part One*
     Gr. 8, E-20
Amasee Gr. 1, 172
Apple Tree Gr. 1, 228
Apples, Peaches, Pears, and Plums
     (speech piece) Gr. 1, 14
Ash Grove, The Gr. 5, 114
Bam, chi, chi, bam Gr. K, 108
Bard of Armagh, The Gr. 4, 296
Bear Dance Gr. K, 126
Bee, Bee Bumblebee (speech piece)
     Gr. 1, 50
Black Snake Gr. 3, 52
Box a-Rockin' Ensemble Gr. 7, D-4
Bundle-Buggy Boogie Woogie (speech
     piece) Gr. 4, 120
California, Here I Come Gr. 4, 286
Canoe Song Gr. 4, 76
*Carnaval, Op. 9, "Valse Noble," Un*
     *poco maestoso* Gr. 3, 200
Charlie over the Water Gr. 1, 66
Children of the Sun Gr. 1, 402
*China Gates* Gr. 7, C-44
Concert for Piano and Orchestra
     Gr. 6, 208
Crayons Gr. K, 74
Cumberland Gap Gr. 4, 138
Deau-deau, ti pitit maman Gr. 2, 306
Der sad to katte Gr. 2, 300
Deux cocodries Gr. 2, 364
*Drums From Around the World*
     Gr. 6, 276
Dry Bones Gr. 4, 162
Eh, cumpari! Gr. 4, 68
El coquí Gr. 2, 292
El mes de abril Gr. 3, 328
Ezekiel Saw the Wheel Gr. 6, 378
Farewell to Tarwathie Gr. 6, 42
Fly and the Bumblebee, The Gr. 1, 384
Follow the Drinkin' Gourd Gr. 4, 266
*Forever, For Now* Gr. 7, B-16
*French Suite No. 5, "Gigue"*
     Gr. 4, 232
Frog Music Gr. 4, 200
*Gapu* Gr. 8, B-38
*Glory Hallelujah Grand March*
     Gr. 8, C-38
*Guitar Tuning* Gr. 7, F-2
Here Comes Valerie Gr. 1, 32
Here I Go! Gr. K, 72

Hi-Dee-Roon Gr. K, 10
Honeybee Song, The Gr. 1, 358
I Can't Spell Hippopotamus Gr. 1, 264
If a Tiger Calls Gr. 3, 354
If You Find a Little Feather Gr. 1, 186
*If You Look* Gr. 7, B-4
If You're Happy Gr. K, 94
It's a Beautiful Day Gr. 3, 338
Jambalaya Gr. 8, F-18
Knock the Cymbals Gr. 1, 174
Kum bachur atzel Gr. 3, 138
La mariposa Gr. 6, 58
Leaves Gr. 1, 26
*"Little" Organ Fugue in G Minor*
     Gr. 6, 128
Little Green Frog, The Gr. 1, 22
Loigratong Gr. 6, 450
Look! Look! The Sun Woke Up!
     Gr. 1, 368
Los maizales Gr. 1, 294
Luna lunera (speech piece) Gr. K, 90
*Mainly Metal Ensemble* Gr. 7, D-26
Mister Ram Goat-O Gr. 3, 54
Morning Has Broken Gr. 5, 28
My Girl Josephine Gr. 8, E-20
My Mama's Calling Me Gr. 1, 260
Nana, Thread Needle Gr. 1, 38
Nani wale na hala Gr. 3, 260
Nanny Goat Gr. K, 160
Never Smile at a Crocodile Gr. 3, 100
Oh, How Lovely is the Evening
     Gr. 4, 216
Oh, Watch the Stars Gr. 2, 144
Oh, Watch the Stars Gr. 5, 216
Old House, Tear It Down! Gr. 4, 178
On a Log, Mister Frog Gr. K, 148
Our Tree (poem) Gr. 1, 184
Painting Song: A Dribble and a Dot
     Gr. K, 174
Pease Porridge Hot Gr. 1, 134
Planets Chant, The Gr. 4, 376
Rabbit Footprints Gr. 2, 304
Rags Gr. 1, 290
Rain, Rain Gr. 1, 54
Rain Sings a Song, The Gr. 1, 100
*Rocky Point Holiday* Gr. 6, 330
*Rundadinella* Gr. 8, I-60
*Rwakanembe* Gr. 8, C-14
Sarika keo Gr. 3, 274
Shoo, Fly Gr. 2, 200
Singin' in the Rain Gr. 4, 360
Snowflakes Gr. 1, 422
Somewhere Out There Gr. 5, 368
Song of the Night, The Gr. 3, 344
Squirrel, The Gr. K, 128
Starlight, Star Bright Gr. 4, 372
Tap It! Rap It! (speech piece)
     Gr. K, 194
This Train Gr. 5, 26
*Toccata and Fugue in D Minor*
     Gr. 7, E-24
Turkey Game, The Gr. 1, 414
*Ue ue* Gr. 8, D-2

Waltzing with Bears Gr. 3, 170
We Are Dear Little Birdies Gr. K, 176
Wheel of the Water, The Gr. 4, 362
*Whirlwind* Gr. 3, 148
*Zomo the Rabbit* Gr. 3, 364

**SOCIAL STUDIES**
Adana ya gidelim Gr. 2, 142
*Aerial Boundaries* Gr. 8, F-20
*Akua Tuta* Gr. 7, D-24
Al tambor Gr. 3, 270
Alabama Gal Gr. 3, 106
Alexander's Ragtime Band Gr. 6, 136
*Ali Pasha* Gr. 5, 218
America Gr. 5, 486
America, the Beautiful Gr. 5, 76
America, the Free Gr. 4, 210
Así es mi tierra Gr. 6, 172
¡Ay, Jalisco no te rajes! Gr. 7, I-6
Banuwa Gr. 6, 294
Basin Street Blues Gr. 5, 354
Bắt kim thang Gr. 6, 12
Battle Cry of Freedom Gr. 5, 272
*Batucada* Parade Ensemble
     Gr. 8, D-22
Big Rock Candy Mountain Gr. 4, 330
Blowin' in the Wind Gr. 5, 382
Bluebonnets of Texas Gr. 3, 332
Bonavist' Harbour Gr. 3, 294
Bonjour, mes amis Gr. 1, 316
Bounce High, Bounce Low Gr. 1, 150
Bus, The Gr. K, 82
By the Waters of Babylon Gr. 6, 310
Camptown Races Gr. 5, 270
Carnaval Calypso Ensemble
     Gr. 7, D-20
*Carolina Sunday Waltz* Gr. 7, F-8
Chairs to Mend Gr. 4, 148
Chang Gr. 1, 154
*Changed My Name* Gr. 6, 338
Chanukah, Chanukah Gr. 1, 418
Cheki, morena Gr. 7, E-12
Cheki, morena Gr. 7, F-10
Cheki, morena Gr. 2, 180
Chicka Hanka Gr. 2, 210
Chrismus a Come Gr. 3, 396
Christmas, Don't Be Late (The
     Chipmunk Song) Gr. 2, 386
Cielito lindo Gr. 4, 270
*Circle of Life (from The Lion King),*
     *The* Gr. 6, 316
Clementine Gr. 4, 340
Con el vito Gr. 7, G-14
Connemara Lullaby Gr. 5, 232
Copyright law Gr. 7, A-8
Cotton Boll Rag Gr. 5, 332
Create a Career Gr. 8, A-32
Crocodile, The Gr. 2, 362
*Dances of Galanta* Gr. 7, C-34
De colores Gr. 8, E-14
Deck the Hall Gr. 5, 474
Deep in the Heart of Texas Gr. 8, E-22

*Diamonds and Rust* Gr. 7, A-4
Ding Dong! Merrily on High Gr. 6, 426
Do Wah Diddy Diddy Gr. 4, 202
Don't Be Cruel Gr. 6, 254
Don't Let Your Watch Run Down
   Gr. 3, 166
Down by the Bay Gr. 1, 18
Down by the Riverside Gr. 8, G-8
Down the Listening Lane Gr. K, 192
Dragon dance Gr. 8, D-26
Draw Me a Bucket of Water Gr. 3, 124
*Drums of the Iroquois and Sioux*
   Gr. 6, 284
Earth Is Our Mother, The Gr. 4, 358
Ee jer ha ba go Gr. K, 132
*El amor brujo, "Danza ritual del*
   *fuego"* Gr. 8, F-20
El juego chirimbolo Gr. 2, 54
El rabel Gr. 3, 362
El rancho grande Gr. 8, I-22
El Tren Gr. 2, 260
El zapatero Gr. 1, 298
*Ev'rybody Ought to Know* Gr. 1, 434
Everybody Says Gr. 1, 286
Fais dodo Gr. K, 158
*Flop-Eared Mule* Gr. 3, 96
Four White Horses Gr. 3, 304
*Free Music #1* Gr. 2, 212
Funwa alafia Gr. 5, 32
*Ghel moma* Gr. 4, 30
Glad to Have a Friend Like You
   Gr. 2, 228
Glendy Burke, The Gr. 4, 262
Glory, Glory, Hallelujah Gr. 6, 52
Go Down, Moses Gr. 5, 190
God Bless the U.S.A. Gr. 8, G-36
Goin' Down the Road Feelin' Bad
   Gr. 5, 282
Going on a Picnic Gr. K, 190
Gonna Build a Mountain Gr. 6, 20
Good Mornin', Blues Gr. 5, 224
Great Big House Gr. 2, 204
Great Big Stars Gr. 1, 60
Green Corn Song Gr. 5, 462
Greenland Whale Fishery, The
   Gr. 5, 230
*Guitar Tuning* Gr. 8, F-2
Habari Gani Gr. 3, 404
Handel, George Frideric Gr. 8, C-8
Happy Wanderer, The Gr. 4, 88
Harambee Gr. 4, 434
Harrison Town Gr. 6, 96
Himmel und Erde Gr. 5, 94
Hop Up, My Ladies Gr. 3, 142
Hosanna, Me Build a House Gr. 5, 132
Hosisipa Gr. 3, 70
How Many Miles to Babylon?
   Gr. 2, 128
I Shall Sing Gr. 8, I-38
I Walk in Beauty Gr. 4, 282
*I Will Survive* Gr. 7, B-10
Ichi-gatsu tsuitachi Gr. 3, 406
Jingle Bells Gr. 2, 388

John Henry Gr. 8, C-34
Karangatia ra Gr. 3, 272
Kelo aba w'ye Gr. 6, 288
Khorovod Gr. 1, 372
Koriko! Gr. K, 154
Kum ba yah Gr. 5, 244
Kwanzaa Gr. 1, 410
Kyrie Gr. 6, 206
L'inverno è passato Gr. 2, 400
La borinqueña Gr. 8, D-18
La calle ancha Gr. 3, 296
La Jesusita Gr. 5, 322
Las estrellitas del cielo Gr. 5, 174
Las velitas Gr. 5, 147
Leila Gr. 1, 258
*Let the Children Play* Gr. 7, B-30
Let Us Sing Together Gr. 6, 156
Li'l Liza Jane Gr. 3, 140
Lift Ev'ry Voice and Sing Gr. 5, 482
Lift Ev'ry Voice and Sing Gr. 8, I-54
Linstead Market Gr. 5, 240
Little Darlin' Gr. 7, F-30
Little Red Wagon Gr. K, 152
*Lluvia* Gr. 6, 332
Loco-Motion, The Gr. 3, 64
*Lohengrin, "Prelude to Act III"*
   Gr. 8, C-22
Look Out for Mother Earth Gr. 3, 340
*Lord of the Dance Medley* Gr. 6, 326
Los días de la semana Gr. 1, 268
Los maizeles Gr. 1, 294
Los reyes de Oriente Gr. 8, I-58
Los trencitos Gr. K, 24
*Lua afe (2000)* Gr. 8, B-24
*Ma Vlast (My Fatherland), "Vltava*
   *(The Moldau)"* Gr. 7, C-32
Magnolia Gr. 6, 16
*Malagueña* Gr. 5, 154
Mammoth Gr. 1, 234
Man of Constant Sorrow Gr. 7, F-28
Mañana Gr. 7, E-14
Mango Walk Gr. 5, 200
*Máru-bihág* Gr. 6, 304
*Men's Fancy Dance* Gr. 7, D-24
*Messiah, "Hallelujah!"* Gr. 8, C-8
Mississippi River Chant (speech piece)
   Gr. 2, 132
*Montage of Historical Styles*
   Gr. 7, C-2
*Musette* Gr. 3, 36
*Music Critic* Gr. 7, A-32
Music promotion Gr. 7, A-26
Music recording media Gr. 7, A-18
My Foot's In My Stirrup Gr. 2, 234
Nampaya omame Gr. 7, D-10
Now Let Me Fly Gr. 3, 178
O, Desayo Gr. 5, 410
O Music Gr. 5, 162
Ocho kandelikas Gr. 4, 428
Oklahoma Gr. 5, 36
Old Abram Brown Gr. 5, 222
Old Man Mosie Gr. 3, 108
Orange Blossom Special Gr. 8, E-6

Over My Head Gr. 4, 118
Pay Me My Money Down Gr. 7, I-46
*Picking Red Chestnuts* Gr. 5, 310
Piñon, pirulín Gr. 2, 174
Pottery Dance Gr. 1, 370
Quâ câù gió bay Gr. 5, 460
*Quality of Seven, A* Gr. 8, B-6
¡Qué bonita bandera! Gr. 5, 294
*Rain* Gr. 8, B-6
*Rhythms of the Cook Islands*
   Gr. 8, B-6
Río, río Gr. 5, 370
Riquir rán Gr. 4, 66
Rockin' Robin Gr. 3, 368
Roll On, Columbia Gr. 5, 116
Route 66 Gr. 4, 276
Sailing to the Sea Gr. 1, 336
*Saltarello detto Trivella* Gr. 7, C-6
*Salute to Sunnyland Slim* Gr. 8, E-32
*Saqian da dhol* Gr. 8, B-20
*Scuttle Buttin'* Gr. 8, F-26
Shalom aleichem Gr. 6, 408
*Shepherd's Hey Sampler* Gr. 7, C-36
Ship that Never Returned, The
   Gr. 5, 402
Shir l'shalom Gr. 4, 418
Si me dan pasteles Gr. 1, 432
Si si si Gr. 7, G-12
Sierra Morena Gr. 3, 296
Simple Gifts Gr. 5, 184
Sing, Sing, Sing! Gr. 5, 340
Sometimes I Feel Like a Motherless
   Child Gr. 6, 240
*Somewhere* Gr. 8, C-44
Song of the Fishes Gr. 3, 244
Song of the Train Gr. K, 152
Star-Spangled Banner, The Gr. 7, I-56
Stille Nacht (Silent Night) Gr. 7, I-54
Sweet Betsy from Pike Gr. 4, 244
Swing Low, Sweet Chariot Gr. 7, C-40
*Symphony No. 3 in E-flat Major*
   Gr. 8, C-16
Take Me Out to the Ball Game
   Gr. 3, 262
*Te dejo Madrid* Gr. 7, B-30
This Land Is Your Land (refrain only)
   Gr. 1, 274
This Little Light of Mine Gr. 6, 232
Tie Me Kangaroo Down, Sport
   Gr. 4, 36
Today Is Your Birthday Gr. 1, 408
Tumba Gr. 5, 161
Turn the Glasses Over Gr. 3, 204
Tuxedo Junction Gr. 8, G-20
*Twist, The* Gr. 7, B-10
Ujima Gr. 1, 430
United Nations on the March, The
   Gr. 6, 442
Vem kan segla? Gr. 6, 416
Video Game Sound Effects Gr. 8, A-2
Voices of Pride, The Gr. 5, 86
*Voiles* Gr. 7, C-38
Wai bamba Gr. 6, 26

*Wandenza* Gr. 8, B-6
We Shall Not be Moved Gr. 4, 436
Wind Blew East, The Gr. 1, 64
Wings of a Dove Gr. 4, 318
World of Difference, A Gr. 5, 386
*Yakety Yak* Gr. 5, 204
Yang wa wa Gr. K, 162
Yellow Rose of Texas, The Gr. 7, I-70
Yonder Come Day Gr. 8, I-68
Yü guang guang Gr. 6, 60

## TECHNOLOGY

Bogando a la luz del sol Gr. 4, 306
Bucket O'Taiko Ensemble Gr. 7, D-16
Corrido de Kansas Gr. 4, 274
*Fire Brigade Water the Road*
    Gr. 7, D-22
Flip, Flop and Fly Gr. 7, I-32
Go-Go Street Ensemble Gr. 8, D-30
*Malê Debalê* Gr. 8, B-16
Rocky Mountain Gr. 2, 98
*Songs from Letters, "So Like Your
    Father"* Gr. 7, C-20
Sound engineering Gr. 7, A-14
This Land Is Your Land Gr. 7, I-66
*Voiles* Gr. 7, C-38

## THEATER

Ama-Lama Gr. 5, 142
Au clair de la lune Gr. 3, 18
Cho'i hát bội Gr. 5, 318
Day-O! (Banana Boat Loader's Song)
    Gr. 5, 18
Down in the Meadow Gr. K, 146
El caracol Gr. K, 130
Feliz Navidad Gr. 7, I-28
Gato Gr. 1, 128
Grizzly Bear Gr. K, 32
How the Kiwi Lost Its Wings Gr. 1, 76
Jack and Jill Gr. K, 46
Johnny Appleseed Gr. 4, 344
Joshua Fought the Battle of Jericho
    Gr. 5, 100
Joshua Fought the Battle of Jericho
    Gr. 8, E-18
*Little Red Hen, The* Gr. 1, 254
My Pony, Macaroni Gr. 1, 158
*Nutcracker Suite, The, "Waltz of the
    Flowers"* Gr. 6, 322
Ōsamu kosamu Gr. 4, 96
Performers Gr. 8, A-16
Pick 'n' Mix Zoo Gr. K, 138
Puff, the Magic Dragon Gr. 2, 350
¡Qué llueva! Gr. K, 80
*Rig-a-Jig-Jig* Gr. K, 98
Scrub Brush Shuffle, The Gr. 1, 118
Skin and Bones Gr. 2, 376
Surfin' U.S.A. Gr. 7, I-58
Tina singu Gr. 4, 300
We've Got Lots in Common Gr. 3, 366
Wooly Bully Gr. 3, 372
World We Love, The Gr. 3, 342
*Yours Forever* Gr. 6, 344

## WRITING

Abiyoyo Gr. 2, 108
Adelita Gr. 5, 50
Adiós, amigos Gr. 6, 56
Aguinaldo Gr. 3, 402
Ah, Poor Bird Gr. 4, 196
Ahora voy a cantarles Gr. 3, 56
Allá en la fuente Gr. 2, 92
Alligator Pie Gr. 3, 12
Amarillo Armadillo Gr. 2, 82
Amefuri Gr. 1, 142
*America* Gr. 7, A-22
America, I Hear You Singing
    Gr. 2, 402
Angels On the Midnight Clear
    Gr. 6, 422
Bananas and Cream (speech piece)
    Gr. 3, 210
Banjo Sam Gr. 2, 314
Bear Dance Gr. 7, I-10
Birthday Gr. 6, 90
*Block Party* Gr. 7, B-12
Bob-a-Needle Gr. 2, 232
Bump! Bump! Bump! Gr. K, 52
*C-Jam Blues* Gr. 8, C-42
*Can't Take My Joy* Gr. 7, B-40
Canto del agua Gr. 8, I-10
*Carry On* Gr. 7, B-2
Children, Go Where I Send Thee
    Gr. 3, 392
Chords and strums Gr. 8, F-4
Ciranda Gr. 2, 272
Coffee Grows on White Oak Trees
    Gr. 3, 168
Cold and Frosty Morning Gr. 2, 139
*Concert No. 4 in E-flat Major for
    French Horn* Gr. 8, B-10
Cookie Gr. 2, 172
Costume Capers Gr. 1, 412
*Dan tranh* Gr. 5, 196
Dance in Tehuantepec (Rivera)
    Gr. 4, 302
*Das Jahr, "Mai"* Gr. 8, C-18
*DJ Premier in Deep Concentration*
    Gr. 7, B-12
Ego sum pauper Gr. 5, 158
Ein Männlein steht im Walde Gr. 2, 90
El florón Gr. 2, 246
El sapito Gr. 3, 336
Electronic keyboard Gr. 8, E-26
Ev'ry Time I Feel the Spirit Gr. 5, 242
Family Tree Gr. 3, 72
*Four Seasons, The, "Spring,"
    Movement 1* Gr. 4, 370
Four Strong Winds (Song to a Seagull)
    Gr. 6, 170
Gift to Share, A Gr. 6, 392
*Glory, Glory, Hallelujah* Gr. 6, 54
Go Around the Corn, Sally Gr. 2, 12
Go-Go Street Ensemble Gr. 8, D-30
Going upon the Mountain Gr. 6, 104
Good Mornin', Blues Gr. 2, 52
Goodbye, Julie Gr. 1, 334

Goodbye, Julie Gr. 8, E-2
Gospel Train, The Gr. 6, 396
Green Corn Song Gr. 5, 462
Green, Green Grass of Home
    Gr. 6, 244
Had to Get Up This Mornin' Soon
    Gr. 3, 114
Haere Gr. 2, 284
Hanuka, Hanuka Gr. 8, I-36
Happy Days Are Here Again
    Gr. 5, 284
He's Got the Whole World in His
    Hands Gr. 3, 230
He's Got the Whole World in His
    Hands Gr. 7, I-36
Heave-Ho!/Going, Going, Gone/The
    Snow Gr. 4, 182
Hej pada pada Gr. 3, 78
*Here Comes My Girl* Gr. 7, F-16
Hey, m'tswala Gr. 4, 78
*Hungarian Rhapsody No. 2 in C
    sharp Minor, S. 244* Gr. 7, E-16
I Believe I Can Fly Gr. 5, 170
I Bought Me a Cat Gr. 2, 308
I Fed My Horse Gr. 2, 94
I'm a Believer Gr. 7, G-32
*Interview with Rick Bassett (Part 2)*
    Gr. 3, 222
Jambalaya Gr. 8, I-46
Johnny Has Gone for a Soldier
    Gr. 5, 188
*Joy* Gr. 7, B-40
*Junk Music Montage* Gr. 1, 73
Kapulu kane Gr. 2, 270
Keep Your Eyes on the Prize
    Gr. 3, 408
Kibungo, Beast of the Forest
    Gr. 2, 352
Kid Like Me, A (speech piece)
    Gr. 2, 394
Knock No More Gr. 3, 386
Kou ri lengay Gr. 2, 216
Kou ri lengay Gr. 7, E-2
Kwanzaa Carol, A Gr. 2, 392
La paloma se fué Gr. 6, 50
La pulga de San José Gr. 3, 40
Las mañanitas Gr. 6, 480
Let Music Surround You Gr. 4, 236
Little Black Bug Gr. 1, 212
*Llactamanta* Gr. 6, 382
Lo yisa Gr. 6, 130
Lone Star Trail Gr. 2, 20
*Malê Debalê* Gr. 8, B-16
Mariposita Gr. 2, 156
Meng Jian Nu Gr. 5, 194
Miss Mary Mack Gr. 2, 42
Morning Comes Early Gr. 5, 13
Morning Is Come Gr. 3, 128
Mubärak Gr. 3, 282
Nana Kru Gr. 6, 280
No quiero plata Gr. 1, 424
Now's the Time Gr. 5, 444
One Family Gr. 7, G-16

One Morning Soon Gr. 3, 68
*Onomatapoiea Study No. 2*
    Gr. 7, E-30
Over There Gr. 5, 278
Paw-Paw Patch Gr. 4, 92
Perot Gr. 2, 378
*Prayer, The* Gr. 7, A-10
*Primitive Fire, "Oya"* Gr. 2, 68
Proud Gr. 7, G-2
Ragupati Ragava Raja Ram Gr. 5, 320
Recording engineer Gr. 7, A-20
*Red Poppy, The, "Russian Sailors'*
    *Dance"* Gr. 4, 222
Riddle Ree (speech piece) Gr. 2, 34
Rise and Shine Gr. 4, 98
Sailing Down My Golden River
    Gr. 4, 332
Sakura Gr. 4, 308
*Same, The* Gr. 6, 268
Same Train Gr. 2, 164
Sea Shell Gr. 2, 100
Sleep, Baby, Sleep Gr. 2, 194
Soldier, Soldier Gr. 4, 10
Sonando Gr. 4, 34
Song of the Eagle Gr. 2, 248
Star Light, Star Bright Gr. 1, 106
Star-Spangled Banner, The Gr. 7, I-56
Star-Spangled Banner, The Gr. 8, I-62
Stopping by Woods on a Snowy
    Evening Gr. 6, 38
Strike Up the Band Gr. 6, 134
Surfin' U.S.A. Gr. 6, 260
Swanee Gr. 6, 118
*Symphony No. 9 in D Minor, Op.*
    *125, "Ode to Joy," Movement 4*
    Gr. 4, 150
T'hola, t'hola Gr. 4, 132
Tancovačka Gr. 4, 230
*This Is Your Night* Gr. 6, 368
*Trash Can Stomp (from Stomp Out*
    *Loud)* Gr. 6, 328
Tsuki Gr. 4, 24
*Two-Part Invention in A Major*
    *(harpsichord)* Gr. 5, 236
Understanding music Gr. 8, C-2
Vamos a la fiesta Gr. 2, 374
Vamos a la mar Gr. 3, 226
*Variations on "America"* Gr. 6, 162
*Variations on "The Carnival of*
    *Venice"* Gr. 6, 160
Vil du? Gr. 1, 92
Wabash Cannon Ball Gr. 5, 136
Waitin' for the Light to Shine Gr. 4, 26
We're All Gonna Shine Tonight
    Gr. 2, 240
When the Train Comes Along
    Gr. 1, 300
Wichita Hand Game Song 1
    Gr. 3, 306
Wichita Hand Game Song 2
    Gr. 3, 306

*Xochipilli* Gr. 8, C-36
*Yertle the Turtle* Gr. 2, 368
Your Friends Shall Be the Tall Wind
    Gr. 6, 200

# Classified Index

**A**

**ACROSS THE CURRICULUM**
*See Curriculum, Across the.*

**AMERICAN FOLK** *See Folk, Traditional, and Regional: United States.*

**ANALYZING** *See also Skills Reinforcement.*
America, the Beautiful Gr. 7, I-4
*Beautiful* Gr. 3, 67
*Cafe Europa* Gr. 7, B-43
*(Can't Live Without Your) Love and Affection* Gr. 7, B-23
*Cantata No. 140 (as performed by The Swingle Singers), "Wachet auf, ruft uns die Stimme," Movement 4* Gr. 7, C-10
Chapel of Love Gr. 7, G-27
*Cheki, morena* Gr. 7, E-13
*Cheki, morena* Gr. 7, I-16
*Chorale Prelude for Organ, BWV 645, "Wachet auf, ruft uns die Stimme"* Gr. 7, C-9
*Crazy Blues* Gr. 7, B-8
*Danses Populaires Francaises, "Branle Double, Branle Simple"* Gr. 7, C-25
Do Wah Diddy Diddy Gr. 7, F-21
*Every Morning* Gr. 7, B-8
*Everything Is Everything* Gr. 7, B-29
Flip, Flop and Fly Gr. 7, I-32
Goin' Down the Road Feelin' Bad Gr. 7, F-13
*If These Walls Could Speak* Gr. 7, B-41
My Home's Across the Blue Ridge Mountains Gr. 7, F-6
Oy, Hanuka Gr. 7, I-45
Pay Me My Money Down Gr. 7, I-49
*Pictures at an Exhibition, "The Great Gate of Kiev"* Gr. 8, A-12
*Plenty o' Nuttin'* Gr. 7, B-45
Proud Gr. 7, G-3
*Shepherd's Hey Sampler* Gr. 7, C-37
Shortnin' Bread Gr. 7, F-27
*Si si si* Gr. 7, G-13
*Simple Gifts* Gr. 8, A-17
*Sonata in C-sharp Minor, Op. 27, No. 2, "Moonlight," Movement 1* Gr. 7, C-19
*Sonata in F Major for Violin and Piano, Op. 24, No. 5, "Spring," Movement 3* Gr. 7, C-19
Sound Processing Gr. 7, A-17
Star-Spangled Banner Gr. 7, I-57

*String Quartet in D Major, Op. 64, No. 5, "The Lark," Allegro moderato* Gr. 7, C-15
Surfin' U.S.A. Gr. 7, E-27
*Symphony No. 47 in G Major, "Menuet"* Gr. 7, C-14
Ten Little Ostinato Pieces Gr. 7, I-62
*That's the Way It Is* Gr. 7, B-23
This Land Is Your Land Gr. 7, I-68
*Well-Tempered Clavier, The, "Be-Bop Bach: Prelude No. 2"* Gr. 7, C-11
*Wings* Gr. 7, C-45
Yellow Rose of Texas, The Gr. 7, I-70

**ARRANGING** *See also Skills Reinforcement.*
At the Top of My Voice Gr. K, 279
Boogie Chant and Dance (speech piece) Gr. 2, 78
Boysie Gr. 2, 195
Bucket O'Taiko Ensemble Gr. 7, D-17
*Bye Bye, Love* Gr. 8, A-15
Cookie Gr. 2, 172
Dance for the Nations Gr. 6, 123
Don't Be Cruel Gr. 6, 255
El coquí Gr. 2, 292
El rancho grande Gr. 8, I-24
Grizzly Bear Gr. K, 33
Harrison Town Gr. 6, 97
He's Got the Whole World in His Hands Gr. 7, I-39
I Am But a Small Voice Gr. 6, 446
I Like Fall Gr. K, 311
Ichi-gatsu tsuitachi Gr. 7, I-43
Leatherwing Bat Gr. 2, 303
My Travel Tree Gr. K, 203
Percussion Fun Rondo Gr. 7, I-53
*Pictures at an Exhibition, "The Great Gate of Kiev"* Gr. 8, A-14
Summertime Gr. 6, 250
*This Is Your Night (Dance Mix)* Gr. 6, 369
Two Little Sausages (speech piece) Gr. 2, 79
What a Wonderful World Gr. 6, 62
Whether It's Cold (proverb) Gr. 2, 118

**ART REPRODUCTIONS** *See Related Arts.*

**ASSESSMENT**

**CHECKPOINT**
Checkpoint Gr. 7, A-11
Checkpoint Gr. 7, A-25
Checkpoint Gr. 7, C-13
Checkpoint Gr. 7, C-31
Checkpoint Gr. 7, D-15
Checkpoint Gr. 7, E-27
Checkpoint Gr. 7, F-25

Checkpoint Gr. 7, F-29
Checkpoint Gr. 7, E-15
Checkpoint Gr. 7, B-11
Checkpoint Gr. 7, B-21
Checkpoint Gr. 7, B-33
Checkpoint Gr. 8, A-19
Checkpoint Gr. 8, B-29
Checkpoint Gr. 8, C-25
Checkpoint Gr. 8, C-41
Checkpoint Gr. 8, D-25
Checkpoint Gr. 8, E-15
Checkpoint Gr. 8, E-23
Checkpoint Gr. 8, F-18

**REVIEW AND ASSESS**
Review and Assess Gr. 7, A-34
Review and Assess Gr. 7, B-46
Review and Assess Gr. 7, C-46
Review and Assess Gr. 7, D-34
Review and Assess Gr. 7, E-34
Review and Assess Gr. 7, F-34
Review and Assess Gr. 7, G-46
Review and Assess Gr. 7, H-30
Review and Assess Gr. 8, A-34
Review and Assess Gr. 8, B-46
Review and Assess Gr. 8, C-48
Review and Assess Gr. 8, D-34
Review and Assess Gr. 8, E-34
Review and Assess Gr. 8, F-34
Review and Assess Gr. 8, G-46
Review and Assess Gr. 8, H-30

**REVIEW, ASSESS, PERFORM, CREATE**
Review, Assess, Perform, Create (Unit 1) Gr. 1, 40
Review, Assess, Perform, Create (Unit 2) Gr. 1, 80
Review, Assess, Perform, Create (Unit 3) Gr. 1, 120
Review, Assess, Perform, Create (Unit 4) Gr. 1, 160
Review, Assess, Perform, Create (Unit 5) Gr. 1, 200
Review, Assess, Perform, Create (Unit 6) Gr. 1, 240
Review, Assess, Perform, Create (Unit 1) Gr. 2, 36
Review, Assess, Perform, Create (Unit 2) Gr. 2, 72
Review, Assess, Perform, Create (Unit 3) Gr. 2, 108
Review, Assess, Perform, Create (Unit 4) Gr. 2, 144
Review, Assess, Perform, Create (Unit 5) Gr. 2, 180
Review, Assess, Perform, Create (Unit 6) Gr. 2, 216

(*Assessment,* continued)

Review, Assess, Perform, Create
(Unit 1) Gr. 3, 42

Review, Assess, Perform, Create
(Unit 2) Gr. 3, 80

Review, Assess, Perform, Create
(Unit 3) Gr. 3, 118

Review, Assess, Perform, Create
(Unit 4) Gr. 3, 156

Review, Assess, Perform, Create
(Unit 5) Gr. 3, 194

Review, Assess, Perform, Create
(Unit 6) Gr. 3, 232

Review, Assess, Perform, Create
(Unit 1) Gr. 4, 42

Review, Assess, Perform, Create
(Unit 2) Gr. 4, 82

Review, Assess, Perform, Create
(Unit 3) Gr. 4, 124

Review, Assess, Perform, Create
(Unit 4) Gr. 4, 164

Review, Assess, Perform, Create
(Unit 5) Gr. 4, 204

Review, Assess, Perform, Create
(Unit 6) Gr. 4, 246

Review, Assess, Perform, Create
(Unit 1) Gr. 5, 40

Review, Assess, Perform, Create
(Unit 2) Gr. 5, 80

Review, Assess, Perform, Create
(Unit 3) Gr. 5, 122

Review, Assess, Perform, Create
(Unit 4) Gr. 5, 164

Review, Assess, Perform, Create
(Unit 5) Gr. 5, 206

Review, Assess, Perform, Create
(Unit 6) Gr. 5, 246

Review, Assess, Perform, Create
(Unit 1) Gr. 6, 32

Review, Assess, Perform, Create
(Unit 2) Gr. 6, 70

Review, Assess, Perform, Create
(Unit 3) Gr. 6, 108

Review, Assess, Perform, Create
(Unit 4) Gr. 6, 146

Review, Assess, Perform, Create
(Unit 5) Gr. 6, 184

Review, Assess, Perform, Create
(Unit 6) Gr. 6, 220

Review, Assess, Perform, Create
(Unit 1) Gr. K, 28

Review, Assess, Perform, Create
(Unit 2) Gr. K, 56

Review, Assess, Perform, Create
(Unit 3) Gr. K, 84

Review, Assess, Perform, Create
(Unit 4) Gr. K, 112

Review, Assess, Perform, Create
(Unit 5) Gr. K, 140

Review, Assess, Perform, Create
(Unit 6) Gr. K, 168

## SHOW WHAT YOU KNOW

Show What You Know (rhythm)
Gr. 2, 17

Show What You Know (rhythm)
Gr. 2, 49

Show What You Know (rhythm)
Gr. 2, 85

Show What You Know (rhythm)
Gr. 2, 123

Show What You Know (rhythm)
Gr. 2, 163

Show What You Know (rhythm)
Gr. 2, 199

Show What You Know (melody)
Gr. 2, 31

Show What You Know (melody)
Gr. 2, 59

Show What You Know (melody)
Gr. 2, 101

Show What You Know (melody)
Gr. 2, 137

Show What You Know (melody)
Gr. 2, 177

Show What You Know (melody)
Gr. 2, 207

Show What You Know (rhythm)
Gr. 3, 15

Show What You Know (rhythm)
Gr. 3, 57

Show What You Know (rhythm)
Gr. 3, 95

Show What You Know (rhythm)
Gr. 3, 133

Show What You Know (rhythm)
Gr. 3, 167

Show What You Know (rhythm)
Gr. 3, 207

Show What You Know (melody)
Gr. 3, 31

Show What You Know (melody)
Gr. 3, 71

Show What You Know (melody)
Gr. 3, 109

Show What You Know (melody)
Gr. 3, 147

Show What You Know (melody)
Gr. 3, 181

Show What You Know (melody)
Gr. 3, 217

Show What You Know (rhythm)
Gr. 4, 17

Show What You Know (rhythm)
Gr. 4, 57

Show What You Know (rhythm)
Gr. 4, 99

Show What You Know (rhythm)
Gr. 4, 139

Show What You Know (rhythm)
Gr. 4, 181

Show What You Know (rhythm)
Gr. 4, 221

Show What You Know (melody)
Gr. 4, 29

Show What You Know (melody)
Gr. 4, 67

Show What You Know (melody)
Gr. 4, 109

Show What You Know (melody)
Gr. 4, 149

Show What You Know (melody)
Gr. 4, 191

Show What You Know (melody)
Gr. 4, 229

Show What You Know (rhythm)
Gr. 5, 17

Show What You Know (rhythm)
Gr. 5, 53

Show What You Know (rhythm)
Gr. 5, 98

Show What You Know (rhythm)
Gr. 5, 141

Show What You Know (rhythm)
Gr. 5, 179

Show What You Know (rhythm)
Gr. 5, 223

Show What You Know (melody)
Gr. 5, 27

Show What You Know (melody)
Gr. 5, 63

Show What You Know (melody)
Gr. 5, 107

Show What You Know (melody)
Gr. 5, 147

Show What You Know (melody)
Gr. 5, 193

Show What You Know (melody)
Gr. 5, 231

Show What You Know (rhythm)
Gr. 6, 13

Show What You Know (rhythm)
Gr. 6, 45

Show What You Know (rhythm)
Gr. 6, 81

Show What You Know (rhythm)
Gr. 6, 120

Show What You Know (rhythm)
Gr. 6, 159

Show What You Know (rhythm)
Gr. 6, 197

Show What You Know (melody)
Gr. 6, 20

Show What You Know (melody)
Gr. 6, 59

Show What You Know (melody)
Gr. 6, 100

Show What You Know (melody)
Gr. 6, 134

Show What You Know (melody)
Gr. 6, 167

Show What You Know (melody)
Gr. 6, 204

## AUDIENCE ETIQUETTE

Applause Gr. 1, 207

Applause Gr. 2, 84

Applause Gr. 3, 51

Applause Gr. 3, 352
Applause Gr. 5, 65
Applause Gr. 6, 478
At School Assemblies Gr. 2, 312
At School Assemblies Gr. 6, 46
At School Assemblies and in the
  Classroom Gr. 4, 185
At School Assemblies or Class
  Performances Gr. 3, 346
Attending a Live Concert Gr. 4, 111
Attending Concerts Gr. 7, F-19
Audience Behavior Gr. 1, 446
Audience Behavior Gr. 3, 281
Audience Behavior Gr. 5, 30
Audience Behavior Gr. 6, 319
Audience Etiquette and Participation
  Gr. 6, 177
Behavior Tips Gr. 2, 139
Critical Listening Gr. 1, 175
Critical Listening Gr. 2, 175
Critical Listening Gr. 2, 175
Critical Listening Gr. 3, 97
Critical Listening Gr. 3, 169
Critical Listening Gr. 4, 347
Critical Listening Gr. 5, 173
Critical Listening Gr. 6, 436
Critical Listening Gr. 7, B-41
Educating the Audience Gr. 3, 316
Educating the Audience Gr. 6, 342
Educating the Audience Gr. 7, I-72
Get There Early! Gr. 1, 429
Get There Early! Gr. 2, 265
Get There Early! Gr. 3, 407
Get There Early! Gr. 5, 357
Get There Early! Gr. 6, 398
Les petites marionettes Gr. K, 237
Museum, A Gr. 1, 271
Museum Visit, A Gr. 2, 387
Museum Visit, A Gr. 3, 259
Museum Visit, A Gr. 5, 103
Museum Visit, A Gr. 6, 67
Performance Behavior Gr. 6, 319
Preparing for an Assembly Concert
  Gr. 1, 328
Preparing for an Assembly Concert
  Gr. K, 186
Preparing to Attend a Performance
  Gr. 1, 289
Preparing to Attend a Performance
  Gr. 2, 219
Preparing to Attend a Performance
  Gr. 4, 295
Preparing to Attend a Performance
  Gr. 5, 275
Preparing to Attend a Performance
  Gr. 6, 203
Rehearsal Etiquette for Performers
  Gr. 1, 103
Rehearsal Etiquette for Performers
  Gr. 2, 339
Rehearsal Etiquette for Performers
  Gr. 3, 147
Rehearsal Etiquette for Performers
  Gr. 4, 401
Rehearsal Etiquette for Performers
  Gr. 5, 235
Rehearsal Etiquette for Performers
  Gr. 7, G-42
Rehearsal Etiquette for Performers
  Gr. 7, I-69
School Assemblies Gr. 5, 422
Specific Venues Gr. 3, 15
Specific Venues and Genres Gr. 1, 37
Specific Venues and Genres
  Gr. 2, 230
Specific Venues and Genres
  Gr. 3, 229
Specific Venues and Genres Gr. 4, 74
Specific Venues and Genres
  Gr. 5, 155
Specific Venues and Genres
  Gr. 6, 259

## B

**BORDUN** *See Texture/Harmony: Borduns.*

## BROADWAY, THEATER, AND FILM *See Genre/Style.*

## C

**CAREERS** *See also Music Makers; Recorded Lessons: Recorded Interviews; Spotlight On.*

### ARCHITECTS
Vangreen, Walter Gr. 6, 331

### ARTISTS/ILLUSTRATORS
Calder, Alexander Gr. 8, F-13
Cassatt, Mary Gr. 8, E-11
Chagall, Marc Gr. 6, 442
Douglas, Aaron Gr. 7, G-10
Johnson, William Gr. 2, 29
Joysmith, Brenda Gr. 1, 332
Marc, Franz Gr. 1, 128
Millet, Jean François Gr. 4, 365
Monet, Claude Gr. 1, 24
Moretto, Gustavo Gr. 1, 96
Moses, Grandma Gr. 6, 454
Picasso, Pablo Gr. 4, 213
Pollock, Jackson Gr. 6, 209
Rivera, Diego Gr. 4, 304
Rivera, Diego Gr. 6, 414
Silverstein, Shel Gr. 1, 74
Stockfleth, Julius Gr. 4, 259

### CHOREOGRAPHERS
Balanchine, George Gr. 6, 323
Cresswell, Luke Gr. 4, 123
McNicholas, Steve Gr. 4, 123
Nikolais, Alwin Gr. 7, C-27

### CHOREOGRAPHERS/DANCERS
Ailey, Alvin Gr. 7, C-27
Graham, Martha Gr. 7, C-27
Taylor, Paul Gr. 7, C-27

### COLLECTORS
Karpeles, Maud Gr. 7, C-35

### DANCERS
American Dance Theater, Alvin
  Ailey Gr. 1, 287
Burke, Liam Gr. 2, 11
Cresswell, Luke Gr. 4, 123
Duncan, Isadora Gr. 7, C-27
McNicholas, Steve Gr. 4, 123

### ETHNOMUSICOLOGISTS
Kodály, Zoltán Gr. 7, C-34

### FILM SCORE COMPOSERS
Bernstein, Elmer Gr. 3, 145
Dun, Tan Gr. 8, A-11
Elfman, Danny Gr. 8, A-11
Rahman, A. R. Gr. 8, B-35
Williams, John Gr. 6, 350

### FILMMAKERS
Alexie, Sherman Gr. 8, B-37

### FOLEY ARTISTS
Keith, Tom Gr. 8, A-9

### INSTRUMENT MAKERS
Blue Man Group Gr. 7, D-5
Cooke, Richard Gr. 8, D-17
Giorgini, Frank Gr. 8, D-5
McGill, Paul Gr. 8, A-28
Moog, Robert Gr. 5, 238
Sand, Kirk Gr. 8, F-11

### JINGLE WRITERS
Louiselle, Brian Gr. 8, A-5

### LYRICISTS
Ephrem, Hidaat Gr. 4, 63
Field, Rachel (lyricist) Gr. 7, G-40

### MOOD MUSICIANS
Collis, Alvin Gr. 8, A-7

### MULTIMEDIA MUSICIANS
Weatherhead, Andrea Gr. 8, A-32

### MUSIC CRITICS
Midgette, Anne Gr. 7, A-33
Sandow, Greg Gr. 7, A-33

### MUSIC EDUCATORS
Amoaku, W. Komla Gr. 8, D-8
Burton, J. Bryan Gr. 4, 285
Dawson, William Gr. 7, C-41
Hammil, Joanne Gr. 7, G-17
Mason, Lowell Gr. 5, 163
Wuytack, Jos Gr. 3, 224

### MUSIC THERAPISTS
Nordoff, Dr. Paul Gr. 8, A-26

### MUSIC VIDEO DIRECTORS
Lambert, Mary Gr. 7, A-29

### MUSICOLOGISTS
Seeger, Ruth Crawford Gr. 8, C-35

(*Careers,* continued)

### ORCHESTRATORS
Besterman, Doug  Gr. 7, A-23

### PIANO TECHNICIAN
Wooten, James  Gr. 8, E-13

### POETS AND WRITERS
Frost, Robert  Gr. 6, 41
George, Chief Dan  Gr. 4, 359
Katz, Bobbi  Gr. 1, 174
Key, Francis Scott  Gr. 5, 488
Lee, Dennis  Gr. 4, 122

### SINGERS/SONGWRITERS
*Have a Little Faith in Me*
    Gr. 8, A-18

### SOUND ENGINEERS
Tillemans, Todd  Gr. 7, A-14

### TECHNO DJs
Calderone, Victor  Gr. 7, A-3
*This Is Your Night (Dance Mix)*
    Gr. 6, 369

### VOCAL COACHES
Garvey, David  Gr. 7, A-13

## CHARACTER EDUCATION

### ADAPTATION
Circle 'Round the Moon  Gr. 4, 406

### AUDIENCE BEHAVIOR
*Concert for Piano and Orchestra*
    Gr. 6, 209
Love Is on Our Side  Gr. 5, 325

### CARING
All Around the Buttercup
    Gr. 2, 171
El coquí  Gr. 2, 293
Fais dodo  Gr. K, 159
Joy to the World  Gr. 3, 21
Leaves  Gr. 1, 29
Lion and the Mouse, The (story)
    Gr. 1, 239
Look Out Below!  Gr. 2, 371
Lullaby (poem)  Gr. 1, 205
Mother, Mother, I Am Sick
    Gr. K, 121
Naranja dulce  Gr. 2, 97
This Little Light of Mine  Gr. 6, 232

### CHARACTER TRAITS
Ise oluwa  Gr. 6, 231
Variations on "America"  Gr. 6, 163
We Shall Not Be Moved  Gr. 4, 437

### CITIZENSHIP
Carpenter, Mary Chapin  Gr. 2, 341
Look Out for Mother Earth
    Gr. 3, 340

### COLLABORATION
Aguinaldo  Gr. 3, 403
Cheki, morena  Gr. 7, I-18
Drill, Ye Tarriers  Gr. 5, 55

Fais do do  Gr. 6, 406
*Lua afe (2000)*  Gr. 8, B-27
Man of Constant Sorrow
    Gr. 7, F-29
Oklahoma  Gr. 5, 39
*Piano Trio in G Minor, Op. 17,
    Allegro*  Gr. 8, C-19
Producer  Gr. 8, A-24

### COMMITMENT
Ain't Gonna Let Nobody Turn Me
    'Round  Gr. 6, 85

### COMPASSION
La Jesusita  Gr. 5, 322
Old House, Tear It Down!
    Gr. 4, 180
There Is Love Somewhere
    Gr. 6, 318

### COOPERATION
Alleluia  Gr. 6, 133
I Know an Old Lady  Gr. 1, 389
John Kanaka  Gr. 3, 63
Knock the Cymbals  Gr. 1, 174
Three Times By She Passes (speech
    piece)  Gr. K, 125
Tree in the Wood, The  Gr. 2, 361
*Ujan mas*  Gr. 2, 105
¡Viva el fútbol!  Gr. 1, 95
*Water Music, "Allegro Maestoso"*
    Gr. 3, 189
Wheel of the Water, The
    Gr. 4, 364

### COURAGE
Battle Cry of Freedom  Gr. 5, 57,
    272
Down the Ohio  Gr. 2, 63
Electronic keyboard  Gr. 8, E-26
Harriet Tubman  Gr. 4, 269
How the Kiwi Lost Its Wings (story)
    Gr. 1, 79
I Shall Sing  Gr. 8, I-40
I'm a Believer  Gr. 7, G-37
Lemonade  Gr. 1, 189
Old Texas  Gr. 3, 77
Run! Run! Hide!  Gr. 6, 343
Sailing to the Sea  Gr. 1, 337
Take Me Out to the Ball Game
    Gr. 3, 263

### COURTESY
Alabama Gal  Gr. 3, 106
Bubble Gum  Gr. K, 38
Mon papa  Gr. 2, 280
Who Has the Penny?  Gr. K, 43

### CREATIVITY
*Kebjar teruna*  Gr. 6, 385

### DIVERSITY
Diversity  Gr. 5, 157
Nie chcę cię znác  Gr. 3, 317
*Soulville*  Gr. 7, B-17
*Ue ue*  Gr. 8, D-2

When Johnny Comes Marching
    Home  Gr. 5, 181
Yonder Come Day  Gr. 8, I-71

### ENVIRONMENTAL AWARENESS
For the Beauty of the Earth
    Gr. 4, 356
Zuni Sunrise Call  Gr. 5, 398

### EXPRESSION OF EMOTIONS
Dancin' in the Street  Gr. 5, 363
Joe Turner Blues  Gr. 4, 57
Love in Any Language  Gr. 6, 479
*Stopping by Woods on a Snowy
    Evening*  Gr. 6, 40
Water Come a Me Eye  Gr. 6, 301

### FAIRNESS
Bonga  Gr. K, 79
*Little Red Hen, The*  Gr. 1, 257
Music Critic  Gr. 7, A-32
Pay Me My Money Down
    Gr. 7, I-47

### FREEDOM
Brand New Day, A  Gr. 6, 8
Lift Ev'ry Voice and Sing
    Gr. 5, 483

### FRIENDSHIP
Lean on Me  Gr. 7, E-22
Sambalele  Gr. 4, 400
Stand By Me  Gr. 5, 47

### GENEROSITY
Chawe chidyo chem'chero
    Gr. 2, 299
I'm Thankful  Gr. 1, 415
Jingle Bells  Gr. 2, 389
Love Will Guide Us  Gr. 4, 329
We Are Dear Little Birdies
    Gr. K, 177

### GOOD JUDGMENT
*(Can't Live Without Your) Love
    and Affection*  Gr. 7, B-22
*Die Walküre, "The Ride of the
    Valkyries"*  Gr. 8, C-23
I Dream a World  Gr. 8, G-45
Jan ken pon  Gr. 3, 302
*Sonata in C-sharp Minor, Op. 27,
    No. 2, "Moonlight," Movement
    1*  Gr. 7, C-19

### HONESTY
A-Tisket, A-Tasket  Gr. 2, 239
Agbekor Ensemble  Gr. 8, D-11
Bob-a-Needle  Gr. 2, 233
Why the Wart Hog Goes About on
    His Knees (story)  Gr. 1, 139
Lost My Gold Ring  Gr. 6, 159

### HUMOR
My Bonnie Lies Over the Ocean
    Gr. 4, 339

### INTEGRITY
Cielito lindo  Gr. 7, I-21

Copyright law  Gr. 7, A-9
Goodbye, Julie  Gr. 8, E-5
If a Tiger Calls  Gr. 3, 355
*Rundadinella*  Gr. 8, I-60

## KINDNESS
El tambor  Gr. 2, 275
En nuestra Tierra tan linda
    Gr. 2, 335
Give a Little Love  Gr. 6, 142
Love Somebody  Gr. 3, 95
Men's Fancy Dance  Gr. 7, D-25
Swing Low, Sweet Chariot
    Gr. 7, C-40
Take a Chance On Me  Gr. 8, G-17
Usagi  Gr. 1, 397

## LOYALTY
America  Gr. 1, 445
Artsa alinu  Gr. 3, 285

## PATIENCE
First-ing (poem)  Gr. 1, 375
Fuzzy Caterpillar  Gr. K, 103
Goin' to the Fair  Gr. K, 157
La tormenta tropical  Gr. 2, 119

## PATRIOTISM
America  Gr. 5, 487
I Vow to You, My Country
    Gr. 5, 420
Star-Spangled Banner, The
    Gr. 6, 486

## PEACE
I Walk in Beauty  Gr. 4, 285
I Walk the Unfrequented Road
    Gr. 6, 78
Shir l'shalom  Gr. 4, 420
Sing a Song of Peace  Gr. 6, 66
This Is My Song  Gr. 6, 78

## PERSEVERANCE
Ain't Gonna Let Nobody Turn Me
    'Round  Gr. 8, F-16
America, the Free  Gr. 4, 211
*Arirang*  Gr. 2, 137
*Caprice No. 1 in E Major*
    Gr. 7, C-22
Corta la caña  Gr. 6, 364
Faith of the Heart  Gr. 8, G-4
Handel, George Frideric  Gr. 8, C-8
I Can't Spell Hippopotamus
    Gr. 1, 266
Oh, Won't You Sit Down  Gr. 3, 29
Same Train  Gr. 2, 165
Simple Gifts  Gr. 5, 186
Small Job, A  Gr. 3, 225

## PRIDE
Proud  Gr. 7, G-5
Voices of Pride, The  Gr. 5, 87

## RESPECT
*ABACA Dabble*  Gr. 4, 184
Ala Da'lona  Gr. 4, 137
Ashchav  Gr. 2, 65

Bắt kim thang  Gr. 6, 13
Creating instrumental pieces
    Gr. 1, 125
Day-O!  Gr. 5, 18
Different Beat, A  Gr. 1, 6
*Drums From Around the World
    (Montage)*  Gr. 6, 277
Go Around the Corn, Sally
    Gr. 2, 13
Hound Dog  Gr. 5, 214
It Don't Mean a Thing if It Ain't Got
    that Swing  Gr. 5, 338
Jambalaya  Gr. 8, F-18
Kwa-nu-te  Gr. 3, 215
La bamba  Gr. 5, 131
Luna lunera  Gr. K, 91
Mon son pha (speech piece)  Gr. K,
    91
O ma washi  Gr. K, 13
*Ostinatos Around the World*
    Gr. 8, B-4
Paw-Paw Patch  Gr. 4, 93
Pay Me My Money Down  Gr. 4, 40
Pitter, Patter, Scatter (poem)
    Gr. 1, 54
*Qiugaviit*  Gr. 3, 259
*Scherzo for Wind Quintet, Op. 48*
    Gr. 1, 328
See-Saw Sacradown  Gr. 2, 208
Shika no Tone  Gr. 5, 112
Shoo, Fly  Gr. 2, 201
Shri Ram, jai Ram  Gr. 4, 311
Song of the Night, The  Gr. 3, 347
Star-Spangled Banner, The
    Gr. 7, I-56
T'hola, t'hola  Gr. 4, 133
*Twist and Shout*  Gr. 4, 239
World of Difference, A  Gr. 5, 387

## RESPONSIBILITY
Don't Let Your Watch Run Down
    Gr. 3, 167
Draw Me a Bucket of Water
    Gr. 3, 127
Ev'ry Time I Feel the Spirit
    Gr. 5, 288
Ev'ry Time I Feel the Spirit
    Gr. 5, 242
Friends Today  Gr. 7, D-12
Haul Away, Joe  Gr. 4, 13
Los maizeles  Gr. 1, 295
*Mass, "Responsory: Alleluia"*
    Gr. 6, 217
Mmmmm mmmmmmmm  Gr. K,
    71
Noah's Shanty  Gr. 1, 345
One Family  Gr. 7, G-19
Playing in ensembles  Gr. 4, 75
Big Book/Student Text  Gr. 1,
    86–87
Turn the World Around  Gr. 4, 117

## SELF-DISCIPLINE
All for One  Gr. 7, E-11

Bubbles  Gr. K, 185
He's Got the Whole World in His
    Hands  Gr. 7, I-38
I'll Fly Away  Gr. 8, I-45
Interview with Liam Burke  Gr. 2, 9
*Zomo the Rabbit*  Gr. 3, 364

## SERVICE
Ding Dong! Merrily on High
    Gr. 6, 430
St. Patrick Was a Gentleman
    Gr. 3, 291

## TAKING TIME FOR YOURSELF
Take Time in Life  Gr. 6, 291

## TOLERANCE
Each of Us Is a Flower  Gr. 3, 155
Families  Gr. 1, 280
Kid Like Me, A  Gr. 2, 397

## VALUES
Beriozka  Gr. 4, 295
Haliwa-Saponi Canoe Song
    Gr. 5, 303
Ríu chíu chíu  Gr. 5, 438

# CHORAL SINGING
## 2-PART
Abraham, Martin, and John
    Gr. 6, 466
Alexander's Ragtime Band
    Gr. 6, 136
America  Gr. 7, I-2
Angels On the Midnight Clear
    Gr. 6, 423
Así es mi tierra  Gr. 6, 172
Book of Love  Gr. 8, G-27
Canción Mixteca  Gr. 5, 326
Canto del agua  Gr. 8, I-10
Circle 'Round the Moon  Gr. 4, 403
Come, Ye Thankful People, Come
    Gr. 5, 459
De colores  Gr. 8, I-14
Ding Dong! Merrily on High
    Gr. 6, 427
Down by the Riverside  Gr. 8, G-8
Einini  Gr. 4, 391
Ev'ry Time I Feel the Spirit
    Gr. 5, 242
For Children Safe and Strong
    Gr. 5, 484
Gift to Share, A  Gr. 6, 393
Goin' to Boston  Gr. 6, 433
Hine mah tov  Gr. 5, 430
I Am But a Small Voice  Gr. 6, 446
I Shall Sing  Gr. 8, I-38
I Vow to You, My Country
    Gr. 5, 418
I'll Fly Away  Gr. 8, I-42
Light Up the World with a Song
    Gr. 8, G-25
Little David, Play on Your Harp
    Gr. 4, 394
Loch Lomond  Gr. 5, 140

**(Choral Singing, continued)**

Lullaby and Dance Gr. 4, 387
Mary Ann Gr. 6, 180
Merry Modal Christmas, A
    Gr. 4, 411
Now's the Time Gr. 5, 445
O, Desayo Gr. 5, 411
On My Way Gr. 6, 313
Osamu kosamu Gr. 4, 96
Oy, Hanuka Gr. 7, I-44
Peace Round Gr. 4, 348
Río, río Gr. 5, 370
Ríu ríu chíu Gr. 5, 435
Sail Away Gr. 5, 404
Seagull, Seagull, Sit on the Shore
    Gr. 4, 383
Shalom aleichem Gr. 6, 409
Sing, Sing, Sing! Gr. 5, 340
Star-Spangled Banner, The
    Gr. 5, 488
Star-Spangled Banner, The
    Gr. 8, I-62
Stille Nacht (Silent Night)
    Gr. 7, I-54
Sweet Betsy from Pike Gr. 4, 244
Take a Chance On Me Gr. 8, G-15
This Little Light of Mine Gr. 6, 232
Tina singu Gr. 4, 300
Uno, dos, y tres Gr. 5, 427
Water Is Wide, The Gr. 6, 228
Yellow Rose of Texas, The
    Gr. 7, I-70
You Were on My Mind Gr. 7, G-23

**3-PART**

Blues with a Feeling Gr. 8, I-6
California Dreamin' Gr. 8, G-31
Caroling, Caroling Gr. 6, 458
Chairs to Mend Gr. 4, 149
Chapel of Love Gr. 7, G-27
Cindy Gr. 4, 384
Fais do do Gr. 6, 403
Freedom Is Coming Gr. 5, 415
I Dream a World Gr. 8, G-40
I'm a Believer Gr. 7, G-33
Ja-Da Gr. 7, G-20
Just a Snap-Happy Blues
    Gr. 6, 388
Kum ba yah Gr. 5, 244
Lion Sleeps Tonight, The
    Gr. 8, I-56
Oh, Freedom Gr. 7, G-30
Shake the Papaya Down
    Gr. 4, 378
Siyahamba Gr. 6, 212
Tuxedo Junction Gr. 8, G-21
'-Ulili E Gr. 5, 441
Vem kan segla? Gr. 6, 417
Wheel of the Water, The
    Gr. 4, 362
Winter Gr. 8, G-11
Yonder Come Day Gr. 8, I-68

**4-PART**

Certainly, Lord Gr. 7, I-13
Let Music Surround You Gr. 4, 236

**CALL AND RESPONSE**

ABC Rock Gr. 1, 262
Ain't Gonna Let Nobody Turn Me
    'Round Gr. 8, F-16
Certainly, Lord Gr. 7, I-13
Down by the Bay Gr. 1, 18
Great Day Gr. 3, 58
He's Got the Whole World in His
    Hands Gr. 7, I-36
I'm on My Way Gr. 3, 76
Shine, Shine, Shine Gr. 1, 42
Shoo, Turkey Gr. 1, 104
Shortnin' Bread Gr. 1, 57
Wade in the Water Gr. 8, I-64

**CANONS AND ROUNDS**

A Ram Sam Sam Gr. 3, 208
Ah, Poor Bird Gr. 4, 196
Alleluia Gr. 6, 133
Autumn Canon Gr. 5, 148
Da pacem, Domine Gr. 5, 62
Dona nobis pacem Gr. 6, 125
Ego sum pauper Gr. 5, 158
Gloria, Gloria Gr. 6, 459
Himmel und Erde Gr. 5, 94
Kyrie Gr. 6, 206
Like a Bird Gr. 6, 167
O Music Gr. 5, 162
Oh, How Lovely Is the Evening
    Gr. 4, 217
Scattin' A-Round (Variations on
    Row 3) Gr. 6, 160
Tender Shepherd (Count Your
    Sheep) Gr. 3, 116
This Pretty Planet Gr. 4, 355

**CHILDREN'S CLASSICS**

Christmas, Don't Be Late (The
    Chipmunk Song) Gr. 2, 386
Don Gato Gr. 3, 352
Heigh-Ho Gr. 2, 6
I'd Like To Teach the World to Sing
    (In Perfect Harmony) Gr. 3, 198
It's a Small World Gr. 3, 268
Let's Go Fly a Kite Gr. 2, 327
Never Smile at a Crocodile
    Gr. 3, 100
Puff, the Magic Dragon Gr. 2, 350
Supercalifragilisticexpialidocious
    (from Mary Poppins) Gr. 3, 7
This Land Is Your Land (refrain
    only) Gr. 1, 274
We've Got Lots in Common
    Gr. 3, 366
Zip-a-Dee-Doo-Dah Gr. 2, 330

**DESCANTS AND
COUNTERMELODIES**

America, the Beautiful Gr. 7, I-4
Ash Grove, The Gr. 5, 114

Battle Hymn of the Republic
    Gr. 5, 274
Cycle Song of Life (The River Song)
    Gr. 4, 370
Eres tú Gr. 6, 473
Going Upon the Mountain
    Gr. 6, 105
Gospel Train, The Gr. 6, 398
Love in Any Language Gr. 6, 476
Oklahoma Gr. 5, 36
Pay Me My Money Down
    Gr. 7, I-46
Roll On, Columbia Gr. 5, 116
This Land Is Your Land Gr. 7, I-66
This Land Is Your Land Gr. K..8,
Winter Song Gr. 6, 455

**ECHO SONGS**

I'd Like To Teach the World to
    Sing (In Perferct Harmony)
    Gr. 3, 198
I'm on My Way Gr. 3, 76
Over My Head Gr. 7, G-9

**EXPRESSIVE SINGING**

Al ánimo Gr. 3, 322
America Gr. 8, I-2
America, I Hear You Singing
    Gr. 2, 402
America, the Beautiful Gr. 3, 413
America, the Beautiful Gr. 8, I-4
Artsa alinu Gr. 3, 285
¡Ay, Jalisco no te rajes! Gr. 7, I-6
Big Beautiful Planet Gr. 3, 326
Connemara Lullaby Gr. 5, 232
Deep in the Heart of Texas
    Gr. 8, I-18
Do, Lord Gr. 3, 164
Dok djampa Gr. 8, I-20
El barquito Gr. 3, 358
El rancho grande Gr. 8, I-22
Erdö, erdö de magos Gr. 3, 182
Every Night When the Sun Goes In
    Gr. 8, I-28
Faith of the Heart Gr. 8, G-3
Feliz Navidad Gr. 7, I-28
For the Beauty of the Earth
    Gr. 4, 356
Go, My Son Gr. K..8,
God Bless the U.S.A. Gr. 8, G-37
Groundhog Blues, The Gr. 3, 122
Guantanamera Gr. 8, I-32
Habemos llegado Gr. 6, 174
Hanuka, Hanuka Gr. 8, I-36
Happy Feet Gr. 2, 252
Happy Wanderer, The Gr. 4, 89
Hello to All the Children of the
    World Gr. 3, 4
How Can I Keep from Singing?
    Gr. 4, 261
I Love the Mountains Gr. 5, 34
It's a Beautiful Day Gr. 3, 338
Ja-Da Gr. 2, 188
Jambalaya Gr. 8, I-46

Karangatia ra  Gr. 3, 272
La golondrina  Gr. 8, I-50
Let's Celebrate!  Gr. 3, 374
Let's Get the Rhythm of the Band
    Gr. 3, 84
Lift Ev'ry Voice and Sing
    Gr. 8, I-54
Los reyes de Oriente  Gr. 8, I-58
Ode to Joy  Gr. 4, 152
Oh, Danny Boy  Gr. 4, 48
Over the Rainbow (from The Wizard
    of Oz)  Gr. 4, 140
Ragtime Cowboy Joe  Gr. 2, 250
Rockin' Robin  Gr. 3, 368
Shir l'shalom  Gr. 4, 419
Sing a Rainbow  Gr. 2, 166
Sing, America, Sing!  Gr. 3, 238
Sing Your Story  Gr. 3, 350
Song That's Just for You, A
    Gr. 2, 126
Stand By Me  Gr. 8, E-25
Star-Spangled Banner, The
    Gr. 7, I-56
Starlight, Star Bright  Gr. 4, 373
Straighten Up and Fly Right
    Gr. 4, 128
Swing Low, Sweet Chariot
    Gr. 7, C-41
There Is Love Somewhere
    Gr. 6, 318
This Is My Song  Gr. 6, 77
Waitin' for the Light to Shine
    Gr. 4, 26
World We Love, The  Gr. 3, 342
You're a Grand Old Flag  Gr. 3, 264

**PARTNER SONGS**
Each of Us Is a Flower  Gr. 3, 154
Let Freedom Ring/America, the
    Beautiful  Gr. 5, 77
Live in the City/Home on the
    Range  Gr. 5, 71
Michael Finnigan/This Old Man
    Gr. 3, 153
Play a Simple Melody  Gr. 5, 72
Sambalele  Gr. 4, 397
Sing a Song of Peace/This Is My
    Country  Gr. 6, 66
Turn the World Around/So Is
    Life/Do You Know Who I Am?
    Gr. 4, 114
Winter Fantasy/Jingle Bells
    Gr. 4, 424

**VERSE AND REFRAIN**
Everybody Says  Gr. 1, 287
Look Out for Mother Earth
    Gr. 3, 341

**COMMUNITY INVOLVEMENT**
Article: Audience Behavior  Gr. 7, E-10
Article: Audience Behavior  Gr. 8, E-10
Attending a performance  Gr. 8, B-37
Celebrations  Gr. 8, B-19

Community Performance  Gr. 7, I-26
Community sing-along  Gr. 8, I-40
Dance Event  Gr. 7, B-10
Fairy Tales  Gr. 7, G-36
Glory, Glory, Hallelujah  Gr. 8, B-14
Guest Musicians  Gr. 7, C-42
Host a Day of Percussion  Gr. 7, I-52
Instrument Players and Collectors
    Gr. 7, B-5
Intergenerational Communication
    Gr. 7, B-29
Interview  Gr. 7, G-39
Interviewing  Gr. 7, B-20
Interviewing adults  Gr. 8, A-5
Interviewing local jazz musicians
    Gr. 8, C-42
Interviews  Gr. 8, C-12
Interviews  Gr. 8, I-33
Inviting Community Participation
    Gr. 7, D-8
Live Performances  Gr. 7, E-19
Local musical theater  Gr. 8, A-22
Locating Instrumentalists  Gr. 7, D-31
Mariachi USA Festival  Gr. 7, B-33
Multicultural celebration  Gr. 8, I-49
Multicultural fair  Gr. 8, B-21
Musical groups  Gr. 8, G-30
Old Phone Books Become Percussion
    Instruments  Gr. 7, D-5
Out and about  Gr. 8, F-5
Performing for Others  Gr. 7, E-13
Performing in the community
    Gr. 8, A-25
Rock 'n' Roll memorabilia  Gr. 8, G-34
Song Writing  Gr. 7, G-25
Sound engineering field trip
    Gr. 7, A-16
Sponsor a Public Festival  Gr. 7, I-31
Technology Time Line  Gr. 7, A-19
Urban art  Gr. 8, F-13
Weave a cultural connection
    Gr. 8, D-12

**COMPOSING** See also Skills
    Reinforcement.
Angry Anymore  Gr. 8, F-32
Boston Ball Game 1967  Gr. 8, F-32
Concert for Piano and Orchestra
    Gr. 6, 209
Dance for the Nations  Gr. 6, 122
Down the Ohio  Gr. 2, 60
Dry Bones Come Skipping  Gr. 4, 219
El Salón México  Gr. 6, 199
Face of Love, The  Gr. 8, B-15
Frère Jacques  Gr. 2, 125
Gamelan angklung  Gr. 6, 384
Glory, Glory, Hallelujah  Gr. 6, 52
Go Around the Corn, Sally  Gr. 2, 12
Going on a Picnic  Gr. K, 190
Gonna Ride Up in the Chariot
    Gr. 4, 21
I Got Rhythm  Gr. 6, 101
It's Time  Gr. 6, 274

John Wayne's Teeth  Gr. 8, B-37
Joy of Kwanzaa, The  Gr. 6, 462
Kebjar teruna  Gr. 6, 385
Lyric Suite, "Allegretto gioviale,"
    Movement 1  Gr. 6, 169
Magnolia  Gr. 6, 16
Mary Ann  Gr. K, 253
Nana Kru  Gr. 6, 282
New Hungarian Folk Song  Gr. 6, 196
One Family  Gr. 7, G-17
Plant Four Seeds  Gr. 2, 130
Radio City Christmas Spectacular
    Jingle  Gr. 8, A-5
Riendo el río corre  Gr. 6, 267
Sha Sha Sha  Gr. 6, 328
Six Little Ducks  Gr. K, 234
Spring Rain  Gr. 2, 294
Sun, The  Gr. K, 143
Sun Seeks Shadow (White)
    Gr. 7, D-28
Syrinx  Gr. 5, 113
Take Time in Life  Gr. 6, 292
Theme and Variations for Percussion
    Gr. 5, 66
T'hola, t'hola  Gr. 4, 133
This Little Light of Mine  Gr. 6, 232
Trouble Is a Mountain  Gr. 2, 202
Xiao yin chuan  Gr. 2, 14

**CREATING** See also Skills
    Reinforcement.
Add-On Machine, The  Gr. K, 298
Aguinaldo  Gr. 3, 402
Ain't Gonna Let Nobody Turn Me
    'Round  Gr. 6, 85
Angry Anymore  Gr. 8, F-32
Boston Ball Game 1967  Gr. 8, F-32
Box a-Rockin' Ensemble  Gr. 7, D-4
Chicken on the Fence Post  Gr. 3, 92
Concert for Piano and Orchestra
    Gr. 6, 209
Create a Career  Gr. 8, A-33
Day-O!  Gr. 5, 21
Dinner Music  Gr. K, 70
Dry Bones Come Skipping  Gr. 4, 219
Éliza Kongo  Gr. 5, 17
Free at Last  Gr. 6, 468
From Sea to Shining Sea  Gr. 2, 342
Glad to Have a Friend Like You
    Gr. 2, 228
Gotta Find a Footprint  Gr. 4, 221
I See With My Hands  Gr. 2, 148
I Vow to You, My Country  Gr. 5, 422
I've Been Everywhere  Gr. 6, 226
I've Been Working on the Railroad
    Gr. 3, 242
Ida Red  Gr. 3, 30
Jambalaya  Gr. 8, I-47
Jig Along Home  Gr. 2, 366
Joy of Kwanzaa, The  Gr. 6, 462
Kum bachur atzel  Gr. 3, 138
Lean on Me  Gr. 7, E-22

(*Creating,* continued)

Little Darlin' Gr. 7, F-30
Look Out for Mother Earth Gr. 3, 341
Make a Music Video! Gr. 7, A-29
Miss Susie Anna Sue Gr. K, 242
Mister Rabbit Gr. K, 128
Monster Stomp, The (poem) Gr. 1, 133
Movie sound effects Gr. 8, A-9
Oh, Watch the Stars Gr. 2, 144
One Family Gr. 7, G-17
Orange Blossom Special Gr. 5, 268
Over in the Meadow Gr. 1, 347
Oy, Hanuka Gr. 7, I-45
Pay Me My Money Down Gr. 7, I-48
Play a Simple Melody Gr. 5, 74
Playing Ball (poem) Gr. 1, 153
Producer Gr. 8, A-25
See-Saw Sacradown Gr. 2, 208
Simple Gifts Gr. 5, 185
Singin' in the Rain Gr. 4, 360
Sometimes I Feel Like a Motherless
    Child Gr. 6, 241
*Song Writing with Technology*
    Gr. 7, A-6
Sun Gonna Shine Gr. 6, 242
Sun Seeks Shadow Gr. 7, D-28
*Symphony No. 1, Movement 3*
    Gr. 4, 237
Table Manners (speech piece)
    Gr. 3, 190
There Was an Old Man (speech piece)
    Gr. 3, 191
This Little Light of Mine Gr. 6, 232
Un elefante Gr. 2, 160
Un pajarito Gr. 2, 16
Until I Saw the Sea Gr. 3, 245
*Watermelon Man* Gr. 6, 271
*Work It Out (Blow Your Horn Dub
    Mix)* Gr. 7, A-3
Yibane amenu Gr. 4, 316

## CULTURAL CONNECTION

1930s-1940s Gr. 5, 284
1950s, Music of Gr. 7, F-31
1950s, The Gr. 5, 356
Aboriginal Music and Culture of
    Australia Gr. 8, B-39
Aborigines of Austrailia Gr. 6, 270
Accordion in Cajun Music, The
    Gr. 8, E-21
Advertising Gr. 4, 148
African American Contributions
    Gr. 8, I-65
African American Music Gr. 2, 182
African American "Plays" Gr. 1, 38
African American Singing Games
    Gr. 1, 8
African American Spirituals Gr. 2, 19
African American Spirituals Gr. 3, 162
African American Spirituals Gr. 5, 101
African American Spirituals Gr. 6, 191
African Children's Games Gr. 3, 287
African Lullabies Gr. 4, 133

African Music Gr. 8, B-29
African Musical Bows Gr. 5, 197
African Singing Gr. 5, 32
African Storytelling Gr. 1, 140
Afro-Brazilian Music Gr. 6, 362
Ah! Les jolis papillons Gr. 1, 362
Akan of Ghana Gr. 5, 308
America Gr. 6, 484
American Cowhand, The Gr. 2, 20
*American Idol* Gr. 7, B-23
American Indian Dance Theater
    Gr. 5, 398
American Popular Dance Gr. 5, 345
American West, Settling the Gr. 3, 175
*Andalusian Music* Gr. 8, B-44
Andean Instruments Gr. 6, 46
Andean Instruments Gr. 6, 58
Animals in Japanese Culture Gr. 1, 186
Appalachia Gr. 3, 16
Appalachian Folk Song Gr. 3, 216
Appalachian Style Gr. 6, 121
Apple Tree Gr. 1, 228
Apples Gr. 1, 230
Arbor Day Gr. 5, 115
Architecture in New Orleans Gr. 2, 205
Argentina and Its Music Gr. 3, 56
Art of Mexico, The Gr. 5, 91
Aural Tradition Gr. 8, I-30
Australia Gr. 2, 10
Ba-Benzélé Pygmies Gr. 6, 268
Bahia, Brazil Gr. 6, 164
*Bairagi* Gr. 8, A-19
Balalaika Gr. 4, 222
Bamboo Gr. 5, 317
Bamboo Instruments Gr. 6, 382
Banjo, The Gr. 2, 314
Bantu Gr. 5, 410
Bantu, The Gr. 2, 108
Bells in English Carols Gr. 1, 426
*Bernstein's "Mass"* Gr. 6, 217
Big Ben Gr. 5, 419
Birthday Celebrations Gr. 1, 410
Blues Gr. 7, F-15
Blues Gr. 8, I-6
Blues Era, The Gr. 5, 355
Blues Style Gr. 5, 225
Bomba and Highlife Gr. 8, B-3
Bora Bora Boom Ensemble Gr. 8, D-3
Brazil Gr. 1, 112
Brazil Gr. 3, 309
Bring in Da Noise, Bring in Da Funk
    Gr. 6, 321
British Brass Band, The Gr. 6, 137
Cajun Culture Gr. 1, 316
Cajun Culture Gr. 2, 86
Cajun Culture Gr. 2, 332
Cajun Culture Gr. 4, 387
Cajun Culture Gr. 8, I-48
Cajun Food Gr. 6, 404
Cajuns of Louisiana Gr. 6, 247
Cakewalk, The Gr. 5, 334
Call and Response Gr. 5, 470

Call and Response Style Gr. 3, 76
Calypso Gr. 2, 173
Calypso style Gr. 5, 200
Calypso Style Gr. 6, 298
Canoes Gr. 4, 77
Caribbean Crafts Gr. 5, 16
Caribbean Culinary Customs Gr. 5, 240
Caribbean Islands Gr. 4, 114
Caribbean music Gr. 5, 132
Caribbean, Music of the Gr. 6, 264
Caribbean, Music of the Gr. 6, 264
Caroling Gr. 6, 426
Celebrating the Landscape of North
    America Gr. 7, I-67
Celtic Music Gr. 4, 260
Chant Today Gr. 7, C-4
Chanukah Gr. 4, 428
Chanukah Gr. 5, 465
Chanukah, Chanukah Gr. 1, 420
Chanukah History Gr. 2, 382
Chawe chidyo chem'chero Gr. 2, 297
Chiapas Gr. 5, 92
Children in China Gr. 1, 324
Chile and Its Music Gr. 3, 362
China Gr. 4, 315
China, Language in Gr. 3, 276
Chinese Folk Art Gr. 2, 158
Chinese Moon Festival Gr. 2, 14
Chinese New Year Gr. 3, 104
Chinese String Instruments Gr. 6, 102
Chinese Writing Gr. 4, 337
Chippewa Music Gr. 4, 284
Chippewa (Ojibwa) Nation Gr. 3, 335
Christmas Caroling Gr. 6, 458
Christmas Customs Gr. 4, 411
Christmas in Catatonia and Puerto
    Rico Gr. 5, 472
Christmas in Mexico Gr. 4, 431
Christmas in Mexico Gr. 5, 146
Civil Rights Movement Gr. 4, 436
Clocks That "Ring the Time"
    Gr. 1, 246
Cockney Dialect Gr. 3, 8
Coded Messages Gr. 7, G-11
Colombia Gr. 5, 307
Community Dance, A Gr. 1, 326
Comparing Cultural Preferences
    Gr. 6, 170
Conga Drum, The Gr. 5, 426
Connemara Gr. 5, 232
Corridos Gr. 5, 11
Cotswolds, The Gr. 5, 423
Countries Have Nicknames, Too
    Gr. K, 91
Country Music Roots Gr. 5, 348
Court Ball at the Palais du Louvre (De
    Médicis) Gr. 2, 278
Creole Lullabies Gr. 2, 194
Crossover Tune, A Gr. 6, 52
Crusades, The Gr. 8, C-4
Cultural Influences in Brazil and Mexico
    Gr. 8, C-37

Culture's Treat to the World, A Gr. 1, 378
Cuna People, The Gr. 4, 145
Customs of Purim, The Gr. 1, 439
Czech Culture Gr. 4, 228
Dakota Sioux, The Gr. 3, 71
Day at the Races, A Gr. 5, 271
Didgeridoo Gr. 4, 37
Different Cultures, Different Timbres Gr. 6, 329
Different Singing Games Gr. K, 91
Divided Country, A Gr. 6, 341
Dixie Cups, The Gr. 7, G-27
Dixieland Jazz Gr. 2, 179
¿Dónde lo escondí? Gr. K, 209
Down the Ohio Gr. 2, 61
Dreydl, Make a Gr. 3, 389
Drum Ensemble, Origin of Gr. 3, 270
Drummer's Role, The Gr. 2, 65
Duck Dance Gr. 2, 248
E-mail Cards Gr. 6, 472
El día de mamita Gr. K, 325
El salvador Gr. 1, 216
El Salvador Gr. 1, 216
Ellis Island Gr. 6, 228
Eritrea Gr. 4, 62
Estampie Gr. 8, I-26
European history Gr. 8, C-17
European Renaissance Gr. 7, C-6
European settlement of Australia, The Gr. 5, 22
Everybody Says Gr. 1, 287
Everyday People Gr. 5, 389
Evolution of Ladino Language Gr. 8, I-36
Evolving African Music Gr. 7, I-24
Fabergé Eggs Gr. 4, 292
Families Gr. 1, 282
Favorite Animals Gr. K, 41
Feasts of Light Gr. 1, 418
Finding Food Gr. 4, 345
Finding Food for Dinner Gr. K, 70
Finland Gr. 6, 77
Flutes Around the World Gr. 5, 112
Folk Dancing Gr. 4, 303
Folk Instruments Gr. 5, 380
Folk Music History Gr. 6, 467
Folk Songs Gr. 6, 433
Foods of the Caribbean Gr. 6, 181
Forty-niners, The Gr. 4, 264
Four Seasons, Concerto No. 2, The, "Summer," Movement 3, "La Tempesta" Gr. 6, 102
Freedom Songs Gr. 2, 396
Freedom Songs Gr. 6, 232
French Culture Gr. 6, 176
Friendly Invasion, A Gr. 6, 258
Gaelic Culture Gr. 4, 391
Gahu, drumming and social dance Gr. 7, D-27
Game Songs Gr. 4, 109
Gamelan Montage Gr. 2, 104
Gavotte, The Gr. 3, 87

Georgia Sea Islands Gr. 4, 38
Georgia Sea Islands Gr. 7, F-7
Georgia Sea Islands Gr. 8, I-69
German school songs Gr. 8, C-20
Ghana Gr. 3, 286
Ghana Gr. 6, 288
Giving Thanks Gr. 3, 384
Glossary for "Jambalaya" Gr. 6, 245
Go Around the Corn, Sally Gr. 2, 12
God Save the Queen (British National Anthem) Gr. 5, 486
Gospel Music Gr. 2, 24
Gospel Music Gr. 3, 165
Gospel Music Gr. 6, 234
Gospel Music Gr. 7, G-31
Gospel Music Gr. 7, I-36
Grand Ole Opry, The Gr. 5, 351
Greetings Gr. 6, 8
Growing Audience, The Gr. 2, 253
Growing Rice in China Gr. 1, 88
Guatemala Gr. 3, 227
Guatemalan Marimbas Gr. 8, D-16
Guitarrón, The Gr. 8, I-52
Gullah Culture Gr. 3, 180
Habitat for Humanity Gr. 7, E-10
Haliwa-Saponi Indians Gr. 5, 302
Halloween Gr. 6, 448
Hana-mi, Cherry-blossom Viewing Gr. 4, 308
Hanging Gardens of Babylon Gr. 2,
Hawaiian culture Gr. 5, 440
Hebrew Language Gr. 3, 139
History and Sailing Ships Gr. 5, 22
History of Pitch Syllables, A Gr. 5, 38
Hmong People, The Gr. 4, 368
Holiday Celebrations Gr. 6, 423
Holiday for Elephants Gr. 1, 154
Holiday Music Gr. 7, I-28
How to Make a Diddley Bow Gr. 6, 364
Humoreque and Old Folks at Home Gr. 5, 72
Hungarian Folk Songs Gr. 3, 183
Hungary, Folk Music of Gr. 6, 197
Imbabura Gr. 5, 202
Immigration's Influence on Culture Gr. 6, 482
Indian Classical Music Gr. 4, 195
Indian Ragas Gr. 4, 310
Information about "Arirang" Gr. 5, 25
Information about sunrises Gr. 5, 29
Instruments: Ennanga Gr. 3, 126
Instruments: Mountain Dulcimer Gr. 3, 16
Instruments of the Middle East Gr. 4, 136
Inuit Culture Gr. 3, 258
Inventions and Innovations Gr. 7, E-18
Iran Gr. 3, 282
Irish Culture Gr. 6, 326
Irish Emigrants, Songs of Gr. 4, 296
Irish Words Gr. 4, 298
Island Drums Gr. K, 108
Israel Gr. 3, 285

Israel Gr. 4, 316
Israel Gr. 4, 418
Israel Gr. 5, 298
Israel Gr. 6, 306
Israeli Folk Dances Gr. 1, 180
Israeli Folk Music Gr. 5, 400
Italian: The Language of Music Gr. 4, 68
Jack-o-Lanterns Gr. 3, 382
Jamaica Gr. 5, 18
Jamaican Christmas Gr. 3, 396
Jamaican Folklore Gr. 4, 321
Jamaican Ska Gr. 6, 143
Japanese Foods Gr. 1, 143
Japanese Game Gr. 3, 303
Japanese Music Gr. 7, D-17
Japanese New Year Gr. 7, I-40
Japanese Noh Theater Gr. 4, 96
Japanese Primary School Gr. 3, 331
Jarocho Ensemble Gr. 5, 129
Jazz Gr. 7, G-20
Jazz and Jewish Folk Song Gr. 6, 101
Je m'endors Gr. K, 219
Jewish Americans Gr. 6, 153
Jewish Culture Gr. 6, 409
Jewish/Israeli Culture Gr. 5, 431
Jota Gr. 3, 252
Kente Cloth from Ghana Gr. 6, 295
King, Martin Luther Jr. Gr. 6, 469
Korea Gr. 3, 134
Korean Pottery Gr. 3, 135
Korean Traditional Music Gr. 4, 175
Koriko! Gr. K, 154
Kum ba yah Gr. 5, 244
Kwanzaa Gr. 2, 393
"La vibora," a Beloved Singing Game Gr. 1, 322
Lakota People, The Gr. 3, 254
Languages Gr. 3, 133
Laotian Culture Gr. 8, I-20
Las posadas Gr. 3, 398
Latin America, Markets of Gr. 3, 40
Latin American Music Gr. 3, 359
Latin Language Gr. 6, 126
Latin Pop Gr. 6, 348
Legacy of Songs, The Gr. 5, 181
Legend of the Bear Dance, The Gr. 7, I-11
Legend of the Poinsettia Gr. 4, 433
Liberia Gr. 6, 280
Life on the Westward Trail Gr. 2, 235
Line Dances Gr. 3, 318
Lions in Art Gr. 4, 131
Little Mermaid, The Gr. 5, 373
Little Mouse, The Gr. 1, 349
Llama, The Gr. 5, 152
Los californios, The Legacy of Gr. 4, 241
Lullabies and Work Songs Gr. 4, 226
Lullabies in Music and Art Gr. K, 135
Lullaby Customs Gr. K, 181
Luogu Ensemble Gr. 4, 156
Má Teodora Gr. 6, 301

**(Cultural Connection, continued)**

Mandarin  Gr. 5, 194
Mandarin  Gr. 5, 314
Many Places, Many Dogs  Gr. K, 132
Maori People  Gr. 2, 284
Maori People, The  Gr. 1, 76
Marketplaces  Gr. 3, 90
Mbira, African instrument  Gr. 7, D-27
Mexican Ceramic Crafts  Gr. 2, 192
Mexican History and Culture
    Gr. 5, 326
Mexican Influences  Gr. 6, 199
Micmac People, The  Gr. 3, 214
Miss Mary Mack  Gr. 2, 42
Modern Day Egypt  Gr. 5, 297
Mohawk Nation  Gr. 3, 335
*Moon Mirrored in the Pool, The*
    Gr. 6, 103
Moors in Spain  Gr. 4, 176
Moravia  Gr. 3, 78
Motivational Songs  Gr. 4, 98
Multicultural Music  Gr. 8, F-7
Music and Singing in Scandinavia
    Gr. 6, 417
Music Dramas from Indonesia
    Gr. 8, C-25
*Music for Harvest Dance*  Gr. 1, 416
Music in African Culture  Gr. 5, 66
Music of Africans and African
    Americans  Gr. 7, D-3
Music of Chile  Gr. 2, 160
Music of Pow-Wows, The  Gr. 6, 444
Music of Puerto Rico  Gr. 6, 175
Music of Southern Appalachia
    Gr. 6, 23
Music Traditions  Gr. 8, B-36
Música Norteña  Gr. 6, 172
Musical Onomatopoeia  Gr. 6, 384
Mythology  Gr. 4, 334
Nanticoke People, The  Gr. 3, 256
National Anthems  Gr. 7, I-2
National Clothing  Gr. 4, 230
Native American Culture  Gr. 3, 214
Native American Flute  Gr. 5, 396
Native American Flutes  Gr. 5, 110
Native American Hand Game
    Gr. 3, 306
Native American Lullabies  Gr. K, 110
Native American Music  Gr. 4, 282
Native Americans of Bolivia
    Gr. 5, 150
Natural Resources  Gr. 6, 277
Navajo Art  Gr. 5, 108
Navajo, The  Gr. 6, 286
New Year's Day in Japan  Gr. 3, 407
New Zealand  Gr. 3, 272
Non-African American Rhythm &
    Blues Performers  Gr. 7, B-38
Nutcrackers  Gr. 6, 324
"Ode to Joy", Op. 125, "Ode to Joy,"
    *Movement 4*  Gr. 4, 151
Oh, Freedom  Gr. 5, 392
Old West, Children in the  Gr. 3, 251

Opera Around the World  Gr. 7, C-30
Oral Traditions  Gr. 3, 364
Origin of Rap  Gr. 7, A-5
Origin of Santa Claus  Gr. 2, 384
Origin of the banjo  Gr. 5, 198
Origins of Salsa  Gr. 6, 335
Origins of the Cha-Cha  Gr. 6, 332
Origins of the Charro Uniform
    Gr. 7, I-7
Oshogatsu (Japanese New Year)
    Gr. 5, 478
Panama  Gr. 3, 270
Passamaquoddy People, The
    Gr. 3, 256
Passover  Gr. 4, 438
Patriotism  Gr. 8, G-39
Percussion Origins  Gr. 8, B-7
Philippines, Music in the  Gr. 4, 173
Pima People, The  Gr. 2, 356
Pizza, Pizza, Daddy-o  Gr. 2, 31
Play-Party Games  Gr. 2, 81
Polynesian culture  Gr. 8, B-28
Pop Culture  Gr. 6, 92
Prairie  Gr. 5, 11
Pre-Revolutionary Russia  Gr. 7, E-5
Puerto Rico  Gr. 8, D-19
Puerto Rico  Gr. 5, 294
Puerto Rico's Music  Gr. 6, 50
Rabbit in the Moon, The  Gr. 1, 396
Ragtime  Gr. 5, 332
Ragupati Ragava Raja Ram  Gr. 5, 320
Ranch Life  Gr. 4, 215
Ranchera  Gr. 8, I-23
Red Cedar Tree  Gr. 2, 322
Reggae Look, The  Gr. 7, B-35
Regional Dress  Gr. 3, 317
Renaissance, The  Gr. 5, 435
Ring Games  Gr. 3, 312
Road to Opportunity (Route 66)
    Gr. 4, 277
Roaring Twenties, The  Gr. 6, 88
Roaring Twenties, The  Gr. 8, G-22
Rock 'n' Roll Music  Gr. 3, 368
Rodrigo, Joaquín  Gr. 6, 199
Rounds in English Tradition  Gr. 4, 197
Rumba  Gr. 6, 333
Russia  Gr. 1, 372
Salsa  Gr. 6, 266
Sambas and Carnaval  Gr. 4, 397
Same Train  Gr. 2, 165
Santiago de Compostela  Gr. 5, 175
Sawatdee tuh jah  Gr. 2, 265
Scat Singers  Gr. 6, 161
Scottish Language  Gr. 5, 140
Sea Shanties  Gr. 4, 258
Secret Code  Gr. 6, 338
See the Children Playin'  Gr. 4, 106
Seeing Patterns  Gr. 4, 305
Seven Principles of Kwanzaa
    Gr. 4, 434
Seven Principles of Kwanzaa (Nguzo
    Saba)  Gr. 6, 462

Seven Principles of Kwanzaa, The
    Gr. 5, 476
Shakers, The  Gr. 5, 184
*Shchedryk, "Carol of the Bells"*
    Gr. 6, 103
Shortnin' Bread  Gr. 1, 56
Signs of friendship  Gr. 5, 47
Sing About Martin  Gr. K, 321
Singing Game  Gr. K, 54
Singing Movie Cowboys  Gr. 6, 236
Sixteenth-Century Elizabethan England
    Gr. 6, 48
Slavonic Dances  Gr. 4, 228
Slovakia  Gr. 3, 78
Social Dancing  Gr. 6, 434
Social Issues (1960s-1970s)
    Gr. 5, 286
Somebody Waiting  Gr. 2, 282
Son Clave  Gr. 7, D-18
Son Montuno Style  Gr. 4, 34
Song Lyrics and History  Gr. 4, 330
Song of the Eagle  Gr. 2, 248
Songs of the Civil War  Gr. 6, 343
South Korea  Gr. 2, 134
Spain, History of Bullfighting in
    Gr. 7, F-15
Spanish Influence in the United States
    Gr. 4, 271
Spanish Influences  Gr. 6, 199
Spanish Instruments  Gr. 2, 16
Spanish Language Songs  Gr. 2, 97
Spike Fiddle  Gr. 5, 310
Spirituals  Gr. 3, 249
Spirituals  Gr. 4, 394
Spirituals  Gr. 6, 397
Spirituals, African American  Gr. 4, 20,
    179, 267
Spirituals, Types of  Gr. 8, G-9
St. Helena Island  Gr. 5, 217
Star Festival, The  Gr. 2, 336
Stonehenge  Gr. 5, 425
String Instruments  Gr. 4, 111
Sukkot  Gr. 2, 378
Surf Scene, The  Gr. 6, 261
Swing  Gr. 5, 337
Swing Era (1930-1940), The
    Gr. 5, 447
Switching Cultures  Gr. 6, 240
Symbolism in Spirituals  Gr. 4, 52
Tahiti  Gr. 6, 24
Taiko (Japanese drum)  Gr. 5, 156
Taiwan  Gr. K, 162
Take Time in Life  Gr. 6, 292
Tarantella, The  Gr. 8, C-46
Technological Advances  Gr. 5, 340
Teen Idols  Gr. 6, 255
Tejano  Gr. 6, 262
*Tema de maimara*  Gr. 1, 297
Tex-Mex Music  Gr. 8, B-25
Textiles  Gr. 2, 70
Thai Arts  Gr. 2, 263
Thai Language  Gr. 6, 450
Thanksgiving  Gr. 2, 380

Three Kings' Day  Gr. 3, 403
Three Kings Day  Gr. 8, I-59
Tibetan Monasteries  Gr. 6, 24
*Tihore Mai*  Gr. 8, B-12
Tin Pan Alley  Gr. 5, 75
Tina singu  Gr. 4, 300
Torah, The  Gr. 5, 107
Tour of Turkey, A  Gr. 2, 142
Tres Reyes Magos  Gr. 5, 480
Trick Roping  Gr. 5, 68
Trinidad  Gr. 3, 55
Trinidad and Tobago  Gr. 1, 195
Trinidad, Steel Drums of  Gr. 3, 12
*Troldhaugen*  Gr. 6, 6
Tu b'Shvat  Gr. 3, 206
Two Caribbean Nations  Gr. 6, 300
Underground Railroad Code Words
    Gr. 5, 26
United Nations  Gr. 3, 378
Venezuela  Gr. 5, 304
Venezuelan Dance Music  Gr. 8, I-10
Vietnam  Gr. 5, 460
Vietnamese music  Gr. 6, 12
Vihuela  Gr. 5, 324
Visiting Spain  Gr. 6, 413
Vocal Forms  Gr. 5, 62
Wabanaki, The  Gr. 5, 462
Wales  Gr. 5, 104
*Way Down Yonder in the Brickyard*
    Gr. 2, 51
*Way of Life*  Gr. 6, 284
Wayang Kulit  Gr. 5, 318
West Indies, The  Gr. 4, 318
Western Swing  Gr. 5, 134
What Makes Jamaica Special  Gr. K,
    10
White Cliffs of Dover  Gr. 5, 421
Winter Olympics, 1998  Gr. 4, 152
Wiz (musical), The  Gr. 6, 6
Work Songs  Gr. 5, 13
Work Songs  Gr. 7, I-48
Work Songs  Gr. K, 70
Work Songs, African American
    Gr. 4, 179
World Food Fest, A  Gr. 6, 60
World Peace Bell  Gr. 6, 454
Yellow Bell (Huang-chung)  Gr. 8, D-27
Yiddish  Gr. 7, I-44
Yoruba, The  Gr. 2, 102
Yule Log  Gr. 5, 474
Yup'ik Culture and Language
    Gr. 8, D-21
Zimbabwe Greeting Song  Gr. 1, 312
Zulu  Gr. 4, 30
Zulu Culture  Gr. 8, I-57
Zulu People, The  Gr. 8, E-8
Zulu, The  Gr. 1, 136
Zulu, The  Gr. 6, 212
Zydeco  Gr. 6, 403

# CURRICULUM, ACROSS THE

## ART

*ABACA Dabble*  Gr. 4, 184
Aguinaldo  Gr. 3, 402
A la rurru niño  Gr. K, 180
Al quebrar la piñata  Gr. 4, 432
America, the Beautiful  Gr. 3, 412
America, the Beautiful  Gr. 7, I-5
Animals Find Water, The
    Gr. 2, 218
Bam, chi, chi, bam  Gr. K, 109
Banjo Sam  Gr. 2, 314
*Cafe Europa*  Gr. 7, B-43
Canción de cuna  Gr. 4, 144
Cho'i hát bội  Gr. 5, 318
Circle 'Round the Moon  Gr. 4, 405
Court Ball at the Palais du Louvre
    (De Médicis)  Gr. 2, 278
*Cowboys' Christmas Ball*
    Gr. 6, 238
De colores  Gr. 5, 90
Dinah  Gr. 2, 120
Draw Me a Bucket of Water
    Gr. 3, 124
Eensy Weensy Spider  Gr. K, 187
Ég a gyertya  Gr. K, 96
Ego sum pauper  Gr. 5, 158
Eighteenth-century coverlet
    Gr. 5, 395
El barquito  Gr. 3, 361
El cóndor pasa  Gr. 6, 48
Farewell to the Warriors  Gr. 4, 285
*Fingerprints*  Gr. 7, B-43
Five Little Chickadees  Gr. K, 179
Follow the Drinkin' Gourd
    Gr. 4, 268
Four in a Boat  Gr. 2, 46
Funwa alafia  Gr. 5, 32
Heri za Kwanzaa  Gr. 5, 476
Hey, m'tswala  Gr. 4, 78
If You're Happy  Gr. K, 94
Ikhanda, maslombe  Gr. K, 15
I'm a Believer  Gr. 7, G-33
Inuit soapstone sculpture
    Gr. 3, 259
It Don't Mean a Thing (If It Ain't
    Got That Swing)  Gr. 5, 336
Jasmine Flowers  Gr. 5, 316
Jig Along Home  Gr. 2, 366
Kangaroo Song, The  Gr. K, 44
Kapulu kane  Gr. 2, 270
Kibungo, Beast of the Forest
    Gr. 2, 352
Kuma san  Gr. K, 40
La piñata  Gr. 3, 399
La pulga de San José  Gr. 3, 40
La tormenta tropical  Gr. 2, 116
Let It Snow! Let It Snow! Let It
    Snow!  Gr. 4, 427
Li'l Liza Jane  Gr. 3, 141
Look Out for Mother Earth
    Gr. 3, 341
Madonna with Flowers (Joysmith)
    Gr. K, 134
Mister Rabbit  Gr. K, 129
Modern Painting with Clef
    (Lichtenstein)  Gr. 2, 79
Music promotion  Gr. 7, A-27
Nitty Gritty Sand Song  Gr. K, 191
Oliver Twist  Gr. K, 139
On a Log, Mister Frog  Gr. K, 149
*Open the Kingdom*  Gr. 6, 30
Ōsamu kosamu  Gr. 4, 96
Painting Song: A Dribble and a Dot
    Gr. K, 175
Party Tonight!  Gr. 2, 153
Peace Round  Gr. 4, 348
*Picking Red Chestnuts*  Gr. 5, 310
Pon, pon, pon  Gr. K, 50
Puff, the Magic Dragon  Gr. 2, 350
Put a Little Love in Your Heart
    Gr. 4, 7
*Rabbit Dance, The*  Gr. 3, 334
Rattlesnake, The (Remington)
    Gr. 3, 176
*Rippa Medley, The, "Block-Block,
    One Leg Up, Let the Beat Go,
    Uh-Oh"*  Gr. 8, D-32
Ríu chíu chíu  Gr. 5, 438
*Riverdance Suite*  Gr. 2, 141
Santa Clara  Gr. 4, 173
Star-Spangled Banner, The
    Gr. 4, 440
Starry Night (Van Gogh),
    1923–1945  Gr. 2, 144
Starry Night (Van Gogh)  Gr. 1, 107
Strike Up the Band  Gr. 6, 134
Sun Seeks Shadow  Gr. 7, D-29
Sweet Potatoes  Gr. 3, 228
*Symphony No. 47 in G Major,
    "Menuet"*  Gr. 7, C-14
Tsuki  Gr. 4, 25
Turn the World Around  Gr. 4, 116
Turn, Turn, Turn (To Everything
    There Is a Season)  Gr. 5, 378
Vamos a la fiesta  Gr. 2, 374
*Voiles*  Gr. 7, C-39
White Water Lilies (Monet)  Gr. 1,
    23
Woman in Black at the Opera
    (Cassatt)  Gr. 8, E-11
Woman Standing, Child on Back
    (Charlot)  Gr. K, 134
Wooly Bully  Gr. 3, 372
Your Friends Shall Be the Tall Wind
    Gr. 6, 201

## HEALTH EDUCATION

Apples, Peaches, Pears, and Plums
    (speech piece)  Gr. 1, 14
Mood Music  Gr. 8, A-7

## LANGUAGE ARTS

*A mi querido Austin*  Gr. 8, B-24
ABC Blues  Gr. K, 281
ABC Rock  Gr. 1, 262
Abiyoyo  Gr. 2, 109
About Buttons  Gr. 1, 211

(*Across the Curriculum,* continued)

Addams Family, The  Gr. 5, 456

Adelita  Gr. 5, 50

Adventures of Isabel, The
    Gr. 3, 173

Ah, eu entrei na roda  Gr. 3, 309

Aiken Drum  Gr. 1, 398

*Ali Pasha*  Gr. 5, 218

All for One  Gr. 7, E-9

Alle meine Entchen  Gr. 1, 98

Alphabet Song  Gr. K, 280

Ama-Lama  Gr. 5, 142

Amarillo Armadillo  Gr. 2, 82

Amefuri  Gr. 1, 143

America  Gr. 5, 486

*America*  Gr. 7, A-25

America, the Beautiful  Gr. 3, 412

America, the Beautiful  Gr. 4, 158

America, the Beautiful  Gr. 5, 76

America, the Beautiful  Gr. 7, I-5

America, the Beautiful  Gr. 8, I-4

America, the Free  Gr. 4, 210

America, the Free  Gr. 4, 212

American Dance Theater/Alvin
    Ailey  Gr. 1, 287

And My Heart Soars  Gr. 2, 240

Angry Anymore  Gr. 8, F-33

Ants Go Marching, The  Gr. 1, 249

Apple, The  Gr. 1, 231

Ash Grove, The  Gr. 5, 114

Autumn Canon  Gr. 5, 149

Away to America  Gr. 5, 57

Ayelivi  Gr. 2, 71

Ayii, Ayii, Ayii  Gr. K, 11

B-A, Bay  Gr. 1, 220

Baby Beluga  Gr. K, 272

Baby Chick  Gr. K, 167

Back to School  Gr. K, 5

Banana Splits  Gr. 1, 318

*Banjo*  Gr. 5, 198

Banjo Sam  Gr. 2, 314

Banuwa  Gr. 6, 294

Beach Rap (speech piece)  Gr. 1,
    352

Bee, Bee Bumblebee (speech piece)
    Gr. 1, 50

Bereleh  Gr. K, 150

Big Old Storm a-Comin'  Gr. K,
    257

Big Rock Candy Mountain
    Gr. 4, 330

Bingo  Gr. 1, 168

Birthday, Birthday, Birthday
    Gr. K, 306

Black Snake  Gr. 3, 52

Blow Ye Winds  Gr. 4, 254

Blowin' in the Wind  Gr. 5, 382

Blowin' in the Wind  Gr. 5, 384

Blue Mountain Lake  Gr. 6, 204

Bluebird  Gr. K, 104

Bluebird, Bluebird  Gr. K, 105

*Bombay Dreams*  Gr. 8, B-35

Bonjour, mes amis  Gr. 1, 316

*Boston Ball Game 1967*
    Gr. 8, F-32

Bounce High, Bounce Low
    Gr. 1, 152

Bridges  Gr. 6, 86

Bubble Trouble  Gr. K, 184

Bubbles  Gr. K, 185

Bump! Bump! Bump!  Gr. K, 53

Bury Me Not on the Lone Prairie
    Gr. 6, 18

Caballito blanco  Gr. 2, 192

Cacophony  Gr. K, 82

Canoe Song  Gr. 4, 76

Cantando mentiras  Gr. 4, 146

Carelessly Crafted Raft, A
    Gr. 6, 416

*Carnival of the Animals,*
    "Aquarium"  Gr. 5, 376

*Carolina Sunday Waltz*  Gr. 7, F-9

Cat's Menu  Gr. 2, 301

Caterpillar, The  Gr. 2, 157

Certainly, Lord  Gr. 7, I-15

Cha yang wu  Gr. 1, 88

Chag Purim  Gr. 1, 438

Chanukah Is Here!  Gr. 2, 382

Chawe chidyo chem'chero
    Gr. 2, 296

Chicka Hanka  Gr. 2, 211

Chickens, The  Gr. 3, 92

Children, Go Where I Send Thee
    Gr. 3, 392

Children Learn What They Live
    Gr. 5, 381

*Children's Corner Suite, "Jimbo's*
    *Lullaby"*  Gr. 1, 272

Cho'i hát bội  Gr. 5, 318

Chrismus a Come  Gr. 3, 396

Chuhwuht  Gr. 2, 356

Chums (poem)  Gr. 1, 290

Cielito lindo  Gr. 4, 271

Cinderella Dressed in Green
    Gr. K, 137

Ciranda  Gr. 2, 273

Circle 'Round the Moon  Gr. 4, 403

Cirmos cica  Gr. 1, 128

*Clair de lune*  Gr. K, 165

Clap, Wiggle, and Stomp  Gr. K, 34

Clouds of Gray  Gr. 2, 56

Colorado Trail  Gr. 5, 276

Come and Go With Me to That
    Land  Gr. 5, 391

Come, Ye Thankful People, Come
    Gr. 5, 458

*Concert for Piano and Orchestra*
    Gr. 6, 208

*Concerto for Orchestra,*
    *"Presentation of Pairs"*
    Gr. 4, 72

Connemara Lullaby  Gr. 5, 234

Cookie  Gr. 2, 172

*Copycat*  Gr. K, 9

Corn Grinding Song  Gr. K, 67

Corta la caña  Gr. 6, 364

Costume Capers  Gr. 1, 412

*Country Dance*  Gr. 3, 211

Cow, The  Gr. 4, 273

Cow's Woc Backward  Gr. 1, 390

Crab Dance  Gr. 2, 307

Crawfish  Gr. 2, 88

Crayons  Gr. K, 75

Crocodile, The  Gr. 2, 362

Cuando pa' Chile me voy
    Gr. 6, 376

Cuckoo, Cuckoo  Gr. 1, 110

Cycle Song of Life (The River Song)
    Gr. 4, 370

Da pacem, Domine  Gr. 5, 63

Dance for the Nations  Gr. 6, 122

Dancin' in the Street  Gr. 5, 361

*Dancin' in the Street*  Gr. 5, 360

Dancin' in the Street  Gr. 5, 362

*Dancing Tree, The*  Gr. K, 202

De colores  Gr. 5, 90

Deck the Hall  Gr. 5, 474

Deep in the Heart of Texas
    Gr. 8, E-22

*Die Walküre, "The Ride of the*
    *Valkyries"*  Gr. 8, C-23

Different Beat, A  Gr. 1, 4

Dinah  Gr. 2, 120

Dinosaur Dance  Gr. 2, 166

Do Wah Diddy Diddy  Gr. 4, 202

Dok djampa  Gr. 8, I-21

Don Gato  Gr. 3, 353

Don't Be Cruel  Gr. 6, 254

Don't Let Your Watch Run Down
    Gr. 3, 166

Don't You Hear the Lambs?
    Gr. 5, 96

¿Dónde lo escondí?  Gr. K, 209

Down by the Bay  Gr. 1, 18

Down by the Riverside  Gr. 5, 257

Down by the Riverside  Gr. 8, G-8

Down, Down, Baby  Gr. 2, 32

Down in the Meadow  Gr. K, 147

Down the Listening Lane  Gr. K,
    192

Dream Keeper, The  Gr. 2, 397

*Dreydl Song, The*  Gr. 3, 391

Drum, A (story)  Gr. 1, 116

*Drums From Around the World*
    Gr. 6, 278

Dry Bones Come Skipping
    Gr. 4, 218

*Dusty Rag*  Gr. K, 165

Ee jer ha ba go  Gr. K, 133

Eensy Weensy Spider  Gr. K, 187

Ein Männlein steht im Walde
    Gr. 2, 90

Einini  Gr. 4, 392

El barquito  Gr. 3, 358

El burrito enfermo  Gr. K, 271

El caracol  Gr. K, 130

El chocolate  Gr. 1, 380

El cóndor pasa  Gr. 6, 46

El gallo pinto  Gr. 3, 86

El rancho grande  Gr. 4, 214
El rancho grande  Gr. 8, I-24
El sapito  Gr. 3, 336
Eletelephony  Gr. 2, 161
En nuestra Tierra tan linda
    Gr. 2, 334
End, The (poem)  Gr. 1, 408
Eres tú  Gr. 6, 474
Ev'rybody Ought to Know
    Gr. 1, 434
Every Morning When I Wake Up
    Gr. 2, 320
Faith of the Heart  Gr. 8, G-3
Family Tree  Gr. 3, 73
Farewell to Tarwathie  Gr. 6, 43
Farewell to the Warriors  Gr. 4, 285
Farmer in the Dell, The  Gr. K, 232
Feng yang hua gu  Gr. 4, 313
First Snowflake  Gr. K, 259
Five Little Chickadees  Gr. K, 179
Flies  Gr. 2, 201
Flowers at Night  Gr. 2, 246
Fly and the Bumblebee, The
    Gr. 1, 384
Follow the Drinkin' Gourd
    Gr. 4, 266
For Children Safe and Strong
    Gr. 5, 485
For the Beauty of the Earth
    Gr. 4, 356
Four Seasons  Gr. 2, 56
Four Seasons "Winter," (Largo),
    Movement 2, The  Gr. 3, 110
Four Strong Winds (Song to a
    Seagull)  Gr. 6, 170
Fourth of July Night (poem)
    Gr. 1, 444
Freight Train  Gr. 1, 46
Frog (poem)  Gr. 1, 25
Frog Music  Gr. 4, 200
Frostiana (from Stopping by
    Woods on a Snowy Evening)
    Gr. 6, 40
Galoshes  Gr. K, 63
Get on Your Feet  Gr. 5, 6
Gift to Share, A  Gr. 6, 392
Glad to Have a Friend Like You
    Gr. 2, 228
Glendy Burke, The  Gr. 4, 263
Gloria In Excelsis  Gr. 6, 211
Go Around the Corn, Sally
    Gr. 2, 12
Go Down, Moses  Gr. 5, 190
God Bless the U.S.A.  Gr. 8, G-38
Going on a Picnic  Gr. K, 190
Golden Ring Around the Susan
    Girl  Gr. 3, 17
Goldilocks and the Three Bears
    Gr. K, 49
Good Mornin' Blues  Gr. 2, 53
Good Mornin' Blues  Gr. 5, 226
Goodbye, Julie  Gr. 1, 334
Gospel Train, The  Gr. 6, 397

Great Big Stars  Gr. 1, 61
Great Day  Gr. 3, 58
Greenland Whale Fishery, The
    Gr. 5, 231
Groundhog Jig, The  Gr. 1, 436
Guitar Tuning  Gr. 7, F-3
Guitar Tuning  Gr. 8, F-3
Habari Gani  Gr. 3, 405
Had to Get Up This Mornin' Soon
    Gr. 3, 114
Haere  Gr. 2, 285
Halley Came to Jackson
    Gr. 2, 340
Halloween Song  Gr. K, 309
Hama chi dori  Gr. 3, 330
Hambone  Gr. 7, D-3
Happy Birthday!  Gr. K, 306
Happy Birthday To You (poem)
    Gr. 1, 411
Happy Wanderer, The  Gr. 4, 88
Harambee  Gr. 4, 434
Hard Day Blues  Gr. 7, B-9
Haul Away, Joe  Gr. 4, 13
He's Got the Whole World in His
    Hands  Gr. 3, 230
Heads Carolina, Tails California
    Gr. 7, B-25
Hearts Like Doors  Gr. K, 188
Heigh-Ho  Gr. 2, 6
Hej pada pada  Gr. 3, 79
Hello!  Gr. 2, 262
Here I Am  Gr. K, 149
Hi Heidi Ho  Gr. 1, 394
Hickory, Dickory, Dock (so-mi-la-so
    version)  Gr. 1, 350
Higglety, Pigglety, Pop!  Gr. K, 23
Himmel und Erde  Gr. 5, 95
His Wife Said… (poem)  Gr. 1, 343
Hokey Pokey  Gr. K, 296
Home on the Range  Gr. 5, 70
Hop Up, My Ladies  Gr. 3, 142
Hot Cross Buns (Version 2)
    Gr. 3, 221
Hound Dog  Gr. 5, 213
How Can I Keep from Singing?
    Gr. 4, 261
How the Kiwi Lost Its Wings (story)
    Gr. 1, 78
Hungarian Dance No. 19
    Gr. 4, 171
Hurt No Living Thing (poem)
    Gr. 1, 226
Hurt No Living Thing  Gr. 4, 32
Hwa yuan li-de young wa wa
    Gr. 3, 102
I Believe I Can Fly  Gr. 5, 170
I Can't Spell Hippopotamus
    Gr. 1, 265
I Don't Care If the Rain Comes
    Down  Gr. 3, 24
I Dream a World  Gr. 8, G-43
I Fed My Horse  Gr. 2, 94

I Got a Letter This Morning
    Gr. K, 68
I Like You  Gr. 6, 7
I Love Peanuts  Gr. 7, E-21
I See the Moon  Gr. 2, 58
I Vow to You, My Country
    Gr. 5, 420
I'm a Believer  Gr. 7, G-34
I'm a Dreydl  Gr. K, 315
I'm a Very Fine Turkey  Gr. K, 310
If I Had a Hammer  Gr. 5, 287
Ikhanda, maslombe  Gr. K, 15
Interview with Rick Bassett (Part 2)
    Gr. 3, 222
Ise oluwa  Gr. 2, 102
It's a Beautiful Day  Gr. 3, 339
Jack and Jill  Gr. K, 46
Jambalaya  Gr. 8, I-46
James Brown  Gr. K, 206
Jellyfish Walk (poem)  Gr. 1, 32
Jig Along Home  Gr. 2, 366
John Kanaka  Gr. 3, 60
Johnny Mister Brown  Gr. K, 36
Jolly Old St. Nicholas  Gr. K, 316
Joshua Fought the Battle
    Gr. 5, 102
Joy to the World  Gr. 3, 22
Juanito  Gr. K, 300
Jump or Jiggle  Gr. 2, 26
Jump Rope Jingle  Gr. K, 211
Jump That Jody  Gr. K, 212
Junk Music Montage  Gr. 1, 73
Just from the Kitchen  Gr. K, 55
Just Watch  Gr. K, 295
Kangaroo Song, The  Gr. K, 44
Karangatia ra  Gr. 3, 272
Keep a Cool Head  Gr. 7, B-34
Khorovod  Gr. 1, 373
Kid Like Me, A (speech piece)
    Gr. 2, 394
Kingston Market  Gr. 3, 90
Knock No More  Gr. 3, 386
Koriko!  Gr. K, 155
Kuma san  Gr. K, 40
Kwanzaa Carol, A  Gr. 2, 392
La bamba  Gr. 5, 128
La golondrina  Gr. 8, I-51
La piñata  Gr. 3, 399
La piñata  Gr. 3, 401
La pulga de San José  Gr. 3, 40
La raspa  Gr. 4, 302
La Tarara  Gr. 4, 176
Lap Time  Gr. K, 101
Las horas  Gr. 1, 246
Last Night I Dreamed of Chickens
    (poem)  Gr. 1, 141
Leatherwing Bat, The  Gr. 2, 302
Leaves  Gr. 1, 26
Lemonade  Gr. 1, 191
Les petites marionettes  Gr. K, 237
Let Freedom Ring  Gr. 5, 77
Let Music Surround You  Gr. 4, 236
Let's Get Ready  Gr. K, 312

**(Across the Curriculum, continued)**

Let's Pretend  Gr. K, 227
Li'l Liza Jane  Gr. 3, 141
Light Up the World with a Song
 Gr. 8, G-25
Like a Bird  Gr. 6, 166
Linstead Market  Gr. 5, 240
Lion Sleeps Tonight, The
 Gr. 4, 130
Little and Lots  Gr. K, 323
Little David  Gr. 1, 232
Little Mouse, The  Gr. 1, 348
Little Red Caboose  Gr. K, 229
*Little Red Hen, The* (story)
 Gr. 1, 255
Little Red Wagon  Gr. K, 152
Little Shop of Horrors  Gr. 4, 422
Little Snail  Gr. K, 131
Little Spider  Gr. K, 93
Lo yisa  Gr. 6, 130
Loch Lomond  Gr. 5, 141
Loco-Motion, The  Gr. 3, 64
London Bridge  Gr. K, 244
Lone Star Trail  Gr. 2, 23
Long Way Home, A  Gr. 1, 383
Looby Loo  Gr. K, 210
Look! Look! The Sun Woke Up!
 Gr. 1, 368
Look Out Below!  Gr. 2, 370
Los maizales  Gr. 1, 296
Los pollitos  Gr. K, 166
Los trencitos  Gr. K, 25
Lots of Worms  Gr. 2, 313
Love in Any Language  Gr. 6, 477
Love Somebody  Gr. 3, 94
Lullaby (poem)  Gr. 1, 205
Lullaby and Dance  Gr. 4, 387
Má Teodora  Gr. 6, 298
*Mad…Sad…Glad: A Piece in
 Three Mood-ments*  Gr. K, 249
Make a Music Video!  Gr. 7, A-28
*Malagueña*  Gr. 5, 154
Mango Walk  Gr. 5, 200
Mary Ann  Gr. 6, 182
Mary Ann  Gr. K, 253
Mashed Potatoes (speech piece)
 Gr. 1, 21
Merry-Go-Round  Gr. K, 290
Mi chacra  Gr. 1, 365
Miss Susie Anna Sue  Gr. K, 242
Missy-La, Massa-La  Gr. 4, 190
Mister Rabbit  Gr. K, 129
Modern Dragon, A  Gr. 3, 242
Mon papa  Gr. 2, 279
Mon papa  Gr. 2, 281
Morning Is Come  Gr. 3, 128
Mother Sent Me to the Store
 Gr. K, 137
Mother to Son  Gr. 2, 203
Mozart, Wolfgang Amadeus
 Gr. 4, 110
Music Critic  Gr. 7, A-33
Must Be Santa  Gr. K, 318

My Bonnie Lies Over the Ocean
 Gr. 4, 338
My Father's House  Gr. 2, 25
My Pony, Macaroni  Gr. 1, 158
My Shadow  Gr. K, 19
Name, Name, What's Your Name?
 (speech piece)  Gr. 3, 10
Nampaya omame  Gr. 1, 137
Nana Kru  Gr. 6, 283
Nani wale na hala  Gr. 3, 260
New Shoes  Gr. 2, 242
New Way to Walk, A  Gr. K, 117
Night, The  Gr. 1, 63
Niño querido  Gr. 1, 308
Noah's Shanty  Gr. 1, 344
*Noah's Zoo in the Big, Big Rain*
 Gr. K, 274
*North Carolina Breakdown*
 Gr. 5, 334
Now Let Me Fly  Gr. 3, 178
*Nruab hnub thiab hmo ntuj*
 Gr. 4, 366
O Music  Gr. 5, 162
Oh, Danny Boy  Gr. 4, 49
Oh, How Lovely Is the Evening
 Gr. 4, 217
Oh, Watch the Stars  Gr. 5, 216
Old House, Tear It Down!
 Gr. 4, 179
Old Mother Goose  Gr. K, 247
Old Mother Hubbard  Gr. 1, 118
On a Log, Mister Frog  Gr. K, 149
One Morning in May  Gr. 6, 120
One Morning Soon  Gr. 3, 68
One, Two, Three, Four, Five
 (rhyme)  Gr. 1, 67
*Onomatapoiea Study No. 2*
 Gr. 7, E-31
Orange Blossom Special
 Gr. 5, 268
Our Washing Machine (poem)
 Gr. 1, 35
Over My Head  Gr. 7, G-9
Over My Head  Gr. 4, 119
Over the River and Through the
 Wood  Gr. 3, 385
Overture to "Candide"  Gr. 6, 218
Panther, The  Gr. 3, 354
Paper  Gr. K, 195
Parade Came Marching, The
 Gr. 1, 166
Patty Cake Polka  Gr. 2, 279
Peace Like a River  Gr. 3, 246
Peace Round  Gr. 4, 348
*Penny Lane*  Gr. 6, 257
Perot  Gr. 2, 378
Peter, Peter, Sugar Eater (poem)
 Gr. 1, 285
*Piano Trio No. 2 in E-flat Major,
 Op. 100, Scherzo*  Gr. 4, 192
Piñon, pirulín  Gr. 2, 177
Pizza, Pizza, Daddy-o  Gr. 2, 28

Plant Four Seeds  Gr. 2, 130
Play a Simple Melody  Gr. 5, 72
Playing Ball (poem)  Gr. 1, 151
Poem  Gr. 3, 163
Poem to Mud  Gr. 3, 34
Polly Wee  Gr. K, 119
Pon, pon, pon  Gr. K, 50
Primitive Fire, "Oya"  Gr. 2, 69
Prism in the Window  Gr. 4, 142
Promised Land, The  Gr. 5, 258
Proud  Gr. 7, G-4
Ptashky u babusi sadochku
 Gr. 1, 193
Puff, the Magic Dragon  Gr. 2, 350
Pumpkin Picking  Gr. 2, 376
Purple People Eater, The
 Gr. 6, 448
Put Your Hand in My Hand
 Gr. 1, 330
Quâ câu gió bay  Gr. 5, 461
¡Qué gusto!  Gr. 3, 132
¡Qué llueva!  Gr. K, 81
Quiet Night  Gr. 4, 336
Rabbit Skip, The  Gr. 2, 305
Rain  Gr. 3, 79
Rain, Rain  Gr. 1, 54
Rain Sings a Song, The  Gr. 1, 102
Rain Sizes  Gr. K, 261
*Rainbow in the Sky*  Gr. 7, B-35
Raindrops  Gr. 1, 100
Reading Glasses  Gr. K, 325
Riendo el río corre  Gr. 6, 263
Riqui rán  Gr. 4, 66
Rise and Shine  Gr. 4, 98
*Rise Up, Shepherd, and Follow*
 Gr. 5, 470
River  Gr. 4, 60
Rockin' Robin  Gr. 3, 369
Rolling Rice Cake, The (story)
 Gr. 1, 90
Roll Over  Gr. K, 288
Rope Rhyme  Gr. 1, 320
Rosie, Darling Rosie  Gr. 2, 214
Route 66  Gr. 4, 278
Rudolph, the Red-Nosed Reindeer
 Gr. 1, 429
Run, Molly, Run  Gr. 1, 8
Sailboat in the Sky  Gr. 4, 375
Sailing to the Sea  Gr. 1, 336
Sambalele  Gr. 4, 398
Sansaw akroma  Gr. 3, 287
Santa Clara  Gr. 4, 173
Santana, Carlos  Gr. 2, 255
Sea Shell  Gr. 2, 100
Seagull, Seagull, Sit on the Shore
 Gr. 4, 382
See-Saw Sacradown  Gr. 2, 208
*Serenade, Op. 3, No. 5*  Gr. 4, 90
Sh'ney dubim  Gr. K, 268
Shady Grove  Gr. 5, 260
Shake Them 'Simmons Down
 Gr. 2, 244

Shalom aleichem  Gr. 6, 410
*Shenandoah*  Gr. 2, 62
Shenandoah  Gr. 5, 265
Shir l'shalom  Gr. 4, 420
Shoo, Fly  Gr. 2, 200
Simple Gifts  Gr. 5, 185
*Simple Gifts*  Gr. 8, A-17
Sing a Song!  Gr. 7, A-11
Sing a Song of Peace  Gr. 6, 69
Singin' in the Rain  Gr. 4, 360
Singing-Time  Gr. 3, 201
Sioux Lullaby  Gr. K, 111
*Sister Rosa*  Gr. 3, 411
Six Little Ducks  Gr. K, 234
Siyahamba  Gr. 6, 214
Sky, Sea, Shore  Gr. 2, 343
Sleep, Baby, Sleep  Gr. 2, 197
Sleep, Baby, Sleep  Gr. 2, 194
Snail (poem)  Gr. 1, 222
Snowflakes (poem)  Gr. 1, 423
Somebody Waiting  Gr. 2, 282
Somebody's Knockin' at Your Door
    Gr. 4, 53
Something Told the Wild *Geese*
    Gr. 7, G-41
*Somewhere*  Gr. 8, C-44
Somewhere Out There  Gr. 5, 368
Song of the Fishes  Gr. 3, 244
Sorida  Gr. 1, 313
Sound engineering field trip
    Gr. 7, A-17
*Sounds of the Circus*  Gr. K, 241
Spring  Gr. 2, 400
Spring! Spring! (poem)  Gr. 1, 419
Stand By Me  Gr. 5, 46
Star Light, Star Bright  Gr. 1, 108
Starlight, Star Bright  Gr. 4, 372
Stars (poem)  Gr. 1, 61
Still, Still, Still  Gr. 5, 468
Stopping by Woods on a Snowy
    Evening  Gr. 2, 388
Stopping by Woods on a Snowy
    Evening  Gr. 6, 40
Sugar "Shuga" Bee  Gr. K, 64
*Suite in E-flat Major for Cello, S.
    1010, "Gigue"*  Gr. 7, C-11
Summertime  Gr. 6, 251
Supercalifragilisticexpialidocious
    (from Mary Poppins)  Gr. 3, 6, 9
Sweet Betsy from Pike  Gr. 4, 244
Take Me Out to the Ball Game
    Gr. 3, 262
Take Time in Life  Gr. 6, 291
Take Your Feet Out 'the Sand
    Gr. K, 231
Texas Cowboy  Gr. 3, 250
There Was an Old Man (speech
    piece)  Gr. 3, 191
*This Is Your Night*  Gr. 6, 368
This Land Is Your Land  Gr. 5, 120
This Land Is Your Land (refrain
    only)  Gr. 1, 274
This Little Light of Mine  Gr. 6, 232

This Old Man  Gr. 3, 152
This Train  Gr. 5,
*Three Little Piggies*  Gr. K, 56
Tic, tac  Gr. 1, 252
Tide in the River, The  Gr. 2, 133
Tideo  Gr. 2, 80
Time to Move  Gr. 1, 244
Time to Sing  Gr. 2, 8
*Toccata and Tango*  Gr. 2, 154
Together in Unity  Gr. K, 320
Tom Dooley  Gr. 6, 375
Tongue Twister Medley, A (speech
    piece)  Gr. K, 283
Train Is A-Comin'  Gr. 3, 50
Trains (poem)  Gr. 1, 300
Trains  Gr. 2, 211
Tree House  Gr. 3, 207
Tree in the Wood, The  Gr. 2, 360
Turn, Turn, Turn (To Everything
    There Is a Season)  Gr. 5, 378
Twelve Days of Christmas, The
    Gr. 4, 430
Twist with a Burger, Jitter with a
    Bug (speech piece)  Gr. 1, 132
Un, deux, trois  Gr. 2, 198
Under the Sea  Gr. 5, 374
Valentines  Gr. 2, 398
Vamos a cantar  Gr. K, 278
Vem kan segla?  Gr. 6, 419
Vil du?  Gr. 1, 92
¡Viva el fútbol!  Gr. 1, 94
Viva Jujuy  Gr. 5, 229
Voices of Pride, The  Gr. 5, 86
Wade in the Water  Gr. 8, I-66
Wai bamba  Gr. 6, 27
Waitin' for a Train  Gr. 7, B-25
*Waitin' for a Train*  Gr. 7, B-25
Waitin' for the Light to Shine
    Gr. 4, 28
Way Down in the Schoolyard
    Gr. 2, 50
We Are Dear Little Birdies
    Gr. K, 177
We're Making Popcorn (speech
    piece)  Gr. 1, 85
We've Got Lots in Common
    Gr. 3, 366
*Wedding Qawwali*  Gr. 8, B-35
*Whale of a Tale, A*  Gr. K, 272
What Do We Plant?  Gr. 2, 130
What Do You Suppose?  Gr. K, 265
What to Do  Gr. K, 43
What Will You Be on Halloween?
    Gr. K, 308
Who Has Seen the Wind?
    Gr. 2, 325
Why the Wart Hog Goes About on
    His Knees (story)  Gr. 1, 138
Willoughby, Wallaby, Woo
    Gr. K, 282
Wind Blew East, The  Gr. 1, 65
Wind, The  Gr. 6, 170
Wings of a Dove  Gr. 4, 318

Winter Fantasy  Gr. 4, 424
*Wioste Olowan Inkpa Ta-Ya*
    Gr. 3, 255
*Wipe Out*  Gr. 7, F-33
Wonderful Wizard of Oz, The
    Gr. 6, 8
World of Difference, A  Gr. 5, 388
World We Love, The  Gr. 3, 343
Worm, The  Gr. 2, 311
*Wu Long*  Gr. 4, 156
Yakety Yak  Gr. 5, 205
Yang wa wa  Gr. K, 162
*Yaudachi*  Gr. 5, 156
Ye jaliya da  Gr. 5, 67
Yellow Butter (poem)  Gr. 1, 124
Yellow Rose of Texas, The
    Gr. 7, I-71
*Yertle the Turtle*  Gr. 2, 368
Yesh lanu taish  Gr. 1, 182
Yo-shi nai  Gr. 6, 286
Yonder Come Day  Gr. 8, I-70
You Were on My Mind  Gr. 7, G-23
Your Friends Shall Be the Tall Wind
    Gr. 6, 201
Yüe liang wan wan  Gr. 5, 315
Zip-a-Dee-Doo-Dah  Gr. 2, 331
Zuni Sunrise Call  Gr. 5, 397

## MATH

About Buttons (poem)  Gr. 1, 211
Achshav  Gr. 2, 64
Alexander's Ragtime Band
    Gr. 6, 138
Alleluia  Gr. 6, 133
Ants Go Marching, The  Gr. 1, 249
Artsa alinu  Gr. 3, 284
At the Same Time  Gr. 6, 116
*Brandenburg Concerto No. 4,
    BWV 1049, Allegro*  Gr. 5, 111
Dinosaur Dance  Gr. 2, 168
Do, Re, Mi, Fa  Gr. 6, 80
Don't Let Your Watch Run Down
    Gr. 3, 166
Earth Is Our Mother, The
    Gr. 8, F-25
Good Morning  Gr. 3, 192
Here I Go!  Gr. K, 72
How Many Miles to Babylon?
    Gr. 2, 128
I Bought Me a Cat  Gr. 2, 308
Ida Red  Gr. 3, 30
Las horas  Gr. 1, 246
Las horas  Gr. 1, 247
Lost My Gold Ring  Gr. 6, 159
Lots of Worms  Gr. 2, 313
*Lyric Suite, "Allegretto gioviale,"
    Movement 1*  Gr. 6, 169
Make New Friends  Gr. 3, 37
Mary Ann  Gr. K, 253
Mary Came a-Running  Gr. K, 294
O pião entrou  Gr. 2, 355
Old Abram Brown  Gr. 5, 222
One Green Jelly Bean  Gr. K, 287

**(Across the Curriculum, continued)**

Pay Me My Money Down  Gr. 4, 40
Rinsho, rinsho  Gr. K, 285
Roll Over  Gr. K, 288
'Round and 'Round  Gr. 1, 148
Route 66  Gr. 4, 277
Shu ha mo  Gr. 3, 277
Time to Move  Gr. 1, 244
Today Is Your Birthday  Gr. 1, 409
Un, deux, trois  Gr. 2, 198
Vive l'amour  Gr. 6, 176
Wabash Cannon Ball  Gr. 5, 136
Weevily Wheat  Gr. 4, 104
Zudio  Gr. 2, 268

## RELATED ARTS

ABC Blues  Gr. K, 281
Abiyoyo  Gr. 2, 109
About Buttons (poem)  Gr. 1, 211
Add-On Machine, The  Gr. K, 298
Ah, Jolis Papillons  Gr. 1, 360
Ai, Dunaii moy  Gr. 4, 292
America, the Beautiful  Gr. 7, I-5
Apple, The  Gr. 1, 231
Avocational musician  Gr. 8, A-31
Awa ewe iwoyi  Gr. 8, D-9
Backstage Careers  Gr. 8, A-23
Bambodansarna  Gr. 8, B-20
Barb'ry Allen  Gr. 6, 44
Big Old Storm a-Comin'  Gr. K, 257
California Dreamin'  Gr. 8, G-33
Cantando mentiras  Gr. 4, 146
Canzon in Echo Duodecimi Toni a
    10  Gr. 8, C-7
Celebrating Our Flag  Gr. K, 327
Certainly, Lord  Gr. 7, I-15
Chag Purim  Gr. 1, 438
Ciranda  Gr. 2, 272
Circle of Life (from The Lion
    King), The  Gr. 6, 317
Circle 'Round the Moon  Gr. 4, 403
Circle Round the Zero  Gr. K, 293
Clair de lune  Gr. K, 165
Come, Ye Thankful People, Come
    Gr. 5, 458
Computer, The  Gr. 4, 198
Cookie Crew, The  Gr. K, 197
Crayons  Gr. K, 75
De colores  Gr. 8, E-15
Doctor Knickerbocker (speech
    piece)  Gr. 1, 302
Dusty Rag  Gr. K, 165
Everything Grows  Gr. K, 267
Feliz Navidad  Gr. 7, I-30
Glory, Glory, Hallelujah  Gr. 6, 54
Glory Hallelujah Grand March
    Gr. 8, C-38
Grass Game  Gr. 1, 371
Hush-a-bye Baby  Gr. 1, 270
Knock the Cymbals  Gr. 1, 176
La golondrina  Gr. 8, I-51
Las copetonas  Gr. 7, B-33
Les petites marionettes  Gr. K, 237

Lion Sleeps Tonight, The  Gr. 4, 132
Little Shop of Horrors  Gr. 4, 422
Loch Lomond  Gr. 5, 141
London Bridge  Gr. K, 244
Los maizales  Gr. 1, 296
Mañana  Gr. 7, E-15
Merry Modal Christmas, A
    Gr. 4, 412
Merry-Go-Round  Gr. K, 290
My Dear Companion  Gr. 6, 22
Nutcracker Suite, The, "Trepak"
    Gr. 3, 281
Nutcracker Suite, The, "Waltz of
    the Flowers"  Gr. 6, 322
Oliver Twist  Gr. K, 139
One Green Jelly Bean  Gr. K, 287
Over the Rainbow  Gr. 4, 140
Painting Song: A Dribble and a Dot
    Gr. K, 175
Penny Lane  Gr. 6, 257
Plow That Broke the Plains, The,
    "Cattle"  Gr. 3, 176
Pottery Dance  Gr. 1, 371
Ptashky u babusi sadochku
    Gr. 1, 193
Red Poppy, The, "Russian Sailors'
    Dance"  Gr. 4, 224
Riqui rán  Gr. 1, 48
Rock It  Gr. 7, B-11
Sailing Down My Golden River
    Gr. 4, 332
Same, The  Gr. 6, 268
Serenade, Op. 3, No. 5  Gr. 4, 90
Silver Apples of the Moon  Gr. 1, 12
Slow Hora/Freylekhs  Gr. 8, B-25
Some Silly Animals (poem)
    Gr. 1, 392
Song That's Just For You, A
    Gr. 2, 127
South African Ensemble  Gr. 7, D-11
Spaceworms  Gr. 1, 401
Storm Dance (speech piece)
    Gr. K, 145
String Quartet No. 5, Movement
    4: Andante  Gr. 3, 177
Stuart, Gilbert  Gr. 2, 386
Surfin' U.S.A.  Gr. 7, I-59
Taiwan Suite, "Lantern Festival"
    Gr. 3, 105
Ten Little Ostinato Pieces  Gr. 7, I-64
Tender Shepherd (from Peter Pan)
    Gr. 3, 117
This Land Is Your Land (refrain
    only)  Gr. 1, 276
Thula, thula, ngoana  Gr. 4, 226
Time to Move  Gr. 1, 244
Toccata and Tango  Gr. 2, 154
Today Is Your Birthday  Gr. 1, 409
Tommy Peoples  Gr. 8, B-20
Troldhaugen trolls  Gr. 6, 8
Tsuki  Gr. 4, 25
Turn the Glasses Over  Gr. 3, 204
Twist, The  Gr. 7, B-11

Udu Pot  Gr. 8, D-4
Watermelon Man  Gr. 1, 12
We're Making Popcorn (speech
    piece)  Gr. 1, 85
What a Wonderful World  Gr. 6, 63
When I'm an Astronaut  Gr. 1, 402
Winter Song  Gr. 6, 455
Wooten, Jim  Gr. 8, E-12
World Winds  Gr. 8, B-8

## SCIENCE

Add-On Machine, The  Gr. K, 298
Adiós, amigos  Gr. 6, 56
Allá en la fuente  Gr. 2, 92
Amarillo Armadillo  Gr. 2, 83
Apple, The  Gr. 1, 231
Apples, Peaches, Pears, and Plums
    (speech piece)  Gr. 1, 14
Banjo Sam  Gr. 2, 314
Bat, The  Gr. 2, 302
Beach Rap (speech piece)  Gr. 1, 352
Bear Dance  Gr. K, 127
Bereleh  Gr. K, 150
Bird's Nest, The  Gr. K, 239
Bonjour, mes amis  Gr. 1, 316
Brush Your Teeth  Gr. 1, 284
Bubble Trouble  Gr. K, 184
California Dreamin'  Gr. 8, G-33
Canto del agua  Gr. 8, I-13
Canzon in Echo Duodecimi Toni a
    10  Gr. 8, C-7
Carnival of the Animals, "Fossils"
    Gr. 4, 221
Carolina Sunday Waltz  Gr. 7, F-9
Cement Mixer  Gr. 4, 102
Chag Purim  Gr. 1, 438
Children of the Sun (poem)
    Gr. 1, 404
Close Encounters of the Third
    Kind  Gr. 4, 235
Clouds  Gr. K, 254
Come Out and Play  Gr. 5, 238
Corta la caña  Gr. 6, 367
Cotton Boll Rag  Gr. 5, 332
Counting-Out Rhyme (speech piece)
    Gr. 1, 357
Crawfish  Gr. 2, 87
Create a Career  Gr. 8, A-33
Crouching Tiger, Hidden Dragon
    Gr. 8, A-11
Cycle Song of Life (The River Song)
    Gr. 4, 370
Dan tranh  Gr. 5, 196
Dancing Tree, The  Gr. K, 202
Den III. Ende VI. Ronde & Quatre
    Branles  Gr. 8, C-7
Ding, Dong, Diggidiggidong
    Gr. 3, 14
Down by the Bay  Gr. 1, 18
Down in the Meadow  Gr. K, 147
Drums From Around the World
    Gr. 6, 276
Each of Us Is a Flower  Gr. 3, 154

Eensy Weensy Spider  Gr. K, 187
Eh, cumpari!  Gr. 4, 69
El carite  Gr. 5, 305
El coquí  Gr. 2, 292
El mes de abril  Gr. 3, 328
El sapito  Gr. 3, 336
Erdö, erdö de magos  Gr. 3, 182
Ezekiel Saw the Wheel  Gr. 6, 378
Fais do do  Gr. 6, 402
Falling Rain  Gr. 2, 328
Feng yang hua gu  Gr. 4, 313
First-ing (poem)  Gr. 1, 374
Fish (poem)  Gr. 1, 177
Five Little Chickadees  Gr. K, 179
Fossils  Gr. 1, 235
Four in a Boat  Gr. 2, 46
Four White Horses  Gr. 3, 304
*Free Music #1*  Gr. 2, 212
*Frère Jacques*  Gr. 3, 112
Frère Jacques  Gr. 2, 124
Frog in the Millpond  Gr. 2, 44
*Frosty, the Snowman*  Gr. 2, 391
Galoshes  Gr. K, 63
Gonna Build a Mountain  Gr. 6, 20
Great Big Stars  Gr. 1, 61
Had to Get Up This Mornin' Soon
    Gr. 3, 114
Hato popo  Gr. 1, 186
Heave-Ho!/Going, Going, Gone/
    The Snow  Gr. 4, 182
Heigh-Ho  Gr. 2, 6
Honeybee Song, The  Gr. 1, 358
Hosanna, Me Build a House
    Gr. 5, 133
I Don't Care If the Rain Comes
    Down  Gr. 3, 25
I Love Peanuts  Gr. 7, E-21
I Love the Mountains  Gr. 5, 34
I See the Moon  Gr. 2, 58
I'm on My Way  Gr. 7, A-15
If a Tiger Calls  Gr. 3, 356
In the Pumpkin Patch  Gr. 3, 380
*Is the Sound High or Low?*  Gr. K, 17
Jambalaya  Gr. 6, 247
Johnny Appleseed  Gr. 4, 344
Juanito  Gr. K, 300
Juniper Tree, The  Gr. 3, 130
*Junk Music Montage*  Gr. 1, 73
Kangaroo Song, The  Gr. K, 44
*Kargiraa-style Song*  Gr. 8, B-40
Khorovod  Gr. 1, 373
*Kitchen Stomp*  Gr. 4, 122
Knock the Cymbals  Gr. 1, 176
La mar estaba serena  Gr. 2, 344
Leatherwing Bat, The  Gr. 2, 302
Leaves  Gr. 1, 26
Let's Get Ready  Gr. K, 312
*Linus and Lucy*  Gr. 8, A-29
Listen to the Water  Gr. 2, 294
Little Mouse, The  Gr. 1, 348
Little Spider  Gr. K, 93
Los pececitos  Gr. 1, 178
Mary Ann  Gr. K, 253

Mashed Potatoes (speech piece)
    Gr. 1, 21
Mi chacra  Gr. 1, 365
Mi cuerpo hace música  Gr. K, 107
Mister Ram Goat-O  Gr. 3, 54
Morning Has Broken  Gr. 5, 28
Mud  Gr. 3, 32
Music  Gr. K, 107
Musical classification of instruments
    Gr. 6, 362
My Shadow  Gr. K, 19
Nani wale na hala  Gr. 3, 260
Never Smile at a Crocodile  Gr. 3, 100
Niu lang zhi nü  Gr. 4, 334
*Nruab hnub thiab hmo ntuj*
    Gr. 4, 368
Ochimbo  Gr. 4, 134
*Onomatapoiea Study No. 2*
    Gr. 7, E-31
Ōsamu kosamu  Gr. 4, 96
Over the Rainbow  Gr. 4, 140
Planets Chant, The  Gr. 4, 376
*Planets, The, "Jupiter"*  Gr. 5, 424
Rain Sizes  Gr. K, 261
Rainbow, The  Gr. 2, 332
Riendo el río corre  Gr. 6, 264
Rockin' Around the Christmas Tree
    Gr. 5, 466
Rockin' Robin  Gr. 3, 369
*Rocky Point Holiday*  Gr. 6, 330
*Rodeo, "Hoedown"*  Gr. 5, 312
Sarika keo  Gr. 3, 274
*Scrub-a-dub*  Gr. 1, 305
Sea Shell  Gr. 2, 100
Ship that Never Returned, The
    Gr. 5, 402
Shoo, Fly  Gr. 2, 200
Shortnin' Bread  Gr. 1, 57
Singin' in the Rain  Gr. 4, 360
Singin' in the Tub  Gr. K, 220
Singing Scales  Gr. 8, B-11
Six Little Ducks  Gr. K, 234
Small Job, A  Gr. 3, 224
Snowflakes (poem)  Gr. 1, 423
Something Told the Wild Geese
    Gr. 7, G-41
Something Told the Wild Geese
    Gr. 7, G-43
Song of the Night, The  Gr. 3, 345
Sorida  Gr. 1, 313
Sound engineering field trip
    Gr. 7, A-17
*Sound Waves Montage*  Gr. 6, 354
Starlight, Star Bright  Gr. 4, 372
Starry Night (Van Gogh)  Gr. 1, 107
Stars (poem)  Gr. 1, 61
Storm Dance (speech piece)
    Gr. K, 145
*Suite No. 3 in C Major for
    Unaccompanied Cello,
    "Bourrée 1"*  Gr. 3, 38
*Symphony No. 5 in C Minor, Op.
    67, Movement 1*  Gr. 7, C-16

Tanabata-sama  Gr. 2, 338
This Is My Song  Gr. 6, 76
Three Little Birds  Gr. 8, F-7
Tic, tac  Gr. 1, 252
Time to Move  Gr. 1, 244
Time to Sing  Gr. 2, 8
*Toccata and Fugue in D Minor*
    Gr. 7, E-25
*Toccata for Percussion, Movement
    3*  Gr. 4, 155
*Two-Part Invention in A Major
    (Harpsichord)*  Gr. 5, 236
Under the Sea  Gr. 5, 372
Vamos a la mar  Gr. 3, 227
Vil du?  Gr. 1, 92
¡Viva el fútbol!  Gr. 1, 94
Waltzing with Bears  Gr. 3, 171
Water Music, Allegro Maestoso
    Gr. 3, 187
We Are Dear Little Birdies
    Gr. K, 177
We're Making Popcorn (speech
    piece)  Gr. 1, 86
What a Wonderful World  Gr. 6, 62
Wheel of the Water, The  Gr. 4, 362
*Whirlwind*  Gr. 3, 149
Wind Blew East, The  Gr. 1, 65
Winter Fantasy  Gr. 4, 424
Yesh lanu taish  Gr. 1, 182
Your changing voice  Gr. 7, G-7
*Yours Forever*  Gr. 6, 344

## SOCIAL STUDIES

A-Tisket, A-Tasket  Gr. 2, 238
A la puerta del cielo  Gr. 5, 60
A Ram Sam Sam  Gr. 3, 209
ABC Rock  Gr. 1, 262
Abraham, Martin, and John
    Gr. 6, 466
Achshav  Gr. 2, 64
Ahora voy a cantarles  Gr. 3, 56
Ai, Dunaii moy  Gr. 4, 292
Ain't Gonna Let Nobody Turn Me
    'Round  Gr. 6, 85
*Ajaja*  Gr. 8, B-3
*Akua Tuta*  Gr. 7, D-25
Al citrón  Gr. 3, 320
Al tambor  Gr. 3, 270
Alexander's Ragtime Band
    Gr. 6, 136
*Ali Pasha*  Gr. 5, 218
All Around the Country (poem)
    Gr. 1, 446
Alumot  Gr. 6, 306
Amazing Grace  Gr. 4, 160
Ambos a dos  Gr. 3, 21
America  Gr. 1, 446
America  Gr. K, 326
America, I Hear You Singing
    Gr. 2, 402
America, the Beautiful  Gr. 4, 158
America, the Beautiful  Gr. 7, I-5

**(Across the Curriculum, continued)**

America, the Beautiful  Gr. 8, I-4
Angels On the Midnight Clear
    Gr. 6, 424
Arirang  Gr. 5, 25
Artsa alinu  Gr. 3, 284
Así es mi tierra  Gr. 6, 172
Avaz-e dashti  Gr. 8, B-43
Awa ewe iwoyi  Gr. 8, D-9
Away to America  Gr. 5, 57
Ayii, Ayii, Ayii  Gr. K, 11
Bantama kra kro  Gr. 5, 308
Bard of Armagh, The  Gr. 4, 296
Basin Street Blues  Gr. 5, 354
Battle Cry of Freedom  Gr. 5, 273
Battle Hymn of the Republic
    Gr. 5, 274
Bear Dance  Gr. 7, I-11
Bling Blang  Gr. 3, 240
Blow the Wind Southerly  Gr. 5, 178
Blow Ye Winds  Gr. 4, 254
Blower's Daughter, The  Gr. 8, B-13
Blue Danube, The  Gr. 6, 192
Bob-a-Needle  Gr. 2, 232
Bogando a la luz del sol  Gr. 4, 307
Brass Rap  Gr. 3, 189
Bridges  Gr. 6, 86
By the Waters of Babylon  Gr. 6, 310
California  Gr. 5, 52
California, Here I Come  Gr. 4, 286
Can You Canoe?  Gr. 4, 171
Canción de cuna  Gr. 4, 144
Cantaré, cantarás  Gr. 6, 412
Canto del agua  Gr. 8, I-13
Carnaval, Op. 9, "Valse Noble,"
    Un poco maestoso  Gr. 3, 202
Cattle Call  Gr. 5, 344
Celebrating Our Flag  Gr. K, 327
Changed My Name  Gr. 6, 338
Chanukah Games  Gr. 3, 388
Che che koolay  Gr. 2, 266
Cielito lindo  Gr. 4, 271
Cinderella Dressed in Green
    Gr. K, 137
Cindy  Gr. 4, 384
Ciranda  Gr. 2, 273
Clementine  Gr. 4, 340
Come and Go With Me to That
    Land  Gr. 5, 391
Coming Home from the Sea
    Gr. 6, 347
Concerto for Flute and Harp in C,
    K. 299, Movement 2  Gr. 8, C-10
Concerto for Viola and Orchestra,
    Movement 3  Gr. 7, C-35
Corn Grinding Song  Gr. K, 67
Cuando pa' Chile me voy  Gr. 6, 376
Dancing Pig, The (story)  Gr. 1, 196
Danses Populaires Francaises,
    "Branle Double, Branle
    Simple"  Gr. 7, C-27
Day-O!  Gr. 5, 19
Dayenu  Gr. 4, 438

De colores  Gr. 8, I-16
Deep in the Heart of Texas  Gr. 4, 22
Ding Dong! Merrily on High
    Gr. 6, 426
Diou shou juan'er  Gr. 2, 276
Dippermouth Blues  Gr. 7, B-14
Doctor Knickerbocker (speech
    piece)  Gr. 1, 302
Dok djampa  Gr. 8, I-21
Doong gul ge  Gr. 3, 136
Down the Ohio  Gr. 2, 60
Drill, Ye Tarriers  Gr. 5, 54
Drums of the Iroquois and Sioux
    Gr. 6, 284
Duck Dance  Gr. 2, 249
Dundai  Gr. 5, 106
Earth Is Our Mother, The  Gr. 4, 358
Ég a gyertya  Gr. K, 96
El borrego  Gr. 4, 242
El carite  Gr. 5, 305
El carnavalito humahuaqueño
    Gr. 6, 483
El cóndor pasa  Gr. 6, 46
El juego chirimbolo  Gr. 2, 54
El tren  Gr. 2, 261
El zapatero  Gr. 1, 298
Elegua  Gr. 7, D-8
Éliza Kongo  Gr. 5, 15
Erie Canal  Gr. 5, 262
Ev'ry Time I Feel the Spirit
    Gr. 5, 242
Every Night When the Sun Goes In
    Gr. 8, I-29
Family Tree  Gr. 3, 73
Farewell to Tarwathie  Gr. 6, 43
Fascinatin' Rhythm (Ella
    Fitzgerald)  Gr. 7, E-11
Fascinatin' Rhythm (Frances Veri)
    Gr. 7, E-11
Fiddler on the Roof  Gr. 7, E-4
Follow the Drinkin' Gourd  Gr. 4, 266
Free at Last  Gr. 6, 468
Freedom Is Coming  Gr. 5, 414
Freight Train  Gr. 1, 44
French Suite No. 5, "Gigue"
    Gr. 4, 232
Friends Today  Gr. 7, D-15
Funwa alafia  Gr. 5, 32
Gakavik  Gr. 4, 14
Gamelan angklung  Gr. 6, 384
Gamelan Montage  Gr. 2, 104
Get on Board  Gr. K, 89
Give a Little Love  Gr. 6, 141
Glad to Have a Friend Like You
    Gr. 2, 231
Glendy Burke, The  Gr. 4, 263
Go Around the Corn, Sally  Gr. 2, 12
God Bless the Child  Gr. 7, B-28
God Bless the U.S.A.  Gr. 8, G-37
Goin' Down the Road Feelin' Bad
    Gr. 5, 283
Goin' to Boston  Gr. 6, 432

Gonna Ride Up in the Chariot
    Gr. 4, 21
Good Old Happy Song, A  Gr. K, 201
Goodbye, Julie  Gr. 1, 334
Gospel Train, The  Gr. 6, 400
Grass Game  Gr. 1, 371
Greenland Whale Fishery, The
    Gr. 5, 231
Habemos llegado  Gr. 6, 172
Hama chi dori  Gr. 3, 330
Hambone  Gr. 7, D-3
Happy Days Are Here Again
    Gr. 5, 285
Hava nagila  Gr. 6, 152
Hava nashira  Gr. 6, 82
He's Got the Whole World in His
    Hands  Gr. 7, I-39
Hearts Like Doors  Gr. K, 188
Hello!  Gr. 2, 264
Here I Go!  Gr. K, 72
Heri za Kwanzaa  Gr. 5, 476
Hine mah tov  Gr. 5, 430
Hot Cross Buns (Version 1)
    Gr. 3, 218
How Can I Keep from Singing?
    Gr. 4, 261
How Many Miles to Babylon?
    Gr. 2, 128
Hungarian Rhapsody No. 2 in C
    sharp Minor, S. 244  Gr. 7, E-17
I Got a Letter This Morning  Gr. K, 68
I Got Shoes  Gr. 2, 242
I Have a Dog  Gr. K, 262
I Saw Three Ships  Gr. 1, 427
I Vow to You, My Country  Gr. 5, 418
I Walk in Beauty  Gr. 4, 283
I'm a Dreydl  Gr. K, 315
I'm Flying Home  Gr. 2, 286
I've Been Working on the Railroad
    Gr. 3, 242
Ichi-gatsu tsuitachi  Gr. 7, I-43
Ichi-gatsu tsuitachi  Gr. 3, 406
Ida Red  Gr. 3, 30
If I Had a Hammer  Gr. 5, 287
If You're Happy  Gr. K, 94
In the Pumpkin Patch  Gr. 3, 380
Ise oluwa  Gr. 2, 102
Ise oluwa  Gr. 6, 230
Jambalaya (On The Bayou)
    Gr. 6, 244
Jan ken pon  Gr. 3, 302
Jelly Roll, The  Gr. 7, B-37
Joe Turner Blues  Gr. 4, 56
Johnny Appleseed  Gr. 4, 346
Johnny Has Gone for a Soldier
    Gr. 5, 189
Joshua Fought the Battle  Gr. 5, 101
Joshua Fought the Battle of Jericho
    Gr. 8, E-18
Joy of Kwanzaa, The  Gr. 6, 463
Jump for Joy  Gr. K, 212
Just Watch  Gr. K, 295
Karangatia ra  Gr. 3, 272

Keel Row, The  Gr. 4, 240
Keep Your Eyes on the Prize
    Gr. 3, 408
Keep Your Eyes on the Prize
    Gr. 8, E-16
Kelo aba w'ye  Gr. 6, 288
Martin Luther King  Gr. 1, 434
Kookaburra  Gr. 4, 186
Kou ri lengay  Gr. 7, E-2
Kwa-nu-te  Gr. 3, 214
Kyrie  Gr. 6, 206
La bamba  Gr. 5, 130
La calle ancha  Gr. 3, 296
La ciudad de Juaja  Gr. 5, 58
La Jesusita  Gr. 5, 322
La paloma se fué  Gr. 6, 51
La Tarara  Gr. 4, 176
Las Navidades  Gr. 5, 472
Lemonade  Gr. 1, 191
Let's Pretend  Gr. K, 227
Linstead Market  Gr. 5, 240
Lion Sleeps Tonight, The  Gr. 4, 130
"Little" Organ Fugue in G Minor
    Gr. 6, 129
Little Red Caboose  Gr. K, 229
Llactamanta  Gr. 6, 383
Lone Star Trail  Gr. 2, 21
Los maizales  Gr. 1, 296
Lost My Gold Ring  Gr. 6, 159
Mad...Sad...Glad: A Piece in
    Three Mood-ments  Gr. K, 249
Magnificent Seven, The  Gr. 3, 144
Make New Friends  Gr. 3, 37
Malagueña  Gr. 5, 154
Malê Debalê  Gr. 8, B-16
Máru-bihág  Gr. 6, 304
Mary Came a-Running  Gr. K, 294
Mass, "Responsory Alleluia"
    Gr. 6, 216
Midnight Special, The  Gr. 7, F-22
Miniature Odyssey, A  Gr. 8, E-29
Morning Comes Early  Gr. 5, 13
Mother Sent Me to the Store
    Gr. K, 137
Mozart, Wolfgang Amadeus
    Gr. 4, 110
Mubärak  Gr. 3, 283
My Father's House (Gospel Style)
    Gr. 2, 24
My Foot's In My Stirrup  Gr. 2, 234
Nana Kru  Gr. 6, 281
Nie chcę cię znác  Gr. 3, 314
No quiero plata  Gr. 1, 425
Now's the Time  Gr. 5, 450
O pião entrou  Gr. 2, 355
Ochimbo  Gr. 4, 134
Oh, Freedom  Gr. 5, 393
Oklahoma  Gr. 5, 36
Old Brass Wagon  Gr. 2, 122
Old Chisholm Trail, The  Gr. 6, 236
Old Dan Tucker  Gr. 3, 97
On Mother's Day (poem)  Gr. 1, 443
One Family  Gr. 7, G-18

One Morning Soon  Gr. 3, 68
Orange Blossom Special  Gr. 5, 266
Orange Blossom Special  Gr. 8, E-6
Ostinatos Around the World
    Gr. 8, B-4
Our Family Comes from 'Round the
    World (poem)  Gr. 1, 299
Over My Head  Gr. 4, 119
Over There  Gr. 5, 279
Oye  Gr. 6, 336
Party Tonight!  Gr. 2, 153
Pat Works on the Railway  Gr. 5, 182
Paths of Victory  Gr. 6, 194
Paw-Paw Patch  Gr. 4, 92
Pay Me My Money Down  Gr. 4, 39
Pennsylvania 6-5000  Gr. 5, 342
Pictures at an Exhibition
    Gr. 8, A-13
Pollerita  Gr. 5, 151
Pottery Dance  Gr. 1, 371
Primitive Fire, "Oya"  Gr. 2, 69
Proud  Gr. 7, G-3
Put Your Hand in My Hand
    Gr. 1, 330
Quâ câu gió bay  Gr. 5, 461
¡Qué bonita bandera!  Gr. 5, 295
Ragtime Cowboy Joe  Gr. 2, 250
Ragupati Ragava Raja Ram
    Gr. 5, 320
Railroad Corral  Gr. 3, 174
Raindrops  Gr. 7, D-23
Red River Valley  Gr. 6, 11
Rig-a-Jig-Jig  Gr. K, 99
Rinsho, rinsho  Gr. K, 285
Rio Grande  Gr. 4, 256
Río, río  Gr. 5, 370
River  Gr. 4, 58
Rock Around the Clock  Gr. 5, 356
Rocky Mountain  Gr. 2, 98
Roll On, Columbia  Gr. 5, 116
Roll Over  Gr. K, 288
Rondo for Lunch, A (speech piece)
    Gr. 3, 212
Route 66  Gr. 4, 277
Run, Molly, Run  Gr. 1, 8
Run! Run! Hide!  Gr. 6, 340
S'vivon  Gr. 6, 452
Sabhyatâ  Gr. 8, B-43
Sakura  Gr. 4, 308
Sambalele  Gr. 4, 398
Scarborough Fair  Gr. 6, 94
Scotland the Brave  Gr. 5, 139
Scrub-a-dub  Gr. 1, 306
See the Children Playin'  Gr. 4, 106
She Is Like the Swallow  Gr. 8, B-12
She'll Be Comin' 'Round the
    Mountain  Gr. 2, 358
Shenandoah  Gr. 2, 62
Shir l'shalom  Gr. 4, 418
Shri Ram, jai Ram  Gr. 4, 310
Shumba  Gr. 8, B-12
Sierra Morena  Gr. 3, 296
Sing a Song of Peace  Gr. 6, 66

Sing About Martin  Gr. K, 321
Siyahamba  Gr. 6, 213
Slow Hora/Freylekhs  Gr. 8, B-25
Sometimes I Feel Like a Motherless
    Child  Gr. 6, 240
Sorida  Gr. 1, 312
Sourwood Mountain  Gr. 4, 64
South African Ensemble  Gr. 7, D-11
St. Patrick Was a Gentleman
    Gr. 3, 290
Star-Spangled Banner, The
    Gr. 3, 414
Star-Spangled Banner, The
    Gr. 4, 440
Star-Spangled Banner, The
    Gr. 5, 489
Star-Spangled Banner, The
    Gr. 6, 485
Stephen Foster and copyright law
    Gr. 7, A-9
Sugar "Shuga" Bee  Gr. K, 64
Suite in E-flat Major for Cello, S.
    1010, "Gigue"  Gr. 7, C-11
Surfin' U.S.A.  Gr. 7, I-59
Swanee  Gr. 6, 118
Sweet Betsy from Pike  Gr. 4, 244
Swing Low, Sweet Chariot
    Gr. 6, 234
Symphony No. 5 in C Minor,
    Movement 1  Gr. 6, 98
Symphony No. 5 in C Minor, Op.
    67, Movement 1  Gr. 7, C-16
Take Time in Life  Gr. 6, 292
Tanabata-sama  Gr. 2, 336
Thanksgiving Is Near  Gr. 2, 380
This Land Is Your Land  Gr. 5, 118
This Land Is Your Land (refrain
    only)  Gr. 1, 274
This Pretty Planet  Gr. 4, 354
Three Little Birds  Gr. 4, 320
Tihore Mai  Gr. 8, B-12
Time to Move  Gr. 1, 244
Time to Sing  Gr. 2, 10
Together  Gr. 3, 147
Together in Unity  Gr. K, 320
Train Is A-Comin'  Gr. 3, 49
Turn the World Around  Gr. 4, 115
Twist and Shout  Gr. 4, 238
Tzena, tzena  Gr. 5, 298
Udu Pot  Gr. 8, D-4
Udu Pot  Gr. 8, D-5
'Ūlili E  Gr. 5, 443
United Nations on the March, The
    Gr. 6, 442
Variations on "America"  Gr. 6, 162
¡Viva el fútbol!  Gr. 1, 96
Vonjeo  Gr. 8, B-12
Wabash Cannon Ball  Gr. 5, 136
Wai bamba  Gr. 6, 27
Waiting for the Traffic Light
    Gr. 2, 106
Walk in Jerusalem  Gr. 4, 101

(*Across the Curriculum,* continued)

Walk Together, Children  Gr. 3, 147
We Shall Not be Moved  Gr. 4, 436
We're All Gonna Shine Tonight
    Gr. 2, 240
When Johnny Comes Marching
    Home  Gr. 5, 180
Wings of a Dove  Gr. 4, 318
World of Difference, A  Gr. 5, 386
World We Love, The  Gr. 3, 343
*Wu Long*  Gr. 4, 156
Yankee Doodle  Gr. 2, 404
Ye jaliya da  Gr. 5, 64
Yellow Rose of Texas, The
    Gr. 7, I-71
Yü guang guang  Gr. 6, 61
Zum gali gali  Gr. 5, 400

## DESCRIBING *See Skills Reinforcement.*

## DRAMATIZATIONS/ PANTOMIMES *See Movement; Skills Reinforcement: Moving.*

## ENSEMBLES, PERFORMING IN *See also Playing Instruments.*
Agbekor Ensemble  Gr. 8, D-12
America  Gr. 7, I-2
America  Gr. 8, I-2
America, the Beautiful  Gr. 7, I-4
America, the Beautiful  Gr. 8, I-4
¡Ay, Jalisco no te rajes!  Gr. 7, I-6
*Batucada* Parade Ensemble
    Gr. 8, D-23
Bear Dance  Gr. 7, I-10
Blues with a Feeling  Gr. 8, I-6
Boomin' Bamboo Ensemble
    Gr. 7, D-22
Bora Bora Boom Ensemble
    Gr. 8, D-23
Box a-Rockin' Ensemble  Gr. 7, D-4
Bucket O'Taiko Ensemble
    Gr. 7, D-17
Canto del agua  Gr. 8, I-10
Caribbean Island Ensemble
    Gr. 7, D-19
Carnaval Calypso Ensemble
    Gr. 7, D-21
Certainly, Lord  Gr. 7, I-13
Chapel of Love  Gr. 7, G-27
Checki, morena  Gr. 7, F-11
Cheki, morena  Gr. 7, I-16
Cielito lindo  Gr. 7, I-20
*Crunchy, Crunchy, Crunchy*
    Gr. 8, D-15
Cuban Rumba Ensemble  Gr. 7, D-7
De colores  Gr. 8, I-14

Deep in the Heart of Texas
    Gr. 8, I-18
Do Wah Diddy Diddy  Gr. 7, F-21
Dok djampa  Gr. 8, I-20
Doumbek or Hand Drum Exercises
    Gr. 7, D-31
El rancho grande  Gr. 8, I-22
Ev'rybody Loves Saturday Night
    Gr. 7, I-24
Every Night When the Sun Goes In
    Gr. 8, I-28
Feliz Navidad  Gr. 7, I-28
Flip, Flop and Fly  Gr. 7, F-15
Flip, Flop and Fly  Gr. 7, I-32
Friends Today  Gr. 7, D-12
Go-Go Street Ensemble  Gr. 8, D-31
Guantanamera  Gr. 8, I-32
Hand Clap Ensemble  Gr. 7, D-2
Hanuka, Hanuka  Gr. 8, I-36
He's Got the Whole World in His
    Hands  Gr. 7, I-36
Highlife Ensemble  Gr. 8, D-7
*Hsù chu* (Prelude) Ensemble
    Gr. 8, D-26
I Shall Sing  Gr. 8, I-38
I'll Fly Away  Gr. 8, I-42
Ichi-gatsu tsuitachi  Gr. 7, I-40
Island Ensemble  Gr. 8, D-18
Jambalaya  Gr. 8, I-46
Kpanlogo Highlife Ensemble
    Gr. 7, D-13
La golondrina  Gr. 8, I-50
Let's Get the Rhythm of the Band
    Gr. 7, E-29
Lift Ev'ry Voice and Sing  Gr. 8, I-54
Lion Sleeps Tonight, The  Gr. 8, I-56
Los reyes de Oriente  Gr. 8, I-58
Mainly Metal Ensemble  Gr. 7, D-26
Nampaya omame  Gr. 7, D-10
Oy, Hanuka  Gr. 7, I-44
Panamam tombé  Gr. 7, D-18
Pay Me My Money Down  Gr. 7, I-46
Percussion Fun Rondo  Gr. 7, I-50
Producer  Gr. 8, A-25
South African Ensemble  Gr. 7, D-11
Star-Spangled Banner, The
    Gr. 7, I-56
Star-Spangled Banner, The
    Gr. 8, I-62
Stille Nacht (Silent Night)  Gr. 7, I-54
Surfin' U.S.A.  Gr. 7, I-58
Ten Little Ostinato Pieces  Gr. 7, I-62
This Land Is Your Land  Gr. 7, I-66
Wade in the Water  Gr. 8, I-64
Wood Works Ensemble  Gr. 8, D-28
Yellow Rose of Texas, The
    Gr. 7, I-70
Yonder Come Day  Gr. 8, I-68

## EVALUATING *See Skills Reinforcement.*

## EXPRESSION

### ARTICULATION
*Aerial Boundaries*  Gr. 8, F-20
Alleluia, Amen  Gr. 7, A-12
America  Gr. 3, 412
America  Gr. 6, 484
America, the Beautiful  Gr. 3, 413
*America, the Beautiful*  Gr. 3, 413
Angels On the Midnight Clear
    Gr. 6, 423
*California Counterpoint: The
    Twittering Machine*  Gr. 8, C-47
Ding Dong! Merrily on High
    Gr. 6, 427
Dok djampa  Gr. 8, I-20
Earth Is Our Mother, The  Gr. 8, F-25
*El amor brujo, "Danza ritual del
    fuego"*  Gr. 8, F-20
*Etude Fantasy for Piano, "Etude
    No 3: Fifths to Thirds"*
    Gr. 8, C-46
Faith of the Heart  Gr. 8, G-3
*Firebird, The, "Finale"*  Gr. 8, C-30
*Frostiana (from Stopping by
    Woods on a Snowy Evening)*
    Gr. 6, 40
Give My Regards to Broadway
    Gr. 6, 39
*I Am a Man of Constant Sorrow*
    Gr. 7, F-29
*If You Asked Me To*  Gr. 8, G-5
Ja-Da  Gr. 7, G-20
*Jo'ashila, "Walking Together"*
    Gr. 6, 286
Karangatia ra  Gr. 8, F-23
*Key to the Highway*  Gr. 8, F-28
*Le Sacre de Printemps (The
    Rite of Spring), "Dance of
    the Youths and Maidens"*
    Gr. 8, C-30
*Native Stepson*  Gr. 7, F-26
One Family  Gr. 7, G-17
Purple People Eater, The  Gr. 6, 448
*Roll Over Vaughan Williams*
    Gr. 8, F-22
*Scuttle Buttin'*  Gr. 8, F-26
*Sextet for Winds and Piano,
    Movement 1*  Gr. 8, C-29
Shalom aleichem  Gr. 6, 409
*Shika no Tone*  Gr. 5, 112
*Sister Rosa*  Gr. 3, 411
Siyahamba  Gr. 6, 212
Star-Spangled Banner, The
    Gr. 6, 486
Stopping by Woods on a Snowy
    Evening  Gr. 6, 41
*Transcendental Etude, No. 3 in G-
    sharp Minor, "La Campanella"*
    Gr. 7, C-23

*Widmung, Op. 25, No. 1*
Gr. 7, C-20
Winter  Gr. 8, G-11

**accents**
A Ram Sam Sam  Gr. 3, 208
*America (from West Side Story)*
Gr. 8, C-45
America, the Free  Gr. 4, 210
Boogie Chant and Dance (speech
piece)  Gr. 2, 78
Book of Love  Gr. 8, G-27
Caribbean Island Ensemble
Gr. 7, D-19
*Carol of the Bells*  Gr. 8, G-10
Chapel of Love  Gr. 7, G-27
*Die forelle*  Gr. 7, C-20
Down by the Riverside  Gr. 8, G-8
*Ev'ry Time I Feel the Spirit*
Gr. 7, C-40
*Firebird, The, "Infernal Dance"*
Gr. 5, 173
*Gazebo Dances, "Tarantella"*
Gr. 8, C-46
God Bless the U.S.A.  Gr. 8, G-37
*I Will Survive*  Gr. 7, B-10
Just a Snap-Happy Blues
Gr. 6, 388
*Las copetonas*  Gr. 7, B-33
*Men's Fancy Dance*  Gr. 7, D-24
Now's the Time  Gr. 5, 445
Paths of Victory  Gr. 6, 195
*Prayer, The*  Gr. 7, A-10
¡Qué bonita bandera!  Gr. 5, 295
*Rods and Cones*  Gr. 7, D-5
Run! Run! Hide!  Gr. 6, 340
*Sha Sha Sha*  Gr. 6, 328
*Simple Song, A, (from Mass)*
Gr. 8, C-45
Something Told the Wild Geese
Gr. 7, G-39
Step in Time  Gr. 2, 74
*Study War No More*  Gr. 7, C-40
*Suite No. 2 in F, Op. 28b,*
*Movement 1, "March"*
Gr. 6, 139
Swing Low, Sweet Chariot
Gr. 7, C-41
*Thunder and Lightning Polka*
Gr. 4, 213
Two Little Sausages (speech
piece)  Gr. 2, 79
Wai bamba  Gr. 8, G-13
Yo-shi nai  Gr. 6, 286
You Were on My Mind
Gr. 7, G-23

**legato**
America, the Beautiful
Gr. 6, 485
Ayliluli, num tsipor  Gr. 1, 204
Cantaré, cantarás  Gr. 6, 413
*Carol of the Bells*  Gr. 8, G-10
*Diamonds and Rust*  Gr. 7, A-4

*Die forelle*  Gr. 7, C-20
Disco Worm  Gr. 2, 312
Einini  Gr. 4, 391
El gallo pinto  Gr. 3, 86
*Ev'ry Time I Feel the Spirit*
Gr. 7, C-40
Falling Rain  Gr. 2, 328
For Children Safe and Strong
Gr. 5, 484
*Gavotte*  Gr. 3, 88
Goin' to Boston  Gr. 6, 433
*Gymnopedie No. 1*  Gr. K, 175
Happy Wanderer, The  Gr. 4, 89
Hine mah tov  Gr. 5, 430
I Dream a World  Gr. 8, G-40
I Vow to You, My Country
Gr. 5, 418
I'm a Believer  Gr. 7, G-33
La golondrina  Gr. 8, I-50
*Le tombeau de Couperin,*
*"Prelude"*  Gr. 8, C-28
Light Up the World with a Song
Gr. 8, G-25
Lots of Worms  Gr. 2, 310
Party Tonight!  Gr. 2, 152
*Prayer, The*  Gr. 7, A-10
Proud  Gr. 7, G-3
*Pupu hinu hinu, "Shiny Shell*
*Lullaby"*  Gr. 1, 109
Scattin' A-Round (Variations on
Row 3)  Gr. 6, 160
*Serenade, Op. 3, No. 5*  Gr. 4, 90
Something Told the Wild Geese
Gr. 7, G-39
*Study War No More*  Gr. 7, C-40
*Suite No. 2 in F, Op. 28b,*
*"March," Movement 1*
Gr. 6, 139
Swing Low, Sweet Chariot
Gr. 7, C-41
*Toccata and Tango*  Gr. 2, 154
United Nations on the March,
The  Gr. 6, 443
Vem kan segla?  Gr. 6, 417
Voices of Pride, The  Gr. 5, 87
*When Johnny Comes Marching*
*Home*  Gr. 5, 88
You Were on My Mind
Gr. 7, G-23

**marcato**
Voices of Pride, The  Gr. 5, 87
*When Johnny Comes Marching*
*Home*  Gr. 5, 88

**slurs**
I Believe I Can Fly  Gr. 5, 170

**staccato**
Ayliluli, num tsipor  Gr. 1, 204
*Carol of the Bells*  Gr. 8, G-10
*Die forelle*  Gr. 7, C-20
Disco Worm  Gr. 2, 312
El gallo pinto  Gr. 3, 86

*Ev'ry Time I Feel the Spirit*
Gr. 7, C-40
Falling Rain  Gr. 2, 328
*Gavotte*  Gr. 3, 88
Goin' to Boston  Gr. 6, 433
Happy Wanderer, The  Gr. 4, 89
Lots of Worms  Gr. 2, 310
*Minstrels*  Gr. K, 175
Party Tonight!  Gr. 2, 152
*Prayer, The*  Gr. 7, A-10
Run! Run! Hide!  Gr. 6, 340
*Rundadinella*  Gr. 8, I-60
Scattin' A-Round (Variations on
Row 3)  Gr. 6, 160
*Serenade, Op. 3, No. 5*
Gr. 4, 90
*Sha Sha Sha*  Gr. 6, 328
Something Told the Wild Geese
Gr. 7, G-39
*String Quartet No. 4,*
*Movement 4, "Allegretto*
*pizzicato"*  Gr. 4, 90
*Study War No More*  Gr. 7, C-40
Swing Low, Sweet Chariot
Gr. 7, C-41
Take a Chance On Me
Gr. 8, G-15
*Toccata and Tango*  Gr. 2, 154
United Nations on the March,
The  Gr. 6, 443
Voices of Pride, The  Gr. 5, 87
*When Johnny Comes Marching*
*Home*  Gr. 5, 88
You Were on My Mind
Gr. 7, G-23

**DYNAMICS**
A la rurru niño  Gr. K, 180
Alleluia, Amen  Gr. 7, A-12
America  Gr. 2, 403
America  Gr. 3, 412
America  Gr. 6, 484
America, I Hear You Singing
Gr. 2, 402
America, the Beautiful  Gr. 3, 413
*America, the Beautiful*  Gr. 3, 413
America, the Beautiful  Gr. 6, 485
Angels On the Midnight Clear
Gr. 6, 423
Back of the Bus  Gr. 3, 410
*Beat of My Heart, The*  Gr. 4, 9
Brand New Day, A  Gr. 6, 7
But the Cat Came Back  Gr. 2, 190
By the Waters of Babylon  Gr. 6, 311
*California Counterpoint: The*
*Twittering Machine*  Gr. 8, C-47
California Dreamin'  Gr. 8, G-31
Cantaré, cantarás  Gr. 6, 413
*Canzon in Echo Duodecimi Toni a*
*10*  Gr. 8, C-7
*Carnaval, Op. 9, "Valse Noble,"*
*Un poco maestoso*  Gr. 3, 202

(*Expression,* continued)

Carnival of the Animals, "Aquarium" Gr. 5, 376
Carol of the Bells Gr. 8, G-10
Cat's Tongue Gr. 2, 190
Chag Purim Gr. 1, 438
Checkerboard Gr. 1, 7
Chippewa Lullaby Gr. K, 181
Circle 'Round the Moon Gr. 4, 403
Clouds Gr. K, 254
Concert for Piano and Orchestra Gr. 6, 209
Concerto for Marimba and String Orchestra, "Saudação" Gr. 2, 119
Concierto Madrigal for Two Guitars and Orchestra, "Fanfarre" Gr. 2, 150
Country Gardens Gr. 1, 440
Dance Suite, "Waltz" Gr. K, 145
Das Jahr, "Mai" Gr. 8, C-18
Die forelle Gr. 7, C-20
Die Walküre, "The Ride of the Valkyries" Gr. 8, C-23
Ding Dong! Merrily on High Gr. 6, 427
Do, Lord Gr. 3, 164
Einini Gr. 4, 391
Ev'ry Time I Feel the Spirit Gr. 7, C-40
Fais do do Gr. 6, 403
Fanfare for Freedom Gr. 6, 139
Finlandia Gr. 6, 78
Frostiana (from Stopping by Woods on a Snowy Evening) Gr. 6, 40
Gazebo Dances, "Tarantella" Gr. 8, C-46
Get on Your Feet Gr. 5, 6
Give My Regards to Broadway Gr. 6, 39
God Bless the U.S.A. Gr. 8, G-37
Goin' to Boston Gr. 6, 433
Gospel Train, The Gr. 6, 398
Grizzly Bear Gr. K, 33
Haere Gr. 2, 285
Hard Day Blues Gr. 7, B-9
Hava nagila Gr. 6, 153
Heigh-Ho Gr. 2, 6
Hello, There! Gr. K, 6
Huagu ge, "Flower Drum song" Gr. 8, D-27
Hungarian Dance No. 3 in F Major Gr. 1, 206
Hush, Hush Gr. 3, 162
Hush Up the Baby Gr. K, 222
I Got Shoes Gr. 2, 242
I Walk the Unfrequented Road Gr. 6, 79
I'm a Believer Gr. 7, G-33
If You Asked Me To Gr. 8, G-5
In My Own Little Corner Gr. 3, 9
La golondrina Gr. 8, I-50

La tormenta tropical Gr. 2, 116
Le tombeau de Couperin, "Prelude" Gr. 8, C-28
Lion Sleeps Tonight, The Gr. 4, 131
Lion Sleeps Tonight, The Gr. 4, 132
Look! Look! The Sun Woke Up! Gr. 1, 368
Loud (poem) Gr. 1, 7
Louder Than a Clap of Thunder (poem) Gr. 1, 87
Louds and Softs of the Seasons Gr. K, 4
Lucy Locket Gr. 2, 27
Lullaby (poem) Gr. 1, 208
Lyric Suite, Op. 65, No. 6, "Wedding Day at Troldhaugen" Gr. 6, 9
Ma Vlast (My Fatherland), "Vltava (The Moldau)" Gr. 7, C-33
Make Your Own Kind of Music Gr. 8, G-30
Marche Militaire, Op. 51, No. 1 Gr. 6, 17
Mass for the 21st Century, "Alleluia" Gr. 3, 163
Niño querido Gr. 1, 308
Noises Gr. K, 305
Nutcracker Suite, The, "Waltz of the Flowers" Gr. 6, 325
Owl and the Pumpkin, The Gr. 2, 377
Parade Came Marching, The Gr. 1, 166
Peer Gynt Suite No. 1, "Morning" Gr. 1, 369
Percussion Fun Rondo Gr. 7, I-51
Pictures at an Exhibition, "The Great Gate of Kiev" Gr. 6, 154
Poem Gr. 3, 163
Prayer, The Gr. 7, A-10
Proud Gr. 7, G-3
Pumpkin Picking Gr. 2, 376
Purple People Eater, The Gr. 6, 448
Put a Little Love in Your Heart Gr. 4, 6
Put a Little Love in Your Heart Gr. 4, 8
Quiet (poem) Gr. 1, 7
Rain Song, The Gr. 2, 323
Raindrops Gr. 7, D-23
Rhapsody in Blue Gr. 7, C-42
Rigoletto, "Bella figlia dell'amore" Gr. 7, C-29
Run! Run! Hide! Gr. 6, 340
Sakura Gr. 4, 308
Seasons Gr. K, 4
Shake the Papaya Down Gr. 4, 378
Shalom aleichem Gr. 6, 409
Shepherds Hey Gr. 1, 208
Sidewalk Sounds Gr. K, 115
Singing-Time Gr. 3, 201
Skin and Bones Gr. 2, 376
Snowflakes Gr. 1, 422

Something Told the Wild Geese Gr. 7, G-39
Somewhere Out There Gr. 5, 369
Sonata in F Major for Violin and Piano, Op. 24, No. 5, "Spring," Movement 3 Gr. 7, C-19
Song of the Night, The Gr. 3, 346
Song of the Nightingale, "The Nightingale" Gr. 8, C-32
Soundings, "Fanfare" Gr. 8, C-47
Spring Has Sprung! Gr. K, 142
Stand By Me Gr. 5, 46
Stars and Stripes Forever, The Gr. 1, 167
Stille Nacht (Silent Night) Gr. 7, I-54
Stopping by Woods on a Snowy Evening Gr. 6, 41
Storm Dance (speech piece) Gr. K, 145
Study War No More Gr. 7, C-40
Suite in F, Op. 28b, No. 2, "Fantasia on the Dargason," Movement 4 Gr. 7, C-36
Suo gan Gr. 1, 309
Supercalifragilisticexpialidocious Gr. 3, 7
Swing Low, Sweet Chariot Gr. 7, C-41
Symphony No. 3 in E-flat Major, "Allegro con brio," Movement 1 Gr. 8, C-17
Symphony No. 3 in E-flat Major, "Marcia funebre," Movement 2 Gr. 8, C-17
Symphony No. 47 in G Major, "Menuet" Gr. 7, C-14
Symphony No. 94 in G Major, No. 94, ("Surprise"), Andante Gr. 1, 86
Symphony No. 94 in G Major, ("Surprise"), Andante Gr. 7,
T'hola, t'hola Gr. 4, 132
Table Manners (speech piece) Gr. 3, 190
Tall Cedar Tree Gr. 2, 322
Theme and Variations for Percussion Gr. 5, 65
There Was an Old Man (speech piece) Gr. 3, 191
This Is My Song Gr. 6, 77
This Little Light of Mine Gr. 6, 232
Toccata and Fugue in D Minor Gr. 7, E-25
United Nations on the March, The Gr. 6, 443
Vem kan segla? Gr. 6, 417
Violin Concerto in E Minor, Op. 64, Movement 1 Gr. 8, C-18
Voices of Pride, The Gr. 5, 86
We Are Dear Little Birdies Gr. K, 176
We're Making Popcorn (speech piece) Gr. 1, 86

*When Johnny Comes Marching Home* Gr. 5, 88
*Whether It's Cold* (proverb) Gr. 2, 118
*Widmung, Op. 25, No. 1* Gr. 7, C-20
Wind Song Gr. K, 7
Winter Gr. 8, G-11
Winter Song Gr. 6, 455
*Woodlands* Gr. K, 254
Yonder Come Day Gr. 8, I-68
*You Were on My Mind* Gr. 7, G-23
*Yours Forever* Gr. 6, 344

## EXPRESSIVE SINGING

Achshav Gr. 2, 64
Alleluia, Amen Gr. 7, A-12
America Gr. 1, 446
America Gr. 2, 403
America Gr. 6, 484
America Gr. 8, I-2
America, I Hear You Singing Gr. 2, 402
America, the Beautiful Gr. 6, 485
America, the Beautiful Gr. 8, I-4
*America, the Beautiful (Gospel)* Gr. 6, 485
Angels On the Midnight Clear Gr. 6, 423
At the Same Time Gr. 6, 115
*Blue Eyes Crying in the Rain* Gr. 7, B-28
Book of Love Gr. 8, G-27
Brand New Day, A Gr. 6, 7
California Dreamin' Gr. 8, G-31
*(Can't Live Without Your) Love and Affection* Gr. 7, B-23
*Can't Take My Joy* Gr. 7, B-40
*Carol of the Bells* Gr. 8, G-10
*Carry On* Gr. 7, B-2
*Carry On Wayward Son* Gr. 7, B-20
Certainly, Lord Gr. 7, I-13
*Changed My Name* Gr. 6, 338
Chapel of Love Gr. 7, G-27
*Crazy Blues* Gr. 7, B-8
*Die forelle* Gr. 7, C-20
*Die Zauberflöte, "Pa-pa-pa-pa-pa-pa-pagena"* Gr. 8, C-13
Eres tú Gr. 6, 473
Ev'ry Kind of Music Gr. 2, 226
Ev'ry Time I Feel the Spirit Gr. 5, 242
*Ev'ry Time I Feel the Spirit* Gr. 7, C-40
*Ev'rybody Ought to Know* Gr. 1, 434
*Everything Is Everything* Gr. 7, B-29
*Face of Love, The* Gr. 8, B-15
Fais do do Gr. 6, 403
Faith of the Heart Gr. 8, G-3
*Forever, For Now* Gr. 7, B-16
Freedom Is Coming Gr. 5, 415

Gift to Share, A Gr. 6, 393
*Go Down, Moses* Gr. 7, G-10
*God Bless the Child* Gr. 7, B-26
God Bless the Child Gr. 7, B-27
God Bless the U.S.A. Gr. 8, G-37
Harambee Gr. 4, 434
*How High the Moon* Gr. 5, 341
Hush Up the Baby Gr. K, 222
I Vow to You, My Country Gr. 5, 418
*I Walk the Line* Gr. 7, B-28
I Walk the Unfrequented Road Gr. 6, 79
I'm a Believer Gr. 7, G-33
I'm in the Mood Gr. K, 86
*If You Asked Me To* Gr. 8, G-5
*It's Time* Gr. 6, 319
Ja-Da Gr. 7, G-20
*John Wayne's Teeth* Gr. 8, B-37
*Joy* Gr. 7, B-40
Joy of Kwanzaa, The Gr. 6, 462
*Keep a Cool Head* Gr. 7, B-34
*Les pêcheurs des perles, "Au fond du temple saint"* Gr. 7, C-30
Lift Ev'ry Voice and Sing Gr. 5, 482
Light Up the World with a Song Gr. 8, G-25
Love Is on Our Side Gr. 5, 324
*Magic Flute, The, "Queen of the Night Aria"* Gr. 7, C-31
*Make Your Own Kind of Music* Gr. 8, G-30
Martin Luther King Gr. 1, 434
Music (poem) Gr. 1, 3
Now's the Time Gr. 5, 445
Oh, Freedom Gr. 7, G-30
On My Way Gr. 6, 313
One Family Gr. 7, G-17
Over My Head Gr. 7, G-9
*Oye mi canto,* Gr. 6, 114
Peace Like a River Gr. 6, 190
*Prayer, The* Gr. 7, A-10
Proud Gr. 7, G-3
Purple People Eater, The Gr. 6, 448
Put a Little Love in Your Heart Gr. 4, 6
Put Your Hand in My Hand Gr. 1, 330
*Rainbow in the Sky* Gr. 7, B-35
*Seasons of Love* Gr. 8, A-22
Rhythm Is Gonna Get You, The Gr. 6, 348
*Rigoletto, "Bella figlia dell'amore"* Gr. 7, C-29
Rock Around the Clock Gr. 7, B-18
Sakura Gr. 4, 308
Shalom aleichem Gr. 6, 409
Sharing Gr. K, 198
*Shed a Little Light* Gr. 8, E-17
Shine, Shine, Shine Gr. 1, 42
Si si si Gr. 7, G-13
Something Told the Wild Geese Gr. 7, G-39

*Sometimes I Feel Like a Motherless Child* Gr. 5, 193
*Somewhere* Gr. 8, C-44
Somewhere Out There Gr. 5, 368
*Soulville* Gr. 7, B-17
Stand By Me Gr. 5, 46
Star-Spangled Banner, The Gr. 6, 486
Star-Spangled Banner, The Gr. 7, I-56
*Stille Nacht (Silent Night)* Gr. 7, I-54
*Study War No More* Gr. 7, C-40
Summertime Gr. 6, 250
Swing Low, Sweet Chariot Gr. 7, C-41
Tall Cedar Tree Gr. 2, 322
*Tears of a Clown, The* Gr. 7, B-39
*That's the Way It Is* Gr. 7, B-23
*Tosca, "Vissi d'arte"* Gr. 7, C-31
*Treaties* Gr. 8, B-36
*Tutti Frutti* Gr. 7, B-29
Twelve Gates to the City Gr. 5, 280
United Nations on the March, The Gr. 6, 443
Vem kan segla? Gr. 6, 417
Voice Choice Gr. K, 27
*Wedding Qawwali* Gr. 8, B-35
*What's Going On?* Gr. 7, B-38
*Why Walk When You Can Fly* Gr. 7, B-28
*Widmung, Op. 25, No. 1* Gr. 7, C-20
Wir hatten gebauet Gr. 8, C-21
Yonder Come Day Gr. 8, I-68
*You Are My Sunshine* Gr. 6, 247
You Were on My Mind Gr. 7, G-23
*You've Got a Friend* Gr. 5, 364

## MOOD

*Aida, "Gloria all'Egitto (Grand March)"* Gr. 8, C-24
Alleluia, Amen Gr. 7, A-12
America Gr. 2, 403
America Gr. 6, 484
America, I Hear You Singing Gr. 2, 402
America, the Beautiful Gr. 6, 485
America, the Beautiful Gr. 8, I-4
Back of the Bus Gr. 3, 410
*Carol of the Bells* Gr. 8, G-10
*Catalana, "Andante"* Gr. K, 134
*Children's Garden, The* Gr. K, 267
*Clair de lune* Gr. K, 165
Clouds Gr. K, 254
*Coming Home from the Sea–I* Gr. 6, 345
*Coming Home from the Sea–II* Gr. 6, 345
Dancing Girl Gr. K, 249
*Das Jahr, "Mai"* Gr. 8, C-18
*Die forelle* Gr. 7, C-20
*Dusty Rag* Gr. K, 165
*Étude in E Major* Gr. K, 241

(*Expression,* continued)

*Ev'ry Time I Feel the Spirit*
Gr. 7, C-40
*Frostiana (from Stopping by
Woods on a Snowy Evening)*
Gr. 6, 40
*Game of the Mechanical
Nightingale, "The Nightingale"*
Gr. 8, C-33
Gaudeamus igitur Gr. 8, C-20
Glory, Glory, Hallelujah Gr. 6, 52
*Haere* Gr. 2, 285
*Hard Day Blues* Gr. 7, B-9
*How High the Moon* Gr. 5, 341
*Hungarian Rhapsody No. 2
in C sharp Minor, S. 244*
Gr. 7, E-17
*Hush, Little Baby* Gr. K, 222
I'm in the Mood Gr. K, 86
*Illusions* Gr. 6, 347
It's a Celebration! Gr. 2, 372
*Jungle Beat* Gr. 6, 347
*Kebjar teruna* Gr. 6, 385
*Keep a Cool Head* Gr. 7, B-34
*La mer, "Jeux de vagues"*
Gr. 7, C-39
*Le tombeau de Couperin,
"Prelude"* Gr. 8, C-28
*Ma Vlast (My Fatherland), "Vltava
(The Moldau)"* Gr. 7, C-33
*Mad...Sad...Glad: A Piece in
Three Mood-ments* Gr. K, 249
Me voy para la luna Gr. 1, 397
*New York State of Mind*
Gr. 7, E-19
Niño querido Gr. 1, 308
*Nutcracker Suite, The, "Waltz of
the Flowers"* Gr. 6, 325
Oh, Freedom Gr. 7, G-30
*Olympic Spirit* Gr. 6, 350
*Ombrose e care selve* Gr. 8, C-5
*On Christmas Morning* Gr. K, 316
On My Way Gr. 6, 313
*One Fine Day* Gr. 6, 347
Owl and the Pumpkin, The
Gr. 2, 377
*Pennsylvania 6-5000* Gr. 5, 342
*Planxty Madame Maxwell*
Gr. K, 134
Poem [2] Gr. 2, 285
*Prelude in G-sharp Minor, No. 12*
Gr. 7, E-4
*Prelude to the Afternoon of a
Faun* Gr. 5, 113
*Princess Hundred Flowers,
The, "Falling in the Trap"*
Gr. 8, C-25
Purple People Eater, The Gr. 6, 448
*Rainbow in the Sky* Gr. 7, B-35
*Reservation Blues* Gr. 8, B-37
*Rhapsody in Blue* Gr. 7, C-42
Rhythm Is Gonna Get You, The
Gr. 6, 348

*Rose, (from the Motion Picture
Titanic)* Gr. 8, B-34
*Run! Run! Hide!* Gr. 6, 340
*Shed a Little Light* Gr. 8, E-17
*Silverly* Gr. K, 135
Sing a Little Song Gr. K, 30
Skin and Bones Gr. 2, 376
*Somewhere* Gr. 8, C-44
*Sonata in C-sharp Minor, Op. 27,
No. 2, (Moonlight), Movement
1* Gr. 7, C-19
*Sonata No. 11, K. 331, "Turkish
Rondo"* Gr. K, 165
Song of the Night, The Gr. 3, 346
*Song of the Nightingale, "The
Nightingale"* Gr. 8, C-32
*Soundings, "Fanfare"* Gr. 8, C-47
Sounds of the Circus Gr. K, 241
Star-Spangled Banner, The
Gr. 6, 486
Stille Nacht (Silent Night) Gr. 7, I-54
*Study War No More* Gr. 7, C-40
Swing Low, Sweet Chariot
Gr. 7, C-41
*Symphony No. 3 in E-flat Major,
"Marcia funebre," Movement 2*
Gr. 8, C-17
*Syrinx* Gr. 5, 113
*Usagi* Gr. 1, 396
*Voiles* Gr. 7, C-39
*Wedding Qawwali* Gr. 8, B-35
*Widmung, Op. 25, No. 1*
Gr. 7, C-20
Winter Gr. 8, G-11
*Woodlands* Gr. K, 254
*Xochipilli, An Imagined Aztec
Music* Gr. 8, C-37
*Yemaya* Gr. 8, G-24
*Yours Forever* Gr. 6, 344

## Tempo

*Add-On Machine, The* Gr. K, 298
*Adzogbo-Ovitse* Gr. 8, D-13
*African Suite, "Mbira"* Gr. K, 61
Alleluia, Amen Gr. 7, A-12
Alumot Gr. 6, 306
America Gr. 2, 403
America Gr. 3, 412
*America (from West Side Story)*
Gr. 8, C-45
America, the Beautiful Gr. 3, 413
*America, the Beautiful* Gr. 3, 413
America, the Beautiful Gr. 8, I-4
*Apu Min'Tan* Gr. 8, D-21
At the Same Time Gr. 6, 115
¡Ay, Jalisco no te rajes! Gr. 7, I-6
Back of the Bus Gr. 3, 410
*Beggar's Opera, The, "Constant
Billy"* Gr. 7, C-24
*Bembe de Plena* Gr. 8, D-18
Bethena Waltz Gr. 6, 157
*Blue Danube, The, Op. 314*
Gr. 6, 192

Bob-a-Needle Gr. 2, 232
Book of Love Gr. 8, G-27
Can You Canoe? Gr. 4, 170
*Carmina Burana, "Chramer, gip
die Varwe mir"* Gr. K, 62
Cat's Tongue Gr. 2, 190
*Cauyaqa Nauwa? (Where's My
Drum?)* Gr. 8, D-20
Chanukah, Chanukah Gr. 1, 420
Chanukiyah li yesh Gr. 1, 421
*Checkerboard* Gr. 1, 7
*Cheki, morena* Gr. 7, I-16
*Chicken Dance, The* Gr. 4, 51
Choo Choo Boogaloo Gr. 1, 127
*Choo-Choo Joubert* Gr. 3, 51
*Cielito lindo* Gr. 4, 270
*Circle of Life (from The Lion
King), The* Gr. 6, 316
Circle 'Round the Moon Gr. 4, 403
*Concert for Piano and Orchestra*
Gr. 6, 209
*Concerto for Flute and Harp
in C, K. 299, Movement 2*
Gr. 8, C-10
*Cotton-Eye Joe* Gr. 4, 290
*Country Gardens* Gr. 1, 440
*Cow Barn Cha Cha* Gr. 8, D-33
*Das Jahr, "Mai"* Gr. 8, C-18
*Die forelle* Gr. 7, C-20
Ding Dong! Merrily on High
Gr. 6, 427
Don't Cry for Me, Argentina
Gr. 6, 74
Draw Me a Bucket of Water
Gr. 3, 124
Eensy Weensy Spider Gr. K, 187
El juego chirimbolo Gr. 2, 54
El rancho grande Gr. 8, I-22
*El Salón México* Gr. 6, 199
*El siquisirí* Gr. 4, 273
*Elegguá* Gr. 8, D-13
*Ennanga, Movement 3* Gr. 3, 127
*Ev'ry Time I Feel the Spirit*
Gr. 7, C-40
*Fanfare for Freedom* Gr. 6, 139
*Forked Deer/Fisher's Hornpipe*
Gr. 4, 343
Freight Train Gr. 1, 44
Galoshes Gr. K, 63
Geef jij mij die schoen Gr. 1, 126
Get on Board Gr. K, 89
*Get on Board* Gr. K, 89
Gospel Train, The Gr. 6, 398
*Guaguancó pá las tumbadoras*
Gr. 7, D-9
*Hard Day Blues* Gr. 7, B-9
Hava nagila Gr. 6, 153
Hey, Diddle, Diddle Gr. K, 246
*Hey, Diddle, Diddle* Gr. K, 247
*Hungarian Dance No. 19*
Gr. 4, 171
*Hungarian Dance No. 3 in F Major*
Gr. 1, 206

*Hungarian Dance No. 6* Gr. 4, 50
I Shall Sing Gr. 8, I-38
*I Shall Sing* Gr. 8, I-41
I'm in the Mood Gr. K, 86
I'm Thankful Gr. 1, 414
Inkpataya Gr. 3, 254
*Irish Tune from County Derry*
Gr. 4, 49
*Itsy Bitsy Spider, The* Gr. K, 187
Joy of Kwanzaa, The Gr. 6, 462
Just Watch Gr. K, 295
La borinqueña Gr. 8, D-19
La piñata Gr. 3, 399
*Las mañanitas* Gr. K, 325
Locomoto-vation Gr. K, 61
*Lord of the Dance Medley*
Gr. 6, 326
*Love for Three Oranges, "March"*
Gr. K, 117
*Lyric Suite, Op. 65, No. 6,*
*"Wedding Day at Troldhaugen"*
Gr. 6, 9
*Ma Vlast (My Fatherland), "Vltava*
*(The Moldau)"* Gr. 7, C-33
*Mambo UK* Gr. 7, D-9
Mary Came a-Running Gr. K, 294
Mbombera Gr. K, 24
Me voy para la luna Gr. 1, 397
Miss Mary Mack Gr. 2, 42
New Way to Walk, A Gr. K, 117
Now's the Time Gr. 5, 445
O hal'lwe Gr. 3, 256
Oh, Danny Boy Gr. 4, 48
*On Parade* Gr. K, 326
*Oye mi canto, " "* Gr. 6, 114
Pavo, pavo Gr. 1, 416
Peace Like a River Gr. 6, 190
Percussion Fun Rondo Gr. 7, I-51
*Pictures at an Exhibition, "The*
*Great Gate of Kiev"* Gr. 6, 154
Planets Chant, The Gr. 4, 377
Race You Down the Mountain
Gr. 1, 127
Ragupati Ragava Raja Ram
Gr. 5, 321
*Raindrops* Gr. 7, D-23
*Rhapsody in Blue* Gr. 7, C-42
Ríu ríu chíu Gr. 5, 435
*Rodeo, "Saturday Night Waltz"*
Gr. 4, 342
S'vivon Gr. 6, 452
Sakura Gr. 4, 308
*Semper Fidelis* Gr. K, 326
*Shadow Dancer* Gr. K, 253
Shalom aleichem Gr. 6, 409
*Sindhi-Bhairavi* Gr. 5, 320
*Slow Hora/Freylekhs* Gr. 8, B-25
Something Told the Wild Geese
Gr. 7, G-39
*Sonata in F Major for Violin and*
*Piano, Op. 24, No. 5, "Spring,"*
*Movement 3* Gr. 7, C-19
Song of the Night, The Gr. 3, 346

Song of the Train Gr. K, 153
*Sorochintsy Fair, "Gopak No. 5"*
Gr. 1, 417
Star-Spangled Banner, The
Gr. 6, 486
Star-Spangled Banner, The
Gr. 7, I-56
Streets of Laredo Gr. 4, 272
*Study War No More* Gr. 7, C-40
Swing Low, Sweet Chariot
Gr. 7, C-41
*Symphony No. 3 in E-flat Major,*
*"Marcia funebre," Movement 2*
Gr. 8, C-17
Take a Chance On Me Gr. 8, G-15
Take Your Feet Out 'the Sand
Gr. K, 231
This Little Light of Mine Gr. 6, 232
Train Is A-Comin' Gr. 3, 48
United Nations on the March, The
Gr. 6, 443
Usagi Gr. 1, 396
Vem kan segla? Gr. 6, 417
*Violin Concerto in E Minor, Op.*
*64, Movement 1* Gr. 8, C-18
*Widmung, Op. 25, No. 1*
Gr. 7, C-20
*Wild Horseman, The* Gr. 1, 159
Windshield Wipers (poem) Gr. 1, 11
Winter Song Gr. 6, 455
*Wioste Olowan Inkpa Ta-Ya*
Gr. 3, 255
*Xochipilli, An Imagined Aztec*
*Music* Gr. 8, C-37
Yellow Butter (poem) Gr. 1, 124
*Yellow Cake Review, The,*
*"Farewell to Stromness"*
Gr. K, 61
*Yellow Rose of Texas, The*
Gr. 7, I-73
*You Sang to Me* Gr. 6, 335
*Yours Forever* Gr. 6, 344
*Zoila* Gr. 8, D-18
Zumba, zumba Gr. 3, 400

## TONE COLOR

*Children's Corner Suite, "Doctor*
*Gradus ad Parnassum"*
Gr. 8, C-27
*Dziban* Gr. 7, F-18
*Elias* Gr. 7, B-21
*Everything Is Everything*
Gr. 7, B-29
*Forever, For Now* Gr. 7, B-16
*God Bless the Child* Gr. 7, B-26
*I Can't Get Started* Gr. 7, B-26
*I Walk the Line* Gr. 7, B-28
*Le tombeau de Couperin,*
*"Prelude"* Gr. 8, C-28
*Native Stepson* Gr. 7, F-26
Oh, Freedom Gr. 7, G-30
One Family Gr. 7, G-17

*Pulcinella Suite, "Serenata"*
Gr. 8, C-32
*Rising of the Mourning Sun*
Gr. 7, F-19
*Soulville* Gr. 7, B-17
*Take Me There* Gr. 7, F-26
*Tutti Frutti* Gr. 7, B-29

## FOLK, TRADITIONAL, AND REGIONAL SELECTIONS
(Listening selections appear in italics.)

### AFRICA

*African Suite, "Mbira"* Gr. K, 61
Dinner Music Gr. K, 70
Enjoy the Earth Gr. 4, 81
Hey, m'tswala Gr. 4, 79
*Hindewhu (whistle) solo*
Gr. 6, 269
*Lost River* Gr. 6, 283
Night, The Gr. 4, 81
Omo Gr. 1, 443
*One Fine Mama* Gr. 8, B-41

**Algeria**
*Hai wedi* Gr. 8, B-13
*Recitation of Verses of the*
*Qu'ran* Gr. 7, C-5
*Sabhyatâ* Gr. 8, B-4

**Angola**
O, Desayo Gr. 5, 411

**Benin**
*Gahu* Gr. 7, D-27
*Tumba* Gr. 7, D-14

**Congo**
*Kyrie, "Missa Luba"* Gr. 7, G-13
Si si si Gr. 7, G-13

**Eritrea**
Hashewie Gr. 4, 62

**Gabon**
*Bombé/Ruht wohl, ruht wohl,*
*ihr heilegen Gebeine, BWV*
*245* Gr. 8, B-39
Bombé/Ruht wohl, ruht
wohl, ihr heilegen Gebeine
Gr. 8, B-39
*Inongo* Gr. 8, B-9
*Mayingo* Gr. 8, B-11

**Gambia**
Nu wahtan Gr. 1, 279

**Ghana**
*Adzogbo-Ovitse* Gr. 8, D-13
*Awakening* Gr. 3, 289
*Awakening* Gr. 7, D- 14
Ayelivi Gr. 2, 70
Bantama kra kro Gr. 5, 308
*Bawa* Gr. 7, D-32
Che che koolay Gr. 2, 266
*Ekombi* Gr. 8, B-31
Ev'rybody Loves Saturday Night
Gr. 7, I-24

**(Folk, Traditional, and Regional Selections, continued)**

Everybody Loves Saturday Night Gr. 6, 296
Friends Today Gr. 7, D-12
James Brown Gr. K, 206
Kébé Mama Gr. 1, 442
Kelo aba w'ye Gr. 6, 290
*Kpanlogo for 2* Gr. 6, 296
*Kpanlogo Highlife Ensemble* Gr. 7, D-13
*Mensu* Gr. 8, D-6
*Obokete* Gr. 6, 291
*Samanfo, begye nsa nom* Gr. 8, D-6
*Samanfo, begye nsa nom* Gr. 8, D-6
Sansaw akroma Gr. 3, 286
*Wo ba wo ba shue* Gr. 8, B-31

**Kenya**
Ochimbo Gr. 4, 134

**Liberia**
African Noel Gr. 1, 427
Banuwa Gr. 6, 294
Kokoleoko Gr. 5, 33
Nana Kru Gr. 6, 282
Take Time in Life Gr. 6, 292

**Madagascar**
*Vonjeo* Gr. 8, B-12

**Mali**
*Karaw* Gr. 8, B-31

**Morocco**
A Ram Sam Sam Gr. 3, 208

**Nigeria**
*Awa ewe iwoyi* Gr. 8, D-9
Ise oluwa Gr. 2, 102
Ise oluwa Gr. 6, 230

**Senegal**
*Fatou yo, "I am Fatou"* Gr. K, 155
Koriko! Gr. K, 154
*Wildlife* Gr. 1, 345

**Shona**
Wai bamba Gr. 6, 26
Wai bamba Gr. 8, G-13

**South Africa**
Abiyoyo Gr. 2, 108
*Be Still, My Child* Gr. 1, 39
*Evening Samba* Gr. 6, 297
Freedom Is Coming Gr. 5, 415
Ikhanda, maslombe Gr. K, 14
*Imbube* Gr. 8, B-30
Kum ba yah Gr. 5, 244
*Lion Sleeps Tonight, The* Gr. 4, 132
Nampaya omame Gr. 1, 138
Nampaya omame Gr. 7, D-10
*Nyamphemphe* Gr. 8, B-3
*Rain, Rain, Beautiful Rain* Gr. 4, 32
*Sikelela* Gr. 1, 139
Siyahamba Gr. 6, 212

South African Ensemble Gr. 7, D-11
T'hola, t'hola Gr. 4, 132
Thula, thula, ngoana Gr. 4, 227
Tina singu Gr. 4, 300
*Vulani ringi ring* Gr. 1, 139
*Welcome to Our World* Gr. 6, 272
Why the Wart Hog Goes About on His Knees (story) Gr. 1, 139
*Zulu Lullaby* Gr. K, 158

**Tanzania**
Kou ri lengay Gr. 2, 217
Kou ri lengay Gr. 7, E-2

**Uganda**
*Rwakanembe* Gr. 8, C-14
*Wandenza* Gr. 8, B-6

**West Africa**
*Ajaja* Gr. 8, B-3
*Badenma* Gr. 8, B-28
*Duniya* Gr. 8, B-7
Funwa alafia Gr. 5, 32
*Primitive Fire, "Oya"* Gr. 2, 68
*Primitive Fire, "Oya"* Gr. 5, 67
Ye jaliya da Gr. 5, 67
*Yo Lé Lé (Fulani Groove)* Gr. 5, 33
*Zomo the Rabbit* Gr. 3, 364

**Zaire**
*Same, The* Gr. 6, 268

**Zimbabwe**
Chawe chidyo chem'chero Gr. 2, 296
*Chigamba* Gr. 6, 27
*Katura* Gr. 7, D-27
*Mai varamba* Gr. 8, B-39
Mbombera Gr. K, 24
*Nyoka* Gr. 7, D-33
*Shumba* Gr. 8, B-12
Sorida Gr. 1, 312

**AFRICAN AMERICAN** *For American selections, see Caribbean Islands: Puerto Rico; Native American; United States.*
ABC Blues Gr. K, 281
Abraham, Martin, and John Gr. 6, 466
Ain't Gonna Let Nobody Turn Me 'Round Gr. 6, 85
Ain't Gonna Let Nobody Turn Me 'Round Gr. 8, F-16
*Ain't That Love* Gr. 5, 20
All Night, All Day Gr. 4, 180
Back of the Bus Gr. 3, 410
Basin Street Blues Gr. 5, 354
*Battle of Jericho, The* Gr. 6, 234
*Bethena Waltz* Gr. 6, 157
Bob-a-Needle Gr. 2, 232
Brand New Day, A Gr. 6, 7
*C-Jam Blues* Gr. 8, C-43
Certainly, Lord Gr. 7, I-13

*Changed My Name* Gr. 6, 338
Chicka Hanka Gr. 2, 211
Chicka Hanka Gr. 8, F-15
Children, Go Where I Send Thee Gr. 3, 392
*Choo-Choo Joubert* Gr. 3, 51
Circle Round the Zero Gr. K, 293
Come and Go with Me to That Land Gr. 5, 390
*Country Blues* Gr. 5, 225
Dancin' in the Street Gr. 5, 363
*Dancin' in the Street* Gr. 5, 360
Do, Lord Gr. 3, 164
*Don't Get Around Much Anymore* Gr. 1, 33
Down by the Riverside Gr. 5, 256
Down by the Riverside Gr. 8, G-8
Down, Down, Baby Gr. 2, 32
Draw Me a Bucket of Water Gr. 3, 124
Dry Bones Gr. 4, 162
*Elite Syncopations* Gr. 6, 159
*Entertainer, The* Gr. 2, 76
*Ev'ry Time I Feel the Spirit* Gr. 3, 248
Ev'ry Time I Feel the Spirit Gr. 5, 242
*Ev'ry Time I Feel the Spirit* Gr. 7, C-40
*Everyday People* Gr. 5, 389
*Everyday People* Gr. 7, G-16
Ezekiel Saw the Wheel Gr. 6, 379
Flat Foot Floogee, The Gr. 3, 160
*Flat Foot Floogee, The* Gr. 3, 158
Flip, Flop and Fly Gr. 7, I-32
*Flip, Flop and Fly* Gr. 7, F-15
Follow the Drinkin' Gourd Gr. 4, 266
For Children Safe and Strong Gr. 5, 484
Free at Last Gr. 2, 396
Free at Last Gr. 6, 468
Get on Board Gr. K, 89
*Get on Board* Gr. K, 89
Gift to Share, A Gr. 6, 393
Glory, Glory, Hallelujah Gr. 6, 52
*Glory, Glory, Hallelujah* Gr. 6, 54
*Glory, Glory, Hallelujah* Gr. 8, B-14
Go Around the Corn, Sally Gr. 2, 12
Go Down, Moses Gr. 5, 190
*Go Down, Moses* Gr. 7, G-10
*Go, Tell It on the Mountain* Gr. 3, 393º
God Bless the Child Gr. 7, B-27
Gonna Ride Up in the Chariot Gr. 4, 20
*Good Golly, Miss Molly* Gr. 8, E-10
Good Mornin', Blues Gr. 2, 52
Good Mornin', Blues Gr. 5, 224

Goodbye, Ev'rybody (Farewell Shout)  Gr. 7, D-2
Goodbye, Julie  Gr. 8, E-2
Gospel Train, The  Gr. 6, 398
Great Day  Gr. 3, 58
Habari Gani  Gr. 3, 404
Had to Get Up This Mornin' Soon  Gr. 3, 114
Hambone  Gr. 7, D-3
Harambee  Gr. 4, 434
Harriet Tubman  Gr. 4, 269
He's Got the Whole World in His Hands  Gr. 3, 230
*He's Got the Whole World in His Hands*  Gr. 3, 249
He's Got the Whole World in His Hands  Gr. 7, I-36
Head, Shoulders, Baby  Gr. 1, 82
Heri za Kwanzaa  Gr. 5, 476
Hit Me with a Hot Note and Watch Me Bounce  Gr. 6, 112
Hold My Mule  Gr. 1, ºº-14
Hush, Hush  Gr. 3, 162
I Am But a Small Voice  Gr. 6, 446
I Got Shoes  Gr. 2, 242
I Love Peanuts  Gr. 1, 162
*I Love Peanuts*  Gr. 1, 163
I Love Peanuts  Gr. 7, E-20
I Wish I Knew How It Would Feel to Be Free  Gr. 6, 470
*I Wish I Knew How It Would Feel To Be Free*  Gr. 6, 470
I'll Fly Away  Gr. 8, I-43
*I'll Fly Away*  Gr. 8, I -43
I'm Gonna Sing  Gr. 4, 33
I'm on My Way  Gr. 3, 76
I'm on My Way  Gr. 7, A-15
If You're Happy  Gr. K, 94
It Don't Mean a Thing (If It Ain't Got That Swing)  Gr. 5, 336
*It Don't Mean a Thing if It Ain't Got that Swing*  Gr. 6, 386
Joe Turner Blues  Gr. 4, 56
Johnny Mister Brown  Gr. K, 37
*Jonah*  Gr. 6, 235
Joshua Fought the Battle of Jericho  Gr. 5, 100
Joshua Fought the Battle of Jericho  Gr. 8, E-18
Joy of Kwanzaa, The  Gr. 6, 462
Juba  Gr. K, 13
*Juba*  Gr. K, 12
Jump That Jody  Gr. K, 212
Just a Snap-Happy Blues  Gr. 6, 388
Just from the Kitchen  Gr. K, 55
Keep Your Eyes on the Prize  Gr. 3, 408
Keep Your Eyes on the Prize  Gr. 8, E-16
*Key to the Highway*  Gr. 6, 243
Key to the Highway  Gr. 6, 243
Key to the Highway  Gr. 8, F-29

Key to the Highway  Gr. 8, F-28
Kid Like Me, A (speech piece)  Gr. 2, 394
Kwanzaa Carol, A  Gr. 2, 392
Let's Get the Rhythm of the Band  Gr. 3, 84
Let's Get the Rhythm of the Band  Gr. 7, E-29
Let's Go Barefoot (poem)  Gr. 1, 440
*Lifetime*  Gr. 7, B-39
Lift Ev'ry Voice and Sing  Gr. 5, 482
Lift Ev'ry Voice and Sing  Gr. 8, I-54
Little David  Gr. 1, 232
Little David, Play on Your Harp  Gr. 4, 394
*Little David, Play on Your Harp*  Gr. 4, 395
Little Johnny Brown  Gr. 3, 313
*Little Pearls, The*  Gr. K, 215
Little Red Caboose  Gr. K, 229
*Little Red Caboose*  Gr. K, 228
Martin Luther King  Gr. 1, 434
Mary Came a-Running  Gr. K, 294
Michael, Row the Boat Ashore  Gr. 2, 18
Midnight Special, The  Gr. 7, F-23
Miss Mary Mack  Gr. 2, 42
Miss Susie Anna Sue  Gr. K, 242
Mister Rabbit  Gr. K, 128
*My Father's House (Gospel Style)*  Gr. 2, 24
My Mama's Calling Me  Gr. 1, 260
Nana, Thread Needle  Gr. 1, 38
*Nobody Knows the Trouble I've Seen*  Gr. 3, 249
Now Let Me Fly  Gr. 3, 178
Now's the Time  Gr. 5, 445
*Now's the Time*  Gr. 5, 451
Oh, Freedom  Gr. 5, 392
Oh, Freedom  Gr. 7, G-30
*Oh, Freedom and Come and Go with Me*  Gr. 5, 394
Oh, Won't You Sit Down  Gr. 3, 28
Old House, Tear It Down!  Gr. 4, 178
One Morning Soon  Gr. 3, 68
Over My Head  Gr. 4, 118
Over My Head  Gr. 7, G- 9
*Pay Me*  Gr. 7, F-5
Pay Me My Money Down  Gr. 4, 38
*Pay Me My Money Down*  Gr. 4, 39
Pay Me My Money Down  Gr. 7, I-46
Peace Like a River  Gr. 3, 246
Peace Like a River  Gr. 6, 190
Polly Wee  Gr. K, 119
*Queen's Suite, The, "Sunset and the Mocking Bird"*  Gr. 8, E-10

*Railroad Bill*  Gr. 8, F-14
Rise Up, Shepherd, and Follow  Gr. 5, 471
*Rise Up, Shepherd, and Follow*  Gr. 5, 470
Rosie, Darling Rosie  Gr. 2, 215
Run! Run! Hide!  Gr. 6, 340
Same Train  Gr. 2, 164
*Scott Joplin's New Rag*  Gr. 5, 335
See the Children Playin'  Gr. 4, 107
Shanghai Chicken  Gr. 1, 140
Shoo, Turkey  Gr. 1, 104
Shortnin' Bread  Gr. 1, 57
Shortnin' Bread  Gr. 7, F-27
Sing About Martin  Gr. K, 321
*Sister Rosa*  Gr. 3, 411
Somebody's Knockin' at Your Door  Gr. 4, 53
*Sometimes I Feel Like a Motherless Child*  Gr. 5, 193
Sometimes I Feel Like a Motherless Child  Gr. 6, 241
*Soulville*  Gr. 7, B-17
*St. Louis Blues*  Gr. 4, 57
*St. Louis Blues*  Gr. 5, 353
St. Louis Blues  Gr. 5, 352
*Standin' in the Need of Prayer*  Gr. 5, 103
*Study War No More*  Gr. 7, C-40
Sun Gonna Shine  Gr. 6, 242
*Sun Gonna Shine*  Gr. 7, F-14
*Swing Low, Sweet Chariot*  Gr. 6, 234
Swing Low, Sweet Chariot  Gr. 7, C-41
*Take the "A" Train*  Gr. 8, C-42
Take Your Feet Out 'the Sand  Gr. K, 231
*Tears of a Clown, The*  Gr. 7, B-39
There Is Love Somewhere  Gr. 6, 318
*This Little Light of Mine*  Gr. 2, 241
This Little Light of Mine  Gr. 6, 232
This Train  Gr. 5, 26
Together in Unity  Gr. K, 320
Train Is A-Comin'  Gr. 3, 48
*Traveling Shoes*  Gr. 3, 248
Twelve Gates to the City  Gr. 5, 280
Ujima  Gr. 1, 430
Wade in the Water  Gr. 4, 268
Wade in the Water  Gr. 8, I-64
Wake Me, Shake Me  Gr. 1, 278
Walk in Jerusalem  Gr. 4, 100
Walk Together, Children  Gr. 3, 146
*Walkin' Blues*  Gr. 5, 227
Way Down in the Schoolyard  Gr. 2, 50

*Way Down Yonder in the Brickyard* Gr. 2, 51
We Shall Not Be Moved Gr. 4, 437
We Shall Overcome Gr. 4, 326
*We Shall Overcome* Gr. 5, 485
*What Kind of Land?* Gr. 4, 327
*When a Man's a Long Way from Home* Gr. 2, 53
When the Saints Go Marching In Gr. 2, 178
*When the Saints Go Marching In* Gr. 2, 179
When the Train Comes Along Gr. 1, 300
Woke Up This Morning Gr. 5, 288
Worried Man Blues Gr. 6, 371
Yonder Come Day Gr. 8, I-68

**AMERICA** *For American selections, see African American; Caribbean Islands: Puerto Rico; Native American; United States; Genre/Style: American.*

**AMERICAN** *For American selections, see African American; Caribbean Islands: Puerto Rico; Native American; United States; Genre/Style: American.*

**ARGENTINA** *See South America.*

**ARMENIA**
Gakavik Gr. 4, 14

**ASIA** *See China, India, Japan, Southeast Asia, Turkey.*

**AUSTRALIA**
*Brolga One* Gr. 4, 36
Kookaburra Gr. 4, 186
*Shepherd's Hey, No. 1* Gr. 7, C-37
*Shepherd's Hey, No. 2* Gr. 7, C-37
*Shepherd's Hey, No. 3* Gr. 7, C-37
Tie Me Kangaroo Down, Sport Gr. 4, 37
**Aboriginee**
 Brolga Gr. 6, 271
 *Dharpa, "Tree"* Gr. 8, B-38
 *Gapu* Gr. 8, B-10
 *Gapu* Gr. 8, B-38

**AUSTRIA**
*Blue Danube, The, Op. 314* Gr. 6, 192
*Die forelle* Gr. 7, C-20
*Magic Flute, The, "Queen of the Night Aria"* Gr. 7, C-31

*Marche Militaire, Op. 51, No. 1* Gr. 6, 17
Still, Still, Still Gr. 5, 468
*String Quartet in D Major, Op. 64, No. 5, "The Lark," Allegro moderato* Gr. 7, C-15
*Symphony No. 47 in G Major, "Menuet"* Gr. 7, C-15

**BOLIVIA** *See South America.*

**BULGARIA**
*Byala stala* Gr. 8, B-13
*Ghel moma* Gr. 4, 31

**BRAZIL** *See South America.*

**CAMBODIA** *See Southeast Asia.*

**CANADA**
Ah! Les Jolis Papillons Gr. 1, 362
*Apu Min'Tan* Gr. 8, D-21
*Drift* Gr. 8, B-42
Frog Music Gr. 4, 200
*Les saluts* Gr. 1, 361
**Newfoundland**
 Bonavist' Harbour Gr. 3, 294
 Greenland Whale Fishery, The Gr. 5, 230

**CARIBBEAN ISLANDS**
*Brisad del Zulia* Gr. 4, 19
By the Waters of Babylon Gr. 6, 311
*Caribbean Leaps* Gr. K, 148
*Eine kleine Nachtmusik (calypso)* Gr. 4, 41
Four White Horses Gr. 3, 304
*Jump in the Line* Gr. 4, 117
Limbo Like Me Gr. 4, 18
Missy-La, Massa-La Gr. 4, 188
*Panamam tombé* Gr. 7, D-18
Shake the Papaya Down Gr. 4, 378
*Somebody* Gr. 4, 41
Three Little Birds Gr. 8, F-7
Turn the World Around Gr. 4, 114
Wings of a Dove Gr. 4, 318
**Bahamas**
 Wind Blew East, The Gr. 1, 64
**Cuba**
 *Ayer, "Yesterday"* Gr. 6, 266
 Cuban Rumba Ensemble Gr. 7, D-7
 ¿Dónde lo escondí? Gr. K, 209
 *El dulcerito llego, "The Sweets Vendor Is Here"* Gr. K, 124
 *Elegguá* Gr. 8, D-13
 *Guaguancó pá las tumbadoras* Gr. 7, D-9

Luna lunera (speech piece) Gr. K, 90
*Má Teodora* Gr. 6, 301
*Mambo UK* Gr. 7, D-9
*Night in Tunisia, A* Gr. 4, 35
*Saludo de Matanzas* Gr. 5, 17
Sonando Gr. 4, 34
Tic, tac Gr. 1, 252
Uno, dos, y tres Gr. 5, 427
Vamos a hacer la ronda Gr. K, 124
**Dominica**
 *Éliza Kongo* Gr. 5, 14
 *Mwen boyko samba* Gr. 4, 319
**Haiti**
 Bonga Gr. K, 78
 Deau-deau, ti pitit maman Gr. 2, 306
 *Retounen* Gr. 8, B-17
**Jamaica**
 Bam, chi, chi, bam Gr. K, 109
 Chrismus a Come Gr. 3, 396
 *Day-O!* Gr. 5, 21
 Day-O! (Banana Boat Loader's Song) Gr. 5, 18
 Give a Little Love Gr. 6, 140
 Hi-Dee-Roon Gr. K, 10
 Hosanna, Me Build a House Gr. 5, 132
 *John B. Sails* Gr. K, 11
 Kingston Market Gr. 3, 90
 Linstead Market Gr. 5, 241
 Lost My Gold Ring Gr. 6, 158
 Mango Walk Gr. 5, 200
 Nanny Goat Gr. K, 161
 *Rainbow in the Sky* Gr. 7, B-35
 *Reggae Is Now* Gr. 6, 143
 Three Little Birds Gr. 4, 320
**Nevis**
 *A-Cling, A-Cling* Gr. 4, 190
**Puerto Rico**
 Aguinaldo Gr. 3, 402
 *Bembe de Plena* Gr. 8, D-18
 *Bomba te traigo yo* Gr. 8, B-3
 Cheki, morena Gr. 2, 180
 Cheki, morena Gr. 7, I-16
 Corta la caña Gr. 6, 364
 *Danzas Puertorriqueñas, "Vano Empeno"* Gr. 7, E-13
 El coquí Gr. 2, 292
 El florón Gr. 2, 246
 El zapatero Gr. 1, 298
 Habemos llegado Gr. 6, 172
 La borinqueña Gr. 8, D-19
 La calle ancha Gr. 3, 297
 La paloma se fué Gr. 6, 51
 Las Navidades Gr. 5, 472
 Los pollitos Gr. K, 166
 Los reyes de Oriente Gr. 5, 480
 Los reyes de Oriente Gr. 8, I-58
 Mi cuerpo hace música Gr. K, 106
 *Pasodoble* Gr. 7, F-11

¡Qué bonita bandera! Gr. 5, 294
¡Qué llueva! Gr. K, 81
Si me dan pasteles Gr. 1, 432
*Zoila* Gr. 8, D-18
**Trinidad**
Boomin' Bamboo Ensemble
Gr. 7, D-22
Boysie Gr. 2, 195
*Fire Brigade Water the Road*
Gr. 7, D-22
*Gidden Riddum* Gr. 6, 299
Gypsy in the Moonlight Gr. 3, 12
*Hard Times* Gr. 1, 194
Hush Up the Baby Gr. K, 222
*Jump for Joy* Gr. 7, D-20
*Love You Forever* Gr. 8, B-23
Mister Ram Goat-O Gr. 3, 54
*Poco, Le' Me 'Lone* Gr. 3, 300
*Raindrops* Gr. 7, D-23
*Shashee* Gr. K, 109
Water Come a Me Eye
Gr. 6, 300
**West Indies**
Cookie Gr. 2, 172
Mary Ann Gr. 6, 180
Mary Ann Gr. K, 253
'Round and 'Round Gr. 1, 148

**CELTIC**
How Can I Keep from Singing?
Gr. 4, 261
*How Can I Keep from Singing?*
Gr. 4, 260

**CENTRAL AMERICA**
Piñon, pirulín Gr. 2, 174
**Costa Rica**
El sapito Gr. 3, 336
Los pececitos Gr. 1, 178
Mariposita Gr. 2, 156
**El Salvador**
¡Jeu! ¡Jeu! Gr. 1, 216
**Guatemala**
*San Miguel Jolonicapan*
Gr. 8, D-16
Vamos a la mar Gr. 3, 226
**Nicaragua**
Banana Gr. 2, 114

**CHILE** *See South America.*

**CHINA** *See also Taiwan.*
*Birds in the Forest* Gr. 4, 315
*Bumper Harvest Celebration*
Gr. 4, 337
Cha yang wu Gr. 1, 90
Diou shou juan'er Gr. 2, 277
*Drift* Gr. 8, B-7
Ee jer ha ba go Gr. K, 133
Feng yang hua gu Gr. 4, 313
*Huagu ge, "Flower Drum Song"*
Gr. 8, D-27

Hui jia qü Gr. 2, 158
*Lian xi qu (étude)* Gr. 4, 157
Meng Jian Nu Gr. 5, 194
*Mido Mountain* Gr. 8, B-42
*Moon Mirrored in the Pool, The*
Gr. 6, 103
News of Home Gr. 4, 336
Niu lang zhi nü Gr. 4, 335
Pai pi qiu Gr. 1, 324
*Seven Tunes Heard in China,*
*"Guessing Song"* Gr. 7, C-3
Shu ha mo Gr. 3, 276
Traveler's Song Gr. 4, 336
*Winter Birds Flying over the*
*Water* Gr. 1, 91
*Wu long* Gr. 4, 156
Xiao Gr. 4, 314
Xiao yin chuan Gr. 2, 14
Yüe liang wan wan Gr. 5, 314
**Hong Kong**
*Colours of the World* Gr. 6, 271
Yü guang guang Gr. 6, 60
**Mongolia**
*Mongolian Long Song*
Gr. 8, B-14
**Taiwan**
Hwa yuan li-de young wa wa
Gr. 3, 102
Jasmine Flowers Gr. 5, 316
Lahk gei mohlee Gr. 5, 317
*Taiwan Suite, "Lantern*
*Festival"* Gr. 3, 104
Yang wa wa Gr. K, 162
**Tibet**
*Gi pai pa yul chola* Gr. 8, B-40
*Kui.Kyon.pan* Gr. 6, 25

**COLOMBIA** *See South America.*

**CUBA** *See Caribbean Islands.*

**CZECH**
Let Us Sing Together Gr. 6, 156
*Ma Vlast (My Fatherland), "Vltava*
*(The Moldau)"* Gr. 7, C-33
*Moravian Dances, "Kalamajka"*
Gr. 3, 79
*Slavonic Dance, Op. 46, No. 1,*
*"Presto"* Gr. 1, 6
*Slavonic Dance, "Presto"*
Gr. 4, 227

**DENMARK**
Der sad to katte Gr. 2, 300
Vil du? Gr. 1, 92

**ECUADOR** *See South America.*

**ENGLAND**
*Abbots Bromley Horn Dance*
Gr. 7, C-24

Ah, Poor Bird Gr. 4, 196
Aiken Drum Gr. 1, 398
*Baa-Baa Black Sheep* Gr. K, 102
Barb'ry Allen Gr. 6, 44
*Beggar's Opera, The, "Constant*
*Billy"* Gr. 7, C-24
Birthday Gr. 6, 90
Blow the Wind Southerly
Gr. 5, 178
Chairs to Mend Gr. 4, 149
Cobbler, Cobbler (speech piece)
Gr. 1, 299
*Cold and Frosty Morning*
Gr. 2, 139
*Danses Populaires Francaises,*
*"Branle Double, Branle Simple"*
Gr. 7, C-25
*Fantasia on the Dargason, Op. 28,*
*No. 2, "Suite in F," Movement*
*4* Gr. 7, C-3
*Farmer in the Dell* Gr. K, 233
Fly and the Bumblebee, The
Gr. 1, 384
*Four Scottish Dances, Op. 59,*
*"Allegretto"* Gr. 6, 43
Good King Wenceslas Gr. 6, 460
Greensleeves Gr. 6, 49
Haul Away, Joe Gr. 4, 13
Hey, Diddle, Diddle Gr. K, 246
*Hey, Diddle, Diddle* Gr. K, 247
Hey, Ho! Nobody Home Gr. 6, 28
Hickory, Dickory, Dare (speech
piece) Gr. K, 20
Higglety, Pigglety, Pop! Gr. K, 22
Hot Cross Buns (Version 1)
Gr. 3, 218
Hot Cross Buns (Version 2)
Gr. 3, 221
How Many Miles to Babylon?
Gr. 2, 128
*Humpty Dumpty* Gr. K, 23
Humpty Dumpty Gr. K, 47
I Saw Three Ships Gr. 1, 426
I Vow to You, My Country
Gr. 5, 418
Kangaroo Song, The Gr. K, 44
Leatherwing Bat Gr. 2, 303
London Bridge Gr. K, 244
Merry Modal Christmas, A
Gr. 4, 411
Morning Is Come Gr. 3, 128
*Old King Cole* Gr. K, 245
Oliver Twist Gr. K, 138
One, Two, Three, Four, Five
(rhyme) Gr. 1, 67
*Penny Lane* Gr. 6, 257
*Planets, The, Op. 32, "Jupiter"*
Gr. 1, 405
Rig-a-Jig-Jig Gr. K, 99
*Saqian da dhol* Gr. 8, B-22
Scarborough Fair Gr. 6, 95
*Search for the Hero* Gr. 7, G-5

**(Folk, Traditional, and Regional Selections, continued)**

Sellenger's Round  Gr. 6, 44

Shepherd's Hey Sampler
Gr. 7, C-37

Six Metamorphoses After Ovid,
Op. 49, "Bacchus"  Gr. 7, C-13

Soldier, Soldier  Gr. 4, 11

Suite in F, Op. 28b, No. 2,
"Fantasia on the Dargason,"
Movement 4  Gr. 7, C-36

Suite No. 2 in F, Op. 28b,
Movement 1, "March"
Gr. 6, 139

Sumer Is Icumen In  Gr. 5, 35

Suo gan  Gr. 1, 309

There's a Place  Gr. 5, 210

This Old Man  Gr. 3, 152

Tree in the Wood, The  Gr. 2, 360

Twelve Days of Christmas, The
Gr. 4, 430

Two Dances for Three
Xylophones, "Hornpipe and
Jig"  Gr. 8, D-17

Water Is Wide, The  Gr. 6, 228

We Wish You a Merry Christmas
Gr. 3, 395

## FINLAND

Bambodansarna  Gr. 8, B-20

Eriskummainen kantele
Gr. 5, 199

Finlandia  Gr. 6, 78

Kerenski  Gr. 6, 78

This Is My Song  Gr. 6, 77

This Is My Song  Gr. 6, 76

Vem kan segla?  Gr. 6, 417

## FRANCE

Ahi! Amours  Gr. 8, C-4

Alle psallite cum luya  Gr. 7, C-5

Alphabet Song  Gr. K, 280

Au clair de la lune  Gr. 3, 18

Bonjour, mes amis  Gr. 1, 316

Ding Dong! Merrily on High
Gr. 6, 427

Fais dodo  Gr. K, 158

Frère Jacques  Gr. 3, 113

Frère Jacques  Gr. 2, 125

La mer, "Jeux de vagues"
Gr. 7, C-39

Les pêcheurs des perles, "Au fond
du temple saint"  Gr. 7, C-30

Les petites marionettes  Gr. K, 237

Merry Modal Christmas, A
Gr. 4, 411

Mon papa  Gr. 2, 280

O tocius Asie gloria, "Oh, Glory of
All Asia"  Gr. 8, C-4

Sonata for Clarinet and Piano,
Op. 167, "Allegro animato,"
Movement 2  Gr. 7, C-12

Three Times By She Passes (speech
piece) Gr. K, 125

Un, deux, trois  Gr. 2, 198

Voiles  Gr. 7, C-39

## GERMANY

Alle meine Entchen  Gr. 1, 98

Brandenburg Concerto No. 2,
Movement 3 Allegro Assai
Gr. 7, C-8

Brandenburg Concerto No. 2, "
Allegro Assai," Movement 3
Gr. 7, C-3

Cantata No. 140 (as performed
by American Bach Solosists),
"Wachet auf, ruft uns die
Stimme," Movement 4
Gr. 7, C-9

Cantata No. 140 (as performed by
The Swingle Singers), "Wachet
auf, ruft uns die Stimme,"
Movement 4  Gr. 7, C-10

Chorale Prelude for Organ, BWV
645, "Wachet auf, ruft uns die
Stimme "  Gr. 7, C-9

Concerto for Trumpet and
Orchestra in E-flat Major,
Rondo: Allegro Molto
Gr. 1, 256

Ein Männlein steht im Walde
Gr. 2, 90

Gaudeamus Igitur  Gr. 8, C-20

Hänsel und Gretel, "Ein Männlein
steht im Walde"  Gr. 2, 91

Himmel und Erde  Gr. 5, 94

Liebe ist ein Ring  Gr. 4, 193

O ignis spiritus Paracliti
Gr. 7, C-4

O ignis spiritus Paracliti
Gr. 7, C-3

O Laufet, ihr Hirten  Gr. 2, 384

Oh, How Lovely Is the Evening
Gr. 4, 217

Sonata in A Minor, "Allegro"
Gr. 7, C-12

Sonata in C-sharp Minor, Op. 27,
No. 2, "Moonlight," Movement
1  Gr. 7, C-19

Sonata in F Major for Violin and
Piano, Op. 24, No. 5, "Spring,"
Movement 3  Gr. 7, C-19

Sonata in G Minor, Op. 1, No. 1,
Movement 2  Gr. 7, C-12

Stille Nacht  Gr. 7, I-54

Suite in E-flat Major for Cello, S.
1010, "Gigue"  Gr. 7, C-11

Symphony No. 5 in C Minor, Op.
67, Movement 1  Gr. 7, C-16

Symphony No. 5 in C Minor, Op.
67, Movement 4  Gr. 7, C-18

Symphony No. 5 in C Minor, Op.
67, Movement 1  Gr. 7, C-3

Toccata and Fugue in D Minor
Gr. 7, E-25

Valentine Dance  Gr. 1, 437

Wachet auf, ruft uns die
Stimme, BWV 140, "Cantata,"
Movement 4  Gr. 7, C-9

Was kommt dort von der Höh'?
Gr. 8, C-21

Well-Tempered Clavier, Book
1, "Prelude and Fugue in C
Minor"  Gr. 7, E-16

Who Has Seen the Wind?
Gr. 2, 324

Widmung, Op. 25, No. 1
Gr. 7, C-20

Wir hatten gebauet  Gr. 8, C-21

## GREECE

Istanbul Coffee House (Kafe neio)
Gr. 8, B-34

Perná, perná, i mélissá  Gr. K, 264

Stalia, stalia  Gr. 8, B-21

## HUNGARY

Cirmos cica  Gr. 1, 130

Concerto for Viola and Orchestra,
Movement 3  Gr. 7, C-35

Dances of Galanta  Gr. 7, C-34

Ég a gyertya  Gr. K, 96

Erdö, erdö de magos  Gr. 3, 182

Fifteen Hungarian Peasant Songs
Gr. 7, C-35

Fifteen Hungarian Peasant Songs,
No. 7, "Old Dance Times,"
Allegro  Gr. 7, C-35

Fifteen Hungarian Peasant Songs,
No. 14, "Old Dance Times
– Allegro"  Gr. 7, C-35

Fifteen Hungarian Peasant Songs,
No. 10, "Old Dance Times –
L'istesso Tempo (Quasi Trio)"
Gr. 7, C-35

Fifteen Hungarian Peasant Songs,
No. 13, "Old Dance Times –
Poco Più Vivo. Allegretto"
Gr. 7, C-35

Hungarian Rhapsody No. 2
in C sharp Minor, S. 244
Gr. 7, E-17

Intermezzo, "Háry János Suite,"
Movement 5  Gr. 7, C-34

La campanella, No. 3  Gr. 7, C-3

Little Spider  Gr. K, 93

Lullaby (poem)  Gr. 1, 208

New Hungarian Folk Song
Gr. 6, 196

Ten Easy Pieces, "Bear Dance"
Gr. 3, 172

Transcendental Etude, No. 3 in G-
sharp Minor, "La Campanella"
Gr. 7, C-23

## India

*Bairagi* Gr. 8, B-10
*Bombay Dreams* Gr. 8, B-35
*Charukeshi* Gr. 4, 311
*Dham dhamak dham samelu* Gr. 6, 305
*Maha ganapathim* Gr. 6, 305
*Máru-bihág* Gr. 6, 304
*Neend koyi* Gr. 8, B-43
*Quality of Seven, A* Gr. 8, B-6
*Rag puria kalyan-gat in tintal* Gr. 4, 192
Ragupati Ragava Raja Ram Gr. 5, 321
*Shri Ram, jai Ram* Gr. 4, 311
*Sindhi-Bhairavi* Gr. 5, 320
*Tabla Solo* Gr. 8, B-32
*Terian gulabi buliyam* Gr. 8, B-26
*Wedding Qawwali* Gr. 8, B-35

## Indonesia *See Southeast Asia.*

## Iran

*Avaz-e dashti* Gr. 8, B-42
Mubärak Gr. 3, 282

## Ireland

Bard of Armagh, The Gr. 4, 296
*Blower's Daughter, The* Gr. 8, B-13
Connemara Lullaby Gr. 5, 232
*Crowley's Reel* Gr. 4, 297
*Crowley's/Jackson's* Gr. 4, 298
*Crowley's/Jackson's* Gr. 8, B-7
*Dúlamán* Gr. 4, 299
*Eanáir* Gr. 8, B-10
*Einini* Gr. 4, 391
*Faerie Stories* Gr. 8, B-5
*Flowing Bowl, The* Gr. 8, B-29
*Geese in the Bog, The* Gr. 8, B-9
*Highway to Kilkenny* Gr. 6, 43
*Irish Tune from County Derry* Gr. 4, 49
*Kerry Dance, The* Gr. 5, 28
*Lord of the Dance Medley* Gr. 6, 326
*MacAllistrum's March-Mairseail Alasdroim* Gr. 4, 297
*Mill Pond, The* Gr. 8, B-8
*O'Sullivan's March* Gr. 5, 157
Oh, Danny Boy Gr. 4, 48
*Paddy Whack* Gr. 6, 327
Pat Works on the Railway Gr. 5, 182
*Planxty Madame Maxwell* Gr. K, 134
*Roddy McCaulay* Gr. 3, 292
*She Is Like the Swallow* Gr. 8, B-12
*Siuil á ruin* Gr. 8, B-13
St. Patrick Was a Gentleman Gr. 3, 290

*Tommy Peoples* Gr. 8, B-20
### Gaelic
Morning Has Broken Gr. 5, 28

## Israeli/Jewish/Hebrew

Achshav Gr. 2, 64
Alumot Gr. 6, 306
Artsa alinu Gr. 3, 285
Ayliluli, num tsipor Gr. 1, 204
Bereleh Gr. K, 151
Chag Purim Gr. 1, 438
Chanukah, Chanukah Gr. 1, 420
Chanukah Games Gr. 3, 389
Chanukah Is Here! Gr. 2, 382
Chanukiyah li yesh Gr. 1, 421
Dayenu Gr. 4, 439
*Dreydl Song, The* Gr. 3, 391
Dundai Gr. 5, 106
*Fantasy for Chanukah* Gr. 1, 421
*Gimpel the Fool* Gr. 8, B-8
Hanuka, Hanuka Gr. 3, 390
Hanuka, Hanuka Gr. 8, I-36
Hashkediya Gr. 3, 206
Hava nagila Gr. 6, 153
Hava nashira Gr. 6, 82
Hevenu shalom aleichem Gr. 3, 378
Hine mah tov Gr. 5, 430
Kum bachur atzel Gr. 3, 138
Lo yisa Gr. 6, 130
My Dreydl Gr. K, 314
Ner li Gr. 2, 383
Ocho kandelikas Gr. 4, 429
Oy, Hanuka Gr. 5, 464
Oy, Hanuka Gr. 7, I-44
Perot Gr. 2, 378
S'vivon Gr. 6, 452
Sh'ney dubim Gr. K, 269
Shalom aleichem Gr. 6, 409
Shir l'shalom Gr. 4, 419
*Slow Hora/Freylekhs* Gr. 8, B-25
Tumba Gr. 5, 161
Tzena, tzena Gr. 5, 298
*Tzlil Zugim* Gr. 3, 139
Uga uga uga Gr. K, 305
*Ve'David Y'Fey Enayiam* Gr. 4, 317
Yesh lanu taish Gr. 1, 182
Yibane amenu Gr. 4, 316
Zum gali gali Gr. 5, 400

## Italy

*Caprice No. 1 in E Major* Gr. 7, C-22
*Danza* Gr. 7, C-7
*Il trovatore, "Anvil Chorus"* Gr. 6, 25
Like a Bird Gr. 6, 167
*Rigoletto, "Bella figlia dell' amore"* Gr. 7, C-3
*Rigoletto, "Bella figlia dell'amore"* Gr. 7, C-29

*Saltarello detto Trivella* Gr. 7, C-6
*Tosca, "Vissi d'arte"* Gr. 7, C-31
Vive l'amour Gr. 6, 176
*Viva la musica* Gr. 5, 95

## Japan

*Akita kusakari uta* Gr. 8, B-13
Amefuri Gr. 1, 144
Bucket O'Taiko Ensemble Gr. 7, D-17
Hama chi dori Gr. 3, 330
*Hannya-Shingyo* Gr. 7, C-5
Haru ga kita Gr. 2, 401
*Harukoma, "Spring Horse Dance"* Gr. 1, 145
Hato popo Gr. 1, 186
Hitotsu toya Gr. 5, 478
House of Spring Gr. 4, 309
I Like You Gr. 6, 7
Ichi-gatsu tsuitachi Gr. 3, 406
Ichi-gatsu tsuitachi Gr. 7, I-40
Jan ken pon Gr. 3, 302
Kaeru no uta Gr. K, 183
Kuma san Gr. K, 40
*Lion* Gr. 6, 303
*Memories of the Seashore* Gr. 3, 150
*Nanafushi* Gr. 7, D-16
O ma washi Gr. K, 13
Osamu kosamu Gr. 4, 96
Rinsho, rinsho Gr. K, 285
Rolling Rice Cake, The (story) Gr. 1, 91
Sakura Gr. 4, 308
*Shika no Tone* Gr. 5, 112
Tanabata-sama Gr. 2, 336
Tsuki Gr. 4, 25
Usagi Gr. 1, 396
*Yamaji* Gr. 3, 407
*Yaudachi* Gr. 5, 156
### Okinawa
Asadoya Gr. 6, 303

## Korea

Arirang Gr. 5, 25
Doong gul ge Gr. 3, 134
*Doraji* Gr. 4, 175
Doraji Gr. 4, 174
Ha'kyo jong Gr. 2, 135
*Kayagum pyongch'ang-sae t'aryug* Gr. 3, 137
*Kayagum pyongch'ang-sae t'aryug* Gr. 8, B-13
Sailboat in the Sky Gr. 4, 374
*Sanjo* Gr. 4, 175

## Ladino

Ocho kandelikas Gr. 4, 429

**(Folk, Traditional, and Regional Selections, continued)**

LAOS *See Southeast Asia.*

## LATIN AMERICA

Ambos a dos  Gr. 3, 20
Buenos días  Gr. 1, 13
Canción de cuna  Gr. 4, 144
Cantando mentiras  Gr. 4, 146
*Conga Kings Grand Finale*
   Gr. 5, 156
Debajo el botón  Gr. 1, 210
Duérmete, mi niño  Gr. 1, 292
El barquito  Gr. 3, 358
La pulga de San José  Gr. 3, 40
Las horas  Gr. 1, 246
Naranja dulce  Gr. 2, 97
*Picadillo*  Gr. 3, 361
Pin Pon  Gr. 1, 146
Riqui rán  Gr. 1, 48
Riqui rán  Gr. 1, 48
Riqui rán  Gr. 4, 66

## MEXICO

A la rurru niño  Gr. K, 180
Adelita  Gr. 5, 50
Al quebrar la piñata  Gr. 4, 432
Allá en la fuente  Gr. 2, 92
Así es mi tierra  Gr. 6, 172
Canción Mixteca  Gr. 5, 326
Chiapanecas  Gr. 5, 92
Cielito lindo  Gr. 4, 270
Cielito lindo  Gr. 7, I-20
*Contigo otra vez*  Gr. 7, B-32
Corrido de Kansas  Gr. 4, 274
Counting Song  Gr. 1, 253
De colores  Gr. 5, 90
Don Gato  Gr. 3, 352
El borrego  Gr. 4, 242
El chocolate  Gr. 1, 380
El Jarabe Tapatío  Gr. K, 215
*El mariachi*  Gr. 4, 303
El payo  Gr. 6, 145
El rancho grande  Gr. 4, 215
El rancho grande  Gr. 8, I-22
*El siquisirí*  Gr. 4, 273
El tambor  Gr. 2, 274
*El tilingo lingo*  Gr. 2, 176
*Good Morning, Aztlán*  Gr. 7, B-7
*Happy Mariachi Band, "Mariachi alegre"*  Gr. 1, 210
*Jarabe tapatío*  Gr. 7, I-7
Juan pirulero  Gr. K, 215
*La bamba*  Gr. 5, 130
La ciudad de Juaja  Gr. 5, 58
La golondrina  Gr. 8, I-50
La Jesusita  Gr. 5, 322
La piñata  Gr. 3, 399
La raspa  Gr. 4, 302
La víbora  Gr. 1, 322
Laredo  Gr. 5, 10

*Las copetonas*  Gr. 7, B-33
Las mañanitas  Gr. 6, 481
*Las mañanitas*  Gr. K, 325
Las velitas  Gr. 5, 147
*Los machetes*  Gr. 8, I-22
Los niños en España cantan
   Gr. 4, 197
*Los pollitos*  Gr. K, 166
*Mexican Hat Dance*  Gr. K, 214
My Song  Gr. 4, 305
No quiero plata  Gr. 1, 424
Pon, pon, pon  Gr. K, 50
Sierra Morena  Gr. 3, 296
Sol, solecito  Gr. 1, 367
*Toccata for Percussion, Movement 3*  Gr. 4, 155
Vamos a cantar  Gr. K, 278
¡Viva el fútbol!  Gr. 1, 97

## MIDDLE EAST *See also Israeli/ Jewish/Hebrew.*

Al yadee  Gr. 6, 308
Drum, A (story)  Gr. 1, 116
### Arabia
Ah ya Zane  Gr. 5, 297
Ala Da'lona  Gr. 4, 136
Ala Da'lona  Gr. 5, 301
### Yemen
*Galbi*  Gr. 1, 183

## NATIVE AMERICAN *For more American selections, see African American; Caribbean Islands: Puerto Rico; United States.*

And My Heart Soars  Gr. 2, 240
And My Heart Soars  Gr. 4, 359
Birds of Fire (poem)  Gr. 3, 257
Butterfly Song  Gr. 1, 363
*Cafe Europa*  Gr. 7, B-43
Corn Grinding Song  Gr. K, 67
*Daybreak Vision*  Gr. 5, 398
Go, My Son  Gr. 6, 188
*Kokopelli Wandering Song*
   Gr. 5, 110
*Mahk jchi*  Gr. 7, D-25
*Reservation Blues*  Gr. 8, B-37
*Round Dance*  Gr. 3, 257
*Round Dance*  Gr. 8, B-15
Sioux Lullaby  Gr. K, 111
There is Joy (poem)  Gr. 3, 258
*Through My Eyes*  Gr. 8, B-8
*Watchers of the Canyon*
   Gr. 6, 270
### Blackfeet
*Intertribal Song*  Gr. 8, B-18
### Cherokee
*Cherokee Morning Song*
   Gr. 8, B-19
Earth Is Our Mother, The
   Gr. 4, 358
Earth Is Our Mother, The
   Gr. 8, F-25

### Chippewa
Chippewa Lullaby  Gr. K, 181
Farewell to the Warriors
   Gr. 4, 284
Song of Greatness, A  Gr. 3, 335
### Coeur d'Alene
*John Wayne's Teeth*  Gr. 8, B-37
*On Fire Suite*  Gr. 8, B-36
*Treaties*  Gr. 8, B-36
### Cree
*Men's Fancy Dance*  Gr. 7, D-24
### Haliwa-Saponi
Haliwa-Saponi Canoe Song
   Gr. 5, 302
*Haliwa-Saponi Canoe Song*
   Gr. 5, 303
### Hopi
Mos Mos  Gr. 1, 130
### Inuit
*Cauyaqa Nauwa? (Where's My Drum?)*  Gr. 8, D-20
*Qiugaviit*  Gr. 3, 259
### Iroquois
*Drums of the Iroquois and Sioux*  Gr. 6, 285
*Light Up the World*  Gr. 2, 196
### Lakota
Inkpataya  Gr. 3, 254
*Wioste Olowan Inkpa Ta-Ya*
   Gr. 3, 255
### Lummi
Tall Cedar Tree  Gr. 2, 322
### Micmac
Kwa-nu-te  Gr. 3, 214
### Mohawk
*Rabbit Dance, The*  Gr. 3, 334
### Montagnais
*Akua Tuta*  Gr. 7, D-24
### Nanticoke
O hal'lwe  Gr. 3, 256
### Navajo
*Corn Grinding Song*  Gr. 6, 10
*Corn Grinding Song*  Gr. K, 66
*Dinéh Round Dance*  Gr. 6, 186
I Walk in Beauty  Gr. 4, 282
Jo'ashila  Gr. 5, 108
*Jo'ashila, "Walking Together"*
   Gr. 6, 286
*Rain Song, The*  Gr. 2, 323
Yo-shi nai  Gr. 6, 286
*Yo-shi nai (Circle Dance)*
   Gr. 6, 287
### Oneida
Kunolounkwa  Gr. K, 110
*Kunolounkwa, "Contemporary"*
   Gr. K, 110
### Pima (Akimel O'Odham)
Chuhwuht  Gr. 2, 356
### Saponi
Bear Dance  Gr. K, 127
### Seminole and Choctaw
Duck Dance  Gr. 2, 249

**Sioux**
*Drums of the Iroquois and Sioux* Gr. 6, 285
Hosisipa Gr. 3, 70
**Southern Plains**
*Malagueña* Gr. 7, 18
*Powwow Song* Gr. 4, 32
*Round Dance* Gr. 6, 445
**Southern Ute**
Bear Dance Gr. 7, I-10
*Bear Dance* Gr. 7, C-5
*Bear Dance Song* Gr. K, 127
**Wabanaki**
Green Corn Song Gr. 5, 462
**Wechihit-Yokuts**
Song of the Eagle Gr. 2, 248
**Wichita**
Wichita Hand Game Song 1 Gr. 3, 306
Wichita Hand Game Song 2 Gr. 3, 306
**Zuni**
Pottery Dance Gr. 1, 370
Zuni Sunrise Call Gr. 5, 396

**NETHERLANDS**
Geef jij mij die schoen Gr. 1, 126

**NEW ZEALAND**
Haere Gr. 2, 285
How the Kiwi Lost Its Wings (story) Gr. 1, 78
Karangatia ra Gr. 3, 272
*Karangatia ra* Gr. 3, 273
*Karangatia ra* Gr. 8, F-23
*Ki mua* Gr. 8, B-27
*Lua afe (2000)* Gr. 8, B-27
*Piki mai* Gr. 1, 79
*Rhythms of the Cook Islands* Gr. 8, B-6
*Tahi* Gr. 8, B-14
*Tarakihi* Gr. 3, 273
*Tihore Mai* Gr. 8, B-12
To'ia mai te waka Gr. 1, 77
*Vaka atua* Gr. 8, B-11

**NORWAY**
*Lyric Suite, Op. 65, No. 6, "Wedding Day at Troldhaugen"* Gr. 6, 9

**PACIFIC ISLANDS**
**Tahiti**
*Tamaiti hunahia* Gr. 6, 24

**PACIFIC RIM**
**Bora Bora**
*Ue ue* Gr. 8, D-2
**Singapore**
*Rice Bowl* Gr. 8, B-30

**PAKISTAN**
*Chang on the Jew's Harp* Gr. 8, B-9
*Face of Love, The* Gr. 8, B-11

**PANAMA**
Al tambor Gr. 3, 270

**PERU** *See South America.*

**POLAND**
Greetings (speech piece) Gr. 3, 316
*Mazurka, Op. 30, No. 3* Gr. 3, 317
Nie chcę cię znać Gr. 3, 314
*Prelude in B-flat Minor, Op. 28, No. 16* Gr. 7, C-22

**PUERTO RICO** *See Caribbean Islands.*

**RUSSIA**
Ai, Dunaii moy Gr. 4, 293
*Bai, bai, bai, bai* Gr. 2, 197
Beriozka Gr. 4, 294
*Garden of the Earth* Gr. 5, 399
*Kargiraa-style Song* Gr. 8, B-15
Khorovod Gr. 1, 372
*Lieutenant Kijé, Op. 60, "Troika"* Gr. 6, 457
*Na rechenki* Gr. 1, 375
*Nutcracker, The, "Arabian Dance"* Gr. 7, C-26
*Nutcracker, The, "Chinese Dance"* Gr. 7, C-26
*Prelude in G-sharp Minor, No. 12* Gr. 7, E-4
Pust' 'vsegda budet sonse Gr. 3, 278
*Red Poppy, The, "Russian Sailors' Dance"* Gr. 4, 224
*Sorochintsy Fair, "Gopak No. 5"* Gr. 1, 417
**Tuva**
*Kargyraa-Style Song* Gr. 8, B-40
*Khöömei* Gr. 8, B-10
*Sigit "Alash" (Tuva)* Gr. 4, 31

**SCANDINAVIA**
*Who Can Sail?* Gr. 5, 30

**SCOTLAND**
*Alasdair mhic cholla ghasda* Gr. 8, B-44
Farewell to Tarwathie Gr. 6, 43
Loch Lomond Gr. 5, 140
Scotland the Brave Gr. 5, 138

*Sealwoman/Yundah: A Guest Artist* Gr. 8, B-14
Skye Boat Song Gr. 6, 372
**Northumbria**
Keel Row, The Gr. 4, 240

**SLOVAKIA**
Hej pada pada Gr. 3, 78
Morning Comes Early Gr. 5, 13
Tancovačka Gr. 4, 230

**SOUTH AMERICA**
**Andes**
El cóndor pasa Gr. 6, 46
**Argentina**
Ahora voy a cantarles Gr. 3, 56
El carnavalito humahuaqueño Gr. 6, 482
Viva Jujuy Gr. 5, 228
*Viva Jujuy* Gr. 8, B-22
**Bolivia**
*Camino de piedra* Gr. 5, 152
La mariposa Gr. 6, 58
Pollerita Gr. 5, 151
**Brazil**
Ah, eu entrei na roda Gr. 3, 308
*Bate-papo* Gr. 4, 401
*Capoeira Na Vila* Gr. 8, D-25
*Chica chica boom chic* Gr. 2, 112
Ciranda Gr. 2, 272
*Concerto for Marimba and String Orchestra, "Saudação"* Gr. 2, 119
*Ijexá, Filhos de Gandhi* Gr. 8, B-31
Kibungo Gr. 2, 354
Kibungo, Beast of the Forest Gr. 2, 352
*Little Train of the Caipira, The, No. 2* Gr. K, 25
*Malê Debalê* Gr. 8, B-16
O lê lê O Bahía Gr. 6, 165
O pião entrou Gr. 2, 355
*Sai da frente* Gr. 8, D-24
Sambalele Gr. 4, 397
Serra, serra, serrador Gr. 1, 112
*Talaque talaque o romance da Maria* Gr. 8, D-24
*Uma história de Ifá* Gr. 3, 311
*Uma história de Ifá* Gr. 6, 362
*Vale do Javari* Gr. 8, B-31
**Chile**
Amores hallarás Gr. 5, 153
Cuando pa' Chile me voy Gr. 6, 376
El rabel Gr. 3, 362
*Fiesta, "Tarantella"* Gr. K, 134
Pavo, pavo Gr. 1, 416
Río, río Gr. 5, 370
Un elefante Gr. 2, 160

**(Folk, Traditional, and Regional Selections, continued)**

**Columbia**

El gallo pinto  Gr. 3, 86

*El nuevo caiman*  Gr. 8, B-17

Se va el caimán  Gr. 5, 306

**Ecuador**

El juego chirimbolo  Gr. 2, 54

Imbabura  Gr. 5, 202

*Llactamanta*  Gr. 6, 382

*Peñas*  Gr. 2, 54

*Peshte longuita*  Gr. 1, 217

**Peru**

Cuculí  Gr. K, 238

Los maizales  Gr. 1, 296

*Tema de maimara*  Gr. 1, 297

*Tema de maimara*  Gr. 8, B-8

**Venezuela**

Bogando a la luz del sol Gr. 4, 306

Canto del agua  Gr. 8, I-10

*Carnaval llanero*  Gr. 4, 307

El carite  Gr. 5, 305

El día de mamita  Gr. K, 325

El Tren  Gr. 2, 260

La mar estaba serena  Gr. 2, 344

*Lluvia*  Gr. 6, 332

Los trencitos  Gr. K, 24

*Luna hermosa*  Gr. 8, I-13

*Si tú no estás*  Gr. 6, 267

## SOUTHEAST ASIA

**Cambodia**

Leak kanseng  Gr. 1, 156

*Mea haarit*  Gr. 3, 274

*Phleng pradall*  Gr. 1, 157

Sarika keo  Gr. 3, 275

**Indonesia**

Dancing Pig, The (story) Gr. 1, 196

*Gamelan angklung*  Gr. 6, 384

*Kebjar teruna*  Gr. 6, 385

*Patalon*  Gr. 5, 319

*Ujan mas*  Gr. 2, 105

**Laos**

Dok djampa  Gr. 8, I-20

*Toei khong*  Gr. 8, B-9

**Philippines**

Santa Clara  Gr. 4, 172

**Thailand**

Chang  Gr. 1, 156

Loigratong  Gr. 6, 451

Mon son pha (speech piece) Gr. K, 91

Sawatdee tuh jah  Gr. 2, 265

*Toei khong*  Gr. 8, B-21

**Vietnam**

Cho'i hát bội  Gr. 5, 318

*Cô hàng xóm*  Gr. 8, B-15

*Quâ câù gió bay*  Gr. 5, 460

*Spring Walk, "Du xuân"* Gr. 1, 440

## SPAIN

A la puerta del cielo  Gr. 5, 60

Al ánimo  Gr. 3, 322

*Bebiendo al Alba*  Gr. 8, B-7

Caballito blanco  Gr. 2, 193

*Catalana, "Andante"*  Gr. K, 134

Con el vito  Gr. 7, G-15

*Concierto de Aranjuez, Movement 1, "Allegro con spirito"* Gr. 6, 199

Don Alfonso  Gr. 5, 177

El burrito enfermo  Gr. K, 271

El caracol  Gr. K, 130

El mes de abril  Gr. 3, 328

Hanuka, Hanuka  Gr. 3, 390

Hanuka, Hanuka  Gr. 8, I-36

Juanito  Gr. K, 300

*La Rosa*  Gr. K, 134

La Tarara  Gr. 4, 176

Las estrellitas del cielo  Gr. 5, 175

*Lorca*  Gr. 1, 49

*Malagueña*  Gr. 5, 154

Mañana  Gr. 7, E-14

*Mi humilde corazón*  Gr. 7, B-32

*Nights in the Gardens of Spain, "En el generalife"*  Gr. 2, 145

Niño querido  Gr. 1, 308

*Puente de los Alunados* Gr. 8, B-7

Ríu ríu chíu  Gr. 5, 435

*Ríu ríu chíu*  Gr. 5, 439

*Suite Española, Op. 47, No. 3, "Sevilla"*  Gr. 7, C-23

Un pajarito  Gr. 2, 16

Zumba, zumba  Gr. 3, 400

**Catalonia**

El desembre congelat  Gr. 5, 473

## SWEDEN

Take a Chance On Me  Gr. 8, G-15

## SWITZERLAND

L'inverno è passato  Gr. 2, 400

## THAILAND *See Southeast Asia.*

## TURKEY

Adana ya gidelim  Gr. 2, 142

*Ali Pasha*  Gr. 5, 218

*Makam sehnaz*  Gr. 2, 142

*Yemeni baglamis telli basina* Gr. 6, 309

## UKRAINE

*Kazak*  Gr. 1, 193

Minka  Gr. 4, 222

Ptashky u babusi sadochku Gr. 1, 192

*Shchedryk, "Carol of the Bells"* Gr. 6, 103

## UNITED STATES *For more American selections, see African American; Caribbean Islands: Puerto Rico; Native American. Additional listings by specific state or region begin on p. 134.*

1, 2, 3, 4 (speech piece)  Gr. K, 15

2, 4, 6, 8 (speech piece)  Gr. K, 67

A-Tisket, A-Tasket  Gr. 2, 238

*A-Tisket, A-Tasket*  Gr. 2, 239

*Acadian Songs, "Walking Song"* Gr. 4, 347

Ackabacka, Soda Cracker (speech piece)  Gr. 1, 303

Addams Family, The  Gr. 5, 456

*Aerial Boundaries*  Gr. 8, F-20

Alexander's Ragtime Band Gr. 6, 136

Alison's Camel  Gr. K, 289

All Around the Buttercup Gr. 2, 170

All for One  Gr. 7, E-8

Alleluia, Amen  Gr. 7, A-12

Almost Day  Gr. 3, 397

Ama-Lama  Gr. 5, 142

Amazing Grace  Gr. 4, 160

*Amazing Grace*  Gr. 4, 161

*Amazing Grace*  Gr. 5, 259

America  Gr. 1, 446

America  Gr. 2, 403

America  Gr. 3, 412

America  Gr. 4, 440

America  Gr. 5, 486

America  Gr. 6, 484

America  Gr. 7, I-2

*America*  Gr. 7, A-22

America  Gr. 8, I-2

America  Gr. K, 326

*America (from West Side Story)* Gr. 8, C-45

America, I Hear You Singing Gr. 2, 402

America (N. Diamond)  Gr. 4, 206

America, the Beautiful  Gr. 3, 413

*America, the Beautiful*  Gr. 3, 413

America, the Beautiful  Gr. 3, 412

America, the Beautiful  Gr. 5, 76

America, the Beautiful  Gr. 6, 485

America, the Beautiful  Gr. 7, I-4

America, the Beautiful  Gr. 8, I-4

*America, the Beautiful (Gospel)* Gr. 6, 485

America, the Free  Gr. 4, 210

*American Salute*  Gr. 5, 275

Andy Pandy  Gr. K, 46

Ants Go Marching, The  Gr. 1, 248

*Appalachian Spring, "Variations on Simple Gifts"*  Gr. 5, 185

Apple Tree  Gr. 1, 228

Apple Tree  Gr. 1, 228

Apples and Bananas  Gr. 1, 390

Apples, Peaches, Pears, and Plums (speech piece)  Gr. 1, 14

*Arkansas Traveler/Angeline the Baker* Gr. K, 114
At the Hop Gr. 4, 168
*At the Hop* Gr. 4, 166
At the Same Time Gr. 6, 115
Autumn Gr. 6, 193
Autumn Canon Gr. 5, 148
Away to America Gr. 5, 57
Baby Beluga Gr. K, 273
*Bamboula* Gr. 3, 229
Banana Splits Gr. 1, 318
Battle Cry of Freedom Gr. 5, 273
Battle Hymn of the Republic Gr. 5, 274
*Beat of the Tango, The* Gr. K, 106
*Beautiful* Gr. 3, 67
Bee, Bee Bumblebee (speech piece) Gr. 1, 50
Big Beautiful Planet Gr. 3, 326
Big Corral, The Gr. 2, 230
Big Rock Candy Mountain Gr. 4, 330
*Billy the Kid, "Celebration"* Gr. 3, 251
Bingo Gr. 1, 170
Black Snake Gr. 3, 53
Bling Blang Gr. 3, 240
Blow, Ye Winds Gr. 4, 255
Blowin' in the Wind Gr. 5, 382
*Blowin' in the Wind* Gr. 5, 384
*Blue Eyes Crying in the Rain* Gr. 7, B-28
Blue Skies Gr. 6, 88
Bluebird, Bluebird Gr. K, 105
Blues with a Feeling Gr. 8, I-6
Bo-bo-skee, Watten-tatten (speech piece) Gr. 1, 259
Boil Them Cabbage Down Gr. 6, 370
*Bonaparte's Retreat* Gr. 4, 385
Boogie Chant and Dance (speech piece) Gr. 2, 78
Book of Love Gr. 8, G-27
*Boston Ball Game 1967* Gr. 8, F-32
*Both Sides Now* Gr. 5, 385
Bounce High, Bounce Low Gr. 1, 152
Bumble Bee, The (speech piece) Gr. K, 74
Bury Me Not on the Lone Prairie Gr. 6, 19
Bus, The Gr. K, 82
Busy Buzzy Bee Gr. K, 77
But the Cat Came Back Gr. 2, 190
Button, You Must Wander Gr. 2, 172
*Bye, Bye Love* Gr. 5, 357
Bye Bye, Love Gr. 8, F-9
*Bye Bye, Love* Gr. 8, A-15
California Gr. 5, 52
California Dreamin' Gr. 8, G-31

California, Here I Come Gr. 4, 287q
Camptown Races Gr. 5, 270
*(Can't Live Without Your) Love and Affection* Gr. 7, B-23
*Candy Man, Salty Dog* Gr. K, 27
Canoe Song Gr. 4, 76
*Carolina Sunday Waltz* Gr. 7, F-9
*Carry On* Gr. 7, B-2
*Carry On Wayward Son* Gr. 7, B-20
*Cattle Call* Gr. 5, 347
Chapel of Love Gr. 7, G-27
Charlie over the Water Gr. 1, 68
Chicken on the Fence Post Gr. 3, 92
*Choo Choo Boogaloo* Gr. 1, 126
Christmas, Don't Be Late (The Chipmunk Song) Gr. 2, 386
*Circle of Life (from The Lion King), The* Gr. 3, 367
*Circle of Life (from The Lion King), The* Gr. 6, 316
Clementine Gr. 4, 341
*Close Encounters of the Third Kind* Gr. 8, B-34
Coffee Grows on White Oak Trees Gr. 3, 168
Colorado Trail Gr. 5, 276
*Colorado Trail* Gr. 5, 277
Come, Ye Thankful People, Come Gr. 5, 459
*Coming Home from the Sea–I* Gr. 6, 345
Costume Capers Gr. 1, 412
Cow's Woc Backward Gr. 1, 390
Crocodile, The Gr. 2, 362
*Dancing in the Street* Gr. 2, 254
*Dancing Queen* Gr. 8, G-19
*Daphne of the Dunes* Gr. 8, D-29
*Diamonds and Rust* Gr. 7, A-4
Different Beat, A Gr. 1, 6
Dinah Gr. 2, 120
Dinosaur Dance Gr. 2, 168
*Dippermouth Blues* Gr. 7, B-14
Do, Re, Mi, Fa Gr. 6, 80
Do Wah Diddy Diddy Gr. 4, 203
Do Wah Diddy Diddy Gr. 7, F-21
*Do-Re-Mi* Gr. 5, 38
Doctor Knickerbocker (speech piece) Gr. 1, 302
Don't Be Cruel Gr. 6, 255
*Don't Look Down* Gr. 6, 249
Down by the Bay Gr. 1, 18
Down the Listening Lane Gr. K, 192
Down the Ohio Gr. 2, 60
Downtown Gr. 6, 258
Drill, Ye Tarriers Gr. 5, 54
Dry Bones Come Skipping Gr. 4, 218
*Dusty Miller* Gr. 4, 291

Earth Is My Mother, The Gr. 1, 340
Eensy Weensy Spider Gr. K, 187
Ego sum pauper Gr. 5, 158
*Elias* Gr. 7, B-21
*Ennanga, Movement 3* Gr. 3, 127
Erie Canal Gr. 5, 262
Ev'ry Kind of Music Gr. 2, 226
*Ev'ry Time I Feel the Spirit* Gr. 7, C-3
*Every Morning* Gr. 7, B-8
Every Morning When I Wake Up Gr. 2, 320
Every Morning When I Wake Up Gr. 2, 320
*Every Night When the Sun Goes In* Gr. 8, I-29
*Everything Grows* Gr. K, 267
Faith of the Heart Gr. 8, G-3
Family Tree Gr. 3, 72
*Fanfare for Freedom* Gr. 6, 139
Farmer in the Dell, The Gr. K, 232
Farmer's Dairy Key, The Gr. 2, 182
*Fascinatin' Rhythm (Ella Fitzgerald)* Gr. 7, E-11
*Fascinatin' Rhythm (Frances Veri)* Gr. 7, E-11
Fiddler on the Roof Gr. 7, E-5
Fifty Nifty United States Gr. 5, 251
Five Little Chickadees Gr. K, 179
Five Little Snowmen Gr. K, 313
*Flop-Eared Mule* Gr. 3, 99
*Flying Home* Gr. 7, B-15
*Footloose* Gr. 7, B-11
*Forever, For Now* Gr. 7, B-16
*Forked Deer/Fisher's Hornpipe* Gr. 4, 343
Four Strong Winds (Song to a Seagull) Gr. 6, 170
Fourth of July Night (poem) Gr. 1, 444
*Fourth of July, The* Gr. 5, 489
Frog in the Millpond Gr. 2, 44
From Sea to Shining Sea Gr. 2, 342
*Frostiana (from Stopping by Woods on a Snowy Evening)* Gr. 6, 40
*Frosty, the Snowman* Gr. 2, 391
Fuzzy Caterpillar Gr. K, 102
*Give Me Your Tired, Your Poor* Gr. 5, 166
Give My Regards to Broadway Gr. 6/RB, 38
Glendy Burke, The Gr. 4, 262
*Glory Hallelujah Grand March* Gr. 8, C-38
God Bless America Gr. 5, 4
*God Bless the Child* Gr. 7, B-26
*God Bless the Child* Gr. 7, B-27
God Bless the Grass Gr. 8, F-13

**(Folk, Traditional, and Regional Selections, continued)**

Goin' Down the Road Feelin' Bad Gr. 5, 282

*Goin' Down the Road Feelin' Bad* Gr. 5, 283

Goin' Down the Road Feelin' Bad Gr. 7, F-13

Goin' to Boston  Gr. 6, 433

Goin' to the Fair  Gr. K, 156

Going to the Zoo  Gr. K, 216

Gonna Build a Mountain  Gr. 6, 21

*Gonna Move*  Gr. 7, F-12

Good Morning  Gr. 3, 192

*Good Vibrations*  Gr. 8, E-28

*Grand Canyon Suite, "Cloudburst"* Gr. K, 261

*Grand Canyon Suite, "On the Trail"*  Gr. 3, 77

*Great Pretender, The*  Gr. 5, 358

Grizzly Bear  Gr. K, 33

*Groundhog Jig, The*  Gr. 1, 436

*Guide Right*  Gr. 1, 447

*Halley Came to Jackson* Gr. 2, 340

Halloween Song  Gr. K, 309

Happy Birthday to You  Gr. K, 304

Happy Days Are Here Again Gr. 5, 284

Happy Feet  Gr. 2, 252

*Hard Way*  Gr. 7, E-33

Heigh-Ho  Gr. 2, 7

Hello, There!  Gr. K, 6

Here Comes Valerie  Gr. 1, 32

*Hermit Songs, Op. 29, "The Monk and His Cat"*  Gr. 7, C-21

Hey, Hey, Look at Me  Gr. 1, 70

Home on the Range  Gr. 5, 69

Honeybee Song, The  Gr. 1, 358

Hop Up, My Ladies  Gr. 3, 142

Hound Dog  Gr. 5, 212

How Much Wood Could a Woodchuck Chuck (speech piece)  Gr. 3, 120

*Howjidoo*  Gr. 1, 315

I Believe I Can Fly  Gr. 5, 170

*I Can't Get Started*  Gr. 7, B-26

I Don't Care If the Rain Comes Down  Gr. 3, 24

*I Don't Want to Feel Like That* Gr. 4, 31

I Dream a World  Gr. 8, G-40

I Fed My Horse  Gr. 2, 94

I Got Rhythm  Gr. 6, 101

I Have a Dog  Gr. K, 262

*I Know You Mardi Gras* Gr. 8, B-17

*I Love a Rainy Night (line dance)* Gr. 5, 350

I Love the Mountains  Gr. 5, 34

I See the Moon  Gr. 2, 58

*I Shall Sing*  Gr. 8, I-41

I Shall Sing  Gr. 8, I-38

*I Walk the Line*  Gr. 7, B-28

I Walk the Unfrequented Road Gr. 6, 79

I'm a Believer  Gr. 7, G-33

I'm a Believer  Gr. 7, G-33

*I'm a Believer*  Gr. 7, G-32

I'm a Dreydl  Gr. K, 315

I'm a Very Fine Turkey  Gr. K, 310

*I'm a Yankee Doodle Dandy* Gr. 5, 278

I'm Curious  Gr. K, 276

I'm Flying Home  Gr. 2, 286

I'm Flying Home  Gr. 2, 286

*I'm Gonna Sing a Silly Song* Gr. K, 225

I'm in the Mood  Gr. K, 86

I'm Tall, I'm Small  Gr. K, 18

I'm Thankful  Gr. 1, 414

I've Been Everywhere  Gr. 6, 226

*I've Been Everywhere*  Gr. 6, 224

I've Been Working on the Railroad Gr. 3, 242

If a Tiger Calls  Gr. 3, 356

*If I Had a Hammer*  Gr. 3, 241

*If These Walls Could Speak* Gr. 7, B-41

*In My Own Little Corner*  Gr. 3, 9

In the Pumpkin Patch  Gr. 3, 380

*In the Still of the Night*  Gr. 4, 47

It's a Small World  Gr. 3, 268

It's Time  Gr. 6, 274

*Itsy Bitsy Spider, The*  Gr. K, 187

Ja-Da  Gr. 2, 188

*Ja-Da*  Gr. 2, 187

Ja-Da  Gr. 7, G-20

Jambalaya (On The Bayou) Gr. 8, F-18

*Jazz in the Box*  Gr. 8, F-11

Jelly in a Dish (speech piece) Gr. 2, 83

Jig Along Home  Gr. 2, 366

*John Henry*  Gr. 8, C-34

Johnny Appleseed  Gr. 4, 344

Johnny Caught a Flea  Gr. 1, 226

Johnny Has Gone for a Soldier Gr. 5, 188

Jolly Old St. Nicholas  Gr. K, 316

*Kansas City Stomp*  Gr. 2, 251

Lady, Lady  Gr. 1, 62

Land of a Thousand Dances Gr. 5, 330

*Last Thing on My Mind, The* Gr. 7, F-7

*Lazy John*  Gr. 4, 11

Lean on Me  Gr. 7, E-22

Lemonade  Gr. 1, 190

Let Freedom Ring  Gr. 5, 77

*Let It Snow! Let It Snow! Let It Snow!*  Gr. 4, 427

Let Music Surround You  Gr. 4, 236

Let the Music Begin!  Gr. 1, 2

Let's Celebrate!  Gr. 3, 374

*Let's Face the Music*  Gr. 7, B-14

Let's Go Fly a Kite  Gr. 2, 327

*Let's Twist Again*  Gr. 6, 257

Li'l Liza Jane  Gr. 3, 140

*Liberty/Chicken Reel*  Gr. 2, 38

Light Up the World with a Song Gr. 8, G-25

*Linus and Lucy*  Gr. 8, A-29

Lion Sleeps Tonight, The Gr. 4, 131

Lion Sleeps Tonight, The Gr. 8, I-57

*Lion Sleeps Tonight, The* Gr. 8, E-8

Little and Lots  Gr. K, 323

Little Black Bug  Gr. 1, 214

Little Black Bug  Gr. 1, 214

Little Darlin'  Gr. 7, F-30

Little Green Frog, The  Gr. 1, 24

Little Red Wagon  Gr. K, 152

Little Shop of Horrors  Gr. 4, 422

Live in the City  Gr. 5, 71

Loco-Motion, The  Gr. 3, 64

Locomoto-vation  Gr. K, 61

Long Way Home, A  Gr. 1, 382

Looby Loo  Gr. K, 210

Look Out Below!  Gr. 2, 370

Look Out for Mother Earth Gr. 3, 341

Love Is on Our Side  Gr. 5, 324

Love Somebody  Gr. 3, 94

Love Will Guide Us  Gr. 4, 328

Lucy Locket  Gr. 2, 27

Lullaby and Dance  Gr. 4, 387

*Lullaby for Strings*  Gr. 1, 293

*Mack the Knife*  Gr. 7, B-26

Make New Friends  Gr. 3, 36

*Make Your Own Kind of Music* Gr. 8, G-30

Mama, Buy Me a Chiney Doll Gr. K, 120

*Manteca*  Gr. 7, B-3

*Marines' Hymn, The*  Gr. 8, C-39

Marines' Hymn, The  Gr. 8, C-39

Mary Wore Her Red Dress Gr. K, 74

Mashed Potatoes (speech piece) Gr. 1, 20

Merry-Go-Round  Gr. K, 290

Michael Finnigan  Gr. 3, 153

Michael Finnigan/This Old Man Gr. 3, 153

*Mr. Bojangles (excerpt 1)* Gr. 7, F-7

*Mr. Bojangles (excerpt 2)* Gr. 7, F-7

Mr. Tambourine Man  Gr. 6, 150

*Mr. Tambourine Man*  Gr. 6, 148

Mud  Gr. 3, 32

Music's in Me, The  Gr. 2, 40

Must Be Santa  Gr. K, 318

My Bonnie Lies Over the Ocean Gr. 4, 338

*My Girl Josephine*  Gr. 8, E-21

My Pony, Macaroni Gr. 1, 158
*Native Stepson* Gr. 7, F-26
Never Smile at a Crocodile
    Gr. 3, 100
*Noah's Zoo in the Big, Big Rain*
    Gr. K, 274
*North Carolina Breakdown*
    Gr. 5, 334
Number One, Touch Your Tongue
    (speech piece) Gr. K, 204
O Music Gr. 5, 162
Oh, Susanna Gr. 4, 264
Old Abram Brown Gr. 5, 222
*Old American Songs, "The
    Boatman's Dance"* Gr. 4, 61
Old Brass Wagon Gr. 2, 122
Old Dan Tucker Gr. 3, 96
Old Man Mosie Gr. 3, 108
Oliver Jump (speech piece)
    Gr. K, 205
On a Log, Mister Frog Gr. K, 148
On My Way Gr. 6, 313
*On Parade* Gr. K, 326
*On the Mall* Gr. 5, 2
One Family Gr. 7, G-17
One Green Jelly Bean Gr. K, 287
One Moment in Time Gr. 6, 352
*Orange Blossom Special* Gr. 1, 47
Orange Blossom Special
    Gr. 5, 269
*Orange Blossom Special*
    Gr. 5, 268
Orange Blossom Special Gr. 8, E-6
*Over and Under a Theme of Mark
    Isham's* Gr. 8, B-4
Over in the Meadow Gr. 1, 346
Over the Rainbow (from The
    Wizard of Oz) Gr. 4, 140
*Over the Rainbow (from The
    Wizard of Oz)* Gr. 4, 143
*Over the Rainbow (from The
    Wizard of Oz)* Gr. 4, 143
Over the River and Through the
    Wood Gr. 3, 384
Over There Gr. 5, 279
*Overture/All That Jazz (from
    Chicago)* Gr. 7, A-23
*Ozark Mountain Jubilee* Gr. 4, 86
Party Tonight! Gr. 2, 152
Paths of Victory Gr. 6, 195
*Patty Cake Polka* Gr. 2, 281
Peace Round Gr. 4, 348
*Peak Moments* Gr. 8, E-4
Peanut Butter (speech piece)
    Gr. 1, 173
Pease Porridge Hot Gr. 1, 134
*Pennsylvania 6-5000* Gr. 5, 342
Peppermint Twist Gr. 3, 46
Pizza, Pizza, Daddy-o Gr. 2, 28
Play a Simple Melody Gr. 5, 72
*Plenty o' Nuttin'* Gr. 7, B-45
*Plow That Broke the Plains, The,
    "Cattle"* Gr. 3, 177

Popcorn Gr. 8, E-27
*Prayer, The* Gr. 7, A-10
*Pride and Joy* Gr. 7, B-9
*Pride and Joy* Gr. 7, B-9
Promised Land, The Gr. 5, 258
Proud Gr. 7, G-3
Puff, the Magic Dragon Gr. 2, 350
Pumpkin, Pumpkin Gr. 1, 413
Put a Little Love in Your Heart
    Gr. 4, 6
*Put a Little Love in Your Heart*
    Gr. 4, 8
Put Your Finger in the Air
    Gr. K, 114
Rabbit Footprints Gr. 2 , 304
Race You Down the Mountain
    Gr. 1, 127
*Ragtime Annie* Gr. 2, 122
Ragtime Cowboy Joe Gr. 2, 250
*Rain* Gr. 8, B-6
Rain on the Green Grass (speech
    piece) Gr. K, 10
Rain, Rain Gr. 1, 54
Rain (Stevenson) Gr. 3, 43
Rainbow, The Gr. 2, 332
Red River Valley Gr. 6, 11
*Reuben's Train* Gr. 1, 334
*Rhapsody in Blue* Gr. 7, C-42
*Rhapsody in Blue* Gr. K, 75
Rio Grande Gr. 4, 256
Rise and Shine Gr. 1, 122
Rise and Shine Gr. 4, 98
*Rising of the Mourning Sun*
    Gr. 7, F-19
River Gr. 4, 58
River Gr. 4, 61
*River Suite, The, "Finale"*
    Gr. 5, 121
*Riverdance Suite* Gr. 2, 141
Rock and Roll Is Here to Stay
    Gr. 6, 36
*Rock Around the Clock*
    Gr. 5, 357
Rock Around the Clock
    Gr. 7, B-18
Rock Island Line Gr. 4, 54
Rockin' Around the Christmas Tree
    Gr. 5, 466
Rockin' Robin Gr. 3, 368
Rocky Top Gr. 5, 348
*Rodeo, "Buckaroo Holiday"*
    Gr. 2, 23
*Rodeo, "Hoedown"* Gr. 1, 6
*Rodeo, "Hoedown"* Gr. 5, 312
*Rodeo, "Hoedown"* Gr. 8, B-42
*Rodeo, "Saturday Night Waltz"*
    Gr. 4, 343
Roll On, Columbia Gr. 5, 116
Roll Over Gr. K, 288
*Rose (from the Motion Picture
    Titanic)* Gr. 8, B-34
'Round the Bay of Mexico
    Gr. 4, 258

Route 66 Gr. 4, 276
*Route 66* Gr. 4, 279
*Route 66* Gr. 4, 279
Rudolph, the Red-Nosed Reindeer
    Gr. 1, 428
Sail Away Gr. 5, 404
Sailing Down My Golden River
    Gr. 4, 332
Sailing to the Sea Gr. 1, 336
Scattin' A-Round (Variations on
    Row 3) Gr. 6, 160
Scattin' A-Round (Variations on
    Row 3) Gr. 6, 160
Seagull, Seagull, Sit on the Shore
    Gr. 4, 383
Seasons Gr. K, 4
Seasons of Love Gr. 8, A-22
See and Touch Gr. K, 172
*Semper Fidelis* Gr. K, 326
*Semper Fidelis* Gr. K, 165
Setting the Thanksgiving Table
    Gr. 2, 381
Shady Grove Gr. 5, 260
Sharing Gr. K, 198
*She'll Be Coming 'Round the
    Mountain When She Comes*
    Gr. 4, 333
*Shed a Little Light* Gr. 3, 409
*Shed a Little Light* Gr. 8, E-17
*Shenandoah* Gr. 2, 62
Shenandoah Gr. 5, 264
*Shenandoah* Gr. 5, 265
Ship that Never Returned, The
    Gr. 5, 402
Ship that Never Returned, The
    Gr. 5, 402
*Shoveling* Gr. 1, 423
Silly Street Gr. K, 224
Simple Gifts Gr. 5, 184
Simple Gifts Gr. 8, A-17
*Simple Gifts* Gr. 8, A-17
Sing a Song of Peace Gr. 6, 66
Sing a Song of Peace/This Is My
    Country Gr. 6, 66
Sing, America, Sing! Gr. 3, 238
Sing Me a Story Gr. 2, 346
Sing! Speak! Whisper! Shout!
    Gr. 1, 36
Sing Your Story Gr. 3, 350
Singin' in the Rain Gr. 4, 360
Skip to My Lou Gr. K, 58
*Sleigh Ride* Gr. 2, 390
Snail, Snail Gr. 1, 190
Snowflakes Gr. 1, 422
*Solsbury Hill* Gr. 8, E-29
Somebody Waiting Gr. 2, 283
Something Told the Wild Geese
    Gr. 7, G-39
*Somewhere (from West Side
    Story)* Gr. 8, C-44
Somewhere Out There Gr. 5, 368
*Somewhere Out There* Gr. 5, 369

**(Folk, Traditional, and Regional Selections, continued)**

Song of One, A  Gr. 3, 344
Song of the Fishes  Gr. 3, 244
Song That's Just for You, A
  Gr. 2, 126
*Songs from Letters, "So Like Your Father"*  Gr. 7, C-21
*Souvenirs L'Amerique, Op. 17, "Yankee Doodle"*  Gr. 2, 405
Spring Has Sprung!  Gr. K, 142
Stand By Me  Gr. 5, 46
*Stand By Me*  Gr. 5, 49
Stand By Me  Gr. 8, E-25
*Stand By Me*  Gr. 8, E-24
Star Light, Star Bright  Gr. 1, 108
Star-Spangled Banner, The
  Gr. 3, 415
Star-Spangled Banner, The
  Gr. 4, 441
Star-Spangled Banner, The
  Gr. 5, 488
Star-Spangled Banner, The
  Gr. 6, 486
Star-Spangled Banner, The
  Gr. 7, I-56
Star-Spangled Banner, The
  Gr. 8, I-63
*Stars and Stripes Forever, The*
  Gr. 1, 167
*Stars and Stripes Forever, The*
  Gr. 4, 159
Step in Time  Gr. 2, 74
Stopping by Woods on a Snowy Evening  Gr. 6, 41
Storm Dance (speech piece)
  Gr. K, 145
Straighten Up and Fly Right
  Gr. 4, 128
Strike Up the Band  Gr. 6, 135
*Suite for Wind Quintet, Movement 1*  Gr. 8, C-34
Summertime  Gr. 6, 253
*Summertime*  Gr. 6, 252
Supercalifragilisticexpialidocious
  Gr. 3, 7
*Surfin' Safari*  Gr. 6, 261
Surfin' U.S.A.  Gr. 6, 260
Surfin' U.S.A.  Gr. 7, I-58
Swanee  Gr. 6, 118
Sweet Betsy from Pike  Gr. 4, 244
*Take Five*  Gr. 5, 220
*Take Five*  Gr. 7, B-15
Take Me Out to the Ball Game
  Gr. 3, 263
*Take Me There*  Gr. 7, F-26
Tender Shepherd (Count Your Sheep)  Gr. 3, 116
*Tennessee River*  Gr. 5, 349
Thanksgiving Is Near  Gr. 2, 380
*That'll Be the Day*  Gr. 6, 256
*That's the Way It Is*  Gr. 7, B-23

That's What's New with Me!
  Gr. K, 2
*Theme and Variations for Percussion*  Gr. 5, 65
This Land Is Your Land  Gr. 5, 118
This Land Is Your Land (refrain only)  Gr. 1, 274
This Pretty Planet  Gr. 4, 355
Those Magic Changes  Gr. 8, E-30
Three Little Pigs  Gr. K, 21
*Thunderer, The*  Gr. 5, 79
Time to Sing  Gr. 2, 8
*Times They Are A-Changin', The*
  Gr. 5, 384
Today Is Your Birthday  Gr. 1, 410
Tom Dooley  Gr. 6, 374
Turn the Glasses Over  Gr. 3, 204
Turn, Turn, Turn (To Everything There Is a Season)  Gr. 5, 378
*Tutti Frutti*  Gr. 7, B-29
Tuxedo Junction  Gr. 8, G-21
*Twist and Shout*  Gr. 4, 238
*Twist, The*  Gr. 5, 358
*Twist, The*  Gr. 7, B-10
Two Little Sausages (speech piece)
  Gr. 2, 79
Under the Same Sun  Gr. 6, 440
Under the Sea  Gr. 5, 372
Until I Saw the Sea  Gr. 3, 245
*Variations on "America"*
  Gr. 6, 163
Vive l'amour  Gr. 6, 176
Voice Choice  Gr. K, 27
Voices of Pride, The  Gr. 5, 86
Wabash Cannon Ball  Gr. 5, 136
*Waitin' for a Train*  Gr. 7, B-24
Waitin' for the Light to Shine
  Gr. 4, 26
*Walkin' to New Orleans*
  Gr. 3, 371
*Washington Post, The*  Gr. 1, 175
*Washington Post, The*  Gr. 8, C-40
*Watermelon Man*  Gr. 1, 12
*Watermelon Man*  Gr. 6, 270
Way Down in the Music  Gr. 2, 227
We Go Together  Gr. 4, 44
We're All Gonna Shine Tonight
  Gr. 2, 240
We've Got Lots in Common
  Gr. 3, 366
Weevily Wheat  Gr. 4, 105
What Do Animals Need?
  Gr. 2, 288
*What's Going On?*  Gr. 7, B-38
Wheel of the Water, The
  Gr. 4, 362
When Johnny Comes Marching Home  Gr. 5, 180
*When Johnny Comes Marching Home*  Gr. 5, 88
*Where Have All the Flowers Gone?*  Gr. 5, 287
Who Has the Penny?  Gr. K, 42

Willoughby, Wallaby, Woo
  Gr. K, 282
Willowbee  Gr. 1, 222
Wind Up the Apple Tree
  Gr. 1, 184
*Wings*  Gr. 7, C-45
Winter  Gr. 8, G-11
Winter Fantasy  Gr. 4, 424
Winter Fantasy/Jingle Bells
  Gr. 4, 424
Winter Wonderland  Gr. 5, 454
*Wipe Out*  Gr. 5, 155
*Wipe Out*  Gr. 7, F-33
*Wooly Bully*  Gr. 3, 372
World We Love, The  Gr. 3, 342
*Would?*  Gr. 8, F-30
Written in March  Gr. 4, 354
Yakety Yak  Gr. 5, 205
Yankee Doodle  Gr. 2, 389
Yankee Doodle  Gr. 2, 405
Yankee Doodle  Gr. 3, 414
*Yankee Doodle Boy, The*
  Gr. 3, 265
You Are My Sunshine  Gr. 6, 246
*You Are My Sunshine*  Gr. 6, 247
*You Are My Sunshine*  Gr. 7, B-7
You Were on My Mind  Gr. 7, G-25
*You Were on My Mind*
  Gr. 7, G-25
*You're a Grand Old Flag*
  Gr. 1, 276
You're a Grand Old Flag
  Gr. 3, 264
You've Got a Friend  Gr. 5, 366
*You've Got a Friend*  Gr. 5, 364
Your Life Is Now  Gr. 6, 4
Zip-a-Dee-Doo-Dah  Gr. 2, 330
Zudio  Gr. 2, 269

**Alabama**

Alabama Gal  Gr. 3, 106
Amasee  Gr. 1, 172

**Appalachia**

*Cedar Swamp*  Gr. 5, 261
*College Hornpipe*  Gr. 4, 95
Four in a Boat  Gr. 2, 46
Golden Ring Around Susan Girl
  Gr. 3, 16
*Golden Ring Around the Susan Girl*  Gr. 3, 17
*I Am a Man of Constant Sorrow*  Gr. 7, F-29
Man of Constant Sorrow
  Gr. 7, F-28
My Dear Companion  Gr. 6, 23
One Morning in May  Gr. 6, 121
*Soldier's Joy*  Gr. 8, B-29
Sourwood Mountain  Gr. 4, 65

**Arkansas**

Harrison Town  Gr. 6, 97
Juniper Tree, The  Gr. 3, 131

**California**

John Kanaka  Gr. 3, 60

**Creole**
Sleep, Baby, Sleep Gr. 2, 197
Sweet Potatoes Gr. 3, 228
**Florida**
Hokey Pokey Gr. K, 296
**Hawaii**
Kapulu kane Gr. 2, 270
Nani wale na hala Gr. 3, 260
'Ūlili E Gr. 5, 441
**Kentucky**
Cumberland Gap Gr. 4, 138
Down in the Valley Gr. 6, 375
*Down in the Valley* Gr. 7, A-23
I Bought Me a Cat Gr. 2, 308
I Wonder Where Maria's Gone Gr. 3, 318
Ida Red Gr. 3, 30
Pretty Saro Gr. 3, 216
Skin and Bones Gr. 2, 376
**Louisiana**
Great Big House Gr. 2, 204
**Louisiana Cajun**
*Allons danser, Colinda* Gr. K, 218
*Bon jour!* Gr. 1, 3
Crawfish! Gr. 2, 86
Deux cocodries Gr. 2, 364
Fais do do Gr. 6, 403
*Jambalaya (On The Bayou)* Gr. 6, 245
Jambalaya (On The Bayou) Gr. 6, 244
Jambalaya (On The Bayou) Gr. 8, I-46
*Je m'endors* Gr. K, 219
*Jolie Blonde* Gr. 4, 389
*L'arc en ciel* Gr. 2, 333
*Le Hoogie Boogie* Gr. K, 296
*P'tit galop pour mamou* Gr. 1, 317
Sugar "Shuga" Bee Gr. K, 64
**Maryland**
Six Little Ducks Gr. K, 234
**Midwest**
*Four Potatoes Medley* Gr. 6, 205
**Mississippi**
Mississippi River Chant (speech piece) Gr. 2, 132
**Missouri**
Jinny Go 'Round Gr. K, 228
**New Mexico**
Adiós, amigos Gr. 6, 57
Magnolia Gr. 6, 16
Riendo el río corre Gr. 6, 263
Tengo, tengo, tengo Gr. 4, 228
**New York**
Blue Mountain Lake Gr. 6, 205
*Fanfare for the Common Man* Gr. 7, C-43
Theme from New York, New York Gr. 4, 250

**North Carolina**
Banjo Sam Gr. 2, 314
*Cookie Crew, The* Gr. K, 196
I Fed My Horse Gr. 2, 94
Leila Gr. 1, 258
Let Us Chase the Squirrel Gr. 2, 98
Phoebe Gr. 1, 30
Phoebe Gr. 1, 30
**Oklahoma**
Jim Along, Josie Gr. K, 39
Oklahoma Gr. 5, 36
Old Texas Gr. 3, 77
**Ozarks**
*Battle of New Orleans, The* Gr. 6, 105
Going Upon the Mountain Gr. 6, 105
*Rumblin' On* Gr. 2, 315
**South Carolina**
I Got a Letter This Morning Gr. K, 68
Oh, Watch the Stars Gr. 2, 144
Oh, Watch the Stars Gr. 5, 216
**Southern Appalachia**
Every Night When the Sun Goes In Gr. 8, I-28
**Southern United States**
B-A, Bay Gr. 1, 220
Cindy Gr. 4, 384
Don't You Hear the Lambs? Gr. 5, 97
*Don't You Hear the Lambs?* Gr. 5, 99
Down in the Meadow Gr. K, 147
*Ev'rybody Ought to Know* Gr. 1, 434
Goodbye, Julie Gr. 1, 334
Great Big Stars Gr. 1, 60
Green, Green, Rocky Gr. 1, 321
Hambone Gr. 1, 202
*Hush, Little Baby* Gr. K, 222
Mama Don't 'Low Gr. 6, 358
My Father's House Gr. 2, 25
My Home's Across the Blue Ridge Mountains Gr. 4, 84
My Home's Across the Blue Ridge Mountains Gr. 7, F-6
Old Blue Gr. K, 122
Paw-Paw Patch Gr. 4, 93
Rocky Mountain Gr. 2, 98
She'll Be Comin' 'Round the Mountain Gr. 2, 358
Shoo, Fly Gr. 2, 200
**Southwestern United States**
¡Qué gusto! Gr. 3, 132
**St. Helena Island**
Don't Let the Wind Gr. 3, 180
**Tennessee**
Cotton-Eye Joe Gr. 4, 288
*Cotton-Eye Joe* Gr. 4, 290
My Foot's In My Stirrup Gr. 2, 234

**Texas**
Bluebonnets of Texas Gr. 3, 333
Cattle Call Gr. 5, 344
Cowboys' Christmas Ball Gr. 6, 239
*Cowboys' Christmas Ball* Gr. 6, 238
Deep in the Heart of Texas Gr. 4, 22
Deep in the Heart of Texas Gr. 8, I-18
Don't Let Your Watch Run Down Gr. 3, 166
God Bless the U.S.A. Gr. 8, G-37
Knock the Cymbals Gr. 1, 176
Lone Star Trail Gr. 2, 21
*New San Antonio Rose* Gr. 5, 135
Old Chisholm Trail, The Gr. 6, 237
*Old Chisholm Trail, The* Gr. 6, 236
Pastures of Plenty Gr. 4, 280
Railroad Corral Gr. 3, 174
San Antonio Rose Gr. 5, 134
*Scuttle Buttin'* Gr. 8, F-26
Shake Them 'Simmons Down Gr. 2, 244
Streets of Laredo Gr. 4, 272
Texas Cowboy Gr. 3, 250
*This Land Is Your Land* Gr. 5, 120
This Land Is Your Land Gr. 7, I-68
Tideo Gr. 2, 80
Toodala Gr. 1, 326
Yellow Rose of Texas, The Gr. 7, I-70
*Yellow Rose of Texas, The* Gr. 7, I-73
**Vermont**
*Northfield* Gr. 6, 25

**VENEZUELA** *See South America.*

**VIETNAM** *See Southeast Asia.*

**WALES**
All Through the Night Gr. 5, 105
*All Through the Night* Gr. 5, 104
Ash Grove, The Gr. 5, 114
Deck the Hall Gr. 5, 474
*Deck the Hall* Gr. 5, 475

# FORM

## 12-BAR BLUES
Birthday Gr. 6, 90
*Birthday* Gr. 6, 92
*Boogie Woogie* Gr. 6, 93
*C-Jam Blues* Gr. 8, C-43
*Country Blues* Gr. 5, 225

*(Form, continued)*

Fingerprints Gr. 7, B-42
Flip, Flop and Fly Gr. 7, I-32
Flip, Flop and Fly Gr. 7, E-32
*Flip, Flop and Fly* Gr. 7, F-15
Good Mornin', Blues Gr. 5, 224
Good Mornin', Blues Gr. 5, 224
*Hard Way* Gr. 7, E-33
*I Know You Mardi Gras* Gr. 8, B-17
Rock Around the Clock Gr. 7, B-18
*Scuttle Buttin'* Gr. 8, F-26
St. Louis Blues Gr. 5, 352
*Sun Gonna Shine* Gr. 7, F-14
*Walkin' Blues* Gr. 5, 227
*Would?* Gr. 8, F-30

## AAB

Sun Gonna Shine Gr. 6, 242
*Sun Gonna Shine* Gr. 7, F-14

## AABA

Bridges Gr. 6, 86
By the Waters of Babylon Gr. 6, 311
Cement Mixer Gr. 4, 102
Hine mah tov Gr. 5, 430
Ja-Da Gr. 7, G-20
*Jesu, Joy of Man's Desiring*
    Gr. 6, 87
*Marines' Hymn, The* Gr. 8, C-39
*MasqueradeSuite, "Galop"* Gr. 4, 16
*Nutcracker Suite, The, "Trepak"*
    Gr. 3, 280
Ode to Joy Gr. 4, 152
Over the Rainbow Gr. 4, 140
*Over the Rainbow* Gr. 4, 143
Railroad Corral Gr. 3, 174
Rockin' Around the Christmas Tree
    Gr. 5, 466
*Take the "A" Train* Gr. 8, C-42
What a Wonderful World Gr. 6, 62

## AABB

Angels On the Midnight Clear
    Gr. 6, 423
El carnavalito humahuaqueño
    Gr. 6, 482
El cóndor pasa Gr. 6, 46
Greensleeves Gr. 6, 49
La paloma se fué Gr. 6, 51
S'vivon Gr. 6, 452

## AB

Abraham, Martin, and John
    Gr. 6, 466
Al quebrar la piñata Gr. 4, 432
Ambos a dos Gr. 3, 20
Amefuri Gr. 1, 144
Big Rock Candy Mountain
    Gr. 4, 330
Dayenu Gr. 4, 439
Dinosaur Dance Gr. 2, 168
Each of Us Is a Flower Gr. 3, 154
El borrego Gr. 4, 242
El carnavalito humahuaqueño
    Gr. 6, 482

El florón Gr. 2, 246
El rabel Gr. 3, 362
*Flop-Eared Mule* Gr. 3, 99
*Harukoma, "Spring Horse Dance"*
    Gr. 1, 145
*Illusions* Gr. 6, 347
Joy to the World Gr. 3, 22
La paloma se fué Gr. 6, 51
Los pececitos Gr. 1, 178
*Old American Songs, "The
    Boatman's Dance"* Gr. 4, 61
Old Dan Tucker Gr. 3, 96
River Gr. 4, 58
*Rodeo, "Saturday Night Waltz"*
    Gr. 4, 342
S'vivon Gr. 6, 452
Shalom aleichem Gr. 6, 409
Shanghai Chicken Gr. 1, 140
*Sikelela* Gr. 1, 139
Uno, dos y tres Gr. 5, 429
*Vulani ringi ring* Gr. 1, 139
Zip-a-Dee-Doo-Dah Gr. 2, 330

## ABA

All Night, All Day Gr. 4, 180
Banana Splits Gr. 1, 318
Blum (poem) Gr. 1, 221
By the Waters of Babylon
    Gr. 6, 311
Con el vito Gr. 7, G-15
*Danses Populaires Francaises,
    "Branle Double, Branle
    Simple"* Gr. 7, C-25
Doong gul ge Gr. 3, 134
Dry Bones Come Skipping
    Gr. 4, 218
*Eccosaise in E-flat Major*
    Gr. 1, 223
*Estancia, "Danza del trigo"*
    Gr. 5, 229
*Flying Home* Gr. 7, B-15
Follow the Drinkin' Gourd Gr. 4, 266
Had to Get Up This Mornin' Soon
    Gr. 3, 114
Hotaru koi Gr. 1, 356
I Got Rhythm Gr. 6, 101
I Vow to You, My Country
    Gr. 5, 418
Joshua Fought the Battle Gr. 5, 101
La Tarara Gr. 4, 176
Lean on Me Gr. 6, 14
Lion Sleeps Tonight, The Gr. 4, 131
Little David, Play on Your Harp
    Gr. 4, 394
*Lohengrin, "Prelude to Act III"*
    Gr. 8, C-22
Magnolia Gr. 6, 16
*Marche Militaire, Op. 51, No. 1*
    Gr. 6, 17
Marines' Hymn, The Gr. 8, C-39
*Messiah, "Hallelujah!"* Gr. 8, C-8
Mubärak Gr. 3, 282

My Home's Across the Blue Ridge
    Mountains Gr. 4, 84
Never Smile at a Crocodile
    Gr. 3, 100
*Nutcracker Suite, The, "Waltz of
    the Flowers"* Gr. 6, 325
Panamam tombé Gr. 7, D-18
Put Your Hand in My Hand
    Gr. 1, 330
Rock Island Line Gr. 4, 54
Shoo, Fly Gr. 2, 200
Sing a Rainbow Gr. 2, 166
Soldier, Soldier Gr. 4, 11
Somos el barco Gr. 4, 352
*Sonata in C-sharp Minor, Op. 27,
    No. 2, "Moonlight," Movement
    1* Gr. 7, C-19
*Standin' in the Need of Prayer*
    Gr. 5, 103
*String Quartet in D Major, Op.
    64, No. 5, "The Lark," Allegro
    moderato* Gr. 7, C-15
*Symphony No. 47 in G Major,
    "Menuet"* Gr. 7, C-14
*Take Five* Gr. 5, 220
Three Little Birds Gr. 4, 320
Wade in the Water Gr. 4, 268
Walk in Jerusalem Gr. 4, 100
Willowbee Gr. 1, 222
Wings of a Dove Gr. 4, 318

## ABABA

Starlight, Star Bright Gr. 4, 373

## ABABAB

*Water Music, "Hornpipe"*
    Gr. 8, C-9

## ABABABA

Gospel Train, The Gr. 6, 398

## ABAC

But the Cat Came Back Gr. 2, 190
Colorado Trail Gr. 5, 276

## ABACA (RONDO)

*ABACA Dabble* Gr. 4, 184
*Acadian Songs, "Walking Song"*
    Gr. 4, 347
Ama-Lama Gr. 5, 142
Bananas and Cream (speech piece)
    Gr. 3, 210
*Carnival of the Animals, "Fossils"*
    Gr. 4, 220
*Concerto for French Horn in
    E-flat Major, K. 495, No. 4,
    Movement 3* Gr. 8, C-11
*Country Dance* Gr. 3, 211
Heave-Ho!/Going, Going, Gone/
    The Snow Gr. 4, 182
How to Be a Friend (poem)
    Gr. 1, 331
La raspa Gr. 4, 302
*Orfferondo* Gr. 4, 194
*Pulcinella Suite, "Minuetto"*
    Gr. 8, C-15

Rondo for Lunch, A (speech piece)
Gr. 3, 212
*Sonata No. 11, K. 331, "Turkish Rondo"* Gr. K, 165
Trouble Is a Mountain Gr. 2, 202

## ABBA
*Pictures at an Exhibition, "The Hut of Baba Yaga (The Hut on Fowl's Legs)"* Gr. 4, 103

## ABC
*Bachianas brasileiras No. 5, "Aria"* Gr. 8, C-37
Dry Bones Gr. 4, 162
Hava nashira Gr. 6, 82
I've Been Working on the Railroad Gr. 3, 242
*Xochipilli, An Imagined Aztec Music* Gr. 8, C-37

## ABCA
Birthday Gr. 6, 90

## ABCAB
Achshav Gr. 2, 64
*Suite No. 2 in F, Op. 28b, Movement 1, "March"* Gr. 6, 139

## BALLADS AND STORY SONGS
Green, Green Grass of Home Gr. 6, 248

## CALL AND RESPONSE
ABC Rock Gr. 1, 262
Ain't Gonna Let Nobody Turn Me 'Round Gr. 8, F-16
*Ajaja* Gr. 8, B-3
All Night, All Day Gr. 4, 180
Amasee Gr. 1, 172
*Awakening* Gr. 7, D-14
Banana Gr. 2, 114
Bantama kra kro Gr. 5, 308
Bob-a-Needle Gr. 2, 232
Bound for South Australia Gr. 5, 22
*Carrament News* Gr. 8, B-22
Certainly, Lord Gr. 7, I-13
Che che koolay Gr. 2, 266
Chicka Hanka Gr. 2, 211
Chicka Hanka Gr. 8, F-15
Cookie Gr. 2, 172
Day-O! (Banana Boat Loader's Song) Gr. 5, 18
Dinner Music Gr. K, 70
Down by the Bay Gr. 1, 18
Earth Is My Mother, The Gr. 1, 340
Ezekiel Saw the Wheel Gr. 6, 379
Free at Last Gr. 2, 396
Free at Last Gr. 6, 468
Go Down, Moses Gr. 5, 190
*Go Down, Moses* Gr. 7, G-10
*Goodbye, Ev'rybody (Farewell Shout)* Gr. 7, D-2
Goodbye, Julie (Miss Julie Ann Johnson) Gr. 1, 334

Goodbye, Julie (Miss Julie Ann Johnson) Gr. 8, E-2
Gospel Train, The Gr. 6, 398
Great Big Stars Gr. 1, 60
Great Day Gr. 3, 58
Green, Green, Rocky Gr. 1, 321
Hambone Gr. 1, 202
Hambone Gr. 7, D-3
Hashewie Gr. 4, 63
He's Got the Whole World in His Hands Gr. 7, I-36
I Got a Letter This Morning Gr. K, 68
I'm on My Way Gr. 3, 76
I'm on My Way Gr. 7, A-15
*If You Can Walk* Gr. 1, 19
Ise oluwa Gr. 6, 230
It Don't Mean a Thing (If It Ain't Got That Swing) Gr. 5, 336
*It's Time* Gr. 6, 319
It's Time Gr. 6, 274
Just from the Kitchen Gr. K, 55
Koriko! Gr. K, 154
Kum ba yah Gr. 5, 244
La copa de la vida Gr. 4, 414
Lemonade Gr. 1, 190
Limbo Like Me Gr. 4, 18
Little Johnny Brown Gr. 3, 313
Mashed Potatoes (speech piece) Gr. 1, 20
Michael, Row the Boat Ashore Gr. 2, 18
Mister Ram Goat-O Gr. 3, 54
My Mama's Calling Me Gr. 1, 260
Pay Me My Money Down Gr. 4, 38
*Pay Me My Money Down* Gr. 4, 39
Pay Me My Money Down Gr. 7, I-46
*PIZZ Ah!* Gr. 1, 105
Ptashky u babusi sadochku Gr. 1, 192
*Reggae Is Now* Gr. 6, 143
Rise Up, Shepherd, and Follow Gr. 5, 471
Shenandoah Gr. 5, 264
Shine, Shine, Shine Gr. 1, 42
Shoo, Turkey Gr. 1, 104
Shortnin' Bread Gr. 1, 57
Shortnin' Bread Gr. 7, F-27
Shri Ram, jai Ram Gr. 4, 311
Sing About Martin Gr. K, 321
Siyahamba Gr. 6, 212
Three Little Birds Gr. 4, 320
Wade in the Water Gr. 8, I-64
Water Come a Me Eye Gr. 6, 300
When I Grow Up Gr. 2, 397

## CANONS AND ROUNDS
*Canon for Violin and Cello* Gr. 6, 126
Dance for the Nations Gr. 6, 122
Dona nobis pacem Gr. 6, 125

## CANTATA
*Cantata No. 140 (as performed by American Bach Solosists), "Wachet auf, ruft uns die Stimme," Movement 4* Gr. 7, C-9
*Cantata No. 140 (as performed by The Swingle Singers), "Wachet auf, ruft uns die Stimme," Movement 4* Gr. 7, C-10

## CODA
All for One Gr. 7, E-8
¡Ay, Jalisco no te rajes! Gr. 7, I-6
Beyond Borders Gr. 5, 292
California Dreamin' Gr. 8, G-31
Canto del agua Gr. 8, I-10
Cement Mixer Gr. 4, 102
Chapel of Love Gr. 7, G-27
Dinosaur Dance Gr. 2, 168
*Dúlamán* Gr. 4, 299
Feliz Navidad Gr. 7, I-28
Go, My Son Gr. 6, 188
God Bless the U.S.A. Gr. 8, G-37
I Believe I Can Fly Gr. 5, 170
I See With My Hands Gr. 2, 148
If a Tiger Calls Gr. 3, 354
Ja-Da Gr. 7, G-20
Kum bachur atzel Gr. 3, 138
La copa de la vida Gr. 4, 414
La mar estaba serena Gr. 2, 344
Little Shop of Horrors Gr. 4, 422
Love Can Build a Bridge Gr. 4, 324
*Nanafushi* Gr. 7, D-16
*Nutcracker Suite, The, "Trepak"* Gr. 3, 280
*Old American Songs, "The Boatman's Dance"* Gr. 4, 61
One Family Gr. 7, G-17
Over the Rainbow Gr. 4, 140
*Over the Rainbow* Gr. 4, 143
*Peak Moments* Gr. 8, E-4
Proud Gr. 7, G-3
*Search for the Hero* Gr. 7, G-5
Silly Street Gr. K, 224
Sing, America, Sing! Gr. 3, 238
Something Told the Wild Geese Gr. 7, G-39
Straighten Up and Fly Right Gr. 4, 128
Surfin' U.S.A. Gr. 7, I-58
*Symphony No. 40 in G Minor, K. 550, Movement 1* Gr. 8, C-12
Take a Chance On Me Gr. 8, G-15
Teach Me to Swing Gr. 5, 84
Theme from New York, New York Gr. 4, 250
There's a Place Gr. 5, 210
This World Gr. 5, 168
*Tzlil Zugim* Gr. 3, 139
Yesh lanu taish Gr. 1, 182
You've Got a Friend Gr. 5, 366

(*Form*, continued)

## CONCERTO

*Brandenburg Concerto No. 2, Movement 3 Allegro Assai* Gr. 7, C-8
*Concerto for Flute and Harp in C, K. 299, Movement 2* Gr. 8, C-10
*Concerto for French Horn in E-flat Major, K. 495, No. 4, Movement 3* Gr. 8, C-11
*Concerto for Viola and Orchestra, Movement 3* Gr. 7, C-35
*Piano Concerto in A Minor, Op. 16, Movement 1* Gr. 8, E-11
*Piano Concerto in E-flat Major, Op. 73, No. 5, "Emperor," Movement 3* Gr. 7, C-18
*Violin Concerto in E Minor, Op. 64, Movement 1* Gr. 8, C-18

## CUMULATIVE SONGS

I Know an Old Lady  Gr. 1, 388
Must Be Santa  Gr. K, 318
Parade Came Marching, The  Gr. 1, 166
Sailing to the Sea  Gr. 1, 336
Tree in the Wood, The  Gr. 2, 360

## D.C.

It's Time  Gr. 6, 274

## D.C. AL CODA

Beyond Borders  Gr. 5, 292
Little Shop of Horrors  Gr. 4, 422
My Home's Across the Blue Ridge Mountains  Gr. 7, F-6
Riendo el río corre  Gr. 6, 263
Teach Me to Swing  Gr. 5, 84

## D.C. AL FINE

Al tambor  Gr. 3, 270
Ala Da'lona  Gr. 4, 136
All Night, All Day  Gr. 4, 180
¡Ay, Jalisco no te rajes!  Gr. 7, I-6
Banana  Gr. 2, 114
Birthday  Gr. 6, 90
Con el vito  Gr. 7, G-15
Dry Bones Come Skipping  Gr. 4, 218
Ezekiel Saw the Wheel  Gr. 6, 379
Flat Foot Floogee, The  Gr. 3, 160
Follow the Drinkin' Gourd  Gr. 4, 266
Free at Last  Gr. 6, 468
Gonna Have a Good Time  Gr. 2, 4
Great Day  Gr. 3, 58
Hashewie  Gr. 4, 63
Hello to All the Children of the World  Gr. 3, 4
Hit Me with a Hot Note and Watch Me Bounce  Gr. 6, 112
I Believe I Can Fly  Gr. 5, 170
I've Been Everywhere  Gr. 6, 226
Joshua Fought the Battle of Jericho  Gr. 8, E-18

La Tarara  Gr. 4, 176
Lion Sleeps Tonight, The  Gr. 4, 131
Little David, Play on Your Harp  Gr. 4, 394
Loco-Motion, The  Gr. 3, 64
Mr. Tambourine Man  Gr. 6, 150
Mud  Gr. 3, 32
My Home's Across the Blue Ridge Mountains  Gr. 4, 84
Never Smile at a Crocodile  Gr. 3, 100
Oh, Won't You Sit Down  Gr. 3, 28
Rock Island Line  Gr. 4, 54
S'vivon  Gr. 6, 452
Shine, Shine, Shine  Gr. 1, 42
Shoo, Fly  Gr. 2, 200
Shortnin' Bread  Gr. 7, F-27
Soldier, Soldier  Gr. 4, 11
Starlight, Star Bright  Gr. 4, 373
Supercalifragilisticexpialidocious  Gr. 3, 7
Three Little Birds  Gr. 4, 320
Three Little Birds  Gr. 8, F-7
Under the Same Sun  Gr. 6, 440
Wade in the Water  Gr. 4, 268
Wake Me, Shake Me  Gr. 1, 278
Walk in Jerusalem  Gr. 4, 100
Wings of a Dove  Gr. 4, 318
Woodland Chorus  Gr. K, 250
You Are My Sunshine  Gr. 6, 246
Zumba, zumba  Gr. 3, 400

## D.S. AL FINE

Abraham, Martin, and John  Gr. 6, 466
I Am But a Small Voice  Gr. 6, 446
Rhythm Is Gonna Get You, The  Gr. 6, 348

## DAL SEGNO

Canto del agua  Gr. 8, I-10
Joy of Kwanzaa, The  Gr. 6, 462
Proud  Gr. 7, G-3

## ECHO (IMITATION)

ABC Rock  Gr. 1, 262
Banuwa  Gr. 6, 294
Bear Dance  Gr. 7, I-10
California Dreamin'  Gr. 8, G-31
*Canzon in Echo Duodecimi Toni a 10*  Gr. 8, C-7
Cuckoo, Cuckoo  Gr. 1, 110
Down by the Bay  Gr. 1, 18
*Ev'rybody Ought to Know*  Gr. 1, 434
*Evening Chaconne*  Gr. 6, 202
*Every Night When the Sun Goes In*  Gr. 8, I-29
Everybody Loves Saturday Night  Gr. 6, 296
Feliz Navidad  Gr. 7, I-28
Four Strong Winds (Song to a Seagull)  Gr. 6, 170
Hello, There!  Gr. K, 6

*If You Can Walk*  Gr. 1, 19
*Jarabe tapatío*  Gr. 7, I-7
Kelo aba w'ye  Gr. 6, 290
*Máru-bihág*  Gr. 6, 304
Mashed Potatoes (speech piece)  Gr. 1, 20
Mashed Potatoes (poem)  Gr. 1, 21
*Men's Fancy Dance*  Gr. 7, D-24
Over My Head  Gr. 7, G-9
Sing a Little Song  Gr. K, 30
Sing About Martin  Gr. K, 321
Vem kan segla?  Gr. 6, 417
What to Do  Gr. K, 43
Who Has the Penny?  Gr. K, 42

## FUGUE

*"Little" Organ Fugue in G Minor*  Gr. 6, 129

## INTERLUDE

Canto del agua  Gr. 8, I-10
Ja-Da  Gr. 7, G-20
One Family  Gr. 7, G-17

## INTRODUCTION

Canto del agua  Gr. 8, I-10
*Galbi*  Gr. 1, 183
Ja-Da  Gr. 7, G-20
Koriko!  Gr. K, 154
Kum bachur atzel  Gr. 3, 138
La copa de la vida  Gr. 4, 414
La mar estaba serena  Gr. 2, 344
*Old American Songs, "The Boatman's Dance"*  Gr. 4, 61
One Family  Gr. 7, G-17
*Peak Moments*  Gr. 8, E-4
Something Told the Wild Geese  Gr. 7, G-39
*Tzlil Zugim*  Gr. 3, 139
Yesh lanu taish  Gr. 1, 182

## MINUET

*Symphony No. 47 in G Major, "Menuet"*  Gr. 7, C-14

## MOTIVE

Birthday  Gr. 6, 90
*L'union*  Gr. 6, 487
*Sonata in F Major for Violin and Piano, Op. 24, No. 5, "Spring," Movement 3*  Gr. 7, C-19
*String Quartet in D Major, Op. 64, No. 5, "The Lark," Allegro moderato*  Gr. 7, C-15
*Symphony No. 3 in E-flat Major, "Allegro con brio," Movement 1*  Gr. 8, C-17
*Symphony No. 3 in E-flat Major, "Marcia funebre," Movement 2*  Gr. 8, C-17
*Symphony No. 5 in C Minor, Op. 67, Movement 1*  Gr. 7, C-16
*Symphony No. 5 in C Minor, Op. 67, Movement 4*  Gr. 7, C-18
Vem kan segla?  Gr. 6, 417

## Part Songs

### 2-part
Angels On the Midnight Clear Gr. 6, 423
Oye Gr. 6, 336

## Phrases
Bluebonnets of Texas Gr. 3, 332
Chanukah Is Here! Gr. 2, 382
Children, Go Where I Send Thee Gr. 3, 392
Ciranda Gr. 2, 272
Gift to Share, A Gr. 6, 393
I'll Fly Away Gr. 8, I-42
*L'arc en ciel* Gr. 2, 333
*Marines' Hymn, The* Gr. 8, C-39
Perot Gr. 2, 378
Rainbow, The Gr. 2, 332
Shalom aleichem Gr. 6, 409
Shu ha mo Gr. 3, 276
Who Has Seen the Wind? Gr. 2, 324
Zip-a-Dee-Doo-Dah Gr. 2, 330

### aab
Good Mornin', Blues Gr. 2, 52
*When a Man's a Long Way from Home* Gr. 2, 53

### aaba
*12 Variations in C Major, K. 265/300e, "Ah, vous dirai-je, Maman"* Gr. 3, 19
Au clair de la lune Gr. 3, 18
Blue Skies Gr. 6, 88
Bridges Gr. 6, 86
Ein Männlein steht im Walde Gr. 2, 90
*Hänsel und Gretel, "Ein Männlein steht im Walde"* Gr. 2, 91
*Jesu, Joy of Man's Desiring* Gr. 6, 87
Song That's Just for You, A Gr. 2, 126

### aabb
Deux cocodries Gr. 2, 364

### aabc
Good King Wenceslas Gr. 6, 460

### ab
America Gr. 5, 486
America Gr. 6, 484

### aba
Hotaru koi Gr. 1, 356
Rain Sings a Song, The Gr. 1, 102

### abac
*You're a Grand Old Flag* Gr. 1, 276

## Question and Answer Phrases
All Around the Buttercup Gr. 2, 170
*Dances from Terpsichore, "Bransle de la Torche"* Gr. 3, 63
Der sad to katte Gr. 2, 300
*Drums From Around the World (Montage)* Gr. 6, 277
El rancho grande Gr. 8, I-22
Farewell to Tarwathie Gr. 6, 43
John Kanaka Gr. 3, 60
Kelo aba w'ye Gr. 6, 290
*Return to Misty Mountain* Gr. 7, D-28
Same Train Gr. 2, 164

## Rondo *See ABACA.*

## Same and Different Phrases
Ah! Les jolis papillons Gr. 1, 362
Au clair de la lune Gr. 3, 18
Bear Dance Gr. K, 127
Chapel of Love Gr. 7, G-27
*Dancing Tree, The* Gr. K, 202
Fais dodo Gr. K, 158
Fly and the Bumblebee, The Gr. 1, 384
Goin' to the Fair Gr. K, 156
Good Mornin', Blues Gr. 2, 52
Hevenu shalom aleichem Gr. 3, 378
Honeybee Song, The Gr. 1, 358
Joy of Kwanzaa, The Gr. 6, 462
Looby Loo Gr. K, 210
Magnolia Gr. 6, 16
*Marche Militaire, Op. 51, No. 1* Gr. 6, 17
S'vivon Gr. 6, 452
Three Times By She Passes (speech piece) Gr. K, 125
Vamos a hacer la ronda Gr. K, 124
*When a Man's a Long Way from Home* Gr. 2, 53
Winter Song Gr. 6, 455

## Scherzo
*Sonata in F Major for Violin and Piano, Op. 24, No. 5, "Spring," Movement 3* Gr. 7, C-19

## Solo/Chorus *See also Call and Response.*
*Aida, "Gloria all'Egitto (Grand March)"* Gr. 8, C-24
Ain't Gonna Let Nobody Turn Me 'Round Gr. 8, F-16
*Ajaja* Gr. 8, B-3
*Awakening* Gr. 7, D-14
*Carrament News* Gr. 8, B-22
Chicka Hanka Gr. 8, F-15
Crawfish! Gr. 2, 86
*Die Walküre, "The Ride of the Valkyries"* Gr. 8, C-23
Dinner Music Gr. K, 70
Free at Last Gr. 6, 468
From Sea to Shining Sea Gr. 2, 342
*Goodbye, Ev'rybody (Farewell Shout)* Gr. 7, D-2
Goodbye, Julie Gr. 8, E-2
Hambone Gr. 7, D-3
I Got Shoes Gr. 2, 242
Little Johnny Brown Gr. 3, 313
O lê lê O Bahía Gr. 6, 165
Ochimbo Gr. 4, 134
Oh, Won't You Sit Down Gr. 3, 28
Oye Gr. 6, 336
Pizza, Pizza, Daddy-o Gr. 2, 28
*Princess Hundred Flowers, The, "Falling in the Trap"* Gr. 8, C-25
Rise Up, Shepherd, and Follow Gr. 5, 471
Rosie, Darling Rosie Gr. 2, 215
'Round the Bay of Mexico Gr. 4, 258
Somebody Waiting Gr. 2, 283
Sugar "Shuga" Bee Gr. K, 64
*Talaque talaque o romance da Maria* Gr. 8, D-24
Who Has the Penny? Gr. K, 42

## Sonata
*Sonata for Clarinet and Piano, Op. 167, "Allegro animato," Movement 2* Gr. 7, C-12
*Sonata in C-sharp Minor, Op. 27, No. 2, "Moonlight," Movement 1* Gr. 7, C-19
*Symphony No. 40 in G Minor, K. 550, Movement 1* Gr. 8, C-12

## Strophic
*America* Gr. 7, A-22

## Theme and Variations
*Choo-Choo Joubert* Gr. 3, 51
Minka Gr. 4, 222
*Red Poppy, The, "Russian Sailors' Dance"* Gr. 4, 224
Scattin' A-Round (Variations on Row 3) Gr. 6, 160
Simple Gifts Gr. 5, 184
*Sonata in F Major for Violin and Piano, Op. 24, No. 5, "Spring," Movement 3* Gr. 7, C-19
Ten Little Ostinato Pieces Gr. 7, I-62
*Theme and Variations for Percussion* Gr. 5, 65
*Variations on "America"* Gr. 6, 162
*Variations on "The Carnival of Venice"* Gr. 6, 161

## Through-composed Form
I Dream a World Gr. 8, G-40
*Ma Vlast (My Fatherland), "Vltava (The Moldau)"* Gr. 7, C-33
Something Told the Wild Geese Gr. 7, G-39

(*Form,* continued)
    Your Friends Shall Be the Tall Wind
      Gr. 6, 201

## VERSE AND REFRAIN

Abraham, Martin, and John
    Gr. 6, 466
All for One Gr. 7, E-8
All the Way Around the World
    Gr. 2, 258
Amefuri Gr. 1, 144
At the Hop Gr. 4, 168
Away to America Gr. 5, 57
Bam, chi, chi, bam Gr. K, 109
Banana Gr. 2, 114
Basin Street Blues Gr. 5, 354
Battle Cry of Freedom Gr. 5, 272
Beach Rap (speech piece)
    Gr. 1, 352
Big Rock Candy Mountain
    Gr. 4, 330
Bling Blang Gr. 3, 240
Blow, Ye Winds Gr. 4, 255
Boil Them Cabbage Down
    Gr. 6, 370
Bonga Gr. K, 78
Brush Your Teeth Gr. 1, 284
But the Cat Came Back Gr. 2, 190
Camptown Races Gr. 5, 270
Cantaré, cantarás Gr. 6, 413
Cattle Call Gr. 5, 344
Children, Go Where I Send Thee
    Gr. 3, 392
Choo Choo Ch'Boogie Gr. 5, 44
Cielito lindo Gr. 4, 270
Cielito lindo Gr. 7, I-20
Cindy Gr. 4, 384
Clementine Gr. 4, 341
Coffee Grows on White Oak Trees
    Gr. 3, 168
Crawfish! Gr. 2, 86
Cuando pa' Chile me voy Gr. 6, 376
Cuculí Gr. K, 238
Cumberland Gap Gr. 4, 138
Cycle Song of Life (The River Song)
    Gr. 4, 370
*Dancing Tree, The* Gr. K, 202
Dayenu Gr. 4, 439
Ding Dong! Merrily on High
    Gr. 6, 427
Dinosaur Dance Gr. 2, 168
Doctor Knickerbocker (speech
    piece) Gr. 1, 302
*Domna, pos vos ay chausida
    (Lady, For You)* Gr. 8, C-6
Don't Cry for Me, Argentina
    Gr. 6, 74
Don't Let Your Watch Run Down
    Gr. 3, 166
Down the Ohio Gr. 2, 60
*Dúlamán* Gr. 4, 299
El coquí Gr. 2, 292
El rancho grande Gr. 4, 215

El rancho grande Gr. 8, I-22
Eres tú Gr. 6, 473
Erie Canal Gr. 5, 262
Everybody Says Gr. 1, 287
*Everything Grows* Gr. K, 267
Falling Rain Gr. 2, 328
Family Tree Gr. 3, 72
Feng yang hua gu Gr. 4, 313
Flip, Flop and Fly Gr. 7, I-32
Four Strong Winds (Song to a
    Seagull) Gr. 6, 170
Free at Last Gr. 2, 396
Free at Last Gr. 6, 468
Freight Train Gr. 1, 44
From Sea to Shining Sea Gr. 2, 342
Get on Your Feet Gr. 5, 6
Give a Little Love Gr. 6, 140
Glad to Have a Friend Like You
    Gr. 2, 228
Glendy Burke, The Gr. 4, 262
*Go, Tell It on the Mountain*
    Gr. 3, 393
Goin' to Boston Gr. 6, 433
Going Upon the Mountain
    Gr. 6, 105
Gonna Have a Good Time Gr. 2, 4
Gonna Ride Up in the Chariot
    Gr. 4, 20
Gospel Train, The Gr. 6, 398
Green, Green Grass of Home
    Gr. 6, 248
Guantanamera Gr. 8, I-32
Happy Wanderer, The Gr. 4, 89
Harambee Gr. 4, 434
Haul Away, Joe Gr. 4, 13
Hello! Gr. 2, 262
Hello to All the Children of the
    World Gr. 3, 4
*Hippopotamus Song, The*
    Gr. 3, 33
Honeybee Song, The Gr. 1, 358
Hop Up, My Ladies Gr. 3, 142
I Love Peanuts Gr. 1, 162
I See With My Hands Gr. 2, 148
I Shall Sing Gr. 8, I-38
*I Shall Sing* Gr. 8, I-41
I'll Fly Away Gr. 8, I-42
I'm a Believer Gr. 7, G-33
I'm Flying Home Gr. 2, 286
I'm in the Mood Gr. K, 86
I've Been Everywhere Gr. 6, 226
It's Time Gr. 6, 274
Jambalaya Gr. 8, I-46
Jambalaya (On The Bayou)
    Gr. 6, 244
Jig Along Home Gr. 2, 366
Joy to the World Gr. 3, 22
Kangaroo Song, The Gr. K, 44
Keel Row, The Gr. 4, 240
Keep Your Eyes on the Prize
    Gr. 3, 408
Kwanzaa Carol, A Gr. 2, 392
La paloma se fué Gr. 6, 51

La pulga de San José Gr. 3, 40
La tormenta tropical Gr. 2, 116
La víbora Gr. 1, 322
Land of a Thousand Dances
    Gr. 5, 330
Leatherwing Bat Gr. 2, 303
Let It Snow! Let It Snow! Let It
    Snow! Gr. 4, 426
Li'l Liza Jane Gr. 3, 140
Linstead Market Gr. 5, 241
Lion Sleeps Tonight, The Gr. 8, I-56
Listen to the Water Gr. 2, 294
Loch Lomond Gr. 5, 140
Looby Loo Gr. K, 210
Look Out for Mother Earth
    Gr. 3, 341
Los pececitos Gr. 1, 178
Love Can Build a Bridge Gr. 4, 324
Love in Any Language Gr. 6, 476
Mi cuerpo hace música Gr. K, 106
Midnight Special, The Gr. 7, F-23
Mister Rabbit Gr. K, 128
Mr. Tambourine Man Gr. 6, 150
Mud Gr. 3, 32
Music's in Me, The Gr. 2, 40
Must Be Santa Gr. K, 318
My Bonnie Lies Over the Ocean
    Gr. 4, 338
My Home's Across the Blue Ridge
    Mountains Gr. 7, F-6
Nampaya omame Gr. 1, 138
New Way to Walk, A Gr. K, 117
Noah's Shanty Gr. 1, 342
O, Desayo Gr. 5, 411
O pião entrou Gr. 2, 355
Ocho kandelikas Gr. 4, 429
Oh, Susanna Gr. 4, 264
Oh, Won't You Sit Down Gr. 3, 28
*Old American Songs, "The
    Boatman's Dance"* Gr. 4, 61
Old Blue Gr. K, 122
Old Chisholm Trail, The Gr. 6, 237
Old Dan Tucker Gr. 3, 96
Oye Gr. 6, 336
Pat Works on the Railway Gr. 5, 182
Paths of Victory Gr. 6, 195
Pay Me My Money Down Gr. 4, 38
*Pay Me My Money Down* Gr. 4, 39
Pay Me My Money Down Gr. 7, I-46
Peanut Butter (speech piece)
    Gr. 1, 173
Polly Wee Gr. K, 119
Proud Gr. 7, G-3
Puff, the Magic Dragon Gr. 2, 350
Purple People Eater, The Gr. 6, 448
Put a Little Love in Your Heart
    Gr. 4, 6
Rags Gr. 1, 290
Rhythm Is Gonna Get You, The
    Gr. 6, 348
Riendo el río corre Gr. 6, 263
Rig-a-Jig-Jig Gr. K, 99
Rio Grande Gr. 4, 256

Rise and Shine  Gr. 1, 122
River  Gr. 4, 58
Rock and Roll Is Here to Stay
    Gr. 6, 36
Scotland the Brave  Gr. 5, 138
*Search for the Hero*  Gr. 7, G-5
See and Touch  Gr. K, 172
Shady Grove  Gr. 5, 260
Shanghai Chicken  Gr. 1, 140
Ship that Never Returned, The
    Gr. 5, 402
Shoo, Turkey  Gr. 1, 104
Shortnin' Bread  Gr. 1, 57
Shortnin' Bread  Gr. 7, F-27
Si me dan pasteles  Gr. 1, 432
Sing, Sing, Sing!  Gr. 5, 340
Singin' in the Tub  Gr. K, 220
Skye Boat Song  Gr. 6, 372
Song of the Fishes  Gr. 3, 244
Spaceworms  Gr. 1, 400
Sweet Betsy from Pike  Gr. 4, 244
Tancovačka  Gr. 4, 230
Tie Me Kangaroo Down, Sport
    Gr. 4, 37
Time to Sing  Gr. 2, 8
Turn, Turn, Turn (To Everything
    There Is a Season)  Gr. 5, 378
Twelve Gates to the City  Gr. 5, 280
Under the Same Sun  Gr. 6, 440
United Nations on the March, The
    Gr. 6, 443
Valentines  Gr. 2, 398
Vamos a hacer la ronda  Gr. K, 124
¡Viva el fútbol!  Gr. 1, 96
Wade in the Water  Gr. 8, I-64
Waitin' for the Light to Shine
    Gr. 4, 26
Wake Me, Shake Me  Gr. 1, 278
Water Come a Me Eye  Gr. 6, 300
Way Down in the Schoolyard
    Gr. 2, 50
We Wish You a Merry Christmas
    Gr. 3, 395
We're Making Popcorn (speech
    piece)  Gr. 1, 86
When the Train Comes Along
    Gr. 1, 300
Willowbee  Gr. 1, 222
Winter Song  Gr. 6, 455
Woodland Chorus  Gr. K, 250
*Wooly Bully*  Gr. 3, 372
Wooly Bully  Gr. 3, 373
Worried Man Blues  Gr. 6, 371
You Are My Sunshine  Gr. 6, 246
You've Got a Friend  Gr. 5, 366
Your Life Is Now  Gr. 6, 4
Zudio  Gr. 2, 269

# G

**GAMES** *See Genre/Style: Game
Songs.*

## GENRE/STYLE

*(Listening selections appear in italics.)*

### ACTION SONGS

Che che koolay  Gr. 2, 266
Clap, Wiggle, and Stomp  Gr. K, 34
*Copycat*  Gr. K, 9
Dinosaur Dance  Gr. 2, 168
*Doing the Penguin*  Gr. K, 35
Goin' to the Fair  Gr. K, 156
Here I Go!  Gr. K, 73
Hi-Dee-Roon  Gr. K, 10
Hokey Pokey  Gr. K, 296
If You're Happy  Gr. K, 94
Jim Along, Josie  Gr. K, 39
Johnny Mister Brown  Gr. K, 37
Kangaroo Song, The  Gr. K, 44
Kuma san  Gr. K, 40
Miss Susie Anna Sue  Gr. K, 242
Nanny Goat  Gr. K, 161
Number One, Touch Your Tongue
    (speech piece)  Gr. K, 204
Oliver Jump (speech piece)
    Gr. K, 205
Oliver Twist  Gr. K, 138
One Green Jelly Bean  Gr. K, 287
Pon, pon, pon  Gr. K, 50
Put Your Finger in the Air  Gr. K, 114
Twist with a Burger, Jitter with a
    Bug (speech piece)  Gr. 1, 132
Uga uga uga  Gr. K, 305
Vamos a cantar  Gr. K, 278
Vamos a hacer la ronda  Gr. K, 124

### AMERICAN (COMPOSED)

Addicott, Fran Smartt: Let Music
    Surround You  Gr. 4, 236
Ager, Milton: Happy Days Are Here
    Again  Gr. 5, 284
Ager, Milton: Happy Feet
    Gr. 2, 252
Allison/Petty/Holly: *That'll Be the
    Day*  Gr. 6, 256
Amos, Tori: *Sorta Fairytale, A*
    Gr. 7, A-5
Anderson, Leroy: *Sleigh Ride*
    Gr. 2, 390
Andersson/Anderson/Ulvaeus:
    *Dancing Queen*  Gr. 8, G-19
Appell/Mann: *Let's Twist Again*
    Gr. 6, 257
Arlen, Harold: Over the Rainbow
    (from The Wizard of Oz)
    Gr. 4, 140
Austin, Mary: Song of Greatness, A
    Gr. 3, 334
Baez, Joan: *Diamonds and Rust*
    Gr. 7, A-4
Bagdasarian, Ross: Christmas, Don't
    Be Late (The Chipmunk Song)
    Gr. 2, 386
Ballard, Henry: *Twist, The*
    Gr. 5, 358
Ballard, Henry: *Twist, The*
    Gr. 7, B-10
Banana Slug String Band: What Do
    Animals Need?  Gr. 2, 288
Barber, Samuel: *Hermit Songs, Op.
    29, "The Monk and His Cat"*
    Gr. 7, C-21
Barry/Greenwich: Do Wah Diddy
    Diddy  Gr. 4, 203
Barry/Greenwich: Do Wah Diddy
    Diddy  Gr. 7, F-21
Bassett, Rick: See and Touch
    Gr. K, 172
Bassett, Rick: Sing! Speak!
    Whisper! Shout!  Gr. 1, 36
Bassett, Rick: Storm Dance (speech
    piece)  Gr. K, 145
Batchelder, W. K.: *Glory Hallelujah
    Grand March*  Gr. 8, C-38
Berlin, Irving: Alexander's Ragtime
    Band  Gr. 6, 136
Berlin, Irving: Blue Skies  Gr. 6, 88
Berlin, Irving: God Bless America
    Gr. 5, 4
Berlin, Irving: *Let's Face the Music*
    Gr. 7, B-14
Berlin, Irving: Play a Simple Melody
    Gr. 5, 72
Berlin/Lazarus: Give Me Your
    Tired, Your Poor  Gr. 5, 166
Bernard, Felix: Winter Wonderland
    Gr. 5, 454
Bernstein, Leonard: *America (from
    West Side Story)*  Gr. 8, C-45
Bernstein, Leonard: *Somewhere
    (from West Side Story)*
    Gr. 8, C-44
Berry, Chuck: Surfin' U.S.A.
    Gr. 6, 260
Berry, Chuck: Surfin' U.S.A.
    Gr. 7, I-58
Berryhill/Connolly/Fuller/Wilson:
    *Wipe Out*  Gr. 5, 155
Berryhill/Connolly/Fuller/Wilson:
    *Wipe Out*  Gr. 7, F-33
Besterman, Doug: *Overture/All
    That Jazz (from Chicago)*
    Gr. 7, A-23
Blackwell/Presley: Don't Be Cruel
    Gr. 6, 255
Bo, Eddie: *I Know You Mardi Gras*
    Gr. 8, B-17
Bock, Jerry: Fiddler on the Roof
    Gr. 7, E-5
Boshkoff, Ruth: Little Black Bug
    Gr. 1, 214
Boshkoff, Ruth: Little Black Bug
    Gr. 1, 214
Boyd/Alexie: *Treaties*  Gr. 8, B-36
Bozzio, Terry: *Over and Under
    a Theme of Mark Isham's*
    Gr. 8, B-4

(*Genre/Style*, continued)

Bricusse/Newley: Gonna Build a Mountain Gr. 6, 21

Britten, Benjamin: Old Abram Brown Gr. 5, 22

Broonzy/Segar: Key to the Highway Gr. 6, 243

Broonzy/Segar: *Key to the Highway* Gr. 6, 243

Broonzy/Segar: Key to the Highway Gr. 8, F-29

Broonzy/Segar: *Key to the Highway* Gr. 8, F-28

Brown, Nacio Herb: Singin' in the Rain Gr. 4, 360

Bruce, Jack: *Boston Ball Game 1967* Gr. 8, F-32

Bruchac, Joseph: *Rabbit Dance, The* Gr. 3, 334

Brumley, Albert E.: I'll Fly Away Gr. 8, I-43

Brumley, Albert E.: *I'll Fly Away* Gr. 8, I-43

Bryant/Bryant: Bye Bye, Love Gr. 8, F-9

Bryant/Bryant: *Bye Bye, Love* Gr. 8, A-15

Bryant/Bryant: *Bye, Bye Love* Gr. 5, 357

Bryant/Bryant: Rocky Top Gr. 5, 348

Burch, Sharon: *Rain Song, The* Gr. 2, 323

Burrough, Roslyn: I Love Peanuts Gr. 1, 162

Burrough, Roslyn: I Love Peanuts Gr. 7, E-20

Burrough, Roslyn: *I Love Peanuts* Gr. 1, 163

Burson-Nofchissey: Go, My Son Gr. 6, 188

Cahn/Styne: *Let It Snow! Let It Snow! Let It Snow!* Gr. 4, 427

Calhoun/Turner: *Flip, Flop and Fly* Gr. 7, F-15

Calhoun/Turner: Flip, Flop and Fly Gr. 7, I-33

Callaway, Ann: At the Same Time Gr. 6, 115

Campbell-Towell, Lee: Mashed Potatoes (speech piece) Gr. 1, 20

Cantrell, Jerry: *Would?* Gr. 8, F-30

Carleton, Bob: Ja-Da Gr. 2, 188

Carleton, Bob: *Ja-Da* Gr. 2, 187

Carleton, Bob: Ja-Da Gr. 7, G-20

Carpenter, Mary Chapin: *Halley Came to Jackson* Gr. 2, 340

Carter, Clifford: Under the Same Sun Gr. 6, 440

Casey, Thomas: Drill, Ye Tarriers Gr. 5, 54

Casey/Jacobs: Those Magic Changes Gr. 8, E-30

Casey/Jacobs: We Go Together Gr. 4, 44

Cash, Johnny: *I Walk the Line* Gr. 7, B-28

Chapin, Tom: *Shoveling* Gr. 1, 423

Charlap, Mark: Tender Shepherd (Count Your Sheep) Gr. 3, 116

Charles, Ray: *Ain't That Love* Gr. 5, 20

Charles, Ray: Fifty Nifty United States Gr. 5, 251

Churchill, Frank: Heigh-Ho Gr. 2, 6

Churchill, Frank: Never Smile at a Crocodile Gr. 3, 100

Cleveland/Gaye/Benson: *What's Going On?* Gr. 7, B-38

Cohan, George M.: *I'm a Yankee Doodle Dandy* Gr. 5, 278

Cohan, George M.: Over There Gr. 5, 279

Cohan, George M.: *Yankee Doodle Boy, The* Gr. 3, 265

Cohan, George M.: *You're a Grand Old Flag* Gr. 1, 276

Cohan, George M.: You're a Grand Old Flag Gr. 3, 264

Cole/Mills: Straighten Up and Fly Right Gr. 4, 128

Connick, Jr./McLean: *Forever, For Now* Gr. 7, B-16

Cook, Victor: Heri za Kwanzaa Gr. 5, 476

Copland, Aaron: *Appalachian Spring, "Variations on Simple Gifts"* Gr. 5, 185

Copland, Aaron: *Billy the Kid, "Celebration"* Gr. 3, 251

Copland, Aaron: *El Salón México* Gr. 6, 199

Copland, Aaron: *Fanfare for the Common Man* Gr. 7, C-43

Copland, Aaron: *Old American Songs, "The Boatman's Dance"* Gr. 4, 61

Copland, Aaron: *Rodeo, "Buckaroo Holiday"* Gr. 2, 23

Copland, Aaron: *Rodeo, "Hoedown"* Gr. 1, 6

Copland, Aaron: *Rodeo, "Hoedown"* Gr. 5, 312

Copland, Aaron: *Rodeo, "Hoedown"* Gr. 8, B-42

Copland, Aaron: *Rodeo, "Saturday Night Waltz"* Gr. 4, 342

Crosby/Stills/Nash/Young: *Carry On* Gr. 7, B-2

Curtis, Natalie: Chuhwuht Gr. 2, 356

Cytrynbaum, Jackie: I'm a Dreydl Gr. K, 315

Dalglish, Malcolm: Sail Away Gr. 5, 404

Davis/Malone/Patrick: Book of Love Gr. 8, G-27

Davis/Mitchell: You Are My Sunshine Gr. 6, 246

Davis/Mitchell: *You Are My Sunshine* Gr. 6, 247

Davis/Mitchell: *You Are My Sunshine* Gr. 7, B-7

DeKnight/Friedman: *Rock Around the Clock* Gr. 5, 357

Desmond, Paul: *Take Five* Gr. 5, 220

Desmond, Paul: *Take Five* Gr. 7, B-15

Diamond, Neil: America (N. Diamond) Gr. 4, 206

Diamond, Neil: I'm a Believer Gr. 7, G-33

Diamond, Neil: *I'm a Believer* Gr. 7, G-32

Diller/Page: Who Has the Penny? Gr. K, 42

Domino/Bartholomew: *My Girl Josephine* Gr. 8, E-21

Domino/Bartholomew/Guidry: *Walkin' to New Orleans* Gr. 3, 371

Doucet, Sharon Arms: *L'arc en ciel* Gr. 2, 333

Driftwood, Jimmie: *Battle of New Orleans, The* Gr. 6, 105

Duke/Gershwin: *I Can't Get Started* Gr. 7, B-26

Dykes, Doyle: *Jazz in the Box* Gr. 8, F-11

Dylan, Bob: Blowin' in the Wind Gr. 5, 382

Dylan, Bob: *Blowin' in the Wind* Gr. 5, 384

Dylan, Bob: *Mr. Tambourine Man* Gr. 6, 148

Dylan, Bob: Mr. Tambourine Man Gr. 6, 150

Dylan, Bob: Paths of Victory Gr. 6, 195

Dylan, Bob: *Times They Are A-Changin', The* Gr. 5, 384

Eaglebear Singers/Sherman Alexie: *John Wayne's Teeth* Gr. 8, B-37

Eddleman, David: *Beat of the Tango, The* Gr. K, 106

Eddleman, David: *Cookie Crew, The* Gr. K, 196

Eddleman, David: Down the Listening Lane Gr. K, 192

Eddleman, David: Ev'ry Kind of Music Gr. 2, 226

Eddleman, David: *I'm Gonna Sing a Silly Song* Gr. K, 225

Eddleman, David: I'm Flying Home Gr. 2, 286

Eddleman, David: Mud Gr. 3, 32

Eddleman, David: *Noah's Zoo in the Big, Big Rain* Gr. K, 274

Eddleman, David: Rabbit Footprints Gr. 2, 304

Eddleman, David: Snowflakes Gr. 1, 422

Ellington, Duke: *C-Jam Blues* Gr. 8, C-43

Ellington, Duke: *Don't Get Around Much Anymore* Gr. 1, 33

Ellington, Duke: Hit Me with a Hot Note and Watch Me Bounce Gr. 6, 112

Ellington, Duke: *It Don't Mean a Thing if It Ain't Got that Swing* Gr. 6, 386

Ellington, Duke: It Don't Mean a Thing (If It Ain't Got That Swing) Gr. 5, 336

Ellington, Duke: *Queen's Suite, The, "Sunset and the Mocking Bird"* Gr. 8, E-10

Elvey, George: Come, Ye Thankful People, Come Gr. 5, 459

Fink/Marxer: Kid Like Me, A (speech piece) Gr. 2, 394

Forbes, James A.: For Children Safe and Strong Gr. 5, 484

Forster/Chapin: Family Tree Gr. 3, 72

Forster/Chapin: Long Way Home, A Gr. 1, 382

Forster/Chapin: Sailing to the Sea Gr. 1, 336

Forster/Chapin: Song of One, A Gr. 3, 344

Forster/Chapin: This Pretty Planet Gr. 4, 355

Forster/Chapin: Wheel of the Water, The Gr. 4, 362

Forster/Chapin: Wheel of the Water, The Gr. 4, 362

Foster, Stephen: Camptown Races Gr. 5, 270

Foster, Stephen: Glendy Burke, The Gr. 4, 262

Foster, Stephen: Oh, Susanna Gr. 4, 264

Foster/Sager: *Prayer, The* Gr. 7, A-10

Freedman/DeKnight: Rock Around the Clock Gr. 7, B-18

Fricker, Sylvia: You Were on My Mind Gr. 7, G-23

Gabriel, Peter: *Solsbury Hill* Gr. 8, E-29

Gaillard/Stewart/Green: Flat Foot Floogee, The Gr. 3, 160

Gaillard/Stewart/Green: *Flat Foot Floogee, The* Gr. 3, 158

Gallina, Jill: Costume Capers Gr. 1, 412

Gallina, Jill: Honeybee Song, The Gr. 1, 358

Gallina, Jill: Honeybee Song, The Gr. 1, 358

Gallina, Jill: Let the Music Begin! Gr. 1, 2

Gallina, Jill: Let's Celebrate! Gr. 3, 374

Gallina, Jill: Music's in Me, The Gr. 2, 40

Gallina, Jill: Party Tonight! Gr. 2, 152

Gallina, Jill: Silly Street Gr. K, 224

Gallina, Jill: Sing Me a Story Gr. 2, 346

Gallina, Jill: Sing, America, Sing! Gr. 3, 238

Gallina, Jill: Winter Fantasy Gr. 4, 424

Gallina, Jill: Winter Fantasy/Jingle Bells Gr. 4, 424

Gaye/Hunter/Stevenson: Dancin' in the Street Gr. 5, 363

Gaye/Hunter/Stevenson: *Dancin' in the Street* Gr. 5, 360

Gaye/Hunter/Stevenson: *Dancing in the Street* Gr. 2, 254

Gershwin, George: *Fascinatin' Rhythm (Frances Veri)* Gr. 7, E-11

Gershwin, George: I Got Rhythm Gr. 6, 101

Gershwin, George: *Lullaby for Strings* Gr. 1, 293

Gershwin, George: *Plenty o' Nuttin'* Gr. 7, B-45

Gershwin, George: *Rhapsody in Blue* Gr. 7, C-42

Gershwin, George: *Rhapsody in Blue* Gr. K, 75

Gershwin, George: Strike Up the Band Gr. 6, 135

Gershwin, George: Summertime Gr. 6, 250

Gershwin, George: *Summertime* Gr. 6, 252

Gershwin, George: Swanee Gr. 6, 118

Gershwin, George and Ira: *Fascinatin' Rhythm (Ella Fitzgerald)* Gr. 7, E-11

Gillespie, Avon: Every Morning When I Wake Up Gr. 2, 320

Gillespie/Fuller/Pozo: *Manteca* Gr. 7, B-3

Gilmore, Patrick S.: Ants Go Marching, The Gr. 1, 248

Gilmore, Patrick S.: When Johnny Comes Marching Home Gr. 5, 180

Gilmore/Harris: *When Johnny Comes Marching Home* Gr. 5, 88

Gilpatrick, Elizabeth: Good Morning Gr. 3, 192

Gilpatrick, Elizabeth: If a Tiger Calls Gr. 3, 356

Gilpatrick, Elizabeth: In the Pumpkin Patch Gr. 3, 380

Ginsburg, Ned: Dinosaur Dance Gr. 2, 168

Ginsburg, Ned: *Groundhog Jig, The* Gr. 1, 436

Ginsburg, Ned: Voices of Pride, The Gr. 5, 86

Glover/Dee: Peppermint Twist Gr. 3, 46

Goffin/King: Loco-Motion, The Gr. 3, 64

Goldman, Edwin: *On the Mall* Gr. 5, 2

Goodman, Benny: *Flying Home* Gr. 7, B-15

Gottschalk, Louis Moreau: *Bamboula* Gr. 3, 229

Gould, Morton: *American Salute* Gr. 5, 275

Gould, Morton: *Fanfare for Freedom* Gr. 6, 139

Gould, Morton: *Fourth of July, The* Gr. 5, 489

Greenfield, Eloise: Way Down in the Music Gr. 2, 227

Greenwood, Lee: God Bless the U.S.A. Gr. 8, G-37

Grier/Everspm: From Sea to Shining Sea Gr. 2, 342

Grofé, Ferde: *Grand Canyon Suite, "On the Trail"* Gr. 3, 77

Guaraldi, Vincent: *Linus and Lucy* Gr. 8, A-29

Gunn, Trey: *Dziban* Gr. 7, F-18

Guthrie, Woody: Bling Blang Gr. 3, 240

Guthrie, Woody: Bling Blang Gr. 3, 240

Guthrie, Woody: *Howjidoo* Gr. 1, 315

Guthrie, Woody: Jig Along Home Gr. 2, 366

Guthrie, Woody: Jig Along Home Gr. 2, 366

Guthrie, Woody: Pastures of Plenty Gr. 4, 280

Guthrie, Woody: Put Your Finger in the Air Gr. K, 114

Guthrie, Woody: *This Land Is Your Land* Gr. 5, 120

Guthrie, Woody: This Land Is Your Land Gr. 5, 118

(*Genre/Style,* continued)

Guthrie, Woody: This Land Is Your Land Gr. 7, I-66

Guthrie, Woody: This Land Is Your Land (refrain only) Gr. 1, 274

Guthrie/Hays: *Goin' Down the Road Feelin' Bad* Gr. 5, 283

Guthrie/Mazia: Race You Down the Mountain Gr. 1, 127

Hammil, Joanne: One Family Gr. 7, G-17

Hammond/Bettis: One Moment in Time Gr. 6, 352

Hancock, Herbie: *Watermelon Man* Gr. 1, 12

Hancock, Herbie: *Watermelon Man* Gr. 6, 270

Handy, W.C.: *St. Louis Blues* Gr. 4, 57

Handy, W.C.: St. Louis Blues Gr. 5, 352

Handy, W.C.: *St. Louis Blues* Gr. 5, 353

Harburg/Arlen: *Over the Rainbow (from The Wizard of Oz)* Gr. 4, 143

Harburg/Arlen: *Over the Rainbow (from The Wizard of Oz)* Gr. 4, 143

Hatch, Tony: Downtown Gr. 6, 258

Hawkins/Johnson/Dash: Tuxedo Junction Gr. 8, G-21

Hayden, John: Autumn Gr. 6, 193

Hedges, Michael: *Aerial Boundaries* Gr. 8, F-20

Hellmer, Jeff: *Peak Moments* Gr. 8, E-4

Hill, Mildred and Patty: Happy Birthday to You Gr. K, 304

Hillaire, Joseph: Tall Cedar Tree Gr. 2, 322

Hinojosa, Tish: Magnolia Gr. 6, 16

Hinojosa, Tish: Riendo el río corre Gr. 6, 263

Holiday / Herzog Jr.: *God Bless the Child* Gr. 7, B-27

Holiday/Herzog: *Elias* Gr. 7, B-21

Holiday/Herzog Jr.: *God Bless the Child* Gr. 7, B-26

Holiday/Myers/ DeShannon: *Put a Little Love in Your Heart* Gr. 4, 8

Holiday/Myers/De Shannon: Put a Little Love in Your Heart Gr. 4, 6

Holler, Dick: Abraham, Martin, and John Gr. 6, 466

Holliday/Herzog Jr.: God Bless the Child Gr. 7, B-27

Horner, James: *Rose (from the Motion Picture Titanic)* Gr. 8, B-34

Horner/Mann/Weil: Somewhere Out There Gr. 5, 368

Horner/Mann/Weil: *Somewhere Out There* Gr. 5, 369

Horner/Mellencamp and Green: *Coming Home from the Sea–I* Gr. 6, 345

Hot Butter: *Popcorn* Gr. 8, E-27

Ingalls, Jeremiah: *Northfield* Gr. 6, 25

Ives, Charles: *Variations on "America"* Gr. 6, 164

Jacobs, Al: Sing a Song of Peace Gr. 6, 66

Jacobs, Al: Sing a Song of Peace/ This Is My Country Gr. 6, 66

Jacobs, Walter: Blues with a Feeling Gr. 8, I-6

John, Elton: *Circle of Life (from The Lion King), The* Gr. 3, 367

John, Elton: *Circle of Life (from The Lion King), The* Gr. 6, 316

Johnson, Carl: Earth Is My Mother, The Gr. 1, 340

Johnson, J. Rosamond: Lift Ev'ry Voice and Sing Gr. 5, 482

Johnson, Robert: *Walkin' Blues* Gr. 5, 227

Jolson/Desylva/Meyer: California, Here I Come Gr. 4, 287

Jones Little, Lessie: Let's Go Barefoot (poem) Gr. 1, 440

Jones, Bessie: Jump That Jody Gr. K, 212

Jones, Bessie: Nana, Thread Needle Gr. 1, 38

Jones, Bessie: Shoo, Turkey Gr. 1, 104

Joplin, Scott: *Bethena Waltz* Gr. 6, 157

Joplin, Scott: *Elite Syncopations* Gr. 6, 159

Joplin, Scott: *Entertainer, The* Gr. 2, 76

Joplin, Scott: *Scott Joplin's New Rag* Gr. 5, 335

Joubert, Joseph: *Choo-Choo Joubert* Gr. 3, 51

Kander, John: Theme from New York, New York Gr. 4, 250

Kelly, R.: I Believe I Can Fly Gr. 5, 170

Kennedy, X.J.: Setting the Thanksgiving Table Gr. 2, 381

Kenner/Domino: Land of a Thousand Dances Gr. 5, 330

King, Carole: *Beautiful* Gr. 3, 67

King, Carole: *You've Got a Friend* Gr. 5, 364

King, Carole: You've Got a Friend Gr. 5, 366

King/Leiber/Stoller: Stand By Me Gr. 5, 46

King/Leiber/Stoller: *Stand By Me* Gr. 5, 49

King/Leiber/Stoller: Stand By Me Gr. 8, E-25

King/Leiber/Stoller: *Stand By Me* Gr. 8, E-24

Kraft, William: *Theme and Variations for Percussion* Gr. 5, 65

Krone, Beatrice: Bluebonnets of Texas Gr. 3, 333

Krumm, John: Winter Gr. 8, G-11

Landreth, Sonny: *Native Stepson* Gr. 7, F-26

Larsen, Libby: *Songs from Letters, "So Like Your Father"* Gr. 7, C-21

Larson, Jonathan: Seasons of Love Gr. 8, A-22

Lebo M./Tongeren/Rifkin: It's Time Gr. 6, 274

Lebo M./Tongeren/Rifkin: *It's Time* Gr. 6, 319

Ledbetter, Huddie: Good Mornin', Blues Gr. 2, 52

Ledbetter, Huddie: Good Mornin', Blues Gr. 5, 224

Ledbetter, Huddie: Midnight Special, The Gr. 7, F-23

Ledbetter, Huddie: Polly Wee Gr. K, 119

Ledbetter/Lomax: Roll On, Columbia Gr. 5, 116

Legg, Adrian: *Carolina Sunday Waltz* Gr. 7, F-9

Lieber/Stoller: Hound Dog Gr. 5, 212

Lieber/Stoller: Yakety Yak Gr. 5, 205

Lieber/Stoller: *Yakety Yak* Gr. 5, 204

Little Richard: *Good Golly, Miss Molly* Gr. 8, E-10

Livgren, Kerry: *Carry On Wayward Son* Gr. 7, B-20

Locke, Lawrence: River Gr. 4, 61

Loggins/Pitchford: *Footloose* Gr. 7, B-11

Lomax, John A. and Alan: Goin' Down the Road Feelin' Bad Gr. 5, 282

Louiselle, Bryan: All for One Gr. 7, E-8

Louiselle, Bryan: Different Beat, A Gr. 1, 6

Louiselle, Bryan: Live in the City Gr. 5, 71

Louiselle, Bryan: Locomoto-vation Gr. K, 61

Louiselle, Bryan: Look Out Below! Gr. 2, 370

Louiselle, Bryan: Look Out for Mother Earth Gr. 3, 341

**(Genre/Style, continued)**

Root, George F.: Battle Cry of Freedom  Gr. 5, 272

Rose, Fred: *Blue Eyes Crying in the Rain*  Gr. 7, B-28

Rouse, Ervin T.: *Orange Blossom Special*  Gr. 1, 47

Rouse, Ervin T.: *Orange Blossom Special*  Gr. 5, 266

Rouse, Ervin T.: *Orange Blossom Special*  Gr. 5, 268

Rouse, Ervin T.: *Orange Blossom Special*  Gr. 8, E-6

Royal, Reggie: Kwanzaa Carol, A  Gr. 2, 392

Royal, Reggie: Ujima  Gr. 1, 430

Samudio, Domingo: *Wooly Bully*  Gr. 3, 373

Schiltz/Radigan: *I Don't Want to Feel Like That*  Gr. 4, 31

Seeger, Pete: *If I Had a Hammer*  Gr. 3, 241

Seeger, Pete: Sailing Down My Golden River  Gr. 4, 332

Seeger, Pete: *Where Have All the Flowers Gone?*  Gr. 5, 287

Seeger, Pete; adapted by: Turn, Turn, Turn (To Everything There Is a Season)  Gr. 5, 378

Seeger, Ruth: *Suite for Wind Quintet, Movement 1*  Gr. 8, C-34

Seeger/Hays: If I Had a Hammer  Gr. 5, 287

Seeger/Hays: If I Had a Hammer  Gr. 5, 287

Sharon, Lois, and Bram: Way Down in the Schoolyard  Gr. 2, 50

Shenandoah, Joanne: *Light Up the World*  Gr. 2, 196

Sherman/Sherman: It's a Small World  Gr. 3, 268

Sherman/Sherman: Let's Go Fly a Kite  Gr. 2, 327

Sherman/Sherman: *Reservation Blues*  Gr. 8, B-37

Sherman/Sherman: Step in Time  Gr. 2, 74

Sherman/Sherman: Supercalifragili sticexpialidocious  Gr. 3, 7

Sherman/Sherman: We've Got Lots in Common  Gr. 3, 366

Shuler, Eddie: Sugar "Shuga" Bee  Gr. K, 64

Sigman/Gray: *Pennsylvania 6-5000*  Gr. 5, 342

Singer/Medora/White: At the Hop  Gr. 4, 168

Small/Vettese: Proud  Gr. 7, G-3

Smith, John Stafford: Star-Spangled Banner, The  Gr. 3, 415

Smith, John Stafford: Star-Spangled Banner, The  Gr. 4, 441

Smith, John Stafford: Star-Spangled Banner, The  Gr. 5, 488

Smith, John Stafford: Star-Spangled Banner, The  Gr. 6, 486

Smith, John Stafford: Star-Spangled Banner, The  Gr. 7, I-56

Smith, John Stafford: Star-Spangled Banner, The  Gr. 8, I-63

Smith, Leroy: *North Carolina Breakdown*  Gr. 5, 334

Smith/Picard: *On Fire Suite*  Gr. 8, B-37

Solomon, Linda: *Lion Sleeps Tonight, The*  Gr. 8, E-8

Sousa, John Philip: *Guide Right*  Gr. 1, 447

Sousa, John Philip: *On Parade*  Gr. K, 326

Sousa, John Philip: *Semper Fidelis*  Gr. K, 326

Sousa, John Philip: *Stars and Stripes Forever, The*  Gr. 1, 167

Sousa, John Philip: *Thunderer, The*  Gr. 5, 79

Sousa, John Philip: *Washington Post, The*  Gr. 1, 175

Sousa, John Philip: *Washington Post, The*  Gr. 8, C-40

Sousa, John Philip: *Stars and Stripes Forever, The*  Gr. 4, 159

Spector/Greenwich/Barry: Chapel of Love  Gr. 7, G-27

Staines, Bill: *River*  Gr. 4, 58

Steffe, William: Battle Hymn of the Republic  Gr. 5, 274

Stewart, Sylvester: *Everyday People*  Gr. 5, 389

Still, William Grant: *Ennanga, Movement 3*  Gr. 3, 127

Stone, Sly: *Everyday People*  Gr. 7, G-16

Strayhorn, Billy: *Take the "A" Train*  Gr. 8, C-42

Styne, Jule: Let It Snow! Let It Snow! Let It Snow!  Gr. 4, 426

Swander/Hershey: Deep in the Heart of Texas  Gr. 4, 22

Taylor, Billy: I Wish I Knew How It Would Feel to Be Free  Gr. 6, 470

Taylor, Billy: *I Wish I Knew How It Would Feel To Be Free*  Gr. 6, 470

Taylor, Brian: *Good Vibrations*  Gr. 8, E-28

Taylor, James: *Shed a Little Light*  Gr. 3, 409

Taylor, James: *Shed a Little Light*  Gr. 8, E-17

Tesori, Jeanine: *On My Way*  Gr. 6, 313

Tesori, Jeanine: Seasons  Gr. K, 4

Tesori, Jeanine: Spring Has Sprung!  Gr. K, 142

Tesori, Jeanine: That's What's New with Me!  Gr. K, 2

Thomas, André: I Dream a World  Gr. 8, G-40

Thompson, Randall: *Frostiana (from Stopping by Woods on a Snowy Evening)*  Gr. 6, 40

Thomson, Virgil: *Acadian Songs, "Walking Song"*  Gr. 4, 347

Thomson, Virgil: *Plow That Broke the Plains, The, "Cattle"*  Gr. 3, 177

Thomson, Virgil: *River Suite, The, "Finale"*  Gr. 5, 121

Tower, Joan: *Wings*  Gr. 7, C-45

Troup, Bobby: Route 66  Gr. 4, 276

Troup, Bobby: *Route 66*  Gr. 4, 279

Troup, Bobby: *Route 66*  Gr. 4, 279

Tucker, Judith Cook: Yonder Come Day  Gr. 8, I-68

Turner/Levy/Glover/Washington: *Soulville*  Gr. 7, B-17

Twine, Linda: ABC Blues  Gr. K, 280

Twine, Linda: *Changed My Name*  Gr. 6, 338

Twine, Linda: Run! Run! Hide!  Gr. 6, 340

Tyson, Ian: Four Strong Winds (Song to a Seagull)  Gr. 6, 170

Ulali: *Mahk jchi*  Gr. 7, D-25

Vallant/McKenzie/Poirier: *Akua Tuta*  Gr. 7, D-24

Vandross, Luther: Brand New Day, A  Gr. 6, 7

Vasquez, Andrew: *Through My Eyes*  Gr. 8, B-8

Vaughan, Stevie Ray: *Pride and Joy*  Gr. 7, B-9

Vaughan, Stevie Ray: *Pride and Joy*  Gr. 7, B-9

Vaughan, Stevie Ray: *Scuttle Buttin'*  Gr. 8, F-26

Velez, Glen: *Rain*  Gr. 8, B-6

Vieuxtemps, Henri: *Souvenirs L'Amerique, Op. 17, "Yankee Doodle"*  Gr. 2, 405

von Tilzer, Albert: Take Me Out to the Ball Game  Gr. 3, 263

Waldman/Buckingham: *Don't Look Down*  Gr. 6, 249

Walker, Jerry J.: *Mr. Bojangles (excerpt 1)*  Gr. 7, F-7

Walker, Jerry J.: *Mr. Bojangles (excerpt 2)*  Gr. 7, F-7

Walker, T. Bone: *Hard Way*  Gr. 7, E-33

Ward/Bates: *America, the Beautiful* Gr. 3, 413

Ward/Bates: America, the Beautiful Gr. 3, 413

Ward/Bates: America, the Beautiful Gr. 3, 412

Ward/Bates: America, the Beautiful Gr. 4, 158

Ward/Bates: America, the Beautiful Gr. 5, 76

Ward/Bates: America, the Beautiful Gr. 6, 485

Ward/Bates: America, the Beautiful Gr. 7, I-4

Ward/Bates: America, the Beautiful Gr. 8, I-4

Ward/Bates: *America, the Beautiful (Gospel)* Gr. 6, 485

Ward/Bates: America, the Free Gr. 4, 210

Warren, Diane: Faith of the Heart Gr. 8, G-3

Warren-Mattox, Cheryl: Let's Get the Rhythm of the Band Gr. 3, 84

Warren-Mattox, Cheryl: Let's Get the Rhythm of the Band Gr. 7, E-29

Waskewitch, Irvin: *Men's Fancy Dance* Gr. 7, D-24

Waters: *Country Blues* Gr. 5, 225

Webb, Jimmy: *If These Walls Could Speak* Gr. 7, B-41

Weill, Kurt: *Mack the Knife* Gr. 7, B-26

Weiss/Peretti/Creatore: Lion Sleeps Tonight, The Gr. 4, 131

Weiss/Peretti/Creatore: Lion Sleeps Tonight, The Gr. 8, I-56

Weissman, "Miss Jackie": Sing About Martin Gr. K, 321

Whelan, Bill: *Riverdance Suite* Gr. 2, 141

White, David: Rock and Roll Is Here to Stay Gr. 6, 36

Whittaker, Roger: I Am But a Small Voice Gr. 6, 446

Wiedman, Lillian: I'm a Very Fine Turkey Gr. K, 310

Williams, Arliene Nofchissey: I Walk in Beauty Gr. 4, 282

Williams, Hank: Jambalaya (On The Bayou) Gr. 6, 244

Williams, Hank: *Jambalaya (On The Bayou)* Gr. 6, 245

Williams, Hank: Jambalaya (On The Bayou) Gr. 8, I-46

Williams, Hank: Jambalaya (On The Bayou) Gr. 8, F-18

Williams, John: *Close Encounters of the Third Kind* Gr. 8, B-34

Williams, Linda: Away to America Gr. 5, 57

Williams, Maurice: Little Darlin' Gr. 7, F-30

Williams, Spencer: Basin Street Blues Gr. 5, 354

Wills, Bob: *New San Antonio Rose* Gr. 5, 135

Wills, Bob: San Antonio Rose Gr. 5, 134

Withers, Bill: Lean on Me Gr. 7, E-22

Wordsworth, William: Written in March Gr. 4, 354

Work, Henry: Ship that Never Returned, The Gr. 5, 402

Workman, Lyle: *Rising of the Mourning Sun* Gr. 7, F-19

Wrubel, Allie: Zip-a-Dee-Doo-Dah Gr. 2, 330

Yarrow/Lipton: Puff, the Magic Dragon Gr. 2, 350

## AMERICAN FOLK AND TRADITIONAL

1, 2, 3, 4 (speech piece) Gr. K, 15

2, 4, 6, 8 (speech piece) Gr. K, 67

A-Tisket, A-Tasket Gr. 2, 238

*A-Tisket, A-Tasket* Gr. 2, 239

Ackabacka, Soda Cracker (speech piece) Gr. 1, 303

Ain't Gonna Let Nobody Turn Me 'Round Gr. 6, 85

Ain't Gonna Let Nobody Turn Me 'Round Gr. 8, F-16

Alabama Gal Gr. 3, 106

Alison's Camel Gr. K, 289

All Around the Buttercup Gr. 2, 170

All Night, All Day Gr. 4, 180

Alleluia, Amen Gr. 7, A-12

*Allons danser, Colinda* Gr. K, 218

Almost Day Gr. 3, 397

Ama-Lama Gr. 5, 142

Amasee Gr. 1, 172

Amazing Grace Gr. 4, 160

*Amazing Grace* Gr. 4, 161

*Amazing Grace* Gr. 5, 259

*Amazing Grace* Gr. 5, 259

America Gr. 1, 446

America Gr. 2, 403

America Gr. 3, 412

America Gr. 4, 440

America Gr. 5, 487

America Gr. 6, 487

America Gr. 7, I-2

*America* Gr. 7, A-25

America Gr. 8, I-2

America Gr. K, 326

America Gr. K, 326

And My Heart Soars Gr. 2, 240

And My Heart Soars Gr. 4, 359

Andy Pandy Gr. K, 46

Apple Tree Gr. 1, 228

Apple Tree Gr. 1, 228

Apples and Bananas Gr. 1, 390

Apples, Peaches, Pears, and Plums (speech piece) Gr. 1, 14

*Arkansas Traveler/Angeline the Baker* Gr. K, 114

B-A, Bay Gr. 1, 220

Back of the Bus Gr. 3, 410

Banana Splits Gr. 1, 320

Banjo Sam Gr. 2, 314

*Battle of Jericho, The* Gr. 6, 234

Bear Dance Gr. 7, I-10

*Bear Dance* Gr. 7, C-5

Bear Dance Gr. K, 127

*Bear Dance Song* Gr. K, 126

Bee, Bee Bumblebee (speech piece) Gr. 1, 50

Big Corral, The Gr. 2, 230

Big Rock Candy Mountain Gr. 4, 330

Bingo Gr. 1, 170

Black Snake Gr. 3, 53

Blow, Ye Winds Gr. 4, 255

Blue Mountain Lake Gr. 6, 205

Bluebird, Bluebird Gr. K, 105

Bo-bo-skee, Watten-tatten (speech piece) Gr. 1, 259

Bob-a-Needle Gr. 2, 232

Boil Them Cabbage Down Gr. 6, 370

*Bonaparte's Retreat* Gr. 4, 385

Boogie Chant and Dance (speech piece) Gr. 2, 78

Bounce High, Bounce Low Gr. 1, 152

Bumble Bee, The (speech piece) Gr. K, 74

Bury Me Not on the Lone Prairie Gr. 6, 19

Bus, The Gr. K, 83

Busy Buzzy Bee Gr. K, 77

Butterfly Song Gr. 1, 363

Button, You Must Wander Gr. 2, 172

California Gr. 5, 52

*Candy Man, Salty Dog* Gr. K, 27

*Cauyaqa Nauwa? (Where's My Drum?)* Gr. 8, D-20

*Cedar Swamp* Gr. 5, 261

Certainly, Lord Gr. 7, I-13

Charlie over the Water Gr. 1, 68

*Cherokee Morning Song* Gr. 8, B-19

Chicka Hanka Gr. 2, 211

Chicka Hanka Gr. 8, F-14

Chicken on the Fence Post Gr. 3, 92

Children, Go Where I Send Thee Gr. 3, 392

Chippewa Lullaby Gr. K, 181

Cindy Gr. 4, 384

Circle Round the Zero Gr. K, 293

Johnny Appleseed  Gr. 4, 344
Johnny Caught a Flea  Gr. 1, 226
Johnny Has Gone for a Soldier
    Gr. 5, 188
Johnny Mister Brown  Gr. K, 37
*Jolie Blonde*  Gr. 4, 389
Jolly Old St. Nicholas  Gr. K, 316
*Jonah*  Gr. 6, 235
Joshua Fought the Battle of Jericho
    Gr. 5, 100
Joshua Fought the Battle of Jericho
    Gr. 8, E-18
Juba  Gr. K, 13
*Juba*  Gr. K, 12
Juniper Tree, The  Gr. 3, 131
Just from the Kitchen  Gr. K, 55
Keep Your Eyes on the Prize
    Gr. 3, 408
Keep Your Eyes on the Prize
    Gr. 8, E-16
Knock the Cymbals  Gr. 1, 176
*Kokopelli Wandering Song*
    Gr. 5, 110
Kunolounkwa  Gr. K, 110
*Kunolounkwa, "Contemporary"*
    Gr. K, 110
Kwa-nu-te  Gr. 3, 214
Lady, Lady  Gr. 1, 62
*Le Hoogie Boogie*  Gr. K, 296
Leila  Gr. 1, 258
Lemonade  Gr. 1, 190
Let Us Chase the Squirrel  Gr. 2, 98
Li'l Liza Jane  Gr. 3, 140
*Liberty/Chicken Reel*  Gr. 2, 38
Lift Ev'ry Voice and Sing
    Gr. 8, I-54
Little and Lots  Gr. K, 323
Little and Lots  Gr. K, 323
Little David  Gr. 1, 232
Little David, Play on Your Harp
    Gr. 4, 394
*Little David, Play on Your Harp*
    Gr. 4, 395
Little Green Frog, The  Gr. 1, 24
Little Johnny Brown  Gr. 3, 313
*Little Pearls, The*  Gr. K, 215
Little Red Caboose  Gr. K, 229
*Little Red Caboose*  Gr. K, 228
Little Red Wagon  Gr. K, 152
Little Shop of Horrors  Gr. 4, 422
Lone Star Trail  Gr. 2, 21
Looby Loo  Gr. K, 210
Love Somebody  Gr. 3, 94
Love Will Guide Us  Gr. 4, 328
Lucy Locket  Gr. 2, 27
Lullaby and Dance  Gr. 4, 387
Make New Friends  Gr. 3, 36
Mama, Buy Me a Chiney Doll
    Gr. K, 120
Mama Don't 'Low  Gr. 6, 358
Man of Constant Sorrow
    Gr. 7, F-28
Marines' Hymn, The  Gr. 8, C-39

*Marines' Hymn, The*  Gr. 8, C-39
Mary Came a-Running  Gr. K, 294
Mary Wore Her Red Dress
    Gr. K, 74
Michael Finnigan  Gr. 3, 153
Michael Finnigan/This Old Man
    Gr. 3, 153
Michael, Row the Boat Ashore
    Gr. 2, 18
Miss Mary Mack  Gr. 2, 42
Miss Susie Anna Sue  Gr. K, 242
Mister Rabbit  Gr. K, 128
Mos Mos  Gr. 1, 130
My Bonnie Lies Over the Ocean
    Gr. 4, 338
My Father's House  Gr. 2, 25
*My Father's House (Gospel Style)*
    Gr. 2, 24
My Foot's In My Stirrup  Gr. 2, 234
My Home's Across the Blue Ridge
    Mountains  Gr. 4, 84
My Home's Across the Blue Ridge
    Mountains  Gr. 7, F-6
My Mama's Calling Me  Gr. 1, 260
*Nobody Knows the Trouble I've
    Seen*  Gr. 3, 249
Now Let Me Fly  Gr. 3, 178
Number One, Touch Your Tongue
    (speech piece)  Gr. K, 204
O hal'lwe  Gr. 3, 256
Oh, Freedom  Gr. 5, 392
Oh, Freedom  Gr. 7, G-30
*Oh, Freedom and Come and Go
    with Me*  Gr. 5, 394
Oh, Watch the Stars  Gr. 2, 144
Oh, Watch the Stars  Gr. 5, 216
Oh, Won't You Sit Down  Gr. 3, 28
Old Blue  Gr. K, 122
Old Brass Wagon  Gr. 2, 122
Old Chisholm Trail, The  Gr. 6, 237
*Old Chisholm Trail, The*
    Gr. 6, 236
Old Dan Tucker  Gr. 3, 96
Old House, Tear It Down!
    Gr. 4, 178
Old Man Mosie  Gr. 3, 108
Old Texas  Gr. 3, 77
Oliver Jump (speech piece)
    Gr. K, 205
On a Log, Mister Frog  Gr. K, 148
One Morning in May  Gr. 6, 121
One Morning Soon  Gr. 3, 68
Over in the Meadow  Gr. 1, 346
Over My Head  Gr. 4, 118
Over My Head  Gr. 7, G-9
Over the River and Through the
    Wood  Gr. 3, 384
*P'tit galop pour mamou*
    Gr. 1, 317
*Patty Cake Polka*  Gr. 2, 281
Paw-Paw Patch  Gr. 4, 93
*Pay Me*  Gr. 7, F-5
Pay Me My Money Down  Gr. 4, 38

*Pay Me My Money Down*
    Gr. 4, 39
Pay Me My Money Down
    Gr. 7, I-47
Peace Like a River  Gr. 3, 246
Peace Like a River  Gr. 6, 190
Peace Round  Gr. 4, 348
Peanut Butter (speech piece)
    Gr. 1, 173
Pease Porridge Hot  Gr. 1, 134
Phoebe  Gr. 1, 30
Phoebe  Gr. 1, 30
Pizza, Pizza, Daddy-o  Gr. 2, 28
Pottery Dance  Gr. 1, 370
*Powwow Song*  Gr. 4, 32
Pretty Saro  Gr. 3, 216
Promised Land, The  Gr. 5, 258
Pumpkin, Pumpkin  Gr. 1, 413
*Qiugaviit*  Gr. 3, 259
*Ragtime Annie*  Gr. 2, 122
*Railroad Bill*  Gr. 8, F-14
Railroad Corral  Gr. 3, 174
Rain on the Green Grass (speech
    piece)  Gr. K, 10
Rain, Rain  Gr. 1, 54
Rain (Stevenson)  Gr. 3, 43
Rainbow, The  Gr. 2, 332
Red River Valley  Gr. 6, 10
*Reuben's Train*  Gr. 1, 334
Rio Grande  Gr. 4, 256
Rise and Shine  Gr. 4, 98
Rise Up, Shepherd, and Follow
    Gr. 5, 471
*Rise Up, Shepherd, and Follow*
    Gr. 5, 470
Rock Island Line  Gr. 4, 54
Rocky Mountain  Gr. 2, 98
Roll Over  Gr. K, 288
Rosie, Darling Rosie  Gr. 2, 215
*Round Dance*  Gr. 3, 257
*Round Dance*  Gr. 6, 445
*Round Dance*  Gr. 8, B-15
'Round the Bay of Mexico
    Gr. 4, 258
*Rumblin' On*  Gr. 2, 315
Same Train  Gr. 2, 164
Scattin' A-Round (Variations on
    Row 3)  Gr. 6, 160
Seagull, Seagull, Sit on the Shore
    Gr. 4, 383
See the Children Playin'  Gr. 4, 107
Shady Grove  Gr. 5, 260
Shake Them 'Simmons Down
    Gr. 2, 244
Shanghai Chicken  Gr. 1, 140
She'll Be Comin' 'Round the
    Mountain  Gr. 2, 358
*She'll Be Coming 'Round the
    Mountain When She Comes*
    Gr. 4, 333
*Shenandoah*  Gr. 2, 62
Shenandoah  Gr. 5, 264
*Shenandoah*  Gr. 5, 265

**Classified Index**

(*Genre/Style,* continued)

Shoo, Fly  Gr. 2, 200
Shortnin' Bread  Gr. 1, 57
Shortnin' Bread  Gr. 7, F-27
Simple Gifts  Gr. 5, 184
Simple Gifts  Gr. 8, A-17
*Simple Gifts*  Gr. 8, A-17
Six Little Ducks  Gr. K, 234
Skin and Bones  Gr. 2, 376
Skip to My Lou  Gr. K, 58
Sleep, Baby, Sleep  Gr. 2, 197
Snail, Snail  Gr. 1, 190
*Soldier's Joy*  Gr. 8, B-29
Somebody Waiting  Gr. 2, 283
Somebody's Knockin' at Your Door
    Gr. 4, 53
*Sometimes I Feel Like a
    Motherless Child*  Gr. 5, 193
Sometimes I Feel Like a Motherless
    Child  Gr. 6, 241
Song of the Eagle  Gr. 2, 248
Song of the Fishes  Gr. 3, 244
Sourwood Mountain  Gr. 4, 65
*Standin' in the Need of Prayer*
    Gr. 5, 103
Star Light, Star Bright  Gr. 1, 108
Streets of Laredo  Gr. 4, 272
*Study War No More*  Gr. 7, C-40
Sun Gonna Shine  Gr. 6, 242
*Sun Gonna Shine*  Gr. 7, F-14
*Sun Gonna Shine*  Gr. 7, F-14
Sweet Betsy from Pike  Gr. 4, 244
Sweet Potatoes  Gr. 3, 228
*Swing Low, Sweet Chariot*
    Gr. 6, 234
Swing Low, Sweet Chariot
    Gr. 7, C-41
Take Your Feet Out 'the Sand
    Gr. K, 230
Texas Cowboy  Gr. 3, 250
There is Joy (poem)  Gr. 3, 258
There Is Love Somewhere
    Gr. 6, 318
*This Little Light of Mine*
    Gr. 2, 241
This Little Light of Mine  Gr. 6, 232
This Train  Gr. 5, 26
Three Little Pigs  Gr. K, 21
Tideo  Gr. 2, 80
Tom Dooley  Gr. 6, 374
Toodala  Gr. 1, 326
Train Is A-Comin'  Gr. 3, 48
*Traveling Shoes*  Gr. 3, 248
Turn the Glasses Over  Gr. 3, 204
Turn, Turn, Turn (To Everything
    There Is a Season)  Gr. 5, 378
Twelve Gates to the City
    Gr. 5, 280
Two Little Sausages (speech piece)
    Gr. 2, 79
Vive l'amour  Gr. 6, 176
Wabash Cannon Ball  Gr. 5, 136
Wade in the Water  Gr. 4, 268

Wade in the Water  Gr. 8, I-64
Wake Me, Shake Me  Gr. 1, 278
Walk in Jerusalem  Gr. 4, 100
Walk Together, Children  Gr. 3, 146
*Watchers of the Canyon*
    Gr. 6, 270
*Way Down Yonder in the
    Brickyard*  Gr. 2, 51
We Shall Not Be Moved  Gr. 4, 437
We Shall Overcome  Gr. 4, 326
*We Shall Overcome*  Gr. 5, 485
We're All Gonna Shine Tonight
    Gr. 2, 240
Weevily Wheat  Gr. 4, 105
*What Kind of Land?*  Gr. 4, 327
*When a Man's a Long Way from
    Home*  Gr. 2, 53
When the Saints Go Marching In
    Gr. 2, 178
*When the Saints Go Marching In*
    Gr. 2, 179
When the Train Comes Along
    Gr. 1, 300
Wichita Hand Game Song 1
    Gr. 3, 306
Wichita Hand Game Song 2
    Gr. 3, 306
Willowbee  Gr. 1, 222
Wind Up the Apple Tree
    Gr. 1, 184
*Wioste Olowan Inkpa Ta-Ya*
    Gr. 3, 255
Woke Up This Morning  Gr. 5, 288
Worried Man Blues  Gr. 6, 371
Yankee Doodle  Gr. 2, 389
Yankee Doodle  Gr. 2, 405
Yankee Doodle  Gr. 3, 414
Yellow Rose of Texas, The
    Gr. 7, I-40
*Yellow Rose of Texas, The*
    Gr. 7, I-73
Yo-shi nai  Gr. 6, 286
*Yo-shi nai (Circle Dance)*
    Gr. 6, 287
Zudio  Gr. 2, 269
Zuni Sunrise Call  Gr. 5, 396

## Art Songs

*Die forelle*  Gr. 7, C-20
*Hermit Songs, Op. 29, "The Monk
    and His Cat"*  Gr. 7, C-21
*Songs from Letters, "So Like Your
    Father"*  Gr. 7, C-21
*Widmung, Op. 25, No. 1*
    Gr. 7, C-20

## Ballads and Story Songs

Animals Find Water, The  Gr. 2, 216
Ayelivi  Gr. 2, 70
Baby Beluga  Gr. K, 272
Baby Chick  Gr. K, 167
Barb'ry Allen  Gr. 6, 44
But the Cat Came Back  Gr. 2, 190

Chawe chidyo chem'chero
    Gr. 2, 296
*Cookie Crew, The*  Gr. K, 197
Corrido de Kansas  Gr. 4, 274
*Dancing Tree, The*  Gr. K, 202
Don Gato  Gr. 3, 352
El burrito enfermo  Gr. K, 271
El carite  Gr. 5, 305
Farmer in the Dell, The  Gr. K, 232
Five Little Chickadees  Gr. K, 179
Five Little Snowmen  Gr. K, 313
Fly and the Bumblebee, The
    Gr. 1, 384
Go Down, Moses  Gr. 5, 190
Goin' to Boston  Gr. 6, 433
*Goldilocks and the Three Bears*
    Gr. K, 49
Good King Wenceslas  Gr. 6, 460
Haliwa-Saponi Canoe Song
    Gr. 5, 302
Higglety, Pigglety, Pop!  Gr. K, 22
I Know an Old Lady  Gr. 1, 388
I'm a Very Fine Turkey  Gr. K, 310
*John Henry*  Gr. 8, C-34
Kibungo, Beast of the Forest
    Gr. 2, 352
Laredo  Gr. 5, 10
*Lazy John*  Gr. 4, 11
Long Way Home, A  Gr. 1, 382
Lots of Worms  Gr. 2, 310
Meng Jian Nu  Gr. 5, 194
My Dear Companion  Gr. 6, 23
*Noah's Zoo in the Big, Big Rain*
    Gr. K, 274
One Morning in May  Gr. 6, 121
Puff, the Magic Dragon  Gr. 2, 350
Purple People Eater, The  Gr. 6, 448
Scrub Brush Shuffle, The  Gr. 1, 118
Se va el caimán  Gr. 5, 306
*Shoveling*  Gr. 1, 423
Silly Street  Gr. K, 224
Sing Me a Story  Gr. 2, 346
Six Little Ducks  Gr. K, 234
Streets of Laredo  Gr. 4, 272
*Three Little Piggies*  Gr. K, 56
Water Is Wide, The  Gr. 6, 228
*You Sang to Me*  Gr. 6, 335

## Bluegrass

*Cotton-Eye Joe*  Gr. 4, 290
*Dusty Miller*  Gr. 4, 291
*I'll Fly Away*  Gr. 8, I-43
My Home's Across the Blue Ridge
    Mountains  Gr. 7, F-6
*Orange Blossom Special*  Gr. 5, 268
*Ragtime Annie*  Gr. 2, 122
*Reuben's Train*  Gr. 1, 334

## Blues

ABC Blues  Gr. K, 281
Basin Street Blues  Gr. 5, 354
Blues with a Feeling  Gr. 8, I-6
*Country Blues*  Gr. 5, 225

*Crazy Blues* Gr. 7, B-8

*Diamonds and Rust* Gr. 7, A-4

*Don't Get Around Much Anymore* Gr. 1, 33

*Every Morning* Gr. 7, B-8

*Every Night When the Sun Goes In* Gr. 8, I-29

Flip, Flop and Fly Gr. 7, I-32

*Flip, Flop and Fly* Gr. 7, F-15

Flip, Flop and Fly Gr. 7, E-32

Good Mornin', Blues Gr. 2, 52

Good Mornin', Blues Gr. 5, 224

Groundhog Blues, The Gr. 3, 122

*Hard Way* Gr. 7, E-33

Joe Turner Blues Gr. 4, 56

Just a Snap-Happy Blues Gr. 6, 388

*Key to the Highway* Gr. 6, 243

Key to the Highway Gr. 6, 243

*Key to the Highway* Gr. 8, F-28

Key to the Highway Gr. 8, F-29

Midnight Special, The Gr. 7, F-23

Polly Wee Gr. K, 119

*Pride and Joy* Gr. 7, B-9

*Railroad Bill* Gr. 8, F-14

*Rainy Day Blues* Gr. 2, 328

*Salute to Sunnyland Slim* Gr. 8, E-33

*Scuttle Buttin'* Gr. 8, F-26

*Soulville* Gr. 7, B-17

*St. Louis Blues* Gr. 4, 57

St. Louis Blues Gr. 5, 352

*St. Louis Blues* Gr. 5, 353

Sun Gonna Shine Gr. 6, 242

*Sun Gonna Shine* Gr. 7, F-14

Take Your Feet Out 'the Sand Gr. K, 231

*Walkin' Blues* Gr. 5, 227

*When a Man's a Long Way from Home* Gr. 2, 53

Worried Man Blues Gr. 6, 371

## Bomba

*Bomba te traigo yo* Gr. 8, B-3

La borinqueña Gr. 8, D-19

*Zoila* Gr. 8, D-18

## Boogie Woogie

*Boogie Woogie* Gr. 6, 93

*Rock It* Gr. 7, B-11

*Salute to Sunnyland Slim* Gr. 8, E-33

## Broadway, Theater, and Film

*America (from West Side Story)* Gr. 8, C-45

*Backstage with Jeanine Tesori (Interview)* Gr. 8, A-20

Big Country, The Gr. 2, 236

*Bombay Dreams* Gr. 8, B-35

Cho'i hát bôi Gr. 5, 318

*Circle of Life, The (from The Lion King)* Gr. 3, 367

*Circle of Life, The (from The Lion King)* Gr. 6, 316

*Close Encounters of the Third Kind* Gr. 4, 235

*Close Encounters of the Third Kind* Gr. 8, B-34

*Colorado Trail (from the Motion Picture The West)* Gr. 5, 277

*Coming Home from the Sea– I (from The Perfect Storm)* Gr. 6, 345

*Coming Home from the Sea– II (from The Perfect Storm)* Gr. 6, 345

*Crouching Tiger, Hidden Dragon* Gr. 8, A-11

*Dance at the Gym (from West Side Story)* Gr. 5, 9

*Do-Re-Mi (from the Sound of Music)* Gr. 5, 38

Don't Cry for Me, Argentina *(from Evita)* Gr. 6, 74

*Main Titles (from Edward Scissorhands)* Gr. 8, A-10

*Fascinatin' Rhythm* (as performed by Ella Fitzgerald) Gr. 7, E-11

Fiddler on the Roof Gr. 7, E-5

*Footloose* Gr. 7, B-11

Four Strong Winds *(from Song to a Seagull)* Gr. 6, 170

Gonna Build a Mountain *(from Stop the World I Want to Get Off)* Gr. 6, 21

Happy Feet *(from the Motion Picture The King of Jazz)* Gr. 2, 252

Heigh-Ho *(from Snow White and the Seven Dwarfs)* Gr. 2, 6

Hit Me with a Hot Note and Watch Me Bounce *(from Swing)* Gr. 6, 112

*I'm a Yankee Doodle Dandy (from George M)* Gr. 5, 278

*Illusions* Gr. 6, 347

*In My Own Little Corner (from Cinderella)* Gr. 3, 9

*Istanbul Coffee House (Kafe neio) (from My Big Fat Greek Wedding)* Gr. 8, B-34

It's a Small World Gr. 3, 268

*John Wayne's Teeth (Smoke Signals)* Gr. 8, B-37

*Jungle Beat* Gr. 6, 347

*Kitchen Stomp (from Stomp Out Loud)* Gr. 4, 122

Let's Go Fly a Kite *(from Mary Poppins)* Gr. 2, 327

*Magnificent Seven, The* Gr. 3, 144

Never Smile at a Crocodile *(from Peter Pan)* Gr. 3, 100

Now That's Tap (speech piece) *(from Bring in Da Noise, Bring in Da Funk)* Gr. 6, 320

Oklahoma Gr. 5, 36

*On Fire Suite (from Smoke Signals)* Gr. 8, B-36

On My Way *(from Violet)* Gr. 6, 313

*One Fine Day* Gr. 6, 347

Over the Rainbow *(from the Wizard of Oz)* Gr. 4, 140

*Over the Rainbow (from the Wizard of Oz)* (as performed by Judy Garland) Gr. 4, 143

*Over the Rainbow (from the Wizard of Oz)* (as performed by Aretha Franklin) Gr. 4, 143

*Overture/All That Jazz (fromChicago)* Gr. 7, A-23

*Reservation Blues (from Smoke Signals)* Gr. 8, B-37

Riverdance Suite Gr. 2, 141

*Rose (from the Motion Picture Titanic)* Gr. 8, B-34

Seasons of Love *(from Rent)* Gr. 8, A-22

*Simple Song, A (from Mass)* Gr. 8, C-45

Singin' in the Rain Gr. 4, 360

*Slow Hora/Freylekhs* Gr. 8, B-25

*Somewhere (from West Side Story)* Gr. 8, C-44

Somewhere Out There *(from An American Tail)* Gr. 5, 368

*Somewhere Out There (from An American Tail)* Gr. 5, 369

*Stalia, stalia* Gr. 8, B-21

Step in Time *(from Mary Poppins)* Gr. 2, 74

Strike Up the Band Gr. 6, 135

*Summertime (from Porgy and Bess)* Gr. 6, 250

*Summertime (from Porgy and Bess)* Gr. 6, 252

Supercalifragilisticexpialidocious *(from Mary Poppins)* Gr. 3, 7

Tender Shepherd *(from Peter Pan)* Gr. 3, 116

Theme from New York, New York Gr. 4, 250

*This World (from The Me Nobody Knows)* Gr. 5, 168

*Those Magic Changes (from Grease)* Gr. 8, E-30

*Trash Can Stomp (from Stomp Out Loud)* Gr. 6, 328

*Treaties (from Smoke Signals)* Gr. 8, B-36

Under the Sea *(from The Little Mermaid)* Gr. 5, 372

*Waitin' for the Light to Shine (from Big River)* Gr. 4, 26

We Go Together (from Grease)
  Gr. 4, 44
We've Got Lots in Common (from
  Charlotte's Web) Gr. 3, 366
Wedding Qawwali (from Bombay
  Dreams) Gr. 8, B-35
Who Will Buy? (from Oliver)
  Gr. 1, 16
Yankee Doodle Boy, The (from
  Little Johnny Jones) Gr. 3, 265
Yours Forever (from The Perfect
  Storm) Gr. 6, 34

## CAJUN
Bon jour! Gr. 1, 3
Crawfish! Gr. 2, 86
Deux cocodries Gr. 2, 364
Jambalaya Gr. 6, 245
L'arc en ciel Gr. 2, 333
Sugar "Shuga" Bee Gr. K, 64

## CALYPSO
Bam, chi, chi, bam Gr. K, 109
Brisad del Zulia Gr. 4, 19
Body Song, The Gr. 6, 438
Caribbean Island Ensemble
  Gr. 7, D-19
Carnaval Calypso Ensemble
  Gr. 7, D-21
Cookie Gr. 2, 172
Day-O! Gr. 5, 21
Eine kleine Nachtmusik Gr. 4, 41
Four White Horses Gr. 3, 304
Hi-Dee-Roon Gr. K, 10
Hosanna, Me Build a House
  Gr. 5, 132
John B. Sails Gr. K, 11
Jump in the Line Gr. 4, 117
Limbo Like Me Gr. 4, 18
Linstead Market Gr. 5, 241
Mango Walk Gr. 5, 200
Mary Ann Gr. 6, 180
Mwen boyko samba Gr. 4, 319
Nanny Goat Gr. K, 161
Panamam tombé Gr. 7, D-18
Shake the Papaya Down Gr. 4, 378
Shashee Gr. K, 109
Somebody Gr. 4, 41
Turn the World Around Gr. 4, 114
Water Come a Me Eye Gr. 6, 300

## CHILDREN'S CLASSICS
Beat of the Tango, The Gr. K, 106
Big Rock Candy Mountain
  Gr. 4, 330
Bling Blang Gr. 3, 240
Circle of Life (from The Lion
  King), The Gr. 3, 367
Ev'ry Kind of Music Gr. 2, 226
Everything Grows Gr. K, 267
Family Tree Gr. 3, 72
Glad to Have a Friend Like You
  Gr. 2, 228
Gonna Have a Good Time Gr. 2, 4

Heigh-Ho Gr. 2, 6
Hippopotamus Song, The Gr. 3, 33
I See With My Hands Gr. 2, 148
I'd Like To Teach the World to Sing
  (In Perfect Harmony) Gr. 3, 198
I'm Gonna Sing a Silly Song
  Gr. K, 225
It's a Small World Gr. 3, 268
Itsy Bitsy Spider, The Gr. K, 187
Jingle Bells Gr. 2, 388
Let's Go Fly a Kite Gr. 2, 327
Listen to the Water Gr. 2, 294
Look Out Below! Gr. 2, 370
Mad...Sad...Glad: A Piece in
  Three Mood-ments Gr. K, 249
Music's in Me, The Gr. 2, 40
Never Smile at a Crocodile
  Gr. 3, 100
Parade Came Marching, The
  Gr. 1, 166
Rabbit Footprints Gr. 2 , 304
Rudolph, the Red-Nosed Reindeer
  Gr. 1, 428
Sailing to the Sea Gr. 1, 336
Sing a Rainbow Gr. 2, 166
Song That's Just for You, A
  Gr. 2, 126
Step in Time Gr. 2, 74
Supercalifragilisticexpialidocious
  Gr. 3, 7
Tender Shepherd (Count Your
  Sheep) Gr. 3, 116
This Land Is Your Land (refrain
  only) Gr. 1, 274
This Old Man Gr. 3, 152
Time to Sing Gr. 2, 8
Waltzing with Bears Gr. 3, 170
Way Down in the Schoolyard
  Gr. 2, 50
Zip-a-Dee-Doo-Dah Gr. 2, 330
Zudio Gr. 2, 269

## CHORAL MUSIC
Angels On the Midnight Clear
  Gr. 6, 423
Cantaré, cantarás Gr. 6, 413
Choral Music Gr. 6, 210
Ding Dong! Merrily on High
  Gr. 6, 427
Fais do do Gr. 6, 403
Gift to Share, A Gr. 6, 393
Give Us Hope Gr. 6, 337
Goin' to Boston Gr. 6, 433
Gospel Train, The Gr. 6, 398
Just a Snap-Happy Blues Gr. 6, 388
Lo, How a Rose E'er Blooming
  Gr. 6, 210
Oye Gr. 6, 336
Shalom aleichem Gr. 6, 409
Vem kan segla? Gr. 6, 417

## CONJUNTO
A mi querido Austin Gr. 8, B-24
Mi humilde corazon Gr. 7, B-32

## COUNTING SONGS
Ants Go Marching, The Gr. 1, 248
Counting Song Gr. 1, 253
Five Little Chickadees Gr. K, 179
Five Little Snowmen Gr. K, 313
Number One, Touch Your Tongue
  (speech piece) Gr. K, 204
Rinsho, rinsho Gr. K, 285
Roll Over Gr. K, 288
Serra, serra, serrador Gr. 1, 112
Un elefante Gr. 2, 160

## COUNTRY
Blue Eyes Crying in the Rain
  Gr. 7, B-28
Cattle Call Gr. 5, 344
Cattle Call Gr. 5, 347
Don't Look Down Gr. 6, 249
Forked Deer/Fisher's Hornpipe
  Gr. 4, 343
Green, Green Grass of Home
  Gr. 6, 248
Have a Little Faith in Me
  Gr. 8, A-18
Heads Carolina, Tails California
  Gr. 7, B-25
I Don't Want to Feel Like That
  Gr. 4, 31
I Walk the Line Gr. 7, B-28
I've Been Everywhere Gr. 6, 224
I've Been Everywhere Gr. 6, 226
Jambalaya (On The Bayou)
  Gr. 6, 244
Ozark Mountain Jubilee Gr. 4, 86
Rocky Top Gr. 5, 348
Soppin' the Gravy Gr. 4, 385
Tennessee River Gr. 5, 349
Waitin' for a Train Gr. 7, B-24
Why Walk When You Can Fly
  Gr. 7, B-28
Yellow Rose of Texas, The
  Gr. 7, I-73
You Are My Sunshine Gr. 6, 247

## COWBOY SONGS
Bury Me Not on the Lone Prairie
  Gr. 6, 19
Colorado Trail Gr. 5, 277
Colorado Trail Gr. 5, 276
Corrido de Kansas Gr. 4, 274
Cowboys' Christmas Ball
  Gr. 6, 238
Cowboys' Christmas Ball
  Gr. 6, 239
Deep in the Heart of Texas
  Gr. 8, I-18
El payo Gr. 6, 145
Home on the Range Gr. 5, 69
Lone Star Trail Gr. 2, 21
Old Chisholm Trail, The
  Gr. 6, 236
Old Chisholm Trail, The Gr. 6, 237
Old Texas Gr. 3, 77
Railroad Corral Gr. 3, 174

Red River Valley  Gr. 6, 11
Streets of Laredo  Gr. 4, 272
Texas Cowboy  Gr. 3, 250
You Are My Sunshine  Gr. 6, 246
*You Are My Sunshine*  Gr. 6, 247

## CUBAN
*Ayer, "Yesterday"*  Gr. 6, 266

## CUMBIA STYLE
*El nuevo caiman*  Gr. 8, B-17

## DISCO
*I Will Survive*  Gr. 7, B-10
Turn the Beat Around  Gr. 4, 2

## ELECTRONICA
*7th Guest, The, "Themes"*
    Gr. 8, A-3
*If You Look*  Gr. 7, B-5
*Miniature Odyssey, A*  Gr. 8, E-29
Party Tonight!  Gr. 2, 152
*Solsbury Hill*  Gr. 8, E-29
*X-Beats*  Gr. 7, B-5

## FINGER PLAYS
Birthday Cake  Gr. K, 307
Eensy Weensy Spider  Gr. K, 187
Fuzzy Caterpillar  Gr. K, 102
Ten Little Teddy Bears  Gr. K, 301

## FLAMENCO
Don Alfonso  Gr. 5, 177
*Río de la miel*  Gr. 5, 296

## FUSION
*Akua Tuta*  Gr. 7, D-24
*Alasdair mhic cholla ghasda*
    Gr. 8, B-44
*Avaz-e dashti*  Gr. 8, B-42
*Cafe Europa*  Gr. 7, B-43
*Drift*  Gr. 8, B-42
*Elias*  Gr. 7, B-21
*Face of Love, The*  Gr. 8, B-15
*Ki mua*  Gr. 8, B-27
*Maitreem*  Gr. 8, B-42
*Mido Mountain*  Gr. 8, B-42
*Quiet City*  Gr. 8, E-29
*Sabhyatâ*  Gr. 8, B-43

## GAME SONGS
A-Tisket, A-Tasket  Gr. 2, 238
Ah, eu entrei na roda  Gr. 3, 308
Al ánimo  Gr. 3, 322
Al citrón  Gr. 3, 320
All Around the Buttercup
    Gr. 2, 170
Andy Pandy  Gr. K, 46
Banana Splits  Gr. 1, 318
Bantama kra kro  Gr. 5, 308
Bereleh  Gr. K, 151
Bluebird, Bluebird  Gr. K, 105
Bob-a-Needle  Gr. 2, 232
Bonga  Gr. K, 78
Chanukah Games  Gr. 3, 389
Cheki, morena  Gr. 2, 180
Ciranda  Gr. 2, 272

Circle Round the Zero  Gr. K, 293
Deux cocodries  Gr. 2, 364
Diou shou juan'er  Gr. 2, 277
Doong gul ge  Gr. 3, 134
Draw Me a Bucket of Water
    Gr. 3, 124
El florón  Gr. 2, 246
El juego chirimbolo  Gr. 2, 54
Farmer in the Dell, The  Gr. K, 232
Geef jij mij die schoen  Gr. 1, 126
Grass Game  Gr. 1, 371
Green, Green, Rocky  Gr. 1, 321
Hosisipa  Gr. 3, 70
How Many Miles to Babylon?
    Gr. 2, 128
James Brown  Gr. K, 206
Jan ken pon  Gr. 3, 302
Juba  Gr. K, 13
Just from the Kitchen  Gr. K, 55
Kapulu kane  Gr. 2, 270
Kou ri lengay  Gr. 2, 217
Kuma san  Gr. K, 40
Lemonade  Gr. 1, 190
Little Johnny Brown  Gr. 3, 313
London Bridge  Gr. K, 244
Lucy Locket  Gr. 2, 27
Mary Came a-Running  Gr. K, 294
Miss Mary Mack  Gr. 2, 42
Miss Susie Anna Sue  Gr. K, 242
Missy-La, Massa-La  Gr. 4, 188
Mister Rabbit  Gr. K, 128
Mon son pha (speech piece)
    Gr. K, 91
My Mama's Calling Me  Gr. 1, 260
Naranja dulce  Gr. 2, 97
Nie chce cie znác  Gr. 3, 314
O ma washi  Gr. K, 13
O pião entrou  Gr. 2, 355
Paw-Paw Patch  Gr. 4, 93
Perná, perná, i mélissá  Gr. K, 264
Pizza, Pizza, Daddy-o  Gr. 2, 28
Raccoon Dance Song  Gr. 1, 260
Roll Over  Gr. K, 288
Rosie, Darling Rosie  Gr. 2, 215
'Round and 'Round  Gr. 1, 148
Run, Molly, Run  Gr. 1, 8
Sansaw akroma  Gr. 3, 286
Son macaron  Gr. 4, 109
Un, deux, trois  Gr. 2, 198
Weevily Wheat  Gr. 4, 105
Wichita Hand Game Song 1
    Gr. 3, 306
Wichita Hand Game Song 2
    Gr. 3, 306

## HIGHLIFE
*Awakening*  Gr. 7, D-14
Friends Today  Gr. 7, D-12
Kpanlogo Highlife Ensemble
    Gr. 7, D-13
*Mensu*  Gr. 8, D-6
*Tumba*  Gr. 7, D-14

## HIP-HOP
*Block Party*  Gr. 7, B-13
*Everything Is Everything*
    Gr. 7, B-29

## HOUSE MUSIC
*Work It Out (Blow Your Horn Dub
    Mix)*  Gr. 7, A-3

## JAZZ
*A-Tisket, A-Tasket*  Gr. 2, 239
*April Joy*  Gr. 8, A-18
*Beat of My Heart, The*  Gr. 4, 9
*Birdland*  Gr. 5, 155
*Boogie Woogie*  Gr. 1, 256
*C-Jam Blues*  Gr. 8, C-43
*Choo Choo Ch'Boogie*  Gr. 5, 44
*Diamonds and Rust*  Gr. 7, A-4
*Dippermouth Blues*  Gr. 7, B-14
*Fascinatin' Rhythm (Frances Veri)*
    Gr. 7, E-11
*Fingerprints*  Gr. 7, B-42
*Flat Foot Floogee, The*  Gr. 3, 158
Flat Foot Floogee, The  Gr. 3, 160
*God Bless the Child*  Gr. 7, B-26
*God Bless the Child*  Gr. 7, B-26
God Bless the Child  Gr. 7, B-26
God Bless the Child  Gr. 7, B-27
Hit Me with a Hot Note and Watch
    Me Bounce  Gr. 6, 112
*Hotter Than That*  Gr. 6, 65
*I Can't Get Started*  Gr. 7, B-26
I Love Peanuts  Gr. 1, 162
*In the Mood*  Gr. 6, 110
*Into the Faddisphere*  Gr. K, 21
It Don't Mean a Thing (If It Ain't
    Got That Swing)  Gr. 5, 336
*It Don't Mean a Thing (If It Ain't
    Got that Swing)*  Gr. 5, 338
*It Don't Mean a Thing (If It Ain't
    Got that Swing)*  Gr. 6, 386
*Ja-Da*  Gr. 7, G-20
*Jazz in the Box*  Gr. 8, F-11
*Knozz-Moe-King*  Gr. 4, 75
*Let It Snow! Let It Snow! Let It
    Snow!*  Gr. 4, 427
*Let's Dance*  Gr. 1, 256
*Let's Face the Music*  Gr. 7, B-14
*Little Birdie*  Gr. 4, 75
*Mack the Knife*  Gr. 7, B-26
*Moment So Close, A*  Gr. 8, B-40
*Now's the Time*  Gr. 5, 451
*On Green Dolphin Street*
    Gr. 4, 126
*Overture/All That Jazz (from
    Chicago)*  Gr. 7, A-23
*Peak Moments*  Gr. 8, E-4
*Pick-a-Rib*  Gr. 3, 151
*Queen's Suite, The, "Sunset and
    the Mocking Bird"*  Gr. 8, E-10
*Quiet City*  Gr. 8, E-29
*Rhapsody in Blue*  Gr. 7, C-42
*Route 66*  Gr. 4, 279

(*Genre/Style,* continued)

Summertime Gr. 6, 250
*Summertime* Gr. 6, 252
*Take Five* Gr. 5, 220
*Take Five* Gr. 7, B-15
*Take Me There* Gr. 7, F-26
*Take the "A" Train* Gr. 8, C-42
*Watermelon Man* Gr. 1, 12
*Watermelon Man* Gr. 6, 270
*What a Wonderful World* Gr. 6, 63
*When the Saints Go Marching In* Gr. 2, 179

## KLEZMER
*Slow Hora/Freylekhs* Gr. 8, B-25

## LATIN
Gaudeamus igitur Gr. 8, C-20

## LATIN MUSIC
*Bachianas brasileiras No. 5, "Aria"* Gr. 8, C-37
*Caravan* Gr. 7, B-31
*Good Morning, Aztlán* Gr. 7, B-7
Guantanamera Gr. 8, I-32
Guantanamera Gr. 8, I-33
*Let the Children Play* Gr. 7, B-30
*Night in Tunisia, A* Gr. 4, 35
*Oye como va* Gr. 2, 255
Sonando Gr. 4, 34
*Sube* Gr. 7, B-31
*Te dejo Madrid* Gr. 7, B-30

## LULLABIES
A la puerta del cielo Gr. 5, 60
A la rurru niño Gr. K, 180
Abiyoyo Gr. 2, 108
Adiós, amigos Gr. 6, 57
All Through the Night Gr. 5, 105
*All Through the Night* Gr. 5, 104
Ayliluli, num tsipor Gr. 1, 204
*Bai, bai, bai, bai* Gr. 2, 197
*Be Still, My Child* Gr. 1, 39
Boysie Gr. 2, 195
Canción de cuna Gr. 4, 144
Chippewa Lullaby Gr. K, 181
*Cradle Song* Gr. K, 97
Deau-deau, ti pitit maman Gr. 2, 306
Duérmete, mi niño Gr. 1, 292
Einini Gr. 4, 391
*En prière* Gr. K, 158
Fais dodo Gr. K, 158
Hej pada pada Gr. 3, 78
*Hush, Little Baby* Gr. K, 222
Hush Up the Baby Gr. K, 222
Hwa yuan li-de young wa wa Gr. 3, 102
Kunolounkwa Gr. K, 110
Lady, Lady Gr. 1, 62
*Light Up the World* Gr. 2, 196
*Lullaby* Gr. 3, 188
Lullaby and Dance Gr. 4, 387
*Lullaby for Strings* Gr. 1, 293
Niño querido Gr. 1, 308

*Omo* Gr. 1, 443
*Pupu hinu hinu, "Shiny Shell Lullaby"* Gr. 1, 109
*Putting Baby to Bed* Gr. 1, 63
Sleep, Baby, Sleep Gr. 2, 197
*Suo gan* Gr. 1, 309
T'hola, t'hola Gr. 4, 132
Tender Shepherd (Count Your Sheep) Gr. 3, 116
Thula, thula, ngoana Gr. 4, 227
*Wioste Olowan Inkpa Ta-Ya* Gr. 3, 255
Xiao yin chuan Gr. 2, 14
Yang wa wa Gr. K, 162
Zulu Lullaby Gr. K, 158

## MADRIGAL
*Silver Swan, The* Gr. 8, C-5
*Sing We and Chant It* Gr. 8, C-5

## MARCHES
*Glory Hallelujah Grand March* Gr. 8, C-38
*Guide Right* Gr. 1, 447
*Love for Three Oranges, "March"* Gr. K, 117
*Marines' Hymn, The* Gr. 8, C-39
On Parade Gr. K, 326
*On the Mall* Gr. 5, 2
Parade Came Marching, The Gr. 1, 166
*Semper Fidelis* Gr. K, 326
*Stars and Stripes Forever, The* Gr. 1, 167
*Stars and Stripes Forever, The* Gr. 4, 159
*Thunderer, The* Gr. 5, 79
*Washington Post, The* (march) Gr. 1, 175
*Washington Post, The* (march) Gr. 8, C-40

## MARIACHI
Al citrón Gr. 3, 320
¡Ay, Jalisco no te rajes! Gr. 7, I-6
Cielito lindo Gr. 4, 270
Cielito lindo Gr. 7, I-20
De colores Gr. 8, I-14
*El mariachi* Gr. 4, 303
El rancho grande Gr. 8, I-22
*Jarabe tapatío* Gr. 7, I-7
La golondrina Gr. 8, I-50
*Las copetonas* Gr. 7, B-33
Los machetes Gr. 8, I-22

## MINIMALIST
*China Gates* Gr. 7, C-45
*Seven Tunes Heard in China, "Guessing Song"* Gr. 7, C-45
*Wings* Gr. 7, C-45

## MUSICAL THEATER *See Genre/ Style: Broadway, Theater and Film.*

## NEWGRASS
*Last Thing on My Mind, The* Gr. 7, F-7

## NURSERY RHYMES
*Baa-Baa Black Sheep* Gr. K, 102
*Farmer in the Dell* Gr. K, 233
*Hey, Diddle, Diddle* Gr. K, 246
*Humpty Dumpty* Gr. K, 23
*Old King Cole* Gr. K, 245

## PROGRAM MUSIC
*1812 Overture* Gr. 4, 293
*Birds in the Forest* Gr. 4, 315
*Carnival of the Animals, "Aviary"* Gr. 4, 70
*Carnival of the Animals, "Fossils"* Gr. 1, 236
*Carnival of the Animals, "Fossils"* Gr. 4, 220
*Carnival of the Animals, "Royal March of the Lion"* Gr. 3, 357
*Carnival of the Animals, "The Aviary"* Gr. K, 44
*Carnival of the Animals, "The Elephant"* Gr. K, 45
*Fontane di Roma, "La fontana di Trevi al meriggio (Fountains of Rome)"* Gr. 2, 93
*Four Seasons, The, "Spring," Movement 1* Gr. 1, 29
*Four Seasons, The, "Spring," Movement 1* Gr. 4, 371
*Grand Canyon Suite, "Cloudburst"* Gr. K, 261
*Grand Canyon Suite, "On the Trail"* Gr. 3, 77
*La mer, "Jeux de vagues"* Gr. 7, C-39
*Ma Vlast (My Fatherland), "Vltava (The Moldau)"* Gr. 7, C-33
*Nutcracker Suite, The, "Chinese Dance"* Gr. K, 105
*Nutcracker Suite, The, "Waltz of the Flowers"* Gr. 6, 325
*Pictures at an Exhibition, "Ballet of the Unhatched Chicks"* Gr. K, 167
*Pictures at an Exhibition, "The Great Gate of Kiev"* Gr. 6, 154
*Pictures at an Exhibition, "The Hut of Baba Yaga"* Gr. 4, 103
*Raindrop Prelude* Gr. 3, 26
*Sounds of the Circus* Gr. K, 241
*Symphony No. 6, Op. 68, "The Storm," Movement 4* Gr. 4, 365
*The Planets, "Mars, the Bringer of War"* Gr. 4, 377
*Voiles* Gr. 7, C-39

## RAGTIME
Alexander's Ragtime Band Gr. 6, 136
*Bethena Waltz* Gr. 6, 157

*Cotton Boll Rag* Gr. 5, 333
*Dusty Rag* Gr. K, 165
*Elite Syncopations* Gr. 6, 159
*Entertainer, The* Gr. 2, 76
*Kansas City Stomp* Gr. 2, 251

## RAP
*Black Suits Comin' (Nod Ya Head)*
   Gr. 7, A-5
*Brass Rap* Gr. 3, 189
Kid Like Me, A (speech piece)
   Gr. 2, 394
Look Out for Mother Earth
   Gr. 3, 341
Mister Snow Rap (speech piece)
   Gr. 2, 391
*Rap Intro* Gr. 8, B-32
School Bus Rap Gr. 1, 83
*Sister Rosa* Gr. 3, 411
*Tabla Solo* Gr. 8, B-32
*Tahi* Gr. 8, B-14
*Yertle the Turtle* Gr. 2, 368

## REGGAE
All the Way Around the World
   Gr. 2, 258
*Can't Take My Joy* Gr. 7, B-40
*Gidden riddum* Gr. 6, 299
Give a Little Love Gr. 6, 140
*I Get Out* Gr. 8, F-6
*Rainbow in the Sky* Gr. 7, B-35
*Reggae Is Now* Gr. 6, 143
Three Little Birds Gr. 4, 320

## RHYTHM & BLUES
*Hard Day Blues* Gr. 7, B-9
*Jelly Roll, The* Gr. 7, B-36
*Rock 'n' Roll Doctor* Gr. 7, B-38
*Tears of a Clown, The* Gr. 7, B-39
*What's Going On?* Gr. 7, B-38

## ROCK 'N' ROLL
At the Hop Gr. 4, 168
*At the Hop* Gr. 4, 166
*Beautiful* Gr. 3, 67
Birthday Gr. 6, 90
Book of Love Gr. 8, G-27
*Bye Bye, Love* Gr. 5, 357
*Bye Bye, Love* Gr. 8, A-15
*Cafe Europa* Gr. 7, B-43
*(Can't Live Without Your) Love
   and Affection* Gr. 7, B-23
*Carry On* Gr. 7, B-2
*Carry On Wayward Son* Gr. 7, B-20
Chapel of Love Gr. 7, G-27
Do Wah Diddy Diddy Gr. 4, 203
*Do Wah Diddy Diddy* Gr. 7, F-21
Don't Be Cruel Gr. 6, 255
Downtown Gr. 6, 258
*Elias* Gr. 7, B-21
*Everyday People* Gr. 7, G-16
*Good Golly, Miss Molly* Gr. 8, E-10
*Great Pretender, The* Gr. 5, 358
*Hold On* Gr. 8, G-35
Hound Dog Gr. 5, 212

I'm a Believer Gr. 7, G-33
*In the Still of the Night* Gr. 4, 47
La bamba Gr. 5, 128
Land of a Thousand Dances
   Gr. 5, 330
Lean on Me Gr. 6, 14
Lean on Me Gr. 7, E-22
*Let's Twist Again* Gr. 6, 257
*Lion Sleeps Tonight, The* Gr. 4, 132
Little Darlin' Gr. 7, F-30
Loco-Motion, The Gr. 3, 64
*Lost River* Gr. 6, 283
*Make Your Own Kind of Music*
   Gr. 8, G-30
*New York State of Mind*
   Gr. 7, E-19
*Penny Lane* Gr. 6, 257
Peppermint Twist Gr. 3, 46
*Pride and Joy* Gr. 7, B-9
Proud Gr. 7, G-3
Rock and Roll Is Here to Stay
   Gr. 6, 36
*Rock Around the Clock* Gr. 5, 356
Rock Around the Clock Gr. 7, B-18
*Rockin' Robin* Gr. 3, 368
*Search for the Hero* Gr. 7, G-5
*Shed a Little Light* Gr. 3, 409
*Shed a Little Light* Gr. 8, E-17
*Solsbury Hill* Gr. 8, E-29
*Stand By Me* Gr. 5, 49
Stand By Me Gr. 5, 46
Stand By Me Gr. 8, E-25
*Stand By Me* Gr. 8, E-24
*Surfin' Safari* Gr. 6, 261
Surfin' U.S.A. Gr. 6, 260
Surfin' U.S.A. Gr. 7, I-58
Surfin' U.S.A. Gr. 7, E-27
*That'll Be the Day* Gr. 6, 256
Time to Move Gr. 1, 244
*Tutti Frutti* Gr. 7, B-29
*Twist and Shout* Gr. 4, 238
*Twist, The* Gr. 5, 359
*Twist, The* Gr. 7, B-10
*Walkin' to New Orleans* Gr. 3, 371
We Go Together Gr. 4, 44
*Wipe Out* Gr. 5, 155
*Wipe Out* Gr. 7, F-33
*Wooly Bully* Gr. 3, 372
Wooly Bully Gr. 3, 373
*Would?* Gr. 8, F-30
*Yakety Yak* Gr. 5, 204
Yakety Yak Gr. 5, 205
You Were on My Mind Gr. 7, G-23
*You Were on My Mind* Gr. 7, G-25

## RUMBA
Cuban Rumba Ensemble Gr. 7, D-7
Elegua Gr. 7, D-8
*Guaguancó pá las tumbadoras*
   Gr. 7, D-9
*Saludo de Matanzas* Gr. 5, 17

## SALSA
*Ayer, "Yesterday"* Gr. 6, 266

*Billie* Gr. 8, B-23
*Guantanamera* Gr. 8, I-33
*Loco bossa nova* Gr. 2, 247
*Picadillo* Gr. 3, 361
Rhythm Is Gonna Get You, The
   Gr. 6, 348
*Riendo el río corre* Gr. 6, 263
*Vaya Puente* Gr. 2, 181

## SAMBA
*Bate-papo* Gr. 4, 401
*Chica chica boom chic* Gr. 2, 112
*Divertimento for Orchestra,
   "Samba"* Gr. 5, 9
*Talaque talaque o romance da
   Maria* Gr. 8, D-24

## SCAT
Cement Mixer Gr. 4, 102
*Flat Foot Floogee, The* Gr. 3, 158
*How High the Moon* Gr. 5, 341
*It Don't Mean a Thing (If It Ain't
   Got that Swing)* Gr. 6, 386
Ja-Da Gr. 7, G-20
Just a Snap-Happy Blues Gr. 6, 388
Now's the Time Gr. 5, 445
Scattin' A-Round (Variations on
   Row 3) Gr. 6, 160
Sing, Sing, Sing! Gr. 5, 340
Teach Me to Swing Gr. 5, 84

## SHANTIES/SEA SONGS
Blow, Ye Winds Gr. 4, 255
Bound for South Australia Gr. 5, 22
Down the Ohio Gr. 2, 60
Haul Away, Joe Gr. 4, 13
John Kanaka Gr. 3, 60
*Pay Me* Gr. 7, F-5
Pay Me My Money Down Gr. 7, I-46
Rio Grande Gr. 4, 256
'Round the Bay of Mexico Gr. 4, 258
Sea Shell Gr. 2, 100
*Shenandoah* Gr. 2, 62
Shenandoah Gr. 5, 264
*Shenandoah* Gr. 5, 265
Song of the Fishes Gr. 3, 244
Turn the Glasses Over Gr. 3, 204

## SKA
*Keep a Cool Head* Gr. 7, B-34

## SOCA
*Love You Forever* Gr. 8, B-23

## SOUL
Dancin' in the Street Gr. 5, 361
*Dancin' in the Street* Gr. 5, 360
*Dancing in the Street* Gr. 2, 254
*Everyday People* Gr. 5, 389

## SPIRITUALS AND GOSPEL SONGS
Ain't Gonna Let Nobody Turn Me
   'Round Gr. 6, 85
All Night, All Day Gr. 4, 180
*Amazing Grace* Gr. 5, 259
*America, the Beautiful* Gr. 3, 413

**(Genre/Style, continued)**

*America, the Beautiful* (Gospel)
Gr. 6, 485

*Battle of Jericho, The* Gr. 6, 234

Certainly, Lord Gr. 7, I-13

*Changed My Name* Gr. 6, 338

Children, Go Where I Send Thee
Gr. 3, 392

Come and Go with Me to That
Land Gr. 5, 390

Do, Lord Gr. 3, 164

Down by the Riverside Gr. 5, 256

Down by the Riverside Gr. 8, G-8

Dry Bones Gr. 4, 162

*Ev'ry Time I Feel the Spirit*
Gr. 3, 248

Ev'ry Time I Feel the Spirit
Gr. 5, 242

*Ev'ry Time I Feel the Spirit*
Gr. 7, C-40

Ezekiel Saw the Wheel Gr. 6, 379

Follow the Drinkin' Gourd Gr. 4, 266

Free at Last Gr. 2, 396

Get on Board Gr. K, 89

*Get on Board* Gr. K, 89

Gift to Share, A Gr. 6, 393

Glory, Glory, Hallelujah Gr. 6, 52

*Glory, Glory, Hallelujah* Gr. 6, 54

*Glory, Glory, Hallelujah*
Gr. 8, B-14

*Go Down, Moses* Gr. 7, G-10

*Go, Tell It on the Mountain*
Gr. 3, 393

Gonna Ride Up in the Chariot
Gr. 4, 20

Gospel Train, The Gr. 6, 398

Great Big Stars Gr. 1, 60

Great Day Gr. 3, 58

He's Got the Whole World in His
Hands Gr. 3, 230

*He's Got the Whole World in His
Hands* Gr. 3, 249

He's Got the Whole World in His
Hands Gr. 7, I-36

Hush, Hush Gr. 3, 162

I Got Shoes Gr. 2, 242

I'll Fly Away Gr. 8, I-42

*I'll Fly Away* Gr. 8, I-43

I'm Gonna Sing Gr. 4, 33

I'm on My Way Gr. 3, 76

I'm on My Way Gr. 7, A-15

*Jonah* Gr. 6, 235

Joshua Fought the Battle of Jericho
Gr. 8, E-18

*Joy* Gr. 7, B-40

*Joy to the World* Gr. 7, A-27

Kum ba yah Gr. 5, 244

Little David Gr. 1, 232

Little David, Play on Your Harp
Gr. 4, 394

*Little David, Play on Your Harp*
Gr. 4, 395

Michael, Row the Boat Ashore
Gr. 2, 18

*My Father's House* (Gospel Style)
Gr. 2, 24

*Nobody Knows the Trouble I've
Seen* Gr. 3, 249

Now Let Me Fly Gr. 3, 178

Oh, Freedom Gr. 7, G-30

*Oh, Freedom and Come and Go
with Me* Gr. 5, 394

Oh, Won't You Sit Down Gr. 3, 28

One Morning Soon Gr. 3, 68

Over My Head Gr. 4, 118

Over My Head Gr. 7, G-9

Peace Like a River Gr. 3, 246

Peace Like a River Gr. 6, 190

Promised Land, The Gr. 5, 258

Rise Up, Shepherd, and Follow
Gr. 5, 471

Run! Run! Hide! Gr. 6, 340

Somebody's Knockin' at Your Door
Gr. 4, 53

Sometimes I Feel Like a Motherless
Child Gr. 6, 241

*Standin' in the Need of Prayer*
Gr. 5, 103

*Study War No More* Gr. 7, C-40

*Swing Low, Sweet Chariot*
Gr. 6, 234

Swing Low, Sweet Chariot
Gr. 7, C-41

*This Little Light of Mine* Gr. 2, 241

This Little Light of Mine Gr. 6, 232

This Train Gr. 5, 26

Train Is A-Comin' Gr. 3, 48

*Traveling Shoes* Gr. 3, 248

Twelve Gates to the City Gr. 5, 280

Wade in the Water Gr. 4, 268

Wade in the Water Gr. 8, I-64

Walk in Jerusalem Gr. 4, 100

Walk Together, Children Gr. 3, 146

*What Could I Do* Gr. 5, 281

When the Saints Go Marching In
Gr. 2, 178

Yonder Come Day Gr. 8, I-68

**SWING**

*After You've Gone* Gr. 2, 189

*Flying Home* Gr. 7, B-15

*Forever, For Now* Gr. 7, B-16

Ja-Da Gr. 2, 188

*Ja-Da* Gr. 2, 187

*On Green Dolphin Street*
Gr. 4, 126

*Pennsylvania 6-5000* Gr. 5, 342

Ragtime Cowboy Joe Gr. 2, 250

Route 66 Gr. 4, 276

*Route 66* Gr. 4, 279

Sing, Sing, Sing! Gr. 5, 340

Straighten Up and Fly Right
Gr. 4, 128

Tuxedo Junction Gr. 8, G-21

**TECHNO**

*Believer* Gr. 7, A-2

*DJ Premier in Deep Concentration*
Gr. 7, B-13

*El cóndor pasa* Gr. 7, A-2

*Suzuki* Gr. 7, A-2

*Think* Gr. 6, 367

*This Is Your Night* Gr. 6, 368

*This Is Your Night* (Dance Mix)
Gr. 6, 369

*Work It Out* (Blow Your Horn Dub
Mix) Gr. 7, A-3

**TEJANO**

*Contigo otra vez* Gr. 7, B-32

Magnolia Gr. 6, 16

Riendo el río corre Gr. 6, 263

**THROAT SINGING**

*Kargyraa-style Song* Gr. 8, B-15

*Kargyraa-style Song* Gr. 8, B-40

*Moment So Close, A* Gr. 8, B-40

**WORK SONGS**

Chicka Hanka Gr. 2, 211

Dinner Music Gr. K, 70

Go Around the Corn, Sally Gr. 2, 12

Miss Susie Anna Sue Gr. K, 242

Same Train Gr. 2, 164

She'll Be Comin' 'Round the
Mountain Gr. 2, 358

**ZYDECO**

Jambalaya Gr. 8, I-46

*My Girl Josephine* Gr. 8, E-21

*Native Stepson* Gr. 7, F-26

*Zydeco dancing* Gr. 1, 21

## GIFTED AND TALENTED See
Meeting Individual Needs.

**H**

# HOLIDAY, SEASONAL, AND SPECIAL OCCASIONS

## ARBOR DAY

Ash Grove, The Gr. 5, 114

*Dancing Tree, The* Gr. K, 202

Tall Cedar Tree Gr. 2, 322

## AUTUMN

Alumot Gr. 6, 306

*Bumper Harvest Celebration*
Gr. 4, 337

Erdö, erdö de magos Gr. 3, 182

In the Pumpkin Patch Gr. 3, 380

In the Pumpkin Patch Gr. 3, 380

Owl and the Pumpkin, The
Gr. 2, 377

Pumpkin Picking Gr. 2, 376

Pumpkin Poem Gr. 3, 381

Pumpkin, Pumpkin Gr. 1, 413

Pumpkins Gr. 3, 381

Quâ câù gió bay Gr. 5, 460

## BIRTHDAYS

Birthday, Birthday, Birthday
  Gr. K, 306
Birthday Cake  Gr. K, 307
End, The (poem)  Gr. 1, 408
Happy Birthday!  Gr. K, 306
Happy Birthday to You  Gr. K, 304
Happy Birthday To You (poem)
  Gr. 1, 411
*Las mañanitas*  Gr. K, 325
Today Is Your Birthday  Gr. 1, 410
Uga uga uga  Gr. K, 305

## BLACK HISTORY MONTH

Abraham, Martin, and John
  Gr. 6, 466
Back of the Bus  Gr. 3, 410
*Ev'rybody Ought to Know*
  Gr. 1, 434
Flat Foot Floogee, The  Gr. 3, 160
*Flat Foot Floogee, The*  Gr. 3, 158
For Children Safe and Strong
  Gr. 5, 484
Free at Last  Gr. 2, 396
Free at Last  Gr. 6, 468
I Am But a Small Voice  Gr. 6, 446
I Got Shoes  Gr. 2, 242
I Wish I Knew How It Would Feel to
  Be Free  Gr. 6, 470
*I Wish I Knew How It Would Feel
  To Be Free*  Gr. 6, 470
Keep Your Eyes on the Prize
  Gr. 3, 408
Keep Your Eyes on the Prize
  Gr. 8, E-16
Kid Like Me, A (speech piece)
  Gr. 2, 394
Lift Ev'ry Voice and Sing
  Gr. 5, 482
Lift Ev'ry Voice and Sing
  Gr. 8, I-54
Martin Luther King  Gr. 1, 434
Oh, Freedom  Gr. 5, 392
Oh, Freedom  Gr. 7, G-30
*Oh, Freedom and Come and Go
  with Me*  Gr. 5, 394
*Shed a Little Light*  Gr. 3, 409
*Shed a Little Light*  Gr. 8, E-17
Sing About Martin  Gr. K, 321
*Sister Rosa*  Gr. 3, 411
We Shall Not Be Moved  Gr. 4, 437
We Shall Overcome  Gr. 4, 326
*We Shall Overcome*  Gr. 5, 485
*What Kind of Land?*  Gr. 4, 327
Woke Up This Morning  Gr. 5, 288
Yonder Come Day  Gr. 8, I-68

## CELEBRATIONS

*Body Song, The*  Gr. 6, 438
Celebrate!  Gr. 1, 406
Celebrate (poem)  Gr. 1, 407
De colores  Gr. 8, I-14
El carnavalito humahuaqueño
  Gr. 6, 482

It's a Celebration!  Gr. 2, 372
La copa de la vida  Gr. 4, 414
Las mañanitas  Gr. 6, 481
Let's Celebrate!  Gr. 3, 374
Loigratong  Gr. 6, 451
Oh, What a Day!  Gr. K, 302
*Round Dance*  Gr. 6, 445
Vamos a la fiesta  Gr. 2, 374
Waiting (poem)  Gr. 1, 413

## CHANUKAH *See also Folk, Traditional, and Regional Selections: Israeli/Jewish/Hebrew.*

Chanukah, Chanukah  Gr. 1, 420
Chanukah Games  Gr. 3, 389
Chanukah Is Here!  Gr. 2, 382
Chanukiyah li yesh  Gr. 1, 421
*Dreydl Song, The*  Gr. 3, 391
*Fantasy for Chanukah*  Gr. 1, 421
Hanuka, Hanuka  Gr. 3, 390
Hanuka, Hanuka  Gr. 8, I-36
I'm a Dreydl  Gr. K, 315
*Klezmer Dances, "Freilachs"*
  Gr. K, 314
My Dreydl  Gr. K, 314
Ner li  Gr. 2, 383
Ocho kandelikas  Gr. 4, 429
Oy, Hanuka  Gr. 5, 464
Oy, Hanuka  Gr. 7, I-44
S'vivon  Gr. 6, 452

## CHINESE NEW YEAR

*Taiwan Suite, "Lantern Festival"*
  Gr. 3, 104
*Wu long*  Gr. 4, 156

## CHRISTMAS

African Noel  Gr. 1, 427
Al quebrar la piñata  Gr. 4, 432
Almost Day  Gr. 3, 397
*Amahl and the Night Visitors,
  "This Is My Box"*  Gr. 1, 433
Angels On the Midnight Clear
  Gr. 6, 423
*Carol of the Bells*  Gr. 8, G-10
Caroling, Caroling  Gr. 6, 458
Children, Go Where I Send Thee
  Gr. 3, 392
Chrismus a Come  Gr. 3, 396
Christmas, Don't Be Late (The
  Chipmunk Song)  Gr. 2, 386
Cowboys' Christmas Ball
  Gr. 6, 239
*Cowboys' Christmas Ball*
  Gr. 6, 238
Deck the Hall  Gr. 5, 474
*Deck the Hall*  Gr. 5, 475
Ding Dong! Merrily on High
  Gr. 6, 427
*Feliz Navidad*  Gr. 4, 433
Feliz Navidad  Gr. 7, I-28
Gloria, Gloria  Gr. 6, 459
*Go, Tell It on the Mountain*
  Gr. 3, 393

*Good King Wenceslas*  Gr. 4, 431
Good King Wenceslas  Gr. 6, 460
*Good King Wenceslas*  Gr. 6, 461
I Saw Three Ships  Gr. 1, 426
It's Santa—Again!  Gr. 2, 385
Jolly Old St. Nicholas  Gr. K, 316
*Joy to the World*  Gr. 7, A-27
La piñata  Gr. 3, 399
Las Navidades  Gr. 5, 472
*Lo, How a Rose E'er Blooming*
  Gr. 6, 210
Merry Modal Christmas, A
  Gr. 4, 411
*Messiah, "Hallelujah!"*  Gr. 8, C-8
Must Be Santa  Gr. K, 318
No quiero plata  Gr. 1, 424
*Nutcracker Suite, The, "Waltz of
  the Flowers"*  Gr. 6, 325
*O Christmas Tree*  Gr. 6, 24
O Laufet, ihr Hirten  Gr. 2, 384
Ode to la piñata (poem)  Gr. 1, 424
*On Christmas Morning*
  Gr. K, 316
*Rise Up, Shepherd, and Follow*
  Gr. 5, 470
Rockin' Around the Christmas Tree
  Gr. 5, 466
Rudolph, the Red-Nosed Reindeer
  Gr. 1, 428
Silent Night  Gr. 3, 394
*Song for Bells, A*  Gr. 1, 427
Still, Still, Still  Gr. 5, 468
Stille Nacht  Gr. 7, I-54
Stille Nacht  Gr. 7, F-24
Twelve Days of Christmas, The
  Gr. 4, 430
We Wish You a Merry Christmas
  Gr. 3, 395
Winter Fantasy/Jingle Bells
  Gr. 4, 424
Zumba, zumba  Gr. 3, 400

## CINCO DE MAYO

Adelita  Gr. 5, 50
Ahora voy a cantarles  Gr. 3, 56
Al citrón  Gr. 3, 323
Buenos días  Gr. 1, 13
Cantaré, cantarás  Gr. 6, 413
Cheki, morena  Gr. 2, 180
Cheki, morena  Gr. 7, I-16
Chiapanecas  Gr. 5, 93
Cielito lindo  Gr. 4, 270
Cielito lindo  Gr. 7, I-23
De colores  Gr. 5, 90
De colores  Gr. 8, I-14
El Jarabe Tapatio  Gr. K, 215
El tambor  Gr. 2, 274
*Happy Mariachi Band, "Mariachi
  alegre"*  Gr. 1, 210
*Jarabe tapatio*  Gr. 7, I-7
*La bamba*  Gr. 5, 130
*La bamba*  Gr. 5, 131
La Jesusita  Gr. 5, 323

(*Holiday, Seasonal, and Special Occasions,* continued)

La raspa  Gr. 4, 302
Las mañanitas  Gr. 6, 481
*Las mañanitas*  Gr. K, 324
*Mexican Hat Dance*  Gr. K, 214
Mi cuerpo hace música  Gr. K, 106
Naranja dulce  Gr. 2, 97
Ode to la piñata (poem)  Gr. 1, 424
Oye  Gr. 6, 337
¡Qué gusto!  Gr. 3, 132
Sonando  Gr. 4, 34
Uno, dos, y tres  Gr. 5, 427
Vamos a cantar  Gr. K, 278
Vamos a la fiesta  Gr. 2, 374

## DIEZ Y SEIS DE SEPTIEMBRE

Adelita  Gr. 5, 50
Ahora voy a cantarles  Gr. 3, 56
Al citrón  Gr. 3, 323
Buenos días  Gr. 1, 13
Cantaré, cantarás  Gr. 6, 413
Cheki, morena  Gr. 2, 180
Cheki, morena  Gr. 7, I-16
Chiapanecas  Gr. 5, 93
Cielito lindo  Gr. 4, 270
Cielito lindo  Gr. 7, I-23
De colores  Gr. 5, 90
De colores  Gr. 8, I-14
El Jarabe Tapatio  Gr. K, 215
El tambor  Gr. 2, 274
*Happy Mariachi Band, "Mariachi alegre"*  Gr. 1, 210
*Jarabe tapatio*  Gr. 7, I-7
*La bamba*  Gr. 5, 130
*La bamba*  Gr. 5, 131
La Jesusita  Gr. 5, 323
La raspa  Gr. 4, 302
Las mañanitas  Gr. 6, 481
*Las mañanitas*  Gr. K, 324
*Mexican Hat Dance*  Gr. K, 214
Mi cuerpo hace música  Gr. K, 106
Naranja dulce  Gr. 2, 97
Ode to la piñata (poem)  Gr. 1, 424
Oye  Gr. 6, 337
¡Qué gusto!  Gr. 3, 132
Sonando  Gr. 4, 34
Uno, dos, y tres  Gr. 5, 427
Vamos a cantar  Gr. K, 278
Vamos a la fiesta  Gr. 2, 374

## EARTH DAY

America, the Beautiful  Gr. 6, 485
And My Heart Soars  Gr. 2, 240
And My Heart Soars  Gr. 4, 359
Baby Beluga  Gr. K, 272
Beach Rap (speech piece)  Gr. 1, 352
Big Beautiful Planet  Gr. 3, 326
Bluebird, Bluebird  Gr. K, 105
Breaks Free  Gr. 2, 319
Butterfly Song  Gr. 1, 363
Chuhwuht  Gr. 2, 356
Clouds  Gr. K, 254

Cycle Song of Life (The River Song)  Gr. 4, 370
*Daybreak Vision*  Gr. 5, 399
*Disco Worm*  Gr. 2, 312
Don't Dump Trash  Gr. 2, 318
Each of Us Is a Flower  Gr. 3, 154
Earth Is My Mother, The  Gr. 1, 340
Earth Is Our Mother, The  Gr. 4, 358
Earth Is Our Mother, The  Gr. 8, F-25
En nuestra Tierra tan linda  Gr. 2, 335
Enjoy the Earth  Gr. 4, 81
*Everything Grows*  Gr. K, 267
For the Beauty of the Earth  Gr. 4, 356
From Sea to Shining Sea  Gr. 2, 342
*Garden of the Earth*  Gr. 5, 399
I Love the Mountains  Gr. 5, 34
It's a Beautiful Day  Gr. 3, 338
Little Shell  Gr. 1, 355
Little Spider  Gr. K, 93
Look Out for Mother Earth  Gr. 3, 341
Mary Ann  Gr. K, 253
*Memories of the Seashore*  Gr. 3, 150
Morning Has Broken  Gr. 5, 29
Plant Four Seeds  Gr. 2, 130
Prayer for Earth  Gr. 4, 350
*Rain Song, The*  Gr. 2, 323
Rise and Shine  Gr. 1, 122
River, The  Gr. 5, 121
See and Touch  Gr. K, 172
Sh'ney dubim  Gr. K, 268
Sing a Little Song  Gr. K, 30
Sky, Sea, Shore  Gr. 2, 343
Somos el barco  Gr. 4, 352
Song of One, A  Gr. 3, 344
*Song of the Night, The*  Gr. 3, 346
Spring Has Sprung!  Gr. K, 142
Starlight, Star Bright  Gr. 4, 373
Stars Streaming in the Sky, The  Gr. 2, 357
Sun, The  Gr. K, 143
Things That Sing  Gr. K, 87
This Pretty Planet  Gr. 4, 355
Turn the World Around  Gr. 4, 114
Valentine for Earth, A  Gr. 3, 324
*Watchers of the Canyon*  Gr. 6, 270
What a Wonderful World  Gr. 6, 62
Wheel of the Water, The  Gr. 4, 362
Woodland Chorus  Gr. K, 250
World We Love, The  Gr. 3, 342
Written in March  Gr. 4, 354
Your Friends Shall Be the Tall Wind  Gr. 6, 201
Zuni Sunrise Call  Gr. 5, 396

## GROUNDHOG DAY

Groundhog Blues, The  Gr. 3, 122
*Groundhog Jig, The*  Gr. 1, 436

## HALLOWEEN

Addams Family, The  Gr. 5, 456
Costume Capers  Gr. 1, 412
*Danse macabre*  Gr. 5, 457
Halloween Is a Very Unusual Night  Gr. 3, 382
Halloween Song  Gr. K, 309
Let's Get Ready  Gr. K, 312
Little Shop of Horrors  Gr. 4, 422
Old Abram Brown  Gr. 5, 222
Owl and the Pumpkin, The  Gr. 2, 377
Pumpkin, Pumpkin  Gr. 1, 413
Purple People Eater, The  Gr. 6, 448
Skin and Bones  Gr. 2, 376
What Will You Be on Halloween?  Gr. K, 308

## KWANZAA

Habari Gani  Gr. 3, 404
Harambee  Gr. 4, 434
Heri za Kwanzaa  Gr. 5, 476
Joy of Kwanzaa, The  Gr. 6, 462
Kwanzaa Carol, A  Gr. 2, 392
Kwanzaa (poem)  Gr. 1, 431
Together in Unity  Gr. K, 320
Ujima  Gr. 1, 430

## MARTIN LUTHER KING DAY *See Black History Month.*

## MOTHER'S DAY

El día de mamita  Gr. K, 325
Kébé Mama  Gr. 1, 442
On Mother's Day (poem)  Gr. 1, 443

## NEW YEAR'S

Hitotsu toya  Gr. 5, 478
Ichi-gatsu tsuitachi  Gr. 3, 406
Ichi-gatsu tsuitachi  Gr. 7, I-40

## PASSOVER *See also Folk, Traditional, and Regional Selections: Israeli/Jewish/Hebrew.*

Dayenu  Gr. 4, 439

## PATRIOTIC

America  Gr. 1, 446
America  Gr. 2, 403
America  Gr. 3, 412
America  Gr. 4, 440
America  Gr. 5, 486
America  Gr. 6, 484
America  Gr. 7, I-2
*America*  Gr. 7, A-22
America  Gr. 8, I-2
America  Gr. K, 326
America, I Hear You Singing  Gr. 2, 402
America (N. Diamond)  Gr. 4, 206

America, the Beautiful  Gr. 3, 413
*America, the Beautiful*  Gr. 3, 413
America, the Beautiful  Gr. 4, 158
America, the Beautiful  Gr. 5, 76
America, the Beautiful  Gr. 6, 485
America, the Beautiful  Gr. 7, I-4
America, the Beautiful  Gr. 8, I-4
*America, the Beautiful (Gospel)*
  Gr. 6, 485
America, the Free  Gr. 4, 210
*American Salute*  Gr. 5, 275
Battle Cry of Freedom  Gr. 5, 272
Battle Hymn of the Republic
  Gr. 5, 274
*Common Ground*  Gr. 3, 379
Deep in the Heart of Texas
  Gr. 4, 22
*Fanfare for Freedom*  Gr. 6, 139
Fifty Nifty United States  Gr. 5, 251
Fifty Nifty United States  Gr. 5, 251
Fourth of July Night (poem)
  Gr. 1, 444
*Fourth of July, The*  Gr. 5, 489
From Sea to Shining Sea
  Gr. 2, 342
*Give Me Your Tired, Your Poor*
  Gr. 5, 166
*Give Me Your Tired, Your Poor*
  Gr. 5, 16
*Glory Hallelujah Grand March*
  Gr. 8, C-38
God Bless America  Gr. 5, 4
God Bless the U.S.A.  Gr. 8, G-37
God Bless the U.S.A.  Gr. 8, G-37
*Guide Right*  Gr. 1, 447
*I'm a Yankee Doodle Dandy*
  Gr. 5, 278
*L'union*  Gr. 6, 487
Let Freedom Ring  Gr. 5, 77
*Marines' Hymn, The*  Gr. 8, C-39
*Olympic Spirit*  Gr. 6, 350
On Parade  Gr. K, 326
Over There  Gr. 5, 279
*Semper Fidelis*  Gr. K, 326
Sing a Song of Peace/This Is My
  Country  Gr. 6, 66
Sing, America, Sing!  Gr. 3, 238
*Souvenirs L'Amerique, Op. 17,*
  *"Yankee Doodle"*  Gr. 2, 405
Star-Spangled Banner, The
  Gr. 3, 415
Star-Spangled Banner, The
  Gr. 4, 441
Star-Spangled Banner, The
  Gr. 5, 488
Star-Spangled Banner, The
  Gr. 6, 486
Star-Spangled Banner, The
  Gr. 7, I-56
Star-Spangled Banner, The
  Gr. 8, I-62
*Stars and Stripes Forever, The*
  Gr. 1, 167

*Stars and Stripes Forever, The*
  Gr. 4, 159
*This Land Is Your Land*
  Gr. 5, 120
This Land Is Your Land  Gr. 5, 118
This Land Is Your Land  Gr. 7, I-66
This Land Is Your Land (refrain
  only)  Gr. 1, 274
*Thunderer, The*  Gr. 5, 79
Voices of Pride, The  Gr. 5, 86
*Washington Post, The*  Gr. 1, 175
*Washington Post, The*  Gr. 8, C-40
Yankee Doodle  Gr. 2, 389
Yankee Doodle  Gr. 2, 405
Yankee Doodle  Gr. 3, 414
*Yankee Doodle Boy, The*
  Gr. 3, 265
*Yellow Rose of Texas, The*
  Gr. 7, I-73
Yellow Rose of Texas, The
  Gr. 7, I-70
*You're a Grand Old Flag*
  Gr. 1, 276
You're a Grand Old Flag
  Gr. 3, 264

**SHAVUOT (DAY OF
HONORING THE TORA)**
Dayenu  Gr. 4, 439
Dundai  Gr. 5, 106

**SPRING**
Bear Dance  Gr. K, 127
*Bear Dance Song*  Gr. K, 127
*Country Gardens*  Gr. 1, 440
De colores  Gr. 5, 90
De colores  Gr. 8, I-14
De colores  Gr. 8, E-14
El mes de abril  Gr. 3, 328
Falling Rain  Gr. 2, 328
*Four Seasons, The, "Spring,"*
  *Movement 1*  Gr. 1, 29
*Four Seasons, The, "Spring,"*
  *Movement 1*  Gr. 4, 371
Haru ga kita  Gr. 2, 401
L'inverno è passato  Gr. 2, 400
Let's Go Barefoot (poem)
  Gr. 1, 440
One Morning in May  Gr. 6, 120
Over the Rainbow (from The
  Wizard of Oz)  Gr. 4, 140
*Over the Rainbow (from The*
  *Wizard of Oz)*  Gr. 4, 143
*Over the Rainbow (from The*
  *Wizard of Oz)*  Gr. 4, 143
Popcorn Popping  Gr. 1, 440
Rain, Rain  Gr. 1, 54
*Rain Song, The*  Gr. 2, 323
Rain (Stevenson)  Gr. 3, 43
Rainbow, The  Gr. 2, 332
Sakura  Gr. 4, 308
Singin' in the Rain  Gr. 4, 360
Spring! Spring! (poem)  Gr. 1, 419

*Spring Walk, "Du xuân"*
  Gr. 1, 440

**ST. PATRICK'S DAY**
St. Patrick Was a Gentleman
  Gr. 3, 290

**SUMMER**
Big Old Storm a-Comin'
  Gr. K, 257
Jasmine Flowers  Gr. 5, 316
Lahk gei mohlee  Gr. 5, 317
*Sumer Is Icumen In*  Gr. 5, 35

**THANKSGIVING**
Come, Ye Thankful People, Come
  Gr. 5, 459
I'm a Very Fine Turkey  Gr. K, 310
I'm Glad (poem)  Gr. 1, 415
I'm Thankful  Gr. 1, 414
Over the River and Through the
  Wood  Gr. 3, 384
Pavo, pavo  Gr. 1, 416
Setting the Thanksgiving Table
  Gr. 2, 381
Thanksgiving Is Near  Gr. 2, 380
Turkey Game, The  Gr. 1, 416

**THREE KING'S DAY**
Aguinaldo  Gr. 3, 402
Los reyes de Oriente  Gr. 5, 480
Los reyes de Oriente  Gr. 8, I-58
Si me dan pasteles  Gr. 1, 432

**UNITED NATIONS DAY**
All the Way Around the World
  Gr. 2, 258
Cantaré, cantarás  Gr. 6, 413
Down by the Riverside  Gr. 5, 256
Green, Green Grass of Home
  Gr. 6, 248
He's Got the Whole World in His
  Hands  Gr. 3, 230
Hello to All the Children of the
  World  Gr. 3, 4
Hello to the World  Gr. 3, 2
Hevenu shalom aleichem
  Gr. 3, 378
Hine mah tov  Gr. 5, 430
It's a Small World  Gr. 3, 268
*It's Time*  Gr. 6, 319
Jingle Bells  Gr. 2, 388
Let It Snow! Let It Snow! Let It
  Snow!  Gr. 4, 426
Let Freedom Ring  Gr. 5, 77
One Small Step  Gr. 5, 126
Shir l'shalom  Gr. 4, 419
Shri Ram, jai Ram  Gr. 4, 311
Siyahamba  Gr. 6, 212
This World  Gr. 5, 168
United Nations on the March, The
  Gr. 6, 443
Walk Together, Children  Gr. 3, 146
World of Difference, A  Gr. 5, 386

## VALENTINE'S DAY

Chapel of Love  Gr. 7, G-27
Cielito lindo  Gr. 4, 270
Eres tú  Gr. 6, 473
Friend of Mine  Gr. 1, 310
Friends Today  Gr. 7, D-12
Glad to Have a Friend Like You
    Gr. 2, 228
How to Be a Friend  Gr. 1, 331
Li'l Liza Jane  Gr. 3, 140
Little and Lots  Gr. K, 323
Love in Any Language  Gr. 6, 476
Love Somebody  Gr. 3, 94
Make New Friends  Gr. 3, 37
Making Valentines  Gr. 1, 437
My Valentine  Gr. K, 323
Put a Little Love in Your Heart
    Gr. 4, 6
Seasons of Love  Gr. 8, A-22
Somewhere Out There  Gr. 5, 368
Valentine Dance  Gr. 1, 437
Valentine Feelings  Gr. K, 322
Valentine for Earth, A  Gr. 3, 324
Valentines  Gr. 2, 398
Valentines  Gr. 2, 398
Very Special Friend, A  Gr. 1, 147
You've Got a Friend  Gr. 5, 366
*You've Got a Friend*  Gr. 5, 364

## WINTER

*Cold and Frosty Morning*
    Gr. 2, 139
Dragon Smoke (poem)  Gr. 3, 387
El desembre congelat  Gr. 5, 473
*Four Seasons, The, "Winter,"*
    *Movement 2*  Gr. 3, 113
*Frosty, the Snowman*  Gr. 2, 391
Jingle Bells  Gr. 2, 388
Knock No More  Gr. 3, 386
Let It Snow! Let It Snow! Let It
    Snow!  Gr. 4, 426
*Let It Snow! Let It Snow! Let It
    Snow!*  Gr. 4, 427
*Lieutenant Kijé, Op. 60, "Troika"*
    Gr. 6, 457
Mister Snow Rap (speech piece)
    Gr. 2, 391
*Musical Sleigh Ride, A,
    "Divertimento in F"*  Gr. 5, 455
*Shoveling*  Gr. 1, 423
*Sleigh Ride*  Gr. 2, 390
Snow Flakes  Gr. 1, 423
Snowflakes  Gr. 1, 422
Winter  Gr. 8, G-11
Winter Fantasy  Gr. 4, 424
Winter Fantasy/Jingle Bells
    Gr. 4, 424
Winter Song  Gr. 6, 455
Winter Wonderland  Gr. 5, 454

## IMPROVISING See also Skills
    Reinforcement.

*7th Guest, The, "Themes"*  Gr. 8, A-3
Add-On Machine, The  Gr. K, 298
Almost Day  Gr. 3, 397
Animals Find Water, The  Gr. 2, 216
Around the World  Gr. 2, 256
Asadoya  Gr. 6, 303
Big Old Storm a-Comin'  Gr. K, 257
Blues with a Feeling  Gr. 8, I-6
*Boogie Woogie*  Gr. 6, 93
Chawe chidyo chem'chero  Gr. 2, 296
Che che koolay  Gr. 2, 266
Cheki, morena  Gr. 7, I-16
Chicka Hanka  Gr. 2, 211
*Circle of Life (from The Lion King),
    The*  Gr. 6, 317
*Concert for Piano and Orchestra*
    Gr. 6, 209
*Danses Populaires Francaises,
    "Branle Double, Branle Simple"*
    Gr. 7, C-25
*Dham dhamak dham samelu*
    Gr. 6, 305
*Drums From Around the World
    (Montage)*  Gr. 6, 277
El caracol  Gr. K, 130
*Flying Home*  Gr. 7, B-15
Frog in the Millpond  Gr. 2, 44
*Glory, Glory, Hallelujah*  Gr. 6, 54
Go, My Son  Gr. 6, 188
Habemos llegado  Gr. 6, 174
He's Got the Whole World in His
    Hands  Gr. 7, I-36
Hit Me with a Hot Note and Watch Me
    Bounce  Gr. 6, 112
*Hotter Than That*  Gr. 6, 65
Juanito  Gr. K, 300
Just a Snap-Happy Blues  Gr. 6, 388
Just from the Kitchen  Gr. K, 55
Key to the Highway  Gr. 8, F-29
Kibungo, Beast of the Forest  Gr. 2, 352
Koriko!  Gr. K, 154
Kunolounkwa  Gr. K, 110
*Let's Pretend*  Gr. K, 227
*Lion*  Gr. 6, 303
Los pollitos  Gr. K, 166
Lots of Worms  Gr. 2, 310
Luna lunera (speech piece)  Gr. K, 90
*Malê Debalê*  Gr. 8, B-16
*Máru-bihág*  Gr. 6, 304
Mary Came a-Running  Gr. K, 294
*Messiah, "Hallelujah!"*  Gr. 8, C-8
Mississippi River Chant (speech piece)
    Gr. 2, 132
*On Christmas Morning*  Gr. K, 316
On My Way  Gr. 6, 313
Over in the Meadow  Gr. 1, 347
*Return to Misty Mountain*  Gr. 7, D-28
Rock and Roll Is Here to Stay  Gr. 6, 36

*Slow Hora/Freylekhs*  Gr. 8, B-25
Squirrel, The  Gr. K, 129
Strike Up the Band  Gr. 6, 135
Summertime  Gr. 6, 250
Surfin' U.S.A.  Gr. 6, 260
Tap It! Rap It! (speech piece)  Gr. K, 194
Un pajarito  Gr. 2, 16
Under the Same Sun  Gr. 6, 440
Vamos a la fiesta  Gr. 2, 374
Yang wa wa  Gr. K, 162
Your Life Is Now  Gr. 6, 4

## INSTRUMENTS, IDENTIFYING
    See also Timbre.

Sound Bank  Gr. 1, 468
Sound Bank  Gr. 2, 420
Sound Bank  Gr. 3, 434
Sound Bank  Gr. 4, 466
Sound Bank  Gr. 5, 514
Sound Bank  Gr. 6, 512

## INSTRUMENTS, MAKING

Bear Dance  Gr. 7, I-10
Boomin' Bamboo Ensemble  Gr. 7, D-22
Box a-Rockin' Ensemble  Gr. 7, D-4
Bucket O'Taiko Ensemble  Gr. 7, D-17
*Cauyaqa Nauwa? (Where's My
    Drum?)*  Gr. 8, D-20
*Crunchy, Crunchy, Crunchy*
    Gr. 8, D-15
*Four Seasons, Concerto No. 2, The,
    "Summer," Movement 3, "La
    Tempesta"*  Gr. 6, 102
Hose-a-phone, Create Your Own
    Gr. 6, 381
How to Make a Diddley Bow
    Gr. 6, 364
*Llactamanta*  Gr. 6, 382
Mainly Metal Ensemble  Gr. 7, D-26
Making a Gutbucket (Washtub Bass)
    Gr. 6, 359
Making Musical Spoons  Gr. 6, 360
McGill, Paul  Gr. 8, A-28
Mi cuerpo hace música  Gr. K, 106
*Rods and Cones*  Gr. 7, D-5
*Udu Pot*  Gr. 8, D-4
*Ue ue*  Gr. 8, D-2

## L

## LISTENING See also Skills
    Reinforcement.

*5 Stücke im Volkston, Op. 102, No.
    1, "Mit Humor"*  Gr. 3, 39
*7th Guest, The, "Themes"*  Gr. 8, A-3
*A mi querido Austin*  Gr. 8, B-24
*Abbots Bromley Horn Dance*
    Gr. 7, C-24
*Academic Festival Overture, Op. 80*
    Gr. 8, C-20
*Adzogbo-Ovitse*  Gr. 8, D-13
*Aerial Boundaries*  Gr. 8, F-20
*Ahi! Amours*  Gr. 8, C-4

Aida, "Gloria all'Egitto (Grand March)" Gr. 8, C-24

Ajaja Gr. 8, B-3

Akua Tuta Gr. 7, D-24

Alasdair mhic cholla ghasda Gr. 8, B-44

Allah hoo Allah hoo Gr. 8, B-13

Alle psallite cum luya Gr. 7, C-5

Altered Landscapes: Part One Gr. 8, E-21

America Gr. 7, A-22

America (from West Side Story) Gr. 8, C-45

America, the Beautiful Gr. 3, 413

America, the Beautiful Gr. 3, 413

Angry Anymore Gr. 8, F-32

April Joy Gr. 8, A-18

Apu Min'Tan Gr. 8, D-21

Avaz-e dashti Gr. 8, B-42

Avaz-e dashti Gr. 8, B-43

Awakening Gr. 3, 289

Awakening Gr. 7, D-14

Bachianas brasileiras No. 5, "Aria" Gr. 8, C-37

Badenma Gr. 8, B-28

Baila caporal Gr. 8, B-22

Bairagi Gr. 8, A-19

Bambodansarna Gr. 8, B-20

Basse danse bergeret sans roch & reprise Gr. 7, C-7

Bawa Gr. 7, D-32

Beggar's Opera, The, "Constant Billy" Gr. 7, C-24

Believer Gr. 7, A-2

Bembe de Plena Gr. 8, D-18

Black Suits Comin' (Nod Ya Head) Gr. 7, A-5

Block Party Gr. 7, B-12

Blower's Daughter, The Gr. 8, B-13

Blue Eyes Crying in the Rain Gr. 7, B-28

Bluebonnets of Texas Gr. 3, 332

Bomba te traigo yo Gr. 8, B-3

Bombay Dreams Gr. 8, B-35

Bombé/Ruht wohl, ruht wohl, ihr heiligen Gebeine, BWV 245 Gr. 8, B-39

Boogie Down Gr. 8, G-29

Boston Ball Game 1967 Gr. 8, F-32

Brandenburg Concerto No. 2, Movement 3 Allegro Assai Gr. 7, C-8

Brass Rap Gr. 3, 189

Bye Bye, Love Gr. 8, A-15

C-Jam Blues Gr. 8, C-43

Cafe Europa Gr. 7, B-43

California Counterpoint: The Twittering Machine Gr. 8, C-47

Can't Take My Joy Gr. 7, B-40

Cantata No. 140 (as performed by American Bach Solosists), "Wachet auf, ruft uns die Stimme," Movement 4 Gr. 7, C-9

Cantata No. 140 (as performed by The Swingle Singers), "Wachet auf, ruft uns die Stimme," Movement 4 Gr. 7, C-10

Canzon in Echo Duodecimi Toni a 10 Gr. 8, C-7

Capoeira Na Vila Gr. 8, D-25

Caprice No. 1 in E Major Gr. 7, C-22

Caravan Gr. 7, B-31

Carnaval, Op. 9, "Valse Noble," Un poco maestoso Gr. 3, 202

Carol of the Bells Gr. 8, G-10

Carolina Sunday Waltz Gr. 7, F-9

Carrament News Gr. 8, B-22

Carry On Gr. 7, B-2

Carry On Wayward Son Gr. 7, B-20

Cauyaqa Nauwa? (Where's My Drum?) Gr. 8, D-20

Cherokee Morning Song Gr. 8, B-19

Children's Corner Suite, "Doctor Gradus ad Parnassum" Gr. 8, C-27

China Gates Gr. 7, C-45

Chorale Prelude for Organ, BWV 645, "Wachet auf, ruft uns die Stimme " Gr. 7, C-9

Close Encounters of the Third Kind Gr. 8, B-34

Common Ground Gr. 3, 379

Concerto for Flute and Harp in C, K. 299, Movement 2 Gr. 8, C-10

Concerto for French Horn in E-flat Major, K. 495, No. 4, Movement 3 Gr. 8, C-11

Concerto for Viola and Orchestra, Movement 3 Gr. 7, C-35

Contigo otra vez Gr. 7, B-32

Cow Barn Cha Cha Gr. 8, D-33

Crazy Blues Gr. 7, B-8

Crouching Tiger, Hidden Dragon Gr. 8, A-11

Dances of Galanta Gr. 7, C-34

Dancing Queen Gr. 8, G-19

Danserye, "Ronde" Gr. 8, C-7

Danses Populaires Francaises, "Branle Double, Branle Simple" Gr. 7, C-25

Danza Gr. 7, C-7

Danzas Puertorriqueñas, "Vano Empeno" Gr. 7, E-13

Daphne of the Dunes Gr. 8, D-29

Das Jahr, "Mai" Gr. 8, C-18

Dharpa, "Tree" Gr. 8, B-38

Diamonds and Rust Gr. 7, A-4

Die forelle Gr. 7, C-20

Die Walküre, "The Ride of the Valkyries" Gr. 8, C-23

Die Zauberflöte, "Pa-pa-pa-pa-pa-pagena" Gr. 8, C-13

Dippermouth Blues Gr. 7, B-14

DJ Premier in Deep Concentration Gr. 7, B-12

Domna, pos vos ay chausida (Lady, For You) Gr. 8, C-6

Down in the Valley Gr. 7, A-23

Dziban Gr. 7, F-18

Ekombi Gr. 8, B-31

El amor brujo, "Danza ritual del fuego" Gr. 8, F-20

El cóndor pasa Gr. 7, A-2

El nuevo caiman Gr. 8, B-17

Elegguá Gr. 8, D-13

Elias Gr. 7, B-21

Eternal Flame Gr. 7, B-6

Etude Fantasy for Piano, "Etude No 3: Fifths to Thirds" Gr. 8, C-46

Ev'ry Time I Feel the Spirit Gr. 3, 248

Ev'ry Time I Feel the Spirit Gr. 7, C-40

Every Morning Gr. 7, B-8

Every Night When the Sun Goes In Gr. 8, I-29

Everyday People Gr. 7, G-16

Everything Is Everything Gr. 7, B-29

Face of Love, The Gr. 8, B-15

Faerie Stories Gr. 8, B-5

Fanfare for the Common Man Gr. 7, C-43

Fascinatin' Rhythm (Ella Fitzgerald) Gr. 7, E-11

Fascinatin' Rhythm (Frances Veri) Gr. 7, E-11

Fifteen Hungarian Peasant Songs Gr. 7, C-35

Fingerprints Gr. 7, B-42

Fire Brigade Water the Road Gr. 7, D-22

Flight of the Bumblebee Gr. 3, 189

Flight of the Ibis Gr. 8, D-16

Flip, Flop and Fly Gr. 7, F-15

Flop-Eared Mule Gr. 3, 99

Flowing Bowl, The Gr. 8, B-29

Flying Home Gr. 7, B-15

Footloose Gr. 7, B-11

Forever, For Now Gr. 7, B-16

Frère Jacques Gr. 3, 113

Gahu Gr. 7, D-27

Galliard Battaglia Gr. 8, C-14

Game of the Mechanical Nightingale, "The Nightingale" Gr. 8, C-33

Gapu Gr. 8, B-38

Gazebo Dances, "Tarantella" Gr. 8, C-46

Gi pai pa yul chola Gr. 8, B-40

Glory Hallelujah Grand March Gr. 8, C-38

Go Down, Moses Gr. 7, G-10

God Bless the Child Gr. 7, B-26

God Bless the Child Gr. 7, B-26

Golden Ring Around the Susan Girl Gr. 3, 17

Good Golly, Miss Molly Gr. 8, E-10

Good Morning, Aztlán Gr. 7, B-7

Good Vibrations Gr. 8, E-28

(*Listening,* continued)

*Goodbye, Ev'rybody (Farewell Shout)* Gr. 7, D-2

*Guaguancó pá las tumbadoras* Gr. 7, D-9

*Guitar Tuning* Gr. 7, F-2

*Guitar Tuning* Gr. 8, F-2

*Hard Day Blues* Gr. 7, B-9

*Hard Way* Gr. 7, E-33

*Have a Little Faith in Me* Gr. 8, A-18

*He's Got the Whole World in His Hands* Gr. 3, 249

*Heads Carolina, Tails California* Gr. 7, B-25

*Hermit Songs, Op. 29, "The Monk and His Cat"* Gr. 7, C-21

*Huagu ge, "Flower Drum song"* Gr. 8, D-27

*Hungarian Rhapsody No. 2 in C sharp Minor, S. 244* Gr. 7, E-17

*I Am a Man of Constant Sorrow* Gr. 7, F-29

*I Can't Get Started* Gr. 7, B-26

*I Get Out* Gr. 8, F-6

*I Know You Mardi Gras* Gr. 8, B-17

*I Shall Sing* Gr. 8, I-41

*I Walk the Line* Gr. 7, B-28

*I Will Survive* Gr. 7, B-10

*I'll Fly Away* Gr. 8, I-43

*Ichi-gatsu tsuitachi* Gr. 3, 406

*If I Had a Hammer* Gr. 3, 241

*If These Walls Could Speak* Gr. 7, B-41

*If You Asked Me To* Gr. 8, G-5

*If You Look* Gr. 7, B-4

*Imbube* Gr. 8, B-30

*Intermezzo, "Háry János Suite," Movement 5* Gr. 7, C-34

*Intertribal Song* Gr. 8, B-18

*Interview with Rick Bassett (Part 2)* Gr. 3, 223

*Istanbul Coffee House (Kefe neio)* Gr. 8, B-34

*Jarabe tapatío* Gr. 7, I-7

*Jazz in the Box* Gr. 8, F-11

*Jelly Roll, The* Gr. 7, B-36

*John Henry* Gr. 8, C-34

*John Wayne's Teeth* Gr. 8, B-37

*Joy* Gr. 7, B-40

*Joy to the World* Gr. 7, A-27

*Jump for Joy* Gr. 7, D-20

*Junk Music Montage* Gr. 1, 73

*Kargiraa-Style Song* Gr. 8, B-40

*Katura* Gr. 7, D-27

*Keep a Cool Head* Gr. 7, B-34

*Key to the Highway* Gr. 8, F-28

*Ki mua* Gr. 8, B-27

*Kyrie, "Missa Luba"* Gr. 7, G-13

*La mer, "Jeux de vagues"* Gr. 7, C-39

*La tierche estampie real* Gr. 8, C-6

*Las copetonas* Gr. 7, B-33

*Last Thing on My Mind, The* Gr. 7, F-7

*Le Sacre de Printemps (The Rite of Spring), "Dance of the Youths and Maidens"* Gr. 8, C-30

*Le tombeau de Couperin, "Prelude"* Gr. 8, C-28

*Les pêcheurs des perles, "Au fond du temple saint"* Gr. 7, C-30

*Let the Children Play* Gr. 7, B-30

*Let's Face the Music* Gr. 7, B-14

*Linus and Lucy* Gr. 8, A-29

*Lion Sleeps Tonight, The* Gr. 8, F-5

*Lion Sleeps Tonight, The* Gr. 8, E-8

*Lohengrin, "Prelude to Act III"* Gr. 8, C-22

*Los machetes* Gr. 8, I-22

*Love You Forever* Gr. 8, B-23

*Lua afe (2000)* Gr. 8, B-27

*Luna hermosa* Gr. 8, I-13

*Ma Vlast (My Fatherland), "Vltava (The Moldau)"* Gr. 7, C-33

*Mack the Knife* Gr. 7, B-26

*Magic Flute, The, "Queen of the Night Aria"* Gr. 7, C-31

*Mahk jchi* Gr. 7, D-25

*Maitreem* Gr. 8, B-42

*Make Your Own Kind of Music* Gr. 8, G-30

*Malê Debalê* Gr. 8, B-16

*Mambo UK* Gr. 7, D-9

*Marines' Hymn, The* Gr. 8, C-39

*Mass for the 21st Century, "Alleluia"* Gr. 3, 163

*Mea haarit* Gr. 3, 274

*Memories of the Seashore* Gr. 3, 150

*Men's Fancy Dance* Gr. 7, D-24

*Mensu* Gr. 8, D-6

*Messiah, "Hallelujah!"* Gr. 8, C-8

*Mi humilde corazon* Gr. 7, B-32

*Mido Mountain* Gr. 8, B-42

*Miniature Odyssey, A* Gr. 8, E-29

*Moment So Close, A* Gr. 8, B-40

*Mongolian Long Song* Gr. 8, B-14

*Mr. Bojangles (excerpt 1)* Gr. 7, F-7

*Mr. Bojangles (excerpt 2)* Gr. 7, F-7

Mud Gr. 3, 32

Musette Gr. 3, 39

*My Adidas* Gr. 7, B-12

*My Girl Josephine* Gr. 8, E-21

*Nanafushi* Gr. 7, D-16

*Native Stepson* Gr. 7, F-26

*Neend koyi* Gr. 8, B-43

*New York State of Mind* Gr. 7, E-19

*Nobody Knows the Trouble I've Seen* Gr. 3, 249

*Nutcracker Suite, The, "Trepak"* Gr. 3, 280

*Nutcracker, The, "Arabian Dance"* Gr. 7, C-26

*Nyamphemphe* Gr. 8, B-3

*Nyoka* Gr. 7, D-33

*O ignis spiritus Paracliti* Gr. 7, C-4

*O tocius Asie gloria, "Oh, Glory of All Asia"* Gr. 8, C-4

*Old Dan Tucker* Gr. 3, 96

*Ombrose e care selve* Gr. 8, C-5

*On Fire Suite* Gr. 8, B-36

*One Family* Gr. 7, G-17

*Onomatapoiea Study No. 2* Gr. 7, E-31

*Orff-Schulwerk, Vol. 1, "Ding, Dong, Diggidiggidong"* Gr. 3, 15

*Overture/All That Jazz (from Chicago)* Gr. 7, A-23

*Partita in A Minor, "Sarabande"* Gr. 3, 185

*Pasodoble* Gr. 7, F-11

*Pay Me* Gr. 7, F-5

*Peak Moments* Gr. 8, E-4

*Piano Concerto in A Minor, Op. 16, Movement 1* Gr. 8, E-11

*Piano Trio in G Minor, Op. 17, Allegro* Gr. 8, C-19

*Pick-a-Rib* Gr. 3, 151

*Pictures at an Exhibition, "The Great Gate of Kiev"* Gr. 8, A-12

*Plenty o' Nuttin'* Gr. 7, B-45

*Popcorn* Gr. 8, E-27

*Prayer, The* Gr. 7, A-10

*Prelude in B-flat Minor, Op. 28, No. 16* Gr. 7, C-22

*Prelude in G-sharp Minor, Op. 32, No. 12* Gr. 7, E-4

*Pride and Joy* Gr. 7, B-9

*Princess Hundred Flowers, The, "Falling in the Trap"* Gr. 8, C-25

*Pulcinella Suite, "Minuetto"* Gr. 8, C-15

*Pulcinella Suite, "Serenata"* Gr. 8, C-32

*Qiugaviit* Gr. 3, 259

*Quality of Seven, A* Gr. 8, B-6

*Queen's Suite, The, "Sunset and the Mocking Bird"* Gr. 8, E-10

*Quiet City* Gr. 8, E-29

*Quintet for Piano and Strings in E-flat Major, Op. 44, Movement 1* Gr. 8, C-19

*Radio City Christmas Spectacular Jingle* Gr. 8, A-5

*Railroad Bill* Gr. 8, F-14

*Rainbow in the Sky* Gr. 7, B-35

*Raindrop Prelude* Gr. 3, 26

*Raindrops* Gr. 7, D-23

*Rap Intro* Gr. 8, B-32

*Reservation Blues* Gr. 8, B-37

*Retounen* Gr. 8, B-17

*Return to Misty Mountain* Gr. 7, D-28

*Rhapsody in Blue* Gr. 7, C-42

*Rhythms of the Cook Islands* Gr. 8, B-6

*Rice Bowl* Gr. 8, B-30

*Rigoletto, "Bella figlia dell'amore"* Gr. 7, C-29

Rippa Medley, The, "Block-Block, One Leg Up, Let the Beat Go, Uh-Oh" Gr. 8, D-32

Rising of the Mourning Sun Gr. 7, F-19

Rock It Gr. 7, B-11

Rock 'n' Roll Doctor Gr. 7, B-38

Roddy McCaulay Gr. 3, 292

Rodeo, "Hoedown" Gr. 8, B-45

Rods and Cones Gr. 7, D-5

Roll Over Vaughan Williams Gr. 8, F-22

Rose, "from the Motion Picture Titanic" Gr. 8, B-34

Rundadinella Gr. 8, I-60

Rwakanembe Gr. 8, C-14

Sabhyatâ Gr. 8, B-43

Sai da Frente Gr. 8, D-24

Saltarello detto Trivella Gr. 7, C-6

Salute to Sunnyland Slim Gr. 8, E-33

Samanfo, begye nsa nom Gr. 8, D-6

San Miguel Jolonicapan Gr. 8, D-16

Saqian da dhol Gr. 8, B-22

Scaramouche, "Brasiliera," Movement 3 Gr. 8, C-29

Scuttle Buttin' Gr. 8, F-26

Sealwoman/Yundah Gr. 8, B-14

Search for the Hero Gr. 7, G-5

Sensemaya Gr. 8, C-15

Seven Tunes Heard in China, "Guessing Song" Gr. 7, C-45

Sevilla Gr. 8, F-22

Sextet for Winds and Piano, Movement 1 Gr. 8, C-29

She Is Like the Swallow Gr. 8, B-12

Shed a Little Light Gr. 8, E-17

Shepherd's Hey Sampler Gr. 7, C-37

Shumba Gr. 8, B-12

Silver Swan, The Gr. 8, C-5

Simple Gifts Gr. 8, A-17

"Simple Song, A," (from Mass) Gr. 8, C-45

Sing We and Chant It Gr. 8, C-5

Six Metamorphoses After Ovid, Op. 49, "Bacchus" Gr. 7, C-13

Slow Hora/Freylekhs Gr. 8, B-25

Soldier's Joy Gr. 8, B-29

Solo de Concours Gr. 8, A-19

Solsbury Hill Gr. 8, E-29

Somewhere Gr. 8, C-44

Sonata for Clarinet and Piano, Op. 167, "Allegro animato," Movement 2 Gr. 7, C-12

Sonata for Violin and Piano, Allegro Gr. 8, C-46

Sonata in A Minor, "Allegro" Gr. 7, C-12

Sonata in C-sharp Minor, Op. 27, No. 2, "Moonlight," Movement 1 Gr. 7, C-19

Sonata in F Major for Violin and Piano, Op. 24, No. 5, "Spring," Movement 3 Gr. 7, C-19

Sonata in G Minor, Op. 1, No. 1, Movement 2 Gr. 7, C-12

Sonatina for Bassoon and Piano, "Allegro con moto," Movement 1 Gr. 7, C-13

Song for George Gr. 8, F-8

Song of the Nightingale, "The Nightingale" Gr. 8, C-32

Songs from Letters, "So Like Your Father" Gr. 7, C-21

Soulville Gr. 7, B-17

Soundings, "Fanfare" Gr. 8, C-47

Spain Gr. 7, B-42

St. Patrick Was a Gentleman Gr. 3, 290

Stalia, stalia Gr. 8, B-21

Stand By Me Gr. 8, E-24

String Quartet in D Major, Op. 64, No. 5, "The Lark," Allegro moderato Gr. 7, C-15

Study War No More Gr. 7, C-40

Sube Gr. 7, B-31

Suite Española, Op. 47, No. 3, "Sevilla" Gr. 7, C-23

Suite for Wind Quintet, Movement 1 Gr. 8, C-34

Suite in E-flat Major for Cello, S. 1010, "Gigue" Gr. 7, C-11

Suite in F, Op. 28b, No. 2, "Fantasia on the Dargason," Movement 4 Gr. 7, C-36

Suite No. 3 in C Major for Unaccompanied Cello, "Bourrée 1" Gr. 3, 38

Suzuki Gr. 7, A-2

Symphony No. 3 in E-flat Major, "Allegro con brio," Movement 1 Gr. 8, C-17

Symphony No. 3 in E-flat Major, "Marcia funebre," Movement 2 Gr. 8, C-17

Symphony No. 40 in G Minor, K. 550, Movement 1 Gr. 8, C-12

Symphony No. 40 in G Minor, K. 550, Movement 1 Gr. 8, B-30

Symphony No. 40 in G Minor, K. 550, Movement 1 Gr. 8, C-13

Symphony No. 47 in G Major, "Menuet" Gr. 7, C-14

Symphony No. 5 in C Minor, Op. 67, Movement 1 Gr. 7, C-16

Symphony No. 94 in G Major, "Surprise," Andante Gr. 7,

Tahi Gr. 8, B-14

Take Five Gr. 7, B-15

Take Me There Gr. 7, F-26

Take the "A" Train Gr. 8, C-42

Talaque talaque o romance da Maria Gr. 8, D-24

Te dejo Madrid Gr. 7, B-30

Tears of a Clown, The Gr. 7, B-39

Ten Easy Pieces, "Bear Dance" Gr. 3, 172

Terian gulabi buliyam Gr. 8, B-26

That's the Way It Is Gr. 7, B-23

Tihore Mai Gr. 8, B-12

Toccata and Fugue in D Minor Gr. 7, E-25

Toei khong Gr. 8, B-21

Tommy Peoples Gr. 8, B-20

Tosca, "Vissi d'arte" Gr. 7, C-31

Train Is A-Comin' Gr. 3, 48

Transcendental Etude, No. 3 in G-sharp Minor, "La Campanella" Gr. 7, C-23

Traveling Shoes Gr. 3, 248

Treaties Gr. 8, B-36

Tumba Gr. 7, D-14

Tutti Frutti Gr. 7, B-29

Twist, The Gr. 7, B-10

Two Dances for Three Xylophones, "Hornpipe and Jig" Gr. 8, D-17

Udu Pot Gr. 8, D-4

Ue ue Gr. 8, D-2

Violin Concerto in E Minor, Op. 64, Movement 1 Gr. 8, C-18

Voiles Gr. 7, C-39

Vonjeo Gr. 8, B-12

Waitin' for a Train Gr. 7, B-24

Walkin' to New Orleans Gr. 3, 371

Washington Post, The Gr. 8, C-40

Water Music, "Allegro Maestoso" Gr. 3, 189

Water Music, "Hornpipe" Gr. 8, C-9

Wedding Qawwali Gr. 8, B-35

Well-Tempered Clavier, Book 1, "Prelude and Fugue in C Minor" Gr. 7, E-16

Well-Tempered Clavier, The, "Be-Bop Bach: Prelude No. 2" Gr. 7, C-11

What's Going On? Gr. 7, B-38

Whirlwind Gr. 3, 149

Why Walk When You Can Fly Gr. 7, B-28

Wichita Lineman Gr. 7, B-41

Widmung, Op. 25, No. 1 Gr. 7, C-20

Wilder Reiter, Gr. 8, D-17

Wings Gr. 7, C-45

Wipe Out Gr. 7, F-33

Wooly Bully Gr. 3, 372

Work It Out (Blow Your Horn Dub Mix) Gr. 7, A-3

Would? Gr. 8, F-30

X-Beats Gr. 7, B-5

Xochipilli, An Imagined Aztec Music Gr. 8, C-37

Yamaji Gr. 3, 407

Yellow Rose of Texas, The Gr. 7, I-73

Yemaya Gr. 8, G-24

You Are My Sunshine Gr. 7, B-7

You Were on My Mind Gr. 7, G-25

You Were on My Mind Gr. 7, G-25

Zahrafat al Sa'id Gr. 7, D-30

Zoila Gr. 8, D-18

**LISTENING MAPS** See
*Technology/Media: Transparencies*

# LITERATURE

## POETRY

*A-You're Adorable* Gr. 1, 263
About Buttons Gr. 1, 211
Adventures of Isabel, The Gr. 3, 173
Advice for a Frog (Concerning a
    Crane) Gr. 4, 200
Advice to Small Children Gr. 3, 109
Ahi! Amours Gr. 8, C-4
All Around the Country Gr. 1, 445
America's Music Gr. 6, 225
And My Heart Soars Gr. 2, 240
And My Heart Soars Gr. 4, 359
Animals Went In One By One, The
    Gr. K, 275
Apple, The Gr. 1, 231
Apples Gr. 1, 16
Around the World Gr. 2, 256
At the Top of My Voice Gr. K, 279
Autumn Gr. 6, 193
Autumn Fires Gr. 5, 149
Ayii, Ayii, Ayii Gr. K, 11
Baby Chick Gr. K, 167
Back to School Gr. K, 5
Bananas and Cream Gr. 1, 49
Bat, The Gr. 2, 302
Be Bop Gr. 5, 42
Beavers in November Gr. 5, 142
Bedtime Gr. K, 159
Beginning on Paper Gr. K, 69
Bird's Nest, The Gr. K, 239
Birds of Fire Gr. 3, 257
Birthday, Birthday, Birthday
    Gr. K, 306
Birthday Cake Gr. K, 307
Bitter Morning, A Gr. K, 177
Blast Off! Gr. 1, 377
Bluebird Gr. K, 104
Blum Gr. 1, 221
Bones Gr. 4, 219
Boogie Chant and Dance (speech
    piece) Gr. 2, 78
Breaks Free Gr. 2, 319
Bubble Trouble Gr. K, 184
Bubbles Gr. K, 185
Bumble Bee Gr. 1, 385
Bump! Bump! Bump! Gr. K, 53
Butterfly Song Gr. 1, 363
By Myself Gr. 1, 43
Cacophony Gr. K, 83
Carelessly Crafted Raft, A
    Gr. 6, 416
Cat Gr. K, 13
Cat's Menu Gr. 2, 301
Cat's Tongue Gr. 2, 190
Caterpillar, The Gr. 2, 157
Caterpillar, The Gr. K, 103
Cats (excerpt) Gr. 3, 15
Celebrate Gr. 1, 407
Celebrating Our Flag Gr. K, 327

Celebration Gr. 6, 122
Changing Gr. K, 199
Chickens, The Gr. 3, 92
Children Learn What They Live
    Gr. 5, 381
Children of Long Ago Gr. 1, 31
Children of the Sun Gr. 1, 402
Chocolate Dreams Gr. 1, 381
Chums Gr. 1, 290
Circle of Sun, A Gr. K, 3
Circus Fare Gr. K, 157
Clouds Gr. K, 255
Cookie Magic Gr. K, 197
Cow, The Gr. 4, 273
Cowboy's Dream Gr. 4, 339
Crab Dance Gr. 2, 307
Crayons Gr. K, 75
Crunch and Lick Gr. 1, 381
Dance Gr. K, 59
Dance of Death Gr. 5, 456
Dancin' in the Rain Gr. 1, 366
Dancing Girl Gr. K, 249
De Beat Gr. 2, 67
Dogs Gr. K, 123
Downpour Gr. K, 51
Dragon Smoke Gr. 3, 387
Dragon Smoke Gr. K, 258
Dream Keeper, The Gr. 2, 397
Dreams Gr. K, 276
Duck, The Gr. 1, 99
Ducks Gr. 1, 99
Ducks in the Rain Gr. K, 235
El chocolate Gr. 1, 380
Eletelephony Gr. 2, 161
End, The Gr. 1, 408
Enjoy the Earth Gr. 4, 81
Extremes Gr. 4, 409
Firefly Gr. 1, 356
First Snowflake Gr. K, 259
First-ing Gr. 1, 375
Fish Gr. 1, 177
Fishes of Kempenfelt Bay, The
    Gr. 1, 19
Flies Gr. 2, 201
Flowering Umbrellas Gr. 1, 145
Flowers at Night Gr. 2, 246
Four Horses, The Gr. 1, 159
Four Seasons Gr. 2, 56
Fourth of July Night Gr. 1, 444
Frog Gr. 1, 25
Frog (haiku) Gr. K, 182
Frog Lullaby Gr. K, 149
Galoshes Gr. K, 63
Gato Gr. 1, 131
Going Places Gr. 3, 323
Goodnight, Sun Gr. 1, 367
Gotta Find a Footprint Gr. 4, 221
Grasshoppers Gr. 3, 35
Growing Corn Gr. 1, 297
Hands Gr. 1, 203
Happiness Gr. K, 62
Happy Birthday! Gr. K, 306
Happy Birthday To You Gr. 1, 411

Harriet Tubman Gr. 4, 269
Hearts Like Doors Gr. K, 189
Hello to the World Gr. 3, 2
Henry Wadsworth Longfellow
    Quote Gr. 5, 364
Here Comes The Band Gr. 1, 167
Hey, Bug! Gr. 1, 215
Hinges Gr. K, 52
His Wife Said… Gr. 1, 343
House of Spring Gr. 4, 309
How Doth the Little Crocodile
    Gr. 2, 363
How to Be a Friend Gr. 1, 331
How to Be Angry Gr. K, 249
Hurt No Living Thing Gr. 4, 32
I Hear America Singing Gr. 3, 236
I Like Fall Gr. K, 311
I Like You Gr. 6, 7
I Was Walking in a Circle Gr. 3, 321
I'm Glad Gr. 1, 415
If You Find a Little Feather
    Gr. 1, 187
In Music Meeting Gr. 5, 162
In the Morning Gr. 1, 217
It Is Fun to Sing (One fish, two fish,
    red fish, blue fish) Gr. 1, 65
It Rains and It Pours Gr. K, 243
Jellyfish Walk Gr. 1, 33
Jump or Jiggle Gr. 2, 26
Jump Rope Jingle Gr. K, 211
Just Me Gr. 1, 71
Just Watch Gr. K, 295
Kangaroo, The Gr. K, 45
Keys Gr. K, 188
Kwanzaa Gr. 1, 431
Lap Time Gr. K, 101
Las estrellas Gr. 1, 109
Last Night I Dreamed of Chickens
    Gr. 1, 141
Leaves Gr. 1, 27
Let's Do the Flip-Flop Frolic!
    Gr. K, 23
Let's Go Barefoot Gr. 1, 440
Lion, The Gr. K, 217
Little Black Train, The Gr. 4, 268
Little Ming, Little Ming Gr. 1, 325
Little Snail Gr. K, 131
Llama, The Gr. 5, 152
Looking for the Mother Birds
    Gr. 3, 331
Los pescaditos Gr. 1, 69
Loud Gr. 1, 7
Louder Than a Clap of Thunder
    Gr. 1, 87
Love Is Gr. K, 180
Lullaby Gr. 1, 205
Lullaby Lady, The Gr. 1, 273
Lumberjack, The Gr. 1, 113
Manhattan Lullaby Gr. K, 193
Maps Gr. 4, 278
Marbles Gr. 1, 75
Mashed Potatoes Gr. 1, 21
Merry-Go-Round Gr. K, 291

Min  Gr. K, 263
Mississippi River Chant (speech piece)  Gr. 2, 132
Mmmmmm mmmmmmm  Gr. K, 71
Modern Dragon, A  Gr. 3, 242
Monster Stomp, The  Gr. 1, 133
Moon, The  Gr. 1, 399
Moon's the North Wind's Cooky, The  Gr. 4, 375
More It Snows, The  Gr. K, 259
Mother to Son  Gr. 2, 203
Music  Gr. 1, 3
Music  Gr. 5, 95
Music  Gr. K, 107
My Legs and I  Gr. 1, 9
My People  Gr. 1, 233
My Shadow  Gr. K, 19
My Song  Gr. 4, 305
My Travel Tree  Gr. K, 203
New Colossus, The  Gr. 5, 166
New Shoes  Gr. 2, 242
News of Home  Gr. 4, 336
Night, The  Gr. 1, 63
Night, The  Gr. 4, 81
Night Will Never Stay, The  Gr. 3, 183
Night-light  Gr. K, 223
Nightdance  Gr. K, 219
Nitty Gritty Sand Song  Gr. K, 191
Noises  Gr. K, 305
Ode to la piñata  Gr. 1, 424
Old Mother Goose  Gr. K, 247
On Mother's Day  Gr. 1, 443
On the Ning Nang Nong  Gr. 1, 395
On This Day  Gr. 3, 69
Oranges and Lemons  Gr. 4, 217
Orchestra  Gr. 1, 74
Orchestra, The  Gr. 1, 328
Our Family Comes from 'Round the World  Gr. 1, 299
Our Mr. Toad  Gr. 3, 337
Our Tree  Gr. 1, 185
Our Washing Machine  Gr. 1, 35
Panther, The  Gr. 3, 354
Paper  Gr. K, 195
Pease Porridge Not  Gr. 1, 135
Pete at the Zoo  Gr. 1, 272
Peter, Peter, Sugar Eater  Gr. 1, 284
Pick 'n' Mix Zoo  Gr. K, 139
Pinwheels  Gr. 1, 149
Pitter Patter Scatter  Gr. 1, 55
Playing Ball  Gr. 1, 153
Poem  Gr. 3, 163
Poem [2]  Gr. 2, 285
Poem to Help You Figure Out What Bone the Patella Is, A  Gr. 4, 219
Poem to Mud  Gr. 3, 34
Prayer for Earth  Gr. 4, 350
Prism in the Window  Gr. 4, 143
Pumpkin Picking  Gr. 2, 376
Pumpkin Poem  Gr. 3, 381

"Quack!" Said the Billy Goat  Gr. K, 233
Quiet  Gr. 1, 7
Rabbit Skip, The  Gr. 2, 305
Rabbits  Gr. 2, 305
Ragtime  Gr. 5, 334
Rain (Livingston)  Gr. 3, 79
Rain Sizes  Gr. K, 261
Rain (Stevenson)  Gr. 3, 43
Rain, The  Gr. 1, 52
Raindrops  Gr. 1, 12
Raindrops  Gr. 1, 100
Reading Glasses  Gr. K, 325
River  Gr. 4, 61
River, The  Gr. 5, 121
River Winding  Gr. 4, 60
Roads Go Ever Ever On  Gr. 6, 214
Rope Rhyme  Gr. 1, 320
School Bus Rap  Gr. 1, 83
Sea Wolf, The  Gr. 4, 257
Setting the Thanksgiving Table  Gr. 2, 381
Shake-'n'-Bake a Jelly  Gr. K, 95
Sheep, Sheep  Gr. 1, 309
Shepherd, The  Gr. 5, 98
Si me pongo yo a cantar  Gr. 3, 133
Sidewalk Songs  Gr. K, 207
Sidewalk Sounds  Gr. K, 115
Sidewalks  Gr. 1, 311
Silverly  Gr. K, 135
Since Hanna Moved Away  Gr. 1, 335
Singing-Time  Gr. 3, 201
Sioux Lullaby  Gr. K, 111
Sir Barks-A-Lot  Gr. 1, 171
Sky, Sea, Shore  Gr. 2, 343
Snail, Snail  Gr. 1, 191
Snow Flakes  Gr. 1, 423
So Many Children  Gr. 1, 333
Some Silly Animals  Gr. 1, 392
Song of Greatness, A  Gr. 3, 335
Song of the Night, The  Gr. 3, 346
Song of the Train  Gr. K, 153
Spring  Gr. 2, 400
Spring Rain  Gr. 2, 294
Spring! Spring!  Gr. 1, 419
Squirrel, The  Gr. K, 129
Stars  Gr. 1, 61
Stars Streaming in the Sky, The  Gr. 2, 357
Stopping by Woods on a Snowy Evening  Gr. 2, 388
Stopping by Woods on a Snowy Evening  Gr. 6, 41
Summer Jazz  Gr. 1, 175
Sun, The  Gr. K, 143
Teddy Bears  Gr. K, 163
Ten Little Teddy Bears  Gr. K, 301
Ten Tom-Toms  Gr. K, 79
There is Joy  Gr. 3, 258
Things That Sing  Gr. K, 87
Think Positive  Gr. 7, A-6
Tide in the River, The  Gr. 2, 133

To a Peanut  Gr. 1, 163
To a Red Kite  Gr. 2, 326
Toaster Time  Gr. K, 17
Together  Gr. 3, 147
Tony Chestnut (poem)  Gr. 2,
Toodala  Gr. 1, 326
Tracks  Gr. K, 299
Trains  Gr. 1, 301
Trains  Gr. 2, 211
Traveler's Song  Gr. 4, 336
Treaties  Gr. 8, B-36
Tree House  Gr. 3, 207
Trees  Gr. 5, 114
Until I Saw the Sea  Gr. 3, 245
Until I Saw the Sea  Gr. 4, 13
Up and Down Kitten, The  Gr. K, 100
Upside Down and Inside Out  Gr. K, 297
Uptown, Downtown  Gr. K, 204
Us Two  Gr. 1, 93
Valentine Feelings  Gr. K, 322
Valentine for Earth, A  Gr. 3, 324
Valentines  Gr. 2, 398
Very Special Friend, A  Gr. 1, 147
Waiting  Gr. 1, 413
Way Down in the Music  Gr. 2, 227
We Moved About a Week Ago  Gr. 2, 230
What Do We Plant?  Gr. 2, 130
What Do You Suppose?  Gr. K, 265
What to Do  Gr. K, 43
When I Dance  Gr. 1, 327
When I Grow Up  Gr. 2, 397
When I'm an Astronaut  Gr. 1, 402
When the Train Comes Along  Gr. 1, 300
Who Has Seen the Wind?  Gr. 5, 207
Wind Has Shaken Autumn Down  Gr. 2, 57
Wind Song  Gr. K, 7
Wind, The  Gr. 6, 170
Windshield Wipers  Gr. 1, 11
Worm, The  Gr. 2, 311
Written in March  Gr. 4, 354
Yellow Butter  Gr. 1, 124
You and I  Gr. 5, 388
Youth  Gr. 6, 6

**PROVERB**
Whether It's Cold  Gr. 2, 118
Zuni Proverb  Gr. 5, 397

**QUOTES**
Alexie, Sherman  Gr. 8, B-37
Armstrong, Neil  Gr. 5, 124
Baez, Joan  Gr. 7, A-4
Balanchine, George  Gr. 7, C-26
Barnabas, Andrew  Gr. 8, A-2
Bates, Katharine Lee  Gr. 7, I-4
Beethoven, Ludwig van  Gr. 7, C-19
Bernstein, Leonard  Gr. 8, C-45
Bienvenu, Marcelle  Gr. 8, I-47
Cage, John  Gr. 6, 209

(*Literature*, continued)

Dancing in the Street: Confessions of a Motown Diva Gr. 5, 360
Diamond, Neil Gr. 7, G-32
DiFranco, Ani Gr. 8, F-32
DuBois, W.E.B. Gr. 7, C-40
Ellington, Duke Gr. 8, C-42
Ephrem, Hidaat Gr. 4, 63
Friedrich, Bonet Gr. 8, C-9
Guthrie, Woody Gr. 8, C-34
Haydn, Franz Joseph Gr. 8, C-11
Hell, Felix Gr. 7, E-24
Hughes, Langston Gr. 8, I-65
Landreth, Sonny Gr. 7, F-26
Legg, Adrian Gr. 7, F-9
Longfellow, Henry Wadsworth Gr. 5, 364
Luther, Martin Gr. 7, C-6
Plato Gr. 8, A-27
Rahman, A. R. Gr. 8, B-35
Raitt, Bonnie Gr. 7, F-26
Schumann, Clara Gr. 8, C-19
Schumann, Robert Gr. 8, C-19
Shabalala, Joseph Gr. 4, 32
Shaw, George Bernard Gr. 7, E-16
Villa-Lobos, Heitor Gr. 8, C-36
Walcha, Helmut Gr. 7, C-11
Wilson, Cassandra Gr. 7, B-14

### RHYMES

1, 2, 3, 4 (speech piece) Gr. K, 15
A la víbora Gr. 1, 323
Andy Pandy Gr. K, 46
*Baa-Baa Black Sheep* Gr. K, 102
Burnie Bee Gr. 1, 51
California Oranges Gr. 1, 15
Cinderella Dressed in Green Gr. K, 136
Doctor Foster Gr. K, 137
Engine, Engine, No. 9 Gr. K, 49
Every Morning at Eight O'Clock Gr. 1, 36
Farmer in the Dell, The Gr. K, 232
Giddy Up Gr. K, 137
Here I Am Gr. K, 149
Hey, Diddle, Diddle Gr. K, 246
Hickory, Dickory, Dare (speech piece) Gr. K, 20
Higglety, Pigglety, Pop! Gr. K, 22
Humpty Dumpty Gr. K, 47
Jack and Jill Gr. K, 47
Leg Over Leg Gr. K, 132
Little Miss Muffet (speech piece) Gr. K, 92
London Bridge Gr. K, 244
*Mother Goose Bounce* Gr. K, 247
Mother, Mother, I Am Sick Gr. K, 121
Mother Sent Me to the Store Gr. K, 136
Old King Cole Gr. K, 245
Old Mother Hubbard Gr. 1, 118
Oliver Twist Gr. K, 138

One, Two, Three, Four, Five Gr. 1, 67
Pai pi qiu Gr. 1, 324
Planting Watermelons Gr. 1, 10
Rain on the Green Grass (speech piece) Gr. K, 10
Sheep in the Meadow Gr. 1, 17
Six Little Ducks Gr. K, 234

### STORIES AND FOLK TALES

Animals Find Water, The Gr. 2, 216
Chawe chidyo chem'chero Gr. 2, 296
Dancing Pig, The Gr. 1, 196
Drum, A Gr. 1, 116
Fantastic Fossil Finds Gr. 1, 237
How the Kiwi Lost Its Wings Gr. 1, 78
Kibungo, Beast of the Forest Gr. 2, 352
Legend of the Bluebonnet, The Gr. 3, 9
Lion and the Mouse, The Gr. 1, 239
Little Red Hen, The Gr. 1, 256
Music from Junk Gr. 1, 72
*Nruab hnub thiab hmo ntuj* Gr. 4, 366
Play About Ayelivi, A Gr. 2,
*Rabbit Dance, The* Gr. 3, 334
Rolling Rice Cake, The Gr. 1, 91
Rose Is a Rose Gr. 3, 10
When I Was a Little Boy Gr. 4, 322
Why the Warthog Goes About on His Knees Gr. 1, 139
*Zomo the Rabbit* Gr. 3, 364

## M

# MEETING INDIVIDUAL NEEDS

### AIDING COMPREHENSION

*Crunchy, Crunchy, Crunchy* Gr. 8, D-14
Glendy Burke, The Gr. 4, 262

### ART MATERIALS

Windshield Wipers (poem) Gr. 1, 10

### ASSIGNING PARTS

*Orfferondo* Gr. 4, 194

### ASSIGNING THE DESCANT

Oh, Freedom Gr. 7, G-31

### BODY/KINESTHETIC

*Orchestral Suite No. 3, BWV 1068, "Air in D," Movement 2* Gr. 4, 23
*Symphony No. 9 in D Minor, Op. 125, "Ode to Joy," Movement 4* Gr. 4, 150

### BOYS' CHANGING VOICES

Cattle Call Gr. 5, 344

### CHALLENGE

*Two-Part Invention in A Major (piano)* Gr. 5, 237

### CHANGING VOICE, THE

Blues with a Feeling Gr. 8, I-8

### CLASSROOM MANAGEMENT

*Edward Scissorhands, "Main Titles"* Gr. 8, A-10
*That'll Be the Day* Gr. 6, 256

### COLOR IDENTIFICATION

Ida Red Gr. 3, 31

### COMBINING DIFFERENT ABILITY LEVELS

Agbekor Ensemble Gr. 8, D-11

### COMPOSING

Gonna Build a Mountain Gr. 6, 21

### COOPERATION

Heave-Ho!/Going, Going, Gone/ The Snow Gr. 4, 183

### COOPERATIVE LEARNING

*When Johnny Comes Marching Home* Gr. 5, 89

### COORDINATION

Feng yang hua gu Gr. 4, 312

### DECODING CHORD FRAMES

Jambalaya Gr. 8, F-19

### DEVELOPING INTEREST

Ala Da'lona Gr. 4, 136

### DEVELOPING PERCUSSION SKILLS

Surfin' U.S.A. Gr. 7, I-59

### DIFFERENT DRUMMERS

*Birdland* Gr. 5, 155

### ENCOURAGING INDIVIDUAL PERFORMANCE

*Frère Jacques* Gr. 3, 113

### ENCOURAGING PARTICIPATION

Chawe chidyo chem'chero Gr. 2, 299
*Chicken Dance, The* Gr. 4, 51
Oh, Freedom Gr. 5, 392

### ENGLISH LANGUAGE LEARNERS

Abraham, Martin, and John Gr. 6, 466
Alphabet Soup (speech piece) Gr. 1, 219
America, the Free Gr. 4, 210
Apples, Peaches, Pears, and Plums (speech piece) Gr. 1, 16
At the Same Time Gr. 6, 117
Baby Beluga Gr. K, 272
Blow Ye Winds Gr. 4, 254
Bluebonnets of Texas Gr. 3, 332
Bundle-Buggy Boogie Woogie Gr. 4, 121

Canción de cuna  Gr. 4, 144

Children, Go Where I Send Thee
    Gr. 3, 393

*Circle of Life (from The Lion
    King), The*  Gr. 6, 316

Crawfish!  Gr. 2, 86

Doctor Knickerbocker (speech
    piece)  Gr. 1, 302

Don Giovanni  Gr. 8,

Down by the Riverside  Gr. 5, 256

Down the Ohio  Gr. 2, 60

Eensy Weensy Spider  Gr. K, 186

El coquí  Gr. 2, 292

Erie Canal  Gr. 5, 262

Family Tree  Gr. 3, 73

From Sea to Shining Sea  Gr. 2, 342

Great Big House  Gr. 2, 204

Ha'kyo jong  Gr. 2, 135

Had to Get Up This Mornin' Soon
    Gr. 3, 114

Honeybee Song, The  Gr. 1, 358

I Bought Me a Cat  Gr. 2, 308

I Fed My Horse  Gr. 2, 94

I Walk the Unfrequented Road
    Gr. 6, 79

I'm Thankful  Gr. 1, 414

Kou ri lengay  Gr. 2, 216

Let's Go Fly a Kite  Gr. 2, 327

Little Black Bug  Gr. 1, 212

Live in the City  Gr. 5, 71

Lone Star Trail  Gr. 2, 22

Los días de la semana  Gr. 1, 268

Lots of Worms  Gr. 2, 310

Love in Any Language  Gr. 6, 477

Love Will Guide Us  Gr. 4, 329

Magnolia  Gr. 6, 16

Michael, Row the Boat Ashore
    Gr. 2, 18

Missy-La, Massa-La  Gr. 4, 188

My Foot's In My Stirrup  Gr. 2, 234

My Pony, Macaroni  Gr. 1, 158

Noah's Shanty  Gr. 1, 342

Old House, Tear It Down!
    Gr. 4, 178

Over in the Meadow  Gr. 1, 346

Painting Song: A Dribble and a Dot
    Gr. K, 175

Parade Came Marching, The
    Gr. 1, 165

Peace Like a River  Gr. 6, 190

Polly Wee  Gr. K, 118

Puff, the Magic Dragon  Gr. 2, 350

Rags  Gr. 1, 290

*Rig-a-Jig-Jig*  Gr. K, 98

River  Gr. 4, 58

Rocky Mountain  Gr. 2, 99

Route 66  Gr. 4, 279

Sambalele  Gr. 4, 396

Same Train  Gr. 2, 164

Sansaw akroma  Gr. 3, 286

Scrub Brush Shuffle, The  Gr. 1, 118

Shoo, Turkey  Gr. 1, 104

Singin' in the Tub  Gr. K, 220

Song of the Fishes  Gr. 3, 244

Song of the Night, The  Gr. 3, 346

St. Patrick Was a Gentleman
    Gr. 3, 293

Summertime  Gr. 6, 251

Train Is A-Comin'  Gr. 3, 48

Tree in the Wood, The  Gr. 2, 360

Turn the World Around  Gr. 4, 117

Twelve Days of Christmas, The
    Gr. 4, 430

We're Making Popcorn (speech
    piece)  Gr. 1, 84

Wheel of the Water, The  Gr. 4, 362

Winter Fantasy  Gr. 4, 424

Zip-a-Dee-Doo-Dah  Gr. 2, 330

## EXPRESSIVE MOVEMENT
Loco-Motion, The  Gr. 3, 65

## FEELING SOUND
Longer Sounds, Longer Rests
    Gr. 7, H-2

Rhythm Basics  Gr. 7, H-2

Rock Around the Clock  Gr. 7, H-2

Syncopation  Gr. 7, H-2

## GIFTED AND TALENTED
Ah, eu entrei na roda  Gr. 3, 308

Connemara Lullaby  Gr. 5, 232

Dance of the Youths and Maidens
    Gr. 8, C-33

Dona nobis pacem  Gr. 6, 124

El cóndor pasa  Gr. 6, 47

Kum bachur atzel  Gr. 3, 138

*Le tombeau de Couperin,
    "Prelude"*  Gr. 8, C-28

Put a Little Love in Your Heart
    Gr. 4, 8

Ten Little Ostinato Pieces  Gr. 7, I-65

*Vocal Olympics*  Gr. 8, B-15

Waitin' for the Light to Shine
    Gr. 4, 26

## IMPROVISING
*Danses Populaires Francaises,
    "Branle Double, Branle
    Simple"*  Gr. 7, C-25

## INCLUDING EVERYONE/
## INCLUSION
Ama-Lama  Gr. 5, 145

Ants Go Marching, The  Gr. 1, 248

Ayliluli, num tsipor  Gr. 1, 204

Big Old Storm a-Comin'  Gr. K, 257

Bingo  Gr. 1, 169

Bluebird, Bluebird  Gr. K, 105

Busy Buzzy Bee  Gr. K, 176

But the Cat Came Back  Gr. 2, 190

Can You Canoe?  Gr. 4, 170

*Chorale Prelude for Organ, BWV
    645, "Wachet auf, ruft uns die
    Stimme "*  Gr. 7, C-9

Cirmos cica  Gr. 1, 130

Cobbler, Cobbler (speech piece)
    Gr. 1, 299

Coffee Grows on White Oak Trees
    Gr. 3, 168

Cuando pa' Chile me voy  Gr. 6, 376

Dance for the Nations  Gr. 6, 122

*Danses Populaires Francaises,
    "Branle Double, Branle
    Simple"*  Gr. 7, C-25

Different Beat, A  Gr. 1, 6

Don Gato  Gr. 3, 352

*Drums From Around the World*
    Gr. 6, 279

Éliza Kongo  Gr. 5, 17

Everybody Loves Saturday Night
    Gr. 6, 294

Five Little Chickadees  Gr. K, 178

Four in a Boat  Gr. 2, 47

Freedom Is Coming  Gr. 5, 416

Freight Train  Gr. 1, 45

*French Suite No. 5, "Gigue"*
    Gr. 4, 232

Fuzzy Caterpillar  Gr. K, 102

Geef jij mij die schoen  Gr. 1, 126

Glory, Glory, Hallelujah  Gr. 6, 52

Grizzly Bear  Gr. K, 32

Happy Wanderer, The  Gr. 4, 88

He's Got the Whole World in His
    Hands  Gr. 7, I-38

Heigh-Ho  Gr. 2, 7

Hey, Hey, Look at Me  Gr. 1, 71

Hickory, Dickory, Dock  Gr. 1, 351

Hound Dog  Gr. 5, 214

How to Be a Friend (poem)
    Gr. 1, 331

I Can't Spell Hippopotamus
    Gr. 1, 265

I Can't Spell Hippopotamus
    Gr. 1, 264

I Got Rhythm  Gr. 6, 100

I Love the Mountains  Gr. 5, 34

Ikhanda, maslombe  Gr. K, 15

Jambalaya  Gr. 6, 249

Jig Along Home  Gr. 2, 366

Jim Along, Josie  Gr. K, 39

Kapulu kane  Gr. 2, 270

Kelo aba w'ye  Gr. 6, 289

La mar estaba serena  Gr. 2, 345

Lean on Me  Gr. 6, 14

Leatherwing Bat, The  Gr. 2, 302

Leaves  Gr. 1, 28

Let Freedom Ring  Gr. 5, 78

Let's Pretend  Gr. K, 227

Li'l Liza Jane  Gr. 3, 140

Lift Ev'ry Voice and Sing  Gr. 5, 482

Like a Bird  Gr. 6, 167

Lion Sleeps Tonight, The  Gr. 4, 132

Lucy Locket  Gr. 2, 26

Mainly Metal Ensemble  Gr. 7, D-28

Mary Wore Her Red Dress  Gr. K, 74

*Memories of the Seashore*
    Gr. 3, 150

Mi chacra  Gr. 1, 364

Name, Name, What's Your Name?
    (speech piece)  Gr. 3, 10

**(*Meeting Individual Needs,* continued)**

Nanny Goat Gr. K, 161
New Way to Walk, A Gr. K, 116
Noah's Shanty Gr. 1, 344
Oh, How Lovely is the Evening
    Gr. 4, 216
Old Blue Gr. K, 122
Old Brass Wagon Gr. 2, 123
Old Dan Tucker Gr. 3, 99
Orange Blossom Special Gr. 5, 267
Orfferondo Gr. 4, 192
Over the Rainbow Gr. 4, 140
Painting Song: A Dribble and a Dot
    Gr. K, 175
Pat Works on the Railway
    Gr. 5, 183
Paths of Victory Gr. 6, 195
Peace Like a River Gr. 3, 247
Peanut Butter (speech piece)
    Gr. 1, 173
Pin Pon Gr. 1, 146
Producer Gr. 8, A-24
Pumpkin Picking Gr. 2, 376
Put a Little Love in Your Heart
    Gr. 4, 6
Rain Sings a Song, The Gr. 1, 103
Ríu ríu chíu Gr. 5, 437
Run, Molly, Run Gr. 1, 9
*Samanfo, begye nsa nom*
    Gr. 8, D-7
Scotland the Brave Gr. 5, 139
*Shepherd's Hey Sampler*
    Gr. 7, C-37
Skin and Bones Gr. 2, 376
Stopping by Woods on a Snowy
    Evening Gr. 6, 40
Storm Dance (speech piece)
    Gr. K, 145
*String Quartet No. 5, Movement
    4: Andante* Gr. 3, 111
Take Your Feet Out 'the Sand
    Gr. K, 231
Tie Me Kangaroo Down, Sport
    Gr. 4, 36
Tina singu Gr. 4, 300
*Toy Symphony, Movement 4*
    Gr. 1, 111
Trouble Is a Mountain Gr. 2, 202
Turn the World Around Gr. 4, 115
Uno, dos y tres Gr. 5, 429
*Vaya Puente* Gr. 2, 181
Waiting for the Traffic Light
    Gr. 2, 106
We Shall Overcome Gr. 4, 327
What a Wonderful World Gr. 6, 64
Who Has Seen the Wind?
    Gr. 2, 324
World of Difference, A Gr. 5, 388
Wu long Gr. 4, 157
Yesh lanu taish Gr. 1, 181
Your Friends Shall Be the Tall Wind
    Gr. 6, 200

**INDEPENDENT SINGING**
Going upon the Mountain
    Gr. 6, 104

**INVENTION**
Amarillo Armadillo Gr. 2, 83

**JAZZ INSTRUMENTS**
Tuxedo Junction Gr. 8, G-22

**LEARNING A NEW LANGUAGE**
At the Same Time Gr. 6, 115

**LEARNING FOREIGN TERMS**
*Jambalaya* Gr. 6, 245

**LEARNING IDIOMS**
Water Come a Me Eye Gr. 6, 299

**LEARNING STYLES**
Canto del agua Gr. 8, I-12

**LOW RANGE**
Book of Love Gr. 8, G-28

**MNEMONIC DEVICES**
*Do-Re-Mi* Gr. 5, 38

**MOTIVATION**
Make a Music Video! Gr. 7, A-29

**MOTOR SKILLS**
*Carnaval, Op. 9, "Valse Noble,"
    Un poco maestoso* Gr. 3, 200
Ding, Dong, Diggidiggidong
    Gr. 3, 15
Frog in the Millpond Gr. 2, 44
Pizza, Pizza, Daddy-o Gr. 2, 30

**NONVOCAL COMMUNICATION**
*Nutcracker Suite, The, "Waltz of
    the Flowers"* Gr. 6, 322

**OSTINATO HINTS**
Yibane amenu Gr. 4, 316

**PAIRING STUDENTS**
Gakavik Gr. 4, 15

**PART SINGING AND GROUP
ASSIGNMENTS**
John Kanaka Gr. 3, 61
Wai bamba Gr. 8, G-12

**PEER TUTORING**
Hey, m'tswala Gr. 4, 78

**PERFORMING**
Ah ya zane Gr. 5, 296
California Gr. 5, 53
*Symphony No. 40 in G Minor, K.
    550, Movement 1* Gr. 8, C-13

**PHYSICAL COORDINATION**
If a Tiger Calls Gr. 3, 354

**PIANO SKILLS**
Minor Practice Plus Gr. 8, H-27
Reading Chord Symbols Gr. 8, H-27

**PITCH ACCURACY**
Now's the Time Gr. 5, 449

**PLAYERS WITH DIVERSE PLAYING
ABILITIES**
Flip, Flop and Fly Gr. 7, I-34

**PLAYING PIANO**
Chords in F Gr. 7, H-26
Reading Chord Symbols
    Gr. 7, H-26
Three Major Chords Gr. 7, H-26
What Makes A Chord Major?
    Gr. 7, H-26

**PLAYING RHYTHM PATTERNS**
La calle ancha Gr. 3, 297
Sierra Morena Gr. 3, 297

**PROVIDING ALTERNATIVES**
Waltzing with Bears Gr. 3, 171

**READING POETRY**
Advice to Small Children Gr. 3, 109

**RECORDER TIPS**
Riqui rán Gr. 4, 67

**RELUCTANT SINGERS**
Dry Bones Come Skipping
    Gr. 4, 219

**RESPONDING TO MUSIC**
Understanding music Gr. 8, C-2

**ROLE-PLAYING MUSICIANS**
Eh, cumpari! Gr. 4, 69

**SCORE READING**
Vem kan segla? Gr. 6, 420

**SELF-ESTEEM**
Hot Cross Buns (Version 1)
    Gr. 3, 220
Music promotion Gr. 7, A-26
*Vocal Olympics* Gr. 8, B-15

**SIGN LANGUAGE**
Make New Friends Gr. 3, 37

**SINGING FOR ALL STUDENTS**
*Hippopotamus Song, The*
    Gr. 3, 33

**SINGING IN HARMONY**
Let Freedom Ring Gr. 5, 77

**SINGING IN PARTS**
Bogando a la luz del sol Gr. 4, 306

**SINGING/PHRASING**
Oklahoma Gr. 5, 37

**SOLO AND GROUP SINGING**
Glad to Have a Friend Like You
    Gr. 2, 230
Hello, There! Gr. K, 7
Pay Me My Money Down Gr. 4, 39

**STUDENTS WITH DIVERSE SKILLS**
This Land Is Your Land Gr. 7, I-68

**SUCCESS FOR ALL**
All for One Gr. 7, E-8
Bananas and Cream (speech piece)
    Gr. 3, 210

Chapel of Love  Gr. 7, G-28
Cheki, morena  Gr. 7, E-12
Deep in the Heart of Texas
    Gr. 8, E-23
El rancho grande  Gr. 8, I-24
Fiddler on the Roof  Gr. 7, E-7
Goodbye, Julie  Gr. 8, E-3
I'm a Believer  Gr. 7, G-35
Joshua Fought the Battle of Jericho
    Gr. 8, E-19
Lean on Me  Gr. 7, E-23
Let's Get the Rhythm of the Band
    Gr. 7, E-29
Orange Blossom Special  Gr. 8, E-7

### Syncopated Lyrics
Give a Little Love  Gr. 6, 140

### Teaching to Multiple Levels
Composing with Sixteenth Notes
    Gr. 7, H-18
Eighth and Sixteenth Combinations
    Gr. 7, H-18
Move It: Sixteenth Notes
    Gr. 7, H-18

### Teaching with Visuals
Pastures of Plenty  Gr. 4, 280

### Thinking Skills
Oh, Danny Boy  Gr. 4, 48

### Transcription help
America  Gr. 7, A-23

### Using Direction Words
Andy Pandy  Gr. K, 47

### Using Technology
Fais do do  Gr. 6, 407

### Utilizing Strengths
Pust' 'vsegda budet sonse  Gr. 3, 279

### Very High/Very Low
Andy Pandy  Gr. K, 47

### Visual Aids
Flight of the Bumblebee  Gr. 3, 186

### Visual/Motor Coordination
Nana Kru  Gr. 6, 280

### Vocabulary Building
Under the Sea  Gr. 5, 372

### Working in Groups
Quiet Night  Gr. 4, 336

### Working Together
Blow, Ye Winds  Gr. 4, 255

## MELODY

### Intervals
Blue Mountain Lake  Gr. 6, 205
Like a Bird  Gr. 6, 167
Lo yisa  Gr. 6, 130
O lê lê O Bahía  Gr. 6, 165
Scarborough Fair  Gr. 6, 95
Shalom aleichem  Gr. 6, 409

### Legato Phrases
Ding Dong! Merrily on High
    Gr. 6, 427

### Melodic Contour
Glory, Glory, Hallelujah  Gr. 6, 52
My Dear Companion  Gr. 6, 23

### Melody Patterns
Addams Family, The  Gr. 5, 456
Bury Me Not on the Lone Prairie
    Gr. 6, 19

### Motive
Changed My Name  Gr. 6, 338
I Got Rhythm  Gr. 6, 101
New Horizons in Music
    Appreciation—Beethoven's
    Fifth Symphony, Movement 1
    Gr. 6, 98
Symphony No. 5 in C Minor,
    Movement 1  Gr. 6, 98

### Patterns
C-Jam Blues  Gr. 8, C-43

**layered patterns**
Badenma  Gr. 8, B-28
Believer  Gr. 7, A-2
Brandenburg Concerto No. 2,
    Movement 3 Allegro Assai
    Gr. 7, C-8
Les pêcheurs des perles, "Au
    fond du temple saint"
    Gr. 7, C-30
Nyoka  Gr. 7, D-33
Rigoletto, "Bella figlia
    dell'amore "  Gr. 7, C-29
Shalom aleichem  Gr. 6, 409

**melodic direction**
Morning Has Broken  Gr. 5, 29

**melodic sequence**
Caroling, Caroling  Gr. 6, 458
Winter Song  Gr. 6, 455

**melody patterns**
A la puerta del cielo  Gr. 5, 60
All Through the Night  Gr. 5, 105
Alle psallite cum luya  Gr. 7, C-5
Allons danser, Colinda
    Gr. K, 218
America, the Beautiful  Gr. 8, I-4
Asadoya  Gr. 6, 303
Ash Grove, The  Gr. 5, 114
Autumn Canon  Gr. 5, 148
Bachianas brasileiras No. 5,
    "Aria"  Gr. 8, C-37
Bird Calls, Bird Songs  Gr. K, 178
Birthday  Gr. 6, 90
Boil Them Cabbage Down
    Gr. 6, 370
Boston Ball Game 1967
    Gr. 8, F-32
Cantando mentiras  Gr. 4, 146
Cantaré, cantarás  Gr. 6, 413

Circle 'Round the Moon
    Gr. 4, 403
Close Encounters of the Third
    Kind  Gr. 8, B-34
Concerto for Flute and Harp
    in C, K. 299, Movement 2
    Gr. 8, C-10
Crocodile, The  Gr. 2, 362
Crunchy, Crunchy, Crunchy
    Gr. 8, D-15
Da pacem, Domine  Gr. 5, 62
Danse macabre  Gr. 5, 457
Deau-deau, ti pitit maman
    Gr. 2, 306
Ding Dong! Merrily on High
    Gr. 6, 427
Dundai  Gr. 5, 106
El día de mamita  Gr. K, 325
El sapito  Gr. 3, 336
Ev'ry Time I Feel the Spirit
    Gr. 7, C-40
Fifty Nifty United States
    Gr. 5, 251
Funwa alafia  Gr. 5, 32
Glad to Have a Friend Like You
    Gr. 2, 228
Goin' to Boston  Gr. 6, 433
Goodbye, Julie (Miss Julie Ann
    Johnson)  Gr. 1, 334
Gospel Train, The  Gr. 6, 398
Happy Birthday to You
    Gr. K, 304
Happy Days Are Here Again
    Gr. 5, 284
Hard Times  Gr. 1, 194
Hound Dog  Gr. 5, 212
I Got Rhythm  Gr. 6, 101
I See the Moon  Gr. 2, 58
Jo'ashila  Gr. 5, 108
Katura  Gr. 7, D-27
Los días de la semana  Gr. 1, 268
Messiah, "Hallelujah!"  Gr. 8, C-8
Missy-La, Massa-La  Gr. 4, 188
Now's the Time  Gr. 5, 445
Nutcracker Suite, The, "Waltz
    of the Flowers"  Gr. 6, 325
Nyoka  Gr. 7, D-32
Oh, Susanna  Gr. 4, 264
One Family  Gr. 7, G-17
Over My Head  Gr. 7, G-9
P'tit galop pour mamou
    Gr. 1, 317
Pastures of Plenty  Gr. 4, 280
Phoebe  Gr. 1, 30
Pollerita  Gr. 5, 151
Proud  Gr. 7, G-3
Roll Over  Gr. K, 288
Skye Boat Song  Gr. 6, 372
Sonata in C Major for Recorder
    and Basso Continuo, Op. 1,
    No. 7, "Gavotte"  Gr. K, 75
Spring Has Sprung!  Gr. K, 142
Study War No More  Gr. 7, C-40

**(Melody, continued)**

    *Suite for Wind Quintet,*
      *Movement 1* Gr. 8, C-34

    This Train Gr. 5, 26

    *Toei khong* Gr. 8, B-21

    'Ūlili E Gr. 5, 441

    *Vem kan segla?* Gr. 6, 417

    *Well-Tempered Clavier, Book*
      *1, "Prelude and Fugue in C*
      *Minor"* Gr. 7, E-16

    Worried Man Blues Gr. 6, 371

    You Were on My Mind
      Gr. 7, G-23

**motives**

    Alleluia Gr. 6, 133

    *Bachianas brasileiras No. 5,*
      *"Aria"* Gr. 8, C-37

    *Cantata No. 140 (as performed*
      *by American Bach Solosists),*
      *"Wachet auf, ruft uns die*
      *Stimme," Movement 4*
      Gr. 7, C-9

    *Children's Corner Suite,*
      *"Doctor Gradus ad*
      *Parnassum"* Gr. 8, C-27

    *Close Encounters of the Third*
      *Kind* Gr. 8, B-34

    *Coming Home from the Sea–I*
      Gr. 6, 345

    *Coming Home from the Sea–II*
      Gr. 6, 345

    *Crunchy, Crunchy, Crunchy*
      Gr. 8, D-15

    *Domna, pos vos ay chausida*
      *(Lady, For You)* Gr. 8, C-6

    Fais do do Gr. 6, 403

    For Children Safe and Strong
      Gr. 5, 484

    *I'm a Yankee Doodle Dandy*
      Gr. 5, 278

    *Invention No. 5 in E-flat*
      Gr. 5, 59

    La ciudad de Juaja Gr. 5, 58

    *La tierche estampie real*
      Gr. 8, C-6

    Over There Gr. 5, 279

    *Return to Misty Mountain*
      Gr. 7, D-28

    Run! Run! Hide! Gr. 6, 340

    *Sonata in F Major for Violin*
      *and Piano, Op. 24, No.*
      *5, "Spring," Movement 3*
      Gr. 7, C-19

    Strike Up the Band Gr. 6, 135

    *Symphony No. 3 in E-flat*
      *Major, "Allegro con brio,"*
      *Movement 1* Gr. 8, C-17

    *Symphony No. 3 in E-flat*
      *Major, "Marcia funebre,"*
      *Movement 2* Gr. 8, C-17

    *Symphony No. 5 in C Minor,*
      *Op. 67, Movement 4*
      Gr. 7, C-18

    Yours Forever Gr. 6, 344

**retrograde patterns**

    *Sonata in F Major for Violin*
      *and Piano, Op. 24, No.*
      *5, "Spring," Movement 3*
      Gr. 7, C-19

    *Symphony No. 47 in G Major,*
      *"Menuet"* Gr. 7, C-14

**same and different patterns**

    Bridges Gr. 6, 86

    Cantaré, cantarás Gr. 6, 413

    Con el vito Gr. 7, G-15

    Dance for the Nations
      Gr. 6, 122

    *Daybreak Vision* Gr. 5, 398

    El carite Gr. 5, 305

    Fifty Nifty United States
      Gr. 5, 251

    God Bless the U.S.A. Gr. 8, G-37

    *I Am a Man of Constant*
      *Sorrow* Gr. 7, F-29

    *I Shall Sing* Gr. 8, I-41

    I'll Fly Away Gr. 8, I-42

    La ciudad de Juaja Gr. 5, 58

    *"Little" Organ Fugue in G*
      *Minor* Gr. 6, 129

    *Messiah, "Hallelujah!"* Gr. 8, C-8

    Nanny Goat Gr. K, 161

    *Nutcracker Suite, The, "Waltz*
      *of the Flowers"* Gr. 6, 325

    Oy, Hanuka Gr. 7, I-44

    Phoebe Gr. 1, 30

    Play a Simple Melody Gr. 5, 72

    Proud Gr. 7, G-3

    Se va el caimán Gr. 5, 306

    Shake the Papaya Down
      Gr. 4, 378

    *Sonata in F Major for Violin*
      *and Piano, Op. 24, No.*
      *5, "Spring," Movement 3*
      Gr. 7, C-19

    Take a Chance On Me
      Gr. 8, G-15

    This Train Gr. 5, 26

    *Two Dances for Three*
      *Xylophones, "Hornpipe and*
      *Jig"* Gr. 8, D-17

    *Washington Post, The*
      Gr. 8, C-40

    *Wilder Reiter,* Gr. 8, D-17

    Winter Gr. 8, G-11

    Yang wa wa Gr. K, 162

    Yellow Rose of Texas, The
      Gr. 7, I-70

## PITCH AND DIRECTION

**high and low**

    Ah ya Zane Gr. 5, 297

    Andy Pandy Gr. K, 46

    *Apu Min'Tan* Gr. 8, D-21

    *Bachianas brasileiras No. 5,*
      *"Aria"* Gr. 8, C-37

    Book of Love Gr. 8, G-27

    *Carnival of the Animals, "The*
      *Elephant"* Gr. K, 45

    *Cauyaqa Nauwa? (Where's My*
      *Drum?)* Gr. 8, D-20

    Chapel of Love Gr. 7, G-27

    Charlie over the Water Gr. 1, 68

    *Close Encounters of the Third*
      *Kind* Gr. 8, B-34

    *Concert for Piano and*
      *Orchestra* Gr. 6, 209

    *Crunchy, Crunchy, Crunchy*
      Gr. 8, D-15

    *Die forelle* Gr. 7, C-20

    *Domna, pos vos ay chausida*
      *(Lady, For You)* Gr. 8, C-6

    Elegua Gr. 7, D-8

    *Ev'ry Time I Feel the Spirit*
      Gr. 7, C-40

    Ev'rybody Loves Saturday Night
      Gr. 7, I-24

    Everybody Loves Saturday Night
      Gr. 6, 296

    *Face of Love, The* Gr. 8, B-15

    *Fanfare for the Common Man*
      Gr. 7, C-43

    Feliz Navidad Gr. 7, I-28

    Friends Today Gr. 7, D-12

    *Goldilocks and the Three Bears*
      Gr. K, 49

    Good Vibrations Gr. 8, E-28

    *Guitar Tuning* Gr. 7, F-2

    Here I Go! Gr. K, 73

    Hickory, Dickory, Dare (speech
      piece) Gr. K, 20

    Humpty Dumpty Gr. K, 47

    I'm a Believer Gr. 7, G-33

    I'm Tall, I'm Small Gr. K, 18

    Ichi-gatsu tsuitachi Gr. 7, I-40

    *Intertribal Song* Gr. 8, B-18

    *Into the Faddisphere* Gr. K, 21

    *Is the Sound High or Low?*
      Gr. K, 17

    It Is Fun to Sing (One fish, two
      fish, red fish, blue fish) (poem)
      Gr. 1, 65

    Jack and Jill Gr. K, 47

    *Jump for Joy* Gr. 7, D-20

    *Kangaroo Song, The* Gr. K, 44

    Kou ri lengay Gr. 7, E-2

    Leg Over Leg Gr. K, 132

    *Lion* Gr. 6, 303

    Little Green Frog, The Gr. 1, 24

    Lone Star Trail Gr. 2, 21

    *Magic Flute, The, "Queen of*
      *the Night Aria"* Gr. 7, C-31

    *Magic Flute, The, "In diesen*
      *heil'gen Hallen (In These*
      *Bright Halls)"* Gr. K, 9

    *Magnificent Seven, The*
      Gr. 3, 144

    *Malê Debalê* Gr. 8, B-16

    Oh, Freedom Gr. 7, G-30

    One Family Gr. 7, G-17

Panamam tombé  Gr. 7, D-18
*Pupu hinu hinu, "Shiny Shell Lullaby"*  Gr. 1, 109
*Return to Misty Mountain*  Gr. 7, D-28
*Rodeo, "Buckaroo Holiday"*  Gr. 2, 23
S'vivon  Gr. 6, 452
Si si si  Gr. 7, G-13
Something Told the Wild Geese  Gr. 7, G-39
Strike Up the Band  Gr. 6, 135
*Study War No More*  Gr. 7, C-40
Take a Chance On Me  Gr. 8, G-15
*Three Little Piggies*  Gr. K, 56
Tuxedo Junction  Gr. 8, G-21
*Widmung, Op. 25, No. 1*  Gr. 7, C-20
*Yemeni baglamis telli basina*  Gr. 6, 309
You Were on My Mind  Gr. 7, G-23

**intervals (steps, skips, repeated pitches)**
A la puerta del cielo  Gr. 5, 60
All Through the Night  Gr. 5, 105
Allá en la fuente  Gr. 2, 92
Arirang  Gr. 5, 25
Blow, Ye Winds  Gr. 4, 255
Book of Love  Gr. 8, G-27
Canción de cuna  Gr. 4, 144
*Caprice No. 1 in E Major*  Gr. 7, C-22
Certainly, Lord  Gr. 7, I-13
Chairs to Mend  Gr. 4, 149
Chanukah Games  Gr. 3, 389
Cielito lindo  Gr. 7, I-20
*Concerto for French Horn in E-flat Major, K. 495, No. 4, Movement 3*  Gr. 8, C-11
Deep in the Heart of Texas  Gr. 4, 22
*Die forelle*  Gr. 7, C-20
Don Alfonso  Gr. 5, 177
Down the Ohio  Gr. 2, 60
*Dreydl Song, The*  Gr. 3, 391
*Etude Fantasy for Piano, "Etude No 3: Fifths to Thirds"*  Gr. 8, C-46
*Fanfare for the Common Man*  Gr. 7, C-43
Go Down, Moses  Gr. 5, 190
Goin' to Boston  Gr. 6, 433
Gonna Ride Up in the Chariot  Gr. 4, 20
Green Corn Song  Gr. 5, 462
Greenland Whale Fishery, The  Gr. 5, 230
Habari Gani  Gr. 3, 404
Hanuka, Hanuka  Gr. 3, 390

Heri za Kwanzaa  Gr. 5, 476
Hop Up, My Ladies  Gr. 3, 142
It Don't Mean a Thing (If It Ain't Got That Swing)  Gr. 5, 336
It's a Beautiful Day  Gr. 3, 338
Ja-Da  Gr. 7, G-20
Johnny Has Gone for a Soldier  Gr. 5, 188
Kookaburra  Gr. 4, 186
Kou ri lengay  Gr. 7, E-2
Las mañanitas  Gr. 6, 481
Las velitas  Gr. 5, 147
*Le cou cou*  Gr. 3, 329
Let It Snow! Let It Snow! Let It Snow!  Gr. 4, 426
Like a Bird  Gr. 6, 167
Loco-Motion, The  Gr. 3, 64
*Magnificent Seven, The*  Gr. 3, 144
O lê lê O Bahía  Gr. 6, 165
*Orchestral Suite No. 3, BWV 1068, "Air in D," Movement 2*  Gr. 4, 23
Over My Head  Gr. 7, G-9
Over the River and Through the Wood  Gr. 3, 384
Pin Pon  Gr. 1, 146
Ptashky u babusi sadochku  Gr. 1, 192
*Rhapsody in Blue*  Gr. 7, C-42
Sailing Down My Golden River  Gr. 4, 332
Shalom aleichem  Gr. 6, 409
*Shenandoah*  Gr. 2, 62
Something Told the Wild Geese  Gr. 7, G-39
*Sometimes I Feel Like a Motherless Child*  Gr. 5, 193
*Sonata for Violin and Piano, Allegro*  Gr. 8, C-46
Star-Spangled Banner, The  Gr. 7, I-56
Take Me Out to the Ball Game  Gr. 3, 263
This Land Is Your Land  Gr. 7, I-66
Tuxedo Junction  Gr. 8, G-21
Vive l'amour  Gr. 6, 176
*Widmung, Op. 25, No. 1*  Gr. 7, C-20

**letter names for pitches**
Alleluia  Gr. 6, 133
Autumn Canon  Gr. 5, 148
Book of Love  Gr. 8, G-27
Bound for South Australia  Gr. 5, 22
Da pacem, Domine  Gr. 5, 62
El payo  Gr. 6, 145
Erie Canal  Gr. 5, 262
*Evening Chaconne*  Gr. 6, 202
Feliz Navidad  Gr. 7, I-28
Greenland Whale Fishery, The  Gr. 5, 230

*Guitar Tuning*  Gr. 8, F-2
Hot Cross Buns (Version 1)  Gr. 3, 218
Like a Bird  Gr. 6, 167
Ode to Joy  Gr. 4, 152
Oh, Freedom  Gr. 7, G-30
Pollerita  Gr. 5, 151
Riqui rán  Gr. 4, 66
Sailing Down My Golden River  Gr. 4, 332
Ten Little Ostinato Pieces  Gr. 7, I-62

**melodic contour**
Ai, Dunaii moy  Gr. 4, 293
*Carol of the Bells*  Gr. 8, G-10
*Diamonds and Rust*  Gr. 7, A-4
*Die Walküre, "The Ride of the Valkyries"*  Gr. 8, C-23
*Ev'ry Time I Feel the Spirit*  Gr. 7, C-40
*Fanfare for the Common Man*  Gr. 7, C-43
*Galliard Battaglia*  Gr. 8, C-14
Gonna Build a Mountain  Gr. 6, 21
*Intertribal Song*  Gr. 8, B-18
*Nruab hnub thiab hmo ntuj*  Gr. 4, 366
Over the River and Through the Wood  Gr. 3, 384
*Qiugaviit*  Gr. 3, 259
*Quintet for Piano and Strings in E-flat Major, Op. 44, Movement 1*  Gr. 8, C-19
*Return to Misty Mountain*  Gr. 7, D-28
*Rhapsody in Blue*  Gr. 7, C-42
Rockin' Robin  Gr. 3, 368
Seagull, Seagull, Sit on the Shore  Gr. 4, 383
*Soundings, "Fanfare"*  Gr. 8, C-47
*Study War No More*  Gr. 7, C-40
*Symphony No. 4, Movement 4*  Gr. 4, 295
This Land Is Your Land  Gr. 7, I-66
This Little Light of Mine  Gr. 6, 232
*Walkin' to New Orleans*  Gr. 3, 371
We've Got Lots in Common  Gr. 3, 366
*Wings*  Gr. 7, C-45
World We Love, The  Gr. 3, 342

**melodic direction**
Allá en la fuente  Gr. 2, 92
Arirang  Gr. 5, 25
Autumn Canon  Gr. 5, 148
*Baa-Baa Black Sheep*  Gr. K, 102
Baby Beluga  Gr. K, 272

**(Melody, continued)**

Beriozka  Gr. 4, 294

Bonjour, mes amis  Gr. 1, 316

Charlie over the Water  Gr. 1, 68

Chuhwuht  Gr. 2, 356

*College Hornpipe*  Gr. 4, 95

*Daybreak Vision*  Gr. 5, 398

Down the Ohio  Gr. 2, 60

Farewell to Tarwathie  Gr. 6, 43

Fly and the Bumblebee, The
  Gr. 1, 384

*Garden of the Earth*  Gr. 5, 399

Gift to Share, A  Gr. 6, 393

Glory, Glory, Hallelujah
  Gr. 6, 52

*Glory, Glory, Hallelujah*
  Gr. 6, 54

Gonna Build a Mountain
  Gr. 6, 21

*Greeting Prelude*  Gr. 2, 264

Haru ga kita  Gr. 2, 401

Hato popo  Gr. 1, 186

Hello!  Gr. 2, 262

Hey, Hey, Look at Me  Gr. 1, 70

I Don't Care If the Rain Comes
  Down  Gr. 3, 24

Kookaburra  Gr. 4, 186

Kwanzaa Carol, A  Gr. 2, 392

L'inverno è passato  Gr. 2, 400

Lady, Lady  Gr. 1, 62

Leatherwing Bat  Gr. 2, 303

Let the Music Begin!  Gr. 1, 2

Má Teodora  Gr. 6, 301

*Nutcracker Suite, The, "Waltz
  of the Flowers"*  Gr. 6, 325

Ode to Joy  Gr. 4, 152

Painting Song: A Dribble and a
  Dot  Gr. K, 175

*Peer Gynt Suite No. 1,
  "Morning"*  Gr. 1, 369

*Raindrop Prelude*  Gr. 3, 26

Rise and Shine  Gr. 1, 122

Sawatdee tuh jah  Gr. 2, 265

*Scherzo for Wind Quintet, Op.
  48*  Gr. 1, 328

Sing a Little Song  Gr. K, 30

Skip to My Lou  Gr. K, 58

*Symphony No. 9 in D Minor,
  Op. 125, "Ode to Joy,"
  Movement 4*  Gr. 4, 151

Tancovačka  Gr. 4, 230

This Land Is Your Land (refrain
  only)  Gr. 1, 274

Thula, thula, ngoana  Gr. 4, 227

Water Come a Me Eye
  Gr. 6, 300

Wind Blew East, The  Gr. 1, 64

Wings of a Dove  Gr. 4, 318

Your Friends Shall Be the Tall
  Wind  Gr. 6, 201

Zuni Sunrise Call  Gr. 5, 396

**melodic sequence**

Alleluia  Gr. 6, 133

Autumn Canon  Gr. 5, 148

California, Here I Come
  Gr. 4, 287

*Canon No. 110 in G*  Gr. 6, 133

Come, Ye Thankful People,
  Come  Gr. 5, 459

*Concerto for French Horn in
  E-flat Major, K. 495, No. 4,
  Movement 3*  Gr. 8, C-11

Corta la caña  Gr. 6, 364

I Got Rhythm  Gr. 6, 101

*Invention No. 5 in E-flat*
  Gr. 5, 59

La ciudad de Juaja  Gr. 5, 58

La golondrina  Gr. 8, I-50

*La tierche estampie real*
  Gr. 8, C-6

O lê lê O Bahía  Gr. 6, 165

Si si si  Gr. 7, G-13

*Slavonic Dance, Op. 46, No. 1*
  Gr. 4, 227

*Sonata in F Major for Violin
  and Piano, Op. 24, No.
  5, "Spring," Movement 3*
  Gr. 7, C-19

Strike Up the Band  Gr. 6, 135

Tancovačka  Gr. 4, 230

Tengo, tengo, tengo  Gr. 4, 228

Thula, thula, ngoana  Gr. 4, 227

Wings of a Dove  Gr. 4, 318

**ornamentation**

*Abbots Bromley Horn Dance*
  Gr. 7, C-24

*Brandenburg Concerto No. 2,
  Movement 3 Allegro Assai*
  Gr. 7, C-8

*Chorale Prelude for Organ,
  BWV 645, "Wachet auf, ruft
  uns die Stimme "*  Gr. 7, C-9

*Danza*  Gr. 7, C-7

*Den III. Ende VI. Ronde &
  Quatre Branles*  Gr. 7, C-7

Dok djampa  Gr. 8, I-20

*Every Night When the Sun
  Goes In*  Gr. 8, I-29

*Face of Love, The*  Gr. 8, B-15

*Glory, Glory, Hallelujah*
  Gr. 6, 54

*God Bless the Child*  Gr. 7, B-26

Goodbye, Julie  Gr. 8, E-2

*How High the Moon*  Gr. 5, 341

*I Can't Get Started*  Gr. 7, B-26

*John Henry*  Gr. 8, C-34

*Messiah, "Hallelujah!"*  Gr. 8, C-8

*Prince of Denmark's March*
  Gr. 6, 55

*Slow Hora/Freylekhs*  Gr. 8, B-25

*Song of the Nightingale, "The
  Nightingale"*  Gr. 8, C-32

Swing Low, Sweet Chariot
  Gr. 7, C-41

*Tahi*  Gr. 8, B-14

**range**

Chapel of Love  Gr. 7, G-27

*China Gates*  Gr. 7, C-45

*Fanfare for the Common Man*
  Gr. 7, C-43

I'm a Believer  Gr. 7, G-33

Jambalaya  Gr. 8, I-46

One Family  Gr. 7, G-17

Something Told the Wild Geese
  Gr. 7, G-39

Star-Spangled Banner, The
  Gr. 8, I-62

Take a Chance On Me
  Gr. 8, G-15

*Widmung, Op. 25, No. 1*
  Gr. 7, C-20

Winter  Gr. 8, G-11

You Were on My Mind
  Gr. 7, G-23

**retrograde patterns**

I Got Rhythm  Gr. 6, 101

**scales**

I Love Peanuts  Gr. 7, E-20

Si si si  Gr. 7, G-13

**upward and downward**

A la puerta del cielo  Gr. 5, 60

*Aida, "Gloria all'Egitto (Grand
  March)"*  Gr. 8, C-24

Alleluia  Gr. 6, 133

America  Gr. 1, 446

Baby Beluga  Gr. K, 272

Bluebird, Bluebird  Gr. K, 105

Bumble Bee, The (speech piece)
  Gr. K, 74

Busy Buzzy Bee  Gr. K, 77

Cattle Call  Gr. 5, 344

*Concerto for French Horn in
  E-flat Major, K. 495, No. 4,
  Movement 3*  Gr. 8, C-11

Cow's Woc Backward  Gr. 1, 390

Day-O! (Banana Boat Loader's
  Song)  Gr. 5, 18

*Don't Get Around Much
  Anymore*  Gr. 1, 33

Down by the Riverside  Gr. 8, G-8

Duérmete, mi niño  Gr. 1, 292

Ee jer ha ba go  Gr. K, 133

El caracol  Gr. K, 130

*Evening Chaconne*  Gr. 6, 202

Fuzzy Caterpillar  Gr. K, 102

*Galliard Battaglia*  Gr. 8, C-14

Go With the Music and Sing
  Gr. 3, 376

Gonna Build a Mountain  Gr. 6, 21

Hello!  Gr. 2, 262

Here Comes Valerie  Gr. 1, 32

Honeybee Song, The  Gr. 1,
  358

I Can't Spell Hippopotamus
  Gr. 1, 264

It's Santa—Again! Gr. 2, 385
*L'Enfant et les sortilèges,*
*"Love for Two Cats"*
Gr. K, 101
Las velitas Gr. 5, 147
Light Up the World with a Song
Gr. 8, G-25
*Lullaby for Strings* Gr. 1, 293
Mary Wore Her Red Dress
Gr. K, 74
*Masquerade Suite, "Galop"*
Gr. 4, 16
Merry-Go-Round Gr. K, 290
Mister Rabbit Gr. K, 128
My Father's House Gr. 2, 25
*Nutcracker Suite, The,*
*"Chinese Dance"* Gr. K, 105
O, Desayo Gr. 5, 411
O Laufet, ihr Hirten Gr. 2, 384
Perná, perná, i mélissá
Gr. K, 264
Proud Gr. 7, G-3
*Return to Misty Mountain*
Gr. 7, D-28
*Scherzo for Wind Quintet, Op.*
*48* Gr. 1, 328
Si me dan pasteles Gr. 1, 432
Someday Very Soon Gr. 1, 376
*Sonata in C Major for Recorder*
*and Basso Continuo, Op. 1,*
*No. 7, "Gavotte"* Gr. K, 75
This Land Is Your Land (refrain
only) Gr. 1, 274
This Train Gr. 5, 26
Tuxedo Junction Gr. 8, G-21
'Ūlili E Gr. 5, 441
Up and Down Kitten, The
Gr. K, 100
*Widmung, Op. 25, No. 1*
Gr. 7, C-20
*Wings* Gr. 7, C-45
Winter Gr. 8, G-11

## SAME AND DIFFERENT PHRASES
El carnavalito humahuaqueño
Gr. 6, 482

## TONALITY
*Pulcinella Suite, "Serenata"*
Gr. 8, C-32
*Sonata for Violin and Piano,*
*Allegro* Gr. 8, C-46
*Tahi* Gr. 8, B-14

### aeolian
Scarborough Fair Gr. 6, 95

### atonal
*Songs from Letters, "So Like*
*Your Father"* Gr. 7, C-21

### blue notes
*Rhapsody in Blue* Gr. 7, C-42
Just a Snap-Happy Blues
Gr. 6, 388
Surfin' U.S.A. Gr. 6, 260

### dorian
Connemara Lullaby Gr. 5, 232
*Fantasia on Greensleeves*
Gr. 5, 235
Scarborough Fair Gr. 6, 95

### harmonic minor
S'vivon Gr. 6, 452
Shalom aleichem Gr. 6, 409

### key change
Chapel of Love Gr. 7, G-27
You Were on My Mind
Gr. 7, G-23

### major
Adiós, amigos Gr. 6, 57
Alleluia Gr. 6, 133
America, the Beautiful Gr. 7, I-4
Deep in the Heart of Texas
Gr. 8, I-18
Dona nobis pacem Gr. 6, 125
El carite Gr. 5, 305
Erie Canal Gr. 5, 262
*Estancia, "Danza del trigo"*
Gr. 5, 229
*Firebird, The, "Finale"*
Gr. 8, C-30
Go, My Son Gr. 6, 188
Gonna Build a Mountain Gr. 6, 21
Hosanna, Me Build a House
Gr. 5, 132
I Love Peanuts Gr. 7, E-20
*I'm a Yankee Doodle Dandy*
Gr. 5, 278
La Jesusita Gr. 5, 322
Las velitas Gr. 5, 147
Let's Get the Rhythm of the
Band Gr. 7, E-29
Like a Bird Gr. 6, 167
Lo yisa Gr. 6, 131
Merry Modal Christmas, A
Gr. 4, 411
Missy-La, Massa-La Gr. 4, 188
*Nyoka* Gr. 7, D-33
Over There Gr. 5, 279
Red River Valley Gr. 6, 11
Scattin' A-Round (Variations on
Row 3) Gr. 6, 160
Sing, Sing, Sing! Gr. 5, 340
*Sonata in F Major for Violin*
*and Piano, Op. 24, No.*
*5, "Spring," Movement 3*
Gr. 7, C-19
*Tabla Solo* Gr. 8, B-32
Take a Chance On Me
Gr. 8, G-15
Ten Little Ostinato Pieces
Gr. 7, I-62
Tzena, tzena Gr. 5, 298
Viva Jujuy Gr. 5, 228
*Voiles* Gr. 7, C-39
We Shall Not Be Moved
Gr. 4, 437

### minor
Alumot Gr. 6, 306
Con el vito Gr. 7, G-15
Dance for the Nations Gr. 6, 122
*Diamonds and Rust* Gr. 7, A-4
El carite Gr. 5, 305
Erie Canal Gr. 5, 262
*Estancia, "Danza del trigo"*
Gr. 5, 229
Go Down, Moses Gr. 5, 190
God Bless the Grass Gr. 8, F-13
Johnny Has Gone for a Soldier
Gr. 5, 188
Joshua Fought the Battle of
Jericho Gr. 8, E-18
Keep Your Eyes on the Prize
Gr. 8, E-16
La mariposa Gr. 6, 58
Let's Get the Rhythm of the
Band Gr. 7, E-29
*"Little" Organ Fugue in G*
*Minor* Gr. 6, 129
Lo yisa Gr. 6, 130
Man of Constant Sorrow
Gr. 7, F-28
Merry Modal Christmas, A
Gr. 4, 411
Oy, Hanuka Gr. 7, I-44
*Piano Trio in G Minor, Op. 17,*
*Allegro* Gr. 8, C-19
Run! Run! Hide! Gr. 6, 340
Scattin' A-Round (Variations on
Row 3) Gr. 6, 160
Shortnin' Bread Gr. 7, F-27
*Slow Hora/Freylekhs* Gr. 8, B-25
Something Told the Wild Geese
Gr. 7, G-39
*Sometimes I Feel Like a*
*Motherless Child* Gr. 5, 193
*Sonata in A Minor, "Allegro"*
Gr. 7, C-12
*Sonata in C-sharp Minor, Op.*
*27, No. 2, "Moonlight,"*
*Movement 1* Gr. 7, C-19
*Sonata in G Minor, Op. 1, No.*
*1, Movement 2* Gr. 7, C-12
*Symphony No. 3 in E-flat*
*Major, "Marcia funebre,"*
*Movement 2* Gr. 8, C-17
*Symphony No. 5 in C Minor,*
*Op. 67, Movement 1*
Gr. 7, C-16
*Symphony No. 5 in C Minor,*
*Op. 67, Movement 4*
Gr. 7, C-18
*Tabla Solo* Gr. 8, B-32
Ten Little Ostinato Pieces
Gr. 7, I-62
*Toccata in D Minor* Gr. 4, 233
Viva Jujuy Gr. 5, 228
Wade in the Water Gr. 8, I-64
Winter Gr. 8, G-11

(*Melody*, continued)

**Mixolydian**

Greenland Whale Fishery, The
Gr. 5, 230

Harrison Town  Gr. 6, 97

Surfin' U.S.A.  Gr. 6, 260

**modulation**

Gift to Share, A  Gr. 6, 393

Joy of Kwanzaa, The  Gr. 6, 462

Love in Any Language
Gr. 6, 476

One Moment in Time  Gr. 6, 352

**pentatonic**

A la puerta del cielo  Gr. 5, 60

Adiós, amigos  Gr. 6, 57

Arirang  Gr. 5, 25

Asadoya  Gr. 6, 303

*Badenma*  Gr. 8, B-28

Bặt kim thang  Gr. 6, 13

Canción de cuna  Gr. 4, 144

Colorado Trail  Gr. 5, 276

Dok djampa  Gr. 8, I-20

Don't Let the Wind  Gr. 3, 180

*Drift*  Gr. 8, B-42

*Dúlamán*  Gr. 4, 299

Erdö, erdö de magos  Gr. 3, 182

Farewell to Tarwathie  Gr. 6, 43

Hashewie  Gr. 4, 63

Hitotsu toya  Gr. 5, 478

Ida Red  Gr. 3, 30

Meng Jian Nu  Gr. 5, 194

My Dear Companion  Gr. 6, 23

Now Let Me Fly  Gr. 3, 178

Old Man Mosie  Gr. 3, 108

One Morning in May  Gr. 6, 121

Pastures of Plenty  Gr. 4, 280

Pretty Saro  Gr. 3, 216

See the Children Playin'
Gr. 4, 107

Son macaron  Gr. 4, 109

Sourwood Mountain  Gr. 4, 65

Summertime  Gr. 6, 250

This Train  Gr. 5, 26

*Toei khong*  Gr. 8, B-21

Tsuki  Gr. 4, 25

*Two Dances for Three
Xylophones, "Hornpipe and
Jig"*  Gr. 8, D-17

*Voiles*  Gr. 7, C-39

Wade in the Water  Gr. 8, I-64

Weevily Wheat  Gr. 4, 105

*Would?*  Gr. 8, F-30

**tonal center**

All Around the Buttercup
Gr. 2, 170

Banuwa  Gr. 6, 294

Don't Let the Wind  Gr. 3, 180

Erdö, erdö de magos  Gr. 3, 182

Go, My Son  Gr. 6, 188

Joy of Kwanzaa, The  Gr. 6, 462

Kwa-nu-te  Gr. 3, 214

"Little" Organ Fugue in G
Minor  Gr. 6, 129

Lo yisa  Gr. 6, 130

Lost My Gold Ring  Gr. 6, 158

One Moment in Time  Gr. 6, 352

Pretty Saro  Gr. 3, 216

Ragupati Ragava Raja Ram
Gr. 5, 321

See the Children Playin'
Gr. 4, 107

Son macaron  Gr. 4, 109

Surfin' U.S.A.  Gr. 6, 260

This Little Light of Mine
Gr. 6, 232

Waitin' for the Light to Shine
Gr. 4, 26

Water Is Wide, The  Gr. 6, 228

**tone row**

*Lyric Suite, "Allegretto
gioviale," Movement 1*
Gr. 6, 169

**whole tone**

*Children's Corner Suite,
"Doctor Gradus ad
Parnassum"*  Gr. 8, C-27

*Voiles*  Gr. 7, C-39

## MOVEMENT *See also Moving; Skills Reinforcement: Moving.*

### BODY PERCUSSION

Ah ya Zane  Gr. 5, 297

Ain't Gonna Let Nobody Turn Me
'Round  Gr. 6, 85

*America (from West Side Story)*
Gr. 8, C-45

Ayelivi  Gr. 2, 70

Banuwa  Gr. 6, 294

*Bembe de Plena*  Gr. 8, D-18

De colores  Gr. 5, 90

Do, Re, Mi, Fa  Gr. 6, 80

*Drums From Around the World
(Montage)*  Gr. 6, 277

Families  Gr. 1, 282

Friend of Mine  Gr. 1, 310

Hava nagila  Gr. 6, 153

*Imbube*  Gr. 8, B-30

Let Us Sing Together  Gr. 6, 156

*Lion Sleeps Tonight, The*  Gr. 8, E-8

Oliver Twist  Gr. K, 138

¡Qué bonita bandera!  Gr. 5, 295

*Rice Bowl*  Gr. 8, B-30

*Saqian da dhol*  Gr. 8, B-22

Scattin' A-Round (Variations on
Row 3)  Gr. 6, 160

Si si si  Gr. 7, G-13

*Stalia, stalia*  Gr. 8, B-21

Swanee  Gr. 6, 118

### CHORAL CHOREOGRAPHY

Circle 'Round the Moon  Gr. 4, 407

Einini  Gr. 4, 391

Flip, Flop and Fly  Gr. 7, I-35

Lullaby and Dance  Gr. 4, 389

Merry Modal Christmas, A
Gr. 4, 413

Stille Nacht (Silent Night)  Gr. 7, I-54

### CONDUCTING

Alleluia  Gr. 6, 133

America  Gr. 7, I-2

Bặt kim thang  Gr. 6, 13

*Den III. Ende VI. Ronde & Quatre
Branles*  Gr. 8, C-7

Do, Re, Mi, Fa  Gr. 6, 80

Don't You Hear the Lambs?
Gr. 5, 97

Farewell to Tarwathie  Gr. 6, 43

*Four Scottish Dances, Op. 59,
"Allegretto"*  Gr. 6, 43

*Glory Hallelujah Grand March*
Gr. 8, C-38

*Highway to Kilkenny*  Gr. 6, 43

I Dream a World  Gr. 8, G-40

*Le Sacre de Printemps (The
Rite of Spring), "Dance of
the Youths and Maidens"*
Gr. 8, C-30

Like a Bird  Gr. 6, 167

*Marines' Hymn, The*  Gr. 8, C-39

Old Blue  Gr. K, 122

*Orchestral Suite No. 2 in B Minor,
"Minuet"*  Gr. 6, 192

Red River Valley  Gr. 6, 11

Star-Spangled Banner, The
Gr. 8, I-62

Swanee  Gr. 6, 118

Wir hatten gebauet  Gr. 8, C-21

### CREATIVE AND INTERPRETIVE MOVEMENT

*Abbots Bromley Horn Dance*
Gr. 7, C-26

*All in One*  Gr. 1, 12

Ama-Lama  Gr. 5, 143

Au clair de la lune  Gr. 3, 18

Banjo Sam  Gr. 2, 315

Banuwa  Gr. 6, 294

Beach Rap  Gr. 1, 353

Bingo  Gr. 1, 170

Black Snake  Gr. 3, 53

*Bon jour!*  Gr. 1, 3

Brand New Day, A  Gr. 6, 7

Bubbles  Gr. K, 185

Buenos días  Gr. 1, 13

Bundle-Buggy Boogie Woogie
Gr. 4, 120

*California Counterpoint: The
Twittering Machine*  Gr. 8, C-47

California Oranges  Gr. 1, 15

*Capoeira Na Vila*  Gr. 8, D-25

Celebrate  Gr. 1, 407

Cha yang wu  Gr. 1, 90

Changing  Gr. K, 199

Chanukah, Chanukah  Gr. 1, 418

Chawe chidyo chem'chero
Gr. 2, 298

Children of Long Ago  Gr. 1, 31

Children of the Sun  Gr. 1, 405
Children of the Sun  Gr. 1, 403
*Clair de lune*  Gr. K, 164
Clap, Wiggle, and Stomp  Gr. K, 34
Clementine  Gr. 4, 340
Clouds  Gr. K, 254
Costume Capers  Gr. 1, 412
Crab Dance  Gr. 2, 307
*Crowley's/Jackson's*  Gr. 4, 299
Cumberland Gap  Gr. 4, 139
Dance of the Youths and Maidens
    Gr. 8, C-33
*Dancing Tree, The*  Gr. K, 202
Different Beat, A  Gr. 1, 4
Don't Dump Trash  Gr. 2, 318
Draw Me a Bucket of Water
    Gr. 3, 125
*Dusty Rag*  Gr. K, 164
Ein Männlein steht im Walde
    Gr. 2, 90
El cóndor pasa  Gr. 6, 46
Everybody Says  Gr. 1, 287
*Faerie Stories*  Gr. 8, B-5
Fifty Nifty United States  Gr. 5, 251
Fish  Gr. 1, 177
Freight Train  Gr. 1, 45
Friend of Mine  Gr. 1, 310
Frosty, the Snowman  Gr. 2, 390
Funwa alafia  Gr. 5, 32
*Galliard Battaglia*  Gr. 8, C-14
Geef jij mij die schoen  Gr. 1, 126
Glory, Glory, Hallelujah  Gr. 6, 52
Goin' Down the Road Feelin' Bad
    Gr. 7, F-13
Going Upon the Mountain
    Gr. 6, 105
Gonna Build a Mountain  Gr. 6, 21
Groundhog Jig  Gr. 1, 436
*Groundhog Jig, The*  Gr. 1, 436
Happiness  Gr. K, 62
*Harukoma, "Spring Horse Dance"*
    Gr. 1, 145
Hi Heidi Ho  Gr. 1, 393
Hickory, Dickory, Dock (so-la-so-mi
    Version)  Gr. 1, 224
*Highway to Kilkenny*  Gr. 6, 43
Howjidoo  Gr. 1, 315
I Believe I Can Fly  Gr. 5, 170
I Can't Spell Hippopotamus
    Gr. 1, 267
*I Know You Mardi Gras*  Gr. 8, B-17
I'm Tall, I'm Small  Gr. K, 18
In the Morning (poem)  Gr. 1, 217
Inkpataya  Gr. 3, 255
*Janitzio*  Gr. 5, 91
Jo'ashila  Gr. 5, 108
Juniper Tree, The  Gr. 3, 131
Kibungo, Beast of the Forest
    Gr. 2, 353
Knock No More  Gr. 3, 387
Kou ri lengay  Gr. 2, 217
La mar estaba serena  Gr. 2, 344

Let It Snow! Let It Snow! Let It
    Snow!  Gr. 4, 426
Let's Go Barefoot (poem)
    Gr. 1, 440
Let's Pretend  Gr. K, 227
Los maizales  Gr. 1, 294
Lots of Worms  Gr. 2, 310
Love Is  Gr. K, 180
Love Will Guide Us  Gr. 4, 328
*Lyric Pieces, Op. 43, No. 1,*
    *"Butterfly"*  Gr. 1, 363
Mary Ann  Gr. 6, 180
Mary Came a-Running  Gr. K, 294
Mbombera  Gr. K, 24
Min  Gr. K, 263
My Dear Companion  Gr. 6, 23
Nana Kru  Gr. 6, 282
Nana, Thread Needle  Gr. 1, 38
Niu lang zhi nü  Gr. 4, 335
Oh, What a Day!  Gr. K, 302
Over My Head  Gr. 4, 118
Over the Rainbow  Gr. 4, 141
Overture to "Candide"  Gr. 6, 219
Painting Song: A Dribble and a Dot
    Gr. K, 175
Parade Came Marching, The
    Gr. 1, 166
Pat Works on the Railway  Gr. 5, 182
Pease Porridge Hot  Gr. 1, 135
*Piki mai*  Gr. 1, 76
Pin Pon  Gr. 1, 146
Pitter Patter Scatter (poem)
    Gr. 1, 55
*Popcorn*  Gr. 8, E-27
Rabbit Skip, The  Gr. 2, 305
Rain Sings a Song, The  Gr. 1, 101
*Rap Intro*  Gr. 8, B-33
*Retounen*  Gr. 8, B-17
Riqui rán  Gr. 1, 49
River  Gr. 4, 61
'Round the Bay of Mexico
    Gr. 4, 258
Run! Run! Hide!  Gr. 6, 341
Sailboat in the Sky  Gr. 4, 374
Sailing to the Sea  Gr. 1, 338
*Scrub-a-dub*  Gr. 1, 306
Seagull, Seagull, Sit on the Shore
    Gr. 4, 382
Seasons of Love  Gr. 8, A-21
Serra, serra, serrador  Gr. 1, 112
*Shake Your Brain*  Gr. 1, 250
Shir l'shalom  Gr. 4, 419
Sidewalk Songs  Gr. K, 207
Sidewalks (poem)  Gr. 1, 311
Silly Street  Gr. K, 224
*Silver Apples of the Moon*
    Gr. 1, 12
Sing a Song of Peace  Gr. 6, 67
Singin' in the Rain  Gr. 4, 360
Siyahamba  Gr. 6, 215
Snow Flakes (poem)  Gr. 1, 423
Song of the Night, The  Gr. 3, 344

Song That's Just for You, A
    Gr. 2, 126
Spaceworms  Gr. 1, 400
*St. Louis Blues*  Gr. 4, 57
*Standin' in the Need of Prayer*
    Gr. 5, 103
Summertime  Gr. 6, 250
*Suo gan*  Gr. 1, 309
*Symphony No. 40 in G Minor, K.*
    *550, Movement 1*  Gr. 8, C-13
Take Me Out to the Ball Game
    Gr. 3, 263
Take Your Feet Out 'the Sand
    Gr. K, 231
Tanabata-sama  Gr. 2, 337
Teach Me to Swing  Gr. 5, 84
*This Little Light of Mine*  Gr. 2, 241
This Pretty Planet  Gr. 4, 354
Time to Sing  Gr. 2, 8
*Two Heads Are Better Than One*
    Gr. 1, 333
Valentine Feelings  Gr. K, 322
Vamos a la mar  Gr. 3, 226
Voice Choice  Gr. K, 27
Wade in the Water  Gr. 4, 269
Walk Together, Children  Gr. 3, 146
*Walkin' to New Orleans*  Gr. 3, 370
*Watermelon Man*  Gr. 1, 12
We Wish You a Merry Christmas
    Gr. 3, 395
We're All Gonna Shine Tonight
    Gr. 2, 240
We're Making Popcorn (speech
    piece)  Gr. 1, 86
When the Train Comes Along
    Gr. 1, 300
Who Has Seen the Wind?
    Gr. 2, 325
With the Sea Snake (rhyme)
    Gr. 1, 323
Woke Up This Morning  Gr. 5, 288
Woodland Chorus  Gr. K, 250
Yertle the Turtle  Gr. 2, 371
You're a Grand Old Flag  Gr. 3, 264
Zudio  Gr. 2, 269

## CREATIVE DRAMATIZATION
Johnny Caught a Flea  Gr. 1, 227
Mammoth (poem)  Gr. 1, 235

## CREATIVE MOVEMENT
*A-You're Adorable*  Gr. 1, 263
Down, Down, Baby  Gr. 2, 33
El chocolate  Gr. 1, 380
Éliza Kongo  Gr. 5, 16
For Children Safe and Strong
    Gr. 5, 484
Four in a Boat  Gr. 2, 49
Hickory, Dickory, Dock  Gr. 1, 351
I Vow to You, My Country
    Gr. 5, 423
Kangaroo Song, The  Gr. K, 44

**(Movement, continued)**

Magic Flute, The, "In diesen heil'gen Hallen (In These Bright Halls)" Gr. K, 9
Morning Has Broken Gr. 5, 28
My Fathers' House Gr. 2, 24
Now's the Time Gr. 5, 445
Pizza, Pizza, Daddy-o Gr. 2, 30
Seasons Gr. K, 5
Simple Gifts Gr. 5, 186
Spaceworms Gr. 1, 400
Tony Chestnut Gr. 2, 35
Wabash Cannon Ball Gr. 5, 136

## DRAMATIZATIONS/PANTOMIMES

Alle meine Entchen Gr. 1, 98
Amahl and the Night Visitors Gr. 1, 432
Animals Went In One By One, The Gr. K, 275
Ayelivi Gr. 2, 70
Banuwa Gr. 6, 294
Bear Dance Gr. K, 127
Bound for South Australia Gr. 5, 22
Bus, The Gr. K, 82
Busy Buzzy Bee Gr. K, 77
Caribbean Leaps Gr. K, 148
Chang Gr. 1, 155
Chanukiyah li yesh Gr. 1, 421
Chums Gr. 1, 291
Cookie Crew, The Gr. K, 197
Cookie Magic Gr. K, 197
Corn Grinding Song Gr. K, 66
Dancin' in the Rain Gr. 1, 366
Dancing Pig, The (story) Gr. 1, 196
Dancing Pig, The (story) Gr. 1, 197
Dinosaur Dance Gr. 2, 169
Doctor Foster Gr. K, 136
Down in the Meadow Gr. K, 146
Dreams Gr. K, 276
Ducks in the Rain Gr. K, 235
Fais dodo Gr. K, 158
First Snowflake Gr. K, 259
Fish (poem) Gr. 1, 177
Fourth of July Night (poem) Gr. 1, 444
Galoshes Gr. K, 62
Giddy Up Gr. K, 136
Glad to Have a Friend Like You Gr. 2, 229
Going on a Picnic Gr. K, 191
Goldilocks and the Three Bears Gr. K, 49
Hey, Diddle, Diddle Gr. K, 246
Hickory, Dickory, Dare (speech piece) Gr. K, 20
I Know an Old Lady Gr. 1, 388
It Rains and It Pours Gr. K, 243
It's Time Gr. 6, 319
Itsy Bitsy Spider, The Gr. K, 186
Jolly Old St. Nicholas Gr. K, 316
Les petites marionettes Gr. K, 237
Lion, The Gr. K, 217

Little Red Caboose Gr. K, 229
Los pececitos Gr. 1, 178
Los trencitos Gr. K, 24
Love for Two Cats Gr. K, 100
Music Gr. K, 107
Night-light Gr. K, 223
Noah's Zoo in the Big, Big Rain Gr. K, 274
Ode to la piñata (poem) Gr. 1, 424
On a Log, Mister Frog Gr. K, 148
Orchestra (poem) Gr. 1, 74
Paper Gr. K, 195
Pick 'n' Mix Zoo Gr. K, 138
Pictures at an Exhibition, "Ballet of the Unhatched Chicks" Gr. K, 167
Ptashky u babusi sadochku Gr. 1, 192
Purple People Eater, The Gr. 6, 448
Rope Rhyme (poem) Gr. 1, 321
Shake-'n'-Bake a Jelly Gr. K, 94
Sharing Gr. K, 198
She'll Be Comin' 'Round the Mountain Gr. 2, 358
Shoo, Turkey Gr. 1, 105
Sing! Speak! Whisper! Shout! Gr. 1, 36
Six Little Ducks Gr. K, 234
Someday Very Soon Gr. 1, 376
Song of the Train Gr. K, 152
Squirrel, The Gr. K, 129
Ten Tom-Toms Gr. K, 78
Toaster Time Gr. K, 17
Today Is Your Birthday Gr. 1, 409
Vamos a cantar Gr. K, 278
Wake Me, Shake Me Gr. 1, 278
We Are Dear Little Birdies Gr. K, 176
Wind Up the Apple Tree Gr. 1, 184

## FOLK DANCES

Ala Da'lona Gr. 5, 301
Chag Purim Gr. 1, 438
Chanukiyah li yesh Gr. 1, 421
Cheki, morena Gr. 7, I-17
Circle Round the Zero Gr. K, 293
Dham dhamak dham samelu Gr. 6, 305
Hanuka, Hanuka Gr. 8, I-37
Hava nagila Gr. 6, 153
Kerenski Gr. 6, 78
Khorovod Gr. 1, 372
Kpanlogo for 2 Gr. 6, 296
Morning Comes Early Gr. 5, 13
My Dreydl Gr. K, 314
Scottish Medley Gr. 5, 139
Yemeni baglamis telli basina Gr. 6, 309

## GAME SONGS

A-Tisket, A-Tasket Gr. 2, 239
Al ánimo Gr. 3, 322
All Around the Buttercup Gr. 2, 170
Ambos a dos Gr. 3, 20

Apple Tree Gr. 1, 230
Bantama kra kro Gr. 5, 309
Bluebird, Bluebird Gr. K, 105
Bob-a-Needle Gr. 2, 232
Cakewalk Game Gr. 5, 333
Charlie over the Water Gr. 1, 66
Che che koolay Gr. 2, 266
Circle Round the Zero Gr. K, 293
Cirmos cica Gr. 1, 129
Deux cocodries Gr. 2, 365
Diou shou juan'er Gr. 2, 277
Dry Bones Come Skipping Gr. 4, 219
Ég a gyertya Gr. K, 97
El caracol Gr. K, 130
El Floron (The Flower) Gr. 2, 247
El juego chirimbolo Gr. 2, 54
El rabel Gr. 3, 363
Farmer in the Dell, The Gr. K, 232
Farmer's Dairy Key, The Gr. 2, 182
Grass Game Gr. 1, 371
Great Big House Gr. 2, 205
Gypsy in the Moonlight Gr. 3, 13
Here Comes Valerie Gr. 1, 32
Hosisipa Gr. 3, 70
La víbora Gr. 1, 322
Leak kanseng Gr. 1, 156
Lemonade Gr. 1, 190
Little Johnny Brown Gr. 3, 313
London Bridge Gr. K, 244
Lost My Gold Ring Gr. 6, 158
Missy-La, Massa-La Gr. 4, 189
Mon son pha Gr. K, 90
Mother, Mother, I Am Sick Gr. K, 120
My Mama's Calling Me Gr. 1, 261
Naranja dulce Gr. 2, 97
Ochimbo Gr. 4, 135
Old Man Mosie Gr. 3, 108
Pavo, pavo Gr. 1, 416
Perná, perná, i mélissá Gr. K, 264
Piñon, pirulín Gr. 2, 174
Serpent, The Gr. 1, 323
Shortnin' Bread Gr. 1, 58
Snail, Snail Gr. 1, 188
Sorida Gr. 1, 312
Sorida Gr. 1, 313
Three Times By She Passes (speech piece) Gr. K, 125
Toodala Gr. 1, 326
Turkey Game, The Gr. 1, 416
Turn the Glasses Over Gr. 3, 205
Un, deux, trois Gr. 2, 198
Vulani ringi ring Gr. 1, 137
Weevily Wheat Gr. 4, 104

## LOCOMOTOR MOVEMENT

Birthday, Birthday, Birthday Gr. K, 306
Chag Purim Gr. 1, 438
Do, Re, Mi, Fa Gr. 6, 81
Dona nobis pacem Gr. 6, 125
Doong gul ge Gr. 3, 137

Get on Board  Gr. K, 89
Ha'kyo jong  Gr. 2, 136
Hava nashira  Gr. 6, 82
Hey, Hey, Look at Me  Gr. 1, 70
James Brown  Gr. K, 206
Jim Along, Josie  Gr. K, 39
Jinny Go 'Round  Gr. K, 228
Johnny Mister Brown  Gr. K, 36
Juanito  Gr. K, 300
Jump That Jody  Gr. K, 212
Karangatia ra  Gr. 3, 273
La piñata  Gr. 3, 399
La tormenta tropical  Gr. 2, 117
Leaves  Gr. 1, 27
Lemonade  Gr. 1, 190
Little David  Gr. 1, 232
Little Green Frog, The  Gr. 1, 23
Looby Loo  Gr. K, 210
Mary Ann  Gr. K, 253
Oliver Jump (speech piece)
    Gr. K, 205
Over the Rainbow  Gr. 4, 141
Pacific 231  Gr. 2, 287
Popcorn Popping  Gr. 1, 440
Rinsho, rinsho  Gr. K, 285
Rockin' Robin  Gr. 3, 369
Sansaw akroma  Gr. 3, 288
Take Your Feet Out 'the Sand
    Gr. K, 231
Tancovačka  Gr. 4, 230
Tracks  Gr. K, 299
Uptown, Downtown  Gr. K, 204
¡Viva el fútbol!  Gr. 1, 95
Wai bamba  Gr. 8, G-12
Waltzing with Bears  Gr. 3, 172
What Will You Be on Halloween?
    Gr. K, 308

## NONLOCOMOTOR MOVEMENT

America, the Beautiful  Gr. 3, 412
Bo-bo-skee, Watten-tatten (speech
    piece)  Gr. 1, 259
Boysie  Gr. 2, 197
Bump! Bump! Bump!  Gr. K, 52
Children's Corner Suite, "Jimbo's
    Lullaby"  Gr. 1, 272
Cielito lindo  Gr. 7, I-23
Clap, Wiggle, and Stomp  Gr. K, 34
Copycat  Gr. K, 9
Downpour  Gr. K, 50
Earth Is My Mother, The  Gr. 1, 340
Fais do do  Gr. 6, 405
Fais dodo  Gr. K, 158
Fanfare for the Common Man
    Gr. 7, C-43
Fanfare for the Common Man
    Gr. 7, C-43
Get on Your Feet (salsa)  Gr. 5, 7
Gift to Share, A  Gr. 6, 395
Go-Go Street Ensemble  Gr. 8, D-31
Goin' to Boston  Gr. 6, 436
Gospel Train, The  Gr. 6, 399
Great Big House  Gr. 2, 205

Habemos llegado  Gr. 6, 174
Haru ga kita  Gr. 2, 400
Hey, Hey, Look at Me  Gr. 1, 70
Hungarian Dance No. 6  Gr. 4, 50
Ikhanda, maslombe  Gr. K, 14
Imbabura  Gr. 5, 202
Ja-Da  Gr. 7, G-21
Je m'endors  Gr. K, 219
Juanito  Gr. K, 300
Key to the Highway  Gr. 8, F-28
Kid Like Me, A  Gr. 2, 394
L'inverno è passato  Gr. 2, 400
Looby Loo  Gr. K, 210
Merry-Go-Round  Gr. K, 290
Must Be Santa  Gr. K, 318
Nanny Goat  Gr. K, 161
Number One, Touch Your Tongue
    (speech piece)  Gr. K, 204
Oh, Danny Boy  Gr. 4, 48
Oliver Jump (speech piece)
    Gr. K, 205
Pay Me My Money Down  Gr. 4, 38
Polly Wee  Gr. K, 119
Rain, Rain  Gr. 1, 68
Riendo el río corre  Gr. 6, 265
River  Gr. 4, 59
Sleep, Baby, Sleep  Gr. 2, 197
Sonata in C-sharp Minor, Op. 27,
    No. 2, "Moonlight," Movement
    1  Gr. 7, C-19
There's a Place  Gr. 5, 210
Tuxedo Junction  Gr. 8, G-23
Wake Me, Shake Me  Gr. 1, 278
World We Love, The  Gr. 3, 342

## PATTERNED DANCES

Abbots Bromley Horn Dance
    Gr. 7, C-26
Adelita  Gr. 5, 51
Ain't Gonna Let Nobody Turn Me
    'Round  Gr. 6, 85
Al yadee  Gr. 6, 309
Ala Da'lona  Gr. 5, 300
Ali Pasha  Gr. 5, 219
Alleluia, Amen  Gr. 7, A-13
Alumot  Gr. 6, 307
Amasee  Gr. 1, 172
Ayer  Gr. 6, 266
B-A Bay  Gr. 1, 218
Batucada Parade Ensemble
    Gr. 8, D-25
Black Suits Comin' (Nod Ya Head)
    Gr. 7, A-7
Block Party  Gr. 7, B-13
Bonavist' Harbour  Gr. 3, 294
Cement Mixer  Gr. 4, 101
Chanukah, Chanukah  Gr. 1, 420
Chapel of Love  Gr. 7, G-29
Chiapanecas  Gr. 5, 93
Chicka Hanka  Gr. 8, F-15
Chicken on the Fence Post  Gr. 3, 93
Coffee Grows on White Oak Trees
    Gr. 3, 169

Cold and Frosty Morning
    Gr. 2, 139
Contigo otra vez  Gr. 7, B-32
Cumberland Gap  Gr. 4, 139
De colores  Gr. 8, I-17
Dham dhamak dham samelu
    Gr. 6, 305
Don Alfonso  Gr. 5, 177
Dotted-Half Note and Whole Note
    Gr. 8, H-5
Drill, Ye Tarriers  Gr. 5, 54
Elegua  Gr. 7, D-9
Ev'rybody Loves Saturday Night
    Gr. 7, I-27
Every Night When the Sun Goes In
    Gr. 8, I-31
Everybody Loves Saturday Night
    Gr. 6, 296
Families  Gr. 1, 282
Families  Gr. 1, 281
Forked Deer/Fisher's Hornpipe
    Gr. 4, 342
Four Potatoes Medley  Gr. 6, 205
Frère Jacques  Gr. 2, 124
Give My Regards to Broadway
    Gr. 6, 39
Glendy Burke, The  Gr. 4, 265
Goin' to the Fair  Gr. K, 157
Going Upon the Mountain
    Gr. 6, 105
Groundhog Jig, The  Gr. 1, 436
Hava nagila  Gr. 6, 154
He's Got the Whole World in His
    Hands  Gr. 7, I-38
Hey, Ho! Nobody Home  Gr. 6, 28
Hine mah tov  Gr. 5, 433
Hit Me with a Hot Note and Watch
    Me Bounce  Gr. 6, 112
Hop Up, My Ladies  Gr. 3, 143
How Do You Doo-tee?  Gr. 4, 186
Hungarian Dance No. 3 in F Major
    Gr. 1, 206
I Don't Care If the Rain Comes
    Down  Gr. 3, 26
I Fed My Horse  Gr. 2, 94
I Know You Mardi Gras  Gr. 8, B-18
John Kanaka  Gr. 3, 62
Karangatia ra  Gr. 8, F-23
La mariposa  Gr. 6, 58
Lean on Me  Gr. 6, 15
Les saluts  Gr. 1, 361
Limbo Like Me  Gr. 4, 19
Lion Sleeps Tonight, The  Gr. 4, 130
Loco-Motion, The  Gr. 3, 65
Love You Forever  Gr. 8, B-23
Mama Don't 'Low  Gr. 6, 360
Mañana  Gr. 7, E-15
Mary Ann  Gr. 6, 180
Minka  Gr. 4, 222
Move up to so  Gr. 8, H-8
My Bonnie Lies Over the Ocean
    Gr. 4, 338
Nani wale na hala  Gr. 3, 261

**(Movement, continued)**

Nie chcę cię znác  Gr. 3, 315
*North Carolina Breakdown*
   Gr. 5, 334
Now's the Time  Gr. 5, 448
Ochimbo  Gr. 4, 135
Oh, Susanna  Gr. 4, 265
Old Dan Tucker  Gr. 3, 97
Orange Blossom Special  Gr. 5, 269
Our Family Comes from 'Round the
   World  Gr. 1, 299
*Paddy Whack*  Gr. 6, 327
Party Tonight!  Gr. 2, 153
Pay Me My Money Down  Gr. 7, F-6
Pease Porridge Hot  Gr. 1, 135
Pollerita  Gr. 5, 151
Pottery Dance  Gr. 1, 370
Pust' 'vsegda budet sonse  Gr. 3, 279
Red River Valley  Gr. 6, 10
*Retounen*  Gr. 8, B-18
Ríu ríu chíu  Gr. 5, 436
Rock Around the Clock  Gr. 7, B-19
Rondo for Lunch, A  Gr. 3, 213
Sambalele  Gr. 4, 399
Scotland the Brave  Gr. 5, 138
*Scott Joplin's New Rag*  Gr. 5, 335
*Sellenger's Round*  Gr. 6, 44
Shortnin' Bread  Gr. 7, F-27
*Sing We and Chant It*  Gr. 8, C-5
St. Patrick Was a Gentleman
   Gr. 3, 290
Stand By Me  Gr. 5, 48
Stand By Me  Gr. 8, E-25
Sun Gonna Shine  Gr. 6, 242
*Take Five*  Gr. 5, 220
*Take Five*  Gr. 7, B-15
*Take the "A" Train*  Gr. 8, C-43
Take Time in Life  Gr. 6, 292
Tancovačka  Gr. 4, 230
Tumba  Gr. 5, 161
Tzena, tzena  Gr. 5, 299
Uno, dos, y tres  Gr. 5, 428
Valentine Dance  Gr. 1, 436
*Viva Jujuy*  Gr. 8, B-22
Willowbee  Gr. 1, 223
Winter  Gr. 8, G-11
Wooly Bully  Gr. 3, 373
Yankee Doodle  Gr. 3, 415
*Yo-shi nai (Circle Dance)*
   Gr. 6, 287
You Were on My Mind  Gr. 7, G-24
Zudio  Gr. 2, 269

### POPULAR DANCES

¡Ay, Jalisco no te rajes!  Gr. 7, I-9
Bye Bye, Love  Gr. 8, F-9
(Chi Chi Chi) Cha Cha Cha
   Gr. 6, 334
*Chicken Dance, The*  Gr. 4, 50
Crawfish  Gr. 2, 87
*Dancing in the Street*  Gr. 2, 254
Dinosaur Dance  Gr. 2, 167
Fais do do  Gr. 6, 405

Fatou yo, "I am Fatou"  Gr. K, 154
Get on Your Feet (salsa)  Gr. 5, 7
Goin' to Boston  Gr. 6, 434
Happy Feet  Gr. 2, 252
*I Love a Rainy Night* (line dance)
   Gr. 5, 350
Pennsylvania 6-5000 (swing)
   Gr. 5, 342
Surfin' U.S.A.  Gr. 7, F-33
Surfin' U.S.A.  Gr. 7, I-61
*Twist, The*  Gr. 5, 359

### SIGNING

ABC Rock  Gr. 1, 263
Adiós, amigos  Gr. 6, 57
Ah, Jolis Papillons  Gr. 1, 361
Ain't Gonna Let Nobody Turn Me
   'Round  Gr. 6, 85
All Through the Night  Gr. 5, 105
America  Gr. 5, 486
Ants Go Marching, The  Gr. 1, 248
Apple Tree  Gr. 1, 230
El barquito  Gr. 3, 360
*Ev'rybody Ought to Know*
   Gr. 1, 434
Everybody Loves Saturday Night
   Gr. 6, 297
Farmer in the Dell, The  Gr. K, 232
Freedom Is Coming  Gr. 5, 415
Great Big Stars  Gr. 1, 60
Greetings  Gr. 3, 315
Hey, Ho! Nobody Home  Gr. 6, 28
I Am But a Small Voice  Gr. 6, 445
I Can't Spell Hippopotamus
   Gr. 1, 264
I See the Moon  Gr. 2, 58
Kum ba yah  Gr. 5, 244
Lean on Me  Gr. 6, 14
Love in Any Language  Gr. 6, 476
Mister Snow Rap  Gr. 2, 390
My Valentine  Gr. K, 323
Oh, Watch the Stars  Gr. 2, 144
Peace Like a River  Gr. 6, 190
Pust' 'vsegda budet sonse  Gr. 3, 279
Rain, Rain  Gr. 1, 54
Sharing  Gr. K, 198
Star Light, Star Bright  Gr. 1, 106
There Is Love Somewhere
   Gr. 6, 318
Yang wa wa  Gr. K, 162
You're a Grand Old Flag  Gr. 3, 264
You've Got a Friend  Gr. 5, 366

### MOVING  *See also Movement; Skills Reinforcement.*

### BODY PERCUSSION

Ackabacka, Soda Cracker (speech
   piece)  Gr. 1, 303
Al yadee  Gr. 6, 308
Caballito blanco  Gr. 2, 193
*Carnival of the Animals, "Fossils"*
   Gr. 4, 220
Certainly, Lord  Gr. 7, I-15

*Circlesong Five*  Gr. 1, 239
Draw Me a Bucket of Water
   Gr. 3, 124
*Evening Chaconne*  Gr. 6, 202
Ezekiel Saw the Wheel  Gr. 6, 379
Families  Gr. 1, 282
Hambone  Gr. 1, 202
Hand Clap Ensemble  Gr. 7, D-2
Hava nashira  Gr. 6, 82
Head, Shoulders, Baby  Gr. 1, 82
Hinges  Gr. K, 52
How Much Wood Could a
   Woodchuck Chuck (speech piece)
   Gr. 3, 120
*John Wayne's Teeth*  Gr. 8, B-37
*Kitchen Stomp*  Gr. 4, 123
Loigratong  Gr. 6, 451
Music's in Me, The  Gr. 2, 40
New Hungarian Folk Song
   Gr. 6, 196
Now That's Tap (speech piece)
   Gr. 6, 320
Old Brass Wagon  Gr. 2, 122
Paths of Victory  Gr. 6, 195
Paw-Paw Patch  Gr. 4, 93
Peanut Butter (speech piece)
   Gr. 1, 173
Planets Chant, The  Gr. 4, 377
*Red Poppy, The, "Russian Sailors'
   Dance"*  Gr. 4, 224
Spring Has Sprung!  Gr. K, 142
Summer Jazz (poem)  Gr. 1, 175
There Was an Old Man (speech
   piece)  Gr. 3, 191
To'ia mai te waka  Gr. 1, 77
Turn the Beat Around  Gr. 4, 2
Yonder Come Day  Gr. 8, I-68
*You Sang to Me*  Gr. 6, 335

### CONDUCTING

Ah! Les jolis papillons  Gr. 1, 362
America, the Beautiful  Gr. 8, I-4
*Blue Danube, The, Op. 314*
   Gr. 6, 192
*El Salón México*  Gr. 6, 199
Ichi-gatsu tsuitachi  Gr. 7, I-40
New Hungarian Folk Song
   Gr. 6, 196
One Morning in May  Gr. 6, 121
Peace Like a River  Gr. 6, 190
*Pictures at an Exhibition, "The
   Great Gate of Kiev"*  Gr. 6, 154
Sailboat in the Sky  Gr. 4, 374
Star-Spangled Banner, The
   Gr. 3, 415
Yankee Doodle  Gr. 3, 414

### CREATIVE AND INTERPRETIVE MOVEMENT

*ABACA Dabble*  Gr. 4, 184
Aiken Drum  Gr. 1, 399
Ambos a dos  Gr. 3, 20
Angels On the Midnight Clear
   Gr. 6, 423

Arkansas Traveler/Angeline the Baker  Gr. K, 114
Ayii, Ayii, Ayii  Gr. K, 11
Beginning on Paper  Gr. K, 69
Bubble Gum (speech piece) Gr. K, 38
By Myself (poem)  Gr. 1, 43
Carmina Burana, "Chramer, gip die Varwe mir"  Gr. K, 62
Checkerboard  Gr. 1, 7
Children, Go Where I Send Thee  Gr. 3, 392
Christmas, Don't Be Late (The Chipmunk Song)  Gr. 2, 386
Cobbler, Cobbler (speech piece) Gr. 1, 299
Concerto for Marimba and String Orchestra, "Saudação" Gr. 2, 119
Cow's Woc Backward  Gr. 1, 391
Dance for the Nations  Gr. 6, 122
Dinosaur Dance  Gr. 2, 168
Disco Worm  Gr. 2, 312
Don't Cry for Me, Argentina Gr. 6, 74
El gallo pinto  Gr. 3, 86
Entertainer, The  Gr. 2, 76
Ev'ry Kind of Music  Gr. 2, 226
Falling Rain  Gr. 2, 328
Free at Last  Gr. 6, 468
Free Music #1  Gr. 2, 212
Frog (poem)  Gr. 1, 25
Frosty, the Snowman  Gr. 2, 391
Gakavik  Gr. 4, 15
Go, My Son  Gr. 6, 188
Gymnopedie No. 1  Gr. K, 175
Hambone  Gr. 1, 202
Hevenu shalom aleichem  Gr. 3, 378
Hit Me with a Hot Note and Watch Me Bounce  Gr. 6, 112
Honeybee Song, The  Gr. 1, 359
How to Be a Friend (poem) Gr. 1, 331
Humpty Dumpty  Gr. K, 47
I Can't Spell Hippopatamus Gr. 1, 267
I'd Like To Teach the World to Sing (In Perfect Harmony)  Gr. 3, 198
I'm in the Mood  Gr. K, 86
It's a Celebration!  Gr. 2, 372
It's Time  Gr. 6, 274
Ja-Da  Gr. 2, 188
Jig Along Home  Gr. 2, 366
Joy to the World  Gr. 3, 22
Juba  Gr. K, 13
Jump for Joy  Gr. K, 212
Just a Snap-Happy Blues Gr. 6, 388
Let's Get the Rhythm of the Band Gr. 3, 84
Let's Twist Again  Gr. 6, 257
Loco bossa nova  Gr. 2, 247
Locomoto-vation  Gr. K, 61

Los maizales  Gr. 1, 296
Los pescaditos  Gr. 1, 69
Love Can Build a Bridge  Gr. 4, 324
Mad...Sad...Glad: A Piece in Three Mood-ments  Gr. K, 249
Minstrels  Gr. K, 175
Mississippi River Chant (speech piece)  Gr. 2, 132
Monster Stomp, The (poem) Gr. 1, 133
Music's in Me, The  Gr. 2, 40
My People (poem)  Gr. 1, 233
New Hungarian Folk Song Gr. 6, 196
Noah's Shanty  Gr. 1, 344
Now That's Tap (speech piece) Gr. 6, 320
Nutcracker Suite, The, "Waltz of the Flowers"  Gr. 6, 325
On My Way  Gr. 6, 313
Overture to "Candide"  Gr. 6, 218
Pacific 231  Gr. 2, 286
Pai pi qiu  Gr. 1, 325
Rags  Gr. 1, 291
Rainbow, The  Gr. 2, 332
Rise and Shine  Gr. 1, 122
Rock and Roll Is Here to Stay Gr. 6, 36
Rundadinella  Gr. 8, I-60
Santa Clara  Gr. 4, 172
Sha Sha Sha  Gr. 6, 328
Shine, Shine, Shine  Gr. 1, 42
Silent Night  Gr. 3, 394
Snowflakes (poem)  Gr. 1, 423
Sometimes I Feel Like a Motherless Child  Gr. 6, 241
Step in Time  Gr. 2, 74
Strike Up the Band  Gr. 6, 135
Sun, The  Gr. K, 143
Supercalifragilisticexpialidocious Gr. 3, 7
That'll Be the Day  Gr. 6, 256
This Is Your Night  Gr. 6, 368
Tree in the Wood, The  Gr. 2, 360
Ujima  Gr. 1, 431
Under the Same Sun  Gr. 6, 440
Walk in Jerusalem  Gr. 4, 101
Walk in the Room  Gr. 1, 12
Way Down in the Schoolyard Gr. 2, 50
Wheel of the Water, The  Gr. 4, 364
Wind Blew East, The  Gr. 1, 64

## CREATIVE MOVEMENT
Blum (poem)  Gr. 1, 221
Eccosaise in E-flat Major  Gr. 1, 223
Johnny Caught a Flea  Gr. 1, 227

## DRAMATIZATIONS/PANTOMIMES
Back to School  Gr. K, 5
Bluebird  Gr. K, 104
Circle of Sun, A  Gr. K, 3
Crocodile, The  Gr. 2, 362
Dance  Gr. K, 59

Dinner Music  Gr. K, 70
Grizzly Bear  Gr. K, 33
Here Comes The Band (poem) Gr. 1, 167
Here I Go!  Gr. K, 73
Hey, Bug!  Gr. 1, 215
I'm Gonna Sing a Silly Song Gr. K, 225
Jellyfish Walk (poem)  Gr. 1, 33
L'Enfant et les sortilèges, "Love for Two Cats"  Gr. K, 101
Look! Look! The Sun Woke Up! Gr. 1, 369
Mashed Potatoes(poem)  Gr. 1, 21
Mashed Potatoes (speech piece) Gr. 1, 20
My Legs and I (poem)  Gr. 1, 9
My Shadow  Gr. K, 19
See and Touch  Gr. K, 172
Sing! Speak! Whisper! Shout! (poem)  Gr. 1, 36
Sounds of the Circus  Gr. K, 241
Summer Jazz  Gr. 1, 175
Three Little Piggies  Gr. K, 56
Time to Move  Gr. 1, 244
Up and Down Kitten, The Gr. K, 100
Usagi  Gr. 1, 397
Wind Song  Gr. K, 7

## FOLK DANCES
Adana ya gidelim  Gr. 2, 142
Al yadee  Gr. 6, 308
Alumot  Gr. 6, 306
Artsa alinu  Gr. 3, 285
Bambodansarna  Gr. 8, B-20
Canto del agua  Gr. 8, I-10
Cha yang wu  Gr. 1, 90
Cindy  Gr. 4, 384
Ciranda  Gr. 2, 272
Danzas Puertorriqueñas, "Vano Empeno"  Gr. 7, E-13
First Night Quadrille  Gr. 4, 343
Forked Deer/Fisher's Hornpipe Gr. 4, 343
Goin' to Boston  Gr. 6, 433
How Many Miles to Babylon? Gr. 2, 128
Jambalaya  Gr. 6, 245
Johnny Mister Brown  Gr. K, 37
Juba  Gr. K, 13
Kalvelis  Gr. 2, 42
La raspa  Gr. 4, 305
O ma washi  Gr. K, 13
Old Brass Wagon  Gr. 2, 122
Patty Cake Polka  Gr. 2, 281
Phoebe  Gr. 1, 30
Round Dance  Gr. 6, 445
Saqian da dhol  Gr. 8, B-22
Shake Them 'Simmons Down Gr. 2, 244
Skip to My Lou  Gr. K, 58
Somebody Waiting  Gr. 2, 283

(*Moving,* continued)

Tideo  Gr. 2, 80

*Toei khong*  Gr. 8, B-21

*Ve'David Y'Fey Enayiam*
Gr. 4, 317

Yo-shi nai  Gr. 6, 286

## GAME SONGS

Bounce High, Bounce Low
Gr. 1, 152

Cheki, morena  Gr. 2, 180

Ciranda  Gr. 2, 272

Four White Horses  Gr. 3, 304

Green, Green, Rocky  Gr. 1, 321

How Many Miles to Babylon?
Gr. 2, 128

Jan ken pon  Gr. 3, 302

Juba  Gr. K, 13

Just from the Kitchen  Gr. K, 55

Kapulu kane  Gr. 2, 270

*Limbo Rock (limbo)*  Gr. 3, 298

Lucy Locket  Gr. 2, 27

Miss Mary Mack  Gr. 2, 42

Poco, Le' Me 'Lone  Gr. 3, 300

Sailboat in the Sky  Gr. 4, 375

Sansaw akroma  Gr. 3, 286

Snail, Snail  Gr. 1, 190

Who Has the Penny?  Gr. K, 42

Wichita Hand Game Song 1
Gr. 3, 306

Wichita Hand Game Song 2
Gr. 3, 306

## LOCOMOTOR MOVEMENT

Apples (poem)  Gr. 1, 15

Bonjour, mes amis  Gr. 1, 317

Boysie  Gr. 2, 195

*Choo Choo Boogaloo*  Gr. 1, 127

Doong gul ge  Gr. 3, 134

El barquito  Gr. 3, 358

*For Children (Sz 42), Volume II,
No. 33, Allegro non troppo*
Gr. 2, 49

Hi-Dee-Roon  Gr. K, 10

Johnny Mister Brown  Gr. K, 37

Khorovod  Gr. 1, 374

La tormenta tropical  Gr. 2, 116

*Little Pearls, The*  Gr. K, 215

My Legs and I (poem)  Gr. 1, 9

Nampaya omame  Gr. 1, 138

New Way to Walk, A  Gr. K, 117

Pottery Dance  Gr. 1, 371

Railroad Corral  Gr. 3, 174

Rig-a-Jig-Jig  Gr. K, 99

Shortnin' Bread  Gr. 1, 57

Skip to My Lou  Gr. K, 58

Song That's Just for You, A
Gr. 2, 126

Time to Move  Gr. 1, 244

Vil du?  Gr. 1, 92

*Washington Post, The* (march)
Gr. 1, 175

When the Train Comes Along
Gr. 1, 301

Yonder Come Day  Gr. 8, I-68

## NONLOCOMOTOR MOVEMENT

A la rurru niño  Gr. K, 180

*Country Dance*  Gr. 3, 211

Great Day  Gr. 3, 58

Hands  Gr. 1, 203

Haul Away, Joe  Gr. 4, 12

He's Got the Whole World in His
Hands  Gr. 3, 230

Head, Shoulders, Baby  Gr. 1, 82

Hi-Dee-Roon  Gr. K, 10

Johnny Mister Brown  Gr. K, 37

Lady, Lady  Gr. 1, 62

*Le Hoogie Boogie*  Gr. K, 296

Michael, Row the Boat Ashore
Gr. 2, 18

Put Your Finger in the Air
Gr. K, 114

*Putting Baby to Bed*  Gr. 1, 63

Riendo el río corre  Gr. 6, 263

Shine, Shine, Shine  Gr. 1, 42

Shortnin' Bread  Gr. 1, 57

Song That's Just for You, A
Gr. 2, 126

Spaceworms  Gr. 1, 401

That's What's New with Me!  Gr. K, 2

Turn the World Around  Gr. 4, 116

Wind Blew East, The  Gr. 1, 64

## PATTERNED DANCES

Ah, eu entrei na roda  Gr. 3, 308

Alabama Gal  Gr. 3, 106

*Allons danser, Colinda*  Gr. K, 218

Ants Go Marching, The  Gr. 1, 250

Así es mi tierra  Gr. 6, 172

*Ayer, "Yesterday"*  Gr. 6, 266

B-A, Bay  Gr. 1, 220

*Baila caporal*  Gr. 8, B-22

Bye Bye, Love  Gr. 8, F-9

*Capoeira Na Vila*  Gr. 8, D-25

Cha yang wu  Gr. 1, 90

Chicka Hanka  Gr. 8, F-15

Down the Ohio  Gr. 2, 60

Duck Dance  Gr. 2, 249

Flat Foot Floogee, The  Gr. 3, 160

Here I Go!  Gr. K, 73

I Wonder Where Maria's Gone
Gr. 3, 318

Just from the Kitchen  Gr. K, 55

Loco-Motion, The  Gr. 3, 64

My Home's Across the Blue Ridge
Mountains  Gr. 4, 84

*Pavane et Gaillarde*  Gr. 2, 279

Perot  Gr. 2, 378

Phoebe  Gr. 1, 30

*Sai da Frente*  Gr. 8, D-24

Sing Your Story  Gr. 3, 350

*Stalia, stalia*  Gr. 8, B-21

Theme from New York, New York
Gr. 4, 250

Winter  Gr. 8, G-11

## PLAY-PARTIES

Four in a Boat  Gr. 2, 46

Great Big House  Gr. 2, 204

Lullaby and Dance  Gr. 4, 387

Old Brass Wagon  Gr. 2, 122

Paw-Paw Patch  Gr. 4, 94

Shake Them 'Simmons Down
Gr. 2, 244

Somebody Waiting  Gr. 2, 283

Tideo  Gr. 2, 80

## POPULAR DANCES

At the Hop (rock 'n' roll)  Gr. 4, 168

*Carrament News*  Gr. 8, B-22

*Footloose*  Gr. 7, B-11

*I Will Survive*  Gr. 7, B-10

*Limbo Rock (limbo)*  Gr. 3, 298

*Rock It*  Gr. 7, B-11

Rockin' Around the Christmas Tree
(swing)  Gr. 5, 466

*Twist, The*  Gr. 7, B-10

## SIGNING

Ég a gyertya  Gr. K, 96

Eres tú  Gr. 6, 473

Everybody Loves Saturday Night
Gr. 6, 296

Falling Rain  Gr. 2, 329

I Am But a Small Voice  Gr. 6, 446

I Got Shoes  Gr. 2, 242

Kuma san  Gr. K, 40

Mama Don't 'Low  Gr. 6, 360

Mariposita  Gr. 2, 156

Name, Name, What's Your Name?
(speech piece)  Gr. 3, 11

Peace Like a River  Gr. 3, 246

Put a Little Love in Your Heart
Gr. 4, 8

Rainbow, The  Gr. 2, 332

Siyahamba  Gr. 6, 214

Sometimes I Feel Like a Motherless
Child  Gr. 6, 243

This Train  Gr. 5, 26

Under the Same Sun  Gr. 6, 440

Yang wa wa  Gr. K, 163

# MUSIC MAKERS *See also Spotlight On.*

## COMPOSERS

Abe, Keiko  Gr. 3, 150

Adams, John  Gr. 7, C-44

Bach, Johann Sebastian  Gr. 3, 36

Bach, Johann Sebastian  Gr. 4, 233

Bach, Johann Sebastian  Gr. 7, C-9

Bach, Johann Sebastian  Gr. 7, E-24

Bartók, Béla  Gr. 3, 172

Bartók, Béla  Gr. 4, 73

Bartók, Béla  Gr. 6, 196

Beach, Amy  Gr. 2, 338

Beethoven, Ludwig van  Gr. 4, 153

Beethoven, Ludwig van  Gr. 6, 99

Berg, Alban  Gr. 6, 169

Berlin, Irving  Gr. 5, 74

Bernstein, Elmer  Gr. 3, 144

Bizet, Georges  Gr. 6, 68
Brahms, Johannes  Gr. 4, 171
Britten, Benjamin  Gr. 5, 223
Cage, John  Gr. 6, 209
Chávez, Carlos  Gr. 8, C-36
Chopin, Frédéric  Gr. 3, 26
Chopin, Frédéric  Gr. 3, 316
Cohan, George M.  Gr. 3, 265
Cohan, George M.  Gr. 5, 278
Copland, Aaron  Gr. 2, 22
Copland, Aaron  Gr. 3, 250
Copland, Aaron  Gr. 4, 343
Copland, Aaron  Gr. 5, 187
Copland, Aaron  Gr. 6, 198
Cunningham, Arthur  Gr. 2, 203
Daquin, Louis-Claude  Gr. 3, 329
Debussy, Claude  Gr. 5, 113
Debussy, Claude  Gr. 7, C-38
Dibdin, Charles  Gr. 3, 212
Dorsey, Thomas A.  Gr. 5, 281
Ellington, Duke  Gr. 5, 339
Foster, Stephen  Gr. 5, 271
Gershwin, George  Gr. 6, 251
Gershwin, George  Gr. 7, C-42
Gershwin, George and Ira
     Gr. 7, E-10
Ginastera, Alberto  Gr. 5, 228
Glass, Philip  Gr. 6, 30
Gliére, Reinhold  Gr. 4, 225
Gossec, François-Joseph  Gr. 3, 86
Gottschalk, Louis Moreau  Gr. 3, 229
Gould, Morton  Gr. 6, 138
Grainger, Percy  Gr. 7, C-37
Grofé, Ferde  Gr. 3, 76
Handel, George Frideric  Gr. 2, 348
Handel, George Frideric  Gr. 8, C-9
Haydn, Franz Joseph  Gr. 2, 84
Haydn, Franz Joseph  Gr. 4, 91
Haydn, Franz Joseph  Gr. 5, 105
Haydn, Franz Joseph  Gr. 6, 132
Haydn, Franz Joseph  Gr. 7, C-15
Holst, Gustav  Gr. 1, 403
Holst, Gustav  Gr. 4, 376
Holst, Gustav  Gr. 5, 424
Holst, Gustav  Gr. 6, 139
Horner, James  Gr. 6, 345
Hunter, Charles  Gr. 5, 333
Ives, Charles  Gr. 6, 162
Jones, Bessie  Gr. K, 54
Joplin, Scott  Gr. 5, 335
Joplin, Scott  Gr. 6, 157
Khachaturian, Aram  Gr. 4, 17
Larsen, Libby  Gr. 7, C-21
Leiber, Jerry  Gr. 5, 49
Liszt, Franz  Gr. 7, E-18
Louiselle, Brian  Gr. 8, A-5
Ma Shui-Long  Gr. 3, 104
Moore, Carman  Gr. 3, 163
Mozart, Wolfgang Amadeus
     Gr. 3, 18
Mozart, Wolfgang Amadeus
     Gr. 4, 111

Mozart, Wolfgang Amadeus
     Gr. 5, 145
Mozart, Wolfgang Amadeus
     Gr. 8, C-10
Nelson, Ron  Gr. 6, 331
Niccoló Paganini  Gr. 7, C-23
Papoulis, Jim  Gr. 6, 337
Partch, Harry  Gr. 8, D-29
Porterfield, Sherri  Gr. 7, G-45
Praetorius, Michael  Gr. 6, 210
Prokofiev, Sergei  Gr. 6, 457
Puccini, Giacomo  Gr. 7, C-31
Ravel, Maurice  Gr. 8, A-13
Rodrigo, Joaquín  Gr. 6, 199
Rossini, Gioacchino  Gr. 7, C-31
Saint-Saëns, Camille  Gr. 3, 357
Saint-Saëns, Camille  Gr. 4, 220
Samuel Barber  Gr. 7, C-21
Schoenberg, Arnold  Gr. 6, 168
Schuman, William  Gr. 6, 83
Schumann, Robert  Gr. 3, 203
Sheng, Bright  Gr. 7, C-44
Sherman, Robert B. and Richard M.
     Gr. 3, 8
Shostakovich, Dimitri  Gr. 6, 442
Sibelius, Jean  Gr. 6, 76
Smetana, Bedrich  Gr. 7, C-33
Sousa, John Philip  Gr. 1, 447
Sousa, John Philip  Gr. 1, 174
Stoller, Mike  Gr. 5, 49
Strauss, Jr., Johann  Gr. 6, 192
Stravinsky, Igor  Gr. 2, 264
Subotnick, Morton  Gr. 6, 366
Swann, Donald  Gr. 3, 33
Tchaikovsky, Piotr  Gr. 4, 295
Tchaikovsky, Piotr Ilyich  Gr. 3, 281
Tchaikovsky, Piotr Ilyich  Gr. 3, 278
Tchaikovsky, Piotr Ilyich  Gr. 6, 324
Thomson, Virgil  Gr. 3, 175
Thomson, Virgil  Gr. 4, 346
Tomita, Isao  Gr. 8, A-14
Tower, Joan  Gr. 7, C-44
Vaughan Williams, Ralph  Gr. 5, 235
Verdi, Giuseppe  Gr. 7, C-31
Villa-Lobos, Heitor  Gr. 8, C-36
Vivaldi, Antonio  Gr. 6, 211
von Bingen, Hildegard  Gr. 7, C-4
Warren, Diane  Gr. 8, G-5
Webber, Andrew Lloyd  Gr. 6, 179

## COMPOSERS/ARRANGERS
Anderson, Leroy  Gr. 2, 390
Bassett, Rick  Gr. 1, 34
Cotton, Elizabeth  Gr. 1, 46
Dawson, William  Gr. 7, C-41
Harris, Roy  Gr. 5, 88
Joubert, Joseph  Gr. 3, 50
Joubert, Joseph  Gr. 3, 49
Rodgers, Richard  Gr. 5, 39
Rodrigo, Joaquín  Gr. 2, 151
Royal, Reggie  Gr. 6, 465
Still, William Grant  Gr. 3, 126
Tesori, Jeanine  Gr. 6, 312

Tomita, Isao  Gr. 5, 239
Twine, Linda  Gr. 6, 339

## COMPOSERS/CONDUCTORS
Bernstein, Leonard  Gr. 5, 9
Bernstein, Leonard  Gr. 6, 216
Sousa, John Philip  Gr. 5, 79
Sousa, John Philip  Gr. 8, C-40

## CONDUCTORS
Ashkenazy, Vladimir  Gr. 4, 234
Falletta, JoAnn  Gr. 3, 200
Goodman, Benny  Gr. 2, 189
Harth-Bedoya, Miguel  Gr. 1, 207
Mehta, Zubin  Gr. 6, 154
Thomas, Andre J.  Gr. 8, G-41
Williams, John  Gr. 6, 350

## LYRICISTS
Crawley, Brian  Gr. 6, 312
Flanders, Michael  Gr. 3, 34
Hammerstein, Oscar  Gr. 5, 39

## MUSIC DIRECTORS
Hogan, Moses  Gr. 4, 395
Leck, Henry  Gr. 6, 435
Rafter, Michael  Gr. 6, 113
Twine, Linda  Gr. 4, 29

## PERFORMERS
Abe, Keiko  Gr. 3, 150
Alabama  Gr. 5, 349
Amoco Renegades  Gr. 4, 41
Anderson, Marian  Gr. 3, 248
Andrews, Julie  Gr. 3, 9
Anthony, Marc  Gr. 6, 335
Armstrong, Louis  Gr. 2, 179
Armstrong, Louis  Gr. 5, 446
Armstrong, Louis  Gr. 6, 65
Ashkenazy, Vladimir  Gr. 4, 234
Asleep at the Wheel  Gr. 4, 278
B.E.A.T.  Gr. 8, D-33
Baker, Etta  Gr. 8, F-14
Banana Slug String Band, The
     Gr. 2, 291
Beach Boys, The  Gr. 6, 260
Beach Boys, The  Gr. 7, E-26
Beatles, The  Gr. 6, 256
Belafonte, Harry  Gr. 5,
Bennett, Tony  Gr. 4, 9
Bliss, Julian  Gr. 8, A-19
Blue Man Group  Gr. 7, D-5
Boys Choir of Harlem, The
     Gr. 5, 393
Broonzy, Big Bill  Gr. 6, 224
Brubeck, Dave  Gr. 5, 220
Burrough, Roslyn  Gr. 7, E-21
Byrds, The  Gr. 6, 149
Cassidy, Eva  Gr. 6, 63
Century Men, The  Gr. 5, 471
Checker, Chubby  Gr. 5, 358
Checker, Chubby  Gr. 6, 258
Chenier, Clifton  Gr. 6, 403
Church, Charlotte  Gr. 6, 178
Clancy Brothers, The  Gr. 3, 292
Clark, Petula  Gr. 6, 259

**(Music Makers, continued)**

Coasters, The  Gr. 5, 204
Cody, Robert Tree  Gr. 5, 111
Corea, Chick  Gr. 7, B-42
Cresswell, Luke  Gr. 4, 123
Danny & the Juniors  Gr. 4, 166
Davis, Miles  Gr. 6, 252
Dawson, William  Gr. 7, C-41
Day, Howie  Gr. 8, A-19
Deep Forest  Gr. 7, B-43
Dispatch  Gr. 7, B-21
Dorsey, Tommy  Gr. 6, 93
Doucet/Beausoleil, Michael
    Gr. K, 65
Ellington, Edward Kennedy "Duke"
    Gr. 8, C-43
Estefan, Gloria  Gr. 5, 8
Estefan, Gloria  Gr. 6, 348
Feliciano, José  Gr. 7, I-29
Fisk Jubilee Singers, The  Gr. 6, 234
Fitzgerald, Ella  Gr. 2, 239
Fitzgerald, Ella  Gr. 5, 341
Fitzgerald, Ella  Gr. 5, 448
Five Satins, The  Gr. 4, 47
Flisher, Leon  Gr. 7, C-18
Franklin, Aretha  Gr. 4, 143
Franklin, Aretha  Gr. 5, 363
Franklin, Aretha  Gr. 7, B-17
Gaillard, Bulee "Slim"  Gr. 3, 161
Galway, James  Gr. 4, 297
Garland, Judy  Gr. 4, 142
Gloria Estefan  Gr. 6, 348
Golden Gate Quartet, The
    Gr. 6, 235
Gómez, Francisco Sánchez
    Gr. 5, 296
Goodman, Benny  Gr. 2, 189
Groban, Josh  Gr. 7, A-10
Guy, Buddy  Gr. 8, F-28
Hackson, Mahalia  Gr. 6, 394
Haliwa-Saponi Singers  Gr. 5, 303
Hampton, Lionel  Gr. 3, 151
Haza, Ofra  Gr. 1, 182
Hell, Felix  Gr. 7, E-25
Hellmer, Jeff  Gr. 8, E-5
Holiday, Billy  Gr. 7, B-27
Holly, Buddy  Gr. 6, 258
Hood, Marilyn  Gr. 6, 287
Houghton, Steve  Gr. 2, 154
Indianapolis Children's Choir
    Gr. 5, 31
Isley Brothers, The  Gr. 4, 239
Ivers, Eileen  Gr. 2, 141
Jackson, Mahalia  Gr. 5, 193
James, Harry  Gr. 4, 279
Johnson, Emma  Gr. 7, C-13
Jolson, Al  Gr. 4, 286
Joubert, Joseph  Gr. 3, 49
Juilliard String Quartet  Gr. 3, 111
Kavina, Lydia  Gr. 2, 212
Kidjo, Angélique  Gr. 7, D-15
King, Ben E.  Gr. 5, 49

Klucevsek, Guy  Gr. 8, E-21
Kodo  Gr. 7, D-16
Landreth, Sonny  Gr. 7, F-26
Lebo M.  Gr. 4, 132
Ledbetter, Huddie  Gr. 2, 53
Lee, CoCo  Gr. 6, 270
Legg, Adrian  Gr. 7, F-9
Los Angeles Guitar Quartet
    Gr. 8, F-20
Los Lobos  Gr. 7, B-7
Louis Armstrong and the Hot 5
    Gr. 6, 64
Ma, Yo-Yo  Gr. 3, 38
Ma, Yo-Yo  Gr. 8, A-16
Mannheim Steamroller  Gr. 5, 475
Mannheim Steamroller  Gr. 6, 461
Mariachi Cobre  Gr. 7, B-33
Marley, Ziggy  Gr. 6, 143
Marsalis, Branford  Gr. 4, 74
Marsalis, Delfeayo  Gr. 4, 74
Marsalis, Ellis  Gr. 4, 74
Marshall, George  Gr. 3, 319
Martin, Mary  Gr. 3, 117
McNicholas, Steve  Gr. 4, 123
Mellencamp, John  Gr. 6, 2
Mensah, Sowah  Gr. 6, 291
Messina, Jo Dee  Gr. 7, B-25
Miller, Glenn  Gr. 5, 342
Nakai, R. Carlos  Gr. 3, 255
Nakai, R. Carlos  Gr. 3, 254
Naranjo, Valerie Dee  Gr. 6, 186
Nelson, Ricky  Gr. 7, B-23
Oakridge Boys, The  Gr. 4, 86
Odetta  Gr. 5, 394
Olatunji, Babatunde  Gr. 2, 69
Olatunji, Babatunde  Gr. 5, 67
Palmieri, Eddie  Gr. 7, B-31
Parker, Charlie  Gr. 5, 451
Parker, Charlie "Bird"  Gr. 6, 225
Platters, The  Gr. 5, 358
Pratt, Awadagin  Gr. 7, E-4
Presley, Elvis  Gr. 5, 212
Presley, Elvis  Gr. 6, 254
Puente, Tito  Gr. 3, 360
Puente, Tito  Gr. 6, 262
Ramone, Joey  Gr. 6, 63
Rampal, Jean-Pierre  Gr. 3, 185
Rimes, LeAnn  Gr. 5, 347
Rockapella  Gr. 4, 193
Rogers, Sally  Gr. 4, 329
Romero Family, The  Gr. 5, 176
Sanchez, David "Dakota"  Gr. 6, 319
Santana, Carlos  Gr. 2, 255
Santana, Carlos  Gr. 6, 262
Seeger Family, The  Gr. 5, 99
Seeger, Pete  Gr. 8, C-35
Selena  Gr. 6, 262
Shakira  Gr. 7, B-32
Shankar, Anoushka  Gr. 4, 310
Shankar, Anoushka  Gr. 8, A-19
Shankar, Ravi  Gr. 5, 320
Singers Unlimited, The  Gr. 4, 126

Sly and the Family Stone  Gr. 5, 389
Smith, Bessie  Gr. 5, 353
Smith, Warren  Gr. 2, 33
Smith, Will  Gr. 7, A-5
Stern, Isaac  Gr. 5, 159
Stewart, Leroy "Slam"  Gr. 3, 161
Sweethearts of the Rodeo
    Gr. 6, 249
Swoboda, Deanna  Gr. 3, 188
Sykes, Jubilant  Gr. 7, G-10
Taylor, Billy  Gr. 6, 471
Teague, Liam  Gr. 7, D-23
Tharpe, Sister Rosetta  Gr. 7, I-13
Tormé, Mel  Gr. 6, 386
Tudjaat  Gr. 3, 258
Turtle Island String Quartet
    Gr. 5, 311
Ulali  Gr. 7, D-25
United States Marine Corps Band,
    The  Gr. 5, 78
Vandellas, The  Gr. 5, 361
Waters, Muddy  Gr. 5, 225
Waters, Muddy  Gr. 7, B-9
Weavers, The  Gr. 3, 241
Winter, Paul  Gr. 3, 378
Winter, Paul  Gr. 5, 399
Yoo, Hi-za  Gr. 4, 175
Yothu Yindi  Gr. 8, B-38

**SINGERS/SONGWRITERS**

Baez, Joan  Gr. 7, A-4
Barry, Jeff  Gr. 7, G-29
Bruce, Jack  Gr. 8, F-32
Burch, Sharon  Gr. 2, 323
Callaway, Ann Hampton  Gr. 6, 113
Carpenter, Mary Chapin  Gr. 2, 341
Chapin, Tom  Gr. 3, 75
Chapin, Tom  Gr. 3, 74
Connick, Harry, Jr.  Gr. 4, 427
de Vita, Franco  Gr. 6, 267
Diamond, Neil  Gr. 7, G-32
DiFranco, Ani  Gr. 8, F-32
Domino, Antoine "Fats"  Gr. 3, 370
Durst, James  Gr. 4, 372
Dylan, Bob  Gr. 5, 384
Dylan, Bob  Gr. 6, 195
Fricker, Sylvia  Gr. 7, G-25
Greenwich, Ellie  Gr. 7, G-29
Guthrie, Woody  Gr. 1, 275
Guthrie, Woody  Gr. 3, 241
Guthrie, Woody  Gr. 4, 281
Guthrie, Woody  Gr. 5, 118
Guthrie, Woody  Gr. 5, 283
Hinojosa, Tish  Gr. 6, 264
Joel, Billy  Gr. 7, E-19
King, Carole  Gr. 3, 66
King, Carole  Gr. 5, 364
Krauss, Alison  Gr. 4, 291
Lennon, John  Gr. 5, 208
Mac Davis  Gr. 2,
Mahal, Taj  Gr. 7, E-33
Marley, Bob  Gr. 8, F-6
McCartney, Paul  Gr. 5, 208

McFerrin, Bobby  Gr. 4, 80
Miller, Roger  Gr. 4, 29
Mitchell, Joni  Gr. 5, 385
N'Dour, Youssou  Gr. 6, 268
Papillion  Gr. 2, 89
Ritchie, Jean  Gr. 3, 16
Ritchie, Jean  Gr. 4, 349
Ritchie, Jean  Gr. 6, 23
Seeger, Mike  Gr. 5, 99
Seeger, Pete  Gr. 5, 380
Shocked, Michelle  Gr. 7, B-40
Small, Heather  Gr. 7, G-5
Swann, Donald  Gr. 3, 34
Valens, Ritchie  Gr. 5, 130
Vandross, Luther  Gr. 6, 9
Vaughan, Stevie Ray  Gr. 8, F-27
Webb, Jimmy  Gr. 7, B-41
Williams, Hank, III  Gr. 8, F-19
Williams, Hank, Jr.  Gr. 8, F-19
Williams, Hank, Sr.  Gr. 8, F-19
Wills, Bob  Gr. 5, 135

## MUSICAL PERIODS *See also Genre/Style.*

### BAROQUE

*Bombé/Ruht wohl, ruht wohl, ihr heiligen Gebeine, BWV 245* Gr. 8, B-39
*Brandenburg Concerto No. 2, Movement 3 Allegro Assai* Gr. 7, C-8
*Brandenburg Concerto No. 4, BWV 1049, Allegro* Gr. 5, 111
*Cantata No. 140 (as performed by American Bach Solosists), "Wachet auf, ruft uns die Stimme," Movement 4* Gr. 7, C-9
*Cantata No. 140 (as performed by The Swingle Singers), "Wachet auf, ruft uns die Stimme," Movement 4* Gr. 7, C-10
*Chorale Prelude for Organ, BWV 645, "Wachet auf, ruft uns die Stimme "* Gr. 7, C-9
*Concerto for Two Trumpets in C Major, Rv. 537, Movement 1, "Allegro"* Gr. 4, 75
*Dances from Terpsichore, "Bransle de la Torche"* Gr. 3, 63
*Four Seasons, Concerto No. 2, The, "Summer," Movement 3, "La Tempesta"* Gr. 6, 102
*Four Seasons, The, "Spring," Movement 1* Gr. 1, 29
*Four Seasons, The, "Spring," Movement 1* Gr. 4, 371
*Four Seasons, The, "Winter," Movement 2* Gr. 3, 113
*French Suite No. 5, "Gigue"* Gr. 4, 232
*Galliard battaglia* Gr. 6, 362
*Gloria In Excelsis* Gr. 6, 210
*Invention No. 5 in E-flat* Gr. 5, 59

*Jesu, Joy of Man's Desiring* Gr. 6, 87
*Le cou cou* Gr. 3, 329
*"Little" Organ Fugue in G Minor* Gr. 6, 129
*"Little" Organ Fugue in G Minor (brass)* Gr. 6, 129
*Messiah, "Behold, I Tell You a Mystery"* Gr. 8, C-8
*Messiah, "Hallelujah!"* Gr. 8, C-8
*Messiah, "The Trumpet Shall Sound"* Gr. 8, C-8
*Musette* Gr. 3, 39
*Musical Offering, BWV 1079, No. 11, "Canon a 4"* Gr. 3, 193
*Orchestral Suite No. 2 in B Minor, "Minuet"* Gr. 6, 192
*Orchestral Suite No. 3, BWV 1068, "Air in D," Movement 2* Gr. 4, 23
*Partita in A Minor, "Sarabande"* Gr. 3, 185
*Sonata in A Minor, "Allegro"* Gr. 7, C-12
*Sonata in C Major for Recorder and Basso Continuo, Op. 1, No. 7, Gavotte* Gr. K, 75
*Sonata in G Minor, Op. 1, No. 1, Movement 2* Gr. 7, C-12
*Sonata Seconda* Gr. 3, 431
*Suite in E-flat Major for Cello, S. 1010, "Gigue"* Gr. 7, C-11
*Suite No. 3 in C Major for Unaccompanied Cello, "Bourrée 1"* Gr. 3, 38
*Toccata and Fugue in D Minor* Gr. 7, E-25
*Toccata in D Minor* Gr. 4, 233
*Water Music, "Allegro Maestoso"* Gr. 3, 189
*Water Music, "Hornpipe"* Gr. 8, C-9
*Well-Tempered Clavier, Book 1, "Prelude and Fugue in C Minor"* Gr. 7, E-16
*Well-Tempered Clavier, The, "Be-Bop Bach: Prelude No. 2"* Gr. 7, C-11

### CLASSICAL

*12 Variations in C Major, K. 265/300e, "Ah, vous dirai-je, Maman"* Gr. 3, 19
Alleluia Gr. 6, 133
*Arrival of the Queen of Sheba (Solomon), The* Gr. 2, 348
*Canon for Violin and Cello* Gr. 6, 126
*Canon No. 110 in G* Gr. 6, 133
*Concerto for Flute and Harp in C, K. 299, Movement 2* Gr. 8, C-10

*Concerto for French Horn in E-flat Major, K. 495, No. 4, Movement 3* Gr. 8, C-11
*Concerto for French Horn in E-flat Major* Gr. 8, C-3
*Concerto in D Major for Flute and Orchestra, K. 314, Movement 3, Allegro* Gr. K, 123
*Concerto No. 1 for Horn and Orchestra, "Rondo," Allegro* Gr. 5, 145
*Country Dance* Gr. 3, 211
*Die Zauberflöte, "Pa-pa-pa-pa-pa-pa-pagena"* Gr. 8, C-13
*Eccosaise in E-flat Major* Gr. 1, 223
*Eine kleine Nachtmusik, Minuet* Gr. 4, 111
*Gavotte* Gr. 3, 88
*Magic Flute, The, "In diesen heil'gen Hallen (In These Bright Halls)"* Gr. K, 9
*Piano Concerto in A Minor, Op. 16, Movement 1* Gr. 8, E-11
*Piano Concerto in E-Flat Major, Op. 73, No. 5, "Emperor," Movement 3* Gr. 7, C-18
*Quartetto buffo di gatti, "Comic Quartet for Cats"* Gr. 1, 131
*Quintet for Piano and Strings in A Major, "Trout," Movement 3, Scherzo* Gr. 1, 179
*Serenade, Op. 3, No. 5* Gr. 4, 90
*Sonata in C Major for Recorder and Basso Continuo, Op. 1, No. 7, "Gavotte"* Gr. K, 75
*Sonata in C-sharp Minor, Op. 27, No. 2, "Moonlight," Movement 1* Gr. 7, C-19
*Sonata in F Major for Violin and Piano, Op. 24, No. 5, "Spring," Movement 3* Gr. 7, C-19
*Sonata No. 11, K. 331, "Turkish Rondo"* Gr. K, 165
*Sonatina for Bassoon and Piano, "Allegro con moto," Movement 1* Gr. 7, C-13
*String Quartet in D Major, Op. 64, No. 5, "The Lark," Allegro moderato* Gr. 7, C-15
*Symphony in G, No. 88, Movement 4* Gr. 2, 84
*Symphony No. 3 in E-flat Major, "Allegro con brio," Movement 1* Gr. 8, C-17
*Symphony No. 3 in E-flat Major, "Marcia funebre," Movement 2* Gr. 8, C-17
*Symphony No. 40 in G Minor, K. 550, Movement 1* Gr. 8, C-12
*Symphony No. 40 in G Minor, K. 550, Movement 1,* Gr. 8, B-30

(*Musical Periods,* continued)

*Symphony No. 47 in G Major,*
   *"Menuet"* Gr. 7, C-14
*Symphony No. 5 in C Minor,*
   *Movement 1* Gr. 6, 98
*Symphony No. 5 in C Minor, Op.*
   *67, Movement 1* Gr. 7, C-16
*Symphony No. 5 in C Minor, Op.*
   *67, Movement 4* Gr. 7, C-18
*Symphony No. 94 in G Major,*
   *No. 94, "Surprise," Andante*
   Gr. 1, 86
*Symphony No. 94 in G Major,*
   *"Surprise," Andante*
   Gr. 7, C-14
*Toy Symphony, Movement 4*
   Gr. 1, 111

## IMPRESSIONISTIC

*Chansons madecasses,*
   *"Nahandove"* Gr. 4, 32
*Children's Corner, "Jimbo's*
   *Lullaby"* Gr. 1, 270
*Children's Corner Suite, "Doctor*
   *Gradus ad Parnassum"*
   Gr. 8, C-27
*Clair de lune* Gr. K, 165
*En prière* Gr. K, 158
*La mer, "Jeux de vagues"*
   Gr. 7, C-39
*Le tombeau de Couperin,*
   *"Prelude"* Gr. 8, C-28
*Little Shepherd, The* Gr. 1, 256
*Minstrels* Gr. K, 175
*Prelude to the Afternoon of a*
   *Faun* Gr. 5, 113
*Syrinx* Gr. 5, 113
*Voiles* Gr. 7, C-39

## MEDIEVAL

*Abbots Bromley Horn Dance*
   Gr. 7, C-24
*Ahi! Amours* Gr. 8, C-4
*Alle psallite cum luya* Gr. 7, C-5
*Beggar's Opera, The, "Constant*
   *Billy"* Gr. 7, C-24
*Domna, pos vos ay chausida*
   *(Lady, For You)* Gr. 8, C-6
*La tierche estampie real* Gr. 8, C-6
*O ignis spiritus Paracliti* Gr. 7, C-4
*O tocius Asie gloria, "Oh, Glory of*
   *All Asia"* Gr. 8, C-4
*O tocius Asie gloria* Gr. 8, C-3
*Sumer Is Icumen In* Gr. 5, 35

## MODERN

*Altered Landscapes: Part One*
   Gr. 8, E-21
*Bachianas brasileiras No. 5, "Aria"*
   Gr. 8, C-3
*Bombé/Ruht wohl, ruht wohl, ihr*
   *heiligen Gebeine, BWV 245*
   Gr. 8, B-39
*C-Jam Blues* Gr. 8, C-3

*California Counterpoint: The*
   *Twittering Machine* Gr. 8, C-47
*China Gates* Gr. 7, C-45
*Dances of Galanta* Gr. 7, C-34
*Etude Fantasy for Piano, "Etude*
   *No 3: Fifths to Thirds"*
   Gr. 8, C-46
*Fanfare for the Common Man*
   Gr. 7, C-43
*Fifteen Hungarian Peasant Songs*
   Gr. 7, C-35
*Game of the Mechanical*
   *Nightingale, "The Nightingale"*
   Gr. 8, C-33
*Gazebo Dances, "Tarantella"*
   Gr. 8, C-46
*Gazebo Dances, "Tarantella"*
   Gr. 8, C-46
I Dream a World  Gr. 8, G-40
*Intermezzo, "Háry János Suite,"*
   *Movement 5* Gr. 7, C-34
*Le Sacre de Printemps (The Rite of*
   *Spring), "Dance of the Youths*
   *and Maidens"* Gr. 8, C-30
*Le tombeau de Couperin,*
   *"Prélude"* Gr. 8, C-3
*Peak Moments* Gr. 8, E-4
*Prelude in G-sharp Minor, No. 12*
   Gr. 7, E-4
*Pulcinella Suite, "Minuetto"*
   Gr. 8, C-15
*Pulcinella Suite, "Serenata"*
   Gr. 8, C-32
*Queen's Suite, The, "Sunset and*
   *the Mocking Bird"* Gr. 8, E-10
*Rhapsody in Blue* Gr. 7, C-42
*Rodeo, "Hoedown"* Gr. 8, B-45
*Scaramouche, "Brasiliera,"*
   *Movement 3* Gr. 8, C-29
*Sensemaya* Gr. 8, C-15
*Seven Tunes Heard in China,*
   *"Guessing Song"* Gr. 7, C-45
*Sevilla* Gr. 8, F-22
*Sextet for Winds and Piano,*
   *Movement 1* Gr. 8, C-29
*Shepherd's Hey Sampler*
   Gr. 7, C-37
*Simple Song, A, "from Mass"*
   Gr. 8, C-45
*Sonata for Violin and Piano,*
   *Allegro* Gr. 8, C-46
*Song of the Nightingale, "The*
   *Nightingale"* Gr. 8, C-32
*Soundings, "Fanfare"* Gr. 8, C-47
*Soundings* Gr. 8, C-3
*Suite in F, Op. 28b, No. 2,*
   *"Fantasia on the Dargason,"*
   *Movement 4* Gr. 7, C-36
*Well-Tempered Clavier, The, "Be-*
   *Bop Bach: Prelude No. 2"*
   Gr. 7, C-11
*Wings* Gr. 7, C-45

## NATIONALIST

*¡Ay, Jalisco no te rajes!* Gr. 7, I-6
*Bachianas brasileiras No. 5, "Aria"*
   Gr. 8, C-37
*Intermezzo, "Háry János Suite,"*
   *Movement 5* Gr. 7, C-34
*Ma Vlast (My Fatherland), "Vltava*
   *(The Moldau)"* Gr. 7, C-33
*Star-Spangled Banner, The*
   Gr. 7, I-56
*Suite in F, Op. 28b, No. 2,*
   *"Fantasia on the Dargason,"*
   *Movement 4* Gr. 7, C-36
*Xochipilli, An Imagined Aztec*
   *Music* Gr. 8, C-37

## RENAISSANCE

*Canzon in Echo Duodecimi Toni a*
   *10* Gr. 8, C-7
*Canzoni et Sonate, "Canzoni*
   *prima a 5"* Gr. 4, 193
*Danses Populaires Francaises,*
   *"Branle Double, Branle*
   *Simple"* Gr. 7, C-25
*Danza* Gr. 7, C-7
*Den III. Ende VI. Ronde & Quatre*
   *Branles* Gr. 7, C-7
*Den III. Ende VI. Ronde & Quatre*
   *Branles* Gr. 8, C-7
*Galliard Battaglia* Gr. 8, C-14
*Ombrose e care selve* Gr. 8, C-3
*Pavane et Gaillarde* Gr. 2, 279
*Ríu ríu chíu* Gr. 5, 435
*Rundadinella* Gr. 8, I-60
*Saltarello detto Trivella* Gr. 7, C-6
*Silver Swan, The* Gr. 8, C-5
*Sing We and Chant It* Gr. 8, C-5

## ROMANTIC

*1812 Overture* Gr. 4, 293
*5 Stücke im Volkston, Op. 102,*
   *No. 1, "Mit Humor"* Gr. 3, 39
*Academic Festival Overture, Op.*
   *80* Gr. 8, C-20
*Aida, "Gloria all'Egitto (Grand*
   *March)"* Gr. 8, C-24
*Bamboula* Gr. 3, 229
*Blue Danube, The, Op. 314*
   Gr. 6, 192
*Caprice No. 1 in E Major*
   Gr. 7, C-22
*Carnaval, Op. 9, "Valse Noble,"*
   *Un poco maestoso* Gr. 3, 202
*Carnival of the Animals, "Fossils"*
   Gr. 1, 236
*Carnival of the Animals, "Royal*
   *March of the Lion"* Gr. 3, 357
*Carnival of the Animals, "The*
   *Aviary"* Gr. K, 44
*Carnival of the Animals, "The*
   *Elephant"* Gr. K, 45
*Das Jahr, "Mai"* Gr. 8, C-18
*Die forelle* Gr. 7, C-20

*Die Walküre,* "The Ride of the Valkyries" Gr. 8, C-23
*Erlkönig,* "The Erlking" Gr. K, 164
*Étude in E Major* Gr. K, 241
*Flight of the Bumblebee* Gr. 1, 385
*Flight of the Bumblebee* (from *Tsar Sultan*) Gr. 3, 189
*Flight of the Bumblebee* Gr. K, 76
*For Children (Sz 42), Volume II, No. 33, Allegro non troppo* Gr. 2, 49
*Grand Canyon Suite,* "Cloudburst" Gr. K, 261
*Hungarian Dance No. 19* Gr. 4, 171
*Hungarian Dance No. 3 in F Major* Gr. 1, 206
*Hungarian Rhapsody No. 2 in C sharp Minor, S. 244* Gr. 7, E-17
*L'Arlésienne Suite No. 2,* "Farandole" Gr. 6, 68
*Lohengrin,* "Prelude to Act III" Gr. 8, C-22
*Lullaby* Gr. 3, 188
*Lyric Pieces, Op. 43, No. 1,* "Butterfly" Gr. 1, 363
*Lyric Pieces, Op. 43, No. 4,* "Little Bird" Gr. 1, 346
*Lyric Suite, Op. 65, No. 6,* "Wedding Day at Troldhaugen" Gr. 6, 9
*Ma Vlast (My Fatherland),* "Vltava (The Moldau)" Gr. 7, C-33
*Marche Militaire, Op. 51, No. 1* Gr. 6, 17
*Mazurka, Op. 30, No. 3* Gr. 3, 317
*Moravian Dances,* "Kalamajka" Gr. 3, 79
*Nutcracker Suite, The,* "Chinese Dance" Gr. K, 105
*Nutcracker Suite, The,* "Trepak" Gr. 3, 280
*Nutcracker Suite, The,* "Trepak" Gr. 6, 207
*Nutcracker Suite, The,* "Waltz of the Flowers" Gr. 6, 325
*Nutcracker, The,* "Arabian Dance" Gr. 7, C-26
*Nutcracker, The,* "Chinese Dance" Gr. 7, C-26
*Peer Gynt Suite No. 1,* "Morning" Gr. 1, 369
*Piano Trio in G Minor, Op. 17, Allegro* Gr. 8, C-19
*Piano Trio in G Minor, Op. 17, Allegro* Gr. 8, C-3
*Piano Trio No. 2 in E-flat Major, Op. 100, Scherzo* Gr. 4, 192
*Pictures at an Exhibition,* "Ballet of the Unhatched Chicks" Gr. K, 167

*Pictures at an Exhibition,* "The Great Gate of Kiev" Gr. 6, 154
*Pictures at an Exhibition,* "The Hut of Baba Yaga" Gr. 4, 103
*Prelude in A Major* Gr. 4, 234
*Prelude in B-flat Minor, Op. 28, No. 16* Gr. 7, C-22
*Prelude in E Minor, Op. 28, No. 4* Gr. 3, 27
*Quintet for Piano and Strings in E-flat Major, Op. 44, Movement 1* Gr. 8, C-19
*Raindrop Prelude* Gr. 3, 26
*Rigoletto,* "Bella figlia dell'amore" Gr. 7, C-29
*Serenade for Strings in C, Op. 48,* "Finale" Gr. 6, 363
*Sonata for Clarinet and Piano, Op. 167,* "Allegro animato," *Movement 2* Gr. 7, C-12
*Sorochintsy Fair,* "Gopak No. 5" Gr. 1, 417
*Spinning Song* Gr. K, 164
*Suite Española, Op. 47, No. 3,* "Sevilla" Gr. 7, C-23
*Symphony No. 1, Movement 3* Gr. 4, 237
*Symphony No. 4, Movement 4* Gr. 4, 295
*Symphony No. 4 in F Minor, Movement 4, Finale: Allegro con fuoco* Gr. 1, 175
*Symphony No. 7, Op. 92, No. 7, Movement 2* Gr. 1, 97
*Symphony No. 9 in D Minor, Op. 125,* "Ode to Joy," *Movement 4* Gr. 4, 151
*Transcendental Etude, No. 3 in G-sharp Minor,* "La Campanella" Gr. 7, C-23
*Violin Concerto in E Minor, Op. 64, Movement 1* Gr. 8, C-18
*Waltz in D-flat* ("Minute" Waltz) Gr. 4, 234
*Widmung, Op. 25, No. 1* Gr. 7, C-20
*Wild Horseman, The* Gr. 1, 159

## TWENTIETH CENTURY

*Allegretto* Gr. 2, 131
*Amahl and the Night Visitors,* "This Is My Box" Gr. 1, 433
*Appalachian Spring,* "Variations on Simple Gifts" Gr. 5, 185
*Billy the Kid,* "Celebration" Gr. 3, 251
*Caprice Basque, Op. 24* Gr. 1, 256
*Catalana,* "Andante" Gr. K, 134
*Circlesong Five* Gr. 1, 239
*Concert for Piano and Orchestra* Gr. 6, 209

*Concerto for Marimba and String Orchestra,* "Saudação" Gr. 2, 119
*Concerto for Orchestra,* "Presentation of Pairs" Gr. 4, 72
*Concerto for Trumpet and Orchestra in E-flat Major, Rondo: Allegro Molto* Gr. 1, 256
*Country Gardens* Gr. 1, 440
*Cradle Song* Gr. K, 97
*Dance Suite,* "Waltz" Gr. K, 145
*Ennanga, Movement 3* Gr. 3, 127
*Fanfare for Freedom* Gr. 6, 139
*Fantasia on Greensleeves* Gr. 5, 235
*Firebird, The,* "Finale" Gr. 8, C-30
*Firebird, The,* "Infernal Dance" Gr. 5, 173
*Fish Food* Gr. 2, 212
*Free Music #1* Gr. 2, 212
*Grand Canyon Suite,* "On the Trail" Gr. 3, 77
*Greeting Prelude* Gr. 2, 264
*Harukoma,* "Spring Horse Dance" Gr. 1, 145
*Hermit Songs, Op. 29,* "The Monk and His Cat" Gr. 7, C-21
*Ionisation* Gr. 6, 357
*L'Enfant et les sortilèges,* "Love for Two Cats" Gr. K, 101
*La Peri,* "Fanfare" Gr. 4, 71
*Les Rêves de Columbine, Op. 65,* "Sous les étoiles" Gr. 2, 338
*Lieutenant Kijé, Op. 60,* "Troika" Gr. 6, 457
*Love for Three Oranges,* "March" Gr. K, 117
*Lullaby for Strings* Gr. 1, 293
*Lyric Suite,* "Allegretto gioviale," *Movement 1* Gr. 6, 169
*Mars Suite,* "Orbital View," *Movement 1* Gr. 4, 199
*Mass for the 21st Century,* "Alleluia" Gr. 3, 163
*Memories of the Seashore* Gr. 3, 150
*Pacific 231* Gr. 2, 286
*Planets, The,* "Jupiter" Gr. 1, 405
*Planxty Madame Maxwell* Gr. K, 134
*Plow That Broke the Plains, The,* "Cattle" Gr. 3, 177
*Rhapsody in Blue* Gr. K, 75
*Rodeo,* "Buckaroo Holiday" Gr. 2, 23
*Rodeo,* "Hoedown" Gr. 5, 312
*Rodeo,* "Saturday Night Waltz" Gr. 4, 342
*Scherzo for Wind Quintet, Op. 48* Gr. 1, 328
*Shepherds Hey* Gr. 1, 208

(*Musical Periods,* continued)

    *Sinfonia Antarctica, "Epilogue"*
      Gr. 2, 326
    *Six Metamorphoses After Ovid,*
      *Op. 49, "Bacchus"* Gr. 7, C-13
    *Soldier's Tale, The, "Waltz"*
      Gr. K, 237
    *Songs from Letters, "So Like Your*
      *Father"* Gr. 7, C-21
    *Souvenirs L'Amerique, Op. 17,*
      *"Yankee Doodle"* Gr. 2, 405
    *Stravinsky Interview and Lullaby*
      *from The Firebird* Gr. 8, C-33
    *String Quartet No. 4, Movement*
      *4, "Allegretto pizzicato"*
      Gr. 4, 90
    *String Quartet No. 5, Movement*
      *4: Andante* Gr. 3, 113
    *Suite No. 2 in F, Op. 28b,*
      *Movement 1, "March"*
      Gr. 6, 139
    *Summertime* Gr. 6, 252
    *Ten Easy Pieces, "Bear Dance"*
      Gr. 3, 172
    *The Planets, "Mars, the Bringer of*
      *War"* Gr. 4, 377
    *Toccata and Tango* Gr. 2, 154
    *Variations on "America"*
      Gr. 6, 162
    *Vocalise* Gr. K, 123
    *Whirlwind* Gr. 3, 149
    *Wild Bull* Gr. 6, 366
    *Yellow Cake Review, The,*
      *"Farewell to Stromness"*
      Gr. K, 61

## MUSIC READING PRACTICE

### GRADE 1

Reading Sequence 1 (rhythm)
  Gr. 1, 448
Reading Sequence 2 (rhythm)
  Gr. 1, 448
Reading Sequence 3 (melody)
  Gr. 1, 449
Reading Sequence 4 (melody)
  Gr. 1, 450
Reading Sequence 5 (rhythm)
  Gr. 1, 451
Reading Sequence 6 (rhythm)
  Gr. 1, 452
Reading Sequence 7 (melody)
  Gr. 1, 452
Reading Sequence 8 (melody)
  Gr. 1, 453
Reading Sequence 9 (rhythm)
  Gr. 1, 454
Reading Sequence 10 (rhythm)
  Gr. 1, 454
Reading Sequence 11 (melody)
  Gr. 1, 455
Reading Sequence 12 (melody)
  Gr. 1, 456
Reading Sequence 13 (rhythm)
  Gr. 1, 457
Reading Sequence 14 (rhythm)
  Gr. 1, 458
Reading Sequence 15 (melody)
  Gr. 1, 459
Reading Sequence 16 (melody)
  Gr. 1, 459
Reading Sequence 17 (rhythm)
  Gr. 1, 460
Reading Sequence 18 (melody)
  Gr. 1, 461
Reading Sequence 19 (melody)
  Gr. 1, 462
Reading Sequence 20 (rhythm)
  Gr. 1, 463
Reading Sequence 21 (melody)
  Gr. 1, 464
Reading Sequence 22 (melody)
  Gr. 1, 465

### GRADE 2

Reading Sequence 1 (rhythm)
  Gr. 2, 406
Reading Sequence 2 (rhythm)
  Gr. 2, 406
Reading Sequence 3 (melody)
  Gr. 2, 407
Reading Sequence 4 (melody)
  Gr. 2, 407
Reading Sequence 5 (rhythm)
  Gr. 2, 408
Reading Sequence 6 (rhythm)
  Gr. 2, 408
Reading Sequence 7 (melody)
  Gr. 2, 409
Reading Sequence 8 (melody)
  Gr. 2, 409
Reading Sequence 9 (rhythm)
  Gr. 2, 410
Reading Sequence 10 (rhythm)
  Gr. 2, 410
Reading Sequence 11 (melody)
  Gr. 2, 411
Reading Sequence 12 (melody)
  Gr. 2, 411
Reading Sequence 13 (rhythm)
  Gr. 2, 412
Reading Sequence 14 (rhythm)
  Gr. 2, 412
Reading Sequence 15 (melody)
  Gr. 2, 413
Reading Sequence 16 (melody)
  Gr. 2, 413
Reading Sequence 17 (rhythm)
  Gr. 2, 414
Reading Sequence 18 (rhythm)
  Gr. 2, 414
Reading Sequence 19 (melody)
  Gr. 2, 415
Reading Sequence 20 (melody)
  Gr. 2, 415
Reading Sequence 21 (rhythm)
  Gr. 2, 416
Reading Sequence 22 (rhythm)
  Gr. 2, 416
Reading Sequence 23 (melody)
  Gr. 2, 417
Reading Sequence 24 (melody)
  Gr. 2, 417

### GRADE 3

Reading Sequence 1 (rhythm)
  Gr. 3, 416
Reading Sequence 2 (rhythm)
  Gr. 3, 416
Reading Sequence 3 (melody)
  Gr. 3, 417
Reading Sequence 4 (melody)
  Gr. 3, 417
Reading Sequence 5 (rhythm)
  Gr. 3, 418
Reading Sequence 6 (rhythm)
  Gr. 3, 418
Reading Sequence 7 (melody)
  Gr. 3, 419
Reading Sequence 8 (melody)
  Gr. 3, 419
Reading Sequence 9 (rhythm)
  Gr. 3, 420
Reading Sequence 10 (rhythm)
  Gr. 3, 420
Reading Sequence 11 (melody)
  Gr. 3, 421
Reading Sequence 12 (melody)
  Gr. 3, 421
Reading Sequence 13 (rhythm)
  Gr. 3, 422
Reading Sequence 14 (rhythm)
  Gr. 3, 422
Reading Sequence 15 (melody)
  Gr. 3, 423
Reading Sequence 16 (melody)
  Gr. 3, 423
Reading Sequence 17 (rhythm)
  Gr. 3, 424
Reading Sequence 18 (rhythm)
  Gr. 3, 424
Reading Sequence 19 (melody)
  Gr. 3, 425
Reading Sequence 20 (melody)
  Gr. 3, 425
Reading Sequence 21 (rhythm)
  Gr. 3, 426
Reading Sequence 22 (rhythm)
  Gr. 3, 426
Reading Sequence 23 (melody)
  Gr. 3, 427
Reading Sequence 24 (melody)
  Gr. 3, 427

### GRADE 4

Reading Sequence 1 (rhythm)
  Gr. 4, 442
Reading Sequence 2 (rhythm)
  Gr. 4, 442
Reading Sequence 3 (melody)
  Gr. 4, 443
Reading Sequence 4 (melody)
  Gr. 4, 443
Reading Sequence 5 (rhythm)
  Gr. 4, 444

Reading Sequence 6 (rhythm)
Gr. 4, 444
Reading Sequence 7 (melody)
Gr. 4, 445
Reading Sequence 8 (melody)
Gr. 4, 445
Reading Sequence 9 (rhythm)
Gr. 4, 446
Reading Sequence 10 (rhythm)
Gr. 4, 446
Reading Sequence 11 (melody)
Gr. 4, 447
Reading Sequence 12 (melody)
Gr. 4, 447
Reading Sequence 13 (rhythm)
Gr. 4, 448
Reading Sequence 14 (rhythm)
Gr. 4, 448
Reading Sequence 15 (melody)
Gr. 4, 449
Reading Sequence 16 (melody)
Gr. 4, 449
Reading Sequence 17 (rhythm)
Gr. 4, 450
Reading Sequence 18 (rhythm)
Gr. 4, 450
Reading Sequence 19 (melody)
Gr. 4, 451
Reading Sequence 20 (melody)
Gr. 4, 451
Reading Sequence 21 (rhythm)
Gr. 4, 452
Reading Sequence 22 (rhythm)
Gr. 4, 452
Reading Sequence 23 (melody)
Gr. 4, 453
Reading Sequence 24 (melody)
Gr. 4, 453

## GRADE 5

Reading Sequence 1 (rhythm)
Gr. 5, 490
Reading Sequence 2 (rhythm)
Gr. 5, 490
Reading Sequence 3 (melody)
Gr. 5, 491
Reading Sequence 4 (melody)
Gr. 5, 491
Reading Sequence 5 (rhythm)
Gr. 5, 492
Reading Sequence 6 (rhythm)
Gr. 5, 492
Reading Sequence 7 (melody)
Gr. 5, 493
Reading Sequence 8 (melody)
Gr. 5, 493
Reading Sequence 9 (rhythm)
Gr. 5, 494
Reading Sequence 10 (rhythm)
Gr. 5, 494
Reading Sequence 11 (melody)
Gr. 5, 495
Reading Sequence 12 (melody)
Gr. 5, 495
Reading Sequence 13 (rhythm)
Gr. 5, 496

Reading Sequence 14 (rhythm)
Gr. 5, 496
Reading Sequence 15 (melody)
Gr. 5, 497
Reading Sequence 16 (melody)
Gr. 5, 497
Reading Sequence 17 (rhythm)
Gr. 5, 498
Reading Sequence 18 (rhythm)
Gr. 5, 498
Reading Sequence 19 (melody)
Gr. 5, 499
Reading Sequence 20 (melody)
Gr. 5, 499
Reading Sequence 21 (rhythm)
Gr. 5, 500
Reading Sequence 22 (rhythm)
Gr. 5, 500
Reading Sequence 23 (melody)
Gr. 5, 501
Reading Sequence 24 (melody)
Gr. 5, 501

## GRADE 6

Reading Sequence 1 (rhythm)
Gr. 6, 488
Reading Sequence 2 (rhythm)
Gr. 6, 488
Reading Sequence 3 (melody)
Gr. 6, 489
Reading Sequence 4 (melody)
Gr. 6, 489
Reading Sequence 5 (rhythm)
Gr. 6, 490
Reading Sequence 6 (rhythm)
Gr. 6, 490
Reading Sequence 7 (melody)
Gr. 6, 491
Reading Sequence 8 (melody)
Gr. 6, 491
Reading Sequence 9 (rhythm)
Gr. 6, 492
Reading Sequence 10 (rhythm)
Gr. 6, 492
Reading Sequence 11 (melody)
Gr. 6, 493
Reading Sequence 12 (melody)
Gr. 6, 493
Reading Sequence 13 (rhythm)
Gr. 6, 494
Reading Sequence 14 (rhythm)
Gr. 6, 494
Reading Sequence 15 (melody)
Gr. 6, 495
Reading Sequence 16 (melody)
Gr. 6, 495
Reading Sequence 17 (rhythm)
Gr. 6, 496
Reading Sequence 18 (rhythm)
Gr. 6, 496
Reading Sequence 19 (melody)
Gr. 6, 497
Reading Sequence 20 (melody)
Gr. 6, 497
Reading Sequence 21 (rhythm)
Gr. 6, 498

Reading Sequence 22 (rhythm)
Gr. 6, 498
Reading Sequence 23 (melody)
Gr. 6, 499
Reading Sequence 24 (melody)
Gr. 6, 499

## MUSIC THEORY AND FUNDAMENTALS

### GRADE 7

1st and 2nd Endings  Gr. 7, H-5
Anacrusis  Gr. 7, H-12
Basics of Melody  Gr. 7, H-6
Chords in F  Gr. 7, H-26
Composing with Sixteenth Notes
Gr. 7, H-19
Conducting in 2/4  Gr. 7, H-12
Conducting Meter  Gr. 7, H-10
A Different Minor Scale  Gr. 7, H-29
Dotted Quarter Note  Gr. 7, H-13
Dotted Rhythms with Sixteenth Notes
Gr. 7, H-20
Dynamics  Gr. 7, H-10
Eighth and Sixteenth Combinations
Gr. 7, H-18
Eighth Rests  Gr. 7, H-11
Five Notes in Two Places  Gr. 7, H-9
Going Up: High *do* and *ti*  Gr. 7, H-16
How Low Can You Go?  Gr. 7, H-16
Intervals - Seconds and Thirds
Gr. 7, H-24
Key Signature Check  Gr. 7, H-17
Longer Sounds, Longer Rests
Gr. 7, H-2
Low *la-la*1  Gr. 7, H-15
Low *ti-ti*1  Gr. 7, H-15
A Major Formula  Gr. 7, H-22
Major Scales with Flats  Gr. 7, H-23
Melodic Sequence  Gr. 7, H-24
Melody Review  Gr. 7, H-8
Meter and Measure  Gr. 7, H-4
*mi-re-do*  Gr. 7, H-6
Minor Chords  Gr. 7, H-28
The Minor iv Chord  Gr. 7, H-29
Minor Scales  Gr. 7, H-28
More Composing with Sixteenth Notes
Gr. 7, H-21
More Intervals - Fourths, Fifths, Sixths,
and Sevenths  Gr. 7, H-25
More Melody: *fa*  Gr. 7, H-7
More Meter and Rhythm  Gr. 7, H-4
Move It: Sixteenth Notes  Gr. 7, H-18
Moving Up to *la*  Gr. 7, H-14
Reading Chord Symbols  Gr. 7, H-27
Repeat Signs  Gr. 7, H-5
Reverse the Rhythm  Gr. 7, H-20
Rhythm Basics  Gr. 7, H-2
Scales: They're Major!  Gr. 7, H-22
The Slur  Gr. 7, H-14
Step Up to *so*  Gr. 7, H-8
Syncopation  Gr. 7, H-3
Three Major Chords  Gr. 7, H-26
Ties and More Ties  Gr. 7, H-11

(*Music Theory and Fundamentals,* continued)

What Makes A Chord Major? Gr. 7, H-27
When do is F Gr. 7, H-9

## GRADE 8

Accidentals Gr. 8, H-24
And Now for the Rest Gr. 8, H-4
Conducting the Beat Gr. 8, H-3
Dot the Eighth Note Gr. 8, H-18
Dotted-Half Note and Whole Note Gr. 8, H-4
Dotted-Quarter Notes and Anacrusis Gr. 8, H-11
Dotted-Quarter and Eighth Note– Backwards! Gr. 8, H-11
Dotted Rhythm and Syncopation Practice Gr. 8, H-12
Dynamics Gr. 8, H-5
Eighth Rest Gr. 8, H-10
*fa* with 1st and 2nd Endings Gr. 8, H-7
Get Down to Low *la* Gr. 8, H-12
Get Down to Low *so* Gr. 8, H-13
Going Up: la Gr. 8, H-8
Harmonic Minor Gr. 8, H-24
Intervals: 3rd, 4th, 5th Gr. 8, H-8
Key of D Major Gr. 8, H-20
Key of F Major Gr. 8, H-20
The Key of G Major Gr. 8, H-19
Major Chords Gr. 8, H-25
Major Review Gr. 8, H-19
The Major Scale Gr. 8, H-17
Melody by Ear Gr. 8, H-5
Meter in Three Plus Repeats Gr. 8, H-3
Meters, Measures, and More Gr. 8, H-2
*mi-re-do* Gr. 8, H-6
Minor Keys Gr. 8, H-22
Minor Practice Plus Gr. 8, H-27
More Minor Seconds Gr. 8, H-15
Move up to so Gr. 8, H-8
One Eighth and Two Sixteenth Notes Gr. 8, H-18
Pitch Notation Fundamentals Gr. 8, H-6
Practice Plus Gr. 8, H-15
Read the Signs Gr. 8, H-9
Reading Chord Symbols Gr. 8, H-26
Rhythm Fundamentals Gr. 8, H-2
Scale Degrees Gr. 8, H-23
Second or Third? Gr. 8, H-7
Sight Reading Practice Gr. 8, H-14
Sixteenth Notes in the Rhythm Gr. 8, H-17
Subdominant in Minor Gr. 8, H-29
Syncopation Gr. 8, H-10
*ti* on the Move Gr. 8, H-16
*ti*$_1$ Time Gr. 8, H-14
Tie Two to Get a Half Gr. 8, H-3
Tonic and Dominant Chords in Minor Gr. 8, H-28
The Top do Gr. 8, H-16

Transposing Practice Gr. 8, H-9
Two More Keys with Flats: B♭ and E♭ Major Gr. 8, H-22
Two More Keys with Sharps: A Major and E Major Gr. 8, H-21
V or V$_7$ Gr. 8, H-25

## N

## NON-ENGLISH LANGUAGE SELECTIONS *See also Pronunciation Practice, Recorded.*

### AKAN
Bantama kra kro Gr. 5, 308

### ANGOLAN
O, Desayo Gr. 5, 411

### ARABIC
Ah ya Zane Gr. 5, 297
Ala Da'lona Gr. 4, 136
Tzena, tzena Gr. 5, 298

### ARMENIAN
Gakavik Gr. 4, 14

### BA-BENZELE
*Hindewhu (whistle) solo* Gr. 6, 269

### BAMBARA
Ye jaliya da Gr. 5, 67

### BANTU
Abiyoyo Gr. 2, 108
T'hola, t'hola Gr. 4, 132
Thula, thula, ngoana Gr. 4, 227

### CAJUN FRENCH
*Allons danser, Colinda* Gr. K, 218
*Bon jour!* Gr. 1, 3
Deux cocodries Gr. 2, 364
Fais do do Gr. 6, 403
*Je m'endors* Gr. K, 219
*Jolie Blonde* Gr. 4, 389
*L'arc en ciel* Gr. 2, 333
*Le Hoogie Boogie* Gr. K, 296
*P'tit galop pour mamou* Gr. 1, 317
Sugar "Shuga" Bee Gr. K, 64

### CANTONESE
Yü guang guang Gr. 6, 60

### CATALAN
El desembre congelat Gr. 5, 473

### CELTIC
*Dúlamán* Gr. 4, 299

### CHINESE
*Colours of the World* Gr. 6, 271
Lahk gei mohlee Gr. 5, 317
Meng Jian Nu Gr. 5, 194
Yüe liang wan wan Gr. 5, 314

### CHIPPEWA
Chippewa Lullaby Gr. K, 181
Farewell to the Warriors Gr. 4, 284

### DANISH
Der sad to katte Gr. 2, 300

### DUTCH
Geef jij mij die schoen Gr. 1, 126

### EWE
Ayelivi Gr. 2, 70

### FANTE
Sansaw akroma Gr. 3, 286

### FARSI
Mubärak Gr. 3, 282

### FRENCH
Ah! Les jolis papillons Gr. 1, 362
Au clair de la lune Gr. 3, 18
Bonjour, mes amis Gr. 1, 316
Éliza Kongo Gr. 5, 14
Fais dodo Gr. K, 158
Frère Jacques Gr. 2, 125
Les petites marionettes Gr. K, 237
Merry Modal Christmas, A Gr. 4, 411
Mon papa Gr. 2, 280
Un, deux, trois Gr. 2, 198
Vil du? Gr. 1, 92

### FULANI
Nu wahtan Gr. 1, 279

### GA
Kelo aba w'ye Gr. 6, 290
*Kpanlogo for 2* Gr. 6, 296

### GAELIC
Einini Gr. 4, 391

### GERMAN
Alle meine Entchen Gr. 1, 98
Ein Männlein steht im Walde Gr. 2, 90
*Hänsel und Gretel, "Ein Männlein steht im Walde"* Gr. 2, 91
Himmel und Erde Gr. 5, 94
O Laufet, ihr Hirten Gr. 2, 384
Ode to Joy Gr. 4, 152
Still, Still, Still Gr. 5, 468

### GREEK
Perná, perná, i mélissá Gr. K, 264

### GUJURATI
*Dham dhamak dham samelu* Gr. 6, 305

### HAITIAN CREOLE
Deau-deau, ti pitit maman Gr. 2, 306

### HAWAIIAN
Kapulu kane Gr. 2, 270
Nani wale na hala Gr. 3, 260
'Ūlili E Gr. 5, 441

### HEBREW
Achshav Gr. 2, 64
Alumot Gr. 6, 306
Artsa alinu Gr. 3, 285

Ayliluli, num tsipor  Gr. 1, 204
Bereleh  Gr. K, 151
Chag Purim  Gr. 1, 438
Chanukah, Chanukah  Gr. 1, 420
Chanukiyah li yesh  Gr. 1, 421
Dayenu  Gr. 4, 439
Dundai  Gr. 5, 106
Hashkediya  Gr. 3, 206
Hava nagila  Gr. 6, 153
Hava nashira  Gr. 6, 82
Hevenu shalom aleichem
     Gr. 3, 378
Hine mah tov  Gr. 5, 430
Kum bachur atzel  Gr. 3, 138
Lo yisa  Gr. 6, 130
Ner li  Gr. 2, 383
Perot  Gr. 2, 378
S'vivon  Gr. 6, 452
Sh'ney dubim  Gr. K, 268
Shalom aleichem  Gr. 6, 409
Shir l'shalom  Gr. 4, 419
Tzena, tzena  Gr. 5, 298
Uga uga uga  Gr. K, 305
*Ve'David Y'Fey Enayiam*
     Gr. 4, 317
Yesh lanu taish  Gr. 1, 182
Yibane amenu  Gr. 4, 316
Zum gali gali  Gr. 5, 401

### HINDI
Ragupati Ragava Raja Ram
     Gr. 5, 321
Shri Ram, jai Ram  Gr. 4, 311

### HMONG
*Nruab hnub thiab hmo ntuj*
     Gr. 4, 366

### HUNGARIAN
Cirmos cica  Gr. 1, 130
Ég a gyertya  Gr. K, 96
Erdö, erdö de magos  Gr. 3, 182

### ITALIAN
Don Giovanni  Gr. 8,
Eh, cumpari!  Gr. 4, 68
*Il trovatore, "Anvil Chorus"*
     Gr. 6, 25
L'inverno è passato  Gr. 2, 400

### JAPANESE
Amefuri  Gr. 1, 144
Asadoya  Gr. 6, 303
Hama chi dori  Gr. 3, 330
Haru ga kita  Gr. 2, 401
Hato popo  Gr. 1, 186
Hitotsu toya  Gr. 5, 478
Hotaru koi  Gr. 1, 356
Ichi-gatsu tsuitachi  Gr. 3, 406
Jan ken pon  Gr. 3, 302
Kaeru no uta  Gr. K, 183
Kuma san  Gr. K, 40
O ma washi  Gr. K, 13
Ōsamu kosamu  Gr. 4, 96
Rinsho, rinsho  Gr. K, 285
Sakura  Gr. 4, 308

Tanabata-sama  Gr. 2, 336
Tsuki  Gr. 4, 25
Usagi  Gr. 1, 396

### KHMER
Leak kanseng  Gr. 1, 156
Sarika keo  Gr. 3, 275

### KIKUYU
Kou ri lengay  Gr. 2, 217

### KOREAN
Arirang  Gr. 5, 25
Doong gul ge  Gr. 3, 134
*Doraji*  Gr. 4, 175
Doraji  Gr. 4, 174
Ha'kyo jong  Gr. 2, 135
Sailboat in the Sky  Gr. 4, 374

### LADINO
Hanuka, Hanuka  Gr. 3, 390
Ocho kandelikas  Gr. 4, 429

### LAKOTA
Inkpataya  Gr. 3, 254

### LATIN
Da pacem, Domine  Gr. 5, 62
Dona nobis pacem  Gr. 6, 125
Ego sum pauper  Gr. 5, 158
Gloria, Gloria  Gr. 6, 459
*Gloria In Excelsis*  Gr. 6, 210
Kyrie  Gr. 6, 206
*Requiem, "Pie Jesu"*  Gr. 6, 178

### LIBERIAN
Banuwa  Gr. 6, 294
Kokoleoko  Gr. 5, 33

### MANDARIN
Cha yang wu  Gr. 1, 90
Diou shou juan'er  Gr. 2, 277
Ee jer ha ba go  Gr. K, 133
Feng yang hua gu  Gr. 4, 313
Hui jia qü  Gr. 2, 158
Hwa yuan li-de young wa wa
     Gr. 3, 102
Niu lang zhi nü  Gr. 4, 335
Pai pi qiu  Gr. 1, 324
Xiao  Gr. 4, 314
Xiao yin chuan  Gr. 2, 14
Yang wa wa  Gr. K, 162

### MAORI
Haere  Gr. 2, 285
Karangatia ra  Gr. 3, 272
*Piki mai*  Gr. 1, 79
To'ia mai te waka  Gr. 1, 77

### MICMAC
Kwa-nu-te  Gr. 3, 214

### NAVAJO
*Dinéh Round Dance*  Gr. 6, 186
I Walk in Beauty  Gr. 4, 282
*Rain Song, The*  Gr. 2, 323
Yo-shi nai  Gr. 6, 286

### ONEIDA
Kunolounkwa  Gr. K, 110
*Kunolounkwa, "Contemporary"*
     Gr. K, 110

### PIMA (AKIMEL O'ODHAM)
Chuhwuht  Gr. 2, 356

### POLISH
Greetings (speech piece)  Gr. 3, 316
Nie chcę cię znác  Gr. 3, 314

### PORTUGUESE
Ah, eu entrei na roda  Gr. 3, 308
*Chica chica boom chic*  Gr. 2, 112
Ciranda  Gr. 2, 272
Kibungo  Gr. 2, 354
O lê lê O Bahía  Gr. 6, 165
O pião entrou  Gr. 2, 355
Sambalele  Gr. 4, 397
Serra, serra, serrador  Gr. 1, 112
*Uma história de Ifá*  Gr. 6, 362

### RUSSIAN
Ai, Dunaii moy  Gr. 4, 293
*Bai, bai, bai, bai*  Gr. 2, 197
Beriozka  Gr. 4, 294
Pust' 'vsegda budet sonse
     Gr. 3, 278

### SETSWANA
Hey, m'tswala  Gr. 4, 79

### SHONA
Chawe chidyo chem'chero
     Gr. 2, 296
Sorida  Gr. 1, 312
Wai bamba  Gr. 6, 26

### SIOUX
Hosisipa  Gr. 3, 70

### SLOVAK
Tancovačka  Gr. 4, 230
Hej pada pada  Gr. 3, 78

### SPANISH
A la puerta del cielo  Gr. 5, 60
A la rurru niño  Gr. K, 180
Adelita  Gr. 5, 50
Adiós, amigos  Gr. 6, 57
Aguinaldo  Gr. 3, 402
Ahora voy a cantarles  Gr. 3, 56
Al citrón  Gr. 3, 320
Al quebrar la piñata  Gr. 4, 432
Al tambor  Gr. 3, 270
Allá en la fuente  Gr. 2, 92
Ambos a dos  Gr. 3, 20
Así es mi tierra  Gr. 6, 172
*Ayer, "Yesterday"*  Gr. 6, 266
Bogando a la luz del sol  Gr. 4, 306
Canción de cuna  Gr. 4, 144
Canción Mixteca  Gr. 5, 326
Cantando mentiras  Gr. 4, 146
Cantaré, cantarás  Gr. 6, 413
Cheki, morena  Gr. 2, 180
Chiapanecas  Gr. 5, 92

**(Non-English Lanugage Selections, continued)**

(Chi Chi Chi) Cha Cha Cha Gr. 6, 334
Cielito lindo Gr. 4, 270
Corrido de Kansas Gr. 4, 274
Corta la caña Gr. 6, 364
Counting Song Gr. 1, 253
Cuando pa' Chile me voy Gr. 6, 376
De colores Gr. 5, 90
Debajo el botón Gr. 1, 210
Don Alfonso Gr. 5, 177
Don Gato Gr. 3, 352
¿Dónde lo escondí? Gr. K, 209
Duérmete, mi niño Gr. 1, 292
El barquito Gr. 3, 358
El burrito enfermo Gr. K, 271
El caracol Gr. K, 130
El carite Gr. 5, 305
El carnavalito humahuaqueño Gr. 6, 482
El cóndor pasa Gr. 6, 46
El coquí Gr. 2, 292
El día de mamita Gr. K, 325
El florón Gr. 2, 246
El gallo pinto Gr. 3, 86
El juego chirimbolo Gr. 2, 54
El mariachi Gr. 4, 303
El mes de abril Gr. 3, 328
El payo Gr. 6, 145
El rabel Gr. 3, 362
El rancho grande Gr. 4, 215
El sapito Gr. 3, 336
En nuestra Tierra tan linda Gr. 2, 335
Eres tú Gr. 6, 473
Feliz Navidad Gr. 4, 433
Gato Gr. 1, 131
Habemos llegado Gr. 6, 174
Imbabura Gr. 5, 203
¡Jeu! ¡Jeu! Gr. 1, 216
Juan pirulero Gr. K, 215
Juanito Gr. K, 300
La bamba Gr. 5, 128
La calle ancha Gr. 3, 297
La ciudad de Juaja Gr. 5, 58
La copa de la vida Gr. 4, 414
La Jesusita Gr. 5, 322
La mariposa Gr. 6, 58
La paloma blanca Gr. 3, 252
La paloma se fué Gr. 6, 51
La piñata Gr. 3, 399
La pulga de San José Gr. 3, 40
La raspa Gr. 4, 302
La Tarara Gr. 4, 176
La tormenta tropical Gr. 2, 116
La víbora Gr. 1, 322
Laredo Gr. 5, 10
Las estrellas Gr. 1, 109
Las estrellitas del cielo Gr. 5, 175
Las mañanitas Gr. 6, 481
Las mañanitas Gr. K, 325
Las Navidades Gr. 5, 472

Las velitas Gr. 5, 147
Llactamanta Gr. 6, 382
Lluvia Gr. 6, 332
Los días de la semana Gr. 1, 268
Los maizales Gr. 1, 296
Los niños en España cantan Gr. 4, 197
Los pececitos Gr. 1, 178
Los pescaditos Gr. 1, 69
Los pollitos Gr. K, 166
Los pollitos Gr. K, 166
Los reyes de Oriente Gr. 5, 480
Los trencitos Gr. K, 24
Luna lunera (speech piece) Gr. K, 90
Má Teodora Gr. 6, 301
Magnolia Gr. 6, 16
Mariposita Gr. 2, 156
Me voy para la luna Gr. 1, 397
Mi cuerpo hace música Gr. K, 106
Mi tierra Gr. 6, 365
Naranja dulce Gr. 2, 97
Niño querido Gr. 1, 308
No quiero plata Gr. 1, 424
Oye Gr. 6, 336
Oye mi canto, Gr. 6, 114
Pavo, pavo Gr. 1, 416
Pin Pon Gr. 1, 146
Piñon, pirulín Gr. 2, 174
Pollerita Gr. 5, 151
Pon, pon, pon Gr. K, 50
¡Qué bonita bandera! Gr. 5, 294
¡Qué gusto! Gr. 3, 132
¡Qué llueva! Gr. K, 81
Riendo el río corre Gr. 6, 263
Río, río Gr. 5, 370
Riqui rán Gr. 1, 48
Riqui rán Gr. 4, 66
Ríu ríu chíu Gr. 5, 435
Se va el caimán Gr. 5, 306
Si me dan pasteles Gr. 1, 432
Si me pongo yo a cantar Gr. 3, 133
Si tú no estás Gr. 6, 267
Sierra Morena Gr. 3, 296
Sol, solecito Gr. 1, 367
Somos el barco Gr. 4, 352
Sonando Gr. 4, 34
Tengo, tengo, tengo Gr. 4, 228
Tic, tac Gr. 1, 252
Un elefante Gr. 2, 160
Un pajarito Gr. 2, 16
Uno, dos y tres Gr. 5, 429
Vamos a cantar Gr. K, 278
Vamos a hacer la ronda Gr. K, 124
Vamos a la fiesta Gr. 2, 374
Vamos a la mar Gr. 3, 226
¡Viva el fútbol! Gr. 1, 96
Viva Jujuy Gr. 5, 228
Zumba, zumba Gr. 3, 400

**SWEDISH**
Vem kan segla? Gr. 6, 417

**SZECHUAN**
Shu ha mo Gr. 3, 276

**TAGALOG**
Santa Clara Gr. 4, 172

**TAHITIAN**
Tamaiti hunahia Gr. 6, 24

**THAI**
Chang Gr. 1, 156
Loigratong Gr. 6, 451
Mon son pha (speech piece) Gr. K, 91
Sawatdee tuh jah Gr. 2, 265

**TIBETAN**
Kui.Kyon.pan Gr. 6, 25

**TIGRINYA**
Hashewie Gr. 4, 63

**TURKISH**
Adana ya gidelim Gr. 2, 142
Ali Pasha Gr. 5, 218

**TWI**
Kébé Mama Gr. 1, 442

**UKRAINIAN**
Minka Gr. 4, 222
Ptashky u babusi sadochku Gr. 1, 192

**VIETNAMESE**
Bắt kim thang Gr. 6, 13
Cho'i hát bội Gr. 5, 318
Quâ câù gió bay Gr. 5, 460

**VOCABLES**
A Ram Sam Sam Gr. 3, 208
Che che koolay Gr. 2, 266
Duck Dance Gr. 2, 249
Grass Game Gr. 1, 371
Green Corn Song Gr. 5, 462
Haliwa-Saponi Canoe Song Gr. 5, 302
Haliwa-Saponi Canoe Song Gr. 5, 303
Jo'ashila Gr. 5, 108
O hal'lwe Gr. 3, 256
Pottery Dance Gr. 1, 370
Raccoon Dance Song Gr. 1, 260
Sikelela Gr. 1, 139
Song of the Eagle Gr. 2, 248
Zuni Sunrise Call Gr. 5, 396

**WELSH**
All Through the Night Gr. 5, 104

**WICHITA**
Wichita Hand Game Song 1 Gr. 3, 306
Wichita Hand Game Song 2 Gr. 3, 306

**YEMENITE-JEWISH**
Galbi Gr. 1, 183

**YIDDISH**
Oy, Hanuka Gr. 5, 464

**Y**ORUBA
Ise oluwa  Gr. 2, 102
Ise oluwa  Gr. 6, 230
*Omo*  Gr. 1, 443

**Z**IMBABWE
*Chigamba*  Gr. 6, 27

**Z**ULU
Nampaya omame  Gr. 1, 138
Siyahamba  Gr. 6, 212
Tina singu  Gr. 4, 300

## NOTATING *See also Skills Reinforcement.*

*America*  Gr. 7, A-22
Bam, chi, chi, bam  Gr. K, 109
Chang  Gr. 1, 155
Clap, Wiggle, and Stomp  Gr. K, 34
Corn Grinding Song  Gr. K, 67
Down the Listening Lane  Gr. K, 192
El chocolate  Gr. 1, 378
Hickory, Dickory, Dare (speech piece)
      Gr. K, 20
Lions  Gr. 1, 238
Little Darlin'  Gr. 7, F-30
Little Miss Muffet (speech piece)
      Gr. K, 92
Locomoto-vation  Gr. K, 60
Mary Wore Her Red Dress  Gr. K, 74
New Way to Walk, A  Gr. K, 117
*Omo*  Gr. 1, 443
To'ia mai te waka  Gr. 1, 77
Today Is Your Birthday  Gr. 1, 408
Ujima  Gr. 1, 430
Vamos a hacer la ronda  Gr. K, 124
Voice Choice  Gr. K, 27

## ORFF ACCOMPANIMENTS

Adana ya gidelim  Gr. 2, 142
Ah ya Zane  Gr. 5, 297
Alabama Gal  Gr. 3, 106
All Night, All Day  Gr. 4, 180
Ama-Lama  Gr. 5, 144
Amefuri  Gr. 1, 144
Andy Pandy  Gr. K, 46
Apple Tree  Gr. 1, 228
Asadoya  Gr. 6, 303
Ayelivi  Gr. 2, 70
Bam, chi, chi, bam  Gr. K, 109
Barb'ry Allen  Gr. 6, 44
Bard of Armagh, The  Gr. 4, 296
Beriozka  Gr. 4, 294
Bob-a-Needle  Gr. 2, 232
Bury Me Not on the Lone Prairie
      Gr. 6, 19
Busy Buzzy Bee  Gr. K, 77
Camptown Races  Gr. 5, 270
Charlie over the Water  Gr. 1, 68
Che che koolay  Gr. 2, 266
Cindy  Gr. 4, 384
Circle Round the Zero  Gr. K, 293

Cirmos cica  Gr. 1, 130
Clementine  Gr. 4, 341
Clouds of Gray  Gr. 2, 56
Connemara Lullaby  Gr. 5, 234
Cuckoo, Cuckoo  Gr. 1, 110
Dayenu  Gr. 4, 439
Don Alfonso  Gr. 5, 177
Don't Let the Wind  Gr. 3, 180
Don't Let Your Watch Run Down
      Gr. 3, 166
Down by the Riverside  Gr. 5, 256
Dundai  Gr. 5, 106
El carnavalito humahuaqueño
      Gr. 6, 482
El cóndor pasa  Gr. 6, 46
El mes de abril  Gr. 3, 328
El payo  Gr. 6, 145
Erdö, erdö de magos  Gr. 3, 182
Every Morning When I Wake Up
      Gr. 2, 320
Everybody Loves Saturday Night
      Gr. 6, 296
Ezekiel Saw the Wheel  Gr. 6, 379
Farewell to Tarwathie  Gr. 6, 43
Farmer's Dairy Key, The  Gr. 2, 182
Feng yang hua gu  Gr. 4, 313
Frère Jacques  Gr. 2, 125
Frog in the Millpond  Gr. 2, 44
Get on Board  Gr. K, 89
Go Around the Corn, Sally  Gr. 2, 13
Hashkediya  Gr. 3, 206
Here I Go!  Gr. K, 73
Hey, Hey, Look at Me  Gr. 1, 70
Hey, Ho! Nobody Home  Gr. 6, 28
Hi-Dee-Roon  Gr. K, 10
Hop Up, My Ladies  Gr. 3, 142
Hush, Hush  Gr. 3, 162
I Don't Care If the Rain Comes Down
      Gr. 3, 24
I'm Tall, I'm Small  Gr. K, 18
It's Santa—Again!  Gr. 2, 385
Jelly in a Dish (speech piece)  Gr. 2, 83
Jim Along, Josie  Gr. K, 39
Johnny Caught a Flea  Gr. 1, 226
Kangaroo Song, The  Gr. K, 44
Kookaburra  Gr. 4, 186
La Jesusita  Gr. 5, 322
La paloma se fué  Gr. 6, 51
Las estrellitas del cielo  Gr. 5, 175
Leatherwing Bat  Gr. 2, 303
Lemonade  Gr. 1, 190
Li'l Liza Jane  Gr. 3, 140
Little Spider  Gr. K, 93
Lo yisa  Gr. 6, 130
Locomoto-vation  Gr. K, 61
Lone Star Trail  Gr. 2, 21
Lost My Gold Ring  Gr. 6, 158
Love Somebody  Gr. 3, 94
Lucy Locket  Gr. 2, 27
Mary Wore Her Red Dress  Gr. K, 74
Miss Mary Mack  Gr. 2, 42
Missy-La, Massa-La  Gr. 4, 188

Mister Snow Rap (speech piece)
      Gr. 2, 391
Morning Comes Early  Gr. 5, 13
My Mama's Calling Me  Gr. 1, 260
Now Let Me Fly  Gr. 3, 178
Oh, Won't You Sit Down  Gr. 3, 28
Old Blue  Gr. K, 122
Old Man Mosie  Gr. 3, 108
Oliver Twist  Gr. K, 138
On a Log, Mister Frog  Gr. K, 148
One Morning in May  Gr. 6, 121
Paths of Victory  Gr. 6, 195
Peace Round  Gr. 4, 348
Pretty Saro  Gr. 3, 216
Pumpkin, Pumpkin  Gr. 1, 413
Roll On, Columbia  Gr. 5, 116
Roll Over  Gr. K, 288
*Rundadinella*  Gr. 8, I-60
Sakura  Gr. 4, 308
Same Train  Gr. 2, 164
Se va el caimán  Gr. 5, 306
Seasons  Gr. K, 4
See the Children Playin'  Gr. 4, 107
See-Saw Sacradown  Gr. 2, 208
Serra, serra, serrador  Gr. 1, 112
Shake Them 'Simmons Down
      Gr. 2, 244
Shenandoah  Gr. 5, 264
Siyahamba  Gr. 6, 212
Skin and Bones  Gr. 2, 376
Sleep, Baby, Sleep  Gr. 2, 197
Snail, Snail  Gr. 1, 190
Soldier, Soldier  Gr. 4, 11
Somebody's Knockin' at Your Door
      Gr. 4, 53
Song of the Eagle  Gr. 2, 248
St. Louis Blues  Gr. 5, 352
Star Light, Star Bright  Gr. 1, 108
Storm Dance (speech piece)  Gr. K, 145
Take Time in Life  Gr. 6, 292
Thanksgiving Is Near  Gr. 2, 380
This Land Is Your Land (refrain only)
      Gr. 1, 274
Tina singu  Gr. 4, 300
Tom Dooley  Gr. 6, 374
Turn the Glasses Over  Gr. 3, 204
Two Little Sausages (speech piece)
      Gr. 2, 79
Wabash Cannon Ball  Gr. 5, 136
Water Come a Me Eye  Gr. 6, 300
Water Is Wide, The  Gr. 6, 228
Weevily Wheat  Gr. 4, 105
Who Has the Penny?  Gr. K, 42
Willowbee  Gr. 1, 222
Wind Up the Apple Tree  Gr. 1, 184
Wings of a Dove  Gr. 4, 318
Woke Up This Morning  Gr. 5, 288
Worried Man Blues  Gr. 6, 371
Yibane amenu  Gr. 4, 316
You Are My Sunshine  Gr. 6, 246

**P**

# PENTATONIC SONGS

Ah! Les jolis papillons  Gr. 1, 362
Ain't Gonna Let Nobody Turn Me 'Round  Gr. 6, 85
Al citrón  Gr. 3, 320
Alabama Gal  Gr. 3, 106
All Around the Buttercup  Gr. 2, 170
Amarillo Armadillo  Gr. 2, 82
Amasee  Gr. 1, 172
Amazing Grace  Gr. 4, 160
Amefuri  Gr. 1, 144
Andy Pandy  Gr. K, 46
Apple Tree  Gr. 1, 228
Arirang  Gr. 5, 25
Asadoya  Gr. 6, 303
*Badenma*  Gr. 8, B-28
Bam, chi, chi, bam  Gr. K, 109
Banana Splits  Gr. 1, 318
Bắt kim thang  Gr. 6, 13
Big Old Storm a-Comin'  Gr. K, 257
Black Snake  Gr. 3, 53
Bluebonnets of Texas  Gr. 3, 332
Bob-a-Needle  Gr. 2, 232
Bounce High, Bounce Low  Gr. 1, 152
Bound for South Australia  Gr. 5, 22
Brush Your Teeth  Gr. 1, 284
Bury Me Not on the Lone Prairie  Gr. 6, 19
Canoe Song  Gr. 4, 76
Chang  Gr. 1, 156
Charlie over the Water  Gr. 1, 68
Chicka Hanka  Gr. 2, 211
Chicken on the Fence Post  Gr. 3, 92
Chippewa Lullaby  Gr. K, 181
Circle Round the Zero  Gr. K, 293
Clouds of Gray  Gr. 2, 56
Colorado Trail  Gr. 5, 276
Come and Go with Me to That Land  Gr. 5, 390
Cookie  Gr. 2, 172
Corn Grinding Song  Gr. K, 67
Cuckoo, Cuckoo  Gr. 1, 110
Cuculí  Gr. K, 238
Ding, Dong, Diggidiggidong  Gr. 3, 14
Dinner Music  Gr. K, 70
Diou shou juan'er  Gr. 2, 277
Dok djampa  Gr. 8, I-20
Don't Let the Wind  Gr. 3, 180
Don't Let Your Watch Run Down  Gr. 3, 166
Doraji  Gr. 4, 174
Down in the Meadow  Gr. K, 147
Draw Me a Bucket of Water  Gr. 3, 124
Dry Bones Come Skipping  Gr. 4, 218
Einini  Gr. 4, 391
El burrito enfermo  Gr. K, 271
Erdö, erdö de magos  Gr. 3, 182
Every Morning When I Wake Up  Gr. 2, 320

Farewell to Tarwathie  Gr. 6, 43
Farmer in the Dell, The  Gr. K, 232
Farmer's Dairy Key, The  Gr. 2, 182
Feng yang hua gu  Gr. 4, 313
Five Little Snowmen  Gr. K, 313
Get on Board  Gr. K, 89
Glory, Glory, Hallelujah  Gr. 6, 52
Go Around the Corn, Sally  Gr. 2, 12
Go, My Son  Gr. 6, 188
Goin' to the Fair  Gr. K, 156
Going on a Picnic  Gr. K, 190
Gonna Ride Up in the Chariot  Gr. 4, 20
Good Morning  Gr. 3, 192
Good Old Happy Song, A  Gr. K, 201
Great Big House  Gr. 2, 204
Great Day  Gr. 3, 58
Green, Green, Rocky  Gr. 1, 321
Ha'kyo jong  Gr. 2, 135
Had to Get Up This Mornin' Soon  Gr. 3, 114
Hama chi dori  Gr. 3, 330
Hambone  Gr. 1, 202
Hashewie  Gr. 4, 63
Hashkediya  Gr. 3, 206
Hato popo  Gr. 1, 186
Here Comes Valerie  Gr. 1, 32
Hey, Hey, Look at Me  Gr. 1, 70
Hey, m'tswala  Gr. 4, 79
Hop Up, My Ladies  Gr. 3, 142
Hosisipa  Gr. 3, 70
Hot Cross Buns (Version 1)  Gr. 3, 218
How Can I Keep from Singing?  Gr. 4, 261
How Many Miles to Babylon?  Gr. 2, 128
Hui jia qü  Gr. 2, 158
Hush, Hush  Gr. 3, 162
Hush Up the Baby  Gr. K, 222
Hwa yuan li-de young wa wa  Gr. 3, 102
I Fed My Horse  Gr. 2, 94
I'm Gonna Sing  Gr. 4, 33
Ida Red  Gr. 3, 30
Inkpataya  Gr. 3, 254
Jasmine Flowers  Gr. 5, 316
Jim Along, Josie  Gr. K, 39
Jinny Go 'Round  Gr. K, 228
John Kanaka  Gr. 3, 60
Johnny Caught a Flea  Gr. 1, 226
Johnny Mister Brown  Gr. K, 37
Juniper Tree, The  Gr. 3, 131
Just from the Kitchen  Gr. K, 55
Keep Your Eyes on the Prize  Gr. 3, 408
Knock the Cymbals  Gr. 1, 176
Kwa-nu-te  Gr. 3, 214
Lahk gei mohlee  Gr. 5, 317
Leatherwing Bat  Gr. 2, 303
Leila  Gr. 1, 258
Lemonade  Gr. 1, 190
Let's Get the Rhythm of the Band  Gr. 3, 84

Li'l Liza Jane  Gr. 3, 140
Little Black Bug  Gr. 1, 214
Little David  Gr. 1, 232
Little Shell  Gr. 1, 355
Little Spider  Gr. K, 93
Locomoto-vation  Gr. K, 61
Loigratong  Gr. 6, 451
Love Will Guide Us  Gr. 4, 328
Mama, Buy Me a Chiney Doll  Gr. K, 120
Mary Came a-Running  Gr. K, 294
Mary Wore Her Red Dress  Gr. K, 74
Miss Mary Mack  Gr. 2, 42
Mister Rabbit  Gr. K, 128
My Dear Companion  Gr. 6, 23
My Mama's Calling Me  Gr. 1, 260
My Pony, Macaroni  Gr. 1, 158
Nana, Thread Needle  Gr. 1, 38
Nanny Goat  Gr. K, 161
New Hungarian Folk Song  Gr. 6, 196
New Way to Walk, A  Gr. K, 117
Now Let Me Fly  Gr. 3, 178
Ochimbo  Gr. 4, 134
Oh, Susanna  Gr. 4, 264
Oh, Watch the Stars  Gr. 2, 144
Oh, Watch the Stars  Gr. 5, 216
Oh, Won't You Sit Down  Gr. 3, 28
Old Brass Wagon  Gr. 2, 122
Old Dan Tucker  Gr. 3, 96
Old House, Tear It Down!  Gr. 4, 178
Oliver Twist  Gr. K, 138
On a Log, Mister Frog  Gr. K, 148
One Morning Soon  Gr. 3, 68
Ōsamu kosamu  Gr. 4, 96
Over My Head  Gr. 4, 118
Pai pi qiu  Gr. 1, 324
Pastures of Plenty  Gr. 4, 280
Paths of Victory  Gr. 6, 195
Peace Like a River  Gr. 3, 246
Pease Porridge Hot  Gr. 1, 134
Perná, perná, i mélissá  Gr. K, 264
Phoebe  Gr. 1, 30
Piñon, pirulín  Gr. 2, 174
Plant Four Seeds  Gr. 2, 130
Pottery Dance  Gr. 1, 370
Pretty Saro  Gr. 3, 216
Pumpkin, Pumpkin  Gr. 1, 413
Put a Little Love in Your Heart  Gr. 4, 6
Rain, Rain  Gr. 1, 54
Rise and Shine  Gr. 4, 98
Rocky Mountain  Gr. 2, 98
Roll Over  Gr. K, 288
Rosie, Darling Rosie  Gr. 2, 215
'Round and 'Round  Gr. 1, 148
Run, Molly, Run  Gr. 1, 8
Sailboat in the Sky  Gr. 4, 374
Same Train  Gr. 2, 164
Sawatdee tuh jah  Gr. 2, 265
See the Children Playin'  Gr. 4, 107
See-Saw Sacradown  Gr. 2, 208
Serra, serra, serrador  Gr. 1, 112
Shake Them 'Simmons Down  Gr. 2, 244

Shoo, Turkey Gr. 1, 104
Shortnin' Bread Gr. 1, 57
Shu ha mo Gr. 3, 276
Sing About Martin Gr. K, 321
Skin and Bones Gr. 2, 376
Skye Boat Song Gr. 6, 372
Sleep, Baby, Sleep Gr. 2, 197
Snail, Snail Gr. 1, 190
Sol, solecito Gr. 1, 367
Soldier, Soldier Gr. 4, 11
Somebody's Knockin' at Your Door
     Gr. 4, 53
Sourwood Mountain Gr. 4, 65
Star Light, Star Bright Gr. 1, 108
Sugar "Shuga" Bee Gr. K, 64
Take Your Feet Out 'the Sand
     Gr. K, 231
Tanabata-sama Gr. 2, 336
Thanksgiving Is Near Gr. 2, 380
This Train Gr. 5, 26
Tideo Gr. 2, 80
Today Is Your Birthday Gr. 1, 410
Tom Dooley Gr. 6, 374
Train Is A-Comin' Gr. 3, 48
Tsuki Gr. 4, 25
Turn the Glasses Over Gr. 3, 204
*Two Dances for Three Xylophones,*
     *"Hornpipe and Jig"* Gr. 8, D-17
Ujima Gr. 1, 430
Vamos a la mar Gr. 3, 226
Wade in the Water Gr. 4, 268
Wade in the Water Gr. 8, I-64
Waiting for the Traffic Light Gr. 2, 107
Wake Me, Shake Me Gr. 1, 278
Walk in Jerusalem Gr. 4, 100
Walk Together, Children Gr. 3, 146
We're All Gonna Shine Tonight
     Gr. 2, 240
Weevily Wheat Gr. 4, 105
When the Train Comes Along
     Gr. 1, 300
Willowbee Gr. 1, 222
Wind Up the Apple Tree Gr. 1, 184
Woodland Chorus Gr. K, 250
Worried Man Blues Gr. 6, 371
Xiao yin chuan Gr. 2, 14
Yang wa wa Gr. K, 162
Yüe liang wan wan Gr. 5, 314

## PERFORMING *See also Skills*
     *Reinforcement.*
Banjo Sam Gr. 2, 314
*DJ Premier in Deep Concentration*
     Gr. 7, B-12
Sing a Song! Gr. 7, A-11

### PERFORMANCE PIECES
*Crunchy, Crunchy, Crunchy*
     Gr. 8, D-15
*Evening Chaconne* Gr. 6, 202
*Nyoka* Gr. 7, D-33
*Orfferondo* Gr. 4, 194
*Sha Sha Sha* Gr. 6, 328

## PLAYING *See also Playing*
     *Instruments.*
*Abbots Bromley Horn Dance*
     Gr. 7, C-24
Bananas and Cream (speech piece)
     Gr. 3, 210
Chicka Hanka Gr. 8, F-14
Coffee Grows on White Oak Trees
     Gr. 3, 168
*Danses Populaires Francaises,*
     *"Branle Double, Branle Simple"*
     Gr. 7, C-25
De colores Gr. 8, I-17
Deep in the Heart of Texas Gr. 8, I-19
Ha'kyo jong Gr. 2, 136
La calle ancha Gr. 3, 297
Lean on Me Gr. 7, E-22
*Ma Vlast (My Fatherland),* *"Vltava*
     *(The Moldau)"* Gr. 7, C-33
Noah's Shanty Gr. 1, 344
*Rhapsody in Blue* Gr. 7, C-42
Rondo for Lunch, A (speech piece)
     Gr. 3, 212
Sierra Morena Gr. 3, 296
*Suite in F, Op. 28b, No. 2, "Fantasia*
     *on the Dargason," Movement 4*
     Gr. 7, C-36
*Symphony No. 5 in C Minor, Op. 67,*
     *Movement 1* Gr. 7, C-16
Walk Together, Children Gr. 3, 146

## PLAYING INSTRUMENTS

### AUTOHARP
Bridges Gr. 6, 86
Clementine Gr. 4, 341
Cotton-Eye Joe Gr. 4, 288
Cuando pa' Chile me voy
     Gr. 6, 376
Down in the Valley Gr. 6, 375
El sapito Gr. 3, 336
Jambalaya (On The Bayou)
     Gr. 6, 244
Keel Row, The Gr. 4, 240
Key to the Highway Gr. 6, 243
Loigratong Gr. 6, 451
Mon papa Gr. 2, 280
Mr. Tambourine Man Gr. 6, 150
My Home's Across the Blue Ridge
     Mountains Gr. 4, 84
Paths of Victory Gr. 6, 195
She'll Be Comin' 'Round the
     Mountain Gr. 2, 358
Song of the Fishes Gr. 3, 244
Sweet Potatoes Gr. 3, 228
Tom Dooley Gr. 6, 374
Vive l'amour Gr. 6, 176
You Are My Sunshine Gr. 6, 246

### BASS INSTRUMENTS
America, the Beautiful Gr. 7, I-5
¡Ay, Jalisco no te rajes! Gr. 7, I-8
Blues with a Feeling Gr. 8, I-8
Canto del agua Gr. 8, I-12

Certainly, Lord Gr. 7, I-14
Cheki, morena Gr. 7, I-18
Cielito lindo Gr. 7, I-23
De colores Gr. 8, I-15
El rancho grande Gr. 8, I-23
Ev'rybody Loves Saturday Night
     Gr. 7, I-27
Feliz Navidad Gr. 7, I-30
Flip, Flop and Fly Gr. 7, I-34
He's Got the Whole World in His
     Hands Gr. 7, I-38
I Shall Sing Gr. 8, I-40
I'll Fly Away Gr. 8, I-44
La golondrina Gr. 8, I-52
Los reyes de Oriente Gr. 8, I-59
Oy, Hanuka Gr. 7, I-45
Pay Me My Money Down Gr. 7, I-48
*Rundadinella* Gr. 8, I-60
Surfin' U.S.A. Gr. 7, I-61
This Land Is Your Land Gr. 7, I-68
Yellow Rose of Texas, The
     Gr. 7, I-71
Yonder Come Day Gr. 8, I-71

### BOOMWHACKER®
Whacky Wheel Ensemble, The
     Gr. 6, 381

## CLASSROOM INSTRUMENTS
A-Tisket, A-Tasket Gr. 2, 238
Aguinaldo Gr. 3, 402
Ah, eu entrei na roda Gr. 3, 308
Ahora voy a cantarles Gr. 3, 56
*Ain't That Love* Gr. 5, 20
Allá en la fuente Gr. 2, 92
America Gr. 5, 486
*Arkansas Traveler/Angeline the*
     *Baker* Gr. K, 114
Around the World Gr. 2, 256
Bam, chi, chi, bam Gr. K, 109
Banana Gr. 2, 114
Big Old Storm a-Comin' Gr. K, 257
Blast Off! (poem) Gr. 1, 377
Boysie Gr. 2, 195
*Chica chica boom chic* Gr. 2, 112
Chrismus a Come Gr. 3, 396
Cuculí Gr. K, 238
Deep in the Heart of Texas
     Gr. 4, 22
Do, Lord Gr. 3, 164
Dok djampa Gr. 8, I-21
Drill, Ye Tarriers Gr. 5, 54
*Ekombi* Gr. 8, B-31
El borrego Gr. 4, 243
El carite Gr. 5, 304
El rancho grande Gr. 4, 215
El sapito Gr. 3, 336
Éliza Kongo Gr. 5, 16
*Eriskummainen kantele*
     Gr. 5, 199
Estampie Gr. 8, I-26
Ev'ry Kind of Music Gr. 2, 226
Families Gr. 1, 282
Farmer in the Dell, The Gr. K, 232

**(Playing Instruments, continued)**

Feng yang hua gu  Gr. 4, 313

Fly and the Bumblebee, The
    Gr. 1, 385

*Frosty, the Snowman*  Gr. 2, 391

Get on Board  Gr. K, 89

Gloria, Gloria  Gr. 6, 459

Go With the Music and Sing
    Gr. 3, 376

Gonna Have a Good Time  Gr. 2, 4

Good King Wenceslas  Gr. 6, 460

Greetings (speech piece)  Gr. 3, 316

Guantanamera  Gr. 8, I-35

Halloween Is a Very Unusual Night
    Gr. 3, 382

Hama chi dori  Gr. 3, 330

Hambone  Gr. 1, 202

Hava nashira  Gr. 6, 82

Head, Shoulders, Baby  Gr. 1, 82

Hej pada pada  Gr. 3, 78

Hello, There!  Gr. K, 6

Hey, m'tswala  Gr. 4, 79

Hi Heidi Ho  Gr. 1, 392

Hush Up the Baby  Gr. K, 222

I Like Fall  Gr. K, 311

Ise oluwa  Gr. 6, 230

It's Santa—Again!  Gr. 2, 385

It's Time  Gr. 6, 274

Jasmine Flowers  Gr. 5, 316

*John B. Sails*  Gr. K, 11

Joshua Fought the Battle of Jericho
    Gr. 5, 100

Kébé Mama  Gr. 1, 443

Koriko!  Gr. K, 154

Kuma san  Gr. K, 40

Kunolounkwa  Gr. K, 110

Kwanzaa Carol, A  Gr. 2, 392

Kyrie  Gr. 6, 206

La paloma blanca  Gr. 3, 252

La pulga de San José  Gr. 3, 40

Las mañanitas  Gr. 6, 481

London Bridge  Gr. K, 244

Los días de la semana  Gr. 1, 269

Los pollitos  Gr. K, 166

Los reyes de Oriente  Gr. 8, I-59

*Love You Forever*  Gr. 8, B-23

Luna lunera (speech piece)  Gr. K, 90

Making Valentines  Gr. 1, 437

Mango Walk  Gr. 5, 201

Me voy para la luna  Gr. 1, 396

Mi chacra  Gr. 1, 365

Mr. Tambourine Man  Gr. 6, 150

Name Game, The (speech piece)
    Gr. 1, 315

No quiero plata  Gr. 1, 425

*Noah's Zoo in the Big, Big Rain*
    Gr. K, 274

Old Brass Wagon  Gr. 2, 122

*Orfferondo*  Gr. 4, 194

Ōsamu kosamu  Gr. 4, 97

Oy, Hanuka  Gr. 5, 465

Parade Came Marching, The
    Gr. 1, 166

Pat Works on the Railway
    Gr. 5, 183

Piñon, pirulín  Gr. 2, 174

Poco, Le' Me 'Lone  Gr. 3, 300

Rabbit Footprints  Gr. 2, 304

Rocky Top  Gr. 5, 350

Rudolph, the Red-Nosed Reindeer
    Gr. 1, 428

S'vivon  Gr. 6, 452

Sailing Down My Golden River
    Gr. 4, 333

Same Train  Gr. 2, 164

See the Children Playin'  Gr. 4, 107

Shake Them 'Simmons Down
    Gr. 2, 244

Shine, Shine, Shine  Gr. 1, 42

Sidewalk Sounds  Gr. K, 115

Sing a Little Song  Gr. K, 30

Sing Me a Story  Gr. 2, 346

Singin' in the Tub  Gr. K, 220

*Slow Hora/Freylekhs*  Gr. 8, B-25

Somebody Waiting  Gr. 2, 283

Someday Very Soon  Gr. 1, 376

Sonando  Gr. 4, 34

Song of One, A  Gr. 3, 344

Spaceworms  Gr. 1, 400

Streets of Laredo  Gr. 4, 272

Summertime  Gr. 6, 250

Tengo, tengo, tengo  Gr. 4, 229

Texas Cowboy  Gr. 3, 250

That's What's New with Me!  Gr. K, 2

Time to Move  Gr. 1, 244

Tumba  Gr. 5, 161

Ujima  Gr. 1, 430

Under the Sea  Gr. 5, 373

Valentine Dance  Gr. 1, 437

Vamos a la mar  Gr. 3, 226

Vive l'amour  Gr. 6, 176

Wake Me, Shake Me  Gr. 1, 278

Walk Together, Children  Gr. 3, 146

We're All Gonna Shine Tonight
    Gr. 2, 240

When the Train Comes Along
    Gr. 1, 300

Wings of a Dove  Gr. 4, 318

Woodland Chorus  Gr. K, 250

## ENVIRONMENTAL SOUNDS

*3 + 2*  Gr. 2, 316

From Sea to Shining Sea  Gr. 2, 342

Just from the Kitchen  Gr. K, 55

Keys  Gr. K, 188

Paper  Gr. K, 195

Parade Came Marching, The
    Gr. 1, 166

*Sha Sha Sha*  Gr. 6, 328

Tap It! Rap It! (speech piece)
    Gr. K, 194

## FLUTE

Cheki, morena  Gr. 7, I-17

Ev'rybody Loves Saturday Night
    Gr. 7, I-26

Pay Me My Money Down  Gr. 7, I-48

Stille Nacht (Silent Night)  Gr. 7, I-55

This Land Is Your Land  Gr. 7, I-69

## GUITAR

12-Bar Blues  Gr. 7, F-14

Adelita  Gr. 5, 50

Adiós, amigos  Gr. 6, 57

¡Ay, Jalisco no te rajes!  Gr. 7, I-8

Banuwa  Gr. 6, 294

Big Rock Candy Mountain
    Gr. 4, 331

Blowin' in the Wind  Gr. 5, 384

Blue Skies  Gr. 6, 88

Bridges  Gr. 6, 86

Canción de cuna  Gr. 4, 147

Cantando mentiras  Gr. 4, 147

Checki, morena  Gr. 7, F-11

Cielito lindo  Gr. 4, 270

Cielito lindo  Gr. 7, I-23

Colorado Trail  Gr. 5, 277

Cotton-Eye Joe  Gr. 4, 288

Cowboys' Christmas Ball  Gr. 6, 239

Cuando pa' Chile me voy  Gr. 6, 376

Dancin' in the Street  Gr. 5, 361

Don Alfonso  Gr. 5, 177

Down in the Valley  Gr. 6, 375

Dry Bones  Gr. 4, 162

El payo  Gr. 6, 144

El rancho grande  Gr. 4, 214

El Salón México  Gr. 6, 198

Ev'ry Time I Feel the Spirit
    Gr. 5, 243

Ezekiel Saw the Wheel  Gr. 6, 379

Fais do do  Gr. 6, 404

Feliz Navidad  Gr. 7, I-30

Flip, Flop and Fly  Gr. 7, I-33

Four Strong Winds  Gr. 6, 171

Four Strong Winds (Song to a
    Seagull)  Gr. 6, 170

Give a Little Love  Gr. 6, 140

Goin' Down the Road Feelin' Bad
    Gr. 5, 283

Goin' Down the Road Feelin' Bad
    Gr. 7, F-13

Greensleeves  Gr. 6, 49

*Guitar Tuning*  Gr. 7, F-2

Habemos llegado  Gr. 6, 174

He's Got the Whole World in His
    Hands  Gr. 7, I-37

Ise oluwa  Gr. 6, 230

Jambalaya (On The Bayou)
    Gr. 6, 244

Key to the Highway  Gr. 6, 243

La Jesusita  Gr. 5, 323

La mariposa  Gr. 6, 58

Las mañanitas  Gr. 6, 480

Linstead Market  Gr. 5, 241

Little David, Play on Your Harp
    Gr. 4, 395

Loigratong  Gr. 6, 451

Los reyes de Oriente  Gr. 5, 480

Mama Don't 'Low  Gr. 6, 358

Mama Don't 'Low  Gr. 6, 361

Mr. Tambourine Man  Gr. 6, 150
My Home's Across the Blue Ridge
    Mountains  Gr. 7, F-6
Old House, Tear It Down!
    Gr. 4, 178
Paths of Victory  Gr. 6, 195
Pay Me My Money Down  Gr. 7, F-5
Pay Me My Money Down  Gr. 7, I-48
¡Qué bonita bandera!  Gr. 5, 295
Riendo el río corre  Gr. 6, 263
*Rock Around the Clock*  Gr. 5, 357
Roll On, Columbia  Gr. 5, 117
Scattin' A-Round (Variations on
    Row 3)  Gr. 6, 160
Shady Grove  Gr. 5, 261
Still, Still, Still  Gr. 5, 469
Stille Nacht (Silent Night)  Gr. 7, I-55
Surfin' U.S.A.  Gr. 7, I-61
*This Land Is Your Land*  Gr. 5, 120
This Land Is Your Land  Gr. 5, 120
This Little Light of Mine  Gr. 6, 233
This Pretty Planet  Gr. 4, 355
Tie Me Kangaroo Down, Sport
    Gr. 4, 36
Tom Dooley  Gr. 6, 374
'Ūlili E  Gr. 5, 442
Vive l'amour  Gr. 6, 176
*Waitin' for a Train*  Gr. 7, B-24
Water Come a Me Eye  Gr. 6, 300
You Are My Sunshine  Gr. 6, 246

**chords**
12-Bar Blues Rock  Gr. 8, F-31
Ain't Gonna Let Nobody Turn
    Me 'Round  Gr. 8, F-16
Blues with a Feeling  Gr. 8, I-8
Canto del agua  Gr. 8, I-11
Chicka Hanka  Gr. 8, F-15
De colores  Gr. 8, I-15
Deep in the Heart of Texas
    Gr. 8, I-19
Do Wah Diddy Diddy  Gr. 7, F-21
Earth Is Our Mother, The
    Gr. 8, F-25
*El amor brujo, "Danza ritual
    del fuego"*  Gr. 8, F-20
El rancho grande  Gr. 8, I-23
Every Night When the Sun Goes
    In  Gr. 8, I-30
God Bless the Grass  Gr. 8, F-13
Guantanamera  Gr. 8, I-34
*I Get Out*  Gr. 8, F-6
I Shall Sing  Gr. 8, I-39
I'll Fly Away  Gr. 8, I-44
Karangatia ra  Gr. 8, F-23
Key to the Highway  Gr. 8, F-29
*Key to the Highway*  Gr. 8, F-28
La golondrina  Gr. 8, I-51
Little Darlin'  Gr. 7, F-30
Man of Constant Sorrow
    Gr. 7, F-28
*Scuttle Buttin'*  Gr. 8, F-26
Shortnin' Bread  Gr. 7, F-27

Surfin' U.S.A.  Gr. 7, F-32
Three Little Birds  Gr. 8, F-7
Wade in the Water  Gr. 8, I-66
*Would?*  Gr. 8, F-30
Yonder Come Day  Gr. 8, I-71

**fingerpicking**
Aerial Boundaries  Gr. 8, F-21

**melodies**
12-Bar Blues Rock  Gr. 8, F-31
Surfin' U.S.A.  Gr. 7, F-33

**progressions**
12-Bar Blues Rock  Gr. 8, F-31
Ain't Gonna Let Nobody Turn
    Me 'Round  Gr. 8, F-16
Chicka Hanka  Gr. 8, F-15
Do Wah Diddy Diddy
    Gr. 7, F-21
Earth Is Our Mother, The
    Gr. 8, F-25
*El amor brujo, "Danza ritual
    del fuego"*  Gr. 8, F-20
El rancho grande  Gr. 8, I-23
Every Night When the Sun Goes
    In  Gr. 8, I-30
God Bless the Grass  Gr. 8, F-13
Guantanamera  Gr. 8, I-34
*I Get Out*  Gr. 8, F-6
I Shall Sing  Gr. 8, I-39
Karangatia ra  Gr. 8, F-23
Key to the Highway  Gr. 8, F-29
*Key to the Highway*  Gr. 8, F-28
Man of Constant Sorrow
    Gr. 7, F-28
*Scuttle Buttin'*  Gr. 8, F-26
Shortnin' Bread  Gr. 7, F-27
Three Little Birds  Gr. 8, F-7
*Would?*  Gr. 8, F-30

**strums**
Ain't Gonna Let Nobody Turn
    Me 'Round  Gr. 8, F-16
Chicka Hanka  Gr. 8, F-15
Earth Is Our Mother, The
    Gr. 8, F-25
*El amor brujo, "Danza ritual
    del fuego"*  Gr. 8, F-20
El rancho grande  Gr. 8, I-23
Every Night When the Sun Goes
    In  Gr. 8, I-30
God Bless the Grass  Gr. 8, F-13
Guantanamera  Gr. 8, I-34
*Guitar Tuning*  Gr. 8, F-2
*I Get Out*  Gr. 8, F-6
I'll Fly Away  Gr. 8, I-44
Karangatia ra  Gr. 8, F-23
Key to the Highway  Gr. 8, F-29
*Key to the Highway*  Gr. 8, F-28
Man of Constant Sorrow
    Gr. 7, F-29
Midnight Special, The
    Gr. 7, F-23
*Scuttle Buttin'*  Gr. 8, F-26

Shortnin' Bread  Gr. 7, F-27
Stille Nacht (Silent Night)
    Gr. 7, F-24
Surfin' U.S.A.  Gr. 7, F-32
This Land is Your Land
    Gr. 7, F-24
Three Little Birds  Gr. 8, F-7
*Would?*  Gr. 8, F-30

## HAND BELLS
Kyrie  Gr. 6, 207

## INSTRUMENTAL ENSEMBLES
El rancho grande  Gr. 8, I-24

## JUG BAND
Mama Don't 'Low  Gr. 6, 358

## KEYBOARD
Adana ya gidelim  Gr. 2, 143
Adelita  Gr. 5, 50
Ah! Les jolis papillons  Gr. 1, 363
Al ánimo  Gr. 3, 322
Al citrón  Gr. 3, 320
Al quebrar la piñata  Gr. 4, 431
Ala Da'lona  Gr. 4, 137
All for One  Gr. 7, E-8
All Through the Night  Gr. 5, 104
Alphabet Song  Gr. K, 280
America, the Beautiful  Gr. 6, 487
America, the Beautiful  Gr. 6, 485
Andy Pandy  Gr. K, 46
Apple Tree  Gr. 1, 228
Apples and Bananas  Gr. 1, 390
Así es mi tierra  Gr. 6, 173
*Badenma*  Gr. 8, B-28
Battle Hymn of the Republic
    Gr. 5, 274
Big Beautiful Planet  Gr. 3, 326
Big Old Storm a-Comin'  Gr. K, 257
*Birthday*  Gr. 6, 92
Birthday  Gr. 6, 90
Blow the Wind Southerly
    Gr. 5, 179
Blowin' in the Wind  Gr. 5, 383
Blue Skies  Gr. 6, 89
Boil Them Cabbage Down
    Gr. 6, 371
*Boogie-Woogie*  Gr. 6, 92
Bridges  Gr. 6, 86
Bury Me Not on the Lone Prairie
    Gr. 6, 19
Bus, The  Gr. K, 83
Camptown Races  Gr. 5, 270
Cattle Call  Gr. 5, 346
Cheki, morena  Gr. 7, E-12
Chicka Hanka  Gr. 2, 210
Chrismus a Come  Gr. 3, 397
Circle Round the Zero  Gr. K, 293
Clementine  Gr. 4, 341
Coffee Grows on White Oak Trees
    Gr. 3, 168
Computer, The  Gr. 4, 198
Corta la caña  Gr. 6, 366
Dance for the Nations  Gr. 6, 123

**(*Playing Instruments,* continued)**

De colores  Gr. 5, 91

Do Wah Diddy Diddy  Gr. 4, 203

Don't Be Cruel  Gr. 6, 255

Down by the Riverside  Gr. 5, 257

Ein Männlein steht im Walde
    Gr. 2, 90

El florón  Gr. 2, 246

Éliza Kongo  Gr. 5, 14

Ev'rybody Loves Saturday Night
    Gr. 7, I-27

Ezekiel Saw the Wheel  Gr. 6, 379

Fiddler on the Roof  Gr. 7, E-5

Flip, Flop and Fly  Gr. 7, E-32

Flip, Flop and Fly  Gr. 7, I-33

For the Beauty of the Earth
    Gr. 4, 357

*Frog in the Millpond*  Gr. 2, 45

From Sea to Shining Sea
    Gr. 2, 342

Give a Little Love  Gr. 6, 140

Give My Regards to Broadway
    Gr. 6, 39

Gloria, Gloria  Gr. 6, 459

Glory, Glory, Hallelujah  Gr. 6, 52

Go, My Son  Gr. 6, 188

Going on a Picnic  Gr. K, 190

Going upon the Mountain
    Gr. 6, 104

Goldilocks and the Three Bears
    Gr. K, 48

Good King Wenceslas  Gr. 6, 460

Good Mornin' Blues  Gr. 5, 226

Good Morning  Gr. 3, 193

Green, Green, Rocky  Gr. 1, 319

Habemos llegado  Gr. 6, 174

Haru ga kita  Gr. 2, 401

Haul Away, Joe  Gr. 4, 12

He's Got the Whole World in His
    Hands  Gr. 3, 231

He's Got the Whole World in His
    Hands  Gr. 7, I-37

Hey, Ho! Nobody Home  Gr. 6, 28

Home on the Range  Gr. 5, 68

Hop Up, My Ladies  Gr. 3, 145

Hosisipa  Gr. 3, 70

Hot Cross Buns (Version 1)
    Gr. 3, 220

How Many Miles to Babylon?
    Gr. 2, 129

I Bought Me a Cat  Gr. 2, 309

I Fed My Horse  Gr. 2, 95

I Got Rhythm  Gr. 6, 100

I Have a Dog  Gr. K, 262

I Love Peanuts  Gr. 7, E-20

I'm Gonna Sing  Gr. 4, 30

I'm Tall, I'm Small  Gr. K, 18

Ichi-gatsu tsuitachi  Gr. 7, I-43

If a Tiger Calls  Gr. 3, 355

If You're Happy  Gr. K, 94

Ikhanda, maslombe  Gr. K, 14

Imbabura  Gr. 5, 202

It Don't Mean a Thing (If It Ain't
    Got That Swing)  Gr. 5, 338

It Don't Mean a Thing (If It Ain't
    Got That Swing)  Gr. 5, 339

Jambalaya (On The Bayou)
    Gr. 6, 244

Jinny Go 'Round  Gr. K, 228

Joe Turner Blues  Gr. 4, 56

John Kanaka  Gr. 3, 62

Johnny Has Gone for a Soldier
    Gr. 5, 188

Johnny Mister Brown  Gr. K, 37

Kaeru no uta  Gr. K, 183

Kapulu kane  Gr. 2, 271

Keel Row, The  Gr. 4, 240

Key to the Highway  Gr. 6, 243

Khorovod  Gr. 1, 372

Knock No More  Gr. 3, 386

Kou ri lengay  Gr. 7, E-2

Kyrie  Gr. 6, 207

*L'Arlésienne Suite No. 2,
    "Farandole"*  Gr. 6, 68

La Jesusita  Gr. 5, 324

La Tarara  Gr. 4, 177

Las mañanitas  Gr. 6, 480

Lean on Me  Gr. 7, E-22

Lemonade  Gr. 1, 190

Let's Get the Rhythm of the Band
    Gr. 7, E-29

Like a Bird  Gr. 6, 167

Limbo Like Me  Gr. 4, 18

Linstead Market  Gr. 5, 241

Lions  Gr. 1, 238

Little David, Play on Your Harp
    Gr. 4, 395

*"Little" Organ Fugue in G Minor*
    Gr. 6, 129

Little Green Frog, The  Gr. 1, 24

Little Red Wagon  Gr. K, 152

*Lo, How a Rose E'er Blooming*
    Gr. 6, 210

Loigratong  Gr. 6, 451

Looby Loo  Gr. K, 210

Love Somebody  Gr. 3, 95

Lucy Locket  Gr. 2, 27

*Lyric Suite, "Allegretto gioviale,"
    Movement 1*  Gr. 6, 169

Mañana  Gr. 7, E-14

Mary Ann  Gr. 6, 180

Mister Rabbit  Gr. K, 128

Mon papa  Gr. 2, 280

Morning Has Broken  Gr. 5, 30

Mos Mos  Gr. 1, 131

Mr. Tambourine Man  Gr. 6, 150

My Bonnie Lies Over the Ocean
    Gr. 4, 339

Name, Name, What's Your Name?
    Gr. 3, 11

Nana Kru  Gr. 6, 282

Nani wale na hala  Gr. 3, 260

Naranja dulce  Gr. 2, 97

Now's the Time  Gr. 5, 449

Ode to Joy  Gr. 4, 152

Oh, Freedom  Gr. 5, 393

Oh, Susanna  Gr. 4, 264

Oh, Watch the Stars  Gr. 5, 216

Oklahoma  Gr. 5, 36

Orange Blossom Special
    Gr. 5, 266

Over My Head  Gr. 4, 118

Oy, Hanuka  Gr. 5, 464

Oy, Hanuka  Gr. 7, I-45

Paths of Victory  Gr. 6, 194

Pay Me My Money Down  Gr. 7, I-49

Peace Like a River  Gr. 3, 246

Peace Like A River  Gr. 6, 193

Play a Simple Melody  Gr. 5, 75

Promised Land, The  Gr. 5, 258

Puff, the Magic Dragon  Gr. 2, 351

Put a Little Love in Your Heart
    Gr. 4, 8

¡Qué bonita bandera!  Gr. 5, 296

Rabbit Footprints  Gr. 2, 304

Reviewing keyboard skills  Gr. 6, 7

Rice Planting Song  Gr. 1, 89

Ríu ríu chíu  Gr. 5, 437

*Rock Around the Clock*  Gr. 5, 357

Rosie, Darling Rosie  Gr. 2, 214

'Round and 'Round  Gr. 1, 149

S'vivon  Gr. 6, 452

Sakura  Gr. 4, 309

Sambalele  Gr. 4, 398

Sarika keo  Gr. 3, 274

Scarborough Fair  Gr. 6, 94

Scotland the Brave  Gr. 5, 138

Sea Shell  Gr. 2, 101

Serra, serra, serrador  Gr. 1, 113

Ship that Never Returned, The
    Gr. 5, 402

Si me dan pasteles  Gr. 1, 433

Sing a Song of Peace  Gr. 6, 67

Singin' in the Tub  Gr. K, 220

Snowflakes  Gr. 1, 422

Sometimes I Feel Like a Motherless
    Child  Gr. 6, 241

Sorida  Gr. 1, 314

St. Louis Blues  Gr. 5, 353

Stand By Me  Gr. 5, 48

Star Light, Star Bright  Gr. 1, 106

Streets of Laredo  Gr. 4, 272

Summertime  Gr. 6, 250

Supercalifragilisticexpialidocious
    Gr. 3, 7

Surfin' U.S.A.  Gr. 7, E-27

Surfin' U.S.A.  Gr. 7, I-59

Swanee  Gr. 6, 118

Sweet Betsy from Pike  Gr. 4, 245

Tender Shepherd (Count Your
    Sheep)  Gr. 3, 116

There's a Place  Gr. 5, 210

This Land Is Your Land  Gr. 5, 120

This Land Is Your Land (refrain
    only)  Gr. 1, 276

This Little Light of Mine  Gr. 6, 233

Tic, tac  Gr. 1, 252

To'ia mai te waka  Gr. 1, 78

Train Is A-Comin' Gr. 3, 51
Tree in the Wood, The Gr. 2, 361
Tumba Gr. 5, 161
Twelve Gates to the City Gr. 5, 281
Vem kan segla? Gr. 6, 417
Vive l'amour Gr. 6, 176
Walk Together, Children Gr. 3, 146
Way Down in the Schoolyard
    Gr. 2, 50
We Go Together Gr. 4, 44
We're All Gonna Shine Tonight
    Gr. 2, 241
Weevily Wheat Gr. 4, 105
Wheel of the Water, The
    Gr. 4, 363
Wichita Hand Game Song 2
    Gr. 3, 307
Wind Up the Apple Tree Gr. 1, 184
Work It Out (Blow Your Horn Dub
    Mix) Gr. 7, A-3
World We Love, The Gr. 3, 342
Xiao Gr. 4, 314
Xiao yin chuan Gr. 2, 15
Yakety Yak Gr. 5, 205
Yang wa wa Gr. K, 163
Yankee Doodle Gr. 2, 405
You Are My Sunshine Gr. 6, 246

**chords**
    De colores Gr. 8, I-15
    Deep in the Heart of Texas
        Gr. 8, I-18
    El rancho grande Gr. 8, I-24
    Every Night When the Sun Goes
        In Gr. 8, I-30
    Goodbye, Julie Gr. 8, E-2
    I'll Fly Away Gr. 8, I-44
    Lion Sleeps Tonight, The
        Gr. 8, I-56
    Los reyes de Oriente Gr. 8, I-58
    Orange Blossom Special
        Gr. 8, E-6
    Wade in the Water Gr. 8, I-66
    Yonder Come Day Gr. 8, I-71

**I-IV-V(7)**
    Blues with a Feeling Gr. 8, I-8

**melodies**
    Face of Love, The Gr. 8, B-15
    Sealwoman/Yundah
        Gr. 8, B-14

**progressions**
    Deep in the Heart of Texas
        Gr. 8, I-18
    Every Night When the Sun Goes
        In Gr. 8, I-30
    Goodbye, Julie Gr. 8, E-2
    I Shall Sing Gr. 8, I-39
    Los reyes de Oriente Gr. 8, I-58
    Orange Blossom Special
        Gr. 8, E-6
    Wade in the Water Gr. 8, I-66

**MALLETS·**
    A Ram Sam Sam Gr. 3, 208
    Abiyoyo Gr. 2, 108
    Adana ya gidelim Gr. 2, 143
    Addams Family, The Gr. 5, 457
    Adiós, amigos Gr. 6, 57
    Ah, eu entrei na roda Gr. 3, 308
    Ah, Poor Bird Gr. 4, 196
    Ai, Dunaii moy Gr. 4, 293
    Alabama Gal Gr. 3, 107
    All Night, All Day Gr. 4, 180
    Alleluia Gr. 6, 133
    Amefuri Gr. 1, 142
    Andy Pandy Gr. K, 46
    Apple Tree Gr. 1, 230
    Arirang Gr. 5, 25
    Artsa alinu Gr. 3, 285
    Asadoya Gr. 6, 302
    At the Hop Gr. 4, 168
    Autumn Canon Gr. 5, 148
    Ayelivi Gr. 2, 70
    Baby Beluga Gr. K, 272
    Baby Elephant Walk Gr. 2, 163
    Barb'ry Allen Gr. 6, 45
    Bard of Armagh, The Gr. 4, 297
    Beach Rap Gr. 1, 353
    Blast Off! (poem) Gr. 1, 377
    Bluebonnets of Texas Gr. 3, 332
    Bob-a-Needle Gr. 2, 233
    Bounce High, Bounce Low
        Gr. 1, 152
    Brush Your Teeth Gr. 1, 284
    Bury Me Not on the Lone Prairie
        Gr. 6, 19
    Caballito blanco Gr. 2, 193
    Camptown Races Gr. 5, 270
    Canción de cuna Gr. 4, 145
    Canoe Song Gr. 4, 76
    Canto del agua Gr. 8, I-13
    Celebrate! Gr. 1, 406
    Charlie over the Water Gr. 1, 68
    Cheki, morena Gr. 7, I-19
    Cinderella Dressed in Green
        Gr. K, 136
    Cindy Gr. 4, 384
    Cirmos cica Gr. 1, 129
    Clementine Gr. 4, 341
    Clouds Gr. K, 254
    Corrido de Kansas Gr. 4, 275
    Counting-Out Rhyme (speech piece)
        Gr. 1, 357
    Crocodile, The Gr. 2, 363
    Cuckoo, Cuckoo Gr. 1, 110
    Dayenu Gr. 4, 439
    De colores Gr. 5, 90
    Deau-deau, ti pitit maman
        Gr. 2, 306
    Ding, Dong, Diggidiggidong
        Gr. 3, 14
    Do, Lord Gr. 3, 164
    Do Wah Diddy Diddy Gr. 4, 203
    Don Alfonso Gr. 5, 176
    Don't Let the Wind Gr. 3, 180

    Don't Let Your Watch Run Down
        Gr. 3, 167
    Dona nobis pacem Gr. 6, 125
    ¿Dónde lo escondí? Gr. K, 209
    Down by the Riverside Gr. 5, 257
    Draw Me a Bucket of Water
        Gr. 3, 124
    Dry Bones Come Skipping
        Gr. 4, 218
    Dundai Gr. 5, 106
    Earth Is My Mother, The Gr. 1, 340
    Ein Männlein steht im Walde
        Gr. 2, 90
    El borrego Gr. 4, 243
    El caracol Gr. K, 130
    El carite Gr. 5, 305
    El carnavalito humahuaqueño
        Gr. 6, 482
    El cóndor pasa Gr. 6, 47
    El mes de abril Gr. 3, 328
    El payo Gr. 6, 144
    El sapito Gr. 3, 337
    En nuestra Tierra tan linda
        Gr. 2, 335
    Erdö, erdö de magos Gr. 3, 182
    Estampie Gr. 8, I-27
    Ev'ry Time I Feel the Spirit
        Gr. 5, 243
    Evening Chaconne Gr. 6, 202
    Every Morning When I Wake Up
        Gr. 2, 320
    Every Night When the Sun Goes In
        Gr. 8, I-31
    Everybody Loves Saturday Night
        Gr. 6, 297
    Ezekiel Saw the Wheel Gr. 6, 379
    Farewell to Tarwathie Gr. 6, 42
    Farmer's Dairy Key, The
        Gr. 2, 183
    Feliz Navidad Gr. 7, I-31
    Flip, Flop and Fly Gr. 7, I-34
    Follow the Drinkin' Gourd
        Gr. 4, 266
    Four White Horses Gr. 3, 304
    Frère Jacques Gr. 2, 125
    Friend of Mine Gr. 1, 310
    Frog in the Millpond Gr. 2, 45
    Frog Music Gr. 4, 200
    Go Around the Corn, Sally
        Gr. 2, 13
    Going Upon the Mountain
        Gr. 6, 105
    Gonna Build a Mountain Gr. 6, 21
    Goodbye, Julie Gr. 1, 335
    Gospel Train, The Gr. 6, 398
    Great Big House Gr. 2, 204
    Great Big House Gr. 2, 207
    Great Big Stars Gr. 1, 60
    Great Day Gr. 3, 59
    Ha'kyo jong Gr. 2, 135
    Habemos llegado Gr. 6, 174
    Hama chi dori Gr. 3, 330
    Hanuka, Hanuka Gr. 8, I-37

**(*Playing Instruments,* continued)**

Hashkediya  Gr. 3, 206
Hato Popo  Gr. 1, 187
He's Got the Whole World in His Hands  Gr. 3, 231
Hej pada pada  Gr. 3, 78
Hey, Hey, Look at Me  Gr. 1, 70
Hey, Ho! Nobody Home  Gr. 6, 28
Hit Me with a Hot Note and Watch Me Bounce  Gr. 6, 112
Hitotsu toya  Gr. 5, 478
Home on the Range  Gr. 5, 68
Home on the Range  Gr. 5, 70
Honeybee Song, The  Gr. 1, 359
Hop Up, My Ladies  Gr. 3, 145
Hosanna, Me Build a House  Gr. 5, 133
Hound Dog  Gr. 5, 214
Hui jia qü  Gr. 2, 158
Hush, Hush  Gr. 3, 164
I Bought Me a Cat  Gr. 2, 308
I Can't Spell Hippopatamus  Gr. 1, 266
I Don't Care If the Rain Comes Down  Gr. 3, 27
I Got a Letter This Morning  Gr. K, 68
I Have a Dog  Gr. K, 262
I Know an Old Lady  Gr. 1, 388
I Saw Three Ships  Gr. 1, 426
I Shall Sing  Gr. 8, I-41
I'm Curious  Gr. K, 276
Ichi-gatsu tsuitachi  Gr. 7, I-41
Ichi-gatsu tsuitachi  Gr. 7, I-42
If a Tiger Calls  Gr. 3, 354
If I Had a Hammer  Gr. 5, 287
It's Santa—Again!  Gr. 2, 385
Jambalaya  Gr. 8, I-49
Jelly in a Dish  Gr. 2, 84
Joe Turner Blues  Gr. 4, 56
John Kanaka  Gr. 3, 60
Johnny Mister Brown  Gr. K, 37
Joshua Fought the Battle  Gr. 5, 102
Knock No More  Gr. 3, 386
Kookaburra  Gr. 4, 187
Kou ri lengay  Gr. 2, 217
Kum ba yah  Gr. 5, 245
Kum bachur atzel  Gr. 3, 138
L'Arlésienne Suite No. 2, "Farandole"  Gr. 6, 68
La paloma se fué  Gr. 6, 50
Las estrellitas del cielo  Gr. 5, 174
Leak kanseng  Gr. 1, 156
Leatherwing Bat  Gr. 2, 303
Lemonade  Gr. 1, 189
Let the Music Begin!  Gr. 1, 2
Li'l Liza Jane  Gr. 3, 140
Little Shell  Gr. 1, 355
Lo yisa  Gr. 6, 130
Loco-Motion, The  Gr. 3, 66
Long Way Home, A  Gr. 1, 382
Lost My Gold Ring  Gr. 6, 158

Love Somebody  Gr. 3, 94
Lucy Locket  Gr. 2, 27
Make New Friends  Gr. 3, 36
Mango Walk  Gr. 5, 201
Mary Ann  Gr. 6, 180
Meng Jian Nu  Gr. 5, 195
Miss Mary Mack  Gr. 2, 42
Mississippi River Chant (speech piece)  Gr. 2, 132
Missy-La, Massa-La  Gr. 4, 189
Mister Snow Rap  Gr. 2, 389
Morning Comes Early  Gr. 5, 13
Mother Sent Me to the Store  Gr. K, 136
My Foot's in My Stirrup  Gr. 2, 236
My Home's Across the Blue Ridge Mountains  Gr. 4, 84
My Mama's Calling Me  Gr. 1, 260
My Pony, Macaroni  Gr. 1, 159
Nana, Thread Needle  Gr. 1, 39
Now Let Me Fly  Gr. 3, 179
*Nruab hnub thiab hmo ntuj*  Gr. 4, 368
Oh, Watch the Stars  Gr. 2, 144
Old Man Mosie  Gr. 3, 108
Oliver Twist  Gr. K, 138
One Morning in May  Gr. 6, 120
One Morning Soon  Gr. 3, 68
*Orfferondo*  Gr. 4, 194
Ōsamu kosamu  Gr. 4, 97
Over in the Meadow  Gr. 1, 346
Pai pi qiu  Gr. 1, 324
Party Tonight!  Gr. 2, 154
Pastures of Plenty  Gr. 4, 280
Paths of Victory  Gr. 6, 194
Paw-Paw Patch  Gr. 4, 94
Pay Me My Money Down  Gr. 7, I-49
Peace Round  Gr. 4, 349
Pin Pon  Gr. 1, 147
Plant Four Seeds  Gr. 2, 130
Pretty Saro  Gr. 3, 217
Pumpkin, Pumpkin  Gr. 1, 412
Put Your Hand in My Hand  Gr. 1, 330
¡Qué bonita bandera!  Gr. 5, 295
Rabbits  Gr. 2, 305
Rain, Rain  Gr. 1, 53
Río, río  Gr. 5, 371
Riqui rán  Gr. 1, 48
Rise and Shine  Gr. 1, 122
Rock Island Line  Gr. 4, 54
Roll On, Columbia  Gr. 5, 117
Rosie, Darling Rosie  Gr. 2, 215
Rundadinella  Gr. 8, I-61
Sakura  Gr. 4, 309
Same Train  Gr. 2, 164
San Antonio Rose  Gr. 5, 135
Scattin' A-Round (Variations on Row 3)  Gr. 6, 160
Se va el caimán  Gr. 5, 305
See the Children Playin'  Gr. 4, 107
See-Saw Sacradown  Gr. 2, 208

Serra, serra, serrador  Gr. 1, 113
Shake Them 'Simmons Down  Gr. 2, 245
Shenandoah  Gr. 5, 264
Shoo, Turkey  Gr. 1, 104
Shu ha mo  Gr. 3, 276
Siyahamba  Gr. 6, 212
Skin and Bones  Gr. 2, 377
Skip to My Lou  Gr. K, 58
Skye Boat Song  Gr. 6, 372
Sleep, Baby, Sleep  Gr. 2, 196
Small Job, A  Gr. 3, 224
Snail, Snail  Gr. 1, 189
Soldier, Soldier  Gr. 4, 10
Somebody's Knockin' at Your Door  Gr. 4, 52
Someday Very Soon  Gr. 1, 376
Spring Has Sprung!  Gr. K, 142
St. Louis Blues  Gr. 5, 353
Star Light, Star Bright  Gr. 1, 108
Storm Dance (speech piece)  Gr. K, 145
Sweet Potatoes  Gr. 3, 228
Take Time in Life  Gr. 6, 289
Tanabata-sama  Gr. 2, 336
Ten Little Ostinato Pieces  Gr. 7, I-62
Tender Shepherd (Count Your Sheep)  Gr. 3, 116
Tengo, tengo, tengo  Gr. 4, 229
Thanksgiving is Near  Gr. 2, 381
There's a Place  Gr. 5, 210
This Land Is Your Land  Gr. 5, 119
This Land Is Your Land (refrain only)  Gr. 1, 275
Three Little Birds  Gr. 4, 320
Tina singu  Gr. 4, 301
Today Is Your Birthday  Gr. 1, 410
Tom Dooley  Gr. 6, 374
Tree in the Wood, The  Gr. 2, 361
Turn the Glasses Over  Gr. 3, 204
*Twist and Shout*  Gr. 4, 238
Wabash Cannon Ball  Gr. 5, 137
Wade in the Water  Gr. 8, I-66
Wai bamba  Gr. 6, 26
Waiting for the Traffic Light  Gr. 2, 107
Water Come a Me Eye  Gr. 6, 299
Water Is Wide, The  Gr. 6, 230
We Go Together  Gr. 4, 44
Weevily Wheat  Gr. 4, 105
What Do Animals Need?  Gr. 2, 288
*Whirlwind*  Gr. 3, 150
Willowbee  Gr. 1, 222
Wind Blew East, The  Gr. 1, 64
Worried Man Blues  Gr. 6, 370
Xiao  Gr. 4, 314
Yakety Yak  Gr. 5, 205
Yellow Rose of Texas, The  Gr. 7, I-73
Yertle the Turtle  Gr. 2, 369
Yesh lanu taish  Gr. 1, 180

Yibane amenu  Gr. 4, 317
You Are My Sunshine  Gr. 6, 246
Yüe liang wan wan  Gr. 5, 315
*Zomo the Rabbit*  Gr. 3, 364
Zum gali gali  Gr. 5, 401

## PERCUSSION

Abiyoyo  Gr. 2, 108
*Add-On Machine, The*  Gr. K, 298
African Noel  Gr. 1, 427
Ah ya Zane  Gr. 5, 297
Al tambor  Gr. 3, 270
Ala Da'lona  Gr. 4, 137
Alligator Pie (speech piece)
     Gr. 3, 13
America (N. Diamond)  Gr. 4, 206
America, the Beautiful  Gr. 7, I-5
Así es mi tierra  Gr. 6, 172
*Ayer, "Yesterday"*  Gr. 6, 266
Bam, chi, chi, bam  Gr. K, 109
*Batucada* Parade Ensemble
     Gr. 8, D-23
Banuwa  Gr. 6, 294
Bear Dance  Gr. 7, I-11
Bereleh  Gr. K, 151
Billie  Gr. 8, B-23
Blue Mountain Lake  Gr. 6, 205
Bonga  Gr. K, 78
Boogie Chant and Dance (speech
     piece)  Gr. 2, 78
Boomin' Bamboo Ensemble
     Gr. 7, D-22
Bora Bora Boom Ensemble
     Gr. 8, D-3
Box a-Rockin' Ensemble  Gr. 7, D-4
Bucket O'Taiko Ensemble
     Gr. 7, D-17
By the Waters of Babylon
     Gr. 6, 311
Can You Canoe?  Gr. 4, 170
Canto del agua  Gr. 8, I-13
Caribbean Island Ensemble
     Gr. 7, D-19
Carnaval Calypso Ensemble
     Gr. 7, D-21
*Cauyaqa Nauwa? (Where's My
     Drum?)*  Gr. 8, D-20
Chanukah, Chanukah  Gr. 1, 420
Chawe chidyo chem'chero
     Gr. 2, 296
Che che koolay  Gr. 2, 266
Cheki, morena  Gr. 7, I-18
*Cherokee Morning Song*
     Gr. 8, B-19
Ciranda  Gr. 2, 272
*Circle of Life, The*  Gr. 6, 316
*Crunchy, Crunchy, Crunchy*
     Gr. 8, D-15
Cuban Rumba Ensemble  Gr. 7, D-7
Day-O!  Gr. 5, 20
Diou shou juan'er  Gr. 2, 277
Dok djampa  Gr. 8, I-21
Don't Be Cruel  Gr. 6, 255

Doumbek or Hand Drum Exercises
     Gr. 7, D-31
Downtown  Gr. 6, 258
*Drums From Around the World
     (Montage)*  Gr. 6, 277
El burrito enfermo  Gr. K, 271
El caracol  Gr. K, 130
*El nuevo caiman*  Gr. 8, B-17
Elegua  Gr. 7, D-8
En nuestra Tierra tan linda
     Gr. 2, 335
Estampie  Gr. 8, I-26
Ev'rybody Loves Saturday Night
     Gr. 7, I-25
*Evening Chaconne*  Gr. 6, 202
Everybody Loves Saturday Night
     Gr. 6, 296
Ezekiel Saw the Wheel  Gr. 6, 379
*Faerie Stories*  Gr. 8, B-5
Feliz Navidad  Gr. 7, I-30
Five Little Chickadees  Gr. K, 179
Give a Little Love  Gr. 6, 140
Going Upon the Mountain
     Gr. 6, 105
Good King Wenceslas  Gr. 6, 460
Good Old Happy Song, A
     Gr. K, 201
Gospel Train, The  Gr. 6, 398
Habemos llegado  Gr. 6, 174
Hanuka, Hanuka  Gr. 8, I-37
Hava nagila  Gr. 6, 153
He's Got the Whole World in His
     Hands  Gr. 7, I-38
Heave-Ho!/Going, Going, Gone/
     The Snow  Gr. 4, 182
Heigh-Ho  Gr. 2, 6
Hey, Ho! Nobody Home  Gr. 6, 28
Highlife Ensemble  Gr. 8, D-7
I Shall Sing  Gr. 8, I-39
Ichi-gatsu tsuitachi  Gr. 7, I-42
Ise oluwa  Gr. 6, 230
It's Time  Gr. 6, 274
Jambalaya  Gr. 8, I-47
*Jo'ashila, "Walking Together"*
     Gr. 6, 286
John Kanaka  Gr. 3, 60
Joy of Kwanzaa, The  Gr. 6, 462
Juan pirulero  Gr. K, 215
Kelo aba w'ye  Gr. 6, 290
*Kitchen Stomp*  Gr. 4, 122
Kou ri lengay  Gr. 2, 217
Kpanlogo Highlife Ensemble
     Gr. 7, D-13
Kwa-nu-te  Gr. 3, 214
*L'union*  Gr. 6, 487
La mariposa  Gr. 6, 58
La paloma se fué  Gr. 6, 51
La tormenta tropical  Gr. 2, 116
Let Us Sing Together  Gr. 6, 156
Lift Ev'ry Voice and Sing
     Gr. 8, I-55
Lion Sleeps Tonight, The
     Gr. 4, 131

Little and Lots  Gr. K, 323
Lone Star Trail  Gr. 2, 21
Los maizales  Gr. 1, 296
Lost My Gold Ring  Gr. 6, 158
*Lost River*  Gr. 6, 283
Má Teodora  Gr. 6, 301
Mainly Metal Ensemble  Gr. 7, D-26
*Máru-bihág*  Gr. 6, 304
Mary Ann  Gr. 6, 180
Mary Came a-Running  Gr. K, 294
Mi cuerpo hace música  Gr. K, 106
*Mi tierra*  Gr. 6, 365
Music's in Me, The  Gr. 2, 40
My Valentine  Gr. K, 323
Name, Name, What's Your Name?
     (speech piece)  Gr. 3, 10
Nampaya omame  Gr. 7, D-10
Nana Kru  Gr. 6, 282
*Nruab hnub thiab hmo ntuj*
     Gr. 4, 368
*Nyoka*  Gr. 7, D-33
O lê lê O Bahía  Gr. 6, 165
*O'Sullivan's March*  Gr. 5, 157
Ochimbo  Gr. 4, 135
*Oye como va*  Gr. 2, 255
Panamam tombé  Gr. 7, D-18
*Penny Lane*  Gr. 6, 257
Percussion Fun Rondo  Gr. 7, I-50
Pottery Dance  Gr. 1, 370
*Return to Misty Mountain*
     Gr. 7, D-28
Rhythm Is Gonna Get You, The
     Gr. 6, 348
Rondo for Lunch, A (speech piece)
     Gr. 3, 212
Rosie, Darling Rosie  Gr. 2, 215
S'vivon  Gr. 6, 452
Sing a Little Song  Gr. K, 30
Song of the Eagle  Gr. 2, 248
South African Ensemble
     Gr. 7, D-11
Star-Spangled Banner  Gr. 7, I-57
Stille Nacht (Silent Night)
     Gr. 7, I-55
Surfin' U.S.A.  Gr. 7, I-60
Take Time in Life  Gr. 6, 292
Ten Little Ostinato Pieces
     Gr. 7, I-62
*That'll Be the Day*  Gr. 6, 256
There Is Love Somewhere
     Gr. 6, 318
*This Is Your Night*  Gr. 6, 368
Today Is Your Birthday  Gr. 1, 410
Tree in the Wood, The  Gr. 2, 360
Turn the World Around  Gr. 4, 116
*Ue ue*  Gr. 8, D-2
Water Come a Me Eye  Gr. 6, 300
What Do Animals Need?
     Gr. 2, 288
When Johnny Comes Marching
     Home  Gr. 5, 181
Winter Song  Gr. 6, 455
Wu long  Gr. 4, 157

**(Playing Instruments, continued)**

Yellow Rose of Texas, The
Gr. 7, I-71

Yü guang guang  Gr. 6, 60

Zumba, zumba  Gr. 3, 400

## RECORDER

A la puerta del cielo  Gr. 5, 60

A Ram Sam Sam  Gr. 3, 208

Abraham, Martin, and John
Gr. 6, 466

Abraham, Martin, and John
Gr. 6, 471

Addams Family, The  Gr. 5, 457

Aguinaldo  Gr. 3, 402

Ahora voy a cantarles  Gr. 3, 57

Ai, Dunaii moy  Gr. 4, 293

Ain't Gonna Let Nobody Turn Me
'Round  Gr. 6, 84

Al citrón  Gr. 3, 320

Al quebrar la piñata  Gr. 4, 431

Al tambor  Gr. 3, 271

Alabama Gal  Gr. 3, 107

All Night, All Day  Gr. 4, 180

Ama-Lama  Gr. 5, 144

Ambos a dos  Gr. 3, 20

Ash Grove, The  Gr. 5, 114

Bear Dance  Gr. 7, I-11

Big Rock Candy Mountain
Gr. 4, 331

Blow the Wind Southerly
Gr. 5, 178

Blue Mountain Lake  Gr. 6, 204

Blue Skies  Gr. 6, 89

Bluebonnets of Texas  Gr. 3, 332

Bogando a la luz del sol  Gr. 4, 306

Boil Them Cabbage Down
Gr. 6, 370

Bonavist' Harbour  Gr. 3, 295

Bound for South Australia
Gr. 5, 22

Brandenburg Concerto No. 4,
BWV 1049, Allegro  Gr. 5, 111

Bridges  Gr. 6, 86

Bury Me Not on the Lone Prairie
Gr. 6, 19

Bury Me Not on the Lone Prairie
Gr. 6, 18

California  Gr. 5, 52

Camptown Races  Gr. 5, 270

Canoe Song  Gr. 4, 76

Canto del agua  Gr. 8, I-12

Cattle Call  Gr. 5, 346

Chairs to Mend  Gr. 4, 148

Cheki, morena  Gr. 7, I-17

Circle of Life, The  Gr. 6, 317

Clementine  Gr. 4, 341

Coffee Grows on White Oak Trees
Gr. 3, 168

Colorado Trail  Gr. 5, 276

Come and Go with Me to That
Land  Gr. 5, 390

Connemara Lullaby  Gr. 5, 233

Corrido de Kansas  Gr. 4, 275

Corta la caña  Gr. 6, 363

De colores  Gr. 5, 91

Do, Lord  Gr. 3, 164

Do, Re, Mi, Fa  Gr. 6, 80

Don Gato  Gr. 3, 353

Don't Cry for Me, Argentina
Gr. 6, 74

Don't You Hear the Lambs?
Gr. 5, 98

Down by the Riverside  Gr. 5, 257

Drill, Ye Tarriers  Gr. 5, 54

Dry Bones Come Skipping
Gr. 4, 218

Dundai  Gr. 5, 106

Ego sum pauper  Gr. 5, 158

Einini  Gr. 4, 393

El gallo pinto  Gr. 3, 87

El mes de abril  Gr. 3, 328

El payo  Gr. 6, 144

El sapito  Gr. 3, 336

Erdö, erdö de magos  Gr. 3, 182

Eres tú  Gr. 6, 474

Everybody Loves Saturday Night
Gr. 6, 296

Family Tree  Gr. 3, 75

Farewell to Tarwathie  Gr. 6, 42

Feng yang hua gu  Gr. 4, 313

Flip, Flop and Fly  Gr. 7, I-35

For the Beauty of the Earth
Gr. 4, 357

Four Strong Winds  Gr. 6, 171

Four White Horses  Gr. 3, 304

Frog Music  Gr. 4, 201

Give a Little Love  Gr. 6, 140

Give My Regards to Broadway
Gr. 6, 39

Glendy Burke, The  Gr. 4, 263

Go Down, Moses  Gr. 5, 190

Going upon the Mountain
Gr. 6, 104

Gonna Ride Up in the Chariot
Gr. 4, 20

Good Morning  Gr. 3, 193

Great Day  Gr. 3, 59

Greensleeves  Gr. 6, 47

Hanuka, Hanuka  Gr. 3, 390

Harrison Town  Gr. 6, 96

Hava nagila  Gr. 6, 152

He's Got the Whole World in His
Hands  Gr. 3, 231

Hop Up, My Ladies  Gr. 3, 145

Hot Cross Buns (Version 2)
Gr. 3, 221

Hound Dog  Gr. 5, 215

How Can I Keep from Singing?
Gr. 4, 260

I Am But a Small Voice  Gr. 6, 444

I Believe I Can Fly  Gr. 5, 172

I Don't Care If the Rain Comes
Down  Gr. 3, 24

I Walk the Unfrequented Road
Gr. 6, 77

I'm Gonna Sing  Gr. 4, 32

I've Been Working on the Railroad
Gr. 3, 243

Ichi-gatsu tsuitachi  Gr. 7, I-43

In the Pumpkin Patch  Gr. 3, 380

It's a Beautiful Day  Gr. 3, 338

Jambalaya  Gr. 6, 248

Joe Turner Blues  Gr. 4, 56

John Kanaka  Gr. 3, 60

Johnny Appleseed  Gr. 4, 344

Joy to the World  Gr. 3, 22

Juniper Tree, The  Gr. 3, 130

Knock No More  Gr. 3, 386

Kokopelli Wandering Song
Gr. 5, 110

Kum ba yah  Gr. 5, 244

La ciudad de Juaja  Gr. 5, 58

La Jesusita  Gr. 5, 323

La paloma blanca  Gr. 3, 252

La raspa  Gr. 4, 303

Laredo  Gr. 5, 10

Lean on Me  Gr. 6, 14

Let Music Surround You  Gr. 4, 236

Let Us Sing Together  Gr. 6, 156

Limbo Like Me  Gr. 4, 18

Linstead Market  Gr. 5, 241

Lion Sleeps Tonight, The
Gr. 4, 131

Little Shop of Horrors  Gr. 4, 423

Love Somebody  Gr. 3, 95

Magnolia  Gr. 6, 16

Mama Don't 'Low  Gr. 6, 361

Mary Ann  Gr. 6, 183

Missy-La, Massa-La  Gr. 4, 189

Morning Comes Early  Gr. 5, 13

Morning Has Broken  Gr. 5, 29

Morning Is Come  Gr. 3, 129

My Bonnie Lies Over the Ocean
Gr. 4, 339

Nie chcę cię znác  Gr. 3, 314

Ode to Joy  Gr. 4, 152

Oh, Watch the Stars  Gr. 5, 216

Old Dan Tucker  Gr. 3, 96

Ōsamu kosamu  Gr. 4, 97

Over the Rainbow  Gr. 4, 143

Over There  Gr. 5, 279

Oy, Hanuka  Gr. 7, I-45

Pat Works on the Railway
Gr. 5, 182

Paw-Paw Patch  Gr. 4, 92

Peace Like a River  Gr. 3, 248

Peace Round  Gr. 4, 349

Piñon, pirulín  Gr. 2, 174

Pretty Saro  Gr. 3, 216

Purple People Eater, The
Gr. 6, 449

Pust' 'vsegda budet sonse
Gr. 3, 278

¡Qué bonita bandera!  Gr. 5, 296

Railroad Corral  Gr. 3, 174

Red River Valley  Gr. 6, 10

Rio Grande  Gr. 4, 256

Riqui rán  Gr. 4, 66

Rise and Shine  Gr. 4, 99
River  Gr. 4, 59
Rock Island Line  Gr. 4, 54
Rockin' Robin  Gr. 3, 368
Rocky Top  Gr. 5, 349
Run! Run! Hide!  Gr. 6, 342
Sailing Down My Golden River
    Gr. 4, 332
Sakura  Gr. 4, 308
Scotland the Brave  Gr. 5, 138
Shady Grove  Gr. 5, 261
Shenandoah  Gr. 5, 264
Simple Gifts  Gr. 5, 185
Sing a Song of Peace  Gr. 6, 67
Sing, Sing, Sing!  Gr. 5, 340
Skye Boat Song  Gr. 6, 372
*Slow Hora/Freylekhs*  Gr. 8, B-25
Somos el barco  Gr. 4, 352
St. Louis Blues  Gr. 5, 352
St. Patrick Was a Gentleman
    Gr. 3, 292
Starlight, Star Bright  Gr. 4, 373
Stille Nacht (Silent Night)
    Gr. 7, I-55
Streets of Laredo  Gr. 4, 272
Strike Up the Band  Gr. 6, 135
Summertime  Gr. 6, 250
Sun Gonna Shine  Gr. 6, 241
Sweet Betsy from Pike  Gr. 4, 245
Take Me Out to the Ball Game
    Gr. 3, 262
Take Time in Life  Gr. 6, 293
Tender Shepherd (Count Your
    Sheep)  Gr. 3, 116
This Land Is Your Land  Gr. 7, I-69
Tie Me Kangaroo Down, Sport
    Gr. 4, 36
Tom Dooley  Gr. 6, 374
Train Is A-Comin'  Gr. 3, 48
Tumba  Gr. 5, 161
Turn the Beat Around  Gr. 4, 2
Turn the World Around  Gr. 4, 116
Tzena, tzena  Gr. 5, 301
Vamos a la mar  Gr. 3, 228
Vem kan segla?  Gr. 6, 420
Vem kan segla?  Gr. 6, 417
Wabash Cannon Ball  Gr. 5, 137
Waitin' for the Light to Shine
    Gr. 4, 29
Water Come a Me Eye  Gr. 6, 300
We've Got Lots in Common
    Gr. 3, 367
Weevily Wheat  Gr. 4, 105
What a Wonderful World  Gr. 6, 62
Winter Fantasy  Gr. 4, 425
Worried Man Blues  Gr. 6, 370
Yellow Rose of Texas, The
    Gr. 7, I-72
Yibane amenu  Gr. 4, 317
You're a Grand Old Flag  Gr. 3, 264
Zum gali gali  Gr. 5, 401

## RESONATOR BELLS
El payo  Gr. 6, 145

## STRINGS
Estampie  Gr. 8, I-27

## TRUMPET
¡Ay, Jalisco no te rajes!  Gr. 7, I-9
Cielito lindo  Gr. 7, I-22

## VIOLIN
¡Ay, Jalisco no te rajes!  Gr. 7, I-9
Cielito lindo  Gr. 7, I-22

## WINDS
Estampie  Gr. 8, I-27
Every Night When the Sun Goes In
    Gr. 8, I-30
Guantanamera  Gr. 8, I-35
I Shall Sing  Gr. 8, I-40
I'll Fly Away  Gr. 8, I-45
Jambalaya  Gr. 8, I-48
Los reyes de Oriente  Gr. 8, I-59
Wade in the Water  Gr. 8, I-65
Yonder Come Day  Gr. 8, I-71

## POETRY *See Literature; Recorded Lessons: Recorded Poems and Stories.*

## PROGRAM IDEAS
Bring Your Passport  Gr. 4, 288
Chasing a Dream  Gr. 4, 322
Earth, Sea, and Sky  Gr. 4, 350
Fun and Games  Gr. 3, 298
Going Places U.S.A.  Gr. 4, 250
Our World of Music  Gr. 3, 266
Singing America  Gr. 3, 236
This Beautiful Planet  Gr. 3, 324
Tuneful Tales  Gr. 3, 348
*Why Is There Day and Night?*
    Gr. 4, 366

## PRONUNCIATION PRACTICE, RECORDED
A la puerta del cielo  Gr. 5, 60
A la rurru niño  Gr. K, 180
Achshav  Gr. 2, 64
Adana ya gidelim  Gr. 2, 142
Adelita  Gr. 5, 50
Adiós, amigos  Gr. 6, 57
Aguinaldo  Gr. 3, 402
Ah, eu entrei na roda  Gr. 3, 308
Ah! Les jolis papillons  Gr. 1, 362
Ah ya Zane  Gr. 5, 297
Ahora voy a cantarles  Gr. 3, 56
Ai, Dunaii moy  Gr. 4, 293
Al ánimo  Gr. 3, 322
Al citrón  Gr. 3, 320
Al quebrar la piñata  Gr. 4, 432
Al tambor  Gr. 3, 270
Ala Da'lona  Gr. 4, 136
Allá en la fuente  Gr. 2, 92
Alle meine Entchen  Gr. 1, 98
Alumot  Gr. 6, 306
Ambos a dos  Gr. 3, 20

Amefuri  Gr. 1, 144
Arirang  Gr. 5, 25
Asadoya  Gr. 6, 303
Así es mi tierra  Gr. 6, 172
Au clair de la lune  Gr. 3, 18
¡Ay, Jalisco no te rajes!  Gr. 7, I-6
Ayelivi  Gr. 2, 70
Ayliluli, num tsipor  Gr. 1, 204
Bantama kra kro  Gr. 5, 308
Banuwa  Gr. 6, 294
Bặt kim thang  Gr. 6, 13
Bereleh  Gr. K, 151
Beriozka  Gr. 4, 294
Bogando a la luz del sol  Gr. 4, 306
Bonjour, mes amis  Gr. 1, 316
Buenos días  Gr. 1, 13
Canción de cuna  Gr. 4, 144
Canción Mixteca  Gr. 5, 326
Cantando mentiras  Gr. 4, 146
Cantaré, cantarás  Gr. 6, 413
Canto del agua  Gr. 8, I-10
Cha yang wu  Gr. 1, 90
Chag purim  Gr. 1, 438
Chang  Gr. 1, 156
Chanukah, Chanukah  Gr. 1, 420
Chanukiyah li yesh  Gr. 1, 421
Chawe chidyo chem'chero  Gr. 2, 296
Cheki, morena  Gr. 2, 180
Cheki, morena  Gr. 7, I-16
Chiapanecas  Gr. 5, 92
Cho'i hát bội  Gr. 5, 318
Chuhwuht  Gr. 2, 356
Cielito lindo  Gr. 4, 270
Cielito lindo  Gr. 7, I-20
Cirmos cica  Gr. 1, 130
Con el vito  Gr. 7, G-15
Corrido de Kansas  Gr. 4, 274
Corta la caña  Gr. 6, 364
Counting Song  Gr. 1, 253
Cuando pa' Chile me voy  Gr. 6, 376
Da pacem, Domine  Gr. 5, 62
Dayenu  Gr. 4, 439
De colores  Gr. 5, 90
De colores  Gr. 8, I-14
Deau-deau, ti pitit maman  Gr. 2, 306
Debajo el botón  Gr. 1, 210
Der sad to katte  Gr. 2, 300
Deux cocodries  Gr. 2, 364
Dinner Music  Gr. K, 70
Diou shou juan'er  Gr. 2, 277
Dok djampa  Gr. 8, I-20
Don Alfonso  Gr. 5, 177
Don Gato  Gr. 3, 352
Dona nobis pacem  Gr. 6, 125
Doong gul ge  Gr. 3, 134
Doraji  Gr. 4, 174
Duck Dance  Gr. 2, 249
Duérmete, mi niño  Gr. 1, 292
Dundai  Gr. 5, 106
Ee jer ha ba go  Gr. K, 133
Ég a gyertya  Gr. K, 96
Ego sum pauper  Gr. 5, 158
Eh, cumpari!  Gr. 4, 68

(*Pronunciation Practice, Recorded,*
continued)

Ein Männlein steht im Walde  Gr. 2, 90
Einini  Gr. 4, 391
El barquito  Gr. 3, 358
El borrego  Gr. 4, 242
El burrito enfermo  Gr. K, 271
El caracol  Gr. K, 130
El carite  Gr. 5, 305
El carnavalito humahuaqueño
    Gr. 6, 482
El chocolate  Gr. 1, 380
El cóndor pasa  Gr. 6, 46
El coquí  Gr. 2, 292
El desembre congelat  Gr. 5, 473
El día de mamita  Gr. K, 325
El florón  Gr. 2, 246
El gallo pinto  Gr. 3, 86
El juego chirimbolo  Gr. 2, 54
El mes de abril  Gr. 3, 328
El payo  Gr. 6, 145
El rabel  Gr. 3, 362
El rancho grande  Gr. 4, 215
El rancho grande  Gr. 8, I-22
El sapito  Gr. 3, 336
El tambor  Gr. 2, 274
El Tren  Gr. 2, 260
El zapatero  Gr. 1, 298
Elegua  Gr. 7, D-8
Éliza Kongo  Gr. 5, 14
En nuestra Tierra tan linda  Gr. 2, 335
Erdö, erdö de magos  Gr. 3, 182
Eres tú  Gr. 6, 473
Fais do do  Gr. 6, 403
Fais dodo  Gr. K, 158
Farewell to the Warriors  Gr. 4, 284
Feliz Navidad  Gr. 7, I-28
Feng yang hua gu  Gr. 4, 313
Frère Jacques  Gr. 2, 125
Funwa alafia  Gr. 5, 32
Gakavik  Gr. 4, 14
Gaudeamus igitur  Gr. 8, C-20
Geef jij mij die schoen  Gr. 1, 126
Gloria, Gloria  Gr. 6, 459
Greetings (speech piece)  Gr. 3, 316
Guantanamera  Gr. 8, I-32
Ha'kyo jong  Gr. 2, 135
Habemos llegado  Gr. 6, 174
Haere  Gr. 2, 285
Hama chi dori  Gr. 3, 330
Hanuka, Hanuka  Gr. 3, 390
Hanuka, Hanuka  Gr. 8, I-36
Haru ga kita  Gr. 2, 401
Hashewie  Gr. 4, 63
Hashkediya  Gr. 3, 206
Hato popo  Gr. 1, 186
Hava nagila  Gr. 6, 153
Hava nashira  Gr. 6, 82
Hej pada pada  Gr. 3, 78
Hevenu shalom aleichem  Gr. 3, 378
Hey, m'tswala  Gr. 4, 79
Himmel und Erde  Gr. 5, 94
Hine mah tov  Gr. 5, 430

Hitotsu toya  Gr. 5, 478
Hotaru koi  Gr. 1, 356
Hui jia qù  Gr. 2, 158
Hwa yuan li-de young wa wa
    Gr. 3, 102
Ichi-gatsu tsuitachi  Gr. 3, 406
Ichi-gatsu tsuitachi  Gr. 7, I-40
Imbabura  Gr. 5, 203
Inkpataya  Gr. 3, 254
Ise oluwa  Gr. 2, 102
Ise oluwa  Gr. 6, 230
Jan ken pon  Gr. 3, 302
¡Jeu! ¡Jeu!  Gr. 1, 216
Jo'ashila  Gr. 5, 108
Kaeru no uta  Gr. K, 183
Kapulu kane  Gr. 2, 270
Karangatia ra  Gr. 3, 272
Karangatia ra  Gr. 8, F-23
Kébé Mama  Gr. 1, 442
Kibungo  Gr. 2, 354
Koriko!  Gr. K, 154
Kou ri lengay  Gr. 2, 217
Kou ri lengay  Gr. 7, E-2
Kum bachur atzel  Gr. 3, 138
Kuma san  Gr. K, 40
Kunolounkwa  Gr. K, 110
L'inverno è passato  Gr. 2, 400
La bamba  Gr. 5, 128
La borinqueña  Gr. 8, D-19
La calle ancha  Gr. 3, 297
La ciudad de Juaja  Gr. 5, 58
La copa de la vida  Gr. 4, 414
La golondrina  Gr. 8, I-50
La Jesusita  Gr. 5, 322
La mar estaba serena  Gr. 2, 344
La mariposa  Gr. 6, 58
La paloma blanca  Gr. 3, 252
La paloma se fué  Gr. 6, 51
La piñata  Gr. 3, 399
La pulga de San José  Gr. 3, 40
La raspa  Gr. 4, 302
La Tarara  Gr. 4, 176
La tormenta tropical  Gr. 2, 116
La víbora  Gr. 1, 322
Lahk gei mohlee  Gr. 5, 317
Laredo  Gr. 5, 10
Las estaciones  Gr. 1, 29
Las estrellitas del cielo  Gr. 5, 175
Las horas  Gr. 1, 246
Las mañanitas  Gr. 6, 481
Las Navidades  Gr. 5, 472
Las velitas  Gr. 5, 147
Leak kanseng  Gr. 1, 156
Liebe ist ein Ring  Gr. 4, 193
Lo yisa  Gr. 6, 130
Loigratong  Gr. 6, 451
Los maizales  Gr. 1, 296
Los niños en España cantan
    Gr. 4, 197
Los pececitos  Gr. 1, 178
Los pollitos  Gr. K, 166
Los reyes de Oriente  Gr. 5, 480
Los reyes de Oriente  Gr. 8, I-58

Los trencitos  Gr. K, 24
Má Teodora  Gr. 6, 301
Magnolia  Gr. 6, 16
Mañana  Gr. 7, E-14
Mariposita  Gr. 2, 156
Mbombera  Gr. K, 24
Me voy para la luna  Gr. 1, 397
Meng Jian Nu  Gr. 5, 194
Merry Modal Christmas, A  Gr. 4, 411
Mi cuerpo hace música  Gr. K, 106
Minka  Gr. 4, 222
Mon papa  Gr. 2, 280
Mubärak  Gr. 3, 282
Nampaya omame  Gr. 1, 138
Nampaya omame  Gr. 7, D-10
Nani wale na hala  Gr. 3, 260
Naranja dulce  Gr. 2, 97
Ner li  Gr. 2, 383
Nie chcę cię znác  Gr. 3, 314
Niño querido  Gr. 1, 308
Niu lang zhi nü  Gr. 4, 335
No quiero plata  Gr. 1, 424
Nu wahtan  Gr. 1, 279
O, Desayo  Gr. 5, 411
O Laufet, ihr Hirten  Gr. 2, 384
O lê lê O Bahía  Gr. 6, 165
O ma washi  Gr. K, 13
O pião entrou  Gr. 2, 355
Ocho kandelikas  Gr. 4, 429
Ode to Joy  Gr. 4, 152
Ōsamu kosamu  Gr. 4, 96
Oy, Hanuka  Gr. 5, 464
Oy, Hanuka  Gr. 7, I-44
Oye  Gr. 6, 336
Pai pi qiu  Gr. 1, 324
Panamam tombé  Gr. 7, D-18
Pavo, pavo  Gr. 1, 416
Perná, perná, i mélissá  Gr. K, 264
Perot  Gr. 2, 378
Pin Pon  Gr. 1, 146
Piñon, pirulín  Gr. 2, 174
Pollerita  Gr. 5, 151
Pon, pon, pon  Gr. K, 50
Ptashky u babusi sadochku  Gr. 1, 192
Pust' 'vsegda budet sonse  Gr. 3, 278
Quâ câù gió bay  Gr. 5, 460
¡Qué bonita bandera!  Gr. 5, 294
¡Qué gusto!  Gr. 3, 132
¡Qué llueva!  Gr. K, 81
Ragupati Ragava Raja Ram  Gr. 5, 321
Riendo el río corre  Gr. 6, 263
Rinsho, rinsho  Gr. K, 285
Río, río  Gr. 5, 370
Riqui rán  Gr. 1, 48
Riqui rán  Gr. 4, 66
Ríu ríu chíu  Gr. 5, 435
S'vivon  Gr. 6, 452
Sailboat in the Sky  Gr. 4, 374
Sakura  Gr. 4, 308
Sambalele  Gr. 4, 397
Sansaw akroma  Gr. 3, 286
Santa Clara  Gr. 4, 172
Sarika keo  Gr. 3, 275

Sawatdee tuh jah  Gr. 2, 265
Se va el caimán  Gr. 5, 306
Serra, serra, serrador  Gr. 1, 112
Shalom aleichem  Gr. 6, 409
Shir l'shalom  Gr. 4, 419
Shu ha mo  Gr. 3, 276
Si me dan pasteles  Gr. 1, 432
Si si si  Gr. 7, G-13
Sierra Morena  Gr. 3, 296
Siyahamba  Gr. 6, 212
Sol, solecito  Gr. 1, 367
Somos el barco  Gr. 4, 352
Son macaron  Gr. 4, 109
Sonando  Gr. 4, 34
Song of the Eagle  Gr. 2, 248
Still, Still, Still  Gr. 5, 468
Stille Nacht (Silent Night)  Gr. 7, I-54
T'hola, t'hola  Gr. 4, 132
Tanabata-sama  Gr. 2, 336
Tancovačka  Gr. 4, 230
Tengo, tengo, tengo  Gr. 4, 228
Thula, thula, ngoana  Gr. 4, 227
Tic, tac  Gr. 1, 252
Tina singu  Gr. 4, 300
To'ia mai te waka  Gr. 1, 77
Tsuki  Gr. 4, 25
Tzena, tzena  Gr. 5, 298
Uga uga uga  Gr. K, 305
'Ūlili E  Gr. 5, 441
Un, deux, trois  Gr. 2, 198
Un elefante  Gr. 2, 160
Un pajarito  Gr. 2, 16
Uno, dos y tres  Gr. 5, 429
Usagi  Gr. 1, 396
Vamos a cantar  Gr. K, 278
Vamos a hacer la ronda  Gr. K, 124
Vamos a la fiesta  Gr. 2, 374
Vamos a la mar  Gr. 3, 226
Vem kan segla?  Gr. 6, 417
Vil du?  Gr. 1, 92
¡Viva el fútbol!  Gr. 1, 96
Viva Jujuy  Gr. 5, 228
Was kommt dort von der Höh'?
    Gr. 8, C-21
Wir hatten gebauet  Gr. 8, C-21
Xiao  Gr. 4, 314
Xiao yin chuan  Gr. 2, 14
Ye jaliya da  Gr. 5, 67
Yesh lanu taish  Gr. 1, 182
Yibane amenu  Gr. 4, 316
Yü guang guang  Gr. 6, 60
Yüe liang wan wan  Gr. 5, 314
Zum gali gali  Gr. 5, 401
Zumba, zumba  Gr. 3, 400

**R**

**READING** See also Skills
    Reinforcement.
Amarillo Armadillo  Gr. 2, 82
America, the Beautiful  Gr. 7, I-4
¡Ay, Jalisco no te rajes!  Gr. 7, I-6
Banjo Sam  Gr. 2, 314

Black Snake  Gr. 3, 53
Caballito blanco  Gr. 2, 193
Caribbean Island Ensemble
    Gr. 7, D-19
Chapel of Love  Gr. 7, G-27
Charleston, The  Gr. 7, B-10
Cheki, morena  Gr. 7, I-16
Ding, Dong, Diggidiggidong  Gr. 3, 14
Do Wah Diddy Diddy  Gr. 7, F-21
Don't Let the Wind  Gr. 3, 180
Edward Scissorhands, "Main Titles"
    Gr. 8, A-10
Ev'rybody Loves Saturday Night
    Gr. 7, I-24
Golden Ring Around Susan Girl
    Gr. 3, 16
Highlife Ensemble  Gr. 8, D-7
Hosisipa  Gr. 3, 70
Hwa yuan li-de young wa wa
    Gr. 3, 102
Ja-Da  Gr. 7, G-20
Lean on Me  Gr. 7, E-22
Morning Is Come  Gr. 3, 128
My Home's Across the Blue Ridge
    Mountains  Gr. 7, F-6
Oh, Freedom  Gr. 7, G-30
Old Man Mosie  Gr. 3, 108
One Morning Soon  Gr. 3, 68
Over My Head  Gr. 7, G-9
Pictures at an Exhibition  Gr. 8, A-13
Rainbow in the Sky  Gr. 7, B-35
Rhapsody in Blue  Gr. 7, C-42
Slow Hora/Freylekhs  Gr. 8, B-25
Something Told the Wild Geese
    Gr. 7, G-39
Stille Nacht (Silent Night)  Gr. 7, F-24
Symphony No. 47 in G Major,
    "Menuet"  Gr. 7, C-14
Symphony No. 5 in C Minor, Op. 67,
    Movement 1  Gr. 7, C-16
This Land is Your Land  Gr. 7, F-24
Turn the Beat Around  Gr. 4, 2
You Were on My Mind  Gr. 7, G-23

**RECORDED LESSONS** See also
    Pronunciation Practice, Recorded.

### RECORDED ASSESSMENTS
African Talking Drum  Gr. 1, 120
Bob-a-Needle  Gr. 2, 72
Cymbals  Gr. 1, 240
Down by the Bay  Gr. K, 56
Machine Music, "Garbage Truck"
    Gr. K, 84
Melody Pattern 1  Gr. 1, 160
Rain Sounds  Gr. K, 84
Rhythm Pattern 1  Gr. 1, 120
Rhythm Pattern 1  Gr. 1, 160

### RECORDED INTERVIEWS
Backstage with Jeanine Tesori
    Gr. 8, A-20
Bassett, Rick (Part 1)  Gr. 3, 222
Bassett, Rick (Part 2)  Gr. 3, 223

Burke, Liam  Gr. 2, 11
Burrough, Roslyn  Gr. 1, 163
Burton, J. Bryan  Gr. 4, 285
Callaway, Ann Hampton
    Gr. 6, 113
Clark, Petula  Gr. 6, 259
Copland, Aaron  Gr. 5, 187
Crawley, Brian  Gr. 6, 312
Glennie, Evelyn  Gr. 3, 149
Hogan, Moses  Gr. 4, 395
Interview with Carlos Chavez
    Gr. 8, C-37
Interview with Pete Seeger
    Gr. 8, C-35
Joubert, Joseph  Gr. 3, 50
Luker, Rebecca  Gr. 5, 38
Moore, Carman  Gr. 3, 163
Naranjo, Valerie Dee  Gr. 6, 186
Rafter, Michael  Gr. 6, 113
Rashad, Phylicia  Gr. 7, A-27
Red, Buryl  Gr. 7, A-21
Ritchie, Jean  Gr. 4, 349
Rodgers, Richard  Gr. 5, 39
Sanchez, David "Dakota"
    Gr. 6, 319
Schuman, William  Gr. 6, 83
Seeger, Pete  Gr. 5, 380
Stravinsky, Igor  Gr. 2, 264
Stravinsky Interview and
    "Barceuse" from The Firebird
    Gr. 8, C-33
Swoboda, Deanna  Gr. 3, 188
Tesori, Jeanine  Gr. 6, 312
Twine, Linda  Gr. 6, 339

### RECORDED POEMS AND STORIES
Bubble Trouble  Gr. K, 184
Bubbles  Gr. K, 185
Cacophony  Gr. K, 83
Chawe chidyo chem'chero
    Gr. 2, 296
Children Learn What They Live
    Gr. 5, 381
De Beat  Gr. 2, 67
Dragon Smoke  Gr. K, 258
End, The  Gr. 1, 408
First Snowflake  Gr. K, 259
Galoshes  Gr. K, 63
Happiness  Gr. K, 62
Harriet Tubman  Gr. 4, 269
It Is Fun to Sing (One fish, two fish,
    red fish, blue fish)  Gr. 1, 65
Kibungo, Beast of the Forest
    Gr. 2, 352
Little Red Hen, The  Gr. 1, 254
Louder Than a Clap of Thunder
    Gr. 1, 87
Manhattan Lullaby  Gr. K, 193
Mmmmmm mmmmmmm
    Gr. K, 71
New Colossus, The  Gr. 5, 166
Paper  Gr. K, 195
Rabbit Dance, The  Gr. 3, 334

(*Recorded Poems and Stories,* continued)
Sea Wolf, The  Gr. 4, 257
Shake-'n'-Bake a Jelly  Gr. K, 95
Song of the Night, The  Gr. 3, 346
Song of the Train  Gr. K, 153
Stopping by Woods on a Snowy
  Evening  Gr. 6, 41
Toaster Time  Gr. K, 17
Wind Song  Gr. K, 7
Windshield Wipers  Gr. 1, 11
Yellow Butter  Gr. 1, 124
*Zomo the Rabbit*  Gr. 3, 364

## RELATED ARTS

### ART REPRODUCTIONS

Alom (Vasarely)  Gr. 6, 134
America (Ong)  Gr. 4, 209
B126 (Tadasky)  Gr. 6, 122
Ballet Rehearsal (Degas)  Gr. 6, 323
Banjo Lesson (Cassatt), The
  Gr. 2, 121
Beethoven while composing the
  Missa Solemnis (Joseph Karl
  Stielere)  Gr. 8, C-16
Beloved Grandchildren, The (Li Mei-
  Shu)  Gr. 3, 105
Bonaparte crossing the Alps at
  Grand-Saint-Bernard (Louis
  David)  Gr. 8, C-16
Bridge Across the Moon  Gr. 6, 302
California Vaqueros  Gr. 4, 275
Calla Lily Vendor (Rivera)
  Gr. 6, 415
Caricature of Liszt (Brennglass)
  Gr. 7, E-18
Carved Memorial Stone  Gr. 6, 416
Cat (Foujita)  Gr. K, 12
Cat Lying on a Yellow Pillow (Marc)
  Gr. 1, 128
Chasm of the Colorade (Moran),
  The  Gr. K, 260
Children Dancing (Gwathmey)
  Gr. 4, 106
Children Playing London Bridge
  (Johnson)  Gr. 2, 29
Chinese ink painting of a panda
  (Zhoren)  Gr. 5, 315
Clipper Ship (Ross), The
  Gr. 5, 265
Computer-generated fractal image
  Gr. 4, 198
Concert, A  Gr. 5, 439
Concert (Gabbiani), The  Gr. 6, 102
Continentals (Mayer), The
  Gr. 2, 404
Court Ball at the Palais du Louvre
  (De Médicis)  Gr. 2, 278
Court Ball at the Palais du Louvre
  (de Medicis)  Gr. 7, C-6
Cowboy Dance (Magafan)
  Gr. 6, 238
Creatures in the Night (Miro)
  Gr. 5, 174

Cuna Indian Molas  Gr. 1, 212
Dakota Sioux doll and cradle board
  Gr. 3, 70
Dance in Tehuantepec (Rivera)
  Gr. 4, 304
Daniel Boone Escorting Pioneers
  (Bingham)  Gr. 4, 139
Danse dans un Pavillion (Watteau)
  Gr. 4, 112
Dawn till Dusk (Johnson)
  Gr. 7, I-49
Detail of a funeral procession
  (Zihong)  Gr. 8, D-27
Eighteenth-century coverlet
  Gr. 5, 395
Empanadas (Garza)  Gr. 6, 173
Engraving of Franz Joseph Haydn
  conducting a string quartet
  Gr. 6, 132
Fabergé egg  Gr. 4, 293
Fiddler (Chagall), The  Gr. 7, E-6
Fiddling Sailor (Pierre)  Gr. 4, 386
Flamingo (Calder)  Gr. 8, F-12
Fourteenth Century painting
  of a monk transribing music
  Gr. 7, A-22
Freedom from Want (Rockwell)
  Gr. 3, 385
Friends (Ong)  Gr. 5, 382
Girl with a Guitar (Vermeer)
  Gr. 4, 177
Going to Church (Johnson)
  Gr. 5, 102
Hand-colored engraving
  (Remington)  Gr. 5, 277
Hanetsuki (Sadahide)  Gr. 7, I-42
Harriet and the Freedom Train
  (Olsen)  Gr. 6, 397
Harriet Tubman Series Number One
  (Lawrence), The  Gr. 8, I-66
Holiday Sleigh Ride (Scott)
  Gr. 2, 389
Horse and Rider weather vane
  Gr. 4, 388
Hungarian painting of Zoltán
  Kodály  Gr. 7, C-34
I See Rhythm (Wood)  Gr. 4, 161
Illumination from sheet music of
  Francesco Landini  Gr. 8, C-6
Illustration of Flag Art (Stutzman)
  Gr. 8, G-36
Impression: Soleil levant (Monet)
  Gr. 8, C-26
Indonesian shadow puppets
  Gr. 5, 319
Into Bondage (Douglas)  Gr. 7, G-11
Inuit soapstone carving  Gr. 3, 258
Jeunes Filles au Piano (Renoir)
  Gr. 8, C-27
Jinshan Peasant Painting
  Gr. 2, 159
Kente Cloth  Gr. 8, D-12
Korean porcelain jar  Gr. 3, 136

Koru, The  Gr. 8, F-23
La piñata (Rivera)  Gr. 3, 398
La Ronde (Picasso)  Gr. 6, 127
Lift Up Thy Voice and Sing
  (Johnson)  Gr. 7, I-12
Lighting the Chanukah Lamp
  (Holzhandler)  Gr. 5, 465
London, England (Griffier)
  Gr. 8, C-8
Madonna with Flowers (Joysmith)
  Gr. K, 134
Man with Kilaut (Nanogak)
  Gr. 8, D-21
Maori wood carvings  Gr. 3, 273
Map (Johns)  Gr. 5, 250
Marilyn Monroe (Warhol)
  Gr. 7, I-63
Masa (Gorman)  Gr. K, 66
Mayan pottery  Gr. 4, 305
Micmac beadwork  Gr. 3, 215
Modern Painting with Clef
  (Lichtenstein)  Gr. 2, 79
Mola textile pattern of the Cuna
  people  Gr. 4, 145
Moonlight on Sebu River (Hiroshige)
  Gr. 4, 24
Mosaic of Jerusalem (Orti)
  Gr. 5, 160
Mother and Child (Walter)
  Gr. 4, 181
Mullet Friday (Green)  Gr. 8, I-71
Mural of musicians playing
  traditional Caribbean instruments
  (Anonymous)  Gr. 4, 191
Navajo rugs  Gr. 7, D-25
Night at the Silver Slipper
  (Burnside/Beadle)  Gr. 5, 16
Nightingale (Fekete), The
  Gr. 8, C-32
Oedipus' Riddle (Kappel)  Gr. 8, G-6
Old Oaken Bucket in Winter
  (Moses), The  Gr. 6, 454
Ozark Mountain folk art carving
  Gr. 4, 92
Painting of Alban Berg  Gr. 6, 169
Painting of Musicians  Gr. 5, 63
Painting of Richard Wagner
  (Beckmann)  Gr. 8, C-22
Paj ntaub (Lor)  Gr. 4, 367
Patticake (Joysmith)  Gr. 1, 330
Piano Lesson (Beardon), The
  Gr. 8, A-27
Pianoforte Cantata (1835)
  (Anonymous)  Gr. 4, 234
Port of Galveston, The (Stockfleth)
  Gr. 4, 259
Procession of Notre Dame de Salon
  (Alsloot), A  Gr. 7, C-7
Puddle Jumpers (Goodacre)
  Gr. K, 38
Rattlesnake, The (Remington)
  Gr. 3, 177

Reflections of the Big Dipper
(Pollack) Gr. 6, 208
Regatta at Argenteuil (Monet)
Gr. 7, C-38
Reunion of Artists in Studio of
Jean-Baptiste Isabey (Boilly)
Gr. 8, C-17
Rhythmical (Klee) Gr. 2, 48
Russian nesting dolls Gr. 4, 224
Sally Walker (Joysmith) Gr. 2, 273
Sankofa Gr. 7, D-13
Scéne de cabaret (Boilly)
Gr. 8, C-17
Schubert at the Piano (Schwind)
Gr. 7, C-20
Sculling at Sunset (Beasley)
Gr. 6, 191
Sergei Prokofiev (Konchalosky)
Gr. 6, 457
Serpentine Wedding Dancers
(anonymous) Gr. 8, G-13
Shepherd (Whiteside), The
Gr. 5, 96
Singing Round Campfire Gr. 5, 68
Snow Palace Gr. 6, 41
Sopron (Nemeth) Gr. 6, 197
Sous les Pins a Carqueiranne
(Gaidan) Gr. 3, 89
Spirit of '76 (Willard), The
Gr. 8, C-38
Stained glass window (U.N.
Building) (Chagall) Gr. 6, 442
Starry Night, 1923–1924 (Munch)
Gr. 2, 145
Starry Night (Van Gogh) Gr. 1, 107
Strike Up the Band Gr. 6, 135
Sun Seeks Shadow (White)
Gr. 7, D-28
Sunsets (Rivera) Gr. 2, 334
Surprised! (Rousseau) Gr. 3, 356
Swing (Wood) Gr. 5, 337
Swing Your Partner Gr. 6, 104
Tapestry (Roy) Gr. 8, D-28
Three Musicians (Picasso)
Gr. 4, 212
Trail Herd to Abilene (Koerner)
Gr. 6, 237
Trees (Derain), The Gr. K, 174
Trío Musical Gr. 6, 50
Tucanos com Bananeíras (Felga)
Gr. 3, 309
Twittering Machine (Klee), The
Gr. 8, C-47
Two Norse ships at sea Gr. 6, 419
Untitled (Haring) Gr. 2, 43
Untitled (Marstall) Gr. 1, 361
Untitled (Saul) Gr. 2, 307
Untitled (Wyeth) Gr. 2, 235
View of the Bombardment of Fort
McHenry (Bower), A Gr. 7, I-57
Watercolor Ripple (Greve)
Gr. 4, 77

Wharf of Venice (Puelma)
Gr. K, 144
Whirl, The (Kupka) Gr. 3, 89
White Water Lilies (Monet)
Gr. 1, 23
Woman in Black at the Opera
(Cassatt) Gr. 8, E-12
Woman playing shakuhachi (Ong)
Gr. 5, 112
Woman Standing, Child on Back
(Charlot) Gr. K, 134
Wooded Landscape (Millet)
Gr. 4, 365
Wooden Medieval kite shield from
the 1400s Gr. 8, C-4
Yankee Volunteers Marching to
Dixie Gr. 5, 273

## BALLET

Billy the Kid, "Celebration"
Gr. 3, 251
Firebird, The, "Finale" Gr. 8, C-30
Le Sacre de Printemps (The Rite
of Spring), "Dance of the Youths
and Maidens" Gr. 8, C-30
Nutcracker Suite, The, "Trepak"
Gr. 3, 280
Nutcracker Suite, The, "Trepak"
Gr. 6, 207
Nutcracker Suite, The, "Waltz of
the Flowers" Gr. 6, 325
Nutcracker, The, "Arabian Dance"
Gr. 7, C-26
Nutcracker, The, "Chinese Dance"
Gr. 7, C-26
Red Poppy, The, "Russian Sailors'
Dance" Gr. 4, 224
Rodeo, "Hoedown" Gr. 5, 312
Rodeo, "Saturday Night Waltz"
Gr. 4, 342

## DANCE

America (from West Side Story)
Gr. 8, C-45
Burke, Liam Gr. 2, 11
Dance at the Gym Gr. 5, 9
Danses Populaires Francaises,
"Branle Double, Branle
Simple" Gr. 7, C-25
Danzas Puertorriqueñas, "Vano
Empeno" Gr. 7, E-13
Estancia, "Danza del trigo"
Gr. 5, 229
Gamelan angklung Gr. 6, 384
Going Upon the Mountain
Gr. 6, 105
Kebjar teruna Gr. 6, 385
Khorovod Gr. 1, 372
Lord of the Dance Medley
Gr. 6, 326
Mon papa Gr. 2, 280
Na rechenki Gr. 1, 375
Riverdance Suite Gr. 2, 141
Sha Sha Sha Gr. 6, 328

Somewhere Gr. 8, C-44
Tommy Peoples Gr. 8, B-20
Trash Can Stomp (from Stomp
Out Loud) Gr. 6, 328
Twist with a Burger, Jitter with a
Bug (speech piece) Gr. 1, 132
Yesh lanu taish Gr. 1, 182

## OPERA

Aida, "Gloria all'Egitto (Grand
March)" Gr. 8, C-24
Die Walküre, "The Ride of the
Valkyries" Gr. 8, C-23
Die Zauberflöte, "Pa-pa-pa-pa-pa-
pa-pagena" Gr. 8, C-13
Hänsel und Gretel, "Ein Männlein
steht im Walde" Gr. 2, 91
Il trovatore, "Anvil Chorus"
Gr. 6, 25
Les pêcheurs des perles, "Au fond
du temple saint" Gr. 7, C-30
Lohengrin, "Prelude to Act III"
Gr. 8, C-22
Magic Flute, The, "Queen of the
Night Aria" Gr. 7, C-31
Magic Flute, The, "In diesen
heil'gen Hallen (In These Bright
Halls)" Gr. K, 9
Overture to "Candide" Gr. 6, 218
Princess Hundred Flowers,
The, "Falling in the Trap"
Gr. 8, C-25
Rigoletto, "Bella figlia dell'amore"
Gr. 7, C-29
Tosca, "Vissi d'arte" Gr. 7, C-31

## THEATER AND FILM

America (from West Side Story)
Gr. 8, C-45
Backstage with Jeanine Tesori
(Interview) Gr. 8, A-20
Big Country, The Gr. 2, 236
Bombay Dreams Gr. 8, B-35
Cho'i hát bôi Gr. 5, 318
Circle of Life, The (from The Lion
King) Gr. 3, 367
Circle of Life, The (from The Lion
King) Gr. 6, 316
Close Encounters of the Third
Kind Gr. 4, 235
Close Encounters of the Third
Kind Gr. 8, B-34
Colorado Trail (from the Motion
Picture The West) Gr. 5, 277
Coming Home from the Sea–I
(from The Perfect Storm)
Gr. 6, 345
Coming Home from the Sea–II
(from The Perfect Storm)
Gr. 6, 345
Crouching Tiger, Hidden Dragon
Gr. 8, A-11
Dance at the Gym (from West
Side Story) Gr. 5, 9

# RHYMES *See Literature.*

# RHYTHM

## BEAT

### anacrusis

### backbeat

### beat/no beat

### beat/rhythm

*Le jig Français* Gr. K, 64
Little Spider Gr. K, 93
*Lorca* Gr. 1, 49
Love Somebody Gr. 3, 94
Luna lunera (speech piece)
   Gr. K, 90
Mon son pha (speech piece)
   Gr. K, 91
Morning Is Come Gr. 3, 128
Pitter Patter Scatter Gr. 1, 55
Rain, Rain Gr. 1, 54
Riqui rán Gr. 1, 48
Sh'ney dubim Gr. K, 268
Shake Them 'Simmons Down
   Gr. 2, 244
Somebody's Knockin' at Your
   Door Gr. 4, 53
Sugar "Shuga" Bee Gr. K, 64
Swanee Gr. 6, 118
Time to Sing Gr. 2, 8
Your Life Is Now Gr. 6, 4

**dotted rhythm**
   Ama-Lama Gr. 5, 142

**off-beat**
   ¡Ay, Jalisco no te rajes!
      Gr. 7, I-6
   Gospel Train, The Gr. 6, 398
   Hound Dog Gr. 5, 212
   Surfin' U.S.A. Gr. 7, I-58
   Three Little Birds Gr. 8, F-7

**silent beat**
   Alle meine Entchen Gr. 1, 98
   Cirmos cica Gr. 1, 130
   Ég a gyertya Gr. K, 96
   If You're Happy Gr. K, 94
   ¡Jeu! ¡Jeu! Gr. 1, 216
   *Peshte longuita* Gr. 1, 217
   *Symphony No. 7, Op. 92, No.*
      *7, Movement 2* Gr. 1, 97
   Twist with a Burger, Jitter
      with a Bug (speech piece)
      Gr. 1, 132
   ¡Viva el fútbol! Gr. 1, 96
   Xiao yin chuan Gr. 2, 14

**steady beat**
   1, 2, 3, 4 (speech piece)
      Gr. K, 15
   Ackabacka, Soda Cracker
      (speech piece) Gr. 1, 303
   Aiken Drum Gr. 1, 398
   Al yadee Gr. 6, 308
   Alumot Gr. 6, 306
   Amasee Gr. 1, 172
   Ants Go Marching, The
      Gr. 1, 248
   Apples Gr. 1, 16
   *Arkansas Traveler/Angeline the*
      *Baker* Gr. K, 114
   At the Hop Gr. 4, 168
   *At the Hop* Gr. 4, 166
   *Awakening* Gr. 3, 289

¡Ay, Jalisco no te rajes!
   Gr. 7, I-6
Bắt kim thang Gr. 6, 13
*Billy the Kid, "Celebration"*
   Gr. 3, 251
Bling Blang Gr. 3, 240
Bo-bo-skee, Watten-tatten
   (speech piece) Gr. 1, 259
*Bon jour!* Gr. 1, 3
Bubble Gum (speech piece)
   Gr. K, 38
Bubble Trouble Gr. K, 184
*Caribbean Leaps* Gr. K, 148
*Cherokee Morning Song*
   Gr. 8, B-19
Chickety, Chickety, Chop
   (speech piece) Gr. K, 41
Clap, Wiggle, and Stomp
   Gr. K, 34
*Copycat* Gr. K, 9
*Corn Grinding Song* Gr. K, 66
Costume Capers Gr. 1, 412
*Cotton Boll Rag* Gr. 5, 333
*Cradle Song* Gr. K, 97
Dance Gr. K, 59
*Danses Populaires Francaises,*
   *"Branle Double, Branle*
   *Simple"* Gr. 7, C-25
Debajo 'el botón Gr. 1, 210
Do, Re, Mi, Fa Gr. 6, 80
Doctor Knickerbocker (speech
   piece) Gr. 1, 302
*Doing the Penguin* Gr. K, 35
Duck Dance Gr. 2, 249
*Elegguá* Gr. 8, D-13
*Entertainer, The* Gr. 2, 76
Families Gr. 1, 282
Farewell to the Warriors
   Gr. 4, 284
Five Little Snowmen Gr. K, 313
Flat Foot Floogee, The
   Gr. 3, 160
Friend of Mine Gr. 1, 310
Gakavik Gr. 4, 14
Get on Board Gr. K, 89
Goin' to Boston Gr. 6, 433
Gonna Have a Good Time
   Gr. 2, 4
Green Corn Song Gr. 5, 462
Haliwa-Saponi Canoe Song
   Gr. 5, 302
Happy Days Are Here Again
   Gr. 5, 284
Haul Away, Joe Gr. 4, 13
Hava nashira Gr. 6, 82
Head, Shoulders, Baby
   Gr. 1, 82
Hi-Dee-Roon Gr. K, 10
Hokey Pokey Gr. K, 296
*Hungarian Dance No. 6*
   Gr. 4, 50
I Love Peanuts Gr. 1, 162
I Walk in Beauty Gr. 4, 282

I'm a Dreydl Gr. K, 315
I'm in the Mood Gr. K, 86
*If I Had a Hammer* Gr. 3, 241
Ikhanda, maslombe Gr. K, 14
It Don't Mean a Thing (If It Ain't
   Got That Swing) Gr. 5, 336
It's a Celebration! Gr. 2, 372
Jack, Be Nimble (speech piece)
   Gr. K, 97
James Brown Gr. K, 206
Jan ken pon Gr. 3, 302
Jim Along, Josie Gr. K, 39
*John B. Sails* Gr. K, 11
Johnny Mister Brown Gr. K, 37
Joshua Fought the Battle of
   Jericho Gr. 8, E-18
Juan pirulero Gr. K, 215
Juanito Gr. K, 300
*Juba* Gr. K, 12
Juba Gr. K, 13
*Jump for Joy* Gr. K, 212
Jump That Jody Gr. K, 212
Kapulu kane Gr. 2, 270
Karangatia ra Gr. 3, 272
Kébé Mama Gr. 1, 442
Khorovod Gr. 1, 372
Kou ri lengay Gr. 7, E-2
Kuma san Gr. K, 40
Leila Gr. 1, 258
Les petites marionettes
   Gr. K, 237
Let the Music Begin! Gr. 1, 2
Let Us Sing Together Gr. 6, 156
Let's Get Ready Gr. K, 312
Little Miss Muffet (speech piece)
   Gr. K, 92
Little Red Wagon Gr. K, 152
*Little Train of the Caipira, The,*
   *No. 2* Gr. K, 25
London Bridge Gr. K, 244
Los maizales Gr. 1, 296
Los trencitos Gr. K, 24
*Lost River* Gr. 6, 283
Love Will Guide Us Gr. 4, 328
Lumberjack, The Gr. 1, 113
Mary Ann Gr. K, 253
*Masquerade Suite, "Galop"*
   Gr. 4, 16
Mbombera Gr. K, 24
Miss Susie Anna Sue Gr. K, 242
Music (poem) Gr. 1, 3
Must Be Santa Gr. K, 318
*Mwen boyko samba* Gr. 4, 319
My Dreydl Gr. K, 314
My Mama's Calling Me
   Gr. 1, 260
Nana Kru Gr. 6, 282
Nani wale na hala Gr. 3, 260
New Hungarian Folk Song
   Gr. 6, 196
Noah's Shanty Gr. 1, 342

**(Rhythm, continued)**

Number One, Touch Your Tongue (speech piece) Gr. K, 204

*Nyoka* Gr. 7, D-32

*O ma washi* Gr. K, 13

Oh, What a Day! Gr. K, 302

Oliver Jump (speech piece) Gr. K, 205

One Green Jelly Bean Gr. K, 287

*Orchestral Suite No. 2 in B Minor, "Minuet"* Gr. 6, 192

Paw-Paw Patch Gr. 4, 93

Pick 'n' Mix Zoo Gr. K, 139

Pottery Dance Gr. 1, 370

Pumpkin, Pumpkin Gr. 1, 413

Put Your Finger in the Air Gr. K, 114

Raccoon Dance Song Gr. 1, 260

Rain on the Green Grass (speech piece) Gr. K, 10

Rockin' Robin Gr. 3, 368

Rocky Top Gr. 5, 348

*Round Dance* Gr. 3, 257

*Round Dance* Gr. 6, 445

Run, Molly, Run Gr. 1, 8

Sailboat in the Sky Gr. 4, 374

Sansaw akroma Gr. 3, 286

School Bus Rap Gr. 1, 83

*Scott Joplin's New Rag* Gr. 5, 335

*Shadow Dancer* Gr. K, 253

Sharing Gr. K, 198

Shine, Shine, Shine Gr. 1, 42

Sidewalk Songs Gr. K, 207

Sidewalk Sounds Gr. K, 115

Sing a Little Song Gr. K, 30

Skip to My Lou Gr. K, 58

Soldier, Soldier Gr. 4, 11

*Soldier's Tale, The, "Waltz"* Gr. K, 237

Somebody Waiting Gr. 2, 283

Someday Very Soon Gr. 1, 376

*Tarakihi* Gr. 3, 273

Texas Cowboy Gr. 3, 250

*That'll Be the Day* Gr. 6, 256

Things That Sing Gr. K, 87

This Land Is Your Land Gr. 7, I-66

Tic, tac Gr. 1, 252

Time to Move Gr. 1, 244

Time to Sing Gr. 2, 8

Tina singu Gr. 4, 300

To'ia mai te waka Gr. 1, 77

Turn the Beat Around Gr. 4, 2

Ujima Gr. 1, 430

Vamos a cantar Gr. K, 278

Wake Me, Shake Me Gr. 1, 278

*Washington Post, The* (march) Gr. 1, 175

*Watermelon Man* Gr. 1, 12

Way Down in the Schoolyard Gr. 2, 50

What Will You Be on Halloween? Gr. K, 308

Yibane amenu Gr. 4, 316

*Zoila* Gr. 8, D-18

**strong beat**

Bonavist' Harbour Gr. 3, 294

Jolly Old St. Nicholas Gr. K, 316

Jump That Jody Gr. K, 212

Karangatia ra Gr. 3, 272

Knock the Cymbals Gr. 1, 176

No quiero plata Gr. 1, 424

**techno beat**

*This Is Your Night* Gr. 6, 368

*This Is Your Night (Dance Mix)* Gr. 6, 369

**upbeat**

A Ram Sam Sam Gr. 3, 208

Bắt kim thang Gr. 6, 13

Einini Gr. 4, 391

Farewell to Tarwathie Gr. 6, 43

Freedom Is Coming Gr. 5, 415

Hashkediya Gr. 3, 206

Hosanna, Me Build a House Gr. 5, 132

Let's Get the Rhythm of the Band Gr. 7, E-29

Ochimbo Gr. 4, 134

Over There Gr. 5, 279

¡Qué gusto! Gr. 3, 132

San Antonio Rose Gr. 5, 134

Star-Spangled Banner, The Gr. 4, 441

## DURATION

**augmentation/diminution**

Do, Re, Mi, Fa Gr. 6, 80

Hava nashira Gr. 6, 82

Lost My Gold Ring Gr. 6, 158

*New England Triptych, "Chester"* Gr. 6, 83

Old Abram Brown Gr. 5, 222

*Raindrops* Gr. 7, D-23

*Sonata in F Major for Violin and Piano, Op. 24, No. 5, "Spring," Movement 3* Gr. 7, C-19

Ten Little Ostinato Pieces Gr. 7, I-62

**dotted rhythm**

America Gr. 5, 486

Don't You Hear the Lambs? Gr. 5, 97

Loch Lomond Gr. 5, 140

Scotland the Brave Gr. 5, 138

**fermata**

¡Ay, Jalisco no te rajes! Gr. 7, I-6

But the Cat Came Back Gr. 2, 190

Haere Gr. 2, 285

Star-Spangled Banner, The Gr. 7, I-56

Star-Spangled Banner, The Gr. 8, I-62

**long/short**

California Gr. 5, 52

*Concerto in D Major for Flute and Orchestra, K. 314, Movement 3, Allegro* Gr. K, 123

Ding Dong! Merrily on High Gr. 6, 427

¿Dónde lo escondí? Gr. K, 209

Éliza Kongo Gr. 5, 14

Halloween Song Gr. K, 309

Let Us Sing Together Gr. 6, 156

Long Way Home, A Gr. 1, 382

Mama, Buy Me a Chiney Doll Gr. K, 120

*Mongolian Long Song* Gr. 8, B-14

Morning Comes Early Gr. 5, 13

Old Blue Gr. K, 122

Polly Wee Gr. K, 119

Scotland the Brave Gr. 5, 138

*Vocalise* Gr. K, 123

Wabash Cannon Ball Gr. 5, 136

**rubato**

Peace Like a River Gr. 6, 190

*Slow Hora/Freylekhs* Gr. 8, B-25

**tie**

Book of Love Gr. 8, G-27

Bury Me Not on the Lone Prairie Gr. 6, 19

Cielito lindo Gr. 7, I-20

*Elite Syncopations* Gr. 6, 159

Éliza Kongo Gr. 5, 14

Erie Canal Gr. 5, 262

Fais do do Gr. 6, 403

Feliz Navidad Gr. 7, I-28

Frère Jacques Gr. 2, 125

Happy Days Are Here Again Gr. 5, 284

I'm a Believer Gr. 7, G-33

Mariposita Gr. 2, 156

Now's the Time Gr. 5, 445

Proud Gr. 7, G-3

Red River Valley Gr. 6, 11

Tuxedo Junction Gr. 8, G-21

## MELODIC RHYTHM *See also Beat/ rhythm.*

Bee, Bee Bumblebee (speech piece) Gr. 1, 50

Ding Dong! Merrily on High Gr. 6, 427

Goin' to Boston Gr. 6, 433

*Luna hermosa* Gr. 8, I-13

Wind Has Shaken Autumn Down Gr. 2, 57

## METER

*Nanafushi* Gr. 7, D-16
*San Miguel Jolonicapan*
    Gr. 8, D-16
*Sonata in F Major for Violin and
    Piano, Op. 24, No. 5, "Spring,"
    Movement 3* Gr. 7, C-19
*Two Dances for Three
    Xylophones, "Hornpipe and
    Jig"* Gr. 8, D-17
*Wilder Reiter, "The Wild Rider"*
    Gr. 8, D-17
*Zoila* Gr. 8, D-18

### $\frac{12}{8}$

God Bless the Child Gr. 7, B-27
Lift Ev'ry Voice and Sing
    Gr. 5, 482
Lift Ev'ry Voice and Sing
    Gr. 8, I-54

### $\frac{2}{2}$

All for One Gr. 7, E-8
Alleluia Gr. 6, 133
Blue Skies Gr. 6, 88
Boomin' Bamboo Ensemble
    Gr. 7, D-22
Cuban Rumba Ensemble
    Gr. 7, D-7
Deck the Hall Gr. 5, 474
*Den III. Ende VI. Ronde &
    Quatre Branles* Gr. 8, C-7
Do Wah Diddy Diddy
    Gr. 7, F-21
Don't Be Cruel Gr. 6, 255
Down by the Riverside
    Gr. 5, 256
Down by the Riverside
    Gr. 8, G-8
Elegua Gr. 7, D-8
Good King Wenceslas
    Gr. 6, 460
Jambalaya Gr. 8, I-46
Kpanlogo Highlife Ensemble
    Gr. 7, D-13
Like a Bird Gr. 6, 167
Rockin' Around the Christmas
    Tree Gr. 5, 466
*Rundadinella* Gr. 8, I-60
Surfin' U.S.A. Gr. 7, I-58
Surfin' U.S.A. Gr. 7, E-27
Swanee Gr. 6, 118
This Land Is Your Land
    Gr. 5, 118
Under the Sea Gr. 5, 372
Yellow Rose of Texas, The
    Gr. 7, I-70

### $\frac{2}{4}$

A la puerta del cielo Gr. 5, 60
Adelita Gr. 5, 50
Ah! Les jolis papillons Gr. 1,
    362

Al citrón Gr. 3, 320
¡Ay, Jalisco no te rajes!
    Gr. 7, I-6
*Bai, bai, bai, bai* Gr. 2, 197
Bắt kim thang Gr. 6, 13
Cho'i hát bội Gr. 5, 318
Crawfish! Gr. 2, 86
Da pacem, Domine Gr. 5, 62
Don't Let Your Watch Run Down
    Gr. 3, 166
Drill, Ye Tarriers Gr. 5, 54
El rancho grande Gr. 4, 215
Faith of the Heart Gr. 8, G-3
Gakavik Gr. 4, 14
*Glory Hallelujah Grand March*
    Gr. 8, C-38
Goin' to Boston Gr. 6, 433
Gospel Train, The Gr. 6, 398
Ichi-gatsu tsuitachi Gr. 7, I-40
Jasmine Flowers Gr. 5, 316
Knock the Cymbals Gr. 1, 176
La mariposa Gr. 6, 58
La Tarara Gr. 4, 176
Lahk gei mohlee Gr. 5, 317
Las Navidades Gr. 5, 472
*Le Sacre de Printemps (The
    Rite of Spring), "Dance of
    the Youths and Maidens"*
    Gr. 8, C-30
*Masquerade Suite, "Galop"*
    Gr. 4, 16
Morning Comes Early Gr. 5, 13
Orange Blossom Special
    Gr. 8, E-6
Paw-Paw Patch Gr. 4, 93
Peanut Butter (speech piece)
    Gr. 1, 173
Percussion Fun Rondo
    Gr. 7, I-50
*Scott Joplin's New Rag*
    Gr. 5, 335
Sierra Morena Gr. 3, 296
Sleep, Baby, Sleep Gr. 2, 197
South African Ensemble
    Gr. 7, D-11
*Stalia, stalia* Gr. 8, B-21
*Symphony No. 3 in E-flat
    Major, "Marcia funebre,"
    Movement 2* Gr. 8, C-17
Take a Chance On Me
    Gr. 8, G-15
*Ten Easy Pieces, "Bear Dance"*
    Gr. 3, 172
Ten Little Ostinato Pieces
    Gr. 7, I-62
Wabash Cannon Ball Gr. 5, 136
*Washington Post, The* (march)
    Gr. 8, C-40
Yankee Doodle Gr. 3, 414
Yo-shi nai Gr. 6, 286
Yüe liang wan wan Gr. 5, 314

### $\frac{3}{4}$

*A mi querido Austin*
    Gr. 8, B-24
America Gr. 4, 440
America Gr. 7, I-2
*America* Gr. 7, A-22
America Gr. 8, I-2
Angels On the Midnight Clear
    Gr. 6, 423
*Bambodansarna* Gr. 8, B-20
Barb'ry Allen Gr. 6, 44
*Blue Danube, The, Op. 314*
    Gr. 6, 192
Boysie Gr. 2, 195
Cattle Call Gr. 5, 344
Chiapanecas Gr. 5, 92
Christmas, Don't Be Late (The
    Chipmunk Song) Gr. 2, 386
Cielito lindo Gr. 4, 270
Cielito lindo Gr. 7, I-20
Clementine Gr. 4, 341
*Concierto de Aranjuez,
    Movement 1, "Allegro con
    spirito"* Gr. 6, 199
De colores Gr. 5, 90
*Doraji* Gr. 4, 175
Doraji Gr. 4, 174
*Eine kleine Nachtmusik,
    Minuet* Gr. 4, 111
El coquí Gr. 2, 292
*El Salón México* Gr. 6, 199
*El siquisirí* Gr. 4, 273
En nuestra Tierra tan linda
    Gr. 2, 335
*Evening Chaconne* Gr. 6, 202
Fais do do Gr. 6, 403
Farewell to Tarwathie Gr. 6, 43
*Four Scottish Dances, Op. 59,
    "Allegretto"* Gr. 6, 43
Gaudeamus igitur Gr. 8, C-20
Gloria, Gloria Gr. 6, 459
Haere Gr. 2, 285
Hama chi dori Gr. 3, 330
*Highway to Kilkenny* Gr. 6, 43
Himmel und Erde Gr. 5, 94
Home on the Range Gr. 5, 69
*Janitzio* Gr. 5, 91
Juniper Tree, The Gr. 3, 131
La calle ancha Gr. 3, 297
La golondrina Gr. 8, I-50
La paloma blanca Gr. 3, 252
*Light Up the World* Gr. 2, 196
Live in the City Gr. 5, 71
Love Will Guide Us Gr. 4, 328
Mañana Gr. 7, E-14
*Mazurka, Op. 30, No. 3*
    Gr. 3, 317
Morning Is Come Gr. 3, 128
My Bonnie Lies Over the Ocean
    Gr. 4, 338
Nie chcę cię znać Gr. 3, 314

(*Rhythm,* continued)

*Nutcracker Suite, The,* "Waltz
of the Flowers" Gr. 6, 325
Oh, How Lovely Is the Evening
Gr. 4, 217
*Orchestral Suite No. 2 in B
Minor,* "Minuet" Gr. 6, 192
*Prelude in A Major* Gr. 4, 234
¡Qué gusto! Gr. 3, 132
River Gr. 4, 58
*Rodeo,* "Saturday Night Waltz"
Gr. 4, 342
Santa Clara Gr. 4, 172
Something Told the Wild Geese
Gr. 7, G-39
Star-Spangled Banner, The
Gr. 3, 415
Star-Spangled Banner, The
Gr. 4, 441
Star-Spangled Banner, The
Gr. 7, I-56
Star-Spangled Banner, The
Gr. 8, I-62
Streets of Laredo Gr. 4, 272
*Suite in F, Op. 28b, No. 2,*
"Fantasia on the Dargason,"
*Movement 4* Gr. 7, C-36
*Symphony No. 3 in E-flat
Major,* "Allegro con brio,"
*Movement 1* Gr. 8, C-17
*Symphony No. 47 in G Major,*
"Menuet" Gr. 7, C-14
*Waltz in D-flat ("Minute" Waltz)*
Gr. 4, 234
Waltzing with Bears Gr. 3, 170

### 3/8

Con el vito Gr. 7, G-15
One Morning in May Gr. 6, 121
*Pulcinella Suite,* "Minuetto"
Gr. 8, C-15

### 4/4

Ain't Gonna Let Nobody Turn
Me 'Round Gr. 6, 85
All Night, All Day Gr. 4, 180
Alleluia Gr. 6, 133
America (N. Diamond)
Gr. 4, 206
America, the Beautiful Gr. 7, I-4
America, the Beautiful Gr. 8, I-4
*Badenma* Gr. 8, B-28
Battle Cry of Freedom
Gr. 5, 272
Box a-Rockin' Ensemble
Gr. 7, D-4
Bucket O'Taiko Ensemble
Gr. 7, D-17
Caribbean Island Ensemble
Gr. 7, D-19
Carnaval Calypso Ensemble
Gr. 7, D-21
Certainly, Lord Gr. 7, I-13

*Cow Barn Cha Cha* Gr. 8, D-33
Don't You Hear the Lambs?
Gr. 5, 97
Doumbek or Hand Drum
Exercises Gr. 7, D-31
Dry Bones Come Skipping
Gr. 4, 218
Faith of the Heart Gr. 8, G-3
Feliz Navidad Gr. 7, I-28
Fiddler on the Roof Gr. 7, E-5
God Bless America Gr. 5, 4
Hambone Gr. 7, D-3
Hand Clap Ensemble Gr. 7, D-2
He's Got the Whole World in His
Hands Gr. 7, I-36
Hound Dog Gr. 5, 212
I Dream a World Gr. 8, G-40
I Shall Sing Gr. 8, I-38
I Walk in Beauty Gr. 4, 282
I Wonder Where Maria's Gone
Gr. 3, 318
I'll Fly Away Gr. 8, I-42
Joe Turner Blues Gr. 4, 56
Joshua Fought the Battle of
Jericho Gr. 8, E-18
*Keep a Cool Head* Gr. 7, B-34
Keep Your Eyes on the Prize
Gr. 8, E-16
Laredo Gr. 5, 10
*Lion Sleeps Tonight, The*
Gr. 8, E-8
Loch Lomond Gr. 5, 140
Mainly Metal Ensemble
Gr. 7, D-26
Man of Constant Sorrow
Gr. 7, F-28
*Mi tierra* Gr. 6, 365
Old House, Tear It Down!
Gr. 4, 178
Over My Head Gr. 7, G-9
Oy, Hanuka Gr. 7, I-44
Paths of Victory Gr. 6, 195
Pay Me My Money Down
Gr. 7, I-46
Peace Like a River Gr. 6, 190
*Rap Intro* Gr. 8, B-32
*Rippa Medley, The,* "Block-
Block, One Leg Up, Let
the Beat Go, Uh-Oh"
Gr. 8, D-32
Rise and Shine Gr. 4, 98
Rock Island Line Gr. 4, 54
*Saqian da dhol* Gr. 8, B-22
Scotland the Brave Gr. 5, 138
Si si si Gr. 7, G-13
Soldier, Soldier Gr. 4, 11
Somebody's Knockin' at Your
Door Gr. 4, 53
Somewhere Out There
Gr. 5, 368
*St. Louis Blues* Gr. 4, 57
Still, Still, Still Gr. 5, 468

Take a Chance On Me
Gr. 8, G-15
Teach Me to Swing Gr. 5, 84
Three Little Birds Gr. 8, F-7
*Tommy Peoples* Gr. 8, B-20
Turn the Glasses Over
Gr. 3, 204
Voices of Pride, The Gr. 5, 86
Wir hatten gebauet Gr. 8, C-21
Yonder Come Day Gr. 8, I-68
You Were on My Mind
Gr. 7, G-23

### 5/4

*Ali Pasha* Gr. 5, 218
*Eriskummainen kantele*
Gr. 5, 199
*Take Five* Gr. 5, 220
*Take Five* Gr. 7, B-15
*The Planets,* "Mars, the Bringer
of War" Gr. 4, 377
Turn the World Around
Gr. 4, 114

### 5/8

Goin' to Boston Gr. 6, 433

### 6/8

*Abbots Bromley Horn Dance*
Gr. 7, C-24
Away to America Gr. 5, 57
Blow the Wind Southerly
Gr. 5, 178
Blue Mountain Lake Gr. 6, 205
Can You Canoe? Gr. 4, 170
*Concierto de Aranjuez,
Movement 1,* "Allegro con
spirito" Gr. 6, 199
*Concierto Madrigal,* "Caccia a
la española" Gr. 5, 176
Connemara Lullaby Gr. 5, 232
*El Salón México* Gr. 6, 199
*Galliard Battaglia* Gr. 8, C-14
Haul Away, Joe Gr. 4, 13
Heave-Ho!/Going, Going,
Gone/The Snow Gr. 4, 182
La ciudad de Juaja Gr. 5, 58
Las estrellitas del cielo
Gr. 5, 175
*Nyoka* Gr. 7, D-33
One Morning in May Gr. 6, 121
Pat Works on the Railway
Gr. 5, 182
Rio Grande Gr. 4, 256
Sailboat in the Sky Gr. 4, 374
Skye Boat Song Gr. 6, 372
Stille Nacht (Silent Night)
Gr. 7, I-54
Ten Little Ostinato Pieces
Gr. 7, I-63
*Viva Jujuy* Gr. 8, B-22

Classified Index

When Johnny Comes Marching
  Home Gr. 5, 180
Winter Song Gr. 6, 455

**⁹⁄₈**

Down in the Valley Gr. 6, 375

**changing meter**
Al quebrar la piñata Gr. 4, 432
Bear Dance Gr. 7, I-10
Beyond Borders Gr. 5, 292
Coffee Grows on White Oak
  Trees Gr. 3, 168
*Concierto de Aranjuez,*
  *Movement 1, "Allegro con*
  *spirito"* Gr. 6, 199
Eh, cumpari! Gr. 4, 68
El desembre congelat Gr. 5, 473
*El Salón México* Gr. 6, 199
Faith of the Heart Gr. 8, G-3
Farewell to the Warriors
  Gr. 4, 284
Goin' to Boston Gr. 6, 433
*Istanbul Coffee House (Kefe*
  *Neio)* Gr. 8, B-34
Kwa-nu-te Gr. 3, 214
Love in Any Language
  Gr. 6, 476
New Hungarian Folk Song
  Gr. 6, 196
One Small Step Gr. 5, 126
Ríu ríu chíu Gr. 5, 435
*Rock 'n' Roll Doctor*
  Gr. 7, B-38
Rondo for Lunch, A (speech
  piece) Gr. 3, 212
Run! Run! Hide! Gr. 6, 340
Sail Away Gr. 5, 404
Take a Chance On Me
  Gr. 8, G-15
Twelve Days of Christmas, The
  Gr. 4, 430

**triplets**
*Havanaise for Violin and*
  *Orchestra, Op. 83*
  Gr. 5, 217
Oh, Watch the Stars Gr. 5, 216

**OSTINATOS, MELODY** *See also*
*Rhythm: Ostinatos, Rhythm.*

**vocal**
*La bamba* Gr. 5, 130

**OSTINATOS, RHYTHM** *See also*
*Texture/Harmony: Ostinatos,*
*Melody.*
Al yadee Gr. 6, 308
Así es mi tierra Gr. 6, 172
*Bomba te traigo yo* Gr. 8, B-3
*Cauyaqa Nauwa? (Where's My*
  *Drum?)* Gr. 8, D-20
*Circle of Life (from The Lion*
  *King), The* Gr. 6, 317

*Danses Populaires Francaises,*
  *"Branle Double, Branle*
  *Simple"* Gr. 7, C-25
El tambor Gr. 2, 274
Habemos llegado Gr. 6, 174
Jambalaya Gr. 8, I-47
*Jungle Beat* Gr. 6, 347
Kyrie Gr. 6, 206
La paloma se fué Gr. 6, 51
My Foot's In My Stirrup Gr. 2, 234
*Nyamphemphe* Gr. 8, B-3
Simple Gifts Gr. 8, A-17
*Tabla Solo* Gr. 8, B-32
*This Is Your Night (Dance Mix)*
  Gr. 6, 369

**body percussion**
Ackabacka, Soda Cracker
  (speech piece) Gr. 1, 303
*Bethena Waltz* Gr. 6, 157
Bo-bo-skee, Watten-tatten
  (speech piece) Gr. 1, 259
*Cookie Crew, The* Gr. K, 197
Der sad to katte Gr. 2, 300
Down, Down, Baby Gr. 2, 32
*El Salón México* Gr. 6, 199
Faith of the Heart Gr. 8, G-2
*For Children (Sz 42), Volume II,*
  *No. 33, Allegro non troppo*
  Gr. 2, 49
*Gahu* Gr. 7, D-27
*Goodbye, Ev'rybody (Farewell*
  *Shout)* Gr. 7, D-2
Green, Green, Rocky Gr. 1, 321
Haere Gr. 2, 285
Hambone Gr. 7, D-3
Hava nagila Gr. 6, 153
Hello to the World Gr. 3, 2
I Am But a Small Voice
  Gr. 6, 446
Joe Turner Blues Gr. 4, 56
Karangatia ra Gr. 8, F-23
Laredo Gr. 5, 10
Leila Gr. 1, 258
Lift Ev'ry Voice and Sing
  Gr. 8, I-55
Lions Gr. 1, 238
Loigratong Gr. 6, 451
Mama Don't 'Low Gr. 6, 358
Mary Ann Gr. 6, 180
Morning Is Come Gr. 3, 128
*My Girl Josephine* Gr. 8, E-21
Oliver Twist Gr. K, 138
On the Ning Nang Nong (poem)
  Gr. 1, 395
Peanut Butter (speech piece)
  Gr. 1, 173
Pease Porridge Not Gr. 1, 135
*Rap Intro* Gr. 8, B-32
*Saqian da dhol* Gr. 8, B-22
Si si si Gr. 7, G-13
Somebody Waiting Gr. 2, 283
To'ia mai te waka Gr. 1, 77

Turn the Glasses Over
  Gr. 3, 204
Vil du? Gr. 1, 92
Yonder Come Day Gr. 8, I-68
Yonder Come Day Gr. 8, I-70

**instrumental**
Abiyoyo Gr. 2, 108
Achshav Gr. 2, 64
Adana ya gidelim Gr. 2, 142
Ahora voy a cantarles Gr. 3, 56
*Ajaja* Gr. 8, B-3
Al tambor Gr. 3, 270
Ala Da'lona Gr. 4, 136
Ayelivi Gr. 2, 70
Banana Gr. 2, 114
Bear Dance Gr. 7, I-10
Brush Your Teeth Gr. 1, 284
Can You Canoe? (speech piece)
  Gr. 4, 170
*Capoeira Na Vila* Gr. 8, D-25
Chawe chidyo chem'chero
  Gr. 2, 296
*Chica chica boom chic*
  Gr. 2, 112
Chicka Hanka Gr. 8, F-15
*Circle of Life (from The Lion*
  *King), The* Gr. 6, 316
*Circlesong 7* Gr. 4, 80
*Concierto de Aranjuez,*
  *Movement 1, "Allegro con*
  *spirito"* Gr. 6, 199
*Cow Barn Cha Cha* Gr. 8, D-33
*Daphne of the Dunes*
  Gr. 8, D-29
Diou shou juan'er Gr. 2, 277
Dragon Smoke Gr. 3, 387
*Drums From Around the World*
  *(Montage)* Gr. 6, 277
El rancho grande Gr. 4, 215
*El Salón México* Gr. 6, 199
Éliza Kongo Gr. 5, 14
En nuestra Tierra tan linda
  Gr. 2, 335
Ev'ry Kind of Music Gr. 2, 226
*Faerie Stories* Gr. 8, B-5
Families Gr. 1, 282
Feng yang hua gu Gr. 4, 313
Five Little Chickadees
  Gr. K, 179
Funwa alafia Gr. 5, 32
*Gamelan angklung* Gr. 6, 384
Give a Little Love Gr. 6, 140
Go With the Music and Sing
  Gr. 3, 376
Good King Wenceslas
  Gr. 6, 460
Gospel Train, The Gr. 6, 398
Gypsy in the Moonlight
  Gr. 3, 12
Halloween Is a Very Unusual
  Night Gr. 3, 382
Hava nagila Gr. 6, 153

(*Rhythm*, continued)

Hey, Ho! Nobody Home
Gr. 6, 28
Hey, m'tswala  Gr. 4, 79
Hi Heidi Ho  Gr. 1, 394
I Am But a Small Voice
Gr. 6, 446
If a Tiger Calls  Gr. 3, 354
In the Pumpkin Patch
Gr. 3, 380
Ise oluwa  Gr. 6, 230
*It's Time*  Gr. 6, 319
It's Time  Gr. 6, 274
Kaeru no uta  Gr. K, 183
*Katura*  Gr. 7, D-27
Kébé Mama  Gr. 1, 442
*Kebjar teruna*  Gr. 6, 385
Kelo aba w'ye  Gr. 6, 290
Khorovod  Gr. 1, 372
Kokoleoko  Gr. 5, 33
Kou ri lengay  Gr. 2, 217
La mariposa  Gr. 6, 58
La paloma blanca  Gr. 3, 252
La pulga de San José  Gr. 3, 40
Laredo  Gr. 5, 10
*Lion*  Gr. 6, 303
Lion Sleeps Tonight, The
Gr. 4, 131
Lions  Gr. 1, 238
Loigratong  Gr. 6, 451
Lone Star Trail  Gr. 2, 21
Los maizales  Gr. 1, 296
Los reyes de Oriente  Gr. 8, I-58
Love Somebody  Gr. 3, 94
Mama Don't 'Low  Gr. 6, 358
*Mi tierra*  Gr. 6, 365
Miss Mary Mack  Gr. 2, 42
*Nruab hnub thiab hmo ntuj*
Gr. 4, 368
O lê lê O Bahía  Gr. 6, 165
O pião entrou  Gr. 2, 355
Ochimbo  Gr. 4, 134
Oliver Twist  Gr. K, 138
One Family  Gr. 7, G-17
One Morning in May  Gr. 6, 121
One Morning Soon  Gr. 3, 68
*Open the Kingdom*  Gr. 6, 31
Pai pi qiu  Gr. 1, 324
Paths of Victory  Gr. 6, 195
Piñon, pirulín  Gr. 2, 174
*Primitive Fire, "Oya"*  Gr. 2, 68
Pumpkin Poem  Gr. 3, 381
Rabbit Footprints  Gr. 2, 304
*Rippa Medley, The, "Block-
Block, One Leg Up, Let
the Beat Go, Uh-Oh"*
Gr. 8, D-32
Riqui rán  Gr. 4, 66
Rock Island Line  Gr. 4, 54
Rosie, Darling Rosie  Gr. 2, 215
Route 66  Gr. 4, 276
*Sai da Frente*  Gr. 8, D-24
Sakura  Gr. 4, 308

See the Children Playin'
Gr. 4, 107
*Sha Sha Sha*  Gr. 6, 328
Somebody's Knockin' at Your
Door  Gr. 4, 53
Sonando  Gr. 4, 34
Streets of Laredo  Gr. 4, 272
*Talaque Talaque o Romance da
Maria*  Gr. 8, D-24
Ten Little Ostinato Pieces
Gr. 7, I-62
*This Is Your Night*  Gr. 6, 368
Tie Me Kangaroo Down, Sport
Gr. 4, 37
Tina singu  Gr. 4, 300
Together in Unity  Gr. K, 320
Train Is A-Comin'  Gr. 3, 48
Turn the World Around
Gr. 4, 116
*Twist and Shout*  Gr. 4, 238
Un pajarito  Gr. 2, 16
*Viva Jujuy*  Gr. 8, B-22
Wai bamba  Gr. 6, 26
Wake Me, Shake Me  Gr. 1, 278
Walk Together, Children
Gr. 3, 146
We're All Gonna Shine Tonight
Gr. 2, 240
We're Making Popcorn (speech
piece)  Gr. 1, 86
What Do Animals Need?
Gr. 2, 288
Wings of a Dove  Gr. 4, 318
*Yo Lé Lé (Fulani Groove)*
Gr. 5, 33
*You Sang to Me*  Gr. 6, 335
Your Life Is Now  Gr. 6, 4
Yüe liang wan wan  Gr. 5, 314

layered patterns
Ev'rybody Loves Saturday Night
Gr. 7, I-25

vocal
Funwa alafia  Gr. 5, 32
Going on a Picnic  Gr. K, 190
Kokoleoko  Gr. 5, 33
Lions  Gr. 1, 238
Lone Star Trail  Gr. 2, 21
Lots of Worms  Gr. 2, 310
Magnolia  Gr. 6, 16
One Morning in May  Gr. 6, 121
*Open the Kingdom*  Gr. 6, 31
Riddle Ree (speech piece)
Gr. 2, 34
Scattin' A-Round (Variations on
Row 3)  Gr. 6, 160
Scrub Brush Shuffle, The
Gr. 1, 118
Wai bamba  Gr. 6, 26
We're Making Popcorn (speech
piece)  Gr. 1, 86

**PATTERNS**

America, the Beautiful  Gr. 8, I-4
*Circle of Life (from The Lion
King), The*  Gr. 6, 316
Doumbek or Hand Drum Exercises
Gr. 7, D-31
*Drums of the Iroquois and Sioux*
Gr. 6, 285
Hanuka, Hanuka  Gr. 8, I-36
*Malê Debalê*  Gr. 8, B-16
*Sabhyatâ*  Gr. 8, B-43
Simple Gifts  Gr. 8, A-17
There Is Love Somewhere
Gr. 6, 318

2/4
*Fifteen Hungarian Peasant
Songs*  Gr. 7, C-35

accents
*Las copetonas*  Gr. 7, B-33

counter-rhythm
Bặt kim thang  Gr. 6, 13

dotted rhythm
Fais do do  Gr. 6, 403
Gospel Train, The  Gr. 6, 398
Joshua Fought the Battle
Gr. 5, 101
Lion Sleeps Tonight, The
Gr. 8, I-56
Shady Grove  Gr. 5, 260
Star-Spangled Banner, The
Gr. 6, 486
Under the Same Sun  Gr. 6, 440
Uno, dos y tres  Gr. 5, 429

Latin rhythms
*(Chi Chi Chi) Cha Cha Cha*
Gr. 6, 334
*Lluvia*  Gr. 6, 332

layered patterns
*Ajaja*  Gr. 8, B-3
All for One  Gr. 7, E-8
*Awa ewe iwoyi*  Gr. 8, D-9
*Badenma*  Gr. 8, B-28
*Bawa*  Gr. 7, D-32
*Believer*  Gr. 7, A-2
*Billie*  Gr. 8, B-23
*Bombé/Ruht wohl, ruht wohl,
ihr heilegen Gebeine, BWV
245*  Gr. 8, B-39
Boomin' Bamboo Ensemble
Gr. 7, D-22
Box a-Rockin' Ensemble
Gr. 7, D-4
Bucket O'Taiko Ensemble
Gr. 7, D-17
*Capoeira Na Vila*  Gr. 8, D-25
Caribbean Island Ensemble
Gr. 7, D-19
Carnaval Calypso Ensemble
Gr. 7, D-21
*Cauyaqa Nauwa? (Where's My
Drum?)*  Gr. 8, D-20

*Cow Barn Cha Cha* Gr. 8, D-33

*Crunchy, Crunchy, Crunchy*
Gr. 8, D-15

Cuban Rumba Ensemble
Gr. 7, D-7

*Daphne of the Dunes*
Gr. 8, D-29

*Dham dhamak dham samelu*
Gr. 6, 305

*Ekombi* Gr. 8, B-31

*El cóndor pasa* Gr. 7, A-2

Elegua Gr. 7, D-8

Feliz Navidad Gr. 7, I-28

*Fire Brigade Water the Road*
Gr. 7, D-22

Friends Today Gr. 7, D-12

*Gahu* Gr. 7, D-27

*Guaguancó pá las tumbadoras*
Gr. 7, D-9

Guantanamera Gr. 8, I-32

Hand Clap Ensemble Gr. 7, D-2

*Huagu ge, "Flower Drum song"*
Gr. 8, D-27

I Shall Sing Gr. 8, I-38

*Jump for Joy* Gr. 7, D-20

*Katura* Gr. 7, D-27

Kelo aba w'ye Gr. 6, 290

Kpanlogo Highlife Ensemble
Gr. 7, D-13

*Maha ganapathim* Gr. 6, 305

Mainly Metal Ensemble
Gr. 7, D-26

*Mambo UK* Gr. 7, D-9

*Máru-bihág* Gr. 6, 304

Name, Name, What's Your
Name? (speech piece)
Gr. 3, 10

Nampaya omame Gr. 7, D-10

Nana Kru Gr. 6, 282

*Nanafushi* Gr. 7, D-16

*Nyoka* Gr. 7, D-33

Panamam tombé Gr. 7, D-18

Percussion Fun Rondo
Gr. 7, I-50

Rabbit Dance, The Gr. 3, 334

Rhythm Is Gonna Get You, The
Gr. 6, 348

*Rippa Medley, The, "Block-
Block, One Leg Up, Let
the Beat Go, Uh-Oh"*
Gr. 8, D-32

*Rock 'n' Roll Doctor*
Gr. 7, B-38

*Rods and Cones* Gr. 7, D-5

*Sai da Frente* Gr. 8, D-24

*Samanfo, begye nsa nom*
Gr. 8, D-6

*San Miguel Jolonicapan*
Gr. 8, D-16

*Saqian da dhol* Gr. 8, B-22

*Si si si* Gr. 7, G-13

*Si tú no estás* Gr. 6, 267

Song of Greatness, A
Gr. 3, 335

South African Ensemble
Gr. 7, D-11

*Spaceville* Gr. 7, D-30

Take Time in Life Gr. 6, 292

*Talaque Talaque o Romance da
Maria* Gr. 8, D-24

*Udu Pot* Gr. 8, D-4

Wai bamba Gr. 8, G-13

*Wilder Reiter, "The Wild Rider"*
Gr. 8, D-17

*Zoila* Gr. 8, D-18

## melody patterns

Jasmine Flowers Gr. 5, 316

## motives

*Ahi! Amours* Gr. 8, C-4

Alexander's Ragtime Band
Gr. 6, 136

*Boston Ball Game 1967*
Gr. 8, F-32

*Crunchy, Crunchy, Crunchy*
Gr. 8, D-15

*Imbube* Gr. 8, B-30

Jambalaya (On The Bayou)
Gr. 6, 244

*Katura* Gr. 7, D-27

*Rap Intro* Gr. 8, B-32

*Return to Misty Mountain*
Gr. 7, D-28

*Rice Bowl* Gr. 8, B-30

*Symphony No. 3 in E-flat
Major, "Marcia funebre,"
Movement 2* Gr. 8, C-17

Woke Up This Morning
Gr. 5, 288

## repeated patterns

*X-Beats* Gr. 7, B-5

## repetition and contrast

America, the Beautiful Gr. 7, I-4

## rhythmic patterns

You Were on My Mind
Gr. 7, G-23

## rock rhythms

Don't Be Cruel Gr. 6, 255

Downtown Gr. 6, 258

*Let's Twist Again* Gr. 6, 257

## same and different patterns

*Adzogbo-Ovitse* Gr. 8, D-13

Ala Da'lona Gr. 4, 136

Alexander's Ragtime Band
Gr. 6, 136

All Night, All Day Gr. 4, 180

Alleluia Gr. 6, 133

Alligator Pie (speech piece)
Gr. 3, 13

Almost Day Gr. 3, 397

America Gr. 6, 484

America, the Beautiful
Gr. 6, 485

Bắt kim thang Gr. 6, 13

Book of Love Gr. 8, G-27

Cantaré, cantarás Gr. 6, 413

*Carnival of the Animals,
"Fossils"* Gr. 4, 220

*Cauyaqa Nauwa? (Where's My
Drum?)* Gr. 8, D-20

Chapel of Love Gr. 7, G-27

Cheki, morena Gr. 7, I-16

*China Gates* Gr. 7, C-45

Chrismus a Come Gr. 3, 396

*College Hornpipe* Gr. 4, 95

Come and Go with Me to That
Land Gr. 5, 390

Con el vito Gr. 7, G-15

Corta la caña Gr. 6, 364

*Cow Barn Cha Cha* Gr. 8, D-33

Don Gato Gr. 3, 352

Down by the Riverside
Gr. 8, G-8

El barquito Gr. 3, 358

El carite Gr. 5, 305

*Éliza Kongo* Gr. 5, 14

*Evening Samba* Gr. 6, 297

Feliz Navidad Gr. 7, I-28

Four in a Boat Gr. 2, 46

Glendy Burke, The Gr. 4, 262

God Bless the U.S.A.
Gr. 8, G-37

Goodbye, Julie Gr. 8, E-2

Gypsy in the Moonlight
Gr. 3, 12

He's Got the Whole World in His
Hands Gr. 7, I-36

*How Can I Keep from Singing?*
Gr. 4, 260

How Can I Keep from Singing?
Gr. 4, 261

I Am But a Small Voice
Gr. 6, 446

*I Shall Sing* Gr. 8, I-41

I Wonder Where Maria's Gone
Gr. 3, 318

*Istanbul Coffee House (Kefe
Neio)* Gr. 8, B-34

Jan ken pon Gr. 3, 302

*Jesu, Joy of Man's Desiring*
Gr. 6, 87

Kookaburra Gr. 4, 186

La Tarara Gr. 4, 176

*Lieutenant Kijé, Op. 60,
"Troika"* Gr. 6, 457

Light Up the World with a Song
Gr. 8, G-25

*Lion Sleeps Tonight, The*
Gr. 8, E-8

Magnolia Gr. 6, 16

*Nanafushi* Gr. 7, D-16

Oh, Susanna Gr. 4, 264

Old House, Tear It Down!
Gr. 4, 178

On My Way Gr. 6, 313

Ōsamu kosamu Gr. 4, 96

**(Rhythm, continued)**

Over My Head  Gr. 7, G-9

Paw-Paw Patch  Gr. 4, 93

Proud  Gr. 7, G-3

*Rippa Medley, The, "Block-Block, One Leg Up, Let the Beat Go, Uh-Oh"*  Gr. 8, D-32

*San Miguel Jolonicapan*  Gr. 8, D-16

*Scrub-a-dub*  Gr. 1, 306

Se va el caimán  Gr. 5, 306

*Sha Sha Sha*  Gr. 6, 328

Shir l'shalom  Gr. 4, 419

Soldier, Soldier  Gr. 4, 11

Somebody's Knockin' at Your Door  Gr. 4, 53

Star-Spangled Banner, The  Gr. 6, 486

*Symphony No. 40 in G Minor, K. 550, Movement 1, K. 550, Movement 1*  Gr. 8, B-30

Take a Chance On Me  Gr. 8, G-15

Ten Little Ostinato Pieces  Gr. 7, I-62

This Land Is Your Land  Gr. 5, 118

Those Magic Changes  Gr. 8, E-30

*Trash Can Stomp (from Stomp Out Loud)*  Gr. 6, 328

*Two Dances for Three Xylophones, "Hornpipe and Jig"*  Gr. 8, D-17

*Viva la musica*  Gr. 5, 95

*Wilder Reiter, "The Wild Rider"*  Gr. 8, D-17

Winter  Gr. 8, G-11

Winter Song  Gr. 6, 455

Worried Man Blues  Gr. 6, 371

Your Friends Shall Be the Tall Wind  Gr. 6, 201

**shuffle rhythms**

Don't Be Cruel  Gr. 6, 255

*Hard Day Blues*  Gr. 7, B-9

*Keep a Cool Head*  Gr. 7, B-34

*Penny Lane*  Gr. 6, 257

*Pride and Joy*  Gr. 7, B-9

**steady beat**

Jambalaya (On The Bayou)  Gr. 6, 244

**swing rhythms**

He's Got the Whole World in His Hands  Gr. 7, I-36

I Love Peanuts  Gr. 7, E-20

Ja-Da  Gr. 7, G-20

Midnight Special, The  Gr. 7, F-23

**syncopation**

Ahora voy a cantarles  Gr. 3, 56

¡Ay, Jalisco no te rajes!  Gr. 7, I-6

Basin Street Blues  Gr. 5, 354

*Bethena Waltz*  Gr. 6, 157

Beyond Borders  Gr. 5, 292

Black Snake  Gr. 3, 53

Book of Love  Gr. 8, G-27

Caribbean Island Ensemble  Gr. 7, D-19

Carnaval Calypso Ensemble  Gr. 7, D-21

*Changed My Name*  Gr. 6, 338

Cheki, morena  Gr. 7, I-16

Cielito lindo  Gr. 7, I-20

Come and Go with Me to That Land  Gr. 5, 390

*Concierto de Aranjuez, Movement 1, "Allegro con spirito"*  Gr. 6, 199

Corta la caña  Gr. 6, 364

*Cotton Boll Rag*  Gr. 5, 333

*Dances of Galanta*  Gr. 7, C-34

Down by the Riverside  Gr. 5, 256

Down by the Riverside  Gr. 8, G-8

Draw Me a Bucket of Water  Gr. 3, 124

*El nuevo caiman*  Gr. 8, B-17

*El Salón México*  Gr. 6, 199

*Elite Syncopations*  Gr. 6, 159

Erie Canal  Gr. 5, 262

Every Night When the Sun Goes In  Gr. 8, I-28

Everybody Loves Saturday Night  Gr. 6, 296

*Everyday People*  Gr. 5, 389

Fais do do  Gr. 6, 403

Flat Foot Floogee, The  Gr. 3, 160

For Children Safe and Strong  Gr. 5, 484

Four White Horses  Gr. 3, 304

Give a Little Love  Gr. 6, 140

God Bless the U.S.A.  Gr. 8, G-37

Gospel Train, The  Gr. 6, 398

Happy Days Are Here Again  Gr. 5, 284

He's Got the Whole World in His Hands  Gr. 7, I-36

Hit Me with a Hot Note and Watch Me Bounce  Gr. 6, 112

Hosanna, Me Build a House  Gr. 5, 132

I'm a Believer  Gr. 7, G-33

If I Had a Hammer  Gr. 5, 287

It Don't Mean a Thing (If It Ain't Got That Swing)  Gr. 5, 336

It's Time  Gr. 6, 274

*Jonah*  Gr. 6, 235

Joshua Fought the Battle of Jericho  Gr. 8, E-18

Just a Snap-Happy Blues  Gr. 6, 388

Kingston Market  Gr. 3, 90

*Kyrie, "Missa Luba"*  Gr. 7, G-13

La bamba  Gr. 5, 128

*La bamba*  Gr. 5, 130

Let Us Sing Together  Gr. 6, 156

Let's Get the Rhythm of the Band  Gr. 7, E-29

Look Out for Mother Earth  Gr. 3, 341

*Lost River*  Gr. 6, 283

*Luna hermosa*  Gr. 8, I-13

Mainly Metal Ensemble  Gr. 7, D-26

*Mass, "Responsory Alleluia"*  Gr. 6, 217

Mister Ram Goat-O  Gr. 3, 54

Morning Comes Early  Gr. 5, 13

New Hungarian Folk Song  Gr. 6, 196

Now That's Tap (speech piece)  Gr. 6, 320

Now's the Time  Gr. 5, 445

*Now's the Time*  Gr. 5, 451

O, Desayo  Gr. 5, 411

Oh, Freedom  Gr. 5, 392

Oh, Freedom  Gr. 7, G-30

One Family  Gr. 7, G-17

Paths of Victory  Gr. 6, 195

Pay Me My Money Down  Gr. 7, I-46

*Pennsylvania 6-5000*  Gr. 5, 342

Proud  Gr. 7, G-3

*Rhapsody in Blue*  Gr. 7, C-42

Rhythm Is Gonna Get You, The  Gr. 6, 348

Riendo el río corre  Gr. 6, 263

Rock Island Line  Gr. 4, 54

Route 66  Gr. 4, 276

Sail Away  Gr. 5, 404

*Saludo de Matanzas*  Gr. 5, 17

*Scott Joplin's New Rag*  Gr. 5, 335

Si si si  Gr. 7, G-13

Somebody's Knockin' at Your Door  Gr. 4, 53

*Study War No More*  Gr. 7, C-40

Surfin' U.S.A.  Gr. 7, E-27

Swing Low, Sweet Chariot  Gr. 7, C-41

Take a Chance On Me  Gr. 8, G-15

Teach Me to Swing  Gr. 5, 84

Turn the Beat Around  Gr. 4, 2

Under the Same Sun  Gr. 6, 440

Wade in the Water  Gr. 8, I-64

Wai bamba  Gr. 8, G-13
Woke Up This Morning
    Gr. 5, 288
World of Difference, A
    Gr. 5, 386
*You Sang to Me*  Gr. 6, 335
You're a Grand Old Flag
    Gr. 3, 264
Your Life Is Now  Gr. 6, 4

**tie**
Somebody's Knockin' at Your
    Door  Gr. 4, 53

**triplets**
Green Corn Song  Gr. 5, 462

**world beat**
*Same, The*  Gr. 6, 268

## S

# SCHOOL TO HOME CONNECTION

1960s, The  Gr. 6, 195
A Silly Song Search  Gr. 1, 395
American Immigration  Gr. 6, 163
American Visuals  Gr. 4, 159
Ancestry  Gr. 6, 79
Art Object from Other Lands
    Gr. 4, 225
Beat/Rhythm Rhymes  Gr. 1, 17
Beatles Memorabilia  Gr. 6, 91
Bird Research  Gr. 4, 187
Birds in the Neighborhood  Gr. 3, 275
Caring for the Earth  Gr. 4, 359
Caroling  Gr. 6, 461
Causes  Gr. 6, 343
CD-ROM Encyclopedia  Gr. 6, 451
Chanukah Traditions  Gr. 1, 421
Civil War Research  Gr. 5, 275
Class project about waterways
    Gr. 5, 117
Collecting Examples  Gr. 1, 13
Collecting Leaves  Gr. 3, 261
Collecting Memories  Gr. 4, 143
Community Involvement  Gr. 5, 301
Community Strings  Gr. 6, 103
Conducting a Survey  Gr. 6, 89
Country Performers  Gr. 5, 351
Create a Drum  Gr. 3, 271
Creating Letters  Gr. K, 69
Creating Poetry  Gr. 3, 321
Cultural Exploration  Gr. 5, 321
Culture  Gr. 5, 297
Cultures  Gr. 5, 109
Customs and Traditions  Gr. 3, 257
Decorating Stones  Gr. 5, 309
Describing Dogs  Gr. 1, 291
Describing Dogs  Gr. K, 123
Discovering Family Heritage  Gr. 3, 15
Discussion  Gr. 1, 55
Drumming Clinic  Gr. 6, 283
Environmental Awareness  Gr. 3, 341
Everyday Heroes  Gr. 5, 389

Exploring Friendships  Gr. 3, 39
Families on the Move  Gr. 4, 245
Family Anecdotes  Gr. 6, 15
Family Fun with Chocolate  Gr. 1, 381
Family Heritage  Gr. 1, 259
Family Sayings  Gr. 3, 101
Family Support During Change
    Gr. 1, 335
Family Ties  Gr. 3, 297
Family Trip, A  Gr. 5, 377
Fast Activities  Gr. K, 61
Favorite Bugs  Gr. 1, 215
Favorite Songs  Gr. 2, 127
Field Recordings  Gr. 4, 107
Fifty Plus  Gr. 5, 359
Fish Stories  Gr. 3, 295
Folk Styles  Gr. 6, 121
Folk Tales  Gr. 4, 369
Found Sounds  Gr. 1, 75
Found Sounds  Gr. 1, 117
Friendships  Gr. 2, 174
Fun from Season to Season  Gr. 1, 29
Getting Back to Nature  Gr. 6, 205
Going on a Sun Hunt  Gr. 1, 369
Gospel Performers  Gr. 6, 55
Gospel Scrapbook  Gr. 6, 235
Great Depression to World War II
    Gr. 5, 285
Here a Vowel, There a Vowel
    Gr. 1, 221
Holidays at Home  Gr. 3, 393
Home "Found Sounds"  Gr. 6, 361
Home Performance  Gr. 6, 373
Homeless, The  Gr. 5, 283
Homemade Instruments  Gr. 6, 367
Immigrants  Gr. 5, 57
Instruments at home  Gr. 4, 71
*Interactive Bulletin Board*  Gr. 6, 279
Interview  Gr. 6, 41
Interview  Gr. 6, 83
Interview and Report  Gr. 6, 145
Interviews  Gr. 6, 139
Involving the Audience  Gr. 2, 391
Keys  Gr. K, 189
Kitchen Patterns  Gr. 1, 177
Kwanzaa Foods  Gr. 6, 465
Latin Influence  Gr. 6, 267
Latin Influence  Gr. 6, 335
Listening List, A  Gr. 1, 97
Local Bagpipers  Gr. 5, 141
Making Props  Gr. 2, 247
Meet the Gardener  Gr. 4, 347
Memories  Gr. 4, 11
Mini-piñata  Gr. 6, 481
Movie Memories  Gr. 4, 361
Music Festival  Gr. 6, 123
Music in Nature  Gr. 2, 17
Music Videos from Home  Gr. 6, 349
Musical Greeting Cards  Gr. 1, 443
My Foot's in My Stirrup  Gr. 2, 235
Need for Peace  Gr. 6, 69
Neighborhood Trees  Gr. 2, 323
Old-Fashioned Popcorn  Gr. 5, 463

On the Trail of Fossils  Gr. 1, 237
Our Wonderful World  Gr. 6, 65
Pets Make Loyal Pals  Gr. 1, 171
Pictures of America  Gr. 5, 489
Pictures of America  Gr. 6, 487
Piñata Game  Gr. 3, 401
Pride  Gr. 5, 89
Pumpkin Faces  Gr. 1, 413
Question-and-Answer Game  Gr. 3, 63
Radio  Gr. 6, 369
Railroads  Gr. 5, 137
Read a Book  Gr. 4, 281
Recording Class Performances
    Gr. K, 53
Repetition and Contrast  Gr. 6, 15
Research  Gr. 6, 49
Rhymes and Games  Gr. 1, 153
Rock in the '50s and '60s  Gr. 6, 259
Rock 'n' Roll Era, The  Gr. 4, 203
SATB Choir  Gr. 6, 211
Science  Gr. 5, 217
Science Project  Gr. 3, 53
Seashore Memories  Gr. 1, 355
Shared Celebration, A  Gr. 2, 393
Sharing  Gr. 3, 339
Sharing Families  Gr. 1, 283
Sharing Games  Gr. 1, 303
Sharing Music  Gr. 2, 381
Sharing Music Learning  Gr. 2, 19
Sharing Traditions  Gr. 1, 425
Sharing with Family  Gr. 4, 239
Singing and Ring Games  Gr. 1, 9
Singing at Home  Gr. 2, 11
Singing at Home  Gr. 5, 31
Singing Games  Gr. 3, 23
Song for Family Get-Togethers, A
    Gr. 1, 105
Songs of the Underground Railroad
    Gr. 3, 51
Sound Around Us  Gr. K, 193
Speaking of Bread  Gr. 1, 59
Special Activities on Special Days
    Gr. 1, 269
Spring Blossoms  Gr. 1, 441
Star Gazing  Gr. 1, 109
Star Gazing  Gr. 2, 145
Student Goals  Gr. 6, 9
Style Wherever We Go  Gr. 1, 7
Sunrise  Gr. 3, 129
Take a Trip  Gr. 5, 369
Tales of Wisdom  Gr. 3, 365
Tap Dance Demonstration  Gr. 6, 321
Tempo Changes  Gr. 1, 127
Timbre Search  Gr. 6, 25
Traditional Games  Gr. 3, 313
Travel Adventures  Gr. 1, 277
Tree Research  Gr. 3, 207
Valentine Greetings  Gr. 2, 399
Water Conservation  Gr. 4, 365
Way Down in the Schoolyard
    Gr. 2, 51
Word Hunt  Gr. 1, 391
World is Our Orchestra  Gr. K, 107

**SIGNING** *See Moving: Signing; Skills Reinforcement.*

**SINGING** *See also Skills Reinforcement.*
Ahora voy a cantarles  Gr. 3, 56
Alleluia, Amen  Gr. 7, A-13
Alleluia, Amen  Gr. 7, A-12
America  Gr. 7, I-2
America, the Beautiful  Gr. 7, I-4
Au clair de la lune  Gr. 3, 18
Back of the Bus  Gr. 3, 410
Bear Dance  Gr. 7, I-10
Certainly, Lord  Gr. 7, I-13
Chanukah Games  Gr. 3, 389
Cheki, morena  Gr. 7, I-16
Con el vito  Gr. 7, G-15
Don Gato  Gr. 3, 352
Each of Us Is a Flower  Gr. 3, 154
Family Tree  Gr. 3, 72
Feliz Navidad  Gr. 7, I-28
Flip, Flop and Fly  Gr. 7, E-32
Friends Today  Gr. 7, D-12
Give My Regards to Broadway  Gr. 6, 39
Good Morning  Gr. 3, 192
Groundhog Blues, The  Gr. 3, 122
Hanuka, Hanuka  Gr. 3, 390
He's Got the Whole World in His Hands  Gr. 7, I-36
Hotter Than That  Gr. 6, 65
I Love Peanuts  Gr. 7, E-20
I'd Like To Teach the World to Sing (In Perfect Harmony)  Gr. 3, 198
I'm a Believer  Gr. 7, G-33
I'm on My Way  Gr. 3, 76
Ichi-gatsu tsuitachi  Gr. 7, I-40
Inkpataya  Gr. 3, 254
It's a Beautiful Day  Gr. 3, 338
Karangatia ra  Gr. 3, 272
Keep Your Eyes on the Prize  Gr. 3, 408
Kou ri lengay  Gr. 7, E-2
La piñata  Gr. 3, 399
Let's Celebrate!  Gr. 3, 374
Man of Constant Sorrow  Gr. 7, F-28
Michael Finnigan  Gr. 3, 153
Midnight Special, The  Gr. 7, F-23
Morning Has Broken  Gr. 5, 30
Mubärak  Gr. 3, 282
Never Smile at a Crocodile  Gr. 3, 100
Now Let Me Fly  Gr. 3, 178
O hal'lwe  Gr. 3, 256
Oh, Freedom  Gr. 7, G-30
Old Texas  Gr. 3, 77
Over the River and Through the Wood  Gr. 3, 384
Proud  Gr. 7, G-3
Si si si  Gr. 7, G-13
Sing Your Story  Gr. 3, 350
Something Told the Wild Geese  Gr. 7, G-39
Song of One, A  Gr. 3, 344

Song of the Fishes  Gr. 3, 244
Star-Spangled Banner, The  Gr. 7, I-56
Stille Nacht (Silent Night)  Gr. 7, I-54
Surfin' U.S.A.  Gr. 7, I-58
Surfin' U.S.A.  Gr. 7, I-59
Take Me Out to the Ball Game  Gr. 3, 263
This Land Is Your Land  Gr. 7, I-66
This Old Man  Gr. 3, 152
What a Wonderful World  Gr. 6, 62
Yellow Rose of Texas, The  Gr. 7, I-70
You're a Grand Old Flag  Gr. 3, 264
Your changing voice  Gr. 7, G-7

**HARMONY**
Book of Love  Gr. 8, G-27
California Dreamin'  Gr. 8, G-31
Down by the Riverside  Gr. 8, G-8
God Bless the U.S.A.  Gr. 8, G-37
I Dream a World  Gr. 8, G-40
Lion Sleeps Tonight, The  Gr. 8, I-57
Take a Chance On Me  Gr. 8, G-15
Tuxedo Junction  Gr. 8, G-21
Wai bamba  Gr. 8, G-13
Winter  Gr. 8, G-11

# SKILLS REINFORCEMENT

**ANALYZING**
Adiós, amigos  Gr. 6, 57
America  Gr. 7, A-22
Blues with a Feeling  Gr. 8, E-33
Blues with a Feeling  Gr. 8, I-7
Bye Bye, Love  Gr. 8, F-8
Con el vito  Gr. 7, G-14
Dancin' in the Street  Gr. 5, 362
Each of Us Is a Flower  Gr. 3, 154
El rancho grande  Gr. 8, I-22
Fiddler on the Roof  Gr. 7, E-6
Flip, Flop and Fly  Gr. 7, E-32
Home on the Range  Gr. 5, 70
Hound Dog  Gr. 5, 215
I Love Peanuts  Gr. 7, E-20
Intervals - Seconds and Thirds  Gr. 7, H-24
Istanbul Coffee House (Kefe Neio)  Gr. 8, B-34
Linus and Lucy  Gr. 8, A-28
Love Is on Our Side  Gr. 5, 324
Make a Music Video!  Gr. 7, A-28
Melodic Sequence  Gr. 7, H-24
Messiah, "Hallelujah!"  Gr. 8, C-8
Minor Chords  Gr. 7, H-28
The Minor iv Chord  Gr. 7, H-28
Minor Keys  Gr. 8, H-22
Minor Scales  Gr. 7, H-28
Montage of Historical Styles  Gr. 7, C-2
Mood Music  Gr. 8, A-6
More Intervals - Fourths, Fifths, Sixths, and Sevenths  Gr. 7, H-24
Movie Sound Effects  Gr. 8, A-8

Planet Drone  Gr. 8, B-10
Retrograde and inversion of motives  Gr. 6, 99
Rigoletto, "Bella figlia dell'amore"  Gr. 7, C-28
Ríu ríu chíu  Gr. 5, 434
Santa Clara  Gr. 4, 172
Star-Spangled Banner, The  Gr. 7, I-56
Surfin' U.S.A.  Gr. 7, I-60
Take Five  Gr. 5, 221
Tommy Peoples  Gr. 8, B-20
Twist, The  Gr. 5, 358
Two-Part Invention in A Major (piano)  Gr. 5, 237
Tzena, tzena  Gr. 5, 299
Viva Jujuy  Gr. 5, 229

**ARRANGING**
Amazing Grace  Gr. 4, 161
Blues with a Feeling  Gr. 8, E-33
Cat's Tongue  Gr. 2, 191
Cookie  Gr. 2, 172
Good Morning  Gr. 3, 193
I Believe I Can Fly  Gr. 5, 171
Leatherwing Bat  Gr. 2, 303
Nyoka  Gr. 7, D-33
Reading Chord Symbols  Gr. 8, H-26
Suite in F, Op. 28b, No. 2, "Fantasia on the Dargason," Movement 4  Gr. 7, C-36

**COMPOSING**
Abbots Bromley Horn Dance  Gr. 7, C-24
All Night, All Day  Gr. 4, 180
America, the Free  Gr. 4, 212
Believer  Gr. 7, A-2
China Gates  Gr. 7, C-44
Compose melodies  Gr. 7, A-8
Country Dance  Gr. 3, 211
Create a Career  Gr. 8, A-32
Draw Me a Bucket of Water  Gr. 3, 127
Farmer's Dairy Key, The  Gr. 2, 183
Fifteen Hungarian Peasant Songs  Gr. 7, C-35
Harmonic Minor  Gr. 8, H-24
Imbube  Gr. 8, B-30
Jelly in a Dish  Gr. 2, 84
Jesu, Joy of Man's Desiring  Gr. 6, 87
Juniper Tree, The  Gr. 3, 130
Listen to the Water  Gr. 2, 294
The Major Scale  Gr. 8, H-16
Rice Bowl  Gr. 8, B-30
Sixteenth Notes in the Rhythm  Gr. 8, H-17
Sonata for Violin and Piano, Allegro  Gr. 8, C-46
Subdominant in Minor  Gr. 8, H-29

*Theme and Variations for Percussion* Gr. 5, 66
*Toccata in D Minor* Gr. 4, 233
The Top *do* Gr. 8, H-16
*Un elefante* Gr. 2, 160
*Vamos a la fiesta* Gr. 2, 374
*Voiles* Gr. 7, C-38
*Whirlwind* Gr. 3, 148

## CONDUCTING
America Gr. 7, I-3
Estampie Gr. 8, I-27
Ichi-gatsu tsuitachi Gr. 7, I-42
Knock the Cymbals Gr. 1, 176
Morning Has Broken Gr. 5, 29
Something Told the Wild Geese Gr. 7, G-39
Voices of Pride, The Gr. 5, 86

## CREATING
Ain't Gonna Let Nobody Turn Me 'Round Gr. 8, F-16
Al quebrar la piñata Gr. 4, 432
Al tambor Gr. 3, 271
Al yadee Gr. 6, 308
Ali Pasha Gr. 5, 219
Alle meine Entchen Gr. 1, 99
Ama-Lama Gr. 5, 142
Amefuri Gr. 1, 144
Ants Go Marching, The Gr. 1, 250
Apple Tree Gr. 1, 230
Apples, Peaches, Pears, and Plums (speech piece) Gr. 1, 14
Arirang Gr. 5, 25
Ayelivi Gr. 2, 70
Back of the Bus Gr. 3, 410
*Batucada* Parade Ensemble Gr. 8, D-24
Beach Rap Gr. 1, 354
Bear Dance Gr. 7, I-10
*Block Party* Gr. 7, B-12
Boogie Chant and Dance (speech piece) Gr. 2, 78
Boysie Gr. 2, 195
Bubble Gum (speech piece) Gr. K, 38
Bubble Trouble Gr. K, 184
Bump! Bump! Bump! Gr. K, 52
Butterfly Song Gr. 1, 361
*C-Jam Blues* Gr. 8, C-42
Cafe Europa Gr. 7, B-43
Canoe Song Gr. 4, 76
*Carnaval, Op. 9, "Valse Noble," Un poco maestoso* Gr. 3, 202
*Carry On* Gr. 7, B-2
Caterpillar, The Gr. K, 102
*Changed My Name* Gr. 6, 338
Chanukiyah li yesh Gr. 1, 421
Chawe chidyo chem'chero Gr. 2, 296
Che che koolay Gr. 2, 267
Cheki, morena Gr. 2, 180

*Children's Corner Suite, "Doctor Gradus ad Parnassum"* Gr. 8, C-27
Cinderella Dressed in Green Gr. K, 136
*Circle of Life (from The Lion King), The* Gr. 6, 317
*Circlesong 7* Gr. 4, 81
*Coming Home from the Sea–I* Gr. 6, 345
Concert for Piano and Orchestra Gr. 6, 208
Cookie Crew, The Gr. K, 196
Cuckoo, Cuckoo Gr. 1, 110
Cumberland Gap Gr. 4, 138
Cuna Indian Molas Gr. 1, 213
Cycle Song of Life (The River Song) Gr. 4, 370
Day-O! Gr. 5, 19
Deau-deau, ti pitit maman Gr. 2, 306
Deep in the Heart of Texas Gr. 8, E-22
*Diamonds and Rust* Gr. 7, A-4
Different Beat, A Gr. 1, 5
Different Beat, A Gr. 1, 7
Ding, Dong, Diggidiggidong Gr. 3, 14
*Doing the Penguin* Gr. K, 35
Don Gato Gr. 3, 353
Don't Let Your Watch Run Down Gr. 3, 167
Don't You Hear the Lambs? Gr. 5, 96
Doraji Gr. 4, 174
Down in the Meadow Gr. K, 146
Downpour Gr. K, 51
*El nuevo caiman* Gr. 8, B-17
Everybody Says Gr. 1, 286
Fais do do Gr. 6, 402
Families Gr. 1, 281
Family Tree Gr. 3, 75
Feliz Navidad Gr. 7, F-24
*Fingerprints* Gr. 7, B-42
Firefly Gr. 1, 356
Flight of the Bumblebee Gr. 3, 186
Flip, Flop and Fly Gr. 7, E-32
Free at Last Gr. 2, 396
Free Music #1 Gr. 2, 213
Freight Train Gr. 1, 47
Frère Jacques Gr. 2, 125
*Frog in the Millpond* Gr. 2, 45
Gavotte Gr. 3, 88
Get on Your Feet Gr. 5, 8
Goin' to the Fair Gr. K, 156
Gonna Ride Up in the Chariot Gr. 4, 20
Goodnight, Sun (poem) Gr. 1, 367
Green, Green, Rocky Gr. 1, 320
Grizzly Bear Gr. K, 32
Halloween Is a Very Unusual Night Gr. 3, 382

Hama chi dori Gr. 3, 330
Harambee Gr. 4, 435
Hashewie Gr. 4, 62
Hava nagila Gr. 6, 154
*Heads Carolina, Tails California* Gr. 7, B-24
Hearts Like Doors Gr. K, 189
Heave-Ho!/Going, Going, Gone/ The Snow Gr. 4, 184
Hej pada pada Gr. 3, 78
Hello! Gr. 2, 262
Hi Heidi Ho Gr. 1, 394
Hurt No Living Thing (poem) Gr. 1, 293
I Bought Me a Cat Gr. 2, 309
I Know an Old Lady Gr. 1, 388
*I Know You Mardi Gras* Gr. 8, B-17
I Love the Mountains Gr. 5, 34
I Walk in Beauty Gr. 4, 283
*I Will Survive* Gr. 7, B-10
If a Tiger Calls Gr. 3, 356
It's a Beautiful Day Gr. 3, 338
*Jazz in the Box* Gr. 8, F-10
Jig Along Home Gr. 2, 367
Jingle Writing Gr. 8, A-4
Johnny Appleseed Gr. 4, 346
Joshua Fought the Battle Gr. 5, 102
Joshua Fought the Battle of Jericho Gr. 5, 100
Keel Row, The Gr. 4, 240
*Keep a Cool Head* Gr. 7, B-34
Kelo aba w'ye Gr. 6, 290
Key to the Highway Gr. 6, 243
Khorovod Gr. 1, 373
Kibungo, Beast of the Forest Gr. 2, 353
*Kitchen Stomp* Gr. 4, 121
Knock the Cymbals Gr. 1, 176
Kookaburra Gr. 4, 187
Koriko! Gr. K, 155
Kwanzaa Carol, A Gr. 2, 392
La bamba Gr. 5, 128
La mar estaba serena Gr. 2, 345
Las estaciones Gr. 1, 29
Las horas Gr. 1, 247
Leaves Gr. 1, 27
Lion Sleeps Tonight, The Gr. 8, I-56
Lion Sleeps Tonight, The Gr. 8, E-9
*Little Red Hen*, The (story) Gr. 1, 256
Locomoto-vation Gr. K, 60
*Lohengrin, "Prelude to Act III"* Gr. 8, C-22
Loigratong Gr. 6, 450
Look Out Below! Gr. 2, 370
Los trencitos Gr. K, 24
Lullaby (poem) Gr. 1, 208

**(Skills Reinforcement, continued)**

*Lyric Suite, "Allegretto gioviale,"
Movement 1* Gr. 6, 168

Magnolia Gr. 6, 16

Mainly Metal Ensemble Gr. 7, D-26

Mama Don't 'Low Gr. 6, 359

Man of Constant Sorrow
Gr. 7, F-28

Manhattan Lullaby Gr. K, 193

Mashed Potatoes (speech piece)
Gr. 1, 20

*Men's Fancy Dance* Gr. 7, D-24

*Mi tierra* Gr. 6, 365

Missy-La, Massa-La Gr. 4, 190

Moon, The (poem) Gr. 1, 399

Morning Is Come Gr. 3, 129

Name, Name, What's Your Name?
Gr. 3, 11

Nana, Thread Needle Gr. 1, 39

*Nutcracker Suite, The, "Trepak"*
Gr. 3, 280

O hal'lwe Gr. 3, 257

Ochimbo Gr. 4, 134

Ode to la piñata (poem) Gr. 1, 424

Oh, Susanna Gr. 4, 264

Oh, Watch the Stars Gr. 2, 145

Old Brass Wagon Gr. 2, 122

One Family Gr. 7, G-18

*Open the Kingdom* Gr. 6, 31

Orange Blossom Special
Gr. 5, 268

*Ostinatos Around the World*
Gr. 8, B-4

Painting Song: A Dribble and a Dot
Gr. K, 174

Parade Came Marching, The
Gr. 1, 166

Pastures of Plenty Gr. 4, 280

Pay Me My Money Down Gr. 4, 40

Pay Me My Money Down
Gr. 7, F-4

Perot Gr. 2, 379

Phoebe Gr. 1, 30

*Planets, The,* "Jupiter" Gr. 1, 405

Planets Chant, The Gr. 4, 376

Play a Simple Melody Gr. 5, 73

Polly Wee Gr. K, 118

*Prelude in E Minor, Op. 28, No. 4*
Gr. 3, 27

Pumpkin Poem Gr. 3, 382

¡Qué llueva! Gr. K, 80

Ragtime Cowboy Joe Gr. 2, 251

Ragupati Ragava Raja Ram
Gr. 5, 321

Rain Sings a Song, The Gr. 1, 100

Rainbow, The Gr. 2, 333

Recording engineer Gr. 7, A-20

*Retounen* Gr. 8, B-17

Rhythm Is Gonna Get You, The
Gr. 6, 348

Rio Grande Gr. 4, 256

River Gr. 4, 61

Sambalele Gr. 4, 397

Scarborough Fair Gr. 6, 94

*Scherzo for Wind Quintet, Op. 48*
Gr. 1, 329

Scotland the Brave Gr. 5, 138

Scrub Brush Shuffle, The
Gr. 1, 119

Scrub-a-dub Gr. 1, 304

See the Children Playin' Gr. 4, 107

Setting the Thanksgiving Table
Gr. 2, 381

Shoo, Turkey Gr. 1, 104

Shortnin' Bread Gr. 1, 58

Shu ha mo Gr. 3, 276

*Silver Apples of the Moon*
Gr. 1, 11

Simple Gifts Gr. 5, 185

Sing! Speak! Whisper! Shout!
Gr. 1, 35

*Slavonic Dance, Op. 46, No. 1,*
Gr. 4, 229

Soldier, Soldier Gr. 4, 10

Son macaron Gr. 4, 108

Sonando Gr. 4, 35

Song of Greatness, A Gr. 3, 334

*Songs from Letters, "So Like Your
Father"* Gr. 7, C-20

Sourwood Mountain Gr. 4, 64

Spaceworms Gr. 1, 400

Stopping By Woods on a Snowy
Evening Gr. 2, 389

Storm Dance Gr. K, 144

*String Quartet No. 5, Movement
4: Andante* Gr. 3, 112

*Symphony No. 3 in E-flat Major*
Gr. 8, C-16

*Tahi* Gr. 8, B-14

Ten Tom-Toms Gr. K, 78

*Theme and Variations for
Percussion* Gr. 5, 64

This Land Is Your Land Gr. 7, I-66

Those Magic Changes Gr. 8, E-31

Three Little Birds Gr. 8, F-6

Thula, thula, ngoana Gr. 4, 227

Today Is Your Birthday Gr. 1, 410

*Twist, The* Gr. 7, B-10

'Ūlili E Gr. 5, 441

Un pajarito Gr. 2, 17

Under the Sea Gr. 5, 375

Up and Down Kitten, The
Gr. K, 100

*Variations on "America"*
Gr. 6, 162

Wade in the Water Gr. 8, I-64

*Waitin' for a Train* Gr. 7, B-24

Waiting for the Traffic Light
Gr. 2, 107

Water Is Wide, The Gr. 6, 229

*Watermelon Man* Gr. 1, 11

We Shall Overcome Gr. 4, 326

Weevily Wheat Gr. 4, 105

Wind Song (poem) Gr. K, 6

Wood Works Ensemble Gr. 8, D-28

*Wu long* Gr. 4, 155

*Xochipilli* Gr. 8, C-36

Yellow Butter (speech piece)
Gr. 1, 124

**DESCRIBING**

*Eternal Flame* Gr. 7, B-6

Plenty o' Nuttin' Gr. 7, B-44

Riverdance Suite Gr. 2, 140

**EVALUATING**

*Voiles* Gr. 7, C-38

**IDENTIFYING**

Guitar Tuning Gr. 7, F-3

Guitar Tuning Gr. 8, F-3

*World Percussion Sounds*
Gr. 8, B-6

**IMPROVISING**

Abiyoyo Gr. 2, 108

Ahora voy a cantarles Gr. 3, 57

America, the Free Gr. 4, 212

Blues with a Feeling Gr. 8, I-9

Chanukah Games Gr. 3, 388

Chicka Hanka Gr. 8, F-14

Create a Career Gr. 8, A-32

*Danza* Gr. 7, C-6

Dot the Eighth Note Gr. 8, H-18

Doumbek or Hand Drum Exercises
Gr. 7, D-30

Ev'rybody Loves Saturday Night
Gr. 7, I-25

*Firebird, The, "Finale"* Gr. 8, C-30

Flip, Flop and Fly Gr. 7, I-33

Give a Little Love Gr. 6, 142

Good Mornin', Blues Gr. 5, 224

Hambone Gr. 7, D-2

Heave-Ho!/Going, Going, Gone/
The Snow Gr. 4, 182

Hevenu shalom aleichem
Gr. 3, 379

*Hungarian Dance No. 6* Gr. 4, 50

Joe Turner Blues Gr. 4, 56

Johnny Appleseed Gr. 4, 344

Kou ri lengay Gr. 2, 217

Kum bachur atzel Gr. 3, 138

La paloma blanca Gr. 3, 252

Las mañanitas Gr. 6, 481

*mi-re-do* Gr. 8, H-6

Lullaby Lady, The (poem)
Gr. 1, 273

Mississippi River Chant (speech
piece) Gr. 2, 132

Old Dan Tucker Gr. 3, 98

One Eighth and Two Sixteenth
Notes Gr. 8, H-18

Over There Gr. 5, 278

Performers Gr. 8, A-16

Railroad Corral Gr. 3, 176

Rhythm Basics Gr. 7, H-2

Rock Around the Clock Gr. 7, H-2

*Slow Hora/Freylekhs* Gr. 8, B-26

Summertime Gr. 6, 252

Tap It! Rap It! (speech piece)
Gr. K, 194

*ti,* Time Gr. 8, H-14
*Twist and Shout* Gr. 4, 238
Un pajarito Gr. 2, 17
Video Game Sound Effects
    Gr. 8, A-2
*Zomo the Rabbit* Gr. 3, 365

## LISTENING

*12 Variations in C Major, K.
    265/300e, "Ah, vous dirai-je,
    Maman"* Gr. 3, 19
*1st and 2nd Endings* Gr. 7, H-4
*Aerial Boundaries* Gr. 8, F-20
Alexander's Ragtime Band
    Gr. 6, 136
*All in One* Gr. 1, 12
Alleluia, Amen Gr. 7, A-12
America Gr. 7, I-3
At the Same Time Gr. 6, 114
*Aviary, The* Gr. K, 45
*Aweigh, Santy Ano* Gr. 1, 338
*Ayliluli, num tsipor* Gr. 1, 204
*Baa-Baa Black Sheep* Gr. K, 102
*Bear Dance Song* Gr. K, 126
*Bethena Waltz* Gr. 6, 157
*Bird Calls, Bird Songs* Gr. K, 178
*Brandenburg Concerto No. 2*
    Gr. 7, E-25
*Can't Take My Joy* Gr. 7, B-40
*Canto del agua* Gr. 8, I-11
*Caprice No. 1 in E Major*
    Gr. 7, C-22
*Carmina Burana, "Chramer, gip
    die Varwe mir"* Gr. K, 62
*Carnival of the Animals, "Fossils"*
    Gr. 1, 236
*Carnival of the Animals, "The
    Elephant"* Gr. K, 45
*Carolina Sunday Waltz* Gr. 7, F-8
Che che koolay Gr. 2, 267
*Chinese Instruments Montage*
    Gr. 2, 276
Circle 'Round the Moon Gr. 4, 402
*Coming Home from the Sea*
    Gr. 6, 346
*Concerto for Trumpet and
    Orchestra in E-flat* Gr. 1, 254
Concerto in D Major for Flute and
    Orchestra Gr. K, 122
*Crazy Blues* Gr. 7, B-8
*Dance Suite, "Waltz"* Gr. K, 144
Day-O! Gr. 5, 20
Debajo el botón Gr. 1, 210
Dinosaur Dance Gr. 2, 168
*Dippermouth Blues* Gr. 7, B-14
*Don't Get Around Much Anymore*
    Gr. 1, 33
Don't You Hear the Lambs?
    Gr. 5, 96
Doong gul ge Gr. 3, 134
Doumbek or Hand Drum Exercises
    Gr. 7, D-30
*Drift* Gr. 8, B-42

Dry Bones Gr. 4, 162
Dynamics Gr. 7, H-11
Eine kleine Nachtmusik Gr. 4, 112
*El amor brujo, "Danza ritual del
    fuego"* Gr. 8, F-20
*El dulcerito llego, "The Sweets
    Vendor Is Here"* Gr. K, 124
El Tren Gr. 2, 260
Electronic keyboard Gr. 8, E-26
*Erlkönig, "The Erlking"*
    Gr. K, 164
*Every Morning* Gr. 7, B-8
*Fantasy for Chanukah* Gr. 1, 418
*Fiesta, "Tarantella"* Gr. K, 134
*Flight of the Bumblebee (from
    Tsar Sultan)* Gr. 1, 385
*Flight of the Bumblebee* Gr. K, 76
*Florida Suite, "Everglades"*
    Gr. 1, 413
*Four Seasons, The, Concerto No.
    2, "Summer," Movement 3, "La
    Tempesta"* Gr. 6, 102
*Four Seasons, The, "Winter,"
    (Largo), Movement 2*
    Gr. 3, 110
*Galbi* Gr. 1, 183
*Gavotte* Gr. 3, 88
Gift to Share, A Gr. 6, 393
Give My Regards to Broadway
    Gr. 6, 39
Gospel Train, The Gr. 6, 396
*Halley Came to Jackson*
    Gr. 2, 340
*Hänsel und Gretel, "Ein Männlein
    steht im Walde"* Gr. 2, 91
*Hard Times* Gr. 1, 194
*Here Comes My Girl* Gr. 7, F-16
*Hindewhu (whistle) solo*
    Gr. 6, 269
*Hippopotamus Song, The*
    Gr. 3, 34
*Hotter Than That* Gr. 6, 65
*Humpty Dumpty* Gr. K, 22
*Hungarian Dance No. 3 in F Major*
    Gr. 1, 206
I'm on My Way Gr. 7, A-14
I'm Thankful Gr. 1, 415
Jo'ashila Gr. 5, 108
*Joy* Gr. 7, B-40
Joy to the World Gr. 3, 22
*Juba* Gr. K, 12
*Julie-O* Gr. 5, 311
Just from the Kitchen Gr. K, 55
Koriko! Gr. K, 155
Kunolounkwa Gr. K, 110
*La Rosa* Gr. K, 134
La Tarara Gr. 4, 177
La tormenta tropical Gr. 2, 118
Las estaciones Gr. 1, 29
Le jig Français Gr. K, 64
Let Freedom Ring Gr. 5, 79
Let Us Sing Together Gr. 6, 157
*Let's Face the Music* Gr. 7, B-14

Let's Get the Rhythm of the Band
    Gr. 7, E-28
*Light Up the World* Gr. 2, 196
*Little Birdie* Gr. 4, 75
*Llactamanta* Gr. 6, 382
*Lo, How a Rose E'er Blooming*
    Gr. 6, 210
*Love for Three Oranges, "March"*
    Gr. K, 116
Lullaby Gr. 3, 188
*Lyric Pieces, Op. 43, No. 4, "Little
    Bird"* Gr. 1, 346
*Ma Vlast (My Fatherland), "Vltava
    (The Moldau)"* Gr. 7, C-32
Mainly Metal Ensemble Gr. 7, D-26
*Malagueña* Gr. 5, 154
*Masquerade Suite, "Galop"*
    Gr. 4, 16
Meter and Measure Gr. 7, H-4
*Montage of Historical Styles*
    Gr. 7, C-2
*Moon Mirrored in the Pool, The*
    Gr. 6, 103
More Meter and Rhythm
    Gr. 7, H-4
Music Critic Gr. 7, A-32
Music delivery Gr. 7, A-30
Music recording media Gr. 7, A-18
*Nights in the Gardens of Spain,
    "En el generalife"* Gr. 2, 145
Now That's Tap (speech piece)
    Gr. 6, 320
*Nruab hnub thiab hmo ntuj*
    Gr. 4, 367
Nutcracker Suite, The, "Chinese
    Dance" Gr. K, 104
*Nutcracker Suite, The, "Waltz of
    the Flowers"* Gr. 6, 325
*Nutcracker Suite, The, "Waltz of
    the Flowers"* Gr. 6, 323
*Nyoka* Gr. 7, D-33
*Oh, Freedom and Come and Go
    with Me* Gr. 5, 394
Old Chisholm Trail, The Gr. 6, 237
Old House, Tear It Down!
    Gr. 4, 178
*Omo* Gr. 1, 442
*Onomatapoiea Study No. 2*
    Gr. 7, E-30
*P'tit galop pour mamou*
    Gr. 1, 317
Peace Like a River Gr. 6, 190
*PIZZ Ah!* Gr. 1, 104
*Planxty Madame Maxwell*
    Gr. K, 134
Pollerita Gr. 5, 151
*Prelude to the Afternoon of a
    Faun* Gr. 5, 113
*Primitive Fire, "Oya"* Gr. 2, 68
Pumpkin, Pumpkin Gr. 1, 412
*Quartetto buffo di gatti* Gr. 1, 131
*Rain Song, The* Gr. 2, 323
*Raindrop Prelude* Gr. 3, 19

**(Skills Reinforcement, continued)**

Repeat Signs  Gr. 7, H-4
*Reuben's Train*  Gr. 1, 334
*Rhythm of the Heat, The*
 Gr. 7, E-30
Riendo el río corre  Gr. 6, 265
Riverdance Suite  Gr. 2, 140
*Rocky Point Holiday*  Gr. 6, 330
Sawatdee tuh jah  Gr. 2, 264
*Scaramouche, "Brasiliera,"*
 *Movement 3*  Gr. 8, C-29
*Scuttle Buttin'*  Gr. 8, F-26
*Shchedryk, "Carol of the Bells"*
 Gr. 6, 103
*She Is Like the Swallow*
 Gr. 8, B-12
*Shumba*  Gr. 8, B-12
*Sikelela*  Gr. 1, 138
Silver Apples of the Moon
 Gr. 1, 11
*Silver Apples of the Moon*
 Gr. 1, 12
Soldier, Soldier  Gr. 4, 10
Something Told the Wild Geese
 Gr. 7, H-4
Somewhere Out There  Gr. 5, 368
*Sonata in C Major for Recorder*
 *and Basso Continuo, Op. 1,*
 *No. 7, Gavotte*  Gr. K, 75
*Song for Bells, A*  Gr. 1, 427
Song That's Just for You, A
 Gr. 2, 126
*Sorochintsy Fair, "Gopak No. 5"*
 Gr. 1, 417
Sound Waves Montage  Gr. 6, 357
*Spinning Song*  Gr. K, 164
*Spring Walk, "Du xuân"*
 Gr. 1, 440
Stand By Me  Gr. 5, 46
Star Light, Star Bright  Gr. 1, 108
*Stars and Stripes Forever*
 Gr. 1, 167
*String Quartet No. 5, Movement*
 *4: Andante*  Gr. 3, 110
Surfin' U.S.A.  Gr. 7, I-60
*Symphony No. 47 in G Major,*
 *"Menuet"*  Gr. 7, C-15
*Symphony No. 7, Op. 92, No. 7,*
 *Movement 2*  Gr. 1, 96
*That's the Way*  Gr. 4, 193
This Land Is Your Land  Gr. 7, I-66
*Tihore Mai*  Gr. 8, B-12
*Toccata and Fugue in D Minor*
 Gr. 7, E-25
*Trout Quintet*  Gr. 1, 179
*Turkish Rondo*  Gr. K, 116
Understanding music  Gr. 8, C-2
*Vonjeo*  Gr. 8, B-12
*Wachet auf, ruft uns die Stimme*
 Gr. 7, E-25
Waitin' for the Light to Shine
 Gr. 4, 27
*Watermelon Man*  Gr. 1, 11

*Watermelon Man*  Gr. 1, 12
We Shall Not Be Moved  Gr. 4, 437
We're Making Popcorn (speech
 piece)  Gr. 1, 85
*Well-Tempered Clavier, Book*
 *1, "Prelude and Fugue in C*
 *Minor"*  Gr. 7, E-16
Wild Horsemen, The  Gr. 1, 159
Willowbee  Gr. 1, 222
*Winter Birds Flying over the Water*
 Gr. 1, 91
*Xochipilli*  Gr. 8, C-36
Yellow Rose of Texas, The
 Gr. 7, I-70
Your Friends Shall Be the Tall Wind
 Gr. 6, 200
Zip-a-Dee-Doo-Dah  Gr. 2, 330
*Zulu Lullaby*  Gr. K, 158

## MOVING  *See also Movement;*
*Moving*

Ama-Lama  Gr. 5, 143
Blues with a Feeling  Gr. 8, I-7
Box a-Rockin' Ensemble  Gr. 7, D-4
California  Gr. 5, 52
Chiapanecas  Gr. 5, 92
*Cho'i hát bội*  Gr. 5, 319
*Cotton-Eye Joe*  Gr. 4, 290
*Danses Populaires Francaises,*
 *"Branle Double, Branle*
 *Simple"*  Gr. 7, C-25
De colores  Gr. 8, I-15
Earth Is Our Mother, The
 Gr. 4, 358
El rabel  Gr. 3, 362
Fuzzy Caterpillar  Gr. K, 102
*Good Golly, Miss Molly*
 Gr. 8, E-13
I've Been Working on the Railroad
 Gr. 3, 243
Jambalaya  Gr. 8, F-18
Jasmine Flowers  Gr. 5, 316
Just from the Kitchen  Gr. K, 55
Kaeru no uta  Gr. K, 183
Laredo  Gr. 5, 10
Look Out for Mother Earth
 Gr. 3, 340
Mubärak  Gr. 3, 282
*Nutcracker, The, "Arabian Dance"*
 Gr. 7, C-26
*Nutcracker, The, "Chinese Dance"*
 Gr. 7, C-26
Over the River and Through the
 Wood  Gr. 3, 384
*Piano Concerto in A Minor, Op.*
 *16, Movement 1*  Gr. 8, E-13
*Queen's Suite, The, "Sunset and*
 *the Mocking Bird"*  Gr. 8, E-13
Rain on the Green Grass (speech
 piece)  Gr. K, 10
*Siyayilanda*  Gr. 8, B-40
Sonando  Gr. 4, 35
Three Little Birds  Gr. 8, F-6

Uno, dos y tres  Gr. 5, 429
Waltzing with Bears  Gr. 3, 170

## NOTATING

A la puerta del cielo  Gr. 5, 60
All Around the Buttercup
 Gr. 2, 170
All Through the Night  Gr. 5, 105
Alleluia  Gr. 6, 132
Autumn Canon  Gr. 5, 148
¡Ay, Jalisco no te rajes!  Gr. 7, I-6
Banuwa  Gr. 6, 295
Basics of Melody  Gr. 7, H-6
Bắt kim thang  Gr. 6, 13
Beach Rap  Gr. 1, 353
Birthday  Gr. 6, 90
Clouds of Gray  Gr. 2, 56
Come, Ye Thankful People, Come
 Gr. 5, 459
Dundai  Gr. 5, 106
Earth Is Our Mother, The
 Gr. 8, F-24
*Firebird, The, "Finale"*  Gr. 8, C-30
Go-Go Street Ensemble
 Gr. 8, D-30
Ha'kyo jong  Gr. 2, 135
Hashkediya  Gr. 3, 206
Hui jia qù  Gr. 2, 159
Intervals - Seconds and Thirds
 Gr. 7, H-25
*Jelly Roll, The*  Gr. 7, B-36
Kelo aba w'ye  Gr. 6, 289
Key of D Major  Gr. 8, H-20
Key of F Major  Gr. 8, H-20
La golondrina  Gr. 8, I-50
A Major Formula  Gr. 7, H-22
Lion Sleeps Tonight, The  Gr. 8, I-56
Little Black Bug  Gr. 1, 214
Lucy Locket  Gr. 2, 27
Major Scales with Flats  Gr. 7, H-22
Melodic Sequence  Gr. 7, H-25
*mi-re-do*  Gr. 7, H-6
Minor Scales  Gr. 7, H-28
Mississippi River Chant (speech
 piece)  Gr. 2, 132
More Intervals - Fourths,
 Fifths, Sixths, and Sevenths
 Gr. 7, H-25
More Melody: *fa*  Gr. 7, H-6
Over in the Meadow  Gr. 1, 346
Pizza, Pizza, Daddy-o  Gr. 2, 28
Rocky Mountain  Gr. 2, 98
*Samanfo, begye nsa nom*
 Gr. 8, D-6
Scales: They're Major!  Gr. 7, H-22
Sea Shell  Gr. 2, 101
Sourwood Mountain  Gr. 4, 64
Stille Nacht (Silent Night)
 Gr. 7, I-55
Syncopation  Gr. 8, H-10
This Land Is Your Land  Gr. 7, I-68
Twist, The  Gr. 5, 358

Two More keys with Sharps: A Major and E Major  Gr. 8, H-20
Un, deux, trois  Gr. 2, 199
Valentines  Gr. 2, 399
Was kommt dort von der Höh'?  Gr. 8, C-21
Yellow Rose of Texas, The  Gr. 7, I-70

## PERFORMING

All Around the Country (poem)  Gr. 1, 445
*Batucada* Parade Ensemble  Gr. 8, D-22
Can You Canoe?  Gr. 4, 170
*(Can't Live Without Your) Love and Affection*  Gr. 7, B-22
Carnaval Calypso Ensemble  Gr. 7, D-20
De colores  Gr. 8, E-14
Dok djampa  Gr. 8, I-20
Don Alfonso  Gr. 5, 176
Dotted Rhythm and Syncopation Practice  Gr. 8, H-13
Every Night When the Sun Goes In  Gr. 8, I-28
Flip, Flop and Fly  Gr. 7, I-33
God Bless the U.S.A.  Gr. 8, G-36
Haul Away, Joe  Gr. 4, 12
He's Got the Whole World in His Hands  Gr. 7, I-37
I Shall Sing  Gr. 8, I-41
Kokoleoko  Gr. 5, 33
Music Therapist/Teacher  Gr. 8, A-26
O, Desayo  Gr. 5, 411
Proud  Gr. 7, G-2
Put a Little Love in Your Heart  Gr. 4, 8
Somebody's Knockin' at Your Door  Gr. 4, 52
*That's the Way It Is*  Gr. 7, B-22
This Land Is Your Land  Gr. 5, 119

## PLAYING

12-Bar Blues Rock  Gr. 8, F-30
*Abbots Bromley Horn Dance*  Gr. 7, C-24
Achshav  Gr. 2, 64
*Aerial Boundaries*  Gr. 8, F-20
Agbekor Ensemble  Gr. 8, D-10
Ain't Gonna Let Nobody Turn Me 'Round  Gr. 8, F-16
All for One  Gr. 7, E-8
Allá en la fuente  Gr. 2, 93
*Alle psallite cum luya*  Gr. 7, C-5
Amarillo Armadillo  Gr. 2, 82
*America*  Gr. 7, A-22
America  Gr. 8, I-3
*America (from West Side Story)*  Gr. 8, C-45
America, the Beautiful  Gr. 7, I-4
America, the Beautiful  Gr. 8, I-5
*Angry Anymore*  Gr. 8, F-32

Animals Find Water, The  Gr. 2, 218
Arirang  Gr. 5, 25
Ash Grove, The  Gr. 5, 114
Así es mi tierra  Gr. 6, 173
Avocational musicians  Gr. 8, A-30
Bam, chi, chi, bam  Gr. K, 108
Bard of Armagh, The  Gr. 4, 297
Bear Dance  Gr. 7, I-10
*Beat of the Tango, The*  Gr. K, 106
Bee, Bee Bumblebee (speech piece)  Gr. 1, 50
Bereleh  Gr. K, 150
Bingo  Gr. 1, 169
Bling Blang  Gr. 3, 240
Boomin' Bamboo Ensemble  Gr. 7, D-22
Bounce High, Bounce Low  Gr. 1, 152
Bound for South Australia  Gr. 5, 22
Bubble Trouble  Gr. K, 184
Bucket O'Taiko Ensemble  Gr. 7, D-16
By the Waters of Babylon  Gr. 6, 310
Caballito blanco  Gr. 2, 193
California, Here I Come  Gr. 4, 287
Canoe Song  Gr. 4, 76
Caribbean Island Ensemble  Gr. 7, D-19
Carnaval Calypso Ensemble  Gr. 7, D-20
*Carolina Sunday Waltz*  Gr. 7, F-8
Certainly, Lord  Gr. 7, I-14
Che che koolay  Gr. 2, 267
Checki, morena  Gr. 7, F-11
Cheki, morena  Gr. 7, E-12
Cheki, morena  Gr. 7, I-16
Chicka Hanka  Gr. 8, F-14
Chords and strums  Gr. 8, F-5
Cielito lindo  Gr. 7, I-20
Ciranda  Gr. 2, 272
*Circlesong 7*  Gr. 4, 81
Clementine  Gr. 4, 343
Cold and Frosty Morning  Gr. 2, 139
Connemara Lullaby  Gr. 5, 234
Corrido de Kansas  Gr. 4, 275
*Crunchy, Crunchy, Crunchy*  Gr. 8, D-15
Cuban Rumba Ensemble  Gr. 7, D-6
Dayenu  Gr. 4, 439
De colores  Gr. 8, I-15
Deep in the Heart of Texas  Gr. 8, I-19
Der sad to katte  Gr. 2, 300
Deux cocodries  Gr. 2, 364
Do Wah Diddy Diddy  Gr. 7, F-20
Dot the Eighth Note  Gr. 8, H-18
Dotted Quarter Note  Gr. 7, H-13
Dotted Rhythm and Syncopation Practice  Gr. 8, H-13

Dotted Rhythms with Sixteenth Notes  Gr. 7, H-20
Dotted-Half Note and Whole Note  Gr. 8, H-4
Down the Ohio  Gr. 2, 61
*Drums From Around the World*  Gr. 6, 276
Earth Is Our Mother, The  Gr. 4, 358
Earth Is Our Mother, The  Gr. 8, F-24
Eighth and Sixteenth Combinations  Gr. 7, H-19
Ein Männlein steht im Walde  Gr. 2, 91
El barquito  Gr. 3, 358
El borrego  Gr. 4, 243
El carnavalito humahuaqueño  Gr. 6, 482
El chocolate  Gr. 1, 381
El desembre congelat  Gr. 5, 473
El juego chirimbolo  Gr. 2, 55
El sapito  Gr. 3, 336
Elegua  Gr. 7, D-6
Éliza Kongo  Gr. 5, 14
Every Morning When I Wake Up  Gr. 2, 321
Ezekiel Saw the Wheel  Gr. 6, 380
Feliz Navidad  Gr. 7, I-30
Fiddler on the Roof  Gr. 7, E-6
*Fifteen Hungarian Peasant Songs*  Gr. 7, C-35
Flip, Flop and Fly  Gr. 7, F-14
Flip, Flop and Fly  Gr. 7, I-33
Fly and the Bumblebee, The  Gr. 1, 385
Four in a Boat  Gr. 2, 46
Four in a Boat  Gr. 2, 48
From Sea to Shining Sea  Gr. 2, 342
*Gershwin's Rhapsody in Blue*  Gr. K, 75
Get on Board  Gr. K, 88
Get on Your Feet  Gr. 5, 6
Glad to Have a Friend Like You  Gr. 2, 229
Go-Go Street Ensemble  Gr. 8, D-30
God Bless the Grass  Gr. 8, F-12
Goin' Down the Road Feelin' Bad  Gr. 5, 282
Good Mornin', Blues  Gr. 2, 52
Goodbye, Julie  Gr. 8, E-4
Gospel Train, The  Gr. 6, 398
Greenland Whale Fishery, The  Gr. 5, 230
Grizzly Bear  Gr. K, 32
Guitar Tuning  Gr. 7, F-3
Gypsy in the Moonlight  Gr. 3, 12
Ha'kyo jong  Gr. 2, 135
Hambone  Gr. 7, D-2
Hanuka, Hanuka  Gr. 3, 390
Hanuka, Hanuka  Gr. 8, I-36

**(Skills Reinforcement, continued)**

Happy Feet Gr. 2, 252
He's Got the Whole World in His Hands Gr. 7, I-37
Hi Heidi Ho Gr. 1, 392
Hickory, Dickory, Dock (so-la-so-mi Version) Gr. 1, 224
Hitotsu toya Gr. 5, 478
Hsù chu (Prelude) Ensemble Gr. 8, D-26
Hush, Hush Gr. 3, 162
I Got a Letter This Morning Gr. K, 68
I Love Peanuts Gr. 7, E-20
I Love the Mountains Gr. 5, 34
I Shall Sing Gr. 8, I-39
I Wonder Where Maria's Gone Gr. 3, 318
Ichi-gatsu tsuitachi Gr. 7, I-42
If a Tiger Calls Gr. 3, 356
If You Look Gr. 7, B-4
Imbabura Gr. 5, 203
Interview with Rick Bassett (Part 2) Gr. 3, 222
Island Ensemble Gr. 8, D-18
It's Santa—Again! Gr. 2, 385
Jambalaya Gr. 8, I-48
Jan ken pon Gr. 3, 302
Jazz in the Box Gr. 8, F-10
Jig Along Home Gr. 2, 367
Jo'ashila Gr. 6, 285
Junk Music Montage Gr. 1, 73
Keel Row, The Gr. 4, 240
Keep Your Eyes on the Prize Gr. 3, 408
Keep Your Eyes on the Prize Gr. 8, E-17
Key to the Highway Gr. 8, F-28
Ki mua Gr. 8, B-26
Kingston Market Gr. 3, 91
Kookaburra Gr. 4, 187
Kou ri lengay Gr. 7, E-3
Kpanlogo Highlife Ensemble Gr. 7, D-12
Kuma san Gr. K, 40
L'Arlésienne Suite No. 2, "Farandole" Gr. 6, 68
L'union Gr. 6, 485
La mar estaba serena Gr. 2, 345
La mariposa Gr. 6, 58
La pulga de San José Gr. 3, 41
Las horas Gr. 1, 247
Let the Children Play Gr. 7, B-30
Let's Twist Again Gr. 6, 257
Lieutenant Kijé, Op. 60, "Troika" Gr. 6, 456
Lion Sleeps Tonight, The Gr. 8, E-9
Lion Sleeps Tonight, The Gr. 8, F-6
Little Spider Gr. K, 92
Los maizales Gr. 1, 297
Los reyes de Oriente Gr. 8, I-58

Lost My Gold Ring Gr. 6, 158
Love Will Guide Us Gr. 4, 328
Luna lunera (speech piece) Gr. K, 90
Mañana Gr. 7, E-14
Marines' Hymn, The Gr. 8, C-39
Mariposita Gr. 2, 156
Máru-bihág Gr. 6, 304
Me voy para la luna Gr. 1, 396
Meng Jian Nu Gr. 5, 195
Meters, Measures, and More Gr. 8, H-2
Mi chacra Gr. 1, 365
Mi tierra Gr. 6, 365
Michael Finnigan Gr. 3, 152
Midnight Special, The Gr. 7, F-22
Minka Gr. 4, 223
Miss Mary Mack Gr. 2, 42
Mon papa Gr. 2, 279
Monster Stomp, The (poem) Gr. 1, 133
Mubärak Gr. 3, 282
Nana Kru Gr. 6, 282
Nangapè Gr. 2, 103
Nanny Goat Gr. K, 160
New Hungarian Folk Song Gr. 6, 196
Nyoka Gr. 7, D-33
O, Desayo Gr. 5, 413
O lê lê O Bahía Gr. 6, 165
O pião entrou Gr. 2, 354
Oklahoma Gr. 5, 36
Old Blue Gr. K, 122
Old Brass Wagon Gr. 2, 122
Old Dan Tucker Gr. 3, 96
On a Log, Mister Frog Gr. K, 148
One Eighth and Two Sixteenth Notes Gr. 8, H-18
Orfferondo (Performance Piece) Gr. 4, 194
Pai pi qiu Gr. 1, 324
Pay Me My Money Down Gr. 7, F-4
Peace Round Gr. 4, 349
Penny Lane Gr. 6, 257
Percussion Fun Rondo Gr. 7, I-51
Pictures at an Exhibition, "The Great Gate of Kiev" Gr. 8, A-12
Prayer, The Gr. 7, A-10
Pretty Saro Gr. 3, 217
Proud Gr. 7, G-4
Pulcinella Suite, "Minuetto" Gr. 8, C-15
¡Qué gusto! Gr. 3, 132
Quintet for Piano and Strings in E-flat Major Gr. 8, C-18
Red Poppy, The, "Russian Sailors' Dance" Gr. 4, 224
Rhythm Fundamentals Gr. 8, H-2
Riendo el río corre Gr. 6, 263
Riqui rán Gr. 1, 48
Riqui rán Gr. 4, 66

Rise and Shine Gr. 4, 99
Rockin' Around the Christmas Tree Gr. 5, 467
'Round and 'Round Gr. 1, 149
S'vivon Gr. 6, 452
Samanfo, begye nsa nom Gr. 8, D-6
Same Train Gr. 2, 164
San Miguel Jolonicapan Gr. 8, D-16
Sha Sha Sha Gr. 6, 328
Shake Them 'Simmons Down Gr. 2, 245
She'll Be Comin' 'Round the Mountain Gr. 2, 359
Shenandoah Gr. 2, 62
Shortnin' Bread Gr. 1, 56
Si si si Gr. 7, G-12
Sing a Rainbow Gr. 2, 167
Singing-Time Gr. 3, 201
Siyahamba Gr. 6, 214
Small Job, A Gr. 3, 225
Somebody Waiting Gr. 2, 283
Sonata in C Major for Recorder and Basso Continuo, Op. 1, No. 7, Gavotte Gr. K, 75
Song of the Eagle Gr. 2, 248
Song of the Fishes Gr. 3, 245
Song of the Night, The Gr. 3, 344
Sound Waves Montage Gr. 6, 355
South African Ensemble Gr. 7, D-11
St. Patrick Was a Gentleman Gr. 3, 291
Stand By Me Gr. 8, E-24
Star-Spangled Banner, The Gr. 7, I-56
Star-Spangled Banner, The Gr. 8, I-62
Stille Nacht (Silent Night) Gr. 7, F-24
Surfin' U.S.A. Gr. 6, 260
Surfin' U.S.A. Gr. 7, E-27
Surfin' U.S.A. Gr. 7, F-32
Symphony No. 47 in G Major, "Menuet" Gr. 7, C-15
Syncopation Gr. 8, H-10
Table Manners (speech piece) Gr. 3, 190
Take Me Out to the Ball Game Gr. 3, 262
Tanabata-sama Gr. 2, 337
Te dejo Madrid Gr. 7, B-30
Tears of a Clown, The Gr. 7, B-36
Ten Little Ostinato Pieces Gr. 7, I-62
Tender Shepherd (Count Your Sheep) Gr. 3, 116
This Is Your Night Gr. 6, 368
This Land Is Your Land Gr. 7, I-66
This Old Man Gr. 3, 152
Those Magic Changes Gr. 8, E-31
Three Little Birds Gr. 8, F-6

*Toccata in D Minor* Gr. 4, 233
Two Little Sausages Gr. 2, 78
*Uma história de Ifá* Gr. 3, 308
Valentine Dance Gr. 1, 437
Video Game Sound Effects
 Gr. 8, A-2
Wade in the Water Gr. 8, I-64
Wai bamba Gr. 6, 26
We Shall Not Be Moved Gr. 4, 437
Whacky Wheel Ensemble, The
 Gr. 6, 381
Wheel of the Water, The
 Gr. 4, 364
When the Train Comes Along
 Gr. 1, 300
Where's Your Drum? Ensemble
 Gr. 8, D-20
Who Has Seen the Wind?
 Gr. 2, 326
Wood Works Ensemble Gr. 8, D-28
*Wu long* Gr. 4, 155
Yellow Rose of Texas, The
 Gr. 7, I-70
Yertle the Turtle Gr. 2, 369
Yonder Come Day Gr. 8, I-68
*You Sang to Me* Gr. 6, 334
Zudio Gr. 2, 268

## READING

Adiós, amigos Gr. 6, 57
Ala Da'lona Gr. 4, 137
Alabama Gal Gr. 3, 107
Alle meine Entchen Gr. 1, 99
Alleluia Gr. 6, 132
Alleluia, Amen Gr. 7, A-12
America Gr. 8, I-3
America, the Free Gr. 4, 211
Apple Tree Gr. 1, 230
Apples, Peaches, Pears, and Plums
 (speech piece) Gr. 1, 16
Banuwa Gr. 6, 295
Barb'ry Allen Gr. 6, 45
Bắt kim thang Gr. 6, 13
Bee, Bee Bumblebee (speech piece)
 Gr. 1, 50
Bereleh Gr. K, 150
Bingo Gr. 1, 169
Blow the Wind Southerly
 Gr. 5, 178
Blue Mountain Lake Gr. 6, 204
Bluebird, Bluebird Gr. K, 104
Book of Love Gr. 8, G-26
Bubble Gum (speech piece)
 Gr. K, 38
Bury Me Not on the Lone Prairie
 Gr. 6, 19
Canción de cuna Gr. 4, 145
Caroling, Caroling Gr. 6, 458
Charlie over the Water Gr. 1, 68
Checki, morena Gr. 7, F-11
Chicken on the Fence Post
 Gr. 3, 92

Children, Go Where I Send Thee
 Gr. 3, 392
Circle 'Round the Moon Gr. 4, 404
Coffee Grows on White Oak Trees
 Gr. 3, 168
Colorado Trail Gr. 5, 276
Come and Go with Me to That
 Land Gr. 5, 390
*Concerto for French Horn in
 E-flat Major, K. 495, No. 4,
 Movement 3* Gr. 8, C-11
Corn Grinding Song Gr. K, 66
Critical Listening Gr. 2, 175
Cuckoo, Cuckoo Gr. 1, 110
Cumberland Gap Gr. 4, 138
De colores Gr. 8, E-14
Dinah Gr. 2, 120
Do, Re, Mi, Fa Gr. 6, 80
*Don't Get Around Much Anymore*
 Gr. 1, 33
Don't Let Your Watch Run Down
 Gr. 3, 167
Draw Me a Bucket of Water
 Gr. 3, 124
Dry Bones Come Skipping
 Gr. 4, 220
Ég a gyertya Gr. K, 96
Eh, cumpari! Gr. 4, 68
El caracol Gr. K, 130
Erdö, erdö de magos Gr. 3, 182
Eres tú Gr. 6, 473
Erie Canal Gr. 5, 263
Faith of the Heart Gr. 8, G-2
Farewell to Tarwathie Gr. 6, 42
Fiddler on the Roof Gr. 7, E-6
Free at Last Gr. 6, 471
Frère Jacques Gr. 2, 125
Gloria, Gloria Gr. 6, 458
*Glory, Glory, Hallelujah* Gr. 6, 54
Go Around the Corn, Sally
 Gr. 2, 13
Go Down, Moses Gr. 5, 193
Goin' Down the Road Feelin' Bad
 Gr. 7, F-12
Gonna Build a Mountain Gr. 6, 20
Good King Wenceslas Gr. 6, 458
Great Big House Gr. 2, 206
Greenland Whale Fishery, The
 Gr. 5, 230
Gypsy in the Moonlight Gr. 3, 12
Harrison Town Gr. 6, 96
Hashkediya Gr. 3, 206
Hava nashira Gr. 6, 82
Heigh-Ho Gr. 2, 6
Hey, Hey, Look at Me Gr. 1, 70
Himmel und Erde Gr. 5, 94
Hop Up, My Ladies Gr. 3, 142
Hot Cross Buns (Version 1)
 Gr. 3, 220
Hui jia qù Gr. 2, 159
I Am But a Small Voice Gr. 6, 445
I Believe I Can Fly Gr. 5, 172
I Dream a World Gr. 8, G-42

I'll Fly Away Gr. 8, I-43
I'm a Believer Gr. 7, G-32
Ichi-gatsu tsuitachi Gr. 3, 406
If I Had a Hammer Gr. 5, 287
Johnny Caught a Flea Gr. 1, 226
Johnny Has Gone for a Soldier
 Gr. 5, 188
Juniper Tree, The Gr. 3, 130
Kaeru no uta Gr. K, 183
Kyrie Gr. 6, 207
La calle ancha Gr. 3, 296
La mariposa Gr. 6, 58
La paloma blanca Gr. 3, 252
La piñata Gr. 3, 398
Las estrellitas del cielo Gr. 5, 174
Las velitas Gr. 5, 147
Lemonade Gr. 1, 189
Li'l Liza Jane Gr. 3, 140
Lift Ev'ry Voice and Sing
 Gr. 8, I-54
Like a Bird Gr. 6, 166
Little Black Bug Gr. 1, 214
Lo yisa Gr. 6, 131
Love Somebody Gr. 3, 94
Lullaby and Dance Gr. 4, 386
*Magic Flute, The, "In diesen
 heil'gen Hallen (In These Bright
 Halls)"* Gr. K, 9
Marines' Hymn, The Gr. 8, C-39
Mister Ram Goat-O Gr. 3, 54
Ner li Gr. 2, 383
New Hungarian Folk Song
 Gr. 6, 196
Nie chcę cię znác Gr. 3, 314
Noah's Shanty Gr. 1, 343
Oh, Watch the Stars Gr. 5, 216
Oh, Won't You Sit Down Gr. 3, 28
One Morning in May Gr. 6, 120
Paths of Victory Gr. 6, 194
Pay Me My Money Down
 Gr. 7, F-4
Pease Porridge Hot Gr. 1, 134
Pretty Saro Gr. 3, 216
¡Qué gusto! Gr. 3, 132
Ragtime Cowboy Joe Gr. 2, 251
Rain, Rain Gr. 1, 53
Red River Valley Gr. 6, 10
River Gr. 4, 59
*Rundadinella* Gr. 8, I-61
Scarborough Fair Gr. 6, 94
Se va el caimán Gr. 5, 306
Shortnin' Bread Gr. 7, F-26
Snail, Snail Gr. 1, 189
Son macaron Gr. 4, 108
Star Light, Star Bright Gr. 1, 106
Stille Nacht (Silent Night)
 Gr. 7, F-24
Stille Nacht (Silent Night)
 Gr. 7, I-55
Surfin' U.S.A. Gr. 7, I-58
Swanee Gr. 6, 118
Symphony No. 5 in C Minor, Op.
 67, Movement 1 Gr. 7, C-18

**(Skills Reinforcement, continued)**

Tancovačka  Gr. 4, 231
Tsuki  Gr. 4, 24
Turn the Glasses Over  Gr. 3, 204
Vem kan segla?  Gr. 6, 416
Wabash Cannon Ball  Gr. 5, 137
*Wachet auf, ruft uns die Stimme*
    Gr. 7, C-9
Walk in Jerusalem  Gr. 4, 100
We Wish You A Merry Christmas
    Gr. 3, 394
Wind Up the Apple Tree
    Gr. 1, 184
Woke Up This Morning  Gr. 5, 288
*Wu long*  Gr. 4, 155
Zumba, zumba  Gr. 3, 400

## SIGNING

Adiós, amigos  Gr. 6, 57
African Noel  Gr. 1, 428
Ain't Gonna Let Nobody Turn Me
    'Round  Gr. 6, 84
All Night, All Day  Gr. 4, 180
California, Here I Come  Gr. 4, 287
Hevenu shalom aleichem
    Gr. 3, 379
Hush, Hush  Gr. 3, 164
La raspa  Gr. 4, 302
Lion Sleeps Tonight, The
    Gr. 4, 131
Love Somebody  Gr. 3, 94
Ocho kandelikas  Gr. 4, 429
Peace Like a River  Gr. 6, 190
Put a Little Love in Your Heart
    Gr. 4, 8
Scrub-a-dub  Gr. 1, 304
Thula, thula, ngoana  Gr. 4, 227
Toodala  Gr. 1, 327
We Shall Overcome  Gr. 4, 326
You Are My Sunshine  Gr. 6, 246

## SINGING

Abraham, Martin, and John
    Gr. 6, 469
Ah, eu entrei na roda  Gr. 3, 310
*Ahi! Amours*  Gr. 8, C-4
Ain't Gonna Let Nobody Turn Me
    'Round  Gr. 6, 84
Allá en la fuente  Gr. 2, 93
America  Gr. 4, 440
America  Gr. 8, I-3
America, the Beautiful  Gr. 4, 159
Angels On the Midnight Clear
    Gr. 6, 422
Angels On the Midnight Clear
    Gr. 6, 424
Artsa alinu  Gr. 3, 284
At the Same Time  Gr. 6, 116
¡Ay, Jalisco no te rajes!  Gr. 7, I-6
*Backstage with Jeanine Tesori*
    Gr. 8, A-20
Barb'ry Allen  Gr. 6, 45
Bắt kim thang  Gr. 6, 13

Battle Hymn of the Republic
    Gr. 5, 273
Bee, Bee Bumblebee (speech piece)
    Gr. 1, 50
Beriozka  Gr. 4, 294
Birthday  Gr. 6, 90
Blowin' in the Wind  Gr. 5, 382
Blum (poem)  Gr. 1, 220
California Dreamin'  Gr. 8, G-32
Canción de cuna  Gr. 4, 145
Cantaré, cantarás  Gr. 6, 413
Chapel of Love  Gr. 7, G-26
Cheki, morena  Gr. 7, I-18
Chicka Hanka  Gr. 8, F-14
Christmas, Don't Be Late (The
    Chipmunk Song)  Gr. 2, 386
Chords in F  Gr. 7, H-26
*Concerto for Orchestra,*
    *"Presentation of Pairs"*
    Gr. 4, 73
Dance for the Nations  Gr. 6, 123
Deep in the Heart of Texas
    Gr. 4, 22
A Different Minor Scale
    Gr. 7, H-28
Ding, Dong, Diggidiggidong
    Gr. 3, 14
Ding Dong! Merrily on High
    Gr. 6, 428
Dona nobis pacem  Gr. 6, 124
Down by the Riverside  Gr. 8, G-8
Eighth and Sixteenth Combinations
    Gr. 7, H-19
El juego chirimbolo  Gr. 2, 55
El tambor  Gr. 2, 275
El Tren  Gr. 2, 260
Eres tú  Gr. 6, 474
Ev'rybody Loves Saturday Night
    Gr. 7, I-25
Falling Rain  Gr. 2, 329
Five Notes in Two Places
    Gr. 7, H-9
Flip, Flop and Fly  Gr. 7, I-33
*Forever, For Now*  Gr. 7, B-16
Free at Last  Gr. 6, 469
Frog Lullaby  Gr. K, 148
Gakavik  Gr. 4, 15
Give a Little Love  Gr. 6, 142
God Bless the Child  Gr. 7, B-26
God Bless the Grass  Gr. 8, F-12
God Bless the U.S.A.  Gr. 8, G-36
Goin' to Boston  Gr. 6, 433
Green Corn Song  Gr. 5, 463
Guantanamera  Gr. 8, I-35
Had to Get Up This Mornin' Soon
    Gr. 3, 115
Happy Wanderer, The  Gr. 4, 89
Hashewie  Gr. 4, 62
Hava nashira  Gr. 6, 82
*Heads Carolina, Tails California*
    Gr. 7, B-24
Hey, m'tswala  Gr. 4, 79
Hine mah tov  Gr. 5, 432

Hop Up, My Ladies  Gr. 3, 142
Hot Cross Buns (Version 1)
    Gr. 3, 219
Hot Cross Buns (Version 2)
    Gr. 3, 219
Hound Dog  Gr. 5, 213
How Low Can You Go?
    Gr. 7, H-16
I Am But a Small Voice  Gr. 6, 446
I Dream a World  Gr. 8, G-40
I'm Flying Home  Gr. 2, 286
Ida Red  Gr. 3, 30
Ja-Da  Gr. 7, G-20
Jambalaya  Gr. 8, F-18
Jambalaya  Gr. 8, I-48
*John Henry*  Gr. 8, C-34
Johnny Mister Brown  Gr. K, 37
Joy of Kwanzaa, The  Gr. 6, 464
Karangatia ra  Gr. 8, F-22
Kwanzaa Carol, A  Gr. 2, 392
La bamba  Gr. 5, 130
La golondrina  Gr. 8, I-50
La tormenta tropical  Gr. 2, 117
Leg Over Leg  Gr. K, 132
Li'l Liza Jane  Gr. 3, 140
Lift Ev'ry Voice and Sing
    Gr. 5, 482
Lift Ev'ry Voice and Sing
    Gr. 8, I-54
Light Up the World with a Song
    Gr. 8, G-24
Little Darlin'  Gr. 7, F-30
Little David, Play on Your Harp
    Gr. 4, 395
"Little" Organ Fugue in G Minor
    Gr. 6, 128
Little Johnny Brown  Gr. 3, 312
Little Miss Muffet (speech piece)
    Gr. K, 92
Lo yisa  Gr. 6, 131
Loch Lomond  Gr. 5, 140
Loco-Motion, The  Gr. 3, 64
Los niños en España cantan
    Gr. 4, 196
Love in Any Language  Gr. 6, 476
Love Somebody  Gr. 3, 95
Low *la-la*l  Gr. 7, H-14
Low *ti-ti*l  Gr. 7, H-14
Lullaby and Dance  Gr. 4, 388
Má Teodora  Gr. 6, 299
A Major Formula  Gr. 7, H-22
Major Scales with Flats  Gr. 7, H-22
Make New Friends  Gr. 3, 36
Mama, Buy Me a Chiney Doll
    Gr. K, 120
Mashed Potatoes (speech piece)
    Gr. 1, 20
*Mass, "Responsory: Alleluia"*
    Gr. 6, 217
Melody Review  Gr. 7, H-9
*mi-re-do*  Gr. 8, H-6
Minor Scales  Gr. 7, H-28

Mmmmmm mmmmmmm
Gr. K, 70
Moving Up to *la* Gr. 7, H-14
Mud Gr. 3, 32
Naranja dulce Gr. 2, 97
Now's the Time Gr. 5, 450
O Music Gr. 5, 162
Oh, Freedom Gr. 7, G-30
Old Abram Brown Gr. 5, 222
Old Dan Tucker Gr. 3, 96
One Family Gr. 7, G-16
One Morning Soon Gr. 3, 69
Over My Head Gr. 7, G-8
Over the Rainbow Gr. 4, 143
Overture to "Candide" Gr. 6, 218
Oy, Hanuka Gr. 7, I-45
Oye Gr. 6, 337
Paw-Paw Patch Gr. 4, 94
Pay Me My Money Down
Gr. 7, I-46
Performers Gr. 8, A-16
Ptashky u babusi sadochku
Gr. 1, 192
Ragtime Cowboy Joe Gr. 2, 251
Reading Chord Symbols
Gr. 7, H-26
Ríu chíu chíu Gr. 5, 439
Rock Around the Clock Gr. 7, B-18
Rockin' Around the Christmas Tree
Gr. 5, 467
Route 66 Gr. 4, 276
Scales: They're Major! Gr. 7, H-22
Seagull, Seagull, Sit on the Shore
Gr. 4, 383
Seasons Gr. K, 4
Second or Third? Gr. 8, H-6
Shalom aleichem Gr. 6, 408
Shortnin' Bread Gr. 7, F-26
Si me dan pasteles Gr. 1, 433
Skin and Bones Gr. 2, 377
The Slur Gr. 7, H-14
Star-Spangled Banner, The
Gr. 6, 487
Star-Spangled Banner, The
Gr. 8, I-62
Step Up to *so* Gr. 7, H-9
*Suite in F, Op. 28b, No. 2,*
"Fantasia on the Dargason,"
*Movement 4* Gr. 7, C-36
Surfin' U.S.A. Gr. 6, 260
Surfin' U.S.A. Gr. 7, F-32
Swing Low, Sweet Chariot
Gr. 7, C-40
T'hola, t'hola Gr. 4, 131
Take a Chance On Me Gr. 8, G-15
Tall Cedar Tree Gr. 2, 322
Tancovačka Gr. 4, 231
Tender Shepherd (Count Your
Sheep) Gr. 3, 116
Those Magic Changes Gr. 8, E-31
Three Major Chords Gr. 7, H-26
Trouble Is a Mountain Gr. 2, 202
Tuxedo Junction Gr. 8, G-20

United Nations on the March, The
Gr. 6, 443
Us Two (poem) Gr. 1, 93
Valentine Dance Gr. 1, 437
Vem kan segla? Gr. 6, 418
Wade in the Water Gr. 4, 268
Wai bamba Gr. 8, G-12
*Waitin' for a Train* Gr. 7, B-24
Walk Together, Children Gr. 3, 146
Was kommt dort von der Höh'?
Gr. 8, C-21
Water Come a Me Eye Gr. 6, 299
We Are Dear Little Birdies
Gr. K, 176
We Shall Overcome Gr. 4, 326
What Makes A Chord Major?
Gr. 7, H-26
What's Happening to my Voice?
Gr. 8, G-6
When *do* is F Gr. 7, H-9
Who Has the Penny? Gr. K, 42
Winter Gr. 8, G-10
Winter Fantasy Gr. 4, 426
Wir hatten gebauet Gr. 8, C-21
Worms March (speech piece)
Gr. 2, 312
Yakety Yak Gr. 5, 204
You Were on My Mind Gr. 7, G-22
Your changing voice Gr. 7, G-6

## VOCAL DEVELOPMENT

Black Snake Gr. 3, 52
Bonavist' Harbour Gr. 3, 295
Don't Let the Wind Gr. 3, 180
El mes de abril Gr. 3, 328
Family Tree Gr. 3, 72
Good Morning Gr. 3, 192
Habari Gani Gr. 3, 404
Hwa yuan li-de young wa wa
Gr. 3, 103
Kwa-nu-te Gr. 3, 215
Never Smile at a Crocodile
Gr. 3, 100
Now Let Me Fly Gr. 3, 179
Old Texas Gr. 3, 77
Peace Like a River Gr. 3, 246
Pretty Saro Gr. 3, 216
Put a Little Love in Your Heart
Gr. 4, 7
Qiugaviit Gr. 3, 258
Song of the Night, The Gr. 3, 346
Supercalifragilisticexpialidocious
Gr. 3, 7
Vamos a la mar Gr. 3, 226
Wichita Hand Game Song 2
Gr. 3, 307
You're a Grand Old Flag Gr. 3, 264

## SPEECH PIECES

1, 2, 3, 4 Gr. K, 15
2, 4, 6, 8 Gr. K, 67
Ackabacka, Soda Cracker Gr. 1, 303
Alligator Pie Gr. 3, 13

Apples, Peaches, Pears, and Plums
Gr. 1, 14
Bananas and Cream Gr. 3, 210
Beach Rap Gr. 1, 352
Bee, Bee Bumblebee Gr. 1, 50
Bo-bo-skee, Watten-tatten Gr. 1, 259
Boogie Chant and Dance Gr. 2, 78
Bubble Gum Gr. K, 38
Bumble Bee, The Gr. K, 74
Bundle-Buggy Boogie Woogie
Gr. 4, 120
Can You Canoe? Gr. 4, 170
Chickety, Chickety, Chop Gr. K, 41
Continents, The Gr. 4, 357
Counting-Out Rhyme Gr. 1, 357
Greetings Gr. 3, 316
Heave-Ho!/Going, Going, Gone/The
Snow Gr. 4, 182
Hickory, Dickory, Dare Gr. K, 20
How Do You Doo-tee? Gr. 4, 510
How Much Wood Could a Woodchuck
Chuck Gr. 3, 120
Jack, Be Nimble Gr. K, 97
Jelly in a Dish Gr. 2, 83
Little Miss Muffet Gr. K, 92
Luna lunera Gr. K, 90
Mississippi River Chant Gr. 2, 132
Name Game, The Gr. 1, 315
Name, Name, What's Your Name?
Gr. 3, 10
Now That's Tap Gr. 6, 320
Planets Chant, The Gr. 4, 377
Rain on the Green Grass Gr. K, 10
Riddle Ree Gr. 2, 34
Rondo for Lunch, A Gr. 3, 212
Storm Dance Gr. K, 145
Table Manners Gr. 3, 190
Tap It! Rap It! Gr. K, 194
There Was an Old Man Gr. 3, 191
Three Times By She Passes
Gr. K, 125
Tongue Twister Medley, A Gr. K, 283
Twist with a Burger, Jitter with a Bug
Gr. 1, 132
Two Little Sausages Gr. 2, 79
We're Making Popcorn Gr. 1, 86

## SPOTLIGHT ON

### ANIMALS/BUGS/INSECTS

Butterflies Gr. 1, 362
Cats Gr. 2, 300
Cats Gr. K, 12
Celebrating Bears Through Music
Gr. K, 126
Dogs Gr. 1, 291
Earthworms Gr. 2, 311
Fireflies Gr. 1, 356
Fly and the Bumblebee, The
Gr. 1, 384
Froggie Facts Gr. 1, 22
Frogs Gr. 4, 200
Mice Gr. 1, 349

(*Spotlight On,* continued)
Rabbits Gr. 2, 304
'Ülili Bird Gr. 5, 442

## ARRANGERS
Dawson, William Gr. 7, C-41
Joubert, Joseph Gr. 3, 49
Still, William Grant Gr. 3, 126
Twine, Linda Gr. 3, 164
Twine, Linda Gr. 4, 100

## ARTISTS/ILLUSTRATORS
Calder, Alexander Gr. 8, F-13
Cassatt, Mary Gr. 2, 121
Cassatt, Mary Gr. 8, E-11
Chagall, Marc Gr. 6, 442
Children Playing Lond Bridge
   (Johnson) Gr. 2, 29
Degas, Edgar Gr. 6, 323
Douglas, Aaron Gr. 7, G-10
Felga de Moraes, João Baptista
   Gr. 3, 311
Joan Miro Gr. 5, 175
Joysmith, Brenda Gr. 1, 332
Klee, Paul Gr. 2, 48
Lichtenstein, Roy Gr. 2, 78
Marc, Franz Gr. 1, 128
Marstall, Bob Gr. 1, 360
Mayer, Frank Blackwell Gr. 2, 404
Millet, Jean François Gr. 4, 365
Monet, Claude Gr. 1, 24
Moses, Grandma Gr. 6, 454
Paul Klee Gr. 8, C-47
Picasso, Pablo Gr. 4, 213
Pollock, Jackson Gr. 6, 209
Remington, Frederic Gr. 3, 177
Remington, Frederic Gr. 5, 277
Rivera, Diego Gr. 2, 334
Rivera, Diego Gr. 4, 304
Rivera, Diego Gr. 6, 414
Rousseau, Henri Gr. 3, 357
Saul, Audes Gr. 2, 306
Scott, Jane Wooster Gr. 2, 388
Stockfleth, Julius Gr. 4, 259
Walker, Sally Gr. 2, 272
Warhol, Andy Gr. 7, I-63
Whiteside, Frank Reed Gr. 5, 97
Wood, Michele Gr. 5, 336
Wyeth, N. C. Gr. 2, 236

## CAREERS
Ailey, Alvin (choreographer)
   Gr. 1, 288
AMTA (American Music Therapy
   Association) Gr. 8, A-27
Careers in Music Gr. 3, 223
Cooke, Richard (instrument maker)
   Gr. 8, D-17
Ephrem, Hidaat (lyricist) Gr. 4, 63
Ethnomusicology as a Career
   Gr. 5, 379
Field, Rachel (lyricist) Gr. 7, G-40
Flanders, Michael (lyricist) Gr. 3, 33

Graham, Martha (dancer;
   choreographer) Gr. 5, 187
Kodály, Zoltán (Ethnomusicologist)
   Gr. 7, C-34
Schickele, Peter (musicalologist)
   Gr. 6, 98

## COMPOSERS
Abe, Keiko Gr. 3, 149
Anderson, Leroy Gr. 2, 390
Babatunde Olatunji Gr. 8, B-2
Bach, Johann Sebastian Gr. 3, 36
Bach, Johann Sebastian Gr. 4, 112
Bach, Johann Sebastian Gr. 6, 128
Bach, Johann Sebastian
   Gr. 7, E-24
Bárdos, Lajos Gr. 5, 148
Bartók, Béla Gr. 3, 172
Bartók, Béla Gr. 6, 196
Berlin, Irving Gr. 5, 74
Bernstein, Elmer Gr. 3, 144
Bizet, Georges Gr. 6, 68
Brumley, Albert E. Gr. 8, I-42
Cage, John Gr. 6, 209
Chávez, Carlos Gr. 4, 154
Chopin, Frédéric Gr. 3, 26
Chopin, Frédéric Gr. 3, 316
Chopin, Frédéric Gr. 4, 233
Cohan, George M. Gr. 5, 278
Copland, Aaron Gr. 2, 22
Copland, Aaron Gr. 3, 250
Copland, Aaron Gr. 4, 60
Copland, Aaron Gr. 5, 312
Copland, Aaron Gr. 6, 198
Daquin, Louis-Claude Gr. 3, 329
Dawson, William Gr. 7, C-41
De Vita, Franco Gr. 6, 332
Debussy, Claude Gr. 7, C-38
Dibdin, Charles Gr. 3, 212
Dvorák, Antonín Gr. 4, 227
Foster, Stephen Gr. 4, 262
Foster, Stephen Gr. 5, 270
Gershwin, George and Ira
   Gr. 7, E-10
Gillespie, Avon Gr. 2, 320
Ginastera, Alberto Gr. 5, 228
Gossec, François-Joseph Gr. 3, 86
Gottschalk, Louis Moreau
   Gr. 3, 229
Gould, Morton Gr. 6, 138
Grainger, Percy Gr. 4, 72
Grofé, Ferde Gr. 3, 76
Handy, W.C. Gr. 4, 57
Haydn, Franz Joseph Gr. 2, 85
Haydn, Franz Joseph Gr. 4, 89
Haydn, Franz Joseph Gr. 6, 132
Holst, Gustav Gr. 1, 404
Holst, Gustav Gr. 5, 424
Honegger, Arthur Gr. 2, 286
Horner, James Gr. 6, 345
Hunter, Charles Gr. 5, 333
Johnson, James Weldon and John
   Rosamond Gr. 8, I-55

Jones, Bessie Gr. K, 54
Kraft, William Gr. 5, 65
Leiber, Jerry and Mike Stoller
   Gr. 5, 204
Ma Shui-Long Gr. 3, 104
Menken, Alan and Howard Ashman
   Gr. 5, 373
Mozart, Wolfgang Amadeus
   Gr. 3, 18
Mussorgsky, Modest Gr. 4, 103
Nakai, R. Carlos Gr. 5, 397
Narciso Serradell Gr. 8, I-53
Nelson, Ron Gr. 6, 331
Niccoló Paganini Gr. 7, C-23
Paul, Barberi Gr. 2, 402
Praetorius, Michael Gr. 6, 210
Prokofiev, Sergei Gr. 6, 457
Puccini, Giacomo Gr. 7, C-31
Puente, Tito Gr. 6, 334
Respighi, Ottorino Gr. 2, 92
Rodrigo, Joaquín Gr. 5, 176
Rossini, Gioacchino Gr. 7, C-31
Royal, Reggie Gr. 6, 465
Samuel Barber Gr. 7, C-21
Schoenberg, Arnold Gr. 6, 168
Schubert, Franz Gr. 6, 17
Schumann, Robert Gr. 3, 203
Shenandoah, Joanne Gr. 2, 195
Sherman, Robert B. and Richard M.
   Gr. 3, 8
Shostakovich, Dimitri Gr. 6, 442
Sibelius, Jean Gr. 6, 76
Smetana, Bedrich Gr. 7, C-33
Sousa, John Philip Gr. 1, 174
Sousa, John Philip Gr. 1, 447
Still, William Grant Gr. 3, 126
Strauss, Jr., Johann Gr. 6, 192
Stravinsky, Igor Gr. 2, 263
Stravinsky in America Gr. 8, C-32
Swann, Donald Gr. 3, 33
Tchaikovsky, Piotr Ilyich Gr. 3, 278
Thomson, Virgil Gr. 3, 175
Ulloa-Newland, Juanita Gr. 2, 116
Vaughan Williams, Ralph
   Gr. 5, 234
Verdi, Giuseppe Gr. 7, C-31
Vivaldi, Antoino Gr. 4, 371
Wagner, Richard and Giuseppe
   Verdi Gr. 8, C-24
Williams, John Gr. 4, 234
Winter, Paul Gr. 5, 399

## COMPOSERS/ARRANGERS
Bassett, Rick Gr. 1, 34
Cotton, Elizabeth Gr. 1, 46
Louiselle, Bryan Gr. 1, 251
Puente, Ernesto "Tito" Gr. 2, 180
Thomson, Virgil Gr. 5, 121

## CONDUCTORS
Bernstein, Leonard Gr. 6, 218
Falletta, JoAnn Gr. 3, 200
Harth-Bedoya, Miguel Gr. 1, 209
Hogan, Moses Gr. 6, 400

Mehta, Zubin Gr. 6, 155
Ozawa, Seiji Gr. 4, 153
Thomas, Andre J. Gr. 8, G-41

## CULTURES

African American Spirituals
  Gr. 3, 28
African American Spirituals
  Gr. 6, 233
African storytelling Gr. 1, 136
Bahamas, The Gr. 1, 64
Bawa Gr. 7, D-32
*Bhangra* Gr. 8, B-22
Brush Painting Gr. 4, 314
Cajuns, The Gr. 2, 364
Carnaval in Rio de Janeiro
  Gr. 8, D-23
Celebrating Women Gr. 1, 442
Chanukah Gr. 3, 389
Dreydl Game Gr. 6, 452
English Ballad, The Gr. 6, 229
Fabric on the Big Book Page, The
  Gr. 1, 212
Festival of Loi Krathong, The
  Gr. 6, 451
Fólklorico Dance Traditions
  Gr. 5, 129
Gaelic Language Gr. 4, 390
Great Sioux Nation, The
  Gr. 6, 285
Ha'kyo jong Gr. 2, 134
Hebrew Tradition Gr. 6, 409
Huayno Dance Style Gr. 2, 375
Jamaica Gr. 5, 132
Japan Gr. 1, 142
Japanese Language Gr. 4, 24
Juju Style Gr. 6, 231
Kente Cloth Gr. 8, D-13
Klezmer Music Gr. 8, B-27
Kwanzaa Gr. 1, 431
Kwanzaa Gr. 3, 405
Ladino Gr. 3, 390
Language, Tagalog and Korean
  Gr. 4, 172
Las posadas Gr. 1, 424
Legend of Kokopelli, The
  Gr. 5, 110
*Lehara* Gr. 8, B-31
"Magnolia" and Tejano Music
  Gr. 6, 17
Mandarin Dialect Gr. 3, 102
Maori Music Gr. 2, 284
Mariachi Ensembles Gr. 4, 302
Mbira Gr. 6, 26
Mexican Rhythms Gr. 7, I-22
Moon in Chinese Art, The
  Gr. 5, 315
Morocco Gr. 3, 208
Motown Sound, The Gr. 2, 254
Music All Around Us Gr. 5, 94
Music in the Kwanzaa Ceremony
  Gr. 6, 463

Musical influences from India
  Gr. 8, B-28
Name-drawing Gr. 6, 475
Nasrudin, Mulla Gr. 2, 142
Pa ndau (Flower Cloth), The
  Gr. 4, 369
Piñatas Gr. 6, 480
Pinpeat Orchestra, The Gr. 3, 275
Popcorn Gr. 1, 84
Popcorn Popping Gr. 1, 440
Powwows Gr. 3, 256
Puerto Rico Gr. 7, F-10
Rasgueado Gr. 7, F-25
Russian nesting boxes Gr. 4, 225
Shiloh Gr. 1, 150
Spanish language Gr. 3, 20
St. Patrick's Day Gr. 3, 291
St. Valentine's Day Traditions
  Gr. 2, 398
Swing Dancing Gr. 5, 337
Thai Greeting Gr. 2, 265
Thanksgiving Gr. 1, 414
The Ashanti People of Ghana
  Gr. 2, 68
The Polka Gr. 2, 280
Throat Singers of Tuva Gr. 4, 31
Valentine Traditions Gr. 6, 478
Valentine's Day Gr. 6, 472
Vocables Gr. 5, 302
West African countries Gr. 8, D-8
West African Griot Gr. 7, D-20
West African textiles Gr. 8, D-7
Why Chanukah Is Celebrated
  Gr. 1, 419
Zimbabwe Gr. 2, 297
Zimbabwean Marimba Ensembles
  Gr. 7, D-32

## DANCES

Dances, from "Twist with a Burger,
  Jitter with a Bug" Gr. 1, 132
Debke, The Gr. 6, 308
Everybody Says Gr. 1, 286
Highlife Gr. 6, 294
Hora, The Gr. 6, 153
Hora, The Gr. 6, 307
Khorovod Gr. 1, 372
Legong, The Gr. 1, 196
Pottery Dance Gr. 1, 370
Raccoon Dance Song Gr. 1, 260
Tap Dancing Gr. 6, 320
Toodala Gr. 1, 327
Yesh lanu taish, the Dance
  Gr. 1, 181

## FOLK MUSIC

Early American Dance Music
  Gr. 3, 97
Fiddle Tune, The Gr. 3, 96
Use in formal compositions
  Gr. 3, 18

## GAMES

Banana Splits Gr. 1, 318

## GENRE/STYLE

Appalacia Gr. 1, 258
Call and Response Gr. 1, 57
Canons Versus Rounds Gr. 6, 125
Gospel Gr. 6, 392
Gospel Music Gr. 6, 396
Mariachi Music Gr. 1, 210
Minimalism Gr. 6, 30
Musical Theater Gr. 6, 318
Popular vs. Folk Style Music
  Gr. 2, 166
Ragtime Gr. 6, 156
*Requiems* Gr. 6, 178
Sacred Harp Singing Gr. 6, 25
Salsa Gr. 8, I-32
Zydeco Music Gr. 1, 20

## HOLIDAYS AND SPECIAL OCCASIONS

Groundhog Day Gr. 1, 436
Three Kings' Day Gr. 1, 432
Why Purim Is Celebrated
  Gr. 1, 439

## INSTRUMENTS

12-String Guitar Gr. 7, F-23
Acoustic Steel-string Fingerstyle
  Guitar Gr. 8, F-21
Bagpipes Gr. 2, 384
Banjo, The Gr. 2, 121
Baroque to Modern Instruments
  Gr. 7, C-8
Bells in Music Gr. 6, 429
Brass Gr. 3, 187
Chinese Musical Instruments
  Gr. 4, 335
Clarinet Gr. 7, C-45
Classical Fingerstyle Guitar
  Gr. 8, F-21
Conga, The Gr. 5, 426
Cowboy Instruments Gr. 6, 237
Drum, The Gr. 2, 274
Flute and Clarinet Gr. 1, 255
Flutes Gr. 3, 185
Folk Instruments of Brazil
  Gr. 2, 354
Gamelan Gr. 1, 196
Guitar Manufacturers Gr. 6, 377
Guitar, The Gr. 6, 374
Guitars Gr. 6, 248
Guitars Gr. 6, 377
Guitars Gr. K, 135
Harp, The Gr. 5, 199
Harpsichord, The Gr. 5, 236
Instrument demonstrations
  Gr. 4, 70
Instrument Sound Groups
  Gr. 6, 363
Irish Instruments Gr. 6, 326
Kayagum Gr. 3, 136
Keyboard instruments Gr. 5, 197
Kpanlogo Drums Gr. 7, D-14
Leadbelly's Guitar Gr. 7, F-23
Lute Gr. 7, C-7

(*Spotlight On,* continued)

Making a Gutbucket (Washtub Bass) Gr. 6, 359
Making Instruments Gr. 2, 352
Making Musical Spoons Gr. 6, 360
*Making Percussion Instruments* Gr. 2, 105
Mountain dulcimer Gr. 5, 260
Musical instruments of South America Gr. 5, 304
Musical spoons Gr. 4, 65
Nontraditional Instruments Gr. 6, 246
Orchestral and Concert Band Percussion Gr. 1, 116
Orff Instruments Gr. 6, 202
Piano, The Gr. 5, 73
Piano, The Gr. 5, 238
Pipe Organs Gr. 6, 128
Playing the Spoons Gr. 6, 360
Recorder, The Gr. 3, 23
Steel Drums Gr. 1, 195
Taiko Gr. 6, 303
Thai Instruments Gr. 1, 156
Trumpet and Trombone Gr. 1, 254
Ukulele Gr. 5, 441
Vibrations and Sand Gr. 6, 355
Violin Gr. 1, 255
Washboard, The Gr. 2, 88
Woodwind Instruments Gr. 7, C-12

## LANGUAGE ARTS
Folklore Gr. 4, 367
Kyrie Eleison Gr. 6, 207
Verne, Jules Gr. 5, 376
Yiddish Gr. 5, 464

## LISTENING SELECTIONS
*1812 Overture* Gr. 4, 294
*Carnaval* Gr. 3, 203
*Carnival of the Animals* Gr. 3, 355
*Carnival of the Animals* Gr. 4, 220
*Dúlamán* Gr. 4, 298
*Four Seasons, The* Gr. 4, 371
*Kerenski* Gr. 6, 78
*Lieutenant Kijé Suite* Gr. 6, 456
Pictures at an Exhibition Gr. 8, A-15
*Pictures at an Exhibition, "The Hut of Baba Yaga"* Gr. 4, 103
*Prince of Denmark's March* Gr. 6, 55
*Red Poppy, The* Gr. 4, 223
*Rocky Point Holiday* Gr. 6, 331
*Rodeo* Gr. 4, 342
Rodeo, the ballet Gr. 5, 312
*Symphony No. 9 in D Minor, Op. 125, "Ode to Joy," Movement 4* Gr. 4, 151
*Wilder Reiter,* Gr. 8, D-17

## MUSIC EDUCATORS
Dawson, William Gr. 7, C-41
Hammil, Joanne Gr. 7, G-17
Wuytack, Jos Gr. 3, 224

## MUSIC HISTORY
1930s, Music of the Gr. 5, 284
1950s music: Ice Cream Changes, The Gr. 7, F-30
1950s, The Gr. 8, E-30
Antiphonal Singing Gr. 5, 460
Big Band Era, The Gr. 4, 278
Blues, Classic Gr. 6, 241
Blues, Different Kinds of Gr. 5, 225
Blues, The Gr. 7, B-9
Blues, The Gr. 8, E-32
Blues, The Gr. 8, F-27
Blues, Urban Gr. 6, 242
Concert Band, The Gr. 6, 137
Concerto, The Gr. 5, 143
Country and Western Gr. 6, 244
Country Blues Gr. 6, 241
Country Music Gr. 5, 349
Early Carol, The Gr. 6, 422
Gospel Music, History of, The Gr. 5, 280
Gospel Singers, Early Gr. 6, 396
Handel and the Baroque Oratorio Gr. 8, C-9
How music travels Gr. 8, B-38
Joplin's Rag Gr. 5, 335
Latin Music Legends Gr. 6, 262
Má Teodora Gr. 6, 301
Mariachi Women Gr. 7, I-8
Melody, History of a Gr. 8, I-2
Music Recording, History of Gr. 7, B-45
Musical Theater Gr. 2, 11
Nationalism in Music Gr. 7, C-37
New Orleans Jazz Gr. 5, 354
Recording Techniques, The Beginnings of Gr. 6, 380
Roaring Twenties, The Gr. 7, A-24
Rock, Easy Gr. 8, G-31
Rock 'n' Roll Gr. 5, 359
Rock, Revolution vs. Evolution of Gr. 7, B-21
Scat Singing Gr. 5, 444
Techno Historical Benchmarks Gr. 6, 369
Tin Pan Alley Gr. 8, G-21
Venezuelan Music, Traditional Gr. 6, 267
Women in Music Gr. 8, C-19

## MUSIC DIRECTORS
Leck, Henry Gr. 6, 435

## MUSICAL STYLES
Calypso Gr. 3, 305
Gospel and Soul Styles Gr. 3, 230
Highlife Music Gr. 3, 289
Mariachi Gr. 3, 321
Mazurka, The Gr. 3, 316
Rap Gr. 3, 340
Rock 'n' Roll Music Gr. 3, 372
Sea Shanties Gr. 3, 60
Waltz, The Gr. 3, 170

## MUSICAL TERMS/VOCABULARY
Ballad Gr. 6, 432
Blues Lyrics Gr. 8, I-7
Call and Response Gr. 7, D-2
Cantata, The Gr. 6, 338
Choral Music Gr. 6, 210
Conductor's Baton, The Gr. 6, 191
Contra Dance Gr. 6, 205
Effects, Guitar Gr. 7, F-17
Harmony Gr. 6, 141
Hornpipe and Jig Gr. 8, D-17
Metronome Gr. 7, C-17
Metronome, The Gr. 6, 115
Modes Gr. 4, 412
Operatic voices Gr. 7, C-29
Oscilloscope Waveforms Gr. 6, 355
Program Music Gr. 4, 363
Rondo Gr. 4, 183
Sounds and Rhythms Named After Performers Gr. 7, B-39
Train Sounds Gr. 6, 399
Types of Ensembles Gr. 4, 193
Voice Classification Gr. 5, 394
Word Painting Gr. 4, 404
World Beat Music Around the World Gr. 6, 268

## OTHER TOPICS
Angels Gr. 6, 425
Apples Gr. 1, 229
Baths Gr. 1, 305
Bays Gr. 1, 18
Bells in English Carols Gr. 1, 426
Big Ben Gr. 1, 225
Corn Gr. 1, 294
Diversity Gr. 6, 60
Echoes Gr. K, 6
Folk Process, The Gr. 5, 380
Keys Gr. K, 188
Tool for mixing hot chocolate (*molinillo*) Gr. 1, 379
Music Education Gr. 5, 163
Pease Porridge Gr. 1, 134
Phoebe, A Gr. 1, 30
Pronunciation Gr. 5, 431
End, The (poem) Gr. 1, 408
Tooth Care Gr. 1, 284
Tuxedos and Tuxedo Junction Gr. 8, G-21

## PERFORMERS
ABBA Gr. 8, G-16
Abe, Keiko Gr. 3, 149
Anderson, Marian Gr. 3, 248
Andes Manta Gr. 5, 153
Armstrong, Louis Gr. 2, 178
Armstrong, Louis Gr. 5, 446
Arnold, Eddy Gr. 5, 347

Beach Boys, The  Gr. 6, 260
Beach Boys, The  Gr. 7, E-26
Beatles, The  Gr. 6, 91
Beatles, The  Gr. 6, 256
Belafonte, Harry  Gr. 5, 20
Bennett, Tony  Gr. 4, 9
Boys Choir of Harlem, The
    Gr. 5, 393
Canadian Brass  Gr. 3, 188
Canadian Brass, The  Gr. 6, 55
Capella Cantabile  Gr. 5, 62
Capercaillie  Gr. 8, B-44
Cassidy, Eva  Gr. 6, 63
Century Men, The  Gr. 5, 471
Chang, Sarah  Gr. 4, 113
Checker, Chubby  Gr. 5, 358
Checker, Chubby  Gr. 6, 258
Chenier, Clifton  Gr. 6, 403
Chieftains, The  Gr. 4, 297
Clancy Brothers, The  Gr. 3, 292
Davis, Miles  Gr. 6, 252
Dawson, William  Gr. 7, C-41
Diallo, Yaya  Gr. 2, 103
Domino, Antoine "Fats"  Gr. 3, 370
Doucet, Michael and Beausoleil
    Gr. K, 65
Eileen Ivers  Gr. 2, 140
Fitzgerald, Ella  Gr. 5, 448
Flisher, Leon  Gr. 7, C-18
Franklin, Aretha  Gr. 7, B-17
Glennie, Evelyn  Gr. 3, 148
Golden Gate Quartet, The
    Gr. 6, 235
Hackson, Mahalia  Gr. 6, 394
Hambone Artist, The  Gr. 2, 32
Hampton, Lionel  Gr. 3, 151
Hancock, Herbie  Gr. 4, 113
Haza, Ofra  Gr. 1, 182
Holiday, Billy  Gr. 7, B-27
Holly, Buddy  Gr. 6, 258
Horowitz, Vladimir  Gr. 8, A-12
Houghton, Steve  Gr. 2, 155
Indianapolis Children's Choir
    Gr. 4, 402
Jackson, Mahalia  Gr. 4, 9
Jolson, Al  Gr. 4, 286
Joubert, Joseph  Gr. 3, 49
Juilliard String Quartet  Gr. 3, 111
Kelly, Gene  Gr. 4, 361
King, B.B.  Gr. 2, 328
King, Ben E.  Gr. 5, 49
Kingston Trio, The  Gr. 5, 403
Kodo  Gr. 7, D-17
Lee, CoCo  Gr. 6, 270
Los Lobos  Gr. 7, B-7
Ma, Yo-Yo  Gr. 3, 38
Makeba, Miriam  Gr. 8, I-38
Mamas and the Papas, The
    Gr. 8, G-34
Mannheim Steamroller  Gr. 5, 475
Mannheim Steamroller  Gr. 6, 461
Marsalis, Wynton  Gr. 4, 74
Marshall, George  Gr. 3, 319

Master Drummer  Gr. 6, 290
Mellencamp, John  Gr. 6, 345
Mensah, Sowah  Gr. 6, 292
Miller, Glenn  Gr. 5, 342
Moses Hogan Chorale  Gr. 6, 400
Moses Hogan Chorale, The
    Gr. 5, 103
Nakai, R. Carlos  Gr. 3, 254
Nusrat Fateh Ali Khan  Gr. 8,
O'Connor, Mark  Gr. 4, 385
Palmieri, Eddie  Gr. 7, B-31
Paracumbé  Gr. 8, D-19
Parker, Charlie  Gr. 5, 451
Perlman, Itzhak  Gr. 4, 113
Presley, Elvis  Gr. 5, 212
Presley, Elvis  Gr. 6, 254
Princeton Footnotes  Gr. 8, G-27
Puente, Tito  Gr. 3, 360
Puente, Tito  Gr. 6, 262
Queen Ida  Gr. 8, E-20
Queen Ida  Gr. 8, I-47
Ramone, Joey  Gr. 6, 63
Sanchez, Poncho  Gr. 4, 34
Santana, Carlos  Gr. 6, 262
Schuur, Diane  Gr. 5, 341
Seeger Family, The  Gr. 4, 333
Seegers, The  Gr. 8, C-35
Selena  Gr. 6, 262
Shakira  Gr. 7, B-32
Shankar, Ravi and Anoushka
    Gr. 4, 311
Smith, Bessie  Gr. 5, 352
String Quartet, The  Gr. 4, 110
Tharpe, Sister Rosetta  Gr. 7, I-13
The Tokens  Gr. 8, I-56
Tokens, The  Gr. 8, I-56
Turtle Island String Quartet
    Gr. 5, 311
United States Marine Corps Band,
    The  Gr. 5, 78
Vandellas, The  Gr. 5, 361
Winter, Paul  Gr. 3, 378
Young People's Chorus of New
    York City  Gr. 6, 336

### POETS AND WRITERS
Bates, Katharine Lee  Gr. 5, 76
Carroll, Lewis  Gr. 2, 362
Chittenden, Lawrence  Gr. 6, 238
Deibler, Sean  Gr. 5, 148
Francis Scott Key  Gr. 8, I-63
Geisel, Theodor Seuss (Dr. Seuss)
    Gr. 2, 368
George, Chief Dan  Gr. 4, 359
Hughes, Langston  Gr. 6, 6
Hughes, Langston  Gr. 8, G-43
Key, Francis Scott  Gr. 6, 486
Key, Francis Scott  Gr. 8, I-63
Lear, Edward  Gr. 3, 190
Lee, Dennis  Gr. 4, 122
McCord, David  Gr. 3, 210
McDermott, Gerald  Gr. 3, 364
Nichols, Grace  Gr. 2, 67

Whiteman, Paul  Gr. 2, 253

### RELATED ARTS
Arts Connection  Gr. 2, 404
Balinese Dance  Gr. 6, 384
Community Dances  Gr. 6, 405
Movie Soundtracks  Gr. 6, 346
Music and Film  Gr. 6, 344
Music Videos  Gr. 6, 349
Nutcracker Ballet, The  Gr. 6, 324
Nutcracker, The  Gr. 3, 280
Pointillism  Gr. 3, 89
Roots of Impressionist art
    Gr. 8, C-26
Stomp  Gr. 6, 328
Trees, The (Derain)  Gr. K, 174
Victor Hartmann and Modest
    Mussorgsky  Gr. 8, A-14
Wharf of Venice (Puelma)
    Gr. K, 144

### SCIENCE
Acoustic Performance  Gr. 7, A-21
Changing Seasons, The  Gr. 1, 26
Clocks Throughout Time
    Gr. 1, 246
Clouds of Gray  Gr. 2, 57
Corn  Gr. 5, 462
Cousteau, Jacques  Gr. 5, 374
Carnival of the Animals, "Fossils"
    Gr. 1, 234
Great Barrier Reef  Gr. 5, 375
Halley and the Comet  Gr. 2, 341
Man in the Moon, The (poem)
    Gr. 1, 398
Planets, The "Jupiter"  Gr. 1, 403
Paw-Paw Tree, The  Gr. 4, 94
Persimmons  Gr. 2, 244
Planets, The  Gr. 4, 377
Rainbows  Gr. 4, 142
Recycling  Gr. 1, 73
Science of Music  Gr. 6, 379
Seashells  Gr. 1, 352
Snowflakes  Gr. 1, 422
Sound Production: Scraping
    Gr. 1, 114
Sound Production: Shaking
    Gr. 1, 115
Sound Production: Striking
    Gr. 1, 115
Stars and Astronomy  Gr. 4, 372
Theremin, The  Gr. 2, 212
Water Sounds  Gr. K, 80
Whale songs  Gr. 1, 69
Wind, The  Gr. 2, 326

### SINGERS/SONGWRITERS
Bruce, Jack  Gr. 8, F-32
Chapin, Tom  Gr. 3, 74
Chapin, Tom  Gr. 4, 355
Diamond, Neil  Gr. 7, G-32
Domino, Antoine "Fats"  Gr. 3, 371
Driftwood, Jimmy  Gr. 6, 105
Estefan, Gloria  Gr. 6, 365

**(Spotlight On, continued)**

Guthrie, Woody Gr. 1, 275
Guthrie, Woody Gr. 3, 241
Guthrie, Woody Gr. 4, 281
Guthrie, Woody Gr. 5, 118
Guthrie, Woody Gr. 5, 282
King, Carole Gr. 3, 66
Ledbetter, Huddie Gr. 8, E-2
Mahal, Taj Gr. 7, E-33
McFerrin, Bobby Gr. 4, 80
Rabbitt, Eddie Gr. 5, 350
Ritchie, Jean Gr. 3, 16
Ritchie, Jean Gr. 4, 11

## SOCIAL STUDIES

1700s Gr. 4, 90
1960s, The Gr. 5, 289
*Ali Pasha* Gr. 5, 218
America's Flag Gr. 7, I-57
American Cowboys Gr. 5, 69
American flag, The Gr. 3, 265
Angola Gr. 5, 410
Appleseed, Johnny Gr. 4, 345
Bequia Gr. 6, 311
Cattle Drives Gr. 4, 274
Civil Rights and the U.S.
   Constitution Gr. 4, 326
Civil Rights Songs Gr. 6, 84
Clearwater Gr. 5, 286
Community Involvement Gr. 2, 260
Costa Rica Gr. 2, 156
Cumberland Gap Gr. 4, 138
Ellis Island Gr. 5, 57
Frog Songs Gr. K, 183
Glad to Have a Friend Like You
   Gr. 2, 230
Grammy Awards, The Gr. 5, 7
Heroes Gr. 5, 192
History of Railroads, A Gr. 2, 210
Hot Cross Buns Gr. 3, 219
Kennedy, John F. Gr. 6, 467
Kennedy, Robert Gr. 6, 470
King, Martin Luther Jr. Gr. 2, 395
King, Martin Luther Jr. Gr. 3, 409
King, Martin Luther Jr. Gr. 5, 484
King, Martin Luther Jr. Gr. 6, 468
King Wenceslas I Gr. 6, 459
Korea Gr. 2, 136
Korea Gr. 4, 174
Kwanzaa Gr. 5, 4
Long Ship, The Gr. 6, 417
Mexico Gr. 2, 176
Mississippi River Gr. 2, 132
Navajo Nation, The Gr. 5, 109
Newfoundland Gr. 3, 294
Nigeria Gr. 6, 231
Orange Blossom Special, The
   Gr. 5, 267
Ozark Mountains, The Gr. 6, 96
Parks, Rosa Gr. 3, 410
Peacemakers Gr. 4, 419
Peacemakers Gr. 4, 420
Pumpkins Gr. 3, 381

Radio Playlists Gr. 7, A-31
Roadside Architecture Gr. 4, 276
San Antonio Gr. 5, 134
Scandinavia and the Sea Gr. 6, 419
Sixties, The Gr. 5, 383
South Africa Gr. 5, 414
Spain in the Sixteenth Century
   Gr. 5, 436
Temple bells Gr. 5, 478
Thanksgiving Holiday, The
   Gr. 5, 458
Transcontinental railroad
   Gr. 3, 242
Treaty of Guadalupe Hidalgo
   Gr. 4, 272
Trinidad Gr. 4, 188
Truth, Sojourner Gr. 6, 340
Tubman, Harriet Gr. 4, 267
Tubman, Harriet Gr. 6, 342
Tubman, Harriet Gr. 8, I-67
West Indies, The Gr. 6, 180

## SONGS

Ackabacka, Soda Cracker (speech
   piece) Gr. 1, 303
African American Spirituals
   Gr. 5, 256
African American Spirituals
   Gr. 5, 191
America Gr. 6, 163
Asadoya Gr. 6, 303
Ballads Gr. 4, 270
Barb'ry Allen Gr. 6, 44
*Believer* Gr. 7, A-2
Brand New Day, A Gr. 6, 6
Cantaré, cantarás (I Will Sing, You
   Will Sing) Gr. 6, 412
*Carnival of the Animals*, "Fossils"
   Gr. 1, 236
Caroling Gr. 4, 410
Carols Gr. 5, 434
Carols Gr. 5, 468
Chester Gr. 6, 83
*Children's Corner*, "Jimbo's
   Lullaby" Gr. 1, 271
*Daphne of the Dunes* Gr. 8, D-29
Deep in the Heart of Texas
   Gr. 8, I-18
Do Wah Diddy Diddy Gr. 4, 202
Duérmete, mi niño Gr. 1, 292
*El cóndor pasa* Gr. 7, A-2
Éliza Kongo Gr. 5, 14
Farewell to the Warriors Gr. 4, 284
Feng Yang Songs Gr. 4, 312
Freedom songs Gr. 5, 416
Get on Board Gr. K, 88
Good Mornin', Blues Gr. 2, 52
Gospel Singing Gr. 4, 162
Haul Away, Joe Gr. 4, 12
I Am But a Small Voice Gr. 6, 447
I Walk in Beauty Gr. 4, 282
Johnny Has Gone for a Soldier
   Gr. 5, 188

Lullabies Gr. 1, 62
Lullaby Gr. 4, 386
Marines' Hymn, The Gr. 8, C-40
Meng Jian Nu Gr. 5, 194
Mos Mos Gr. 1, 130
National Anthem, The Gr. 4, 158
National Anthem, The Gr. 4, 441
Noah's Shanty Gr. 1, 342
Ocho kandelikas Gr. 4, 428
Old Abram Brown Gr. 5, 223
Over the Rainbow Gr. 4, 141
Partner Songs Gr. 4, 396
Pay Me My Money Down Gr. 4, 41
Play Parties Gr. 4, 388
Rock Island Line Gr. 4, 55
Round Singing Gr. 3, 128
Sacred Harp Spirituals Gr. 5, 259
Shanties Gr. 4, 255
Shanties Gr. 5, 264
Simple Gifts Gr. 5, 184
Strike Up the Band Gr. 6, 134
Turn the World Around Gr. 4, 114
Winter Gr. 8, G-11
Yankee Doodle Gr. 3, 414

## THEATER AND FILM

Addams Family, The Gr. 5, 456
American Tail, An Gr. 5, 369
Broadway Musicals Gr. 4, 26
Lion King Story, The Gr. 6, 316
Little Shop of Horrors Gr. 4, 422
Mary Poppins Gr. 3, 7
Musical Theater Gr. 8, C-45
Oklahoma, The Musical Gr. 5, 37
Peter Pan Gr. 3, 116
Rent Gr. 8, A-22
Riverdance Gr. 4, 298
West Side Story Gr. 5, 9

## STORIES AND FOLK TALES

*See Literature; Recorded Lessons:
Recorded Poems and Stories.*

## STYLE *See Genre/Style.*

## TEACHER TO TEACHER

### ACHIEVING ENSEMBLE STABILITY
Kpanlogo Highlife Ensemble
   Gr. 7, D-13

### ACKNOWLEDGING SIMILARITIES
### AND DIFFERENCES
Our Family Comes from 'Round the
   World (poem) Gr. 1, 282

### ADDITIONAL PRACTICE
De colores Gr. 8, E-14

### ARP AS A TEACHING TOOL
*Copycat* Gr. K, 9
*Un pajarito* Gr. 2, 16

### ASSESSING AURAL SKILLS
Shortnin' Bread Gr. 7, F-26

**ASSIGNING PARTS**
Canción Mixteca Gr. 5, 326
Gloria, Gloria Gr. 6, 459
Over My Head Gr. 7, G-10

**AURAL PERCEPTION**
Greenland Whale Fishery, The
Gr. 5, 230

**AWARENESS**
Sorida Gr. 1, 314

**BEAT MAINTENANCE**
Sorida Gr. 1, 314

**BIG BAND INSTRUMENTATION**
Sing, Sing, Sing! Gr. 5, 341

**BODY PERCUSSION**
Bonga Gr. K, 79
Bundle-Buggy Boogie Woogie
Gr. 4, 120

**BOUNCING BALLS IN A MUSICAL CONTEXT**
Pai pi qiu Gr. 1, 325

**BUILDING A MOVEMENT VOCABULARY**
Rain Sings a Song, The Gr. 1, 101

**BUILDING CONFIDENCE IN IMPROVISING**
I'll Fly Away Gr. 8, I-44

**BUILDING LEADERSHIP SKILLS**
Sansaw akroma Gr. 3, 288

**BUILDING PRIOR KNOWLEDGE**
Los maizales Gr. 1, 295

**BUILDING TEXT-READING AND SPELLING SKILLS**
I Can't Spell Hippopotamus
Gr. 1, 264

**BULLETIN BOARD IDEA**
Water Is Wide, The Gr. 6, 228

**CARE OF INSTRUMENTS**
*Guitar Tuning* Gr. 7, F-2
*Guitar Tuning* Gr. 8, F-2

**CAREERS IN MUSIC**
Corta la caña Gr. 6, 366

**CELEBRATING BIRTHDAYS**
Birthday Gr. 6, 90

**CHANGING CHORDS**
Goin' Down the Road Feelin' Bad
Gr. 7, F-12

**CHANGING VOICE TECHNIQUES**
I Am But a Small Voice Gr. 6, 446

**CHANGING VOICES**
Hey, Ho! Nobody Home Gr. 6, 29
*Vive l'amour* Gr. 6, 177

**CHARACTER MOTIVES**
*E. T.'s Theme* Gr. 6, 99

**CHASE GAMES**
Charlie over the Water Gr. 1, 66

**CHORAL TEACHING TIPS**
Einini Gr. 4, 392

**CHORD FUNCTION**
Lion Sleeps Tonight, The
Gr. 8, F-4

**CHORD ROOTS**
Dry Bones Gr. 4, 163

**CLAPPING**
¡Qué bonita bandera! Gr. 5, 294

**CLASS SPIRIT**
Pay Me My Money Down
Gr. 7, I-49

**CLASSROOM MANAGEMENT**
Elegua Gr. 7, D-7
I Don't Care If the Rain Comes
Down Gr. 3, 25
It's a Beautiful Day Gr. 3, 338
My Foot's in My Stirrup Gr. 2, 237
Never Smile at a Crocodile
Gr. 3, 101
Pumpkin Poem Gr. 3, 381
Summertime Gr. 6, 253
Supercalifragilisticexpialidocious
Gr. 3, 6
Time to Sing Gr. 2, 9

**CLASSROOM MUSIC CORNER, A**
Doctor Foster Gr. K, 137

**CLASSROOM PROJECT**
Rocky Top Gr. 5, 348

**CLASSROOM SOUNDS**
Tap It! Rap It! (speech piece)
Gr. K, 194

**CODA**
God Bless the U.S.A. Gr. 8, G-38

**COMPARE SEQUENCES**
Tengo, tengo, tengo Gr. 4, 228

**COMPARING AND CONSTRUCTING INSTRUMENTS**
Moon Mirrored in the Pool, The
Gr. 6, 102

**COMPARISON CHART**
Gonna Ride Up in the Chariot
Gr. 4, 21

**CONCEPT DEVELOPMENT**
Little Green Frog, The Gr. 1, 22

**CONDUCTING**
Ah! Les jolis papillons Gr. 1, 362
I Dream a World Gr. 8, G-44
Morning Has Broken Gr. 5, 31

**CONSTELLATION CONNECTION**
Follow the Drinkin' Gourd
Gr. 4, 266

**COOPERATION**
Faith of the Heart Gr. 8, G-4
Riddle Ree (speech piece) Gr. 2, 34
Song of the Night, The Gr. 3, 345
*World instrument families*
Gr. 8, B-9

**COUNTERMELODIES**
Roll On, Columbia Gr. 5, 116

**CREATING MELODIES**
Bounce High, Bounce Low
Gr. 1, 150

**CREATING RELEVANCE**
Kid Like Me, A (speech piece)
Gr. 2, 394

**CREATING SOUNDSCAPES**
Rain Sings a Song, The Gr. 1, 102

**CREATIVE AND INTERPRETIVE MOVEMENT**
Everybody Says Gr. 1, 288

**CREATIVE DECISION-MAKING**
Locomoto-vation Gr. K, 61

**CREATIVE PERFORMANCE**
*Nruab hnub thiab hmo ntuj*
Gr. 4, 366

**CROSS-CURRICULUM**
*Den III. Ende VI. Ronde & Quatre
Branles* Gr. 8, C-7

**CULTURAL DIVERSITY, PROMOTING**
Al ánimo Gr. 3, 323

**DANCE HINTS**
Nie chcę cię znác Gr. 3, 315

**DATA PORTFOLIOS**
Low *la-la*₁ Gr. 7, H-15
Low *ti-ti*₁ Gr. 7, H-15
Moving Up to *la* Gr. 7, H-15
The Slur Gr. 7, H-15

**DEGRESS OF BODILY MOVEMENT**
Habemos llegado Gr. 6, 173

**DESCRIBING MUSIC**
One Morning Soon Gr. 3, 68

**DESCRIBING TEMPO**
Freight Train Gr. 1, 44

**DEVELOPING AUTOHARP SKILLS**
Clementine Gr. 4, 341

**DEVELOPING GOOD INTONATION**
Sioux Lullaby Gr. K, 111

**DEVELOPING INTEREST IN SINGING**
I'm Gonna Sing Gr. 4, 33

(*Teacher to Teacher,* continued)

**DEVELOPING LISTENING SKILLS**
Four in a Boat Gr. 2, 47

**DEVELOPING SOUND CLASSIFICATION SKILLS**
Seasons Gr. K, 4

**DEVELOPING VOICES**
Sing! Speak! Whisper! Shout! Gr. 1, 36

**DICTION**
*America* Gr. 7, A-25

**DICTION-VOWELS**
Missy-La, Massa-La Gr. 4, 191

**DIFFERENT MODES**
Connemara Lullaby Gr. 5, 233

**DIFFERENT VOICES FOR DIFFERENT SITUATIONS**
Voice Choice Gr. K, 27

**DIVIDING THE CLASS**
At the Same Time Gr. 6, 114

**DO VIBRATIONS EXIST**
*Sound Waves Montage* Gr. 6, 354

**DOUBLE MALLETS**
Going upon the Mountain Gr. 6, 106

**EAR TRAINING**
Lemonade Gr. 1, 188

**EDUCATIONAL GOALS**
*Batucada* Parade Ensemble Gr. 8, D-24

**EFFECTIVE SEATING ARRANGEMENTS**
Surfin' U.S.A. Gr. 7, F-32

**ELEMENTAL SONGS**
Wind Up the Apple Tree Gr. 1, 184

**ELEMENTS OF MOVEMENT**
¡Viva el fútbol! Gr. 1, 94

**ELICITING IDEAS**
Cookie Crew, The Gr. K, 196

**ELIMINATING MUFFLED OR BUZZY STRINGS**
God Bless the Grass Gr. 8, F-12

**ENCOURAGING STUDENTS TO SING**
Do Wah Diddy Diddy Gr. 7, F-21

**ENHARMONIC TONES**
Tuxedo Junction Gr. 8, G-20

**FEEDBACK**
I'm on My Way Gr. 7, A-16

**FEELING CONTOUR**
Mister Rabbit Gr. K, 128

**FINDING PARTNERS**
Hickory, Dickory, Dock (*so-mi-la-so* Version) Gr. 1, 350

**FLAT PICKS**
God Bless the Grass Gr. 8, F-12

**FOCUS HELP**
*Toccata for Percussion, Movement 3* Gr. 4, 154

**FOCUSING ON INDIVIDUAL TIMBRES**
*Symphony No. 4 in F Minor, Movement 4, Finale: Allegro con fuoco* Gr. 1, 175

**FOSTERING MUSICALITY**
Dotted Rhythms with Sixteenth Notes Gr. 7, H-20
More Composing with Sixteenth Notes Gr. 7, H-20
Reverse the Rhythm Gr. 7, H-20

**GIVING DIRECTIONS**
Happy Wanderer, The Gr. 4, 91

**GLISSANDI AND TONAL QUALITY**
Duérmete, mi niño Gr. 1, 292

**GRAPHIC ORGANIZERS**
*7th Guest, The, "Themes"* Gr. 8, A-3

**GROUPS IN CONCENTRIC CIRCLES**
Let Music Surround You Gr. 4, 237

**GUEST PERFORMERS**
Waitin' for the Light to Shine Gr. 4, 28

**GUITAR CAPO**
Good Mornin', Blues Gr. 5, 224

**GUITAR CHORDS**
Se va el caimán Gr. 5, 306
Tzena, tzena Gr. 5, 300

**GUITAR DRONE**
Yüe liang wan wan Gr. 5, 314

**GUITAR MANAGEMENT TIPS**
Tom Dooley Gr. 6, 375

**GUITAR STRUM**
Good Mornin' Blues Gr. 5, 226

**HAND BELLS AND CHIMES**
America Gr. 8, I-3

**HEARING CHORD CHANGES**
Joshua Fought the Battle of Jericho Gr. 5, 100

**HEARING THE DIATONIC SCALE**
Chairs to Mend Gr. 4, 149

**HIDDEN RHYTHMS**
Rock Island Line Gr. 4, 54

**HIGH, MIDDLE, AND LOW REGISTERS**
Five Little Chickadees Gr. K, 179

**HIGHER-ORDER THINKING SKILLS**
*Hard Times* Gr. 1, 194
Long Way Home, A Gr. 1, 382

**HISTORICAL RESEARCH**
When Johnny Comes Marching Home Gr. 5, 180

**HOW TO IMPROVISE**
Good Mornin', Blues Gr. 5, 224

**HOW TO SING A DESCANT**
Hine mah tov Gr. 5, 432

**IDENTIFYING HISTORICAL STYLES**
*Samples of Historical Styles* Gr. 8, C-3

**IDENTIFYING SOUNDS**
Who Has the Penny? Gr. K, 42

**IDIOMS**
World of Difference, A Gr. 5, 387

**IMPROVISING**
12-Bar Blues Rock Gr. 8, F-31
Cement Mixer Gr. 4, 102
Great Big House Gr. 2, 206
Yang wa wa Gr. K, 163

**INCLUDING EVERYONE**
Little David Gr. 1, 233

**INDIANAPOLIS CHILDREN'S CHOIR**
Goin' to Boston Gr. 6, 435

**INNER HEARING DEVELOPMENT**
Engine, Engine, Number Nine Gr. K, 121
Get Down to Low *la* Gr. 8, H-12
Get Down to Low *so* Gr. 8, H-12
Gift to Share, A Gr. 6, 393

**INSPIRING SPONTANEITY**
Come and Go with Me to That Land Gr. 5, 390

**INSTRUMENT TIPS**
Adiós, amigos Gr. 6, 56
*Symphony No. 9 in D Minor, Op. 125, "Ode to Joy," Movement 4* Gr. 4, 150

**INSTRUMENTS**
*Dan tranh* Gr. 5, 196

**INTERVALS**
All Night, All Day Gr. 4, 181
Go Down, Moses Gr. 5, 191
Las velitas Gr. 5, 147
Lo yisa Gr. 6, 130

**INTONATION**
Take a Chance on Me Gr. 8, G-14

**INTRODUCING EXPLORATORY MOVEMENT**
Scrub-a-dub Gr. 1, 304

**INTRODUCING ORCHESTRAL INSTRUMENTS**
Concerto for Trumpet and Orchestra in E♭ Gr. 1, 256

**INTRODUCING SCULPTURE**
Hush-a-bye Baby Gr. 1, 270

**INVENTION**
La ciudad de Juaja Gr. 5, 58

**JOBS AND CLASSROOM MANAGEMENT**
Hickory, Dickory, Dock (so-mi-la-so Version) Gr. 1, 225

**KEY SIGNATURE PRACTICE**
Two More Keys with Sharps: A Major and E Major Gr. 8, H-21

**KEY SIGNATURES IN GRADE 1**
Lemonade Gr. 1, 188

**KEYBOARD ACCOMPANIMENTS**
America Gr. 6, 484
I Vow to You, My Country Gr. 5, 418

**KWANZAA FREQUENTLY ASKED QUESTIONS**
Joy of Kwanzaa, The Gr. 6, 462

**LAYERING PARTS**
Caribbean Island Ensemble Gr. 7, D-19

**LEADING IMPROVISATION ACTIVITIES**
Doumbek or Hand Drum Exercises Gr. 7, D-31

**LEADING MOVEMENT ACTIVITIES**
(Can't Live Without Your) Love and Affection Gr. 7, B-23
That's the Way It Is Gr. 7, B-23

**LEARNING A NEW LANGUAGE**
Las estaciones Gr. 1, 29

**LEARNING NEW CHORDS**
Bye Bye, Love Gr. 8, F-8

**LEARNING STYLES**
Tabla Solo Gr. 8, B-32

**LEGATO PHRASES**
Angels On the Midnight Clear Gr. 6, 423

**LEGEND BEHIND THE SONG, THE**
Yellow Rose of Texas, The Gr. 7, I-73

**LISTENING**
Alexander's Ragtime Band Gr. 6, 139
Ghel moma Gr. 4, 31
O lê lê O Bahía Gr. 6, 164
Requiem, "Pie Jesu" Gr. 6, 178

**LISTENING MAPS**
Choo-Choo Joubert Gr. 3, 50
Magnificent Seven, The Gr. 3, 143
Masquerade Suite, "Galop" Gr. 4, 16
Uma história de Ifá Gr. 3, 310
Walkin' to New Orleans Gr. 3, 370

**LISTENING TIPS**
5 Stücke im Volkston, Op. 102, No. 1, "Mit Humor" Gr. 3, 39
Battle Cry of Freedom Gr. 5, 272

**LIVE DEMONSTRATIONS**
Concerto for Orchestra, "Presentation of Pairs" Gr. 4, 73

**LOCAL LAWS**
Rainbow in the Sky Gr. 7, B-35

**LONG PHRASES**
Eres tú Gr. 6, 473

**LYRICS**
Cobbler, Cobbler (speech piece) Gr. 1, 298
I Vow to You, My Country Gr. 5, 422

**MAKE A DIDGERIDOO**
Brolga Gr. 6, 271

**MAKING A WATER DRUM**
Spring Rain Gr. 2, 295

**MAKING CURRICULUM CONNECTIONS**
Breathe Gr. 1, 402

**MAKING FRIENDS**
Glad to Have a Friend Like You Gr. 2, 228

**MAKING SONGS FROM RHYMES**
Burnie Bee Gr. 1, 51

**MAKING THE PAST CONCRETE**
Carnival of the Animals, "Fossils" Gr. 1, 234

**MALLET INSTRUMENTS**
La Jesusita Gr. 5, 323

**MALLETS**
Dona nobis pacem Gr. 6, 126
We've Got Lots in Common Gr. 3, 366

**MANAGEMENT TIPS**
Cielito lindo Gr. 7, I-21

Drums From Around the World Gr. 6, 278
Feliz Navidad Gr. 7, I-29
I Got Shoes Gr. 2, 242
Ichi-gatsu tsuitachi Gr. 7, I-41
Nana Kru Gr. 6, 281
Obokete Gr. 6, 291
Rio Grande Gr. 4, 257
Sleep, Baby, Sleep Gr. 2, 196
Ten Little Ostinato Pieces Gr. 7, I-62
Udu Pot Gr. 8, D-4

**MANAGING COMPOSITION ACTIVITIES**
Éliza Kongo Gr. 5, 15

**MANAGING GAME PLAYING**
Yellow Butter (speech piece) Gr. 1, 125

**MANAGING IMPROVISED OSTINATOS**
Circlesong 7 Gr. 4, 80

**MANAGING INSTUMENT PLAYING**
Shortnin' Bread Gr. 1, 59

**MANAGING MOVEMENT ACTIVITIES**
Different Beat, A Gr. 1, 5

**MANAGING THE CREATING ACTIVITY**
Eh, cumpari! Gr. 4, 70

**MEANINGFUL REPETITION**
Conducting Meter Gr. 7, H-10
Dynamics Gr. 7, H-10
Eighth Rests Gr. 7, H-10
Ties and More Ties Gr. 7, H-10

**MEDIEVAL RESOURCE**
Beggar's Opera, The Gr. 7, C-26

**MELISMAS**
Ding Dong! Merrily on High Gr. 6, 428

**MEMORIZING STRING AND FINGER NUMBERS**
Pay Me My Money Down Gr. 7, F-5

**METER**
Las estrellitas del cielo Gr. 5, 174

**METER CHANGES**
Ríu ríu chíu Gr. 5, 435

**METER IN 5**
Take Five Gr. 5, 220

**MINOR KEY**
Winter Gr. 8, G-10

(*Teacher to Teacher*, continued)

**MODELING**
Draw Me a Bucket of Water
Gr. 3, 125
Ichi-gatsu tsuitachi  Gr. 7, I-41

**MODELING AN INSTRUMENTAL PART**
Mary Ann  Gr. 6, 182

**MORE TECHNOLOGY**
*Children's Corner Suite,
"Snowflakes Are Dancing"*
Gr. 5, 239

**MOTIVATION**
Movie sound effects  Gr. 8, A-9

**MOVEMENT MANAGEMENT**
Chawe chidyo chem'chero
Gr. 2, 298
Doong gul ge  Gr. 3, 135

**MOVING**
Party Tonight!  Gr. 2, 152
*Rig-a-Jig-Jig*  Gr. K, 98

**MULTIPLE PERFORMANCE PARTS, ORGANIZING**
La paloma blanca  Gr. 3, 253

**MUSIC JOURNALS**
Chicka Hanka  Gr. 8, F-14

**NAMING GUITARS**
*Guitar Tuning*  Gr. 7, F-2
*Guitar Tuning*  Gr. 8, F-2

**NATIVE AMERICAN MUSIC**
Zuni Sunrise Call  Gr. 5, 396

**NEW METER, A**
Lift Ev'ry Voice and Sing
Gr. 5, 483

**NO-FAULT IMPROVISATION**
Man of Constant Sorrow
Gr. 7, F-29

**NON-ENGLISH LANGUAGE SONGS, TEACHING**
Au clair de la lune  Gr. 3, 19

**NOT ENOUGH DRUMS?**
El tambor  Gr. 2, 274

**NOTATING**
A la puerta del cielo  Gr. 5, 61

**NOTATION PREPARATION**
Cantando mentiras  Gr. 4, 146

**ONE-MINUTE REPORTS**
*Piano Concerto in A Minor, Op.
16, Movement 1*  Gr. 8, E-12

**ONOMATOPOEIA**
Parade Came Marching, The
Gr. 1, 166

**ORAL LANGUAGE DEVELOPMENT**
Going on a Picnic  Gr. K, 191
¡Qué llueva!  Gr. K, 81

**ORFF INSTRUMENTS**
Corrido de Kansas  Gr. 4, 274

**ORFF TERMINOLOGY**
Lone Star Trail  Gr. 2, 20
Rosie, Darling Rosie  Gr. 2, 215

**OSTINATOS**
Bingo  Gr. 1, 168

**OTHER LANGUAGES**
Viva Jujuy  Gr. 5, 228

**PART SINGING**
Sambalele  Gr. 4, 400

**PARTNER SONGS**
Michael Finnigan  Gr. 3, 153
Play a Simple Melody  Gr. 5, 74
Winter Fantasy  Gr. 4, 425

**PEACE, TEACHING ABOUT**
Peace Like a River  Gr. 3, 247

**PEER ASSESSMENT**
Conducting the Beat  Gr. 8, H-3
Meter in Three Plus Repeats
Gr. 8, H-3
Meters, Measures, and More
Gr. 8, H-3
Rhythm Fundamentals  Gr. 8, H-3
Tie Two to Get a Half  Gr. 8, H-3

**PEER COACHING**
America, the Beautiful  Gr. 7, I-4
Peace Round  Gr. 4, 348

**PEER TUTORING**
Basics of Melody  Gr. 7, H-7
*mi-re-do*  Gr. 7, H-7
More Melody: *fa*  Gr. 7, H-7

**PERCEPTION**
Concerto No. 4 in E-flat Major for
French horn  Gr. 8, B-12

**PERCUSSION**
Box a-Rockin' Ensemble  Gr. 7, D-5
Mary Ann  Gr. 6, 180
Percussion Fun Rondo  Gr. 7, I-50

**PERFORMANCE TIPS**
Freedom Is Coming  Gr. 5, 415
Winter Song  Gr. 6, 455

**PHONEMIC AWARENESS**
On the Ning Nang Nong (poem)
Gr. 1, 393

**PITCH**
Cha yang wu  Gr. 1, 88
Fais dodo  Gr. K, 159
Hound Dog  Gr. 5, 212
Loco-Motion, The  Gr. 3, 67
*Roll Over Vaughan Williams*
Gr. 8, F-22
*Sevilla*  Gr. 8, F-22

**PLAN A PERFORMANCE**
Hey, m'tswala  Gr. 4, 79

**PLAY-PARTY INSTRUCTIONS**
Paw-Paw Patch  Gr. 4, 93

**PLAYING**
Bound for South Australia
Gr. 5, 23
Kum bachur atzel  Gr. 3, 139
Los días de la semana  Gr. 1, 268
Mary Ann  Gr. 6, 182
Nampaya omame  Gr. 7, D-10
*Six Metamorphoses After Ovid,
Op. 49, "Bacchus"*  Gr. 7, C-13

**POEM PERFORMANCE TIPS**
Grasshoppers  Gr. 3, 35

**POP STYLE**
Carry On  Gr. 7, B-3

**POSITIVE ROLE MODELING**
Alleluia, Amen  Gr. 7, A-12

**PREPARING FOR fa**
Son macaron  Gr. 4, 108

**PREPARING HANDS FOR PLAYING GUITAR**
Chords and strums  Gr. 8, F-4

**PREPARING TO PLAY**
Hush, Hush  Gr. 3, 163

**PREPARING TO READ A NEW PITCH**
'Round and 'Round  Gr. 1, 148

**PROGRAM MUSIC**
Don't You Hear the Lambs?
Gr. 5, 97

**PROGRAM PERFORMANCE**
Soldier, Soldier  Gr. 4, 10

**PROGRAM VS. ABSOLUTE MUSIC**
*Ma Vlast (My Fatherland), "Vltava
(The Moldau)"*  Gr. 7, C-32

**PROMOTIONAL BUDGET**
Music promotion  Gr. 7, A-27

**PRONUNCIATION ACCURACY**
Uno, dos, y tres  Gr. 5, 428

**PROVIDING STOPPING CUES**
Locomoto-vation  Gr. K, 61

**QUESTION-AND-ANSWER FORM**
Farewell to Tarwathie  Gr. 6, 42

**RAISING THE LEVEL OF YOUR CHOIR**
Ding Dong! Merrily on High
Gr. 6, 427

**REACHING OUT**
Five Notes in Two Places
Gr. 7, H-8
Melody Review  Gr. 7, H-8

Step Up to *so* Gr. 7, H-8
When *do* is F Gr. 7, H-8

## READING
Don't You Hear the Lambs?
    Gr. 5, 99
Skye Boat Song Gr. 6, 373

## RECORDER, TEACHING
I Believe I Can Fly Gr. 5, 171
John Kanaka Gr. 3, 61
Worried Man Blues Gr. 6, 371

## REHEARSAL AIDS
Canto del agua Gr. 8, I-11
De colores Gr. 8, I-14
Deep in the Heart of Texas
    Gr. 8, I-19
El rancho grande Gr. 8, I-22
Feliz Navidad Gr. 7, I-29
Guantanamera Gr. 8, I-34
Lift Ev'ry Voice and Sing
    Gr. 8, I-55
Pay Me My Money Down
    Gr. 7, I-49
This Land Is Your Land Gr. 7, I-68
Yonder Come Day Gr. 8, I-71

## REINFORCING BEAT AWARENESS
Little Red Wagon Gr. K, 153

## REINFORCING TEXT-READING SKILLS
I Know an Old Lady Gr. 1, 387

## REINFORCING TONALITY
Merry Modal Christmas, A
    Gr. 4, 410

## RELUCTANT SINGERS
Limbo Like Me Gr. 4, 18

## RESEARCH AND PERFORM
Where's Your Drum? Ensemble
    Gr. 8, D-20

## RESONANCE
What's Happening to my Voice?
    Gr. 8, G-7

## RESONATOR BELLS AND HAND CHIMES
Blowin' in the Wind Gr. 5, 385
El payo Gr. 6, 145

## RESOURCE MATERIALS
Cattle Call Gr. 5, 346

## RESPONSE SONGS
Ego sum pauper Gr. 5, 159

## RHYTHM
Don't Let Your Watch Run Down
    Gr. 3, 166
El chocolate Gr. 1, 379
Kaeru no uta Gr. K, 183

## RIBBON OF HIGHWAY
This Land Is Your Land Gr. 5, 119

## ROUND REINFORCEMENT
Computer, The Gr. 4, 199

## SAFETY
Hui jia qù Gr. 2, 158
Mama Don't 'Low Gr. 6, 358

## SCHOOL PERFORMANCES
Give My Regards to Broadway
    Gr. 6, 38
*Rundadinella* Gr. 8, I-61

## SCIENCE
Ezekiel Saw the Wheel Gr. 6, 378
Under the Sea Gr. 5, 377

## SEEING AND HEARING DIRECTION
Apple Tree Gr. 1, 228

## SELF-ESTEEM
Rudolph, the Red-Nosed Reindeer
    Gr. 1, 428

## SELF-EVALUATION
Key of D Major Gr. 8, H-21
Key of F Major Gr. 8, H-21

## SEQUENCING EVENTS
Sailing to the Sea Gr. 1, 337

## SHAPING MUSICAL PLAYLETS
Mi chacra Gr. 1, 364

## SHARING
Families Gr. 1, 280
More Meter and Rhythm
    Gr. 7, H-4

## SHIFTING MODES
Con el vito Gr. 7, G-15

## SINGING
Amazing Grace Gr. 4, 160
Ah, Poor Bird Gr. 4, 196
Alabama Gal Gr. 3, 106
Apples, Peaches, Pears, and Plums
    (speech piece) Gr. 1, 15
Banana Splits Gr. 1, 319
Bereleh Gr. K, 151
Cattle Call Gr. 5, 345
Don't Let the Wind Gr. 3, 181
Each of Us Is a Flower Gr. 3, 155
Ee jer ha ba go Gr. K, 133
El barquito Gr. 3, 359
El borrego Gr. 4, 242
Eres tú Gr. 6, 475
Going Up: High *do* and *ti*
    Gr. 7, H-16
Going upon the Mountain
    Gr. 6, 106
Guantanamera Gr. 8, I-34
How Low Can You Go?
    Gr. 7, H-16
Hwa yuan li-de young wa wa
    Gr. 3, 103
Keel Row, The Gr. 4, 241
Key Signature Check Gr. 7, H-16

Kum ba yah Gr. 5, 245
Little Black Bug Gr. 1, 214
Little David, Play on Your Harp
    Gr. 4, 394
Los reyes de Oriente Gr. 5, 481
Nanny Goat Gr. K, 160
O, Desayo Gr. 5, 412
Piñon, pirulín Gr. 2, 176
Scattin' A-Round (Variations on
    Row 3) Gr. 6, 160
Shalom aleichem Gr. 6, 408
Star-Spangled Banner, The
    Gr. 5, 488
*Three Little Piggies* Gr. K, 56
To'ia mai te waka Gr. 1, 77
Tuxedo Junction Gr. 8, G-20
Twelve Gates to the City
    Gr. 5, 280
Vem kan segla? Gr. 6, 418
Your changing voice Gr. 7, G-6

## SLOW VS. FAST METER
Home on the Range Gr. 5, 69

## SMALL GROUP PROJECTS
*Le sacre du printemps (The Rite of*
    *Spring)* Gr. 8, C-31

## SONG FORM
O, Desayo Gr. 5, 411

## SOUND CENTER
*Silver Apples of the Moon*
    Gr. 1, 10
*Watermelon Man* Gr. 1, 10
Windshield Wipers (poem)
    Gr. 1, 10

## SOUND-EXPLORATION ACTIVITIES
Orchestra (poem) Gr. 1, 74

## STAYING FOCUSED
Get on Your Feet Gr. 5, 8

## STEADY BEAT AND STYLE
Jim Along, Josie Gr. K, 38

## STRING GAME
Lost My Gold Ring Gr. 6, 158

## STRING INSTRUMENTS
Rodeo, Hoedown Gr. 5, 313

## STUDENT FOUND INSTRUMENTS
Go-Go Street Ensemble
    Gr. 8, D-33

## SUBSTITUTING INSTRUMENTS
Ama-Lama Gr. 5, 144

## SUCCESSFUL MUSIC-READING EXPERIENCES
Rain, Rain Gr. 1, 53

## SYNCOPATION
Now's the Time Gr. 5, 445

## SYNTHESIZER SHARING
Electronic keyboard Gr. 8, E-28

(*Teacher to Teacher*, continued)

**TEACHING TIPS**
Ain't Gonna Let Nobody Turn Me
'Round Gr. 8, F-17
Angry Anymore Gr. 8, F-33
Bắt kim thang Gr. 6, 12
Book of Love Gr. 8, G-28
Cheki, morena Gr. 7, I-19, F-10
Circle 'Round the Moon Gr. 4, 407
Day-O! Gr. 5, 21
Einini Gr. 4, 390
Éliza Kongo Gr. 5, 15
Gakavik Gr. 4, 14
Hot Cross Buns (Version 1)
Gr. 3, 218
I Wish I Knew How It Would Feel to
Be Free Gr. 6, 470
*Jazz in the Box* Gr. 8, F-11
La raspa Gr. 4, 304
La tormenta tropical Gr. 2, 118
Laredo Gr. 5, 10
Merry Modal Christmas, A
Gr. 4, 410
Nana Kru Gr. 6, 281
Now's the Time Gr. 5, 446
*Nyoka* Gr. 7, D-32
O ma washi Gr. K, 13
Pizza, Pizza, Daddy-o Gr. 2, 29
Plant Four Seeds Gr. 2, 130
Put a Little Love in Your Heart
Gr. 4, 6
Río, río Gr. 5, 370
Silent Night Gr. 3, 394
Star Light, Star Bright Gr. 1, 107
Tumba Gr. 5, 161
Xiao yin chuan Gr. 2, 14

**TETRACHORDS**
Major Formula, A Gr. 7, H-23
Major Review Gr. 8, H-19
Major Scales with Flats Gr. 7, H-23
Key of G Major, The Gr. 8, H-19
Scales: They're Major! Gr. 7, H-23

**TIED RHYTHMS**
I'm a Believer Gr. 7, G-34

**TIPS**
Sing a Song of Peace Gr. 6, 66

**TONE LADDERS**
Harrison Town Gr. 6, 97
Scarborough Fair Gr. 6, 95

**TRANSPOSING**
Key to the Highway Gr. 8, F-29

**TUNING**
*Guitar Tuning* Gr. 7, F-2
*Guitar Tuning* Gr. 8, F-2

**UNDERSTANDING THE STORY
LINE**
Circle 'Round the Moon Gr. 4, 403

**UNUSUAL VOCAL SOUNDS**
*Kui.Kyon.pan* Gr. 6, 24

**USING A STORY MAP**
Napping House, The (story)
Gr. 1, 198

**USING GRAPHIC ORGANIZERS**
Six-Inch Boots in a Nine-Inch
Puddle Gr. 1, 366

**USING LOOPS**
*Work It Out (Blow Your Horn Dub
Mix)* Gr. 7, A-3

**USING ONE PIECE FOR SEVERAL
ELEMENTS**
*Shepherds Hey* Gr. 1, 208

**USING PROPS**
This Land Is Your Land (refrain
only) Gr. 1, 274

**USING RECORDINGS**
Certainly, Lord Gr. 7, I-12

**USING THE SONG RECORDINGS**
Shoo, Fly Gr. 2, 200

**USING THE SPEAKING VOICE**
Ikhanda, maslombe Gr. K, 14

**VENN DIAGRAMS**
*America, the Beautiful* Gr. 3, 413
America, the Beautiful Gr. 3, 413
*Irish Tune from County Derry*
Gr. 4, 49
La piñata Gr. 3, 400
*Waltz in D-flat ("Minute" Waltz)*
Gr. 4, 234
Zumba, zumba Gr. 3, 400

**VISUAL AIDS**
More Minor Seconds Gr. 8, H-15
Sight Reading Practice Gr. 8, H-15

**VISUAL SENSE OF WORLD
DRUMMING**
Nampaya omame Gr. 7, D-10

**VOCABLES**
Pottery Dance Gr. 1, 370

**VOCABULARY DEVELOPMENT**
Ants Go Marching, The Gr. 1, 248
Niño querido Gr. 1, 308

**VOCAL DEVELOPMENT**
Amefuri Gr. 1, 144
Apples, Peaches, Pears, and Plums
(speech piece) Gr. 1, 15
Bluebonnets of Texas Gr. 3, 333
Fuzzy Caterpillar Gr. K, 103
Vil du? Gr. 1, 92

**VOCAL EXPLORATION**
Andy Pandy Gr. K, 47
Busy Buzzy Bee Gr. K, 77
Engine, Engine, No. 9 Gr. K, 49
Here I Go! Gr. K, 72
Mmmmmm mmmmmmm
Gr. K, 71
Polly Wee Gr. K, 119

**VOCAL STYLES**
Wichita Hand Game Song 1
Gr. 3, 306
Wichita Hand Game Song 2
Gr. 3, 306

**WAVEFORM, THE ROPE TRICK**
*Sound Waves Montage* Gr. 6, 356

**WHEN CHILDREN LEAD AN
ACTIVITY**
Nanny Goat Gr. K, 160

**WORD ACCENTS**
Book of Love Gr. 8, G-28

**WORKING TOGETHER**
*Gavotte* Gr. 3, 88
*New York State of Mind*
Gr. 7, E-18
Voices of Pride, The Gr. 5, 88
Wheel of the Water, The
Gr. 4, 364

## TECHNOLOGY/MEDIA
## CD-ROM

*Band-in-a-Box*
12-Bar Blues Gr. 7, F-15
12-Bar Blues Rock Gr. 8, F-31
Accidentals Gr. 8, H-25
Aerial Boundaries Gr. 8, F-21
All for One Gr. 7, E-11
Blowin' in the Wind Gr. 5, 385
*Boogie Woogie* Gr. 6, 93
*Boston Ball Game 1967*
Gr. 8, F-32
Box a-Rockin' Ensemble
Gr. 7, D-5
Cantando mentiras Gr. 4, 147
Carnaval Calypso Ensemble
Gr. 7, D-21
Cuando pa' Chile me voy
Gr. 6, 377
Cuban Rumba Ensemble
Gr. 7, D-7
Deck the Hall Gr. 5, 475
Deep in the Heart of Texas
Gr. 8, I-19
A Different Minor Scale
Gr. 7, H-29
Do Wah Diddy Diddy
Gr. 7, F-21
Don't Be Cruel Gr. 6, 259
Elegua Gr. 7, D-9
Flip, Flop and Fly Gr. 7, E-33
*Flying Home* Gr. 7, B-15
Free at Last Gr. 6, 471
Frog Music Gr. 4, 201
Give a Little Love Gr. 6, 143
God Bless the Grass Gr. 8, F-13
Good Mornin' Blues Gr. 2, 53
Good Mornin' Blues Gr. 5, 227
Goodbye, Julie Gr. 8, E-5
Habemos llegado Gr. 6, 175

Hine mah tov  Gr. 5, 433
Hound Dog  Gr. 5, 215
I Got Rhythm  Gr. 6, 101
I Shall Sing  Gr. 8, I-41
Imbabura  Gr. 5, 203
Island Ensemble  Gr. 8, D-19
Jingle Bells  Gr. 2, 391
*John Wayne's Teeth*
    Gr. 8, B-37
Key to the Highway  Gr. 6, 243
Kou ri lengay  Gr. 7, E-3
Las mañanitas  Gr. 6, 481
Limbo Like Me  Gr. 4, 19
Loco-Motion, The  Gr. 3, 67
Má Teodora  Gr. 6, 301
Major Chords  Gr. 8, H-25
Man of Constant Sorrow
    Gr. 7, F-29
Mango Walk  Gr. 5, 201
The Minor iv Chord  Gr. 7, H-29
Now's the Time  Gr. 5, 451
Oh, Freedom  Gr. 5, 395
Pastures of Plenty  Gr. 4, 281
Play a Simple Melody  Gr. 5, 75
Purple People Eater, The
    Gr. 6, 449
*Radio City Music Hall Jingle*
    Gr. 8, A-5
Rhythm Is Gonna Get You, The
    Gr. 6, 349
Riendo el río corre  Gr. 6, 267
River  Gr. 4, 61
Rockin' Around the Christmas
    Tree  Gr. 5, 467
*Rodeo, "Hoedown"*  Gr. 8, B-45
S'vivon  Gr. 6, 453
Scattin' A-Round  Gr. 6, 161
Shortnin' Bread  Gr. 7, F-27
Sing, Sing, Sing!  Gr. 5, 343
St. Louis Blues  Gr. 5, 353
Stand By Me  Gr. 5, 49
Still, Still, Still  Gr. 5, 469
Subdominant in Minor
    Gr. 8, H-28
Summertime  Gr. 6, 253
Surfin' U.S.A.  Gr. 7, E-27
Sweet Potatoes  Gr. 3, 229
Those Magic Changes
    Gr. 8, E-31
Tonic and Dominant Chords in
    Minor  Gr. 8, H-28
Turn, Turn, Turn  Gr. 5, 381
V or V$_7$  Gr. 8, H-25
*Vocal Olympics*  Gr. 8, B-15
Water Come a Me Eye
    Gr. 6, 301
*Watermelon Man*  Gr. 6, 271

## Encyclopedia
Love in Any Language
    Gr. 6, 479

## Essentials of Music Theory
A Major Formula  Gr. 7, H-23

Adiós, amigos  Gr. 6, 57
America  Gr. 8, I-3
Anacrusis  Gr. 7, H-13
And Now for the Rest
    Gr. 8, H-5
Blues with a Feeling  Gr. 8, I-9
Conducting in 2/4  Gr. 7, H-13
Deep in the Heart of Texas
    Gr. 8, E-23
Dok djampa  Gr. 8, I-21
Dotted Quarter Note
    Gr. 7, H-13
Dotted-Half Note and Whole
    Note  Gr. 8, H-5
Dotted-Quarter and Eighth Note–
    Backwards!  Gr. 8, H-11
Dotted-Quarter Notes and
    Anacrusis  Gr. 8, H-11
Eighth Rest  Gr. 8, H-11
Feliz Navidad  Gr. 7, I-31
Going Up: *la*  Gr. 8, H-8
Joe Turner Blues  Gr. 4, 57
Lift Ev'ry Voice and Sing
    Gr. 8, I-55
Major Scales with Flats
    Gr. 7, H-23
Minor Chords  Gr. 7, H-29
Minor Keys  Gr. 8, H-23
Minor Scales  Gr. 7, H-29
More Minor Seconds
    Gr. 8, H-14
Move up to *so*  Gr. 8, H-8
O lê lê O Bahía  Gr. 6, 165
Scale Degrees  Gr. 8, H-23
Scales: They're Major!
    Gr. 7, H-23
Star-Spangled Banner, The
    Gr. 8, I-63
Stille Nacht (Silent Night)
    Gr. 7, I-55
Surfin' U.S.A.  Gr. 7, I-61
T'hola, t'hola  Gr. 4, 133
The Minor iv Chord  Gr. 7, H-29
*Twist and Shout*  Gr. 4, 239
Two More Keys with Sharps:
    A Major and E Major
    Gr. 8, H-21

## Making More Music
*A-Cling, A-Cling*  Gr. 4, 191
Basics of Melody  Gr. 7, H-7
*Carnival of the Animals,
    "Royal March of the Lion"*
    Gr. 3, 357
Dynamics  Gr. 7, H-11
La Tarara  Gr. 4, 177
*Llactamanta*  Gr. 6, 383
*mi-re-do*  Gr. 7, H-7
More Melody: *fa*  Gr. 7, H-7
Morning Is Come  Gr. 3, 129
Tancovačka  Gr. 4, 231

## Making Music
Ah! Les jolis papillons
    Gr. 1, 363
Amefuri  Gr. 1, 145
Bluebonnets of Texas  Gr. 3, 333
Bounce High, Bounce Low
    Gr. 1, 153
Busy Buzzy Bee  Gr. K, 77
Chuhwuht  Gr. 2, 357
Deux cocodries  Gr. 2, 365
Down the Ohio  Gr. 2, 63
Ég a gyertya  Gr. K, 97
Erdö, erdö de magos  Gr. 3, 183
Falling Rain  Gr. 2, 329
Farmer's Dairy Key, The
    Gr. 2, 183
Four in a Boat  Gr. 2, 49
Freight Train  Gr. 1, 47
Ha'kyo jong  Gr. 2, 137
Haru ga kita  Gr. 2, 401
Hato Popo  Gr. 1, 187
Here I Go!  Gr. K, 73
Honeybee Song, The  Gr. 1, 359
Hosisipa  Gr. 3, 71
¡Jeu! ¡Jeu!  Gr. 1, 217
Lady, Lady  Gr. 1, 63
Lap Time  Gr. K, 101
Le jig Français  Gr. K, 64
Let's Go Fly a Kite  Gr. 2, 327
Li'l Liza Jane  Gr. 3, 141
Los días de la semana
    Gr. 1, 269
Los pececitos  Gr. 1, 179
Michael Finnigan  Gr. 3, 153
Now Let Me Fly  Gr. 3, 179
Old Brass Wagon  Gr. 2, 123
Oliver Twist  Gr. K, 139
Phoebe  Gr. 1, 31
Pin Pon  Gr. 1, 147
Pottery Dance  Gr. 1, 371
Ptashky u babusi sadochku
    Gr. 1, 193
Race You Down the Mountain
    Gr. 1, 127
Rain, Rain  Gr. 1, 55
Rainbow, The  Gr. 2, 333
*Rodeo, "Saturday Night Waltz"*
    Gr. 4, 343
Sansaw akroma  Gr. 3, 289
Song That's Just For You, A
    Gr. 2, 127
*Sous les étoiles*  Gr. 2, 339
Star Light, Star Bright  Gr. 1,
    109
Valentines  Gr. 2, 399
¡Viva el fútbol!  Gr. 1, 97
*Vulani ringi ring*  Gr. 1, 139
Willowbee  Gr. 1, 223
Zip-a-Dee-Doo-Dah  Gr. 2, 331
*Zomo the Rabbit*  Gr. 3, 365

(*Technology/Media,* **continued**)

## DIGITAL AUDIO

Alleluia, Amen  Gr. 7, A-13
Angry Anymore  Gr. 8, F-33
Avocational musician  Gr. 8, A-31
*Footloose*  Gr. 7, B-11
Going upon the Mountain
    Gr. 6, 107
*Good Morning, Aztlán*  Gr. 7, B-7
I Dream a World  Gr. 8, G-43
I'm on My Way  Gr. 7, A-17
*Jelly Roll, The*  Gr. 7, B-39
*Joy to the World*  Gr. 7, A-27
Music promotion  Gr. 7, A-27
*Onomatapoiea Study No. 2*
    Gr. 7, E-31
*Paddy Whack*  Gr. 6, 327
*Rock It*  Gr. 7, B-11
Tuxedo Junction  Gr. 8, G-23

## DIGITAL STILL PHOTOGRAPHY

*Paddy Whack*  Gr. 6, 327

## ELECTRONIC KEYBOARD

ABC Rock  Gr. 1, 263
Abiyoyo  Gr. 2, 109
Alabama Gal  Gr. 3, 107
Alexander's Ragtime Band
    Gr. 6, 139
All Night, All Day  Gr. 4, 181
America  Gr. 1, 447
America  Gr. 4, 441
Ants Go Marching, The  Gr. 1, 251
Apples, Peaches, Pears, and Plums
    (speech piece)  Gr. 1, 17
Birds of Fire  Gr. 3, 257
Black Snake  Gr. 3, 53
Blow the Wind Southerly
    Gr. 5, 179
Bounce High, Bounce Low
    Gr. 1, 153
Bound for South Australia
    Gr. 5, 23
Buenos días  Gr. 1, 13
Caballito blanco  Gr. 2, 193
Chag Purim  Gr. 1, 441
Charlie over the Water  Gr. 1, 69
Children of the Sun (poem)
    Gr. 1, 405
*Children's Corner Suite,*
    *"Snowflakes Are Dancing"*
    Gr. 5, 239
Clouds  Gr. K, 254
Cowboys' Christmas Ball
    Gr. 6, 239
*Dancing Tree, The*  Gr. K, 202
Dayenu  Gr. 4, 439
*Debajo el Butón*  Gr. 1, 211
Ding, Dong, Diggidiggidong
    Gr. 3, 17
Do Wah Diddy Diddy  Gr. 4, 203
*Doing the Penguin*  Gr. K, 35
Dona nobis pacem  Gr. 6, 127

Doraji  Gr. 4, 175
Down by the Bay  Gr. 1, 19
El caracol  Gr. K, 131
El carnavalito humahuaqueño
    Gr. 6, 483
El mes de abril  Gr. 3, 329
Frère Jacques  Gr. 2, 125
Frog (poem)  Gr. 1, 25
From Sea to Shining Sea
    Gr. 2, 343
Galoshes  Gr. K, 63
Goodbye, Julie  Gr. 1, 334
Goodbye, Julie  Gr. 1, 335
Grizzly Bear  Gr. K, 33
Habari Gani  Gr. 3, 405
Habemos llegado  Gr. 6, 175
Haere  Gr. 2, 285
*Halley Came to Jackson*
    Gr. 2, 341
Halloween Song  Gr. K, 309
Happy Wanderer, The  Gr. 4, 91
He's Got the Whole World in His
    Hands  Gr. 3, 231
Hello, There!  Gr. K, 7
Hokey Pokey  Gr. K, 296
I Can't Spell Hippopotamus
    Gr. 1, 267
I Got a Letter This Morning
    Gr. K, 69
I Got Shoes  Gr. 2, 243
I'm a Very Fine Turkey  Gr. K, 310
I'm Flying Home  Gr. 2, 287
I'm Tall, I'm Small  Gr. K, 18
I've Been Working on the Railroad
    Gr. 3, 243
In the Pumpkin Patch  Gr. 3, 383
*Interview with Rick Bassett (Part*
    *2)*  Gr. 3, 223
James Brown  Gr. K, 206
Jelly in a Dish  Gr. 2, 85
Jo'ashila  Gr. 5, 109
John Kanaka  Gr. 3, 63
Johnny Caught a Flea  Gr. 1, 227
Juan pirulero  Gr. K, 215
*Junk Music Montage*  Gr. 1, 75
Kangaroo Song, The  Gr. K, 45
*Kansas City Stomp*  Gr. 2, 251
Keel Row, The  Gr. 4, 243
Martin Luther King  Gr. 1, 435
Knock the Cymbals  Gr. 1, 177
Kuma san  Gr. K, 41
La paloma se fué  Gr. 6, 51
La piñata  Gr. 3, 401
La pulga de San José  Gr. 3, 41
Lean on Me  Gr. 6, 15
Leatherwing Bat  Gr. 2, 303
Let's Get Ready  Gr. K, 312
Lion and the Mouse, The (story)
    Gr. 1, 239
Little David  Gr. 1, 233
Little Green Frog, The  Gr. 1, 25
Little Shop of Horrors  Gr. 4, 423
Little Spider  Gr. K, 93

Long Way Home, A  Gr. 1, 383
Making Valentines  Gr. 1, 437
Mary Ann  Gr. 6, 183
Merry-Go-Round  Gr. K, 290
Michael, Row the Boat Ashore
    Gr. 2, 19
*Miniature Odyssey, A*  Gr. 8, E-29
Mon papa  Gr. 2, 281
Must Be Santa  Gr. K, 318
My Mama's Calling Me  Gr. 1, 261
My Pony, Macaroni  Gr. 1, 158
Name Game, The (speech piece)
    Gr. 1, 315
Name, Name, What's Your Name?
    Gr. 3, 11
Nana Kru  Gr. 6, 283
Nana, Thread Needle  Gr. 1, 39
Nani wale na hala  Gr. 3, 261
Night-light  Gr. K, 223
Noah's Shanty  Gr. 1, 345
Ocho kandelikas  Gr. 4, 429
Ode to Joy  Gr. 4, 153
Oh, Won't You Sit Down  Gr. 3, 29
Old Blue  Gr. K, 123
On a Log, Mister Frog  Gr. K, 149
One Green Jelly Bean  Gr. K, 287
Ōsamu kosamu  Gr. 4, 97
Over the River and Through the
    Wood  Gr. 3, 385
Parade Came Marching, The
    Gr. 1, 167
*Percussion Montage*  Gr. 1, 117
*Pick-a-Rib*  Gr. 3, 151
Pizza, Pizza, Daddy-o  Gr. 2, 31
Pon, pon, pon  Gr. K, 51
Put Your Hand in My Hand
    Gr. 1, 333
*Quiet City*  Gr. 8, E-29
Rice Planting Song  Gr. 1, 91
Riddle Ree  Gr. 2, 35
Rig-a-Jig-Jig  Gr. K, 99
Rockin' Robin  Gr. 3, 371
*Rodeo, "Buckaroo Holiday"*
    Gr. 2, 23
'Round and 'Round  Gr. 1, 149
'Round the Bay of Mexico
    Gr. 4, 259
Run, Molly, Run  Gr. 1, 9
Sailing Down My Golden River
    Gr. 4, 333
Sailing to the Sea  Gr. 1, 339
Serra, serra, serrador  Gr. 1, 113
She'll Be Comin' 'Round the
    Mountain  Gr. 2, 359
Shoo, Fly  Gr. 2, 201
*Silver Apples of the Moon*
    Gr. 1, 12
Singin' in the Rain  Gr. 4, 361
Singing Scales  Gr. 8, B-11
*Somebody*  Gr. 4, 41
Somebody's Knockin' at Your Door
    Gr. 4, 53
Song of the Eagle  Gr. 2, 249

Song of the Night, The  Gr. 3, 347
Sound Waves Montage  Gr. 6, 357
Spaceworms  Gr. 1, 401
Star-Spangled Banner, The
    Gr. 4, 441
Thanksgiving is Near  Gr. 2, 381
*Think*  Gr. 6, 367
Time to Sing  Gr. 2, 11
Toccata and Tango  Gr. 2, 155
Today Is Your Birthday  Gr. 1, 411
Tree in the Wood, The  Gr. 2, 361
Twelve Days of Christmas, The
    Gr. 4, 433
Twist with a Burger, Jitter with a
    Bug (speech piece)  Gr. 1, 133
Usagi  Gr. 1, 397
Walk in the Room  Gr. 1, 13
We've Got Lots in Common (from
    Charlotte's Web)  Gr. 3, 367
Weevily Wheat  Gr. 4, 105
What a Wonderful World  Gr. 6, 65
Will You?  Gr. 1, 93
Willoughby, Wallaby, Woo
    Gr. K, 282
Wind Blew East, The  Gr. 1, 65
Wind Up the Apple Tree
    Gr. 1, 184
World of Difference, A  Gr. 5, 389
Yakety Yak  Gr. 5, 205
Yankee Doodle  Gr. 2, 405
Yertle the Turtle  Gr. 2, 371
Zudio  Gr. 2, 269

## INTERNET

Create a Career  Gr. 8, A-33

## MIDI

America  Gr. 8, G-7
*Can't Take My Joy*  Gr. 7, B-41
Dance of the Youths and Maidens
    Gr. 8, C-33
*Das Jahr, "Mai"*  Gr. 8, C-19
*Den III. Ende VI. Ronde & Quatre
    Branles*  Gr. 8, C-7
Down by the Riverside  Gr. 8, G-9
Faith of the Heart  Gr. 8, G-5
He's Got the Whole World in His
    Hands  Gr. 7, G-7
*Heads Carolina, Tails California*
    Gr. 7, B-25
I'm a Believer  Gr. 7, G-37
*Joy*  Gr. 7, B-41
Lohengrin, "Prelude to Act III"
    Gr. 8, C-25
One Family  Gr. 7, G-19
Pictures at an Exhibition
    Gr. 8, A-15
Proud  Gr. 7, G-5
Si si si  Gr. 7, G-13
Something Told the Wild Geese
    Gr. 7, G-41
*Sonatina for Bassoon and Piano,
    "Allegro con moto," Movement
    1*  Gr. 7, C-13

Texture composition  Gr. 8, C-5
*Watitin' for a Train*  Gr. 7, B-25
Winter  Gr. 8, G-11
You Were on My Mind  Gr. 7, G-25

## MIDI/SEQUENCING SOFTWARE

*7th Guest, The, "Themes"*
    Gr. 8, A-3
Abraham, Martin, and John
    Gr. 6, 471
Adelita  Gr. 5, 51
Ah, eu entrei na roda  Gr. 3, 311
Ain't Gonna Let Nobody Turn Me
    'Round  Gr. 6, 85
Al tambor  Gr. 3, 271
All Through the Night  Gr. 5, 105
Alle meine Entchen  Gr. 1, 99
Ambos a dos  Gr. 3, 23
America, the Beautiful  Gr. 7, I-5
America, the Beautiful  Gr. 8, I-5
Apples and Bananas  Gr. 1, 391
Apples and Bananas  Gr. 1, 391
Ash Grove, The  Gr. 5, 115
At the Same Time  Gr. 6, 117
Au clair de la lune  Gr. 3, 19
Au clair de la lune  Gr. 3, 185
Away to America  Gr. 5, 57
¡Ay, Jalisco no te rajes!  Gr. 7, I-9
Ayelivi  Gr. 2, 71
Book of Love  Gr. 8, G-29
Bury Me Not on the Lone Prairie
    Gr. 6, 19
*C-Jam Blues*  Gr. 8, C-43
*Cafe Europa*  Gr. 7, B-43
California Dreamin'  Gr. 8, G-33
Cantaré, cantarás  Gr. 6, 415
*Canzon in Echo Duodecimi Toni a
    10*  Gr. 8, C-7
Chairs to Mend  Gr. 4, 149
Chanukah Games  Gr. 3, 391
Chapel of Love  Gr. 7, G-29
Che che koolay  Gr. 2, 267
Cheki, morena  Gr. 7, F-11
Cheki, morena  Gr. 2, 181
Cheki, morena  Gr. 7, I-19
Cielito lindo  Gr. 7, I-23
Cindy  Gr. 4, 385
Circle 'Round the Moon  Gr. 4, 409
Come and Go With Me to That
    Land  Gr. 5, 391
Con el vito  Gr. 7, G-15
*Crouching Tiger, Hidden Dragon*
    Gr. 8, A-11
Cumberland Gap  Gr. 4, 139
Deck the Hall  Gr. 5, 475
Different Beat, A  Gr. 1, 7
Ding, Dong, Diggidiggidong
    Gr. 3, 39
Do, Lord  Gr. 3, 165
Down, Down, Baby  Gr. 2, 33
Draw Me a Bucket of Water
    Gr. 3, 127
Ego sum pauper  Gr. 5, 159

Eh, cumpari!  Gr. 4, 71
El barquito  Gr. 3, 361
El Floron (The Flower)  Gr. 2, 247
El gallo pinto  Gr. 3, 89
El rancho grande  Gr. 8, I-25
El sapito  Gr. 3, 337
El tren  Gr. 2, 261
En nuestra Tierra tan linda
    Gr. 2, 335
Ev'ry Time I Feel the Spirit
    Gr. 5, 243
Fais do do  Gr. 6, 407
Farewell to Tarwathie  Gr. 6, 43
*Fingerprints*  Gr. 7, B-43
For Children Safe and Strong
    Gr. 5, 485
Freedom Is Coming  Gr. 5, 417
*Frog in the Millpond*  Gr. 2, 45
Gift to Share, A  Gr. 6, 395
Give My Regards to Broadway
    Gr. 6, 41
Glory, Glory, Hallelujah  Gr. 6, 53
Go Around the Corn, Sally
    Gr. 2, 13
God Bless the U.S.A.  Gr. 8, G-39
Gonna Build a Mountain  Gr. 6, 21
Gonna Ride Up in the Chariot
    Gr. 4, 23
Good King Wenceslas  Gr. 6, 461
Good Morning  Gr. 3, 193
Gospel Train, The  Gr. 6, 401
Great Big Stars  Gr. 1, 61
Harrison Town  Gr. 6, 97
Heigh-Ho  Gr. 2, 7
Hej pada pada  Gr. 3, 79
Hey, Ho! Nobody Home  Gr. 6, 29
Hine mah tov  Gr. 5, 433
Hitotsu toya  Gr. 5, 478
Hush, Hush  Gr. 3, 165
I Am But a Small Voice  Gr. 6, 447
I Don't Care If the Rain Comes
    Down  Gr. 3, 27
I Got Shoes  Gr. 2, 243
I Vow to You, My Country
    Gr. 5, 425
I'm on My Way  Gr. 7, A-17
Ichi-gatsu tsuitachi  Gr. 3, 407
Ja-Da  Gr. 7, G-21
Jan ken pon  Gr. 3, 303
Keep Your Eyes on the Prize
    Gr. 8, E-17
Key to the Highway  Gr. 8, F-29
Khorovod  Gr. 1, 375
Knock No More  Gr. 3, 387
Kookaburra  Gr. 4, 187
Kou ri lengay  Gr. 2, 219
Kyrie  Gr. 6, 207
La mariposa  Gr. 6, 58
La raspa  Gr. 4, 305
La tormenta tropical  Gr. 2, 119
Laredo  Gr. 5, 11
Let Us Sing Together  Gr. 6, 157

(*Technology/Media,* continued)

Let's Get the Rhythm of the Band
Gr. 7, E-29

Light Up the World with a Song
Gr. 8, G-25

Linstead Market  Gr. 5, 241

*Lion*  Gr. 6, 303

Lion Sleeps Tonight, The
Gr. 8, E-9

Lion Sleeps Tonight, The
Gr. 8, F-4

Little David, Play on Your Harp
Gr. 4, 395

*"Little" Organ Fugue in G Minor*
Gr. 6, 129

Little Green Frog, The  Gr. 1, 25

Los reyes de Oriente  Gr. 8, I-59

Lots of Worms  Gr. 2, 310

Lots of Worms  Gr. 2, 313

Love Is on Our Side  Gr. 5, 325

Lullaby and Dance  Gr. 4, 389

Make a Music Video!  Gr. 7, A-29

Mary Ann  Gr. 6, 183

*Messiah, "The Trumpet Shall
Sound"*  Gr. 8, C-8

Miss Mary Mack  Gr. 2, 43

Mood Music  Gr. 8, A-7

Morning Has Broken  Gr. 5, 31

Mud  Gr. 3, 35

Music Critic  Gr. 7, A-33

My Dear Companion  Gr. 6, 23

Niño querido  Gr. 1, 309

Niu lang zhi nü  Gr. 4, 337

Now Let Me Fly  Gr. 3, 179

O, Desayo  Gr. 5, 413

Oh, Freedom  Gr. 7, G-31

Oh, Won't You Sit Down  Gr. 3, 29

Old Dan Tucker  Gr. 3, 99

Orange Blossom Special
Gr. 5, 269

Orange Blossom Special  Gr. 8, E-7

Over My Head  Gr. 7, G-11

Over My Head  Gr. 4, 119

Pavo, pavo  Gr. 1, 416

Peace Like a River  Gr. 3, 249

Piñon, pirulín  Gr. 2, 177

Pollerita  Gr. 5, 153

Ptashky u babusi sadochku
Gr. 1, 193

Rabbit Footprints  Gr. 2, 305

Railroad Corral  Gr. 3, 177

Recording engineer  Gr. 7, A-21

Red River Valley  Gr. 6, 11

Riqui rán  Gr. 1, 49

Riqui rán  Gr. 4, 67

Rise Up, Shepherd, and Follow
Gr. 5, 471

Ríu chíu chíu  Gr. 5, 439

Sakura  Gr. 4, 309

Sambalele  Gr. 4, 399

Sarika keo  Gr. 3, 185

Sarika keo  Gr. 3, 275

*Scrub-a-dub*  Gr. 1, 306

Scrub-a-Dub  Gr. 1, 307

Se va el caimán  Gr. 5, 307

Seagull, Seagull, Sit on the Shore
Gr. 4, 383

Seasons of Love  Gr. 8, A-23

Serra, serra, serrador  Gr. 1, 113

Shalom aleichem  Gr. 6, 411

She'll Be Comin' 'Round the
Mountain  Gr. 2, 359

*Shepherd's Hey Sampler*
Gr. 7, C-37

Ship that Never Returned, The
Gr. 5, 403

Shu ha mo  Gr. 3, 277

Simple Gifts  Gr. 8, A-17

Sing a Song!  Gr. 7, A-11

Sing! Speak! Whisper! Shout!
Gr. 1, 37

Siyahamba  Gr. 6, 215

Small Job, A  Gr. 3, 225

Somebody's Knockin' at Your Door
Gr. 4, 53

Sonando  Gr. 4, 35

Song of the Fishes  Gr. 3, 245

St. Patrick Was a Gentleman
Gr. 3, 293

Streets of Laredo  Gr. 4, 273

Strike Up the Band  Gr. 6, 135

Supercalifragilisticexpialidocious
(from Mary Poppins)  Gr. 3, 9

Surfin' U.S.A.  Gr. 6, 261

Take a Chance On Me  Gr. 8, G-17

*That's the Way It Is*  Gr. 7, B-23

This Land Is Your Land  Gr. 5, 121

This Land Is Your Land  Gr. 7, I-69

Three Little Birds  Gr. 4, 321

Tie Me Kangaroo Down, Sport
Gr. 4, 37

Train Is A-Comin'  Gr. 3, 51

Turkey Game, The  Gr. 1, 417

Tuxedo Junction  Gr. 8, G-23

Tzena, tzena  Gr. 5, 301

'Ūlili E  Gr. 5, 443

Uno, dos y tres  Gr. 5, 429

Various Instrumental Performers
Gr. 8, A-19

Wai bamba  Gr. 6, 27

Wai bamba  Gr. 8, G-13

Waiting for the Traffic Light
Gr. 2, 107

Walk Together, Children  Gr. 3, 147

Was kommt dort von der Höh'?
Gr. 8, C-21

*Water Music, "Hornpipe"*
Gr. 8, C-9

When the Train Comes Along
Gr. 1, 301

Wir hatten gebauet  Gr. 8, C-21

*Work It Out (Blow Your Horn Dub
Mix)*  Gr. 7, A-3

*You're a Grand Old Flag*
Gr. 1, 276

Zudio  Gr. 2, 269

## MULTIMEDIA

Allá en la fuente  Gr. 2, 93

America  Gr. 3, 413

America  Gr. 6, 487

America, the Beautiful  Gr. 3, 413

America, the Beautiful  Gr. 6, 487

Angels On the Midnight Clear
Gr. 6, 425

B-A, Bay  Gr. 1, 221

Barb'ry Allen  Gr. 6, 45

Blue Skies  Gr. 6, 89

Coming Home from the Sea
Gr. 6, 347

*Concert for Piano and Orchestra*
Gr. 6, 209

Families  Gr. 1, 282

Families  Gr. 1, 283

Goin' to Boston  Gr. 6, 437

I Bought Me a Cat  Gr. 2, 309

I Know an Old Lady  Gr. 1, 389

Jig Along Home  Gr. 2, 367

Keep Your Eyes on the Prize
Gr. 3, 409

Le sacre du printemps (The Rite of
Spring)  Gr. 8, C-33

Looby Loo  Gr. K, 210

Love in Any Language  Gr. 6, 479

Magnolia  Gr. 6, 17

*Paddy Whack*  Gr. 6, 327

Puff, the Magic Dragon  Gr. 2, 351

*Rags*  Gr. 1, 291

*Riverdance Suite*  Gr. 2, 141

Scarborough Fair  Gr. 6, 95

*Sikelela*  Gr. 1, 139

Skin and Bones  Gr. 2, 377

Snowflakes (poem)  Gr. 1, 423

Star-Spangled Banner, The
Gr. 6, 487

This Land Is Your Land (refrain
only)  Gr. 1, 277

This Train  Gr. 5,

Trouble Is a Mountain  Gr. 2, 203

Waitin' for the Light to Shine
Gr. 4, 29

Yesh lanu taish  Gr. 1, 183

## NOTATION SOFTWARE

A la puerta del cielo  Gr. 5, 61

Ah, Poor Bird  Gr. 4, 197

Ahora voy a cantarles  Gr. 3, 57

Al citrón  Gr. 3, 323

Alleluia  Gr. 6, 133

Alligator Pie (speech piece)
Gr. 3, 13

Ama-Lama  Gr. 5, 145

*America*  Gr. 7, A-25

America  Gr. 7, I-3

*America (from West Side Story)*
Gr. 8, C-45

America, the Free  Gr. 4, 213

Artsa alinu  Gr. 3, 285

Autumn Canon  Gr. 5, 149

Bear Dance  Gr. 7, I-11

Bereleh Gr. K, 151
Big Rock Candy Mountain
    Gr. 4, 331
Blue Mountain Lake Gr. 6, 205
*Boston Ball Game 1967*
    Gr. 8, F-32
Bridges Gr. 6, 87
Brush Your Teeth Gr. 1, 285
Camptown Races Gr. 5, 271
Canto del agua Gr. 8, I-13
Cement Mixer Gr. 4, 103
Chiapanecas Gr. 5, 93
Circle 'Round the Moon Gr. 4, 405
*Circlesong 7* Gr. 4, 81
Clouds of Gray Gr. 2, 57
Computer, The Gr. 4, 199
Conducting the Beat Gr. 8, H-3
Connemara Lullaby Gr. 5, 235
Continents, The (speech piece)
    Gr. 4, 357
Corrido de Kansas Gr. 4, 275
Crawfish Gr. 2, 89
Cycle Song of Life Gr. 4, 371
*Danses Populaires Francaises,*
    *"Branle Double, Branle*
    *Simple"* Gr. 7, C-27
*Danza* Gr. 7, C-7
Der sad to katte Gr. 2, 301
Dinah Gr. 2, 121
Ding, Dong, Diggidiggidong
    Gr. 3, 17
Ding Dong! Merrily on High
    Gr. 6, 431
Do, Re, Mi, Fa Gr. 6, 81
Don Alfonso Gr. 5, 177
Don't Let the Wind Gr. 3, 181
Don't Let Your Watch Run Down
    Gr. 3, 167
Doong gul ge Gr. 3, 137
Doumbek or Hand Drum Exercises
    Gr. 7, D-31
*Dr Gradus ad Parnassum*
    Gr. 8, C-29
Drill, Ye Tarriers Gr. 5, 54
Earth Is Our Mother, The
    Gr. 8, F-25
Ein Männlein steht im Walde
    Gr. 2, 91
El desembre congelat Gr. 5, 473
El rancho grande Gr. 4, 215
El sapito Gr. 3, 337
Éliza Kongo Gr. 5, 14
Éliza Kongo Gr. 5, 17
Evening Chaconne Gr. 6, 203
*fa* with 1st and 2nd Endings
    Gr. 8, H-7
*Fanfare for the Common Man*
    Gr. 7, C-43
*Fifteen Hungarian Peasant Songs*
    Gr. 7, C-35
Five Notes in Two Places
    Gr. 7, H-9
Four Strong Winds Gr. 6, 171

*Gavotte* Gr. 3, 89
Glad to Have a Friend Like You
    Gr. 2, 231
Great Big House Gr. 2, 207
Had to Get Up This Mornin' Soon
    Gr. 3, 115
Halloween Is a Very Unusual Night
    Gr. 3, 383
Harambee Gr. 4, 435
Hashkediya Gr. 3, 207
Heri za Kwanzaa Gr. 5, 477
Himmel und Erde Gr. 5, 95
Hot Cross Buns (Version 2)
    Gr. 3, 221
How Can I Keep from Singing?
    Gr. 4, 261
How Many Miles to Babylon?
    Gr. 2, 129
*Hungarian Dance No. 6* Gr. 4, 51
I Believe I Can Fly Gr. 5, 173
I Love the Mountains Gr. 5, 35
I See the Moon Gr. 2, 59
I Wonder Where Maria's Gone
    Gr. 3, 319
I'll Fly Away Gr. 8, I-45
Ida Red Gr. 3, 31
Jambalaya Gr. 8, I-49
Johnny Has Gone for a Soldier
    Gr. 5, 189
Juniper Tree, The Gr. 3, 131
Karangatia ra Gr. 8, F-23
The Key of G Major Gr. 8, H-18
Kingston Market Gr. 3, 91
La ciudad de Juaja Gr. 5, 58
*La mer, "Jeux de vagues"*
    Gr. 7, C-39
La paloma blanca Gr. 3, 253
Las velitas Gr. 5, 147
Low *la-la*₁ Gr. 7, H-15
Let It Snow! Let It Snow! Let It
    Snow! Gr. 4, 427
Let Music Surround You Gr. 4, 237
Let's Get the Rhythm of the Band
    Gr. 7, E-29
Like a Bird Gr. 6, 167
Lo, How a Rose E'er Blooming
    Gr. 6, 211
Love Somebody Gr. 3, 95
Lucy Locket Gr. 2, 27
*Lyric Suite, "Allegretto gioviale,"*
    *Movement 1* Gr. 6, 169
*Ma Vlast (My Fatherland), "Vltava*
    *(The Moldau)"* Gr. 7, C-33
Malê Debalê Gr. 8, B-19
Melody Review Gr. 7, H-9
Merry Modal Christmas, A
    Gr. 4, 413
Meter in Three Plus Repeats
    Gr. 8, H-3
Meters, Measures, and More
    Gr. 8, H-3
*mi-re-do* Gr. 8, H-7
Minor Keys Gr. 8, H-23

Minor Practice Plus Gr. 8, H-27
Mister Ram Goat-O Gr. 3, 55
More Meter and Rhythm
    Gr. 7, H-5
Morning Comes Early Gr. 5, 13
Mubärak Gr. 3, 283
My Father's House Gr. 2, 25
Notate original compositions
    Gr. 7, A-9
O Music Gr. 5, 163
Oh, Watch the Stars Gr. 5, 217
Old Abram Brown Gr. 5, 223
One Morning in May Gr. 6, 121
One Morning Soon Gr. 3, 69
Over There Gr. 5, 279
Oy, Hanuka Gr. 7, I-45
Paw-Paw Patch Gr. 4, 95
Pay Me My Money Down
    Gr. 7, F-7
Peace Like a River Gr. 6, 193
Peanut Butter (speech piece)
    Gr. 1, 173
Pease Porridge Hot Gr. 1, 135
Perot Gr. 2, 379
*Piano Sonata No. 8 in C Minor*
    *("Pathéthique"), Movement 3,*
    *Rondo: Allegro* Gr. 4, 185
Plant Four Seeds Gr. 2, 131
Play a Simple Melody Gr. 5, 75
Pretty Saro Gr. 3, 217
¡Qué gusto! Gr. 3, 133
*Rap Intro* Gr. 8, B-33
*Red Poppy, The, "Russian Sailors'*
    *Dance"* Gr. 4, 225
Rise and Shine Gr. 4, 99
Rock Island Line Gr. 4, 55
Rocky Mountain Gr. 2, 99
'Round and 'Round Gr. 1, 149
Rhythm Fundamentals Gr. 8, H-3
Sailboat in the Sky Gr. 4, 375
Scale Degrees Gr. 8, H-23
Second or Third? Gr. 8, H-7
*Shepherd's Hey Sampler*
    Gr. 7, C-37
Singing-Time Gr. 3, 203
Skye Boat Song Gr. 6, 373
Soldier, Soldier Gr. 4, 11
Somebody Waiting Gr. 2, 283
Son macaron Gr. 4, 109
*Sonata in C-sharp Minor, Op. 27,*
    *No. 2, "Moonlight," Movement*
    *1* Gr. 7, C-19
*Soundings, "Fanfare"* Gr. 8, C-47
Step Up to *so* Gr. 7, H-9
Swanee Gr. 6, 119
*Symphony No. 40 in G Minor, K.*
    *550, Movement 1* Gr. 8, C-13
*Symphony No. 47 in G Major,*
    *"Menuet"* Gr. 7, C-15
Take Me Out to the Ball Game
    Gr. 3, 263
Ten Little Ostinato Pieces
    Gr. 7, I-65

(*Technology/Media,* continued)

Tengo, tengo, tengo  Gr. 4, 229

Tideo  Gr. 2, 81

Transposing Practice  Gr. 8, H-8

Tsuki  Gr. 4, 25

Un, deux, trois  Gr. 2, 199

Vem kan segla?  Gr. 6, 421

*Vive l'amour*  Gr. 6, 179

*Voiles*  Gr. 7, C-39

Washington Post, The (march)
Gr. 8, C-41

We Shall Not Be Moved  Gr. 4, 437

When *do* is F  Gr. 7, H-9

*Why Is There Day and Night?*
Gr. 4, 369

World We Love, The  Gr. 3, 343

Xiao yin chuan  Gr. 2, 15

You're a Grand Old Flag  Gr. 3, 265

Your Friends Shall Be the Tall Wind
Gr. 6, 201

## SEQUENCING SOFTWARE  *See also MIDI/Sequencing software.*

A Ram Sam Sam  Gr. 3, 209

Abiyoyo  Gr. 2, 109

Addams Family, The  Gr. 5, 457

Aiken Drum  Gr. 1, 399

All Around the Buttercup
Gr. 2, 171

Alleluia, Amen  Gr. 7, A-13

Amazing Grace  Gr. 4, 161

And My Heart Soars  Gr. 2, 241

Animals Find Water, The
Gr. 2, 219

Arirang  Gr. 5, 25

Ashchav  Gr. 2, 67

Banuwa  Gr. 6, 297

Bee, Bee Bumblebee  Gr. 1, 51

*Billie*  Gr. 8, B-23

*Black Suits Comin' (Nod Ya Head)*
Gr. 7, A-7

Bling Blang  Gr. 3, 241

*Block Party*  Gr. 7, B-13

Bonavist' Harbour  Gr. 3, 295

Bonjour, mes amis  Gr. 1, 317

Bundle-Buggy Boogie Woogie
Gr. 4, 123

Bus, The  Gr. K, 83

By the Waters of Babylon
Gr. 6, 311

Bye Bye, Love  Gr. 8, F-9

California, Here I Come  Gr. 4, 287

Canoe Song  Gr. 4, 77

Cat's Tongue  Gr. 2, 191

Chicka Hanka  Gr. 2, 211

Chords in F  Gr. 7, H-27

Chrismus a Come  Gr. 3, 397

Colorado Trail  Gr. 5, 277

Come, Ye Thankful People, Come
Gr. 5, 459

Composing with Sixteenth Notes
Gr. 7, H-19

Cookie  Gr. 2, 173

Cow's Woc Backward  Gr. 1, 390

Crocodile, The  Gr. 2, 363

Da pacem, Domine  Gr. 5, 63

Dance for the Nations  Gr. 6, 123

De colores  Gr. 8, E-15

Deau-deau, ti pitit maman
Gr. 2, 307

Dinosaur Dance  Gr. 2, 169

*DJ Premier in Deep Concentration*
Gr. 7, B-13

Don't You Hear the Lambs?
Gr. 5, 99

Dona nobis pacem  Gr. 6, 127

Down in the Meadow  Gr. K, 147

Dry Bones Come Skipping
Gr. 4, 221

Each of Us Is a Flower  Gr. 3, 155

Eighth and Sixteenth Combinations
Gr. 7, H-19

El juego chirimbolo  Gr. 2, 55

Estampie  Gr. 8, I-27

Ev'rybody Loves Saturday Night
Gr. 7, I-27

Every Morning When I Wake Up
Gr. 2, 321

Everybody Says  Gr. 1, 289

Ezekiel Saw the Wheel  Gr. 6, 381

*Faerie Stories*  Gr. 8, B-5

Faith of the Heart  Gr. 8, G-5

Family Tree  Gr. 3, 75

Flip, Flop and Fly  Gr. 7, I-35

*Forever, for Now*  Gr. 7, B-17

Four Seasons, Concerto No. 2, The
Gr. 6, 103

Gakavik  Gr. 4, 17

Gamelan angklung  Gr. 6, 385

Goin' Down the Road Feelin' Bad
Gr. 5, 283

Going Up: High *do* and *ti*
Gr. 7, H-17

Going upon the Mountain
Gr. 6, 107

Guantanamera  Gr. 8, I-35

Hava nagila  Gr. 6, 155

Hevenu shalom aleichem
Gr. 3, 379

Hey, Hey, Look at Me  Gr. 1, 71

Hi Heidi Ho  Gr. 1, 395

*Higglety, Pigglety, Pop!*  Gr. K, 23

Hop Up, My Ladies  Gr. 3, 145

Hui jia qü  Gr. 2, 159

I Dream a World  Gr. 8, G-43

Ichi-gatsu tsuitachi  Gr. 7, I-43

Intervals - Seconds and Thirds
Gr. 7, H-25

It's a Beautiful Day  Gr. 3, 339

It's Santa—Again!  Gr. 2, 385

*Jazz in the Box*  Gr. 8, F-11

Joshua Fought the Battle
Gr. 5, 103

Kapulu kane  Gr. 2, 271

Kid Like Me, A  Gr. 2, 397

Kokoleoko  Gr. 5, 33

Kum ba yah  Gr. 5, 245

Kum bachur atzel  Gr. 3, 139

La golondrina  Gr. 8, I-53

Let's Get the Rhythm of the Band
Gr. 7, H-3

*Linus and Lucy*  Gr. 8, A-29

Lion Sleeps Tonight, The
Gr. 8, H-57

Listen to the Water  Gr. 2, 295

Little Shell  Gr. 1, 355

Live in the City  Gr. 5, 71

Lo yisa  Gr. 6, 131

Longer Sounds, Longer Rests
Gr. 7, H-3

Look Out for Mother Earth
Gr. 3, 341

Los maizales  Gr. 1, 296

The Major Scale  Gr. 8, H-17

Mariposita  Gr. 2, 157

Mississippi River Chant  Gr. 2, 133

More Composing with Sixteenth
Notes  Gr. 7, H-21

More Intervals - Fourths,
Fifths, Sixths, and Sevenths
Gr. 7, H-25

Move It: Sixteenth Notes
Gr. 7, H-19

Nampaya omame  Gr. 7, D-11

Nanny Goat  Gr. K, 161

Ner li  Gr. 2, 383

Never Smile at a Crocodile
Gr. 3, 101

New Hungarian Folk Song
Gr. 6, 197

Oh, Watch the Stars  Gr. 2, 145

Old Man Mosie  Gr. 3, 109

Old Mother Hubbard (rhyme)
Gr. 1, 119

On the Ning Nang Nong (poem)
Gr. 1, 395

Over in the Meadow  Gr. 1, 346

Oye  Gr. 6, 337

Pai pi qiu  Gr. 1, 325

Panamam tombé  Gr. 7, D-19

Pat Works on the Railway
Gr. 5, 183

Pay Me My Money Down
Gr. 7, I-49

Percussion Fun Rondo  Gr. 7, I-53

Primitive Fire, "Oya"  Gr. 2, 69

Pumpkin, Pumpkin  Gr. 1, 413

Rabbit Footprints  Gr. 2, 305

Rabbit Skip, The  Gr. 2, 305

Reading Chord Symbols
Gr. 7, H-27

Rhythm Basics  Gr. 7, H-3

Río, río  Gr. 5, 371

*Rocky Point Holiday*  Gr. 6, 331

Roll On, Columbia  Gr. 5, 117

Rondo for Lunch, A (speech piece)
Gr. 3, 213

Rosie, Darling Rosie  Gr. 2, 215

Run! Run! Hide!  Gr. 6, 343

*Rundadinella* Gr. 8, I-61
Sea Shell Gr. 2, 101
See-Saw Sacradown Gr. 2, 209
Sha Sha Sha (performance piece)
    Gr. 6, 329
Shenandoah Gr. 5, 265
Shir l'shalom Gr. 4, 421
Sing a Song! Gr. 7, A-11
Six-Inch Boots in a Nine-Inch
    Puddle Gr. 1, 367
Sixteenth Notes in the Rhythm
    Gr. 8, H-17
*Soulville* Gr. 7, B-17
Star-Spangled Banner Gr. 7, I-57
Syncopation Gr. 7, H-3
Table Manners Gr. 3, 191
*Take Five* Gr. 5, 221
*Tap Dance Concerto* Gr. 6, 321
Tender Shepherd (Count Your
    Sheep) Gr. 3, 117
There Is Love Somewhere
    Gr. 6, 319
There Was an Old Man (speech
    piece) Gr. 3, 191
This Is Your Night Gr. 6, 369
This Land is Your Land Gr. 7, F-25
Three Major Chords Gr. 7, H-27
To'ia mai te waka Gr. 1, 79
Trouble Is a Mountain Gr. 2, 203
Tumba Gr. 5, 161
Turn the Glasses Over Gr. 3, 205
Two Little Sausages (speech piece)
    Gr. 2, 79
Un pajarito Gr. 2, 17
Wabash Cannon Ball Gr. 5, 137
Wade in the Water Gr. 8, I-67
Waltzing with Bears Gr. 3, 173
We're Making Popcorn Gr. 1, 87
What Makes A Chord Major?
    Gr. 7, H-27
Wind Up the Apple Tree
    Gr. 1, 184
*Wipe Out* Gr. 7, F-33
Wu Long Gr. 4, 157
*Xochipilli, An Imagined Aztec
    Music* Gr. 8, C-37
Yankee Doodle Gr. 3, 415
Ye jaliya da Gr. 5, 67
Yibane amenu Gr. 4, 317
Yonder Come Day Gr. 8, I-71

## TRANSPARENCIES (LISTENING MAPS)

*12 Variations in C Major, K.
    265/300e, "Ah, vous dirai-je,
    Maman"* Gr. 3, 19
*A-Cling, A-Cling* Gr. 4, 191
*Acadian Songs, "Walking Song"*
    Gr. 4, 347
*Add-On Machine, The* Gr. K, 298
*Amores hallarás* Gr. 5, 153
*Arrival of the Queen of Sheba
    (Solomon), The* Gr. 2, 349

*Baby Elephant Walk* Gr. 2, 163
*Big Country, The* Gr. 2, 237
*Bumper Harvest Celebration*
    Gr. 4, 337
*Carnival of the Animals*, "Fossils"
    Gr. 1, 237
Children's Corner Suite, Jimbo's
    Lullaby Gr. 1, 273
*Choo-Choo Joubert* Gr. 3, 51
*Close Encounters of the Third
    Kind* Gr. 4, 235
*College Hornpipe* Gr. 4, 95
*Concerto for Marimba and
    String Orchestra, "Saudação"*
    Gr. 2, 119
*Concierto Madrigal for Two
    Guitars and Orchestra,
    "Fanfarre"* Gr. 2, 150
Cotton Boll Rag Gr. 5, 335
*Country Dance* Gr. 3, 213
Daybreak Vision Gr. 5, 399
*Dúlamán* Gr. 4, 299
*Edward Scissorhands, "Main
    Titles"* Gr. 8, A-10
*Evening Samba* Gr. 6, 297
Fanfare for the Common Man
    Gr. 7, C-43
Firebird, "Finale," The Gr. 8, C-31
*Firebird, The, "Infernal Dance"*
    Gr. 5, 173
*Flip, Flop and Fly* Gr. 7, F-15
Free Music #1 Gr. 2, 213
*Galbi* Gr. 1, 183
*Gavotte* Gr. 3, 89
Grizzly Bear Gr. K, 33
*Hungarian Dance No. 6* Gr. 4, 51
*Ionisation* Gr. 6, 357
*Jesu, Joy of Man's Desiring*
    Gr. 6, 87
L'Arlésienne Suite No. 2 Gr. 6, 69
*Le jig Français* Gr. K, 64
*Little Red Hen, The* Gr. 1, 257
*Little Train of the Caipira, The,
    No. 2* Gr. K, 25
Lullaby for Strings Gr. 1, 293
*Ma Vlast (My Fatherland), "Vltava
    (The Moldau)"* Gr. 7, C-33
*Magnificent Seven, The (from The
    Magnificent Seven)* Gr. 3, 145
Mass, "Responsory Alleluia"
    Gr. 6, 219
Masquerade Suite, "Gallop"
    Gr. 4, 16
*Nutcracker Suite, The, "Trepak"*
    Gr. 3, 281
*Nutcracker Suite, The, "Waltz of
    the Flowers"* Gr. 6, 325
Ode to Joy Gr. 4, 153
Open the Kingdom Gr. 6, 31
Orange Blossom Special
    Gr. 5, 269
*Orchestral Suite No. 3, BWV
    1068, "Air in D"* Gr. 4, 23

*Overture to "Candide"* Gr. 6, 219
*Pavane et Gaillarde* Gr. 2, 281
*Peer Gynt Suite No. 1, "Morning"*
    Gr. 1, 369
Pennsylvania 6-5000 Gr. 5, 343
*Phleng pradall* Gr. 1, 157
*Piano Sonata No. 8 in C Minor
    ("Pathéthique"), Movement 3,
    Rondo: Allegro* Gr. 4, 185
*Prelude in E Minor, Op. 28, No. 4*
    Gr. 3, 27
*Qiugaviit* Gr. 3, 259
*Requiem, "Pie Jesu"* Gr. 6, 178
*Requiem, "Pie Jesu"* Gr. 6, 179
*Rodeo, "Buckaroo Holiday"*
    Gr. 2, 23
Rodeo, Hoedown Gr. 5, 313
*Rodeo, "Saturday Night Waltz"*
    Gr. 4, 343
*Scherzo for Wind Quintet, Op. 48*
    Gr. 1, 329
*Shenandoah* Gr. 2, 63
Somewhere Out There Gr. 5, 369
*Sonata No. 11, K. 331, "Turkish
    Rondo"* Gr. K, 165
*Sounds of the Circus* Gr. K, 241
*Sous les étoiles* Gr. 2, 339
*Sumer Is Icumen In* Gr. 5, 35
Summertime Gr. 6, 253
*Tema de maimara* Gr. 1, 297
*Ten Easy Pieces, "Bear Dance"*
    Gr. 3, 173
*Thunder and Lightning Polka*
    Gr. 4, 213
*Toy Symphony, Movement 4*
    Gr. 1, 111
*Ujan mas* Gr. 2, 105
*Uma história de Ifá* Gr. 3, 311
Variations on "America" Gr. 6, 163
*Walkin' Blues* Gr. 5, 227
*Walkin' to New Orleans*
    Gr. 3, 371
*When Johnny Comes Marching
    Home* Gr. 5, 89
Ye jaliya da Gr. 5, 67

## VIDEO

Audience etiquette Gr. 8, E-13
Music teacher Gr. 8, A-27
Producer Gr. 8, A-25

## VIDEO LIBRARY

Arpeggio Meets the Brass Family
    Gr. 3, 189
Creating Music: Creating simple
    compositions Gr. 4, 373
Creating Music: Instrumental
    Ensemble (India) Gr. 6, 305
Creating Music: Rimsy–Korsakov:
    The Flight of the Bumblebee
    Gr. 1, 385
Dancing: Classical Dancers
    (Cambodia) Gr. 5, 461

**(*Technology/Media,* continued)**

Dancing: The Cape Fox Dancers
(Alaska) Gr. 4, 359

Dancing: The National Tap Dance
Company (Canada) Gr. 1, 133

Folk Dance: Background
Gr. 2, 245

Folk Dance: Circle dance (Russia)
Gr. 1, 259

Folk Dance: Turkish line dance
Gr. 4, 137

From Mao to Mozart: Isaac Stern in
China (excerpts) Gr. 2, 277

How We Make Music: "Blackbird"
(Bobby McFerrin) Gr. K, 201

How We Make Music: Hambone
Gr. K, 51

How We Make Music: Hambone
(using body percussion)
Gr. 7, D-3

How We Make Music: Sasa-Samoa
Gr. K, 51

How We Make Music: The Story
Gr. 1, 191

Jazz and Improvisation: Sweet
Home Chicago (Eagle Park Slim)
Gr. 5, 355

Keyboards: Marcus Roberts
Gr. 7, E-7

Music for Special Occasions:
Kwanzaa celebration Gr. 1, 431

Music for Special Occasions:
Kwanzaa celebration Gr. 2, 393

Music for Special Occasions:
Sousa: Stars and Stripes Forever
Gr. 1, 447

One Voice, Many Voices: Albert
McNeil Jubilee Singers
Gr. 3, 395

One Voice, Many Voices: "Great
Gettin' Up Morning" Gr. 3, 59

One Voice, Many Voices: "Great
Gettin' Up Morning" Gr. 5, 193

One Voice, Many Voices: "Last Old
Train's A-Leavin' " (Jean Ritchie)
Gr. 4, 349

One Voice, Many Voices: Ostinatos
Gr. 2, 183

One Voice, Many Voices: "Our
Melody" Gr. 3, 403

Percussion Instruments: Batukara–
samba (Brazil) Gr. 4, 401

Percussion Instruments: Bochinche–
Salsa from Latin America/United
States Gr. 3, 361

Percussion Instruments: Dou
Dou Rose Ensemble (Senegal)
Gr. 5, 309

Percussion Instruments: Gamelan
(Indonesia) Gr. 1, 197

Percussion Instruments: Samul Nori
Performers (Korea) Gr. 1, 197

Percussion Instruments: Tuned–
Marimba Ensemble (Zimbabwe)
Gr. 7, D-32

Percussion Instruments:
Tuned–Marimbas (Zimbabwe)
Gr. 8, D-17

Percussion Instruments: Tuned–
Steel Drums Gr. 6, 159

Percussion Instruments: Tuned–
Steel Drums Gr. 6, 301

Percussion Instruments: Tuned–
Steel drums (Trinidad and
Tobago) Gr. 3, 305

Percussion Instruments: Tuned–
Steel Drums (Trinidad and
Tobago) Gr. 7, D-23

Percussion Instruments: Tuned–
Warren Wolf from the United
States Gr. 3, 149

Performing in Groups Gr. 4, 195

Performing in Groups: Mallet
Percussion Ensemble (Canada)
Gr. 8, D-17

Performing in Groups: Turkey
Gr. 2, 143

Rhythm: Kodo (Japan) Gr. 7, D-16

Rhythm: "London Bridge"
Gr. 1, 49

Rhythm: Michael Noschen (juggler)
Gr. 2, 51

Rhythm: Rhythm: Michael Noschen
(juggler) Gr. 2, 197

Singing Games Gr. 1, 321

Singing Games: "Che Che Koolay"
(Ghana) Gr. 3, 307

Singing Games: Different countries
Gr. 2, 233

Singing Games: "Here Comes
Valerie" Gr. 2, 95

Singing Games: "Here Comes
Valerie" (United States)
Gr. 1, 33

Singing Games: "Here Comes
Valerie"(United States)
Gr. 3, 313

Singing Games: Juggling Game
(Japan) Gr. 3, 307

Singing Games: "La Víbora"
(Mexico) Gr. 3, 313

Singing Games: "La víbora"
(Mexico) Gr. 1, 323

Singing Styles Gr. 4, 33

Singing Styles Gr. 4, 143

Singing Styles: Bobby McFerrin
Gr. 6, 25

Singing Styles: Jazz and
Improvisation (Diane Schuur)
Gr. 5, 339

Singing Styles: Pam Tillis
Gr. 6, 249

Singing Styles: Second Edition
(Barbershop) Gr. 1, 47

Singing Styles: Shanghai School of
Music Gr. 3, 105

Singing Styles: Shanghai School of
Music Gr. 3, 277

Singing Styles: The King's Singers
Gr. 1, 253

Singing Styles: The King's Singers
Gr. 1, 389

Singing Styles: Total Experience
Gospel Choir Gr. 4, 269

Singing Styles: Total Experience
Gospel Choir Gr. 4, 9

Singing Styles: Total Experience
Gospel Choir Gr. 6, 55

Singing Styles: Total Experience
Gospel Choir Gr. 6, 395

Singing Styles: Whitney Houston
Gr. 6, 9

Singing Styles: Whitney Houston,
Bobby McFerrin, Pam Tillis, and
Total Experience Gospel Choir
Gr. 6, 61

Storytelling: "Sing a Whale Song"
Gr. 1, 339

Storytelling: "Sing a Whale Song"
Gr. 3, 353

Storytelling: The Nutcracker
Gr. 3, 281

Storytelling: "Trouble" Gr. 1, 141

String Instruments Gr. 4, 113

String Instruments: Bowed—erhu
and yangqin Gr. 5, 317

String Instruments: Bowed–Guarneri
Quartet Gr. 3, 113

String Instruments: Bowed—Kevin
and Joshua Moore Gr. 5, 347

String Instruments: Plucked–Banjo
and Acoustic Guitar Gr. 3, 107

String Instruments: Plucked –
Charango and Ensemble
Gr. 6, 49

String Instruments: Plucked –
Charango and Ensemble
Gr. 6, 58

String Instruments: Plucked –"Koto"
Gr. 3, 331

String Instruments: Plucked (Zheng)
Gr. 3, 105

Technology and Music: Using
MIDI in the Elementary Music
Classroom Gr. 6, 19

Unusual Sound Sources:
Metaphonics (sounds from the
junkyard) Gr. 1, 75

Unusual Sound Sources:
Metaphonics–sounds from the
Junkyard Gr. 8, D-33

Wind Instruments: Wood
Gr. 3, 185

Wind Instruments: Wood–
"Shakuhachi" Gr. 3, 331

## WEB SITE

1930s, Music of the  Gr. 5, 285
1930s, Music of the  Gr. 7, F-13
1950s, Music and performers of
    Gr. 7, F-31
1950s, Music and performing artists
    of the  Gr. 5, 359
1960s, Music and performers of
    Gr. 7, B-21
1960s, Music of the  Gr. 5, 363
African American music
    Gr. 7, B-29
African American music: blues and
    jazz  Gr. 5, 281
African American music: blues and
    jazz  Gr. 7, I-15
African American music: blues and
    jazz  Gr. 8, F-27
African American music: gospel and
    spirituals  Gr. 5, 259
African American music: gospel and
    spirituals  Gr. 7, I-15
African American music: gospel and
    spirituals  Gr. 7, I-39
African American music styles
    Gr. 7, C-43
African American music styles
    Gr. K, 37
African American spirituals
    Gr. 3, 77
African American spirituals
    Gr. 8, G-9
African drumming  Gr. 6, 279
African drumming and music
    ensembles  Gr. 4, 135
African music and instruments
    Gr. 4, 301
African percussion instruments
    Gr. 6, 293
Alvin and the Chipmunks
    Gr. 2, 387
American Civil War period, Music
    and songs of the  Gr. 5, 275
Appalachian music and instruments
    Gr. 1, 31
Appalachian music and instruments
    Gr. 5, 261
Appalachian music and instruments
    Gr. 6, 23
Appalachian music and instruments
    Gr. 8, I-31
Argentina, Music and composers of
    Gr. 5, 229
Argentina, music of  Gr. 8, D-25
Bach, Johann Sebastian
    Gr. 7, C-11
Backstage Careers  Gr. 8, A-23
Baroque instruments  Gr. 7, C-11
Bartók, Béla  Gr. 3, 113
Bartók, Béla  Gr. 4, 75
Bartók, Béla  Gr. 6, 197
Bartók, Béla  Gr. K, 97
Beatles, The  Gr. 6, 93

Beethoven, Ludwig van  Gr. 4, 365
Beethoven, Ludwig van  Gr. 6, 101
Beethoven, Ludwig van  Gr. 8, C-17
Belafonte, Harry  Gr. 4, 117
Bells  Gr. 4, 217
Bernstein, Leonard  Gr. 5, 9
Bernstein, Leonard  Gr. 6, 219
Big River and the Adventures of
    Huckleberry Finn  Gr. 4, 29
Bingo  Gr. 1, 171
Blue notes  Gr. 8, E-33
Blues, The development of
    Gr. 8, F-15
Bora Bora Boom Ensemble
    Gr. 8, D-3
Brahms, Johannes  Gr. 1, 209
Brahms, Johannes  Gr. 4, 171
Brazil, Music and instruments of
    Gr. 2, 355
Brazil, music of  Gr. 8, D-25
Broadway shows  Gr. 7, E-21
Burch, Sharon  Gr. 2, 323
California Gold Rush, Music of the
    Gr. 4, 245
California Gold Rush, Popular music
    of the  Gr. 5, 53
Caribbean and Latin pop
    performers  Gr. 7, E-13
Caribbean instruments  Gr. 3, 305
Caribbean music  Gr. 5, 135
Caribbean, Music and instruments
    of the  Gr. 6, 183
Caribbean music and musicians
    Gr. 4, 319
Caribbean music and musicians
    Gr. 5, 21
Caribbean music and musicians
    Gr. 7, B-35
Caribbean music styles  Gr. 3, 305
Chanukah, Chanukah  Gr. 1, 421
Chanukiyah li yesh  Gr. 1, 421
Chapin, Tom  Gr. 3, 74
China and Taiwan, Music of
    Gr. 5, 195
China and Taiwan, Music of
    Gr. 8, D-27
Chinese and Taiwanese music styles
    Gr. 3, 105
Chinese musical instruments
    Gr. 1, 91
Chopin, Frédéric  Gr. 3, 27
Chopin, Frédéric  Gr. 3, 317
Chopin, Frédéric  Gr. 7, C-22
Chopin, Frédéric  Gr. 7, C-23
Ciranda  Gr. 2, 273
Civil Rights Movement  Gr. 8, F-17
Civil Rights Movement, Songs of
    the  Gr. 3, 411
Civil Rights Movement, Songs of
    the  Gr. 4, 327
Civil Rights Movement, Songs of
    the  Gr. 5, 289

Civil War period, Music of
    Gr. 7, I-73
Conjunto jarocho, Mexican music
    Gr. 5, 131
Copland, Aaron  Gr. 3, 251
Copland, Aaron  Gr. 6, 199
Copland, Aaron  Gr. 7, C-43
Country music  Gr. 8, F-19
Country music  Gr. 8, I-31
Country music and jazz  Gr. 4, 279
Country music and musicians
    Gr. 5, 135
Country music and musicians
    Gr. 5, 351
Country music and musicians
    Gr. 7, B-29
Cuba, Music of  Gr. 7, D-9
Den III. Ende VI. Ronde & Branles
    Gr. 7, C-7
Dylan, Bob  Gr. 6, 195
El tambor  Gr. 2, 275
Estefan, Gloria  Gr. 5, 9
Finland, Music of  Gr. 6, 79
Fitzgerald, Ella  Gr. 2, 239
Flight of the Bumblebee
    Gr. 1, 385
Flowing Bowl, The  Gr. 8, B-29
Flutes around the world  Gr. 5, 113
Foster, Stephen  Gr. 4, 265
Gaelic music  Gr. 4, 393
Gaelic music of Scotland and Ireland
    Gr. 5, 141
Glennie, Evelyn  Gr. 2, 119
Glennie, Evelyn  Gr. 3, 151
Gospel music  Gr. 8, I-31
Grainger, Percy  Gr. 4, 75
Greg & Steve  Gr. K, 9
Guitars and guitar music  Gr. 7, F-3
Guitars and guitar music  Gr. 7, F-9
Guitars and guitar music
    Gr. 7, F-19
Guitars and guitar music  Gr. 8, F-3
Guthrie, Woody  Gr. 1, 275
Guthrie, Woody  Gr. 2, 367
Hawaiian dance, instruments, and
    music  Gr. 5, 443
Haydn, Franz Joseph  Gr. 1, 87
Haydn, Franz Joseph  Gr. 2, 85
Haydn, Franz Joseph  Gr. 7, C-15
Holiday music  Gr. 6, 465
Holst, Gustav  Gr. 1, 405
Holst, Gustav  Gr. 4, 377
Holst, Gustav  Gr. 5, 425
Honegger, Arthur  Gr. 2, 287
Hotaru koi  Gr. 1, 357
Hungary, music of  Gr. K, 97
India, Music and instruments of
    Gr. 6, 305
India, Music instruments of
    Gr. 5, 321
Instruments, Brass  Gr. 3, 189
Instruments, How they produce
    sound  Gr. 6, 367

(*Technology/Media,* continued)

Instruments, Mallet Gr. 3, 151
Instruments of the world Gr. 4, 315
Instruments, Slovakian Gr. 3, 79
Instruments, Woodwind Gr. 3, 23
Internet, Music on the Gr. 7, A-31
Israel and the Middle East, music of
   Gr. 4, 421
Israel, Historical facts on music of
   Gr. 6, 83
Israel, Music of Gr. 6, 411
Israeli folk music Gr. 5, 401
Jamaica, Music and instruments of
   Gr. 8, F-7
Jamaica, Music and instruments of
   Gr. K, 11
Jamaica, Music of Gr. 6, 143
Japan, Music and instruments of
   Gr. 8, D-27
Japanese Music Gr. 7, D-17
Javanese and Balinese gamelans
   Gr. 5, 319
Jazz and blues Gr. 7, B-29
Jewish music Gr. 5, 465
John Lomax and folk music
   Gr. 8, C-35
Jug bands and skiffle music
   Gr. 2, 315
Jug bands and skiffle music
   Gr. 6, 361
Jug bands and skiffle music
   Gr. 8, D-29
Jug bands and skiffle music
   Gr. 8, I-31
Key, Francis Scott Gr. 4, 441
Khorovod Gr. 1, 375
King, B. B. Gr. 2, 329
King, B. B. Gr. 7, B-9
Latin America and the Middle East,
   Music and folk instruments of
   Gr. 5, 297
Latin America, Folk instruments
   from Gr. 4, 307
Latin American instruments
   Gr. 3, 41
Latin American instruments
   Gr. 3, 297
Latin American instruments
   Gr. 3, 363
Latin American instruments
   Gr. 5, 481
Latin American music styles
   Gr. 3, 297
Latin American music styles
   Gr. 3, 363
Latin dance styles Gr. 6, 335
Latin Pop: music, dance styles, and
   performers Gr. 7, B-33
Latin pop performers Gr. 6, 267
Leadbelly and other blues guitarists
   Gr. 7, F-23
Liszt, Franz Gr. K, 97
Lomax, John Gr. 4, 107

Lullaby songs and paintings
   Gr. K, 181
Ma, Yo-Yo Gr. 3, 39
Ma, Yo-Yo Gr. 7, C-11
Ma, Yo-Yo Gr. 7, C-45
Machine music Gr. 7, B-45
Machine music Gr. K, 83
Make a music e-zine Gr. 7, A-32
Maori and Hawaiian cultures
   Gr. 8, D-5
Maori culture Gr. 3, 273
Maori music and dances Gr. 1, 79
Maori music styles Gr. 3, 273
Maraire, Dumisani Gr. 2, 299
Marching bands and band
   instruments Gr. 1, 167
Mariachi songs and instruments
   Gr. 6, 145
Marimba Gr. 8, D-17
Marsalis Family, The Gr. 4, 75
McFerrin, Bobby Gr. 3, 39
Medieval and Renaissance music
   Gr. 7, C-5
Mexican music Gr. 8, I-17
Mexico, Music of Gr. 4, 275
Mexico, Music of Gr. 5, 287
Middle Eastern music Gr. 5, 107
Middle Eastern music Gr. 6, 309
Migration Gr. 7, G-41
Minimalism Gr. 7, C-45
Minimalism in music and painting
   Gr. 6, 31
Movies, Music for the Gr. 5, 377
Mozart, Leopold Gr. 1, 111
Music recording media Gr. 7, A-19
Musical styles Gr. 4, 329
Musical styles and genres
   Gr. 2, 293
*Na rechenki* Gr. 1, 375
Native American dance Gr. 3, 254
Native American dance Gr. 7, D-25
Native American music Gr. 4, 285
Native American music Gr. 5, 463
Native American music Gr. 7, D-25
Native American music and
   instruments Gr. 6, 287
Native American music styles
   Gr. 3, 215
Native American music styles
   Gr. 3, 335
Native American musical
   instruments Gr. 7, D-25
Native American musical
   instruments Gr. 8, D-21
Native American songs Gr. 8, D-21
Niño querido Gr. 1, 309
*O tocius Asie gloria, "Oh, Glory of
   All Asia"* Gr. 8, C-4
Opera performances Gr. 7, C-31
Patriotic songs, History of
   Gr. 5, 489
Percussion instruments Gr. 1, 117

Percussion instruments from around
   the world Gr. 5, 157
Percussion instruments from around
   the world Gr. 8, D-13
Peru, Music of Gr. 8, D-25
Peruvian music and instruments
   Gr. 2, 375
Pipe organs and their history
   Gr. 7, E-25
Pop music, 1950s and 1960s
   Gr. 8, E-25
*Prelude in B-flat Minor, Op. 28,
   No. 16* Gr. 7, C-22
Primitive Fire, "Oya" Gr. 2, 69
Prokofiev, Sergei and other Russian
   composers Gr. 6, 457
*Pulcinella Suite, "Minuetto"*
   Gr. 8, C-15
Recorder and its history, The
   Gr. 6, 373
Reggae music Gr. 4, 321
Renaissance music Gr. 5, 439
Renaissance music Gr. 7, C-7
Ríu chíu chíu Gr. 5, 438
Rock 'n' Roll Gr. 2, 255
Rock 'n' Roll Gr. 3, 371
Rock 'n' Roll, 1960s Gr. 3, 373
Rock 'n' Roll, 1960s Gr. 7, B-29
Rock 'n' Roll, The history of
   Gr. 7, E-23
Rodgers and Hammerstein
   Gr. 5, 39
Rossini, Gioacchino Gr. 1, 131
Same Train Gr. 2, 165
Sawatdee tuh jah Gr. 2, 265
*Scherzo for Wind Quintet, Op. 48*
   Gr. 1, 329
Schuman, William Gr. 6, 83
Schumann, Clara and Robert
   Gr. 3, 203
Schumann, Clara and Robert
   Gr. 7, C-21
Schumann, Robert Gr. 1, 159
Schumann, Robert Gr. 8, D-17
Scientific discoveries and the
   impact on keyboard instruments
   Gr. 7, E-19
Scotland, Music of Gr. 6, 43
Sea shanties and seafaring songs
   Gr. 5, 231
*Sensemaya* Gr. 8, C-15
Shankar, Ravi and Anoushka
   Gr. 4, 311
Shanties and other work songs
   Gr. 4, 257
Shanties and other work songs
   Gr. 4, 13
Shenandoah, Joanne Gr. 2, 197
*Shepherd's Hey Sampler*
   Gr. 7, C-37
Shostakovich, Dmitri and other
   Russian composers Gr. 6, 443
*Simple Gifts* Gr. 8, A-17

Sir Barks-A-Lot  Gr. 1, 171
*Slow Hora/Freylekhs*  Gr. 8, B-25
Smith, Samuel Francis  Gr. 4, 441
*Soldier's Joy*  Gr. 8, B-29
*Song for Bells, A*  Gr. 1, 429
Sousa, John Philip  Gr. 4, 159
Sousa, John Philip  Gr. 5, 79
Spain, Music of  Gr. 2, 345
Spain, Music of  Gr. K, 131
Spanish music and dance
    Gr. 7, E-15
Spirituals and gospel music
    Gr. 4, 163
Spirituals and gospel music
    Gr. 8, E-19
String instruments  Gr. 4, 65
String instruments and composers
    Gr. 4, 113
String instruments from around the
    world  Gr. 5, 199
*Take the "A" Train*  Gr. 8, C-42
Tchaikovsky, Piotr Ilyich  Gr. 3, 281
Tchaikovsky, Piotr Ilyich  Gr. 4, 295
Tejano and zydeco music
    Gr. 8, E-21
Thailand, music of  Gr. 6, 451
Usagi  Gr. 1, 397
*Vocal Olympics*  Gr. 8, B-15
Webber, Andrew Lloyd  Gr. 6, 179
West African drumming and vocal
    styles  Gr. 5, 33
West African drumming and vocal
    styles  Gr. 6, 231
West African drumming and vocal
    styles  Gr. 7, D-15
West African drumming and vocal
    styles  Gr. 7, D-29
West African Drumming and Vocal
    Styles  Gr. 7, D-14
West African drumming and vocal
    styles  Gr. 8, D-9
Westward movement, Songs of the
    Gr. 4, 339
Westward movement, Songs of the
    Gr. 5, 263
When the Saints Go Marching In
    Gr. 2, 179
*World instrument families*
    Gr. 8, B-9
Xylophone  Gr. 8, D-17
*You're a Grand Old Flag*  Gr. 1,
    276
Zoltán, Kodály  Gr. K, 97
Zydeco music  Gr. 8, I-49
Zydeco music and instruments
    Gr. 1, 21

## TEXTURE/HARMONY

### ACCOMPANIMENT/NO
### ACCOMPANIMENT
*5 Stücke im Volkston, Op. 102,
    No. 1, "Mit Humor"*  Gr. 3, 39
All for One  Gr. 7, E-8

America  Gr. 7, I-2
America  Gr. 8, I-2
America  Gr. K, 326
America, the Beautiful  Gr. 6, 485
*Arkansas Traveler/Angeline the
    Baker*  Gr. K, 114
*Bembe de Plena*  Gr. 8, D-18
*Brandenburg Concerto No. 2,
    Movement 3 Allegro Assai*
    Gr. 7, C-8
Bundle-Buggy Boogie Woogie
    Gr. 4, 120
*Circle of Life (from The Lion
    King), The*  Gr. 6, 316
Dance for the Nations  Gr. 6, 122
*Diamonds and Rust*  Gr. 7, A-4
*Die forelle*  Gr. 7, C-20
Do Wah Diddy Diddy  Gr. 4, 203
Don't Be Cruel  Gr. 6, 255
Dry Bones  Gr. 4, 162
Earth Is My Mother, The  Gr. 1, 340
Earth Is Our Mother, The
    Gr. 8, F-25
El carnavalito humahuaqueño
    Gr. 6, 482
El payo  Gr. 6, 145
Ev'ry Kind of Music  Gr. 2, 226
Ev'rybody Loves Saturday Night
    Gr. 7, I-24
Ezekiel Saw the Wheel  Gr. 6, 379
Faith of the Heart  Gr. 8, G-3
Farewell to Tarwathie  Gr. 6, 43
Frog Music  Gr. 4, 200
Give a Little Love  Gr. 6, 140
*Give Us Hope*  Gr. 6, 337
Gloria, Gloria  Gr. 6, 459
*Gloria In Excelsis*  Gr. 6, 210
*Go Down, Moses*  Gr. 7, G-10
Good King Wenceslas  Gr. 6, 460
Hava nashira  Gr. 6, 82
He's Got the Whole World in His
    Hands  Gr. 3, 230
Head, Shoulders, Baby  Gr. 1, 82
Hej pada pada  Gr. 3, 78
Hush Up the Baby  Gr. K, 222
I Bought Me a Cat  Gr. 2, 308
I Dream a World  Gr. 8, G-40
I Have a Dog  Gr. K, 262
I Shall Sing  Gr. 8, I-38
*If These Walls Could Speak*
    Gr. 7, B-41
Ise oluwa  Gr. 6, 230
Ja-Da  Gr. 7, G-20
*Jarabe tapatio*  Gr. 7, I-7
*John Henry*  Gr. 8, C-34
Joshua Fought the Battle of Jericho
    Gr. 8, E-18
Joy of Kwanzaa, The  Gr. 6, 462
*Kayagum pyongch'ang-sae t'aryug*
    Gr. 8, B-13
Keel Row, The  Gr. 4, 240
Kelo aba w'ye  Gr. 6, 290
Kou ri lengay  Gr. 7, E-2

Kunolounkwa  Gr. K, 110
*L'union*  Gr. 6, 487
Las mañanitas  Gr. 6, 481
Let the Music Begin!  Gr. 1, 2
*Lion Sleeps Tonight, The*
    Gr. 8, E-8
Little Darlin'  Gr. 7, F-30
*Little Red Caboose*  Gr. K, 228
*Lo, How a Rose E'er Blooming*
    Gr. 6, 210
Loigratong  Gr. 6, 451
Los maizales  Gr. 1, 296
Má Teodora  Gr. 6, 301
Make New Friends  Gr. 3, 36
Mama Don't 'Low  Gr. 6, 358
Mary Ann  Gr. 6, 180
*Messiah, "Hallelujah!"*  Gr. 8, C-8
*Mi tierra*  Gr. 6, 365
*Musette*  Gr. 3, 39
Nana Kru  Gr. 6, 282
O lê lê O Bahía  Gr. 6, 165
*Open the Kingdom*  Gr. 6, 31
Paths of Victory  Gr. 6, 195
*Penny Lane*  Gr. 6, 257
Rhythm Is Gonna Get You, The
    Gr. 6, 348
'Round the Bay of Mexico
    Gr. 4, 258
S'vivon  Gr. 6, 452
*San Miguel Jolonicapan*
    Gr. 8, D-16
Simple Gifts  Gr. 8, A-17
Sing a Little Song  Gr. K, 30
*Songs from Letters, "So Like Your
    Father"*  Gr. 7, C-21
Stand By Me  Gr. 8, E-25
Star-Spangled Banner, The
    Gr. 7, I-56
Stopping by Woods on a Snowy
    Evening  Gr. 6, 41
*Suite No. 3 in C Major for
    Unaccompanied Cello,
    "Bourrée 1"*  Gr. 3, 38
Sun, The  Gr. K, 143
Sweet Potatoes  Gr. 3, 228
*That'll Be the Day*  Gr. 6, 256
Those Magic Changes  Gr. 8, E-30
Tom Dooley  Gr. 6, 374
*Tommy Peoples*  Gr. 8, B-20
*Two Dances for Three
    Xylophones, "Hornpipe and
    Jig"*  Gr. 8, D-17
Vamos a la mar  Gr. 3, 226
Vem kan segla?  Gr. 6, 417
Wai bamba  Gr. 6, 26
*Widmung, Op. 25, No. 1*
    Gr. 7, C-20
*Wilder Reiter*  Gr. 8, D-17
Worried Man Blues  Gr. 6, 370
*Would?*  Gr. 8, F-30
*Yemaya*  Gr. 8, G-24
*You Sang to Me*  Gr. 6, 335
*Zoila*  Gr. 8, D-18

(*Texture/Harmony,* continued)

**2-part**
God Bless the U.S.A.
Gr. 8, G-37

**ANTIPHONAL**
*Canzon in Echo Duodecimi Toni a
10* Gr. 8, C-7

## BORDUNS
Abiyoyo Gr. 2, 108
Adana ya gidelim Gr. 2, 142
*Alasdair mhic cholla ghasda*
Gr. 8, B-44
Andy Pandy Gr. K, 46
*Bambodansarna* Gr. 8, B-20
Busy Buzzy Bee Gr. K, 77
Circle Round the Zero Gr. K, 293
Every Morning When I Wake Up
Gr. 2, 320
*Kargiraa-style Song* Gr. 8, B-15
Kou ri lengay Gr. 2, 217
Little Spider Gr. K, 93
*Moment So Close, A* Gr. 8, B-40
My Pony, Macaroni Gr. 1, 158
Nanny Goat Gr. K, 161
Noah's Shanty Gr. 1, 342
On a Log, Mister Frog Gr. K, 148
Rain Sings a Song, The Gr. 1, 102
Roll Over Gr. K, 288
Rosie, Darling Rosie Gr. 2, 215
Uga uga uga Gr. K, 305
Waiting for the Traffic Light
Gr. 2, 107

## CANONS AND ROUNDS
A Ram Sam Sam Gr. 3, 208
Adiós, amigos Gr. 6, 57
Ah, Poor Bird Gr. 4, 196
Alleluia Gr. 6, 133
Autumn Canon Gr. 5, 148
*Canon No. 110 in G* Gr. 6, 133
Chairs to Mend Gr. 4, 149
Computer, The Gr. 4, 199
Continents, The Gr. 4, 357
Da pacem, Domine Gr. 5, 62
Dance for the Nations Gr. 6, 122
Do, Re, Mi, Fa Gr. 6, 80
Ego sum pauper Gr. 5, 158
Frog Music Gr. 4, 200
Gloria, Gloria Gr. 6, 459
Good Morning Gr. 3, 192
Hava nashira Gr. 6, 82
Hey, Ho! Nobody Home Gr. 6, 28
Himmel und Erde Gr. 5, 94
Knock No More Gr. 3, 386
Kookaburra Gr. 4, 186
Kyrie Gr. 6, 206
Let Music Surround You Gr. 4, 236
Let Us Sing Together Gr. 6, 156
Like a Bird Gr. 6, 167
Los niños en España cantan
Gr. 4, 197
Make New Friends Gr. 3, 36

Morning Is Come Gr. 3, 128
*Musical Offering, BWV 1079, No.
11, "Canon a 4"* Gr. 3, 193
O Music Gr. 5, 162
Oh, How Lovely Is the Evening
Gr. 4, 217
Old Abram Brown Gr. 5, 222
Peace Round Gr. 4, 348
Riddle Ree (speech piece) Gr. 2, 34
Scattin' A-Round (Variations on
Row 3) Gr. 6, 160
Small Job, A Gr. 3, 224
*Sumer Is Icumen In* Gr. 5, 35
Table Manners (speech piece)
Gr. 3, 190
Ten Little Ostinato Pieces
Gr. 7, I-62
Tender Shepherd (Count Your
Sheep) Gr. 3, 116
There Was an Old Man (speech
piece) Gr. 3, 191
This Pretty Planet Gr. 4, 355
Tumba Gr. 5, 161
*Viva la musica* Gr. 5, 95
Yibane amenu Gr. 4, 316

## CHORD CHANGES
**I**
Kou ri lengay Gr. 7, E-2
**I-IV**
All for One Gr. 7, E-8
Cumberland Gap Gr. 4, 138
Do Wah Diddy Diddy Gr. 4, 203
Do Wah Diddy Diddy
Gr. 7, F-21
Imbabura Gr. 5, 203
Kookaburra Gr. 4, 186
Oh, How Lovely Is the Evening
Gr. 4, 217
Old House, Tear It Down!
Gr. 4, 178
**i-iv₇**
See the Children Playin'
Gr. 4, 107
**I-IV-I-V**
Surfin' U.S.A. Gr. 7, E-27
**I-IV-I-V₇-I**
Birthday Gr. 6, 90
*Boogie Woogie* Gr. 6, 93
**I-IV-V₇**
12-Bar Blues Gr. 7, F-14
Abraham, Martin, and John
Gr. 6, 466
Al quebrar la piñata Gr. 4, 432
Ala Da'lona Gr. 4, 136
All Night, All Day Gr. 4, 180
Amazing Grace Gr. 4, 160
At the Hop Gr. 4, 168
¡Ay, Jalisco no te rajes!
Gr. 7, I-6
Banuwa Gr. 6, 294

Big Rock Candy Mountain
Gr. 4, 330
Bye Bye, Love Gr. 8, F-9
Certainly, Lord Gr. 7, I-13
Cielito lindo Gr. 4, 270
Cindy Gr. 4, 384
Cotton-Eye Joe Gr. 4, 288
Cuando pa' Chile me voy
Gr. 6, 376
De colores Gr. 8, I-14
Dry Bones Come Skipping
Gr. 4, 218
Earth Is Our Mother, The
Gr. 8, F-25
El borrego Gr. 4, 242
El payo Gr. 6, 145
El rancho grande Gr. 4, 215
El rancho grande Gr. 8, I-22
Ev'rybody Loves Saturday Night
Gr. 7, I-24
Every Night When the Sun Goes
In Gr. 8, I-28
Feliz Navidad Gr. 7, I-28
Flip, Flop and Fly Gr. 7, I-32
Flip, Flop and Fly Gr. 7, E-32
For the Beauty of the Earth
Gr. 4, 356
Four Strong Winds (Song to a
Seagull) Gr. 6, 170
Give a Little Love Gr. 6, 140
Goin' Down the Road Feelin'
Bad Gr. 7, F-13
Habemos llegado Gr. 6, 174
Happy Wanderer, The Gr. 4, 89
*Hard Way* Gr. 7, E-33
*I Know You Mardi Gras*
Gr. 8, B-17
I Love Peanuts Gr. 7, E-20
I'll Fly Away Gr. 8, I-42
I'm on My Way Gr. 7, A-15
Joshua Fought the Battle of
Jericho Gr. 8, E-18
Karangatia ra Gr. 8, F-23
Keel Row, The Gr. 4, 240
La raspa Gr. 4, 302
Las mañanitas Gr. 6, 481
Lean on Me Gr. 7, E-22
Linstead Market Gr. 5, 241
Lion Sleeps Tonight, The
Gr. 4, 131
Lion Sleeps Tonight, The
Gr. 8, I-56
*Lion Sleeps Tonight, The*
Gr. 8, E-8
Little David, Play on Your Harp
Gr. 4, 394
Loigratong Gr. 6, 451
Love Will Guide Us Gr. 4, 328
Lullaby and Dance Gr. 4, 387
Mama Don't 'Low Gr. 6, 358
Midnight Special, The
Gr. 7, F-23
Missy-La, Massa-La Gr. 4, 188

O lê lê O Bahía  Gr. 6, 165
Oh, Susanna  Gr. 4, 264
Orange Blossom Special
    Gr. 8, E-6
Rio Grande  Gr. 4, 256
Riqui rán  Gr. 4, 66
Rock Around the Clock
    Gr. 7, B-18
Santa Clara  Gr. 4, 172
Sourwood Mountain  Gr. 4, 65
Streets of Laredo  Gr. 4, 272
*Sun Gonna Shine*  Gr. 7, F-14
This Land Is Your Land
    Gr. 7, I-66
Thula, thula, ngoana  Gr. 4, 227
Tina singu  Gr. 4, 300
*Twist and Shout*  Gr. 4, 238
Vive l'amour  Gr. 6, 176
Walk in Jerusalem  Gr. 4, 100
Weevily Wheat  Gr. 4, 105
Wings of a Dove  Gr. 4, 318
Winter Fantasy  Gr. 4, 424
*Yakety Yak*  Gr. 5, 204
Yakety Yak  Gr. 5, 205
Yellow Rose of Texas, The
    Gr. 7, I-70

**I-IV-V₇-VI-I**
Three Little Birds  Gr. 8, F-7

**i-v**
Keep Your Eyes on the Prize
    Gr. 8, E-16

**I-V₇**
Bard of Armagh, The
    Gr. 4, 296
Cantando mentiras  Gr. 4, 146
Checki, morena  Gr. 7, F-11
Cheki, morena  Gr. 7, I-16
Clementine  Gr. 4, 341
Computer, The  Gr. 4, 199
Corrido de Kansas  Gr. 4, 274
Dayenu  Gr. 4, 439
Deep in the Heart of Texas
    Gr. 8, I-18
Down in the Valley  Gr. 6, 375
Dry Bones  Gr. 4, 162
El mes de abril  Gr. 3, 328
Frog Music  Gr. 4, 200
Glendy Burke, The  Gr. 4, 262
God Bless the Grass  Gr. 8, F-13
Goodbye, Julie  Gr. 8, E-2
He's Got the Whole World in His
    Hands  Gr. 7, I-36
I'm Gonna Sing  Gr. 4, 33
Jambalaya  Gr. 8, I-46
*Jarabe tapatío*  Gr. 7, I-7
Mañana  Gr. 7, E-14
Mango Walk  Gr. 5, 200
Mary Ann  Gr. 6, 180
My Home's Across the Blue
    Ridge Mountains  Gr. 4, 84
My Home's Across the Blue
    Ridge Mountains  Gr. 7, F-6

Old Chisholm Trail, The
    Gr. 6, 237
Over My Head  Gr. 4, 118
Paw-Paw Patch  Gr. 4, 93
Pay Me My Money Down
    Gr. 4, 38
Pay Me My Money Down
    Gr. 7, I-46
Pay Me My Money Down
    Gr. 7, F-5
Seagull, Seagull, Sit on the Shore
    Gr. 4, 383
Singin' in the Rain  Gr. 4, 360
Son macaron  Gr. 4, 109
Sweet Potatoes  Gr. 3, 228
Tancovačka  Gr. 4, 230
Tengo, tengo, tengo  Gr. 4, 228
Tom Dooley  Gr. 6, 374
Vamos a la mar  Gr. 3, 226
Wheel of the Water, The
    Gr. 4, 362
Yonder Come Day  Gr. 8, I-68

**I-V₇-I**
Good Mornin', Blues  Gr. 5, 224

**i-V₇**
Beriozka  Gr. 4, 294
La Tarara  Gr. 4, 176
Ocho kandelikas  Gr. 4, 429

**I-vi-IV-V₇-I**
America  Gr. 8, I-2
Little Darlin'  Gr. 7, F-30
Stand By Me  Gr. 8, E-25
*Stand By Me*  Gr. 8, E-24
Those Magic Changes
    Gr. 8, E-30
We Go Together  Gr. 4, 44

## DESCANTS AND COUNTERMELODIES
Abraham, Martin, and John
    Gr. 6, 466
Ain't Gonna Let Nobody Turn Me
    'Round  Gr. 6, 85
Alexander's Ragtime Band
    Gr. 6, 136
Amazing Grace  Gr. 4, 160
America, the Beautiful  Gr. 4, 158
America, the Beautiful  Gr. 7, I-4
Angels On the Midnight Clear
    Gr. 6, 423
Ash Grove, The  Gr. 5, 114
Battle Hymn of the Republic
    Gr. 5, 274
Blue Skies  Gr. 6, 88
Bogando a la luz del sol  Gr. 4, 306
Bridges  Gr. 6, 86
Cindy  Gr. 4, 384
Cycle Song of Life (The River Song)
    Gr. 4, 370
Ding Dong! Merrily on High
    Gr. 6, 427
Do, Re, Mi, Fa  Gr. 6, 80

Eres tú  Gr. 6, 473
*Every Night When the Sun Goes
    In*  Gr. 8, I-29
Farewell to Tarwathie  Gr. 6, 43
Four Strong Winds (Song to a
    Seagull)  Gr. 6, 170
Gift to Share, A  Gr. 6, 393
Going Upon the Mountain
    Gr. 6, 105
Gospel Train, The  Gr. 6, 398
I Am But a Small Voice  Gr. 6, 446
I Walk the Unfrequented Road
    Gr. 6, 79
Ja-Da  Gr. 7, G-20
Lean on Me  Gr. 6, 14
Like a Bird  Gr. 6, 167
Love in Any Language  Gr. 6, 476
Oh, Freedom  Gr. 7, G-30
Pat Works on the Railway
    Gr. 5, 182
Pay Me My Money Down
    Gr. 7, I-46
Roll On, Columbia  Gr. 5, 116
Sakura  Gr. 4, 308
Somos el barco  Gr. 4, 352
*Stars and Stripes Forever, The*
    Gr. 4, 159
Stille Nacht (Silent Night)
    Gr. 7, I-54
*Symphony No. 1, Movement 3*
    Gr. 4, 237
This Land Is Your Land  Gr. 5, 118
*This Land Is Your Land*
    Gr. 5, 120
This Land Is Your Land  Gr. 7, I-66
Vem kan segla?  Gr. 6, 417
Water Is Wide, The  Gr. 6, 228
Winter Song  Gr. 6, 455

## ECHO SONGS
Every Night When the Sun Goes In
    Gr. 8, I-28
*Every Night When the Sun Goes
    In*  Gr. 8, I-29
I'd Like To Teach the World to Sing
    (In Perfect Harmony)  Gr. 3, 198
I'm on My Way  Gr. 3, 76
Ja-Da  Gr. 7, G-20
*Jarabe tapatío*  Gr. 7, I-7
Old Texas  Gr. 3, 77
Over My Head  Gr. 7, G-9
Siyahamba  Gr. 6, 212

## LIMITED-CHORD SONGS
Ah, Poor Bird  Gr. 4, 196
Bard of Armagh, The  Gr. 4, 296
Beriozka  Gr. 4, 294
Canción de cuna  Gr. 4, 144
Cantando mentiras  Gr. 4, 146
Chairs to Mend  Gr. 4, 149
Clementine  Gr. 4, 341
Computer, The  Gr. 4, 199
Corrido de Kansas  Gr. 4, 274

**(Texture/Harmony, continued)**

Cuando pa' Chile me voy
Gr. 6, 376

Cumberland Gap  Gr. 4, 138

Dayenu  Gr. 4, 439

Deep in the Heart of Texas
Gr. 8, I-18

Down in the Valley  Gr. 6, 375

Down the Ohio  Gr. 2, 60

Every Night When the Sun Goes In
Gr. 8, I-28

*Every Night When the Sun Goes
In*  Gr. 8, I-29

Fiddler on the Roof  Gr. 7, E-5

Four Strong Winds (Song to a
Seagull)  Gr. 6, 170

Frog Music  Gr. 4, 200

Glendy Burke, The  Gr. 4, 262

Good Mornin', Blues  Gr. 2, 52

Habemos llegado  Gr. 6, 174

Ida Red  Gr. 3, 30

Imbabura  Gr. 5, 203

Joshua Fought the Battle of Jericho
Gr. 8, E-18

Keep Your Eyes on the Prize
Gr. 8, E-16

Kookaburra  Gr. 4, 186

Kou ri lengay  Gr. 7, E-2

La Tarara  Gr. 4, 176

Las mañanitas  Gr. 6, 481

Let Music Surround You  Gr. 4, 236

Lion Sleeps Tonight, The
Gr. 8, I-56

Loigratong  Gr. 6, 451

Los niños en España cantan
Gr. 4, 197

Man of Constant Sorrow
Gr. 7, F-28

Mango Walk  Gr. 5, 200

Mary Ann  Gr. 6, 180

Mon papa  Gr. 2, 280

Mr. Tambourine Man  Gr. 6, 150

Ochimbo  Gr. 4, 134

Ocho kandelikas  Gr. 4, 429

Oh, How Lovely Is the Evening
Gr. 4, 217

Old Chisholm Trail, The  Gr. 6, 237

Old House, Tear It Down!
Gr. 4, 178

Pay Me My Money Down
Gr. 7, I-46

Peace Round  Gr. 4, 348

Seagull, Seagull, Sit on the Shore
Gr. 4, 383

Shortnin' Bread  Gr. 7, F-27

Singin' in the Rain  Gr. 4, 360

St. Louis Blues  Gr. 5, 352

T'hola, t'hola  Gr. 4, 132

Tancovačka  Gr. 4, 230

Tengo, tengo, tengo  Gr. 4, 228

*This Is Your Night*  Gr. 6, 368

Three Little Birds  Gr. 8, F-7

Vive l'amour  Gr. 6, 176

Wheel of the Water, The
Gr. 4, 362

Yakety Yak  Gr. 5, 205

Yibane amenu  Gr. 4, 316

Yonder Come Day  Gr. 8, I-68

## OSTINATOS, MELODY  *See also
Rhythm: Ostinatos, Rhythm.*

*Evening Chaconne*  Gr. 6, 202

Ten Little Ostinato Pieces
Gr. 7, I-62

Yüe liang wan wan  Gr. 5, 315

Zum gali gali  Gr. 5, 401

**instrumental**

Adiós, amigos  Gr. 6, 57

Ah, Poor Bird  Gr. 4, 196

Artsa alinu  Gr. 3, 285

Canoe Song  Gr. 4, 76

Chicka Hanka  Gr. 2, 211

Deau-deau, ti pitit maman
Gr. 2, 306

Ding, Dong, Diggidiggidong
Gr. 3, 14

Do Wah Diddy Diddy  Gr. 4, 203

Éliza Kongo  Gr. 5, 14

Every Morning When I Wake Up
Gr. 2, 320

Farewell to Tarwathie  Gr. 6, 43

Farmer's Dairy Key, The
Gr. 2, 182

Feng yang hua gu  Gr. 4, 313

Follow the Drinkin' Gourd
Gr. 4, 266

Funwa alafia  Gr. 5, 32

Ha'kyo jong  Gr. 2, 135

Hey, Ho! Nobody Home
Gr. 6, 28

Hey, m'tswala  Gr. 4, 79

Honeybee Song, The  Gr. 1, 358

I Love the Mountains  Gr. 5, 34

Jasmine Flowers  Gr. 5, 316

Knock No More  Gr. 3, 386

La mariposa  Gr. 6, 58

La paloma blanca  Gr. 3, 252

Morning Is Come  Gr. 3, 128

Niu lang zhi nü  Gr. 4, 335

Noah's Shanty  Gr. 1, 342

*Nruab hnub thiab hmo ntuj*
Gr. 4, 368

Oh, Watch the Stars  Gr. 2, 144

*Open the Kingdom*  Gr. 6, 31

Peace Round  Gr. 4, 348

Plant Four Seeds  Gr. 2, 130

See the Children Playin'
Gr. 4, 107

See-Saw Sacradown  Gr. 2, 208

Small Job, A  Gr. 3, 224

Spring Has Sprung!  Gr. K, 142

*Symphony No. 1, Movement 3*
Gr. 4, 237

Tanabata-sama  Gr. 2, 336

Tender Shepherd (Count Your
Sheep)  Gr. 3, 116

Tina singu  Gr. 4, 300

*Twist and Shout*  Gr. 4, 238

Waiting for the Traffic Light
Gr. 2, 107

Walk Together, Children
Gr. 3, 146

What Do Animals Need?
Gr. 2, 288

Whether It's Cold (proverb)
Gr. 2, 118

Yellow Rose of Texas, The
Gr. 7, I-70

Yibane amenu  Gr. 4, 316

**vocal**

Ah, Poor Bird  Gr. 4, 196

Canoe Song  Gr. 4, 76

*Circlesong 7*  Gr. 4, 80

Gospel Train, The  Gr. 6, 398

Had to Get Up This Mornin'
Soon  Gr. 3, 114

Hey, Ho! Nobody Home
Gr. 6, 28

I Love the Mountains  Gr. 5, 34

Johnny Caught a Flea
Gr. 1, 226

Little David, Play on Your Harp
Gr. 4, 394

Merry Modal Christmas, A
Gr. 4, 411

Oh, How Lovely Is the Evening
Gr. 4, 217

Old Man Mosie  Gr. 3, 108

*Open the Kingdom*  Gr. 6, 31

Scattin' A-Round (Variations on
Row 3)  Gr. 6, 160

*Sumer Is Icumen In*  Gr. 5, 35

Take a Chance On Me
Gr. 8, G-15

## PARALLEL MOTION IN THIRDS
## AND SIXTHS

Abraham, Martin, and John
Gr. 6, 466

Adelita  Gr. 5, 50

Ain't Gonna Let Nobody Turn Me
'Round  Gr. 6, 85

America, the Beautiful  Gr. 8, I-4

Así es mi tierra  Gr. 6, 172

*Bembe de Plena*  Gr. 8, D-18

Birthday  Gr. 6, 90

By the Waters of Babylon
Gr. 6, 311

Camptown Races  Gr. 5, 270

Canción Mixteca  Gr. 5, 326

Cantaré, cantarás  Gr. 6, 413

Day-O! (Banana Boat Loader's
Song)  Gr. 5, 18

De colores  Gr. 8, I-14

Don Alfonso  Gr. 5, 177

Elegua  Gr. 7, D-8

Ezekiel Saw the Wheel  Gr. 6, 379

Friends Today  Gr. 7, D-12

*Good Vibrations*  Gr. 8, E-28

Guantanamera  Gr. 8, I-32
Habemos llegado  Gr. 6, 174
Ise oluwa  Gr. 6, 230
La golondrina  Gr. 8, I-50
La paloma se fué  Gr. 6, 51
Las copetonas  Gr. 7, B-33
Las mañanitas  Gr. 6, 481
Lean on Me  Gr. 6, 14
Loch Lomond  Gr. 5, 140
Los reyes de Oriente  Gr. 8, I-58
Luna hermosa  Gr. 8, I-13
Má Teodora  Gr. 6, 301
Mahk jchi  Gr. 7, D-25
Mary Ann  Gr. 6, 180
Nutcracker Suite, The, "Trepak"
    Gr. 6, 207
Oy, Hanuka  Gr. 7, I-44
Pay Me My Money Down
    Gr. 7, I-46
Requiem, "Pie Jesu"  Gr. 6, 178
Siyahamba  Gr. 6, 212
Surfin' U.S.A.  Gr. 7, E-27
Vive l'amour  Gr. 6, 176
Water Come a Me Eye  Gr. 6, 300
Water Is Wide, The  Gr. 6, 228
Yellow Rose of Texas, The
    Gr. 7, I-70

## PART SONGS

### 2-part

Abraham, Martin, and John
    Gr. 6, 466
Alexander's Ragtime Band
    Gr. 6, 136
Amazing Grace  Gr. 4, 160
America  Gr. 7, I-2
America, the Beautiful
    Gr. 4, 158
America, the Beautiful  Gr. 7, I-4
America, the Free  Gr. 4, 210
Ash Grove, The  Gr. 5, 114
Así es mi tierra  Gr. 6, 172
Bantama kra kro  Gr. 5, 308
Bogando a la luz del sol
    Gr. 4, 306
Book of Love  Gr. 8, G-27
Canción Mixteca  Gr. 5, 326
Cantaré, cantarás  Gr. 6, 413
Canto del agua  Gr. 8, I-10
Changed My Name  Gr. 6, 338
Circle 'Round the Moon
    Gr. 4, 403
Come, Ye Thankful People,
    Come  Gr. 5, 459
Con el vito  Gr. 7, G-15
Cycle Song of Life (The River
    Song)  Gr. 4, 370
De colores  Gr. 8, I-14
Deck the Hall  Gr. 5, 474
Ding Dong! Merrily on High
    Gr. 6, 427
Don Alfonso  Gr. 5, 177
Don Giovanni  Gr. 8, C-13

Down by the Riverside
    Gr. 8, G-8
Earth Is Our Mother, The
    Gr. 4, 358
Earth Is Our Mother, The
    Gr. 8, F-25
Ego sum pauper  Gr. 5, 158
Einini  Gr. 4, 391
Éliza Kongo  Gr. 5, 14
Ev'ry Time I Feel the Spirit
    Gr. 5, 242
Ezekiel Saw the Wheel
    Gr. 6, 379
Feliz Navidad  Gr. 7, I-28
For Children Safe and Strong
    Gr. 5, 484
Four Strong Winds (Song to a
    Seagull)  Gr. 6, 170
Free at Last  Gr. 6, 468
Gift to Share, A  Gr. 6, 393
He's Got the Whole World in His
    Hands  Gr. 7, I-36
Heri za Kwanzaa  Gr. 5, 476
I Am But a Small Voice
    Gr. 6, 446
I Shall Sing  Gr. 8, I-38
I Vow to You, My Country
    Gr. 5, 418
I'll Fly Away  Gr. 8, I-42
I'm on My Way  Gr. 7, A-15
Ise oluwa  Gr. 6, 230
Jarabe tapatio  Gr. 7, I-7
Kelo aba w'ye  Gr. 6, 290
L'Arlésienne Suite No. 2,
    "Farandole"  Gr. 6, 68
La paloma se fué  Gr. 6, 51
Land of a Thousand Dances
    Gr. 5, 330
Las mañanitas  Gr. 6, 481
Lean on Me  Gr. 6, 14
Light Up the World with a Song
    Gr. 8, G-25
Loch Lomond  Gr. 5, 140
Los reyes de Oriente  Gr. 5, 480
Love in Any Language
    Gr. 6, 476
Lullaby and Dance  Gr. 4, 387
Mary Ann  Gr. 6, 180
Merry Modal Christmas, A
    Gr. 4, 411
Now's the Time  Gr. 5, 445
On My Way  Gr. 6, 313
Ōsamu kosamu  Gr. 4, 96
Over My Head  Gr. 4, 118
Over My Head  Gr. 7, G-9
Oy, Hanuka  Gr. 7, I-44
Pay Me My Money Down
    Gr. 7, I-46
Peace Like a River  Gr. 6, 190
Peace Round  Gr. 4, 348
Requiem, "Pie Jesu"  Gr. 6, 178
Río, río  Gr. 5, 370
Roll On, Columbia  Gr. 5, 116

Sail Away  Gr. 5, 404
Scattin' A-Round (Variations on
    Row 3)  Gr. 6, 160
Seagull, Seagull, Sit on the Shore
    Gr. 4, 383
Sing a Song of Peace  Gr. 6, 66
Sing, Sing, Sing!  Gr. 5, 340
Sometimes I Feel Like a
    Motherless Child  Gr. 6, 241
Star-Spangled Banner, The
    Gr. 5, 488
Star-Spangled Banner, The
    Gr. 6, 486
Star-Spangled Banner, The
    Gr. 8, I-62
Stille Nacht (Silent Night)
    Gr. 7, I-54
Sweet Betsy from Pike
    Gr. 4, 244
Take a Chance On Me
    Gr. 8, G-15
This Land Is Your Land
    Gr. 5, 118
This Land Is Your Land
    Gr. 7, I-66
This Little Light of Mine
    Gr. 6, 232
Tina singu  Gr. 4, 300
Uno, dos y tres  Gr. 5, 429
Vive l'amour  Gr. 6, 176
Water Is Wide, The  Gr. 6, 228
Winter Fantasy  Gr. 4, 424
Winter Song  Gr. 6, 455
Yellow Rose of Texas, The
    Gr. 7, I-70
You Are My Sunshine
    Gr. 6, 246
You Were on My Mind
    Gr. 7, G-23

### 3-part

Alleluia  Gr. 6, 133
Banuwa  Gr. 6, 294
Blues with a Feeling  Gr. 8, I-6
California Dreamin'  Gr. 8, G-31
Certainly, Lord  Gr. 7, I-13
Chairs to Mend  Gr. 4, 149
Changed My Name  Gr. 6, 338
Chapel of Love  Gr. 7, G-27
Cindy  Gr. 4, 384
Ding Dong! Merrily on High
    Gr. 6, 427
Fais do do  Gr. 6, 403
Flip, Flop and Fly  Gr. 7, I-32
Free at Last  Gr. 6, 468
Gloria, Gloria  Gr. 6, 459
Gospel Train, The  Gr. 6, 398
How Much Wood Could a
    Woodchuck Chuck (speech
    piece)  Gr. 3, 120
I Dream a World  Gr. 8, G-40
I Wish I Knew How It Would Feel
    to Be Free  Gr. 6, 470

(*Texture/Harmony*, continued)

I'm a Believer Gr. 7, G-33
Ise oluwa Gr. 6, 230
Ja-Da Gr. 7, G-20
Joy of Kwanzaa, The Gr. 6, 462
Just a Snap-Happy Blues
   Gr. 6, 388
Kum ba yah Gr. 5, 244
Kyrie Gr. 6, 206
Lion Sleeps Tonight, The
   Gr. 8, I-56
Little David, Play on Your Harp
   Gr. 4, 394
O Music Gr. 5, 162
Oh, Freedom Gr. 7, G-30
Oh, How Lovely Is the Evening
   Gr. 4, 217
Run! Run! Hide! Gr. 6, 340
Shake the Papaya Down
   Gr. 4, 378
Si si si Gr. 7, G-13
Siyahamba Gr. 6, 212
Something Told the Wild Geese
   Gr. 7, G-39
Surfin' U.S.A. Gr. 7, I-58
Take Time in Life Gr. 6, 292
This Little Light of Mine
   Gr. 6, 232
This Pretty Planet Gr. 4, 355
Turn the World Around
   Gr. 4, 114
Tuxedo Junction Gr. 8, G-21
Vem kan segla? Gr. 6, 417
Wai bamba Gr. 6, 26
Wai bamba Gr. 8, G-13
Wheel of the Water, The
   Gr. 4, 362
Winter Gr. 8, G-11
Yemaya Gr. 8, G-24
Yonder Come Day Gr. 8, I-68
You Were on My Mind
   Gr. 7, G-25

**4-part**

Certainly, Lord Gr. 7, I-13
Let Music Surround You
   Gr. 4, 236
One Family Gr. 7, G-17

## PARTNER SONGS

America, the Beautiful Gr. 5, 76
Each of Us Is a Flower Gr. 3, 154
Home on the Range Gr. 5, 69
Let Freedom Ring Gr. 5, 77
Live in the City Gr. 5, 71
Michael Finnigan Gr. 3, 153
Play a Simple Melody Gr. 5, 72
Sambalele Gr. 4, 397
Seagull, Seagull, Sit on the Shore
   Gr. 4, 383
Sing a Song of Peace Gr. 6, 66
This Old Man Gr. 3, 152
Turn the World Around Gr. 4, 114
Winter Fantasy Gr. 4, 424

## THIN AND THICK TEXTURE

Abiyoyo Gr. 2, 108
Adana ya gidelim Gr. 2, 142
Aguinaldo Gr. 3, 402
Ah, eu entrei na roda Gr. 3, 308
Ah, Poor Bird Gr. 4, 196
*Ahi! Amours* Gr. 8, C-4
*Altered Landscapes: Part One*
   Gr. 8, E-21
*Amazing Grace* Gr. 4, 160
*Amazing Grace* Gr. 4, 161
America, the Beautiful Gr. 4, 158
America, the Beautiful Gr. 5, 76
*Apu Min'Tan* Gr. 8, D-21
*Así es mi tierra* Gr. 6, 172
Banuwa Gr. 6, 294
*Be Still, My Child* Gr. 1, 39
*Bird* Gr. 1, 39
*Bomba te traigo yo* Gr. 8, B-3
*Bombay Dreams* Gr. 8, B-35
*Boogie Down* Gr. 8, G-29
*Brandenburg Concerto No. 2,*
   *Movement 3 Allegro Assai*
   Gr. 7, C-8
Bundle-Buggy Boogie Woogie
   (speech piece) Gr. 4, 120
*Cafe Europa* Gr. 7, B-43
*Capoeira Na Vila* Gr. 8, D-25
*Carol of the Bells* Gr. 8, G-10
*Close Encounters of the Third*
   *Kind* Gr. 8, B-34
*Concert for Piano and Orchestra*
   Gr. 6, 209
*Eine kleine Nachtmusik* Gr. 4, 41
*El payo* Gr. 6, 145
*Evening Chaconne* Gr. 6, 202
*Evening Samba* Gr. 6, 297
*Fanfare for Freedom* Gr. 6, 139
*Firebird, The, "Finale"* Gr. 8, C-30
*Gloria In Excelsis* Gr. 6, 210
Good Morning Gr. 3, 192
Habemos llegado Gr. 6, 174
Hej pada pada Gr. 3, 78
Hey, m'tswala Gr. 4, 79
*Huagu ge, "Flower Drum song"*
   Gr. 8, D-27
I Love the Mountains Gr. 5, 34
*Istanbul Coffee House (Kefe neio)*
   Gr. 8, B-34
*Jug Band Music* Gr. 6, 361
*Kitchen Stomp* Gr. 4, 122
Knock No More Gr. 3, 386
Kunolounkwa Gr. K, 110
Kyrie Gr. 6, 206
*Le tombeau de Couperin,*
   *"Prelude"* Gr. 8, C-28
*Les Rêves de Columbine, Op. 65,*
   *"Sous les étoiles"* Gr. 2, 338
Let Freedom Ring Gr. 5, 77
Let Music Surround You Gr. 4, 236
*Lluvia* Gr. 6, 332
Los maizales Gr. 1, 296

Los niños en España cantan
   Gr. 4, 197
Los pollitos Gr. K, 166
*Ma Vlast (My Fatherland), "Vltava*
   *(The Moldau)"* Gr. 7, C-33
*Mars Suite, "Orbital View,"*
   *Movement 1* Gr. 4, 199
*Mass, "Responsory Alleluia"*
   Gr. 6, 217
*Moment So Close, A* Gr. 8, B-40
*My Girl Josephine* Gr. 8, E-21
Nana Kru Gr. 6, 282
*Nanafushi* Gr. 7, D-16
*Night in Tunisia, A* Gr. 4, 35
*Nights in the Gardens of Spain,*
   *"En el generalife"* Gr. 2, 145
*Nyamphemphe* Gr. 8, B-3
Oklahoma Gr. 5, 36
Oliver Twist Gr. K, 138
*Ombrose e care selve* Gr. 8, C-5
*On Fire Suite* Gr. 8, B-36
One Family Gr. 7, G-17
*Open the Kingdom* Gr. 6, 31
Overture to "Candide" Gr. 6, 218
Pay Me My Money Down Gr. 4, 38
Peace Like a River Gr. 6, 190
*Phleng pradall* Gr. 1, 157
*Piano Trio in G Minor, Op. 17,*
   *Allegro* Gr. 8, C-19
Play a Simple Melody Gr. 5, 72
*Primitive Fire, "Oya"* Gr. 2, 68
*Reggae Is Now* Gr. 6, 143
*Riddle Ree* (speech piece) Gr. 2, 34
*Rose, "from the Motion Picture*
   *Titanic"* Gr. 8, B-34
*Sai da Frente* Gr. 8, D-24
Scrub Brush Shuffle, The
   Gr. 1, 118
*Simple Song (from Mass), A*
   Gr. 8, C-45
*Sing We and Chant It* Gr. 8, C-5
*Somebody* Gr. 4, 41
Sonando Gr. 4, 34
*Stars and Stripes Forever, The*
   Gr. 4, 159
Stille Nacht (Silent Night)
   Gr. 7, I-54
*Sumer Is Icumen In* Gr. 5, 35
*Talaque talaque o romance da*
   *Maria* Gr. 8, D-24
Tanabata-sama Gr. 2, 336
*Tema de maimara* Gr. 1, 297
Ten Little Ostinato Pieces
   Gr. 7, I-62
*This Is Your Night* Gr. 6, 368
Tie Me Kangaroo Down, Sport
   Gr. 4, 37
Turn the World Around Gr. 4, 114
*Uma história de Ifá* Gr. 3, 311
*Violin Concerto in E Minor, Op.*
   *64, Movement 1* Gr. 8, C-18
Vive l'amour Gr. 6, 176
Wai bamba Gr. 6, 26

*Wai bamba*  Gr. 8, G-13
*Watermelon Man*  Gr. 6, 270
Wheel of the Water, The
  Gr. 4, 362
Winter  Gr. 8, G-11
Winter Song  Gr. 6, 455
*You Sang to Me*  Gr. 6, 335
*Zomo the Rabbit*  Gr. 3, 364

## UNISON
America  Gr. 8, I-2
Book of Love  Gr. 8, G-27
*Capoeira Na Vila*  Gr. 8, D-25
*Faith of the Heart*  Gr. 8, G-3
*Mahk jchi*  Gr. 7, D-25
*Nanafushi*  Gr. 7, D-16
Proud  Gr. 7, G-3
*Sai da Frente*  Gr. 8, D-24
Take a Chance On Me  Gr. 8, G-15
*Talaque talaque o romance da
  Maria*  Gr. 8, D-24
You Were on My Mind  Gr. 7, G-23

## TIMBRE
Sound Bank  Gr. K, 328
Sound Bank  Gr. 1, 468
Sound Bank  Gr. 2, 420
Sound Bank  Gr. 3, 434
Sound Bank  Gr. 4, 466
Sound Bank  Gr. 5, 514
Sound Bank  Gr. 6, 512

## BODY PERCUSSION
*Bombé/Ruht wohl, ruht wohl, ihr
  heiligen Gebeine, BWV 245*
  Gr. 8, B-39
Bonga  Gr. K, 78
Bump! Bump! Bump!  Gr. K, 53
*Cauyaqa Nauwa? (Where's My
  Drum?)*  Gr. 8, D-20
*Circlesong Five*  Gr. 1, 239
Down, Down, Baby  Gr. 2, 32
Downpour  Gr. K, 51
Hinges  Gr. K, 52
Orchestra  Gr. 1, 74
Pon, pon, pon  Gr. K, 50
Ten Tom-Toms  Gr. K, 79

## ENVIRONMENTAL SOUNDS
*3 + 2*  Gr. 2, 316
Big Old Storm a-Comin'
  Gr. K, 257
*Bird Calls, Bird Songs*  Gr. K, 178
*Birdcall—Cuckoo*  Gr. 1, 110
*Birdcall—Loon*  Gr. 1, 110
*Birdcall—Mockingbird*  Gr. 1, 110
*Bombay Dreams*  Gr. 8, B-35
Breaks Free  Gr. 2, 319
Cacophony  Gr. K, 83
*Cow Barn Cha Cha*  Gr. 8, D-33
*Cuculí*  Gr. K, 238
Down the Listening Lane
  Gr. K, 192
Farmer in the Dell, The  Gr. K, 232
*Fingerprints*  Gr. 7, B-42

*Fire Brigade Water the Road*
  Gr. 7, D-22
*Is the Sound High or Low?*
  Gr. K, 17
*Istanbul Coffee House (Kafe neio)*
  Gr. 8, B-34
*Jug Band Music*  Gr. 6, 361
*Junk Music Montage*  Gr. 1, 73
Just from the Kitchen  Gr. K, 55
Keys  Gr. K, 188
*Kitchen Stomp*  Gr. 4, 122
*Little Red Caboose*  Gr. K, 228
*Llactamanta*  Gr. 6, 382
*Louds and Softs of the Seasons*
  Gr. K, 4
*Machine Music*  Gr. K, 82
Marbles (poem)  Gr. 1, 75
Noah's Shanty  Gr. 1, 342
*Noah's Zoo in the Big, Big Rain*
  Gr. K, 274
*One Frog, Two Frogs, Three
  Frogs... Sing!*  Gr. K, 182
¡Qué llueva!  Gr. K, 81
*Reuben's Train*  Gr. 1, 334
*Rippa Medley, The, "Block-Block,
  One Leg Up, Let the Beat Go,
  Uh-Oh"*  Gr. 8, D-32
*Rods and Cones*  Gr. 7, D-5
Sailing to the Sea  Gr. 1, 336
Scrub-a-dub  Gr. 1, 306
*Sha Sha Sha (performance piece)*
  Gr. 6, 328
*Sinfonia Antarctica, "Epilogue"*
  Gr. 2, 326
Six Little Ducks  Gr. K, 234
Song of the Train  Gr. K, 153
Storm Dance (speech piece)
  Gr. K, 145
Tap It! Rap It! (speech piece)
  Gr. K, 194
Things That Sing  Gr. K, 87
*Trash Can Stomp (from Stomp
  Out Loud)*  Gr. 6, 328
*Udu Pot*  Gr. 8, D-4
*Whale of a Tale, A*  Gr. K, 272
*Wildlife*  Gr. 1, 345

## INSTRUMENTAL
*Battle of New Orleans, The*
  Gr. 6, 105
*Corta la caña*  Gr. 6, 364
*Cowboys' Christmas Ball*
  Gr. 6, 238
Don't Be Cruel  Gr. 6, 255
*Drums of the Iroquois and Sioux*
  Gr. 6, 285
*Hotter Than That*  Gr. 6, 65
*Jambalaya*  Gr. 6, 245
*L'Arlésienne Suite No. 2,
  "Farandole"*  Gr. 6, 68
*Old Chisholm Trail, The*
  Gr. 6, 236
Old Chisholm Trail, The  Gr. 6, 237

*Si tú no estás*  Gr. 6, 267
*That'll Be the Day*  Gr. 6, 256
What a Wonderful World  Gr. 6, 62
*What a Wonderful World*
  Gr. 6, 63

## aerophones (wind instruments)
*1812 Overture*  Gr. 4, 293
*A mi querido Austin*
  Gr. 8, B-24
*Abbots Bromley Horn Dance*
  Gr. 7, C-24
*Acadian Songs, "Walking
  Song"*  Gr. 4, 347
*Aida, "Gloria all'Egitto (Grand
  March)"*  Gr. 8, C-24
*Alasdair mhic cholla ghasda*
  Gr. 8, B-44
Alexander's Ragtime Band
  Gr. 6, 136
*Altered Landscapes: Part One*
  Gr. 8, E-21
*Avaz-e dashti*  Gr. 8, B-42
*B. B.'s Blues*  Gr. 4, 70
*Bard of Armagh, The*
  Gr. 4, 296
*Bee, The*  Gr. 4, 70
*Beggar's Opera, The, "Constant
  Billy"*  Gr. 7, C-24
*Bembe de Plena*  Gr. 8, D-18
*Billie*  Gr. 8, B-23
*Birds in the Forest*  Gr. 4, 315
*Bombay Dreams*  Gr. 8, B-35
*Boogie Woogie*  Gr. 1, 256
*Brandenburg Concerto No. 2,
  Movement 3 Allegro Assai*
  Gr. 7, C-8
*Brandenburg Concerto No.
  4, BWV 1049, Allegro*
  Gr. 5, 111
*Brass Rap*  Gr. 3, 189
*Brolga One*  Gr. 4, 36
*California Counterpoint:
  The Twittering Machine*
  Gr. 8, C-47
*Canzoni et Sonate, "Canzoni
  prima a 5"*  Gr. 4, 193
*Caravan*  Gr. 7, B-31
*Carnival of the Animals,
  "Aviary"*  Gr. 4, 70
*Carrament News*  Gr. 8, B-22
Cheki, morena  Gr. 2, 180
*China Gates*  Gr. 7, C-45
*Close Encounters of the Third
  Kind*  Gr. 8, B-34
*Concerto for Flute and Harp
  in C, K. 299, Movement 2*
  Gr. 8, C-10
*Concerto for French Horn in
  E-flat Major, K. 495, No. 4,
  Movement 3*  Gr. 8, C-11

(*Timbre,* continued)

Concerto for Orchestra,
    "Presentation of Pairs"
    Gr. 4, 72
Concerto for Trumpet and
    Orchestra in E-flat Major,
    Rondo: Allegro Molto
    Gr. 1, 256
Concerto for Two Trumpets in
    C Major, Rv. 537, Movement
    1, "Allegro" Gr. 4, 75
Concerto for Viola and
    Orchestra, Movement 3
    Gr. 7, C-35
Concerto in E-flat for Horn and
    Orchestra, K. 417, "Rondo"
    Gr. 4, 71
Concierto Madrigal for Two
    Guitars and Orchestra,
    "Fanfare" Gr. 2, 150
Crazy Blues Gr. 7, B-8
Crowley's Reel Gr. 4, 297
Dances of Galanta Gr. 7, C-34
Danses Populaires Francaises,
    "Branle Double, Branle
    Simple" Gr. 7, C-25
Dharpa, "Tree" Gr. 8, B-38
Eh, cumpari! Gr. 4, 68
El mariachi Gr. 4, 303
El nuevo caiman Gr. 8, B-17
Estancia, "Danza del trigo"
    Gr. 5, 229
Fanfare for Freedom
    Gr. 6, 139
Fanfare for the Common Man
    Gr. 7, C-43
Fantasy for Chanukah
    Gr. 1, 421
Flight of the Bumblebee
    Gr. 3, 189
Flowing Bowl, The Gr. 8, B-29
Fourth of July, The Gr. 5, 489
Galliard battaglia Gr. 6, 362
Galliard Battaglia Gr. 8, C-14
Gamelan angklung Gr. 6, 384
Gapu Gr. 8, B-38
Glory Hallelujah Grand March
    Gr. 8, C-38
How Can I Keep from Singing?
    Gr. 4, 260
I Know You Mardi Gras
    Gr. 8, B-17
Ichi-gatsu tsuitachi Gr. 3, 406
In the Mood Gr. 6, 110
Intermezzo, "Háry János
    Suite," Movement 5
    Gr. 7, C-34
Jarabe tapatio Gr. 7, I-7
Knozz-Moe-King Gr. 4, 75
La mariposa Gr. 6, 58
La mer, "Jeux de vagues"
    Gr. 7, C-39
La Peri, "Fanfare" Gr. 4, 71

Le tombeau de Couperin,
    "Prelude" Gr. 8, C-28
Legend of Kokopelli, The
    Gr. 5, 110
Let's Dance Gr. 1, 256
Lincolnshire Posy, "Lord
    Melbourne" Gr. 4, 74
Little Birdie Gr. 4, 75
"Little" Organ Fugue in G
    Minor (brass) Gr. 6, 129
"Little" Organ Fugue in G
    Minor (organ) Gr. 6, 129
Little Red Hen, The Gr. 1, 254
Little Shepherd, The
    Gr. 1, 256
Love You Forever Gr. 8, B-23
Lullaby Gr. 3, 188
Ma Vlast (My Fatherland),
    "Vltava (The Moldau)"
    Gr. 7, C-33
MacAllistrum's March-Mairseail
    Alasdroim Gr. 4, 297
Malagueña Gr. 5, 154
Marines' Hymn, The
    Gr. 8, C-39
Mea haarit Gr. 3, 274
Messiah, "Hallelujah!"
    Gr. 8, C-8
Mi humilde corazón
    Gr. 7, B-32
Mi tierra Gr. 6, 365
Mido Mountain Gr. 8, B-42
My Girl Josephine Gr. 8, E-21
Night in Tunisia, A Gr. 4, 35
Niu lang zhi nü Gr. 4, 335
Olympic Spirit Gr. 6, 350
One Fine Day Gr. 6, 347
Partita in A Minor, "Sarabande"
    Gr. 3, 185
Peak Moments Gr. 8, E-4
Pennsylvania 6-5000
    Gr. 5, 342
Peshte longuita Gr. 1, 217
Phleng pradall Gr. 1, 157
Piano Concerto in A Minor, Op.
    16, Movement 1 Gr. 8, E-11
Piano Concerto in E-Flat Major,
    Op. 73, No. 5, "Emperor,"
    Movement 3 Gr. 7, C-18
Picadillo Gr. 3, 361
Planets, The, Op. 32, "Jupiter"
    Gr. 1, 405
Prelude to the Afternoon of a
    Faun Gr. 5, 113
Pulcinella Suite, "Minuetto"
    Gr. 8, C-15
Pulcinella Suite, "Serenata"
    Gr. 4, 70
Pulcinella Suite Gr. 4, 71
Quartet for Oboe, Clarinet,
    Flute, and Bassoon, "Allegro
    molto" Gr. 4, 70

Queen's Suite, The, "Sunset
    and the Mocking Bird"
    Gr. 8, E-10
Quiet City Gr. 8, E-29
Rhapsody in Blue Gr. 7, C-42
Rocky Point Holiday
    Gr. 6, 331
Rodeo, "Hoedown" Gr. 8, B-45
Rose (from the Motion Picture
    Titanic) Gr. 8, B-34
Rwakanembe Gr. 8, C-14
Scherzo for Wind Quintet, Op.
    48 Gr. 1, 328
Sensemaya Gr. 8, C-15
Sextet for Winds and Piano,
    Movement 1 Gr. 8, C-29
Shepherd's Hey, No. 2
    Gr. 7, C-37
Shepherd's Hey, No. 3
    Gr. 7, C-37
Shika no Tone Gr. 5, 112
Six Metamorphoses After
    Ovid, Op. 49, "Bacchus"
    Gr. 7, C-13
Slow Hora/Freylekhs
    Gr. 8, B-25
Soldier's Joy Gr. 8, B-29
Sonata for Clarinet and Piano,
    Op. 167, "Allegro animato,"
    Movement 2 Gr. 7, C-12
Sonata for Violin and Piano,
    Allegro Gr. 8, C-46
Sonata in A Minor, "Allegro"
    Gr. 7, C-12
Sonata in F Minor for Bassoon,
    Vivace Gr. 4, 70
Sonata in G Minor, Op. 1, No.
    1, Movement 2 Gr. 7, C-12
Sonata Seconda Gr. 3, 431
Sonatina for Bassoon and
    Piano, "Allegro con moto,"
    Movement 1 Gr. 7, C-13
Songs from Letters, "So Like
    Your Father" Gr. 7, C-21
Sound Waves Montage
    Gr. 6, 354
Soundings, "Fanfare"
    Gr. 8, C-47
Sube Gr. 7, B-31
Suite for Wind Quintet,
    Movement 1 Gr. 8, C-34
Suite in F, Op. 28b, No. 2,
    "Fantasia on the Dargason,"
    Movement 4 Gr. 7, C-36
Suite No. 2 in F, Op. 28b,
    Movement 1, "March"
    Gr. 6, 139
Summertime Gr. 6, 252
Sweet Georgia Brown Gr. 4, 71
Symphony No. 40 in G Minor,
    K. 550, Movement 1
    Gr. 8, B-30

*Symphony No. 5 in C Minor, Op. 67, Movement 1* Gr. 7, C-16
*Symphony No. 5 in C Minor, Op. 67, Movement 4* Gr. 7, C-18
*Syrinx* Gr. 5, 113
*Take the "A" Train* Gr. 8, C-42
*Thunder and Lightning Polka* Gr. 4, 213
*Variations on "The Carnival of Venice"* Gr. 6, 161
*Vaya Puente* Gr. 2, 181
*Violin Concerto in E Minor, Op. 64, Movement 1* Gr. 8, C-18
*Viva Jujuy* Gr. 8, B-22
*Walkin' to New Orleans* Gr. 3, 371
*Washington Post, The* Gr. 8, C-40
*Water Music, "Allegro Maestoso"* Gr. 3, 189
*Well-Tempered Clavier, The, "Be-Bop Bach: Prelude No. 2"* Gr. 7, C-11
When the Saints Go Marching In Gr. 2, 178
*When the Saints Go Marching In* Gr. 2, 179
*Whirlwind* Gr. 3, 149
*Wings* Gr. 7, C-45
*Winter Birds Flying over the Water* Gr. 1, 91
*Wioste Olowan Inkpa Ta-Ya* Gr. 3, 255
*World Music Montage* Gr. 3, 266
Worried Man Blues Gr. 6, 371
*Xiao* Gr. 4, 314
*Xochipilli, An Imagined Aztec Music* Gr. 8, C-37
*Yamaji* Gr. 3, 407

**chordophones (strings and keyboards)**
*1812 Overture* Gr. 4, 293
*5 Stücke im Volkston, Op. 102, No. 1, "Mit Humor"* Gr. 3, 39
*A-Cling, A-Cling* Gr. 4, 190
*Abbots Bromley Horn Dance* Gr. 7, C-24
*Acadian Songs, "Walking Song"* Gr. 4, 347
*Aerial Boundaries* Gr. 8, F-20
*Akua Tuta* Gr. 7, D-24
*Ala Da'lona* Gr. 4, 137
*Alasdair mhic cholla ghasda* Gr. 8, B-44
*Angry Anymore* Gr. 8, F-32
*Avaz-e dashti* Gr. 8, B-42
*Awa ewe iwoyi* Gr. 8, D-9
*Badenma* Gr. 8, B-28

*Bairagi* Gr. 8, A-19
*Bambodansarna* Gr. 8, B-20
*Banjo* Gr. 5, 198
*Bard of Armagh, The* Gr. 4, 296
*Beggar's Opera, The, "Constant Billy"* Gr. 7, C-24
*Bembe de Plena* Gr. 8, D-18
*Billie* Gr. 8, B-23
*Birds in the Forest* Gr. 4, 315
*Bomba te traigo yo* Gr. 8, B-3
*Boston Ball Game 1967* Gr. 8, F-32
*Brandenburg Concerto No. 2, Movement 3 Allegro Assai* Gr. 7, C-8
*Bye Bye, Love* Gr. 8, A-15
*(Can't Live Without Your) Love and Affection* Gr. 7, B-23
*Canon for Violin and Cello* Gr. 6, 126
*Caprice Basque, Op. 24* Gr. 1, 256
*Caprice No. 1 in E Major* Gr. 7, C-22
*Caravan* Gr. 7, B-31
*Carnaval llanero* Gr. 4, 307
*Carolina Sunday Waltz* Gr. 7, F-9
*Carrament News* Gr. 8, B-22
*Catalana, "Andante"* Gr. K, 134
*Cedar Swamp* Gr. 5, 261
*Charukeshi* Gr. 4, 311
*China Gates* Gr. 7, C-45
*Chorale Prelude for Organ, BWV 645, "Wachet auf, ruft uns die Stimme "* Gr. 7, C-9
*Clair de lune* Gr. K, 165
*Clavichord* Gr. 5, 197
*Close Encounters of the Third Kind* Gr. 8, B-34
*Cold and Frosty Morning* Gr. 2, 139
*College Hornpipe* Gr. 4, 95
*Concerto for Flute and Harp in C, K. 299, Movement 2* Gr. 8, C-10
*Concerto for Orchestra, "Presentation of Pairs"* Gr. 4, 72
*Concerto for Viola and Orchestra, Movement 3* Gr. 7, C-35
*Concierto Madrigal for Two Guitars and Orchestra, "Fanfarre"* Gr. 2, 150
*Contigo otra vez* Gr. 7, B-32
*Cotton-Eye Joe* Gr. 4, 290
*Country Blues* Gr. 5, 225
*Crouching Tiger, Hidden Dragon* Gr. 8, A-11
*Crowley's Reel* Gr. 4, 297

*Crowley's/Jackson's* Gr. 4, 298
*Dan tranh* Gr. 5, 196
*Dances of Galanta* Gr. 7, C-34
*Danses Populaires Francaises, "Branle Double, Branle Simple"* Gr. 7, C-25
*Danza* Gr. 7, C-7
*Danzas Puertorriqueñas, "Vano Empeno"* Gr. 7, E-13
*Das Jahr, "Mai"* Gr. 8, C-18
*Diamonds and Rust* Gr. 7, A-4
*Die forelle* Gr. 7, C-20
*Drift* Gr. 8, B-42
*Dúlamán* Gr. 4, 299
*Dusty Miller* Gr. 4, 291
*Dusty Rag* Gr. K, 165
*Dziban* Gr. 7, F-18
*Eh, cumpari!* Gr. 4, 68
*Eine kleine Nachtmusik, Minuet* Gr. 4, 111
*El mariachi* Gr. 4, 303
*El nuevo caiman* Gr. 8, B-17
*El siquisirí* Gr. 4, 273
*Ennanga, Movement 3* Gr. 3, 127
*Eriskummainen kantele* Gr. 5, 199
*Erlkönig, "The Erlking"* Gr. K, 164
*Estancia, "Danza del trigo"* Gr. 5, 229
*Etude Fantasy for Piano, "Etude No 3: Fifths to Thirds"* Gr. 8, C-46
*Ezekiel Saw the Wheel* Gr. 6, 379
*Fascinatin' Rhythm (Frances Veri)* Gr. 7, E-11
*Fingerprints* Gr. 7, B-42
*Flip, Flop and Fly* Gr. 7, F-15
*Flowing Bowl, The* Gr. 8, B-29
*Forked Deer/Fisher's Hornpipe* Gr. 4, 343
*Four Seasons, Concerto No. 2, The, "Summer," Movement 3, "La Tempesta"* Gr. 6, 102
*Four Seasons, The, "Spring," Movement 1* Gr. 4, 371
*Four Seasons, The, "Winter," Movement 2* Gr. 3, 113
*French Suite No. 5, "Gigue"* Gr. 4, 232
*Frère Jacques* Gr. 3, 113
*Gazebo Dances, "Tarantella"* Gr. 8, C-46
*Go Down, Moses* Gr. 7, G-10
*Good Vibrations* Gr. 8, E-28
*Guitar* Gr. 5, 198
*Halley Came to Jackson* Gr. 2, 340
*Hammered dulcimer* Gr. 5, 196
*Hard Day Blues* Gr. 7, B-9

**(*Timbre: Instrumental,* continued)**

*Harp* Gr. 5, 198
*Harpsichord* Gr. 5, 197
*Hermit Songs, Op. 29,*
    *"The Monk and His Cat"*
    Gr. 7, C-21
*Hungarian Rhapsody No. 2*
    *in C sharp Minor, S. 244*
    Gr. 7, E-17
*I Am a Man of Constant*
    *Sorrow* Gr. 7, F-29
*I Get Out* Gr. 8, F-6
*I Know You Mardi Gras*
    Gr. 8, B-17
*I Walk the Line* Gr. 7, B-28
Ichi-gatsu tsuitachi Gr. 3, 406
*If These Walls Could Speak*
    Gr. 7, B-41
*If You Look* Gr. 7, B-5
*Illusions* Gr. 6, 347
*Imbube* Gr. 8, B-30
*Intermezzo, "Háry János*
    *Suite,"*
    *Movement 5* Gr. 7, C-34
*Invention No. 5 in E-flat*
    Gr. 5, 59
*Istanbul Coffee House (Kafe*
    *neio)* Gr. 8, B-34
*It Won't Be Wrong* Gr. 7, F-17
*Jamaican Rumba* Gr. 5, 201
*Jarabe tapatío* Gr. 7, I-7
*Jazz in the Box* Gr. 8, F-11
Jingle Bells Gr. 2, 388
*John Henry* Gr. 8, C-34
*Joy to the World* Gr. 7, A-27
*Julie-O* Gr. 5, 311
*Kayagum pyongch'ang-sae*
    *t'aryug* Gr. 3, 137
*Koto* Gr. 4, 110
*Koto* Gr. 5, 196
La mariposa Gr. 6, 58
*La mer, "Jeux de vagues"*
    Gr. 7, C-39
*La Tarara* Gr. 4, 176
*Le Sacre de Printemps (The*
    *Rite of Spring), "Dance of*
    *the Youths and Maidens"*
    Gr. 8, C-30
*Le tombeau de Couperin,*
    *"Prelude"* Gr. 8, C-28
Leila Gr. 1, 258
*Linus and Lucy* Gr. 8, A-29
*Lion Sleeps Tonight, The*
    Gr. 8, E-8
Little Darlin' Gr. 7, F-30
Little Red Hen, The Gr. 1, 254
*Lluvia* Gr. 6, 332
*Love You Forever* Gr. 8, B-23
*Lute* Gr. 4, 110
*Lute* Gr. 5, 198
*Lyric Suite, "Allegretto*
    *gioviale," Movement 1*
    Gr. 6, 169

*Ma Vlast (My Fatherland),*
    *"Vltava (The Moldau)"*
    Gr. 7, C-33
*MacAllistrum's March-Mairseail*
    *Alasdroim* Gr. 4, 297
*Maha ganapathim* Gr. 6, 305
*Maitreem* Gr. 8, B-42
*Messiah, "Hallelujah!"*
    Gr. 8, C-8
*Mi humilde corazón*
    Gr. 7, B-32
*Mi tierra* Gr. 6, 365
*Mido Mountain* Gr. 8, B-42
*Moment So Close, A*
    Gr. 8, B-40
*Moon Mirrored in the Pool,*
    *The* Gr. 6, 103
*Mr. Bojangles (excerpt 1)*
    Gr. 7, F-7
*Mr. Bojangles (excerpt 2)*
    Gr. 7, F-7
*My Girl Josephine* Gr. 8, E-21
*Native Stepson* Gr. 7, F-26
*New York State of Mind*
    Gr. 7, E-19
Niu lang zhi nü Gr. 4, 335
*On Fire Suite* Gr. 8, B-36
*One Fine Day* Gr. 6, 347
Osamu kosamu Gr. 4, 96
*Oud* Gr. 5, 198
*Pasodoble* Gr. 7, F-11
*Peak Moments* Gr. 8, E-4
*Piano* Gr. 5, 197
*Piano Concerto in A Minor, Op.*
    *16, Movement 1* Gr. 8, E-11
*Piano Sonata No. 8 in C Minor*
    *("Pathéthique"), Movement*
    *3, Rondo: Allegro*
    Gr. 4, 185
*Piano Trio in G Minor, Op. 17,*
    *Allegro* Gr. 8, C-19
*Piano Trio No. 2 in E-flat*
    *Major, Op. 100, Scherzo*
    Gr. 4, 192
*Pictures at an Exhibition,*
    *"The Great Gate of Kiev"*
    Gr. 8, A-12
*Planxty Madame Maxwell*
    Gr. K, 134
*Plenty o' Nuttin'* Gr. 7, B-45
*Prelude in A Major* Gr. 4, 234
*Prelude in B-flat Minor, Op. 28,*
    *No. 16* Gr. 7, C-22
*Prelude in G-sharp Minor,*
    *No. 12* Gr. 7, E-4
*Pride and Joy* Gr. 7, B-9
*Queen's Suite, The, "Sunset*
    *and the Mocking Bird"*
    Gr. 8, E-10
*Quintet for Piano and Strings*
    *in E-flat Major, Op. 44,*
    *Movement 1* Gr. 8, C-19

*Rag puria kalyan-gat in tintal*
    Gr. 4, 192
Ragupati Ragava Raja Ram
    Gr. 5, 321
*Railroad Bill* Gr. 8, F-14
*Rap Intro* Gr. 8, B-32
*Rebab* Gr. 4, 110
*Rhapsody in Blue* Gr. 7, C-42
*Río de la miel* Gr. 5, 296
*Rising of the Mourning Sun*
    Gr. 7, F-19
*Riverdance Suite* Gr. 2, 141
*Roddy McCaulay* Gr. 3, 292
*Rodeo, "Hoedown"* Gr. 5, 312
*Rodeo, "Hoedown"* Gr. 8, B-45
*Roll Over Vaughan Williams*
    Gr. 8, F-22
*Rose (from the Motion Picture*
    *Titanic)* Gr. 8, B-34
*Sabhyatâ* Gr. 8, B-43
*Saltarello detto Trivella*
    Gr. 7, C-6
*Sanjo* Gr. 4, 175
*Serenade, Op. 3, No. 5*
    Gr. 4, 90
*Serenade for Strings in C, Op.*
    *48, "Finale"* Gr. 6, 363
*Seven Tunes Heard in*
    *China, "Guessing Song"*
    Gr. 7, C-45
*Sevilla* Gr. 8, F-22
*Shchedryk, "Carol of the Bells"*
    Gr. 6, 103
*She'll Be Coming 'Round the*
    *Mountain When She Comes*
    Gr. 4, 333
*Shed a Little Light* Gr. 8, E-17
*Shepherd's Hey, No. 1*
    Gr. 7, C-37
*Shepherd's Hey, No. 2*
    Gr. 7, C-37
*Shri Ram, jai Ram* Gr. 4, 311
*Sindhi-Bhairavi* Gr. 5, 320
*Sitar* Gr. 4, 110
*Sitar* Gr. 5, 198
*Slow Hora/Freylekhs*
    Gr. 8, B-25
*Soldier's Joy* Gr. 8, B-29
*Sonata for Violin and Piano,*
    *Allegro* Gr. 8, C-46
*Sonata in C-sharp Minor, Op.*
    *27, No. 2, "Moonlight,"*
    *Movement 1* Gr. 7, C-19
*Sonata in F Major for Violin*
    *and Piano, Op. 24, No.*
    *5, "Spring," Movement 3*
    Gr. 7, C-19
*Sonata No. 11, K. 331,*
    *"Turkish Rondo"* Gr. K, 165
*Sonata Seconda* Gr. 3, 431
*Songs from Letters, "So Like*
    *Your Father"* Gr. 7, C-21
*Soppin' the Gravy* Gr. 4, 385

Classified Index

Sorta Fairytale, A Gr. 7, A-5
Sound Waves Montage
    Gr. 6, 354
Spinning Song Gr. K, 164
St. Patrick Was a Gentleman
    Gr. 3, 290
Stalia, stalia Gr. 8, B-21
String Quartet No. 4,
    Movement 4, "Allegretto
    pizzicato" Gr. 4, 90
String Quartet No. 5,
    Movement 4: Andante
    Gr. 3, 113
Sube Gr. 7, B-31
Suite in E-flat Major for
    Cello, S. 1010, "Gigue"
    Gr. 7, C-11
Suite in F, Op. 28b, No. 2,
    "Fantasia on the Dargason,"
    Movement 4 Gr. 7, C-36
Suite No. 3 in C Major for
    Unaccompanied Cello,
    "Bourrée 1" Gr. 3, 38
Symphony No. 40 in G Minor,
    K. 550, Movement 1
    Gr. 8, B-30
Symphony No. 5 in C Minor,
    Op. 67, Movement 1
    Gr. 7, C-16
Symphony No. 5 in C Minor,
    Op. 67, Movement 4
    Gr. 7, C-18
Tabla Solo Gr. 8, B-32
Take Me There Gr. 7, F-26
Take the "A" Train Gr. 8, C-42
Tema de maimara Gr. 1, 297
Terian gulabi buliyam
    Gr. 8, B-26
Thunder and Lightning Polka
    Gr. 4, 213
Toccata and Fugue in D Minor
    Gr. 7, E-25
Toccata and Tango Gr. 2, 154
Toccata in D Minor Gr. 4, 233
Tommy Peoples Gr. 8, B-20
Transcendental Etude, No.
    3 in G-sharp Minor, "La
    Campanella" Gr. 7, C-23
Two-Part Invention in A Major
    (Harpsichord) Gr. 5, 236
Two-Part Invention in A Major
    (piano) Gr. 5, 237
Violin Concerto in E Minor, Op.
    64, Movement 1 Gr. 8, C-18
Voiles Gr. 7, C-39
Waltz in D-flat ("Minute" Waltz)
    Gr. 4, 234
Well-Tempered Clavier, Book
    1, "Prelude and Fugue in C
    Minor" Gr. 7, E-16
Widmung, Op. 25, No. 1
    Gr. 7, C-20

Winter Birds Flying over the
    Water Gr. 1, 91
Wipe Out Gr. 7, F-33
World Music Montage
    Gr. 3, 266
Would? Gr. 8, F-30
Yamaji Gr. 3, 407
You Are My Sunshine
    Gr. 7, B-7

**electrophones (electronic)**
Africa Gr. 7, B-6
Akua Tuta Gr. 7, D-24
Alasdair mhic cholla ghasda
    Gr. 8, B-44
Awa ewe iwoyi Gr. 8, D-9
Bembe de Plena Gr. 8, D-18
Bombay Dreams Gr. 8, B-35
(Can't Live Without Your) Love
    and Affection Gr. 7, B-23
Caravan Gr. 7, B-31
Cherokee Morning Song
    Gr. 8, B-19
Children's Corner Suite,
    "Snowflakes Are Dancing"
    Gr. 5, 239
Close Encounters of the Third
    Kind Gr. 4, 235
Close Encounters of the Third
    Kind Gr. 8, B-34
Come Out and Play Gr. 5, 238
Contigo otra vez Gr. 7, B-32
Daphne of the Dunes
    Gr. 8, D-29
Dziban Gr. 7, F-18
Faerie Stories Gr. 8, B-5
Fish Food Gr. 2, 212
Free Music #1 Gr. 2, 212
Good King Wenceslas
    Gr. 6, 461
Good Vibrations Gr. 8, E-28
Hard Day Blues Gr. 7, B-9
If You Look Gr. 7, B-5
Interview with Rick Bassett
    (Part 2) Gr. 3, 223
It Won't Be Wrong Gr. 7, F-17
Joy to the World Gr. 7, A-27
Love You Forever Gr. 8, B-23
Magnificent Tree, The
    Gr. 7, E-31
Mars Suite, "Orbital View,"
    Movement 1 Gr. 4, 199
Mensu Gr. 8, D-6
Miniature Odyssey, A
    Gr. 8, E-29
Moment So Close, A
    Gr. 8, B-40
Nyamphemphe Gr. 8, B-3
On Fire Suite Gr. 8, B-36
Onomatapoiea Study No. 2
    Gr. 7, E-31
Piano Concerto in A Minor, Op.
    16, Movement 1 Gr. 8, E-11

Popcorn Gr. 8, E-27
Pride and Joy Gr. 7, B-9
Queen's Suite, The, "Sunset
    and the Mocking Bird"
    Gr. 8, E-10
Quiet City Gr. 8, E-29
Radio City Christmas
    Spectacular Jingle
    Gr. 8, A-5
Rice Bowl Gr. 8, B-30
Rising of the Mourning Sun
    Gr. 7, F-19
Rodeo, "Hoedown" Gr. 8, B-45
Sabhyatâ Gr. 8, B-43
Shalom aleichem Gr. 6, 409
Solo Flight Gr. 5, 312
Stalia, stalia Gr. 8, B-21
This Is Your Night Gr. 6, 368
Two-Part Invention in A Major
    (synthesizer) Gr. 5, 237
Wild Bull Gr. 6, 366
X-Beats Gr. 7, B-5

**idiophones (percussion)**
Abbots Bromley Horn Dance
    Gr. 7, C-24
Achshav Gr. 2, 64
Adzogbo-Ovitse Gr. 8, D-13
Africa Gr. 7, B-6
Ajaja Gr. 8, B-3
Al yadee Gr. 6, 308
Ala Da'lona Gr. 4, 137
Alexander's Ragtime Band
    Gr. 6, 136
Allegretto Gr. 2, 131
Alumot Gr. 6, 306
Awa ewe iwoyi Gr. 8, D-9
Axatse Gr. 5, 66
Bachianas brasileiras No. 5,
    "Aria" Gr. 8, C-37
Bam, chi, chi, bam Gr. K, 109
Bawa Gr. 7, D-32
Beggar's Opera, The, "Constant
    Billy" Gr. 7, C-24
Bembe de Plena Gr. 8, D-18
Billie Gr. 8, B-23
Bomba te traigo yo Gr. 8, B-3
Bombay Dreams Gr. 8, B-35
Brisad del Zulia Gr. 4, 19
By the Waters of Babylon
    Gr. 6, 311
Capoeira Na Vila Gr. 8, D-25
Carnival of the Animals,
    "Fossils" Gr. 1, 236
Carnival of the Animals,
    "Fossils" Gr. 4, 220
Chang Gr. 1, 156
Cherokee Morning Song
    Gr. 8, B-19
Cho'i hát bội Gr. 5, 318
Close Encounters of the Third
    Kind Gr. 8, B-34

(*Timbre: Instrumental,* continued)

*Concerto for Marimba and String Orchestra, "Saudação"* Gr. 2, 119

*Concerto for Viola and Orchestra, Movement 3* Gr. 7, C-35

*Cow Barn Cha Cha* Gr. 8, D-33

*Crouching Tiger, Hidden Dragon* Gr. 8, A-11

*Crowley's Reel* Gr. 4, 297

*Dances of Galanta* Gr. 7, C-34

Dancing Pig, The (story) Gr. 1, 196

*Danses Populaires Francaises, "Branle Double, Branle Simple"* Gr. 7, C-25

*Daphne of the Dunes* Gr. 8, D-29

*Dham dhamak dham samelu* Gr. 6, 305

*Drums From Around the World* (Montage) Gr. 6, 277

*Dundun* Gr. 5, 66

*Eine kleine Nachtmusik* Gr. 4, 41

*Ekombi* Gr. 8, B-31

*El dulcerito llego, "The Sweets Vendor Is Here"* Gr. K, 124

*El nuevo caiman* Gr. 8, B-17

*Elegguá* Gr. 8, D-13

*Estancia, "Danza del trigo"* Gr. 5, 229

*Eternal Flame* Gr. 7, B-6

*Evening Samba* Gr. 6, 297

Everybody Loves Saturday Night Gr. 6, 296

*Faerie Stories* Gr. 8, B-5

*Fanfare for Freedom* Gr. 6, 139

*Fanfare for the Common Man* Gr. 7, C-43

*Flight of the Ibis* Gr. 8, D-16

*Fourth of July, The* Gr. 5, 489

*Gahu* Gr. 7, D-27

*Gamelan angklung* Gr. 6, 384

*Guaguancó pá las tumbadoras* Gr. 7, D-9

*Hard Times* Gr. 1, 194

*Huagu ge, "Flower Drum Song"* Gr. 8, D-27

*Hunt, The* Gr. 6, 363

*I Know You Mardi Gras* Gr. 8, B-17

*I Walk the Line* Gr. 7, B-28

*In the Mood* Gr. 6, 110

*Intermezzo, "Háry János Suite," Movement 5* Gr. 7, C-34

*Ionisation* Gr. 6, 357

*Ise oluwa* Gr. 2, 102

*Istanbul Coffee House (Kafe neio)* Gr. 8, B-34

*Jingle Bells* Gr. 2, 388

*Jo'ashila, "Walking Together"* Gr. 6, 286

*Jump for Joy* Gr. 7, D-20

*Junk Music Montage* Gr. 1, 73

*Katura* Gr. 7, D-27

*Kebjar teruna* Gr. 6, 385

*Kelo aba w'ye* Gr. 6, 290

*Kpanlogo for 2* Gr. 6, 296

*La mer, "Jeux de vagues"* Gr. 7, C-39

*Le tombeau de Couperin, "Prelude"* Gr. 8, C-28

*Let the Children Play* Gr. 7, B-30

*Lian xi qu (étude)* Gr. 4, 157

*Limbo Rock* Gr. 3, 298

*Lion* Gr. 6, 303

*Lluvia* Gr. 6, 332

*Lost River* Gr. 6, 283

*Love You Forever* Gr. 8, B-23

*Ma Vlast (My Fatherland), "Vltava (The Moldau)"* Gr. 7, C-33

*Mahk jchi* Gr. 7, D-25

*Malagueña* Gr. 5, 154

*Malê Debalê* Gr. 8, B-16

*Mambo UK* Gr. 7, D-9

*Mbira* Gr. 5, 66

*Mea haarit* Gr. 3, 274

*Memories of the Seashore* Gr. 3, 150

*Men's Fancy Dance* Gr. 7, D-24

*Mensu* Gr. 8, D-6

Mi cuerpo hace música Gr. K, 106

*Mwen boyko samba* Gr. 4, 319

Nana Kru Gr. 6, 282

*Nanafushi* Gr. 7, D-16

Noah's Shanty Gr. 1, 342

*Nyamphemphe* Gr. 8, B-3

*Nyoka* Gr. 7, D-33

*Obokete* Gr. 6, 291

*On Fire Suite* Gr. 8, B-36

*Orfferondo* Gr. 4, 194

*Phleng pradall* Gr. 1, 157

*Piano Concerto in A Minor, Op. 16, Movement 1* Gr. 8, E-11

*Picadillo* Gr. 3, 361

*Pick-a-Rib* Gr. 3, 151

*Pictures at an Exhibition, "The Great Gate of Kiev"* Gr. 8, A-12

*Plenty o' Nuttin'* Gr. 7, B-45

*Queen's Suite, The, "Sunset and the Mocking Bird"* Gr. 8, E-10

*Raindrops* Gr. 7, D-23

*Retounen* Gr. 8, B-17

*Return to Misty Mountain* Gr. 7, D-28

*Rhapsody in Blue* Gr. 7, C-42

*Rice Bowl* Gr. 8, B-30

*Riendo el río corre* Gr. 6, 263

*Rippa Medley, The, "Block-Block, One Leg Up, Let the Beat Go, Uh-Oh"* Gr. 8, D-32

*Rocky Point Holiday* Gr. 6, 331

*Rods and Cones* Gr. 7, D-5

*Rose (from the Motion Picture Titanic)* Gr. 8, B-34

*Sabhyatâ* Gr. 8, B-43

*Sai da frente* Gr. 8, D-24

*San Miguel Jolonicapan* Gr. 8, D-16

*Sekar jepun* Gr. 1, 195

*Shashee* Gr. K, 109

*Shepherd's Hey, No. 2* Gr. 7, C-37

*Shepherd's Hey, No. 3* Gr. 7, C-37

*Somebody* Gr. 4, 41

*Spring Walk, "Du xuân"* Gr. 1, 440

*Sube* Gr. 7, B-31

*Suite in F, Op. 28b, No. 2, "Fantasia on the Dargason," Movement 4* Gr. 7, C-36

*Suite No. 2 in F, Op. 28b, Movement 1, "March"* Gr. 6, 139

*Symphony No. 4 in F Minor, Movement 4, Finale: Allegro con fuoco* Gr. 1, 175

*Take the "A" Train* Gr. 8, C-42

Take Time in Life Gr. 6, 292

*Talaque talaque o romance da Maria* Gr. 8, D-24

*Tema de maimara* Gr. 1, 297

*Thunder and Lightning Polka* Gr. 4, 213

*Toccata and Tango* Gr. 2, 154

*Toccata for Percussion, Movement 3* Gr. 4, 155

*Tumba* Gr. 7, D-14

*Two Dances for Three Xylophones, "Hornpipe and Jig"* Gr. 8, D-17

*Ujan mas* Gr. 2, 105

*Violin Concerto in E Minor, Op. 64, Movement 1* Gr. 8, C-18

*Viva Jujuy* Gr. 8, B-22

*Washington Post, The* (march) Gr. 1, 175

Water Come a Me Eye Gr. 6, 300

*Water Is Wide, The* Gr. 6, 228

*Whirlwind* Gr. 3, 149

*Wilder Reiter* Gr. 8, D-17

*Wildlife* Gr. 1, 345

*World Music Montage* Gr. 3, 266

*Xochipilli, An Imagined Aztec Music* Gr. 8, C-37

*Zoila* Gr. 8, D-18

**jug band**

Mama Don't 'Low Gr. 6, 358

**membranophones (drums)**

*Achshav* Gr. 2, 64

*Adzogbo-Ovitse* Gr. 8, D-13

*Africa* Gr. 7, B-6

*Alasdair mhic cholla ghasda* Gr. 8, B-44

*Awa ewe iwoyi* Gr. 8, D-9

*Badenma* Gr. 8, B-28

*Bambodansarna* Gr. 8, B-20

*Bembe de Plena* Gr. 8, D-18

*Billie* Gr. 8, B-23

*Birdland* Gr. 5, 155

*Bombay Dreams* Gr. 8, B-35

*Capoeira Na Vila* Gr. 8, D-25

*Carrament News* Gr. 8, B-22

*Cauyaqa Nauwa? (Where's My Drum?)* Gr. 8, D-20

*Charukeshi* Gr. 4, 311

*Cherokee Morning Song* Gr. 8, B-19

*Close Encounters of the Third Kind* Gr. 8, B-34

*Concerto for Viola and Orchestra, Movement 3* Gr. 7, C-35

*Conga Kings Grand Finale* Gr. 5, 156

*Cow Barn Cha Cha* Gr. 8, D-33

*Crouching Tiger, Hidden Dragon* Gr. 8, A-11

*Dances of Galanta* Gr. 7, C-34

*Danses Populaires Francaises, "Branle Double, Branle Simple"* Gr. 7, C-25

*Daphne of the Dunes* Gr. 8, D-29

*Dinéh Round Dance* Gr. 6, 186

*Drift* Gr. 8, B-42

*Dúlamán* Gr. 4, 299

*El nuevo caiman* Gr. 8, B-17

*Estancia, "Danza del trigo"* Gr. 5, 229

*Faerie Stories* Gr. 8, B-5

*Fanfare for Freedom* Gr. 6, 139

*Fanfare for the Common Man* Gr. 7, C-43

*Fingerprints* Gr. 7, B-42

*Firebird, The, "Finale"* Gr. 8, C-30

*Gamelan angklung* Gr. 6, 384

*Guaguancó pá las tumbadoras* Gr. 7, D-9

*Hard Day Blues* Gr. 7, B-9

*Huagu ge, "Flower Drum Song"* Gr. 8, D-27

*Hunt, The* Gr. 6, 363

*I Know You Mardi Gras* Gr. 8, B-17

*Intermezzo, "Háry János Suite," Movement 5* Gr. 7, C-34

*John Wayne's Teeth* Gr. 8, B-37

*Jump for Joy* Gr. 7, D-20

*Kayagum pyongch'ang-sae t'aryug* Gr. 3, 137

*Kebjar teruna* Gr. 6, 385

*Le tombeau de Couperin, "Prelude"* Gr. 8, C-28

*Loco bossa nova* Gr. 2, 247

*Love You Forever* Gr. 8, B-23

*Ma Vlast (My Fatherland), "Vltava (The Moldau)"* Gr. 7, C-33

*Mahk jchi* Gr. 7, D-25

*Maitreem* Gr. 8, B-42

*Malagueña* Gr. 5, 154

*Malê Debalê* Gr. 8, B-16

*Mambo UK* Gr. 7, D-9

*Men's Fancy Dance* Gr. 7, D-24

*Mensu* Gr. 8, D-6

Mi cuerpo hace música Gr. K, 106

*Mi tierra* Gr. 6, 365

*Nanafushi* Gr. 7, D-16

*Night in Tunisia, A* Gr. 4, 35

*Niu lang zhi nü* Gr. 4, 335

*Nyamphemphe* Gr. 8, B-3

*O'Sullivan's March* Gr. 5, 157

*Omo* Gr. 1, 443

*On Fire Suite* Gr. 8, B-36

*Peak Moments* Gr. 8, E-4

*Piano Concerto in A Minor, Op. 16, Movement 1* Gr. 8, E-11

*Planets, The, Op. 32, "Jupiter"* Gr. 1, 405

*Primitive Fire, "Oya"* Gr. 5, 67

*Queen's Suite, The, "Sunset and the Mocking Bird"* Gr. 8, E-10

*Rag puria kalyan-gat in tintal* Gr. 4, 192

*Retounen* Gr. 8, B-17

*Rhapsody in Blue* Gr. 7, C-42

Riendo el río corre Gr. 6, 263

*Rippa Medley, The, "Block-Block, One Leg Up, Let the Beat Go, Uh-Oh"* Gr. 8, D-32

*Rocky Point Holiday* Gr. 6, 331

*Sai da frente* Gr. 8, D-24

*Saqian da dhol* Gr. 8, B-22

*Shepherd's Hey, No. 2* Gr. 7, C-37

*Shepherd's Hey, No. 3* Gr. 7, C-37

*Spaceville* Gr. 7, D-30

*Stalia, stalia* Gr. 8, B-21

*Sube* Gr. 7, B-31

*Suite in F, Op. 28b, No. 2, "Fantasia on the Dargason," Movement 4* Gr. 7, C-36

*Suite No. 2 in F, Op. 28b, Movement 1, "March"* Gr. 6, 139

*Symphony No. 40 in G Minor, K. 550, Movement 1* Gr. 8, B-30

*Tabla Solo* Gr. 8, B-32

*Take Me There* Gr. 7, F-26

*Take the "A" Train* Gr. 8, C-42

*Talaque talaque o romance da Maria* Gr. 8, D-24

*Terian gulabi buliyam* Gr. 8, B-26

*Thunder and Lightning Polka* Gr. 4, 213

*Toccata and Tango* Gr. 2, 154

*Tommy Peoples* Gr. 8, B-20

*Tumba* Gr. 7, D-14

*Ue ue* Gr. 8, D-2

*Uma história de Ifá* Gr. 6, 362

*Viva Jujuy* Gr. 8, B-22

*Welcome to Our World* Gr. 6, 272

*Wipe Out* Gr. 5, 155

*Xochipilli, An Imagined Aztec Music* Gr. 8, C-37

*Yaudachi* Gr. 5, 156

*Zoila* Gr. 8, D-18

**unusual sound sources**

*Gidden riddum* Gr. 6, 299

**VOCAL**

*Asadoya* Gr. 6, 303

*Battle of New Orleans, The* Gr. 6, 105

*Dham dhamak dham samelu* Gr. 6, 305

Ezekiel Saw the Wheel Gr. 6, 379

Four Strong Winds (Song to a Seagull) Gr. 6, 170

*Hindewhu (whistle) solo* Gr. 6, 269

*Hotter Than That* Gr. 6, 65

*Il trovatore, "Anvil Chorus"* Gr. 6, 25

*It Don't Mean a Thing if It Ain't Got that Swing* Gr. 6, 386

*Jo'ashila, "Walking Together"* Gr. 6, 286

*Kui.Kyon.pan* Gr. 6, 25

*Mass, "Responsory Alleluia"* Gr. 6, 217

*Northfield* Gr. 6, 25

*Siyahamba* Gr. 6, 212

*Strike Up The Band Medley, "Strike Up The Band, Mardi Gras March, Listen To That Dixie Band"* Gr. 6, 25

*Tamaiti hunahia* Gr. 6, 24

(*Timbre: Vocal,* **continued**)

*This Little Light of Mine* Gr. 6, 232
*Vocal Timbres Around the World*
Gr. 6, 170
What a Wonderful World Gr. 6, 62
*What a Wonderful World*
Gr. 6, 63
Yo-shi nai Gr. 6, 286
*Yü guang guang* Gr. 6, 60

**adult female**

*A-Tisket, A-Tasket* Gr. 2, 239
*Aida, "Gloria all'Egitto (Grand
March)"* Gr. 8, C-24
*Angry Anymore* Gr. 8, F-32
*Bachianas brasileiras No. 5,
"Aria"* Gr. 8, C-37
*Bombay Dreams* Gr. 8, B-35
*Both Sides Now* Gr. 5, 385
*Can't Take My Joy* Gr. 7, B-40
*Carol of the Bells* Gr. 8, G-10
*Chansons madecasses,
"Nahandove"* Gr. 4, 32
*Cherokee Morning Song*
Gr. 8, B-19
*Diamonds and Rust* Gr. 7, A-4
*Die Zauberflöte, "Pa-pa-pa-pa-
pa-pa-pagena"* Gr. 8, C-13
*Ev'ry Time I Feel the Spirit*
Gr. 3, 248
*Everything Is Everything*
Gr. 7, B-29
Family Tree Gr. 3, 72
*Fascinatin' Rhythm (Ella
Fitzgerald)* Gr. 7, E-11
Follow the Drinkin' Gourd
Gr. 4, 266
*Ghel moma* Gr. 4, 31
*Glory, Glory, Hallelujah*
Gr. 8, B-14
*God Bless the Child*
Gr. 7, B-26
*He's Got the Whole World in
His Hands* Gr. 3, 249
*Heads Carolina, Tails
California* Gr. 7, B-25
*Hermit Songs, Op. 29,
"The Monk and His Cat"*
Gr. 7, C-21
*Humpty Dumpty* Gr. K, 23
*I Don't Want to Feel Like That*
Gr. 4, 31
*I Shall Sing* Gr. 8, I-41
*If These Walls Could Speak*
Gr. 7, B-41
*John Henry* Gr. 8, C-34
*Joy* Gr. 7, B-40
*Kayagum pyongch'ang-sae
t'aryug* Gr. 3, 137
*Kayagum pyongch'ang-sae
t'aryug* Gr. 8, B-13

*Les pêcheurs des perles, "Au
fond du temple saint"*
Gr. 7, C-30
*Let the Children Play*
Gr. 7, B-30
*Los pollitos* Gr. K, 166
*Magic Flute, The, "Queen of
the Night Aria"* Gr. 7, C-31
*Make Your Own Kind of Music*
Gr. 8, G-30
*Mass for the 21st Century,
"Alleluia"* Gr. 3, 163
*Mongolian Long Song*
Gr. 8, B-14
*Niño querido* Gr. 1, 308
*Oh, Freedom and Come and
Go with Me* Gr. 5, 394
*Over the Rainbow (from The
Wizard of Oz)* Gr. 4, 143
*Piki mai* Gr. 1, 79
*Powwow Song* Gr. 4, 32
*Requiem, "Pie Jesu"* Gr. 6, 178
*Rigoletto, "Bella figlia
dell'amore"* Gr. 7, C-29
*Rose (from the Motion Picture
Titanic)* Gr. 8, B-34
*She Is Like the Swallow*
Gr. 8, B-12
Shortnin' Bread Gr. 1, 57
*Songs from Letters, "So Like
Your Father"* Gr. 7, C-21
*Soulville* Gr. 7, B-17
*Tahi* Gr. 8, B-14
*That's the Way It Is* Gr. 7, B-23
*Tihore Mai* Gr. 8, B-12
*Tosca, "Vissi d'arte"*
Gr. 7, C-31
*Traveling Shoes* Gr. 3, 248
*Vocal Styles Around the World*
Gr. 6, 61
*What Could I Do* Gr. 5, 281
*Why Walk When You Can Fly*
Gr. 7, B-28
*Widmung, Op. 25, No. 1*
Gr. 7, C-20

**adult male**

*Aida, "Gloria all'Egitto (Grand
March)"* Gr. 8, C-24
*Allah hoo Allah hoo*
Gr. 8, B-13
*At the Hop* Gr. 4, 166
*Blower's Daughter, The*
Gr. 8, B-13
Blowin' in the Wind Gr. 5, 384
*Blue Eyes Crying in the Rain*
Gr. 7, B-28
*Bombay Dreams* Gr. 8, B-35
*Boogie Down* Gr. 8, G-29
*Boston Ball Game 1967*
Gr. 8, F-32
*Candy Man, Salty Dog*
Gr. K, 27

*Circlesong Five* Gr. 1, 239
*Country Blues* Gr. 5, 225
*Die forelle* Gr. 7, C-20
*Die Zauberflöte, "Pa-pa-pa-pa-
pa-pa-pagena"* Gr. 8, C-13
*Erlkönig, "The Erlking"*
Gr. K, 164
*Ev'ry Time I Feel the Spirit*
Gr. 3, 248
*Face of Love, The* Gr. 8, B-15
Family Tree Gr. 3, 72
*Feliz Navidad* Gr. 4, 433
*Forever, For Now* Gr. 7, B-16
*Go Down, Moses* Gr. 7, G-10
*God Bless the Child*
Gr. 7, B-26
*Goin' Down the Road Feelin'
Bad* Gr. 5, 283
*Hippopotamus Song, The*
Gr. 3, 33
*Humpty Dumpty* Gr. K, 23
*I Get Out* Gr. 8, F-6
*I Walk the Line* Gr. 7, B-28
*Intertribal Song* Gr. 8, B-18
*John Henry* Gr. 8, C-34
*John Wayne's Teeth*
Gr. 8, B-37
*Jump for Joy* Gr. 7, D-20
*Kargiraa-style Song* Gr. 8, B-15
*Keep a Cool Head* Gr. 7, B-34
*Kerry Dance, The* Gr. 5, 28
*Les pêcheurs des perles, "Au
fond du temple saint"*
Gr. 7, C-30
*Let It Snow! Let It Snow! Let It
Snow!* Gr. 4, 427
*Lifetime* Gr. 7, B-39
*Lion Sleeps Tonight, The*
Gr. 4, 132
*Lluvia* Gr. 6, 332
*Love You Forever* Gr. 8, B-23
*M.T.A.* Gr. 5, 403
*Mack the Knife* Gr. 7, B-26
*Malê Debalê* Gr. 8, B-16
*Messiah, "Behold, I Tell You a
Mystery"* Gr. 8, C-8
*Messiah, "The Trumpet Shall
Sound"* Gr. 8, C-8
*Mi humilde corazón*
Gr. 7, B-32
*Mr. Tambourine Man*
Gr. 6, 148
*Musette* Gr. 3, 39
*New York State of Mind*
Gr. 7, E-19
*Nyamphemphe* Gr. 8, B-3
*Ozark Mountain Jubilee*
Gr. 4, 86
*Powwow Song* Gr. 4, 32
*Prayer, The* Gr. 7, A-10
*Queen's Suite, The, "Sunset
and the Mocking Bird"*
Gr. 8, E-10

*Rain, Rain, Beautiful Rain*
Gr. 4, 32
*Retounen* Gr. 8, B-17
*Rigoletto, "Bella figlia dell'amore"* Gr. 7, C-29
*Rise Up, Shepherd, and Follow*
Gr. 5, 470
*Route 66* Gr. 4, 279
*Shed a Little Light* Gr. 8, E-17
*Shenandoah* Gr. 5, 265
*Shumba* Gr. 8, B-12
*Sigit "Alash" (Tuva)* Gr. 4, 31
Six-Inch Boots in a Nine-Inch
Puddle Gr. 1, 366
*Tahi* Gr. 8, B-14
*Tears of a Clown, The*
Gr. 7, B-39
*Times They Are A-Changin',
The* Gr. 5, 384
*Tutti Frutti* Gr. 7, B-29
*Vocal Styles Around the World*
Gr. 6, 61
*Vonjeo* Gr. 8, B-12
Wade in the Water Gr. 4, 268
*Waitin' for a Train* Gr. 7, B-24
Where Have All the Flowers
Gone? Gr. 5, 287
*You Sang to Me* Gr. 6, 335

**child/children**
A-Tisket, A-Tasket Gr. 2, 238
America Gr. K, 326
Family Tree Gr. 3, 72
Follow the Drinkin' Gourd
Gr. 4, 266
*Lion Sleeps Tonight, The*
Gr. 8, E-8
*Mass for the 21st Century,
"Alleluia"* Gr. 3, 163
Mud Gr. 3, 32
*Nobody Knows the Trouble I've
Seen* Gr. 3, 249
Peace Like a River Gr. 3, 246
*Requiem, "Pie Jesu"* Gr. 6, 178
Shortnin' Bread Gr. 1, 57
Sing! Speak! Whisper! Shout!
Gr. 1, 36
Six-Inch Boots in a Nine-Inch
Puddle Gr. 1, 366
Voice Choice Gr. K, 27
*Who Can Sail?* Gr. 5, 30

**groups**
*Abbots Bromley Horn Dance*
Gr. 7, C-24
*Aida, "Gloria all'Egitto (Grand
March)"* Gr. 8, C-24
*Alasdair mhic cholla ghasda*
Gr. 8, B-44
*Alle psallite cum luya*
Gr. 7, C-5
*Apu Min'Tan* Gr. 8, D-21
At the Hop Gr. 4, 166

*Beggar's Opera, The, "Constant
Billy"* Gr. 7, C-24
*Bombay Dreams* Gr. 8, B-35
*Boogie Down* Gr. 8, G-29
Bye Bye, Love Gr. 8, A-15
(Can't Live Without Your) Love
and Affection Gr. 7, B-23
*Cantata No. 140 (as performed
by The Swingle Singers),
"Wachet auf, ruft uns die
Stimme," Movement 4*
Gr. 7, C-10
*Carol of the Bells* Gr. 8, G-10
Carry On Wayward Son
Gr. 7, B-20
Changed My Name Gr. 6, 338
Cherokee Morning Song
Gr. 8, B-19
*Circlesong 7* Gr. 4, 80
*Dancing Queen* Gr. 8, G-19
*El nuevo caiman* Gr. 8, B-17
*Elias* Gr. 7, B-21
*Eternal Flame* Gr. 7, B-6
Ev'ry Time I Feel the Spirit
Gr. 3, 248
Ev'ry Time I Feel the Spirit
Gr. 7, C-40
*Everyday People* Gr. 7, G-16
Give Me Your Tired, Your Poor
Gr. 5, 166
Give Us Hope Gr. 6, 337
Gloria In Excelsis Gr. 6, 210
Glory, Glory, Hallelujah
Gr. 8, B-14
Good King Wenceslas
Gr. 4, 431
*Good Vibrations* Gr. 8, E-28
*Hippopotamus Song, The*
Gr. 3, 33
In the Still of the Night
Gr. 4, 47
*John Wayne's Teeth*
Gr. 8, B-37
Joy to the World Gr. 7, A-27
*Karangatia ra* Gr. 3, 273
*Kelo aba w'ye* Gr. 6, 290
*Kerry Dance, The* Gr. 5, 28
*Las copetonas* Gr. 7, B-33
*Lion Sleeps Tonight, The*
Gr. 4, 132
*Lion Sleeps Tonight, The*
Gr. 8, E-8
Little David, Play on Your Harp
Gr. 4, 395
Lo, How a Rose E'er Blooming
Gr. 6, 210
Love You Forever Gr. 8, B-23
*Mahk jchi* Gr. 7, D-25
*Maitreem* Gr. 8, B-42
Make Your Own Kind of Music
Gr. 8, G-30
*Malê Debalê* Gr. 8, B-16

*Messiah, "Hallelujah!"*
Gr. 8, C-8
Mud Gr. 3, 32
*Nobody Knows the Trouble I've
Seen* Gr. 3, 249
*Nyamphemphe* Gr. 8, B-3
*O ignis spiritus Paracliti*
Gr. 7, C-4
*On Green Dolphin Street*
Gr. 4, 126
*Ozark Mountain Jubilee*
Gr. 4, 86
*Rigoletto, "Bella figlia
dell'amore"* Gr. 7, C-29
*Rise Up, Shepherd, and Follow*
Gr. 5, 470
*Rodeo, "Hoedown"* Gr. 8, B-45
*Search for the Hero* Gr. 7, G-5
*Study War No More*
Gr. 7, C-40
*Tahi* Gr. 8, B-14
*That's the Way* Gr. 4, 193
*Tihore Mai* Gr. 8, B-12
*Traveling Shoes* Gr. 3, 248
*Vocal Styles Around the World*
Gr. 6, 61
*Yemaya* Gr. 8, G-24
*Zoila* Gr. 8, D-18

**vocables**
*John Wayne's Teeth*
Gr. 8, B-37
*Men's Fancy Dance* Gr. 7, D-24
*On Fire Suite* Gr. 8, B-36

**vocal sounds (nonsinging)**
Beach Rap (speech piece)
Gr. 1, 352
Big Old Storm a-Comin'
Gr. K, 257
Blum (poem) Gr. 1, 221
*Cantata No. 140 (as performed
by The Swingle Singers),
"Wachet auf, ruft uns die
Stimme," Movement 4*
Gr. 7, C-10
*Cherokee Morning Song*
Gr. 8, B-19
*Circlesong Five* Gr. 1, 239
De Beat Gr. 2, 67
Dogs Gr. K, 123
Down, Down, Baby Gr. 2, 32
Downpour Gr. K, 51
Ducks (poem) Gr. 1, 99
Ducks in the Rain Gr. K, 235
*Face of Love, The* Gr. 8, B-15
*Gapu* Gr. 8, B-38
Harriet Tubman Gr. 4, 269
Higglety, Pigglety, Pop!
Gr. K, 22
Hurt No Living Thing Gr. 4, 32
James Brown Gr. K, 206
Jinny Go 'Round Gr. K, 228
*Kargiraa-style Song* Gr. 8, B-15

(*Timbre: Vocal,* continued)

Let's Pretend  Gr. K, 227
Little Black Train, The
    Gr. 4, 268
Little Red Caboose  Gr. K, 229
Los trencitos  Gr. K, 24
Manhattan Lullaby  Gr. K, 193
Mbombera  Gr. K, 24
Mos Mos  Gr. 1, 130
*Noah's Zoo in the Big, Big Rain*
    Gr. K, 274
Now That's Tap (speech piece)
    Gr. 6, 320
Old King Cole  Gr. K, 245
Our Washing Machine (poem)
    Gr. 1, 35
Parade Came Marching, The
    Gr. 1, 166
*Pay Me My Money Down*
    Gr. 4, 39
*Puppy Love*  Gr. K, 262
"Quack!" Said the Billy Goat
    Gr. K, 233
¡Qué llueva!  Gr. K, 81
*Rods and Cones*  Gr. 7, D-5
Sailing to the Sea  Gr. 1, 336
Scrub-a-dub  Gr. 1, 306
She'll Be Comin' 'Round the
    Mountain  Gr. 2, 358
*Shumba*  Gr. 8, B-12
Sing! Speak! Whisper! Shout!
    Gr. 1, 36
Skin and Bones  Gr. 2, 376
Trains  Gr. 1, 301
Up and Down Kitten, The
    Gr. K, 100
Valentine Feelings  Gr. K, 322
We're Making Popcorn (speech
    piece)  Gr. 1, 86

## VOCAL DEVELOPMENT  *See*
*also Skills Reinforcement:*
*Singing; Texture/Harmony: Part*
*Songs.*
ABC Rock  Gr. 1, 262
All Around the Buttercup  Gr. 2, 170
Alleluia, Amen  Gr. 7, A-12
Alphabet Soup  Gr. 1, 219
Amasee  Gr. 1, 172
America  Gr. 2, 403
America  Gr. 7, I-2
America  Gr. 8, I-2
America, the Beautiful  Gr. 7, I-4
America, the Beautiful  Gr. 8, I-4
Angels On the Midnight Clear
    Gr. 6, 423
Baby Beluga  Gr. K, 272
*Blower's Daughter, The*  Gr. 8, B-13
Blues with a Feeling  Gr. 8, I-6
Book of Love  Gr. 8, G-27
Bounce High, Bounce Low  Gr. 1, 150
Boys' changing voices  Gr. 6, 9
Brand New Day, A  Gr. 6, 7

California Dreamin'  Gr. 8, G-31
Canción Mixteca  Gr. 5, 327
Cantando mentiras  Gr. 4, 147
Cantaré, cantarás  Gr. 6, 413
Canto del agua  Gr. 8, I-10
Certainly, Lord  Gr. 7, I-12
Chapel of Love  Gr. 7, G-27
Charlie over the Water  Gr. 1, 68
Chuhwuht  Gr. 2, 357
Circle 'Round the Moon  Gr. 4, 406
Con el vito  Gr. 7, G-15
Crawfish  Gr. 2, 89
De colores  Gr. 8, I-14
Deep in the Heart of Texas  Gr. 8, I-18
Ding Dong! Merrily on High
    Gr. 6, 427
Dok djampa  Gr. 8, I-20
Dona nobis pacem  Gr. 6, 125
Down by the Bay  Gr. 1, 19
Down by the Riverside  Gr. 8, G-8
El coquí  Gr. 2, 293
Eres tú  Gr. 6, 475
Ev'ry Time I Feel the Spirit  Gr. 5, 243
*Ev'rybody Ought to Know*  Gr. 1, 434
*Every Night When the Sun Goes In*
    Gr. 8, I-29
Every Night When the Sun Goes In
    Gr. 8, I-29
Fais do do  Gr. 6, 403
Feliz Navidad  Gr. 7, I-28
Flip, Flop and Fly  Gr. 7, I-32
*Forever, For Now*  Gr. 7, B-16
Four Strong Winds  Gr. 6, 171
Four Strong Winds (Song to a Seagull)
    Gr. 6, 170
Free at Last  Gr. 6, 468
Friends Today  Gr. 7, D-12
Frog Lullaby  Gr. K, 149
Fuzzy Caterpillar  Gr. K, 102
Gift to Share, A  Gr. 6, 393
Glory, Glory, Hallelujah  Gr. 6, 53
God Bless the Child  Gr. 7, B-27
God Bless the U.S.A.  Gr. 8, G-37
Goin' to Boston  Gr. 6, 433
Gonna Build a Mountain  Gr. 6, 20
Gospel Train, The  Gr. 6, 398
Great Big House  Gr. 2, 204
Ha'kyo jong  Gr. 2, 137
Hanuka, Hanuka  Gr. 8, I-36
He's Got the Whole World in His
    Hands  Gr. 7, I-36
Hey, Ho! Nobody Home  Gr. 6, 28
Himmel und Erde  Gr. 5, 94
Hine mah tov  Gr. 5, 430
I Am But a Small Voice  Gr. 6, 446
I Dream a World  Gr. 8, G-40
I Know an Old Lady  Gr. 1, 387
I Love Peanuts  Gr. 7, E-20
I See the Moon  Gr. 2, 59
I Vow to You, My Country  Gr. 5, 419
I Vow to You, My Country  Gr. 5, 421
I Walk the Unfrequented Road
    Gr. 6, 79

I Wish I Knew How It Would Feel to Be
    Free  Gr. 6, 470
I'll Fly Away  Gr. 8, I-43
I'm a Believer  Gr. 7, G-33
Ichi-gatsu tsuitachi  Gr. 7, I-40
Ja-Da  Gr. 7, G-20
Jambalaya  Gr. 8, I-48
Joy of Kwanzaa, The  Gr. 6, 462
*Kayagum pyongch'ang-sae t'aryug*
    Gr. 8, B-13
Kunolounkwa  Gr. K, 110
La golondrina  Gr. 8, I-50
La mar estaba serena  Gr. 2, 345
Lady, Lady  Gr. 1, 62
Las mañanitas  Gr. 6, 481
Lift Ev'ry Voice and Sing  Gr. 8, I-54
Light Up the World with a Song
    Gr. 8, G-25
Lion Sleeps Tonight, The  Gr. 8, I-57
Lone Star Trail  Gr. 2, 21
Look! Look! The Sun Woke Up!
    Gr. 1, 368
Love in Any Language  Gr. 6, 476
Mañana  Gr. 7, E-14
Mary Ann  Gr. K, 253
Merry Modal Christmas, A  Gr. 4, 411
Michael, Row the Boat Ashore
    Gr. 2, 18
Midnight Special, The  Gr. 7, F-23
*Mongolian Long Song*  Gr. 8, B-14
Nampaya omame  Gr. 7, D-10
Now's the Time  Gr. 5, 450
O, Desayo  Gr. 5, 412
Oh, Freedom  Gr. 7, G-30
Oh, How Lovely is the Evening
    Gr. 4, 216
One Family  Gr. 7, G-17
Oy, Hanuka  Gr. 7, I-44
Panamam tombé  Gr. 7, D-18
Party Tonight!  Gr. 2, 152
Pay Me My Money Down  Gr. 7, I-46
Peace Like a River  Gr. 3, 246
Peace Like a River  Gr. 6, 190
Peace Like a River  Gr. 6, 193
Pin Pon  Gr. 1, 147
Plant Four Seeds  Gr. 2, 131
Proud  Gr. 7, G-3
Red River Valley  Gr. 6, 10
Rent  Gr. 8, A-22
*Requiem, "Pie Jesu"*  Gr. 6, 179
Riddle Ree (speech piece)  Gr. 2, 34
Rocky Mountain  Gr. 2, 98
Sailing to the Sea  Gr. 1, 336
Scattin' A-Round (Variations on Row 3)
    Gr. 6, 160
Sea Shell  Gr. 2, 100
See-Saw Sacradown  Gr. 2, 209
Shalom aleichem  Gr. 6, 409
Shanghai Chicken  Gr. 1, 140
Shenandoah  Gr. 5, 264
Shir l'shalom  Gr. 4, 421
Shoo, Fly  Gr. 2, 201
Si si si  Gr. 7, G-13

Sing a Song of Peace  Gr. 6, 66
Sing! Speak! Whisper! Shout!
    Gr. 1, 36
Singing vocalises  Gr. 6, 7
Siyahamba  Gr. 6, 212
Siyahamba  Gr. 6, 213
Something Told the Wild Geese
    Gr. 7, G-39
*Soulville*  Gr. 7, B-17
Star-Spangled Banner, The  Gr. 6, 486
Star-Spangled Banner, The  Gr. 7, I-56
Star-Spangled Banner, The  Gr. 8, I-62
Stille Nacht (Silent Night)  Gr. 7, I-54
Surfin' U.S.A.  Gr. 7, E-27
Surfin' U.S.A.  Gr. 7, I-59
Swing Low, Sweet Chariot
    Gr. 7, C-41
Tanabata-sama  Gr. 2, 338
This Is My Song  Gr. 6, 77
This Land Is Your Land  Gr. 7, I-66
Tideo  Gr. 2, 80
*Tihore Mai*  Gr. 8, B-12
Tuxedo Junction  Gr. 8, G-21
United Nations on the March, The
    Gr. 6, 443
Uno, dos y tres  Gr. 5, 429
Vem kan segla?  Gr. 6, 417
Voices of Pride, The  Gr. 5, 88
*Vonjeo*  Gr. 8, B-12
Wai bamba  Gr. 8, G-13
Who Has Seen the Wind?  Gr. 2, 324
Wind Blew East, The  Gr. 1, 64
Winter  Gr. 8, G-11
World of Difference, A  Gr. 5, 386
Yellow Rose of Texas, The  Gr. 7, I-70
Yonder Come Day  Gr. 8, I-68
Your changing voice  Gr. 7, G-7

# Pitch and Rhythm Index

*This section provides a listing of songs from MAKING MUSIC that can be used to teach specific pitches and rhythms. The pitch and rhythm patterns are listed in the teaching sequence that is used in this series. Songs that can be used to teach the pitch and rhythm patterns indicated are listed alphabetically.*

*Specific measure numbers are indicated in parentheses when the rhythms or pitches apply to only a portion of the song. The letter a indicates that the anacrusis to the measure is included.*

*An asterisk (\*) next to a song title indicates that the song is used to present the pitch or rhythm in the specific grade level.*

## Pitch Index

### so-mi

#### mi so

A Ram Sam Sam (m. 5–6), Gr. 3, p. 208
Aguinaldo (m. 1–4), Gr. 3, p. 402
Andy Pandy (m. 1–2), Gr. K, p. 46
Apple Tree (m. 1–2, 5–6), Gr. 1, p. 228
Banana (m. 9, 13, 21), Gr. 2, p. 114
Bluebird, Bluebird (m. 1, 5), Gr. K, p. 105
Chanukah, Chanukah (m. 1–2, 9–10), Gr. 1, p. 420
Charlie over the Water, Gr. 1, p. 68
Corn Grinding Song (m. 1, 3), Gr. K, p. 67
Cuckoo, Cuckoo, Gr. 1, p. 110
Cuculí (m. 1–2, 5–6, 16–17, 20–21, 24–25), Gr. K, p. 238
Downtown (m. 18, 20, 22), Gr. 6, p. 258
El zapatero (Melody only, m. 1–2, 5–6), Gr. 1, p. 298
God Bless the Child (m. a7–8, 25–26), Gr. 7, p. 27
Hello, There! (m. 1–2, 7–10), Gr. K, p. 6
Hey, Hey, Look at Me, Gr. 1, p. 70
I'm in the Mood (m. 9–10), Gr. K, p. 86
Ise oluwa (m. 3-4, 15-16), Gr. 2, p. 102
Jim Along, Josie (m. 1, 3), Gr. K, p. 39
L'inverno è passato (m. 9–10), Gr. 2, p. 400
Lady, Lady (m. 1–2, 6, 8–10), Gr. 1, p. 62
Lemonade (m. 1–5), Gr. 1, p. 190
Listen to the Water (m. 1-2), Gr. 2, p. 294
Little Red Caboose (m. 1–4), Gr. K, p. 229
Little Shell (m. 1, 3), Gr. 1, p. 355
Look! Look! The Sun Woke Up! (m. 1–3), Gr. 1, p. 368
Los días de la semana (m. 1–2, 4), Gr. 1, p. 268
Mi cuerpo hace música (m. 1–2, 5–6), Gr. K, p. 106
Oliver Twist (m. 1–2, 5–6), Gr. K, p. 138
Pai pi qiu (m. 1–2), Gr. 1, p. 324
Pease Porridge Hot (m. 1–7), Gr. 1, p. 134
Pizza, Pizza, Daddy-o (m. 3, 5, 7, 9, 11, 13, 15, 17–18), Gr. 2, p. 28
Rain, Rain (m. 1–2), Gr. 1, p. 54
Riquirrán (m. 1–2), Gr. 1, p. 48
Serra, serra, serrador, Gr. 1, p. 112
Snail, Snail (m. 1–2), Gr. 1, p. 190
\*Star Light, Star Bright, Gr. 1, p. 108
This Old Man (m. 1–2), Gr. 3, p. 152
Tic, tac (m. 1–2, 4–5), Gr. 1, p. 252
Turn the Glasses Over (m. 9–10), Gr. 3, p. 204
Vamos a la fiesta (m. 1–2), Gr. 2, p. 374

### la

#### mi so la

A-Tisket, A-Tasket (m. 1–4, 9–12), Gr. 2, p. 238
Abiyoyo (m. 1, 3), Gr. 2, p. 108
Ahora voy a cantarles (m. 1–2), Gr. 3, p. 56
Amarillo Armadillo (m. 1-2), Gr. 2, p. 82
Apple Tree (m. 1–7), Gr. 1, p. 228
Bling Blang (m. 1–2, 5–6), Gr. 3, p. 240
Bluebird, Bluebird (m. 1–2, 5–6), Gr. K, p. 105
\*Bounce High, Bounce Low, Gr. 1, p. 152
Busy Buzzy Bee (m. 1–3), Gr. K, p. 77
Camptown Races (m. 1–12, 5–8, 11–12, 17–18), Gr. 5, p. 270
Clouds of Gray (m. 1–3), Gr. 2, p. 56
Cuculí (m. 5–8, 20–25), Gr. K, p. 238
Don't Let the Wind (m. 1–4), Gr. 3, p. 180
El cóndor pasa (m. a3–4, a7–8), Gr. 6, p. 46
El juego chirimbolo (m. 1–12), Gr. 2, p. 54
Elegua (m. 1–8, 11–12), Gr. 7, p. 8
Gakavik (m. 1–2, 9–10), Gr. 4, p. 14
Glendy Burke, The (m. 17–18), Gr. 4, p. 262
Goin' Down the Road Feelin' Bad (m. 1–4), Gr. 7, p. 13
Great Big House (m. 1–2), Gr. 2, p. 204
Great Day (m. 5–6), Gr. 3, p. 58
Ha'kyo jong (m. 1-2, 5-6), Gr. 2, p. 135
Hey, Ho! Nobody Home (m. 1–2, 7–8), Gr. 6, p. 28
I'm in the Mood (m. 7–8), Gr. K, p. 86
Ja-Da (m. 1-2, 5-6, 13-14), Gr. 2, p. 188
Ja-Da (Part I, m. 1–2), Gr. 7, p. 20
Johnny Caught a Flea (m. 1–7), Gr. 1, p. 226
Joy to the World (Melody only, m. 1–4), Gr. 3, p. 22
Karangatia ra (m. 9–12, 17–18), Gr. 8, p. 23
Keep Your Eyes on the Prize (m. a5–6), Gr. 8, p. 16
Kookaburra (m. 1–2), Gr. 4, p. 186
La paloma se fué (m. 1–2, a5–6), Gr. 6, p. 51
Lemonade, Gr. 1, p. 190
Little Darlin' (m. 9–11), Gr. 7, p. 30
Los pollitos (m. 5–6), Gr. K, p. 166
\*Lucy Locket (final: *mi*), Gr. 2, p. 27
My Pony, Macaroni, Gr. 1, p. 158
Oliver Twist, Gr. K, p. 138
On a Log, Mister Frog, Gr. K, p. 148
Osamu kosamu (final: *la*), Gr. 4, p. 96
Pay Me My Money Down (m. 9–10), Gr. 7, p. 46
Perná, perná, i mélissá (m. 1–2), Gr. K, p. 264
Perot (m. 1–2), Gr. 2, p. 378
Pizza, Pizza, Daddy-o (final: *mi*), Gr. 2, p. 28
Pollerita (m. 5–6, 9–10), Gr. 5, p. 151

Rain, Rain, Gr. 1, p. 54
Rio Grande (m. 3–4, 11–12), Gr. 4, p. 256
Rise and Shine (m. 1–2), Gr. 4, p. 98
'Round and 'Round (m. 1–2, 5–6), Gr. 1, p. 148
Same Train (m. 5-8), Gr. 2, p. 164
Si si si (Part I, m. 1–2, 5–6), Gr. 7, p. 13
Silent Night (melody only, m. 1–2), Gr. 3, p. 394
Snail, Snail, Gr. 1, p. 190
Stand By Me (m. a1–2, a9–10), Gr. 8, p. 25
Step in Time (m. 1-2), Gr. 2, p. 74
Stille Nacht (Silent Night) (m. 1–2), Gr. 7, p. 54
Tideo (m. 1-2, 5-6), Gr. 2, p. 80
¡Viva el fútbol! (m. 1), Gr. 1, p. 96
Viva Jujuy (m. 17–20), Gr. 5, p. 228
Who Has Seen the Wind? (m. 1-2), Gr. 2, p. 324
Wind Up the Apple Tree, Gr. 1, p. 184

**so la**

Banana Splits (m. 1–2), Gr. 1, p. 318
Cirmos cica (m. 1–4), Gr. 1, p. 130
Cookie (m. 1-2, 5-6, 10, 12), Gr. 2, p. 172
Ég a gyertya (m. 1–4) (final: *do*), Gr. K, p. 96
Let the Music Begin! (m. 9–12), Gr. 1, p. 2
Old Man Mosie (m. 1–4, 9–14), Gr. 3, p. 108

**mi la**

Joshua Fought the Battle of Jericho (m. a9–14), Gr. 8, p. 18
Owl and the Pumpkin, The (m. 7–8), Gr. 2, p. 377

**do**

**do mi so la**

*Apple Tree (final: *do*), Gr. 1, p. 228
Bonavist' Harbour (m. 1–3, 6–7, 10–12), Gr. 3, p. 294
Clouds of Gray (final: *do*), Gr. 2, p. 56
Coffee Grows on White Oak Trees (m. 1–2, 5–6), Gr. 3, p. 168
Costume Capers (m. 1–2), Gr. 1, p. 412
Counting Song (m. 1–2), Gr. 1, p. 253
Farmer in the Dell, The (m. 5–6) (final: *do*), Gr. K, p. 232
Goin' to the Fair (m. 1–4), Gr. K, p. 156
Hashkediya (m. 1–4), Gr. 3, p. 206
I Fed My Horse (m. 1-2, 5-6), Gr. 2, p. 94
I See With My Hands (m. 3-4), Gr. 2, p. 148
I'm a Believer (m. 16–23, 46–53), Gr. 7, p. 33
Juan pirulero (m. 1–4), Gr. K, p. 215
Knock the Cymbals (m. 1–2, 5–6) (final: *do*), Gr. 1, p. 176
Les petites marionettes (m. 1–2, 4–6), Gr. K, p. 237
Michael, Row the Boat Ashore (m. 1-4), Gr. 2, p. 18
My Foot's In My Stirrup (m. 1-6), Gr. 2, p. 234
Old Chisholm Trail, The (m. 1–4), Gr. 6, p. 237
One Morning Soon (m. 1–2), Gr. 3, p. 68
Piñon, pirulín (m. mm. 1-2, 5-6) (final: *do*), Gr. 2, p. 174
Piñon, pirulín (m. 1–2, 5–6), Gr. 2, p. 174
Plant Four Seeds (m. 1–2) (final: *do*), Gr. 2, p. 130
Rocky Mountain (m. 9-10, 13-14), Gr. 2, p. 98
Vamos a cantar (m. a1–2), Gr. K, p. 278
Willowbee (m. 1–6) (final: *do*), Gr. 1, p. 222
Yesh lanu taish (m. 7–8), Gr. 1, p. 182

**do mi so**

Almost Day (m. 1–2), Gr. 3, p. 397
Ambos a dos (m. 1–2), Gr. 3, p. 20
America (N. Diamond) (m. 1–10), Gr. 4, p. 206

Andy Pandy (final: *do*), Gr. K, p. 46
Bus, The (m. 3–4, 7–8, 11–12) (final: *do*), Gr. K, p. 82
Clouds of Gray (m. 4), Gr. 2, p. 56
Cowboys' Christmas Ball (m. 1–2), Gr. 6, p. 239
Der sad to katte (m. 11-12), Gr. 2, p. 300
Free at Last (m. 1–2), Gr. 2, p. 396
Free at Last (m. 1–2), Gr. 6, p. 468
Going to the Zoo (m. 1–2, 5–6), Gr. K, p. 216
Gypsy in the Moonlight (m. 1–2), Gr. 3, p. 12
Harrison Town (m. a1–2, a5–6, a13–14), Gr. 6, p. 97
He's Got the Whole World in His Hands (m. 1–2, 5–6), Gr. 3, p. 230
He's Got the Whole World in His Hands (Melody only, m. 1–2, 5–6), Gr. 7, p. 36
Hello! (m. 1-2), Gr. 2, p. 262
Hi-Dee-Roon (m. 1, 5), Gr. K, p. 10
I Bought Me a Cat (m. verse 2, ending 2, verse 4, ending 4), Gr. 2, p. 308
*I See the Moon (final: *do*), Gr. 2, p. 58
If I Had a Hammer (m. 1–2, 5–6), Gr. 5, p. 287
Knock the Cymbals (m. 1–2, 5–6), Gr. 1, p. 176
*Little Mouse, The, Gr. 1, p. 348
Looby Loo (m. 1–2, 5–6) (final: *do*), Gr. K, p. 210
Lost My Gold Ring (m. 1–2), Gr. 6, p. 158
Love Somebody (m. 1, 3, 5), Gr. 3, p. 94
Mama Don't 'Low (m. 5–8), Gr. 6, p. 358
Mos Mos, Gr. 1, p. 130
My Foot's In My Stirrup (m. 1-2, 5-6), Gr. 2, p. 234
O Laufet, ihr Hirten (m. 1–2, 5–6, 13–14), Gr. 2, p. 384
One Morning Soon (m. 1), Gr. 3, p. 68
Panamam tombé (m. 1–2, 5), Gr. 7, p. 18
Panamam tombé (m. 1–2, 5), Gr. 7, p. 18
Paw-Paw Patch (m. 1–2, 5–6), Gr. 4, p. 93
Pease Porridge Hot (final: *do*), Gr. 1, p. 134
Pumpkin, Pumpkin (m. 1–4) (final: *do*), Gr. 1, p. 413
Rock Around the Clock (m. 1–8), Gr. 7, p. 18
Rocky Mountain (m. 1-4), Gr. 2, p. 98
Roll Over (m. 2–4) (final: *do*), Gr. K, p. 288
Singin' in the Tub (m. 1–6 of refrain), Gr. K, p. 220
Sorida (final: *do*), Gr. 1, p. 312
Swing Low, Sweet Chariot (m. 3–4, 11–12), Gr. 7, p. 41
Together in Unity (m. 1, 8–9), Gr. K, p. 320
¡Viva el fútbol! (m. 4), Gr. 1, p. 96
Walk in Jerusalem (m. 1–2), Gr. 4, p. 100

**do so**

Johnny Caught a Flea (m. 7–8), Gr. 1, p. 226
Little Mouse, The (m. 13–16), Gr. 1, p. 348
Wind Blew East, The (m. 1–6) (final: *do*), Gr. 1, p. 64

**do mi**

Rock Island Line (m. 11–12), Gr. 4, p. 54
Vamos a la fiesta (m. 5–6), Gr. 2, p. 374

**do so la**

Alphabet Song (m. 1–2, 9–10) (final: *do*), Gr. K, p. 280
Here Comes Valerie (m. 1–3) (final: *do*), Gr. 1, p. 32
Kou ri lengay (m. 1-6), Gr. 2, p. 217
Kou ri lengay (m. 1-6), Gr. 7, p. 2
Little Black Bug (m. 1–4) (final: *do*), Gr. 1, p. 214
Over in the Meadow (m. 9–12), Gr. 1, p. 346
Zudio (m. 1-3, 5-7), Gr. 2, p. 269

## re

### do re

O ma washi, Gr. K, p. 13

### do re mi

Achshav (m. 9-12), Gr. 2, p. 64
Alison's Camel (m. 1–7), Gr. K, p. 289
All Around the Buttercup (m. 3-4, 7-8), Gr. 2, p. 170
All the Way Around the World (m. 7-8), Gr. 2, p. 258
Apples and Bananas (m. 1–3), Gr. 1, p. 390
At the Same Time (m. 1–2), Gr. 6, p. 115
Au clair de la lune (m. 1–8, 13–16), Gr. 3, p. 18
Banjo Sam (m. 1-8), Gr. 2, p. 314
Big Old Storm a-Comin' (m. 7–8), Gr. K, p. 257
Book of Love (m. 7–14, 21–28), Gr. 8, p. 27
Chapel of Love (Part I, m. 13–15), Gr. 7, p. 27
Chrismus a Come (m. 1–2, 5–6), Gr. 3, p. 396
Con el vito (m. 1–4, 9–12), Gr. 7, p. 15
Cookie (m. 3-4, 7-8, 9-10, 11-12, 13-14), Gr. 2, p. 172
Day-O! (Banana Boat Loader's Song) (m. 3–4, 7–8, 11–12, 15–16, 19–20, 23–24), Gr. 5, p. 18
Different Beat, A (m. 7–8), Gr. 1, p. 6
Dinah (m. 7-8), Gr. 2, p. 120
Do, Lord (m. 13–16, 30–33), Gr. 3, p. 164
Don't Dump Trash (m. 14-16), Gr. 2, p. 318
Down by the Bay (m. 13–15), Gr. 1, p. 18
Dry Bones (m. 1–8), Gr. 4, p. 162
En nuestra Tierra tan linda (m. 1-4), Gr. 2, p. 335
Every Night When the Sun Goes In (m. a1–2), Gr. 8, p. 28
Fais do do (m. 1–16, 25–32, part 1–2), Gr. 6, p. 403
Fais dodo (m. 1–8), Gr. K, p. 158
Frère Jacques (m. 1-2), Gr. 2, p. 125
Friend of Mine (m. 7–8), Gr. 1, p. 310
*Frog in the Millpond (final: do), Gr. 2, p. 44
Give My Regards to Broadway (m. 19–32), Gr. 6, p. 39
God Bless the Child (m. 1–2, 19–20), Gr. 7, p. 27
Going Upon the Mountain (Melody only), Gr. 6, p. 105
Gonna Ride Up in the Chariot (m. 1, 3, 5), Gr. 4, p. 20
Hashewie (m. 1–9), Gr. 4, p. 63
Hot Cross Buns (Version 1) (final: do), Gr. 3, p. 218
How Many Miles to Babylon? (m. 1-2, 4-6, 8), Gr. 2, p. 128
I Bought Me a Cat (m. 9-12), Gr. 2, p. 308
I Don't Care If the Rain Comes Down (m. 1–2, 5–8, 11–12, 15–16), Gr. 3, p. 24
I Fed My Horse (m. 9-12), Gr. 2, p. 94
I Got Shoes (m. 1-4, 15-16), Gr. 2, p. 242
I'll Fly Away (m. 7–8, 15–16), Gr. 8, p. 42
I'm a Dreydl (m. 5–8, 13–16), Gr. K, p. 315
I'm Gonna Sing (m. 6–8), Gr. 4, p. 33
It's a Small World (m. 17–20), Gr. 3, p. 268
Jinny Go 'Round (m. 6–8), Gr. K, p. 228
Jolly Old St. Nicholas (m. 1–4, 9–12, 15–16), Gr. K, p. 316
Joy to the World (Melody only, m. 11–12), Gr. 3, p. 22
Kibungo (m. 7-8), Gr. 2, p. 354
Koriko!, Gr. K, p. 154
Kum bachur atzel (m. 1–8), Gr. 3, p. 138
Kuma san, Gr. K, p. 40
*Las horas, Gr. 1, p. 246
Leak kanseng, Gr. 1, p. 156
Leila (m. 7–8, 11–12), Gr. 1, p. 258

Let the Music Begin! (m. 1–2, 17–18), Gr. 1, p. 2
Love Somebody (m. 7–8), Gr. 3, p. 94
Lullaby and Dance (m. 1–4), Gr. 4, p. 387
Michael, Row the Boat Ashore (m. 7–8), Gr. 2, p. 18
Music's in Me , The (m. 1-2, 5-10), Gr. 2, p. 40
Must Be Santa (m. 9–10), Gr. K, p. 318
My Father's House (m. 1-2, 9-10, 13–15), Gr. 2, p. 25
Nanny Goat (m. 1, 3, 5, 7), Gr. K, p. 161
Now Let Me Fly (m. 7–8), Gr. 3, p. 178
Oh, Watch the Stars (m. 1-2, 7-8), Gr. 2, p. 144
Oh, Won't You Sit Down (verse), Gr. 3, p. 28
Over My Head (final: do), Gr. 4, p. 118
Over My Head (Melody) (final: do), Gr. 7, p. 9
Party Tonight! (m. 9-10, 13-14), Gr. 2, p. 152
Piñon, pirulín (m. 3-4), Gr. 2, p. 174
Ragtime Cowboy Joe (m. 18-19), Gr. 2, p. 250
Rio Grande (m. 1-2, 9-10), Gr. 4, p. 256
Rocky Mountain (m. 7-8, 11-12, 15-16), Gr. 2, p. 98
Sail Away (m. 9–14), Gr. 5, p. 404
Scattin' A-Round (Variations on Row 3) (m. 1-2, 9-10, 17–18), Gr. 6, p. 160
See-Saw Sacradown (m. 3–4, 7–8), Gr. 2, p. 208
Shake Them 'Simmons Down (Melody only, m. 7-8), Gr. 2, p. 244
Shortnin' Bread (m. 9–10), Gr. 7, p. 27
Si si si (Part I, m. 3–4, 7–8), Gr. 7, p. 13
Spring Has Sprung! (m. 7–8, 15–16), Gr. K, p. 142
Stand By Me (m. 20–24), Gr. 8, p. 25
Sugar "Shuga" Bee, Gr. K, p. 64
Take Your Feet Out 'the Sand (m. 7–11), Gr. K, p. 231
There Is Love Somewhere (m. 1–4, 13–16), Gr. 6, p. 318
Those Magic Changes (m. 21–22), Gr. 8, p. 30
Three Little Birds (m. a1, verse m. 16–17, 29–31), Gr. 8, p. 7
To'ia mai te waka (m. 7–8), Gr. 1, p. 77
Trouble Is a Mountain (m. 1, 3-4), Gr. 2, p. 202
Wake Me, Shake Me (m. 1–4, 7–8), Gr. 1, p. 278
Way Down in the Schoolyard (m. 3-4, 7-8, 11, 15-16), Gr. 2, p. 50
We Are Dear Little Birdies (m. 1–4), Gr. K, p. 176
We're All Gonna Shine Tonight (m. 15-16), Gr. 2, p. 240
Who Has the Penny? (m. 1–4, 13–16), Gr. K, p. 42
Yibane amenu (m. 9–10), Gr. 4, p. 316

### do re mi so

Ah! Les Jolis Papillons, Gr. 1, p. 362
All Around the Buttercup (final: do), Gr. 2, p. 170
All the Way Around the World (m. 16-17), Gr. 2, p. 258
Amarillo Armadillo (m. 3-4), Gr. 2, p. 82
Banjo Sam (final: mi), Gr. 2, p. 314
Canción de cuna (m. 1–4), Gr. 4, p. 144
Chang (m. 1–4), Gr. 1, p. 156
Chicken on the Fence Post (m. 1-2, 5-6), Gr. 3, p. 92
Circle 'Round the Moon (m. 5–12), Gr. 4, p. 403
Corn Grinding Song (m. 1–4), Gr. K, p. 67
Deux cocodries (m. 1–8), Gr. 2, p. 364
Dinah (final: do), Gr. 2, p. 120
Diou shou juan'er (m. 9-11), Gr. 2, p. 277
Don't Be Cruel (m. a1–8, coda), Gr. 6, p. 255
Doraji (m. 1–4, 9–12), Gr. 4, p. 174
Dry Bones Come Skipping (m. 2, 6), Gr. 4, p. 218
Earth Is My Mother, The (m. 1–2), Gr. 1, p. 340
Einini (m. 1–12, voices 1–2), Gr. 4, p. 391
*El zapatero (Melody only), Gr. 1, p. 298

Families (m. 9–10), Gr. 1, p. 282

Farmer's Dairy Key, The (m. 7-8), Gr. 2, p. 182

Fly and the Bumblebee, The (m. 1–4, 9–12),
  Gr. 1, p. 384

Free at Last (m. 5–8), Gr. 2, p. 396

Free at Last (m. 5–8), Gr. 6, p. 468

From Sea to Shining Sea (m. 1-2, 5-6), Gr. 2, p. 342

Gakavik (m. 21–24), Gr. 4, p. 14

Going on a Picnic (m. 3–4, 7–8), Gr. K, p. 190

Going Upon the Mountain (Melody only), Gr. 6, p. 105

Going Upon the Mountain (m. a9–16), Gr. 6, p. 105

Gonna Ride Up in the Chariot (m. 7–8), Gr. 4, p. 20

Good Morning (m. 5–8), Gr. 3, p. 192

Great Big House (m. 7–8), Gr. 2, p. 204

Great Day (m. 11–12, 15, 16), Gr. 3, p. 58

Gypsy in the Moonlight (m. 1–4), Gr. 3, p. 12

Ha'kyo jong (m. 7-8), Gr. 2, p. 135

Hato popo (m. 1–4), Gr. 1, p. 186

Hey, m'tswala (final: *do*), Gr. 4, p. 79

How Many Miles to Babylon? (final: *do*), Gr. 2, p. 128

Hui jia qù (m. 1-4, 7-8), Gr. 2, p. 158

Hwa yuan li-de young wa wa (m. 1–2), Gr. 3, p. 102

I Have a Dog, Gr. K, p. 262

I'll Fly Away (m. 9–12), Gr. 8, p. 42

I'm Flying Home (m. 1-4), Gr. 2, p. 286

Imbabura (m. 1–8), Gr. 5, p. 202

Ja-Da (m. 3-4, 15-16), Gr. 2, p. 188

Jingle Bells (m. 17–20, 25–28), Gr. 2, p. 388

John Kanaka (m. 1–16), Gr. 3, p. 60

Knock the Cymbals (m. 1–4), Gr. 1, p. 176

Lady, Lady (m. 1–4, 9–12), Gr. 1, p. 62

Let Us Chase the Squirrel (final: *do*), Gr. 2, p. 98

Little Darlin' (m. 1–8, 34–38), Gr. 7, p. 30

Little Spider (final: *do*), Gr. K, p. 93

London Bridge (m. 4), Gr. K, p. 244

Looby Loo (m. 1–6, 15–16), Gr. K, p. 210

Look! Look! The Sun Woke Up! (m. 9–10), Gr. 1, p. 368

Man of Constant Sorrow (Melody, m. 1–4), Gr. 7, p. 28

Mariposita (m. 1-4, 17-20), Gr. 2, p. 156

My Dear Companion (m. 13–16, 29–33), Gr. 6, p. 23

My Home's Across the Blue Ridge Mountains (m. 3–4,
  11–12), Gr. 7, p. 6

Old Blue (refrain), Gr. K, p. 122

Pastures of Plenty (m. 4–6, 7–8), Gr. 4, p. 280

Paths of Victory (m. 5–8), Gr. 6, p. 195

Piñon, pirulín (m. 7-8), Gr. 2, p. 174

Pottery Dance (m. 1–2), Gr. 1, p. 370

Rise and Shine (m. 7–8), Gr. 4, p. 98

*Sea Shell (final: *do*), Gr. 2, p. 100

Seasons of Love (m. 9–10), Gr. 8, p. 22

She'll Be Comin' 'Round the Mountain (m. 4–8),
  Gr. 2, p. 358

Shine, Shine, Shine (m. 1–2, 6–8), Gr. 1, p. 42

Shu ha mo (m. 1–4), Gr. 3, p. 276

Sing a Rainbow (m. 1-2), Gr. 2, p. 166

Sleep, Baby, Sleep (m. 9-12), Gr. 2, p. 197

Song of One, A (m. 9–12), Gr. 3, p. 344

Tanabata-sama (m. 5-8), Gr. 2, p. 336

Three Little Birds (m. 1–2), Gr. 4, p. 320

Three Little Birds (m. a1–2), Gr. 8, p. 7

Today Is Your Birthday (m. 1–8), Gr. 1, p. 410

Turn the Glasses Over (m. 7–8), Gr. 3, p. 204

Valentines (m. 1–4), Gr. 2, p. 398

Was kommt dort von der Höh'? (m. 7–10), Gr. 8, p. 21

Wichita Hand Game Song 2, Gr. 3, p. 306

Willowbee (m. 9–12), Gr. 1, p. 222

Yang wa wa (m. 5–6), Gr. K, p. 162

## do re mi so la

Ahora voy a cantarles (m. 5–8), Gr. 3, p. 56

All Around the Buttercup (final: *do*), Gr. 2, p. 170

All the Way Around the World (m. 1-6), Gr. 2, p. 258

Amarillo Armadillo (final: *do*), Gr. 2, p. 82

Asadoya (m. 1–3), Gr. 6, p. 303

Bam, chi, chi, bam (verse), Gr. K, p. 109

Banana Splits (m. 5–8), Gr. 1, p. 318

Barb'ry Allen (m. a7–8), Gr. 6, p. 44

Black Snake (final: *do*), Gr. 3, p. 53

Bling Blang (m. 1–4), Gr. 3, p. 240

Button, You Must Wander, Gr. 2, p. 172

California (m. 1–8), Gr. 5, p. 52

Camptown Races (m. 1–16), Gr. 5, p. 270

Cha yang wu (m. 5–12), Gr. 1, p. 90

Chicken on the Fence Post (m. 7–8), Gr. 3, p. 92

Coffee Grows on White Oak Trees (m. 3–4, 15–16),
  Gr. 3, p. 168

Cookie (final: *do*), Gr. 2, p. 172

Costume Capers (m. 1–4, 17–20), Gr. 1, p. 412

Cuculí, Gr. K, p. 238

Deep in the Heart of Texas (m. 13–16, 29–32),
  Gr. 8, p. 18

Diou shou juan'er (m. 12-14), Gr. 2, p. 277

Ég a gyertya (m. 7–8), Gr. K, p. 96

Ezekiel Saw the Wheel (m. verse, melody, m. 17–24),
  Gr. 6, p. 379

Farmer's Dairy Key, The (m. 1–4), Gr. 2, p. 182

Gakavik (m. 1–4, 9–12), Gr. 4, p. 14

Goin' to the Fair (final: *do*), Gr. K, p. 156

Great Big House, Gr. 2, p. 204

Great Big Stars (m. 7–10), Gr. 1, p. 60

Ha'kyo jong (final: *do*), Gr. 2, p. 135

Harambee (m. 1–2), Gr. 4, p. 434

Hashkediya (m. 5–8), Gr. 3, p. 206

Hato popo (final: *do*), Gr. 1, p. 186

Here Comes Valerie (final: *do*), Gr. 1, p. 32

Hop Up, My Ladies (verse), Gr. 3, p. 142

I Fed My Horse (final: *do*), Gr. 2, p. 94

I Fed My Horse (final: *do*), Gr. 2, p. 94

I Wonder Where Maria's Gone (final: *re*), Gr. 3, p. 318

Ida Red (final: *do*), Gr. 3, p. 30

Ja-Da (m. 1-4, 13-16), Gr. 2, p. 188

Ja-Da (Part I, m. 1–3), Gr. 7, p. 20

Joy of Kwanzaa, The (m. 1–16), Gr. 6, p. 462

Juan pirulero (final: *do*), Gr. K, p. 215

Knock the Cymbals (final: *do*), Gr. 1, p. 176

Li'l Liza Jane (m. 1–8), Gr. 3, p. 140

Little Black Bug (final: *do*), Gr. 1, p. 214

Little Shell (final: *do*), Gr. 1, p. 355

Los maizales (m. 1–4, 9–12), Gr. 1, p. 296

Mama, Buy Me a Chiney Doll (final: *do*), Gr. K, p. 120

Mary Came a-Running (final: *do*), Gr. K, p. 294

Mister Rabbit (refrain), Gr. K, p. 128

My Dear Companion (m. 5–8, 21–24), Gr. 6, p. 23

My Foot's In My Stirrup (final: *do*), Gr. 2, p. 234

O hal'lwe (m. 9–12), Gr. 3, p. 256

Oh, Susanna (m. 1–16, 21–24) (final: *do*), Gr. 4, p. 264

Old Chisholm Trail, The ( , m. a7–8), Gr. 6, p. 237

Pai pi qiu (final: *do*), Gr. 1, p. 324
Perná, perná, i mélissá (final: *do*), Gr. K, p. 264
Piñon, pirulín (final: *do*), Gr. 2, p. 174
Pumpkin, Pumpkin (final: *do*), Gr. 1, p. 413
*Rocky Mountain (final: *do*), Gr. 2, p. 98
Rocky Top (m. 1–16), Gr. 5, p. 348
'Round and 'Round, Gr. 1, p. 148
Sail Away (m. 15–20), Gr. 5, p. 404
Si si si (Part I, m. 1–8), Gr. 7, p. 13
Sing, Sing, Sing! (m. 17–24), Gr. 5, p. 340
Stand By Me (m. 1–16), Gr. 5, p. 46
Stand By Me (m. a1–16), Gr. 8, p. 25
Three Little Birds (m. 8–10), Gr. 4, p. 320
Tideo (m. 1–8), Gr. 2, p. 80
Tsuki (final: *do*), Gr. 4, p. 25
Under the Same Sun (m. 14–18 of verse), Gr. 6, p. 440
Valentine Dance (final: *do*), Gr. 1, p. 437
When the Train Comes Along (m. 3–4, 6–8), Gr. 1, p. 300
Willowbee (final: *do*), Gr. 1, p. 222
Your Life Is Now (m. 14–18), Gr. 6, p. 4

### do re mi so la do'
Imbabura (m. 9–16), Gr. 5, p. 202

### do re so la
Mister Ram Goat-O (m. 1–2), Gr. 3, p. 54

### re mi so
Don't Let Your Watch Run Down (m. 9–12), Gr. 3, p. 166

### re mi so la
Bear Dance (m. 1–4), Gr. 7, p. 10
Deep in the Heart of Texas (m. 5–8, 21–24), Gr. 8, p. 18
Great Big House (m. 3-4), Gr. 2, p. 204
Jambalaya (m. 1–3), Gr. 8, p. 46
Jambalaya (On The Bayou) (m. a1–3), Gr. 6, p. 244
New Hungarian Folk Song (m. 3–8), Gr. 6, p. 196
Supercalifragilisticexpialidocious (m. 5–8, 25–28), Gr. 3, p. 7
There Is Love Somewhere (m. 5–8), Gr. 6, p. 318
Tsuki (m. 5–8), Gr. 4, p. 25
Turn the Glasses Over (m. 11–12), Gr. 3, p. 204
Yüe liang wan wan (m. 1–6), Gr. 5, p. 314

### mi re do
Swing Low, Sweet Chariot (m. 7–8, 15–16), Gr. 7, p. 41

## mi,

### mi, so, la, do mi
Little Johnny Brown (m. 13–16), Gr. 3, p. 313

## la,

### la, do re
Artsa alinu (m. 13–16), Gr. 3, p. 285
Chicka Hanka (m. 1-4), Gr. 2, p. 211
Chicka Hanka (m. 1–4), Gr. 8, p. 15
Dinner Music, Gr. K, p. 70
Down, Down, Baby (final: *re*), Gr. 2, p. 32
Goin' Down the Road Feelin' Bad (m. 5–8), Gr. 7, p. 13
Hui jia qü (m. 5-6), Gr. 2, p. 158
Rosie, Darling Rosie (m. 7-8), Gr. 2, p. 215
Rosie, Darling Rosie (m. 2, 4, 6, 8), Gr. 2, p. 215
Skin and Bones (m. 1–2), Gr. 2, p. 376
Song of the Eagle (m. 1-4), Gr. 2, p. 248
Straighten Up and Fly Right (m. 9–14), Gr. 4, p. 128

### la, do re mi
Abiyoyo (m. 5-8), Gr. 2, p. 108
Ain't Gonna Let Nobody Turn Me 'Round, Gr. 6, p. 85
Ain't Gonna Let Nobody Turn Me 'Round (final: *la*), Gr. 8, p. 16
Ala Da'lona (m. 1–3, 7–9, 13–15), Gr. 4, p. 136
Amasee (final: *do*), Gr. 1, p. 172
Bear Dance, Gr. K, p. 127
Big Corral, The (m. 1-8), Gr. 2, p. 230
Canoe Song (m. 1–4), Gr. 4, p. 76
Certainly, Lord (Part I, m. 6–8), Gr. 7, p. 13
Chag Purim (m. 9–14), Gr. 1, p. 438
Chicka Hanka (final: *la*), Gr. 2, p. 211
Chicka Hanka (m. 5-12), Gr. 2, p. 211
Chicka Hanka (final: *la*), Gr. 8, p. 15
Crawfish! (m. 11-25), Gr. 2, p. 86
Dancin' in the Street (m. 1–13), Gr. 5, p. 361
Draw Me a Bucket of Water (m. 7–8), Gr. 3, p. 124
Drill, Ye Tarriers (m. 1–4), Gr. 5, p. 54
From Sea to Shining Sea (m. 3-4, 7-8), Gr. 2, p. 342
God Bless the Grass (m. a5–8), Gr. 8, p. 13
Gonna Ride Up in the Chariot (m. 3–4), Gr. 4, p. 20
Green, Green, Rocky (final: *la*), Gr. 1, p. 321
Haere (m. 1-3), Gr. 2, p. 285
Hambone (final: *do*), Gr. 1, p. 202
Hambone (final: *do*), Gr. 7, p. 3
Hosisipa (final: *la,*), Gr. 3, p. 70
I Got a Letter This Morning (m. 1–6) (final: *la,*), Gr. K, p. 68
I've Been Everywhere (m. 1–4), Gr. 6, p. 226
It's a Celebration! (m. 5–6), Gr. 2, p. 372
Keep Your Eyes on the Prize (m. 1–4), Gr. 3, p. 408
Keep Your Eyes on the Prize (m. a1–4), Gr. 8, p. 16
Land of a Thousand Dances (m. 1–8), Gr. 5, p. 330
Little Shop of Horrors (m. 1–16), Gr. 4, p. 422
Lots of Worms (m. 1-2, 7-8), Gr. 2, p. 310
Midnight Special, The (Refrain, m. 7–9), Gr. 7, p. 23
Music's in Me , The (m. 1–4, 9–12), Gr. 2, p. 40
My Home's Across the Blue Ridge Mountains (m. 7–8, 15–16), Gr. 7, p. 6
Nanny Goat, Gr. K, p. 161
New Way to Walk, A (m. 1, 3, 5 of refrain 1–4 of verse), Gr. K, p. 117
Old House, Tear It Down!, Gr. 4, p. 178
Oy, Hanuka (m. 3–6), Gr. 7, p. 44
Pollerita (m. 7–8, 11–12), Gr. 5, p. 151
Rosie, Darling Rosie (m. 3-4), Gr. 2, p. 215
Sail Away (m. 27–29), Gr. 5, p. 404
Same Train (m. 1-4, 11-14), Gr. 2, p. 164
Scrub Brush Shuffle, The (m. 1–8 of verse), Gr. 1, p. 118
See the Children Playin' (m. 1–12), Gr. 4, p. 107
Shortnin' Bread (m. 1–8; verse), Gr. 1, p. 57
Shortnin' Bread (m. 11–12, Verse 2nd ending), Gr. 7, p. 27
Sing About Martin (m. 14–16), Gr. K, p. 321
Skin and Bones (final: *la,*), Gr. 2, p. 376
Skye Boat Song (m. 9–16), Gr. 6, p. 372
Somebody's Knockin' at Your Door (m. 1–2, 7–8), Gr. 4, p. 53
Sometimes I Feel Like a Motherless Child (m. 1–6), Gr. 6, p. 241
Sonando (final: *do*), Gr. 4, p. 34

Tie Me Kangaroo Down, Sport (m. 1–2, 5–6), Gr. 4, p. 37
Time to Sing (m. 13-16 ), Gr. 2, p. 8
Train Is A-Comin' (m. 1–2), Gr. 3, p. 48
Turn the Beat Around (m. 1–14), Gr. 4, p. 2
Walk in Jerusalem (m. 7–8, 11–12, 15–16), Gr. 4, p. 100
Wooly Bully (m. 8–15), Gr. 3, p. 373
Yonder Come Day (m. 1–3, 5–16), Gr. 8, p. 68
Your Life Is Now (m. 13–20), Gr. 6, p. 4

### la, do re mi so

Corn Grinding Song (final: *la₁*), Gr. K, p. 67
Dok djampa (m. 19–22), Gr. 8, p. 20
Don't Let Your Watch Run Down (m. 13–16), Gr. 3, p. 166
Duck Dance (final: *la*), Gr. 2, p. 249
El carnavalito humahuaqueño (Melody only), Gr. 6, p. 482
El carnavalito humahuaqueño (m. 9–16), Gr. 6, p. 482
Go, My Son (final: *mi*), Gr. 6, p. 188
Go With the Music and Sing (m. 1–4), Gr. 3, p. 376
Goin' Down the Road Feelin' Bad (m. 9–12), Gr. 7, p. 13
Golden Ring Around Susan Girl (m. 7–8), Gr. 3, p. 16
Hui jia qù (final: *do*), Gr. 2, p. 158
Jim Along, Josie (final: *do*), Gr. K, p. 39
Leatherwing Bat (m. 5-8, 13-16), Gr. 2, p. 303
Love Can Build a Bridge (m. 1–2), Gr. 4, p. 324
On My Way (m. 1–8, 9–16 uppervoice), Gr. 6, p. 313
One Morning Soon (final: *do*), Gr. 3, p. 68
Pottery Dance (final: *do*), Gr. 1, p. 370
Proud (Refrain, m. 17–20), Gr. 7, p. 3
Tanabata-sama (m. 9-12), Gr. 2, p. 336
Woodland Chorus (m. 9–14), Gr. K, p. 250
Yang wa wa (m. 1–2), Gr. K, p. 162

### la, do re mi so la

Cindy (m. 1–16), Gr. 4, p. 384
Cumberland Gap (m. 1–8), Gr. 4, p. 138
Diou shou juan'er (final do) (final: *do*), Gr. 2, p. 277
Dok djampa (m. 15–18), Gr. 8, p. 20
Don't Let Your Watch Run Down (m. 1–4) (final: *do*), Gr. 3, p. 166
Erdö, erdö de magos, Gr. 3, p. 182
Goin' Down the Road Feelin' Bad (m. 1–11), Gr. 5, p. 282
Keep Your Eyes on the Prize (final: *la₁*), Gr. 3, p. 408
Keep Your Eyes on the Prize (m. a7–8) (final: *la₁*), Gr. 8, p. 16
Let's Get the Rhythm of the Band (m. 1–12), Gr. 3, p. 84
Let's Get the Rhythm of the Band (m. 3–12), Gr. 7, p. 29
Los maizales (final: *do*), Gr. 1, p. 296
Love Can Build a Bridge (m. 5–6), Gr. 4, p. 324
New Hungarian Folk Song, Gr. 6, p. 196
Pollerita (m. 1–12, 21–28), Gr. 5, p. 151
Same Train (m. 1-8), Gr. 2, p. 164
Wade in the Water (m. 1–4, 9–10, 13–14), Gr. 8, p. 64
Yüe liang wan wan (final: *la₁*), Gr. 5, p. 314
Yüe liang wan wan (m. 7–13), Gr. 5, p. 314
Zuni Sunrise Call (final: *do*), Gr. 5, p. 396

### la, do re so

Feng yang hua gu (m. 17–30), Gr. 4, p. 313

### la, do mi

Alabama Gal (m. 1–2), Gr. 3, p. 106
Don't Dump Trash (m. 1-4), Gr. 2, p. 318
Every Morning When I Wake Up (m. 7-8), Gr. 2, p. 320

Farewell to the Warriors (m. 5–6), Gr. 4, p. 284
Had to Get Up This Mornin' Soon (m. 1–4, 7–8), Gr. 3, p. 114
Hambone (m. 1–2), Gr. 7, p. 3
James Brown (m. 1–2) (final: *la₁*), Gr. K, p. 206
Jinny Go 'Round (m. 1–2, 5–6), Gr. K, p. 228
Johnny Mister Brown, Gr. K, p. 37
Rosie, Darling Rosie (m. 1-2, 5–6), Gr. 2, p. 215
Yibane amenu (m. 1–4), Gr. 4, p. 316
Your Life Is Now (m. 1–2 of refrain), Gr. 6, p. 4

### la, do mi so

Big Corral, The (m. 1-9) (final: *do*), Gr. 2, p. 230
My Dear Companion (m. 1–4, 9–12, 25–28), Gr. 6, p. 23

### la, mi la

Owl and the Pumpkin, The (m. 13–16), Gr. 2, p. 377

## so₁

### so, la, do

At the Hop (m. 1–3), Gr. 4, p. 168
Cheki, morena (m. 1-2, 9-10), Gr. 2, p. 180
Down by the Bay (m. 1–4), Gr. 1, p. 18
Dry Bones Come Skipping (m. 1, 3, 5, 7), Gr. 4, p. 218
Earth Is Our Mother, The (m. 6–9), Gr. 8, p. 25
Ev'ry Kind of Music (m. 1, 4-5, 8-9), Gr. 2, p. 226
Flip, Flop and Fly (m. 1–3), Gr. 7, p. 32
Gaudeamus Igitur (m. 1–2), Gr. 8, p. 20
God Bless the Child (m. a7, a27), Gr. 7, p. 27
Had to Get Up This Mornin' Soon (m. 9–12), Gr. 3, p. 114
I'll Fly Away (m. 3–4, 11–12), Gr. 8, p. 42
Little David, Play on Your Harp (m. 24–28, refrain ostinato 3), Gr. 4, p. 394
Love Will Guide Us (m. 1–6), Gr. 4, p. 328
Mama Don't 'Low (m. 13–16), Gr. 6, p. 358
Miss Mary Mack (final: *do*), Gr. 2, p. 42
Noah's Shanty (m. 1, 3–5, 7–9, refrain, 11–13, 15–16), Gr. 1, p. 342
O hal'lwe (m. 13–15), Gr. 3, p. 256
See-Saw Sacradown (m. 1–2), Gr. 2, p. 208
Shake Them 'Simmons Down (m. 3-4), Gr. 2, p. 244
Shortnin' Bread (m. 1–10), Gr. 1, p. 57
Shortnin' Bread (m. 1–8), Gr. 7, p. 27
Sleep, Baby, Sleep (m. 13-20), Gr. 2, p. 197
Ujima (m. 1–2, 5–6), Gr. 1, p. 430
Wade in the Water (m. 5–8, 11–12, 15–16), Gr. 8, p. 64
We're All Gonna Shine Tonight (m. 13-14), Gr. 2, p. 240

### so, la, do re

Bear Dance (m. 5–8), Gr. 7, p. 10
Big Old Storm a-Comin' (final: *do*), Gr. K, p. 257
Chicken on the Fence Post (m. 3–4), Gr. 3, p. 92
Clouds (m. 1–6), Gr. K, p. 254
Coffee Grows on White Oak Trees (m. 11–12), Gr. 3, p. 168
Different Beat, A (final: *do*), Gr. 1, p. 6
El burrito enfermo (final: *do*), Gr. K, p. 271
Faith of the Heart (m. a1–3), Gr. 8, p. 3
Five Little Snowmen (final: *do*), Gr. K, p. 313
Follow the Drinkin' Gourd (m. 1–4, 9–12), Gr. 4, p. 266
Get on Board (final: *do*), Gr. K, p. 89
Go Around the Corn, Sally (final: *do*), Gr. 2, p. 12
Great Big Stars (m. 7–10), Gr. 1, p. 60
Hashewie (m. 10–15), Gr. 4, p. 63

I Got Rhythm (m. 1–4, 17–20), Gr. 6, p. 101

Inkpataya (m. 5–8), Gr. 3, p. 254

Jinny Go 'Round (final: *do*), Gr. K, p. 228

Jolly Old St. Nicholas (m. 1–6, 9–16), Gr. K, p. 316

Just from the Kitchen (final: *do*), Gr. K, p. 55

Let's Get the Rhythm of the Band (m. 13–16), Gr. 3, p. 84

Let's Get the Rhythm of the Band (Melody only, m. 13–16), Gr. 7, p. 29

Locomoto-vation (final: *do*), Gr. K, p. 61

Miss Mary Mack (final: *do*), Gr. 2, p. 42

Miss Susie Anna Sue (m. 1–6), Gr. K, p. 242

Mister Ram Goat-O (m. 5–8) (final: *do*), Gr. 3, p. 54

My Valentine (m. 1–6), Gr. K, p. 323

Oh, Freedom (Melody only), Gr. 7, p. 30

Oh, Won't You Sit Down (final: *do*), Gr. 3, p. 28

Old Brass Wagon (m. 1–4), Gr. 2, p. 122

Pastures of Plenty (m. 1–3), Gr. 4, p. 280

Rock Island Line (m. 9–10), Gr. 4, p. 54

See the Children Playin' (final: *la₁*), Gr. 4, p. 107

See-Saw Sacradown (final: *do*), Gr. 2, p. 208

Sing About Martin (final: *do*), Gr. K, p. 321

Take Your Feet Out 'the Sand (final: *do*), Gr. K, p. 231

Wade in the Water (m. 5–8, 11–12, 15–16), Gr. 4, p. 268

Water Is Wide, The (m. 13–16), Gr. 6, p. 228

We're All Gonna Shine Tonight (final: *do*), Gr. 2, p. 240

Willoughby, Wallaby, Woo (m. 1–4), Gr. K, p. 282

### *so₁ la₁ do re mi*

Asadoya (m. 7–9), Gr. 6, p. 303

At the Same Time (m. 1–8), Gr. 6, p. 115

Bát kim thang (final: *do*), Gr. 6, p. 13

Bear Dance (m. 9–16), Gr. 7, p. 10

Bingo (Melody only, m. 1-4), Gr. 1, p. 170

Blue Skies (m. 1–15, 25–32), Gr. 6, p. 88

Bury Me Not on the Lone Prairie (m. 5–8, 13–16), Gr. 6, p. 19

Cotton-Eye Joe (m. 1–8) (final: *do*), Gr. 4, p. 288

Do, Lord (m. 1–4, 9–12, 17–20, 25–28), Gr. 3, p. 164

Don't Let Your Watch Run Down (m. 5–8), Gr. 3, p. 166

Down by the Riverside (Part III, m. a9–10), Gr. 8, p. 8

Faith of the Heart (m. 38–42), Gr. 8, p. 3

Farewell to Tarwathie (m. a1–8, a13–16), Gr. 6, p. 43

Farewell to the Warriors (m. 7–9), Gr. 4, p. 284

Flip, Flop and Fly (m. 13–20), Gr. 7, p. 32

Four in a Boat (m. 1-2), Gr. 2, p. 46

Glory, Glory, Hallelujah (m. 1–8), Gr. 6, p. 52

Go Around the Corn, Sally (final: *do*), Gr. 2, p. 12

Golden Ring Around Susan Girl (m. 1–6), Gr. 3, p. 16

Gonna Build a Mountain (m. 1–8), Gr. 6, p. 21

Gospel Train, The (Part III), Gr. 6, p. 398

Gospel Train, The (Part II), Gr. 6, p. 398

Hashewie (final: *do*), Gr. 4, p. 63

I Believe I Can Fly (m. 1–9), Gr. 5, p. 170

I Got Shoes (m. 5-8), Gr. 2, p. 242

I'm Gonna Sing (final: *do*), Gr. 4, p. 33

It's a Celebration! (m. 8–12), Gr. 2, p. 372

Jingle Bells (m. 1–4, 9–12), Gr. 2, p. 388

Key to the Highway (m. 1–2), Gr. 6, p. 243

Key to the Highway (m. a1–2), Gr. 8, p. 29

Kwa-nu-te (m. 1–4), Gr. 3, p. 214

Kwanzaa Carol, A (m. 1–4), Gr. 2, p. 392

Little Shop of Horrors (m. 17–27), Gr. 4, p. 422

Loigratong (m. 5–12), Gr. 6, p. 451

Look Out for Mother Earth (final: *do*), Gr. 3, p. 341

Love Will Guide Us (final: *do*), Gr. 4, p. 328

Mister Ram Goat-O (m. 5–8), Gr. 3, p. 54

Nana, Thread Needle (final: *do*), Gr. 1, p. 38

Noah's Shanty (final: *do*), Gr. 1, p. 342

Oh, Freedom (Part I) (final: *do*), Gr. 7, p. 30

Oh, Won't You Sit Down (m. 1–8), Gr. 3, p. 28

Old Brass Wagon (final: *do*), Gr. 2, p. 122

Old Dan Tucker (final: *do*), Gr. 3, p. 96

Pastures of Plenty (m. 9–12), Gr. 4, p. 280

Paths of Victory (m. 1–4, 9–12), Gr. 6, p. 195

Peace Like a River (final: *do*), Gr. 3, p. 246

Peace Like a River (Melody) (final: *do*), Gr. 6, p. 190

Peppermint Twist (Melody only, m. 11–24), Gr. 3, p. 46

Pretty Saro (m. 1–4, 13–16), Gr. 3, p. 216

Sail Away (m. 23–30, voice 2 - melody), Gr. 5, p. 404

Shake Them 'Simmons Down (final: *do*), Gr. 2, p. 244

Shoo, Turkey (m. 13–20, refrain), Gr. 1, p. 104

Shortnin' Bread (final: *la₁*), Gr. 7, p. 27

Somebody Waiting (m. 1-2, 5-6), Gr. 2, p. 283

Song of the Eagle (final: *la*), Gr. 2, p. 248

Song That's Just for You, A (m. 1-8), Gr. 2, p. 126

Swanee (m. 1–7, 17–24), Gr. 6, p. 118

Swing Low, Sweet Chariot (m. 1–2), Gr. 7, p. 41

Tanabata-sama (m. 13-16), Gr. 2, p. 336

This Little Light of Mine (m. 21–36), Gr. 6, p. 232

Tom Dooley (final: *do*), Gr. 6, p. 374

Under the Same Sun (m. 6 –13 of verse), Gr. 6, p. 440

Under the Sea (m. 17–32), Gr. 5, p. 372

Waitin' for the Light to Shine (m. 1–4), Gr. 4, p. 26

Water Is Wide, The (m. 1–4), Gr. 6, p. 228

We're All Gonna Shine Tonight (final: *do*), Gr. 2, p. 240

Worried Man Blues (final: *do*), Gr. 6, p. 371

Yonder Come Day (m. 7–8), Gr. 8, p. 68

Your Life Is Now (m. 1–8), Gr. 6, p. 4

### *so₁ la₁ do re mi so*

*Alabama Gal (final: *do*), Gr. 3, p. 106

All Night, All Day (m. 1–4, 9–12), Gr. 4, p. 180

Amazing Grace (final: *do*), Gr. 4, p. 160

Arirang (final: *do*), Gr. 5, p. 25

Bear Dance (final: *la₁*), Gr. 7, p. 10

Big Corral, The (final: *do*), Gr. 2, p. 230

Coffee Grows on White Oak Trees (verse), Gr. 3, p. 168

Doraji (final: *so₁*), Gr. 4, p. 174

Dry Bones Come Skipping (final: *do*), Gr. 4, p. 218

Four in a Boat (m. 1–4), Gr. 2, p. 46

Glory, Glory, Hallelujah (m. 9–12), Gr. 6, p. 52

Going on a Picnic (final: *do*), Gr. K, p. 190

Good Old Happy Song, A, Gr. K, p. 201

How Can I Keep from Singing? (final: *do*), Gr. 4, p. 261

Hush, Hush (final: *do*), Gr. 3, p. 162

Hwa yuan li-de young wa wa (final: *do*), Gr. 3, p. 102

I'd Like To Teach the World to Sing (In Perfect Harmony) (m. 1–8), Gr. 3, p. 198

Inkpataya, Gr. 3, p. 254

Juniper Tree, The (final: *do*), Gr. 3, p. 131

Love Can Build a Bridge (m. 1–4), Gr. 4, p. 324

Mary Wore Her Red Dress (final: *do*), Gr. K, p. 74

Meng Jian Nu (final: *so*), Gr. 5, p. 194

New Way to Walk, A (final: *do*), Gr. K, p. 117

Pastures of Plenty, Gr. 4, p. 280

Paths of Victory (final: *do*), Gr. 6, p. 195

Pretty Saro (m. 5–8), Gr. 3, p. 216
Sawatdee tuh jah (final: *do*), Gr. 2, p. 265
Shanghai Chicken (verse), Gr. 1, p. 140
Shu ha mo (final: *do*), Gr. 3, p. 276
Skye Boat Song, Gr. 6, p. 372
Sleep, Baby, Sleep (final: *do*), Gr. 2, p. 197
Soldier, Soldier (m. 1–4, 9–12), Gr. 4, p. 11
Sourwood Mountain (m. 1–8), Gr. 4, p. 65
Swing Low, Sweet Chariot, Gr. 7, p. 41
Swing Low, Sweet Chariot (m. 1–4), Gr. 7, p. 41
Tanabata-sama (final: *do*), Gr. 2, p. 336
Toodala (Melody only), Gr. 1, p. 326
Ujima (final: *do*), Gr. 1, p. 430
Woodland Chorus, Gr. K, p. 250
Yang wa wa (final: *do*), Gr. K, p. 162

### so, la, do re mi so la

Bling Blang (m. 1–8), Gr. 3, p. 240
Bluebonnets of Texas (Melody only) (final: *do*), Gr. 3, p. 332
Bury Me Not on the Lone Prairie (Melody only) (final: *do*), Gr. 6, p. 19
Chang (final: *do*), Gr. 1, p. 156
Chicken on the Fence Post (final: *do*), Gr. 3, p. 92
Come and Go with Me to That Land (final: *do*), Gr. 5, p. 390
El carite (m. 1–8), Gr. 5, p. 305
Farewell to Tarwathie (final: *do*), Gr. 6, p. 43
Farewell to the Warriors (final: *la*), Gr. 4, p. 284
Glory, Glory, Hallelujah (m. 13–16), Gr. 6, p. 52
Kwa-nu-te (final: *la*,), Gr. 3, p. 214
Let's Get the Rhythm of the Band (Melody only) (final: *la*,), Gr. 3, p. 84
Little David (final: *do*), Gr. 1, p. 232
Little David, Play on Your Harp (final: *do*), Gr. 4, p. 394
Loco-Motion, The (m. 1–8), Gr. 3, p. 64
Love Is on Our Side (final: *la*), Gr. 5, p. 324
Now Let Me Fly (final: *do*), Gr. 3, p. 178
Oh, Freedom (final: *do*), Gr. 5, p. 392
Old Texas (final: *do*), Gr. 3, p. 77
Pretty Saro (final: *so*,), Gr. 3, p. 216
Sailboat in the Sky (m. 1–12), Gr. 4, p. 374
Soldier, Soldier (final: *do*), Gr. 4, p. 11
Swing Low, Sweet Chariot (m. 1–8, 9–16), Gr. 7, p. 41
Turn the Glasses Over (final: *do*), Gr. 3, p. 204
Wade in the Water (final: *la*), Gr. 4, p. 268
Wade in the Water (final: *la*,), Gr. 8, p. 64
Waitin' for the Light to Shine (m. 9–12), Gr. 4, p. 26
Weevily Wheat (final: *do*), Gr. 4, p. 105
Your Life Is Now (m. 1–11), Gr. 6, p. 4

### so, la, do re mi la

Canoe Song (final: *la*), Gr. 4, p. 76

### so, la, do mi

Alabama Gal (m. 1–4), Gr. 3, p. 106
Brush Your Teeth (final: *do*), Gr. 1, p. 284
Different Beat, A (m. 1–2, 5–6), Gr. 1, p. 6
Down the Ohio (m. 1-2, 5-6), Gr. 2, p. 60
Four White Horses (m. 1–4) (final: *do*), Gr. 3, p. 304
Key to the Highway (m. a5), Gr. 8, p. 29
Mama Don't 'Low (m. 1–4), Gr. 6, p. 358
Rock Island Line (m. 1–2, 5–6), Gr. 4, p. 54
See-Saw Sacradown (m. 5–6), Gr. 2, p. 208
Snowflakes (m. 1–2), Gr. 1, p. 422

### so, la, do mi so

ABC Rock (m. 1–14), Gr. 1, p. 262
Had to Get Up This Mornin' Soon (final: *do*), Gr. 3, p. 114
Snowflakes (m. 1–4), Gr. 1, p. 422

### so, la, re mi

El gallo pinto (m. 1–6), Gr. 3, p. 86

### so, do

Adiós, amigos (m. a9–12), Gr. 6, p. 57
Do Wah Diddy Diddy (m. 9–12), Gr. 7, p. 21
Frère Jacques (m. 7-8), Gr. 2, p. 125
Merry-Go-Round (m. 3, 4), Gr. K, p. 290

### so, do re

Bye Bye, Love (m. 7–8, 15–18), Gr. 8, p. 9
Kapulu kane (final: *do*), Gr. 2, p. 270
Nu wahtan (m. 3–5, 8–10), Gr. 1, p. 279

### so, do re mi

Achshav (m. 1–4), Gr. 2, p. 64
Al citrón, Gr. 3, p. 320
Baby Beluga (m. 1–2), Gr. K, p. 272
Buenos días (Melody only, m. 1-4), Gr. 1, p. 13
But the Cat Came Back (m. 1-2), Gr. 2, p. 190
Chanukiyah li yesh (m. 1–4) (final: *do*), Gr. 1, p. 421
Cow's Woc Backward (m. 1–4), Gr. 1, p. 390
Draw Me a Bucket of Water (m. 1–6), Gr. 3, p. 124
Eensy Weensy Spider (m. 1–4, 9–16), Gr. K, p. 187
Ev'rybody Ought to Know (m. 1–4) (final: *do*), Gr. 1, p. 434
Ezekiel Saw the Wheel (m. refrain, melody, m. 1–16), Gr. 6, p. 379
Five Little Chickadees (refrain), Gr. K, p. 179
Gakavik (m. 17–20), Gr. 4, p. 14
Good Morning (m. 1–4), Gr. 3, p. 192
Hej pada pada (m. 3–4), Gr. 3, p. 78
Hush Up the Baby, Gr. K, p. 222
I Can't Spell Hippopotamus (m. 1–2), Gr. 1, p. 264
Juanito (m. 1–4, 9–12), Gr. K, p. 300
La pulga de San José (m. 1–2), Gr. 3, p. 40
La víbora (m. 1–2, 5–6), Gr. 1, p. 322
*Mi chacra (Melody only, m. 1-2), Gr. 1, p. 364
Must Be Santa (m. 3–4, 7–10), Gr. K, p. 318
Nampaya omame (m. 9–16), Gr. 1, p. 138
Nampaya omame (Countermelody, m. refrain, m. 9–16), Gr. 7, p. 10
Perot (m. 4–5), Gr. 2, p. 378
Pust' 'vsegda budet sonse (m. 1–4), Gr. 3, p. 278
Race You Down the Mountain, Gr. 1, p. 127
Six Little Ducks (m. 1–6), Gr. K, p. 234
Sleep, Baby, Sleep (m. 1-8), Gr. 2, p. 197
This Land Is Your Land (m. 5–8), Gr. 7, p. 66
This Land Is Your Land (refrain only) (m. 4–7), Gr. 1, p. 274
Today Is Your Birthday (m. 1–4), Gr. 1, p. 410
What Will You Be on Halloween? (m. 1–2, 5–6), Gr. K, p. 308
Wichita Hand Game Song 1, Gr. 3, p. 306
You Are My Sunshine (m. 1–2), Gr. 6, p. 246

### so, do re mi so

Ama-Lama (m. 1–4), Gr. 5, p. 142
Bus, The (m. 1–4, 7–12), Gr. K, p. 82
Good Morning (final: *do*), Gr. 3, p. 192
Little Green Frog, The (m. 1–5), Gr. 1, p. 24

Long Way Home, A (m. 13–17), Gr. 1, p. 382
Looby Loo (m. 1–14), Gr. K, p. 210
Today Is Your Birthday, Gr. 1, p. 410
Uga uga uga (m. 1–6), Gr. K, p. 305
Vamos a la mar (final: *do*), Gr. 3, p. 226

### so₁ do re mi so la

Bam, chi, chi, bam (final: *do*), Gr. K, p. 109
Deep in the Heart of Texas (m. 1–8, 17–24), Gr. 4, p. 22
Ezekiel Saw the Wheel (final: *do*), Gr. 6, p. 379
Farmer in the Dell, The (final: *do*), Gr. K, p. 232
Lullaby and Dance (m. 5–10), Gr. 4, p. 387
Mister Rabbit (final: *do*), Gr. K, p. 128

### so₁ do mi

Deep in the Heart of Texas (m. 1–4, 17–20), Gr. 8, p. 18
Deux cocodries (m. 9-10, 13-14), Gr. 2, p. 364
Frog Music (m. 6–9, 14–17), Gr. 4, p. 200
Mon papa (m. 1-2, 5-6), Gr. 2, p. 280
Over There (m. 1–7, 16–23), Gr. 5, p. 279

### so₁ do mi so

Bonjour, mes amis (m. 1–4), Gr. 1, p. 316
El Tren (m. 1–2), Gr. 2, p. 260
La Jesusita (m. 1–2, 9–10), Gr. 5, p. 322
Lone Star Trail (m. 1–8 of verse), Gr. 2, p. 21
Lone Star Trail (m. 9-12), Gr. 2, p. 21
Naranja dulce (m. 1), Gr. 2, p. 97
Roll Over, Gr. K, p. 288

### so₁ do mi la

Ochimbo (final: *do*), Gr. 4, p. 134

### so₁ mi

Bát kim thang (m. 11), Gr. 6, p. 13

### so₁ do so

Hot Cross Buns (Version 2) (m. 1–2), Gr. 3, p. 221

### mi₁ so₁ la₁ do re

Loigratong (m. 1–4), Gr. 6, p. 451

### mi₁ so₁ la₁ do re mi

Put a Little Love in Your Heart (final: *do*), Gr. 4, p. 6

### mi₁ so₁ la₁ do mi

Run! Run! Hide! (m. part 2, 1–8, 18–37), Gr. 6, p. 340

## do'

### do re mi so la do'

Amefuri (final: *do*), Gr. 1, p. 144
Asadoya (m. 4–5), Gr. 6, p. 303
Banana Splits (final: *do*), Gr. 1, p. 318
Bound for South Australia (final: *do*), Gr. 5, p. 22
California (final: *do*), Gr. 5, p. 52
California (m. 9–16), Gr. 5, p. 52
Camptown Races (m. 17–24), Gr. 5, p. 270
Certainly, Lord (Melody, m. 1–5), Gr. 7, p. 13
Certainly, Lord (Part I, m. 1–5), Gr. 7, p. 13
Ding, Dong, Diggidiggidong (final: *do*), Gr. 3, p. 14
Don't Be Cruel (m. 5–12), Gr. 6, p. 255
Don't Let the Wind (final: *do*), Gr. 3, p. 180
Earth Is My Mother, The (m. 1–2, 5–8), Gr. 1, p. 340
Einini (m. 13–20, voices 1–2, 24–28), Gr. 4, p. 391
Every Night When the Sun Goes In (m. 5–8), Gr. 8, p. 28
Farmer's Dairy Key, The (final: *do*), Gr. 2, p. 182
Feng yang hua gu (m. 1–8), Gr. 4, p. 313
Funwa alafia (final: *do*), Gr. 5, p. 32
Going Upon the Mountain (final: *do*), Gr. 6, p. 105
Gonna Ride Up in the Chariot (m. 9–16), Gr. 4, p. 20

Great Day (final: *do*), Gr. 3, p. 58
Hama chi dori, Gr. 3, p. 330
Hashkediya (final: *do*), Gr. 3, p. 206
Hop Up, My Ladies (refrain) (final: *do*), Gr. 3, p. 142
Jo'ashila, Gr. 5, p. 108
Li'l Liza Jane (final: *do*), Gr. 3, p. 140
Look! Look! The Sun Woke Up! (m. 1–4, 7–10),
   Gr. 1, p. 368
My Mama's Calling Me (final: *do*), Gr. 1, p. 260
Oh, Watch the Stars (final: *do*), Gr. 2, p. 144
Oh, Watch the Stars (final: *do*), Gr. 5, p. 216
Old Man Mosie (Melody only) (final: *do*), Gr. 3, p. 108
Plant Four Seeds (final: *do*), Gr. 2, p. 130
Shady Grove (final: *re*), Gr. 5, p. 260
Sourwood Mountain (m. 9–16), Gr. 4, p. 65
Take Me Out to the Ball Game (m. 1–7), Gr. 3, p. 263
Tideo (final: *do*), Gr. 2, p. 80
Walk in Jerusalem, Gr. 4, p. 100
Walk Together, Children (final: *do'*), Gr. 3, p. 146
Way Down in the Schoolyard (m. 1–8), Gr. 2, p. 50
When the Train Comes Along (final: *do*), Gr. 1, p. 300
Xiao (m. 1–16), Gr. 4, p. 314

### do re mi so do'

America, I Hear You Singing (m. 13–16), Gr. 2, p. 402
I Don't Care If the Rain Comes Down (m. 9–16),
   Gr. 3, p. 24
John Kanaka (final: *do*), Gr. 3, p. 60
Leila (m. 1–4) (final: *do*), Gr. 1, p. 258
Take a Chance On Me (m. 1, 10, 32), Gr. 8, p. 15

### do mi so la do'

Joe Turner Blues (m. 1–3), Gr. 4, p. 56
La piñata (m. 1–2), Gr. 3, p. 399
Waiting for the Traffic Light (m. 1-2, 5-8, 13-16),
   Gr. 2, p. 107
Wheel of the Water, The (m. voice 4), Gr. 4, p. 362

### do mi so do'

Farmer's Dairy Key, The (m. 5-6), Gr. 2, p. 182
Star-Spangled Banner, The (m. 1-2, 7–11, 6–17),
   Gr. 6, p. 486
Star-Spangled Banner, The (m. 1), Gr. 7, p. 56
Star-Spangled Banner, The (m. 1–2), Gr. 8, p. 62

### do so la do'

This World (m. 1–15), Gr. 5, p. 168
Way Down in the Schoolyard (m. 1-2, 5-6, 9, 15),
   Gr. 2, p. 50

### re so la do'

Jambalaya (m. 8–11, 24–27), Gr. 8, p. 46

### mi so la do'

Dok djampa (m. 7–10), Gr. 8, p. 20
Down in the Meadow, Gr. K, p. 147
El cóndor pasa (m. a11–12, a15–16), Gr. 6, p. 46
Every Morning When I Wake Up (m. 1-2, 5-6),
   Gr. 2, p. 320
Going Upon the Mountain (m. 1–4), Gr. 6, p. 105
Kelo aba w'ye (final: *mi*), Gr. 6, p. 290
Los días de la semana (m. 5–6), Gr. 1, p. 268
Rudolph, the Red-Nosed Reindeer (m. 9–10, 17–18,
   25–26, 33–34), Gr. 1, p. 428
Somebody's Knockin' at Your Door (m. 3–4), Gr. 4, p. 53
Thanksgiving Is Near (m. 1–7), Gr. 2, p. 380
Xiao yin chuan (final: *mi*), Gr. 2, p. 14

Pitch and Rhythm Index

**mi so do'**
Day-O! (Banana Boat Loader's Song) (m. 9–10, 13–14, 33–34, 37–38), Gr. 5, p. 18
Water Come a Me Eye (m. calls: m. 9–10, 13–14), Gr. 6, p. 300

**so la do'**
All for One (m. 13–16, 17–21), Gr. 7, p. 8
Banuwa (m. 13–16 of melody), Gr. 6, p. 294
Cha yang wu (m. 1–2), Gr. 1, p. 90
Che che koolay (final: *la*), Gr. 2, p. 266
Don't Be Cruel (m. 1–4), Gr. 6, p. 255
Free at Last (m. 9–10), Gr. 6, p. 468
Going Upon the Mountain (m. 1–2, 5–6), Gr. 6, p. 105
Ise oluwa (m. 9–12), Gr. 6, p. 230
It's Santa—Again! (m. 9–10, 13–14), Gr. 2, p. 385
It's Time (m. 5, 7, 9), Gr. 6, p. 274
Karangatia ra (m. 1–4), Gr. 8, p. 23
Waiting for the Traffic Light (m. 1-2, 9-10), Gr. 2, p. 107

**la₁ do re mi so la do'**
By the Waters of Babylon (m. 9–13), Gr. 6, p. 311
Circle Round the Zero (final: *do*), Gr. K, p. 293
Colorado Trail (final: *do*), Gr. 5, p. 276
Cumberland Gap (final: *do*), Gr. 4, p. 138
Gonna Ride Up in the Chariot (final: *do*), Gr. 4, p. 20
Somebody's Knockin' at Your Door (final: *do*), Gr. 4, p. 53
Walk in Jerusalem (final: *do*), Gr. 4, p. 100

**la₁ do mi so la' do'**
Every Morning When I Wake Up (final: *do*), Gr. 2, p. 320

**so₁ la₁ do re mi so la do'**
Asadoya (final: *do*), Gr. 6, p. 303
Sail Away (m. 31–38, voice 1 - melody), Gr. 5, p. 404

**do re mi so la do' re'**
Bound for South Australia (final: *do*), Gr. 5, p. 22
I Walk in Beauty (final: *do*), Gr. 4, p. 282
Xiao (m. 17–29), Gr. 4, p. 314

**mi so la do' re'**
California, Here I Come (m. 1–8), Gr. 4, p. 287
Thanksgiving Is Near (m. 7–8), Gr. 2, p. 380

**so do' re' mi'**
Wheel of the Water, The (m. voice 1), Gr. 4, p. 362

**la do' re' mi'**
Cielito lindo (m. 1st Refrain 17–24, Last Refrain m. 34–41), Gr. 7, p. 20

**re mi so la do' re' mi'**
Jasmine Flowers (final: *so*), Gr. 5, p. 316
Lahk gei mohlee (final: *so*), Gr. 5, p. 317

**re so la do' mi'**
Jambalaya (m. a17–19), Gr. 8, p. 46

**do mi so do' mi'**
Happy Days Are Here Again (m. 1–7), Gr. 5, p. 284

**so₁ la₁ do re mi so la' do'**
Ev'ry Time I Feel the Spirit (final: *do*), Gr. 5, p. 242
Sailboat in the Sky (final: *do*), Gr. 4, p. 374
Sourwood Mountain (final: *do*), Gr. 4, p. 65
This Train (final: *do*), Gr. 5, p. 26

**la do re mi so la do'**
Same Train (final: *do*), Gr. 2, p. 164
Train Is A-Comin' (final: *do*), Gr. 3, p. 48

**re'**
**do re mi fa so la ti do' re'**
Texas Cowboy (final: *do*), Gr. 3, p. 250

**fa**
**do re mi fa**
Achshav (m. 9-16), Gr. 2, p. 64
African Noel (m. 1–4), Gr. 1, p. 427
Aiken Drum (m. 1–6) (final: *do*), Gr. 1, p. 398
America, the Free (m. 1–4), Gr. 4, p. 210
Back of the Bus (m. 1–4, 9–12), Gr. 3, p. 410
Banuwa (m. 1–4), Gr. 6, p. 294
Boil Them Cabbage Down (final: *do*), Gr. 6, p. 370
By the Waters of Babylon (m. 14–17), Gr. 6, p. 311
Bye Bye, Love (m. 1–6, 9–14, 27–28), Gr. 8, p. 9
Chrismus a Come (m. 1–4), Gr. 3, p. 396
Da pacem, Domine (m. 1–4, 9–12), Gr. 5, p. 62
Do, Re, Mi, Fa (m. 1–2), Gr. 6, p. 80
Down by the Riverside (Part II, m. 16–24), Gr. 8, p. 8
Elegua (m. 9–11), Gr. 7, p. 8
Freedom Is Coming (m. voice 1 - melody) (final: *do*), Gr. 5, p. 415
Give a Little Love (m. 1–4, 9–16 of verse), Gr. 6, p. 140
Gonna Have a Good Time (m. 4-5, 10-11), Gr. 2, p. 4
Goodbye, Julie (m. 3–4, 7–8), Gr. 8, p. 2
Hi Heidi Ho (m. 1–4), Gr. 1, p. 394
Honeybee Song, The (m. refrain, 1–6, verse m, 9–16), Gr. 1, p. 358
I'm a Believer (Part I, Melody, m. 1–15, 31–45), Gr. 7, p. 33
Juba, Gr. K, p. 13
Kokoleoko (m. 1–2), Gr. 5, p. 33
Kookaburra (m. 1–4), Gr. 4, p. 186
Lean on Me (m. 1–4, a26–27), Gr. 6, p. 14
Lean on Me, Gr. 6, p. 14
Lean on Me (m. 1–4), Gr. 7, p. 22
Limbo Like Me (m. 25–26), Gr. 4, p. 18
Lion Sleeps Tonight, The (m. 5–8), Gr. 8, p. 56
Love Can Build a Bridge (m. 7–8), Gr. 4, p. 324
Mon papa (m. 3–4), Gr. 2, p. 280
Nampaya omame (m. 1–8), Gr. 1, p. 138
Nampaya omame (m. 1–8), Gr. 7, p. 10
O lê lê O Bahía (m. 1–2), Gr. 6, p. 165
Oh, How Lovely Is the Evening (m. 1–6), Gr. 4, p. 217
Oye (m. 1–3 (verse); 13–18 (refrain)), Gr. 6, p. 336
Riendo el río corre (m. 9–16), Gr. 6, p. 263
'Round the Bay of Mexico (m. 1–2, 7–8), Gr. 4, p. 258
Shoo, Fly (m. 1-2, 5-6), Gr. 2, p. 200
Si me dan pasteles (m. 1–7), Gr. 1, p. 432
Song That's Just for You, A (m. 15-16), Gr. 2, p. 126
Surfin' U.S.A. (m. 15–16, 31–32), Gr. 7, p. 58
Take Time in Life (m. 1–2, 5–6), Gr. 6, p. 292
That's What's New with Me!, Gr. K, p. 2
This Is My Song (m. 1–8, 15–16, 21–24), Gr. 6, p. 77
This Land Is Your Land (m. 1–4, 9–12), Gr. 7, p. 66
Those Magic Changes (m. a24–35), Gr. 8, p. 30
Three Little Birds (m. 16–19), Gr. 8, p. 7
Water Come a Me Eye (m. 7–8, 13–14) (final: *do*), Gr. 6, p. 300
We Shall Not Be Moved (m. 1–8), Gr. 4, p. 437
Zumba, zumba (m. 9–24), Gr. 3, p. 400

### do re mi fa so

All for One (m. 1–4), Gr. 7, p. 8

Ambos a dos (m. 1–8), Gr. 3, p. 20

America (N. Diamond) (m. last 15), Gr. 4, p. 206

America, the Free (m. 1–8), Gr. 4, p. 210

Barb'ry Allen (m. a1–2) (final: do), Gr. 6, p. 44

Beyond Borders (m. 1–8), Gr. 5, p. 292

But the Cat Came Back (m. 16-17), Gr. 2, p. 190

*Canción de cuna, Gr. 4, p. 144

Cantando mentiras (m. 1–9), Gr. 4, p. 146

Cantaré, cantarás (m. 1–13), Gr. 6, p. 413

Da pacem, Domine (final: do), Gr. 5, p. 62

Debajo el botón (m. 1–2, 7–8), Gr. 1, p. 210

¿Dónde lo escondí?, Gr. K, p. 209

Down the Listening Lane, Gr. K, p. 192

Downtown (m. a18–24), Gr. 6, p. 258

Eh, cumpari! (m. 1–11), Gr. 4, p. 68

El barquito (m. 1–8, 18–27), Gr. 3, p. 358

El juego chirimbolo (m. 11-14), Gr. 2, p. 54

El tambor (m. 9-12), Gr. 2, p. 274

En nuestra Tierra tan linda (final: do), Gr. 2, p. 335

Eres tú (Part II, m. 17–20, 25–28), Gr. 6, p. 473

Everybody Says (m. 1–4, 7–8), Gr. 1, p. 287

Fais dodo, Gr. K, p. 158

Freight Train (m. 1, 3, 9), Gr. 1, p. 44

Friends Today (m. 1–7 of uppervoice, 9–15, 16–31), Gr. 7, p. 12

Get on Your Feet (Melody only, m. 1–8), Gr. 5, p. 6

Glad to Have a Friend Like You (m. 9-12), Gr. 2, p. 228

God Bless the U.S.A. (m. 1–5), Gr. 8, p. 37

*Goin' Down the Road Feelin' Bad (m. 13–16), Gr. 7, p. 13

Green, Green Grass of Home (m. a8–10, 16–19), Gr. 6, p. 248

Guantanamera (m. 12–16), Gr. 8, p. 32

Harrison Town (m. 13–16), Gr. 6, p. 97

He's Got the Whole World in His Hands (m. 7–8), Gr. 3, p. 230

He's Got the Whole World in His Hands (m. 7–8), Gr. 7, p. 36

He's Got the Whole World in His Hands (m. 7–8), Gr. 7, p. 36

Hi Heidi Ho (m. 5–16), Gr. 1, p. 394

I Love Peanuts (m. 1–4), Gr. 1, p. 162

I Love Peanuts (m. 1–4), Gr. 7, p. 20

I Shall Sing (m. a1–2), Gr. 8, p. 38

Ise oluwa (m. 1-8, 13–20), Gr. 2, p. 102

Ise oluwa (m. 1-8, 13–20), Gr. 6, p. 230

It's Santa—Again! (m. 1–3, 5–7), Gr. 2, p. 385

Jingle Bells (m. 29–32), Gr. 2, p. 388

Joy of Kwanzaa, The (m. 17–24), Gr. 6, p. 462

Kwanzaa Carol, A (m. 9–24) (final: do), Gr. 2, p. 392

Lady, Lady, Gr. 1, p. 62

Lion Sleeps Tonight, The (final: do), Gr. 4, p. 131

Lion Sleeps Tonight, The (m. 9–12), Gr. 8, p. 56

Listen to the Water (final: do), Gr. 2, p. 294

Lone Star Trail (m. 9-12), Gr. 2, p. 21

Lost My Gold Ring (final: do), Gr. 6, p. 158

Love Somebody (m. 1–2, 5–6), Gr. 3, p. 94

Magnolia (m. 1–4, 9–12), Gr. 6, p. 16

Making Valentines (m. 1–4), Gr. 1, p. 437

Mariposita (m. 1-8, 25-32), Gr. 2, p. 156

Mary Ann (m. 1–4, 9–12), Gr. 6, p. 180

Mary Ann, Gr. K, p. 253

Me voy para la luna (m. 1–6, 8–10), Gr. 1, p. 397

Mi chacra (m. 3–4), Gr. 1, p. 364

Mi cuerpo hace música (refrain), Gr. K, p. 106

Morning Comes Early (m. 1–4, 13–16, 21–24), Gr. 5, p. 13

My Dreydl (m. 1–7), Gr. K, p. 314

Never Smile at a Crocodile (m. 1–2, 9–10), Gr. 3, p. 100

O, Desayo (m. 1–6), Gr. 5, p. 411

O Laufet, ihr Hirten (m. 3–4, 7–8, 15–16), Gr. 2, p. 384

Ode to Joy (m. 1–8), Gr. 4, p. 152

Parade Came Marching, The (m. 5–8), Gr. 1, p. 166

Party Tonight! (m. 7-8), Gr. 2, p. 152

Pavo, pavo (m. 1–8), Gr. 1, p. 416

Pay Me My Money Down (m. 7–8, 15–16) (final: do), Gr. 4, p. 38

Pay Me My Money Down (m. 7–8, 15–16), Gr. 7, p. 46

Put Your Hand in My Hand (m. 1–4, 9–10), Gr. 1, p. 330

Rainbow, The (m. 7-8), Gr. 2, p. 332

Scattin' A-Round (Variations on Row 3) (m. 1–4, 9–12, 17–20), Gr. 6, p. 160

Seasons, Gr. K, p. 4

She'll Be Comin' 'Round the Mountain (m. 6–9), Gr. 2, p. 358

Shoo, Fly (m. 7-8), Gr. 2, p. 200

Si si si (Part II, m. 9–16), Gr. 7, p. 13

Simple Gifts (m. 9–12), Gr. 8, p. 17

Sing a Rainbow (m. 13-16, coda), Gr. 2, p. 166

Sing Me a Story (m. 1-8), Gr. 2, p. 346

Someday Very Soon (m. 13–16), Gr. 1, p. 376

Spring Has Sprung!, Gr. K, p. 142

Surfin' U.S.A. (m. 15–16, 31–32), Gr. 6, p. 260

Surfin' U.S.A. (m. 29–30), Gr. 7, p. 58

Surfin' U.S.A. (m. 29–30), Gr. 7, p. 58

Sweet Betsy from Pike (m. 1–4, 13–16, 21–25), Gr. 4, p. 244

Tancovacka (m. 1–12), Gr. 4, p. 230

Tengo, tengo, tengo (m. 1–4), Gr. 4, p. 228

This Little Light of Mine (m. 11–16), Gr. 6, p. 232

This Old Man (final: do), Gr. 3, p. 152

Thula, thula, ngoana (m. 1–6), Gr. 4, p. 227

Tic, tac, Gr. 1, p. 252

Time to Move (m. 13–29), Gr. 1, p. 244

Tina singu (m. 1–4), Gr. 4, p. 300

Trouble Is a Mountain (m. 1-2, 9–10), Gr. 2, p. 202

Turn the World Around/So Is Life/Do You Know Who I Am? (final: do), Gr. 4, p. 114

Tzena, tzena (m. 1–16), Gr. 5, p. 298

Valentines (m. 7–8, 15–16, 23–24), Gr. 2, p. 398

Waitin' for the Light to Shine (m. 20–23, 2nd ending), Gr. 4, p. 26

Wheel of the Water, The (m. voice 5), Gr. 4, p. 362

Wheel of the Water, The (m. voice 5), Gr. 4, p. 362

When the Saints Go Marching In (final: do), Gr. 2, p. 178

### do re mi fa so la

A-Tisket, A-Tasket (final: do), Gr. 2, p. 238

Abiyoyo (m. 1-4), Gr. 2, p. 108

African Noel, Gr. 1, p. 427

Al ánimo (Melody only), Gr. 3, p. 322

All the Way Around the World (final: do), Gr. 2, p. 258

Alle meine Entchen, Gr. 1, p. 98

Alphabet Song, Gr. K, p. 280

America (m. 7–14) (final: do), Gr. 1, p. 446

America (m. 7–14) (final: *do*), Gr. 2, p. 403
America (m. 7–14), Gr. 6, p. 484
America (m. 7–14), Gr. 7, p. 2
America (m. 7–14), Gr. 8, p. 2
Artsa alinu (m. 9–12), Gr. 3, p. 285
Battle Cry of Freedom (m. 9–12), Gr. 5, p. 272
Blowin' in the Wind (final: *do*), Gr. 5, p. 382
Bonjour, mes amis (m. 5–10), Gr. 1, p. 316
Boysie (m. 1-8) (final: *do*), Gr. 2, p. 195
Chairs to Mend (m. 1–4), Gr. 4, p. 149
Cirmos cica, Gr. 1, p. 130
Coffee Grows on White Oak Trees (m. 1–8), Gr. 3, p. 168
Counting Song, Gr. 1, p. 253
Cowboys' Christmas Ball (m. 9–16), Gr. 6, p. 239
Cycle Song of Life (The River Song) (m. 1–2, 5–6),
    Gr. 4, p. 370
Dayenu (m. 1–4), Gr. 4, p. 439
Do, Re, Mi, Fa (final: *re*), Gr. 6, p. 80
Dona nobis pacem, Gr. 6, p. 125
Dona nobis pacem (m. 9–16), Gr. 6, p. 125
Duérmete, mi niño (m. 1–6), Gr. 1, p. 292
Ee jer ha ba go, Gr. K, p. 133
Ég a gyertya, Gr. K, p. 96
Eh, cumpari! (final: *do*), Gr. 4, p. 68
Ein Männlein steht im Walde (m. 9-16), Gr. 2, p. 90
El juego chirimbolo (final: *do*), Gr. 2, p. 54
Elegua (m. 12–15), Gr. 7, p. 8
Fly and the Bumblebee, The (m. 5–8), Gr. 1, p. 384
Give a Little Love (refrain), Gr. 6, p. 140
Give a Little Love (m. 16–32 of verse), Gr. 6, p. 140
Glad to Have a Friend Like You (m. 1-8), Gr. 2, p. 228
God Bless America (m. 30–39), Gr. 5, p. 4
God Bless the U.S.A. (m. 6–10), Gr. 8, p. 37
Goin' to Boston (m. 9–16, 33–40, 53–60, 69–76),
    Gr. 6, p. 433
Hava nashira (m. 1–4), Gr. 6, p. 82
Hello to All the Children of the World (m. 7–8),
    Gr. 3, p. 4
Here I Go!, Gr. K, p. 73
Hi Heidi Ho, Gr. 1, p. 394
I Love Peanuts (verse), Gr. 1, p. 162
I Love Peanuts (m. 5–8), Gr. 7, p. 20
I'm Flying Home (final: *do*), Gr. 2, p. 286
I'm in the Mood, Gr. K, p. 86
Ichi-gatsu tsuitachi (m. 1–8), Gr. 3, p. 406
Ichi-gatsu tsuitachi (m. 1–8), Gr. 7, p. 40
Kaeru no uta, Gr. K, p. 183
Kum ba yah (final: *do*), Gr. 5, p. 244
Kunolounkwa, Gr. K, p. 110
La golondrina (m. 1–8), Gr. 8, p. 50
La víbora (m. 11–16), Gr. 1, p. 322
Las estaciones (m. 1-3), Gr. 1, p. 29
Les petites marionettes, Gr. K, p. 237
Let the Music Begin!, Gr. 1, p. 2
Light Up the World with a Song (m. 9–16), Gr. 8, p. 25
Little and Lots, Gr. K, p. 323
Little Red Caboose, Gr. K, p. 229
London Bridge, Gr. K, p. 244
Lullaby and Dance (m. 26–37, voices 1–2), Gr. 4, p. 387
Making Valentines, Gr. 1, p. 437
Man of Constant Sorrow (final: *re*), Gr. 7, p. 28
Mariposita (m. 9-24) (final: *do*), Gr. 2, p. 156
Mi chacra (m. 5–12), Gr. 1, p. 364

Michael, Row the Boat Ashore (final: *do*), Gr. 2, p. 18
Mister Ram Goat-O (m. 1–4), Gr. 3, p. 54
Mubärak (m. 9–16), Gr. 3, p. 282
Ner li (m. 3–4, 7–8), Gr. 2, p. 383
O Music (m. 5–12), Gr. 5, p. 162
Oh, How Lovely Is the Evening (final: *do*), Gr. 4, p. 217
Oh, Susanna (m. 17–20), Gr. 4, p. 264
Oh, What a Day!, Gr. K, p. 302
One Small Step (m. 1–11), Gr. 5, p. 126
Over in the Meadow (final: *do*), Gr. 1, p. 346
Oye (m. 17–20 of refrain), Gr. 6, p. 336
Panamam tombé (m. 17–32), Gr. 7, p. 18
Pay Me My Money Down (Melody) (final: *do*), Gr. 7, p. 46
Perot (m. 2–3, 6–7), Gr. 2, p. 378
Poco, Le' Me 'Lone (m. 1–4), Gr. 3, p. 300
¡Qué llueva!, Gr. K, p. 81
Rainbow, The (m. 1-2, 5-6), Gr. 2, p. 332
Seagull, Seagull, Sit on the Shore (Part II, m. voice 2),
    Gr. 4, p. 383
Shine, Shine, Shine (final: *do*), Gr. 1, p. 42
Sing a Song of Peace (Part I, m. 13–16), Gr. 6, p. 66
Sing Me a Story (final: *do*), Gr. 2, p. 346
Starlight, Star Bright (m. 1–10), Gr. 4, p. 373
Strike Up the Band (m. 29–32), Gr. 6, p. 135
There Is Love Somewhere (m. 9–12) (final: *do*),
    Gr. 6, p. 318
This Is My Song (Melody only), Gr. 6, p. 77
Three Little Birds (m. 16–23), Gr. 4, p. 320
To'ia mai te waka (m. 3–8), Gr. 1, p. 77
Together in Unity, Gr. K, p. 320
Tree in the Wood, The (final: *do*), Gr. 2, p. 360
Turn, Turn, Turn (To Everything There Is a Season) (m.
    1–15), Gr. 5, p. 378
Un *elefante* (final: *do*), Gr. 2, p. 160
Valentines (m. 5–20), Gr. 2, p. 398
Vamos a hacer la ronda, Gr. K, p. 124
Voice Choice, Gr. K, p. 27
Wind Blew East, The (m. 1–10), Gr. 1, p. 64
Yesh lanu taish (final: *do*), Gr. 1, p. 182
You Were on My Mind (m. 1–44), Gr. 7, p. 23

## *do re mi fa so la do'*

Big Rock Candy Mountain (final: *do*), Gr. 4, p. 330
Bluebird, Bluebird (final: *do*), Gr. K, p. 105
Bonga, Gr. K, p. 78
Cha yang wu, Gr. 1, p. 90
Deau-deau, ti pitit maman (final: *do*), Gr. 2, p. 306
Earth Is My Mother, The, Gr. 1, p. 340
El florón (final: *do*), Gr. 2, p. 246
Honeybee Song, The (final refrain), Gr. 1, p. 358
Hosanna, Me Build a House (m. 1–10, 29–32),
    Gr. 5, p. 132
I Bought Me a Cat (final: *do*), Gr. 2, p. 308
I'm a Believer (m. 24–30), Gr. 7, p. 33
Ichi-gatsu tsuitachi (m. 9–16) (final: *do*), Gr. 7, p. 40
Ise oluwa, Gr. 2, p. 102
Ise oluwa (final: *do*), Gr. 6, p. 230
It's Santa—Again! (final: *do*), Gr. 2, p. 385
Love Can Build a Bridge (m. 9–25, 33–51), Gr. 4, p. 324
Missy-La, Massa-La (m. 9–16), Gr. 4, p. 188
Pin Pon, Gr. 1, p. 146
Popcorn Popping (m. 1–8, 11–16), Gr. 1, p. 440
Put Your Hand in My Hand (m. 1–12) (final: *do*),
    Gr. 1, p. 330

'Round the Bay of Mexico (m. 1–4), Gr. 4, p. 258
Scotland the Brave (m. 1–8), Gr. 5, p. 138
Sing Your Story (m. 21–34), Gr. 3, p. 350
Tender Shepherd (Count Your Sheep) (final: *do*),
    Gr. 3, p. 116
Three Little Birds (m. 24–32), Gr. 4, p. 320
Trouble Is a Mountain (final: *do*), Gr. 2, p. 202
Uno, dos, y tres (Part I) (final: *do*), Gr. 5, p. 427
Valentines (final: *do*), Gr. 2, p. 398
Wir hatten gebauet (m. 9–12), Gr. 8, p. 21

### *do re mi fa so do'*
I Bought Me a Cat (m. 1–8), Gr. 2, p. 308
I Don't Care If the Rain Comes Down (final: *do*),
    Gr. 3, p. 24
Kum bachur atzel (final: *do*), Gr. 3, p. 138
Marines' Hymn, The (m. 1–16, 25–32), Gr. 8, p. 39
Scattin' A-Round (Variations on Row 3) (final: *do*),
    Gr. 6, p. 160
Stille Nacht (Silent Night) (m. 11–12), Gr. 7, p. 54

### *do re mi fa so la do' re'*
Eres tú (Part II, m. 21–24, 29–32), Gr. 6, p. 473
Texas Cowboy (Melody only, last three measures) (final:
    *do*), Gr. 3, p. 250
Texas Cowboy (Melody only, m. 1-8) (final: *do*),
    Gr. 3, p. 250
Texas Cowboy (Melody only, m. 1-4) (final: *do*),
    Gr. 3, p. 250

### *do re mi fa so la do' re' mi'*
Haru ga kita (final: *do'*), Gr. 2, p. 401
Scotland the Brave (m. 9–16), Gr. 5, p. 138

### *do mi fa so*
All for One (m. 22–25), Gr. 7, p. 8
Cindy (m. 17–24, countermelody 1), Gr. 4, p. 384
Cowboys' Christmas Ball (m. 1–4), Gr. 6, p. 239
Each of Us Is a Flower (m. 9–24), Gr. 3, p. 154
Gonna Build a Mountain (m. 9–10, 13–14) (final: *do*),
    Gr. 6, p. 21
Rock Around the Clock (verse 5, m. a1–4), Gr. 7, p. 18
This Little Light of Mine (m. 1–4), Gr. 6, p. 232
Twelve Gates to the City (m. 1–6), Gr. 5, p. 280

### *do mi fa so la*
Book of Love (m. 1–6, 15–20, 29–34, 51–62),
    Gr. 8, p. 27
Gonna Build a Mountain (m. 9–12), Gr. 6, p. 21
I'm on My Way (m. 9–12), Gr. 7, p. 15
I'm on My Way (m. 9–12), Gr. 7, p. 15
Limbo Like Me (m. 1–2, 17–18), Gr. 4, p. 18
My Dear Companion (m. 17–20), Gr. 6, p. 23
Son macaron (final: *do*), Gr. 4, p. 109
Wir hatten gebauet (m. 5–8), Gr. 8, p. 21

### *do mi fa so do'*
Children, Go Where I Send Thee (m. 1–8), Gr. 3, p. 392

### *do mi fa so la do'*
Crocodile, The (m. 1-2, 5-6, 9-10), Gr. 2, p. 362

### *do fa so la*
All for One (m. 5–8), Gr. 7, p. 8

### *do re fa so la*
Alleluia (m. 1–4), Gr. 6, p. 133

### *re mi fa*
Lion Sleeps Tonight, The (m. 1–4), Gr. 8, p. 56

### *re mi fa so*
El día de mamita (m. 1–4, 9–12), Gr. K, p. 325
Everybody Loves Saturday Night (m. 9–12), Gr. 6, p. 296
Fais do do (m. 17–24, part 1–2), Gr. 6, p. 403
Fais do do (Part III, m. 34–48), Gr. 6, p. 403
Let Us Sing Together (m. 9–12), Gr. 6, p. 156
Niño querido (m. 1–4), Gr. 1, p. 308
Pay Me My Money Down (m. 3–4, 11–12), Gr. 4, p. 38
Pay Me My Money Down (m. 3–4, 11–12), Gr. 7, p. 46
Star-Spangled Banner, The (m. 10–13), Gr. 7, p. 56
Star-Spangled Banner, The (m. 10–13), Gr. 8, p. 62
Take a Chance On Me (m. a13–16, a31), Gr. 8, p. 15

### *re mi fa so la*
Corta la caña (m. 17–24), Gr. 6, p. 364
De colores (m. 1–24), Gr. 8, p. 14
Four Strong Winds (Song to a Seagull) (Harmony),
    Gr. 6, p. 170
He's Got the Whole World in His Hands (m. 3–4),
    Gr. 7, p. 36
Man of Constant Sorrow (m. 5–8), Gr. 7, p. 28
O hal'lwe (m. 1–8), Gr. 3, p. 256
Pay Me My Money Down (m. 5–6, 13–14), Gr. 7, p. 46
Sierra Morena (Melody only) (final: *do*), Gr. 3, p. 296
Take a Chance On Me (m. 33–39), Gr. 8, p. 15
Water Come a Me Eye (m. reprise m. 3–4, 11–12),
    Gr. 6, p. 300

### *re mi fa so la do'*
No quiero plata, Gr. 1, p. 424
*Water Come a Me Eye (m. 1–4), Gr. 6, p. 300

### *re fa so la do'*
Cho'i hát bôi (final: *so*), Gr. 5, p. 318

### *mi fa so*
Book of Love (m. 35–50), Gr. 8, p. 27
Canción de cuna (m. 5–8), Gr. 4, p. 144
Fais do do (Part III, m. 9–16, 25–32, 49–64),
    Gr. 6, p. 403
Gospel Train, The (Part I) (final: *mi*), Gr. 6, p. 398
I Shall Sing (m. 9–10, 13–14, 18–19), Gr. 8, p. 38
Little David, Play on Your Harp (m. 19–23, refrain
    ostinato 2), Gr. 4, p. 394
Má Teodora (m. reprise uppervoice - m. a3–4, a7–8,
    a11–16), Gr. 6, p. 301
Pay Me My Money Down (m. 1–2), Gr. 7, p. 46

### *mi fa so la*
All for One (m. 9–12), Gr. 7, p. 8
Banuwa (m. 5–8), Gr. 6, p. 294
Deau-deau, ti pitit maman (m. 1-2), Gr. 2, p. 306
Do Wah Diddy Diddy (m. 1–8), Gr. 7, p. 21
Dok djampa (m. 11–14), Gr. 8, p. 20
Guantanamera (m. 1–6, 21–26), Gr. 8, p. 32
Orange Blossom Special (m. a7–12), Gr. 8, p. 6
Over the Rainbow (from The Wizard of Oz) (m. 17–19),
    Gr. 4, p. 140
Oye (Melody only), Gr. 6, p. 336
Supercalifragilisticexpialidocious (m. 1–4, 21–24),
    Gr. 3, p. 7
We Shall Overcome (m. 1–4), Gr. 4, p. 326
Yibane amenu (m. 5–8), Gr. 4, p. 316

### *mi fa so la do'*
Do Wah Diddy Diddy (final: *so*), Gr. 4, p. 203
Do Wah Diddy Diddy (final: *do*), Gr. 7, p. 21

Don't Cry for Me, Argentina (m. 1–4 of refrain),
   Gr. 6, p. 74
Lift Ev'ry Voice and Sing (m. 9–10), Gr. 8, p. 54

*mi fa so la do' re' mi'*
Yellow Rose of Texas, The (Melody, m. 1–2, 17–18,
   25–26), Gr. 7, p. 70
Yellow Rose of Texas, The (m. 1–4, 17–20, 25–28),
   Gr. 7, p. 70

*mi fa so do'*
Fiddler on the Roof (m. 1–4, 9–12, 50–53), Gr. 7, p. 5

*fa so la*
Those Magic Changes (m. 1–8), Gr. 8, p. 30

*fa so la do'*
Surfin' U.S.A. (m. 9–12), Gr. 7, p. 58

*fa so la do' re'*
Surfin' U.S.A. (m. 25–28), Gr. 7, p. 58

*mi fa so do'*
Little David, Play on Your Harp (m. 14–18, refrain
   ostinato 1), Gr. 4, p. 394

*so la ti do' re' fa'*
Cielito lindo (Last Refrain, m. 42–49), Gr. 7, p. 20

*la, do re mi fa*
Canto del agua (m. 1–15), Gr. 8, p. 10
Cycle Song of Life (The River Song) (m. 3–4),
   Gr. 4, p. 370
Faith of the Heart (m. a3–5), Gr. 8, p. 3
My Home's Across the Blue Ridge Mountains (m. 1–2,
   5–6, 9–10, 13–14), Gr. 7, p. 6
Under the Same Sun (m. 1–5 of refrain), Gr. 6, p. 440

*la, do re mi fa so*
Book of Love, Gr. 8, p. 27
Land of a Thousand Dances (m. 9–19), Gr. 5, p. 330
My Home's Across the Blue Ridge Mountains (final: *do*),
   Gr. 4, p. 84
My Home's Across the Blue Ridge Mountains (final: *do*),
   Gr. 7, p. 6

*la, do re mi fa so la*
Goin' Down the Road Feelin' Bad (final: *do*), Gr. 5, p. 282
Goin' Down the Road Feelin' Bad (final: *do*), Gr. 7, p. 13
It's Time (m. 1–4), Gr. 6, p. 274
My Dear Companion (final: *do*), Gr. 6, p. 23
Your Friends Shall Be the Tall Wind (final: *so*),
   Gr. 6, p. 201
Your Friends Shall Be the Tall Wind (m. 13–16),
   Gr. 6, p. 201

*so, la , do re mi fa so la do'*
By the Waters of Babylon (final: *do*), Gr. 6, p. 311

*la, do re mi fa so la do'*
It's Time (Melody) (final: *do*), Gr. 6, p. 274
Sail Away (m. 40–83, voice 1 - melody), Gr. 5, p. 404

*la, do re fa so la do'*
T'hola, t'hola (final: *do*), Gr. 4, p. 131

*la, do mi fa so*
Habemos llegado (m. 1–8), Gr. 6, p. 174

*la, do mi fa so do'*
America (N. Diamond) (m. 11–12), Gr. 4, p. 206

*do, la, do re mi fa*
Back of the Bus (m. 5–8, 13–16), Gr. 3, p. 410

*so, do re mi fa so*
Ah, eu entrei na roda (final: *do*), Gr. 3, p. 308
Ama-Lama (Melody only) (final: *do*), Gr. 5, p. 142
Chanukiyah li yesh (m. 1–8) (final: *do*), Gr. 1, p. 421
Clementine (m. 1–4), Gr. 4, p. 341
Deux cocodries (final: *do*), Gr. 2, p. 364
El mes de abril (final: *do*), Gr. 3, p. 328
Fais do do (Part I) (final: *do*), Gr. 6, p. 403
Frog Music (final: *do*), Gr. 4, p. 200
Frog Round (final: *do*), Gr. 4
Hot Cross Buns (Version 2) (final: *do*), Gr. 3, p. 221

*so, la, do re mi fa*
Back of the Bus (m. 5–8, 13–16), Gr. 3, p. 410
*Bingo (Melody only, m. 1-10), Gr. 1, p. 170
Faith of the Heart (m. a9–11, 31–37), Gr. 8, p. 3
I Got Rhythm (m. 5–8), Gr. 6, p. 101
Let's Celebrate! (m. 1–8), Gr. 3, p. 374
River (m. 1–32), Gr. 4, p. 58
Siyahamba (m. 1–8, melody), Gr. 6, p. 212
This Pretty Planet (m. 1–4), Gr. 4, p. 355

*so, do re mi fa so*
I Saw Three Ships, Gr. 1, p. 426
Johnny Appleseed (m. 1–4), Gr. 4, p. 345
Liebe ist ein Ring (final: *so*), Gr. 4, p. 193
Little Green Frog, The, Gr. 1, p. 24
Looby Loo (final: *do*), Gr. K, p. 210
Make New Friends (m. 1–2), Gr. 3, p. 36
Ode to Joy (final: *do*), Gr. 4, p. 152
Pust' 'vsegda budet sonse (final: *do*), Gr. 3, p. 278
Rags (m. 1–8), Gr. 1, p. 290
Shoo, Fly (m. 9-16), Gr. 2, p. 200
Simple Gifts (m. 1–2, 13–16), Gr. 8, p. 17
Sweet Potatoes (m. 1–6), Gr. 3, p. 228
Uga uga uga (final: *do*), Gr. K, p. 305
Vil du? (m. 1–4), Gr. 1, p. 92
Winter Song (m. 9–16), Gr. 6, p. 455
Wir hatten gebauet (m. 1–4), Gr. 8, p. 21

*so, la, do re mi fa so*
Big Beautiful Planet (final: *do*), Gr. 3, p. 326
Four in a Boat (final: *do*), Gr. 2, p. 46
Gypsy in the Moonlight (final: *do*), Gr. 3, p. 12
I Got Rhythm (m. 21–26), Gr. 6, p. 101
It's a Celebration! (final: *do*), Gr. 2, p. 372
Kwanzaa Carol, A (final: *do*), Gr. 2, p. 392
Red River Valley (m. a1–6, a9–14) (final: *do*), Gr. 6, p. 11
River (final: *do*), Gr. 4, p. 58
Shanghai Chicken (final: *do*), Gr. 1, p. 140
Singin' in the Rain (m. 1–12, 17–28), Gr. 4, p. 360
Wai bamba (Part I), Gr. 6, p. 26
Wai bamba (Part II) (final: *re*), Gr. 8, p. 13
Winter Fantasy (m. 17–32), Gr. 4, p. 424

*so, la, do re mi fa so la*
Corta la caña (final: *mi*), Gr. 6, p. 364
Cycle Song of Life (The River Song) (m. 1–8),
   Gr. 4, p. 370
Jingle Bells (final: *do*), Gr. 2, p. 388
Loch Lomond (final: *do*), Gr. 5, p. 140
Love in Any Language (m. 1–18), Gr. 6, p. 476
Mister Ram Goat-O (final: *do*), Gr. 3, p. 54

*so, la, do re fa so la*
Niu lang zhi nü (final: *do*), Gr. 4, p. 335

**so, la, do mi fa**
 Cindy (m. 17–24, countermelody 2), Gr. 4, p. 384

**so, la, mi fa**
 This Pretty Planet (m. 9–12), Gr. 4, p. 355

**so, do re mi fa**
 Achshav (final: *do*), Gr. 2, p. 64
 By the Waters of Babylon (m. 1–8), Gr. 6, p. 311
 Cow's Woc Backward, Gr. 1, p. 390
 I've Been Working on the Railroad (m. 1–8), Gr. 3, p. 242
 Nampaya omame, Gr. 1, p. 138
 Nu wahtan, Gr. 1, p. 279
 Seagull, Seagull, Sit on the Shore (Part I, m. voice 1),
  Gr. 4, p. 383
 This Land Is Your Land (refrain only) (m. 1–10) (final: *do*),
  Gr. 1, p. 274
 Wake Me, Shake Me, Gr. 1, p. 278
 Winter Song (m. 1–4), Gr. 6, p. 455
 Yellow Rose of Texas, The (m. 13–16, 29–32),
  Gr. 7, p. 70

**so, do re mi fa so la**
 A la puerta del cielo (verse) (final: *do*), Gr. 5, p. 60
 Bonjour, mes amis (final: *do*), Gr. 1, p. 316
 Chairs to Mend (final: *do*), Gr. 4, p. 149
 Ein Männlein steht im Walde (final: *do*), Gr. 2, p. 90
 El Tren (final: *do*), Gr. 2, p. 260
 Frère Jacques (final: *do*), Gr. 2, p. 125
 Glendy Burke, The (final: *do*), Gr. 4, p. 262
 I Am But a Small Voice (m. 1–8), Gr. 6, p. 446
 I Can't Spell Hippopotamus (m. 9–16), Gr. 1, p. 264
 Lone Star Trail (final: *do*), Gr. 2, p. 21
 Long Way Home, A (final: *do*), Gr. 1, p. 382
 Lullaby and Dance (m. 38–45, voices 1–2), Gr. 4, p. 387
 *Mi chacra (Melody only), Gr. 1, p. 364
 Naranja dulce (final: *do*), Gr. 2, p. 97
 On My Way (m. a17–26), Gr. 6, p. 313
 One Moment in Time (m. a1–17), Gr. 6, p. 352
 Perot (final: *do*), Gr. 2, p. 378
 Seagull, Seagull, Sit on the Shore (m. voices 1 and 2)
  (final: *do*), Gr. 4, p. 383
 Six Little Ducks (final: *do*), Gr. K, p. 234
 United Nations on the March, The (m. 1–15 of verse),
  Gr. 6, p. 443
 Was kommt dort von der Höh'? (final: *do*), Gr. 8, p. 21
 You Are My Sunshine (m. 5–16), Gr. 6, p. 246

**so, do re mi fa so la do'**
 Wir hatten gebauet (final: *do*), Gr. 8, p. 21

**so, do re mi fa so do'**
 Ama-Lama (m. 5–17), Gr. 5, p. 142
 Make New Friends (final: *do*), Gr. 3, p. 36

**mi, fa, so, la, do re mi fa so la**
 Waitin' for the Light to Shine (final: *do*), Gr. 4, p. 26

**mi, fa, so, ti, do re mi fa so**
 Sambalele (m. 1–46, voices 1–2), Gr. 4, p. 397

**ti,**

**ti, do**
 *El chocolate, Gr. 1, p. 380

**ti, do re**
 Chapel of Love (m. 1–4, 9–12), Gr. 7, p. 27
 Falling Rain (m. coda after verse 3), Gr. 2, p. 328

 I'd Like To Teach the World to Sing (In Perfect Harmony)
  (m. 11–12), Gr. 3, p. 198
 What a Wonderful World (m. 14–15, 34–35), Gr. 6, p. 62

**ti, do re mi**
 Alumot (m. 9–12), Gr. 6, p. 306
 Bye Bye, Love (m. 19–26), Gr. 8, p. 9
 Dona nobis pacem, Gr. 6, p. 125
 En nuestra Tierra tan linda (m. 1–8), Gr. 2, p. 335
 Feliz Navidad (m. 14–17), Gr. 7, p. 28
 Gaudeamus Igitur (m. 3–4, 5–8), Gr. 8, p. 20
 Give a Little Love (m. 5–8 of verse), Gr. 6, p. 140
 Hanuka, Hanuka (m. 1–4, 9–14), Gr. 8, p. 36
 Hey, Ho! Nobody Home (m. 5–6), Gr. 6, p. 28
 I See With My Hands (m. 1-2), Gr. 2, p. 148
 Kyrie (m. 5–8), Gr. 6, p. 206
 *Lean on Me (m. 5–8), Gr. 6, p. 14
 Limbo Like Me (m. 3–4, 7–8, 11–12, 15–16, 19–20,
  23–24, 27–28), Gr. 4, p. 18
 Mary Ann (Harmony) (final: *do*), Gr. 6, p. 180
 O Laufet, ihr Hirten (m. 9–10), Gr. 2, p. 384
 Shoo, Fly (m. 3-4), Gr. 2, p. 200
 What a Wonderful World (m. 6–7, 30–31), Gr. 6, p. 62
 What a Wonderful World (m. a5–7, a13–15, a28–34),
  Gr. 6, p. 62

**ti, do re mi fa**
 Aiken Drum, Gr. 1, p. 398
 America (m. 1–6), Gr. 2, p. 403
 America (m. 1–6), Gr. 6, p. 484
 America (m. 1–6), Gr. 7, p. 2
 America (m. 1–6), Gr. 8, p. 2
 Apples and Bananas (final: *do*), Gr. 1, p. 390
 Chrismus a Come (m. 5–8), Gr. 3, p. 396
 Cycle Song of Life (The River Song) (m. 1–2, refrain),
  Gr. 4, p. 370
 Habemos llegado (Melody only), Gr. 6, p. 174
 Hava nashira (m. 5–8), Gr. 6, p. 82
 Heri za Kwanzaa (m. 1–16, melody lower voice),
  Gr. 5, p. 476
 Kokoleoko (m. 3–4) (final: *do*), Gr. 5, p. 33
 La ciudad de Juaja (final: *do*), Gr. 5, p. 58
 Lean on Me (m. 5–8), Gr. 7, p. 22
 Los reyes de Oriente (m. a1–7), Gr. 8, p. 58
 Magnolia (m. 17–23), Gr. 6, p. 16
 Mary Ann (m. 5–8, 13–16), Gr. 6, p. 180
 Nana Kru (m. 5–8), Gr. 6, p. 282
 Oye (Melody only), Gr. 6, p. 336
 Stille Nacht (Silent Night) (m. 9–10), Gr. 7, p. 54
 Take Time in Life (final: *do*), Gr. 6, p. 292

**ti, do re mi fa so**
 Al tambor (m. 1–8), Gr. 3, p. 270
 Alleluia (m. 5–8), Gr. 6, p. 133
 Ash Grove, The (Countermelody) (final: *do*), Gr. 5, p. 114
 Bantama kra kro (final: *do*), Gr. 5, p. 308
 Cantando mentiras (m. 10–12), Gr. 4, p. 146
 Éliza Kongo (m. voices 1–2) (final: *do*), Gr. 5, p. 14
 En nuestra Tierra tan linda (final: *do*), Gr. 2, p. 335
 Ev'rybody Loves Saturday Night (m. 9–16), Gr. 7, p. 24
 Falling Rain (m. 5-8), Gr. 2, p. 328
 Freight Train, Gr. 1, p. 44
 Grizzly Bear, Gr. K, p. 33
 Heri za Kwanzaa (m. 17–32, melody), Gr. 5, p. 476
 Hi-Dee-Roon, Gr. K, p. 10

Pitch and Rhythm Index

I Shall Sing (m. a1–8), Gr. 8, p. 38
I'm Thankful (m. 5–8), Gr. 1, p. 414
Jig Along Home (m. 7-8), Gr. 2, p. 366
La tormenta tropical (final: *do*), Gr. 2, p. 116
Lift Ev'ry Voice and Sing (m. a1–4), Gr. 8, p. 54
Los niños en España cantan (m. 5–8), Gr. 4, p. 197
Mary Ann (Melody only) (final: *do*), Gr. 6, p. 180
Me voy para la luna, Gr. 1, p. 397
O, Desayo (m. voices 1-2) (final: *do*), Gr. 5, p. 411
O Laufet, ihr Hirten, Gr. 2, p. 384
Sambalele (m. 1–25), Gr. 4, p. 397
Skip to My Lou, Gr. K, p. 58
Tengo, tengo, tengo (Melody only) (final: *do*),
   Gr. 4, p. 228
Thula, thula, ngoana (final: *do*), Gr. 4, p. 227
Wings of a Dove (m. 7–10), Gr. 4, p. 318

### *ti, do re mi so*
I See With My Hands (final: *do*), Gr. 2, p. 148
Jig Along Home (m. 15-16), Gr. 2, p. 366
Seasons of Love (m. 1–8, 13–16), Gr. 8, p. 22
Vamos a la fiesta (m. 3–4), Gr. 2, p. 374

### *ti, do re mi fa so la*
Adiós, amigos (m. 1–4) (final: *do*), Gr. 6, p. 57
America (final: *do*), Gr. 1, p. 446
America (final: *do*), Gr. 2, p. 403
America (final: *do*), Gr. 3, p. 412
America (final: *do*), Gr. 4, p. 440
America (final: *do*), Gr. 5, p. 486
America (final: *do*), Gr. 6, p. 484
America (final: *do*), Gr. 7, p. 2
America (final: *do*), Gr. 8, p. 2
America (final: *do*), Gr. K, p. 326
Ayelivi (m. 5-8), Gr. 2, p. 70
Blowin' in the Wind (final: *do*), Gr. 5, p. 382
Bogando a la luz del sol (m. 11–18), Gr. 4, p. 306
Cowboys' Christmas Ball (final: *do*), Gr. 6, p. 239
Duérmete, mi niño (final: *do*), Gr. 1, p. 292
Einini (m. 24–28, voice 2), Gr. 4, p. 391
El borrego (m. 1–32), Gr. 4, p. 242
Falling Rain (final: *do*), Gr. 2, p. 328
Fuzzy Caterpillar (final: *do*), Gr. K, p. 102
Harambee (final: *do*), Gr. 4, p. 434
He's Got the Whole World in His Hands (final: *do*),
   Gr. 7, p. 36
I See With My Hands (final: *coda*), Gr. 2, p. 148
Las estaciones (final: *do*), Gr. 1, p. 29
Lift Ev'ry Voice and Sing (m. a5–6, a14–15), Gr. 8, p. 54
Má Teodora (m. call m. a5–6), Gr. 6, p. 301
Magnolia (m. 9–16), Gr. 6, p. 16
Put Your Finger in the Air (final: *do*), Gr. K, p. 114
Somos el barco (m. 1–8), Gr. 4, p. 352
'-Ulili E (m. voices 1–2) (final: *do*), Gr. 5, p. 441

### *ti, do re mi fa so la do'*
America, I Hear You Singing (final: *do*), Gr. 2, p. 402
Water Come a Me Eye (Melody) (final: *do*), Gr. 6, p. 300

### *ti, do re mi fa so do'*
Children, Go Where I Send Thee (final: *do*), Gr. 3, p. 392
Still, Still, Still (final: *do*), Gr. 5, p. 468

### *ti, do re mi so do'*
Viva Jujuy (final: *do*), Gr. 5, p. 228

### *ti, do re mi fa so la do' mi'*
Limbo Like Me (final: *do*), Gr. 4, p. 18

### *la, ti, do*
Ev'rybody Loves Saturday Night (m. 1–4, 5–8, 13–16),
   Gr. 7, p. 24
Everybody Loves Saturday Night (m. 1–7, 13–15),
   Gr. 6, p. 296
Sing a Song of Peace (Part I, m. 1–2, 5–6), Gr. 6, p. 66

### *la, ti, do re*
Alumot (m. 1–4), Gr. 6, p. 306
El borrego (m. 33–40), Gr. 4, p. 242
Hej pada pada (m. 7–8, 11–12), Gr. 3, p. 78
Vive l'amour (m. 13–16), Gr. 6, p. 176

### *la, ti, do re mi*
Ala Da'lona (final: *la,*), Gr. 4, p. 136
Ala Da'lona (m. 4–6, 10–12, 16–18), Gr. 4, p. 136
Alumot (m. 13–16) (final: *la,*), Gr. 6, p. 306
Beriozka (m. 1–3, 7–12), Gr. 4, p. 294
Blue Mountain Lake (m. 1–4, a9–10), Gr. 6, p. 205
Connemara Lullaby (m. 1–4), Gr. 5, p. 232
Drill, Ye Tarriers (m. 5–8), Gr. 5, p. 54
Gakavik (m. 5–8, 13–16), Gr. 4, p. 14
God Bless the Grass (final: *la,*), Gr. 8, p. 13
Hanuka, Hanuka (m. 1–8, 9–14), Gr. 3, p. 390
Hanuka, Hanuka (m. 5–8), Gr. 8, p. 36
Hava nagila (m. 17–23), Gr. 6, p. 153
I Got a Letter This Morning (final: *la*), Gr. K, p. 68
La borinqueña (m. 1–5), Gr. 8, p. 19
La mariposa (m. 13–14, 19–26), Gr. 6, p. 58
Scarborough Fair (m. 13–16), Gr. 6, p. 95
Small Job, A (m. 1–4), Gr. 3, p. 224
Something Told the Wild Geese (Part I, m. 7–10),
   Gr. 7, p. 39
Straighten Up and Fly Right (final: *do*), Gr. 4, p. 128
Tumba (m. 9–16), Gr. 5, p. 161
Turn the World Around (final: *do*), Gr. 4, p. 114
Un pajarito (m. 1-6), Gr. 2, p. 16
Winter (m. 9–16), Gr. 8, p. 11
Yibane amenu (m. 11–12), Gr. 4, p. 316
Yo-shi nai (final: *do*), Gr. 6, p. 286
Zip-a-Dee-Doo-Dah (m. 29-32), Gr. 2, p. 330

### *la, ti, do re mi fa*
Don Alfonso (final: *la*), Gr. 5, p. 177
Faith of the Heart (m. a9–15), Gr. 8, p. 3
Gaudeamus Igitur (m. 9–12), Gr. 8, p. 20
Habemos llegado (Melody only), Gr. 6, p. 174
Haere (final: *do*), Gr. 2, p. 285
Halloween Song, Gr. K, p. 309
La copa de la vida (m. 43–54), Gr. 4, p. 414
Lo yisa (m. 9–16), Gr. 6, p. 130
Mon papa (m. 7–8), Gr. 2, p. 280
Oy, Hanuka (m. 7–16), Gr. 7, p. 44
Oye (m. 1–8), Gr. 6, p. 336
Something Told the Wild Geese (Part I, m. 7–14),
   Gr. 7, p. 39
Un pajarito (m. 1–10), Gr. 2, p. 16

### *la, ti, do re mi fa so*
Ai, Dunaii moy, Gr. 4, p. 293
De colores (Countermelody) (final: *mi*), Gr. 5, p. 90
Ev'rybody Loves Saturday Night (final: *do*), Gr. 7, p. 24
Everybody Loves Saturday Night (final: *do*), Gr. 6, p. 296
Habemos llegado (melody) (final: *la,*), Gr. 6, p. 174

Oye (m. 9–12), Gr. 6, p. 336
Strike Up the Band (m. a17–24), Gr. 6, p. 135

### *la, ti, do re mi so*

Beriozka (final: *la,*), Gr. 4, p. 294

### *la, ti, do re mi fa so la*

Dundai (final: *la,*), Gr. 5, p. 106
El borrego (final: *do*), Gr. 4, p. 242
Oye (final: *so*), Gr. 6, p. 336
Yibane amenu (final: *la*), Gr. 4, p. 316

### *la, ti, do re mi so la*

Ah, Poor Bird (final: *la*), Gr. 4, p. 196
Blue Mountain Lake (final: *la*), Gr. 6, p. 205
Hine mah tov (m. 50–62, voice 1 - melody), Gr. 5, p. 430
In the Pumpkin Patch (final: *la*), Gr. 3, p. 380
Oh, Danny Boy (m. 1–8), Gr. 4, p. 48
Promised Land, The (Melody only) (final: *la,*),
    Gr. 5, p. 258
Small Job, A (m. 5–8), Gr. 3, p. 224

### *la, ti, do re mi fa la*

Chanukah Games (final: *la,*), Gr. 3, p. 389
Owl and the Pumpkin, The (final: *la*), Gr. 2, p. 377
Oy, Hanuka (final: *la*), Gr. 5, p. 464
Oy, Hanuka (Melody, uppervoice) (final: *la*), Gr. 7, p. 44

### *la, ti, do re mi la*

Joshua Fought the Battle of Jericho (m. a9–16),
    Gr. 8, p. 18

### *so, la, do mi fa so*

El rabel, Gr. 3, p. 362

### *la, ti, do mi*

Ai, Dunaii moy (m. 5–8, 13–16), Gr. 4, p. 293
Scarborough Fair (m. 1–4), Gr. 6, p. 95

### *so, la, ti, do re mi fa so la do'*

O lê lê O Bahía (final: *do*), Gr. 6, p. 165

### *so, la, ti, do*

Angels On the Midnight Clear (Melody only),
    Gr. 6, p. 423
Artsa alinu (m. 17–20), Gr. 3, p. 285
Cheki, morena (final: *do*), Gr. 2, p. 180
Cheki, morena (final: *do*), Gr. 7, p. 16
Do, Lord, Gr. 3, p. 164
Down by the Bay (m. 1–7, 10–12), Gr. 1, p. 18
Earth Is Our Mother, The (final: *la,*), Gr. 4, p. 358
Fais do do (Part II, m. 17–24), Gr. 6, p. 403
Friend of Mine (m. 1, 3, 5), Gr. 1, p. 310
Friends Today (lowervoice) (final: *so*), Gr. 7, p. 12
Haere (m. 17-20), Gr. 2, p. 285
I Know an Old Lady (m. 5–6), Gr. 1, p. 388
I'm Thankful (m. 1–2), Gr. 1, p. 414
Mubärak (m. 1–8), Gr. 3, p. 282
Railroad Corral (m. 3–4, 7–8, 15–16), Gr. 3, p. 174
Si si si (Part III, m. 17–24), Gr. 7, p. 13
Somebody Waiting (m. 3-4, 7-8), Gr. 2, p. 283
Sweet Potatoes (m. 7–8), Gr. 3, p. 228
Theme from New York, New York (m. 3–4, 9–12),
    Gr. 4, p. 250

### *so, ti, do*

Má Teodora (m. reprise lowervoice m. a3–4, a7–8, a11–
    16), Gr. 6, p. 301
Rinsho, rinsho, Gr. K, p. 285

### *so, la, ti, do re*

Al yadee (final: *la,*), Gr. 6, p. 308
All Through the Night (m. 1–8, 13–16, 25–28),
    Gr. 5, p. 105
Alumot (m. 5–8), Gr. 6, p. 306
Au clair de la lune (m. 9–12), Gr. 3, p. 18
Bingo (m. 9–12), Gr. 1, p. 170
Caroling, Caroling (m. 1–8), Gr. 6, p. 458
Crocodile, The (m. 15-16), Gr. 2, p. 362
Der sad to katte (m. 1-8), Gr. 2, p. 300
Ding Dong! Merrily on High (Part I, m. 9–16, 27–33),
    Gr. 6, p. 427
Earth Is Our Mother, The (Melody only) (final: *la,*),
    Gr. 8, p. 25
Feliz Navidad (m. 1–6), Gr. 7, p. 28
Four Strong Winds (Song to a Seagull) (m. a1–8, refrain
    m. a17–25), Gr. 6, p. 170
Give My Regards to Broadway (m. 1–24), Gr. 6, p. 39
God Bless the U.S.A. (m. a42–43), Gr. 8, p. 37
Good King Wenceslas (m. 1–8), Gr. 6, p. 460
Green, Green Grass of Home (m. 11–15, 20–24),
    Gr. 6, p. 248
I'm on My Way (m. 1–4), Gr. 7, p. 15
L'inverno è passato (m. 5–8, 13–16), Gr. 2, p. 400
La raspa (m. 1–8, 17–24, 33–40), Gr. 4, p. 302
Let Us Sing Together (m. 1–4), Gr. 6, p. 156
Nana Kru (m. 1–4), Gr. 6, p. 282
Tancovacka (m. 29–32), Gr. 4, p. 230
Walk in the Room (Melody only), Gr. 1, p. 12
Yankee Doodle (m. 13–16), Gr. 2, p. 405

### *so, ti, do re*

Gonna Build a Mountain (m. 15–16), Gr. 6, p. 21
This Land Is Your Land (m. 13–16), Gr. 7, p. 66

### *so, la, ti, do re mi*

Angels On the Midnight Clear (Melody only),
    Gr. 6, p. 423
Angels On the Midnight Clear (m. 1–22), Gr. 6, p. 423
Artsa alinu (m. 1–8), Gr. 3, p. 285
Au clair de la lune (m. 9–16) (final: *do*), Gr. 3, p. 18
Ayliluli, num tsipor, Gr. 1, p. 204
Bridges (m. 5–6), Gr. 6, p. 86
Chapel of Love (m. 17–20), Gr. 7, p. 27
Clap, Wiggle, and Stomp, Gr. K, p. 34
Clouds, Gr. K, p. 254
Down the Ohio (m. 9–16 of refrain), Gr. 2, p. 60
Downtown (m. 1–8), Gr. 6, p. 258
El gallo pinto (final: *do*), Gr. 3, p. 86
Eres tú (m. 1–4, 7–8), Gr. 6, p. 473
Ev'ry Kind of Music, Gr. 2, p. 226
Follow the Drinkin' Gourd (m. 5–8, 13–16), Gr. 4, p. 266
Four White Horses (final: *do*), Gr. 3, p. 304
Halloween Is a Very Unusual Night (m. 21–25, 38–40),
    Gr. 3, p. 382
Hine mah tov (m. 1–28, voice 1 - melody), Gr. 5, p. 430
I Got Shoes (final: *do*), Gr. 2, p. 242
I Know an Old Lady, Gr. 1, p. 388
I'm a Dreydl, Gr. K, p. 315
I've Been Everywhere (m. 9–12), Gr. 6, p. 226
I've Been Working on the Railroad (m. 17–28),
    Gr. 3, p. 242
¡Jeu! ¡Jeu!, Gr. 1, p. 216
Jolly Old St. Nicholas, Gr. K, p. 316

Juanito, Gr. K, p. 300
Let's Celebrate! (m. 9–24), Gr. 3, p. 374
Miss Susie Anna Sue, Gr. K, p. 242
My Father's House (final: *do*), Gr. 2, p. 25
My Valentine, Gr. K, p. 323
Old Chisholm Trail, The (m. 5–6), Gr. 6, p. 237
Parade Came Marching, The (m. 1–4), Gr. 1, p. 166
Rabbit Footprints (final: *la*), Gr. 2, p.-304
Race You Down the Mountain, Gr. 1, p. 127
Red River Valley (m. a7–8, a15–16), Gr. 6, p. 11
Roll On, Columbia (final: *do*), Gr. 5, p. 116
Scarborough Fair (m. 13–16), Gr. 6, p. 95
Scrub Brush Shuffle, The (m. 9–12), Gr. 1, p. 118
Somebody Waiting (final: *do*), Gr. 2, p. 283
Willoughby, Wallaby, Woo, Gr. K, p. 282
Yankee Doodle (m. 1–8), Gr. 2, p. 405

**so¸ ti¸ re**
Deep in the Heart of Texas (m. 9–12, 25–28),
    Gr. 8, p. 18

**so¸ la¸ ti¸ do re mi fa**
*Bingo (Melody only), Gr. 1, p. 170
*Buenos días (Melody only), Gr. 1, p. 13
Downtown (m. 9–17), Gr. 6, p. 258
Each of Us Is a Flower (m. 1–8), Gr. 3, p. 154
Families (final: *do*), Gr. 1, p. 282
For the Beauty of the Earth (m. 1–8), Gr. 4, p. 356
Four Strong Winds (Song to a Seagull) (Melody only) (final:
    *so¸*), Gr. 6, p. 170
Four Strong Winds (Song to a Seagull) (m. a9–16, a25–
    32), Gr. 6, p. 170
Gaudeamus Igitur (Melody only) (final: *do*), Gr. 8, p. 20
Heigh-Ho (final: *do*), Gr. 2, p. 6
Higglety, Pigglety, Pop! (final: *do*), Gr. K, p. 22
If You're Happy (final: *do*), Gr. K, p. 94
La bamba (final: *so¸*), Gr. 5, p. 128
La paloma blanca (final: *do*), Gr. 3, p. 252
Let Us Sing Together (m. 5–8), Gr. 6, p. 156
Mañana (m. 9–16), Gr. 7, p. 14
Mon papa (final: *do*), Gr. 2, p. 280
Must Be Santa (final: *do*), Gr. K, p. 318
Nana Kru (final: *do*), Gr. 6, p. 282
O lê lê O Bahía (m. 10–13), Gr. 6, p. 165
Sh'ney dubim, Gr. K, p. 268
Siyahamba (m. 9–16, melody) (final: *do*), Gr. 6, p. 212
Song That's Just for You, A (final: *do*), Gr. 2, p. 126
Uno, dos, y tres (Part II) (final: *do*), Gr. 5, p. 427
Waltzing with Bears (m. 18–21, 44–47), Gr. 3, p. 170
We Shall Not Be Moved (final: *do*), Gr. 4, p. 437
Winter Fantasy (m. 1–8), Gr. 4, p. 424
Yankee Doodle (final: *do*), Gr. 2, p. 389
Yankee Doodle (m. 1–8), Gr. 3, p. 414

**so¸ ti¸ do re mi**
A Ram Sam Sam (m. 1–4), Gr. 3, p. 208
El gallo pinto (m. 7–8), Gr. 3, p. 86
Gonna Have a Good Time (m. 1-2, 7-8, 13-18),
    Gr. 2, p. 4
Goodbye, Julie (m. 1–2, 5–6), Gr. 8, p. 2
I'm on My Way (m. 5–8), Gr. 7, p. 15
La pulga de San José (m. 7–8, verse), Gr. 3, p. 40
La víbora (m. 1–8), Gr. 1, p. 322
Nie chce cie znác (m. 1–8), Gr. 3, p. 314
O lê lê O Bahía (m. 7–8), Gr. 6, p. 165

One Green Jelly Bean, Gr. K, p. 287
Pon, pon, pon, Gr. K, p. 50
Time to Sing (m. 1-2), Gr. 2, p. 8
What Will You Be on Halloween?, Gr. K, p. 308
Yellow Rose of Texas, The (m. 5–8, 21–24), Gr. 7, p. 70

**so¸ la¸ ti¸ do re mi fa so**
A la rurru niño, Gr. K, p. 180
Al tambor (m. 9–16), Gr. 3, p. 270
Blow, Ye Winds (final: *do*), Gr. 4, p. 255
Bridges (final: *do*), Gr. 6, p. 86
Chanukiyah li yesh (final: *do*), Gr. 1, p. 421
Der sad to katte (final: *do*), Gr. 2, p. 300
Ding Dong! Merrily on High (Part I, m. 17–34),
    Gr. 6, p. 427
Downtown (final: *do*), Gr. 6, p. 258
El rabel (final: *do*), Gr. 3, p. 362
El tambor (m. 9-16), Gr. 2, p. 274
For the Beauty of the Earth (final: *do*), Gr. 4, p. 356
Good King Wenceslas (final: *do*), Gr. 6, p. 460
Happy Birthday to You (final: *do*), Gr. K, p. 304
Hey, Diddle, Diddle, Gr. K, p. 246
Home on the Range (final: *do*), Gr. 5, p. 69
I'd Like To Teach the World to Sing (In Perfect Harmony)
    (Melody only, m. 1-8), Gr. 3, p. 198
Johnny Appleseed (final: *do*), Gr. 4, p. 345
La Jesusita (final: *do*), Gr. 5, p. 322
Niño querido, Gr. 1, p. 308
Purple People Eater, The (m. 9–16), Gr. 6, p. 448
Rags (final: *do*), Gr. 1, p. 290
Red River Valley (final: *do*), Gr. 6, p. 11
Sailing Down My Golden River (final: *do*), Gr. 4, p. 332
Shake the Papaya Down (final: *do*), Gr. 4, p. 378
Singin' in the Rain (final: *do*), Gr. 4, p. 360
Sweet Potatoes (final: *do*), Gr. 3, p. 228
Tancovacka (final: *do*), Gr. 4, p. 230
This Pretty Planet (m. 5–8), Gr. 4, p. 355
This Pretty Planet (final: *do*), Gr. 4, p. 355
Wai bamba (Melody only), Gr. 8, p. 13
Water Is Wide, The (final: *do*), Gr. 6, p. 228

**so¸ ti¸ do re mi fa**
Keel Row, The (m. 1–8), Gr. 4, p. 240
La pulga de San José (m. 9–16, refrain), Gr. 3, p. 40
La pulga de San José (final: *do*), Gr. 3, p. 40
Los niños en España cantan (m. 1–4), Gr. 4, p. 197
Shri Ram, jai Ram (final: *do*), Gr. 4, p. 311
This Land Is Your Land (Melody) (final: *do*), Gr. 7, p. 66
This Land Is Your Land (Melody) (final: *do*), Gr. 7, p. 66
This Land Is Your Land (refrain only), Gr. 1, p. 274
Water Is Wide, The (m. 5–8), Gr. 6, p. 228
Zumba, zumba (final: *do*), Gr. 3, p. 400

**so¸ la¸ ti¸ do re mi so**
All Night, All Day (m. 5–8, 13–16), Gr. 4, p. 180
Erie Canal (m. 1–16), Gr. 5, p. 262
Look Out Below! (m. 15–18), Gr. 2, p. 370
Mañana (m. 1–8), Gr. 7, p. 14
Michael Finnigan (final: *do*), Gr. 3, p. 153
Scrub Brush Shuffle, The (m. 13–16), Gr. 1, p. 118
She'll Be Comin' 'Round the Mountain (m. 9–17),
    Gr. 2, p. 358
Snowflakes, Gr. 1, p. 422
You're a Grand Old Flag (m. 1–19), Gr. 3, p. 264

**so, ti, do re mi fa so**
A Ram Sam Sam, Gr. 3,  p. 208
Almost Day (final: *do*), Gr. 3,  p. 397
Bus, The, Gr. K,  p. 82
Clementine, Gr. 4,  p. 341
Dona nobis pacem, Gr. 6,  p. 125
Down in the Valley (final: *do*), Gr. 6,  p. 375
El rancho grande (m. 16–31), Gr. 4,  p. 215
El rancho grande (m. 16–32), Gr. 8,  p. 22
Fais do do (Part II) (final: *do*), Gr. 6,  p. 403
Gonna Build a Mountain (m. 13–16), Gr. 6,  p. 21
Gonna Have a Good Time (final: *do*), Gr. 2,  p. 4
Goodbye, Julie, Gr. 1,  p. 334
Goodbye, Julie (final: *do*), Gr. 8,  p. 2
I Shall Sing (final: *so,*), Gr. 8,  p. 38
I'm on My Way (m. 13–16), Gr. 7,  p. 15
I'm Thankful, Gr. 1,  p. 414
Jan ken pon (final: *do*), Gr. 3,  p. 302
Little Red Wagon, Gr. K,  p. 152
Los niños en España cantan (final: *do*), Gr. 4,  p. 197
Love Somebody (final: *do*), Gr. 3,  p. 94
Merry-Go-Round, Gr. K,  p. 290
Morning Is Come, Gr. 3,  p. 128
Old Blue, Gr. K,  p. 122
Painting Song: A Dribble and a Dot, Gr. K,  p. 175
Panamam tombé (m. 1–16), Gr. 7,  p. 18
Pust' 'vsegda budet sonse (final: *do*), Gr. 3,  p. 278
Shoo, Fly (final: *do*), Gr. 2,  p. 200
Simple Gifts (final: *do*), Gr. 5,  p. 184
Simple Gifts (m. a5–8) (final: *do*), Gr. 8,  p. 17
Streets of Laredo (final: *do*), Gr. 4,  p. 272
Vil du?, Gr. 1,  p. 92

**so, la, ti, do re mi fa so la**
All Through the Night (final: *do*), Gr. 5,  p. 105
Bard of Armagh, The (final: *do*), Gr. 4,  p. 296
Book of Love (final: *mi*), Gr. 8,  p. 27
Caroling, Caroling (final: *do*), Gr. 6,  p. 458
Eres tú (m. 1–16), Gr. 6,  p. 473
Family Tree (final: *do*), Gr. 3,  p. 72
Fifty Nifty United States (m. 1–27) (final: *do*),
    Gr. 5,  p. 251
Gakavik (final: *do*), Gr. 4,  p. 14
God Bless America (final: *do*), Gr. 5,  p. 4
Gonna Build a Mountain (final: *do*), Gr. 6,  p. 21
Guantanamera (final: *so,*), Gr. 8,  p. 32
Guantanamera (m. a7–8, a17–20, a27–28), Gr. 8,  p. 32
Habari Gani (final: *do*), Gr. 3,  p. 404
Himmel und Erde (final: *do*), Gr. 5,  p. 94
I Love the Mountains (final: *do*), Gr. 5,  p. 34
I'm on My Way (final: *do*), Gr. 3,  p. 76
I'm on My Way (final: *do*), Gr. 7,  p. 15
L'inverno è passato (final: *do*), Gr. 2,  p. 400
La mariposa (final: *la,*), Gr. 6,  p. 58
Las Navidades (final: *mi*), Gr. 5,  p. 472
Mubärak (final: *do*), Gr. 3,  p. 282
Nie chce cie znác (final: *do*), Gr. 3,  p. 314
On My Way (final: *do*), Gr. 6,  p. 313
Parade Came Marching, The (final: *do*), Gr. 1,  p. 166
Ptashky u babusi sadochku (final: *do*), Gr. 1,  p. 192
Río, río (final: *do*), Gr. 5,  p. 370
Rock Island Line (final: *do*), Gr. 4,  p. 54
Song of the Fishes (final: *do*), Gr. 3,  p. 244
Tie Me Kangaroo Down, Sport (final: *do*), Gr. 4,  p. 37

**so, ti, do re mi so**
Mañana (m. 1–8), Gr. 7,  p. 14

**so, ti, do re mi fa so la**
Adiós, amigos (final: *do*), Gr. 6,  p. 57
Baby Beluga (final: *do*), Gr. K,  p. 272
Ciranda (final: *do*), Gr. 2,  p. 272
Dona nobis pacem (final: *do*), Gr. 6,  p. 125
El payo (final: *do*), Gr. 6,  p. 145
Jig Along Home (final: *do*), Gr. 2,  p. 366
Kangaroo Song, The (final: *do*), Gr. K,  p. 44
La víbora (final: *do*), Gr. 1,  p. 322
Long Way Home, A (final: *do*), Gr. 1,  p. 382
Mango Walk (final: *do*), Gr. 5,  p. 200
Paw-Paw Patch (final: *do*), Gr. 4,  p. 93
Wind Blew East, The, Gr. 1,  p. 64

**so, ti, do re mi fa so la do'**
Keel Row, The, Gr. 4,  p. 240
'Round the Bay of Mexico (final: *do*), Gr. 4,  p. 258
Wings of a Dove (m. 1–10), Gr. 4,  p. 318

**so, ti, do re mi so la**
Deep in the Heart of Texas (final: *do*), Gr. 4,  p. 22
Deep in the Heart of Texas (final: *do*), Gr. 8,  p. 18
Scarborough Fair (m. 9–12), Gr. 6,  p. 95

**fa, so, la, ti, do**
Light Up the World with a Song (Coda), Gr. 8,  p. 25

**fa, so, la, ti, do re mi**
Lean on Me (Refrains, uppervoice), Gr. 7,  p. 22

**fa, so, la, ti, do re mi fa**
Sharing (final: *do*), Gr. K,  p. 198

**mi, so, la, ti, do re mi so**
She'll Be Comin' 'Round the Mountain (final: *do*),
    Gr. 2,  p. 358

**fa, so, la, ti, do re mi fa so**
Wai bamba (final: *so*), Gr. 8,  p. 13

**fa, so, la, ti, do re mi so**
Ash Grove, The (Melody only, m. 1–8, 17–24),
    Gr. 5,  p. 114
Wabash Cannon Ball (final: *do*), Gr. 5,  p. 136

**mi, fa, so, la, ti,**
Little Darlin' (m. 9–17), Gr. 7,  p. 30

**mi, fa, so, la, ti, do**
Doong gul ge (m. 1–8), Gr. 3,  p. 134
La paloma se fué (m. a3–4, a7–8), Gr. 6,  p. 51
Las estrellitas del cielo (final: *mi*), Gr. 5,  p. 175
Little Darlin' (m. 18–33), Gr. 7,  p. 30
Vive l'amour (Harmony) (final: *mi,*), Gr. 6,  p. 176

**mi, fa, so, la, ti, do re**
Feliz Navidad (m. 1–8), Gr. 7,  p. 28
Karangatia ra, Gr. 3,  p. 272
Pat Works on the Railway (final: *la,*), Gr. 5,  p. 182
Pat Works on the Railway (m. solo male voice 2) (final: *la*),
    Gr. 5,  p. 182
¡Qué gusto! (final: *do'*), Gr. 3,  p. 132
Santa Clara (m. 12–24), Gr. 4,  p. 172
Se va el caimán (final: *do'*), Gr. 5,  p. 306

**mi, fa, so, la, ti, do re mi**
Battle Cry of Freedom (m. 1–8, 13–16), Gr. 5,  p. 272
Battle Hymn of the Republic (final: *do*), Gr. 5,  p. 274
Blow the Wind Southerly (m. 1–8, 17–24), Gr. 5,  p. 178
California Dreamin' (Part III, m. 8–15), Gr. 8,  p. 31

Pitch and Rhythm Index

**mi₁ fa₁ so₁ la₁ ti₁ do re mi fa**
  Christmas, Don't Be Late (The Chipmunk Song) (final: *do*),
    Gr. 2, p. 386
  Doong gul ge (final: *do*), Gr. 3, p. 134
  Vive l'amour (Melody only) (final: *do*), Gr. 6, p. 176
  Yankee Doodle (m. 9–16) (final: *do*), Gr. 3, p. 414
  Yellow Rose of Texas, The (Melody) (final: *do'*),
    Gr. 7, p. 70

**mi₁ fa₁ so₁ la₁ ti₁ do re mi fa so**
  El tambor, Gr. 2, p. 274

**mi₁ fa₁ so₁ la₁ ti₁ do re mi so**
  Little Darlin' (final: *do*), Gr. 7, p. 30

**mi₁ fa₁ so₁ la₁ ti₁ do re mi fa so la**
  Battle Cry of Freedom (final: *do*), Gr. 5, p. 272
  O Music (final: *do*), Gr. 5, p. 162
  Proud (final: *do*), Gr. 7, p. 3

**mi₁ fa₁ la₁ ti₁ do mi fa la**
  Hitotsu toya (final: *ti₁*), Gr. 5, p. 478

**mi₁ so₁ la₁ ti₁ do**
  California Dreamin' (Part III, m. 1–7), Gr. 8, p. 31
  Con el vito (m. 21–24, 29–32), Gr. 7, p. 15
  Pollerita (m. 13–18), Gr. 5, p. 151
  Sometimes I Feel Like a Motherless Child (m. 7–8),
    Gr. 6, p. 241
  Turn the World Around (final: *mi₁*), Gr. 4, p. 115

**mi₁ so₁ la₁ ti₁ do re**
  I Walk the Unfrequented Road (m. 1–2), Gr. 6, p. 79

**mi₁ so₁ la₁ ti₁ do re mi**
  Green, Green Grass of Home (final: *la₁*), Gr. 6, p. 248
  Hey, Ho! Nobody Home (final: *la₁*), Gr. 6, p. 28
  Khorovod, Gr. 1, p. 372
  Sarika keo (final: *do*), Gr. 3, p. 275
  Spaceworms (final: *la*), Gr. 1, p. 400
  Summertime (final: *la₁*), Gr. 6, p. 250
  When Johnny Comes Marching Home (final: *la₁*),
    Gr. 5, p. 180

**mi₁ so₁ la₁ ti₁ do re mi so**
  Yü guang guang (final: *do*), Gr. 6, p. 60

**mi₁ so₁ la₁ ti₁ do re mi fa**
  I Walk the Unfrequented Road, Gr. 6, p. 79

**mi₁ so₁ la₁ ti₁ do re fa**
  I Vow to You, My Country (m. 33–60, voice 1 - melody, C
    - do), Gr. 5, p. 418

**mi₁ la₁ ti₁ do**
  Hej pada pada (m. 1–2), Gr. 3, p. 78
  I Walk the Unfrequented Road (m. 7–8), Gr. 6, p. 79
  Lo yisa (m. a1–2, 5–6), Gr. 6, p. 130
  Zum gali gali (m. 1–4), Gr. 5, p. 400

**mi₁ la₁ ti₁ do re mi**
  Groundhog Blues, The (final: *la*), Gr. 3, p. 122
  I Walk the Unfrequented Road (m. 3–4), Gr. 6, p. 79
  Kyrie (m. 9–12), Gr. 6, p. 206
  Proud (m. 1–3), Gr. 7, p. 3
  S'vivon (m. 1–16), Gr. 6, p. 452

**so₁ la₁ ti₁ do re'mi fa so**
  We Wish You a Merry Christmas (Melody only),
    Gr. 3, p. 395

**mi₁ la₁ ti₁ do re mi**
  Zum gali gali (final: *la₁*), Gr. 5, p. 400

**mi₁ la₁ ti₁ do re mi fa**
  Hej pada pada (final: *la₁*), Gr. 3, p. 78

**do₁ la₁ ti₁ do re mi**
  Purple People Eater, The (m. 9–14), Gr. 6, p. 448

**ti**

**so la ti do'**
  Banuwa (m. 9–12 of melody), Gr. 6, p. 294
  El coquí (m. 13-20, refrain), Gr. 2, p. 292
  Polly Wee, Gr. K, p. 119
  Stand By Me (m. a17–18), Gr. 8, p. 25
  Tzena, tzena (m. 17–32), Gr. 5, p. 298
  Yakety Yak (final: *do'*), Gr. 5, p. 205

**so la ti do' re mi'**
  Hava nashira (m. 9–12), Gr. 6, p. 82

**fa so la ti do'**
  Lean on Me (m. 10–11, 13–14), Gr. 6, p. 14
  Marines' Hymn, The (m. 17–24), Gr. 8, p. 39
  Wai bamba (Part III), Gr. 6, p. 26
  Wai bamba (Part III) (final: *so₁*), Gr. 8, p. 13

**so mi so la ti do'**
  El carnavalito humahuaqueño (Melody only), Gr. 6, p. 482

**mi fa so la ti do'**
  Boysie (m. 9-16), Gr. 2, p. 195
  Light Up the World with a Song (m. 5–8, 17–24),
    Gr. 8, p. 25
  Over the Rainbow (from The Wizard of Oz) (m. 37–40),
    Gr. 4, p. 140
  Step in Time (final: *do'*), Gr. 2, p. 74

**mi so la ti do' re'**
  California, Here I Come (m. 1–12), Gr. 4, p. 287
  Karangatia ra (m. 17–20), Gr. 8, p. 23
  Nani wale na hala (final: *do'*), Gr. 3, p. 260

**mi fa so la ti do' re'**
  Así es mi tierra (m. 28–32), Gr. 6, p. 172
  ¡Ay, Jalisco no te rajes! (Melody, m. 32–56), Gr. 7, p. 6
  Cuando pa' Chile me voy (m. 1–16), Gr. 6, p. 376
  Karangatia ra (final: *do'*), Gr. 8, p. 23
  Puff, the Magic Dragon (final: *do'*), Gr. 2, p. 350

**mi fa so la ti do' re' mi'**
  Kingston Market (final: *do*), Gr. 3, p. 90
  La golondrina (m. 41–48), Gr. 8, p. 50
  Those Magic Changes (m. 9–20), Gr. 8, p. 30

**mi so la ti do' re' mi' fa'**
  Cielito lindo (m. 17–32, 33–48), Gr. 4, p. 270
  Cielito lindo (1st Refrain, m. 25–32), Gr. 7, p. 20
  I Vow to You, My Country (m. 1–32, voice 1 - melody, Bb
    - do), Gr. 5, p. 418

**mi so la ti do'**
  Ahora voy a cantarles (m. 3–4), Gr. 3, p. 56
  La piñata (m. 9–24), Gr. 3, p. 399
  Stille Nacht (Silent Night) (m. 5–8), Gr. 7, p. 54

**mi so la ti**
  Jambalaya (m. 4–7, 20–23), Gr. 8, p. 46

**mi so la ti do' re' mi'**
  Hey, Ho! Nobody Home (final: *mi*), Gr. 6, p. 28
  My Bonnie Lies Over the Ocean (final: *do'*), Gr. 4, p. 338
  Peace Round (final: *la*), Gr. 4, p. 348
  Wheel of the Water, The (m. voice 2), Gr. 4, p. 362

**re mi so la ti**
California Dreamin' (Part III, m. 16–19), Gr. 8, p. 31

**re mi so ti do'**
Barb'ry Allen (m. 3–4), Gr. 6, p. 44

**re mi fa so la ti do'**
(final: *mi*)
Caballito blanco (final: *mi*), Gr. 2, p. 193
Cielito lindo (m. 1–16), Gr. 4, p. 270
El día de mamita (final: *do'*), Gr. K, p. 325
Fais do do (Part III) (final: *mi*), Gr. 6, p. 403
Light Up the World with a Song (m. 1–4), Gr. 8, p. 25
Rig-a-Jig-Jig (verse), Gr. K, p. 99
Riquirrán (final: *do'*), Gr. 4, p. 66

**re mi fa so la ti**
Aguinaldo (m. 1–14), Gr. 3, p. 402
America, the Beautiful (m. 1–4), Gr. 6, p. 485
America, the Beautiful (m. 1–4), Gr. 7, p. 4
America, the Beautiful (m. 1–4), Gr. 8, p. 4
Cielito lindo (m. 9–16), Gr. 7, p. 20

**do re fa so ti**
Tall Cedar Tree (final: *so*), Gr. 2, p. 322

**re fa so la ti do'**
Cielito lindo (m. 1–8), Gr. 7, p. 20

**do re mi fa so la ti**
America, the Beautiful (m. 1–4), Gr. 5, p. 76
¡Ay, Jalisco no te rajes! (Lowervoice - harmony, m. 29–56), Gr. 7, p. 6
We've Got Lots in Common (m. 1–16), Gr. 3, p. 366
Winter Wonderland (m. 1–17, 26–33), Gr. 5, p. 454

**do re mi fa so la ti do'**
Aguinaldo (final: *mi*), Gr. 3, p. 402
Allá en la fuente (final: *do*), Gr. 2, p. 92
Alleluia, Amen (final: *do*), Gr. 7, p. 12
Ambos a dos (final: *do*), Gr. 3, p. 20
Banana (final: *do*), Gr. 2, p. 114
Barb'ry Allen (final: *do*), Gr. 6, p. 44
Bonavist' Harbour (final: *do*), Gr. 3, p. 294
Boysie (final: *do*), Gr. 2, p. 195
Cantaré, cantarás (m. 1–16), Gr. 6, p. 413
Computer, The (final: *do*), Gr. 4, p. 199
Dayenu (m. 5–8), Gr. 4, p. 439
Debajo el botón (final: *do*), Gr. 1, p. 210
Dok djampa (m. 1–6), Gr. 8, p. 20
El barquito (final: *do*), Gr. 3, p. 358
El coquí (final: *do*), Gr. 2, p. 292
El desembre congelat (final: *do*), Gr. 5, p. 473
El sapito (final: *do*), Gr. 3, p. 336
Everybody Says (final: *do*), Gr. 1, p. 287
Glad to Have a Friend Like You (m. 13-20), Gr. 2, p. 228
Happy Wanderer, The (m. 1–8), Gr. 4, p. 89
I Love Peanuts, Gr. 1, p. 162
I Love Peanuts (m. 9–16), Gr. 7, p. 20
Ikhanda, maslombe (final: *do*), Gr. K, p. 14
It's a Beautiful Day (final: *do*), Gr. 3, p. 338
La piñata (final: *do*), Gr. 3, p. 399
Leaves (final: *do*), Gr. 1, p. 28
Light Up the World with a Song (final: *do*), Gr. 8, p. 25
Like a Bird (m. 1–8), Gr. 6, p. 167
Look! Look! The Sun Woke Up! (final: *do*), Gr. 1, p. 368
Los pececitos, Gr. 1, p. 178
Los pollitos (final: *do*), Gr. K, p. 166

Marines' Hymn, The (final: *do*), Gr. 8, p. 39
Mi cuerpo hace música, Gr. K, p. 106
*Missy-La, Massa-La (final: *do*), Gr. 4, p. 188
Mr. Tambourine Man (final: *do*), Gr. 6, p. 150
My Dreydl, Gr. K, p. 314
Ner li (final: *do*), Gr. 2, p. 383
Over the Rainbow (from The Wizard of Oz) (final: *do'*), Gr. 4, p. 140
Over the River and Through the Wood (final: *do*), Gr. 3, p. 384
Pavo, pavo (final: *do*), Gr. 1, p. 416
Popcorn Popping (final: *do*), Gr. 1, p. 440
Put Your Hand in My Hand (final: *do*), Gr. 1, p. 330
Rise and Shine (Melody only), Gr. 1, p. 122
Sailing to the Sea (final: *do*), Gr. 1, p. 336
Sansaw akroma (final: *do*), Gr. 3, p. 286
Scotland the Brave (m. 1–8, 11–12), Gr. 5, p. 138
Sing a Little Song, Gr. K, p. 30
Song of One, A (final: *do*), Gr. 3, p. 344
Sweet Betsy from Pike (final: *do*), Gr. 4, p. 244
Take a Chance On Me (Melody only) (final: *do*), Gr. 8, p. 15
This Little Light of Mine (m. 1–16), Gr. 6, p. 232
To'ia mai te waka (final: *do*), Gr. 1, p. 77
*United Nations on the March, The (m. 16–31), Gr. 6, p. 443
¡Viva el fútbol! (final: *do*), Gr. 1, p. 96
World We Love, The (final: *do*), Gr. 3, p. 342

**do re mi fa so ti do'**
Sweet Betsy from Pike (final: *do*), Gr. 4, p. 244

**do re mi fa so ti do' re' mi'**
Turn, Turn, Turn (To Everything There Is a Season) (final: *do*), Gr. 5, p. 378

**do re mi so la ti**
Jambalaya (m. 12–15, 28–31), Gr. 8, p. 46

**do re mi so la do'**
Stand By Me (m. 17–25), Gr. 5, p. 46

**do re mi so la ti do'**
Abraham, Martin, and John (m. 17–33 of refrain, uppervoice), Gr. 6, p. 466
Jambalaya (On The Bayou) (m. a9–16, 24–32), Gr. 6, p. 244
Johnny Has Gone for a Soldier (final: *la*), Gr. 5, p. 188
Kibungo (final: *do*), Gr. 2, p. 354
Rise and Shine (final: *do*), Gr. 4, p. 98
Stand By Me (final: *do*), Gr. 5, p. 46
Stand By Me (final: *do*), Gr. 8, p. 25

**do mi fa so la ti do' re'**
Sing a Song of Peace (Part II) (final: *mi*), Gr. 6, p. 66

**do mi so la ti do'**
El carnavalito humahuaqueño (m. 1–8), Gr. 6, p. 482
Limbo Like Me (m. 27–28), Gr. 4, p. 18

**do so la ti do'**
Cantaré, cantarás (m. 14–16), Gr. 6, p. 413
I'm a Very Fine Turkey, Gr. K, p. 310

**do re mi fa so la ti do' re'**
Artsa alinu, Gr. 3, p. 285
Crocodile, The (final: *do'*), Gr. 2, p. 362
Cuando pa' Chile me voy (final: *do'*), Gr. 6, p. 376
Hello! (final: *do'*), Gr. 2, p. 262
Las velitas (final: *do*), Gr. 5, p. 147

Pitch and Rhythm Index

Morning Has Broken (final: *do*), Gr. 5, p. 28
O pião entrou (final: *do*), Gr. 2, p. 355
One Moment in Time (m. 18–58), Gr. 6, p. 352
Poco, Le' Me 'Lone (final: *do*), Gr. 3, p. 300
Sing, America, Sing! (final: *do*), Gr. 3, p. 238
Tzena, tzena (m. 33–48), Gr. 5, p. 298
Tzena, tzena (final: *do*), Gr. 5, p. 298
World of Difference, A (final: *do*), Gr. 5, p. 386

*do re mi fa so la ti do' re' mi'*
Happy Wanderer, The, Gr. 4, p. 89
Morning Comes Early (final: *do*), Gr. 5, p. 13
Scotland the Brave (m. 9–10), Gr. 5, p. 138
Ship that Never Returned, The (final: *do*), Gr. 5, p. 402
You've Got a Friend (final: *so*), Gr. 5, p. 366

*do re mi fa so la do' re'*
We Shall Overcome (final: *do*), Gr. 4, p. 326

*do re mi so la ti do' re'*
Green Corn Song (final: *do*), Gr. 5, p. 462
There's a Place (final: *do'*), Gr. 5, p. 210

*do re mi so la ti do' mi'*
Jambalaya (final: *do*), Gr. 8, p. 46
Jambalaya (On The Bayou), Gr. 6, p. 244

*do mi fa so la ti do'*
Barb'ry Allen (m. 5–6), Gr. 6, p. 44
Dayenu (m. 5–12), Gr. 4, p. 439
Kookaburra (m. 5–8), Gr. 4, p. 186
La paloma se fué (m. a9–16), Gr. 6, p. 51
This Little Light of Mine (m. 5–10), Gr. 6, p. 232

*do mi so la ti do' re' mi'*
Wheel of the Water, The (final: *do*), Gr. 4, p. 362

*do so la ti do' re' mi'*
Ego sum pauper (final: *do'*), Gr. 5, p. 158

*re mi fa so la ti do' re'*
Gift to Share, A (m. 5–21), Gr. 6, p. 393

*re mi fa so la ti do' re' mi'*
God Bless the U.S.A. (m. a15–19), Gr. 8, p. 37
Rhythm Is Gonna Get You, The (final: *la*), Gr. 6, p. 348

*re fa so la ti do' re'*
God Bless the U.S.A. (m. 11–14), Gr. 8, p. 37

*so la ti do' re' mi'*
America, the Beautiful (m. 9–16), Gr. 5, p. 76
America, the Beautiful (m. 9–16), Gr. 6, p. 485
America, the Beautiful (m. 9–16), Gr. 7, p. 4
America, the Beautiful (m. 9–16), Gr. 8, p. 4
Let's Go Fly a Kite (m. 17–32), Gr. 2, p. 327

*so la ti do' re' mi' fa' so'*
Star-Spangled Banner, The (m. 25–32), Gr. 6, p. 486
Star-Spangled Banner, The (m. 18–25), Gr. 7, p. 56

*do re mi fa so la ti do' re' mi' fa'*
Hava nashira (final: *do'*), Gr. 6, p. 82
Silent Night (Melody only, m. 1-2) (final: *do*),
   Gr. 3, p. 394
Silent Night (Melody only) (final: *do*), Gr. 3, p. 394
Stille Nacht (Silent Night) (Melody) (final: *do*), Gr. 7, p. 54

*la, do re mi fa so la ti do' re'*
Somewhere Out There (m. 1–16), Gr. 5, p. 368

*la, re mi so la ti*
Quâ câù gió bay (final: *mi*), Gr. 5, p. 460

**ti/ti,**
*so, do re mi fa so la ti do'*
Abraham, Martin, and John (m. 1–16 of verse, uppervoice), Gr. 6, p. 466
Corrido de Kansas (final: *mi*), Gr. 4, p. 274
Shenandoah (final: *do*), Gr. 5, p. 264

*ti, do re mi fa so la ti do'*
Ayelivi (final: *do*), Gr. 2, p. 70
Heri za Kwanzaa (final: *do'*), Gr. 5, p. 476
Heri za Kwanzaa (final: *do'*), Gr. 5, p. 476
Hosanna, Me Build a House (m. 11–28), Gr. 5, p. 132
Hosanna, Me Build a House (m. 11–28), Gr. 5, p. 132
La paloma se fué (final: *mi*), Gr. 6, p. 51
Linstead Market (final: *do*), Gr. 5, p. 241
Linstead Market (final: *do*), Gr. 5, p. 241
Three Little Piggies (final: *do'*), Gr. K, p. 56
Un, deux, trois (final: *do*), Gr. 2, p. 198

*ti, do re mi fa so la ti do' mi'*
Oh, Danny Boy (m. 9–16), Gr. 4, p. 48

*ti, do re fa so la ti do'*
Heri za Kwanzaa (m. 33–37), Gr. 5, p. 476

*ti, do mi fa la ti do'*
Sakura (final: *mi*), Gr. 4, p. 308

*ti, re mi fa so la ti do' re' mi'*
La golondrina (m. 33–40), Gr. 8, p. 50

*ti, fa so la ti do'*
Má Teodora (m. call m. a1–2), Gr. 6, p. 301

*la, ti, do re mi fa so la*
Autumn Canon (final: *la,*), Gr. 5, p. 148
Live in the City (m. 1–16) (final: *do*), Gr. 5, p. 71
Old Abram Brown (final: *la,*), Gr. 5, p. 222

*ti, fa so la ti do' re' mi'*
Má Teodora (m. call m. a9–10), Gr. 6, p. 301

*la, ti, do re mi fa so la ti*
El carite (m. 9–18), Gr. 5, p. 305
Sing a Song of Peace (Part I) (final: *do*), Gr. 6, p. 66

*la, ti, do re mi fa so la ti do' re' mi'*
Oh, Danny Boy, Gr. 4, p. 48

*la, ti, do re mi fa so la ti do' re' mi' fa'*
Those Magic Changes (final: *do'*), Gr. 8, p. 30

*la, ti, do re mi so la ti do'*
Drill, Ye Tarriers (m. 9–18) (final: *la*), Gr. 5, p. 54

*so, la, ti, do re mi fa so la ti*
Cattle Call (final: *do*), Gr. 5, p. 344

*so, la, ti, do re mi so la*
Old Chisholm Trail, The (final: *do*), Gr. 6, p. 237

*so, la, ti, do re mi fa so la ti do'*
Circle 'Round the Moon (m. 29–68, voice 2),
   Gr. 4, p. 403

*so, la, do re mi so la ti do'*
Great Big Stars (final: *do*), Gr. 1, p. 60

*so, ti, do re mi fa so la ti*
¡Ay, Jalisco no te rajes! (Melody, m. 13–24), Gr. 7, p. 6
Las mañanitas (final: *do*), Gr. 6, p. 481
Las mañanitas (final: *do*), Gr. 6, p. 481
Let It Snow! Let It Snow! Let It Snow! (m. 1–10),
   Gr. 4, p. 426

**so, ti, do re mi fa so la ti do'**
Day-O! (Banana Boat Loader's Song) (final: *do*),
  Gr. 5, p. 18
Like a Bird (final: *do*), Gr. 6, p. 167

**so, la ti, do mi so**
Singin' in the Rain (m. 13–16), Gr. 4, p. 360

**ti, fa so la ti do' re' mi'**
Má Teodora (m. call m. a9–10), Gr. 6, p. 301

**la, do re mi fa so la ti do'**
Dok djampa (final: *do*), Gr. 8, p. 20

## si

**mi fa so si la**
Peace Like a River (Harmony, m. 9–12), Gr. 6, p. 190

**mi fa so si la ti do'**
Con el vito (m. 17–32), Gr. 7, p. 15

**mi fa si la**
Chanukah Is Here! (m. 2, 4), Gr. 2, p. 382

**mi si la**
Chanukah Is Here! (m. 1, 3), Gr. 2, p. 382

**mi si la ti do'**
Winter (Melody only) (final: *la,*), Gr. 8, p. 11
Winter (m. 1–2, 5–8), Gr. 8, p. 11

**mi si la do'**
Chanukah Is Here! (m. 5, 7), Gr. 2, p. 382

**si, la, ti, do**
Something Told the Wild Geese (Part II, m. 19–24),
  Gr. 7, p. 39

**si, la, ti, do re mi**
Hanuka, Hanuka (final: *la,*), Gr. 3, p. 390
Hanuka, Hanuka (final: *la*), Gr. 8, p. 36
Hanuka, Hanuka (m. 15–17), Gr. 8, p. 36
Joshua Fought the Battle of Jericho (final: *la,*),
  Gr. 8, p. 18
Joshua Fought the Battle of Jericho (m. 1–8), Gr. 8, p. 18
Minka (final: *la,*), Gr. 4, p. 222
Ríu ríu chíu (m. voices 1–2) (final: *la,*), Gr. 5, p. 435

**si, la, ti, do re mi fa**
Riendo el río corre (final: *la,*), Gr. 6, p. 263
Vamos a la fiesta (final: *la*), Gr. 2, p. 374

**si, la, ti, do re mi fa so**
Habemos llegado (lowervoice) (final: *la*), Gr. 6, p. 174

**si, la, ti, do re mi la**
*Joshua Fought the Battle of Jericho (Melody only) (final:
  *la,*), Gr. 5, p. 100

**si, la, ti, do re mi fa si' la'**
¡Qué bonita bandera! (final: *la,*), Gr. 5, p. 294

**si, la, ti, do re mi si' la' ti' do'**
El cóndor pasa (m. a1–2, a5–6), Gr. 6, p. 46

**si, la, ti, do mi**
Vamos a la fiesta (m. 7–8), Gr. 2, p. 374

**si, la, do re mi**
Feliz Navidad (m. 10–11), Gr. 7, p. 28

**mi, fa, so, si, la, ti, do re mi fa**
Dance for the Nations (final: *la,*), Gr. 6, p. 122

**mi, fa, si, la, ti, do re mi**
Canto del agua (final: *la*), Gr. 8, p. 10
Chanukah Is Here! (final: *la*), Gr. 2, p. 382

**mi, si, la, ti, do re mi**
Con el vito (final: *la,*), Gr. 7, p. 15
Con el vito (m. 5–8, 13–16), Gr. 7, p. 15
Con el vito (m. 17–20, 25–28), Gr. 7, p. 15
*Go Down, Moses (Melody only) (final: *la,*), Gr. 5, p. 190
*Kyrie (final: *la*), Gr. 6, p. 206
Merry Modal Christmas, A (m. 1–17, voice 1),
  Gr. 4, p. 411

**mi, si, la, ti, do re mi fa**
Knock No More, Gr. 3, p. 386
La mar estaba serena (final: *la*), Gr. 2, p. 344
La Tarara, Gr. 4, p. 176
Lo yisa (final: *la,*), Gr. 6, p. 130
Merry Modal Christmas, A (m. 44–61, voices 1–2),
  Gr. 4, p. 411
S'vivon (final: *la,*), Gr. 6, p. 452

**mi, si, la, ti, do re mi fa so la**
Vem kan segla  (Part II) (final: *la,*), Gr. 6, p. 417

**mi, si, la, ti, do mi**
Winter (m. 1–4), Gr. 8, p. 11

**mi, si, la, ti, do re mi fa si**
Canto del agua (Melody only) (final: *la,*), Gr. 8, p. 10

**si, la, ti, do re ma mi so**
St. Louis Blues (final: *do*), Gr. 5, p. 352

**mi si so si la ti do'**
El cóndor pasa (final: *la,*), Gr. 6, p. 46
Greensleeves (m. 1–4, 11–12), Gr. 6, p. 49
Greensleeves (m. a1–47), Gr. 6, p. 49
Hava nagila (m. 23–24), Gr. 6, p. 153
Riendo el río corre (m. 1–8), Gr. 6, p. 263
Riendo el río corre (m. 17–18), Gr. 6, p. 263
Supercalifragilisticexpialidocious (m. 13–16), Gr. 3, p. 7

**mi, so, si, la, ti, do re mi**
Winter (m. 17–24), Gr. 8, p. 11

**mi, si, la, ti, do re mi' si'**
Canto del agua (m. a16–24), Gr. 8, p. 10

**do re mi fa so si la**
Oh, Freedom (Descant) (final: *mi*), Gr. 7, p. 30
Your Life Is Now (m. 14–19), Gr. 6, p. 4

**do re mi so si la ti do' re'**
Imbabura (Melody only) (final: *do*), Gr. 5, p. 202

**re mi fa si la ti do'**
Adana ya gidelim (final: *re*), Gr. 2, p. 142

**re mi so si la**
El carnavalito humahuaqueño (m. 17–20), Gr. 6, p. 482

**re mi fa si la ti do' re' mi'**
Hava nagila (m. 1–8) (final: *la*), Gr. 6, p. 153

**re mi fa so si la ti do' re' mi'**
Who Has Seen the Wind  (final: *la*), Gr. 2, p. 324

**re mi fa so si la ti do' re' mi' fa'**
Shalom aleichem (Part I and II) (final: *la*), Gr. 6, p. 409

**la, ti, do re mi fa si la**
*Un pajarito (final: *la,*), Gr. 2, p. 16

**la, ti, do re mi fa si la ti**
El carite (m. 17–25), Gr. 5, p. 305

**la, do re mi fa si**
Canto del agua (m. 33–40), Gr. 8, p. 10

**so, la, ti, do re mi si la**
St. Patrick Was a Gentleman (m. 1–8), Gr. 3, p. 290

**so, si, la, ti, do re mi fa so la**
Something Told the Wild Geese (final: *la*), Gr. 7, p. 39

**ti, do re mi fa fi si la ti**
Los reyes de Oriente (melody - uppervoice) (final: *la₁*),
Gr. 5, p. 480

**ti, do re mi fa so si la ti**
Play a Simple Melody (m. 9–16), Gr. 5, p. 72

**ti, do re mi fa so si la ti do'**
Rockin' Around the Christmas Tree (final: *do'*),
Gr. 5, p. 466

## fi

**do re mi fa fi so**
Bye Bye, Love (m. 27–35), Gr. 8, p. 9
Ja-Da (m. 9-12), Gr. 2, p. 188
Sing Your Story (m. 1–20), Gr. 3, p. 350

**do re mi fa fi so la**
La calle ancha, Gr. 3, p. 297
La golondrina (m. 9–16, 25–32), Gr. 8, p. 50

**do re mi fa fi so la ti do'**
La golondrina (m. a49–64), Gr. 8, p. 50

**do re mi fa fi so la do'**
Oklahoma (m. 1–7, 17–23), Gr. 5, p. 36

**do re mi fa fi so la ti do' re'**
Hello! (final: *do'*), Gr. 2, p. 262

**re mi fa fi so la ti do'**
Rig-a-Jig-Jig (final: *do*), Gr. K, p. 99

**re mi fa fi so la**
Wings of a Dove (m. 11–18), Gr. 4, p. 318

**mi fa fi so la ti**
Peace Like a River (Harmony, m. 5–8), Gr. 6, p. 190

**mi fa fi so la ti do' re' mi'**
Let's Go Fly a Kite (final: *do'*), Gr. 2, p. 327

**mi fi so la ti do' re' mi' fa'**
Star-Spangled Banner, The (m. 14–17), Gr. 7, p. 56
Star-Spangled Banner, The (m. 14–17), Gr. 8, p. 62

**mi fi so la ti do' re' mi' fa' fi' so'**
El rancho grande (final: *do*), Gr. 8, p. 22

**mi fi so la do' re' mi' fa'**
El rancho grande (m. 7–15), Gr. 4, p. 215
El rancho grande (m. 8–14), Gr. 8, p. 22

**mi fi so do' re' mi'**
Star-Spangled Banner, The (m. 3–4), Gr. 7, p. 56
Star-Spangled Banner, The (m. 3–4), Gr. 8, p. 62

**fi, so, la, do re**
Feliz Navidad (m. 12–13), Gr. 7, p. 28

**so, la, ti, do re mi fi so la**
Scarborough Fair, Gr. 6, p. 95

**do re mi fa fi so si la ti**
Los reyes de Oriente (m. 8–16), Gr. 8, p. 58

**mi fa fi so si la ti do' re' mi'**
Feliz Navidad (final: *do*), Gr. 7, p. 28

**mi, fi, si, la, ti, do re mi**
If a Tiger Calls (final: *la₁*), Gr. 3, p. 354

**mi, fi, so, si, la, ti, do re mi fa**
Greensleeves (m. a5–8), Gr. 6, p. 49

**mi, fi, so, si, la, ti, do re mi fa fi so**
Greensleeves (final: *la₁*), Gr. 6, p. 49

**so, la, ti, do re mi fa so'**
Star-Spangled Banner, The (m. 18–25), Gr. 8, p. 62

**so, la, do re mi fa fi so**
I Got Rhythm (final: *do*), Gr. 6, p. 101

**so, la, do re mi fa fi so la ti do'**
Caroling, Caroling (final: *do*), Gr. 6, p. 458

**so, la, do re mi fa fi so la do'**
Don't Cry for Me, Argentina (final: *do*), Gr. 6, p. 74

**so, ti, do re mi fa fi so**
Bye Bye, Love (final: *do*), Gr. 8, p. 9
El rancho grande (m. 1–5), Gr. 8, p. 22

**so, la, ti, do re mi fa fi so**
Twelve Days of Christmas, The (final: *do*), Gr. 4, p. 430
Winter Fantasy (m. 9–16), Gr. 4, p. 424

**so, la, ti, do re mi fa fi so la**
Blow the Wind Southerly (m. 9–16), Gr. 5, p. 178
Deck the Hall (m. voice 2) (final: *do*), Gr. 5, p. 474
God Bless America (Melody only) (final: *do*), Gr. 5, p. 4
Shir l'shalom (final: *la*), Gr. 4, p. 419

**so, do re mi fa fi so**
El rancho grande (m. 1–6), Gr. 4, p. 215

**so, do re mi fa fi so la**
¡Ay, Jalisco no te rajes! (Melody, m. 1–9), Gr. 7, p. 6

**so, do re mi fa fi so la ti**
Adelita (m. 16–37, uppervoice), Gr. 5, p. 50
Sing a Rainbow (final: *do*), Gr. 2, p. 166

**so, ti, do re mi fa fi so la ti do' re**
¡Ay, Jalisco no te rajes! (Melody - uppervoice) (final: *do'*),
Gr. 7, p. 6

**so, ri mi fa fi so la ti**
Laredo (uppervoice) (final: *mi*), Gr. 5, p. 10

**so, ti, do re mi fa fi so la ti do' re' mi'**
La golondrina (final: *do*), Gr. 8, p. 50

**la, ti, do re mi fa fi so la**
Come, Ye Thankful People, Come (uppervoice, melody)
(final: *do*), Gr. 5, p. 459

**la, ti, do re mi fi la ti**
Connemara Lullaby (Melody only) (final: *la₁*), Gr. 5, p. 232

**la, re mi fi so**
Winter Song (m. 5–8), Gr. 6, p. 455

**ti, do re mi fa fi so**
Erie Canal (m. 17–24), Gr. 5, p. 262

**ti, do re mi fa fi so si la ti**
Los reyes de Oriente (final: *la₁*), Gr. 8, p. 58

**ti, do re mi fa fi so la**
Ash Grove, The (m. 17–24), Gr. 5, p. 114

**ti, do re mi fa fi so la ti do'**
Deck the Hall (m. voice 1 - melody) (final: *do*),
Gr. 5, p. 474
We've Got Lots in Common (m. 17–32), Gr. 3, p. 366

**ti, do re mi fa fi si la ti**
Los reyes de Oriente (melody - uppervoice) (final: *la₁*),
Gr. 5, p. 480

**do re mi fa fi so si re ti do' re'**
Take Me Out to the Ball Game, Gr. 3, p. 263

**fi-si**

**mi fi si la**
Pollerita (m. 19–22), Gr. 5, p. 151

**ta**

**do re mi fa so la ta**
Don't You Hear the Lambs? (final: *do*), Gr. 5, p. 97
Free at Last (final: *do*), Gr. 2, p. 396

**do re mi fa so la ta ti do'**
Circle 'Round the Moon (m. 13–28), Gr. 4, p. 403

**do re mi fa so la ta do'**
Harrison Town (final: *do*), Gr. 6, p. 97
Three Little Birds (final: *so*), Gr. 8, p. 7
Three Little Birds (m. 16–32), Gr. 8, p. 7

**do re mi fa so la ta ti do' re'**
America, the Free (final: *do'*), Gr. 4, p. 210

**do re mi fa so la ta do' re'**
Beyond Borders (m. 9–16), Gr. 5, p. 292
Goin' to Boston (Part I, m. 17–24, 41–48) (final: *do*), Gr. 6, p. 433
Surfin' U.S.A. (final: *do*), Gr. 6, p. 260
Surfin' U.S.A. (final: *do*), Gr. 7, p. 58

**do re mi fa so la ta ti do' re' mi' fa'**
Circle 'Round the Moon (m. 29–68, voice 1), Gr. 4, p. 403

**do re mi so la ta**
Every Night When the Sun Goes In (m. 1–4), Gr. 8, p. 28
God Bless the Child (m. 1–4, 19–22), Gr. 7, p. 27
Rockin' Robin (m. 1–8, 17–24), Gr. 3, p. 368
Seasons of Love (m. a17–23), Gr. 8, p. 22
Three Little Birds (m. 1–15), Gr. 4, p. 320
Three Little Birds (m. a1–15), Gr. 8, p. 7

**do re mi so la ta do'**
Every Night When the Sun Goes In (final: *do*), Gr. 8, p. 28
Rocky Top (final: *do'*), Gr. 5, p. 348

**do mi fa so la ta**
One Small Step (m. 12–15), Gr. 5, p. 126

**do mi fa so la ta do'**
Haul Away, Joe (final: *do*), Gr. 4, p. 13

**do mi so la ta**
Free at Last (m. 1–4), Gr. 6, p. 468
Rock Around the Clock (m. 9–12, 21–24), Gr. 7, p. 18
Rock Around the Clock (m. 9–12, 21–24), Gr. 7, p. 18

**re mi fa so la ta**
Peace Like a River (Harmony, m. 1–4. 13–16), Gr. 6, p. 190

**re mi fa so la ta ti do'**
De colores (melody or uppervoice) (final: *do'*), Gr. 5, p. 90
De colores (Melody only) (final: *do'*), Gr. 8, p. 14

**re so la ta**
Surfin' U.S.A. (m. 1–8, 13–14, 17–24), Gr. 7, p. 58

**mi fa so la ta**
Brand New Day, A (m. 1–8), Gr. 6, p. 7

**mi fa so la ta ti**
De colores (m. 25–41), Gr. 8, p. 14

**mi fa so la ta ti do'**
De colores (m. 25–45), Gr. 8, p. 14

**mi fa so la ta do'**
Teach Me to Swing (m. 1–16), Gr. 5, p. 84

**mi fa so la ta ti do' re' mi'**
Santa Clara (final: *do*), Gr. 4, p. 172

**mi so la ta do'**
Lean on Me (m. 16, 20), Gr. 6, p. 14

**so, la, do re mi fa so la ta ti do'**
Voices of Pride, The (m. 1–16), Gr. 5, p. 86

**so, la, do re mi so la ta do'**
If I Had a Hammer, Gr. 5, p. 287

**so, la, ta, do**
Land of a Thousand Dances (m. 20–30), Gr. 5, p. 330

**so, ta, do re so**
One Family (Part I, m. 5–8, 31–46), Gr. 7, p. 17

**so, la, ta, do re mi fa so**
Greenland Whale Fishery, The, Gr. 5, p. 230

**so, la, ta, do re mi fa so la**
Let Music Surround You (final: *do*), Gr. 4, p. 236

**so, la, ta, ti, do re mi fa so**
Land of a Thousand Dances, Gr. 5, p. 330
Yonder Come Day (final: *do*), Gr. 8, p. 68

**so, ta, ti, do re mi fa so**
Twelve Gates to the City (m. 1–10), Gr. 5, p. 280

**la, ta ti, do re**
Yonder Come Day (m. 3–4), Gr. 8, p. 68

**do re mi fa fi so si la ta ti do re ma'**
Basin Street Blues, Gr. 5, p. 354

**ma**

**do re ma**
Flip, Flop and Fly (m. 5–12, 21–24), Gr. 7, p. 32
Zudio (m. 4, 8), Gr. 2, p. 269

**do re ma mi fa so**
Rock Around the Clock (m. a13–20, a25–32), Gr. 7, p. 18
Rockin' Robin (m. 9–16), Gr. 3, p. 368

**do re ma mi so**
Mama Don't 'Low (m. 9–12), Gr. 6, p. 358
Rent (final: *do*), Gr. 8, p. 22
Seasons of Love (m. 11–12), Gr. 8, p. 22

**do re ma mi fa fi so la**
Ja-Da (m. 1–16), Gr. 7, p. 20

**do re ma mi fa so la ti do'**
Orange Blossom Special (Melody only) (final: *do*), Gr. 5, p. 266

**do re ma mi so la**
Ja-Da (Part I, m. 5–7), Gr. 7, p. 20

**do re ma fa so ti**
Orange Blossom Special (m. a13–19), Gr. 8, p. 6

**do re ma mi so la do'**
Joe Turner Blues (final: *do*), Gr. 4, p. 56

**do re ma so la do'**
Free at Last (m. 13–16), Gr. 6, p. 468

**do re mi fa fi so si la ta ti do re ma'**
Basin Street Blues, Gr. 5, p. 354

**do re ma mi fa so la ti**
Orange Blossom Special (final: *do*), Gr. 8, p. 6

**do re mi fa so la ta do re ma mi fa**
I'm a Believer, Gr. 7, p. 33

***do ma mi fa so***
Sun Gonna Shine (final: *do*), Gr. 6, p. 242

***do ma mi so***
Orange Blossom Special (m. 1–6), Gr. 8, p. 6

***do ma fa so***
Blues with a Feeling (m. 8–12), Gr. 8, p. 6
Key to the Highway (m. a3–4, 7–8), Gr. 8, p. 29

***do ma mi fa so la ta***
Blues with a Feeling (final: *do*), Gr. 8, p. 6

***do ma fa so ta***
Blues with a Feeling (m. 1–7), Gr. 8, p. 6

***do ma so la ta do'***
Blues with a Feeling (m. 22–25), Gr. 8, p. 6

***re ma fi so la ta***
Ah ya Zane (final: *re*), Gr. 5, p. 297

***mi, so, la, ti do re ma mi***
California Dreamin' (m. 20–58), Gr. 8, p. 31

***si, la, ti, do re ma mi so***
St. Louis Blues (final: *do*), Gr. 5, p. 352

***so, la, do re ma***
At the Hop (final: *do*), Gr. 4, p. 168
Hound Dog (final: *do*), Gr. 5, p. 212
Midnight Special, The (m. 5–6), Gr. 7, p. 23
Tuxedo Junction (m. a1–5, 9–14, a18–22), Gr. 8, p. 21

***so, la, do re ma mi***
Choo Choo Ch'Boogie (m. 5–8), Gr. 5, p. 44
Flip, Flop and Fly (final: *do*), Gr. 7, p. 32
Good Mornin', Blues (final: *do*), Gr. 2, p. 52
Good Mornin', Blues (final: *do*), Gr. 5, p. 224
Peppermint Twist (Melody only) (final: *do*), Gr. 3, p. 46

***so, la, do re ma fa so***
Flat Foot Floogee, The (m. 1–8), Gr. 3, p. 160

***so, la, do re ma mi so***
Mama Don't 'Low (final: *do*), Gr. 6, p. 358

***so, la, do re ma so la***
Tuxedo Junction (m. a22–25, a6–8), Gr. 8, p. 21

***so, la, do re ma mi fa so***
Key to the Highway, Gr. 6, p. 243
Key to the Highway (final: *do*), Gr. 8, p. 29

***so, ta, ti, do re ma mi fa so***
Twelve Gates to the City (final: *do*), Gr. 5, p. 280

***so, la, ta, do re ma fa so***
Just a Snap-Happy Blues (m. 13–24), Gr. 6, p. 388

***so, do re ma***
Midnight Special, The (Refrain, m. 1–4), Gr. 7, p. 23

***so, la, do re ma so***
Mud, Gr. 3, p. 32

***la, ti, do re ma mi***
It Don't Mean a Thing (If It Ain't Got That Swing) (m. 21–29), Gr. 5, p. 336

***so, ti, do re ma so***
Route 66 (m. 1–19, 40–51), Gr. 4, p. 276

***la, ta do re ma mi fa***
Dancin' in the Street (final: *mi*), Gr. 5, p. 361
Dancin' in the Street (final: *mi*), Gr. 5, p. 361

***la, do re ma***
Midnight Special, The (m. 1–2), Gr. 7, p. 23

Rock and Roll Is Here to Stay (m. 1–8, 11–12, 15–16, 25–28), Gr. 6, p. 36

***la, do re ma mi***
I've Been Everywhere (m. 1–8), Gr. 6, p. 226
It Don't Mean a Thing (If It Ain't Got That Swing) (m. 1–20), Gr. 5, p. 336
Little Johnny Brown (m. 1–8), Gr. 3, p. 313

***la, do re ma mi fa so***
Choo Choo Ch'Boogie (m. 13–20), Gr. 5, p. 44

***la, do re ma mi so la***
Cindy (m. 17–24, melody), Gr. 4, p. 384
Music's in Me , The (m. 13-23), Gr. 2, p. 40

***ti, do re ma mi fa so la ta do'***
Seasons of Love (final: *do*), Gr. 8, p. 22

## ri

***do re ri mi***
Down by the Riverside (Part II, m. 3–4, 7–8), Gr. 8, p. 8
Lift Ev'ry Voice and Sing (m. a7–8, a16–17), Gr. 8, p. 54
Purple People Eater, The (m. 1–2), Gr. 6, p. 448

***do re ri mi so la ta do'***
Rocky Top (final: *do'*), Gr. 5, p. 348

***do re ri mi fa so la do' mi'***
San Antonio Rose (m. 1–16), Gr. 5, p. 134

***ti, do re ri mi fa so la***
Lift Ev'ry Voice and Sing (m. 1–8), Gr. 5, p. 482

***mi, fa, so, si,la, ti, do re ri mi fa so***
Lift Ev'ry Voice and Sing (Melody only) (final: *do*), Gr. 8, p. 54

***la, ti, do re ri mi fa so la***
Bogando a la luz del sol (final: *la,*), Gr. 4, p. 306

***so, ti, do re ri mi fa so***
¡Ay, Jalisco no te rajes! (Lowervoice - harmony, m. 1–25), Gr. 7, p. 6

***so, do re ri mi***
You Are My Sunshine (m. 1–4), Gr. 6, p. 246

***so, do re ri ma fa so la***
You Are My Sunshine (final: *do*), Gr. 6, p. 246

***so, la, do re ri mi***
Choo Choo Ch'Boogie (m. 1–4), Gr. 5, p. 44

***so, do ri mi fa***
I'll Fly Away (m. 1–2, 5–6), Gr. 8, p. 42

***so, la, do re ri mi***
Woke Up This Morning (m. 1–16), Gr. 5, p. 288

***so, la, do re ri mi fa***
I'll Fly Away (m. 13–16), Gr. 8, p. 42

***so, la, ti, do re ri mi fa so la***
What a Wonderful World (final: *do*), Gr. 6, p. 62

***so ri mi fa fi so la ti***
Laredo (uppervoice) (final: *mi*), Gr. 5, p. 10

***so, la, ti, do di re ri mi fa***
Down by the Riverside, Gr. 5, p. 256

## di

***do di re mi fa***
La borinqueña (m. 7–11), Gr. 8, p. 19

***so, la, do di re mi***
Let Us Sing Together (m. 13–16), Gr. 6, p. 156

*so, do di re mi fa so*
I've Been Working on the Railroad, Gr. 3, p. 242

*ti, do di re mi*
Chapel of Love (m. 1–16), Gr. 7, p. 27

*la, ti, do di re mi fa so*
Don Gato (final: *la*), Gr. 3, p. 352

*so, la, ti, do di re mi*
Chapel of Love (m. 33–48), Gr. 7, p. 27

*so, la, ti, do di re mi fa so*
Let Us Sing Together (final: *do*), Gr. 6, p. 156
Let Us Sing Together (final: *do*), Gr. 6, p. 156

*di re ri mi fa*
La borinqueña (m. 12–15), Gr. 8, p. 19

*so, la, ti, do di re ri mi fa*
Down by the Riverside, Gr. 5, p. 256
Down by the Riverside (Part II) (final: *do*), Gr. 8, p. 8

*do di re ri mi fa fi so si la*
Down by the Riverside (Part I) (final: *mi*), Gr. 8, p. 8

*mi so si la ti do' di' re' mi'*
California, Here I Come (m. 13–32), Gr. 4, p. 287

## *lo*

*mi, fa, so, lo, la, ti, do re ri mi fa so*
Lift Ev'ry Voice and Sing (final: *do*), Gr. 8, p. 54

*mi, fa, so, lo, la, ti, do re ri mi fa so la*
Lift Ev'ry Voice and Sing (m. 9–17), Gr. 5, p. 482

*mi, fi, si, lo, la, ti, do re ri mi fa so la*
Angels On the Midnight Clear (m. a23–30), Gr. 6, p. 423

Pitch and Rhythm Index

# Rhythm Index

♩ ♫

1, 2, 3, 4 (speech piece), Gr. K, p. 15
A la puerta del cielo, Gr. 5, p. 60
Alle meine Entchen (m. 1–2, 5–6), Gr. 1, p. 98
Alleluia, Amen, Gr. 7, p. 12
Alleluia, Amen, Gr. 7, p. 12
Alphabet Song (m. 1–2, 5–6, 9–12), Gr. K, p. 280
Apple Tree, Gr. 1, p. 228
Apples, Peaches, Pears, and Plums (speech piece), Gr. 1, p. 14
Ash Grove, The (Melody, m. a1–7, a9–15, a17–23), Gr. 5, p. 114
Bee, Bee Bumblebee (speech piece), Gr. 1, p. 50
Bereleh, Gr. K, p. 151
Bingo (Melody only, m. 5-8), Gr. 1, p. 170
*Bingo (Melody only, m. 5-8), Gr. 1, p. 170
Bounce High, Bounce Low, Gr. 1, p. 152
Buenos días (Melody only), Gr. 1, p. 13
Buenos días (Melody only, m. 1-4), Gr. 1, p. 13
Busy Buzzy Bee, Gr. K, p. 77
Canción de cuna, Gr. 4, p. 144
Cantando mentiras, Gr. 4, p. 146
Cha yang wu, Gr. 1, p. 90
Chag Purim (m. 1–4), Gr. 1, p. 438
Chanukah Is Here! (m. 1–4), Gr. 2, p. 382
Clouds of Gray, Gr. 2, p. 56
Cuckoo, Cuckoo, Gr. 1, p. 110
Dinner Music (m. 1–2, 5–6, 9–10, 13–14), Gr. K, p. 70
Down in the Meadow (m. 1–3), Gr. K, p. 147
Duérmete, mi niño, Gr. 1, p. 292
El carnavalito humahuaqueño (Melody only), Gr. 6, p. 482
El chocolate (Melody only, m. 2-5), Gr. 1, p. 380
Five Little Chickadees (m. 1, 5, 7), Gr. K, p. 179
Gakavik (m. 1–16), Gr. 4, p. 14
*Go Around the Corn, Sally, Gr. 2, p. 12
Great Big Stars (m. 2, 4, 6–7, 9), Gr. 1, p. 60
Grizzly Bear (m. 5–8), Gr. K, p. 33
Habemos llegado, Gr. 6, p. 174
Hey, Hey, Look at Me, Gr. 1, p. 70
I Have a Dog (m. 1–4), Gr. K, p. 262
I'll Fly Away, Gr. 8, p. 42
Inkpataya (m. 1–4), Gr. 3, p. 254
Jolly Old St. Nicholas (m. 1–2, 5–6, 9–10, 13–14), Gr. K, p. 316
Kébé Mama (m. 1, 3), Gr. 1, p. 442
Knock the Cymbals, Gr. 1, p. 176
Kuma san (m. 1–2, 5–6, 9–10, 13–14), Gr. K, p. 40
Kunolounkwa (m. 1–3, 5–7), Gr. K, p. 110
La víbora (m. 3–4, 9–16), Gr. 1, p. 322
Lemonade, Gr. 1, p. 190
Les petites marionettes, Gr. K, p. 237
Little Green Frog, The (m. 1–3), Gr. 1, p. 24
Little Red Wagon (m. 1–6), Gr. K, p. 152
Little Spider, Gr. K, p. 93
London Bridge (m. 2), Gr. K, p. 244
Los pececitos (m. 3–4, 7–8), Gr. 1, p. 178
Los trencitos, Gr. K, p. 24
Lucy Locket, Gr. 2, p. 27
Luna lunera (speech piece), Gr. K, p. 90
Making Valentines (m. 1–2), Gr. 1, p. 437

Mary Wore Her Red Dress (m. 1–6), Gr. K, p. 74
Mon son pha (speech piece) (m. 1–4), Gr. K, p. 91
My Valentine (m. 1–6), Gr. K, p. 323
Name, Name, What's Your Name? (speech piece) (m. 1–4), Gr. 3, p. 10
Nanny Goat (m. 1–2, 5–6), Gr. K, p. 161
Nu wahtan (m. 1–2), Gr. 1, p. 279
Number One, Touch Your Tongue (speech piece) (m. 1–18), Gr. K, p. 204
O hal'lwe, Gr. 3, p. 256
Old Chisholm Trail, The (Melody only), Gr. 6, p. 237
On a Log, Mister Frog, Gr. K, p. 148
Over in the Meadow (m. 1–4, 9–12), Gr. 1, p. 346
Oy, Hanuka, Gr. 7, p. 44
Pai pi qiu (m. 1–2), Gr. 1, p. 324
Painting Song: A Dribble and a Dot (m. 1–7), Gr. K, p. 175
Perná, perná, i mélissá (m. 1–2), Gr. K, p. 264
Pon, pon, pon (m. 3–4), Gr. K, p. 50
Ptashky u babusi sadochku (m. 1–4, 9–12), Gr. 1, p. 192
*Rain, Rain, Gr. 1, p. 54
Riddle Ree (speech piece) (m. 1–2, 5–12), Gr. 2, p. 34
Riquirrán, Gr. 1, p. 48
Riquirrán, Gr. 4, p. 66
Rock Around the Clock (Melody only), Gr. 7, p. 18
Rock Around the Clock (Melody only), Gr. 7, p. 18
'Round and 'Round (m. 1–2, 5–6), Gr. 1, p. 148
Seasons (m. 1, 3, 5), Gr. K, p. 4
Serra, serra, serrador (m. 1–2, 5–9), Gr. 1, p. 112
Sh'ney dubim (m. 2–6), Gr. K, p. 268
Shake Them 'Simmons Down (Melody only, m. 1, 3, 5), Gr. 2, p. 244
Shake Them 'Simmons Down (Melody only, m. 1, 3, 5), Gr. 2, p. 244
Si me dan pasteles (m. 1–4), Gr. 1, p. 432
Skip to My Lou (m. 2, 4, 6, 8), Gr. K, p. 58
Snail, Snail, Gr. 1, p. 190
Snowflakes (m. 1–3, 5–7), Gr. 1, p. 422
Soldier, Soldier, Gr. 4, p. 11
Something Told the Wild Geese, Gr. 7, p. 39
Something Told the Wild Geese, Gr. 7, p. 39
Son macaron, Gr. 4, p. 109
Star Light, Star Bright, Gr. 1, p. 108
Sugar "Shuga" Bee (m. 2–6), Gr. K, p. 64
This Land Is Your Land, Gr. 7, p. 66
Three Little Piggies, Gr. K, p. 56
Tic, tac, Gr. 1, p. 252
Tsuki, Gr. 4, p. 25
Turn the Glasses Over (m. 1–8), Gr. 3, p. 204
Uga uga uga (m. 1–2), Gr. K, p. 305
Un pajarito (m. 1–4), Gr. 2, p. 16
Was kommt dort von der Höh'?, Gr. 8, p. 21
Was kommt dort von der Höh'?, Gr. 8, p. 21
What Will You Be on Halloween? (m. 1, 5), Gr. K, p. 308
Who Has the Penny? (m. 1–4, 9–12), Gr. K, p. 42
Willoughby, Wallaby, Woo (m. 1, 5), Gr. K, p. 282
Wind Up the Apple Tree (m. 1–2, 5–6), Gr. 1, p. 184
Wings of a Dove, Gr. 4, p. 318
Wir hatten gebauet, Gr. 8, p. 21

♩

ABC Blues (m. 19–22), Gr. K, p. 281

Alle meine Entchen, Gr. 1, p. 98
Alligator Pie (speech piece), Gr. 3, p. 13
Banana Splits (m. 3–4, 9–10), Gr. 1, p. 318
Beach Rap (speech piece) (refrain), Gr. 1, p. 352
Button, You Must Wander (m. 1–8), Gr. 2, p. 172
Canción de cuna, Gr. 4, p. 144
Cantando mentiras, Gr. 4, p. 146
Circle Round the Zero (m. 2–6), Gr. K, p. 293
*Cirmos cica, Gr. 1, p. 130
Ég a gyertya, Gr. K, p. 96
El chocolate, Gr. 1, p. 380
El día de mamita (m. 1–4, 9–12), Gr. K, p. 325
Five Little Snowmen, Gr. K, p. 313
Four in a Boat, Gr. 2, p. 46
*Frog in the Millpond, Gr. 2, p. 44
Gypsy in the Moonlight, Gr. 3, p. 12
Hashkediya (m. 9–16), Gr. 3, p. 206
Here I Go! (m. 9–12), Gr. K, p. 73
Hot Cross Buns (Version 1), Gr. 3, p. 218
Hot Cross Buns (Version 2), Gr. 3, p. 221
I Fed My Horse, Gr. 2, p. 94
I Have a Dog, Gr. K, p. 262
I See the Moon (m. 1–4), Gr. 2, p. 58
I'll Fly Away, Gr. 8, p. 42
Jinny Go 'Round (m. 1–7), Gr. K, p. 228
Johnny Caught a Flea, Gr. 1, p. 226
Kaeru no uta (m. 5–8), Gr. K, p. 183
Kuma san (m. 1–8), Gr. K, p. 40
Let Us Chase the Squirrel, Gr. 2, p. 98
Little Black Bug, Gr. 1, p. 214
Little Red Caboose (m. 1–4, 9–16), Gr. K, p. 229
Little Shell (m. 2, 4), Gr. 1, p. 355
Los pollitos, Gr. K, p. 166
Merry-Go-Round (m. 9–12), Gr. K, p. 290
Mi cuerpo hace música (verse), Gr. K, p. 106
Mon son pha (speech piece) (m. 5–8), Gr. K, p. 91
Mos Mos (m. 1–8), Gr. 1, p. 130
Must Be Santa (m. 1–8), Gr. K, p. 318
Never Smile at a Crocodile (m. 1–16), Gr. 3, p. 100
Over in the Meadow, Gr. 1, p. 346
Pease Porridge Hot, Gr. 1, p. 134
Plant Four Seeds, Gr. 2, p. 130
Polly Wee (m. 8–11), Gr. K, p. 119
Ptashky u babusi sadochku, Gr. 1, p. 192
Pumpkin, Pumpkin, Gr. 1, p. 413
Rinsho, rinsho (m. 1–4, 8–9), Gr. K, p. 285
Rock Around the Clock (Melody only), Gr. 7, p. 18
*Sea Shell, Gr. 2, p. 100
Seasons (m. 1–4), Gr. K, p. 4
Sh'ney dubim (m. 2–8), Gr. K, p. 268
Sing a Little Song (m. 5–8, 13–27), Gr. K, p. 30
Soldier, Soldier, Gr. 4, p. 11
Son macaron, Gr. 4, p. 109
Storm Dance (speech piece) (m. 1–4, 19–22), Gr. K, p. 145
Tanabata-sama, Gr. 2, p. 336
Tap It! Rap It! (speech piece) (m. 1–2, 6–10), Gr. K, p. 194
Tender Shepherd (Count Your Sheep), Gr. 3, p. 116
Tsuki, Gr. 4, p. 25
Twist with a Burger, Jitter with a Bug (speech piece) (m. 2–14), Gr. 1, p. 132
Two Little Sausages (speech piece), Gr. 2, p. 79

Un, deux, trois, Gr. 2, p. 198
Un pajarito, Gr. 2, p. 16
Vamos a hacer la ronda (verse), Gr. K, p. 124
Vamos a la mar, Gr. 3, p. 226
Vil du?, Gr. 1, p. 92
¡Viva el fútbol!, Gr. 1, p. 96
Voice Choice (m. 9–16), Gr. K, p. 27
Wind Up the Apple Tree, Gr. 1, p. 184
Wings of a Dove, Gr. 4, p. 318
Wir hatten gebauet, Gr. 8, p. 21
*Xiao yin chuan, Gr. 2, p. 14
Yang wa wa, Gr. K, p. 162
Yesh lanu taish (m. 1–2), Gr. 1, p. 182
Zumba, zumba (Melody only, m. 9-24), Gr. 3, p. 400

♪ ♩ ♩ ♩

Alphabet Song (m. 1–4), Gr. K, p. 280
*Amarillo Armadillo, Gr. 2, p. 82
Chicken on the Fence Post, Gr. 3, p. 92
Cumberland Gap (m. 1–4), Gr. 4, p. 138
Ding, Dong, Diggidiggidong, Gr. 3, p. 14
*Golden Ring Around Susan Girl, Gr. 3, p. 16
Hanuka, Hanuka, Gr. 8, p. 36
Jelly in a Dish (speech piece), Gr. 2 , p.-83
Keep Your Eyes on the Prize, Gr. 3, p. 408
Khorovod (m. 2, 4), Gr. 1, p. 372
Kookaburra (m. 5–6), Gr. 4, p. 186
Los maizales (m. 1–4), Gr. 1, p. 296
Love Somebody, Gr. 3, p. 94
Old Brass Wagon (m. 1–6), Gr. 2, p. 122
Paw-Paw Patch, Gr. 4, p. 93
Shortnin' Bread (Melody only), Gr. 7, p. 27
Tideo, Gr. 2, p. 80
Toodala (Melody only, m. 1, 5), Gr. 1, p. 326
Winter, Gr. 8, p. 11

𝄾

Al ánimo (Melody only), Gr. 3, p. 322
Bogando a la luz del sol, Gr. 4, p. 306
*Buenos días, Gr. 1, p. 13
Corrido de Kansas, Gr. 4, p. 274
Deep in the Heart of Texas, Gr. 4, p. 22
Deep in the Heart of Texas, Gr. 8, p. 18
Earth Is Our Mother, The, Gr. 8, p. 25
El rancho grande, Gr. 8, p. 22
*El zapatero, Gr. 1, p. 298
God Bless the Grass, Gr. 8, p. 13
Guantanamera, Gr. 8, p. 32
Habemos llegado (Melody only), Gr. 6, p. 174
*Las estaciones, Gr. 1, p. 29
*Mi chacra, Gr. 1, p. 364
Piñon, pirulín, Gr. 2, p. 174
*Toodala, Gr. 1, p. 326

𝅗𝅥

A la puerta del cielo, Gr. 5, p. 60
A la rurru niño (m. 1–7), Gr. K, p. 180
ABC Rock (m. 1–2, 9–10), Gr. 1, p. 262
African Noel, Gr. 1, p. 427
All Around the Buttercup, Gr. 2, p. 170
Alumot, Gr. 6, p. 306

Pitch and Rhythm Index

Angels On the Midnight Clear (Melody only), Gr. 6, p. 423

Au clair de la lune, Gr. 3, p. 18

Ayliluli, num tsipor (m. 7–8), Gr. 1, p. 204

Baby Beluga (m. 9–12), Gr. K, p. 272

Bam, chi, chi, bam, Gr. K, p. 109

Banjo Sam (m. mm. 9-10), Gr. 2, p. 314

Bear Dance, Gr. 7, p. 10

Bluebird, Bluebird, Gr. K, p. 105

Bluebonnets of Texas, Gr. 3, p. 332

Bonjour, mes amis (m. 1–5), Gr. 1, p. 316

Bus, The (m. 3–6), Gr. K, p. 82

Button, You Must Wander, Gr. 2, p. 172

Chanukah, Chanukah, Gr. 1, p. 420

Chanukah Is Here!, Gr. 2, p. 382

Chicka Hanka, Gr. 8, p. 15

Christmas, Don't Be Late (The Chipmunk Song) (m. mm. 1-27), Gr. 2, p. 386

Clouds (m. 1–2, 5–6), Gr. K, p. 254

Costume Capers (m. 1–2), Gr. 1, p. 412

Cow's Woc Backward (m. 1–4), Gr. 1, p. 390

Da pacem, Domine, Gr. 5, p. 62

Dinner Music (m. 1–3, 5–7, 9–15), Gr. K, p. 70

Dona nobis pacem (Melody only), Gr. 6, p. 125

Down in the Meadow (m. 1–4, 7–8), Gr. K, p. 147

Down the Listening Lane, Gr. K, p. 192

Ee jer ha ba go, Gr. K, p. 133

El carnavalito humahuaqueño (Melody only), Gr. 6, p. 482

El día de mamita, Gr. K, p. 325

Everybody Says (m. 11–12), Gr. 1, p. 287

Fais dodo (m. 1–15), Gr. K, p. 158

Five Little Chickadees, Gr. K, p. 179

Frère Jacques, Gr. 2, p. 125

Fuzzy Caterpillar (m. 5–8), Gr. K, p. 102

Good Old Happy Song, A (m. 1), Gr. K, p. 201

Great Big House, Gr. 2, p. 204

Great Big Stars, Gr. 1, p. 60

Green, Green, Rocky, Gr. 1, p. 321

Grizzly Bear, Gr. K, p. 33

Ha'kyo jong, Gr. 2, p. 135

Halloween Song, Gr. K, p. 309

Hama chi dori (m. 1–4, 9–12, 17–20, 25–28), Gr. 3, p. 330

Hato popo, Gr. 1, p. 186

Hava nashira, Gr. 6, p. 82

Here I Go!, Gr. K, p. 73

Hey, m'tswala, Gr. 4, p. 79

*Hui jia qü, Gr. 2, p. 158

I Got a Letter This Morning (m. 3–4), Gr. K, p. 68

I Love Peanuts, Gr. 7, p. 20

I See the Moon, Gr. 2, p. 58

I'm a Dreydl, Gr. K, p. 315

I'm Curious (m. 1–3), Gr. K, p. 276

Imbabura, Gr. 5, p. 202

Inkpataya, Gr. 3, p. 254

Jim Along, Josie, Gr. K, p. 39

Jinny Go 'Round, Gr. K, p. 228

Johnny Mister Brown, Gr. K, p. 37

Jolly Old St. Nicholas, Gr. K, p. 316

Kaeru no uta, Gr. K, p. 183

Kébé Mama, Gr. 1, p. 442

Koriko!, Gr. K, p. 154

Kunolounkwa, Gr. K, p. 110

Kyrie, Gr. 6, p. 206

La paloma se fué (Melody only), Gr. 6, p. 51

Las velitas, Gr. 5, p. 147

Little and Lots (m. 6–8), Gr. K, p. 323

Making Valentines, Gr. 1, p. 437

Merry-Go-Round, Gr. K, p. 290

Must Be Santa (m. 1–18), Gr. K, p. 318

My Pony, Macaroni (m. 1–9), Gr. 1, p. 158

My Valentine, Gr. K, p. 323

Nana, Thread Needle (refrain), Gr. 1, p. 38

Nanny Goat, Gr. K, p. 161

Never Smile at a Crocodile, Gr. 3, p. 100

Nie chce cie znác, Gr. 3, p. 314

Noah's Shanty, Gr. 1, p. 342

O Music, Gr. 5, p. 162

Oh, What a Day! (m. 1–2, 5–6), Gr. K, p. 302

One Green Jelly Bean, Gr. K, p. 287

Over the Rainbow (from The Wizard of Oz), Gr. 4, p. 140

Peace Round, Gr. 4, p. 348

Pin Pon, Gr. 1, p. 146

Polly Wee, Gr. K, p. 119

Pon, pon, pon, Gr. K, p. 50

Riddle Ree (speech piece), Gr. 2, p. 34

Rocky Mountain, Gr. 2, p. 98

Seasons, Gr. K, p. 4

See and Touch, Gr. K, p. 172

Shake Them 'Simmons Down (Melody only), Gr. 2, p. 244

Shu ha mo (m. 1–4), Gr. 3, p. 276

Si me dan pasteles, Gr. 1, p. 432

Six Little Ducks, Gr. K, p. 234

Snowflakes (m. 5–8), Gr. 1, p. 422

Soldier, Soldier, Gr. 4, p. 11

Something Told the Wild Geese, Gr. 7, p. 39

Star-Spangled Banner, The, Gr. 7, p. 56

There Is Love Somewhere (Melody only), Gr. 6, p. 318

This Land Is Your Land, Gr. 7, p. 66

Today Is Your Birthday (m. 3–6), Gr. 1, p. 410

Turn the Glasses Over (m. 9–16), Gr. 3, p. 204

Un elefante, Gr. 2, p. 160

What Will You Be on Halloween?, Gr. K, p. 308

Who Has the Penny?, Gr. K, p. 42

Willowbee (m. 1–7), Gr. 1, p. 222

Wings of a Dove (m. 11–18), Gr. 4, p. 318

Wir hatten gebauet, Gr. 8, p. 21

Woodland Chorus (m. 15–16; verse), Gr. K, p. 250

♪ ♩ ♪

Achshav (m. 9–16), Gr. 2, p. 64

Ahora voy a cantarles, Gr. 3, p. 56

Ain't Gonna Let Nobody Turn Me 'Round (m. 7, 8), Gr. 6, p. 85

Ain't Gonna Let Nobody Turn Me 'Round (m. 7-8), Gr. 8, p. 16

Alabama Gal, Gr. 3, p. 106

Artsa alinu (m. 13–20), Gr. 3, p. 285

¡Ay, Jalisco no te rajes!, Gr. 7, p. 6

*Black Snake, Gr. 3, p. 53

Bling Blang (m. 1–4), Gr. 3, p. 240

Bogando a la luz del sol, Gr. 4, p. 306

Canoe Song, Gr. 4, p. 76

Che che koolay, Gr. 2, p. 266

Cheki, morena, Gr. 2, p. 180
Cheki, morena, Gr. 7, p. 16
Cookie (m. 1–2, 5–6, 9, 11, 13), Gr. 2, p. 172
Cuculí (m. 1–8; refrain), Gr. K, p. 238
Diou shou juan'er, Gr. 2, p. 277
Don't Let the Wind, Gr. 3, p. 180
Dry Bones Come Skipping (m. 1, 3), Gr. 4, p. 218
Duck Dance, Gr. 2, p. 249
El rancho grande, Gr. 8, p. 22
Funwa alafia, Gr. 5, p. 32
Going Upon the Mountain (Melody only), Gr. 6, p. 105
Happy Feet (m. mm. 1-5), Gr. 2, p. 252
He's Got the Whole World in His Hands (Melody only), Gr. 7, p. 36
Hej pada pada, Gr. 3, p. 78
Hi-Dee-Roon (m. 1, 3, 5, 7), Gr. K, p. 10
Hop Up, My Ladies (m. 17–18, 21–22, 25–26, 29–30), Gr. 3, p. 142
Hush Up the Baby, Gr. K, p. 222
I Love Peanuts, Gr. 7, p. 20
I Shall Sing, Gr. 8, p. 38
I'll Fly Away, Gr. 8, p. 42
I'm in the Mood (m. 1–2, 5–6, 9–10, 15–16, 19–20), Gr. K, p. 86
Ja-Da (Melody/Part I), Gr. 7, p. 20
Jambalaya (On The Bayou), Gr. 6, p. 244
Kingston Market (m. 9–12), Gr. 3, p. 90
Kokoleoko, Gr. 5, p. 33
Kou ri lengay, Gr. 7, p. 2
La borinqueña, Gr. 8, p. 19
Laredo, Gr. 5, p. 10
Leila, Gr. 1, p. 258
Let the Music Begin!, Gr. 1, p. 2
Let's Get the Rhythm of the Band, Gr. 3, p. 84
Let's Get the Rhythm of the Band, Gr. 7, p. 29
Li'l Liza Jane (m. 3–4, 7–8, 11–12, 15–16), Gr. 3, p. 140
Little David (m. 1), Gr. 1, p. 232
Little Red Caboose, Gr. K, p. 229
Los pececitos (m. 1–8), Gr. 1, p. 178
Mango Walk, Gr. 5, p. 200
Mbombera (m. 5–12), Gr. K, p. 24
*Mister Ram Goat-O, Gr. 3, p. 54
Morning Comes Early, Gr. 5, p. 13
My Mama's Calling Me (m. 2, 5, 7), Gr. 1, p. 260
Nu wahtan, Gr. 1, p. 279
*One Morning Soon, Gr. 3, p. 68
Pizza, Pizza, Daddy-o (m. 3, 5, 7, 9), Gr. 2, p. 28
Rise and Shine (m. 1–4), Gr. 4, p. 98
Rock and Roll Is Here to Stay (m. 27–28), Gr. 6, p. 36
Rock Island Line, Gr. 4, p. 54
Seagull, Seagull, Sit on the Shore, Gr. 4, p. 383
Shake the Papaya Down (m. 5–12), Gr. 4, p. 378
*Somebody's Knockin' at Your Door (m. 1–4, 7–8), Gr. 4, p. 53
Take Your Feet Out 'the Sand (m. 2–3, 5–6), Gr. K, p. 231
Tancovacka (m. 1–16), Gr. 4, p. 230
Tengo, tengo, tengo, Gr. 4, p. 228
This Train, Gr. 5, p. 26
Twist with a Burger, Jitter with a Bug (speech piece) (m. 2–18), Gr. 1, p. 132
Wade in the Water, Gr. 8, p. 64
Waitin' for the Light to Shine (m. 1–4), Gr. 4, p. 26

Wake Me, Shake Me, Gr. 1, p. 278
Weevily Wheat (m. 1–4), Gr. 4, p. 105
When the Train Comes Along (m. 5–6), Gr. 1, p. 300
Wind Blew East, The (m. 9–11, 13–15, 17–20), Gr. 1, p. 64
Yesh lanu taish (m. 1–6), Gr. 1, p. 182

♩.

All for One (Melody only), Gr. 7, p. 8
America (m. 5–6, 13–14), Gr. 1, p. 446
America (m. 5, 6, 13, 14), Gr. 2, p. 403
America, Gr. 3, p. 412
America, the Beautiful, Gr. 8, p. 4
Angels On the Midnight Clear (Melody only), Gr. 6, p. 423
Artsa alinu, Gr. 3, p. 285
Ash Grove, The (Countermelody), Gr. 5, p. 114
Bonavist' Harbour (refrain), Gr. 3, p. 294
Christmas, Don't Be Late (The Chipmunk Song), Gr. 2, p. 386
Cielito lindo (Melody only), Gr. 7, p. 20
Cookie, Gr. 2, p. 172
Costume Capers (m. 22–24), Gr. 1, p. 412
Dok djampa, Gr. 8, p. 20
Don't Let the Wind, Gr. 3, p. 180
Dona nobis pacem (Melody only), Gr. 6, p. 125
El sapito, Gr. 3, p. 336
Ezekiel Saw the Wheel (m. 10, 16, 20), Gr. 6, p. 379
Fais do do, Gr. 6, p. 403
Fais dodo, Gr. K, p. 158
Fiddler on the Roof (Melody only), Gr. 7, p. 5
Good Mornin', Blues, Gr. 2, p. 52
Haere, Gr. 2, p. 285
Hama chi dori, Gr. 3, p. 330
Home on the Range, Gr. 5, p. 69
I'll Fly Away, Gr. 8, p. 42
I'm Tall, I'm Small, Gr. K, p. 18
I'm Thankful (m. 3–8), Gr. 1, p. 414
I've Been Working on the Railroad (m. 1–16), Gr. 3, p. 242
*Juniper Tree, The, Gr. 3, p. 131
La paloma blanca, Gr. 3, p. 252
Las velitas, Gr. 5, p. 147
Liebe ist ein Ring, Gr. 4, p. 193
Little Shell, Gr. 1, p. 355
Los niños en España cantan, Gr. 4, p. 197
Mary Ann, Gr. K, p. 253
*Morning Is Come, Gr. 3, p. 128
Niño querido, Gr. 1, p. 308
Oh, Freedom, Gr. 5, p. 392
Oh, Freedom (Melody only), Gr. 7, p. 30
Oh, How Lovely Is the Evening (m. 13–18), Gr. 4, p. 217
Old Chisholm Trail, The (Melody only), Gr. 6, p. 237
Over My Head (m. 15), Gr. 4, p. 118
Oy, Hanuka (Melody only), Gr. 7, p. 44
Peace Round, Gr. 4, p. 348
Pretty Saro, Gr. 3, p. 216
Put Your Finger in the Air (m. 1–5, 7–8), Gr. K, p. 114
Put Your Hand in My Hand, Gr. 1, p. 330
Rock and Roll Is Here to Stay (m. 26), Gr. 6, p. 36
'Round the Bay of Mexico, Gr. 4, p. 258

Rudolph, the Red-Nosed Reindeer (m. 5–41), Gr. 1, p. 428
Si si si (Melody only), Gr. 7, p. 13
Sing a Rainbow, Gr. 2, p. 166
Something Told the Wild Geese, Gr. 7, p. 39
That's What's New with Me!, Gr. K, p. 2
This Is My Song (Melody only), Gr. 6, p. 77
Tom Dooley, Gr. 6, p. 374
Vem kan segla?, Gr. 6, p. 417
We're Making Popcorn (speech piece) (m. 1–5), Gr. 1, p. 86
World We Love, The (verse), Gr. 3, p. 342

♩

A Ram Sam Sam, Gr. 3, p. 208
*Adiós, amigos, Gr. 6, p. 57
Amazing Grace, Gr. 4, p. 160
Ambos a dos (refrain), Gr. 3, p. 20
America, the Beautiful, Gr. 6, p. 485
Ash Grove, The (Melody), Gr. 5, p. 114
Ash Grove, The (Countermelody), Gr. 5, p. 114
Big Corral, The (m. a1–a5), Gr. 2, p. 230
Bluebonnets of Texas, Gr. 3, p. 332
Bonjour, mes amis, Gr. 1, p. 316
Bus, The, Gr. K, p. 82
Canción Mixteca, Gr. 5, p. 326
El borrego (m. 1-16), Gr. 4, p. 242
Happy Wanderer, The, Gr. 4, p. 89
Hey, m'tswala, Gr. 4, p. 79
Home on the Range, Gr. 5, p. 69
I Fed My Horse, Gr. 2, p. 94
I Walk the Unfrequented Road, Gr. 6, p. 79
I'm Thankful, Gr. 1, p. 414
Juanito, Gr. K, p. 300
La paloma se fué (Melody only), Gr. 6, p. 51
Laredo, Gr. 5, p. 10
Little Green Frog, The, Gr. 1, p. 24
Lone Star Trail (verse), Gr. 2, p. 21
Los niños en España cantan, Gr. 4, p. 197
My Bonnie Lies Over the Ocean, Gr. 4, p. 338
My Foot's In My Stirrup, Gr. 2, p. 234
O Laufet, ihr Hirten, Gr. 2, p. 384
Pin Pon, Gr. 1, p. 146
Song of the Fishes, Gr. 3, p. 244
Streets of Laredo, Gr. 4, p. 272
Sweet Betsy from Pike, Gr. 4, p. 244
Texas Cowboy (Melody only), Gr. 3, p. 250
Three Little Piggies, Gr. K, p. 56
Tic, tac, Gr. 1, p. 252
Today Is Your Birthday, Gr. 1, p. 410
We Wish You a Merry Christmas, Gr. 3, p. 395
Wir hatten gebauet, Gr. 8, p. 21

♫

A Ram Sam Sam, Gr. 3, p. 208
Ambos a dos (verse), Gr. 3, p. 20
Bát kim thang, Gr. 6, p. 13
Big Old Storm a-Comin', Gr. K, p. 257
Big Rock Candy Mountain, Gr. 4, p. 330
Blow, Ye Winds, Gr. 4, p. 255
Corrido de Kansas, Gr. 4, p. 274

El burrito enfermo, Gr. K, p. 271
El tambor, Gr. 2, p. 274
El Tren, Gr. 2, p. 260
Goin' to the Fair, Gr. K, p. 156
Happy Birthday to You, Gr. K, p. 304
I'm a Very Fine Turkey, Gr. K, p. 310
If You're Happy, Gr. K, p. 94
Lone Star Trail (refrain), Gr. 2, p. 21
Los trencitos, Gr. K, p. 24
Mary Ann, Gr. K, p. 253
Painting Song: A Dribble and a Dot, Gr. K, p. 175
Polly Wee, Gr. K, p. 119
Pust' 'vsegda budet sonse, Gr. 3, p. 278
Put Your Finger in the Air, Gr. K, p. 114
*Red River Valley, Gr. 6, p. 11
Riquirrán, Gr. 1, p. 48
Rudolph, the Red-Nosed Reindeer, Gr. 1, p. 428
Shri Ram, jai Ram, Gr. 4, p. 311
Simple Gifts, Gr. 5, p. 184
Somebody Waiting, Gr. 2, p. 283
Uno, dos, y tres, Gr. 5, p. 427
Vamos a cantar, Gr. K, p. 278
Voice Choice, Gr. K, p. 27
We Are Dear Little Birdies, Gr. K, p. 176

♪

A-Tisket, A-Tasket, Gr. 2, p. 238
Achshav (m. 1–8), Gr. 2, p. 64
Al ánimo, Gr. 3, p. 322
Banana Splits, Gr. 1, p. 318
Barb'ry Allen, Gr. 6, p. 44
*Bingo, Gr. 1, p. 170
Blow, Ye Winds, Gr. 4, p. 255
Buenos días (Melody only), Gr. 1, p. 13
Chanukiyah li yesh, Gr. 1, p. 421
Connemara Lullaby (Melody only), Gr. 5, p. 232
Costume Capers, Gr. 1, p. 412
Dance for the Nations (m. 8), Gr. 6, p. 122
Deep in the Heart of Texas, Gr. 4, p. 22
Doctor Knickerbocker (speech piece), Gr. 1, p. 302
Down Home, Gr. 3, p. 354
Down the Ohio, Gr. 2, p. 60
Earth Is My Mother, The, Gr. 1, p. 340
Earth Is Our Mother, The, Gr. 8, p. 25
Eensy Weensy Spider, Gr. K, p. 187
Ein Männlein steht im Walde, Gr. 2, p. 90
El juego chirimbolo, Gr. 2, p. 54
El mes de abril, Gr. 3, p. 328
El payo, Gr. 6, p. 145
El rancho grande, Gr. 4, p. 215
El rancho grande, Gr. 8, p. 22
Farmer's Dairy Key, The, Gr. 2, p. 182
Frog Music, Gr. 4, p. 200
Get on Board, Gr. K, p. 89
Good Mornin', Blues, Gr. 2, p. 52
Good Morning, Gr. 3, p. 192
Habemos llegado (Melody only), Gr. 6, p. 174
Harrison Town, Gr. 6, p. 97
Hashkediya, Gr. 3, p. 206
Hello, There!, Gr. K, p. 6
How Can I Keep from Singing?, Gr. 4, p. 261
I Wonder Where Maria's Gone, Gr. 3, p. 318

I'm Curious, Gr. K, p. 276
Ikhanda, maslombe, Gr. K, p. 14
James Brown, Gr. K, p. 206
John Kanaka, Gr. 3, p. 60
Keel Row, The, Gr. 4, p. 240
L'inverno è passato, Gr. 2, p. 400
Las estaciones, Gr. 1, p. 29
Magnolia, Gr. 6, p. 16
Mbombera, Gr. K, p. 24
Mon son pha (speech piece), Gr. K, p. 91
My Dreydl, Gr. K, p. 314
My Pony, Macaroni, Gr. 1, p. 158
Oy, Hanuka, Gr. 5, p. 464
Pat Works on the Railway, Gr. 5, p. 182
Perná, perná, i mélissá, Gr. K, p. 264
Piñon, pirulín, Gr. 2, p. 174
¡Qué llueva!, Gr. K, p. 81
Race You Down the Mountain, Gr. 1, p. 127
Railroad Corral (m. 1–8), Gr. 3, p. 174
Rig-a-Jig-Jig, Gr. K, p. 99
Río, río, Gr. 5, p. 370
Shoo, Fly (m. a9–16), Gr. 2, p. 200
Sierra Morena, Gr. 3, p. 296
Silly Street, Gr. K, p. 224
Skin and Bones, Gr. 2, p. 376
Small Job, A, Gr. 3, p. 224
Spring Has Sprung!, Gr. K, p. 142
Tap It! Rap It! (speech piece), Gr. K, p. 194
Thanksgiving Is Near, Gr. 2, p. 380
Three Times By She Passes (speech piece), Gr. K, p. 125
Tree in the Wood, The, Gr. 2, p. 360
When Johnny Comes Marching Home, Gr. 5, p. 180
Willoughby, Wallaby, Woo, Gr. K, p. 282

**o**

All for One (Melody only), Gr. 7, p. 8
Ash Grove, The (Melody), Gr. 5, p. 114
Bear Dance, Gr. 7, p. 10
Bury Me Not on the Lone Prairie (Melody only), Gr. 6, p. 19
Clouds, Gr. K, p. 254
Dinner Music, Gr. K, p. 70
Dok djampa, Gr. 8, p. 20
Earth Is Our Mother, The, Gr. 8, p. 25
Ego sum pauper, Gr. 5, p. 158
Ev'rybody Ought to Know, Gr. 1, p. 434
Falling Rain (m. 1–8), Gr. 2, p. 328
Fuzzy Caterpillar, Gr. K, p. 102
Glory, Glory, Hallelujah, Gr. 6, p. 52
Halloween Song, Gr. K, p. 309
Happy Feet (m. mm. 1-8), Gr. 2, p. 252
Honeybee Song, The (m. 28–31), Gr. 1, p. 358
Hush, Hush (m. 1–4), Gr. 3, p. 162
I'm in the Mood (verse), Gr. K, p. 86
I'm on My Way, Gr. 7, p. 15
Las velitas, Gr. 5, p. 147
Man of Constant Sorrow, Gr. 7, p. 28
Michael, Row the Boat Ashore (m. 3, 5), Gr. 2, p. 18
Mos Mos, Gr. 1, p. 130
Must Be Santa, Gr. K, p. 318
My Dear Companion, Gr. 6, p. 23
My Father's House, Gr. 2, p. 25

Oh, Freedom, Gr. 5, p. 392
Over My Head, Gr. 4, p. 118
Over My Head (Melody only), Gr. 7, p. 9
Panamam tombé (Countermelody), Gr. 7, p. 18
Put Your Hand in My Hand (m. 18–21), Gr. 1, p. 330
Rainbow, The, Gr. 2, p. 332
Rock and Roll Is Here to Stay (m. 25), Gr. 6, p. 36
Scattin' A-Round (Variations on Row 3) (m. 1–8), Gr. 6, p. 160
Sing a Song of Peace (Part I, m. 16, 18), Gr. 6, p. 66
Snowflakes, Gr. 1, p. 422
Somebody's Knockin' at Your Door, Gr. 4, p. 53
Swing Low, Sweet Chariot, Gr. 7, p. 41
There Is Love Somewhere (Melody only), Gr. 6, p. 318
This Is My Song (Melody only), Gr. 6, p. 77
Willowbee (verse), Gr. 1, p. 222

**♩. ♪**

Adana ya gidelim, Gr. 2, p. 142
All Night, All Day, Gr. 4, p. 180
All Through the Night, Gr. 5, p. 105
Alleluia, Gr. 6, p. 133
Amazing Grace (m. 9–12), Gr. 4, p. 160
America, Gr. 1, p. 446
America, Gr. 2, p. 403
America, Gr. 3, p. 412
America, Gr. 4, p. 440
America, Gr. 5, p. 486
America (m. 1–4, 7–12), Gr. 6, p. 484
*America, Gr. 7, p. 2
America, Gr. 8, p. 2
America, Gr. K, p. 326
America, the Beautiful, Gr. 6, p. 485
America, the Beautiful (Melody only), Gr. 7, p. 4
*America, the Beautiful, Gr. 8, p. 4
Angels On the Midnight Clear (Countermelody), Gr. 6, p. 423
Arirang, Gr. 5, p. 25
Barb'ry Allen, Gr. 6, p. 44
Beriozka (m. 7–12), Gr. 4, p. 294
Big Old Storm a-Comin', Gr. K, p. 257
Big Rock Candy Mountain, Gr. 4, p. 330
Bonga, Gr. K, p. 78
Bound for South Australia, Gr. 5, p. 22
Boysie, Gr. 2, p. 195
By the Waters of Babylon (m. 1–2, 7–8), Gr. 6, p. 311
Chairs to Mend (m. 1–4), Gr. 4, p. 149
Chang (m. 1–4), Gr. 1, p. 156
Chiapanecas, Gr. 5, p. 92
Cuculí, Gr. K, p. 238
Dance for the Nations (m. 10), Gr. 6, p. 122
De colores (Melody only), Gr. 5, p. 90
Debajo el botón, Gr. 1, p. 210
Deep in the Heart of Texas, Gr. 4, p. 22
Deep in the Heart of Texas, Gr. 8, p. 18
Deux cocodries (m. 1–8), Gr. 2, p. 364
Don't You Hear the Lambs?, Gr. 5, p. 97
Dona nobis pacem (Melody only), Gr. 6, p. 125
¿Dónde lo escondí?, Gr. K, p. 209
Doraji, Gr. 4, p. 174
Everybody Says (m. 9–12), Gr. 1, p. 287
Ezekiel Saw the Wheel (m. 1–2, 13–14), Gr. 6, p. 379

For the Beauty of the Earth (m. 9–12), Gr. 4, p. 356
Four Strong Winds (Song to a Seagull) (m. a5–7, a11–12), Gr. 6, p. 170
Freight Train, Gr. 1, p. 44
Glad to Have a Friend Like You (refrain), Gr. 2, p. 228
God Bless the Grass, Gr. 8, p. 13
Great Day (m. 1–4), Gr. 3, p. 58
Green, Green Grass of Home (m. 8–15 of verse refrain), Gr. 6, p. 248
Greenland Whale Fishery, The, Gr. 5, p. 230
Happy Wanderer, The (m. 1–8 of verse), Gr. 4, p. 89
Hi Heidi Ho, Gr. 1, p. 394
Himmel und Erde, Gr. 5, p. 94
Home on the Range, Gr. 5, p. 69
How Can I Keep from Singing?, Gr. 4, p. 261
How Much Wood Could a Woodchuck Chuck (speech piece), Gr. 3, p. 120
Hwa yuan li-de young wa wa, Gr. 3, p. 102
I Dream a World, Gr. 8, p. 40
I Fed My Horse (m. mm. 9-12), Gr. 2, p. 94
I Walk the Unfrequented Road, Gr. 6, p. 79
Jambalaya (On The Bayou), Gr. 6, p. 244
John Kanaka (m. 5–8, 13–16, 21–24), Gr. 3, p. 60
Kingston Market (m. 9–16), Gr. 3, p. 90
*La Tarara, Gr. 4, p. 176
Leatherwing Bat (m. 9–16), Gr. 2, p. 303
Let Us Sing Together (m. 5–6), Gr. 6, p. 156
Li'l Liza Jane, Gr. 3, p. 140
*Los reyes de Oriente (Melody only), Gr. 8, p. 58
Magnolia (m. 21), Gr. 6, p. 16
Make New Friends, Gr. 3, p. 36
*Mi chacra (Melody only, m. 1-8), Gr. 1, p. 364
Mister Rabbit (refrain), Gr. K, p. 128
My Bonnie Lies Over the Ocean, Gr. 4, p. 338
My Dreydl, Gr. K, p. 314
My Home's Across the Blue Ridge Mountains, Gr. 4, p. 84
Ner li, Gr. 2, p. 383
Ode to Joy, Gr. 4, p. 152
Oh, Danny Boy, Gr. 4, p. 48
Promised Land, The, Gr. 5, p. 258
¡Qué llueva!, Gr. K, p. 81
River (m. 13–21 of refrain), Gr. 4, p. 58
'Round the Bay of Mexico, Gr. 4, p. 258
San Antonio Rose, Gr. 5, p. 134
Sansaw akroma (m. 5–8, 30–34), Gr. 3, p. 286
Scarborough Fair, Gr. 6, p. 95
Seagull, Seagull, Sit on the Shore, Gr. 4, p. 383
Si si si (Melody only), Gr. 7, p. 13
Simple Gifts (m. 9–16), Gr. 5, p. 184
Somebody's Knockin' at Your Door (m. 5–6), Gr. 4, p. 53
Something Told the Wild Geese, Gr. 7, p. 39
Star-Spangled Banner, The (Melody only), Gr. 7, p. 56
Star-Spangled Banner, The, Gr. 8, p. 62
Storm Dance (speech piece), Gr. K, p. 145
Streets of Laredo, Gr. 4, p. 272
Sweet Betsy from Pike (m. 17–20 of refrain), Gr. 4, p. 244
Sweet Potatoes, Gr. 3, p. 228
Swing Low, Sweet Chariot, Gr. 7, p. 41
Tancovacka (m. 17–32), Gr. 4, p. 230
There Is Love Somewhere (Melody only), Gr. 6, p. 318
This Is My Song (Melody only), Gr. 6, p. 77

This Land Is Your Land, Gr. 7, p. 66
To'ia mai te waka, Gr. 1, p. 77
Twist with a Burger, Jitter with a Bug (speech piece) (m. 1–19), Gr. 1, p. 132
Uga uga uga, Gr. K, p. 305
Vem kan segla?, Gr. 6, p. 417
Wade in the Water, Gr. 8, p. 64
Xiao (m. 27–29), Gr. 4, p. 314
Yellow Rose of Texas, The, Gr. 7, p. 70
You Were on My Mind (Melody only), Gr. 7, p. 23

♪ ♩.

All Night, All Day, Gr. 4, p. 180
Ama-Lama, Gr. 5, p. 142
Barb'ry Allen, Gr. 6, p. 44
Bling Blang (m. 9–12), Gr. 3, p. 240
Certainly, Lord (Melody only), Gr. 7, p. 13
Come and Go with Me to That Land, Gr. 5, p. 390
Cow's Woc Backward, Gr. 1, p. 390
Dayenu (m. 5–8), Gr. 4, p. 439
Deep in the Heart of Texas, Gr. 4, p. 22
Deep in the Heart of Texas, Gr. 8, p. 18
Don't You Hear the Lambs?, Gr. 5, p. 97
El rancho grande (refrain), Gr. 4, p. 215
El rancho grande, Gr. 8, p. 22
Erdö, erdö de magos, Gr. 3, p. 182
Farewell to Tarwathie, Gr. 6, p. 43
Four Strong Winds (Song to a Seagull), Gr. 6, p. 170
Go Down, Moses, Gr. 5, p. 190
Great Day (m. 1–8), Gr. 3, p. 58
Guantanamera, Gr. 8, p. 32
He's Got the Whole World in His Hands (Melody only), Gr. 7, p. 36
Hi-Dee-Roon, Gr. K, p. 10
I Shall Sing, Gr. 8, p. 38
Let's Get the Rhythm of the Band (Melody only), Gr. 3, p. 84
*Los reyes de Oriente (Melody only), Gr. 8, p. 58
Mister Rabbit, Gr. K, p. 128
Mud, Gr. 3, p. 32
*New Hungarian Folk Song, Gr. 6, p. 196
Old Dan Tucker (m. 13–16), Gr. 3, p. 96
*Old House, Tear It Down!, Gr. 4, p. 178
Old Man Mosie (Melody only), Gr. 3, p. 108
Peace Like a River, Gr. 6, p. 190
Ragtime Cowboy Joe (m. mm. 18-19), Gr. 2, p. 250
Rise and Shine (m. 7–8), Gr. 4, p. 98
River (m. 13–21 of refrain), Gr. 4, p. 58
Rudolph, the Red-Nosed Reindeer, Gr. 1, p. 428
Scarborough Fair, Gr. 6, p. 95
Shanghai Chicken, Gr. 1, p. 140
Sing a Little Song, Gr. K, p. 30
Sing a Song of Peace (Part II, m. 1–2, 5–6), Gr. 6, p. 66
Tengo, tengo, tengo, Gr. 4, p. 228
This Little Light of Mine (m. 3–4, 7–8, 11–12), Gr. 6, p. 232
When Johnny Comes Marching Home, Gr. 5, p. 180
Willoughby, Wallaby, Woo (m. 3–4, 7–8), Gr. K, p. 282
Willowbee, Gr. 1, p. 222
World We Love, The (refrain), Gr. 3, p. 342
Yüe liang wan wan, Gr. 5, p. 314

Ai, Dunaii moy, Gr. 4, p. 293
Ala Da'lona, Gr. 4, p. 136
Amefuri, Gr. 1, p. 144
California, Gr. 5, p. 52
Chag Purim, Gr. 1, p. 438
El burrito enfermo, Gr. K, p. 271
El desembre congelat, Gr. 5, p. 473
El rabel (Melody only, m. "B-section" (13-20)), Gr. 3,
    p. 362
Frog Music, Gr. 4, p. 200
Hanuka, Hanuka, Gr. 3, p. 390
Hanuka, Hanuka, Gr. 8, p. 36
How Much Wood Could a Woodchuck Chuck (speech
    piece), Gr. 3, p. 120
Ida Red (m. 1,2), Gr. 3, p. 30
Keep Your Eyes on the Prize, Gr. 3, p. 408
Kookaburra (m. 1-4), Gr. 4, p. 186
La víbora, Gr. 1, p. 322
Li'l Liza Jane (m. 1-4), Gr. 3, p. 140
Mama, Buy Me a Chiney Doll, Gr. K, p. 120
Mama Don't 'Low (m. 1-3, 5-7, 13-15), Gr. 6, p. 358
*Mi chacra (Melody only, m. 1, 3), Gr. 1, p. 364
Number One, Touch Your Tongue (speech piece), Gr. K,
    p. 204
Pottery Dance (m. 3-6), Gr. 1, p. 370
'Round and 'Round, Gr. 1, p. 148
See-Saw Sacradown (m. 1-4), Gr. 2, p. 208
Serra, serra, serrador, Gr. 1, p. 112
Shortnin' Bread (m. 11-14), Gr. 1, p. 57
Shortnin' Bread (Melody only), Gr. 7, p. 27
Skip to My Lou, Gr. K, p. 58
Sourwood Mountain (m. 3-4), Gr. 4, p. 65
Take a Chance On Me, Gr. 8, p. 15
This Train (m. 6), Gr. 5, p. 26
Usagi (m. 5-8), Gr. 1, p. 396
Vamos a la fiesta (m. 1-4), Gr. 2, p. 374

Ai, Dunaii moy, Gr. 4, p. 293
Almost Day, Gr. 3, p. 397
Alphabet Song, Gr. K, p. 280
Ayliluli, num tsipor (m. 5-8), Gr. 1, p. 204
Bubble Gum (speech piece), Gr. K, p. 38
California (m. 13), Gr. 5, p. 52
Cumberland Gap (m. 7-9), Gr. 4, p. 138
Drill, Ye Tarriers, Gr. 5, p. 54
Dry Bones Come Skipping, Gr. 4, p. 218
Goin' to Boston (Part I, m. 17-22, 41-46), Gr. 6, p. 433
Going Upon the Mountain (Melody only), Gr. 6, p. 105
Goodbye, Julie, Gr. 8, p. 2
Hanuka, Hanuka, Gr. 3, p. 390
Hanuka, Hanuka, Gr. 8, p. 36
How Many Miles to Babylon?, Gr. 2, p. 128
Ida Red, Gr. 3, p. 30
Khorovod (m. 1-2), Gr. 1, p. 372
Name, Name, What's Your Name? (speech piece), Gr. 3,
    p. 10
Orange Blossom Special, Gr. 5, p. 266
Pai pi qiu (m. 1-4), Gr. 1, p. 324
See-Saw Sacradown, Gr. 2, p. 208

Shortnin' Bread (Melody only), Gr. 7, p. 27
Sourwood Mountain (m. 1-4), Gr. 4, p. 65
This Old Man, Gr. 3, p. 152
Weevily Wheat (m. 1-2), Gr. 4, p. 105

Al yadee, Gr. 6, p. 308
Ama-Lama, Gr. 5, p. 142
Asadoya (m. 2-3, 5-8), Gr. 6, p. 303
¡Ay, Jalisco no te rajes! (Melody only), Gr. 7, p. 6
Ayliluli, num tsipor, Gr. 1, p. 204
Baby Beluga, Gr. K, p. 272
Bantama kra kro, Gr. 5, p. 308
Bát kim thang, Gr. 6, p. 13
Battle Cry of Freedom, Gr. 5, p. 272
Battle Hymn of the Republic, Gr. 5, p. 274
Bear Dance (m. 1-4), Gr. K, p. 127
Blow, Ye Winds, Gr. 4, p. 255
Chang (m. 6-13), Gr. 1, p. 156
Chanukah Games, Gr. 3, p. 389
Cindy, Gr. 4, p. 384
Circle Round the Zero, Gr. K, p. 293
Clementine, Gr. 4, p. 341
Colorado Trail, Gr. 5, p. 276
Counting Song (m. 1-8), Gr. 1, p. 253
Cowboys' Christmas Ball (Melody only), Gr. 6, p. 239
Doong gul ge (m. 17-32), Gr. 3, p. 134
Drill, Ye Tarriers (m. 15-16), Gr. 5, p. 54
Ein Männlein steht im Walde (m. 9-16), Gr. 2, p. 90
El desembre congelat, Gr. 5, p. 473
Gaudeamus Igitur, Gr. 8, p. 20
Glendy Burke, The (m. 17-24), Gr. 4, p. 262
Gloria, Gloria (m. 1-8), Gr. 6, p. 459
God Bless America, Gr. 5, p. 4
Goin' to Boston (Part I, m. 33-38), Gr. 6, p. 433
Going on a Picnic, Gr. K, p. 190
Going Upon the Mountain (Melody only), Gr. 6, p. 105
Gospel Train, The (Part I, A section), Gr. 6, p. 398
Gospel Train, The, Gr. 6, p. 398
Happy Wanderer, The (m. 9-14 of refrain), Gr. 4, p. 89
Hava nagila (m. 9-16), Gr. 6, p. 153
Here Comes Valerie, Gr. 1, p. 32
I Can't Spell Hippopotamus (m. 1-8), Gr. 1, p. 264
I Dream a World, Gr. 8, p. 40
I Love the Mountains, Gr. 5, p. 34
I Shall Sing, Gr. 8, p. 38
Ichi-gatsu tsuitachi, Gr. 3, p. 406
Jan ken pon, Gr. 3, p. 302
Jingle Bells (m. 17-32), Gr. 2, p. 388
Jo'ashila, Gr. 5, p. 108
Joshua Fought the Battle of Jericho, Gr. 5, p. 100
Joshua Fought the Battle of Jericho, Gr. 8, p. 18
Keel Row, The, Gr. 4, p. 240
Kum ba yah, Gr. 5, p. 244
Kum bachur atzel, Gr. 3, p. 138
La mariposa, Gr. 6, p. 58
Leak kanseng, Gr. 1, p. 156
Lion Sleeps Tonight, The (m. 1-4), Gr. 4, p. 131
Lion Sleeps Tonight, The, Gr. 8, p. 56
Little and Lots, Gr. K, p. 323
Loch Lomond, Gr. 5, p. 140
London Bridge, Gr. K, p. 244

Pitch and Rhythm Index

*Mon papa, Gr. 2, p. 280
My Mama's Calling Me (m. 1–9), Gr. 1, p. 260
Name Game, The (speech piece), Gr. 1, p. 315
Nampaya omame, Gr. 1, p. 138
Nampaya omame (Countermelody), Gr. 7, p. 10
Now Let Me Fly (verse), Gr. 3, p. 178
O ma washi, Gr. K, p. 13
Oh, Susanna, Gr. 4, p. 264
Old Blue, Gr. K, p. 122
Old Brass Wagon, Gr. 2, p. 122
Old Man Mosie (Melody only, m. 1–8), Gr. 3, p. 108
Oye (Melody only), Gr. 6, p. 336
Pai pi qiu, Gr. 1, p. 324
Pavo, pavo (m. 9–11, 13–15), Gr. 1, p. 416
Race You Down the Mountain, Gr. 1, p. 127
Rondo for Lunch, A (speech piece), Gr. 3, p. 212
Scotland the Brave, Gr. 5, p. 138
Scrub Brush Shuffle, The (Introduction), Gr. 1, p. 118
*Shady Grove, Gr. 5, p. 260
Shoo, Fly, Gr. 2, p. 200
Sing About Martin, Gr. K, p. 321
Sourwood Mountain (m. 3–4, 7–8, 11–12, 15–16), Gr. 4, p. 65
Star-Spangled Banner, The (Melody only), Gr. 8, p. 62
*Toodala (Melody only), Gr. 1, p. 326
*Wabash Cannon Ball (m. 1, 3), Gr. 5, p. 136
Way Down in the Schoolyard (m. 1–8 of refrain), Gr. 2, p. 50
When the Train Comes Along, Gr. 1, p. 300
Wind Blew East, The (m. 9–20), Gr. 1, p. 64
Winter, Gr. 8, p. 11
Yankee Doodle (m. 9–16), Gr. 2, p. 389
Yesh lanu taish, Gr. 1, p. 182
Yonder Come Day, Gr. 8, p. 68

♪ ♩.

Blow, Ye Winds, Gr. 4, p. 255
Bridges (m. 5), Gr. 6, p. 86
Camptown Races, Gr. 5, p. 270
Coffee Grows on White Oak Trees (verse), Gr. 3, p. 168
Colorado Trail, Gr. 5, p. 276
Get on Board, Gr. K, p. 89
Goin' Down the Road Feelin' Bad (Melody only), Gr. 7, p. 13
Gospel Train, The, Gr. 6, p. 398
Jo'ashila, Gr. 5, p. 108
Keel Row, The, Gr. 4, p. 240
Keep Your Eyes on the Prize, Gr. 3, p. 408
La borinqueña, Gr. 8, p. 19
Loch Lomond, Gr. 5, p. 140
My Home's Across the Blue Ridge Mountains (m. 7, 15), Gr. 4, p. 84
My Home's Across the Blue Ridge Mountains (Melody only), Gr. 7, p. 6
Rondo for Lunch, A (speech piece), Gr. 3, p. 212
*Shake Them 'Simmons Down, Gr. 2, p. 244

6/8 ♩ ♩ ♩

Blow the Wind Southerly, Gr. 5, p. 178
Blue Mountain Lake (Melody only, m. 1–8), Gr. 6, p. 205
Bonavist' Harbour, Gr. 3, p. 294

Can You Canoe?, Gr. 4, p. 170
Connemara Lullaby, Gr. 5, p. 232
Corrido de Kansas, Gr. 4, p. 274
Down the Ohio, Gr. 2, p. 60
Eh, cumpari! (m. 26), Gr. 4, p. 68
El borrego (m. 17–33), Gr. 4, p. 242
El florón (m. 1–3), Gr. 2, p. 246
Frog Round
Hey, Diddle, Diddle (m. 1–2), Gr. K, p. 246
Higglety, Pigglety, Pop! (m. 1, 5, 7), Gr. K, p. 22
Juan pirulero (m. 1–3, 5–7), Gr. K, p. 215
Kangaroo Song, The (refrain), Gr. K, p. 44
Las estrellitas del cielo, Gr. 5, p. 175
Lift Ev'ry Voice and Sing, Gr. 8, p. 54
Over the River and Through the Wood, Gr. 3, p. 384
Pat Works on the Railway, Gr. 5, p. 182
Railroad Corral (m. 1–8), Gr. 3, p. 174
Río, río, Gr. 5, p. 370
Sailboat in the Sky, Gr. 4, p. 374
Skye Boat Song (m. 1–8 of verse), Gr. 6, p. 372
Viva Jujuy, Gr. 5, p. 228
Vive l'amour, Gr. 6, p. 176

6/8 ♩.

Andy Pandy (m. 3–4), Gr. K, p. 46
Blow the Wind Southerly, Gr. 5, p. 178
Blue Mountain Lake (Melody only, m. 9–10), Gr. 6, p. 205
Bonavist' Harbour, Gr. 3, p. 294
Can You Canoe?, Gr. 4, p. 170
Caroling, Caroling (m. 3–4, 7–8, 13–14), Gr. 6, p. 458
Down the Ohio, Gr. 2, p. 60
Eh, cumpari!, Gr. 4, p. 68
El borrego (m. 17-33), Gr. 4, p. 242
El florón (m. 2–4), Gr. 2, p. 246
Frog Round
Haul Away, Joe, Gr. 4, p. 13
I Know an Old Lady, Gr. 1, p. 388
Kangaroo Song, The (refrain), Gr. K, p. 44
Las estrellitas del cielo, Gr. 5, p. 175
Lift Ev'ry Voice and Sing, Gr. 8, p. 54
Nani wale na hala, Gr. 3, p. 260
Over the River and Through the Wood, Gr. 3, p. 384
Pat Works on the Railway, Gr. 5, p. 182
Sailboat in the Sky, Gr. 4, p. 374
Viva Jujuy, Gr. 5, p. 228
Vive l'amour, Gr. 6, p. 176
When Johnny Comes Marching Home, Gr. 5, p. 180
Winter Song (m. 16–18, 20–21, 26–31), Gr. 6, p. 455

6/8 ♩ ♪

Andy Pandy, Gr. K, p. 46
Ants Go Marching, The, Gr. 1, p. 248
Blow the Wind Southerly, Gr. 5, p. 178
Bonavist' Harbour, Gr. 3, p. 294
Caroling, Caroling (m. 1–12, 15–16), Gr. 6, p. 458
Charlie over the Water, Gr. 1, p. 68
Chickety, Chickety, Chop (speech piece), Gr. K, p. 41
Connemara Lullaby, Gr. 5, p. 232
Corrido de Kansas, Gr. 4, p. 274
Down the Ohio, Gr. 2, p. 60

Eensy Weensy Spider, Gr. K, p. 187
Eh, cumpari!, Gr. 4, p. 68
El borrego (m. 17-33), Gr. 4, p. 242
El florón (m. 1, 7), Gr. 2, p. 246
Farmer in the Dell, The, Gr. K, p. 232
Fly and the Bumblebee, The, Gr. 1, p. 384
Frog Round
Haul Away, Joe, Gr. 4, p. 13
Hey, Diddle, Diddle, Gr. K, p. 246
Hickory, Dickory, Dare (speech piece), Gr. K, p. 20
I Know an Old Lady, Gr. 1, p. 388
I Saw Three Ships (m. 1–7), Gr. 1, p. 426
Jack, Be Nimble (speech piece), Gr. K, p. 97
Kangaroo Song, The (verse), Gr. K, p. 44
Lady, Lady, Gr. 1, p. 62
*Las horas (m. 1-8), Gr. 1, p. 246
Lift Ev'ry Voice and Sing, Gr. 8, p. 54
Looby Loo, Gr. K, p. 210
Martin Luther King, Gr. 1, p. 434
Nani wale na hala, Gr. 3, p. 260
Oliver Twist, Gr. K, p. 138
Over the River and Through the Wood, Gr. 3, p. 384
Pat Works on the Railway, Gr. 5, p. 182
Rig-a-Jig-Jig, Gr. K, p. 99
Río, río, Gr. 5, p. 370
Sailboat in the Sky, Gr. 4, p. 374
Viva Jujuy, Gr. 5, p. 228
Vive l'amour, Gr. 6, p. 176
When Johnny Comes Marching Home, Gr. 5, p. 180
Winter Song (m. 14–15), Gr. 6, p. 455

Blow the Wind Southerly, Gr. 5, p. 178
Greensleeves, Gr. 6, p. 49
Skye Boat Song (m. 1–8 of refrain), Gr. 6, p. 372
Winter Song (m. 1–8), Gr. 6, p. 455

Juan pirulero, Gr. K, p. 215
No quiero plata, Gr. 1, p. 424
Oh, Freedom (m. 9–16), Gr. 5, p. 392
Río, río, Gr. 5, p. 370
Viva Jujuy, Gr. 5, p. 228
When Johnny Comes Marching Home, Gr. 5, p. 180

Arirang (m. 3), Gr. 5, p. 25
Blues with a Feeling, Gr. 8, p. 6
Doong gul ge, Gr. 3, p. 134
Every Night When the Sun Goes In (m. 6), Gr. 8, p. 28
I've Been Working on the Railroad (m. 9–16 of C
    section), Gr. 3, p. 242
Key to the Highway, Gr. 6, p. 243
Key to the Highway, Gr. 8, p. 29
*Oh, Watch the Stars, Gr. 5, p. 216
Oliver Jump (speech piece), Gr. K, p. 205

Don't Cry for Me, Argentina, Gr. 6, p. 74
I Dream a World, Gr. 8, p. 40

I'd Like To Teach the World to Sing (In Perfect Harmony)
    (Melody only, m. 9-16), Gr. 3, p. 198
Sometimes I Feel Like a Motherless Child, Gr. 6, p. 241
Take Time in Life, Gr. 6, p. 292
What a Wonderful World (m. 6–7, 14–15, 30–31, 32–
    35), Gr. 6, p. 62

Camptown Races (m. 23), Gr. 5, p. 270
Counting Song, Gr. 1, p. 253
I Got a Letter This Morning, Gr. K, p. 68
Little Miss Muffet (speech piece), Gr. K, p. 92
Los maizales, Gr. 1, p. 296
*Lost My Gold Ring, Gr. 6, p. 158
Osamu kosamu (m. 3–4), Gr. 4, p. 96
Sambalele, Gr. 4, p. 397
Vamos a hacer la ronda, Gr. K, p. 124
Vamos a la fiesta, Gr. 2, p. 374

# Thematic Index

## A

### ADVENTURES
Around the World (poem) Gr. 2, 256
*Aweigh, Santy Ano* Gr. 1, 338
Ayelivi Gr. 2, 70
Bus, The Gr. K, 82
But the Cat Came Back Gr. 2, 190
Charlie over the Water Gr. 1, 68
Chawe chidyo chem'chero (story) Gr. 2, 296
Circus Fare (poem) Gr. K, 157
Con el vito Gr. 7, G-15
*Cookie Crew, The* Gr. K, 197
Der sad to katte Gr. 2, 300
Don Gato Gr. 3, 352
Down by the Bay Gr. 1, 18
Ein Männlein steht im Walde Gr. 2, 90
*Frosty, the Snowman* Gr. 2, 391
Get on Board Gr. K, 89
Goin' Down the Road Feelin' Bad Gr. 7, F-13
Goin' to the Fair Gr. K, 156
Going on a Picnic Gr. K, 190
*Goldilocks and the Three Bears* Gr. K, 49
Halloween Song Gr. K, 309
Hambone Gr. 1, 202
Happy Wanderer, The Gr. 4, 89
I See the Moon Gr. 2, 58
I See With My Hands Gr. 2, 148
If a Tiger Calls Gr. 3, 354
Jingle Bells Gr. 2, 388
Jinny Go 'Round Gr. K, 228
Kibungo, Beast of the Forest (story) Gr. 2, 352
Lion and the Mouse, The (story) Gr. 1, 239
*Little Red Hen, The* Gr. 1, 254
Little Red Hen, The (story) Gr. 1, 256
Little Red Wagon Gr. K, 152
Lone Star Trail Gr. 2, 21
Long Way Home, A Gr. 1, 382
Lots of Worms Gr. 2, 310
Merry-Go-Round Gr. K, 290
Merry-Go-Round (poem) Gr. K, 291
Mother Sent Me to the Store (rhyme) Gr. K, 136
Nitty Gritty Sand Song (poem) Gr. K, 191
Oh, What a Day! Gr. K, 302
One, Two, Three, Four, Five (rhyme) Gr. 1, 67
Over the River and Through the Wood Gr. 3, 384
Parade Came Marching, The Gr. 1, 166
Phoebe Gr. 1, 30

Pumpkin Picking (poem) Gr. 2, 376
Rig-a-Jig-Jig Gr. K, 99
Rolling Rice Cake, The: A Story from Japan (folk tale) Gr. 1, 91
Rosie, Darling Rosie Gr. 2, 215
Rudolph, the Red-Nosed Reindeer Gr. 1, 428
Sailing to the Sea Gr. 1, 336
*Shenandoah* Gr. 2, 62
Silly Street Gr. K, 224
*Silver Apples of the Moon-Part A* Gr. 1, 12
Sing Me a Story Gr. 2, 346
Sing Your Story Gr. 3, 350
Skin and Bones Gr. 2, 376
*Sleigh Ride* Gr. 2, 390
Someday Very Soon Gr. 1, 376
Song of the Fishes Gr. 3, 244
Song of the Train (poem) Gr. K, 153
*Sounds of the Circus* Gr. K, 241
Spaceworms Gr. 1, 400
Spring Has Sprung! Gr. K, 142
That's What's New with Me! Gr. K, 2
*Three Little Piggies* Gr. K, 56
Un elefante Gr. 2, 160
When I'm an Astronaut (poem) Gr. 1, 402
Why the Warthog Goes About on His Knees (story) Gr. 1, 139
Zomo the Rabbit (story) Gr. 3, 364

### ALPHABET
*A-You're Adorable* Gr. 1, 263
ABC Blues Gr. K, 281
ABC Rock Gr. 1, 262
Alphabet Song Gr. K, 280
I Can't Spell Hippopotamus Gr. 1, 264
I'm Curious Gr. K, 276
Tongue Twister Medley, A (speech piece) Gr. K, 283
Willoughby, Wallaby, Woo Gr. K, 282

### ANIMALS *See also Zoos.*

#### AMPHIBIANS AND REPTILES
Advice for a Frog (Concerning a Crane) (poem) Gr. 4, 200
Black Snake Gr. 3, 53
Cantando mentiras Gr. 4, 146
Crocodile, The Gr. 2, 362
Deux cocodries Gr. 2, 364
Draw Me a Bucket of Water Gr. 3, 124
El coquí Gr. 2, 292
El sapito Gr. 3, 336
Frog (poem) Gr. 1, 25
Frog (haiku) (poem) Gr. K, 182
Frog in the Millpond Gr. 2, 44
Frog Lullaby (poem) Gr. K, 149
Frog Music Gr. 4, 200

How Doth the Little Crocodile (poem) Gr. 2, 363
Jig Along Home Gr. 2, 366
Jump or Jiggle (poem) Gr. 2, 26
Kaeru no uta Gr. K, 183
Little Green Frog, The Gr. 1, 24
Never Smile at a Crocodile Gr. 3, 100
Noah's Shanty Gr. 1, 342
*Noah's Zoo in the Big, Big Rain* Gr. K, 274
On a Log, Mister Frog Gr. K, 148
Our Mr. Toad (poem) Gr. 3, 337
Over in the Meadow Gr. 1, 346
Polly Wee Gr. K, 119
Se va el caimán Gr. 5, 306
Shu ha mo Gr. 3, 276
Spring Rain (poem) Gr. 2, 294
Voice Choice Gr. K, 27
What Do Animals Need? Gr. 2, 288
*Yertle the Turtle* Gr. 2, 368

#### BIRDS
Advice for a Frog (Concerning a Crane) (poem) Gr. 4, 200
Ah, Poor Bird Gr. 4, 196
Alle meine Entchen Gr. 1, 98
*Bai, bai, bai, bai* Gr. 2, 197
Bam, chi, chi, bam Gr. K, 109
*Bird* Gr. 1, 39
*Bird Calls, Bird Songs* Gr. K, 178
Bird's Nest, The (poem) Gr. K, 239
*Birdcall—Phoebe* Gr. 1, 31
Bitter Morning, A (poem) Gr. K, 177
Bluebird (poem) Gr. K, 104
Bluebird, Bluebird Gr. K, 105
*Brolga* Gr. 6, 271
Canoe Song Gr. 4, 76
Cuckoo, Cuckoo Gr. 1, 110
Cuculí Gr. K, 238
De colores Gr. 8, I-14
Duck, The (poem) Gr. 1, 99
Ducks (poem) Gr. 1, 99
El condor pasa Gr. 6, 46
El mes de abril Gr. 3, 328
Erdö, erdö de magos Gr. 3, 182
Farewell to Tarwathie Gr. 6, 43
Five Little Chickadees Gr. K, 179
Gakavik Gr. 4, 14
*Groundhog Jig, The* Gr. 1, 436
Hama chi dori Gr. 3, 330
Hato popo Gr. 1, 186
How the Kiwi Lost Its Wings (story) Gr. 1, 78
Hwa yuan li-de young wa wa Gr. 3, 102
I'm Curious Gr. K, 276

(*Animals,* continued)

If You Find a Little Feather (poem)
Gr. 1, 187
In the Morning (poem) Gr. 1, 217
¡Jeu! ¡Jeu! Gr. 1, 216
Jig Along Home Gr. 2, 366
Jump or Jiggle (poem) Gr. 2, 26
Kokoleoko Gr. 5, 33
Kookaburra Gr. 4, 186
L'inverno è passato Gr. 2, 400
Las mañanitas Gr. 6, 481
Leatherwing Bat Gr. 2, 303
Let's Pretend Gr. K, 227
Like a Bird Gr. 6, 167
Listen to the Water Gr. 2, 294
*Little Birdie* Gr. 4, 75
Looking for the Mother Birds
Gr. 3, 331
Los pececitos Gr. 1, 178
Los pollitos Gr. K, 166
*Lyric Pieces, Op. 43, No. 4, "Little Bird"* Gr. 1, 346
Mary Ann Gr. K, 253
Mary Wore Her Red Dress Gr. K, 74
Morning Has Broken Gr. 5, 28
New Hungarian Folk Song
Gr. 6, 196
Noah's Shanty Gr. 1, 342
Nruab hnub thiab hmo ntuj (story)
Gr. 4, 366
Ochimbo Gr. 4, 134
Over in the Meadow Gr. 1, 346
Owl and the Pumpkin, The
Gr. 2, 377
Party Tonight! Gr. 2, 152
Pavo, pavo Gr. 1, 416
Ptashky u babusi sadochku
Gr. 1, 192
Rockin' Robin Gr. 3, 368
Sarika keo Gr. 3, 275
Shoo, Turkey Gr. 1, 104
Sky, Sea, Shore (poem) Gr. 2, 343
Song of the Eagle Gr. 2, 248
Spring! Spring! (poem) Gr. 1, 419
T'hola, t'hola Gr. 4, 132
There Was an Old Man (speech piece) Gr. 3, 191
Tie Me Kangaroo Down, Sport
Gr. 4, 37
*Toy Symphony, Movement 4*
Gr. 1, 111
Tree in the Wood, The Gr. 2, 360
'Ulili E Gr. 5, 441
Un pajarito Gr. 2, 16
We Are Dear Little Birdies
Gr. K, 176
We've Got Lots in Common
Gr. 3, 366
What Do Animals Need? Gr. 2, 288
World We Love, The Gr. 3, 342

### DINOSAURS AND FOSSILS

*Carnival of the Animals, "Fossils"*
Gr. 4, 220
Dinosaur Dance Gr. 2, 168
Dry Bones Come Skipping
Gr. 4, 218
Gotta Find a Footprint (poem)
Gr. 4, 221

### FARM/RANCH

*Baa-Baa Black Sheep* Gr. K, 102
Baby Chick (poem) Gr. K, 167
Bee, Bee Bumblebee (speech piece)
Gr. 1, 50
Cantando mentiras Gr. 4, 146
Cat's Menu (poem) Gr. 2, 301
Cattle Call Gr. 5, 344
Chicken on the Fence Post Gr. 3, 92
Chickens, The (poem) Gr. 3, 92
Cow, The (poem) Gr. 4, 273
Cow's Woc Backward Gr. 1, 390
Dancing Pig, The (folk tale)
Gr. 1, 196
Der sad to katte Gr. 2, 300
Don't You Hear the Lambs?
Gr. 5, 97
*Don't You Hear the Lambs?*
Gr. 5, 99
Down by the Bay Gr. 1, 18
Down in the Meadow Gr. K, 147
Ducks in the Rain (poem) Gr. K, 235
El burrito enfermo Gr. K, 271
El gallo pinto Gr. 3, 86
*Everything Grows* Gr. K, 267
*Farmer in the Dell* Gr. K, 233
Farmer in the Dell, The Gr. K, 232
Four Horses, The (poem) Gr. 1, 159
Giddy Up (rhyme) Gr. K, 137
*Harukoma, "Spring Horse Dance"*
Gr. 1, 145
Hey, Diddle, Diddle Gr. K, 246
Hi Heidi Ho Gr. 1, 394
Hickory, Dickory, Dare (speech piece) Gr. K, 20
Higglety, Pigglety, Pop! Gr. K, 22
His Wife Said… (poem) Gr. 1, 343
Hop Up, My Ladies Gr. 3, 142
I Bought Me a Cat Gr. 2, 308
I Know an Old Lady Gr. 1, 388
I'm a Very Fine Turkey Gr. K, 310
Juba Gr. K, 13
Jump or Jiggle (poem) Gr. 2, 26
Kum bachur atzel Gr. 3, 138
Last Night I Dreamed of Chickens (poem) Gr. 1, 141
*Little Red Hen, The* Gr. 1, 254
Little Red Hen, The (story)
Gr. 1, 256
Long Way Home, A Gr. 1, 382
*Los pollitos* Gr. K, 166
Luna lunera (speech piece) Gr. K, 90
Mama, Buy Me a Chiney Doll
Gr. K, 120
Mister Rabbit Gr. K, 128
Mister Ram Goat-O Gr. 3, 54
My Pony, Macaroni Gr. 1, 158
Nanny Goat Gr. K, 161

*Noah's Zoo in the Big, Big Rain*
Gr. K, 274
O ma washi Gr. K, 13
Old Mother Goose (poem)
Gr. K, 247
On a Log, Mister Frog Gr. K, 148
*Pictures at an Exhibition, "Ballet of the Unhatched Chicks"*
Gr. K, 167
"Quack!" Said the Billy Goat (poem)
Gr. K, 233
Railroad Corral Gr. 3, 174
Shanghai Chicken Gr. 1, 140
Sheep in the Meadow (rhyme)
Gr. 1, 17
Sheep, Sheep (poem) Gr. 1, 309
Shepherd, The (poem) Gr. 5, 98
Six Little Ducks Gr. K, 234
Squirrel, The (poem) Gr. K, 129
*Three Little Piggies* Gr. K, 56
Tracks (poem) Gr. K, 299
Voice Choice Gr. K, 27
We've Got Lots in Common
Gr. 3, 366
What Do Animals Need? Gr. 2, 288
*Wild Horseman, The* Gr. 1, 159
World We Love, The Gr. 3, 342
Yesh lanu taish Gr. 1, 182

### INSECTS

Ah! Les jolis papillons Gr. 1, 362
Animals Went In One By One, The (poem) Gr. K, 275
Ants Go Marching, The Gr. 1, 248
Bee, Bee Bumblebee (speech piece)
Gr. 1, 50
Bumble Bee (poem) Gr. 1, 385
Bumble Bee, The (speech piece)
Gr. K, 74
Busy Buzzy Bee Gr. K, 77
Butterfly Song (poem) Gr. 1, 363
Caterpillar, The (poem) Gr. K, 103
Counting-Out Rhyme (speech piece)
Gr. 1, 357
Down by the Bay Gr. 1, 18
Firefly (poem) Gr. 1, 356
First-ing (poem) Gr. 1, 375
Flies (poem) Gr. 2, 201
Fly and the Bumblebee, The
Gr. 1, 384
Fuzzy Caterpillar Gr. K, 102
Grasshoppers (poem) Gr. 3, 35
Hi Heidi Ho Gr. 1, 394
Honeybee Song, The Gr. 1, 358
Hotaru koi Gr. 1, 356
Hurt No Living Thing (poem)
Gr. 4, 32
I Know an Old Lady Gr. 1, 388
I'm Curious Gr. K, 276
Jig Along Home Gr. 2, 366
Johnny Caught a Flea Gr. 1, 226
Jump or Jiggle (poem) Gr. 2, 26
Little Black Bug Gr. 1, 214
Lots of Worms Gr. 2, 310

Lyric Pieces, Op. 43, No. 1,
   "Butterfly" Gr. 1, 363
Mariposita Gr. 2, 156
Nightdance (poem) Gr. K, 219
Nitty Gritty Sand Song (poem)
   Gr. K, 191
Noah's Shanty Gr. 1, 342
Over in the Meadow Gr. 1, 346
Riquir rán Gr. 4, 66
Shoo, Fly Gr. 2, 200
Sugar "Shuga" Bee Gr. K, 64
Summer Jazz (poem) Gr. 1, 175
Tree in the Wood, The Gr. 2, 360
Weevily Wheat Gr. 4, 105
What Do You Suppose? (poem)
   Gr. K, 265

## PETS

But the Cat Came Back Gr. 2, 190
Cantando mentiras Gr. 4, 146
Cat (poem) Gr. K, 13
Cat's Tongue (poem) Gr. 2, 190
Cats (excerpt) (poem) Gr. 3, 15
Chums (poem) Gr. 1, 290
Cirmos cica Gr. 1, 130
Dogs (poem) Gr. K, 123
Don Gato Gr. 3, 352
Ee jer ha ba go Gr. K, 133
Farmer in the Dell Gr. K, 233
Farmer in the Dell, The Gr. K, 232
Hey, Bug! (poem) Gr. 1, 215
Hey, Diddle, Diddle Gr. K, 246
Higglety, Pigglety, Pop! Gr. K, 22
Hound Dog Gr. 5, 212
I Have a Dog Gr. K, 262
L'Enfant et les sortilèges, "Love
   for Two Cats" Gr. K, 101
Lap Time (poem) Gr. K, 101
Leak kanseng Gr. 1, 156
Let's Pretend Gr. K, 227
Min (poem) Gr. K, 263
Noah's Zoo in the Big, Big Rain
   Gr. K, 274
Old Blue Gr. K, 122
Old Mother Hubbard (rhyme)
   Gr. 1, 118
Over in the Meadow Gr. 1, 346
Perná, perná, i mélissá Gr. K, 264
Puppy Love Gr. K, 262
Quartetto buffo di gatti, "Comic
   Quartet for Cats" Gr. 1, 131
Rags Gr. 1, 290
Scrub Brush Shuffle, The Gr. 1, 118
Sounds of the Circus Gr. K, 241
Tracks (poem) Gr. K, 299
Up and Down Kitten, The (poem)
   Gr. K, 100
What Do Animals Need? Gr. 2, 288
What to Do (poem) Gr. K, 43

## SNAILS, SPIDERS, AND WORMS

Animals Went In One By One, The
   (poem) Gr. K, 275
Disco Worm Gr. 2, 312
Eensy Weensy Spider Gr. K, 187
El caracol Gr. K, 130
Hurt No Living Thing (poem)
   Gr. 4, 32
Jig Along Home Gr. 2, 366
Jump or Jiggle (poem) Gr. 2, 26
Little Miss Muffet (speech piece)
   Gr. K, 92
Little Snail (poem) Gr. K, 131
Little Spider Gr. K, 93
Lots of Worms Gr. 2, 310
Over in the Meadow Gr. 1, 346
Snail, Snail Gr. 1, 190
Snail, Snail (poem) Gr. 1, 191
Spider's Web Gr. K, 93
Un elefante Gr. 2, 160
What Do Animals Need? Gr. 2, 288
Worm, The (poem) Gr. 2, 311

## WATER ANIMALS

Baby Beluga Gr. K, 272
Blow, Ye Winds Gr. 4, 255
Carnival of the Animals,
   "Aquarium" Gr. 5, 376
Crab Dance (poem) Gr. 2, 307
Crawfish! Gr. 2, 86
Deau-deau, ti pitit maman
   Gr. 2, 306
Doing the Penguin Gr. K, 35
El carite Gr. 5, 305
Farewell to Tarwathie Gr. 6, 43
Fish (poem) Gr. 1, 177
Fishes of Kempenfelt Bay, The
   (poem) Gr. 1, 19
From Sea to Shining Sea
   Gr. 2, 342
George and Gracie Gr. 1, 69
Greenland Whale Fishery, The
   Gr. 5, 230
Hi Heidi Ho Gr. 1, 394
Jellyfish Walk (poem) Gr. 1, 33
Jig Along Home Gr. 2, 366
Kelo aba w'ye Gr. 6, 290
Let's Pretend Gr. K, 227
Los pececitos Gr. 1, 178
Los pescaditos (poem) Gr. 1, 69
Noah's Shanty Gr. 1, 342
One, Two, Three, Four, Five
   (rhyme) Gr. 1, 67
Rio Grande Gr. 4, 256
Sea Wolf, The (poem) Gr. 4, 257
Shanghai Chicken Gr. 1, 140
Song of the Fishes Gr. 3, 244
Under the Sea Gr. 5, 372
Vamos a la mar Gr. 3, 226
What Do Animals Need? Gr. 2, 288
Zomo the Rabbit (story) Gr. 3, 364

## WILD (DESERT, FOREST, AND JUNGLE)

Adventures of Isabel, The (poem)
   Gr. 3, 173
Animals Went In One By One, The
   (poem) Gr. K, 275
Bat, The (poem) Gr. 2, 302
Bear Dance Gr. 7, C-5
Bear Dance Gr. K, 127
Bear Dance Song Gr. K, 127
Bury Me Not on the Lone Prairie
   Gr. 6, 19
Carnival of the Animals, "Royal
   March of the Lion" Gr. 3, 357
Carnival of the Animals, "The
   Elephant" Gr. K, 45
Chang Gr. 1, 156
Chawe chidyo chem'chero (story)
   Gr. 2, 296
Cumberland Gap Gr. 4, 138
Dancing Pig, The (folk tale)
   Gr. 1, 196
Deux cocodries Gr. 2, 364
Eletelephony (poem) Gr. 2, 161
Farmer in the Dell Gr. K, 233
Farmer in the Dell, The Gr. K, 232
Goldilocks and the Three Bears
   Gr. K, 49
Grizzly Bear Gr. K, 33
Groundhog Blues, The Gr. 3, 122
Groundhog Jig, The Gr. 1, 436
Hi Heidi Ho Gr. 1, 394
Hippopotamus Song, The
   Gr. 3, 33
His Wife Said... (poem) Gr. 1, 343
Home on the Range Gr. 5, 69
How Much Wood Could a
   Woodchuck Chuck (speech piece)
   Gr. 3, 120
If a Tiger Calls Gr. 3, 354
Jig Along Home Gr. 2, 366
Jump or Jiggle (poem) Gr. 2, 26
Kangaroo Song, The Gr. K, 44
Kangaroo, The (poem) Gr. K, 45
Kibungo, Beast of the Forest (story)
   Gr. 2, 352
Kou ri lengay Gr. 2, 217
Kuma san Gr. K, 40
Leatherwing Bat Gr. 2, 303
Lion and the Mouse, The (story)
   Gr. 1, 239
Lion Sleeps Tonight, The Gr. 4, 131
Lion Sleeps Tonight, The Gr. 4, 132
Lion, The (poem) Gr. K, 217
Lions Gr. 1, 238
Little Black Bug Gr. 1, 214
Llama, The (poem) Gr. 5, 152
Mos Mos Gr. 1, 130
Mud Gr. 3, 32
Noah's Shanty Gr. 1, 342
Noah's Zoo in the Big, Big Rain
   Gr. K, 274
Nruab hnub thiab hmo ntuj (story)
   Gr. 4, 366

**(Animals,** continued)

Over in the Meadow Gr. 1, 346
Panther, The (poem) Gr. 3, 354
Party Tonight! Gr. 2, 152
Prayer for Earth (poem) Gr. 4, 350
*Prelude to the Afternoon of a
Faun* Gr. 5, 113
Rabbit Dance, The (story) Gr. 3, 334
Rabbit Footprints Gr. 2, 304
Rabbit Skip, The (poem) Gr. 2, 305
Rabbits (poem) Gr. 2, 305
Rolling Rice Cake, The: A Story
from Japan (folk tale) Gr. 1, 91
Rondo for Lunch, A (speech piece)
Gr. 3, 212
Sh'ney dubim Gr. K, 268
Sheep, Sheep (poem) Gr. 1, 309
*Shika no Tone* Gr. 5, 112
Sky, Sea, Shore (poem) Gr. 2, 343
*Sounds of the Circus* Gr. K, 241
Squirrel, The (poem) Gr. K, 129
T'hola, t'hola Gr. 4, 132
Tie Me Kangaroo Down, Sport
Gr. 4, 37
Un elefante Gr. 2, 160
Usagi Gr. 1, 396
Voice Choice Gr. K, 27
Waltzing with Bears Gr. 3, 170
What Do Animals Need? Gr. 2, 288
Why the Warthog Goes About on
His Knees (story) Gr. 1, 139
*Wild Bull* Gr. 6, 366
Woodland Chorus Gr. K, 250
Zomo the Rabbit (story) Gr. 3, 364

**C**

**CALENDARS** *See also Days of the
Week; Seasons.*
Aguinaldo Gr. 3, 402
Almost Day Gr. 3, 397
Birthday, Birthday, Birthday (poem)
Gr. K, 306
Birthday Cake Gr. K, 307
Chag purim Gr. 1, 438
Chanukah, Chanukah Gr. 1, 420
Chanukah Games Gr. 3, 389
Chanukah Is Here! Gr. 2, 382
Chanukiyah li yesh Gr. 1, 421
Chrismus a Come Gr. 3, 396
*Dreydl Song, The* Gr. 3, 391
El día de mamita Gr. K, 325
Feliz Navidad Gr. 7, I-28
Fourth of July Night (poem) Gr. 1, 444
*Frosty, the Snowman* Gr. 2, 391
*Groundhog Jig, The* Gr. 1, 436
Habari Gani Gr. 3, 404
Halloween Is a Very Unusual Night
Gr. 3, 382
Happy Birthday! (poem) Gr. K, 306
Haru ga kita Gr. 2, 401
Hevenu shalom aleichem Gr. 3, 378
I Saw Three Ships Gr. 1, 426

Ichi-gatsu tsuitachi Gr. 3, 406
It's Santa—Again! Gr. 2, 385
Jingle Bells Gr. 2, 388
Jolly Old St. Nicholas Gr. K, 316
Kid Like Me, A (speech piece)
Gr. 2, 394
King, Martin Luther Jr. Gr. 1, 434
Kwanzaa (poem) Gr. 1, 431
Kwanzaa Carol, A Gr. 2, 392
L'inverno è passato Gr. 2, 400
La piñata Gr. 3, 399
*Las mañanitas* Gr. K, 325
Little and Lots Gr. K, 323
Making Valentines Gr. 1, 437
Mary Came a-Running Gr. K, 294
Must Be Santa Gr. K, 318
My Valentine Gr. K, 323
Ner li Gr. 2, 383
No quiero plata Gr. 1, 424
Oh, What a Day! Gr. K, 302
On Mother's Day (poem) Gr. 1, 443
Over the River and Through the Wood
Gr. 3, 384
Pumpkin Picking (poem) Gr. 2, 376
Rudolph, the Red-Nosed Reindeer
Gr. 1, 428
Run, Molly, Run Gr. 1, 8
Setting the Thanksgiving Table (poem)
Gr. 2, 381
Si me dan pasteles Gr. 1, 432
Sing About Martin Gr. K, 321
*Sister Rosa* Gr. 3, 411
Skin and Bones Gr. 2, 376
Spring (poem) Gr. 2, 400
Thanksgiving Is Near Gr. 2, 380
Together in Unity Gr. K, 320
Ujima Gr. 1, 430
Valentine Feelings (poem) Gr. K, 322
Valentines Gr. 2, 398
Valentines (poem) Gr. 2, 398

**CHANGE AND ADAPTATION**
Baby Chick (poem) Gr. K, 167
Caterpillar, The (poem) Gr. 2, 157
Caterpillar, The (poem) Gr. K, 103
Changing (poem) Gr. K, 199
Chawe chidyo chem'chero (story)
Gr. 2, 296
End, The (poem) Gr. 1, 408
*Everything Grows* Gr. K, 267
*Fatou yo, "I am Fatou"* Gr. K, 155
First-ing (poem) Gr. 1, 375
Frog Lullaby (poem) Gr. K, 149
*Frosty, the Snowman* Gr. 2, 391
Fuzzy Caterpillar Gr. K, 102
Grasshoppers (poem) Gr. 3, 35
Growing Corn (poem) Gr. 1, 297
Haru ga kita Gr. 2, 401
How the Kiwi Lost Its Wings (story)
Gr. 1, 78
In the Pumpkin Patch Gr. 3, 380
Khorovod Gr. 1, 372
King, Martin Luther Jr. Gr. 1, 434

Kwanzaa (poem) Gr. 1, 431
L'inverno è passato Gr. 2, 400
Leatherwing Bat Gr. 2, 303
Little Red Hen, The (story) Gr. 1, 256
*Los pollitos* Gr. K, 166
Mariposita Gr. 2, 156
Puff, the Magic Dragon Gr. 2, 350
Pumpkin Poem (poem) Gr. 3, 381
Pumpkin, Pumpkin Gr. 1, 413
Rain, The (poem) Gr. 1, 52
River Winding (poem) Gr. 4, 60
Sheep, Sheep (poem) Gr. 1, 309
Someday Very Soon Gr. 1, 376
*Three Little Piggies* Gr. K, 56
Time to Move Gr. 1, 244
Turn, Turn, Turn (To Everything There
Is a Season) Gr. 5, 378
Ujima Gr. 1, 430
We Moved About a Week Ago (poem)
Gr. 2, 230
When I Dance (poem) Gr. 1, 327
When I Grow Up (poem) Gr. 2, 397
Zomo the Rabbit (story) Gr. 3, 364

**CHARACTER TRAITS**

**CARING**
A la rurru niño Gr. K, 180
*A-You're Adorable* Gr. 1, 263
Achshav Gr. 2, 64
Adiós, amigos Gr. 6, 57
Aguinaldo Gr. 3, 402
All Around the Buttercup
Gr. 2, 170
All Around the Country Gr. 1, 446
All the Way Around the World
Gr. 2, 258
All Through the Night Gr. 5, 105
Amefuri Gr. 1, 144
America, I Hear You Singing
Gr. 2, 402
America, the Beautiful Gr. 3, 413
America, the Beautiful Gr. 5, 76
America, the Beautiful Gr. 6, 485
America, the Beautiful Gr. 7, I-4
And My Heart Soars (poem)
Gr. 2, 240
At the Same Time Gr. 6, 115
¡Ay, Jalisco no te rajes! Gr. 7, I-6
Ayelivi Gr. 2, 70
Ayliluli, num tsipor Gr. 1, 204
*Bai, bai, bai, bai* Gr. 2, 197
Banana Splits Gr. 1, 318
Bassett, Rick (Part 1) Gr. 3, 222
Bassett, Rick (Part 2) Gr. 3, 223
Beach Rap (speech piece)
Gr. 1, 352
*Beautiful* Gr. 3, 67
Big Beautiful Planet Gr. 3, 326
Bling Blang Gr. 3, 240
Blowin' in the Wind Gr. 5, 382
*Blowin' in the Wind* Gr. 5, 384
Bonjour, mes amis Gr. 1, 316
Bridges Gr. 6, 86

Cantaré, cantarás  Gr. 6, 413
Celebration (poem)  Gr. 6, 122
Children Learn What They Live
    (poem)  Gr. 5, 381
Chums (poem)  Gr. 1, 290
Common Ground  Gr. 3, 379
Dance for the Nations  Gr. 6, 122
Dancing Pig, The (folk tale)
    Gr. 1, 196
De colores  Gr. 8, I-14
Don Giovanni  Gr. 8,
Don't Dump Trash  Gr. 2, 318
Drum, A (folk tale)  Gr. 1, 116
Duérmete, mi niño  Gr. 1, 292
Earth Is My Mother, The  Gr. 1, 340
Éliza Kongo  Gr. 5, 14
Ev'rybody Ought to Know
    Gr. 1, 434
Fais dodo  Gr. K, 158
Feliz Navidad  Gr. 7, I-28
Flowering Umbrellas (poem)
    Gr. 1, 145
Friend of Mine  Gr. 1, 310
Funwa alafia  Gr. 5, 32
Gift to Share, A  Gr. 6, 393
Give a Little Love  Gr. 6, 140
Glad to Have a Friend Like You
    Gr. 2, 228
Gonna Have a Good Time  Gr. 2, 4
Guantanamera  Gr. 8, I-32
Gypsy in the Moonlight  Gr. 3, 12
Habari Gani  Gr. 3, 404
Happy Birthday! (poem)  Gr. K, 306
Harambee  Gr. 4, 434
Hato popo  Gr. 1, 186
He's Got the Whole World in His
    Hands  Gr. 3, 230
Hearts Like Doors (poem)
    Gr. K, 189
Hello to All the Children of the
    World  Gr. 3, 4
Hello to the World (poem)  Gr. 3, 2
Hevenu shalom aleichem  Gr. 3, 378
Hey, Bug! (poem)  Gr. 1, 215
Hine mah tov  Gr. 5, 430
Hotaru koi  Gr. 1, 356
How the Kiwi Lost Its Wings (story)
    Gr. 1, 78
How to Be a Friend (poem)
    Gr. 1, 331
Howjidoo  Gr. 1, 315
Hui jia qù  Gr. 2, 158
I Am But a Small Voice  Gr. 6, 446
I Like You (poem)  Gr. 6, 7
I See the Moon  Gr. 2, 58
I See With My Hands  Gr. 2, 148
I'm Glad (poem)  Gr. 1, 415
I'm on My Way  Gr. 3, 76
I'm Thankful  Gr. 1, 414
Ichi-gatsu tsuitachi  Gr. 3, 406
If I Had a Hammer  Gr. 3, 241
If You Find a Little Feather (poem)
    Gr. 1, 187

It's a Beautiful Day  Gr. 3, 338
It's a Celebration!  Gr. 2, 372
It's a Small World  Gr. 3, 268
Joy of Kwanzaa, The  Gr. 6, 462
Kébé mama  Gr. 1, 442
Keep Your Eyes on the Prize
    Gr. 3, 408
Keep Your Eyes on the Prize
    Gr. 8, E-16
Khorovod  Gr. 1, 372
Kibungo, Beast of the Forest (story)
    Gr. 2, 352
Kid Like Me, A (speech piece)
    Gr. 2, 394
King, Martin Luther Jr.  Gr. 1, 434
Kwanzaa Carol, A  Gr. 2, 392
La tormenta tropical  Gr. 2, 116
Lean on Me  Gr. 6, 14
Let the Music Begin!  Gr. 1, 2
Let's Celebrate!  Gr. 3, 374
Li'l Liza Jane  Gr. 3, 140
Light Up the World  Gr. 2, 196
Lion and the Mouse, The (story)
    Gr. 1, 239
Little and Lots  Gr. K, 323
Little Johnny Brown  Gr. 3, 313
Little Red Hen, The  Gr. 1, 254
Little Red Hen, The (story)
    Gr. 1, 256
Lo yisa  Gr. 6, 130
Look Out Below!  Gr. 2, 370
Look Out for Mother Earth
    Gr. 3, 341
Love Can Build a Bridge  Gr. 4, 324
Love in Any Language  Gr. 6, 476
Love Is (poem)  Gr. K, 180
Love Is on Our Side  Gr. 5, 324
Lullaby (poem)  Gr. 1, 205
Lullaby (poem)  Gr. 1, 208
Make New Friends  Gr. 3, 36
Marines' Hymn, The  Gr. 8, C-39
Michael, Row the Boat Ashore
    Gr. 2, 18
Mubärak  Gr. 3, 282
My Father's House  Gr. 2, 25
My Legs and I (poem)  Gr. 1, 9
My People (poem)  Gr. 1, 233
My Valentine  Gr. K, 323
Nampaya omame  Gr. 1, 138
Naranja dulce  Gr. 2, 97
Niño querido  Gr. 1, 308
Nu wahtan  Gr. 1, 279
Ode to Joy (Come and Sing)
    Gr. 4, 152
Ode to la piñata (poem)  Gr. 1, 424
Old Mother Hubbard (rhyme)
    Gr. 1, 118
On Mother's Day (poem)  Gr. 1, 443
On This Day (poem)  Gr. 3, 69
One Small Step  Gr. 5, 126
Our Family Comes from 'Round the
    World (poem)  Gr. 1, 299

Over the River and Through the
    Wood  Gr. 3, 384
Peace Like a River  Gr. 3, 246
Peace Like a River  Gr. 6, 190
Pin Pon  Gr. 1, 146
Plant Four Seeds  Gr. 2, 130
Pretty Saro  Gr. 3, 216
Pumpkin, Pumpkin  Gr. 1, 413
Pust' 'vsegda budet sonse
    Gr. 3, 278
Put a Little Love in Your Heart
    Gr. 4, 6
Put a Little Love in Your Heart
    Gr. 4, 8
Put Your Hand in My Hand
    Gr. 1, 330
Rabbit Footprints  Gr. 2, 304
Rags  Gr. 1, 290
Rise and Shine  Gr. 1, 122
Roddy McCaulay  Gr. 3, 292
Rolling Rice Cake, The: A Story
    from Japan (folk tale)  Gr. 1, 91
Rudolph, the Red-Nosed Reindeer
    Gr. 1, 428
Scrub Brush Shuffle, The  Gr. 1, 118
Sharing  Gr. K, 198
Shed a Little Light  Gr. 3, 409
Shenandoah  Gr. 2, 62
Shine, Shine, Shine  Gr. 1, 42
Shir l'shalom  Gr. 4, 419
Sidewalks (poem)  Gr. 1, 311
Since Hanna Moved Away (poem)
    Gr. 1, 335
Sing a Song of Peace  Gr. 6, 66
Sing About Martin  Gr. K, 321
Sing, America, Sing!  Gr. 3, 238
Sing! Speak! Whisper! Shout!
    Gr. 1, 36
Sleep, Baby, Sleep  Gr. 2, 197
So Many Children (poem)
    Gr. 1, 333
Somewhere Out There  Gr. 5, 368
Somewhere Out There  Gr. 5, 369
Song of the Night, The (poem)
    Gr. 3, 346
St. Patrick Was a Gentleman
    Gr. 3, 290
Stand By Me  Gr. 5, 46
Stand By Me  Gr. 5, 49
Star-Spangled Banner, The
    Gr. 7, I-56
Starlight, Star Bright  Gr. 4, 373
Still, Still, Still  Gr. 5, 468
Swoboda, Deanna  Gr. 3, 188
Symphony No. 9 in D Minor, Op.
    125, "Ode to Joy," Movement 4
    Gr. 4, 151
Tender Shepherd (Count Your
    Sheep)  Gr. 3, 116
This Land Is Your Land  Gr. 7, I-66
This Little Light of Mine
    Gr. 2, 241
Those Magic Changes  Gr. 8, E-30

**(Character Traits, continued)**

Three Little Birds  Gr. 4, 320
Thula, thula, ngoana  Gr. 4, 227
Time to Sing  Gr. 2, 8
Together (poem)  Gr. 3, 147
Together in Unity  Gr. K, 320
Train Is A-Comin'  Gr. 3, 48
*Traveling Shoes*  Gr. 3, 248
*Two Heads Are Better Than One*
  Gr. 1, 333
Tzena, tzena  Gr. 5, 298
Ujima  Gr. 1, 430
Un elefante  Gr. 2, 160
Valentine Feelings (poem)
  Gr. K, 322
Valentine for Earth, A (poem)
  Gr. 3, 324
Walk Together, Children  Gr. 3, 146
We Moved About a Week Ago
  (poem)  Gr. 2, 230
We've Got Lots in Common
  Gr. 3, 366
What a Wonderful World  Gr. 6, 62
What Do Animals Need?  Gr. 2, 288
What Do We Plant? (poem)
  Gr. 2, 130
When the Saints Go Marching In
  Gr. 2, 178
World We Love, The  Gr. 3, 342
*Yankee Doodle Boy, The*
  Gr. 3, 265
Yellow Rose of Texas, The
  Gr. 7, I-70
Yonder Come Day  Gr. 8, I-68
*You're a Grand Old Flag*
  Gr. 1, 276
You're a Grand Old Flag  Gr. 3, 264
You've Got a Friend  Gr. 5, 366
Your Friends Shall Be the Tall Wind
  Gr. 6, 201

## COURAGE

Adventures of Isabel, The (poem)
  Gr. 3, 173
America  Gr. K, 326
America  Gr. 1, 446
America  Gr. 2, 403
America  Gr. 3, 412
America  Gr. 4, 440
America  Gr. 5, 486
America  Gr. 6, 484
America  Gr. 7, I-2
America  Gr. 8, I-2
*Aweigh, Santy Ano*  Gr. 1, 338
Back of the Bus  Gr. 3, 410
Battle Cry of Freedom  Gr. 5, 272
Battle Hymn of the Republic
  Gr. 5, 274
Caterpillar, The (poem)  Gr. 2, 157
Chawe chidyo chem'chero (story)
  Gr. 2, 296
Dancing Pig, The (folk tale)
  Gr. 1, 196
Different Beat, A  Gr. 1, 6

*Finlandia*  Gr. 6, 78
Halloween Is a Very Unusual Night
  Gr. 3, 382
How the Kiwi Lost Its Wings (story)
  Gr. 1, 78
I Vow to You, My Country
  Gr. 5, 418
I'm on My Way  Gr. 3, 76
*If I Had a Hammer*  Gr. 3, 241
Keep Your Eyes on the Prize
  Gr. 3, 408
Keep Your Eyes on the Prize
  Gr. 8, E-16
Kibungo, Beast of the Forest (story)
  Gr. 2, 352
Kid Like Me, A (speech piece)
  Gr. 2, 394
La tormenta tropical  Gr. 2, 116
Lift Ev'ry Voice and Sing  Gr. 5, 482
Lift Ev'ry Voice and Sing  Gr. 5, 482
*Light Up the World*  Gr. 2, 196
Lion and the Mouse, The (story)
  Gr. 1, 239
Lone Star Trail  Gr. 2, 21
Marines' Hymn, The  Gr. 8, C-39
Mother to Son (poem)  Gr. 2, 203
Over There  Gr. 5, 279
*Roddy McCaulay*  Gr. 3, 292
Rudolph, the Red-Nosed Reindeer
  Gr. 1, 428
*Sister Rosa*  Gr. 3, 411
Song of Greatness, A (poem)
  Gr. 3, 335
St. Patrick Was a Gentleman
  Gr. 3, 290
Star-Spangled Banner, The
  Gr. 3, 415
Star-Spangled Banner, The
  Gr. 4, 441
Star-Spangled Banner, The
  Gr. 5, 488
Star-Spangled Banner, The
  Gr. 6, 486
Star-Spangled Banner, The
  Gr. 7, I-56
Supercalifragilisticexpialidocious
  Gr. 3, 7
To'ia mai te waka  Gr. 1, 77
Trouble Is a Mountain  Gr. 2, 202
Voices of Pride, The  Gr. 5, 86
We Moved About a Week Ago
  (poem)  Gr. 2, 230
When I'm an Astronaut (poem)
  Gr. 1, 402
*When Johnny Comes Marching
  Home*  Gr. 5, 88
When Johnny Comes Marching
  Home  Gr. 5, 180
*You're a Grand Old Flag*
  Gr. 1, 276
You're a Grand Old Flag  Gr. 3, 264
Zomo the Rabbit (story)  Gr. 3, 364

## INTEGRITY

*Amazing Grace*  Gr. 4, 161
Amazing Grace  Gr. 4, 160
*Amazing Grace*  Gr. 5, 259
America  Gr. 7, I-2
Beach Rap (speech piece)  Gr. 1, 352
*Changed My Name*  Gr. 6, 338
Children Learn What They Live
  (poem)  Gr. 5, 381
Dancing Pig, The (folk tale)
  Gr. 1, 196
Don Giovanni  Gr. 8,
Drum, A (folk tale)  Gr. 1, 116
Earth Is My Mother, The  Gr. 1, 340
*Ev'rybody Ought to Know*
  Gr. 1, 434
*Frostiana (from Stopping by
  Woods on a Snowy Evening)*
  Gr. 6, 40
Go, My Son  Gr. 6, 188
Habari Gani  Gr. 3, 404
Heri za Kwanzaa  Gr. 5, 476
How the Kiwi Lost Its Wings (story)
  Gr. 1, 78
How to Be a Friend (poem)
  Gr. 1, 331
I'm Thankful  Gr. 1, 414
If a Tiger Calls  Gr. 3, 354
*If I Had a Hammer*  Gr. 3, 241
If I Had a Hammer  Gr. 5, 287
It's Time  Gr. 6, 274
Keep Your Eyes on the Prize
  Gr. 3, 408
Kid Like Me, A (speech piece)
  Gr. 2, 394
Lion and the Mouse, The (story)
  Gr. 1, 239
Long Way Home, A  Gr. 1, 382
My Father's House  Gr. 2, 25
Naranja dulce  Gr. 2, 97
On My Way  Gr. 6, 313
Put Your Hand in My Hand
  Gr. 1, 330
Rolling Rice Cake, The: A Story
  from Japan (folk tale)  Gr. 1, 91
Shoo, Turkey  Gr. 1, 104
Si me dan pasteles  Gr. 1, 432
Simple Gifts  Gr. 8, A-17
Siyahamba  Gr. 6, 212
Song of Greatness, A (poem)
  Gr. 3, 335
Stopping by Woods on a Snowy
  Evening  Gr. 6, 41
This Little Light of Mine  Gr. 6, 232
*Two Heads Are Better Than One*
  Gr. 1, 333
Ujima  Gr. 1, 430
United Nations on the March, The
  Gr. 6, 443
When the Train Comes Along
  Gr. 1, 300
You're a Grand Old Flag  Gr. 3, 264

Your Friends Shall Be the Tall Wind
   Gr. 6, 201
Your Life Is Now  Gr. 6, 4

## PERSEVERANCE

Alle meine Entchen  Gr. 1, 98
Artsa alinu  Gr. 3, 285
Back of the Bus  Gr. 3, 410
Bassett, Rick (Part 1)  Gr. 3, 222
Bassett, Rick (Part 2)  Gr. 3, 223
Battle Cry of Freedom  Gr. 5, 272
*Beautiful*  Gr. 3, 67
Brush Your Teeth  Gr. 1, 284
Burke, Liam  Gr. 2, 11
Burrough, Roslyn  Gr. 1, 163
But the Cat Came Back  Gr. 2, 190
Chawe chidyo chem'chero (story)
   Gr. 2, 296
Children of Long Ago (poem)
   Gr. 1, 31
Children of the Sun (poem)
   Gr. 1, 404
Come and Go with Me to That
   Land  Gr. 5, 390
Dancing Pig, The (folk tale)
   Gr. 1, 196
Different Beat, A  Gr. 1, 6
Drum, A (folk tale)  Gr. 1, 116
End, The (poem)  Gr. 1, 408
For Children Safe and Strong
   Gr. 5, 484
Free at Last  Gr. 6, 468
Freedom Is Coming  Gr. 5, 415
Get on Your Feet  Gr. 5, 6
*Get on Your Feet*  Gr. 5, 8
Go Down, Moses  Gr. 5, 190
Goin' Down the Road Feelin' Bad
   Gr. 5, 282
*Goin' Down the Road Feelin' Bad*
   Gr. 5, 283
Gonna Have a Good Time  Gr. 2, 4
Goodbye, Julie (Miss Julie Ann
   Johnson)  Gr. 1, 334
Growing Corn (poem)  Gr. 1, 297
Ha'kyo jong  Gr. 2, 135
Heigh-Ho  Gr. 2, 6
Heri za Kwanzaa  Gr. 5, 476
I Believe I Can Fly  Gr. 5, 170
I'm on My Way  Gr. 3, 76
*If You Can Walk*  Gr. 1, 19
Joubert, Joseph  Gr. 3, 50
Keep Your Eyes on the Prize
   Gr. 3, 408
Keep Your Eyes on the Prize
   Gr. 8, E-16
Kibungo, Beast of the Forest (story)
   Gr. 2, 352
Kid Like Me, A (speech piece)
   Gr. 2, 394
La copa de la vida  Gr. 4, 414
La piñata  Gr. 3, 399
La tormenta tropical  Gr. 2, 116
*Light Up the World*  Gr. 2, 196

Lion and the Mouse, The (story)
   Gr. 1, 239
*Little Red Hen, The*  Gr. 1, 254
Little Red Hen, The (story)
   Gr. 1, 256
Lone Star Trail  Gr. 2, 21
Louiselle, Bryan  Gr. 1, 251
Lumberjack, The (poem)  Gr. 1, 113
Moore, Carman  Gr. 3, 163
Mother to Son (poem)  Gr. 2, 203
Mud  Gr. 3, 32
Now Let Me Fly  Gr. 3, 178
Ode to la piñata (poem)  Gr. 1, 424
Oh, Freedom  Gr. 5, 392
*Oh, Freedom and Come and Go
   with Me*  Gr. 5, 394
Over There  Gr. 5, 279
Parade Came Marching, The
   Gr. 1, 166
Paths of Victory  Gr. 6, 195
Rock Around the Clock  Gr. 7, B-18
Rope Rhyme (poem)  Gr. 1, 320
Run! Run! Hide!  Gr. 6, 340
Same Train  Gr. 2, 164
Scrub Brush Shuffle, The  Gr. 1, 118
*Shed a Little Light*  Gr. 3, 409
*Shenandoah*  Gr. 2, 62
Sing Your Story  Gr. 3, 350
Singing-Time (poem)  Gr. 3, 201
*Sister Rosa*  Gr. 3, 411
Star-Spangled Banner, The
   Gr. 3, 415
Star-Spangled Banner, The
   Gr. 7, I-56
Swoboda, Deanna  Gr. 3, 188
This World  Gr. 5, 168
Time to Move  Gr. 1, 244
To'ia mai te waka  Gr. 1, 77
Trouble Is a Mountain  Gr. 2, 202
Voices of Pride, The  Gr. 5, 86
Walk Together, Children  Gr. 3, 146
Waltzing with Bears  Gr. 3, 170
We Shall Not Be Moved  Gr. 4, 437
We Shall Overcome  Gr. 4, 326
*We Shall Overcome*  Gr. 5, 485
Yibane amenu  Gr. 4, 316
Zomo the Rabbit (story)  Gr. 3, 364
Zum gali gali  Gr. 5, 400

## RESPECT

Achshav  Gr. 2, 64
All Around the Country  Gr. 1, 446
All the Way Around the World
   Gr. 2, 258
America  Gr. 2, 403
America  Gr. 3, 412
America  Gr. 7, I-2
America, I Hear You Singing
   Gr. 2, 402
¡Ay, Jalisco no te rajes!  Gr. 7, I-6
Banana Splits  Gr. 1, 318
Beach Rap (speech piece)
   Gr. 1, 352
Big Beautiful Planet  Gr. 3, 326

Brand New Day, A  Gr. 6, 7
*Changed My Name*  Gr. 6, 338
Changing (poem)  Gr. K, 199
Children Learn What They Live
   (poem)  Gr. 5, 381
Children of Long Ago (poem)
   Gr. 1, 31
Dancing Pig, The (folk tale)
   Gr. 1, 196
De colores  Gr. 8, I-14
Don't Dump Trash  Gr. 2, 318
Down by the Riverside  Gr. 8, G-8
Drum, A (folk tale)  Gr. 1, 116
Earth Is My Mother, The  Gr. 1, 340
End, The (poem)  Gr. 1, 408
*Ev'rybody Ought to Know*
   Gr. 1, 434
Everybody Says  Gr. 1, 287
*Everyday People*  Gr. 5, 389
Families  Gr. 1, 282
For Children Safe and Strong
   Gr. 5, 484
Friend of Mine  Gr. 1, 310
From Sea to Shining Sea
   Gr. 2, 342
Glad to Have a Friend Like You
   Gr. 2, 228
God Bless the U.S.A.  Gr. 8, G-37
Growing Corn (poem)  Gr. 1, 297
Ha'kyo jong  Gr. 2, 135
Habari Gani  Gr. 3, 404
Happy Birthday To You (poem)
   Gr. 1, 411
Hashewie  Gr. 4, 63
Hato popo  Gr. 1, 186
Hearts Like Doors (poem)
   Gr. K, 189
Hello to the World (poem)  Gr. 3, 2
Honeybee Song, The  Gr. 1, 358
How the Kiwi Lost Its Wings (story)
   Gr. 1, 78
How to Be a Friend (poem)
   Gr. 1, 331
*Howjidoo*  Gr. 1, 315
I'm Thankful  Gr. 1, 414
Ichi-gatsu tsuitachi  Gr. 3, 406
*If I Had a Hammer*  Gr. 3, 241
Just Me (poem)  Gr. 1, 71
Keep Your Eyes on the Prize
   Gr. 3, 408
Kid Like Me, A (speech piece)
   Gr. 2, 394
King, Martin Luther Jr.  Gr. 1, 434
Kwanzaa Carol, A  Gr. 2, 392
Let the Music Begin!  Gr. 1, 2
*Light Up the World*  Gr. 2, 196
Lion and the Mouse, The (story)
   Gr. 1, 239
Little Johnny Brown  Gr. 3, 313
*Little Red Hen, The*  Gr. 1, 254
Little Red Hen, The (story)
   Gr. 1, 256
Look Out Below!  Gr. 2, 370

(*Character Traits,* continued)

Look Out for Mother Earth
Gr. 3, 341

Looking for the Mother Birds
Gr. 3, 331

Los maizales  Gr. 1, 296

Music (poem)  Gr. 1, 3

My Father's House  Gr. 2, 25

My People (poem)  Gr. 1, 233

Naranja dulce  Gr. 2, 97

Ode to Joy (Come and Sing)
Gr. 4, 152

Oh, Freedom  Gr. 7, G-30

One Small Step  Gr. 5, 126

Our Family Comes from 'Round the
World (poem)  Gr. 1, 299

Over in the Meadow  Gr. 1, 346

Peace Like a River  Gr. 3, 246

Peace Round  Gr. 4, 348

Put Your Hand in My Hand
Gr. 1, 330

Rabbit Dance, The (story)  Gr. 3, 334

Rolling Rice Cake, The: A Story
from Japan (folk tale)  Gr. 1, 91

Rudolph, the Red-Nosed Reindeer
Gr. 1, 428

*Shed a Little Light*  Gr. 3, 409

*Shenandoah*  Gr. 2, 62

Shoo, Turkey  Gr. 1, 104

Si me dan pasteles  Gr. 1, 432

Sing, America, Sing!  Gr. 3, 238

Sing! Speak! Whisper! Shout!
Gr. 1, 36

Sleep, Baby, Sleep  Gr. 2, 197

So Many Children (poem)
Gr. 1, 333

Song of Greatness, A (poem)
Gr. 3, 335

Star-Spangled Banner, The
Gr. 3, 415

Star-Spangled Banner, The
Gr. 7, I-56

*Symphony No. 9 in D Minor, Op.
125, "Ode to Joy," Movement 4*
Gr. 4, 151

This Land Is Your Land  Gr. 7, I-66

Together (poem)  Gr. 3, 147

*Two Heads Are Better Than One*
Gr. 1, 333

Ujima  Gr. 1, 430

Under the Same Sun  Gr. 6, 440

United Nations on the March, The
Gr. 6, 443

Valentine for Earth, A (poem)
Gr. 3, 324

We Shall Overcome  Gr. 4, 326

We've Got Lots in Common
Gr. 3, 366

What Do Animals Need?  Gr. 2, 288

World of Difference, A  Gr. 5, 386

World We Love, The  Gr. 3, 342

Yellow Rose of Texas, The
Gr. 7, I-70

You and I (poem)  Gr. 5, 388

*You're a Grand Old Flag*
Gr. 1, 276

You're a Grand Old Flag  Gr. 3, 264

Your Friends Shall Be the Tall Wind
Gr. 6, 201

**RESPONSIBILITY**

Amefuri  Gr. 1, 144

America, I Hear You Singing
Gr. 2, 402

Artsa alinu  Gr. 3, 285

*Bai, bai, bai, bai*  Gr. 2, 197

Beach Rap (speech piece)
Gr. 1, 352

Beyond Borders  Gr. 5, 292

Big Beautiful Planet  Gr. 3, 326

Bling Blang  Gr. 3, 240

Blowin' in the Wind  Gr. 5, 382

*Blowin' in the Wind*  Gr. 5, 384

Bridges  Gr. 6, 86

Brush Your Teeth  Gr. 1, 284

By Myself (poem)  Gr. 1, 43

Caterpillar, The (poem)  Gr. 2, 157

Cha yang wu  Gr. 1, 90

Children, Go Where I Send Thee
Gr. 3, 392

Children of Long Ago (poem)
Gr. 1, 31

Dancing Pig, The (folk tale)
Gr. 1, 196

Don't Dump Trash  Gr. 2, 318

Drum, A (folk tale)  Gr. 1, 116

Earth Is My Mother, The  Gr. 1, 340

*Ev'rybody Ought to Know*
Gr. 1, 434

Flowering Umbrellas (poem)
Gr. 1, 145

For Children Safe and Strong
Gr. 5, 484

From Sea to Shining Sea
Gr. 2, 342

*Garden of the Earth*  Gr. 5, 399

Good Morning  Gr. 3, 192

Growing Corn (poem)  Gr. 1, 297

Ha'kyo jong  Gr. 2, 135

Habari Gani  Gr. 3, 404

Had to Get Up This Mornin' Soon
Gr. 3, 114

Harambee  Gr. 4, 434

Hato popo  Gr. 1, 186

Heri za Kwanzaa  Gr. 5, 476

How the Kiwi Lost Its Wings (story)
Gr. 1, 78

How to Be a Friend (poem)
Gr. 1, 331

Hui jia qù  Gr. 2, 158

I Am But a Small Voice  Gr. 6, 446

I'm Thankful  Gr. 1, 414

*If I Had a Hammer*  Gr. 3, 241

In the Pumpkin Patch  Gr. 3, 380

Joy of Kwanzaa, The  Gr. 6, 462

Keep Your Eyes on the Prize
Gr. 3, 408

Kid Like Me, A (speech piece)
Gr. 2, 394

Kwanzaa Carol, A  Gr. 2, 392

*Light Up the World*  Gr. 2, 196

Lion and the Mouse, The (story)
Gr. 1, 239

*Little Red Hen, The*  Gr. 1, 254

Little Red Hen, The (story)
Gr. 1, 256

Lone Star Trail  Gr. 2, 21

Long Way Home, A  Gr. 1, 382

Look Out Below!  Gr. 2, 370

Look Out for Mother Earth
Gr. 3, 341

Looking for the Mother Birds
Gr. 3, 331

Los maizales  Gr. 1, 296

Louiselle, Bryan  Gr. 1, 251

Lumberjack, The (poem)  Gr. 1, 113

Michael, Row the Boat Ashore
Gr. 2, 18

Moore, Carman  Gr. 3, 163

Mother to Son (poem)  Gr. 2, 203

Mud  Gr. 3, 32

My Legs and I (poem)  Gr. 1, 9

Now Let Me Fly  Gr. 3, 178

Over in the Meadow  Gr. 1, 346

Parade Came Marching, The
Gr. 1, 166

Peter, Peter, Sugar Eater (poem)
Gr. 1, 284

Pin Pon  Gr. 1, 146

Plant Four Seeds  Gr. 2, 130

Rabbit Footprints  Gr. 2, 304

Railroad Corral  Gr. 3, 174

Rise and Shine  Gr. 1, 122

Rolling Rice Cake, The: A Story
from Japan (folk tale)  Gr. 1, 91

Rudolph, the Red-Nosed Reindeer
Gr. 1, 428

Same Train  Gr. 2, 164

*Scrub-a-dub*  Gr. 1, 306

Serra, serra, serrador  Gr. 1, 112

*Shake Your Brain*  Gr. 1, 250

*Shed a Little Light*  Gr. 3, 409

Shine, Shine, Shine  Gr. 1, 42

Shoo, Turkey  Gr. 1, 104

Si me dan pasteles  Gr. 1, 432

Sing! Speak! Whisper! Shout!
Gr. 1, 36

Six-Inch Boots in a Nine-Inch
Puddle  Gr. 1, 366

Song of Greatness, A (poem)
Gr. 3, 335

Star-Spangled Banner, The
Gr. 7, I-56

Sweet Potatoes  Gr. 3, 228

Swoboda, Deanna  Gr. 3, 188

Tender Shepherd (Count Your
Sheep)  Gr. 3, 116

This Pretty Planet  Gr. 4, 355

This World  Gr. 5, 168

Time to Move  Gr. 1, 244

Thematic Index

To'ia mai te waka  Gr. 1, 77
*Traveling Shoes*  Gr. 3, 248
*Two Heads Are Better Than One*
    Gr. 1, 333
Ujima  Gr. 1, 430
Wake Me, Shake Me  Gr. 1, 278
What Do We Plant? (poem)
    Gr. 2, 130
When the Saints Go Marching In
    Gr. 2, 178
When the Train Comes Along
    Gr. 1, 300
Zomo the Rabbit (story)  Gr. 3, 364

## SELF-DISCIPLINE

America, the Beautiful  Gr. 5, 76
America, the Beautiful  Gr. 6, 485
America, the Beautiful  Gr. 7, I-4
Bassett, Rick (Part 1)  Gr. 3, 222
Bassett, Rick (Part 2)  Gr. 3, 223
Beach Rap (speech piece)
    Gr. 1, 352
*Beautiful*  Gr. 3, 67
Brush Your Teeth  Gr. 1, 284
Burke, Liam  Gr. 2, 11
Burrough, Roslyn  Gr. 1, 163
Children of Long Ago (poem)
    Gr. 1, 31
Dancing Pig, The (folk tale)
    Gr. 1, 196
Drum, A (folk tale)  Gr. 1, 116
Earth Is My Mother, The  Gr. 1, 340
Everybody Says  Gr. 1, 287
For Children Safe and Strong
    Gr. 5, 484
*Frostiana (from Stopping by*
    *Woods on a Snowy Evening)*
    Gr. 6, 40
Get on Your Feet  Gr. 5, 6
*Get on Your Feet*  Gr. 5, 8
Gift to Share, A  Gr. 6, 393
Give a Little Love  Gr. 6, 140
Go, My Son  Gr. 6, 188
Gonna Build a Mountain  Gr. 6, 21
Growing Corn (poem)  Gr. 1, 297
Ha'kyo jong  Gr. 2, 135
Habari Gani  Gr. 3, 404
Had to Get Up This Mornin' Soon
    Gr. 3, 114
Heri za Kwanzaa  Gr. 5, 476
How the Kiwi Lost Its Wings (story)
    Gr. 1, 78
How to Be a Friend (poem)
    Gr. 1, 331
Hui jia qü  Gr. 2, 158
Joy of Kwanzaa, The  Gr. 6, 462
Keep Your Eyes on the Prize
    Gr. 3, 408
Kibungo, Beast of the Forest (story)
    Gr. 2, 352
King, Martin Luther Jr.  Gr. 1, 434
La tormenta tropical  Gr. 2, 116
*Light Up the World*  Gr. 2, 196

Lion and the Mouse, The (story)
    Gr. 1, 239
*Little Red Hen, The*  Gr. 1, 254
Little Red Hen, The (story)
    Gr. 1, 256
Long Way Home, A  Gr. 1, 382
Louiselle, Bryan  Gr. 1, 251
Lumberjack, The (poem)  Gr. 1, 113
Moore, Carman  Gr. 3, 163
Mother to Son (poem)  Gr. 2, 203
My Legs and I (poem)  Gr. 1, 9
Ode to la piñata (poem)  Gr. 1, 424
Over There  Gr. 5, 279
Parade Came Marching, The
    Gr. 1, 166
Paths of Victory  Gr. 6, 195
Peter, Peter, Sugar Eater (poem)
    Gr. 1, 284
Pin Pon  Gr. 1, 146
Railroad Corral  Gr. 3, 174
Rise and Shine  Gr. 1, 122
*Roddy McCaulay*  Gr. 3, 292
*Scrub-a-dub*  Gr. 1, 306
Si me dan pasteles  Gr. 1, 432
Sing! Speak! Whisper! Shout!
    Gr. 1, 36
Singing-Time (poem)  Gr. 3, 201
Six-Inch Boots in a Nine-Inch
    Puddle  Gr. 1, 366
Song of Greatness, A (poem)
    Gr. 3, 335
Stopping by Woods on a Snowy
    Evening  Gr. 6, 41
Sweet Potatoes  Gr. 3, 228
Swoboda, Deanna  Gr. 3, 188
Time to Move  Gr. 1, 244
To'ia mai te waka  Gr. 1, 77
Trouble Is a Mountain  Gr. 2, 202
*Two Heads Are Better Than One*
    Gr. 1, 333
Waitin' for the Light to Shine
    Gr. 4, 26
Waiting (poem)  Gr. 1, 413
Wake Me, Shake Me  Gr. 1, 278
When the Saints Go Marching In
    Gr. 2, 178
When the Train Comes Along
    Gr. 1, 300
Your Life Is Now  Gr. 6, 4

## CITIZENSHIP

America  Gr. K, 326
America  Gr. 1, 446
America  Gr. 2, 403
America  Gr. 3, 412
America  Gr. 4, 440
America  Gr. 5, 486
America  Gr. 6, 484
America  Gr. 7, I-2
America  Gr. 8, I-2
America, I Hear You Singing
    Gr. 2, 402
*America, the Beautiful*  Gr. 3, 413

America, the Beautiful  Gr. 3, 413
America, the Beautiful  Gr. 4, 158
America, the Beautiful  Gr. 5, 76
America, the Beautiful  Gr. 6, 485
America, the Beautiful  Gr. 7, I-4
America, the Beautiful  Gr. 8, I-4
At the Same Time  Gr. 6, 115
Beyond Borders  Gr. 5, 292
Blowin' in the Wind  Gr. 5, 382
*Blowin' in the Wind*  Gr. 5, 384
Celebrating Our Flag (poem)  Gr. K, 327
Celebration (poem)  Gr. 6, 122
Children Learn What They Live (poem)
    Gr. 5, 381
Dance for the Nations  Gr. 6, 122
*Ev'rybody Ought to Know*  Gr. 1, 434
Fifty Nifty United States  Gr. 5, 251
For Children Safe and Strong
    Gr. 5, 484
Give a Little Love  Gr. 6, 140
*I'm a Yankee Doodle Dandy*
    Gr. 5, 278
If I Had a Hammer  Gr. 3, 241
If I Had a Hammer  Gr. 5, 287
Kid Like Me, A (speech piece)
    Gr. 2, 394
King, Martin Luther Jr.  Gr. 1, 434
Let Freedom Ring  Gr. 5, 77
Lo yisa  Gr. 6, 130
Los maizales  Gr. 1, 296
Love Can Build a Bridge  Gr. 4, 324
Ode to Joy (Come and Sing)
    Gr. 4, 152
*Olympic Spirit*  Gr. 6, 350
Put a Little Love in Your Heart  Gr. 4, 6
*Put a Little Love in Your Heart*
    Gr. 4, 8
¡Qué bonita bandera!  Gr. 5, 294
Sing a Song of Peace  Gr. 6, 66
Sing, America, Sing!  Gr. 3, 238
Star-Spangled Banner, The  Gr. 3, 415
Star-Spangled Banner, The  Gr. 4, 441
Star-Spangled Banner, The  Gr. 5, 488
Star-Spangled Banner, The  Gr. 6, 486
Star-Spangled Banner, The  Gr. 7, I-56
Star-Spangled Banner, The  Gr. 8, I-62
Strike Up the Band  Gr. 6, 135
*Symphony No. 9 in D Minor, Op.*
    *125, "Ode to Joy," Movement 4*
    Gr. 4, 151
This Land Is Your Land  Gr. 5, 118
*This Land Is Your Land*  Gr. 5, 120
This Land Is Your Land  Gr. 7, I-66
This Land Is Your Land (refrain only)
    Gr. 1, 274
This World  Gr. 5, 168
*Variations on "America"*  Gr. 6, 162
Viva Jujuy  Gr. 5, 228
Voices of Pride, The  Gr. 5, 86
*Yankee Doodle Boy, The*  Gr. 3, 265
*You're a Grand Old Flag*  Gr. 1, 276
You're a Grand Old Flag  Gr. 3, 264
Zum gali gali  Gr. 5, 400

**CLIMATES** *See also Weather.*
Baby Beluga  Gr. K, 272
Cha yang wu  Gr. 1, 90
*Doing the Penguin*  Gr. K, 35
Falling Rain  Gr. 2, 328
I'm Flying Home  Gr. 2, 286
La borinqueña  Gr. 8, D-19
Summertime  Gr. 6, 250
Take Your Feet Out 'the Sand
    Gr. K, 231

**COLORS**
Beach Rap (speech piece)  Gr. 1, 352
Bird's Nest, The (poem)  Gr. K, 239
Bumble Bee (poem)  Gr. 1, 385
Circle of Sun, A (poem)  Gr. K, 3
Corn Grinding Song  Gr. K, 67
Crayons (poem)  Gr. K, 75
El burrito enfermo  Gr. K, 271
Flowering Umbrellas (poem)  Gr. 1, 145
Fourth of July Night (poem)  Gr. 1, 444
I Was Walking in a Circle (poem)
    Gr. 3, 321
I'm Glad (poem)  Gr. 1, 415
Ida Red  Gr. 3, 30
Leatherwing Bat  Gr. 2, 303
Making Valentines  Gr. 1, 437
Mary Wore Her Red Dress  Gr. K, 74
Merry-Go-Round  Gr. K, 290
Oh, Won't You Sit Down  Gr. 3, 28
Painting Song: A Dribble and a Dot
    Gr. K, 175
Pumpkin Picking (poem)  Gr. 2, 376
Rabbits (poem)  Gr. 2, 305
Rainbow, The  Gr. 2, 332
Seasons  Gr. K, 4
Song of One, A  Gr. 3, 344
Spring! Spring! (poem)  Gr. 1, 419
World We Love, The  Gr. 3, 342

**COUNTING AND
    COMPUTATION**
1, 2, 3, 4 (speech piece)  Gr. K, 15
Ah, eu entrei na roda  Gr. 3, 308
Ants Go Marching, The  Gr. 1, 248
Banana Splits  Gr. 1, 318
Bo-bo-skee, Watten-tatten (speech
    piece)  Gr. 1, 259
Chickens, The (poem)  Gr. 3, 92
Chickety, Chickety, Chop (speech
    piece)  Gr. K, 41
Children, Go Where I Send Thee
    Gr. 3, 392
Circle Round the Zero  Gr. K, 293
Counting Song  Gr. 1, 253
Draw Me a Bucket of Water  Gr. 3, 124
El barquito  Gr. 3, 358
End, The (poem)  Gr. 1, 408
Every Morning at Eight O'Clock
    (rhyme)  Gr. 1, 36
Five Little Chickadees  Gr. K, 179
Five Little Snowmen  Gr. K, 313
Gonna Have a Good Time  Gr. 2, 4
Head, Shoulders, Baby  Gr. 1, 82

Johnny Caught a Flea  Gr. 1, 226
Kaeru no uta  Gr. K, 183
Las estrellas (poem)  Gr. 1, 109
Little and Lots  Gr. K, 323
Little David  Gr. 1, 232
Lumberjack, The (poem)  Gr. 1, 113
Making Valentines  Gr. 1, 437
Noah's Shanty  Gr. 1, 342
Number One, Touch Your Tongue
    (speech piece)  Gr. K, 204
Ode to la piñata (poem)  Gr. 1, 424
One Green Jelly Bean  Gr. K, 287
One, Two, Three, Four, Five (rhyme)
    Gr. 1, 67
Over in the Meadow  Gr. 1, 346
Rinsho, rinsho  Gr. K, 285
Roll Over  Gr. K, 288
Rope Rhyme (poem)  Gr. 1, 320
Serra, serra, serrador  Gr. 1, 112
Shu ha mo  Gr. 3, 276
Six Little Ducks  Gr. K, 234
Son macaron  Gr. 4, 109
Song of One, A  Gr. 3, 344
Ten Little Teddy Bears (poem)
    Gr. K, 301
That's What's New with Me!  Gr. K, 2
This Old Man  Gr. 3, 152
Un, deux, trois  Gr. 2, 198
Un elefante  Gr. 2, 160
Weevily Wheat  Gr. 4, 105

**DAYS OF THE WEEK**
Ahora voy a cantarles  Gr. 3, 56
Los días de la semana  Gr. 1, 268
Mary Came a-Running  Gr. K, 294
Oh, What a Day!  Gr. K, 302

**D**

**DIVERSITY (ALIKE AND
    DIFFERENT)**
Adana ya gidelim  Gr. 2, 142
All Around the Country  Gr. 1, 446
Back of the Bus  Gr. 3, 410
Changing (poem)  Gr. K, 199
*Checkerboard*  Gr. 1, 7
Different Beat, A  Gr. 1, 6
*Everyday People*  Gr. 5, 389
Families  Gr. 1, 282
Four Horses, The (poem)  Gr. 1, 159
Hello to All the Children of the World
    Gr. 3, 4
Hello to the World (poem)  Gr. 3, 2
It's a Celebration!  Gr. 2, 372
Keep Your Eyes on the Prize  Gr. 3, 408
Love in Any Language  Gr. 6, 476
Nightdance (poem)  Gr. K, 219
Our Family Comes from 'Round the
    World (poem)  Gr. 1, 299
*Shed a Little Light*  Gr. 3, 409
*Sister Rosa*  Gr. 3, 411
So Many Children (poem)  Gr. 1, 333
We've Got Lots in Common  Gr. 3, 366
World of Difference, A  Gr. 5, 386

You and I (poem)  Gr. 5, 388
**DRAGONS, GIANTS, AND
    MONSTERS** *See also
    Imagination and Fantasy.*
*Danse macabre*  Gr. 5, 457
Halloween Song  Gr. K, 309
Kibungo  Gr. 2, 354
Kibungo, Beast of the Forest (story)
    Gr. 2, 352
Little Shop of Horrors  Gr. 4, 422
Puff, the Magic Dragon  Gr. 2, 350

**E**

**EARTH, THE** *See also Ecology and
    Natural Resources; Environments.*
And My Heart Soars (poem)  Gr. 4, 359
Big Beautiful Planet  Gr. 3, 326
Circle of Sun, A (poem)  Gr. K, 3
Continents, The (speech piece)
    Gr. 4, 357
Don't Dump Trash  Gr. 2, 318
Earth Is My Mother, The  Gr. 1, 340
Earth Is Our Mother, The  Gr. 4, 358
En nuestra Tierra tan linda  Gr. 2, 335
Enjoy the Earth (poem)  Gr. 4, 81
For the Beauty of the Earth  Gr. 4, 356
From Sea to Shining Sea  Gr. 2, 342
*Garden of the Earth*  Gr. 5, 399
It's a Small World  Gr. 3, 268
Look Out for Mother Earth  Gr. 3, 341
Prayer for Earth (poem)  Gr. 4, 350
This Land Is Your Land  Gr. 5, 118
*This Land Is Your Land*  Gr. 5, 120
This Pretty Planet  Gr. 4, 355
Turn the World Around  Gr. 4, 114
Valentine for Earth, A (poem)
    Gr. 3, 324
World We Love, The  Gr. 3, 342

**ECOLOGY AND NATURAL
    RESOURCES** *See also Earth,
    The; Environments.*
3 + 2  Gr. 2, 316
Allá en la fuente  Gr. 2, 92
And My Heart Soars (poem)  Gr. 4, 359
Beach Rap (speech piece)  Gr. 1, 352
Big Beautiful Planet  Gr. 3, 326
Blowin' in the Wind  Gr. 5, 382
*Circle of Life, The*  Gr. 6, 316
Come, Ye Thankful People, Come
    Gr. 5, 459
*Daybreak Vision*  Gr. 5, 398
Don't Dump Trash  Gr. 2, 318
Earth Is My Mother, The  Gr. 1, 340
Earth Is Our Mother, The  Gr. 4, 358
Enjoy the Earth (poem)  Gr. 4, 81
For the Beauty of the Earth  Gr. 4, 356
From Sea to Shining Sea  Gr. 2, 342
*Garden of the Earth*  Gr. 5, 399
Hashkediya  Gr. 3, 206
Hurt No Living Thing (poem)  Gr. 4, 32
I Love the Mountains  Gr. 5, 34

I'm Glad (poem) Gr. 1, 415
Let's Go Fly a Kite Gr. 2, 327
Look Out for Mother Earth Gr. 3, 341
Lots of Worms Gr. 2, 310
Morning Has Broken Gr. 5, 28
Prayer for Earth (poem) Gr. 4, 350
Rabbit Dance, The (story) Gr. 3, 334
*Rain, Rain, Beautiful Rain* Gr. 4, 32
*Rain Song, The* Gr. 2, 323
Starlight, Star Bright Gr. 4, 373
Tall Cedar Tree Gr. 2, 322
This Land Is Your Land Gr. 5, 118
*This Land Is Your Land* Gr. 5, 120
This Pretty Planet Gr. 4, 355
Trees (poem) Gr. 5, 114
Turn the World Around Gr. 4, 114
What a Wonderful World Gr. 6, 62
*Where Have All the Flowers Gone?*
     Gr. 5, 287
Written in March (poem) Gr. 4, 354
Your Friends Shall Be the Tall Wind
     Gr. 6, 201
Zuni Sunrise Call Gr. 5, 396

## ENVIRONMENTS *See also Earth,*
     *The; Ecology and Natural*
     *Resources; Water in Our World.*

### DESERTS
Abiyoyo Gr. 2, 108
Ala Da'lona Gr. 4, 136
Ala Da'lona Gr. 5, 301
Mos Mos Gr. 1, 130
This Land Is Your Land Gr. 5, 118
*This Land Is Your Land*
     Gr. 5, 120
This Land Is Your Land Gr. 7, I-66
Tumba Gr. 5, 161
Zum gali gali Gr. 5, 400

### FORESTS
Erdö, erdö de magos Gr. 3, 182
*Frostiana (from Stopping by*
     *Woods on a Snowy Evening)*
     Gr. 6, 40
How the Kiwi Lost Its Wings (story)
     Gr. 1, 78
Kookaburra Gr. 4, 186
Lion Sleeps Tonight, The Gr. 4, 131
*Lion Sleeps Tonight, The* Gr. 4, 132
Lumberjack, The (poem) Gr. 1, 113
Stopping by Woods on a Snowy
     Evening Gr. 6, 41
Tall Cedar Tree Gr. 2, 322
This Land Is Your Land Gr. 7, I-66
This Land Is Your Land (refrain
     only) Gr. 1, 274
Tree in the Wood, The Gr. 2, 360
Woodland Chorus Gr. K, 250

### JUNGLES
Ayelivi Gr. 2, 70
*Jungle Beat* Gr. 6, 347
Lion Sleeps Tonight, The Gr. 4, 131
*Lion Sleeps Tonight, The* Gr. 4, 132

## MEADOWS
Beriozka Gr. 4, 294
De colores Gr. 5, 90
De colores Gr. 8, I-14
Down in the Meadow Gr. K, 147
*Farmer in the Dell* Gr. K, 233
Farmer in the Dell, The Gr. K, 232
Morning Comes Early Gr. 5, 13
Over in the Meadow Gr. 1, 346
Sky, Sea, Shore (poem) Gr. 2, 343

## MOUNTAINS
Al yadee Gr. 6, 308
Arirang Gr. 5, 25
Ash Grove, The Gr. 5, 114
Away to America Gr. 5, 57
Cielito lindo Gr. 7, I-20
Cumberland Gap Gr. 4, 138
*Doraji* Gr. 4, 175
Doraji Gr. 4, 174
Gonna Build a Mountain Gr. 6, 21
Growing Corn (poem) Gr. 1, 297
Happy Wanderer, The Gr. 4, 89
Harrison Town Gr. 6, 97
I Love the Mountains Gr. 5, 34
I Walk the Unfrequented Road
     Gr. 6, 79
I'm Flying Home Gr. 2, 286
La borinqueña Gr. 8, D-19
Loch Lomond Gr. 5, 140
Los maizales Gr. 1, 296
My Home's Across the Blue Ridge
     Mountains Gr. 4, 84
*Ozark Mountain Jubilee* Gr. 4, 86
Paw-Paw Patch Gr. 4, 93
Red River Valley Gr. 6, 11
Riendo el río corre Gr. 6, 263
Rocky Mountain Gr. 2, 98
Rocky Top Gr. 5, 348
Roll On, Columbia Gr. 5, 116
Sourwood Mountain Gr. 4, 65
*Tennessee River* Gr. 5, 349
This Land Is Your Land Gr. 5, 118
*This Land Is Your Land*
     Gr. 5, 120
Trains (poem) Gr. 1, 301
Trains (poem) Gr. 2, 211
Viva Jujuy Gr. 5, 228
World We Love, The Gr. 3, 342
Yüe liang wan wan Gr. 5, 314

## OCEANS AND SEAS
Al yadee Gr. 6, 308
Baby Beluga Gr. K, 272
Beach Rap (speech piece)
     Gr. 1, 352
Blow the Wind Southerly
     Gr. 5, 178
Blow, Ye Winds Gr. 4, 255
Bound for South Australia
     Gr. 5, 22
Charlie over the Water Gr. 1, 68
*Coming Home from the Sea–I*
     Gr. 6, 345

*Coming Home from the Sea–II*
     Gr. 6, 345
Cuando pa' Chile me voy
     Gr. 6, 376
Down by the Bay Gr. 1, 18
El carite Gr. 5, 305
Farewell to Tarwathie Gr. 6, 43
Fishes of Kempenfelt Bay, The
     (poem) Gr. 1, 19
Four Strong Winds (Song to a
     Seagull) Gr. 6, 170
Four White Horses Gr. 3, 304
From Sea to Shining Sea
     Gr. 2, 342
*George and Gracie* Gr. 1, 69
Hama chi dori Gr. 3, 330
Haul Away, Joe Gr. 4, 13
La borinqueña Gr. 8, D-19
Little Shell Gr. 1, 355
Mary Ann Gr. 6, 180
My Bonnie Lies Over the Ocean
     Gr. 4, 338
*Old American Songs, "The*
     *Boatman's Dance"* Gr. 4, 61
Rio Grande Gr. 4, 256
River Gr. 4, 58
River Winding (poem) Gr. 4, 60
Rocky Mountain Gr. 2, 98
Sail Away Gr. 5, 404
Shenandoah Gr. 5, 264
*Shenandoah* Gr. 5, 265
Sky, Sea, Shore (poem) Gr. 2, 343
Skye Boat Song Gr. 6, 372
Somos el barco Gr. 4, 352
*Surfin' Safari* Gr. 6, 261
Surfin' U.S.A. Gr. 6, 260
This Land Is Your Land Gr. 7, I-66
This Land Is Your Land (refrain
     only) Gr. 1, 274
Under the Sea Gr. 5, 372
Until I Saw the Sea (poem)
     Gr. 4, 13
Vamos a la mar Gr. 3, 226
Vem kan segla? Gr. 6, 417
Wheel of the Water, The
     Gr. 4, 362
World We Love, The Gr. 3, 342
Your Friends Shall Be the Tall Wind
     Gr. 6, 201

## PLAINS
Alumot Gr. 6, 306
America, the Beautiful Gr. 6, 485
Bury Me Not on the Lone Prairie
     Gr. 6, 19
Cattle Call Gr. 5, 344
*Cattle Call* Gr. 5, 347
El rancho grande Gr. 4, 215
Home on the Range Gr. 5, 69
I'm Flying Home Gr. 2, 286
Laredo Gr. 5, 10
Lion and the Mouse, The (story)
     Gr. 1, 239
Lions Gr. 1, 238

**(Environments, continued)**
Ochimbo Gr. 4, 134
Oklahoma Gr. 5, 36
Trains (poem) Gr. 1, 301
Trains (poem) Gr. 2, 211

## RAINFORESTS
Kibungo Gr. 2, 354
Kibungo, Beast of the Forest (story)
    Gr. 2, 352

## RIVERS, LAKES, AND STREAMS
Basin Street Blues Gr. 5, 354
Blue Danube, The, Op. 314
    Gr. 6, 192
Blue Mountain Lake Gr. 6, 205
Canto del agua Gr. 8, I-10
Crawfish! Gr. 2, 86
Crocodile, The Gr. 2, 362
Cuando pa' Chile me voy
    Gr. 6, 376
Cycle Song of Life (The River Song)
    Gr. 4, 370
Deux cocodries Gr. 2, 364
Down by the Riverside Gr. 8, G-8
Erie Canal Gr. 5, 262
Great Big House Gr. 2, 204
Hippopotamus Song, The
    Gr. 3, 33
How Doth the Little Crocodile
    (poem) Gr. 2, 363
I See the Moon Gr. 2, 58
I Walk the Unfrequented Road
    Gr. 6, 79
Janitzio Gr. 5, 91
Listen to the Water Gr. 2, 294
Loigratong Gr. 6, 451
Mary Ann Gr. K, 253
Michael, Row the Boat Ashore
    Gr. 2, 18
Mississippi River Chant (speech
    piece) Gr. 2, 132
Mud Gr. 3, 32
Ochimbo Gr. 4, 134
Peace Like a River Gr. 6, 190
Red River Valley Gr. 6, 11
Riendo el río corre Gr. 6, 263
River Gr. 4, 58
River (poem) Gr. 4, 61
River Suite, The, "Finale"
    Gr. 5, 121
River Winding (poem) Gr. 4, 60
Roll On, Columbia Gr. 5, 116
Sailing Down My Golden River
    Gr. 4, 332
Se va el caimán Gr. 5, 306
Shenandoah Gr. 2, 62
Shenandoah Gr. 5, 264
Shenandoah Gr. 5, 265
Sky, Sea, Shore (poem) Gr. 2, 343
Somos el barco Gr. 4, 352
Swanee Gr. 6, 118
Tennessee River Gr. 5, 349

Tide in the River, The (poem)
    Gr. 2, 133
Trains (poem) Gr. 2, 211
Wheel of the Water, The
    Gr. 4, 362
World We Love, The Gr. 3, 342
Your Friends Shall Be the Tall Wind
    Gr. 6, 201

## F

## FAMILIES
A la puerta del cielo Gr. 5, 60
A la rurru niño Gr. K, 180
Ai, Dunaii moy Gr. 4, 293
All Through the Night Gr. 5, 105
Almost Day Gr. 3, 397
Amefuri Gr. 1, 144
Asadoya Gr. 6, 303
At the Same Time Gr. 6, 115
Away to America Gr. 5, 57
Ayelivi Gr. 2, 70
Ayliluli, num tsipor Gr. 1, 204
Bai, bai, bai, bai Gr. 2, 197
Be Still, My Child Gr. 1, 39
Bereleh Gr. K, 151
Birthday Gr. 6, 90
Bling Blang Gr. 3, 240
Canción de cuna Gr. 4, 144
Chawe chidyo chem'chero (story)
    Gr. 2, 296
Children Learn What They Live (poem)
    Gr. 5, 381
Children of Long Ago (poem)
    Gr. 1, 31
Dancing Pig, The (folk tale) Gr. 1, 196
Deau-deau, ti pitit maman Gr. 2, 306
Dinner Music Gr. K, 70
Down by the Bay Gr. 1, 18
Drum, A (folk tale) Gr. 1, 116
Duérmete, mi niño Gr. 1, 292
El día de mamita Gr. K, 325
Everything Grows Gr. K, 267
Fais do do Gr. 6, 403
Fais dodo Gr. K, 158
Families Gr. 1, 282
Family Tree Gr. 3, 72
Farmer in the Dell Gr. K, 233
Farmer in the Dell, The Gr. K, 232
Flowering Umbrellas (poem) Gr. 1, 145
For the Beauty of the Earth Gr. 4, 356
Gift to Share, A Gr. 6, 393
Green, Green Grass of Home
    Gr. 6, 248
Habari Gani Gr. 3, 404
Hama chi dori Gr. 3, 330
Happy Birthday! (poem) Gr. K, 306
Hey, m'tswala Gr. 4, 79
Hine mah tov Gr. 5, 430
Hui jia qù Gr. 2, 158
Hush Up the Baby Gr. K, 222
Hwa yuan li-de young wa wa
    Gr. 3, 102

I'm Thankful Gr. 1, 414
Ichi-gatsu tsuitachi Gr. 3, 406
It's a Celebration! Gr. 2, 372
Joubert, Joseph Gr. 3, 50
Joy of Kwanzaa, The Gr. 6, 462
Jump That Jody Gr. K, 212
Kunolounkwa Gr. K, 110
Kunolounkwa, "Contemporary"
    Gr. K, 110
Lady, Lady Gr. 1, 62
Las mañanitas Gr. K, 325
Long Way Home, A Gr. 1, 382
Louder Than a Clap of Thunder (folk
    tale) Gr. 1, 87
Love in Any Language Gr. 6, 476
Love Is on Our Side Gr. 5, 324
Lullaby (poem) Gr. 1, 208
Mama, Buy Me a Chiney Doll
    Gr. K, 120
Mama Don't 'Low Gr. 6, 358
Mango Walk Gr. 5, 200
Mon papa Gr. 2, 280
My Father's House Gr. 2, 25
Nampaya omame Gr. 1, 138
New Shoes (poem) Gr. 2, 242
Niño querido Gr. 1, 308
Nu wahtan Gr. 1, 279
O, Desayo Gr. 5, 411
O Laufet, ihr Hirten Gr. 2, 384
Ocho kandelikas Gr. 4, 429
Ode to la piñata (poem) Gr. 1, 424
On Mother's Day (poem) Gr. 1, 443
Our Family Comes from 'Round the
    World (poem) Gr. 1, 299
Over in the Meadow Gr. 1, 346
Over the River and Through the Wood
    Gr. 3, 384
Ptashky u babusi sadochku Gr. 1, 192
Pust' 'vsegda budet sonse Gr. 3, 278
Rabbit Footprints Gr. 2, 304
Reading Glasses (poem) Gr. K, 325
Rockin' Around the Christmas Tree
    Gr. 5, 466
Sailing Down My Golden River
    Gr. 4, 332
See the Children Playin' Gr. 4, 107
Sharing Gr. K, 198
Shortnin' Bread Gr. 1, 57
Sioux Lullaby (poem) Gr. K, 111
Sleep, Baby, Sleep Gr. 2, 197
St. Patrick Was a Gentleman
    Gr. 3, 290
Stand By Me Gr. 5, 46
Stand By Me Gr. 5, 49
Standin' in the Need of Prayer
    Gr. 5, 103
Still, Still, Still Gr. 5, 468
Summertime Gr. 6, 250
Sweet Potatoes Gr. 3, 228
Swing Low, Sweet Chariot
    Gr. 6, 234
Take Time in Life Gr. 6, 292

Thematic Index

Thula, thula, ngoana  Gr. 4, 227
Together in Unity  Gr. K, 320
Traveler's Song (poem)  Gr. 4, 336
*Traveling Shoes*  Gr. 3, 248
Ujima  Gr. 1, 430
Valentine Feelings (poem)  Gr. K, 322
Voice Choice  Gr. K, 27
Wai bamba  Gr. 6, 26
What to Do (poem)  Gr. K, 43
World We Love, The  Gr. 3, 342
Worm, The (poem)  Gr. 2, 311
*Yakety Yak*  Gr. 5, 204
Yakety Yak  Gr. 5, 205
Yü guang guang  Gr. 6, 60

## FAVORITE THINGS  *See also Toys.*

ABC Blues  Gr. K, 281
Bantama kra kro  Gr. 5, 308
Beach Rap (speech piece)  Gr. 1, 352
Birthday  Gr. 6, 90
Birthday, Birthday, Birthday (poem)
    Gr. K, 306
Birthday Cake  Gr. K, 307
Bubble Gum (speech piece)  Gr. K, 38
Bubble Trouble (poem)  Gr. K, 184
Bubbles (poem)  Gr. K, 185
Burrough, Roslyn  Gr. 1, 163
Celebrate!  Gr. 1, 406
Celebration (poem)  Gr. 6, 122
Cho'i hát bội  Gr. 5, 318
Cinderella Dressed in Green (rhyme)
    Gr. K, 136
Circle of Sun, A (poem)  Gr. K, 3
Circus Fare (poem)  Gr. K, 157
*Cookie Crew, The*  Gr. K, 197
Cookie Magic (poem)  Gr. K, 197
Crayons (poem)  Gr. K, 75
Downtown  Gr. 6, 258
Drum, A (folk tale)  Gr. 1, 116
Everybody Loves Saturday Night
    Gr. 6, 296
Fais dodo  Gr. K, 158
Feng yang hua gu  Gr. 4, 313
Friend of Mine  Gr. 1, 310
Glad to Have a Friend Like You
    Gr. 2, 228
Goin' to the Fair  Gr. K, 156
Going on a Picnic  Gr. K, 190
Good Old Happy Song, A  Gr. K, 201
*I Love a Rainy Night (line dance)*
    Gr. 5, 350
I Love Peanuts  Gr. 1, 162
I'm a Dreydl  Gr. K, 315
I'm Thankful  Gr. 1, 414
Jingle Bells  Gr. 2, 388
Jolly Old St. Nicholas  Gr. K, 316
Jump Rope Jingle (poem)  Gr. K, 211
Keys (poem)  Gr. K, 188
Les petites marionettes  Gr. K, 237
Let's Do the Flip-Flop Frolic! (poem)
    Gr. K, 23
*Lion*  Gr. 6, 303
Magnolia  Gr. 6, 16

Mama, Buy Me a Chiney Doll
    Gr. K, 120
Marbles (poem)  Gr. 1, 75
Merry-Go-Round  Gr. K, 290
Merry-Go-Round (poem)  Gr. K, 291
Mmmmmm mmmmmmm (poem)
    Gr. K, 71
Mon papa  Gr. 2, 280
Music (poem)  Gr. K, 107
Must Be Santa  Gr. K, 318
My Dreydl  Gr. K, 314
Nampaya omame  Gr. 1, 138
Night-light (poem)  Gr. K, 223
No quiero plata  Gr. 1, 424
One Green Jelly Bean  Gr. K, 287
Painting Song: A Dribble and a Dot
    Gr. K, 175
*Penny Lane*  Gr. 6, 257
Pick 'n' Mix Zoo (poem)  Gr. K, 139
Poem to Mud (poem)  Gr. 3, 34
Puff, the Magic Dragon  Gr. 2, 350
River  Gr. 4, 58
Rockin' Around the Christmas Tree
    Gr. 5, 466
See and Touch  Gr. K, 172
Sidewalk Songs (poem)  Gr. K, 207
Sidewalks (poem)  Gr. 1, 311
Singin' in the Tub  Gr. K, 220
Song of the Night, The (poem)
    Gr. 3, 346
Song That's Just for You, A
    Gr. 2, 126
*Surfin' Safari*  Gr. 6, 261
Surfin' U.S.A.  Gr. 6, 260
Swanee  Gr. 6, 118
Swoboda, Deanna  Gr. 3, 188
Take Your Feet Out 'the Sand
    Gr. K, 231
Teddy Bears (poem)  Gr. K, 163
Ten Little Teddy Bears (poem)
    Gr. K, 301
*This Is Your Night*  Gr. 6, 368
Tree House (poem)  Gr. 3, 207
Uga uga uga  Gr. K, 305
¡Viva el fútbol!  Gr. 1, 96
Waltzing with Bears  Gr. 3, 170
Yang wa wa  Gr. K, 162
Your Friends Shall Be the Tall Wind
    Gr. 6, 201

## FOLLOWING DIRECTIONS

ABC Blues  Gr. K, 281
All Around the Buttercup  Gr. 2, 170
Amasee  Gr. 1, 172
Andy Pandy  Gr. K, 46
Ants Go Marching, The  Gr. 1, 248
Bo-bo-skee, Watten-tatten (speech
    piece)  Gr. 1, 259
Bonavist' Harbour  Gr. 3, 294
Boogie Chant and Dance (speech
    piece)  Gr. 2, 78
Bubble Gum (speech piece)  Gr. K, 38
Celebrate  Gr. 1, 407

Cheki, morena  Gr. 2, 180
Ciranda  Gr. 2, 272
Circle Round the Zero  Gr. K, 293
Clap, Wiggle, and Stomp  Gr. K, 34
*Copycat*  Gr. K, 9
Crab Dance (poem)  Gr. 2, 307
Dinosaur Dance  Gr. 2, 168
Diou shou juan'er  Gr. 2, 277
*Doing the Penguin*  Gr. K, 35
Down, Down, Baby  Gr. 2, 32
Geef jij mij die schoen  Gr. 1, 126
Go Around the Corn, Sally  Gr. 2, 12
Goin' to the Fair  Gr. K, 156
Head, Shoulders, Baby  Gr. 1, 82
Hi-Dee-Roon  Gr. K, 10
Hokey Pokey  Gr. K, 296
Hop Up, My Ladies  Gr. 3, 142
How to Be Angry (poem)  Gr. K, 249
I Wonder Where Maria's Gone
    Gr. 3, 318
Ikhanda, maslombe  Gr. K, 14
Jim Along, Josie  Gr. K, 39
Johnny Mister Brown  Gr. K, 37
Juan pirulero  Gr. K, 215
Juba  Gr. K, 13
Kangaroo Song, The  Gr. K, 44
Kuma san  Gr. K, 40
La piñata  Gr. 3, 399
Leila  Gr. 1, 258
Let's Get the Rhythm of the Band
    Gr. 3, 84
Let's Pretend  Gr. K, 227
Little Johnny Brown  Gr. 3, 313
Loco-Motion, The  Gr. 3, 64
Looby Loo  Gr. K, 210
Mashed Potatoes (speech piece)
    Gr. 1, 20
Miss Mary Mack  Gr. 2, 42
Miss Susie Anna Sue  Gr. K, 242
Mister Snow Rap (speech piece)
    Gr. 2, 391
Music's in Me , The  Gr. 2, 40
Nie chcę cię znác  Gr. 3, 314
Number One, Touch Your Tongue
    (speech piece)  Gr. K, 204
O pião entrou  Gr. 2, 355
Old Brass Wagon  Gr. 2, 122
Oliver Jump (speech piece)  Gr. K, 205
Oliver Twist  Gr. K, 138
One Green Jelly Bean  Gr. K, 287
Peppermint Twist  Gr. 3, 46
Pizza, Pizza, Daddy-o  Gr. 2, 28
Race You Down the Mountain
    Gr. 1, 127
*Rainy Day Blues*  Gr. 2, 328
Riddle Ree (speech piece)  Gr. 2, 34
Shake Them 'Simmons Down
    Gr. 2, 244
Sheep in the Meadow (rhyme)
    Gr. 1, 17
Somebody Waiting  Gr. 2, 283
Step in Time  Gr. 2, 74
Time to Move  Gr. 1, 244

**(Following Directions, continued)**

Time to Sing  Gr. 2, 8

*Traveling Shoes*  Gr. 3, 248

Uptown, Downtown (poem)
Gr. K, 204

Way Down in the Schoolyard
Gr. 2, 50

*Way Down Yonder in the Brickyard*
Gr. 2, 51

We're Making Popcorn (speech piece)
Gr. 1, 86

What Will You Be on Halloween?
Gr. K, 308

Yellow Butter (poem)  Gr. 1, 124

## FOOD

Adana ya gidelim  Gr. 2, 142

Aiken Drum  Gr. 1, 398

Alligator Pie (speech piece)  Gr. 3, 13

Apples (poem)  Gr. 1, 16

Apples, Peaches, Pears, and Plums
(speech piece)  Gr. 1, 14

Back to School (poem)  Gr. K, 5

Banana  Gr. 2, 114

Bananas and Cream (poem)  Gr. 1, 49

Bananas and Cream (speech piece)
Gr. 3, 210

Bantama kra kro  Gr. 5, 308

Bereleh  Gr. K, 151

Birthday, Birthday, Birthday (poem)
Gr. K, 306

Birthday Cake  Gr. K, 307

Boil Them Cabbage Down  Gr. 6, 370

Bound for South Australia  Gr. 5, 22

Bubble Gum (speech piece)  Gr. K, 38

California Oranges (rhyme)  Gr. 1, 15

Cat's Menu (poem)  Gr. 2, 301

Cha yang wu  Gr. 1, 90

Chag purim  Gr. 1, 438

Chawe chidyo chem'chero (story)
Gr. 2, 296

Chickens, The (poem)  Gr. 3, 92

Children of Long Ago (poem)
Gr. 1, 31

Cinderella Dressed in Green (rhyme)
Gr. K, 136

Circle of Sun, A (poem)  Gr. K, 3

Circus Fare (poem)  Gr. K, 157

Cirmos cica  Gr. 1, 130

Come, Ye Thankful People, Come
Gr. 5, 459

Cookie  Gr. 2, 172

*Cookie Crew, The*  Gr. K, 197

Cookie Magic (poem)  Gr. K, 197

Corn Grinding Song  Gr. K, 67

Day-O! (Banana Boat Loader's Song)
Gr. 5, 18

Dinner Music  Gr. K, 70

Down by the Bay  Gr. 1, 18

Fais dodo  Gr. K, 158

Going on a Picnic  Gr. K, 190

Great Big House  Gr. 2, 204

Green Corn Song  Gr. 5, 462

Hato popo  Gr. 1, 186

Heri za Kwanzaa  Gr. 5, 476

Honeybee Song, The  Gr. 1, 358

Hot Cross Buns (Version 1)  Gr. 3, 218

Hot Cross Buns (Version 2)  Gr. 3, 221

Hush Up the Baby  Gr. K, 222

I Love Peanuts  Gr. 1, 162

I'm Thankful  Gr. 1, 414

Jambalaya (On The Bayou)  Gr. 6, 244

Jelly in a Dish (speech piece)  Gr. 2, 83

Johnny Appleseed  Gr. 4, 345

Just from the Kitchen  Gr. K, 55

Kelo aba w'ye  Gr. 6, 290

La Tarara  Gr. 4, 176

La víbora  Gr. 1, 322

Lemonade  Gr. 1, 190

Linstead Market  Gr. 5, 241

*Little Red Hen, The*  Gr. 1, 254

Little Red Hen, The (story)  Gr. 1, 256

Lone Star Trail  Gr. 2, 21

Los maizales  Gr. 1, 296

Mashed Potatoes (speech piece)
Gr. 1, 20

Mashed Potatoes (poem)  Gr. 1, 21

Mmmmmm mmmmmmm (poem)
Gr. K, 71

Nampaya omame  Gr. 1, 138

Nitty Gritty Sand Song (poem)
Gr. K, 191

No quiero plata  Gr. 1, 424

Nruab hnub thiab hmo ntuj (story)
Gr. 4, 366

O lê lê O Bahía  Gr. 6, 165

Ode to la piñata (poem)  Gr. 1, 424

Our Tree (poem)  Gr. 1, 185

Over the River and Through the Wood
Gr. 3, 384

Peanut Butter (speech piece)
Gr. 1, 173

Pease Porridge Hot  Gr. 1, 134

Pease Porridge Not (poem)  Gr. 1, 135

Perot  Gr. 2, 378

Peter, Peter, Sugar Eater (poem)
Gr. 1, 284

Pick 'n' Mix Zoo (poem)  Gr. K, 139

Pin Pon  Gr. 1, 146

Popcorn Popping  Gr. 1, 440

Rabbit Dance, The (story)  Gr. 3, 334

Rabbit Footprints  Gr. 2, 304

Rabbits (poem)  Gr. 2, 305

Riquir rán  Gr. 1, 48

Rolling Rice Cake, The: A Story from
Japan (folk tale)  Gr. 1, 91

*Salt Peanuts*  Gr. 1, 162

Scrub Brush Shuffle, The  Gr. 1, 118

Setting the Thanksgiving Table (poem)
Gr. 2, 381

Sh'ney dubim  Gr. K, 268

Shake the Papaya Down  Gr. 4, 378

Shake Them 'Simmons Down
Gr. 2, 244

Shake-'n'-Bake a Jelly (poem)
Gr. K, 95

Shoo, Turkey  Gr. 1, 104

Shortnin' Bread  Gr. 1, 57

Si me dan pasteles  Gr. 1, 432

Sweet Potatoes  Gr. 3, 228

Thanksgiving Is Near  Gr. 2, 380

To a Peanut (poem)  Gr. 1, 163

Toaster Time (poem)  Gr. K, 17

Two Little Sausages (speech piece)
Gr. 2, 79

Uga uga uga  Gr. K, 305

Vamos a cantar  Gr. K, 278

Vamos a la mar  Gr. 3, 226

Waiting (poem)  Gr. 1, 413

We Are Dear Little Birdies  Gr. K, 176

We're Making Popcorn (speech piece)
Gr. 1, 86

Weevily Wheat  Gr. 4, 105

World We Love, The  Gr. 3, 342

Worm, The (poem)  Gr. 2, 311

Yellow Butter (poem)  Gr. 1, 124

Yü guang guang  Gr. 6, 60

## FORCE AND MOTION

*Allons danser, Colinda*  Gr. K, 218

Amasee  Gr. 1, 172

Ants Go Marching, The  Gr. 1, 248

Ayii, Ayii, Ayii (poem)  Gr. K, 11

Bard of Armagh, The  Gr. 4, 296

Birthday  Gr. 6, 90

Burke, Liam  Gr. 2, 11

*Caribbean Leaps*  Gr. K, 148

Celebrate  Gr. 1, 407

Celebration (poem)  Gr. 6, 122

Cheki, morena  Gr. 2, 180

Ciranda  Gr. 2, 272

Circle of Sun, A (poem)  Gr. K, 3

Circle Round the Zero  Gr. K, 293

Clap, Wiggle, and Stomp  Gr. K, 34

*Copycat*  Gr. K, 9

Crab Dance (poem)  Gr. 2, 307

Crawfish!  Gr. 2, 86

Cuando pa' Chile me voy  Gr. 6, 376

Dance (poem)  Gr. K, 59

*Dance at the Gym*  Gr. 5, 9

Dancin' in the Street  Gr. 5, 361

Dancing Girl (poem)  Gr. K, 249

*Dancing in the Street*  Gr. 2, 254

*Dancing Tree, The*  Gr. K, 202

Different Beat, A  Gr. 1, 6

Dinosaur Dance  Gr. 2, 168

*Disco Worm*  Gr. 2, 312

*Doing the Penguin*  Gr. K, 35

Down, Down, Baby  Gr. 2, 32

Everybody Says  Gr. 1, 287

Fish (poem)  Gr. 1, 177

Four Horses, The (poem)  Gr. 1, 159

Frog (poem)  Gr. 1, 25

Gato (poem)  Gr. 1, 131

Giddy Up (rhyme)  Gr. K, 137

Goin' to Boston  Gr. 6, 433

Grasshoppers (poem)  Gr. 3, 35

Hands (poem)  Gr. 1, 203

Happy Wanderer, The  Gr. 4, 89

Harukoma, "Spring Horse Dance"
   Gr. 1, 145
Here I Am (rhyme) Gr. K, 149
Here I Go! Gr. K, 73
Hey, Hey, Look at Me Gr. 1, 70
Hi-Dee-Roon Gr. K, 10
Hokey Pokey Gr. K, 296
I Like Fall (poem) Gr. K, 311
I'm a Dreydl Gr. K, 315
I'm in the Mood Gr. K, 86
If You Can Walk Gr. 1, 19
If You're Happy Gr. K, 94
In the Pumpkin Patch Gr. 3, 380
Jack and Jill (rhyme) Gr. K, 47
Jack, Be Nimble (speech piece)
   Gr. K, 97
Jelly in a Dish (speech piece) Gr. 2, 83
Jellyfish Walk (poem) Gr. 1, 33
Jim Along, Josie Gr. K, 39
Jinny Go 'Round Gr. K, 228
Johnny Mister Brown Gr. K, 37
Juba Gr. K, 13
Jump or Jiggle (poem) Gr. 2, 26
Jump That Jody Gr. K, 212
Just Watch (poem) Gr. K, 295
Kangaroo Song, The Gr. K, 44
Kangaroo, The (poem) Gr. K, 45
Kibungo, Beast of the Forest (story)
   Gr. 2, 352
Koriko! Gr. K, 154
Kuma san Gr. K, 40
La bamba Gr. 5, 128
La bamba Gr. 5, 130
La bamba Gr. 5, 131
La Jesusita Gr. 5, 322
La mariposa Gr. 6, 58
La raspa Gr. 4, 302
La Tarara Gr. 4, 176
Les petites marionettes Gr. K, 237
Let's Do the Flip-Flop Frolic! (poem)
   Gr. K, 23
Let's Get the Rhythm of the Band
   Gr. 3, 84
Limbo Like Me Gr. 4, 18
Little David Gr. 1, 232
Loco-Motion, The Gr. 3, 64
Locomoto-vation Gr. K, 61
Loigratong Gr. 6, 451
Looby Loo Gr. K, 210
Los pescaditos (poem) Gr. 1, 69
Má Teodora Gr. 6, 301
Mary Came a-Running Gr. K, 294
Miss Mary Mack Gr. 2, 42
Monster Stomp, The (poem)
   Gr. 1, 133
Music (poem) Gr. 1, 3
Music's in Me , The Gr. 2, 40
My Legs and I (poem) Gr. 1, 9
My Mama's Calling Me Gr. 1, 260
My Pony, Macaroni Gr. 1, 158
Nanny Goat Gr. K, 161
New Way to Walk, A Gr. K, 117
Nightdance (poem) Gr. K, 219

Now That's Tap (speech piece)
   Gr. 6, 320
Number One, Touch Your Tongue
   (speech piece) Gr. K, 204
O pião entrou Gr. 2, 355
Ode to la piñata (poem) Gr. 1, 424
Oliver Jump (speech piece) Gr. K, 205
One Green Jelly Bean Gr. K, 287
Peppermint Twist Gr. 3, 46
Pinwheels (poem) Gr. 1, 149
Pizza, Pizza, Daddy-o Gr. 2, 28
Pollerita Gr. 5, 151
Put Your Finger in the Air Gr. K, 114
Rabbit Skip, The (poem) Gr. 2, 305
Rabbits (poem) Gr. 2, 305
Race You Down the Mountain
   Gr. 1, 127
Riddle Ree (speech piece) Gr. 2, 34
Rig-a-Jig-Jig Gr. K, 99
Rockin' Robin Gr. 3, 368
Rope Rhyme (poem) Gr. 1, 320
Run, Molly, Run Gr. 1, 8
Shake the Papaya Down Gr. 4, 378
Sheep in the Meadow (rhyme)
   Gr. 1, 17
Sidewalk Sounds (poem) Gr. K, 115
Sing a Little Song Gr. K, 30
Skip to My Lou Gr. K, 58
Snowflakes Gr. 1, 422
Song of the Night, The (poem)
   Gr. 3, 346
Step in Time Gr. 2, 74
Sugar "Shuga" Bee Gr. K, 64
Teach Me to Swing Gr. 5, 84
This Is Your Night Gr. 6, 368
Time to Sing Gr. 2, 8
Twist and Shout Gr. 4, 238
Twist with a Burger, Jitter with a Bug
   (speech piece) Gr. 1, 132
Tzena, tzena Gr. 5, 298
Vamos a cantar Gr. K, 278
Vamos a hacer la ronda Gr. K, 124
Vulani ringi ring Gr. 1, 139
Waiting for the Traffic Light
   Gr. 2, 107
Way Down in the Schoolyard
   Gr. 2, 50
Way Down Yonder in the Brickyard
   Gr. 2, 51
When I Dance (poem) Gr. 1, 327
Who Has Seen the Wind? Gr. 2, 324
Wild Horseman, The Gr. 1, 159
Wind Song (poem) Gr. K, 7
Xiao yin chuan Gr. 2, 14
Yo-shi nai Gr. 6, 286
Zudio Gr. 2, 269

## FREEDOM, JUSTICE, AND PEACE See also Citizenship.

Abraham, Martin, and John
   Gr. 6, 466
Ain't Gonna Let Nobody Turn Me
   'Round Gr. 6, 85

All the Way Around the World
   Gr. 2, 258
Amazing Grace Gr. 4, 160
Amazing Grace Gr. 4, 161
Amazing Grace Gr. 5, 259
America Gr. 1, 446
America Gr. 2, 403
America Gr. 3, 412
America Gr. 4, 440
America Gr. 5, 486
America Gr. 6, 484
America Gr. 7, I-2
America Gr. K, 326
America, I Hear You Singing
   Gr. 2, 402
America, the Beautiful Gr. 3, 413
America, the Beautiful Gr. 5, 76
America, the Beautiful Gr. 6, 485
America, the Beautiful Gr. 7, I-4
America, the Beautiful (Gospel)
   Gr. 6, 485
At the Same Time Gr. 6, 115
Battle Cry of Freedom Gr. 5, 272
Battle Hymn of the Republic
   Gr. 5, 274
Battle of Jericho, The Gr. 6, 234
Beyond Borders Gr. 5, 292
Blowin' in the Wind Gr. 5, 382
Blowin' in the Wind Gr. 5, 384
By the Waters of Babylon Gr. 6, 311
Cantaré, cantarás Gr. 6, 413
Changed My Name Gr. 6, 338
Children Learn What They Live (poem)
   Gr. 5, 381
Come and Go with Me to That Land
   Gr. 5, 390
Da pacem, Domine Gr. 5, 62
Da pacem, Domine Gr. 5, 62
Dance for the Nations Gr. 6, 122
Dayenu Gr. 4, 439
Down by the Riverside Gr. 5, 256
Down by the Riverside Gr. 8, G-8
Éliza Kongo Gr. 5, 14
Ev'rybody Ought to Know Gr. 1, 434
Everyday People Gr. 5, 389
Fanfare for Freedom Gr. 6, 139
Follow the Drinkin' Gourd Gr. 4, 266
For Children Safe and Strong
   Gr. 5, 484
Free at Last Gr. 2, 396
Free at Last Gr. 6, 468
Freedom Is Coming Gr. 5, 415
Funwa alafia Gr. 5, 32
Garden of the Earth Gr. 5, 399
Give a Little Love Gr. 6, 140
Give Me Your Tired, Your Poor
   Gr. 5, 166
Go Down, Moses Gr. 5, 190
God Bless the U.S.A. Gr. 8, G-37
Gonna Ride Up in the Chariot
   Gr. 4, 20
Gospel Train, The Gr. 6, 398
Habari Gani Gr. 3, 404

(*Freedom, Justice, and Peace,* continued)

Harambee  Gr. 4, 434
Harriet Tubman (poem)  Gr. 4, 269
Hava nagila  Gr. 6, 153
Hevenu shalom aleichem  Gr. 3, 378
*How Can I Keep from Singing?*
   Gr. 4, 260
How Can I Keep from Singing?
   Gr. 4, 261
I Am But a Small Voice  Gr. 6, 446
I Wish I Knew How It Would Feel to Be
   Free  Gr. 6, 470
I'm on My Way  Gr. 3, 76
*If I Had a Hammer*  Gr. 3, 241
If I Had a Hammer  Gr. 5, 287
It's Time  Gr. 6, 274
*It's Time*  Gr. 6, 319
Joe Turner Blues  Gr. 4, 56
Joy of Kwanzaa, The  Gr. 6, 462
Keep Your Eyes on the Prize  Gr. 3, 408
Keep Your Eyes on the Prize
   Gr. 8, E-16
Kid Like Me, A (speech piece)
   Gr. 2, 394
King, Martin Luther Jr.  Gr. 1, 434
Kum ba yah  Gr. 5, 244
Kwanzaa Carol, A  Gr. 2, 392
*L'union*  Gr. 6, 487
Let Freedom Ring  Gr. 5, 77
Lift Ev'ry Voice and Sing  Gr. 5, 482
Lift Ev'ry Voice and Sing  Gr. 8, I-54
Lo yisa  Gr. 6, 130
Love Is on Our Side  Gr. 5, 324
New Colossus, The (poem)  Gr. 5, 166
Ode to Joy (Come and Sing)
   Gr. 4, 152
Oh, Freedom  Gr. 5, 392
*Oh, Freedom and Come and Go with
   Me*  Gr. 5, 394
Over My Head  Gr. 4, 118
Paths of Victory  Gr. 6, 195
Peace Like a River  Gr. 6, 190
Put a Little Love in Your Heart  Gr. 4, 6
*Put a Little Love in Your Heart*
   Gr. 4, 8
Ríu ríu chíu  Gr. 5, 435
Run! Run! Hide!  Gr. 6, 340
*Shed a Little Light*  Gr. 3, 409
Shir l'shalom  Gr. 4, 419
Sing a Song of Peace  Gr. 6, 66
Sing About Martin  Gr. K, 321
Somebody's Knockin' at Your Door
   Gr. 4, 53
Star-Spangled Banner, The  Gr. 3, 415
Star-Spangled Banner, The  Gr. 4, 441
Star-Spangled Banner, The  Gr. 5, 488
Star-Spangled Banner, The  Gr. 6, 486
Star-Spangled Banner, The  Gr. 7, I-56
Star-Spangled Banner, The  Gr. 8, I-62
Starlight, Star Bright  Gr. 4, 373
*Swing Low, Sweet Chariot*
   Gr. 6, 234

*Symphony No. 9 in D Minor, Op.
   125, "Ode to Joy," Movement 4*
   Gr. 4, 151
*Tennessee River*  Gr. 5, 349
This Little Light of Mine  Gr. 6, 232
This Train  Gr. 5, 26
Tom Dooley  Gr. 6, 374
Turn, Turn, Turn (To Everything There
   Is a Season)  Gr. 5, 378
Tzena, tzena  Gr. 5, 298
United Nations on the March, The
   Gr. 6, 443
*Variations on "America"*  Gr. 6, 162
Voices of Pride, The  Gr. 5, 86
Wade in the Water  Gr. 4, 268
Wade in the Water  Gr. 8, I-64
We Shall Not Be Moved  Gr. 4, 437
We Shall Overcome  Gr. 4, 326
*We Shall Overcome*  Gr. 5, 485
*Welcome to Our World*  Gr. 6, 272
*What Kind of Land?*  Gr. 4, 327
*Where Have All the Flowers Gone?*
   Gr. 5, 287
World of Difference, A  Gr. 5, 386
*Yaudachi*  Gr. 5, 156
Yonder Come Day  Gr. 8, I-68
You and I (poem)  Gr. 5, 388
You're a Grand Old Flag  Gr. 3, 264

## FRIENDSHIP

A-Tisket, A-Tasket  Gr. 2, 238
*A-You're Adorable*  Gr. 1, 263
Adiós, amigos  Gr. 6, 57
Aguinaldo  Gr. 3, 402
Ahora voy a cantarles  Gr. 3, 56
All Around the Buttercup  Gr. 2, 170
All Around the Country  Gr. 1, 446
America, the Beautiful  Gr. 7, I-4
Ash Grove, The  Gr. 5, 114
At the Same Time  Gr. 6, 115
Ayelivi  Gr. 2, 70
Banana Splits  Gr. 1, 318
Birthday  Gr. 6, 90
*Bon jour!*  Gr. 1, 3
Children Learn What They Live (poem)
   Gr. 5, 381
*Common Ground*  Gr. 3, 379
Counting Song  Gr. 1, 253
*Dancing in the Street*  Gr. 2, 254
Dancing Pig, The (folk tale)  Gr. 1, 196
Don Gato  Gr. 3, 352
Eh, cumpari!  Gr. 4, 68
*Ev'rybody Ought to Know*  Gr. 1, 434
Friend of Mine  Gr. 1, 310
Funwa alafia  Gr. 5, 32
Gato (poem)  Gr. 1, 131
Gift to Share, A  Gr. 6, 393
Glad to Have a Friend Like You
   Gr. 2, 228
Gonna Have a Good Time  Gr. 2, 4
Goodbye, Julie (Miss Julie Ann
   Johnson)  Gr. 1, 334
*Groundhog Jig, The*  Gr. 1, 436

Gypsy in the Moonlight  Gr. 3, 12
Habari Gani  Gr. 3, 404
Happy Birthday! (poem)  Gr. K, 306
Hashewie  Gr. 4, 63
Hato popo  Gr. 1, 186
Hello, There!  Gr. K, 6
Hello to All the Children of the World
   Gr. 3, 4
Hello to the World (poem)  Gr. 3, 2
Hevenu shalom aleichem  Gr. 3, 378
Hey, Bug! (poem)  Gr. 1, 215
Hine mah tov  Gr. 5, 430
Honeybee Song, The  Gr. 1, 358
Hotaru koi  Gr. 1, 356
How to Be a Friend (poem)  Gr. 1, 331
*Howjidoo*  Gr. 1, 315
I Like You (poem)  Gr. 6, 7
I'm on My Way  Gr. 3, 76
I'm Thankful  Gr. 1, 414
Ichi-gatsu tsuitachi  Gr. 3, 406
If You Find a Little Feather (poem)
   Gr. 1, 187
It's a Beautiful Day  Gr. 3, 338
It's a Celebration!  Gr. 2, 372
It's a Small World  Gr. 3, 268
Joy of Kwanzaa, The  Gr. 6, 462
Keep Your Eyes on the Prize
   Gr. 8, E-16
King, Martin Luther Jr.  Gr. 1, 434
Lean on Me  Gr. 6, 14
Let the Music Begin!  Gr. 1, 2
Let's Celebrate!  Gr. 3, 374
Love Can Build a Bridge  Gr. 4, 324
Love in Any Language  Gr. 6, 476
Love Is on Our Side  Gr. 5, 324
Make New Friends  Gr. 3, 36
Mary Ann  Gr. 6, 180
Morning Comes Early  Gr. 5, 13
My Father's House  Gr. 2, 25
My Valentine  Gr. K, 323
Naranja dulce  Gr. 2, 97
Nie chcę cię znać  Gr. 3, 314
O, Desayo  Gr. 5, 411
Old Mother Hubbard (rhyme)
   Gr. 1, 118
On This Day (poem)  Gr. 3, 69
Our Family Comes from 'Round the
   World (poem)  Gr. 1, 299
Owl and the Pumpkin, The  Gr. 2, 377
Pai pi qiu  Gr. 1, 324
Peace Round  Gr. 4, 348
Pin Pon  Gr. 1, 146
Puff, the Magic Dragon  Gr. 2, 350
Put Your Hand in My Hand  Gr. 1, 330
*Rainy Day Blues*  Gr. 2, 328
Rise and Shine  Gr. 1, 122
Ríu ríu chíu  Gr. 5, 435
River  Gr. 4, 58
Rockin' Around the Christmas Tree
   Gr. 5, 466
Rocky Mountain  Gr. 2, 98
Rolling Rice Cake, The: A Story from
   Japan (folk tale)  Gr. 1, 91

Rosie, Darling Rosie  Gr. 2, 215
Run, Molly, Run  Gr. 1, 8
Sailing to the Sea  Gr. 1, 336
Scrub Brush Shuffle, The  Gr. 1, 118
Sharing  Gr. K, 198
Sidewalks (poem)  Gr. 1, 311
Since Hanna Moved Away (poem)
    Gr. 1, 335
Sing! Speak! Whisper! Shout!
    Gr. 1, 36
So Many Children (poem)  Gr. 1, 333
Somebody Waiting  Gr. 2, 283
Somewhere Out There  Gr. 5, 368
*Somewhere Out There*  Gr. 5, 369
Stand By Me  Gr. 5, 46
*Stand By Me*  Gr. 5, 49
*Stick Together*  Gr. 2, 231
Those Magic Changes  Gr. 8, E-30
Time to Sing  Gr. 2, 8
Together (poem)  Gr. 3, 147
*Two Heads Are Better Than One*
    Gr. 1, 333
Ujima  Gr. 1, 430
Un elefante  Gr. 2, 160
Under the Same Sun  Gr. 6, 440
Valentine Feelings (poem)  Gr. K, 322
Valentines  Gr. 2, 398
Valentines (poem)  Gr. 2, 398
Very Special Friend, A (poem)
    Gr. 1, 147
Vil du?  Gr. 1, 92
Vive l'amour  Gr. 6, 176
*Vulani ringi ring*  Gr. 1, 139
Waiting (poem)  Gr. 1, 413
We Go Together  Gr. 4, 44
We Moved About a Week Ago (poem)
    Gr. 2, 230
We Shall Overcome  Gr. 4, 326
Yellow Rose of Texas, The  Gr. 7, I-70
You and I (poem)  Gr. 5, 388
*You've Got a Friend*  Gr. 5, 364
You've Got a Friend  Gr. 5, 366

## G

## GAMES AND PLAY

A-Tisket, A-Tasket  Gr. 2, 238
Ackabacka, Soda Cracker (speech
    piece)  Gr. 1, 303
Ah, eu entrei na roda  Gr. 3, 308
Al quebrar la piñata  Gr. 4, 432
Alabama Gal  Gr. 3, 106
All Around the Buttercup  Gr. 2, 170
Ants Go Marching, The  Gr. 1, 248
Apples, Peaches, Pears, and Plums
    (speech piece)  Gr. 1, 14
Banana Splits  Gr. 1, 318
Bantama kra kro  Gr. 5, 308
Bee, Bee Bumblebee (speech piece)
    Gr. 1, 50
Bluebird, Bluebird  Gr. K, 105
Bob-a-Needle  Gr. 2, 232
Bounce High, Bounce Low  Gr. 1, 152

California Oranges (rhyme)  Gr. 1, 15
Chang  Gr. 1, 156
Chanukah Games  Gr. 3, 389
Che che koolay  Gr. 2, 266
Cheki, morena  Gr. 2, 180
Chicken on the Fence Post  Gr. 3, 92
Children of Long Ago (poem)
    Gr. 1, 31
Ciranda  Gr. 2, 272
Debajo 'el botón  Gr. 1, 210
Der sad to katte  Gr. 2, 300
Deux cocodries  Gr. 2, 364
Diou shou juan'er  Gr. 2, 277
Doctor Knickerbocker (speech piece)
    Gr. 1, 302
¿Dónde lo escondí?  Gr. K, 209
Doong gul ge  Gr. 3, 134
Down, Down, Baby  Gr. 2, 32
Draw Me a Bucket of Water  Gr. 3, 124
*Dreydl Song, The*  Gr. 3, 391
El florón  Gr. 2, 246
El juego chirimbolo  Gr. 2, 54
Falling Rain  Gr. 2, 328
Farmer's Dairy Key, The  Gr. 2, 182
Four in a Boat  Gr. 2, 46
Four White Horses  Gr. 3, 304
Friend of Mine  Gr. 1, 310
Geef jij mij die schoen  Gr. 1, 126
Grass Game  Gr. 1, 371
Green, Green, Rocky  Gr. 1, 321
*Groundhog Jig, The*  Gr. 1, 436
Gypsy in the Moonlight  Gr. 3, 12
Here Comes Valerie  Gr. 1, 32
Here I Go!  Gr. K, 73
Hitotsu toya  Gr. 5, 478
Hop Up, My Ladies  Gr. 3, 142
How Many Miles to Babylon?
    Gr. 2, 128
I'm a Dreydl  Gr. K, 315
Ikhanda, maslombe  Gr. K, 14
It Rains and It Pours (poem)
    Gr. K, 243
James Brown  Gr. K, 206
Jan ken pon  Gr. 3, 302
Juba  Gr. K, 13
*Jump for Joy*  Gr. K, 212
Jump Rope Jingle (poem)  Gr. K, 211
Jump That Jody  Gr. K, 212
Juniper Tree, The  Gr. 3, 131
Kapulu kane  Gr. 2, 270
Knock the Cymbals  Gr. 1, 176
La piñata  Gr. 3, 399
La víbora  Gr. 1, 322
Leak kanseng  Gr. 1, 156
Lemonade  Gr. 1, 190
Let's Do the Flip-Flop Frolic! (poem)
    Gr. K, 23
Let's Go Fly a Kite  Gr. 2, 327
Limbo Like Me  Gr. 4, 18
Little Johnny Brown  Gr. 3, 313
Los pececitos  Gr. 1, 178
Lost My Gold Ring  Gr. 6, 158
Lullaby and Dance  Gr. 4, 387

Marbles (poem)  Gr. 1, 75
Miss Mary Mack  Gr. 2, 42
Missy-La, Massa-La  Gr. 4, 188
Mon son pha (speech piece)  Gr. K, 91
My Dreydl  Gr. K, 314
My Mama's Calling Me  Gr. 1, 260
Name Game, The (speech piece)
    Gr. 1, 315
Name, Name, What's Your Name?
    (speech piece)  Gr. 3, 10
Nana, Thread Needle  Gr. 1, 38
Naranja dulce  Gr. 2, 97
Nie chcę cię znác  Gr. 3, 314
Nightdance (poem)  Gr. K, 219
No quiero plata  Gr. 1, 424
Noises (poem)  Gr. K, 305
Number One, Touch Your Tongue
    (speech piece)  Gr. K, 204
O ma washi  Gr. K, 13
O pião entrou  Gr. 2, 355
Ocho kandelikas  Gr. 4, 429
Ode to la piñata (poem)  Gr. 1, 424
Old Brass Wagon  Gr. 2, 122
Oliver Jump (speech piece)  Gr. K, 205
Pai pi qiu  Gr. 1, 324
Pavo, pavo  Gr. 1, 416
Paw-Paw Patch  Gr. 4, 93
Perná, perná, i mélissá  Gr. K, 264
Piñon, pirulín  Gr. 2, 174
Pizza, Pizza, Daddy-o  Gr. 2, 28
Raccoon Dance Song  Gr. 1, 260
Race You Down the Mountain
    Gr. 1, 127
*Rainy Day Blues*  Gr. 2, 328
Riddle Ree (speech piece)  Gr. 2, 34
Rig-a-Jig-Jig  Gr. K, 99
Rope Rhyme (poem)  Gr. 1, 320
'Round and 'Round  Gr. 1, 148
Run, Molly, Run  Gr. 1, 8
S'vivon  Gr. 6, 452
See the Children Playin'  Gr. 4, 107
Shake Them 'Simmons Down
    Gr. 2, 244
She'll Be Comin' 'Round the Mountain
    Gr. 2, 358
Sheep in the Meadow (rhyme)
    Gr. 1, 17
Shoo, Turkey  Gr. 1, 104
Sidewalk Songs (poem)  Gr. K, 207
Snail, Snail  Gr. 1, 190
Somebody Waiting  Gr. 2, 283
Son macaron  Gr. 4, 109
Song That's Just for You, A
    Gr. 2, 126
Spring Has Sprung!  Gr. K, 142
This Old Man  Gr. 3, 152
Three Times By She Passes (speech
    piece)  Gr. K, 125
Tideo  Gr. 2, 80
To a Red Kite (poem)  Gr. 2, 326
Tony Chestnut  Gr. 2, 35
Turn the Glasses Over  Gr. 3, 204
Uga uga uga  Gr. K, 305

**(Games and Play, continued)**

Un, deux, trois  Gr. 2, 198
Un elefante  Gr. 2, 160
Uptown, Downtown (poem)
   Gr. K, 204
Vamos a hacer la ronda  Gr. K, 124
Vil du?  Gr. 1, 92
*Vulani ringi ring*  Gr. 1, 139
Waiting (poem)  Gr. 1, 413
Way Down in the Schoolyard
   Gr. 2, 50
*Way Down Yonder in the Brickyard*
   Gr. 2, 51
Weevily Wheat  Gr. 4, 105
What to Do (poem)  Gr. K, 43
Who Has the Penny?  Gr. K, 42
Wind Up the Apple Tree  Gr. 1, 184
Zudio  Gr. 2, 269

## GREETINGS AND GOODBYES

Adiós, amigos  Gr. 6, 57
Ah, eu entrei na roda  Gr. 3, 308
*Bon jour!*  Gr. 1, 3
Bonjour, mes amis  Gr. 1, 316
Counting Song  Gr. 1, 253
*Feliz Navidad*  Gr. 4, 433
Funwa alafia  Gr. 5, 32
Goin' to Boston  Gr. 6, 433
Good Morning  Gr. 3, 192
Goodbye, Julie (Miss Julie Ann
   Johnson)  Gr. 1, 334
Great Big House  Gr. 2, 204
Greetings (speech piece)  Gr. 3, 316
Hashkediya  Gr. 3, 206
Hearts Like Doors (poem)  Gr. K, 189
Hello!  Gr. 2, 262
Hello, There!  Gr. K, 6
Hello to All the Children of the World
   Gr. 3, 4
Hello to the World (poem)  Gr. 3, 2
*Howjidoo*  Gr. 1, 315
I Wonder Where Maria's Gone
   Gr. 3, 318
Ichi-gatsu tsuitachi  Gr. 3, 406
Jambalaya (On The Bayou)  Gr. 6, 244
Key to the Highway  Gr. 6, 243
Kokoleoko  Gr. 5, 33
Las mañanitas  Gr. 6, 481
Love in Any Language  Gr. 6, 476
Morning Is Come  Gr. 3, 128
Name Game, The (speech piece)
   Gr. 1, 315
Name, Name, What's Your Name?
   (speech piece)  Gr. 3, 10
Nie chcę cię znać  Gr. 3, 314
Nu wahtan  Gr. 1, 279
O, Desayo  Gr. 5, 411
*Piki mai*  Gr. 1, 79
Pretty Saro  Gr. 3, 216
Sawatdee tuh jah  Gr. 2, 265
She'll Be Comin' 'Round the Mountain
   Gr. 2, 358
Sing, America, Sing!  Gr. 3, 238

So Many Children (poem)  Gr. 1, 333
Those Magic Changes  Gr. 8, E-30
Time to Sing  Gr. 2, 8
*Walkin' to New Orleans*  Gr. 3, 371
*Welcome to Our World*  Gr. 6, 272
*Who Can Sail?*  Gr. 5, 30
Yellow Rose of Texas, The  Gr. 7, I-70

## H

## HABITATS AND HOMES

Bat, The (poem)  Gr. 2, 302
Beach Rap (speech piece)  Gr. 1, 352
Big Beautiful Planet  Gr. 3, 326
Bird's Nest, The (poem)  Gr. K, 239
Crab Dance (poem)  Gr. 2, 307
Crawfish!  Gr. 2, 86
De colores  Gr. 8, I-14
El caracol  Gr. K, 130
El sapito  Gr. 3, 336
Éliza Kongo  Gr. 5, 14
Erdö, erdö de magos  Gr. 3, 182
Fishes of Kempenfelt Bay, The (poem)
   Gr. 1, 19
Frog (poem)  Gr. 1, 25
Frog in the Millpond  Gr. 2, 44
Grasshoppers (poem)  Gr. 3, 35
Great Big House  Gr. 2, 204
Groundhog Blues, The  Gr. 3, 122
Hippopotamus Song, The  Gr. 3, 33
Home on the Range  Gr. 5, 69
Honeybee Song, The  Gr. 1, 358
Hosanna, Me Build a House
   Gr. 5, 132
In the Pumpkin Patch  Gr. 3, 380
Kibungo, Beast of the Forest (story)
   Gr. 2, 352
Lion and the Mouse, The (story)
   Gr. 1, 239
Listen to the Water  Gr. 2, 294
Little Red Hen, The (story)  Gr. 1, 256
Little Snail (poem)  Gr. K, 131
Little Spider  Gr. K, 93
Live in the City  Gr. 5, 71
Look Out for Mother Earth  Gr. 3, 341
Los pececitos  Gr. 1, 178
Los pollitos  Gr. K, 166
Lots of Worms  Gr. 2, 310
Mud  Gr. 3, 32
My Home's Across the Blue Ridge
   Mountains  Gr. 4, 84
News of Home (poem)  Gr. 4, 336
Oklahoma  Gr. 5, 36
On a Log, Mister Frog  Gr. K, 148
Our Mr. Toad (poem)  Gr. 3, 337
Over in the Meadow  Gr. 1, 346
Over the River and Through the Wood
   Gr. 3, 384
*Ozark Mountain Jubilee*  Gr. 4, 86
Party Tonight!  Gr. 2, 152
Ptashky u babusi sadochku  Gr. 1, 192
¡Qué gusto!  Gr. 3, 132
Rabbit Footprints  Gr. 2, 304

Rabbits (poem)  Gr. 2, 305
Rocky Top  Gr. 5, 348
Sailing Down My Golden River
   Gr. 4, 332
*She'll Be Coming 'Round the
   Mountain When She Comes*
   Gr. 4, 333
Sheep, Sheep (poem)  Gr. 1, 309
Snail, Snail (poem)  Gr. 1, 191
Spring Rain (poem)  Gr. 2, 294
*Tennessee River*  Gr. 5, 349
Traveler's Song (poem)  Gr. 4, 336
We Are Dear Little Birdies  Gr. K, 176
What Do Animals Need?  Gr. 2, 288
Why the Warthog Goes About on His
   Knees (story)  Gr. 1, 139
World We Love, The  Gr. 3, 342
Zomo the Rabbit (story)  Gr. 3, 364

## HEALTHY LIVING

Apples (poem)  Gr. 1, 16
*Beautiful*  Gr. 3, 67
Brush Your Teeth  Gr. 1, 284
Every Morning When I Wake Up
   Gr. 2, 320
*Loose Tooth Blues*  Gr. 1, 284
One Green Jelly Bean  Gr. K, 287
Pease Porridge Not (poem)  Gr. 1, 135
Peter, Peter, Sugar Eater (poem)
   Gr. 1, 284
Pin Pon  Gr. 1, 146
*Rainy Day Blues*  Gr. 2, 328
*Scrub-a-dub*  Gr. 1, 306
Time to Move  Gr. 1, 244
Wake Me, Shake Me  Gr. 1, 278
What Do Animals Need?  Gr. 2, 288

## HEAT AND LIGHT  See also Space.

Au clair de la lune  Gr. 3, 18
Autumn Fires (poem)  Gr. 5, 149
Big Beautiful Planet  Gr. 3, 326
Each of Us Is a Flower  Gr. 3, 154
Ég a gyertya  Gr. K, 96
En nuestra Tierra tan linda  Gr. 2, 335
*Everything Grows*  Gr. K, 267
Gakavik  Gr. 4, 14
Goodnight, Sun (poem)  Gr. 1, 367
In the Pumpkin Patch  Gr. 3, 380
Jack, Be Nimble (speech piece)
   Gr. K, 97
Las velitas  Gr. 5, 147
My Shadow (poem)  Gr. K, 19
*Primitive Fire, "Oya"*  Gr. 5, 67
Pust' 'vsegda budet sonse  Gr. 3, 278
Seasons  Gr. K, 4
Sol, solecito  Gr. 1, 367
There is Joy (poem)  Gr. 3, 258
Turn the World Around  Gr. 4, 114
Until I Saw the Sea (poem)  Gr. 4, 13
World We Love, The  Gr. 3, 342

## HEROES AND LEADERS  See also
   Citizenship.

Abraham, Martin, and John
   Gr. 6, 466

America  Gr. 1, 446
America, the Beautiful  Gr. 7, I-4
Back of the Bus  Gr. 3, 410
*Battle of Jericho, The*  Gr. 6, 234
*Changed My Name*  Gr. 6, 338
Children Learn What They Live (poem)
    Gr. 5, 381
Follow the Drinkin' Gourd  Gr. 4, 266
Go Down, Moses  Gr. 5, 190
Harriet Tubman (poem)  Gr. 4, 269
Johnny Appleseed  Gr. 4, 345
*Jonah*  Gr. 6, 235
Joshua Fought the Battle of Jericho
    Gr. 5, 100
Joshua Fought the Battle of Jericho
    Gr. 8, E-18
Keep Your Eyes on the Prize  Gr. 3, 408
Kid Like Me, A (speech piece)
    Gr. 2, 394
Lift Ev'ry Voice and Sing  Gr. 5, 482
One Moment in Time  Gr. 6, 352
Rabbit Dance, The (story)  Gr. 3, 334
Run! Run! Hide!  Gr. 6, 340
*Shed a Little Light*  Gr. 3, 409
Sing About Martin  Gr. K, 321
*Sister Rosa*  Gr. 3, 411
Song of Greatness, A (poem)
    Gr. 3, 335
Wade in the Water  Gr. 4, 268
When Johnny Comes Marching Home
    Gr. 5, 180
Yankee Doodle  Gr. 3, 414
Yo-shi nai  Gr. 6, 286

## HOPES AND DREAMS *See also*
*Imagination and Fantasy.*
Abraham, Martin, and John
    Gr. 6, 466
Adelita  Gr. 5, 50
Ain't Gonna Let Nobody Turn Me
    'Round  Gr. 6, 85
Al yadee  Gr. 6, 308
All the Way Around the World
    Gr. 2, 258
America  Gr. 1, 446
America  Gr. 2, 403
America  Gr. 4, 440
America  Gr. 5, 486
America  Gr. 6, 484
America  Gr. 7, I-2
America  Gr. K, 326
America, I Hear You Singing
    Gr. 2, 402
America, the Beautiful  Gr. 3, 413
America, the Beautiful  Gr. 5, 76
America, the Beautiful  Gr. 6, 485
America, the Beautiful  Gr. 7, I-4
*America, the Beautiful (Gospel)*
    Gr. 6, 485
And My Heart Soars (poem)  Gr. 4, 359
Apple, The (poem)  Gr. 1, 231
Arirang  Gr. 5, 25
Around the World (poem)  Gr. 2, 256

At the Same Time  Gr. 6, 115
Away to America  Gr. 5, 57
Back of the Bus  Gr. 3, 410
Basin Street Blues  Gr. 5, 354
Beyond Borders  Gr. 5, 292
Big Rock Candy Mountain  Gr. 4, 330
Birthday, Birthday, Birthday (poem)
    Gr. K, 306
Birthday Cake  Gr. K, 307
Blast Off! (poem)  Gr. 1, 377
Blow the Wind Southerly  Gr. 5, 178
Blowin' in the Wind  Gr. 5, 382
*Blowin' in the Wind*  Gr. 5, 384
Blue Skies  Gr. 6, 88
*Body Song, The*  Gr. 6, 438
*Both Sides Now*  Gr. 5, 385
Brand New Day, A  Gr. 6, 7
Bridges  Gr. 6, 86
Burke, Liam  Gr. 2, 11
Bury Me Not on the Lone Prairie
    Gr. 6, 19
By the Waters of Babylon  Gr. 6, 311
California  Gr. 5, 52
California, Here I Come  Gr. 4, 287
Cantaré, cantarás  Gr. 6, 413
Changing (poem)  Gr. K, 199
Chickens, The (poem)  Gr. 3, 92
Children Learn What They Live (poem)
    Gr. 5, 381
Cielito lindo  Gr. 7, I-20
*Circle of Life, The*  Gr. 6, 316
Come and Go with Me to That Land
    Gr. 5, 390
Come, Ye Thankful People, Come
    Gr. 5, 459
Cotton-Eye Joe  Gr. 4, 288
Cowboy's Dream (poem)  Gr. 4, 339
Cuando pa' Chile me voy  Gr. 6, 376
Do, Lord  Gr. 3, 164
Don Alfonso  Gr. 5, 177
Don Giovanni  Gr. 8,
Don't Be Cruel  Gr. 6, 255
Down by the Riverside  Gr. 5, 256
Down in the Valley  Gr. 6, 375
Downtown  Gr. 6, 258
Dream Keeper, The (poem)  Gr. 2, 397
Dreams (poem)  Gr. K, 276
El condor pasa  Gr. 6, 46
El payo  Gr. 6, 145
Ev'ry Time I Feel the Spirit  Gr. 5, 242
Follow the Drinkin' Gourd  Gr. 4, 266
For Children Safe and Strong
    Gr. 5, 484
For the Beauty of the Earth  Gr. 4, 356
Four Strong Winds (Song to a Seagull)
    Gr. 6, 170
Free at Last  Gr. 6, 468
Freedom Is Coming  Gr. 5, 415
Freight Train  Gr. 1, 44
*Frostiana (from Stopping by Woods*
    *on a Snowy Evening)*  Gr. 6, 40
*Garden of the Earth*  Gr. 5, 399
Get on Board  Gr. K, 89

Get on Your Feet  Gr. 5, 6
*Get on Your Feet*  Gr. 5, 8
Gift to Share, A  Gr. 6, 393
Give a Little Love  Gr. 6, 140
*Give Me Your Tired, Your Poor*
    Gr. 5, 166
Go, My Son  Gr. 6, 188
Goin' Down the Road Feelin' Bad
    Gr. 5, 282
*Goin' Down the Road Feelin' Bad*
    Gr. 5, 283
Goin' Down the Road Feelin' Bad
    Gr. 7, F-13
Gonna Build a Mountain  Gr. 6, 21
Gonna Ride Up in the Chariot
    Gr. 4, 20
Gospel Train, The  Gr. 6, 398
Green, Green Grass of Home
    Gr. 6, 248
*Halley Came to Jackson*  Gr. 2, 340
Hambone  Gr. 1, 202
Happy Days Are Here Again
    Gr. 5, 284
Hava nagila  Gr. 6, 153
Hello to the World (poem)  Gr. 3, 2
Heri za Kwanzaa  Gr. 5, 476
Hosanna, Me Build a House
    Gr. 5, 132
I Am But a Small Voice  Gr. 6, 446
I Believe I Can Fly  Gr. 5, 170
I Got Rhythm  Gr. 6, 101
I Like Fall (poem)  Gr. K, 311
I Like You (poem)  Gr. 6, 7
I Vow to You, My Country  Gr. 5, 418
I Walk the Unfrequented Road
    Gr. 6, 79
I Wish I Knew How It Would Feel to Be
    Free  Gr. 6, 470
If I Had a Hammer  Gr. 5, 287
*Illusions*  Gr. 6, 347
It Rains and It Pours (poem)
    Gr. K, 243
It's Time  Gr. 6, 274
*It's Time*  Gr. 6, 319
Jambalaya (On The Bayou)  Gr. 6, 244
Johnny Appleseed  Gr. 4, 345
Joy of Kwanzaa, The  Gr. 6, 462
*Jump for Joy*  Gr. K, 212
Keel Row, The  Gr. 4, 240
Keep Your Eyes on the Prize  Gr. 3, 408
Keep Your Eyes on the Prize
    Gr. 8, E-16
*Key to the Highway*  Gr. 6, 243
Key to the Highway  Gr. 6, 243
Kid Like Me, A (speech piece)
    Gr. 2, 394
King, Martin Luther Jr.  Gr. 1, 434
Kwanzaa (poem)  Gr. 1, 431
La borinqueña  Gr. 8, D-19
La copa de la vida  Gr. 4, 414
Las estrellitas del cielo  Gr. 5, 175
Lean on Me  Gr. 6, 14
Let Freedom Ring  Gr. 5, 77

**(Hopes and Dreams, continued)**

Lift Ev'ry Voice and Sing  Gr. 5, 482
Lift Ev'ry Voice and Sing  Gr. 8, I-54
*Light Up the World*  Gr. 2, 196
Like a Bird  Gr. 6, 167
Live in the City  Gr. 5, 71
Loch Lomond  Gr. 5, 140
Los reyes de Oriente  Gr. 5, 480
Louiselle, Bryan  Gr. 1, 251
Love Can Build a Bridge  Gr. 4, 324
Love in Any Language  Gr. 6, 476
Love Is on Our Side  Gr. 5, 324
Love Will Guide Us  Gr. 4, 328
Lullaby (poem)  Gr. 1, 208
Lullaby and Dance  Gr. 4, 387
Mama, Buy Me a Chiney Doll
    Gr. K, 120
Moore, Carman  Gr. 3, 163
Mother to Son (poem)  Gr. 2, 203
*Mr. Tambourine Man*  Gr. 6, 148
Mr. Tambourine Man  Gr. 6, 150
My Dear Companion  Gr. 6, 23
My Travel Tree (poem)  Gr. K, 203
New Colossus, The (poem)  Gr. 5, 166
News of Home (poem)  Gr. 4, 336
Now Let Me Fly  Gr. 3, 178
Oh, Freedom  Gr. 5, 392
Oh, Freedom  Gr. 7, G-30
On My Way  Gr. 6, 313
One Moment in Time  Gr. 6, 352
One Small Step  Gr. 5, 126
Over the Rainbow  Gr. 4, 140
*Over the Rainbow*  Gr. 4, 143
Paths of Victory  Gr. 6, 195
Peace Round  Gr. 4, 348
Put a Little Love in Your Heart  Gr. 4, 6
*Put a Little Love in Your Heart*
    Gr. 4, 8
*Rain Song, The*  Gr. 2, 323
Reading Glasses (poem)  Gr. K, 325
Rise and Shine  Gr. 1, 122
*Rise Up, Shepherd, and Follow*
    Gr. 5, 470
Rise Up, Shepherd, and Follow
    Gr. 5, 471
Ríu ríu chíu  Gr. 5, 435
Roads Go Ever Ever On (poem)
    Gr. 6, 214
Rockin' Around the Christmas Tree
    Gr. 5, 466
Route 66  Gr. 4, 276
*Route 66*  Gr. 4, 279
Sail Away  Gr. 5, 404
Sailing Down My Golden River
    Gr. 4, 332
Santa Clara  Gr. 4, 172
Scotland the Brave  Gr. 5, 138
*She'll Be Coming 'Round the
    Mountain When She Comes*
    Gr. 4, 333
*Shed a Little Light*  Gr. 3, 409
Shir l'shalom  Gr. 4, 419
Sioux Lullaby (poem)  Gr. K, 111

*Sister Rosa*  Gr. 3, 411
Siyahamba  Gr. 6, 212
Sol, solecito  Gr. 1, 367
Someday Very Soon  Gr. 1, 376
Somewhere Out There  Gr. 5, 368
*Somewhere Out There*  Gr. 5, 369
Somos el barco  Gr. 4, 352
Stand By Me  Gr. 5, 46
*Stand By Me*  Gr. 5, 49
Star Light, Star Bright  Gr. 1, 108
Star-Spangled Banner, The  Gr. 4, 441
Star-Spangled Banner, The  Gr. 5, 488
Star-Spangled Banner, The  Gr. 6, 486
Star-Spangled Banner, The  Gr. 7, I-56
Starlight, Star Bright  Gr. 4, 373
Still, Still, Still  Gr. 5, 468
Stopping by Woods on a Snowy
    Evening  Gr. 6, 41
Strike Up the Band  Gr. 6, 135
Summertime  Gr. 6, 250
*Summertime*  Gr. 6, 252
Sun Gonna Shine  Gr. 6, 242
*Surfin' Safari*  Gr. 6, 261
Swanee  Gr. 6, 118
*Swing Low, Sweet Chariot*
    Gr. 6, 234
Tanabata-sama  Gr. 2, 336
*Tennessee River*  Gr. 5, 349
There's a Place  Gr. 5, 210
*This Is Your Night*  Gr. 6, 368
This Little Light of Mine  Gr. 6, 232
This World  Gr. 5, 168
*Times They Are A-Changin', The*
    Gr. 5, 384
Together in Unity  Gr. K, 320
Traveler's Song (poem)  Gr. 4, 336
Turn, Turn, Turn (To Everything There
    Is a Season)  Gr. 5, 378
Under the Same Sun  Gr. 6, 440
Under the Sea  Gr. 5, 372
United Nations on the March, The
    Gr. 6, 443
*Variations on "America"*  Gr. 6, 162
Wabash Cannon Ball  Gr. 5, 136
Wade in the Water  Gr. 4, 268
Wade in the Water  Gr. 8, I-64
Waitin' for the Light to Shine
    Gr. 4, 26
We Shall Overcome  Gr. 4, 326
*We Shall Overcome*  Gr. 5, 485
What a Wonderful World  Gr. 6, 62
*What Kind of Land?*  Gr. 4, 327
When I Grow Up (poem)  Gr. 2, 397
When Johnny Comes Marching Home
    Gr. 5, 180
*Where Have All the Flowers Gone?*
    Gr. 5, 287
Wings of a Dove  Gr. 4, 318
Winter Wonderland  Gr. 5, 454
Yellow Rose of Texas, The  Gr. 7, I-70
Yonder Come Day  Gr. 8, I-68
You Are My Sunshine  Gr. 6, 246
*You Are My Sunshine*  Gr. 6, 247

Your Friends Shall Be the Tall Wind
    Gr. 6, 201
Your Life Is Now  Gr. 6, 4
*Yours Forever*  Gr. 6, 344
Youth (poem)  Gr. 6, 6
Zomo the Rabbit (story)  Gr. 3, 364
Zum gali gali  Gr. 5, 400

## HUMOR

Addams Family, The  Gr. 5, 456
Adventures of Isabel, The (poem)
    Gr. 3, 173
Advice for a Frog (Concerning a Crane)
    (poem)  Gr. 4, 200
Aiken Drum  Gr. 1, 398
Animals Went In One By One, The
    (poem)  Gr. K, 275
Ants Go Marching, The  Gr. 1, 248
Apple Tree  Gr. 1, 228
Bát kim thang  Gr. 6, 13
Bat, The (poem)  Gr. 2, 302
Bones (poem)  Gr. 4, 219
Boogie Chant and Dance (speech
    piece)  Gr. 2, 78
Brush Your Teeth  Gr. 1, 284
Bumble Bee, The (speech piece)
    Gr. K, 74
Bump! Bump! Bump! (poem)
    Gr. K, 53
But the Cat Came Back  Gr. 2, 190
Camptown Races  Gr. 5, 270
Can You Canoe? (speech piece)
    Gr. 4, 170
Cantando mentiras  Gr. 4, 146
*Carnival of the Animals, "Royal
    March of the Lion"*  Gr. 3, 357
Cement Mixer  Gr. 4, 102
Chicken on the Fence Post  Gr. 3, 92
*Choo Choo Boogaloo*  Gr. 1, 127
Choo Choo Ch'Boogie  Gr. 5, 44
Chums (poem)  Gr. 1, 290
Cindy  Gr. 4, 384
Counting-Out Rhyme (speech piece)
    Gr. 1, 357
Cow's Woc Backward  Gr. 1, 390
Crocodile, The  Gr. 2, 362
Der sad to katte  Gr. 2, 300
Deux cocodries  Gr. 2, 364
*Disco Worm*  Gr. 2, 312
Don Gato  Gr. 3, 352
Down by the Bay  Gr. 1, 18
Down in the Meadow  Gr. K, 147
Draw Me a Bucket of Water  Gr. 3, 124
*Dreydl Song, The*  Gr. 3, 391
Duck, The (poem)  Gr. 1, 99
Ducks (poem)  Gr. 1, 99
Ducks in the Rain (poem)  Gr. K, 235
Eletelephony (poem)  Gr. 2, 161
Firefly (poem)  Gr. 1, 356
*Frosty, the Snowman*  Gr. 2, 391
Groundhog Blues, The  Gr. 3, 122
*Groundhog Jig, The*  Gr. 1, 436
Haul Away, Joe  Gr. 4, 13

Hi Heidi Ho  Gr. 1, 394
Hippopotamus Song, The  Gr. 3, 33
His Wife Said… (poem)  Gr. 1, 343
Honeybee Song, The  Gr. 1, 358
Hound Dog  Gr. 5, 212
How Much Wood Could a Woodchuck
    Chuck (speech piece)  Gr. 3, 120
I Love Peanuts  Gr. 1, 162
I Was Walking in a Circle (poem)
    Gr. 3, 321
If a Tiger Calls  Gr. 3, 354
Jellyfish Walk (poem)  Gr. 1, 33
Jig Along Home  Gr. 2, 366
Jump or Jiggle (poem)  Gr. 2, 26
Kibungo, Beast of the Forest (story)
    Gr. 2, 352
Kookaburra  Gr. 4, 186
Last Night I Dreamed of Chickens
    (poem)  Gr. 1, 141
*Lazy John*  Gr. 4, 11
Leatherwing Bat  Gr. 2, 303
*Little Red Hen, The*  Gr. 1, 254
Little Red Hen, The (story)  Gr. 1, 256
Llama, The (poem)  Gr. 5, 152
*Loose Tooth Blues*  Gr. 1, 284
Lots of Worms  Gr. 2, 310
Louder Than a Clap of Thunder (folk
    tale)  Gr. 1, 87
Michael Finnigan  Gr. 3, 153
Miss Mary Mack  Gr. 2, 42
Mister Ram Goat-O  Gr. 3, 54
Mother, Mother, I Am Sick (rhyme)
    Gr. K, 121
Mud  Gr. 3, 32
Never Smile at a Crocodile  Gr. 3, 100
*New Horizons in Music
    Appreciation—Beethoven's Fifth
    Symphony, Movement 1*  Gr. 6, 98
Noah's Shanty  Gr. 1, 342
O lê lê O Bahía  Gr. 6, 165
Old Dan Tucker  Gr. 3, 96
Old Mother Hubbard (rhyme)
    Gr. 1, 118
*On Green Dolphin Street*  Gr. 4, 126
On Mother's Day (poem)  Gr. 1, 443
On the Ning Nang Nong (poem)
    Gr. 1, 395
Our Mr. Toad (poem)  Gr. 3, 337
Our Washing Machine (poem)
    Gr. 1, 35
Panther, The (poem)  Gr. 3, 354
Party Tonight!  Gr. 2, 152
Pat Works on the Railway  Gr. 5, 182
Pavo, pavo  Gr. 1, 416
Pease Porridge Not (poem)  Gr. 1, 135
Peter, Peter, Sugar Eater (poem)
    Gr. 1, 284
Poem to Help You Figure Out What
    Bone the Patella Is, A (poem)
    Gr. 4, 219
Poem to Mud (poem)  Gr. 3, 34
Pumpkin Poem (poem)  Gr. 3, 381
Purple People Eater, The  Gr. 6, 448

"Quack!" Said the Billy Goat (poem)
    Gr. K, 233
*Quartetto buffo di gatti, "Comic
    Quartet for Cats"*  Gr. 1, 131
¡Qué llueva!  Gr. K, 81
Rags  Gr. 1, 290
Riquir rán  Gr. 4, 66
Rondo for Lunch, A (speech piece)
    Gr. 3, 212
Rudolph, the Red-Nosed Reindeer
    Gr. 1, 428
Sambalele  Gr. 4, 397
Scrub Brush Shuffle, The  Gr. 1, 118
*Scrub-a-dub*  Gr. 1, 306
Se va el caimán  Gr. 5, 306
Shake-'n'-Bake a Jelly (poem)
    Gr. K, 95
Shanghai Chicken  Gr. 1, 140
*She'll Be Coming 'Round the
    Mountain When She Comes*
    Gr. 4, 333
Silly Street  Gr. K, 224
Six-Inch Boots in a Nine-Inch Puddle
    Gr. 1, 366
Small Job, A  Gr. 3, 224
Soldier, Soldier  Gr. 4, 11
Some Silly Animals (poem)  Gr. 1, 392
Spaceworms  Gr. 1, 400
Straighten Up and Fly Right
    Gr. 4, 128
Summer Jazz (poem)  Gr. 1, 175
Table Manners (speech piece)
    Gr. 3, 190
There Was an Old Man (speech piece)
    Gr. 3, 191
This Old Man  Gr. 3, 152
Tie Me Kangaroo Down, Sport
    Gr. 4, 37
Twist with a Burger, Jitter with a Bug
    (speech piece)  Gr. 1, 132
Two Little Sausages (speech piece)
    Gr. 2, 79
Un elefante  Gr. 2, 160
Upside Down and Inside Out (poem)
    Gr. K, 297
Valentines  Gr. 2, 398
Waltzing with Bears  Gr. 3, 170
Worm, The (poem)  Gr. 2, 311
*Yakety Yak*  Gr. 5, 204
Yakety Yak  Gr. 5, 205
*Yertle the Turtle*  Gr. 2, 368
Zomo the Rabbit (story)  Gr. 3, 364

## IMAGINATION AND FANTASY

*See also Hopes and Dreams.*

A-Tisket, A-Tasket  Gr. 2, 238
Abiyoyo  Gr. 2, 108
About Buttons (poem)  Gr. 1, 211
Addams Family, The  Gr. 5, 456
Adventures of Isabel, The (poem)
    Gr. 3, 173

Aiken Drum  Gr. 1, 398
Animals Went In One By One, The
    (poem)  Gr. K, 275
Ants Go Marching, The  Gr. 1, 248
Arirang  Gr. 5, 25
Around the World (poem)  Gr. 2, 256
*Baa-Baa Black Sheep*  Gr. K, 102
Barb'ry Allen  Gr. 6, 44
Basin Street Blues  Gr. 5, 354
Be Bop (poem)  Gr. 5, 42
Big Rock Candy Mountain  Gr. 4, 330
Blast Off! (poem)  Gr. 1, 377
*Both Sides Now*  Gr. 5, 385
Bridges  Gr. 6, 86
Bump! Bump! Bump! (poem)
    Gr. K, 53
By Myself (poem)  Gr. 1, 43
*Carnival of the Animals, "Aquarium"*
    Gr. 5, 376
*Carnival of the Animals, "Royal
    March of the Lion"*  Gr. 3, 357
*Chawe chidyo chem'chero (story)*
    Gr. 2, 296
*Children's Corner Suite, "Snowflakes
    Are Dancing"*  Gr. 5, 239
*Children's Garden, The*  Gr. K, 267
Circle of Sun, A (poem)  Gr. K, 3
Clementine  Gr. 4, 341
*Coming Home from the Sea–I*
    Gr. 6, 345
*Coming Home from the Sea–II*
    Gr. 6, 345
*Cookie Crew, The*  Gr. K, 197
Costume Capers  Gr. 1, 412
Cowboy's Dream (poem)  Gr. 4, 339
Crab Dance (poem)  Gr. 2, 307
Crocodile, The  Gr. 2, 362
Cuculí  Gr. K, 238
Dance of Death (poem)  Gr. 5, 456
Dancing Girl (poem)  Gr. K, 249
Dancing Pig, The (folk tale)  Gr. 1, 196
*Dancing Tree, The*  Gr. K, 202
*Danse macabre*  Gr. 5, 457
Debajo 'el botón  Gr. 1, 210
Deck the Hall  Gr. 5, 474
Deux cocodries  Gr. 2, 364
Don Alfonso  Gr. 5, 177
Don Gato  Gr. 3, 352
Down by the Bay  Gr. 1, 18
Down in the Meadow  Gr. K, 147
Down in the Valley  Gr. 6, 375
Downtown  Gr. 6, 258
Dragon Smoke (poem)  Gr. 3, 387
*Dreydl Song, The*  Gr. 3, 391
Ducks in the Rain (poem)  Gr. K, 235
Ein Männlein steht im Walde  Gr. 2, 90
El barquito  Gr. 3, 358
Falling Rain  Gr. 2, 328
*Farmer in the Dell*  Gr. K, 233
Farmer in the Dell, The  Gr. K, 232
*Fish Food*  Gr. 2, 212

**(Imagination and Fantasy, continued)**

Flies (poem) Gr. 2, 201
Fly and the Bumblebee, The Gr. 1, 384
Free Music #1 Gr. 2, 212
Frosty, the Snowman Gr. 2, 391
Glad to Have a Friend Like You Gr. 2, 228
Goin' to Boston Gr. 6, 433
Goldilocks and the Three Bears Gr. K, 49
Goodnight, Sun (poem) Gr. 1, 367
Groundhog Jig, The Gr. 1, 436
Halloween Is a Very Unusual Night Gr. 3, 382
Halloween Song Gr. K, 309
Harrison Town Gr. 6, 97
Haul Away, Joe Gr. 4, 13
Hey, Diddle, Diddle Gr. K, 246
Hey, Diddle, Diddle Gr. K, 247
Hickory, Dickory, Dare (speech piece) Gr. K, 20
Higglety, Pigglety, Pop! Gr. K, 22
How Many Miles to Babylon? Gr. 2, 128
Humpty Dumpty (rhyme) Gr. K, 47
I Know an Old Lady Gr. 1, 388
I Walk the Unfrequented Road Gr. 6, 79
If a Tiger Calls Gr. 3, 354
In My Own Little Corner Gr. 3, 9
In the Pumpkin Patch Gr. 3, 380
Jack and Jill (rhyme) Gr. K, 47
Jellyfish Walk (poem) Gr. 1, 33
Jig Along Home Gr. 2, 366
Jinny Go 'Round Gr. K, 228
Johnny Appleseed Gr. 4, 345
Jolly Old St. Nicholas Gr. K, 316
Juan pirulero Gr. K, 215
Jump Rope Jingle (poem) Gr. K, 211
Jungle Beat Gr. 6, 347
Kibungo, Beast of the Forest (story) Gr. 2, 352
Kokopelli Wandering Song Gr. 5, 110
Kou ri lengay Gr. 2, 217
L'Enfant et les sortilèges, "Love for Two Cats" Gr. K, 101
La ciudad de Juaja Gr. 5, 58
Las estrellitas del cielo Gr. 5, 175
Las velitas Gr. 5, 147
Last Night I Dreamed of Chickens (poem) Gr. 1, 141
Les petites marionettes Gr. K, 237
Let's Pretend Gr. K, 227
Like a Bird Gr. 6, 167
Little Black Bug Gr. 1, 214
Little Miss Muffet (speech piece) Gr. K, 92
Little Red Caboose Gr. K, 229
Little Red Caboose Gr. K, 228
Little Red Hen, The (story) Gr. 1, 256
Little Shell Gr. 1, 355

Little Shop of Horrors Gr. 4, 422
London Bridge Gr. K, 244
Long Way Home, A Gr. 1, 382
Los pececitos Gr. 1, 178
Lots of Worms Gr. 2, 310
Love Can Build a Bridge Gr. 4, 324
Lullaby (poem) Gr. 1, 205
Lullaby (poem) Gr. 1, 208
Lullaby and Dance Gr. 4, 387
Luna lunera (speech piece) Gr. K, 90
Mad...Sad...Glad: A Piece in Three Mood-ments Gr. K, 249
Mariposita Gr. 2, 156
Marvelous Toy, The Gr. 1, 382
Mashed Potatoes (poem) Gr. 1, 21
Me voy para la luna Gr. 1, 397
Merry Modal Christmas, A Gr. 4, 411
Miss Susie Anna Sue Gr. K, 242
Mister Snow Rap (speech piece) Gr. 2, 391
Modern Dragon, A (poem) Gr. 3, 242
Monster Stomp, The (poem) Gr. 1, 133
More It Snows, The (poem) Gr. K, 259
Mother, Mother, I Am Sick (rhyme) Gr. K, 121
Mr. Tambourine Man Gr. 6, 148
Mr. Tambourine Man Gr. 6, 150
My Bonnie Lies Over the Ocean Gr. 4, 338
My Travel Tree (poem) Gr. K, 203
News of Home (poem) Gr. 4, 336
Night-light (poem) Gr. K, 223
Niu lang zhi nü Gr. 4, 335
Noah's Zoo in the Big, Big Rain Gr. K, 274
Noises (poem) Gr. K, 305
Nutcracker Suite, The, "Waltz of the Flowers" Gr. 6, 325
O, Desayo Gr. 5, 411
Oh, Watch the Stars Gr. 5, 216
Old Abram Brown Gr. 5, 222
Old Dan Tucker Gr. 3, 96
Old King Cole (rhyme) Gr. K, 245
Old King Cole Gr. K, 245
Old Mother Goose (poem) Gr. K, 247
One Fine Day Gr. 6, 347
One Green Jelly Bean Gr. K, 287
Open the Kingdom Gr. 6, 31
Orchestra (poem) Gr. 1, 74
Over the Rainbow Gr. 4, 140
Over the Rainbow Gr. 4, 143
Owl and the Pumpkin, The Gr. 2, 377
Panther, The (poem) Gr. 3, 354
Party Tonight! Gr. 2, 152
Paths of Victory Gr. 6, 195
Penny Lane Gr. 6, 257
Pin Pon Gr. 1, 146
Planets Chant, The (speech piece) Gr. 4, 377
Prayer for Earth (poem) Gr. 4, 350

Prelude to the Afternoon of a Faun Gr. 5, 113
Puff, the Magic Dragon Gr. 2, 350
Pumpkin Picking (poem) Gr. 2, 376
Pumpkin, Pumpkin Gr. 1, 413
Purple People Eater, The Gr. 6, 448
Quâ câu gió bay Gr. 5, 460
"Quack!" Said the Billy Goat (poem) Gr. K, 233
Rabbit Dance, The (story) Gr. 3, 334
Rain Sings a Song, The Gr. 1, 102
Rainy Day Blues Gr. 2, 328
Riendo el río corre Gr. 6, 263
Roads Go Ever Ever On (poem) Gr. 6, 214
Rockin' Robin Gr. 3, 368
Rolling Rice Cake, The: A Story from Japan (folk tale) Gr. 1, 91
Sail Away Gr. 5, 404
Sailboat in the Sky Gr. 4, 374
Santa Clara Gr. 4, 172
Scarborough Fair Gr. 6, 95
School Bus Rap (poem) Gr. 1, 83
Se va el caimán Gr. 5, 306
Shake Your Brain Gr. 1, 250
Shake-'n'-Bake a Jelly (poem) Gr. K, 95
Shanghai Chicken Gr. 1, 140
She'll Be Coming 'Round the Mountain When She Comes Gr. 4, 333
Ship that Never Returned, The Gr. 5, 402
Silly Street Gr. K, 224
Sing Me a Story Gr. 2, 346
Sing Your Story Gr. 3, 350
Singin' in the Rain Gr. 4, 360
Six Little Ducks Gr. K, 234
Skin and Bones Gr. 2, 376
Sleigh Ride Gr. 2, 390
Some Silly Animals (poem) Gr. 1, 392
Somewhere Out There Gr. 5, 368
Somewhere Out There Gr. 5, 369
Song of the Fishes Gr. 3, 244
Sounds of the Circus Gr. K, 241
Spaceworms Gr. 1, 400
Spring (poem) Gr. 2, 400
Starlight, Star Bright Gr. 4, 373
Summer Jazz (poem) Gr. 1, 175
Summertime Gr. 6, 250
Summertime Gr. 6, 252
Surfin' Safari Gr. 6, 261
Surfin' U.S.A. Gr. 6, 260
Syrinx Gr. 5, 113
Take Your Feet Out 'the Sand Gr. K, 231
Ten Little Teddy Bears (poem) Gr. K, 301
This Pretty Planet Gr. 4, 355
To a Red Kite (poem) Gr. 2, 326
Traveler's Song (poem) Gr. 4, 336
Twelve Days of Christmas, The Gr. 4, 430

Twist with a Burger, Jitter with a Bug (speech piece) Gr. 1, 132
Un elefante Gr. 2, 160
Under the Sea Gr. 5, 372
Usagi Gr. 1, 396
*Variations on "The Carnival of Venice"* Gr. 6, 161
Very Special Friend, A (poem) Gr. 1, 147
What a Wonderful World Gr. 6, 62
What Will You Be on Halloween? Gr. K, 308
When I Dance (poem) Gr. 1, 327
Wings of a Dove Gr. 4, 318
Winter Fantasy Gr. 4, 424
Winter Wonderland Gr. 5, 454
*Yertle the Turtle* Gr. 2, 368
Zomo the Rabbit (story) Gr. 3, 364

## MAP AND GLOBE *See also Places We Live.*

Abiyoyo Gr. 2, 108
Achshav Gr. 2, 64
Adana ya gidelim Gr. 2, 142
Ah, eu entrei na roda Gr. 3, 308
Away to America Gr. 5, 57
*Aweigh, Santy Ano* Gr. 1, 338
¡Ay, Jalisco no te rajes! Gr. 7, I-6
Blue Mountain Lake Gr. 6, 205
Bonavist' Harbour Gr. 3, 294
Bounce High, Bounce Low Gr. 1, 152
Bound for South Australia Gr. 5, 22
Chang Gr. 1, 156
Che che koolay Gr. 2, 266
Chuhwuht Gr. 2, 356
Cumberland Gap Gr. 4, 138
Dancin' in the Street Gr. 5, 361
Doong gul ge Gr. 3, 134
Elegua Gr. 7, D-8
Family Tree Gr. 3, 72
Farewell to Tarwathie Gr. 6, 43
Fifty Nifty United States Gr. 5, 251
Gypsy in the Moonlight Gr. 3, 12
*Hard Times* Gr. 1, 194
Hwa yuan li-de young wa wa Gr. 3, 102
I See the Moon Gr. 2, 58
I'm Flying Home Gr. 2, 286
*I've Been Everywhere* Gr. 6, 224
I've Been Everywhere Gr. 6, 226
Ise oluwa Gr. 2, 102
Jinny Go 'Round Gr. K, 228
Khorovod Gr. 1, 372
Kibungo Gr. 2, 354
Leak kanseng Gr. 1, 156
Los maizales Gr. 1, 296
Marines' Hymn, The Gr. 8, C-39
Mariposita Gr. 2, 156
Mister Ram Goat-O Gr. 3, 54
Nampaya omame Gr. 1, 138
Nani wale na hala Gr. 3, 260

Nie chcę cię znác Gr. 3, 314
O pião entrou Gr. 2, 355
*Orange Blossom Special* Gr. 1, 47
Orange Blossom Special Gr. 5, 266
Panamam tombé Gr. 7, D-18
Roll On, Columbia Gr. 5, 116
Route 66 Gr. 4, 276
Sarika keo Gr. 3, 275
*Sekar jepun* Gr. 1, 195
*Shenandoah* Gr. 2, 62
Shu ha mo Gr. 3, 276
Song of the Fishes Gr. 3, 244
Tall Cedar Tree Gr. 2, 322
This Land Is Your Land Gr. 5, 118
*This Land Is Your Land* Gr. 5, 120
This Land Is Your Land (refrain only) Gr. 1, 274
Train Is A-Comin' Gr. 3, 48
Turn the Glasses Over Gr. 3, 204
Un pajarito Gr. 2, 16
Vamos a la mar Gr. 3, 226
Wabash Cannon Ball Gr. 5, 136
Walk in Jerusalem Gr. 4, 100
Wind Blew East, The Gr. 1, 64
Xiao yin chuan Gr. 2, 14
*Yo Lé Lé (Fulani Groove)* Gr. 5, 33
Yonder Come Day Gr. 8, I-68

## MEASUREMENT

How Many Miles to Babylon? Gr. 2, 128
Just Watch (poem) Gr. K, 295
Let's Go Fly a Kite Gr. 2, 327
Lumberjack, The (poem) Gr. 1, 113
Six-Inch Boots in a Nine-Inch Puddle Gr. 1, 366

## MONEY

Banana Splits Gr. 1, 318
Bantama kra kro Gr. 5, 308
Boil Them Cabbage Down Gr. 6, 370
California Oranges (rhyme) Gr. 1, 15
Corta la caña Gr. 6, 364
Don't Let Your Watch Run Down Gr. 3, 166
Ego sum pauper Gr. 5, 158
El payo Gr. 6, 145
Goin' Down the Road Feelin' Bad Gr. 5, 282
*Goin' Down the Road Feelin' Bad* Gr. 5, 283
Guantanamera Gr. 8, I-32
Hot Cross Buns (Version 1) Gr. 3, 218
Hot Cross Buns (Version 2) Gr. 3, 221
I Bought Me a Cat Gr. 2, 308
James Brown Gr. K, 206
Linstead Market Gr. 5, 241
Mother Sent Me to the Store (rhyme) Gr. K, 136
Oranges and Lemons (poem) Gr. 4, 217
Pay Me My Money Down Gr. 4, 38
*Shake Your Brain* Gr. 1, 250
Worried Man Blues Gr. 6, 371

## MONTHS

Aguinaldo Gr. 3, 402
Apples, Peaches, Pears, and Plums (speech piece) Gr. 1, 14
Chanukah Is Here! Gr. 2, 382
El mes de abril Gr. 3, 328
*Groundhog Jig, The* Gr. 1, 436
Habari Gani Gr. 3, 404
Ichi-gatsu tsuitachi Gr. 3, 406
It's Santa—Again! Gr. 2, 385
Jingle Bells Gr. 2, 388
Kid Like Me, A (speech piece) Gr. 2, 394
Kwanzaa Carol, A Gr. 2, 392
L'inverno è passato Gr. 2, 400
Ner li Gr. 2, 383
Seasons Gr. K, 4
Setting the Thanksgiving Table (poem) Gr. 2, 381
Sheep in the Meadow (rhyme) Gr. 1, 17
*Sister Rosa* Gr. 3, 411
Spring Has Sprung! Gr. K, 142
Thanksgiving Is Near Gr. 2, 380
Valentines Gr. 2, 398
Valentines (poem) Gr. 2, 398
Written in March (poem) Gr. 4, 354

## MUSIC MAKING, POEMS, RHYMES, SONGS, AND STORIES ABOUT

ABC Rock Gr. 1, 262
African Noel Gr. 1, 427
Ahora voy a cantarles Gr. 3, 56
Ai, Dunaii moy Gr. 4, 293
Al tambor Gr. 3, 270
Alexander's Ragtime Band Gr. 6, 136
Alleluia Gr. 6, 133
Alumot Gr. 6, 306
America, I Hear You Singing Gr. 2, 402
*At the Hop* Gr. 4, 166
At the Hop Gr. 4, 168
At the Top of My Voice (poem) Gr. K, 279
Bam, chi, chi, bam Gr. K, 109
Bard of Armagh, The Gr. 4, 296
Be Bop (poem) Gr. 5, 42
Beriozka Gr. 4, 294
Beyond Borders Gr. 5, 292
Bonga Gr. K, 78
Boogie Chant and Dance (speech piece) Gr. 2, 78
Brand New Day, A Gr. 6, 7
Bridges Gr. 6, 86
*Brolga One* Gr. 4, 36
Cantaré, cantarás Gr. 6, 413
*Carnival of the Animals, "Royal March of the Lion"* Gr. 3, 357
Caroling, Caroling Gr. 6, 458
Chanukah, Chanukah Gr. 1, 420
Chawe chidyo chem'chero (story) Gr. 2, 296

**(*Making Music,* continued)**

Cheki, morena  Gr. 2, 180
Cho'i hát bội  Gr. 5, 318
*Choo Choo Boogaloo*  Gr. 1, 127
Cielito lindo  Gr. 4, 270
Cielito lindo  Gr. 7, I-20
*Common Ground*  Gr. 3, 379
Cuando pa' Chile me voy  Gr. 6, 376
Cuckoo, Cuckoo  Gr. 1, 110
Dance (poem)  Gr. K, 59
Dancin' in the Street  Gr. 5, 361
*Dancing in the Street*  Gr. 2, 254
De Beat (poem)  Gr. 2, 67
Deck the Hall  Gr. 5, 474
Different Beat, A  Gr. 1, 6
Ding Dong! Merrily on High
    Gr. 6, 427
*Disco Worm*  Gr. 2, 312
Do, Re, Mi, Fa  Gr. 6, 80
*Do-Re-Mi*  Gr. 5, 38
Doong gul ge  Gr. 3, 134
Down, Down, Baby  Gr. 2, 32
Drum, A (folk tale)  Gr. 1, 116
Eh, cumpari!  Gr. 4, 68
Ev'ry Kind of Music  Gr. 2, 226
Every Morning When I Wake Up
    Gr. 2, 320
Everybody Says  Gr. 1, 287
Extremes (poem)  Gr. 4, 409
*Fatou yo, "I am Fatou"*  Gr. K, 155
Feng yang hua gu  Gr. 4, 313
Go Around the Corn, Sally  Gr. 2, 12
Go With the Music and Sing
    Gr. 3, 376
Gonna Have a Good Time  Gr. 2, 4
Good Old Happy Song, A  Gr. K, 201
*Groundhog Jig, The*  Gr. 1, 436
Growing Corn (poem)  Gr. 1, 297
Gypsy in the Moonlight  Gr. 3, 12
Hanuka, Hanuka  Gr. 3, 390
Happy Wanderer, The  Gr. 4, 89
Hava nagila  Gr. 6, 153
Hava nashira  Gr. 6, 82
Heigh-Ho  Gr. 2, 6
Hello, There!  Gr. K, 6
Here Comes The Band (poem)
    Gr. 1, 167
Himmel und Erde  Gr. 5, 94
*Hindewhu (whistle) solo*  Gr. 6, 269
Hippopotamus Song, The  Gr. 3, 33
Hit Me with a Hot Note and Watch Me
    Bounce  Gr. 6, 112
Hitotsu toya  Gr. 5, 478
*Hotter Than That*  Gr. 6, 65
*How Can I Keep from Singing?*
    Gr. 4, 260
How Can I Keep from Singing?
    Gr. 4, 261
*Howjidoo*  Gr. 1, 315
I Don't Care If the Rain Comes Down
    Gr. 3, 24
I Got Rhythm  Gr. 6, 101
I Got Shoes  Gr. 2, 242

I Wonder Where Maria's Gone
    Gr. 3, 318
I'm Gonna Sing  Gr. 4, 33
I'm in the Mood  Gr. K, 86
I've Been Working on the Railroad
    Gr. 3, 242
*If I Had a Hammer*  Gr. 3, 241
*If You Can Walk*  Gr. 1, 19
In Music Meeting (poem)  Gr. 5, 162
It Don't Mean a Thing (If It Ain't Got
    That Swing)  Gr. 5, 336
*It Don't Mean a Thing if It Ain't Got
    that Swing*  Gr. 5, 338
*It Don't Mean a Thing if It Ain't Got
    that Swing*  Gr. 6, 386
It Is Fun to Sing (One fish, two fish, red
    fish, blue fish) (poem)  Gr. 1, 65
Jig Along Home  Gr. 2, 366
Jingle Bells  Gr. 2, 388
Just a Snap-Happy Blues  Gr. 6, 388
Kaeru no uta  Gr. K, 183
Kibungo, Beast of the Forest (story)
    Gr. 2, 352
Knock the Cymbals  Gr. 1, 176
*Kokopelli Wandering Song*
    Gr. 5, 110
Kwanzaa Carol, A  Gr. 2, 392
La mariposa  Gr. 6, 58
Las mañanitas  Gr. 6, 481
Leila  Gr. 1, 258
Let Music Surround You  Gr. 4, 236
Let the Music Begin!  Gr. 1, 2
Let Us Sing Together  Gr. 6, 156
Let's Celebrate!  Gr. 3, 374
*Lieutenant Kijé, Op. 60, "Troika"*
    Gr. 6, 457
Lift Ev'ry Voice and Sing  Gr. 8, I-54
*Lion*  Gr. 6, 303
Little David  Gr. 1, 232
Little David, Play on Your Harp
    Gr. 4, 394
*Little David, Play on Your Harp*
    Gr. 4, 395
*Little Red Hen, The*  Gr. 1, 254
Lone Star Trail  Gr. 2, 21
Los niños en España cantan
    Gr. 4, 197
Mama Don't 'Low  Gr. 6, 358
Mary Ann  Gr. 6, 180
Merry Modal Christmas, A  Gr. 4, 411
Mi cuerpo hace música  Gr. K, 106
Michael, Row the Boat Ashore
    Gr. 2, 18
Miss Mary Mack  Gr. 2, 42
Mon papa  Gr. 2, 280
Monster Stomp, The (poem)
    Gr. 1, 133
Morning Comes Early  Gr. 5, 13
*Mr. Tambourine Man*  Gr. 6, 148
Mr. Tambourine Man  Gr. 6, 150
Music (poem)  Gr. 1, 3
Music (poem)  Gr. 5, 95
Music (poem)  Gr. K, 107

Music's in Me , The  Gr. 2, 40
My Father's House  Gr. 2, 25
My Song (poem)  Gr. 4, 305
Ner li  Gr. 2, 383
*New Horizons in Music
    Appreciation—Beethoven's Fifth
    Symphony, Movement 1*  Gr. 6, 98
Niño querido  Gr. 1, 308
Now That's Tap (speech piece)
    Gr. 6, 320
Now's the Time  Gr. 5, 445
O, Desayo  Gr. 5, 411
O Laufet, ihr Hirten  Gr. 2, 384
O Music  Gr. 5, 162
Oh, Freedom  Gr. 7, G-30
Oh, How Lovely Is the Evening
    Gr. 4, 217
Oranges and Lemons (poem)
    Gr. 4, 217
Orchestra (poem)  Gr. 1, 74
Orchestra, The (poem)  Gr. 1, 328
Over My Head  Gr. 4, 118
*Oye mi canto, " "*  Gr. 6, 114
Parade Came Marching, The  Gr. 1, 166
Peppermint Twist  Gr. 3, 46
Piñon, pirulín  Gr. 2, 174
Play a Simple Melody  Gr. 5, 72
Pollerita  Gr. 5, 151
*Quartetto buffo di gatti, "Comic
    Quartet for Cats"*  Gr. 1, 131
¡Qué gusto!  Gr. 3, 132
Rabbit Dance, The (story)  Gr. 3, 334
Ragtime (poem)  Gr. 5, 334
Rain Sings a Song, The  Gr. 1, 102
*Rainy Day Blues*  Gr. 2, 328
*Reggae Is Now*  Gr. 6, 143
Rhythm Is Gonna Get You, The
    Gr. 6, 348
Ríu ríu chíu  Gr. 5, 435
Rock and Roll Is Here to Stay
    Gr. 6, 36
*Rock Around the Clock*  Gr. 5, 356
Rock Around the Clock  Gr. 7, B-18
Rockin' Around the Christmas Tree
    Gr. 5, 466
Run, Molly, Run  Gr. 1, 8
Scattin' A-Round (Variations on Row 3)
    Gr. 6, 160
*Sha Sha Sha*  Gr. 6, 328
*Shchedryk, "Carol of the Bells"*
    Gr. 6, 103
Shir l'shalom  Gr. 4, 419
Sidewalk Songs (poem)  Gr. K, 207
Sing a Little Song  Gr. K, 30
Sing a Song of Peace  Gr. 6, 66
Sing, America, Sing!  Gr. 3, 238
Sing Me a Story  Gr. 2, 346
Sing, Sing, Sing!  Gr. 5, 340
Sing! Speak! Whisper! Shout!
    Gr. 1, 36
Sing Your Story  Gr. 3, 350
Singin' in the Tub  Gr. K, 220
Singing-Time (poem)  Gr. 3, 201

Sonando Gr. 4, 34
Song of One, A Gr. 3, 344
Song That's Just for You, A
　　Gr. 2, 126
Spring (poem) Gr. 2, 400
Step in Time Gr. 2, 74
Strike Up the Band Gr. 6, 135
Summer Jazz (poem) Gr. 1, 175
Tall Cedar Tree Gr. 2, 322
Tancovačka Gr. 4, 230
Tap It! Rap It! (speech piece)
　　Gr. K, 194
Teach Me to Swing Gr. 5, 84
Ten Tom-Toms (poem) Gr. K, 79
That's What's New with Me! Gr. K, 2
*This Is Your Night* Gr. 6, 368
This Land Is Your Land Gr. 7, I-66
Those Magic Changes Gr. 8, E-30
Three Little Birds Gr. 4, 320
Time to Sing Gr. 2, 8
Today Is Your Birthday Gr. 1, 410
Turn the Beat Around Gr. 4, 2
*Twist, The* Gr. 5, 359
Twist with a Burger, Jitter with a Bug
　　(speech piece) Gr. 1, 132
Tzena, tzena Gr. 5, 298
Ujima Gr. 1, 430
Un pajarito Gr. 2, 16
Vamos a cantar Gr. K, 278
Vamos a la fiesta Gr. 2, 374
*Viva la musica* Gr. 5, 95
Vive l'amour Gr. 6, 176
Voice Choice Gr. K, 27
Voices of Pride, The Gr. 5, 86
Walk Together, Children Gr. 3, 146
Way Down in the Music (poem)
　　Gr. 2, 227
When the Saints Go Marching In
　　Gr. 2, 178
Willowbee Gr. 1, 222
Wings of a Dove Gr. 4, 318
Winter Song Gr. 6, 455
Woodland Chorus Gr. K, 250
Xiao Gr. 4, 314
Yellow Rose of Texas, The Gr. 7, I-70

## N

### NEIGHBORHOODS

Banana Splits Gr. 1, 318
Children of Long Ago (poem)
　　Gr. 1, 31
Growing Corn (poem) Gr. 1, 297
*Howjidoo* Gr. 1, 315
James Brown Gr. K, 206
Li'l Liza Jane Gr. 3, 140
*Little Red Hen, The* Gr. 1, 254
Little Red Hen, The (story) Gr. 1, 256
Parade Came Marching, The Gr. 1, 166
*Penny Lane* Gr. 6, 257
Pizza, Pizza, Daddy-o Gr. 2, 28
We Moved About a Week Ago (poem)
　　Gr. 2, 230

### NIGHT AND DAY

A la puerta del cielo Gr. 5, 60
A la rurru niño Gr. K, 180
Ah, Poor Bird Gr. 4, 196
Ala Da'lona Gr. 5, 301
All Night, All Day Gr. 4, 180
*All Through the Night* Gr. 5, 104
All Through the Night Gr. 5, 105
Almost Day Gr. 3, 397
Ash Grove, The Gr. 5, 114
Au clair de la lune Gr. 3, 18
Ayliluli, num tsipor Gr. 1, 204
Baby Beluga Gr. K, 272
*Bai, bai, bai, bai* Gr. 2, 197
Bam, chi, chi, bam Gr. K, 109
Bedtime (poem) Gr. K, 159
Blow the Wind Southerly Gr. 5, 178
Bound for South Australia Gr. 5, 22
Boysie Gr. 2, 195
Brush Your Teeth Gr. 1, 284
Canción de cuna Gr. 4, 144
*Catalana, "Andante"* Gr. K, 134
Chippewa Lullaby Gr. K, 181
*Cradle Song* Gr. K, 97
Cycle Song of Life (The River Song)
　　Gr. 4, 370
Dance (poem) Gr. K, 59
Day-O! (Banana Boat Loader's Song)
　　Gr. 5, 18
Deau-deau, ti pitit maman Gr. 2, 306
Dinner Music Gr. K, 70
Each of Us Is a Flower Gr. 3, 154
Ég a gyertya Gr. K, 96
Einini Gr. 4, 391
El caracol Gr. K, 130
El coquí Gr. 2, 292
En nuestra Tierra tan linda Gr. 2, 335
*En prière* Gr. K, 158
*Evening Chaconne* Gr. 6, 202
Every Morning at Eight O'Clock
　　(rhyme) Gr. 1, 36
Every Morning When I Wake Up
　　Gr. 2, 320
Fais do do Gr. 6, 403
Fais dodo Gr. K, 158
Flowers at Night (poem) Gr. 2, 246
For the Beauty of the Earth Gr. 4, 356
Frère Jacques Gr. 2, 125
Frog Lullaby (poem) Gr. K, 149
Goodnight, Sun (poem) Gr. 1, 367
Had to Get Up This Mornin' Soon
　　Gr. 3, 114
Hej pada pada Gr. 3, 78
Hui jia qü Gr. 2, 158
Hush Up the Baby Gr. K, 222
*I Love a Rainy Night (line dance)*
　　Gr. 5, 350
In the Morning (poem) Gr. 1, 217
*In the Still of the Night* Gr. 4, 47
*Je m'endors* Gr. K, 219
*Jump for Joy* Gr. K, 212
Jump That Jody Gr. K, 212
Kum bachur atzel Gr. 3, 138

Kunolounkwa Gr. K, 110
*Kunolounkwa, "Contemporary"*
　　Gr. K, 110
Las mañanitas Gr. 6, 481
*Las mañanitas* Gr. K, 325
Las velitas Gr. 5, 147
Leatherwing Bat Gr. 2, 303
*Light Up the World* Gr. 2, 196
Lion Sleeps Tonight, The Gr. 4, 131
*Lion Sleeps Tonight, The* Gr. 4, 132
Lion, The (poem) Gr. K, 217
*Lo, How a Rose E'er Blooming*
　　Gr. 6, 210
Look! Look! The Sun Woke Up!
　　Gr. 1, 368
Lullaby (poem) Gr. 1, 205
Lullaby (poem) Gr. 1, 208
Lullaby and Dance Gr. 4, 387
Manhattan Lullaby (poem) Gr. K, 193
Mary Wore Her Red Dress Gr. K, 74
Mashed Potatoes (speech piece)
　　Gr. 1, 20
Moon, The (poem) Gr. 1, 399
Morning Comes Early Gr. 5, 13
Morning Has Broken Gr. 5, 28
Morning Is Come Gr. 3, 128
Night, The (poem) Gr. 4, 81
Night Will Never Stay, The (poem)
　　Gr. 3, 183
Night-light (poem) Gr. K, 223
Nightdance (poem) Gr. K, 219
Niño querido Gr. 1, 308
Niu lang zhi nü Gr. 4, 335
Noises (poem) Gr. K, 305
Nruab hnub thiab hmo ntuj (story)
　　Gr. 4, 366
Nu wahtan Gr. 1, 279
Oh, How Lovely Is the Evening
　　Gr. 4, 217
Oh, Watch the Stars Gr. 2, 144
On My Way Gr. 6, 313
*Rain, Rain, Beautiful Rain* Gr. 4, 32
Riquir rán Gr. 4, 66
Rise and Shine Gr. 1, 122
Sheep, Sheep (poem) Gr. 1, 309
Shine, Shine, Shine Gr. 1, 42
Silverly (poem) Gr. K, 135
Sioux Lullaby (poem) Gr. K, 111
Skye Boat Song Gr. 6, 372
Sleep, Baby, Sleep Gr. 2, 197
Song of the Night, The (poem)
　　Gr. 3, 346
Star Light, Star Bright Gr. 1, 108
Star-Spangled Banner, The Gr. 8, I-62
Starlight, Star Bright Gr. 4, 373
Stars (poem) Gr. 1, 61
Still, Still, Still Gr. 5, 468
T'hola, t'hola Gr. 4, 132
*This Is Your Night* Gr. 6, 368
This Pretty Planet Gr. 4, 355
Thula, thula, ngoana Gr. 4, 227
Upside Down and Inside Out (poem)
　　Gr. K, 297

Thematic Index

**(Night and Day, continued)**
Vamos a cantar  Gr. K, 278
Wind Up the Apple Tree  Gr. 1, 184
Winter Song  Gr. 6, 455
World We Love, The  Gr. 3, 342
You Are My Sunshine  Gr. 6, 246
*You Are My Sunshine*  Gr. 6, 247
*Yü guang guang*  Gr. 6, 60
*Zulu Lullaby*  Gr. K, 158

**P**

## PARADES
Celebrating Our Flag (poem)  Gr. K, 327
*Cookie Crew, The*  Gr. K, 197
Here Comes The Band (poem)
    Gr. 1, 167
*Love for Three Oranges, "March"*
    Gr. K, 117
*On Parade*  Gr. K, 326
Parade Came Marching, The  Gr. 1, 166
*Rocky Point Holiday*  Gr. 6, 331
*Semper Fidelis*  Gr. K, 326
*Sounds of the Circus*  Gr. K, 241
Ten Tom-Toms (poem)  Gr. K, 79
What Will You Be on Halloween?
    Gr. K, 308
When Johnny Comes Marching Home
    Gr. 5, 180

## PARTS OF THE BODY
Ayii, Ayii, Ayii (poem)  Gr. K, 11
Bee, Bee Bumblebee (speech piece)
    Gr. 1, 50
Bones (poem)  Gr. 4, 219
Celebrate  Gr. 1, 407
Che che koolay  Gr. 2, 266
Clap, Wiggle, and Stomp  Gr. K, 34
*Copycat*  Gr. K, 9
Debajo 'el botón  Gr. 1, 210
Doctor Knickerbocker (speech piece)
    Gr. 1, 302
Down, Down, Baby  Gr. 2, 32
Dry Bones  Gr. 4, 162
Dry Bones Come Skipping  Gr. 4, 218
El juego chirimbolo  Gr. 2, 54
Frog (poem)  Gr. 1, 25
Gato (poem)  Gr. 1, 131
Hands (poem)  Gr. 1, 203
Head, Shoulders, Baby  Gr. 1, 82
Hinges (poem)  Gr. K, 52
Hokey Pokey  Gr. K, 296
How to Be Angry (poem)  Gr. K, 249
I'm Tall, I'm Small  Gr. K, 18
Ikhanda, maslombe  Gr. K, 14
Juanito  Gr. K, 300
Let's Get the Rhythm of the Band
    Gr. 3, 84
Let's Go Barefoot (poem)  Gr. 1, 440
Little Green Frog, The  Gr. 1, 24
Looby Loo  Gr. K, 210
My Shadow (poem)  Gr. K, 19
New Shoes (poem)  Gr. 2, 242
Oliver Twist  Gr. K, 138

One, Two, Three, Four, Five (rhyme)
    Gr. 1, 67
Poem to Help You Figure Out What
    Bone the Patella Is, A (poem)
    Gr. 4, 219
Pon, pon, pon  Gr. K, 50
Put Your Finger in the Air  Gr. K, 114
*Rainy Day Blues*  Gr. 2, 328
Riddle Ree (speech piece)  Gr. 2, 34
*Scrub-a-dub*  Gr. 1, 306
Shu ha mo  Gr. 3, 276
Singin' in the Tub  Gr. K, 220
Time to Move  Gr. 1, 244
Time to Sing  Gr. 2, 8
Tony Chestnut  Gr. 2, 35
Tracks (poem)  Gr. K, 299
Un, deux, trois  Gr. 2, 198
Zudio  Gr. 2, 269

## PAST AND PRESENT  *See also*
    *Social Studies.*
A-Tisket, A-Tasket  Gr. 2, 238
Away to America  Gr. 5, 57
Bard of Armagh, The  Gr. 4, 296
Blow, Ye Winds  Gr. 4, 255
Bob-a-Needle  Gr. 2, 232
California  Gr. 5, 52
California, Here I Come  Gr. 4, 287
Children of Long Ago (poem)
    Gr. 1, 31
Cindy  Gr. 4, 384
Don't You Hear the Lambs?  Gr. 5, 97
*Don't You Hear the Lambs?*
    Gr. 5, 99
Drill, Ye Tarriers  Gr. 5, 54
Family Tree  Gr. 3, 72
Farewell to the Warriors  Gr. 4, 284
Feng yang hua gu  Gr. 4, 313
Follow the Drinkin' Gourd  Gr. 4, 266
Glendy Burke, The  Gr. 4, 262
Goin' to Boston  Gr. 6, 433
Gotta Find a Footprint (poem)
    Gr. 4, 221
*Halley Came to Jackson*  Gr. 2, 340
Harriet Tubman (poem)  Gr. 4, 269
Haul Away, Joe  Gr. 4, 13
Johnny Appleseed  Gr. 4, 345
Kwanzaa Carol, A  Gr. 2, 392
La ciudad de Juaja  Gr. 5, 58
*Lazy John*  Gr. 4, 11
London Bridge  Gr. K, 244
Mama, Buy Me a Chiney Doll
    Gr. K, 120
Mississippi River Chant (speech piece)
    Gr. 2, 132
Ner li  Gr. 2, 383
Old Abram Brown  Gr. 5, 222
Old Brass Wagon  Gr. 2, 122
Old House, Tear It Down!  Gr. 4, 178
Over My Head  Gr. 4, 118
Pastures of Plenty  Gr. 4, 280
Paw-Paw Patch  Gr. 4, 93
Pease Porridge Hot  Gr. 1, 134

Peppermint Twist  Gr. 3, 46
Phoebe  Gr. 1, 30
Route 66  Gr. 4, 276
*Route 66*  Gr. 4, 279
Sing Your Story  Gr. 3, 350
Soldier, Soldier  Gr. 4, 11
Somebody Waiting  Gr. 2, 283
Streets of Laredo  Gr. 4, 272
Sweet Betsy from Pike  Gr. 4, 244
Thanksgiving Is Near  Gr. 2, 380
This Train  Gr. 5, 26
We Shall Not Be Moved  Gr. 4, 437
We Shall Overcome  Gr. 4, 326
We're Making Popcorn (speech piece)
    Gr. 1, 86
Weevily Wheat  Gr. 4, 105
*What Kind of Land?*  Gr. 4, 327

## PATTERNS
Ants Go Marching, The  Gr. 1, 248
Brush Your Teeth  Gr. 1, 284
Frog (poem)  Gr. 1, 25
I Can't Spell Hippopotamus  Gr. 1, 264
Merry-Go-Round  Gr. K, 290
Orchestra, The (poem)  Gr. 1, 328
Over in the Meadow  Gr. 1, 346
Sailing to the Sea  Gr. 1, 336
Tracks (poem)  Gr. K, 299

## PLACES WE LIVE  *See also Map and*
    *Globe.*

### CITIES
*Aweigh, Santy Ano*  Gr. 1, 338
¡Ay, Jalisco no te rajes!  Gr. 7, I-6
Basin Street Blues  Gr. 5, 354
Blow, Ye Winds  Gr. 4, 255
*Choo Choo Boogaloo*  Gr. 1, 127
Con el vito  Gr. 7, G-15
Cotton-Eye Joe  Gr. 4, 288
Dancin' in the Street  Gr. 5, 361
*Dancing in the Street*  Gr. 2, 254
*El Salón México*  Gr. 6, 199
Goin' to Boston  Gr. 6, 433
Goodbye, Julie (Miss Julie Ann
    Johnson)  Gr. 1, 334
Great Big House  Gr. 2, 204
I'm Flying Home  Gr. 2, 286
*I've Been Everywhere*  Gr. 6, 224
I've Been Everywhere  Gr. 6, 226
Jambalaya (On The Bayou)
    Gr. 6, 244
James Brown  Gr. K, 206
Kingston Market  Gr. 3, 90
La ciudad de Juaja  Gr. 5, 58
Lemonade  Gr. 1, 190
Li'l Liza Jane  Gr. 3, 140
Live in the City  Gr. 5, 71
London Bridge  Gr. K, 244
Manhattan Lullaby (poem)
    Gr. K, 193
Rio Grande  Gr. 4, 256
Rocky Top  Gr. 5, 348
Rondo for Lunch, A (speech piece)
    Gr. 3, 212

Rosie, Darling Rosie  Gr. 2, 215
Route 66  Gr. 4, 276
See-Saw Sacradown  Gr. 2, 208
Sidewalk Songs (poem)  Gr. K, 207
*Sister Rosa*  Gr. 3, 411
Sun Gonna Shine  Gr. 6, 242
Surfin' U.S.A.  Gr. 6, 260
Theme from New York, New York
 Gr. 4, 250
Turn the Glasses Over  Gr. 3, 204
*Variations on "The Carnival of
 Venice"*  Gr. 6, 161
Wabash Cannon Ball  Gr. 5, 136
Walk in Jerusalem  Gr. 4, 100
*Walkin' to New Orleans*
 Gr. 3, 371

## COMMUNITIES (RURAL, SUBURBAN, URBAN)

*Bear Dance*  Gr. 7, C-5
Bury Me Not on the Lone Prairie
 Gr. 6, 19
Children of Long Ago (poem)
 Gr. 1, 31
Cuando pa' Chile me voy
 Gr. 6, 376
Downtown  Gr. 6, 258
El rancho grande  Gr. 4, 215
Farewell to Tarwathie  Gr. 6, 43
Green, Green Grass of Home
 Gr. 6, 248
*Halley Came to Jackson*
 Gr. 2, 340
Harrison Town  Gr. 6, 97
Hey, Ho! Nobody Home  Gr. 6, 28
Home on the Range  Gr. 5, 69
I'm a Very Fine Turkey  Gr. K, 310
*I've Been Everywhere*  Gr. 6, 224
I've Been Everywhere  Gr. 6, 226
Jambalaya (On The Bayou)
 Gr. 6, 244
James Brown  Gr. K, 206
Jinny Go 'Round  Gr. K, 228
Live in the City  Gr. 5, 71
Loch Lomond  Gr. 5, 140
Manhattan Lullaby (poem)
 Gr. K, 193
My Home's Across the Blue Ridge
 Mountains  Gr. 4, 84
News of Home (poem)  Gr. 4, 336
*Ozark Mountain Jubilee*  Gr. 4, 86
*Penny Lane*  Gr. 6, 257
River  Gr. 4, 58
Scarborough Fair  Gr. 6, 95
Sidewalk Songs (poem)  Gr. K, 207
Sidewalk Sounds (poem)
 Gr. K, 115
Sourwood Mountain  Gr. 4, 65
Summertime  Gr. 6, 250
*Summertime*  Gr. 6, 252
*Surfin' Safari*  Gr. 6, 261
Surfin' U.S.A.  Gr. 6, 260

Theme from New York, New York
 Gr. 4, 250
This Land Is Your Land  Gr. 5, 118
*This Land Is Your Land*
 Gr. 5, 120
Walk in Jerusalem  Gr. 4, 100
When the Saints Go Marching In
 Gr. 2, 178

## CONTINENTS

Abiyoyo  Gr. 2, 108
Ayelivi  Gr. 2, 70
Bound for South Australia
 Gr. 5, 22
Chawe chidyo chem'chero (story)
 Gr. 2, 296
Continents, The (speech piece)
 Gr. 4, 357
El juego chirimbolo  Gr. 2, 54
Ise oluwa  Gr. 2, 102
Kibungo  Gr. 2, 354
Kibungo, Beast of the Forest (story)
 Gr. 2, 352
*Primitive Fire, "Oya"*  Gr. 2, 68
*River Suite, The, "Finale"*
 Gr. 5, 121
Usagi  Gr. 1, 396
Xiao yin chuan  Gr. 2, 14

## COUNTRIES

Achshav  Gr. 2, 64
Adana ya gidelim  Gr. 2, 142
African Noel  Gr. 1, 427
Ah, eu entrei na roda  Gr. 3, 308
Ahora voy a cantarles  Gr. 3, 56
Allá en la fuente  Gr. 2, 92
Amefuri  Gr. 1, 144
America  Gr. 1, 446
America  Gr. 2, 403
America  Gr. 3, 412
America  Gr. 4, 440
America  Gr. 5, 486
America  Gr. 6, 484
America  Gr. 7, I-2
America  Gr. K, 326
America, the Beautiful  Gr. 3, 413
Artsa alinu  Gr. 3, 285
Así es mi tierra  Gr. 6, 172
Au clair de la lune  Gr. 3, 18
¡Ay, Jalisco no te rajes!  Gr. 7, I-6
Ayliluli, num tsipor  Gr. 1, 204
Banana  Gr. 2, 114
*Be Still, My Child*  Gr. 1, 39
Bonavist' Harbour  Gr. 3, 294
Bound for South Australia
 Gr. 5, 22
Cha yang wu  Gr. 1, 90
Chang  Gr. 1, 156
Chawe chidyo chem'chero (story)
 Gr. 2, 296
Che che koolay  Gr. 2, 266
*Chica chica boom chic*  Gr. 2, 112
Ciranda  Gr. 2, 272

*Cold and Frosty Morning*
 Gr. 2, 139
Con el vito  Gr. 7, G-15
Counting Song  Gr. 1, 253
Crocodile, The  Gr. 2, 362
Cuando pa' Chile me voy
 Gr. 6, 376
De colores  Gr. 8, I-14
Debajo 'el botón  Gr. 1, 210
Diou shou juan'er  Gr. 2, 277
Don Gato  Gr. 3, 352
Don't Cry for Me, Argentina
 Gr. 6, 74
Doong gul ge  Gr. 3, 134
Drum, A (folk tale)  Gr. 1, 116
Ein Männlein steht im Walde
 Gr. 2, 90
El barquito  Gr. 3, 358
El juego chirimbolo  Gr. 2, 54
El mes de abril  Gr. 3, 328
Elegua  Gr. 7, D-8
Family Tree  Gr. 3, 72
Farewell to Tarwathie  Gr. 6, 43
Feliz Navidad  Gr. 7, I-28
*Finlandia*  Gr. 6, 78
Freedom Is Coming  Gr. 5, 415
Frère Jacques  Gr. 2, 125
Geef jij mij die schoen  Gr. 1, 126
Ha'kyo jong  Gr. 2, 135
Hama chi dori  Gr. 3, 330
*Harukoma, "Spring Horse Dance"*
 Gr. 1, 145
Hato popo  Gr. 1, 186
Hej pada pada  Gr. 3, 78
Hello!  Gr. 2, 262
Hevenu shalom aleichem  Gr. 3, 378
Hotaru koi  Gr. 1, 356
How Doth the Little Crocodile
 (poem)  Gr. 2, 363
How Many Miles to Babylon?
 Gr. 2, 128
How the Kiwi Lost Its Wings (story)
 Gr. 1, 78
Hwa yuan li-de young wa wa
 Gr. 3, 102
I Vow to You, My Country
 Gr. 5, 418
Ichi-gatsu tsuitachi  Gr. 3, 406
Ikhanda, maslombe  Gr. K, 14
Ise oluwa  Gr. 2, 102
Jan ken pon  Gr. 3, 302
¡Jeu! ¡Jeu!  Gr. 1, 216
Khorovod  Gr. 1, 372
Kibungo  Gr. 2, 354
Kibungo, Beast of the Forest (story)
 Gr. 2, 352
Kou ri lengay  Gr. 2, 217
L'inverno è passato  Gr. 2, 400
La borinqueña  Gr. 8, D-19
La piñata  Gr. 3, 399
La víbora  Gr. 1, 322
Leak kanseng  Gr. 1, 156
Los maizales  Gr. 1, 296

(*Places We Live,* continued)

Mariposita Gr. 2, 156
*Mi tierra* Gr. 6, 365
Mubärak Gr. 3, 282
Nampaya omame Gr. 1, 138
Naranja dulce Gr. 2, 97
Nie chcę cię znác Gr. 3, 314
No quiero plata Gr. 1, 424
Nu wahtan Gr. 1, 279
O ma washi Gr. K, 13
O pião entrou Gr. 2, 355
Pai pi qiu Gr. 1, 324
Panamam tombé Gr. 7, D-18
Pavo, pavo Gr. 1, 416
*Piki mai* Gr. 1, 79
Ptashky u babusi sadochku
    Gr. 1, 192
Pust' 'vsegda budet sonse
    Gr. 3, 278
¡Qué bonita bandera! Gr. 5, 294
*Riverdance Suite* Gr. 2, 141
*Roddy McCaulay* Gr. 3, 292
Rolling Rice Cake, The: A Story
    from Japan (folk tale) Gr. 1, 91
Sarika keo Gr. 3, 275
Sawatdee tuh jah Gr. 2, 265
Scotland the Brave Gr. 5, 138
Serra, serra, serrador Gr. 1, 112
Shu ha mo Gr. 3, 276
Si me dan pasteles Gr. 1, 432
Sing, America, Sing! Gr. 3, 238
Sol, solecito Gr. 1, 367
St. Patrick Was a Gentleman
    Gr. 3, 290
Star-Spangled Banner, The
    Gr. 3, 415
Star-Spangled Banner, The
    Gr. 7, I-56
Tanabata-sama Gr. 2, 336
This Land Is Your Land Gr. 7, I-66
To'ia mai te waka Gr. 1, 77
Un, deux, trois Gr. 2, 198
Un elefante Gr. 2, 160
Un pajarito Gr. 2, 16
Vamos a la mar Gr. 3, 226
*Variations on "America"*
    Gr. 6, 162
Vil du? Gr. 1, 92
Viva Jujuy Gr. 5, 228
*Vulani ringi ring* Gr. 1, 139
Why the Warthog Goes About on
    His Knees (story) Gr. 1, 139
Xiao yin chuan Gr. 2, 14
Yankee Doodle Gr. 3, 414
Yibane amenu Gr. 4, 316
Zomo the Rabbit (story) Gr. 3, 364
Zum gali gali Gr. 5, 400

**HOMES**

Así es mi tierra Gr. 6, 172
¡Ay, Jalisco no te rajes! Gr. 7, I-6
By the Waters of Babylon
    Gr. 6, 311

Family Tree Gr. 3, 72
*Frostiana (from Stopping by
    Woods on a Snowy Evening)*
    Gr. 6, 40
God Bless the U.S.A. Gr. 8, G-37
Green, Green Grass of Home
    Gr. 6, 248
Hello to All the Children of the
    World Gr. 3, 4
Home on the Range Gr. 5, 69
I Vow to You, My Country
    Gr. 5, 418
I'm Flying Home Gr. 2, 286
*L'union* Gr. 6, 487
La borinqueña Gr. 8, D-19
Li'l Liza Jane Gr. 3, 140
Loch Lomond Gr. 5, 140
Lumberjack, The (poem) Gr. 1, 113
*Mi tierra* Gr. 6, 365
My Father's House Gr. 2, 25
My Home's Across the Blue Ridge
    Mountains Gr. 4, 84
Oh, Danny Boy Gr. 4, 48
*Ozark Mountain Jubilee* Gr. 4, 86
River Gr. 4, 58
Rocky Top Gr. 5, 348
Scotland the Brave Gr. 5, 138
Scrub Brush Shuffle, The Gr. 1, 118
Stopping by Woods on a Snowy
    Evening Gr. 6, 41
Swanee Gr. 6, 118
*Tennessee River* Gr. 5, 349
Tree House (poem) Gr. 3, 207
World of Difference, A Gr. 5, 386

**ISLANDS**

Aguinaldo Gr. 3, 402
Cheki, morena Gr. 2, 180
Chrismus a Come Gr. 3, 396
Cookie Gr. 2, 172
Dancing Pig, The (folk tale)
    Gr. 1, 196
Deau-deau, ti pitit maman
    Gr. 2, 306
El coquí Gr. 2, 292
El florón Gr. 2, 246
Four White Horses Gr. 3, 304
*Hard Times* Gr. 1, 194
Hi-Dee-Roon Gr. K, 10
Mister Ram Goat-O Gr. 3, 54
Nani wale na hala Gr. 3, 260
Poco, Le' Me 'Lone Gr. 3, 300
'Round and 'Round Gr. 1, 148
*Sekar jepun* Gr. 1, 195
Wind Blew East, The Gr. 1, 64

**NATIONS**

America, I Hear You Singing
    Gr. 2, 402
Banana Gr. 2, 114
Dance for the Nations Gr. 6, 122
Go, My Son Gr. 6, 188
Harrison Town Gr. 6, 97

United Nations on the March, The
    Gr. 6, 443
Yo-shi nai Gr. 6, 286

**REGIONS**

Abiyoyo Gr. 2, 108
*Bear Dance* Gr. 7, C-5
Bury Me Not on the Lone Prairie
    Gr. 6, 19
Cattle Call Gr. 5, 344
*Cattle Call* Gr. 5, 347
Cumberland Gap Gr. 4, 138
El rancho grande Gr. 4, 215
Erie Canal Gr. 5, 262
Farewell to the Warriors Gr. 4, 284
Four in a Boat Gr. 2, 46
God Bless the U.S.A. Gr. 8, G-37
Home on the Range Gr. 5, 69
*I've Been Everywhere* Gr. 6, 224
I've Been Everywhere Gr. 6, 226
Jambalaya (On The Bayou)
    Gr. 6, 244
Laredo Gr. 5, 10
Leila Gr. 1, 258
Loch Lomond Gr. 5, 140
Lullaby and Dance Gr. 4, 387
*New England Triptych, "Chester"*
    Gr. 6, 83
Orange Blossom Special
    Gr. 5, 266
*Ozark Mountain Jubilee* Gr. 4, 86
Pat Works on the Railway
    Gr. 5, 182
Paw-Paw Patch Gr. 4, 93
Piñon, pirulín Gr. 2, 174
Red River Valley Gr. 6, 11
Roll On, Columbia Gr. 5, 116
Route 66 Gr. 4, 276
*Route 66* Gr. 4, 279
*Shenandoah* Gr. 2, 62
Summertime Gr. 6, 250
*Summertime* Gr. 6, 252
This Land Is Your Land Gr. 5, 118
*This Land Is Your Land*
    Gr. 5, 120
Wabash Cannon Ball Gr. 5, 136
*Yo Lé Lé (Fulani Groove)*
    Gr. 5, 33
Yo-shi nai Gr. 6, 286

**STATES**

Alabama Gal Gr. 3, 106
Away to America Gr. 5, 57
*Aweigh, Santy Ano* Gr. 1, 338
Blue Mountain Lake Gr. 6, 205
California, Here I Come Gr. 4, 287
Chuhwuht Gr. 2, 356
Clementine Gr. 4, 341
Colorado Trail Gr. 5, 276
*Colorado Trail* Gr. 5, 277
Crawfish! Gr. 2, 86
Deux cocodries Gr. 2, 364
Family Tree Gr. 3, 72
Fifty Nifty United States Gr. 5, 251

Thematic Index

Glendy Burke, The  Gr. 4, 262
Harrison Town  Gr. 6, 97
I See the Moon  Gr. 2, 58
I Wonder Where Maria's Gone
    Gr. 3, 318
I'm Flying Home  Gr. 2, 286
*I've Been Everywhere*  Gr. 6, 224
I've Been Everywhere  Gr. 6, 226
Kapulu kane  Gr. 2, 270
Lone Star Trail  Gr. 2, 21
My Home's Across the Blue Ridge
    Mountains  Gr. 4, 84
Oklahoma  Gr. 5, 36
*Orange Blossom Special*  Gr. 1, 47
Orange Blossom Special
    Gr. 5, 266
Raccoon Dance Song  Gr. 1, 260
Rocky Top  Gr. 5, 348
*Sister Rosa*  Gr. 3, 411
Surfin' U.S.A.  Gr. 6, 260
Tall Cedar Tree  Gr. 2, 322
This Land Is Your Land  Gr. 5, 118
*This Land Is Your Land*
    Gr. 5, 120
This Land Is Your Land  Gr. 7, I-66
This Land Is Your Land (refrain
    only)  Gr. 1, 274
Tideo  Gr. 2, 80
Yellow Rose of Texas, The
    Gr. 7, I-70
Yonder Come Day  Gr. 8, I-68

## PLANTS AND TREES

Ah ya Zane  Gr. 5, 297
Amefuri  Gr. 1, 144
Apple, The (poem)  Gr. 1, 231
Apple Tree  Gr. 1, 228
Apples (poem)  Gr. 1, 16
Ash Grove, The  Gr. 5, 114
Autumn (poem)  Gr. 6, 193
Autumn Canon  Gr. 5, 148
Autumn Fires (poem)  Gr. 5, 149
Beriozka  Gr. 4, 294
Bird's Nest, The (poem)  Gr. K, 239
Busy Buzzy Bee  Gr. K, 77
*Children's Garden, The*  Gr. K, 267
Cho'i hát bội  Gr. 5, 318
Come, Ye Thankful People, Come
    Gr. 5, 459
*Dancing Tree, The*  Gr. K, 202
Don't Dump Trash  Gr. 2, 318
Doraji  Gr. 4, 174
El día de mamita  Gr. K, 325
El florón  Gr. 2, 246
Erdö, erdö de magos  Gr. 3, 182
*Everything Grows*  Gr. K, 267
First-ing (poem)  Gr. 1, 375
Flowers at Night (poem)  Gr. 2, 246
Grasshoppers (poem)  Gr. 3, 35
Green Corn Song  Gr. 5, 462
Growing Corn (poem)  Gr. 1, 297
Hashkediya  Gr. 3, 206
Hitotsu toya  Gr. 5, 478

House of Spring (poem)  Gr. 4, 309
I Love the Mountains  Gr. 5, 34
In the Pumpkin Patch  Gr. 3, 380
Jasmine Flowers  Gr. 5, 316
Johnny Appleseed  Gr. 4, 345
Juniper Tree, The  Gr. 3, 131
Khorovod  Gr. 1, 372
Kookaburra  Gr. 4, 186
La Tarara  Gr. 4, 176
Lahk gei mohlee  Gr. 5, 317
Let's Get Ready  Gr. K, 312
Listen to the Water  Gr. 2, 294
*Lo, How a Rose E'er Blooming*
    Gr. 6, 210
Lo yisa  Gr. 6, 130
Looking for the Mother Birds
    Gr. 3, 331
Los maizales  Gr. 1, 296
Los pececitos  Gr. 1, 178
Lumberjack, The (poem)  Gr. 1, 113
Magnolia  Gr. 6, 16
Mary Ann  Gr. K, 253
Meng Jian Nu  Gr. 5, 194
Morning Has Broken  Gr. 5, 28
My Travel Tree (poem)  Gr. K, 203
Nani wale na hala  Gr. 3, 260
New Hungarian Folk Song  Gr. 6, 196
News of Home (poem)  Gr. 4, 336
*Nutcracker Suite, The, "Waltz of the
    Flowers"*  Gr. 6, 325
Our Tree (poem)  Gr. 1, 185
Paw-Paw Patch  Gr. 4, 93
Plant Four Seeds  Gr. 2, 130
Popcorn Popping  Gr. 1, 440
Pumpkin Poem (poem)  Gr. 3, 381
Rain, The (poem)  Gr. 1, 52
River Winding (poem)  Gr. 4, 60
Rockin' Around the Christmas Tree
    Gr. 5, 466
Sakura  Gr. 4, 308
Seasons  Gr. K, 4
See and Touch  Gr. K, 172
Sh'ney dubim  Gr. K, 268
Small Job, A  Gr. 3, 224
Spring! Spring! (poem)  Gr. 1, 419
*Sumer Is Icumen In*  Gr. 5, 35
Take Your Feet Out 'the Sand
    Gr. K, 231
Tall Cedar Tree  Gr. 2, 322
Tree in the Wood, The  Gr. 2, 360
Trees (poem)  Gr. 5, 114
Un pajarito  Gr. 2, 16
What Do We Plant? (poem)  Gr. 2, 130
What Do You Suppose? (poem)
    Gr. K, 265
Who Has Seen the Wind? (poem)
    Gr. 5, 207
Wind Up the Apple Tree  Gr. 1, 184
World We Love, The  Gr. 3, 342
Your Friends Shall Be the Tall Wind
    Gr. 6, 201

## PLAYING WITH WORDS

*A-You're Adorable*  Gr. 1, 263
Ackabacka, Soda Cracker (speech
    piece)  Gr. 1, 303
Arirang  Gr. 5, 25
Bling Blang  Gr. 3, 240
Blum (poem)  Gr. 1, 221
Bo-bo-skee, Watten-tatten (speech
    piece)  Gr. 1, 259
Bumble Bee (poem)  Gr. 1, 385
Bundle-Buggy Boogie Woogie (speech
    piece)  Gr. 4, 120
Cantando mentiras  Gr. 4, 146
Cement Mixer  Gr. 4, 102
*Chica chica boom chic*  Gr. 2, 112
*Choo Choo Boogaloo*  Gr. 1, 127
Circle 'Round the Moon  Gr. 4, 403
Cow's Woc Backward  Gr. 1, 390
Ding, Dong, Diggidiggidong  Gr. 3, 14
Do Wah Diddy Diddy  Gr. 4, 203
*Do-Re-Mi*  Gr. 5, 38
Down, Down, Baby  Gr. 2, 32
El gallo pinto  Gr. 3, 86
Eletelephony (poem)  Gr. 2, 161
Extremes (poem)  Gr. 4, 409
Fish (poem)  Gr. 1, 177
Flat Foot Floogee, The  Gr. 3, 160
Frog Lullaby (poem)  Gr. K, 149
*Give Me Your Tired, Your Poor*
    Gr. 5, 166
Grasshoppers (poem)  Gr. 3, 35
Hands (poem)  Gr. 1, 203
How Much Wood Could a Woodchuck
    Chuck (speech piece)  Gr. 3, 120
*Howjidoo*  Gr. 1, 315
I Bought Me a Cat  Gr. 2, 308
I Can't Spell Hippopotamus  Gr. 1, 264
I'm Curious  Gr. K, 276
Jellyfish Walk (poem)  Gr. 1, 33
Jig Along Home  Gr. 2, 366
Jump or Jiggle (poem)  Gr. 2, 26
Loch Lomond  Gr. 5, 140
Lucy Locket  Gr. 2, 27
Mister Ram Goat-O  Gr. 3, 54
Modern Dragon, A (poem)  Gr. 3, 242
Monster Stomp, The (poem)
    Gr. 1, 133
New Colossus, The (poem)  Gr. 5, 166
*Now's the Time*  Gr. 5, 451
On the Ning Nang Nong (poem)
    Gr. 1, 395
Orchestra, The (poem)  Gr. 1, 328
Our Washing Machine (poem)
    Gr. 1, 35
Parade Came Marching, The  Gr. 1, 166
Peace Like a River  Gr. 6, 190
Peppermint Twist  Gr. 3, 46
Poem to Mud (poem)  Gr. 3, 34
Raindrops (poem)  Gr. 1, 100
Riquir rán  Gr. 4, 66
School Bus Rap (poem)  Gr. 1, 83
*Scrub-a-dub*  Gr. 1, 306
Snow Flakes (poem)  Gr. 1, 423

(*Playing with Words,* continued)

Snowflakes  Gr. 1, 422
Song of One, A  Gr. 3, 344
Supercalifragilisticexpialidocious
 Gr. 3, 7
Teach Me to Swing  Gr. 5, 84
Tie Me Kangaroo Down, Sport
 Gr. 4, 37
Tongue Twister Medley, A (speech
 piece)  Gr. K, 283
Tree House (poem)  Gr. 3, 207
Waltzing with Bears  Gr. 3, 170
We Go Together  Gr. 4, 44
Willoughby, Wallaby, Woo  Gr. K, 282
*Yankee Doodle Boy, The*  Gr. 3, 265

## PROBLEM SOLVING

About Buttons (poem)  Gr. 1, 211
Adventures of Isabel, The (poem)
 Gr. 3, 173
Apple, The (poem)  Gr. 1, 231
Ayelivi  Gr. 2, 70
Baby Chick (poem)  Gr. K, 167
Big Rock Candy Mountain  Gr. 4, 330
Bling Blang  Gr. 3, 240
Blowin' in the Wind  Gr. 5, 382
*Blowin' in the Wind*  Gr. 5, 384
Bridges  Gr. 6, 86
But the Cat Came Back  Gr. 2, 190
Chawe chidyo chem'chero (story)
 Gr. 2, 296
Chickens, The (poem)  Gr. 3, 92
Cinderella Dressed in Green (rhyme)
 Gr. K, 136
Cookie  Gr. 2, 172
Dancing Pig, The (folk tale)  Gr. 1, 196
Dreams (poem)  Gr. K, 276
*Dreydl Song, The*  Gr. 3, 391
El carite  Gr. 5, 305
El condor pasa  Gr. 6, 46
Flat Foot Floogee, The  Gr. 3, 160
Frog in the Millpond  Gr. 2, 44
From Sea to Shining Sea  Gr. 2, 342
Goin' Down the Road Feelin' Bad
 Gr. 7, F-13
Gonna Have a Good Time  Gr. 2, 4
Goodbye, Julie (Miss Julie Ann
 Johnson)  Gr. 1, 334
Heigh-Ho  Gr. 2, 6
How the Kiwi Lost Its Wings (story)
 Gr. 1, 78
I Walk the Unfrequented Road
 Gr. 6, 79
I'm Curious  Gr. K, 276
Jasmine Flowers  Gr. 5, 316
Keep Your Eyes on the Prize  Gr. 3, 408
Keep Your Eyes on the Prize
 Gr. 8, E-16
Kibungo, Beast of the Forest (story)
 Gr. 2, 352
Lion and the Mouse, The (story)
 Gr. 1, 239
*Little Red Hen, The*  Gr. 1, 254

Little Red Hen, The (story)  Gr. 1, 256
Look Out Below!  Gr. 2, 370
Look Out for Mother Earth  Gr. 3, 341
Moore, Carman  Gr. 3, 163
Mother Sent Me to the Store (rhyme)
 Gr. K, 136
Mother to Son (poem)  Gr. 2, 203
Must Be Santa  Gr. K, 318
My Legs and I (poem)  Gr. 1, 9
My Mama's Calling Me  Gr. 1, 260
One, Two, Three, Four, Five (rhyme)
 Gr. 1, 67
Parade Came Marching, The  Gr. 1, 166
*Rainy Day Blues*  Gr. 2, 328
Scrub Brush Shuffle, The  Gr. 1, 118
*Shake Your Brain*  Gr. 1, 250
*Sister Rosa*  Gr. 3, 411
Somebody's Knockin' at Your Door
 Gr. 4, 53
Straighten Up and Fly Right
 Gr. 4, 128
Supercalifragilisticexpialidocious
 Gr. 3, 7
Tina singu  Gr. 4, 300
Tree House (poem)  Gr. 3, 207
Trouble Is a Mountain  Gr. 2, 202
*Two Heads Are Better Than One*
 Gr. 1, 333
Under the Sea  Gr. 5, 372
Upside Down and Inside Out (poem)
 Gr. K, 297
We Moved About a Week Ago (poem)
 Gr. 2, 230
*What Kind of Land?*  Gr. 4, 327
Why the Warthog Goes About on His
 Knees (story)  Gr. 1, 139
Yellow Rose of Texas, The  Gr. 7, I-70
*Yertle the Turtle*  Gr. 2, 368
Zomo the Rabbit (story)  Gr. 3, 364

## R

## READING IS FUN

ABC Blues  Gr. K, 281
Alphabet Song  Gr. K, 280
Beginning on Paper (poem)  Gr. K, 69
Bumble Bee (poem)  Gr. 1, 385
Bundle-Buggy Boogie Woogie (speech
 piece)  Gr. 4, 120
Cat's Tongue (poem)  Gr. 2, 190
Children of Long Ago (poem)
 Gr. 1, 31
Counting-Out Rhyme (speech piece)
 Gr. 1, 357
Firefly (poem)  Gr. 1, 356
How the Kiwi Lost Its Wings (story)
 Gr. 1, 78
I Can't Spell Hippopotamus  Gr. 1, 264
I Got a Letter This Morning  Gr. K, 68
I Was Walking in a Circle (poem)
 Gr. 3, 321
I'm Curious  Gr. K, 276
Ida Red  Gr. 3, 30

More It Snows, The (poem)
 Gr. K, 259
Panther, The (poem)  Gr. 3, 354
Reading Glasses (poem)  Gr. K, 325
Rise and Shine  Gr. 4, 98
Scrub Brush Shuffle, The  Gr. 1, 118
Sing Your Story  Gr. 3, 350
Valentine for Earth, A (poem)
 Gr. 3, 324
Willoughby, Wallaby, Woo  Gr. K, 282

## S

## SAFETY

From Sea to Shining Sea  Gr. 2, 342
Lumberjack, The (poem)  Gr. 1, 113
Sleep, Baby, Sleep  Gr. 2, 197
Waiting for the Traffic Light
 Gr. 2, 107
We're Making Popcorn (speech piece)
 Gr. 1, 86

## SCHOOL

Back to School (poem)  Gr. K, 5
Flowering Umbrellas (poem)  Gr. 1, 145
Good Old Happy Song, A  Gr. K, 201
Ha'kyo jong  Gr. 2, 135
Hui jia qù  Gr. 2, 158
I Can't Spell Hippopotamus  Gr. 1, 264
Koriko!  Gr. K, 154
Locomoto-vation  Gr. K, 61
Number One, Touch Your Tongue
 (speech piece)  Gr. K, 204
Oliver Jump (speech piece)  Gr. K, 205
Paper (poem)  Gr. K, 195
Seasons  Gr. K, 4
That's What's New with Me!  Gr. K, 2
Uptown, Downtown (poem)
 Gr. K, 204

## SEASONS

Almost Day  Gr. 3, 397
Alumot  Gr. 6, 306
Autumn (poem)  Gr. 6, 193
Autumn Canon  Gr. 5, 148
Autumn Fires (poem)  Gr. 5, 149
Back to School (poem)  Gr. K, 5
Barb'ry Allen  Gr. 6, 44
Big Old Storm a-Comin'  Gr. K, 257
Blue Mountain Lake  Gr. 6, 205
Chag purim  Gr. 1, 438
Chanukah Games  Gr. 3, 389
Chanukah Is Here!  Gr. 2, 382
Chrismus a Come  Gr. 3, 396
Clouds  Gr. K, 254
Clouds of Gray  Gr. 2, 56
Come, Ye Thankful People, Come
 Gr. 5, 459
Costume Capers  Gr. 1, 412
Cotton-Eye Joe  Gr. 4, 288
Cycle Song of Life (The River Song)
 Gr. 4, 370
Dance (poem)  Gr. K, 59
*Dancing in the Street*  Gr. 2, 254

Dancing Tree, The  Gr. K, 202
De colores  Gr. 5, 90
De colores  Gr. 8, I-14
Deck the Hall  Gr. 5, 474
Dragon Smoke (poem)  Gr. K, 258
Dreydl Song, The  Gr. 3, 391
El mes de abril  Gr. 3, 328
First Snowflake (poem)  Gr. K, 259
First-ing (poem)  Gr. 1, 375
Five Little Snowmen  Gr. K, 313
Four Seasons, Concerto No. 2, The,
     "Summer," Movement 3, "La
     Tempesta"  Gr. 6, 102
Four Seasons, The, "Spring,"
     Movement 1  Gr. 4, 371
Good King Wenceslas  Gr. 6, 460
Good King Wenceslas  Gr. 6, 461
Green Corn Song  Gr. 5, 462
Groundhog Blues, The  Gr. 3, 122
Groundhog Jig, The  Gr. 1, 436
Habari Gani  Gr. 3, 404
Hanuka, Hanuka  Gr. 3, 390
Haru ga kita  Gr. 2, 401
House of Spring (poem)  Gr. 4, 309
I Like Fall (poem)  Gr. K, 311
I Walk the Unfrequented Road
     Gr. 6, 79
I'm a Very Fine Turkey  Gr. K, 310
Irish Tune from County Derry
     Gr. 4, 49
It's Santa—Again!  Gr. 2, 385
Jingle Bells  Gr. 2, 388
Khorovod  Gr. 1, 372
Knock No More  Gr. 3, 386
L'inverno è passato  Gr. 2, 400
La piñata  Gr. 3, 399
Let It Snow! Let It Snow! Let It Snow!
     Gr. 4, 426
Let It Snow! Let It Snow! Let It
     Snow!  Gr. 4, 427
Let's Get Ready  Gr. K, 312
Lieutenant Kijé, Op. 60, "Troika"
     Gr. 6, 457
Lo, How a Rose E'er Blooming
     Gr. 6, 210
Louds and Softs of the Seasons
     Gr. K, 4
Magnolia  Gr. 6, 16
Meng Jian Nu  Gr. 5, 194
Mister Snow Rap (speech piece)
     Gr. 2, 391
More It Snows, The (poem)
     Gr. K, 259
Musical Sleigh Ride, A, "Divertimento
     in F"  Gr. 5, 455
Ner li  Gr. 2, 383
Oh, Danny Boy  Gr. 4, 48
One Morning in May  Gr. 6, 121
Our Tree (poem)  Gr. 1, 185
Over the River and Through the Wood
     Gr. 3, 384
Owl and the Pumpkin, The  Gr. 2, 377
Perot  Gr. 2, 378

Popcorn Popping  Gr. 1, 440
Pumpkin Picking (poem)  Gr. 2, 376
Pumpkin, Pumpkin  Gr. 1, 413
Quả câù gió bay  Gr. 5, 460
Rabbit Footprints  Gr. 2, 304
Rain (Livingston) (poem)  Gr. 3, 79
River  Gr. 4, 58
Roads Go Ever Ever On (poem)
     Gr. 6, 214
Sakura  Gr. 4, 308
Seasons  Gr. K, 4
Setting the Thanksgiving Table (poem)
     Gr. 2, 381
Sheep, Sheep (poem)  Gr. 1, 309
Sidewalk Songs (poem)  Gr. K, 207
Skin and Bones  Gr. 2, 376
Sleigh Ride  Gr. 2, 390
Snow Flakes (poem)  Gr. 1, 423
Snowflakes  Gr. 1, 422
Spring (poem)  Gr. 2, 400
Spring Has Sprung!  Gr. K, 142
Spring Rain (poem)  Gr. 2, 294
Spring! Spring! (poem)  Gr. 1, 419
Sumer Is Icumen In  Gr. 5, 35
Summertime  Gr. 6, 250
Summertime  Gr. 6, 252
Tap It! Rap It! (speech piece)
     Gr. K, 194
Thanksgiving Is Near  Gr. 2, 380
There is Joy (poem)  Gr. 3, 258
Turn, Turn, Turn (To Everything There
     Is a Season)  Gr. 5, 378
Valentines (poem)  Gr. 2, 398
We Are Dear Little Birdies  Gr. K, 176
Wind Has Shaken Autumn Down
     (poem)  Gr. 2, 57
Winter Fantasy  Gr. 4, 424
Winter Song  Gr. 6, 455
Winter Wonderland  Gr. 5, 454
Worm, The (poem)  Gr. 2, 311
Xiao yin chuan  Gr. 2, 14
Yours Forever  Gr. 6, 344

**SELF-ESTEEM**
ABC Blues  Gr. K, 281
Ain't Gonna Let Nobody Turn Me
     'Round  Gr. 6, 85
Amazing Grace  Gr. 4, 160
Amazing Grace  Gr. 4, 161
At the Top of My Voice (poem)
     Gr. K, 279
Beautiful  Gr. 3, 67
Body Song, The  Gr. 6, 438
Both Sides Now  Gr. 5, 385
Burke, Liam  Gr. 2, 11
By Myself (poem)  Gr. 1, 43
Cantaré, cantarás  Gr. 6, 413
Celebrate  Gr. 1, 407
Changing (poem)  Gr. K, 199
Children Learn What They Live (poem)
     Gr. 5, 381
Children of the Sun (poem)  Gr. 1, 404
Circle of Life, The  Gr. 6, 316

Circle of Sun, A (poem)  Gr. K, 3
Copycat  Gr. K, 9
End, The (poem)  Gr. 1, 408
Everybody Says  Gr. 1, 287
Everyday People  Gr. 5, 389
Fatou yo, "I am Fatou"  Gr. K, 155
Get on Your Feet  Gr. 5, 6
Get on Your Feet  Gr. 5, 8
Gift to Share, A  Gr. 6, 393
Glad to Have a Friend Like You
     Gr. 2, 228
Glory, Glory, Hallelujah  Gr. 6, 52
Glory, Glory, Hallelujah  Gr. 6, 54
Gonna Build a Mountain  Gr. 6, 21
Great Big Stars  Gr. 1, 60
Growing Corn (poem)  Gr. 1, 297
Happy Birthday To You (poem)
     Gr. 1, 411
Hey, Hey, Look at Me  Gr. 1, 70
Howjidoo  Gr. 1, 315
I Am But a Small Voice  Gr. 6, 446
I Believe I Can Fly  Gr. 5, 170
I Can't Spell Hippopotamus  Gr. 1, 264
I Got Shoes  Gr. 2, 242
I Walk in Beauty  Gr. 4, 282
I'm Curious  Gr. K, 276
I'm Tall, I'm Small  Gr. K, 18
It's Time  Gr. 6, 319
Jump or Jiggle (poem)  Gr. 2, 26
Just Me (poem)  Gr. 1, 71
Just Watch (poem)  Gr. K, 295
Kwanzaa Carol, A  Gr. 2, 392
La copa de la vida  Gr. 4, 414
Lean on Me  Gr. 6, 14
Leatherwing Bat  Gr. 2, 303
Light Up the World  Gr. 2, 196
Little David  Gr. 1, 232
Little Johnny Brown  Gr. 3, 313
Little Red Hen, The  Gr. 1, 254
Little Red Hen, The (story)  Gr. 1, 256
Love Will Guide Us  Gr. 4, 328
Marines' Hymn, The  Gr. 8, C-39
Mother to Son (poem)  Gr. 2, 203
My Song (poem)  Gr. 4, 305
New Shoes (poem)  Gr. 2, 242
New Way to Walk, A  Gr. K, 117
One Moment in Time  Gr. 6, 352
Our Family Comes from 'Round the
     World (poem)  Gr. 1, 299
Peace Like a River  Gr. 6, 190
Put Your Hand in My Hand  Gr. 1, 330
Rise and Shine  Gr. 1, 122
River  Gr. 4, 58
Rudolph, the Red-Nosed Reindeer
     Gr. 1, 428
Scrub-a-dub  Gr. 1, 306
Shake Your Brain  Gr. 1, 250
Si me dan pasteles  Gr. 1, 432
Simple Gifts  Gr. 5, 184
Simple Gifts  Gr. 8, A-17
Song of Greatness, A (poem)
     Gr. 3, 335
Stand By Me  Gr. 5, 46

**(Self-Esteem, continued)**

*Stand By Me* Gr. 5, 49

Supercalifragilisticexpialidocious Gr. 3, 7

That's What's New with Me! Gr. K, 2

*This Little Light of Mine* Gr. 2, 241

This World Gr. 5, 168

Time to Move Gr. 1, 244

Trouble Is a Mountain Gr. 2, 202

Ujima Gr. 1, 430

Under the Same Sun Gr. 6, 440

Waitin' for the Light to Shine Gr. 4, 26

Waiting (poem) Gr. 1, 413

Wake Me, Shake Me Gr. 1, 278

We're All Gonna Shine Tonight Gr. 2, 240

You and I (poem) Gr. 5, 388

Your Life Is Now Gr. 6, 4

## SENSES

A la rurru niño Gr. K, 180

Ah! Les jolis papillons Gr. 1, 362

Apples (poem) Gr. 1, 16

Beach Rap (speech piece) Gr. 1, 352

Big Beautiful Planet Gr. 3, 326

Big Old Storm a-Comin' Gr. K, 257

*Bird Calls, Bird Songs* Gr. K, 178

Bubble Trouble (poem) Gr. K, 184

Bubbles (poem) Gr. K, 185

Burke, Liam Gr. 2, 11

Celebrate Gr. 1, 407

Chippewa Lullaby Gr. K, 181

Clouds Gr. K, 254

Clouds (poem) Gr. K, 255

*Cookie Crew, The* Gr. K, 197

Cookie Magic (poem) Gr. K, 197

Crayons (poem) Gr. K, 75

Don Gato Gr. 3, 352

Eensy Weensy Spider Gr. K, 187

El mes de abril Gr. 3, 328

First Snowflake (poem) Gr. K, 259

Five Little Chickadees Gr. K, 179

Flowering Umbrellas (poem) Gr. 1, 145

For the Beauty of the Earth Gr. 4, 356

Fourth of July Night (poem) Gr. 1, 444

Frog (haiku) (poem) Gr. K, 182

Going on a Picnic Gr. K, 190

Gonna Have a Good Time Gr. 2, 4

Haru ga kita Gr. 2, 401

Here Comes The Band (poem) Gr. 1, 167

I Like Fall (poem) Gr. K, 311

*I Love a Rainy Night (line dance)* Gr. 5, 350

I See With My Hands Gr. 2, 148

I Walk the Unfrequented Road Gr. 6, 79

I'm Thankful Gr. 1, 414

Just from the Kitchen Gr. K, 55

Kaeru no uta Gr. K, 183

Keys (poem) Gr. K, 188

Kingston Market Gr. 3, 90

L'inverno è passato Gr. 2, 400

Las estrellas (poem) Gr. 1, 109

Let's Get Ready Gr. K, 312

Let's Go Barefoot (poem) Gr. 1, 440

Listen to the Water Gr. 2, 294

Look! Look! The Sun Woke Up! Gr. 1, 368

Loud (poem) Gr. 1, 7

Louder Than a Clap of Thunder (folk tale) Gr. 1, 87

*Lyric Pieces, Op. 43, No. 1, "Butterfly"* Gr. 1, 363

Mary Ann Gr. K, 253

Mmmmmm mmmmmmm (poem) Gr. K, 71

Music's in Me , The Gr. 2, 40

Nampaya omame Gr. 1, 138

Painting Song: A Dribble and a Dot Gr. K, 175

Paper (poem) Gr. K, 195

Peter, Peter, Sugar Eater (poem) Gr. 1, 284

Poem to Mud (poem) Gr. 3, 34

Popcorn Popping Gr. 1, 440

Quiet (poem) Gr. 1, 7

Rain Sizes (poem) Gr. K, 261

Sailing to the Sea Gr. 1, 336

Seasons Gr. K, 4

See and Touch Gr. K, 172

Since Hanna Moved Away (poem) Gr. 1, 335

Song of the Night, The (poem) Gr. 3, 346

Star-Spangled Banner, The Gr. 7, I-56

Take Your Feet Out 'the Sand Gr. K, 231

Tap It! Rap It! (speech piece) Gr. K, 194

Thanksgiving Is Near Gr. 2, 380

That's What's New with Me! Gr. K, 2

We Are Dear Little Birdies Gr. K, 176

We're Making Popcorn (speech piece) Gr. 1, 86

Wind Song (poem) Gr. K, 7

Zudio Gr. 2, 269

## SHAPES

About Buttons (poem) Gr. 1, 211

Ah! Les jolis papillons Gr. 1, 362

Beach Rap (speech piece) Gr. 1, 352

Circle Round the Zero Gr. K, 293

Doong gul ge Gr. 3, 134

Flowering Umbrellas (poem) Gr. 1, 145

I Was Walking in a Circle (poem) Gr. 3, 321

Little Shop of Horrors Gr. 4, 422

Merry-Go-Round (poem) Gr. K, 291

Painting Song: A Dribble and a Dot Gr. K, 175

Tracks (poem) Gr. K, 299

## SOCIAL STUDIES *See also Past and Present.*

### AMERICAN

Abraham, Martin, and John Gr. 6, 466

Ain't Gonna Let Nobody Turn Me 'Round Gr. 6, 85

America Gr. K, 326

America Gr. 1, 446

America Gr. 2, 403

America Gr. 3, 412

America Gr. 4, 440

America Gr. 5, 486

America Gr. 6, 484

America Gr. 7, I-2

America Gr. 8, I-2

*America, the Beautiful* Gr. 3, 413

America, the Beautiful Gr. 3, 158

America, the Beautiful Gr. 5, 76

America, the Beautiful Gr. 6, 485

America, the Beautiful Gr. 7, I-4

America, the Beautiful Gr. 8, I-4

Away to America Gr. 5, 57

*Aweigh, Santy Ano* Gr. 1, 338

Back of the Bus Gr. 3, 410

Bard of Armagh, The Gr. 4, 296

Battle Cry of Freedom Gr. 5, 272

Battle Hymn of the Republic Gr. 5, 274

Big Rock Candy Mountain Gr. 4, 330

Blow, Ye Winds Gr. 4, 255

Blue Mountain Lake Gr. 6, 205

California Gr. 5, 52

California, Here I Come Gr. 4, 287

Camptown Races Gr. 5, 270

Celebrating Our Flag (poem) Gr. K, 327

*Changed My Name* Gr. 6, 338

Cindy Gr. 4, 384

Clementine Gr. 4, 341

Coffee Grows on White Oak Trees Gr. 3, 168

Come and Go with Me to That Land Gr. 5, 390

Come, Ye Thankful People, Come Gr. 5, 459

*Coming Home from the Sea–I* Gr. 6, 345

*Coming Home from the Sea–II* Gr. 6, 345

Down by the Riverside Gr. 5, 256

Drill, Ye Tarriers Gr. 5, 54

Erie Canal Gr. 5, 262

*Ev'ry Time I Feel the Spirit* Gr. 3, 248

Farewell to the Warriors Gr. 4, 284

Fifty Nifty United States Gr. 5, 251

Follow the Drinkin' Gourd Gr. 4, 266

Free at Last Gr. 6, 468

Get on Board Gr. K, 89

Glendy Burke, The  Gr. 4, 262
Go Around the Corn, Sally
    Gr. 2, 12
Goin' Down the Road Feelin' Bad
    Gr. 5, 282
Goin' Down the Road Feelin' Bad
    Gr. 5, 283
Goin' Down the Road Feelin' Bad
    Gr. 7, F-13
Goin' to Boston  Gr. 6, 433
Gonna Ride Up in the Chariot
    Gr. 4, 20
Gospel Train, The  Gr. 6, 398
Greenland Whale Fishery, The
    Gr. 5, 230
Happy Days Are Here Again
    Gr. 5, 284
Harriet Tubman (poem)  Gr. 4, 269
He's Got the Whole World in His
    Hands  Gr. 3, 249
I See the Moon  Gr. 2, 58
I'm a Yankee Doodle Dandy
    Gr. 5, 278
I've Been Working on the Railroad
    Gr. 3, 242
Joe Turner Blues  Gr. 4, 56
Johnny Appleseed  Gr. 4, 345
Johnny Has Gone for a Soldier
    Gr. 5, 188
Keep Your Eyes on the Prize
    Gr. 3, 408
Keep Your Eyes on the Prize
    Gr. 8, E-16
Kid Like Me, A (speech piece)
    Gr. 2, 394
L'union  Gr. 6, 487
La ciudad de Juaja  Gr. 5, 58
Lazy John  Gr. 4, 11
Lift Ev'ry Voice and Sing  Gr. 5, 482
Lone Star Trail  Gr. 2, 21
Marines' Hymn, The  Gr. 8, C-39
Michael, Row the Boat Ashore
    Gr. 2, 18
My Father's House  Gr. 2, 25
New England Triptych, "Chester"
    Gr. 6, 83
Nobody Knows the Trouble I've
    Seen  Gr. 3, 249
Oh, Freedom  Gr. 5, 392
Oh, Freedom  Gr. 7, G-30
Oh, Susanna  Gr. 4, 264
Old American Songs, "The
    Boatman's Dance"  Gr. 4, 61
Orange Blossom Special
    Gr. 5, 266
Over My Head  Gr. 4, 118
Over There  Gr. 5, 279
Pastures of Plenty  Gr. 4, 280
Pat Works on the Railway
    Gr. 5, 182
Paths of Victory  Gr. 6, 195
Peace Like a River  Gr. 3, 246
Peppermint Twist  Gr. 3, 46

Railroad Corral  Gr. 3, 174
Red River Valley  Gr. 6, 11
Rio Grande  Gr. 4, 256
Rock Island Line  Gr. 4, 54
Route 66  Gr. 4, 276
Route 66  Gr. 4, 279
Run! Run! Hide!  Gr. 6, 340
She'll Be Comin' 'Round the
    Mountain  Gr. 2, 358
Shed a Little Light  Gr. 3, 409
Shenandoah  Gr. 2, 62
Shenandoah  Gr. 5, 264
Shenandoah  Gr. 5, 265
Simple Gifts  Gr. 8, A-17
Sister Rosa  Gr. 3, 411
Soldier, Soldier  Gr. 4, 11
Somebody's Knockin' at Your Door
    Gr. 4, 53
Sometimes I Feel Like a Motherless
    Child  Gr. 6, 241
Sourwood Mountain  Gr. 4, 65
Star-Spangled Banner, The
    Gr. 3, 415
Star-Spangled Banner, The
    Gr. 4, 441
Star-Spangled Banner, The
    Gr. 5, 488
Star-Spangled Banner, The
    Gr. 6, 486
Star-Spangled Banner, The
    Gr. 7, I-56
Star-Spangled Banner, The
    Gr. 8, I-62
Streets of Laredo  Gr. 4, 272
Sweet Betsy from Pike  Gr. 4, 244
Thanksgiving Is Near  Gr. 2, 380
This Little Light of Mine  Gr. 6, 232
This Train  Gr. 5, 26
Tideo  Gr. 2, 80
Times They Are A-Changin', The
    Gr. 5, 384
Tom Dooley  Gr. 6, 374
Train Is A-Comin'  Gr. 3, 48
Traveling Shoes  Gr. 3, 248
Wade in the Water  Gr. 8, I-64
We Shall Not Be Moved  Gr. 4, 437
We Shall Overcome  Gr. 4, 326
What Kind of Land?  Gr. 4, 327
When Johnny Comes Marching
    Home  Gr. 5, 180
Worried Man Blues  Gr. 6, 371
Yankee Doodle  Gr. 3, 414
Yankee Doodle Boy, The
    Gr. 3, 265
Yellow Rose of Texas, The
    Gr. 7, I-70

## WORLD

Así es mi tierra  Gr. 6, 172
Bound for South Australia
    Gr. 5, 22
By the Waters of Babylon
    Gr. 6, 311

Carelessly Crafted Raft, A, A (poem)
    Gr. 6, 416
Cow, The (poem)  Gr. 4, 273
Don't Cry for Me, Argentina
    Gr. 6, 74
Feng yang hua gu  Gr. 4, 313
Finlandia  Gr. 6, 78
Freedom Is Coming  Gr. 5, 415
Haliwa-Saponi Canoe Song
    Gr. 5, 302
Haliwa-Saponi Canoe Song
    Gr. 5, 303
How Many Miles to Babylon?
    Gr. 2, 128
I Vow to You, My Country
    Gr. 5, 418
La borinqueña  Gr. 8, D-19
Las estrellitas del cielo  Gr. 5, 175
London Bridge  Gr. K, 244
Lost My Gold Ring  Gr. 6, 158
Má Teodora  Gr. 6, 301
S'vivon  Gr. 6, 452
Scarborough Fair  Gr. 6, 95
To'ia mai te waka  Gr. 1, 77
Tumba  Gr. 5, 161
Tzena, tzena  Gr. 5, 298
Vem kan segla?  Gr. 6, 417
Walk in Jerusalem  Gr. 4, 100
Water Is Wide, The  Gr. 6, 228
Weevily Wheat  Gr. 4, 105
Yibane amenu  Gr. 4, 316

## SOUNDS AROUND US

3 + 2  Gr. 2, 316
Adana ya gidelim  Gr. 2, 142
At the Top of My Voice (poem)
    Gr. K, 279
Bird Calls, Bird Songs  Gr. K, 178
Birdcall—Phoebe  Gr. 1, 31
Brolga  Gr. 6, 271
Bumble Bee (poem)  Gr. 1, 385
Bumble Bee, The (speech piece)
    Gr. K, 74
Bus, The  Gr. K, 82
Cacophony (poem)  Gr. K, 83
Caroling, Caroling  Gr. 6, 458
Celebrate  Gr. 1, 407
Chag purim  Gr. 1, 438
Chairs to Mend  Gr. 4, 149
Cheki, morena  Gr. 2, 180
Choo Choo Boogaloo  Gr. 1, 127
Cold and Frosty Morning  Gr. 2, 139
Common Ground  Gr. 3, 379
Cuckoo, Cuckoo  Gr. 1, 110
Cuculí  Gr. K, 238
De Beat (poem)  Gr. 2, 67
Ding Dong! Merrily on High
    Gr. 6, 427
Down in the Meadow  Gr. K, 147
Down the Listening Lane  Gr. K, 192
El mes de abril  Gr. 3, 328

**(Sounds Around Us, continued)**

El sapito  Gr. 3, 336
Erdö, erdö de magos  Gr. 3, 182
Ev'ry Kind of Music  Gr. 2, 226
*Fish Food*  Gr. 2, 212
Fly and the Bumblebee, The
  Gr. 1, 384
*Free Music #1*  Gr. 2, 212
Freight Train  Gr. 1, 44
Frère Jacques  Gr. 2, 125
Galoshes (poem)  Gr. K, 63
*George and Gracie*  Gr. 1, 69
Gonna Have a Good Time  Gr. 2, 4
Good Old Happy Song, A  Gr. K, 201
Ha'kyo jong  Gr. 2, 135
Hambone  Gr. 1, 202
*Hard Times*  Gr. 1, 194
Here Comes The Band (poem)
  Gr. 1, 167
*Hindewhu (whistle) solo*  Gr. 6, 269
His Wife Said... (poem)  Gr. 1, 343
Honeybee Song, The  Gr. 1, 358
Hwa yuan li-de young wa wa
  Gr. 3, 102
I Bought Me a Cat  Gr. 2, 308
I Saw Three Ships  Gr. 1, 426
I've Been Working on the Railroad
  Gr. 3, 242
*Is the Sound High or Low?*  Gr. K, 17
Ise oluwa  Gr. 2, 102
Jan ken pon  Gr. 3, 302
¡Jeu! ¡Jeu!  Gr. 1, 216
Jingle Bells  Gr. 2, 388
*Jug Band Music*  Gr. 6, 361
*Junk Music Montage*  Gr. 1, 73
Just from the Kitchen  Gr. K, 55
Kaeru no uta  Gr. K, 183
Kapulu kane  Gr. 2, 270
Keys (poem)  Gr. K, 188
Kibungo, Beast of the Forest (story)
  Gr. 2, 352
Kingston Market  Gr. 3, 90
*Kitchen Stomp*  Gr. 4, 122
Kokoleoko  Gr. 5, 33
Kum bachur atzel  Gr. 3, 138
L'inverno è passato  Gr. 2, 400
Leila  Gr. 1, 258
Lion, The (poem)  Gr. K, 217
*Little Red Hen, The*  Gr. 1, 254
Loud (poem)  Gr. 1, 7
Louder Than a Clap of Thunder (folk
  tale)  Gr. 1, 87
*Louds and Softs of the Seasons*
  Gr. K, 4
*Lyric Pieces, Op. 43, No. 4, "Little
  Bird"*  Gr. 1, 346
Mama Don't 'Low  Gr. 6, 358
Manhattan Lullaby (poem)  Gr. K, 193
Marbles (poem)  Gr. 1, 75
Mary Ann  Gr. K, 253
Mississippi River Chant (speech piece)
  Gr. 2, 132

*Noah's Zoo in the Big, Big Rain*
  Gr. K, 274
Noises (poem)  Gr. K, 305
Now That's Tap (speech piece)
  Gr. 6, 320
O pião entrou  Gr. 2, 355
Our Washing Machine (poem)
  Gr. 1, 35
Over in the Meadow  Gr. 1, 346
Owl and the Pumpkin, The  Gr. 2, 377
Paper (poem)  Gr. K, 195
Parade Came Marching, The  Gr. 1, 166
Pat Works on the Railway  Gr. 5, 182
*Penny Lane*  Gr. 6, 257
*Primitive Fire, "Oya"*  Gr. 2, 68
Puff, the Magic Dragon  Gr. 2, 350
*Quartetto buffo di gatti, "Comic
  Quartet for Cats"*  Gr. 1, 131
Quiet (poem)  Gr. 1, 7
Raindrops (poem)  Gr. 1, 12
River Winding (poem)  Gr. 4, 60
*Riverdance Suite*  Gr. 2, 141
Sailing to the Sea  Gr. 1, 336
*Sekar jepun*  Gr. 1, 195
*Sha Sha Sha*  Gr. 6, 328
She'll Be Comin' 'Round the Mountain
  Gr. 2, 358
Sidewalk Sounds (poem)  Gr. K, 115
Skin and Bones  Gr. 2, 376
*Sleigh Ride*  Gr. 2, 390
*Song for Bells, A*  Gr. 1, 427
Song of the Night, The (poem)
  Gr. 3, 346
Spaceworms  Gr. 1, 400
Spring Rain (poem)  Gr. 2, 294
Storm Dance (speech piece)
  Gr. K, 145
*Storm, The*  Gr. 1, 55
Summer Jazz (poem)  Gr. 1, 175
Tanabata-sama  Gr. 2, 336
Tap It! Rap It! (speech piece)
  Gr. K, 194
Things That Sing (poem)  Gr. K, 87
Toaster Time (poem)  Gr. K, 17
*Toy Symphony, Movement 4*
  Gr. 1, 111
*Trash Can Stomp (from Stomp Out
  Loud)*  Gr. 6, 328
Un pajarito  Gr. 2, 16
Vamos a cantar  Gr. K, 278
Wabash Cannon Ball  Gr. 5, 136
Waiting for the Traffic Light
  Gr. 2, 107
We're Making Popcorn (speech piece)
  Gr. 1, 86
When the Saints Go Marching In
  Gr. 2, 178
Wind Blew East, The  Gr. 1, 64
Wind Song (poem)  Gr. K, 7
Windshield Wipers (poem)  Gr. 1, 11
Woodland Chorus  Gr. K, 250

**SPACE**

Aiken Drum  Gr. 1, 398
Big Beautiful Planet  Gr. 3, 326
Birds of Fire (poem)  Gr. 3, 257
Blast Off! (poem)  Gr. 1, 377
Children of the Sun (poem)  Gr. 1, 404
*Clair de lune*  Gr. K, 165
*Close Encounters of the Third Kind*
  Gr. 4, 235
Eres tú  Gr. 6, 473
For the Beauty of the Earth  Gr. 4, 356
*Free Music #1*  Gr. 2, 212
Great Big Stars  Gr. 1, 60
*Halley Came to Jackson*  Gr. 2, 340
La borinqueña  Gr. 8, D-19
Las estrellas (poem)  Gr. 1, 109
Las estrellitas del cielo  Gr. 5, 175
*Les Rêves de Columbine, Op. 65,
  "Sous les étoiles"*  Gr. 2, 338
Like a Bird  Gr. 6, 167
Little Shop of Horrors  Gr. 4, 422
Loigratong  Gr. 6, 451
Los reyes de Oriente  Gr. 5, 480
Luna lunera (speech piece)  Gr. K, 90
*Mars Suite, "Orbital View,"
  Movement 1*  Gr. 4, 199
Me voy para la luna  Gr. 1, 397
*Moon Mirrored in the Pool, The*
  Gr. 6, 109
Moon, The (poem)  Gr. 1, 399
Moon's the North Wind's Cooky, The
  (poem)  Gr. 4, 375
Night, The (poem)  Gr. 4, 81
Niu lang zhi nü  Gr. 4, 335
Nruab hnub thiab hmo ntuj (story)
  Gr. 4, 366
Oh, Watch the Stars  Gr. 2, 144
Oh, Watch the Stars  Gr. 5, 216
Planets Chant, The (speech piece)
  Gr. 4, 377
*Planets, The, "Jupiter"*  Gr. 5, 424
Purple People Eater, The  Gr. 6, 448
Sailboat in the Sky  Gr. 4, 374
See and Touch  Gr. K, 172
*Silver Apples of the Moon-Part A*
  Gr. 1, 12
Silverly (poem)  Gr. K, 135
Sky, Sea, Shore (poem)  Gr. 2, 343
Someday Very Soon  Gr. 1, 376
Somewhere Out There  Gr. 5, 368
*Somewhere Out There*  Gr. 5, 369
Song of the Night, The (poem)
  Gr. 3, 346
Spaceworms  Gr. 1, 400
Star Light, Star Bright  Gr. 1, 108
Starlight, Star Bright  Gr. 4, 373
Stars (poem)  Gr. 1, 61
Stars Streaming in the Sky, The (poem)
  Gr. 2, 357
Sun, The (poem)  Gr. K, 143
Tanabata-sama  Gr. 2, 336
There is Joy (poem)  Gr. 3, 258
This Pretty Planet  Gr. 4, 355

Tsuki  Gr. 4, 25
Usagi  Gr. 1, 396
Valentine for Earth, A (poem)
    Gr. 3, 324
When I'm an Astronaut (poem)
    Gr. 1, 402
World We Love, The  Gr. 3, 342
Xiao yin chuan  Gr. 2, 14
Yü guang guang  Gr. 6, 60
Yüe liang wan wan  Gr. 5, 314

## SPORTS
Bounce High, Bounce Low  Gr. 1, 152
Camptown Races  Gr. 5, 270
Con el vito  Gr. 7, G-15
Four Horses, The (poem)  Gr. 1, 159
Let's Go Fly a Kite  Gr. 2, 327
*Olympic Spirit*  Gr. 6, 350
Playing Ball (poem)  Gr. 1, 153
Take Me Out to the Ball Game
    Gr. 3, 263
Tina singu  Gr. 4, 300
¡Viva el fútbol!  Gr. 1, 96

## TEAMWORK
Bling Blang  Gr. 3, 240
Cha yang wu  Gr. 1, 90
*Common Ground*  Gr. 3, 379
Dancing Pig, The (folk tale)  Gr. 1, 196
Doong gul ge  Gr. 3, 134
Eh, cumpari!  Gr. 4, 68
For Children Safe and Strong
    Gr. 5, 484
Get on Your Feet  Gr. 5, 6
*Get on Your Feet*  Gr. 5, 8
Give a Little Love  Gr. 6, 140
Growing Corn (poem)  Gr. 1, 297
Ha'kyo jong  Gr. 2, 135
Habari Gani  Gr. 3, 404
Harambee  Gr. 4, 434
If I Had a Hammer  Gr. 5, 287
Joy of Kwanzaa, The  Gr. 6, 462
Keep Your Eyes on the Prize  Gr. 3, 408
Keep Your Eyes on the Prize
    Gr. 8, E-16
Kwanzaa Carol, A  Gr. 2, 392
La copa de la vida  Gr. 4, 414
Little Johnny Brown  Gr. 3, 313
Look Out Below!  Gr. 2, 370
Love Can Build a Bridge  Gr. 4, 324
Michael, Row the Boat Ashore
    Gr. 2, 18
Mud  Gr. 3, 32
*Olympic Spirit*  Gr. 6, 350
One Small Step  Gr. 5, 126
Riddle Ree (speech piece)  Gr. 2, 34
Rise and Shine  Gr. 4, 98
*Shed a Little Light*  Gr. 3, 409
Sing, America, Sing!  Gr. 3, 238
Sing! Speak! Whisper! Shout!
    Gr. 1, 36
Sing Your Story  Gr. 3, 350

Somos el barco  Gr. 4, 352
Turn, Turn, Turn (To Everything There
    Is a Season)  Gr. 5, 378
Ujima  Gr. 1, 430
¡Viva el fútbol!  Gr. 1, 96
Vive l'amour  Gr. 6, 176
Walk Together, Children  Gr. 3, 146
World of Difference, A  Gr. 5, 386
*Yertle the Turtle*  Gr. 2, 368
Zum gali gali  Gr. 5, 400

## TIME
Brush Your Teeth  Gr. 1, 284
Cycle Song of Life (The River Song)
    Gr. 4, 370
Deck the Hall  Gr. 5, 474
Don't Let Your Watch Run Down
    Gr. 3, 166
El barquito  Gr. 3, 358
Every Morning at Eight O'Clock
    (rhyme)  Gr. 1, 36
Flowers at Night (poem)  Gr. 2, 246
For the Beauty of the Earth  Gr. 4, 356
Gypsy in the Moonlight  Gr. 3, 12
*Halley Came to Jackson*  Gr. 2, 340
Hanuka, Hanuka  Gr. 3, 390
Hitotsu toya  Gr. 5, 478
How Many Miles to Babylon?
    Gr. 2, 128
Locomoto-vation  Gr. K, 61
Nruab hnub thiab hmo ntuj (story)
    Gr. 4, 366
Oh, Watch the Stars  Gr. 2, 144
One Morning Soon  Gr. 3, 68
Rock Around the Clock  Gr. 7, B-18
Sol, solecito  Gr. 1, 367
Tic, tac  Gr. 1, 252
Trains (poem)  Gr. 2, 211
Turn, Turn, Turn (To Everything There
    Is a Season)  Gr. 5, 378
What to Do (poem)  Gr. K, 43

## TOYS  *See also Favorite Things.*
I'm a Dreydl  Gr. K, 315
Les petites marionettes  Gr. K, 237
Mama, Buy Me a Chiney Doll
    Gr. K, 120
*Marvelous Toy, The*  Gr. 1, 382
My Dreydl  Gr. K, 314
O pião entrou  Gr. 2, 355
Pin Pon  Gr. 1, 146
Pinwheels (poem)  Gr. 1, 149
Puff, the Magic Dragon  Gr. 2, 350
Teddy Bears (poem)  Gr. K, 163
Ten Little Teddy Bears (poem)
    Gr. K, 301
*Toy Symphony, Movement 4*
    Gr. 1, 111
Very Special Friend, A (poem)
    Gr. 1, 147
Yang wa wa  Gr. K, 162

## TRAVEL AND TRANSPORTATION
### BOAT
All the Way Around the World
    Gr. 2, 258
*Aweigh, Santy Ano*  Gr. 1, 338
Blow, Ye Winds  Gr. 4, 255
Bound for South Australia
    Gr. 5, 22
Can You Canoe? (speech piece)
    Gr. 4, 170
Canoe Song  Gr. 4, 76
Carelessly Crafted Raft, A, A (poem)
    Gr. 6, 416
Cotton-Eye Joe  Gr. 4, 288
El barquito  Gr. 3, 358
El carite  Gr. 5, 305
Four in a Boat  Gr. 2, 46
Greenland Whale Fishery, The
    Gr. 5, 230
Haliwa-Saponi Canoe Song
    Gr. 5, 302
*Haliwa-Saponi Canoe Song*
    Gr. 5, 303
Haul Away, Joe  Gr. 4, 13
I Saw Three Ships  Gr. 1, 426
I See the Moon  Gr. 2, 58
Keel Row, The  Gr. 4, 240
Loigratong  Gr. 6, 451
Long Way Home, A  Gr. 1, 382
Michael, Row the Boat Ashore
    Gr. 2, 18
Mississippi River Chant (speech
    piece)  Gr. 2, 132
Nana Kru  Gr. 6, 282
Noah's Shanty  Gr. 1, 342
Rio Grande  Gr. 4, 256
Sailing to the Sea  Gr. 1, 336
Skye Boat Song  Gr. 6, 372
Someday Very Soon  Gr. 1, 376
Somos el barco  Gr. 4, 352
Song of the Fishes  Gr. 3, 244
Vem kan segla?  Gr. 6, 417
Water Is Wide, The  Gr. 6, 228
*Who Can Sail?*  Gr. 5, 30

### BUS
Bus, The  Gr. K, 82
Locomoto-vation  Gr. K, 61
Long Way Home, A  Gr. 1, 382
School Bus Rap (poem)  Gr. 1, 83

### CAR
Cotton-Eye Joe  Gr. 4, 288
Route 66  Gr. 4, 276
*Route 66*  Gr. 4, 279
Sailing to the Sea  Gr. 1, 336

### OTHER
Li'l Liza Jane  Gr. 3, 140
Long Way Home, A  Gr. 1, 382
Me voy para la luna  Gr. 1, 397
Old Brass Wagon  Gr. 2, 122
Over the River and Through the
    Wood  Gr. 3, 384
Sweet Betsy from Pike  Gr. 4, 244

Thematic Index

**(Travel and Transportation, continued)**

When I'm an Astronaut (poem)
Gr. 1, 402

**PLANE**

I'm Flying Home Gr. 2, 286
Long Way Home, A Gr. 1, 382

**TRAIN**

Chicka Hanka Gr. 2, 211
Choo Choo Boogaloo Gr. 1, 127
Choo Choo Ch'Boogie Gr. 5, 44
Drill, Ye Tarriers Gr. 5, 54
Freight Train Gr. 1, 44
Get on Board Gr. K, 89
Get on Board Gr. K, 89
Glendy Burke, The Gr. 4, 262
Goodbye, Julie (Miss Julie Ann
Johnson) Gr. 1, 334
Gospel Train, The Gr. 6, 398
I've Been Working on the Railroad
Gr. 3, 242
Little Red Caboose Gr. K, 229
Little Red Caboose Gr. K, 228
Long Way Home, A Gr. 1, 382
Los trencitos Gr. K, 24
Mbombera Gr. K, 24
Modern Dragon, A (poem)
Gr. 3, 242
Orange Blossom Special Gr. 1, 47
Orange Blossom Special
Gr. 5, 266
Pat Works on the Railway
Gr. 5, 182
Reuben's Train Gr. 1, 334
Rock Island Line Gr. 4, 54
Sailing to the Sea Gr. 1, 336
Same Train Gr. 2, 164
She'll Be Comin' 'Round the
Mountain Gr. 2, 358
Song of the Train (poem)
Gr. K, 153
This Train Gr. 5, 26
Train Is A-Comin' Gr. 3, 48
Trains (poem) Gr. 1, 301
Trains (poem) Gr. 2, 211
Wabash Cannon Ball Gr. 5, 136
When the Train Comes Along
Gr. 1, 300

## W

## WATER IN OUR WORLD See also
Environments.

Allá en la fuente Gr. 2, 92
Aweigh, Santy Ano Gr. 1, 338
Big Old Storm a-Comin' Gr. K, 257
Blue Danube, The, Op. 314
Gr. 6, 192
Bubble Trouble (poem) Gr. K, 184
Bubbles (poem) Gr. K, 185
Canoe Song Gr. 4, 76
Canto del agua Gr. 8, I-10
Cumberland Gap Gr. 4, 138
Doctor Foster (rhyme) Gr. K, 137

Downpour (poem) Gr. K, 51
Ducks in the Rain (poem) Gr. K, 235
Eensy Weensy Spider Gr. K, 187
Eres tú Gr. 6, 473
Falling Rain Gr. 2, 328
Galoshes (poem) Gr. K, 63
I Don't Care If the Rain Comes Down
Gr. 3, 24
I See the Moon Gr. 2, 58
Let's Do the Flip-Flop Frolic! (poem)
Gr. K, 23
Loigratong Gr. 6, 451
Look Out for Mother Earth Gr. 3, 341
Mary Ann Gr. K, 253
Michael, Row the Boat Ashore
Gr. 2, 18
Mississippi River Chant (speech piece)
Gr. 2, 132
Moon Mirrored in the Pool, The
Gr. 6, 109
Old American Songs, "The
Boatman's Dance" Gr. 4, 61
Osamu kosamu Gr. 4, 96
Peace Like a River Gr. 6, 190
Pitter Patter Scatter (poem) Gr. 1, 55
¡Qué llueva! Gr. K, 81
Rain (Livingston) (poem) Gr. 3, 79
Rain Sizes (poem) Gr. K, 261
Rain Song, The Gr. 2, 323
Raindrops (poem) Gr. 1, 100
Rise and Shine Gr. 4, 98
River (poem) Gr. 4, 61
Roll On, Columbia Gr. 5, 116
Sailing Down My Golden River
Gr. 4, 332
Sailing to the Sea Gr. 1, 336
Shenandoah Gr. 2, 62
Singin' in the Rain Gr. 4, 360
Singin' in the Tub Gr. K, 220
Syrinx Gr. 5, 113
Valentine for Earth, A (poem)
Gr. 3, 324
Water Is Wide, The Gr. 6, 228
Wheel of the Water, The Gr. 4, 362

## WEATHER

Amefuri Gr. 1, 144
Animals Went In One By One, The
(poem) Gr. K, 275
Autumn (poem) Gr. 6, 193
Big Old Storm a-Comin' Gr. K, 257
Bitter Morning, A (poem) Gr. K, 177
Bling Blang Gr. 3, 240
Blow the Wind Southerly Gr. 5, 178
Blow, Ye Winds Gr. 4, 255
Bury Me Not on the Lone Prairie
Gr. 6, 19
Carelessly Crafted Raft, A, A (poem)
Gr. 6, 416
Children of Long Ago (poem)
Gr. 1, 31
Children's Corner Suite, "Snowflakes
Are Dancing" Gr. 5, 239

Circle 'Round the Moon Gr. 4, 403
Clouds Gr. K, 254
Clouds (poem) Gr. K, 255
Coming Home from the Sea–I
Gr. 6, 345
Coming Home from the Sea–II
Gr. 6, 345
Crayons (poem) Gr. K, 75
Dancin' in the Rain (poem) Gr. 1, 366
Dancing Tree, The Gr. K, 202
De colores Gr. 5, 90
Doctor Foster (rhyme) Gr. K, 137
Don't Let the Wind Gr. 3, 180
Down in the Valley Gr. 6, 375
Downpour (poem) Gr. K, 51
Dragon Smoke (poem) Gr. 3, 387
Dragon Smoke (poem) Gr. K, 258
Ducks in the Rain (poem) Gr. K, 235
Eensy Weensy Spider Gr. K, 187
El caracol Gr. K, 130
Erdö, erdö de magos Gr. 3, 182
Eres tú Gr. 6, 473
Extremes (poem) Gr. 4, 409
Falling Rain Gr. 2, 328
First Snowflake (poem) Gr. K, 259
Five Little Snowmen Gr. K, 313
Flowering Umbrellas (poem) Gr. 1, 145
Four Strong Winds (Song to a Seagull)
Gr. 6, 170
Four White Horses Gr. 3, 304
Frostiana (from Stopping by Woods
on a Snowy Evening) Gr. 6, 40
Gakavik Gr. 4, 14
Galoshes (poem) Gr. K, 63
Goin' Down the Road Feelin' Bad
Gr. 7, F-13
Good King Wenceslas Gr. 6, 460
Good King Wenceslas Gr. 6, 461
Groundhog Jig, The Gr. 1, 436
Happiness (poem) Gr. K, 62
Hosanna, Me Build a House
Gr. 5, 132
House of Spring (poem) Gr. 4, 309
I Don't Care If the Rain Comes Down
Gr. 3, 24
I Like Fall (poem) Gr. K, 311
I Love a Rainy Night (line dance)
Gr. 5, 350
It Rains and It Pours (poem)
Gr. K, 243
Knock No More Gr. 3, 386
L'arc en ciel Gr. 2, 333
L'inverno è passato Gr. 2, 400
La tormenta tropical Gr. 2, 116
Las mañanitas Gr. 6, 481
Let It Snow! Let It Snow! Let It Snow!
Gr. 4, 426
Let It Snow! Let It Snow! Let It
Snow! Gr. 4, 427
Let's Get Ready Gr. K, 312
Let's Go Barefoot (poem) Gr. 1, 440
Lieutenant Kijé, Op. 60, "Troika"
Gr. 6, 457

*Lluvia* Gr. 6, 332
Look! Look! The Sun Woke Up!
 Gr. 1, 368
*Louds and Softs of the Seasons*
 Gr. K, 4
Magnolia Gr. 6, 16
Mary Ann Gr. K, 253
Mississippi River Chant (speech piece)
 Gr. 2, 132
Mister Snow Rap (speech piece)
 Gr. 2, 391
Moon's the North Wind's Cooky, The
 (poem) Gr. 4, 375
More It Snows, The (poem)
 Gr. K, 259
Morning Has Broken Gr. 5, 28
*Musical Sleigh Ride, A, "Divertimento
 in F"* Gr. 5, 455
My Bonnie Lies Over the Ocean
 Gr. 4, 338
My Shadow (poem) Gr. K, 19
O, Desayo Gr. 5, 411
Oklahoma Gr. 5, 36
*One Fine Day* Gr. 6, 347
Over the River and Through the Wood
 Gr. 3, 384
Parade Came Marching, The Gr. 1, 166
Pitter Patter Scatter (poem) Gr. 1, 55
Quâ câù gió bay Gr. 5, 460
¡Qué llueva! Gr. K, 81
Rabbit Footprints Gr. 2, 304
Rain (Livingston) (poem) Gr. 3, 79
Rain on the Green Grass (speech piece)
 Gr. K, 10
Rain, Rain Gr. 1, 54
*Rain, Rain, Beautiful Rain* Gr. 4, 32
Rain Sings a Song, The Gr. 1, 102
Rain Sizes (poem) Gr. K, 261
*Rain Song, The* Gr. 2, 323
Rain, The (poem) Gr. 1, 52
Rainbow, The Gr. 2, 332
Raindrops (poem) Gr. 1, 12
*Rainy Day Blues* Gr. 2, 328
Rise and Shine Gr. 4, 98
River Winding (poem) Gr. 4, 60
Roads Go Ever Ever On (poem)
 Gr. 6, 214
Sail Away Gr. 5, 404
Seasons Gr. K, 4
See and Touch Gr. K, 172
Sing a Little Song Gr. K, 30
Singin' in the Rain Gr. 4, 360
Six-Inch Boots in a Nine-Inch Puddle
 Gr. 1, 366
Skye Boat Song Gr. 6, 372
Snow Flakes (poem) Gr. 1, 423
Snowflakes Gr. 1, 422
Spring Rain (poem) Gr. 2, 294
Stopping by Woods on a Snowy
 Evening Gr. 6, 41
Storm Dance (speech piece)
 Gr. K, 145
*Storm, The* Gr. 1, 55

Sun, The (poem) Gr. K, 143
T'hola, t'hola Gr. 4, 132
Take Your Feet Out 'the Sand
 Gr. K, 231
Tancovačka Gr. 4, 230
This Land Is Your Land Gr. 5, 118
*This Land Is Your Land* Gr. 5, 120
To a Red Kite (poem) Gr. 2, 326
Traveler's Song (poem) Gr. 4, 336
Until I Saw the Sea (poem) Gr. 4, 13
Valentine for Earth, A (poem)
 Gr. 3, 324
Valentines (poem) Gr. 2, 398
Vem kan segla? Gr. 6, 417
What to Do (poem) Gr. K, 43
When the Train Comes Along
 Gr. 1, 300
Who Has Seen the Wind? Gr. 2, 324
Who Has Seen the Wind? (poem)
 Gr. 5, 207
Wind Blew East, The Gr. 1, 64
Wind Song (poem) Gr. K, 7
Wind, The (poem) Gr. 6, 170
Windshield Wipers (poem) Gr. 1, 11
Winter Fantasy Gr. 4, 424
Winter Song Gr. 6, 455
Winter Wonderland Gr. 5, 454
Written in March (poem) Gr. 4, 354
Your Friends Shall Be the Tall Wind
 Gr. 6, 201
Zip-a-Dee-Doo-Dah Gr. 2, 330

## WORK

### AGRICULTURE

Alumot Gr. 6, 306
Artsa alinu Gr. 3, 285
California Oranges (rhyme)
 Gr. 1, 15
Cha yang wu Gr. 1, 90
Chawe chidyo chem'chero (story)
 Gr. 2, 296
*Corn Grinding Song* Gr. K, 66
Corn Grinding Song Gr. K, 67
Corta la caña Gr. 6, 364
Dinner Music Gr. K, 70
Don't You Hear the Lambs?
 Gr. 5, 97
*Don't You Hear the Lambs?*
 Gr. 5, 99
Erie Canal Gr. 5, 262
*Farmer in the Dell* Gr. K, 233
Farmer in the Dell, The Gr. K, 232
Go Around the Corn, Sally
 Gr. 2, 12
Growing Corn (poem) Gr. 1, 297
I Walk the Unfrequented Road
 Gr. 6, 79
Johnny Appleseed Gr. 4, 345
*Little Red Hen, The* Gr. 1, 254
Little Red Hen, The (story)
 Gr. 1, 256
Los maizales Gr. 1, 296

Mashed Potatoes (speech piece)
 Gr. 1, 20
Pastures of Plenty Gr. 4, 280
Peanut Butter (speech piece)
 Gr. 1, 173
Perot Gr. 2, 378
Ptashky u babusi sadochku
 Gr. 1, 192
See the Children Playin' Gr. 4, 107
Shake the Papaya Down
 Gr. 4, 378
Shepherd, The (poem) Gr. 5, 98
To a Peanut (poem) Gr. 1, 163
Tumba Gr. 5, 161
Weevily Wheat Gr. 4, 105
When I Grow Up (poem)
 Gr. 2, 397
World We Love, The Gr. 3, 342
Yü guang guang Gr. 6, 60

### BAKING, COOKING

Dinner Music Gr. K, 70
Growing Corn (poem) Gr. 1, 297
Hot Cross Buns (Version 1)
 Gr. 3, 218
Hot Cross Buns (Version 2)
 Gr. 3, 221
*Little Red Hen, The* Gr. 1, 254
Little Red Hen, The (story)
 Gr. 1, 256
Mashed Potatoes (speech piece)
 Gr. 1, 20
Peanut Butter (speech piece)
 Gr. 1, 173
Shoo, Turkey Gr. 1, 104
Sweet Potatoes Gr. 3, 228
Vamos a la mar Gr. 3, 226
We're Making Popcorn (speech
 piece) Gr. 1, 86
When I Grow Up (poem)
 Gr. 2, 397

### BOATING, SHIPPING

*Aweigh, Santy Ano* Gr. 1, 338
Blow, Ye Winds Gr. 4, 255
Bound for South Australia
 Gr. 5, 22
*Coming Home from the Sea–I*
 Gr. 6, 345
*Coming Home from the Sea–II*
 Gr. 6, 345
Day-O! (Banana Boat Loader's
 Song) Gr. 5, 18
Glendy Burke, The Gr. 4, 262
Greenland Whale Fishery, The
 Gr. 5, 230
Haliwa-Saponi Canoe Song
 Gr. 5, 302
*Haliwa-Saponi Canoe Song*
 Gr. 5, 303
Haul Away, Joe Gr. 4, 13
I See the Moon Gr. 2, 58
*Old American Songs, "The
 Boatman's Dance"* Gr. 4, 61

Thematic Index

(*Work,* continued)

Pay Me My Money Down  Gr. 4, 38
*Red Poppy, "Russian Sailors' Dance", The, "Russian Sailors' Dance"*  Gr. 4, 224
Rio Grande  Gr. 4, 256
Sailing to the Sea  Gr. 1, 336
*Shenandoah*  Gr. 2, 62
Shenandoah  Gr. 5, 264
*Shenandoah*  Gr. 5, 265
Skye Boat Song  Gr. 6, 372
Someday Very Soon  Gr. 1, 376
To'ia mai te waka  Gr. 1, 77
When I Grow Up (poem)
    Gr. 2, 397

### BUILDING

Bling Blang  Gr. 3, 240
Cement Mixer  Gr. 4, 102
Don't Let Your Watch Run Down
    Gr. 3, 166
London Bridge  Gr. K, 244
Mud  Gr. 3, 32
Old House, Tear It Down!
    Gr. 4, 178
Zum gali gali  Gr. 5, 400

### COWBOY/RANCHER

Bury Me Not on the Lone Prairie
    Gr. 6, 19
Cattle Call  Gr. 5, 344
*Cattle Call*  Gr. 5, 347
Colorado Trail  Gr. 5, 276
*Colorado Trail*  Gr. 5, 277
Cowboy's Dream (poem)
    Gr. 4, 339
El payo  Gr. 6, 145
El rancho grande  Gr. 4, 215
Home on the Range  Gr. 5, 69
Laredo  Gr. 5, 10
Lone Star Trail  Gr. 2, 21
Morning Comes Early  Gr. 5, 13
Railroad Corral  Gr. 3, 174
Sheep in the Meadow (rhyme)
    Gr. 1, 17
Streets of Laredo  Gr. 4, 272

### DOCTOR, NURSE

El burrito enfermo  Gr. K, 271
Mother, Mother, I Am Sick (rhyme)
    Gr. K, 121

### FISHING

Blow, Ye Winds  Gr. 4, 255
Bonavist' Harbour  Gr. 3, 294
Charlie over the Water  Gr. 1, 68
Farewell to Tarwathie  Gr. 6, 43
Ochimbo  Gr. 4, 134
One, Two, Three, Four, Five
    (rhyme)  Gr. 1, 67
Rio Grande  Gr. 4, 256
Sea Wolf, The (poem)  Gr. 4, 257
Song of the Fishes  Gr. 3, 244
Vamos a la mar  Gr. 3, 226

### HOUSEHOLD CHORES

It Rains and It Pours (poem)
    Gr. K, 243
Miss Susie Anna Sue  Gr. K, 242
Scrub Brush Shuffle, The  Gr. 1, 118

### LUMBERING

Blue Mountain Lake  Gr. 6, 205
Erie Canal  Gr. 5, 262
Lumberjack, The (poem)  Gr. 1, 113
Má Teodora  Gr. 6, 301
Riquir rán  Gr. 1, 48
See-Saw Sacradown  Gr. 2, 208
Serra, serra, serrador  Gr. 1, 112
What Do We Plant? (poem)
    Gr. 2, 130

### MILITARY

Battle Cry of Freedom  Gr. 5, 272
Battle Hymn of the Republic
    Gr. 5, 274
Johnny Has Gone for a Soldier
    Gr. 5, 188
*Lazy John*  Gr. 4, 11
One Morning in May  Gr. 6, 121
Over There  Gr. 5, 279
Soldier, Soldier  Gr. 4, 11
When Johnny Comes Marching
    Home  Gr. 5, 180
Yo-shi nai  Gr. 6, 286

### MINING

California  Gr. 5, 52
Clementine  Gr. 4, 341
Erie Canal  Gr. 5, 262
Oh, Susanna  Gr. 4, 264

### MUSICIAN

Bassett, Rick (Part 1)  Gr. 3, 222
Bassett, Rick (Part 2)  Gr. 3, 223
Burrough, Roslyn  Gr. 1, 163
De Beat (poem)  Gr. 2, 67
Joubert, Joseph  Gr. 3, 50
Louiselle, Bryan  Gr. 1, 251
Moore, Carman  Gr. 3, 163
*Piki mai*  Gr. 1, 79
Someday Very Soon  Gr. 1, 376
Swoboda, Deanna  Gr. 3, 188
When the Saints Go Marching In
    Gr. 2, 178

### POSTAL

Every Morning at Eight O'Clock
    (rhyme)  Gr. 1, 36
Ida Red  Gr. 3, 30

### RAILROAD

Chicka Hanka  Gr. 2, 211
Don't Let Your Watch Run Down
    Gr. 3, 166
Drill, Ye Tarriers  Gr. 5, 54
Gospel Train, The  Gr. 6, 398
I've Been Working on the Railroad
    Gr. 3, 242
Little Red Caboose  Gr. K, 229
*Little Red Caboose*  Gr. K, 228

Pat Works on the Railway
    Gr. 5, 182
Rock Island Line  Gr. 4, 54
Same Train  Gr. 2, 164
Trains (poem)  Gr. 1, 301
Trains (poem)  Gr. 2, 211
When the Train Comes Along
    Gr. 1, 300

### SALES

Chairs to Mend  Gr. 4, 149
Feng yang hua gu  Gr. 4, 313
Linstead Market  Gr. 5, 241
Perot  Gr. 2, 378

### TECHNOLOGY

Bassett, Rick (Part 1)  Gr. 3, 222
Bassett, Rick (Part 2)  Gr. 3, 223
Computer, The  Gr. 4, 199
*Think*  Gr. 6, 367
When I Grow Up (poem)
    Gr. 2, 397

## WORLD COMMUNITY, THE

A la puerta del cielo  Gr. 5, 60
A la rurru niño  Gr. K, 180
Abiyoyo  Gr. 2, 108
Achshav  Gr. 2, 64
Adana ya gidelim  Gr. 2, 142
Adelita  Gr. 5, 50
African Noel  Gr. 1, 427
Aguinaldo  Gr. 3, 402
Ah, eu entrei na roda  Gr. 3, 308
Ah ya Zane  Gr. 5, 297
Ahora voy a cantarles  Gr. 3, 56
Ai, Dunaii moy  Gr. 4, 293
Al quebrar la piñata  Gr. 4, 432
Ala Da'lona  Gr. 4, 136
Ala Da'lona  Gr. 5, 301
All the Way Around the World
    Gr. 2, 258
All Through the Night  Gr. 5, 105
Allá en la fuente  Gr. 2, 92
*Allons danser, Colinda*  Gr. K, 218
Amefuri  Gr. 1, 144
Arirang  Gr. 5, 25
Around the World (poem)  Gr. 2, 256
Artsa alinu  Gr. 3, 285
Asadoya  Gr. 6, 303
Así es mi tierra  Gr. 6, 172
At the Same Time  Gr. 6, 115
Au clair de la lune  Gr. 3, 18
Ayelivi  Gr. 2, 70
Ayii, Ayii, Ayii (poem)  Gr. K, 11
Ayliluli, num tsipor  Gr. 1, 204
Bam, chi, chi, bam  Gr. K, 109
Bantama kra kro  Gr. 5, 308
Banuwa  Gr. 6, 294
Barb'ry Allen  Gr. 6, 44
Bard of Armagh, The  Gr. 4, 296
Bát kim thang  Gr. 6, 13
*Be Still, My Child*  Gr. 1, 39
*Bear Dance*  Gr. 7, C-5
Bear Dance  Gr. K, 127
*Bear Dance Song*  Gr. K, 127

Beyond Borders  Gr. 5, 292
Birds of Fire (poem)  Gr. 3, 257
Blow the Wind Southerly  Gr. 5, 178
*Body Song, The*  Gr. 6, 438
Bonavist' Harbour  Gr. 3, 294
Bonga  Gr. K, 78
Bonjour, mes amis  Gr. 1, 316
Bound for South Australia  Gr. 5, 22
Brand New Day, A  Gr. 6, 7
*Brolga One*  Gr. 4, 36
*Brolga*  Gr. 6, 271
Canción de cuna  Gr. 4, 144
Cantaré, cantarás  Gr. 6, 413
Celebrating Our Flag (poem)  Gr. K, 327
Celebration (poem)  Gr. 6, 122
Cha yang wu  Gr. 1, 90
Chang  Gr. 1, 156
Chanukah, Chanukah  Gr. 1, 420
Chanukiyah li yesh  Gr. 1, 421
Chawe chidyo chem'chero (story)
       Gr. 2, 296
Che che koolay  Gr. 2, 266
*Chica chica boom chic*  Gr. 2, 112
Chippewa Lullaby  Gr. K, 181
Cho'i hát bội  Gr. 5, 318
Chrismus a Come  Gr. 3, 396
Chuhwuht  Gr. 2, 356
Cielito lindo  Gr. 4, 270
Cielito lindo  Gr. 7, I-20
Ciranda  Gr. 2, 272
*Cold and Frosty Morning*  Gr. 2, 139
*Common Ground*  Gr. 3, 379
Con el vito  Gr. 7, G-15
*Corn Grinding Song*  Gr. K, 66
Corn Grinding Song  Gr. K, 67
Corta la caña  Gr. 6, 364
Counting Song  Gr. 1, 253
Cuculí  Gr. K, 238
Dance for the Nations  Gr. 6, 122
Dancing Pig, The (folk tale)  Gr. 1, 196
Day-O! (Banana Boat Loader's Song)
       Gr. 5, 18
De colores  Gr. 5, 90
De colores  Gr. 8, I-14
Deau-deau, ti pitit maman  Gr. 2, 306
Debajo 'el botón  Gr. 1, 210
Dinner Music  Gr. K, 70
Diou shou juan'er  Gr. 2, 277
Don Alfonso  Gr. 5, 177
Don Gato  Gr. 3, 352
¿Dónde lo escondí?  Gr. K, 209
Doong gul ge  Gr. 3, 134
*Doraji*  Gr. 4, 175
Doraji  Gr. 4, 174
Drum, A (folk tale)  Gr. 1, 116
Duérmete, mi niño  Gr. 1, 292
Dundai  Gr. 5, 106
Ee jer ha ba go  Gr. K, 133
Ein Männlein steht im Walde  Gr. 2, 90
Einini  Gr. 4, 391
El barquito  Gr. 3, 358
El carite  Gr. 5, 305
El condor pasa  Gr. 6, 46

El coquí  Gr. 2, 292
El día de mamita  Gr. K, 325
El florón  Gr. 2, 246
El juego chirimbolo  Gr. 2, 54
El mes de abril  Gr. 3, 328
Éliza Kongo  Gr. 5, 14
Families  Gr. 1, 282
Farewell to Tarwathie  Gr. 6, 43
Farewell to the Warriors  Gr. 4, 284
*Fatou yo, "I am Fatou"*  Gr. K, 155
*Feliz Navidad*  Gr. 4, 433
Feliz Navidad  Gr. 7, I-28
Feng yang hua gu  Gr. 4, 313
Four White Horses  Gr. 3, 304
Frère Jacques  Gr. 2, 125
Funwa alafia  Gr. 5, 32
*Garden of the Earth*  Gr. 5, 399
Geef jij mij die schoen  Gr. 1, 126
Give a Little Love  Gr. 6, 140
Go Down, Moses  Gr. 5, 190
Go, My Son  Gr. 6, 188
Grass Game  Gr. 1, 371
Green Corn Song  Gr. 5, 462
Greensleeves  Gr. 6, 49
Greetings (speech piece)  Gr. 3, 316
Guantanamera  Gr. 8, I-32
Gypsy in the Moonlight  Gr. 3, 12
Ha'kyo jong  Gr. 2, 135
Haliwa-Saponi Canoe Song
       Gr. 5, 302
*Haliwa-Saponi Canoe Song*
       Gr. 5, 303
Hama chi dori  Gr. 3, 330
Harambee  Gr. 4, 434
*Hard Times*  Gr. 1, 194
*Harukoma, "Spring Horse Dance"*
       Gr. 1, 145
Hashewie  Gr. 4, 63
Hato popo  Gr. 1, 186
Hava nagila  Gr. 6, 153
Hej pada pada  Gr. 3, 78
Hello!  Gr. 2, 262
Hello to All the Children of the World
       Gr. 3, 4
Heri za Kwanzaa  Gr. 5, 476
Hevenu shalom aleichem  Gr. 3, 378
Hey, m'tswala  Gr. 4, 79
Hi-Dee-Roon  Gr. K, 10
*Hindewhu (whistle) solo*  Gr. 6, 269
Hine mah tov  Gr. 5, 430
Hitotsu toya  Gr. 5, 478
Hosanna, Me Build a House
       Gr. 5, 132
Hotaru koi  Gr. 1, 356
*How Can I Keep from Singing?*
       Gr. 4, 260
How Can I Keep from Singing?
       Gr. 4, 261
How Many Miles to Babylon?
       Gr. 2, 128
How the Kiwi Lost Its Wings (story)
       Gr. 1, 78
Hush Up the Baby  Gr. K, 222

Hwa yuan li-de young wa wa
       Gr. 3, 102
I Am But a Small Voice  Gr. 6, 446
I Saw Three Ships  Gr. 1, 426
I Walk in Beauty  Gr. 4, 282
Ichi-gatsu tsuitachi  Gr. 3, 406
Ikhanda, maslombe  Gr. K, 14
Ise oluwa  Gr. 2, 102
Ise oluwa  Gr. 6, 230
*It's Time*  Gr. 6, 319
Jan ken pon  Gr. 3, 302
*Janitzio*  Gr. 5, 91
Jasmine Flowers  Gr. 5, 316
*Je m'endors*  Gr. K, 219
¡Jeu! ¡Jeu!  Gr. 1, 216
Juan pirulero  Gr. K, 215
Juanito  Gr. K, 300
Kaeru no uta  Gr. K, 183
Kelo aba w'ye  Gr. 6, 290
Khorovod  Gr. 1, 372
Kibungo  Gr. 2, 354
Kibungo, Beast of the Forest (story)
       Gr. 2, 352
Kokoleoko  Gr. 5, 33
*Kokopelli Wandering Song*
       Gr. 5, 110
Koriko!  Gr. K, 154
Kou ri lengay  Gr. 2, 217
Kuma san  Gr. K, 40
Kunolounkwa  Gr. K, 110
*Kunolounkwa, "Contemporary"*
       Gr. K, 110
L'inverno è passato  Gr. 2, 400
La bamba  Gr. 5, 128
*La bamba*  Gr. 5, 130
*La bamba*  Gr. 5, 131
La borinqueña  Gr. 8, D-19
La Jesusita  Gr. 5, 322
La mariposa  Gr. 6, 58
La piñata  Gr. 3, 399
La raspa  Gr. 4, 302
La Tarara  Gr. 4, 176
La víbora  Gr. 1, 322
Lahk gei mohlee  Gr. 5, 317
Laredo  Gr. 5, 10
Las estrellitas del cielo  Gr. 5, 175
*Las mañanitas*  Gr. K, 325
Las velitas  Gr. 5, 147
Leak kanseng  Gr. 1, 156
Les petites marionettes  Gr. K, 237
Lift Ev'ry Voice and Sing  Gr. 5, 482
Linstead Market  Gr. 5, 241
*Lion*  Gr. 6, 303
Lo yisa  Gr. 6, 130
Loigratong  Gr. 6, 451
Los días de la semana  Gr. 1, 268
Los maizales  Gr. 1, 296
Los reyes de Oriente  Gr. 5, 480
Los trencitos  Gr. K, 24
Lost My Gold Ring  Gr. 6, 158
Love in Any Language  Gr. 6, 476
Lullaby and Dance  Gr. 4, 387
Luna lunera (speech piece)  Gr. K, 90

**(World Community, The, continued)**

Má Teodora  Gr. 6, 301
Mariposita  Gr. 2, 156
Mary Ann  Gr. 6, 180
Mbombera  Gr. K, 24
Meng Jian Nu  Gr. 5, 194
Merry Modal Christmas, A  Gr. 4, 411
Mi cuerpo hace música  Gr. K, 106
*Mi tierra*  Gr. 6, 365
Minka  Gr. 4, 222
Miss Susie Anna Sue  Gr. K, 242
Missy-La, Massa-La  Gr. 4, 188
Mister Ram Goat-O  Gr. 3, 54
Mon son pha (speech piece)  Gr. K, 91
Morning Comes Early  Gr. 5, 13
Morning Has Broken  Gr. 5, 28
Mos Mos  Gr. 1, 130
Mubärak  Gr. 3, 282
Nampaya omame  Gr. 1, 138
Naranja dulce  Gr. 2, 97
New Hungarian Folk Song  Gr. 6, 196
Nie chcę cię znác  Gr. 3, 314
Nightdance (poem)  Gr. K, 219
Niu lang zhi nü  Gr. 4, 335
No quiero plata  Gr. 1, 424
Nruab hnub thiab hmo ntuj (story)
    Gr. 4, 366
Nu wahtan  Gr. 1, 279
O lê lê O Bahía  Gr. 6, 165
O ma washi  Gr. K, 13
Ochimbo  Gr. 4, 134
Ocho kandelikas  Gr. 4, 429
Oh, Danny Boy  Gr. 4, 48
*Olympic Spirit*  Gr. 6, 350
Our Family Comes from 'Round the
    World (poem)  Gr. 1, 299
Pai pi qiu  Gr. 1, 324
Panamam tombé  Gr. 7, D-18
Pavo, pavo  Gr. 1, 416
Pay Me My Money Down  Gr. 4, 38
Perná, perná, i mélissá  Gr. K, 264
*Piki mai*  Gr. 1, 79
Piñon, pirulín  Gr. 2, 174
Pollerita  Gr. 5, 151
Pon, pon, pon  Gr. K, 50
*Primitive Fire, "Oya"*  Gr. 2, 68
Ptashky u babusi sadochku  Gr. 1, 192
Pust' 'vsegda budet sonse  Gr. 3, 278
Quâ câù gió bay  Gr. 5, 460
¡Qué bonita bandera!  Gr. 5, 294
Rabbit Dance, The (story)  Gr. 3, 334
Raccoon Dance Song  Gr. 1, 260
Ragupati Ragava Raja Ram  Gr. 5, 321
*Rain, Rain, Beautiful Rain*  Gr. 4, 32
Riendo el río corre  Gr. 6, 263
Rinsho, rinsho  Gr. K, 285
*Riverdance Suite*  Gr. 2, 141
*Roddy McCaulay*  Gr. 3, 292
Rolling Rice Cake, The: A Story from
    Japan (folk tale)  Gr. 1, 91
'Round and 'Round  Gr. 1, 148
Sailboat in the Sky  Gr. 4, 374
Sakura  Gr. 4, 308

Sambalele  Gr. 4, 397
Santa Clara  Gr. 4, 172
Sarika keo  Gr. 3, 275
Sawatdee tuh jah  Gr. 2, 265
Scarborough Fair  Gr. 6, 95
Scotland the Brave  Gr. 5, 138
Se va el caimán  Gr. 5, 306
*Sekar jepun*  Gr. 1, 195
Serra, serra, serrador  Gr. 1, 112
Sh'ney dubim  Gr. K, 268
Shake the Papaya Down  Gr. 4, 378
Shalom aleichem  Gr. 6, 409
*Shika no Tone*  Gr. 5, 112
Shir l'shalom  Gr. 4, 419
Shri Ram, jai Ram  Gr. 4, 311
Shu ha mo  Gr. 3, 276
Si me dan pasteles  Gr. 1, 432
Simple Gifts  Gr. 8, A-17
Sioux Lullaby (poem)  Gr. K, 111
Siyahamba  Gr. 6, 212
Skye Boat Song  Gr. 6, 372
So Many Children (poem)  Gr. 1, 333
Sol, solecito  Gr. 1, 367
Somebody's Knockin' at Your Door
    Gr. 4, 53
*Sometimes I Feel Like a Motherless
    Child*  Gr. 5, 193
Son macaron  Gr. 4, 109
Sonando  Gr. 4, 34
Song of Greatness, A (poem)
    Gr. 3, 335
St. Patrick Was a Gentleman
    Gr. 3, 290
Still, Still, Still  Gr. 5, 468
Take Time in Life  Gr. 6, 292
Tanabata-sama  Gr. 2, 336
This World  Gr. 5, 168
Thula, thula, ngoana  Gr. 4, 227
Tic, tac  Gr. 1, 252
Tie Me Kangaroo Down, Sport
    Gr. 4, 37
Tina singu  Gr. 4, 300
To'ia mai te waka  Gr. 1, 77
Tumba  Gr. 5, 161
Tzena, tzena  Gr. 5, 298
Uga uga uga  Gr. K, 305
Un, deux, trois  Gr. 2, 198
Un elefante  Gr. 2, 160
Un pajarito  Gr. 2, 16
Under the Same Sun  Gr. 6, 440
United Nations on the March, The
    Gr. 6, 443
Usagi  Gr. 1, 396
Vamos a cantar  Gr. K, 278
Vamos a hacer la ronda  Gr. K, 124
Vamos a la mar  Gr. 3, 226
Viva Jujuy  Gr. 5, 228
*Vulani ringi ring*  Gr. 1, 139
Wai bamba  Gr. 6, 26
Water Come a Me Eye  Gr. 6, 300
Water Is Wide, The  Gr. 6, 228
*Welcome to Our World*  Gr. 6, 272
*Who Can Sail?*  Gr. 5, 30

Why the Warthog Goes About on His
    Knees (story)  Gr. 1, 139
Wind Blew East, The  Gr. 1, 64
Xiao  Gr. 4, 314
Xiao yin chuan  Gr. 2, 14
Yang wa wa  Gr. K, 162
*Yaudachi*  Gr. 5, 156
Ye jaliya da  Gr. 5, 67
Yibane amenu  Gr. 4, 316
*Yo Lé Lé (Fulani Groove)*  Gr. 5, 33
Yo-shi nai  Gr. 6, 286
Yüe liang wan wan  Gr. 5, 314
Zomo the Rabbit (story)  Gr. 3, 364
Zum gali gali  Gr. 5, 400

**Z**

**ZOOS**  *See also Animals.*
Animals Went In One By One, The
    (poem)  Gr. K, 275
*Carnival of the Animals, "Royal
    March of the Lion"*  Gr. 3, 357
I Love Peanuts  Gr. 1, 162
Lion, The (poem)  Gr. K, 217
Party Tonight!  Gr. 2, 152
Pick 'n' Mix Zoo (poem)  Gr. K, 139

# Bridges to Asia

**Bridges to Asia: Primary Level**

| Title | Language | Credits | Page | CD Track |
|---|---|---|---|---|
| Are You Sleeping Medley (Stereo Vocal) | Mandarin, Cantonese, Thai, and Hmong | Collected by Mary Shamrock | 38 | 2-1 |
| Are You Sleeping Medley (Stereo Performance Track) | English | | 38 | 2-3 |
| Are You Sleeping Medley (English) (Stereo Vocal) | English | English Words by Alice Firgau and Kim Williams | 38 | 2-2 |
| Before Mealtime (Mun pel nhaim) (Pick-A-Track) | English | English Words by David Eddleman; Music by Sam-Ang Sam and Yang Sam | 31 | 1-27 |
| Bird Song (Sarika keo) (Pick-A-Track) | English | Folk Song from Cambodia; English Words by David Eddleman | 34 | 1-30 |
| Bouncing Balls (Pai pi qiu) (Pick-A-Track) | English | English Words by Mary Shamrock; Music by Li-Chin Wong | 12 | 1-11 |
| Chitchiritchit (Pick-A-Track) | English | Folk Song from the Philippines | 60 | 2-22 |
| Cov men-yuam (How Are You, Little Children?) (Pick-A-Track) | Hmong | Hmong American Children's Song | 43 | 2-5 |
| Dam sen (The Lotus in a Pond) (Pick-A-Track) | Vietnamese | Folk Song from Vietnam | 57 | 2-19 |
| Dêm trung thu (A Mid-Autumn Night) (Pick-A-Track) | Vietnamese | Words and Music by Phong Nguyen | 54 | 2-16 |
| Doong gul ge ('Round and Around We Go) (Stereo Vocal) | Korean | Korean Words and Music by Lee Su In | 2 | 1-1 |
| Doong gul ge ('Round and Around We Go) (Stereo Performance Track) | Korean | | 2 | 1-3 |
| Ee jer ha ba go (The Hungry Dog) (Pick-A-Track) | Mandarin | Children's Song from China; Collected by Mary Shamrock | 9 | 1-8 |
| Fan bu ge (Song of the Crow) (Pick-A-Track) | Mandarin | Folk Song from China; English Words Anonymous | 18 | 1-15 |
| Frogs (Shu ha mo) (Pick-A-Track) | English | Folk Song from China; English Words by Dietz and Park | 27 | 1-23 |
| Haathi (poem) (The Elephant) (Stereo Vocal) | Hindi | | 47 | 2-12 |
| Hello Song (Sawatdee tuh jah) (Pick-A-Track) | English | Collected by Mary Shamrock; Folk Song from Thailand | 6 | 1-6 |
| Hide the Scarf (Leak kanseng) (Pick-A-Track) | English | Children's Song from Cambodia; English Words by Mae Vincent | 30 | 1-25 |
| Home from School (Hui jia qù) (Pick-A-Track) | English | English Words by David Eddleman; Folk Song from China | 15 | 1-13 |
| How Are You, Little Children? (Cov men-yuam) (Pick-A-Track) | English | Hmong American Children's Song; English Words by Kim Williams | 43 | 2-6 |
| Hui jia qù (Home from School) (Pick-A-Track) | Mandarin | Folk Song from China | 15 | 1-13 |
| Hungry Dog (Ee jer ha ba go) (Pick-A-Track) | English | English Words by Will Gau; Collected by Mary Shamrock | 9 | 1-8 |
| I Love Mama (Kuv niam) (Pick-A-Track) | English | Hmong American Children's Song; English words by Will Gau | 44 | 2-9 |
| Ichi-gatsu tsuitachi (A New Year's Greeting) (Pick-A-Track) | Japanese | School Song from Japan; Music by Ue Sanemichi; Words by Senge Takatomi | 68 | 2-28 |
| Kuv niam (I Love Mama) (Pick-A-Track) | Hmong | Hmong American Children's Song; Collected by Mary Shamrock; My Vang | 44 | 2-8 |
| Lao kasae (Northern Dance) (Pick-A-Track) | Lao | Folk Song from Laos; English Words by Alice Firgau | 50 | 2-13 |
| Law dai yü (Old Lullaby) (Pick-A-Track) | Cantonese | Folk Song from China; English Words by Mary Shamrock | 21 | 1-18 |
| Leak kanseng (Hide the Scarf) (Pick-A-Track) | Cambodian | Children's Song from Cambodia | 30 | 1-25 |
| Lotus in a Pond (Dam sen) (Pick-A-Track) | English | Folk Song from Vietnam; English Words by David Eddleman | 57 | 2-20 |

| Title | Language | Credits | Page | CD Track |
|---|---|---|---|---|
| Mid-Autumn Night (Dem trung thu) (Pick-A-Track) | English | English Words by Will Gau; Music by Phong Nguyen | 54 | 2-17 |
| Mun pel nhaim (Before Mealtime) (Pick-A-Track) | Cambodian | Words and Music by Sam-Ang Sam and Yang Sam | 31 | 1-27 |
| New Year's Greeting (Ichi-gatsu tsuitachi) (Pick-A-Track) | English | School Song from Japan; Music by Ue Sanemichi; English Words Adapted by Katherine S. Bolt | 68 | 2-28 |
| Northern Dance (Lao kasae) (Pick-A-Track) | English | Folk Song from Laos | 50 | 2-14 |
| Number Song (Yu(t) ee sahm) (Pick-A-Track) | English | Folk Song from China; Collected by Mary Shamrock | 24 | 1-21 |
| Old Lullaby (Law dai yü) (Pick-A-Track) | English | Folk Song from China; As sung by Gong-Bi Yu | 21 | 1-19 |
| Pai pi qiu (Bouncing Balls) (Pick-A-Track) | Mandarin | Words and Music by Li-Chin Wong | 12 | 1-10 |
| 'Round and Around We Go (Doong gul ge) (Stereo Vocal) | English | English Words by Kim Williams | 2 | 1-2 |
| Sarika keo (Bird Song) (Pick-A-Track) | Cambodian | Folk Song from Cambodia | 34 | 1-29 |
| Sawatdee tuh jah (The Hello Song) (Pick-A-Track) | Thai | Collected by Mary Shamrock; Folk Song from Thailand | 6 | 1-5 |
| Shu ha mo (Frogs) (Pick-A-Track) | Szechuan | Folk Song from China; Collected by Mary Shamrock | 27 | 1-23 |
| Song of the Crow (Fan bu ge) (Pick-A-Track) | English | Folk Song from China | 18 | 1-16 |
| Star Festival (Tanabata-sama) (Stereo Vocal) | English | School Song from Japan; Music by Kan-ichi Shimofusa; English Words by Mary Shamrock | 64 | 2-25 |
| Taaray (poem) (Stars) (Stereo Vocal) | Hindi | | 47 | 2-11 |
| Tanabata-sama (Star Festival) (Stereo Vocal) | Japanese | School Song from Japan; Music by Kan-ichi Shimofusa; Words by Hanayo Gondo with Ryuha Hayashi | 64 | 2-24 |
| Tanabata-sama (Star Festival) (Stereo Performance Track) | Japanese | | 64 | 2-26 |
| Yu(t) ee sahm (Number Song) (Pick-A-Track) | Cantonese | Folk Song from China; Collected by Mary Shamrock; As sung by Shin-Pai Li | 24 | 1-21 |

## Bridges to Asia: Intermediate Level

| Title | Language | Credits | Page | CD Track |
|---|---|---|---|---|
| Aksar (Learning Day by Day) (Pick-A-Track) | Cambodian | Folk Song from Cambodia | 26 | 1-21 |
| Asadoya (Pick-A-Track) | English | Folk Song from Okinawa; English Words by D. G. Britton | 9 | 1-7 |
| Asadoya (Pick-A-Track) | Okinawan | Folk Song from Okinawa | 9 | 1-6 |
| Bát kim thang (Setting Up the Golden Ladder) (Pick-A-Track) | Vietnamese | Traditional Song from Vietnam | 37 | 2-1 |
| Chim da da (The Da Da Bird) (Pick-A-Track) | Vietnamese | Traditional Song from Vietnam | 40 | 2-4 |
| Cho'i hát bôi (The Theater Game) (Pick-A-Track) | Vietnamese | Traditional Song from Vietnam; Collected by Phong Nguyen | 34 | 1-28 |
| Cowherd and the Weaving Maid (Niu lang zhi nü) (Pick-A-Track) | English | Folk Song from China; English Words by Mary Shamrock | 12 | 1-10 |
| Crescent Moon (Yüe liang wan wan) (Pick-A-Track) | English | Folk Song from China; English Words by Elaine Nienow | 16 | 1-12 |
| Da Da Bird, The (Chim da da ) (Pick-A-Track) | English | Traditional Song from Vietnam; English Words by Kim Williams | 40 | 2-5 |
| Dok djampa (The White Jasmine Flower) (Stereo Vocal) | Lao | Folk Song from Laos | 30 | 1-24 |
| Dok djampa (The White Jasmine Flower) (Stereo Performance Track) | Lao | | 30 | 1-26 |
| Fandango (Pandangguhan) (Pick-A-Track) | English | Folk Song from the Philippines; English Words by David Eddleman | 66 | 2-21 |

| Title | Language | Credits | Page | CD Track |
|---|---|---|---|---|
| Go hyang eü bohm (Hometown in Spring) (Teach-A-Part) | Korean | Music by Hong Nan Pa; Words by Lee Won Su | 22 | 1-17 |
| Go hyang eü bohm (Hometown in Spring) (Stereo Performance Track) | Korean | | 22 | 1-19 |
| Hitotsu toya (English) (Pick-A-Track) | English | Folk Song from Japan; English Words Anonymous | 5 | 1-4 |
| Hitotsu toya (Japanese) (Pick-A-Track) | Japanese | Folk Song from Japan | 5 | 1-3 |
| Hometown in Spring (Go hyang eü bohm) (Teach-A-Part) | English | Music by Hong Nan Pa; English Words by Aura Kontra | 22 | 1-18 |
| Jan ken pon (Pick-A-Track) | Japanese | Collected by Mary Shamrock at the Nishi Hongwanji Temple Dharma School | 2 | 1-1 |
| Learning Day by Day (Aksar) (Pick-A-Track) | English | Folk Song from Cambodia; English Words by David Eddleman | 26 | 1-22 |
| Loigratong (Stereo Performance Track) | English | | 52 | 2-12 |
| Loigratong (English) (Stereo Vocal) | English | Folk Song from Thailand; English Words by Alice Firgau | 52 | 2-11 |
| Loigratong (Thai) (Stereo Vocal) | Thai | Folk Song from Thailand | 52 | 2-10 |
| Moonlight Lullaby (Yü guang guang) (Pick-A-Track) | English | Folk Song from Hong Kong; English Words by Aura Kontra | 19 | 1-15 |
| Niu lang zhi nü (The Cowherd and the Weaving Maid) (Pick-A-Track) | Mandarin | Folk Song from China | 12 | 1-9 |
| Nruab hnub thiab hmo ntuj (story) (Why Is There Day and Night?) (Stereo Vocal) | Hmong | Hmong Folk Tale | 48 | 2-8 |
| Orphan's Song | Hmong | Hmong Song | 44 | 2-7 |
| Pandangghuan (Fandango) (Pick-A-Track) | Tagalog | Folk Song from the Philippines; As sung by Sonny Alforque | 66 | 2-20 |
| Prarthana (Prayer) (Pick-A-Track) | Hindi | Traditional Hindi Song | 57 | 2-14 |
| Prayer (Prarthana) (Pick-A-Track) | English | Traditional Hindi Song; English Words by Alice Firgau | 57 | 2-15 |
| Santa Clara (English) (Pick-A-Track) | English | Folk Song from the Philippines; English Words by Alice Firgau | 62 | 2-18 |
| Santa Clara (Tagalog) (Pick-A-Track) | Tagalog | Folk Song from the Philippines; As sung by Sonny Alforque | 62 | 2-17 |
| Setting Up the Golden Ladder (Bat kim yhang) (Pick-A-Track) | English | Traditional Song from Vietnam; English Words by Alice Firgau | 37 | 2-2 |
| Theater Game (Cho'i hát bôi) (Pick-A-Track) | English | Traditional Song from Vietnam; English Words by Kim Williams | 34 | 1-29 |
| White Jasmine Flower (Dok djampa) (Stereo Vocal) | English | Folk Song from Laos; Enlgish Words by Alice Firgau | 30 | 1-25 |
| Why Is There Day and Night? (story) (Nruab hnub thiab hmo ntuj) (Stereo Vocal) | English | Hmong Folk Tale | 48 | 2-9 |
| Yü guang guang (Moonlight Lullaby) (Pick-A-Track) | Cantonese | Folk Song from Hong Kong; As sung by Shin-Pai Li | 19 | 1-14 |
| Yüe liang wan wan (Crescent Moon) (Pick-A-Track) | Mandarin | Folk Song from China | 16 | 1-12 |

# Step into Music

## Musical Activities, Rhymes, and Language Development

| Title | Credits | page | CD Track Number |
|---|---|---|---|
| Alexander Pope Quote | | 28 | |
| All Night, All Day | African American Spiritual | 27 | 1 |
| Angel Band, The | Folk Song from South Carolina | 17 | 2 |
| Baby Mice, The | Traditional Finger Play from the United States | 25 | |
| Bobby Shafto | Folk Song from the United States | 37 | |
| Bow-Wow-Wow! | Nursery Rhyme from England | 6 | |
| Chocolate (Bate, bate) | Children's Rhyme from Mexico | 20 | |
| Deedle, Deedle, Dumpling | Mother Goose Rhyme | 46 | |
| Dickery, Dickery, Dare | Mother Goose Rhyme | 30 | |
| Down by the Station | Traditional Rhyme from the United States | 10 | |
| Duermete, mi niña (Sleep My Child) | Rhyme from Latin America | 14 | |
| Elephant | Traditional Finger Play from the United States | 43 | |
| Engine, Engine, Number Nine | Traditional Rhyme from the United States | 18 | |
| Hey, Diddle, Diddle | Mother Goose Rhyme | 42 | |
| Hickory, Dickory, Dock | Nursery Rhyme from England | 6 | |
| Hoddley Poddley | Mother Goose Rhyme | 45 | |
| Humpty Dumpty | Mother Goose Rhyme | 27 | |
| Hush, Little Baby | Folk Song from Southern United States; Collected by Jean Ritchie | 14 | 9 |
| I'm a Little Teapot | Traditional Rhyme from the United States | 3 | |
| Jack and Jill | Mother Goose Rhyme | 37 | |
| Jack, Be Nimble | Mother Goose Rhyme | 53 | |
| Jerry Hall | Oh Where, Oh Where, has my little dog gone? | 30 | |
| Little Marionettes, The | Children's Song from France; English Words by Susan Greene | 39 | 17 |
| Little Mousie | Traditional Finger Play from the United States | 48 | |
| London Bridge | Singing Game from England | 22 | 18 |
| Mary Wore Her Red Dress | Folk Song from the United States | 32 | 20 |
| Miss Mary Mack | African American Clapping Game | 52 | |
| Mix a Pancake | Poem by Christina Rossetti | 41 | |
| Muffin Man | Game Song from England | 7 | 21 |
| My Shadow (excerpt) | Poem by Robert Louis Stevenson | 55 | |
| My Shadow Play (excerpt) | Poem by Robert Louis Stevenson | 55 | |
| Noble Duke of York | Play-Party Game | 93 | 24 |
| One Misty, Moisty Morning | Mother Goose Rhyme | 26 | |
| One, Two, Buckle My Shoe | Traditional Street Rhyme from the United States | 9 | |
| Pat-a-Cake | Traditional Finger Play from England and the United States | 19 | |
| Paw-Paw Patch | Play-Party Song from the United States | 2 | 28 |
| Pretty Trappings | Folk Song from France | 4, 31, 51 | 29 |
| Rig-a-Jig-Jig | Folk Song from England | 13 | 31 |
| Ring-a-Round the Rosy | Mother Goose Rhyme | 40 | |
| Robert Louis Stevenson | Quote | 15 | |
| Sally, Go Round the Sun | Nursery Rhyme from England | 16 | |
| Shakespeare | Quote | 1 | |
| Star Light | Mother Goose Rhyme | 44 | |
| Swing with Me | Poem by Robert Louis Stevenson | 61 | |
| Ten Galloping Horses | Traditional Children's Rhyme from the United States | 29 | |
| Three Little Kittens, The | Mother Goose Rhyme | 58 | |
| To Market, To Market | Mother Goose Rhyme | 21 | |
| Two Little Blackbirds | Mother Goose Rhyme | 48 | |
| Up to the Heavens | Nursery Rhyme from England | 9 | |
| Walter de la Mare | Quote | 47 | |
| Wee Willie Winkie | Mother Goose Rhyme | 53 | |
| What Shall We Do? | Traditional Game Song from the United States | 62 | |
| Where Is Thumbkin? | Traditional Finger Play from the United States | 8 | |
| Whoops, Johnny | Traditional Finger Play from the United States | 5 | |
| You Be Saucer | Written by Eve Merriam | 16 | |

## Pre K - Heritage Song Book

| Title | Credits | page | CD Track Number |
|---|---|---|---|
| Angel Band, The | Folk Song from South Carolina | 16 | 2 |
| Bye'm Bye | Folk Song from Texas | 38 | 4 |
| Clap Your Hands | Folk Song from the United States | 18 | 5 |
| Hello There! | Traditional Children's Song | 4 | 6 |
| Hi-Dee-Roon | Traditional Calypso Song from Jamaica, Adapted | 34 | 7 |
| Hush, Little Baby | Folk Song from the Southern United States; Collected by Jean Ritchie | 24 | 9 |
| If You're Happy | Traditional Children's Song of the United States | 40 | 11 |
| Jimmie Crack Corn | Folk Song from the Southern United States | 32 | 12 |
| Jingle Bells | Words and Music by James Pierpont | 36 | 13 |
| Johnny Mister Brown | African American Children's Song | 8 | 15 |
| Li'l Liza Jane | Dance Song from the United States | 22 | 16 |
| Looby Loo | Traditional Song of the United States and England | 26 | 19 |
| Mary Wore Her Red Dress | Folk Song from the United States | 6 | 20 |
| Mulberry Bush, The | Nursery Rhyme from England | 28 | 22 |
| Paw-Paw Patch | Play-Party Song from the United States | 12 | 28 |
| Put Your Finger in the Air | Words and Music by Woody Guthrie | 10 | 30 |
| Skip to My Lou | Folk Song from the United States | 20 | 32 |
| Teddy Bear | Jump Rope Rhyme | 30 | 33 |
| This Old Man | Folk Song from England | 14 | 34 |

## A Sourcebook of Arts Experiences

| Title | Credits | page | track |
|---|---|---|---|
| All Night, All Day | African American Spiritual | 77 | 1 |
| Angel Band, The | Folk Song from South Carolina | 78 | 2 |
| Battle Hymn of the Republic (refrain) | Words by Julia Ward Howe; Music by William Steffe | 78 | 3 |
| Bye'm Bye | Folk Song from Texas | 79 | 4 |
| Clap Your Hands | Folk Song from the United States | 79 | 5 |
| Hello There! | Traditional Children's Song | 80 | 6 |
| Hi-Dee-Roon | Traditional Calypso Song from Jamaica, Adapted | 81 | 7 |
| Hokey Pokey | Play-Party Song from Florida | 82 | 8 |
| Hush, Little Baby | Folk Song from Southern United States; Collected by Jean Ritchie | 83 | 9 |
| I Bought Me a Cat | Folk Song from Kentucky | 84 | 10 |
| If You're Happy | Traditional Children's Song of the United States | 85 | 11 |
| Jimmie Crack Corn | Folk Song from the Southern United States | 85 | 12 |
| Jingle Bells | Words and Music by James Pierpont | 86 | 13 |
| John the Rabbit | African American Folk Game Song; Collected by John W. Work | 87 | 14 |
| Johnny Mister Brown | African American Children's Song | 88 | 15 |
| Li'l Liza Jane | Dance Song from the United States | 88 | 16 |
| Little Marionettes, The | Children's Song from France; English Words by Susan Greene | 89 | 17 |
| London Bridge | Singing Game from England | 89 | 18 |
| Looby Loo | Traditional Song of the United States and England | 90 | 19 |
| Mary Wore Her Red Dress | Folk Song from the United States | 91 | 20 |
| Muffin Man | Game Song from England | 91 | 21 |
| Mulberry Bush, The | Nursery Rhyme from England | 92 | 22 |
| My Head and My Shoulders | Zulu Children's Game Song | 93 | 23 |
| Noble Duke of York | Play-Party Game | 93 | 24 |
| Old MacDonald | Traditional Children's Song | 94 | 25 |
| Oliver Twist | Traditional Game Song from England and the United States | 94 | 26 |
| One Finger, One Thumb | Traditional Children's Song | 95 | 27 |
| Paw-Paw Patch | Play-Party Song from the United States | 96 | 28 |
| Pretty Trappings | Folk Song from France | 96 | 29 |
| Put Your Finger in the Air | Words and Music by Woody Guthrie | 97 | 30 |
| Rig-a-Jig-Jig | Folk Song from England | 98 | 31 |
| Skip to My Lou | Folk Song from the United States | 99 | 32 |
| Teddy Bear | Jump Rope Rhyme | 99 | 33 |
| This Old Man | Folk Song from England | 101 | 34 |
| Train Is A-Comin' | African American Spiritual | 101 | 35 |

# Technology Resources

| MIDI Song Files Title | Gr. | Pg. | Song file |
|---|---|---|---|
| 12-Bar Blues Rock | 8 | F-31 | 5 |
| Abraham, Martin, and John | 6 | 466 | 35 |
| Adelita | 5 | 50 | 3 |
| Ah, eu entrei na roda (I Came to Try This Game) | 3 | 308 | 30 |
| Ain't Gonna Let Nobody Turn Me 'Round | 6 | 85 | 8 |
| Ain't Gonna Let Nobody Turn Me 'Round | 8 | 16 | 4 |
| Al citrón | 3 | 320 | 31 |
| Al tambor (The Drum Song) | 3 | 270 | 25 |
| Ala Da'lona | 4 | 136 | 10 |
| Alabama Gal | 3 | 106 | 11 |
| All Through the Night | 5 | 105 | 7 |
| Alle Meine Entchen (All My Little Ducklings) | 1 | 98 | 6 |
| Ambos a dos (Go Two by Two) | 3 | 20 | 3 |
| America | 7 | I-2 | 16 |
| America | 8 | I-2 | 17 |
| America, I Hear You Singing | 2 | 402 | 26 |
| America, the Beautiful | 4 | 158 | 13 |
| America, the Beautiful | 6 | 485 | 37 |
| America, the Beautiful | 7 | 4 | 17 |
| America, the Beautiful | 8 | 4 | 18 |
| Angels on the Midnight Clear | 6 | 423 | 31 |
| Apples and Bananas | 1 | 391 | 16 |
| Ash Grove, The | 5 | 114 | 8 |
| Así es mi tierra (This Is My Land) | 6 | 172 | 14 |
| At the Same Time | 6 | 115 | 10 |
| Au clair de la lune (In the Moonlight) | 3 | 18 | 2 |
| Away to America | 5 | 57 | 4 |
| ¡Ay, Jalisco no te rajes! (Oh, Jalisco!) | 7 | I-6 | 18 |
| Ayelivi | 2 | 70 | 6 |
| Banuwa | 6 | 294 | 21 |
| Book of Love | 8 | G-27 | 13 |
| Bury Me Not on the Lone Prairie | 6 | 19 | 1 |
| California Dreamin' | 8 | 31 | 14 |
| Cantaré, cantarás (I Will Sing, You Will Sing) | 6 | 413 | 29 |
| Chairs to Mend | 4 | 149 | 12 |
| Chanukah Games | 3 | 389 | 35 |
| Chapel of Love | 7 | G-27 | 12 |
| Che che koolay | 2 | 266 | 18 |
| Cheki, morena (Shake It!) | 2 | 180 | 12 |
| Cheki, morena (Shake It!) | 7 | 16 | 19 |
| Cielito lindo | 4 | 270 | 19 |
| Cielito lindo | 7 | 20 | 20 |
| Cindy | 4 | 384 | 28 |
| Circle 'Round the Moon | 4 | 403 | 33 |
| Come and Go With Me to That Land | 5 | 390 | 25 |
| Con el vito | 7 | G-15 | 8 |
| Corta la caña (Head for the Canefields) | 6 | 364 | 22 |
| Cumberland Gap | 4 | 138 | 11 |
| De colores | 5 | 90 | 6 |
| De colores | 8 | 14 | 19 |
| Deck the Hall | 5 | 474 | 37 |
| Different Beat, A | 1 | 6 | 1 |
| Ding Dong! Merrily on High | 6 | 427 | 32 |
| Dinosaur Dance | 2 | 168 | 9 |
| Do, Lord | 3 | 164 | 17 |
| Don Alfonso | 5 | 177 | 24 |
| Down by the Riverside | 5 | 256 | 18 |
| Down by the Riverside | 8 | G-8 | 7 |

| MIDI Song Files Title | Gr. | Pg. | Song file |
|---|---|---|---|
| Down, Down, Baby | 2 | 32 | 3 |
| Draw Me a Bucket of Water | 3 | 452 | 12 |
| Dry Bones | 4 | 162 | 14 |
| Ego Sum Pauper (Nothing Do I Own) | 5 | 158 | 11 |
| Eh, cumpari! (Hey, Buddy!) | 4 | 68 | 7 |
| Einini | 4 | 391 | 30 |
| El barquito (The Tiny Boat) | 3 | 358 | 33 |
| El florón (The Flower) | 2 | 246 | 17 |
| El gallo pinto (The Painted Rooster) | 3 | 86 | 9 |
| El sapito (The Little Toad) | 3 | 336 | 32 |
| Elegua (Spanish) | 7 | D-8 | 1 |
| En nuestra Tierra tan linda (On Our Beautiful Planet Earth) | 2 | 335 | 23 |
| Ev'ry Kind of Music | 2 | 226 | 14 |
| Ev'ry Time I Feel the Spirit | 5 | 242 | 17 |
| Fais do do (Go to Sleep) | 6 | 403 | 27 |
| Faith of the Heart | 8 | G-3 | 6 |
| Feliz Navidad | 7 | I-28 | 21 |
| For Children Safe and Strong | 5 | 484 | 41 |
| Freedom Is Coming | 5 | 415 | 29 |
| Gift to Share, A | 6 | 393 | 25 |
| Give My Regards to Broadway | 6 | 39 | 5 |
| Glory, Glory, Hallelujah | 6 | 52 | 6 |
| Go Around the Corn, Sally | 2 | 12 | 2 |
| God Bless the U.S.A. | 8 | G-37 | 15 |
| Goin' Down the Road Feelin' Bad | 7 | F-13 | 4 |
| Goin' to Boston | 6 | 433 | 33 |
| Gonna Build a Mountain | 6 | 21 | 2 |
| Gonna Ride Up in the Chariot | 4 | 20 | 1 |
| Good King Wenceslas | 6 | 460 | 34 |
| Good Morning | 3 | 192 | 20 |
| Gospel Train, The | 6 | 398 | 26 |
| Great Big Stars | 1 | 60 | 5 |
| Habari Gani | 3 | 404 | 36 |
| Harambee | 4 | 434 | 35 |
| Harrison Town | 6 | 97 | 9 |
| Haru ga kita (Springtime Has Come) | 2 | 401 | 25 |
| Hava nagila | 6 | 153 | 12 |
| He's Got the Whole World in His Hands | 3 | 230 | 21 |
| He's Got the Whole World in His Hands | 7 | 36 | 22 |
| Heigh-Ho | 2 | 7 | 1 |
| Hej pada pada (Dewdrops) | 3 | 78 | 8 |
| Hey, Ho! Nobody Home | 6 | 28 | 4 |
| Hine mah tov | 5 | 431 | 32 |
| Hitotsu toya (Temple Bells) | 5 | 478 | 38 |
| Hound Dog | 5 | 212 | 14 |
| Hush, Hush | 3 | 162 | 16 |
| I Don't Care If the Rain Comes Down | 3 | 24 | 4 |
| I Dream a World | 8 | G-40 | 16 |
| I Got Shoes | 2 | 242 | 15 |
| I Vow to You, My Country | 5 | 418 | 30 |
| I'm a Believer | 7 | 33 | 14 |
| I'm Flying Home | 2 | 286 | 20 |
| I'm Gonna Sing | 4 | 33 | 2 |
| Ichi-gatsu tsuitachi (A New Year's Greeting) | 3 | 406 | 37 |
| Ichi-gatsu tsuitachi (A New Year's Greeting) | 7 | 40 | 23 |
| Ja-Da | 7 | G-20 | 10 |
| Jan ken pon | 3 | 302 | 29 |

| Title | Gr. | Pg. | Song file |
|---|---|---|---|
| Joe Turner Blues | 4 | 56 | 5 |
| Just a Snap-Happy Blues | 6 | 388 | 24 |
| Keep Your Eyes on the Prize | 3 | 408 | 38 |
| Keep Your Eyes on the Prize | 8 | 16 | 3 |
| Khorovod (Round Dance) | 1 | 374 | 15 |
| Knock No More | 3 | 386 | 34 |
| Kookaburra | 4 | 186 | 15 |
| Kou ri lengay (The Strength of the Lion) | 2 | 217 | 13 |
| Kou ri lengay (The Strength of the Lion) | 7 | 2 | 13 |
| Kum bachur atzel (Hear the Rooster Crowing) | 3 | 138 | 13 |
| Kyrie | 6 | 206 | 17 |
| La Jesusita | 5 | 322 | 22 |
| La mariposa (The Butterfly) | 6 | 58 | 7 |
| La raspa | 4 | 302 | 21 |
| La tormenta tropical (The Tropical Storm) | 2 | 116 | 8 |
| La víbora (The Serpent) | 1 | 322 | 14 |
| Laredo | 5 | 10 | 1 |
| Las estrellitas del cielo (Stars of the Heavens) | 5 | 175 | 13 |
| Las mañanitas (The Morning) | 6 | 481 | 36 |
| Let Us Sing Together | 6 | 156 | 13 |
| Li'l Liza Jane | 3 | 140 | 14 |
| Lift Ev'ry Voice and Sing | 5 | 482 | 40 |
| Lift Ev'ry Voice and Sing | 8 | 54 | 20 |
| Light Up the World With a Song | 8 | 25 | 12 |
| Linstead Market | 5 | 241 | 16 |
| Little David, Play on Your Harp | 4 | 394 | 31 |
| Little Green Frog, The | 1 | 24 | 2 |
| Los reyes de Oriente (The Kings from the East) | 5 | 480 | 39 |
| Los reyes de Oriente (The Kings from the East) | 8 | 58 | 21 |
| Lots of Worms | 2 | 310 | 22 |
| Lullaby and Dance | 4 | 387 | 29 |
| Mary Ann | 6 | 180 | 15 |
| Merry Modal Christmas, A | 4 | 411 | 34 |
| Minka | 4 | 222 | 16 |
| Miss Mary Mack | 2 | 42 | 5 |
| Morning Has Broken | 5 | 29 | 2 |
| Mud | 3 | 32 | 6 |
| My Dear Companion | 6 | 23 | 3 |
| My Mama's Calling Me | 1 | 261 | 9 |
| Niño querido (Dearest Child) | 1 | 308 | 13 |
| Niu lang zhi nu (The Cowherd and the Weaving Maid) | 4 | 335 | 24 |
| Now Let Me Fly | 3 | 178 | 19 |
| Now's the Time | 5 | 445 | 35 |
| O, Desayo | 5 | 411 | 28 |
| Ochimbo | 4 | 134 | 9 |
| Oh, Freedom | 7 | G-30 | 13 |
| Oh, Won't You Sit Down | 3 | 28 | 5 |
| Old Dan Tucker | 3 | 96 | 10 |
| One Family | 7 | G-17 | 9 |
| Orange Blossom Special | 5 | 266 | 19 |
| Orange Blossom Special | 8 | 6 | 2 |
| Over My Head | 4 | 118 | 8 |
| Over My Head | 7 | 9 | 6 |
| Panamam tombé | 7 | D-18 | 2 |
| Pat Works on the Railway | 5 | 182 | 12 |
| Pavo, pavo (The Turkey Game) | 1 | 416 | 17 |
| Peace Like a River | 3 | 246 | 23 |
| Peace Like a River | 6 | 190 | 16 |
| Pictures at an Exhibition "The Great Gate of Kiev" (excerpt) | 8 | A-14 | 1 |
| Piñon, pirulín | 2 | 174 | 10 |
| Pollerita | 5 | 151 | 10 |
| Proud | 7 | G-3 | 5 |
| Ptashky u babusi sadochku (Birds in Granny's Garden) | 1 | 192 | 8 |

| Title | Gr. | Pg. | Song file |
|---|---|---|---|
| Rabbit Footprints | 2 | 304 | 21 |
| Railroad Corral | 3 | 174 | 18 |
| Riddle Ree | 2 | 34 | 4 |
| Riquirrán | 1 | 48 | 4 |
| Riquirrán | 4 | 66 | 6 |
| Rise Up, Shepherd, and Follow | 5 | 471 | 36 |
| Ríu ríu chíu | 5 | 435 | 33 |
| Sail Away | 5 | 404 | 27 |
| Sailboat in the Sky | 4 | 374 | 25 |
| Sakura | 4 | 308 | 22 |
| Sambalele | 4 | 397 | 32 |
| Sarika keo (Bird Song) | 3 | 275 | 26 |
| Scrub-a-dub | 1 | 306 | 12 |
| Se va el caimán (The Alligator) | 5 | 306 | 21 |
| Seagull, Seagull, Sit on the Shore | 4 | 383 | 60 |
| Serra, serra, serrador (Saw, Saw, Lumberjack) | 1 | 112 | 7 |
| Shake the Papaya Down | 4 | 378 | 26 |
| Shake them 'Simmons Down | 2 | 244 | 16 |
| Shalom aleichem | 6 | 409 | 28 |
| She'll Be Comin' 'Round the Mountain | 2 | 358 | 24 |
| Ship That Never Returned, The | 5 | 402 | 23 |
| Shu ha mo (Frogs) | 3 | 276 | 27 |
| Sing! Speak! Whisper! Shout! | 1 | 36 | 3 |
| Siyahamba | 6 | 212 | 18 |
| Skye Boat Song | 6 | 372 | 23 |
| Something Told the Wild Geese | 7 | G-39 | 15 |
| Sonando | 4 | 34 | 3 |
| Song of the Fishes | 3 | 244 | 22 |
| St. Patrick Was a Gentleman | 3 | 290 | 28 |
| Streets of Laredo | 4 | 272 | 20 |
| Strike Up the Band | 6 | 135 | 11 |
| Sun Gonna Shine | 6 | 242 | 19 |
| Supercalifragilisticexpialidocious | 3 | 7 | 1 |
| Surfin' U.S.A. | 6 | 260 | 20 |
| Surfin' U.S.A. | 7 | 58 | 24 |
| Sweet Betsy from Pike | 4 | 244 | 17 |
| Take a Chance on Me | 8 | 15 | 10 |
| This Land Is Your Land | 5 | 118 | 9 |
| This Land Is Your Land | 7 | 66 | 25 |
| Tie Me Kangaroo Down, Sport | 4 | 37 | 4 |
| Train Is A-Comin' | 3 | 48 | 7 |
| Tuxedo Junction | 8 | G-21 | 11 |
| Tzena, tzena | 5 | 298 | 20 |
| 'Ūlili E | 5 | 441 | 34 |
| Uno, dos, y tres | 5 | 427 | 31 |
| Vem kan segla? (Who Can Sail?) | 6 | 417 | 30 |
| Viva Jujuy | 5 | 228 | 15 |
| Voices of Pride, The | 5 | 86 | 5 |
| Wade in the Water | 4 | 268 | 18 |
| Wade in the Water | 8 | 64 | 22 |
| Wai bamba | 8 | G-13 | 9 |
| Waiting for the Traffic Light | 2 | 107 | 7 |
| Walk Together, Children | 3 | 146 | 15 |
| When the Saints Go Marching In | 2 | 178 | 11 |
| When the Train Comes Along | 1 | 300 | 11 |
| Winter | 8 | G-11 | 8 |
| Xiao (Bamboo Flute) | 4 | 314 | 23 |
| Yellow Rose of Texas, The | 7 | I-70 | 26 |
| You Were on My Mind | 7 | G-23 | 11 |
| You're a Grand Old Flag | 3 | 264 | 24 |
| You're a Grand Old Flag | 1 | 277 | 10 |
| Zudio | 2 | 269 | 19 |
| Zum gali gali | 5 | 401 | 26 |

| Music Reading Practice | Element | TE Page | MIDI Song file | CD Track |
|---|---|---|---|---|
| **Grade 1** | | | | |
| Reading Sequence 1 | Rhythm | 448 | 18 | 1-14 |
| Reading Sequence 2 | Rhythm | 448 | 19 | 1-24 |
| Reading Sequence 3 | Melody | 499 | 20 | 1-47 |
| Reading Sequence 4 | Melody | 450 | 21 | 1-53 |
| Reading Sequence 5 | Rhythm | 451 | 22 | 2-25 |
| Reading Sequence 6 | Rhythm | 452 | 23 | 2-29 |
| Reading Sequence 7 | Melody | 452 | 24 | 2-45 |
| Reading Sequence 8 | Melody | 453 | 25 | 2-51 |
| Reading Sequence 9 | Rhythm | 454 | 26 | 3-9 |
| Reading Sequence 10 | Rhythm | 454 | 27 | 3-28 |
| Reading Sequence 11 | Melody | 455 | 28 | 3-38 |
| Reading Sequence 12 | Melody | 456 | 29 | 3-46 |
| Reading Sequence 13 | Rhythm | 457 | 30 | 4-23 |
| Reading Sequence 14 | Rhythm | 458 | 31 | 4-32 |
| Reading Sequence 15 | Melody | 459 | 32 | 4-55 |
| Reading Sequence 16 | Melody | 459 | 33 | 4-60 |
| Reading Sequence 17 | Rhythm | 460 | 34 | 5-39 |
| Reading Sequence 18 | Melody | 461 | 35 | 6-10 |
| Reading Sequence 19 | Melody | 462 | 36 | 6-19 |
| Reading Sequence 20 | Rhythm | 463 | 37 | 7-3 |
| Reading Sequence 21 | Melody | 464 | 38 | 7-20 |
| Reading Sequence 22 | Melody | 465 | 39 | 7-25 |
| **Grade 2** | | | | |
| Reading Sequence 1 | Rhythm | 406 | 27 | 1-10 |
| Reading Sequence 2 | Rhythm | 406 | 28 | 1-17 |
| Reading Sequence 3 | Melody | 407 | 29 | 1-33 |
| Reading Sequence 4 | Melody | 407 | 30 | 1-38 |
| Reading Sequence 5 | Rhythm | 408 | 31 | 2-10 |
| Reading Sequence 6 | Rhythm | 408 | 32 | 2-15 |
| Reading Sequence 7 | Melody | 409 | 33 | 2-34 |
| Reading Sequence 8 | Melody | 409 | 34 | 2-39 |
| Reading Sequence 9 | Rhythm | 410 | 35 | 3-28 |
| Reading Sequence 10 | Rhythm | 410 | 36 | 3-35 |
| Reading Sequence 11 | Melody | 411 | 37 | 4-9 |
| Reading Sequence 12 | Melody | 411 | 38 | 4-14 |
| Reading Sequence 13 | Rhythm | 412 | 39 | 4-41 |
| Reading Sequence 14 | Rhythm | 412 | 40 | 5-5 |
| Reading Sequence 15 | Melody | 413 | 41 | 5-12 |
| Reading Sequence 16 | Melody | 413 | 42 | 5-26 |
| Reading Sequence 17 | Rhythm | 414 | 43 | 6-9 |
| Reading Sequence 18 | Rhythm | 414 | 44 | 6-16 |
| Reading Sequence 19 | Melody | 415 | 45 | 6-28 |
| Reading Sequence 20 | Melody | 415 | 46 | 6-37 |
| Reading Sequence 21 | Rhythm | 416 | 47 | 6-22 |

| Music Reading Practice | Element | TE Page | MIDI Song file | CD Track |
|---|---|---|---|---|
| Reading Sequence 22 | Rhythm | 416 | 48 | 6-35 |
| Reading Sequence 23 | Melody | 417 | 49 | 6-44 |
| Reading Sequence 24 | Melody | 417 | 50 | 6-51 |

## Grade 3

| Music Reading Practice | Element | TE Page | MIDI Song file | CD Track |
|---|---|---|---|---|
| Reading Sequence 1 | Rhythm | 416 | 39 | 1-12 |
| Reading Sequence 2 | Rhythm | 416 | 40 | 1-17 |
| Reading Sequence 3 | Melody | 417 | 41 | 1-45 |
| Reading Sequence 4 | Melody | 417 | 42 | 1-50 |
| Reading Sequence 5 | Rhythm | 418 | 43 | 2-23 |
| Reading Sequence 6 | Rhythm | 418 | 44 | 2-28 |
| Reading Sequence 7 | Melody | 419 | 45 | 2-45 |
| Reading Sequence 8 | Melody | 419 | 46 | 2-50 |
| Reading Sequence 9 | Rhythm | 420 | 47 | 3-27 |
| Reading Sequence 10 | Rhythm | 420 | 48 | 3-33 |
| Reading Sequence 11 | Melody | 421 | 49 | 4-5 |
| Reading Sequence 12 | Melody | 421 | 50 | 4-11 |
| Reading Sequence 13 | Rhythm | 422 | 51 | 4-37 |
| Reading Sequence 14 | Rhythm | 422 | 52 | 4-42 |
| Reading Sequence 15 | Melody | 423 | 53 | 5-8 |
| Reading Sequence 16 | Melody | 423 | 54 | 5-13 |
| Reading Sequence 17 | Rhythm | 424 | 55 | 6-5 |
| Reading Sequence 18 | Rhythm | 424 | 56 | 6-10 |
| Reading Sequence 19 | Melody | 425 | 57 | 6-24 |
| Reading Sequence 20 | Melody | 425 | 58 | 6-31 |
| Reading Sequence 21 | Rhythm | 426 | 59 | 7-14 |
| Reading Sequence 22 | Rhythm | 426 | 60 | 7-21 |
| Reading Sequence 23 | Melody | 427 | 61 | 7-35 |
| Reading Sequence 24 | Melody | 427 | 62 | 7-40 |

## Grade 4

| Music Reading Practice | Element | TE Page | MIDI Song file | CD Track |
|---|---|---|---|---|
| Reading Sequence 1 | Rhythm | 442 | 36 | 1-9 |
| Reading Sequence 2 | Rhythm | 442 | 37 | 1-21 |
| Reading Sequence 3 | Melody | 443 | 38 | 1-30 |
| Reading Sequence 4 | Melody | 443 | 39 | 1-40 |
| Reading Sequence 5 | Rhythm | 444 | 40 | 3-4 |
| Reading Sequence 6 | Rhythm | 444 | 41 | 3-11 |
| Reading Sequence 7 | Melody | 445 | 42 | 3-25 |
| Reading Sequence 8 | Melody | 445 | 43 | 3-30 |
| Reading Sequence 9 | Rhythm | 446 | 44 | 4-38 |
| Reading Sequence 10 | Rhythm | 446 | 45 | 5-19 |
| Reading Sequence 11 | Melody | 447 | 46 | 5-17 |
| Reading Sequence 12 | Melody | 447 | 47 | 5-24 |
| Reading Sequence 13 | Rhythm | 448 | 48 | 6-13 |
| Reading Sequence 14 | Rhythm | 448 | 49 | 6-24 |
| Reading Sequence 15 | Melody | 449 | 50 | 6-35 |
| Reading Sequence 16 | Melody | 449 | 51 | 7-3 |

| Music Reading Practice | Element | TE Page | MIDI Song file | CD Track |
|---|---|---|---|---|
| Reading Sequence 17 | Rhythm | 450 | 52 | 8-5 |
| Reading Sequence 18 | Rhythm | 450 | 53 | 8-10 |
| Reading Sequence 19 | Melody | 451 | 54 | 8-21 |
| Reading Sequence 20 | Melody | 451 | 55 | 8-27 |
| Reading Sequence 21 | Rhythm | 452 | 56 | 9-12 |
| Reading Sequence 22 | Rhythm | 452 | 57 | 9-17 |
| Reading Sequence 23 | Melody | 453 | 58 | 9-31 |
| Reading Sequence 24 | Melody | 453 | 59 | 9-43 |

## Grade 5

| Music Reading Practice | Element | TE Page | MIDI Song file | CD Track |
|---|---|---|---|---|
| Reading Sequence 1 | Rhythm | 490 | 42 | 1-14 |
| Reading Sequence 2 | Rhythm | 490 | 43 | 1-19 |
| Reading Sequence 3 | Melody | 491 | 44 | 2-3 |
| Reading Sequence 4 | Melody | 491 | 45 | 2-12 |
| Reading Sequence 5 | Rhythm | 492 | 46 | 3-11 |
| Reading Sequence 6 | Rhythm | 492 | 47 | 3-18 |
| Reading Sequence 7 | Melody | 493 | 48 | 3-33 |
| Reading Sequence 8 | Melody | 493 | 49 | 4-1 |
| Reading Sequence 9 | Rhythm | 494 | 50 | 5-15 |
| Reading Sequence 10 | Rhythm | 494 | 51 | 5-21 |
| Reading Sequence 11 | Melody | 495 | 52 | 5-29 |
| Reading Sequence 12 | Melody | 495 | 53 | 5-38 |
| Reading Sequence 13 | Rhythm | 496 | 54 | 7-3 |
| Reading Sequence 14 | Rhythm | 496 | 55 | 7-8 |
| Reading Sequence 15 | Melody | 497 | 56 | 7-22 |
| Reading Sequence 16 | Melody | 497 | 57 | 7-27 |
| Reading Sequence 17 | Rhythm | 498 | 58 | 8-33 |
| Reading Sequence 18 | Rhythm | 498 | 59 | 9-10 |
| Reading Sequence 19 | Melody | 499 | 60 | 9-23 |
| Reading Sequence 20 | Melody | 499 | 61 | 9-28 |
| Reading Sequence 21 | Rhythm | 500 | 62 | 10-31 |
| Reading Sequence 22 | Rhythm | 500 | 63 | 11-1 |
| Reading Sequence 23 | Melody | 501 | 64 | 11-18 |
| Reading Sequence 24 | Melody | 501 | 65 | 11-23 |

## Grade 6

| Music Reading Practice | Element | TE Page | MIDI Song file | CD Track |
|---|---|---|---|---|
| Reading Sequence 1 | Rhythm | 488 | 38 | 1-8 |
| Reading Sequence 2 | Rhythm | 488 | 39 | 1-17 |
| Reading Sequence 3 | Melody | 489 | 40 | 2-3 |
| Reading Sequence 4 | Melody | 489 | 41 | 2-8 |
| Reading Sequence 5 | Rhythm | 490 | 42 | 3-3 |
| Reading Sequence 6 | Rhythm | 490 | 43 | 3-9 |
| Reading Sequence 7 | Melody | 491 | 44 | 4-5 |
| Reading Sequence 8 | Melody | 491 | 45 | 4-12 |
| Reading Sequence 9 | Rhythm | 492 | 46 | 5-10 |
| Reading Sequence 10 | Rhythm | 492 | 47 | 5-19 |
| Reading Sequence 11 | Melody | 493 | 48 | 6-6 |

| Music Reading Practice | Element | TE Page | MIDI Song file | CD Track |
|---|---|---|---|---|
| Reading Sequence 12 | Melody | 493 | 49 | 6-11 |
| Reading Sequence 13 | Rhythm | 494 | 50 | 7-5 |
| Reading Sequence 14 | Rhythm | 494 | 51 | 7-10 |
| Reading Sequence 15 | Melody | 495 | 52 | 7-27 |
| Reading Sequence 16 | Melody | 495 | 53 | 7-32 |
| Reading Sequence 17 | Rhythm | 496 | 54 | 8-30 |
| Reading Sequence 18 | Rhythm | 496 | 55 | 9-3 |
| Reading Sequence 19 | Melody | 497 | 56 | 9-18 |
| Reading Sequence 20 | Melody | 497 | 57 | 9-23 |
| Reading Sequence 21 | Rhythm | 498 | 58 | 10-32 |
| Reading Sequence 22 | Rhythm | 498 | 59 | 10-37 |
| Reading Sequence 23 | Melody | 499 | 60 | 11-6 |
| Reading Sequence 24 | Melody | 499 | 61 | 11-13 |

| Video Title | Video Episode | Episode Title | Episode Focus |
|---|---|---|---|
| **Grade 1** | | | |
| Arpeggio meets the brass family | Episode 1 | Introduction to brass instruments | The brass family |
| | Episode 2 | Ancestors of brass instruments | conch shells, bull's horn and didgeridoo |
| | Episode 3 | Brass Rap, The | classroom instruments |
| | Episode 4 | Flight of the Bumblebee | Practicing and developing a musical skill |
| How We Make Music | Episode 1 | The Story | Making sounds |
| | Episode 2 | Tapa pounding—Tonga | Sounds of work |
| | Episode 3 | Sasa—Samoa | Dancers: Body percussion |
| | Episode 4 | Hambone | Rhythmic accompaniment using body percussion |
| | Episode 5 | "Blackbird"—Bobby McFerrin | Using the body and voice |
| | Episode 6 | Flute, drum, and guitar | |
| | Episode 7 | Panpipe, pipa, and violin | |
| | Episode 8 | "This Is the Day" | Adding clapping and instruments to singing |
| Singing Games | Episode 1 | "Here Comes Valerie"—United States | Folk song from the United States (singing game) |
| | Episode 2 | "La víbora"—Mexico | Folk song from Mexico (singing game) |
| | Episode 3 | Juggling game—Japan | Singing game from Japan (singing game) |
| | Episode 4 | "Che Che Koolay"—Ghana | Folk song from Ghana (singing game) |
| Storytelling | Episode 1 | "Trouble" | Stories and poems |
| | Episode 2 | "I Had an Old Coat" | Telling a story through dramatic movement. |
| | Episode 3 | "Sing a Whale Song" | Singing a story song. |
| | Episode 4 | The Nutcracker | A ballet tells a story through music and dance. |
| **Grade 2** | | | |
| Melody | Episode 1 | The story | Lullabies |
| | Episode 2 | "Chumbara" | Steps, leaps, repeats |
| | Episode 3 | Tracing a contour | Musical contour |
| | Episode 4 | More bells and whistles | Computer animation |
| | Episode 5 | "Hawaiian Rainbows" | Phrases |
| | Episode 6 | Bell peals | bells |
| Music for Special Occasions | Episode 1 | Handel: "Minuet" from Royal Fireworks Music | Celebrations and holidays |
| | Episode 2 | Sousa: The Stars and Stripes Forever | Marches and parades |
| | Episode 3 | Nongak—Korea | Sowing and harvest |
| | Episode 4 | Carnaval—South America | Pre-Lenten festival |
| | Episode 5 | Kwanzaa celebration | African American holiday |
| | Episode 6 | "Arp's Anniversary Song" | Special Occasions |
| Rhythm | Episode 1 | Rhythms around us | rhythm |
| | Episode 2 | Michael Moschen, juggler | Steady beat, strong beat |
| | Episode 3 | Dance—Mexico | Rhythm patterns-Mexico |

| Video Title | Video Episode | Episode Title | Episode Focus |
|---|---|---|---|
| Rhythm (continued) | Episode 4 | "London Bridge" | Melodic rhythm |
| | Episode 5 | Kodo—Japan | Drummers around the world - Japan |
| | Episode 6 | Compagnons D'Akati—Côte d'Ivoire (Ivory Coast) | World of Drums |
| | Episode 7 | Steve Gadd—United States | Rock drumming - United States |
| | Episode 8 | "Zudio" | Moving to a steady beat |

## Grade 3

| Video Title | Video Episode | Episode Title | Episode Focus |
|---|---|---|---|
| Creating music | Episode 1 | Baking sequence | Ingredients of music |
| | Episode 2 | Section elements | Creating simple compositions |
| | Episode 3 | Rondo form | Form |
| | Episode 4 | Rimsky-Korsakov: The Flight of the Bumblebee | Program music |
| | Episode 5 | Instrumental ensemble—India | India |
| | Episode 6 | Gamelan—Indonesia | Improvisation - Indonesia |
| Folk Dance | Episode 1 | Background | Introduction to folk dances |
| | Episode 2 | Folk dance—Columbia | Columbia |
| | Episode 3 | Line dance—Turkey | Turkey |
| | Episode 4 | Square dance—United States | United States |
| | Episode 5 | Circle dance—Russia | Russia |
| | Episode 6 | "La raspa"—Mexico | Mexico |
| One Voice, Many Voices | Episode 1 | The story | Introduction to the video |
| | Episode 2 | "Last Old Train's A-Leavin' " | Unison, harmony |
| | Episode 3 | "A Ram Sam Sam"—Morocco | Ostinatos |
| | Episode 4 | "Sandy Land" and "Skip to My Lou" | Partner songs |
| | Episode 5 | "Row, Row, Row Your Boat" | Rounds |
| | Episode 6 | "Great Gettin' Up Morning" | Call, response; unison, harmony |
| | Episode 7 | "Ballo"—Italy | Voices imitating instruments |
| | Episode 8 | "Our Melody" | Countermelodies |

## Grade 4

| Video Title | Video Episode | Episode Title | Episode Focus |
|---|---|---|---|
| Percussion Instruments | Episode 1 | Dou Dou Rose Ensemble—Senegal | World of Drums |
| | Episode 2 | Batukada: samba—Brazil | Brazil |
| | Episode 3 | Bochinche: salsa—Latin America/United States | Latin America/United States |
| | Episode 4 | Artis: spoon player—United States | United States |
| | Episode 5 | Gamelan—Indonesia | World Drums |
| | Episode 6 | Samul Nori Performers—Korea | Korea |
| | Episode 7 | Center Grove High School Percussion Ensemble—United States | United States |
| Singing Styles | Episode 1 | Whitney Houston | Pop, gospel |
| | Episode 2 | Bobby McFerrin | Folk/country |
| | Episode 3 | Tom Paxton | Folk |
| | Episode 4 | Pam Tillis | Country |
| | Episode 5 | Diane Schuur | Jazz |
| | Episode 6 | Pink Floyd | The Artist - excerpts from Pink Floyd in Concert |
| | Episode 7 | Second Edition | Barbershop |
| | Episode 8 | The King's Singers | Small group |

| Video Title | Video Episode | Episode Title | Episode Focus |
|---|---|---|---|
| Singing Styles | Episode 9 | Hei-Kyung Hong | Opera |
| | Episode 10 | Shanghai School of Music | Vocal production |
| | Episode 11 | Daisy Eagan | Young soloist |
| | Episode 12 | Bambini di Praga | Choral singing |
| | Episode 13 | Oklahoma Collegium Musicum | Choral singing |
| | Episode 14 | Total Experience Gospel Choir | Gospel Choir |
| String Instruments: Bowed | Episode 1 | Zhang Xiaohui, erhu; Li Xiaoyuan, yangqin | erhu/yangqin |
| | Episode 2 | Kevin and Joshua Moore | fiddles |
| | Episode 3 | Orchestra de Camera; Richard Rintoul, conductor | A virtuoso |
| | Episode 4 | Leila Josefowicz | violin; age three |
| | Episode 5 | Leila Josefowicz | violin; age nine |
| | Episode 6 | Leila Josefowicz | violin; age twelve |
| | Episode 7 | Paul Neubauer | viola |
| | Episode 8 | Carter Brey | cello |
| | Episode 9 | Gary Karr | double bass |
| | Episode 10 | Guarneri quartet | String Quartet |
| | Episode 11 | Cleveland Institute of Music Youth Orchestra; Christopher Wilkins, conductor | Youth Orchestra |

# Grade 5

| Video Title | Video Episode | Episode Title | Episode Focus |
|---|---|---|---|
| From Mao to Mozart: Isaac Stern in China (Excerpts) | Episode 1 | Traditional Chinese instruments | Chinese instruments |
| | Episode 2 | Violin and orchestra | violin and orchestra |
| | Episode 3 | Violin and piano | violin and piano |
| | Episode 4 | Erhu | erhu |
| | Episode 5 | Cello and piano | cello and piano |
| | Episode 6 | Piano | piano |
| | Episode 7 | Violin and orchestra | violin and orchestra |
| String Instruments: Plucked | Episode 1 | Electric guitar | electric guitar |
| | Episode 2 | Acoustic guitar | acoustic guitar |
| | Episode 3 | Lute | lute |
| | Episode 4 | Pipa | pipa |
| | Episode 5 | Balalaika | balalaika |
| | Episode 6 | Charango and ensemble | charango |
| | Episode 7 | Ukulele enbsemble | ukulele |
| | Episode 8 | Banjo | banjo |
| | Episode 9 | Banjo and acoustic guitar | banjo and acoustic guitar |
| | Episode 10 | Acoustic guitar | acoustic guitar |
| | Episode 11 | Acoustic guitar and piano | acoustic guitar and piano |
| | Episode 12 | Guitar ensemble | guitar ensemble |
| | Episode 13 | Zheng | zheng |
| | Episode 14 | Koto | koto |
| | Episode 15 | Harp | harp |
| Wind Instruments: Wood | Episode 1 | Bolivian flutes and ensemble | bolivian flutes |
| | Episode 2 | Panpipes and ensemble | panpipes |
| | Episode 3 | Shakuhachi | shakuhachi |

| Video Title | Video Episode | Episode Title | Episode Focus |
|---|---|---|---|
| Wind Instruments: Wood (continued) | Episode 4 | Sáo flute | sáo flute |
| | Episode 5 | Bagpipe | bagpipe |
| | Episode 6 | Shawm | shawm |
| | Episode 7 | Oboe | oboe |
| | Episode 8 | Banjo | banjo |
| | Episode 9 | Bassoon and piano | bassoon and piano |
| | Episode 10 | Sopranino recorder and accordion | sopranino recorder and accordion |
| | Episode 11 | Soprano recorder, cello, and harpsichord | soprano recorder, cello, and harpsichord |
| | Episode 12 | Baroque flute, cello, and harpsichord | Baroque flute, cello, and harpsichord |
| | Episode 13 | Flute and piano | flute and piano |
| | Episode 14 | Clarinet and piano | clarinet  and piano |
| | Episode 15 | Flute and jazz ensemble | flute and jazz ensemble |

# Grade 6

| Video Title | Video Episode | Episode Title | Episode Focus |
|---|---|---|---|
| Dancing | Episode 1 | Compagnons d'Akati–Cote d' Ivoire (Ivory Coast), Africa | World of Drums |
| | Episode 2 | Marcia Merrill, flamenco—Spain | Spain: flamenco |
| | Episode 3 | Classical dancers—Cambodia | Cambodia |
| | Episode 4 | The Cape Fox Dancers—Alaska | Alaska |
| | Episode 5 | Aloha Dalire's dancers, hula—Hawaii | Hawaii: hula |
| | Episode 6 | Slask Dancers—Poland | Poland |
| | Episode 7 | Alexander Godunov—Russia/United States | Russia/United States |
| | Episode 8 | The National Tap Dance Company—Canada | Canada: Tap dancing |
| Percussion Instruments: Tuned | Episode 1 | Marimba Ensemble—Zimbabwe | Marimba - Zimbabwe |
| | Episode 2 | Warren Wolf—United States | United States |
| | Episode 3 | Roneat players—Vietnam | Vietnam |
| | Episode 4 | T'rung and anklung players—Vietnam | Vietnam |
| | Episode 5 | Gamelan—Java | Java |
| | Episode 6 | Steel drums—Trinidad and Tobago | steel drums |
| Wind Instruments: Brass | Episode 1 | The United States Marine Drum and Bugle Corps | World of Drums |
| | Episode 2 | Trumpet demonstration | trumpet |
| | Episode 3 | Wynton Marsalis Quartet | Blues and Swing |
| | Episode 4 | Bryan Lowe | French horn |
| | Episode 5 | Steve Wampler | trombone |
| | Episode 6 | Jay Huntsberger | tuba show |
| | Episode 7 | Ralph Whittle (euphonium) | euphonium |
| | Episode 8 | Euphonium Ensemble of Indiana Univeristy | euphonium |
| | Episode 9 | Canadian Brass | Canadian Brass |
| | Episode 10 | Cleveland Institute of Music Youth Orchestra | Youth Orchestra |

**Technology Resources**

| Video Title | Video Episode | Episode Title | Episode Focus |
|---|---|---|---|
| **Grade 7** | | | |
| Keyboards | Episode 1 | Pae Nwen Tsai | |
| | Episode 2 | Daniel Lee and Annie Laughlin | piano duo |
| | Episode 3 | Robin McCabe and students | piano |
| | Episode 4 | Marcus Roberts | piano |
| | Episode 5 | Virginia Moore | harpsichord |
| | Episode 6 | Clavichord | clavichord |
| | Episode 7 | Fortepiano | fortepiano |
| | Episode 8 | Acoustic piano | acoustic piano |
| | Episode 9 | Matt Kocmieroski | prepared piano |
| | Episode 10 | Michael Bloss | pipe organ |
| | Episode 11 | Chris Halon | electronic organ |
| | Episode 12 | Don Muro | synthesizers |
| Percussion Instruments: Tuned | Episode 1 | The wind harp of Bainbridge Island | wind harp |
| | Episode 2 | Electronic digital sound sampling | digital sound |
| | Episode 3 | Metaphonics—sounds from the junkyard | metaphonic sounds |
| Performing in Groups | Episode 1 | Mallet Percussion Ensemble—Canada | Canada - mallet percussion |
| | Episode 2 | Dvorak Trio—United States | United States |
| | Episode 3 | Haydn Trio—United States | Cello Show |
| | Episode 4 | Yeni Ses Folk Ensemble—Turkey | Turkey |
| | Episode 5 | Taypi Kala Folk Ensemble—Bolivia | Bolivia |
| | Episode 6 | Instrumental ensemble—China | China |
| | Episode 7 | Dou Dou Rose Ensemble—Senegal | Senegal |
| | Episode 8 | Seattle Symphony—United States | American Folk |
| | Episode 9 | Total Experience Gospel Choir—United States | United States |
| | Episode 10 | Pink Floyd—England | Delicate Sound of Thunder - excerpts from Pink Floyd in Concert |
| **Grade 8** | | | |
| Jazz and Improvisation | Episode 1 | Eagle Park Slim sings Sweet Home Chicago | vocal |
| | Episode 2 | Louis Armstrong plays On the Sunny Side of the Street | instrumental |
| | Episode 3 | Wynton Marsalis plays Butter and Egg Man. | trumpet |
| | Episode 4 | Cliff Lenz plays Golden Slippers in ragtime style. | ragtime |
| | Episode 5 | Overton Barry and Bruce Phares improvise on Mary Had a Little Lamb | improvisation on nursery rhymes |
| | Episode 6 | Emily Beaulieu and Bruce Phares improvise on Meet the Flintstones. | improvisation |
| | Episode 7 | Diane Schuur sings and plays It Don't Mean a Thing if It Ain't Got That Swing. | jazz vocal |
| | Episode 8 | Dominant Seventh sings a jazz medley. | jazz medley |
| | Episode 9 | The Canadian Brass plays J. S. Bach's Fugue in C Minor. | Improv on Bach |

| Video Title | Video Episode | Episode Title | Episode Focus |
|---|---|---|---|
| Jazz and Improvisation (continued) | Episode 10 | Rose Jazz Ensemble plays You're Nobody 'Til Somebody Loves You | jazz ensemble |
| Technology and Music | Episode 1 | What Makes Music | |
| | Episode 2 | What Makes Music Happen? | |
| Theater and Film | Episode 1 | Westside Delegation—United States | show choir |
| | Episode 2 | Nongak (Samul Nori musicians) | Korea |
| | Episode 3 | University of Michigan Marching Band—United States | United States— Marching Band |
| | Episode 4 | Vietnam Water Puppets and scene from an Italian opera | Vietnam/Italy |
| | Episode 5 | "Children's Chorus" from Bizet's Carmen | opera |
| | Episode 6 | Silent film—United States | United States—Silent film |
| | Episode 7 | Alligator scene—United States | United States—Silent film |
| | Episode 8 | "Wild About Anchorage" commerical—United States | commerical—silent film |

# Art Series Correlation

**Silver Burdett MAKING MUSIC ©2005**
**Correlated to Scott Foresman Art ©2005**

| Scott Foresman Art | Silver Burdett Making Music | | |
|---|---|---|---|
| **Themes** | **Selections** | **Page** | **CD Track** |
| **Kindergarten** | | | |
| **Unit 1 Art in My World** | | | |
| **Lesson 1**<br>Art Is Everywhere | Cats on the Move<br>Juba<br>Oma washi<br>I Got a Letter This Morning<br>Going to the Zoo<br>Everything Grows | 12<br>13<br>13<br>68<br>216<br>266 | <br>1-13<br>1-16<br>7-36<br>2-57<br>9-17 |
| **Lesson 2**<br>Line | Dribbles, Dots, Lines, and Spots<br>Painting Song: A Dribble and a Dot<br>Across the Curriculum: Art | 174<br>175<br>175 | <br><br>6-26 |
| **Lesson 3**<br>Shape | The Shape of a Bee's Flight<br>Perná, perná, I mélissá<br>Fly By, Fly By<br>The Circle Game<br>Circle Round the Zero | 264<br>264<br>264<br>292<br>293 | <br>9-13<br>9-14<br><br>10-15 |
| **Lesson 4**<br>Senses | Echoes of Loud and Soft<br>Wind Song<br>Sleepytime Soft and Loud<br>Grizzly Bear<br>Storm Sounds Louder and Softer<br>Storm Dance | 6<br>7<br>32<br>33<br>144<br>145 | <br>1-8<br><br>2-3<br><br>5-26 |
| **Lesson 5**<br>Color | Crayons (poem)<br>Birdies Fly Up and Down<br>Bluebird, Bluebird<br>Little Red Wagon | 75<br>105<br>105<br>152 | <br>4-5<br>5-38 |
| **Lesson 6**<br>Warm and Cool Colors | Cinderella Dressed in Green (rhyme)<br>Dribbles, Dots, Lines, and Spots<br>The Trees (Derain) | 136<br>174<br>174 | |
| **Unit 2 Art Nearby** | | | |
| **Lesson 1**<br>Texture | See and Touch | 172 | 6-22 |
| **Lesson 2**<br>Paintings | Cats on the Move<br>Wharf of Venice (Puelma)<br>Musical Paintings, Musical Stories | 12<br>144<br>260 | |

| Themes | Selections | Page | CD Track |
|---|---|---|---|
| **Lesson 3**<br>Colors Together | Merry-Go-Round Colors<br>Merry-Go-Round<br>Merry-Go-Round (poem) | 290<br>290<br>291 | 10-13 |
| **Lesson 4**<br>More Colors | Old Blue | 122 | 4-35 |
| **Lesson 5**<br>Pattern | Patterns for a Picnic<br>Going on a Picnic<br>A Pattern of Puppy Love<br>I Have a Dog<br>Patterns Here, There, Everywhere!<br>Tracks (poem)<br>Nanny Goat's Patterns<br>Nanny Goat<br>Pattern of Toys<br>Yang wa wa<br>Nursery Song | 190<br>190<br>262<br>262<br>298<br>299<br>160<br>161<br>162<br>162<br>162 | 7-1<br><br>9-10<br><br><br><br><br>6-1<br><br>6-3<br>6-4 |
| **Unit 3  Art Forms** | | | |
| **Lesson 2**<br>Animal Forms | Animal Walk, Animal Talk<br>Let's Pretend<br>The Up and Down Kitten<br>Lap Time (poem)<br>Birdies Fly Up and Down<br>Bluebird, Bluebird<br>Frog Fun, Long and Short<br>Polly Wee<br>Long Dogs, Short Dogs<br>Old Blue<br>Dogs (poem) | 226<br>227<br>100<br>101<br>104<br>105<br>118<br>119<br>122<br>122<br>123 | 8-4<br><br><br><br><br>4-5<br><br>4-31<br><br>4-35 |
| **Lesson 4**<br>Puppets | Audience Etiquette<br>A Tale of Puppet Platter<br>Les petites marionettes<br>The Little Marionettes | 236<br><br>237<br>237 | <br><br>8-18<br>8-19 |
| **Lesson 5**<br>Imagination | Timbres for Tellling Tales<br>Mother Sent Me to the Store (rhyme)<br>Halloween Make-Believe<br>What Will You Be on Halloween? | 136<br>136<br>308<br>309 | <br><br><br>11-1 |
| **Unit 4 A World of Art** | | | |
| **Lesson 1**<br>Photographs | Everything Grows | 266 | |
| **Lesson 5**<br>Art and Nature | Spider on the Go<br>Eensy Weensy Spider<br>Animal Walk, Animal Talk<br>Let's Pretend<br>Nature Sounds and Songs<br>Mary Ann<br>The Shape of a Bee's Flight<br>Perná, perná, i mélissá<br>Fly By, Fly By<br>As the Seasons Change<br>Let's Get Ready<br>Five Little Snowmen | 186<br>187<br>226<br>227<br>252<br>253<br>264<br>264<br>264<br>312<br>312<br>313 | <br>6-46<br><br>8-4<br><br>8-40<br><br>9-13<br>9-14<br><br>11-7<br>11-9 |

Art Correlations

Art Correlations: *Scott Foresman Art*  **359**

| Themes | Selections | Page | CD Track |
|---|---|---|---|
| **Lesson 6**<br>Movement | Dancing Tree Just Like Me | 202 | |
| | The Dancing Tree | 203 | 7-14 |
| | Animal Talk, Animal Walk | 226 | |
| | Let's Pretend | 227 | 8-4 |
| | Nature Sounds and Songs | 252 | |
| | Mary Ann | 253 | 8-40 |
| | Jelly Bean Jump | 286 | |
| | One Green Jelly Bean | 287 | 10-7 |
| | The Circle Game | 292 | |
| | Circle 'Round the Zero | 293 | 10-15 |
| **Unit 5 Artists Explore** | | | |
| **Lesson 3**<br>Letters | Groovin' with MY ABCs | 280 | |
| | Alphabet Song | 280 | 9-37 |
| | ABC Blues | 281 | 9-39 |
| | Letters and Sounds and Rhymes | 282 | |
| | Willoughby, Wallaby, Woo | 282 | 10-1 |
| | A Tongue Twister Medley (rhymes) | 283 | |
| **Unit 6 Visual Stories** | | | |
| **Lesson 1**<br>Buildings | Building Up London Bridge | 244 | |
| | London Bridge | 245 | 8-29 |
| **Lesson 2**<br>Spaces at Home | Tapping in the Tub | 220 | |
| | Singin' in the Tub | 220 | 7-40 |
| | Hush, Hush...It's Bedtime | 222 | |
| | Hush Up the Baby | 222 | 7-42 |
| | A Song for Playing House | 242 | |
| | Miss Susie Anna Sue | 242 | 8-27 |
| | Sounds from the Kitchen | 54 | |
| | Just from the Kitchen | 55 | 2-32 |
| **Lesson 5**<br>Games | Everyone Plays Hide and Seek | 208 | |
| | ¿Dónde lo escondí? | 209 | 7-21 |
| | Where did I Hide it? | 209 | 7-22 |
| | A Playful Part that Returns | 211 | |
| | Jump Rope Jingle (rhyme) | 211 | |
| **Lesson 6**<br>**People at Play** | Playground Beat, Playground Rhythms | 90 | |
| | Luna lunera | 90 | 3-36 |
| | Moon, Moonlight | 90 | 3-37 |
| | Mon sa pha | 91 | 3-40 |
| | Mon Hides the Cloth | 91 | 3-41 |
| | Rhymes to Say at Recess | 204 | |
| | Number One, Touch Your Tongue | 204 | 7-15 |
| | Oliver Jump | 205 | 7-17 |
| | Chanukah Play | 314 | |
| | My Dreydl | 314 | 11-11 |
| | I'm a Dreydl | 314 | 11-14 |
| | Patterns of Toys | 162 | |
| | Yang wa wa | 162 | 6-3 |
| | Nursery Song | 162 | 6-4 |

Art Correlations

| Themes | Selections | Page | CD Track |
|---|---|---|---|
| **GRADE 1** | | | |
| **Unit 1 Art in Your World** | | | |
| **Lesson 1**<br>Line | Starry Night | 107 | |
| | Star Light, Star Bright | 106 | |
| | Las estrellas | 106 | |
| | Skills Reinforcement: Creating | 213 | |
| | Teacher to Teacher: Introducing Sculpture | 270 | |
| | Across the Curriculum: Related Arts | 276 | |
| **Lesson 2**<br>Mood | Starry Night | 107 | |
| **Lesson 3**<br>Shape | Across the Curriculum: Science | 107 | |
| | Building Skills Through Music: Math | 136 | |
| | Galbi | 183 | 6-7 |
| | Skills Reinforcement: Listening | 183 | |
| | Building Skills Through Music: Math | 210 | |
| | Dabjo el botón | 210 | 6-44 |
| | Under the button | 210 | 6-45 |
| | Teacher to Teacher: Introducing Sculpture | 270 | |
| | This Land is Your Land | 276 | 9-1 |
| | Across the Curriculum: Related Arts | 276 | |
| **Lesson 4**<br>Artworks of Families | Cultural Connection: African American Singing Games | 8 | |
| | Run, Molly, Run | 8 | 1-11 |
| | School to Home Connection | 29 | |
| | Las estaciones | 29 | 1-40 |
| | The Seasons | 29 | 1-41 |
| | School to Home Connection: A Song for Family Get-Togethers | 105 | |
| | Shoo, Turkey | 104 | 3-33 |
| | School to Home Connection: Special Activities on Special Days | 269 | |
| | Families Around the World | 280 | |
| | Families | 280 | 9-10 |
| | Building Skills Through Music: Visual Arts | 280 | |
| | Families Work and Sing Together | 294 | |
| | Los maizales | 294 | 9-24 |
| | The Cornfields | 294 | 9-25 |
| | Building Skills Through Music: Visual Arts | 312 | 10-1 |
| | Sorida | 314 | |
| **Lesson 5**<br>Color | Starry Night | 107 | |
| | "Pinwheels" (poem) | 149 | |
| | Building Skills Through Music: Math | 206 | |
| | Hungarian Dance No. 3 in F Major | 206 | 6-42 |
| | Building Skills Through Music: Math | 210 | |
| | Debajo el botón | 210 | 6-44 |
| | Under the Button | 210 | 6-45 |
| | Across the Curriculum: Science/Language Arts | 229 | 7-23 |
| | Bright Red Apples (rhyme) | 229 | |
| | Apple Tree | 230 | 7-23 |
| | The Apple (rhyme) | 231 | |
| | Across the Curriculum: Science/Art | 231 | |
| | Across the Curriculum: Related Arts | 276 | |
| | This Land is Your Land | 276 | 9-1 |
| | You're a Grand Old Flag | 277 | 9-3 |

Art Correlations

| Themes | Selections | Page | CD Track |
|---|---|---|---|
| **Lesson 6**<br>Kinds of Color | Starry Night<br>Pinwheels (poem)<br>Across the Curriculum: Science/Language Arts<br>Bright Red Apples (rhyme)<br>Across the Curriculum: Related Arts | 107<br>149<br>229<br>229<br>276 | |
| **Unit 2  Look at Art** | | | |
| **Lesson 1**<br>Animal Textures | Spotlight On: Froggie Facts<br>The Little Green Frog<br>Frog (poem)<br>Cat on a Yellow Pillow<br>Cirmos cica<br>Naughty Tabby Cat<br>Gato (poem)<br>Across the Curriculum: Language Arts<br>My Pony, Macaroni<br>The Wild Horseman<br>The Four Horses (poem)<br>Across the Curriculum: Language Arts<br>Bingo<br>Sir Barks-A-Lot (poem)<br>Hato popo<br>Pigeons<br>If You Find a Little Feather (poem)<br>Rags<br>School to Home Connection: Describing Dogs | 22<br>24<br>25<br>128<br>129<br>129<br><br>158<br>158<br>158<br>159<br>170<br>170<br>171<br>186<br>186<br>187<br>290<br>291 | <br>1-35<br><br><br>4-19<br>4-20<br><br><br>5-10<br>5-12<br><br><br>5-29<br><br>6-13<br>6-14<br><br>9-17 |
| **Lesson 2**<br>Pattern | Across the Curriculum: Related Arts<br>The Rain Sings a Song<br>Same or Different? (Play this pattern)<br>Building Skills Through Music: Math<br>Toy Symphony<br>Woof, Woof, Woof! A Pattern<br>Bingo<br>Building Skills Through Music: Math<br>Hungarian Dance No. 3 in F Major<br>Pottery Dance<br>Across the Curriculum: Social Studies/Related Arts<br>Hi Heidi Ho<br>Skills Reinforcement: Playing<br>Play a Birthday Pattern<br>The End (poem)<br>Today is Your Birthday<br>Happy Birthday to You! (poem) | 48<br>100<br>101<br>110<br>111<br>168<br>170<br>206<br>206<br>370<br>371<br>394<br>392<br>408<br>409<br>410<br>411 | <br>3-31<br><br><br>3-49<br><br>5-29<br><br>6-42<br>11-41<br><br>12-24<br><br><br>13-8<br>13-9 |
| **Lesson 3**<br>Space | Movement: Creative Movement | 4 | |
| **Lesson 4**<br>Warm and Cool Colors | Starry Night<br>Star Light, Star Bright<br>Across the Curriculum: Related Arts<br>This Land is Your Land<br>You're a Grand Old Flag | 107<br>106<br>276 | <br>3-36<br><br>9-1<br>9-3 |

Art Correlations

| Themes | Selections | Page | CD Track |
|---|---|---|---|
| **Lesson 5** Real and Abstract | Building Skills Through Music: Reading | 62 | |
| | Lady, Lady | 62 | 2-37 |
| | The Night (poem) | 63 | |
| | Building Skills Through Music: Reading | 140 | |
| | Last Night I Dreamed of Chickens (poem) | 141 | |
| | Building Skills Through Music: Science | 384 | |
| | The Fly and the Bumblebee | 384 | 12-14 |
| | Flight of the Bumblebee | 384 | 12-16 |
| | Bumble bee (poem) | 385 | |
| | Across the Curriculum: Language Arts | 386 | |
| | I Know an Old Woman | 387 | 12-19 |
| | I Know an Old Lady | 388 | 12-17 |
| | Across the Curriculum: Language Arts | 390 | |
| | Building Skills Through Music: Language | 392 | |
| | Hi Heidi Ho | 394 | 12-24 |
| **Lesson 6** Subjects of Artworks | White Water Lilies | 23 | |
| | Andante quieto | | 1-37 |
| | Starry Night | 107 | |
| | Star Light, Star Bright | 106 | 3-36 |
| | Cat on a Yellow Pillow | 128 | |
| | Cirmos cica | 129 | 4-19 |
| | Naughty Tabby Cat | 129 | 4-20 |
| | Across the Curriculum: Language Arts | 141 | |
| | Spotlight On: The Country | 142 | |
| | Amefuri | 144 | 4-43 |
| | Japanese Rain Song | 144 | 4-44 |
| | Meeting Individual Needs: English-Language Learners | 164 | |
| | The Parade Came Marching | 166 | 5-26 |
| | School to Home Connection: Favorite Bugs | 215 | |
| | Little Black Bug | 214 | 7-1 |
| | Hey, Bug! (poem) | 215 | |
| | Hush-a-Bye-Baby | 270 | |
| | Teacher to Teacher: Introducing Sculpture | 270 | |
| | Jimbo's Lullaby | 271 | 8-34 |
| | Across the Curriculum: Science/Language Arts | 348 | |
| | The Little Mouse | 350 | 11-7 |
| | Hickory, Dickory, Dock (poem) | 351 | |
| | Building Skills Through Music: Visual Arts | 364 | |
| | Mi chacra | 364 | 11-28 |
| | My Farm | 364 | 11-29 |
| **Unit 3  Art Everywhere** | | | |
| **Lesson 1** Form in Nature | Sea Treasures | 352 | |
| | Across the Curriculum: Science/Language Arts | 352 | |
| | Beach Rap | 354 | 11-9 |
| | Little Shell | 355 | 11-11 |
| **Lesson 2** You Are a Form | Across the Curriculum: Language Arts | 151 | |
| | Bounce High, Bounce Low | 152 | 4-58 |
| | Playing Ball | 153 | |
| | Music Makers | 287 | |
| | Pottery Dance | 370 | 11-41 |
| | Across the Curriculum: Social Studies/Related Arts | 371 | |

Art Correlations

| Themes | Selections | Page | CD Track |
|---|---|---|---|
| **Lesson 3**<br>Found-Object Sculpture | What Makes That Sound? | 72 | |
| | Junk Music Montage | 72 | 2-54 |
| | School to Home Connection: Found Sounds | 75 | |
| | Marbles (poem) | 75 | |
| | Across the Curriculum: Related Arts/Science | 176 | |
| | Knock the Cymbals | 176 | 5-37 |
| | Building Skills Through Music: Math | 322 | |
| | La víbora | 322 | 10-15 |
| | The Serpent | 322 | 10-16 |
| **Lesson 4**<br>Movement All Around | On the Move with Loud and Soft | 4 | |
| | Hoedown | 4 | 1-4 |
| | Reverie from Scenes from Childhood | 4 | 1-5 |
| | Slavonic Dance No. 1 | 4 | 1-7 |
| | Reverie | 4 | 1-6 |
| | A Different Beat | 6 | 1-8 |
| | Movement: Creative Movement | 4 | |
| | Teacher to Teacher: Managing Movement Activities | 5 | |
| | Meeting Individual Needs: Including Everyone | 6 | |
| | Run, Molly, Run | 8 | 1-11 |
| | My Legs and I (poem) | 9 | |
| | Building Skills Through Music: Language | 8 | |
| | Across the Curriculum: Related Arts | 12 | |
| | Walk in the Room | 12 | 1-15 |
| | Skills Reinforcement: Listening | 108 | |
| | Pupu hinu hinu | 107 | 3-41 |
| | (Shiny Shell Lullaby) | 107 | |
| **Lesson 5**<br>Puppets in Action | Pin Pon | 146 | 4-48<br>4-49 |
| | Movement: Creative Movement | 146 | |
| | Building Skills Through Music: Visual Arts | 146 | |
| | A Very Special Friend (poem) | 147 | |
| | Rags | 290 | 9-17 |
| | Meeting Individual Needs: English-Language Learners | 290 | |
| **Unit 4  Think Like an Artist** | | | |
| **Lesson 1**<br>Important Parts | "Andante" from Symphony No. 94 in G Major | 85 | 3-3 |
| | Skills Reinforcement: Listening | 85 | |
| | Across the Curriculum: Language Arts | 100 | |
| | Raindrop (poem) | 103 | |
| | Movement: Creative Dramatization | 178 | |
| | Fish (poem) | 179 | |
| | Toodala | 326 | 10-23 |
| | Skills Reinforcement: Speech Patterns and Expressive Singing | 327 | |

Art Correlations

| Themes | Selections | Page | CD Track |
|---|---|---|---|
| **Lesson 2**<br>Senses | Teacher to Teacher: Sound Center | 10 | |
| | Skills Reinforcement: Creating | 14 | |
| | Apples (poem) | 16 | |
| | Apples, Peaches, Pears and Plums (speech piece) | 17 | 1-27 |
| | Mashed Potatoes | 20 | 1-32 |
| | Mashed Potatoes (poem) | 21 | |
| | Across the Curriculum: Language Arts | 21 | |
| | Across the Curriculum: Language Arts/Science | 26 | |
| | "Spring" from The Four Seasons | 26 | 1-44 |
| | Leaves | 28 | 1-38 |
| | Las estaciones | 29 | 1-40 |
| | The Seasons | 29 | 1-41 |
| | Across the Curriculum: Language Arts | 65 | |
| | Building Skills Through Music: Language | 204 | |
| | Ayliluli, num tsipor | 204 | 6-37 |
| | Ayliluli, Sleep, My Bird | 204 | 6-38 |
| **Lesson 3**<br>Balance | Across the Curriculum: Math | 148 | |
| | 'Round and 'Round | 148 | 4-53 |
| | Across the Curriculum: Related Arts | 360 | |
| | Ah! Les jolis papillons | 362 | 11-21 |
| | Ah! The Pretty Butterflies | 362 | 11-22 |
| **Lesson 5**<br>Portraits of People | Across the Curriculum: Language Arts/Social Studies | 8 | |
| | Run, Molly, Run | 8 | 1-11 |
| | Building Skills Through Music: Visual Arts | 442 | |
| | Kébé Mama | 442 | 14-22 |
| | My Dear Mama | 442 | 14-23 |
| **Unit 5  Art, Then and Now** | | | |
| **Lesson 3**<br>Storybook Illustrations | Building Skills Through Music: Language | 84 | |
| | We're Making Popcorn | 86 | 3-1 |
| | Soft Pops, Loud Pops | 84 | |
| | Building Skills Through Music: Visual Arts | 198 | |
| | The Napping House (poem) | 198 | 6-31 |
| | Across the Curriculum: Related Arts | 296 | |
| | Las maizales | 296 | 9-24 |
| | The Cornfields | 296 | 9-25 |
| **Lesson 4**<br>Messages in Art | Building Skills Through Music: Writing | 72 | |
| | Junk Music Montage | 72 | 2-54 |
| | What Makes That Sound? | 72 | |
| | Building Skills Through Music: Language | 84 | |
| | We're Making Popcorn | 86 | 3-1 |
| | Soft Pops, Loud Pops | 84 | |
| **Lesson 5**<br>Still Lifes | Across the Curriculum: Related Arts | 12 | |
| | Watermelon Man | 10 | 1-17 |
| | Silver Apples of the Moon | 10 | 1-18 |

| Themes | Selections | Page | CD Track |
|---|---|---|---|
| **Unit 6  Art for Everyone** | | | |
| **Lesson 1**<br>Decorations | Across the Curriculum: Language Arts/Related Arts<br>We're Making Popcorn<br>Pottery Dance<br>Across the Curriculum: Social Studies/Related Arts | 85<br>86<br>370<br>371 | <br>3-1<br>11-41<br> |
| **Lesson 2**<br>Masks | Pottery Dance<br>Across the Curriculum: Social Studies/Related Arts | 370<br>371 | 11-41<br> |
| **Lesson 3**<br>Special Games | Cultural Connection: African American Singing Games<br>Run, Molly, Run<br>Cultural Connection: African American "Plays,"<br>Nana, Thread Needle<br>Across the Curriculum: Social Studies<br>Viva el fútbol!<br>I Love Soccer!<br>Shoo, Turkey<br>School to Home Connection: A Song for Family Get-Togethers<br>Playing Ball (poem)<br>Musical Games<br>Banana Splits (speech piece)<br>Green, Green, Rocky<br>Spotlight On: The Value of Playing Games<br>Spotlight On: Clapping Games<br>School to Home Connection: Sharing Traditions<br>Ode to la piñata (poem) | 8<br><br>8<br>38<br>38<br>96<br>96<br>96<br>104<br>105<br><br>153<br>318<br>320<br>321<br>318<br>331<br>425<br>425 | <br><br>1-11<br><br>2-1<br><br>3-19<br>3-20<br>3-33<br><br><br><br><br>10-11<br>10-13 |
| **Lesson 4**<br>Fabric Artworks | Spotlight On: The Fabric on the Big Book Page<br>Rug Bug Rhythms<br>Little Black Bug | 212<br>212<br>214 | <br><br>7-1 |
| **Lesson 5**<br>Artworks You Can Use | Spotlight On: Zydeco<br>Zydeco Dancing<br>What Makes That Sound?<br>Junk Music Montage<br>Cultural Connection: The Maori People<br>To'ia mai te waka<br>Pull the Canoe<br>Thump, Rattle, and Scrape<br>Percussion Montage<br>Across the Curriculum: Related Arts/Science<br>Knock the Cymbals<br>Building Skills Through Music: Social Studies,<br>Pottery Dance | 20<br>20<br>72<br>72<br>76<br>77<br>77<br>114<br>114<br>176<br>176<br>370<br>370 | <br>1-34<br><br>2-54<br><br>2-55<br>2-56<br><br>3-54<br><br>5-37<br><br>11-41 |
| **Lesson 6**<br>Signs and Symbols | School to Home Connection: Kitchen Patterns<br>Cultural Connection: Animals in Japanese Culture<br>Hato popo<br>Pigeons<br>Cow's Woc Backward<br>School to Home Connection: Word Hunt | 177<br>186<br>186<br>186<br>390<br>391 | <br><br>6-13<br>6-14<br>12-20 |

Art Correlations

| Themes | Selections | Page | CD Track |
|---|---|---|---|
| **Grade 2** | | | |
| **Unit 1 Art Around You** | | | |
| **Lesson 2**<br>Shape | Ciranda | 273 | 10-1 |
| **Lesson 3**<br>Feeling Texture | Waiting for the Traffic Light<br>Ayelivi<br>Abiyoyo<br>Oh, Watch the Stars<br>Kou ri lengay | 106<br>70<br>108<br>144<br>217 | 4-23<br>3-9<br>4-25<br>5-38<br>8-7 |
| **Lesson 4**<br>Seeing Texture | Riddle Ree<br>Oya<br>Adana ya gidelim<br>The Farmer's Diary Key<br>Rosie, Darling Rosie | 34<br>69<br>142<br>182<br>215 | 1-43<br>3-8<br>5-32<br>7-6<br>8-5 |
| **Lesson 5**<br>Color Families | Modern Painting with Clef (Lichtenstein)<br>Two Little Sausages<br>Ise oluwa<br>The Rainbow<br>L'arc en ciel | 79<br>79<br>102<br>333<br>334 | <br>3-24<br>4-17<br>12-6<br>12-8 |
| **Lesson 6**<br>Warm and Cool Colors | Rhythmical (Klee)<br>Allegro non troppo, no. 33<br>Untitled (Saul)<br>Sunsets (Rivera) | 43<br>49<br>307<br>334 | <br>2-20<br> |
| **Unit 2  Art is Everywhere** | | | |
| **Lesson 1**<br>Patterns and Prints | Arts Connection, 48<br>Finding Patterns in Two Songs<br>Banjo Sam | 48<br>94<br>314 | <br><br>11-22 |
| **Lesson 3**<br>Realistic and Abstract | Court Ball<br>The Banjo Lesson (Ossawa)<br>Rumblin' On | 278<br>315<br>315 | <br><br>11-24 |
| **Lesson 4**<br>Portraits | Children Playing London Bridge (Johnson)<br>The Skater (Stuart)<br>Les patineurs | 29<br>387<br>387 | <br><br>14-29 |
| **Lesson 5**<br>Still Life | Holiday Sleigh Ride (Scott)<br>Jingle Bells | 389<br>388 | <br>14-30 |
| **Lesson 6**<br>Landscape as a Subject | A Mountain of a Form<br>Tall Cedar Tree<br>The Rainbow<br>L'arc en ciel<br>Sunsets (Rivera)<br>En nuestra tierra tan linda | 202<br>322<br>332<br>333<br>334<br>335 | <br>11-30<br>12-6<br>12-8<br><br>12-9 |

Art Correlations

| Themes | Selections | Page | CD Track |
|---|---|---|---|
| **Unit 3 Art You Can Go Around** | | | |
| **Lesson 1**<br>Forms in Places | Michael, Row the Boat Ashore<br>Ein Männlein Steht im Walde<br>*Ein Männlein Steht im Walde*<br>Same Train<br>Shoo, Fly | 18<br>90<br>91<br>164<br>200 | 1-24<br>3-43<br>3-47<br>6-20<br>7-38 |
| **Lesson 2**<br>Playscapes | Un pajarito<br>Bob-a-Needle<br>Shake Them 'Simmons Down<br>Kapulu kane | 16<br>232<br>244<br>270 | 1-20<br>8-19<br>8-32<br>9-37 |
| **Lesson 3**<br>Forms and Space | Good Mornin', Blues<br>A Song That's Just for You<br>Sing a Rainbow | 52<br>126<br>166 | 2-24<br>5-8<br>6-22 |
| **Unit 4 Creative Expression** | | | |
| **Lesson 1**<br>Art and Music | Children Playing London Bridge (Johnson)<br>Rhythmical (Klee)<br>Modern painting with Clef (Lichtenstein)<br>The Banjo Lesson (Ossawa)<br>Jinshan Peasant Painting | 28<br>46<br>78<br>120<br>159 | |
| **Lesson 3**<br>Rhythm as Expression | Time to Sing<br>Frog in the Millpond<br>Tideo<br>Dinah<br>Un Elephante | 8<br>44<br>80<br>120<br>160 | 1-5<br>2-8<br>3-26<br>4-39<br>6-12 |
| **Lesson 6**<br>Symbols | Un, deux, trois | 198 | 7-31 |
| **Unit 6 Types of Artworks** | | | |
| **Lesson 3**<br>Celebrate with Art | Vamos a la fiesta<br>Thanksgiving is Near<br>O laufet, ihr Hirten<br>A Kwanzaa Carol<br>Valentines | 374<br>380<br>384<br>392<br>398 | 14-1<br>14-13<br>14-21<br>14-36<br>14-42 |
| **Lesson 4**<br>Masks for Expression | Ise oluwa<br>*Nangape* | 103<br>104 | 4-17<br>4-20 |
| **Lesson 5**<br>Community Art | Hui jia qü<br>Jinshan Peasant Painting<br>A-Tisket, A-Tasket<br>*A-Tisket, A-Tasket* | 159<br>159<br>238<br>239 | 6-5<br><br>8-24<br>8-25 |
| **Grade 3** | | | |
| **Unit 1 Art All Around You** | | | |
| **Lesson 2**<br>Shape | Little Johnny Brown<br>Al citrón | 313<br>320 | 11-1<br>11-16 |

| Themes | Selections | Page | CD Track |
|---|---|---|---|
| **Lesson 3**<br>Texture | Make New Friends<br>I'm on My Way<br>Tender Shepherd<br>Each of Us is a Flower<br>He's Got the Whole World in His Hands | 36<br>76<br>116<br>154<br>230 | 2-1<br>3-1<br>4-22<br>5-28<br>7-56 |
| **Lesson 4**<br>Symmetry | Railroad Corral<br>Bonavist' Harbour<br>Over the River and Through the Wood | 174<br>294<br>384 | 6-17<br>10-16<br>13-20 |
| **Lesson 6**<br>Space | The World We Love | 342 | 12-1 |
| **Unit 2  Look Closely at Art** | | | |
| **Lesson 1**<br>Color | La paloma blanca<br>Bonavist' Harbour<br>La pinata (Rivera) | 252<br>294<br>398 | 8-22<br>10-16 |
| **Lesson 2**<br>Color Families | *Mea haarit*<br>Sarika keo<br>Tucanos com Bananeíras (de Moraes)<br>If a Tiger Calls<br>Surprised! (Rousseau)<br>The Royal March of the Lion | 274<br>275<br>309<br>354<br>356<br>357 | 9-25<br>9-26<br>12-12<br><br><br>12-14 |
| **Lesson 4**<br>Landscapes | Across the Curriculum, Language Arts<br>¡Qué gusto!<br>Song of the Fishes<br>America, the Beautiful<br>Surprised!, 356 | <br>132<br>132<br>244<br>413 | <br><br>4-45<br>8-11<br>15-6 |
| **Unit 3  Forms in Art** | | | |
| **Lesson 1**<br>Forms All Around | Au clair de la lune<br>Great Day<br>Old Dan Tucker<br>Kum bachur atzel<br>Railroad Corral | 18<br>58<br>96<br>138<br>174 | 1-26<br>2-35<br>3-36<br>5-1<br>6-17 |
| **Lesson 2**<br>Line Direction in Forms | Great Day | 58 | 2-35 |
| **Lesson 4**<br>Pattern | Ding, Dong, Diggidiggidong<br>Ahora voy a cantarles<br>Love Somebody<br>¡Qué gusto!<br>Waltzing with Bears | 14<br>56<br>94<br>132<br>170 | 1-15<br>2-31<br>3-31<br>4-45<br>6-14 |
| **Lesson 5**<br>Ways of Sculpting | Soapstone carving<br>Maori wood carvings<br>Tune In???<br>*Mazurka, Opus 30, No. 3* | 258<br>273<br>317<br>317 | <br><br><br>11-12 |

Art Correlations

| Themes | Selections | Page | CD Track |
|---|---|---|---|
| **Unit 4 Art, Then and Now** | | | |
| **Lesson 1** <br> Contrast | La pinata (Rivera) | 398 | |
| **Lesson 2** <br> Portraits of People | Music Makers: Camille Saint-Saens | 357 | |
| **Lesson 3** <br> Portrait of an Artist | Bear Dance <br> Béla Bartók | 172 <br> 173 | 6-16 |
| **Unit 5 Artists and Expression** | | | |
| **Lesson 2** <br> Expression and Style | Supercalifragilisticexpialidocious <br> Train is A-Comin' <br> El gallo pinto <br> Draw Me a Bucket of Water <br> Hush, Hush | 6 <br> 48 <br> 86 <br> 124 <br> 162 | 1-3 <br> 2-17 <br> 318 <br> 4-31 <br> 5-36 |
| **Lesson 5** <br> Computer Art | Technology/Media Link <br> Technology/Media Link <br> Technology/Media Link <br> Technology/Media Link | 289 <br> 293 <br> 295 <br> 333 | |
| **Lesson 6** <br> Landscape art | ¡Qué gusto! <br> A Song of One <br> Surprised! (Rouseau) | 132 <br> 344 <br> 356 | 4-45 <br> 12-3 |
| **Unit 6 A World of Art** | | | |
| **Lesson 1** <br> Fiber Artworks | Doll and cradle board <br> Hej pada pada | 70 <br> 78 | 3-6 |
| **Lesson 4** <br> Folk Art | The Rabbit Dance <br> Freedom from Want (Rockwell) | 334 <br> 385 | 11-36 |
| # Grade 4 | | | |
| **Unit 1 Art in Your World** | | | |
| **Lesson 3** <br> Shape | Across the Curriculum: Art <br> *ABACA Dabble* <br> Three Musicians (Picasso) | 184 <br> 184 <br> 212 | 8-17 |
| **Lesson 4** <br> Texture | Review, Assess, Perform, Create <br> Bundle-Buggy Boogie Woogie <br> Across the Curriculum: Social Studies/Art <br> Canción de cuna <br> Amazing Grace <br> Lullaby and Dance | 43 <br> 120 <br> 144 <br> 144 <br> 160 <br> 387 | 5-37 <br><br> 6-31 <br> 7-18 <br> 16-26 |
| **Lesson 5** <br> Space and Distance | America | 206 | 9-1 |
| **Lesson 6** <br> Artists See Spaces | America the Beautiful | 158 | 7-15 |

Art Correlations

| Themes | Selections | Page | CD Track |
|---|---|---|---|
| **Unit 2 Cultural Expressions** | | | |
| **Lesson 1**<br>Color | Watercolor Ripple (Greve)<br>Across the Curriculum: Fine Arts/Science<br>Over the Rainbow | 77<br>140<br>140 | <br><br>6-27 |
| **Lesson 2**<br>Color Schemes | Across the Curriculum: Fine Arts/Science<br>Across the Curriculum: Social Studies/Art<br>Canción de cuna | 140<br>144<br>144 | <br><br>6-31 |
| **Lesson 3**<br>Landmarks and Color | Route 66 | 276 | 11-21 |
| **Lesson 5**<br>Pattern | Haul Away Joe<br>Gakavik<br>Tsuki<br>Watercolor Ripple (Greve)<br>Movement: Patterned Dance | 13<br>14<br>25<br>77<br>101 | 1-15<br>1-17<br>1-36 |
| **Unit 3 Expression in Art** | | | |
| **Lesson 2**<br>Rhythm in Forms | Galop<br>Over the Rainbow<br>Minka<br>Russian Sailor's Dance | 16<br>140<br>222<br>224 | 1-24<br>6-27<br>9-21<br>9-26 |
| **Lesson 3**<br>Emphasis in Forms | Spotlight On: Rondo<br>Three Musicians (Picasso) | 183<br>212 | |
| **Lesson 4**<br>Pop Art | Music Makers: The Five Saints<br>Music Makers: Bobby McFerrin<br>Music Makers; Patti LaBelle<br>Cultural Connection: Music in the Philippines<br>Music Makers: Rockapella | 47<br>80<br>143<br>173<br>192 | |
| **Lesson 5**<br>Design in Architecture | Mission San Luis Rey photo<br>The Pyramids | 243<br>438 | |
| **Unit 4 Creative Expression** | | | |
| **Lesson 4**<br>Moving Pictures | Daniel Boone Escorting Pioneers (Bingham)<br>California Vaqueros (Walker) | 139<br>275 | |
| **Lesson 5**<br>Artists See Places | Across the Curriculum: Social Studies/Science<br>Ochimbo<br>Cumberland Gap<br>Santa Clara<br>Across the Curriculum: Social Studies<br>La Tarara | 134<br>134<br>138<br>172<br>176<br>176 | <br>6-11<br>6-22<br>7-32<br><br>8-1 |
| **Lesson 6**<br>Technology as Expression | Technology/Media Link<br>Technology/Media Link<br>Technology/Media Link<br>Technology/Media Link<br>Computer-generated image | 119<br>123<br>149<br>157<br>198 | |

Art Correlations

| Themes | Selections | Page | CD Track |
|---|---|---|---|
| **Unit 5 Art, Old and New** | | | |
| **Lesson 2** <br> Weaving | Mola textile <br> *How Can I Keep from Singing* <br> How Can I Keep from Singing <br> Navajo blanket <br> Niu lang zhi nu | 145 <br> 260 <br> 261 <br> 283 <br> 335 | <br> 10-35 <br> 10-33 <br> <br> 14-15 |
| **Lesson 4** <br> Industrial Design | Cultural Connection: Advertising | 148 | |
| **Lesson 5** <br> Portraits and Proportion | Painting (Wood) <br> Girl with a Guitar (Vermeer) <br> Mother and Child (Walter) | 161 <br> 177 <br> 181 | |
| **Lesson 6** <br> The Human Form | Children Dancing (Gwathmey) <br> Danse dans un Pavillion (Watteau) <br> Over My Head <br> Across the Curriculum: Social Studies | 106 <br> 112 <br> 118 <br> 119 | <br> <br> 5-35 |
| **Unit 6 An Assortment of Art** | | | |
| **Lesson 3** <br> Many Kinds of Folk Art | Tune In: Sourwood Mountain <br> Sourwood Mountain <br> Music Makers: The Oak Ridge Boys <br> See the Children Playin' <br> Across the Curriculum: Language Arts <br> Faberge egg | 65 <br> 65 <br> 86 <br> 107 <br> 176 <br> 293 | <br> 3-28 <br> <br> 5-22 |
| **Lesson 4** <br> Fiber Art | Nruab hnub thiab hmo ntuj <br> Paj ntaub story-telling quilt (Lor) | 366 <br> 367 | 16-4 |
| **Lesson 5** <br> Murals | Mural of musicians playing traditional Caribbean instruments (Anonymous) | 191 | |
| **Grade 5** | | | |
| **Unit 1 Art and You** | | | |
| **Lesson 1** <br> Beauty in Your World | I Love the Mountains <br> Skills Reinforcement: Creating <br> Sumer Is Icumen In <br> Across the Curriculum: Science <br> America, the Beautiful <br> Across the Curriculum: Language Arts <br> De colores <br> This Land Is Your Land | 34 <br> 34 <br> 35 <br> 35 <br> 76 <br> 77 <br> 90 <br> 118 | 2-26 <br> <br> 2-28 <br> <br> 4-19 <br> <br> 5-1 |
| **Lesson 2** <br> Line | Night of the Silver Slipper (Burnside) <br> Texture <br> *The Thunderer* <br> Going to Church (Johnson) <br> Across the Curriculum: Social Studies <br> *Scottish Medley* | 16 <br> 78 <br> 79 <br> 102 <br> 139 <br> 139 | <br> <br> 4-24 <br> <br> <br> 7-11 |

| Themes | Selections | Page | CD Track |
|---|---|---|---|
| **Lesson 3**<br>Line and Design | Night of the Silver Slipper (Burnside) | 16 | |
| | Going to Church (Johnson) | 102 | |
| | Across the Curriculum: Social Studies | 139 | |
| | *Scottish Medley* | 139 | 7-11 |
| | School to Home Connection: Decorating Stones | 309 | |
| **Lesson 4**<br>Balance | Going to Church (Johnson) | 102 | |
| | Skills Reinforcement: Creating | 142 | |
| | Ama-lama | 142 | 7-15 |
| **Lesson 5**<br>Shape | Skills Reinforcement: Creating, 142 | 142 | |
| | Ama-lama | 142 | 7-15 |
| | Across the Curriculum: Art | 336 | |
| | It Don't Mean a Thing (If it Ain't Got That Swing) | 336 | 15-23 |
| **Unit 2  Expression and Art** | | | |
| **Lesson 1**<br>Pattern and Rhythm | Morning Comes Early | 13 | 1-17 |
| | Eliza Kongo | 14 | 1-23 |
| | Funwa Alafia | 32 | 2-19 |
| | California | 52 | 3-9 |
| | Drill, Ye Tarriers | 54 | 3-16 |
| | Don't You Hear the Lambs? | 97 | 5-19 |
| | Scotland the Brave | 138 | 7-6 |
| | Meeting Individual Needs: Including Everyone | 139 | |
| | Autumn Canon | 148 | 7-25 |
| | Pollerita | 151 | 7-30 |
| | *Amores Hallarás* | 153 | 7-35 |
| | Oh, Watch the Stars | 216 | 10-29 |
| **Lesson 4**<br>Say It with Color | Night at the Silver Slipper (Burnside) | 16 | |
| | De colores | 90 | 5-1 |
| | Cultural Connection: The Art of Mexico | 139 | |
| | School to Home Connection: Decorating Stones | 309 | |
| | Across the Curriculum: Art | 336 | |
| | It Don't Mean a Thing (If it Ain't Got That Swing) | 438 | 15-23 |
| | Illustration (Wood) | 336 | |
| | Across the Curriculum: Art History | 337 | |
| | Building Skills Through Music: Art | 438 | |
| | Heri Za Kwanzaa | 476 | 20-32 |
| | A Joyful Sound (Border Art) | 476 | |
| | | 476 | |
| **Lesson 5**<br>Value | Across the Curriculum: Art History | 438 | |
| **Lesson 6**<br>Color Schemes | De colores | 90 | 5-1 |
| | Cultural Connection: The Art of Mexico | 91 | |
| | *Scottish Medley* | 138 | 7-11 |
| | Across the Curriculum: Social Studies | 139 | |
| | School to Home Connection: Decorating Stones | 309 | |
| | Across the Curriculum: Art History | 438 | |
| | Building Skills Through Music | 476 | |
| | Heri Za Kwanzaa | 476 | 20-32 |
| | A Joyful Sound (Border Art) | 476 | |

Art Correlations

| Themes | Selections | Page | CD Track |
|---|---|---|---|
| **Unit 3  Art, Past and Present** | | | |
| **Lesson 1**<br>Texture | Texture | 78 | |
| | The Thunderer | 79 | 4-24 |
| | Skills Reinforcement: Creating | 142 | |
| | Ama-lama | 142 | 7-15 |
| | Across the Curriculum: Art/Language Arts | 318 | |
| | Cho'i hát bôi | 318 | 14-32 |
| | Across the Curriculum: Art | 336 | |
| | It Don't Mean a Thing (If it Ain't Got That Swing) | 336 | 15-23 |
| **Lesson 2**<br>Emphasis | Skills Reinforcement: Creating | 128 | |
| | La Bamba | 128 | 6-20 |
| | Hound Dog | 212 | 10-27 |
| **Lesson 3**<br>Variety and Subjects | Skills Reinforcement: Creating | 142 | |
| | Ama-lama | 142 | 7-15 |
| **Lesson 4**<br>Ceramic Slab Structures | De colores | 90 | 5-1 |
| | Across the Curriculum: Art | 91 | |
| | Cultural Connection: The Art of Mexico | 91 | |
| **Lesson 5**<br>Familiar Forms | De colores | 90 | 5-1 |
| | Across the Curriculum: Art | 90 | |
| | Cultural Connection: The Art of Mexico | 91 | |
| | Cultural Connection: Navajo Art | 108 | |
| | Jo'ashilá | 108 | 5-43 |
| **Unit 4  Art as Self-Expression** | | | |
| **Lesson 1**<br>Pattern | Cultural Connection: The Art of Mexico | 91 | |
| | Jo'ashilá | 108 | 5-43 |
| | Cultural Connection: Navajo Art | 108 | |
| | Across the Curriculum: Social Studies | 139 | |
| | Scottish Medley | 139 | 7-11 |
| | Across the Curriculum: Visual Arts | 158 | |
| | Ego sum pauper | 158 | 8-7 |
| | School to Home Connection: Decorating Stones | 309 | |
| | Across the Curriculum: Art/Language Arts | 318 | |
| | Cho'i hát bôi | 318 | 14-32 |
| | A Joyful Sound (Border Art) | 476 | |
| | Heri Za Kwanzaa | 476 | 20-32 |
| **Lesson 2**<br>Printmaking | Cultural Connection: Akan of Ghana | 308 | |
| | Bantama kra kro | 308 | 14-14 |
| **Lesson 3**<br>Unity and Variety | La ciudad de Juaja | 59 | 3-24 |
| | Going to Church (Johnson) | 102 | |
| | Arts Connection | 108 | |
| | Skills Reinforcement: Creating | 142 | 7-15 |
| | Ama-lama | 142 | |
| **Lesson 4**<br>Artistic Adornment | Arts Connection | 108 | |
| | The Ash Grove | 114 | 6-6 |
| **Lesson 5**<br>Industrial Design | School to Home Connection: Create Instruments | 113 | |

| Themes | Selections | Page | CD Track |
|---|---|---|---|
| **Unit 5  All Kinds of Art** | | | |
| **Lesson 3**<br>Artists as Architects | Meeting Individual Needs: English Language Learners<br>Live in the City<br>Across the Curriculum: Art, 336<br>Cultural Connection: Big Ben, 419<br>Cultural Connection: Stonehenge, 425 | 71<br>71 | 4-13 |
| **Lesson 5**<br>Murals | De colores<br>Cultural Connection: The Art of Mexico<br>Across the Curriculum: Art<br>Turn, Turn, Turn | 90<br>91<br>378<br>378 | 5-1<br><br><br>17-15 |
| **Unit 6  More Ideas for Art** | | | |
| **Lesson 1**<br>Photography | Meeting Individual Needs: English Language Learners<br>Live in the City<br>America, the Beautiful<br>School to Home Connection: Memorabilia<br>Across the Curriculum: Visual Arts<br>Jasmine Flowers<br>Cultural Connection: Everyday People<br>Everyday People<br>Unit Project<br>Across the Curriculum: Language Arts<br>I Vow to You, My Country<br>'Ulili E<br>Big Island, Hawaii<br>Waipio Valley, Hawaii<br>Volcano steam<br>We Shall Overcome<br>Nobel Peace Prize Winners<br>The Star-Spangled Banner<br>School to Home Connection: Pictures of America<br>The Fourth of July | 71<br>71<br>79<br>79<br>316<br>316<br>389<br>389<br>404<br>420<br>420<br>441<br>442<br>443<br>443<br>485<br>485<br>488<br>489<br>489 | <br>4-13<br>4-19<br><br><br>14-27<br><br>18-4<br><br><br>18-27<br>19-13<br><br><br><br>21-14<br><br>21-17<br><br>21-19 |
| **Lesson 2**<br>Photomontage Art | America, the Beautiful<br>School to Home Connection: Memorabilia<br>Yüe liang wan wan<br>Across the Curriculum: Visual Arts<br>Jasmine Flowers<br>Lahk gei mohlee | 79<br>79<br>314<br>316<br>316<br>317 | 4-19<br><br>14-23<br><br>14-27<br>14-29 |
| **Lesson 3**<br>Moving Pictures | I Vow to You, My Country<br>Across the Curriculum: Language Arts, | 418<br>420 | 18-27 |
| **Lesson 4**<br>Surrealism | Creatures in the Night (Miro)<br>Spotlight On: The Artist<br>Across the Curriculum: Social Studies<br>El desembre congelat | 174<br>175<br>472<br>473 | <br><br><br>20-25 |
| **Lesson 6**<br>Jewelry, Old and New | Cultural Connection: Navajo Art<br>Jo'ashilá | 108<br>108 | <br>5-43 |

**Art Correlations:** *Scott Foresman Art*  **375**

Art Correlations

| Themes | Selections | Page | CD Track |
|---|---|---|---|
| **GRADE 6** | | | |
| **Unit 1 The Elements of Art** | | | |
| **Lesson 1** <br> Line | Strike Up the Band <br> *Allegretto gioviale* | 135 <br> 168 | 7-36 <br> 9-26 |
| **Lesson 2** <br> Shape | My Dear Companion <br> B126 (Tadasky) <br> Dance for the Nations | 23 <br> 122 <br> 122 | 2-11 <br> <br> 7-15 |
| **Lesson 3** <br> Form | El condor pasa <br> La paloma se fue <br> Birthday <br> *Birthday* <br> Dance for the Nations <br> Dona nobis pacem <br> "Little" Organ Fugue in G Minor (organ) <br> "Little" Organ Fugue in G Minor (brass) | 46 <br> 50 <br> 90 <br> 92 <br> 122 <br> 124 <br> 128 <br> 128 | 3-16 <br> 3-22 <br> 6-1 <br> 6-1 <br> 7-15 <br> 7-17 <br> 7-21 <br> 7-22 |
| **Lesson 4** <br> Space | Bridge Across the Moon | 302 | |
| **Lesson 5** <br> Space and Distance | Gonna Build a Mountain <br> O le le O Bahia <br> Like a Bird | 21 <br> 164 <br> 166 | 2-6 <br> 9-14 <br> 9-21 |
| **Lesson 7** <br> Color | What a Wonderful World <br> *What a Wonderful World* <br> B126 (Tadasky) | 62 <br> 62 <br> 122 | 4-20 <br> 4-22 <br> |
| **Lesson 8** <br> Color and Colorists | La paloma se fue <br> Alom (Vasarely) | 50 <br> 134 | 3-22 <br> |
| **Lesson 9** <br> Texture | El payo <br> Mary Ann <br> *Responsory: Alleluia* from Mass | 144 <br> 180 <br> 217 | 8-8 <br> 10-10 <br> 11-25 |
| **Unit 2 The Principles of Design** | | | |
| **Lesson 3** <br> Proportion | Sergei Prokofiev, 457 | 457 | |
| **Lesson 4** <br> Pattern | Alom (Vasarely) | 134 | |
| **Lesson 5** <br> Rhythm | Red River Valley <br> Barb'ry Allen <br> Ain't Gonna Let Nobody Turn Me 'Round <br> Syncopated Rhythms, 156 | 11 <br> 44 <br> 85 <br> 156 | 1-6 <br> 3-8 <br> 5-26 <br> |
| **Lesson 7** <br> Variety | Scattin' A-Round <br> The Carnival of Venice <br> *Variations on "America"* | 160 <br> 161 <br> 162 | 9-10 <br> 9-12 <br> 9-13 |

Art Correlations

| Themes | Selections | Page | CD Track |
|---|---|---|---|
| **Unit 3  Media and Methods** | | | |
| **Lesson 2**<br>Painting | Snow Palace (Kuerner)<br>Trio Musical (Gomez)<br>Garden of Eden (Bouttats)<br>The Concert (Gabbiani)<br>Swing Your Partner (Scott) | 41<br>50<br>66<br>102<br>104 | |
| **Lesson 4**<br>Collage | Harriet and the Freedom Train (Olsen)<br>The Gospel Train | 397<br>398 | 19-26 |
| **Lesson 9**<br>Still Photography | Music Maker: John Cage | 209 | |
| **Lesson 10**<br>Computer Art | Technology/Media Link | 415 | |
| **Unit 4   A World of Art and Artists** | | | |
| **Lesson 5**<br>Art in the Middle Ages | Garden of Eden (Bouttats) | 66 | |
| **Lesson 8**<br>Early Eastern Art | Vietnamese folk art, 12<br>Bridge Across the Moon (artist unknown)<br>Maru-bihag<br>Maha ganapathim<br>Dham dhamak dham samelu<br>Alumot | 12<br>302<br>304<br>305<br>305<br>306 | <br><br>15-22<br>15-23<br>15-24<br>15-26 |
| **Lesson 9**<br>Modern Western Art | Red River Valley<br>Swing Your Partner (Scott) | 10<br>104 | 1-6 |
| **Lesson 10**<br>Modern Global Art | Sing a Song of Peace<br>Dance for the Nations<br>The Same<br>Vive l'amour<br>Stained glass window in the UN building (Chagall)<br>The United Nations on the March | 66<br>123<br>268<br>176<br>442<br>443 | 4-26<br>7-15<br>14-3<br>10-6<br><br>21-4 |
| **Unit 5  Subjects and Styles** | | | |
| **Lesson 1**<br>People as Subjects | Cast members from The Wiz<br>The Concert (Gabbiani)<br>Swing Your Partner (Scott)<br>Painting of Alban (Schoenberg)<br>Calla Lily Vendor (Rivera) | 6<br>102<br>104<br>169<br>415 | |
| **Lesson 2**<br>Proportion and Faces | Music Maker: Tchaikovsky<br>Waltz of the Flowers | 324<br>325 | 16-14 |
| **Lesson 3**<br>Animals as Subjects | The Old Oaken Bucket in Winter (Moses) | 454 | |
| **Lesson 4**<br>Still Life as Subject | Empanadas (Garza) | 173 | |

Art Correlations

| Themes | Selections | Page | CD Track |
|---|---|---|---|
| **Lesson 5**<br>Landscape as Subject | Snow Palace (Kuerner)<br>Stopping by Woods on a Snowy Evening<br>Swing Your Partner (Scott)<br>Going upon the Mountain<br>Sculling at Sunset (Beasley)<br>Peace Like a River | 41<br>40<br>104<br>105<br>191<br>190 | 2-36<br><br>6-21<br><br>10-26 |
| **Lesson 9**<br>Pop Art | B126 (Tadasky)<br>Dance for the Nations | 122<br>122 | 7-15 |
| **Unit 6  Expression and Meaning** | | | |
| **Lesson 1**<br>Murals Tell Stories | Trial Herd to Abilene (Koerner)<br>The Old Chisholm Trail | 237<br>237 | 12-12 |
| **Lesson 2**<br>Mosaic Expression | Stained glass window in the UN building (Chagall) | 442 | |
| **Lesson 4**<br>Expressive Points of View | Reflections of the Big Dipper (Pollock)<br>Concert for Piano and Orchestra<br>Calla Lily Vendor (Rivera) | 208<br>209<br>415 | 11-17 |

# GRADE 7

| Themes | Selections | Page | CD Track |
|---|---|---|---|
| **Unit 1  The Elements of Art** | | | |
| **Lesson 2**<br>Shape | Rock Around the Clock | B-18 | 3-3 |
| **Lesson 3**<br>Form | Awakening<br>All for One<br>My Home's Across the Blue Ridge Mountains<br>Ja-Da<br>Cielito lindo | D-14<br>E-8<br>F-6<br>G-20<br>I-20 | 8-31<br>9-21<br>10-22<br>12-13<br>13-18 |
| **Lesson 5**<br>Space and Perspective | He's Got the Whole World in His Hands<br>A View of the Bombardment of Fort McHenry (Bower) | I-36<br>I-57 | 13-29 |
| **Lesson 7**<br>Color | Regatta at Argenteuil (Monet)<br>Into Bondage (Douglas)<br>Yellow Rose of Texas | C-38<br>G-11<br>I-70 | 14-18 |
| **Lesson 8**<br>Color Schemes | Court Ball<br>The Fiddler (Chagall)<br>Fiddler on the Roof<br>Lift Up Thy Voice and Sing (Johnson) | C-6<br>E-6<br>E-5<br>I-12 | 9-19 |
| **Lesson 9**<br>Texture | A Sorta Fairytale<br>Carry On<br>Saltarello detto trivella<br>Prelude in G-sharp Minor<br>Everyday People | A-5<br>B-2<br>C-6<br>E-4<br>G-16 | 1-7<br>2-1<br>5-31<br>9-18<br>12-10 |

Art Correlations

| Themes | Selections | Page | CD Track |
|---|---|---|---|
| **Unit 2  The Principles of Design** | | | |
| **Lesson 1**<br>Balance | Hungarian painting of Zoltán Kodaly (Unknown artist) | C-34 | |
| **Lesson 2**<br>Emphasis | The Fiddler (Chagall)<br>Fiddler on the Roof<br>A View of the Bombardment of Fort McHenry (Bower) | E-6<br>E-5<br>I-57 | 9-19 |
| **Lesson 3**<br>Proportion | Court Ball<br>Into Bondage (Douglas) | C-6<br>G-11 | |
| **Lesson 4**<br>Rhythm | *A Sorta Fairytale*<br>*Footloose*<br>*Rainbow in the Sky*<br>*Die Forelle*<br>*Go Down, Moses* | A-5<br>B-11<br>B-35<br>C-20<br>G-10 | 1-7<br>2-16<br>4-21<br>6-20<br>11-25 |
| **Lesson 5**<br>Pattern | *Black Suits Comin'*<br>Shortnin' Bread<br>Rhythm Basics<br>More Meter and Rhythm<br>Certainly, Lord | A-5<br>F-27<br>H-2<br>H-4<br>I-13 | 1-6<br>11-12<br><br><br>13-12 |
| **Lesson 6**<br>Unity | Lift Up Thy Voice and Sing (Johnson) | I-12 | |
| **Lesson 7**<br>Variety | Dynamics<br>Andante from Ten Little Ostinato Pieces and Variations | H-10<br>I-62 | |
| **Unit 3  Art Media and Techniques** | | | |
| **Lesson 2**<br>Painting | 14th Century Italian painting: a monk transcribing music<br>Court Ball | A-22<br>C-6 | |
| **Lesson 6**<br>Sculpture | Sun Seeks Shadow (White) | D-29 | |
| **Lesson 7**<br>Architecture | Arts Connection | B-12 | |
| **Lesson 9**<br>Photography and Videography | Beyond Categories<br>*Fingerprints*<br>*Spain*<br>*Cafe Europa*<br>Arts Connection | B-42<br>B-42<br>B-42<br>B-43<br>D-11 | <br>5-10<br>5-11<br>5-12 |
| **Lesson 10**<br>Computer Art | Alleluia, Amen<br>*Fingerprints*<br>Flip, Flop and Fly<br>I'm a Believer<br>Cielito lindo | A-12<br>B-42<br>F-15<br>G-33<br>I-20 | 1-9<br>5-10<br>11-2<br>12-23<br>13-18 |

Art Correlations

| Themes | Selections | Page | CD Track |
|---|---|---|---|
| **Unit 4 The Creative Process** | | | |
| **Lesson 2**<br>People as Subjects | 14th Century Italian painting: a monk transcribing music<br>Court Ball<br>Hungarian painting of Zoltán Kodaly (Unknown artist)<br>The Fiddler<br>The Fiddler on the Roof<br>Lift Up Thy Voice and Sing (Johnson) | A-22<br>C-6<br>C-34<br>E-6<br>E-5<br>I-12 | 9-19 |
| **Lesson 4**<br>Subjects in Still Life | Court Ball<br>Schubert at the Piano (Schwind) | C-6<br>C-20 | |
| **Lesson 5**<br>Animals as Subjects | Bear Dance | I-10 | 13-11 |
| **Lesson 6**<br>Landscapes as Subjects | Into Bondage (Douglas)<br>America, the Beautiful | G-11<br>I-4 | 13-3 |
| **Lesson 7**<br>Seascapes as Subjects | Regatta at Argenteuil (Monet)<br>A View of the Bombardment of Fort McHenry (Bower) | C-38<br>I-57 | |
| **Lesson 8**<br>Cityscapes as Subjects | Arts Connection | B-12 | |
| **Unit 5 Styles in Art History** | | | |
| **Lesson 1**<br>Prehistoric Styles | Sonata in G Minor, Op. 1, No. 1<br>Allegro<br>Sonata for Clarinet and Piano<br>Sonatina for Bassoon and Piano<br>Bacchus from Six Metamorphoses After Ovid, Op. 49 | C-12<br>C-12<br>C-12<br>C-13<br>C-13 | 6-7<br>6-8<br>6-9<br>6-10<br>6-11 |
| **Lesson 5**<br>The Roman Style | O Ignis spiritus Paracliti<br>Alle psallite cum luya | C-4<br>C-5 | 5-26<br>5-27 |
| **Lesson 6**<br>The Medieval Style | O ignis spiritus Paracliti<br>Alle psallite cum luya<br>Abbots Bromley Horn Dance | C-4<br>C-5<br>C-24 | 5-26<br>5-27<br>7-5 |
| **Lesson 7**<br>The Renaissance | Saltarello ditto Trivella<br>Procession of Notre Dame de Salon (Alsloot)<br>Branle Double, Branle Simple | C-6<br>C-7<br>C-25 | 5-31<br><br>7-7 |
| **Lesson 9**<br>Eastern Art Styles | Nanafushi<br>Bucket O'Taiko Ensemble<br>Ichi-gatsu tsuitachi | D-16<br>D-17<br>I-40 | <br><br>13-31 |
| **Lesson 10**<br>Modern Art Styles | Carry On<br>Manteca<br>Forever, for Now<br>Soulville<br>Waitin' for a Train<br>Heads Carolina, Tails Carolina<br>Keep a Cool Head<br>Rainbow in the Sky<br>Joy<br>Can't Take My Joy<br>Wichita Lineman<br>If These Walls Could Speak | B-2<br>B-3<br>B-16<br>B-17<br>B-24<br>B-25<br>B-34<br>B-35<br>B-40<br>B-40<br>B-41<br>B-41 | 2-1<br>2-2<br>3-1<br>3-2<br>3-9<br>3-10<br>4-20<br>4-21<br>5-6<br>5-7<br>5-8<br>5-9 |

Art Correlations

| Themes | Selections | Page | CD Track |
|---|---|---|---|
| **Unit 6  Careers in Art** | | | |
| **Lesson 2** <br> Cartoonist | Caricature of Liszt (Brennglass) | E-18 | |
| **Lesson 8** <br> Art Teacher | Alleluia, Amen | A-12 | 1-9 |

# Grade 8

| Themes | Selections | Page | CD Track |
|---|---|---|---|
| **Unit 1  The Elements of Art** | | | |
| **Lesson 1** <br> Line | Analyzing <br> The Twittering Machine (Klee) <br> *California Counterpoint: The Twittering Machine* <br> African Art <br> Meeting Individual Needs <br> *Crunchy, Crunchy, Crunchy* <br> Tapestry (Roy) | C-47 <br> C-47 <br> C-47 <br> D-8 <br> D-14 <br> D-14 <br> D-28 | 8-4 <br><br> 8-19 |
| **Lesson 2** <br> Shape | Analyzing <br> The Twittering Machine (Klee) <br> *California Counterpoint: The Twittering Machine* | C-47 <br> C-47 <br> C-47 | 8-4 |
| **Lesson 3** <br> Form | From Tuba to Sousaphone <br> Careers: Richard Cooke <br> On Your Own <br> Tapestry (Roy) <br> Flamingo (Calder) | C-41 <br> D-17 <br> D-17 <br> D-28 <br> F-12 | |
| **Lesson 4** <br> Space | Drones and Scales <br> *Planet Drone* <br><br><br><br> *Singing Scales* <br><br><br> Skills Reinforcement <br> *Tarantella* <br> *Allegro* | B-10 <br> B-10 <br><br><br><br> B-11 <br><br><br> C-46 <br> C-46 <br> C-46 | <br> 2-25, 2-26, 2-27, 2-28 <br> 2-29, 2-30, 2-31, 2-32 <br> 8-1 <br> 8-2 |
| **Lesson 7** <br> Color | Analyzing <br> The Twittering Machine (Klee) <br> *California Counterpoint: The Twittering Machine* <br> Across the Curriculum <br> *Samanfo, begye nsa nom* <br> Highlife Ensemble <br> Agbekor Ewe Ensemble <br> Kente cloth | C-47 <br> C-47 <br> C-47 <br> D-9 <br> D-6 <br> D-7 <br> D-10 <br> D-12 | 8-4 <br><br> 8-15 |
| **Lesson 8** <br> Color Schemes | Mood Music | A-6 <br> A-7 | |

| Themes | Selections | Page | CD Track |
|---|---|---|---|
| **Lesson 9**<br>Texture | Introduce | C-4 | |
| | Skills Reinforcement: Analyzing | C-8 | |
| | *Hallelujah!* | C-8 | 5-5 |
| | Close | C-35 | |
| | *Suite for Wind Quintet, Movement 1* | C-34 | 7-2 |
| | Spotlight On | D-13 | |
| | *Adzogbo-Ovitse* | D-13 | 8-17 |
| **Unit 2  The Principles of Design** | | | |
| **Lesson 1**<br>Balance | Skills Reinforcement: Creating | C-36 | |
| | Analyzing | C-47 | |
| | The Twittering Machine (Klee) | C-47 | |
| | *California Counterpoint: The Twittering Machine* | C-47 | 8-4 |
| | Close | C-47 | |
| | Tapestry (Roy) | D-28 | |
| | Wood Works Ensemble | D-28 | |
| | Writing a Song: Form and Balance | F-33 | |
| **Lesson 2**<br>Emphasis | Analyzing | C-47 | |
| | The Twittering Machine (Klee) | C-47 | |
| | *California Counterpoint: The Twittering Machine* | C-47 | 8-4 |
| | Singing Tips | G-14 | |
| | Skills Reinforcement | G-15 | |
| | Take a Chance on Me | G-15 | 12-1 |
| | Teacher to Teacher (Word Accents) | G-28 | |
| | Book of Love | G-27 | 12-9 |
| **Lesson 3**<br>Proportion | Flamingo (Calder) | F-12 | |
| **Lesson 4**<br>Rhythm | *Main Titles from Edward Scissorhands* | A-10 | 1-3 |
| | Edward Scissorhands Listening Map | A-10 | |
| | *Ostinatos Around the World* | B-4 | 2-4, 2-5, 2-6 |
| | *Faerie Stories* | B-5 | 2-7 |
| | Skills Reinforcement | B-20 | |
| | *Tommy Peoples* | B-20 | 3-2 |
| | *Toei khong* | B-21 | 3-4 |
| | *Saqian da dhol* | B-22 | 3-5 |
| | *Baila caporal* | B-22 | 3-6 |
| | Cultural Connection | B-29 | |
| | *Badenma (Friendship)* | B-28 | 3-15 |
| | Spotlight On | B-31 | |
| | *Tabla Solo* | B-32 | 3-27 |
| | Close | C-35 | |
| | *Suite for Wind Quintet, Movement 1* | C-34 | 7-2 |
| | Building Skills Through Music | D-10 | |
| | Agbekor Ensemble | D-10 | |
| | Rhythm Fundamentals | H-2 | |

Art Correlations

| Themes | Selections | Page | CD Track |
|---|---|---|---|
| **Lesson 5** <br> Pattern | Edward Scissorhands Listening Map | A-10 | |
| | *Main Titles from Edward Scissorhands* | A-10 | 1-3 |
| | Movement (Patterned Movement) | B-18 | |
| | *Retounen* | B-17 | 2-51 |
| | Building Skills Through Music | B-30 | |
| | *Symphony No. 40 in G Minor, K. 550* | B-30 | 3-18 |
| | African Art, D-8 | D-8 | |
| | Across the Curriculum | D-9 | |
| | *Samanfo, begye nsa nom* | D-6 | |
| | Highlife Ensemble | D-7 | |
| | Agbekor Ewe Ensemble | D-10 | |
| | Building Skills Through Music | D-10 | |
| | Kente cloth | D-12 | |
| | Spotlight On | D-13 | |
| | Tapestry (Roy) | D-28 | |
| | Wood Works Ensemble | D-28 | |
| **Lesson 6** <br> Unity | Analyzing | C-47 | |
| | The Twittering Machine (Klee) | C-47 | |
| | *California Counterpoint: The Twittering Machine* | C-47 | 8-4 |
| | Kente Cloth | D-12 | |
| | Writing a Song: Form and Balance | F-33 | |
| **Lesson 7** <br> Variety | Analyzing | C-47 | |
| | The Twittering Machine (Klee) | C-47 | |
| | *California Counterpoint: The Twittering Machine* | C-47 | 8-4 |
| | Listening | D-27 | |
| | Huagu ge | D-27 | 9-4 |
| | Writing a Song: Form and Balance | F-33 | |
| **Unit 3 Art Media and Techniques** | | | |
| **Lesson 1** <br> Drawing | Spotlight On | C-26 | |
| | Soleil levant (Monet) | C-26 | |
| | *Doctor Gradus ad Parnassum* | C-27 | 6-18 |
| | *Dialogue du vent et de me* | C-27 | 6-19 |
| | *Prelude from Le tombeau de Couperin* | C-28 | 6-20 |
| | Meeting Individual Needs, D-14 | D-14 | |
| | *Crunchy, Crunchy, Crunchy* | D-14 | 8-19 |
| | Across the Curriculum | E-12 | |
| **Lesson 2** <br> Painting | The French Connection | C-26 | |
| | Spotlight On | C-26 | |
| | Soleil levant (Monet) | C-26 | |
| | *Doctor Gradus ad Parnassum* | C-27 | |
| | *Dialogue du vent et de mer* | C-27 | |
| | Jeunes filles au piano (Renoir) | C-27 | |
| | *Prelude from Le tombeau de Couperin* | C-28 | |
| **Lesson 3** <br> Printmaking | African Art | D-8 | |

Art Correlations

| Themes | Selections | Page | CD Track |
|---|---|---|---|
| **Lesson 5** Textiles and Fibers | Spotlight On | D-7 | |
| | African Art | D-8 | |
| | Mensu | D-6 | 8-14 |
| | Samanfo, begye nsa nom | D-6 | 8-15 |
| | Highlife Ensemble | D-7 | |
| | Across the Curriculum | D-9 | |
| | Agbekor Ensemble | D-12 | |
| | Spotlight On, D-13 | D-13 | |
| | Brazilian Percussion | D-24 | |
| | Sai da frente | D-24 | 9-1 |
| | Talaque talaque o romance da María | D-24 | 9-2 |
| **Lesson 6** Sculpture | Great Instrument Makers | A-28, A-29 | |
| | Careers: Paul McGill | A-28 | |
| | *Linus and Lucy* | A-29 | 1-20 |
| | Across the Curriculum | B-8 | |
| | Across the Curriculum | D-4 | |
| | *Ue ue* | D-2 | 8-12 |
| | Bora Bora Boom Ensemble | D-3 | |
| | *Udu Pot* | D-4 | 8-12 |
| | Meeting Individual Needs | D-14 | |
| | *Crunchy, Crunchy, Crunchy* | D-14 | 8-19 |
| | Careers: Richard Cooke | D-17 | |
| | *Flight of the Ibis* | D-16 | 8-21 |
| | On Your Own | D-17 | |
| | Tapestry (Roy) | D-28 | |
| | Wood Works Ensemble | D-28 | |
| | Music Makers: Harry Partch | D-29 | |
| | *Daphne of the Dunes* | D-29 | 9-5 |
| | Across the Curriculum | D-32 | |
| | *The Rippa Medley* | D-32 | 9-6 |
| | Flamingo (Calder) | F-12 | |
| **Lesson 7** Architecture | Chicago, Illinois (photograph) | I-5 | |
| **Lesson 8** Ceramics and Pottery | Across the Curriculum | D-4 | |
| | *Ue ue* | D-2 | 8-12 |
| | Bora Bora Boom Ensemble | D-3 | |
| | *Udu Pot* | D-4 | 8-12 |
| | Clay Gourd Music | D-4 | |
| | Careers: Frank Giorgini | D-5 | |
| **Lesson 10** Computer Art | Multimedia Music | A-2 | |
| | *Themes from the 7th Guest* | A-2 | 1-1 |

| Themes | Selections | Page | CD Track |
|---|---|---|---|
| **Unit 4  The Creative Process** | | | |
| **Lesson 3**<br>People Living and Working | Celebrate! | B-16 | |
| | Across the Curriculum | C-38 | |
| | A Night on the Town | E-10 | |
| | *Goog Golly, Miss Molly* | E-10 | 9-14 |
| | *The Queen's Suite: Sunset and the Mockingbird* | E-10 | 9-15 |
| | *Piano Concerto in A Minor* | E-11 | 9-16 |
| | Across the Curriculum | E-11 | |
| | Woman in Black at the Opera (Cassatt) | E-12 | |
| | Tuxedo Junction | G-21 | 12-4 |
| | I'll Fly Away | I-42 | 14-16 |
| | *I'll Fly Away* | I-43 | 14-18 |
| **Unit 5  Art Through the Ages** | | | |
| **Lesson 1**<br>Prehistoric Beginnings | Cultural Connection | B-39 | |
| | *Gapu* | B-38 | 4-1 |
| | Building Skills Through Music | C-14 | |
| | Brass Fever | C-14 | |
| | *Rwakanembe* | C-14 | 5-14 |
| | *Galliard Battaglia* | C-14 | 5-14 |
| | *Minuetto* | C-15 | 5-16 |
| | *Sensemaya* | C-15 | 5-17 |
| **Lesson 2**<br>Ancient Egypt | A Grand Scene | C-24 | |
| | Grand March "Gloria all 'egitto" | C-24 | 6-16 |
| **Lesson 3**<br>Ancient Greece | Greece | B-21 | |
| | *Stalia, Stalia* | B-21 | 3-3 |
| | Cultural Connection, B-36 | B-36 | |
| | Cultural Connection, C-17 | C-17 | |
| **Lesson 4**<br>Ancient Rome | Cultural Connection | C-17 | |
| | *Symphony No. 3  in E-flat Major, Movement 1* | C-17 | 5-18 |
| | *Symphony No. 3 in E-flat Major, Movement 2* | C-17 | 5-19 |
| **Lesson 5**<br>Art of the Middle Ages | Oldies But Goodies | C-4 | |
| | Wooden Midieval kite shield | C-4 | |
| | *Ahi! Amours* | C-4 | 4-30 |
| | *O tocius Asie* | C-4 | 4-31 |
| | Cultural Connection | C-4 | |
| | What About Instruments? | C-6 | |
| | *Domna, pos vos ay chausida* | C-6 | 5-1 |
| | *La tierce estampie real* | C-6 | 5-2 |
| | *Ronde* | C-7 | 5-3 |
| | *Canzon in Echo Duodecimi Toni a 10* | C-7 | 5-4 |
| | Estampie ??? no listenings | I-26 | |
| | Cultural Connection | I-26 | |

| Themes | Selections | Page | CD Track |
|---|---|---|---|
| **Lesson 6**<br>*The Renaissance* | *Ombrose e care selve* | C-5 | 4-32 |
| | *Ronde* | C-7 | 5-3 |
| | *Canzon in Echo Duodecimi Toni a 10* | C-7 | 5-4 |
| | Across the Curriculum | C-7 | |
| | Teacher to Teacher | C-7 | |
| | *Galliard Battaglia* | C-14 | 5-15 |
| **Lesson 7**<br>Art of the Americas | World Percussion Sounds | B-6 | 2-8,<br>2-9,<br>2-10,<br>2-11 |
| | Listening/Describing | B-7 | |
| | *Carnaval* in Brazil | B-16 | |
| | *Malê Debalê* | B-16 | 2-50 |
| | *Carnaval* in Columbia | B-17 | |
| | *El nuevo caiman* | B-17 | 2-52 |
| | Border Music | B-24 | |
| | *A mi querido Austin* | B-24 | 3-10 |
| | Viva Latin American Music! | C-36 | |
| | *Interview with Carlos Chavez* | C-37 | 7-5 |
| | *Xochipilli* | C-37 | 7-6 |
| | Cultural Connection | C-37 | |
| | Cultural Connection | D-16 | |
| | *Swan Miguel Jolonicapan* | D-16 | 8-20 |
| | *Canto del agua* | I-10 | 13-7 |
| | *Luna hermosa* | I-13 | 13-12 |

Art Correlations

# Reading Correlations

Silver Burdett MAKING MUSIC ©2005
Correlated to Scott Foresman Reading ©2000

| Scott Foresman Reading | Silver Burdett Making Music | | |
|---|---|---|---|
| Themes | Selections | Page | CD Track |
| **Kindergarten** | | | |
| **Volume 1—Getting to Know Us** | | | |
| **LOOK AT ME NOW** (Where do we grow from here?) | That's What's New with Me! | 2 | 1-1 |
| | Hello, There! | 6 | 1-6 |
| | Copycat | 9 | 1-9 |
| | Ayii, Ayii, Ayii (poem) | 11 | |
| | I'm Tall, I'm Small | 18 | 1-26 |
| | My Shadow (poem) | 19 | |
| | Sing a Little Song | 30 | 2-1 |
| | Mary Wore Her Red Dress | 74 | 3-6 |
| | A Good Old Happy Song | 201 | 7-12 |
| | Everything Grows (poem) | 267 | 9-17 |
| | I'm Curious | 276 | 9-31 |
| | Oh, What a Day! | 302 | 10-27 |
| **MEET FAMILY AND FRIENDS** (Who are the people we love?) | What to Do (poem) | 43 | |
| | Rig-a-Jig-Jig | 99 | 3-55 |
| | Teddy Bears (poem) | 163 | |
| | A la rurru niño (Hush, My Little Baby) | 180 | 6-33 |
| | Going on a Picnic | 190 | 7-1 |
| | Nightdance (poem) | 219 | |
| | It Rains and It Pours (poem) | 243 | |
| | Birthday, Birthday, Birthday (poem) | 306 | |
| | El dia de mamita (Mommy's Day) | 325 | 11-29 |
| **Volume 2—A World of Wonders** | | | |
| **CLAWS, PAWS, FINS, AND FEATHERS** (Can a lion and a mouse be friends?) | Three Little Pigs | 21 | 1-28 |
| | Grizzly Bear | 33 | 2-3 |
| | The Kangaroo Song | 44 | 2-18 |
| | The Kangaroo (poem) | 45 | |
| | Goldilocks and the Three Bears (story) | 49 | 2-24 |
| | The Bumble Bee (speech piece) | 74 | |
| | Busy Buzzy Bee | 77 | 3-8 |
| | Things That Sing (poem) | 87 | |
| | Little Spider | 93 | 3-44 |
| | The Up and Down Kitten (poem) | 100 | |
| | Fuzzy Caterpillar | 102 | 4-2 |
| | The Caterpillar (poem) | 103 | |
| | Bam, Chi, Chi, Bam | 109 | 4-13 |
| | Old Blue | 122 | 4-35 |
| | Dogs (poem) | 123 | |

| Themes | Selections | Page | CD Track |
|---|---|---|---|
| (continued) | Bear Dance | 127 | 5-1 |
| | Mister Rabbit | 128 | 5-4 |
| | The Squirrel (poem) | 129 | |
| | El Caracol (The Snail's Dance) | 130 | 5-6 |
| | Ee jer ha ba go (The Hungry Dog) | 133 | 5-10 |
| | Down in the Meadow | 147 | 5-29 |
| | On a Log, Mister Frog | 148 | 5-31 |
| | Frog Lullaby (poem) | 149 | |
| | Los pollitos (Baby Chicks) | 166 | 6-12 |
| | Baby Chick (poem) | 167 | |
| | A Bitter Morning (poem) | 177 | |
| | Kaeru no uta (The Frog Song) | 183 | 6-40 |
| | Going to the Zoo | 216 | 7-36 |
| | Let's Pretend | 227 | 8-4 |
| | "Quack!" Said the Billy Goat (poem) | 233 | |
| | Six Little Ducks | 234 | 8-16 |
| | Ducks in the Rain (poem) | 235 | |
| | Cuculí | 238 | 8-23 |
| | The Bird's Nest (poem) | 239 | |
| | Sounds of the Circus | 241 | 8-25 |
| | Woodland Chorus | 250 | 8-38 |
| | I Have a Dog | 262 | 9-10 |
| | Min (poem) | 263 | |
| | Perná, perná, I mélissá (The Bee Flies By) | 264 | 9-13 |
| | What Do You Suppose? (poem) | 265 | |
| | Sh'ney dubim (Two Bears) | 268 | 9-19 |
| | Let's Go on a Bear Hunt (poem) | 269 | |
| | El burrito enfermo (The Sick Little Donkey) | 271 | 9-23 |
| | Baby Beluga | 272 | 9-28 |
| | Noah's Zoo in the Big, Big Rain | 274 | 9-30 |
| | The Animals Went In One by One (poem) | 275 | |
| | Alison's Camel | 289 | 10-11 |
| | Ten Little Teddy Bears (poem) | 301 | |
| **OUR BIG BACKYARD** (Why is the sky blue?) | Seasons | 4 | 1-4 |
| | What to Do (poem) | 43 | |
| | ¡Que llueva! (It's Raining) | 81 | 3-15 |
| | The Caterpillar (poem) | 103 | |
| | Spring Has Sprung! | 142 | 5-24 |
| | The Dancing Tree | 203 | 7-14 |
| | Take Your Feet Out 'the Sand | 231 | 8-11 |
| | Ducks in the Rain (poem) | 235 | |
| | The Bird's Nest (poem) | 239 | |
| | Mary Ann | 253 | 8-40 |
| | Clouds | 254 | 9-1 |
| | Clouds (poem) | 255 | |
| | Big Old Storm a-Comin' | 257 | 9-4 |
| | First Snowflake (poem) | 259 | 9-7 |
| | The More It Snows (poem) | 259 | |
| | Grand Canyon Suite, Cloudburst | 260 | 9-9 |
| | Rain Sizes (poem) | 261 | |
| | What Do You Suppose? (poem) | 265 | |
| | Everything Grows | 267 | 9-17 |
| | I Like Fall (poem) | 311 | |

Reading Correlations

| Themes | Selections | Page | CD Track |
|---|---|---|---|
| **Volume 3—So Much to Do!** | | | |
| **FINDING OUR WAY** <br> (Where do I fit in?) | Manhattan Lullaby (poem) <br> ¿Dónde lo escondí? (Where Did I Hide It?) <br> London Bridge <br> Upside Down and Inside Out (poem) | 193 <br> 209 <br> 244 <br> 297 | 7-5 <br> 7-21 <br> 8-29 |
| **BUSY PEOPLE** <br> (Where is everybody going?) | Locomoto-vation <br> Goin' to the Fair <br> Going on a Picnic <br> Going to the Zoo | 61 <br> 156 <br> 190 <br> 216 | 2-43 <br> 5-45 <br> 7-1 <br> 7-36 |
| **Volume 4—Every Day Is Special** | | | |
| **ALL TOGETHER** <br> (Why is it better being together?) | That's What's New with Me! <br> Dinner Music <br> Rig-a-Jig-Jig <br> Sharing <br> A Good Old Happy Song <br> Jump for Joy <br> My Valentine | 2 <br> 70 <br> 99 <br> 198 <br> 201 <br> 213 <br> 323 | 1-1 <br> 3-1 <br> 3-55 <br> 7-10 <br> 7-12 <br> 7-29 <br> 11-27 |
| **ONCE UPON A TIME** <br> (What do stories tell us about us?) | Three Little Pigs <br> Goldilocks and the Three Bears (story) <br> Teddy Bears (poem) <br> Hearts Like Doors (poem) | 21 <br> 49 <br> 163 <br> 189 | 1-28 <br> 2-24 |
| **Volume 5—Off We Go!** | | | |
| **LET'S GO** <br> How do we get from here to there?) | Los trencitos (Little Trains) <br> Locomoto-vation <br> The Bus <br> Get on Board <br> Little Red Wagon <br> Little Red Caboose | 24 <br> 61 <br> 82 <br> 89 <br> 152 <br> 229 | 1-34 <br> 2-43 <br> 3-20 <br> 3-33 <br> 5-38 <br> 8-8 |
| **HOW THINGS WORK** <br> (What makes it go?) | A New Way to Walk <br> Song of the Train (poem) <br> Cookie Magic (poem) | 117 <br> 153 <br> 197 | 4-28 <br> 5-40 |
| **Volume 6—Open the Doors** | | | |
| **IMAGINE THAT!** <br> (How do we use our thinking caps?) | A Circle of Sun (poem) <br> My Shadow (poem) <br> Mister Rabbit <br> Little Snail (poem) <br> Singin' in the Tub <br> Let's Pretend <br> Hey, Diddle, Diddle <br> At the Top of My Voice (poem) <br> Noises (poem) <br> I'm a Dreydl | 3 <br> 19 <br> 128 <br> 131 <br> 220 <br> 227 <br> 246 <br> 279 <br> 303 <br> 315 | <br> <br> 5-4 <br> <br> 7-40 <br> 8-4 <br> 8-33 <br> <br> <br> 11-14 |

| Themes | Selections | Page | CD Track |
|---|---|---|---|
| **THAT'S FUNNY**<br>(What makes us giggle?) | Let's Do the Flip-Flop Frolic! (poem) | 23 | |
| | If You're Happy | 94 | 3-47 |
| | Shake-'n'-Bake a Jelly (poem) | 95 | 3-49 |
| | Pick 'n' Mix Zoo (poem) | 139 | |
| | Bubble Trouble (poem) | 184 | 6-44 |
| | Jump Rope Jingle (poem) | 211 | |
| | Silly Street | 224 | 8-1 |
| | Old Mother Goose (poem) | 247 | |
| | The Animals Went In One by One (poem) | 275 | |
| | Willoughby, Wallaby, Woo | 282 | 10-1 |
| | Hokey Pokey | 296 | 10-19 |
| | Upside Down and Inside Out (poem) | 297 | |

# Grade 1

| | | | |
|---|---|---|---|
| **Volume 1—Good Times We Share** | | | |
| **GOOD TIMES WE SHARE**<br>(How are our families and friends special?) | Let the Music Begin! | 2 | 1-1 |
| | Vil Du? (Will You?) | 92 | 3-16 |
| | ¡Viva el fútbol! ( I Love Soccer) | 96 | 3-19 |
| | Families | 282 | 9-10 |
| | Our Family Comes from 'Round the World  (poem) | 299 | |
| | Friend of Mine | 310 | 9-46 |
| | Sidewalks (poem) | 311 | |
| | Celebrate! | 406 | 13-5 |
| | Chanukah, Chanukah | 420 | 13-24 |
| **Volume 2—Take a Closer Look** | | | |
| **TAKE A CLOSER LOOK**<br>(Look closely! Now what can we see?) | The Little Green Frog | 24 | 1-35 |
| | Frog (poem) | 25 | |
| | Jellyfish Walk (poem) | 33 | |
| | Stars (poem) | 61 | |
| | The Wind Blew East | 64 | 2-40 |
| | Cha yang wu (Rice Planting Song) | 90 | 3-5 |
| | Alle meine Entchen (All My Little Ducklings) | 98 | 3-24 |
| | Ducks (poem) | 99 | |
| | Gato (poem) | 131 | |
| | Why the Wart Hog… (story) | 139 | |
| | Hato Popo | 186 | 6-13 |
| | Ptashky u babusi sadochku | 192 | 6-24 |
| | The Lion and the Mouse (story) | 239 | |
| | Rags | 290 | 9-17 |
| | Los maizales (The Cornfields) | 296 | 9-24 |
| | The Earth Is My Mother | 340 | 10-35 |
| | I Look at the World (poem) | 341 | |
| | Noah's Shanty | 344 | 11-1 |
| | Beach Rap (speech piece) | 354 | 11-9 |

| Themes | Selections | Page | CD Track |
|---|---|---|---|
| **Volume 3—Let's Learn Together** | | | |
| **LET'S LEARN TOGETHER**<br>(What can we learn when we all work together?) | Let the Music Begin!<br>We're Making Popcorn<br>*The Little Red Hen (story)*<br>The Honeybee Song<br>Ujima<br>*Ev'rybody Ought to Know* | 2<br>86<br>255<br>358<br>430<br>435 | 1-1<br>3-1<br>8-12<br>11-19<br>13-46<br>14-8 |
| **Volume 4—Favorite Things Old and New** | | | |
| **FAVORITE THINGS OLD AND NEW**<br>(How do things get to be favorites?) | Children of Long Ago (poem)<br>Freight Train<br>A Drum (story)<br>If You Find a Little Feather (poem)<br>Blum (poem) | 31<br>46<br>116<br>187<br>221 | 2-15 |
| **Volume 5—Take Me There** | | | |
| **TAKE ME THERE**<br>(Where will we go? How will we grow?) | A Different Beat<br>Sing! Speak! Whisper! Shout!<br>I Can't Spell Hippopotamus<br>Put Your Hand in My Hand<br>Someday Very Soon<br>Me voy para la luna (I'm Going to the Moon) | 6<br>36<br>266<br>332<br>376<br>397 | 1-8<br>1-57<br>8-30<br>10-26<br>12-5<br>12-29 |
| **Volume 6—Surprise Me!** | | | |
| **SURPRISE ME!**<br>(How do we get all those great ideas?) | A Different Beat<br>School Bus Rap (poem)<br>The Rain Sings a Song<br>Little David | 6<br>83<br>102<br>232 | 1-8<br><br>3-31<br>7-28 |
| # Grade 2 | | | |
| **Volume 1—New Beginnings** | | | |
| **YOU + ME = SPECIAL**<br>(What makes us all special?) | Let the Music Begin!<br>Vil Du? (Will You?)<br>¡Viva el fútbol! ( I Love Soccer)<br>Families<br>Our Family Comes from 'Round the World  (poem)<br>Friend of Mine<br>Sidewalks (poem)<br>Celebrate!<br>Chanukah, Chanukah | 2<br>92<br>96<br>282<br>299<br>310<br>311<br>406<br>420 | 1-1<br>3-16<br>3-19<br>9-10<br><br>9-46<br><br>13-5<br>13-24 |

Reading Correlations

| Themes | Selections | Page | CD Track |
|---|---|---|---|
| **ZOOM IN!** <br> (What can we learn from looking at the world around us?) | Un pajarito (A Little Bird) <br> Clouds of Gray <br> What Do Animals Need? <br> El coquí (The Little Frog) <br> Listen to the Water <br> Rabbits (poem) <br> I Bought Me a Cat <br> The Rainbow <br> The Crocodile | 16 <br> 56 <br> 288 <br> 292 <br> 294 <br> 305 <br> 308 <br> 332 <br> 362 | 1-20 <br> 2-32 <br> 10-34 <br> 10-36 <br> 10-40 <br> <br> 11-17 <br> 12-6 <br> 13-19 |
| **SIDE BY SIDE** <br> (How can we learn and work well together?) | Gonna Have a Good Time <br> Michael, Row the Boat Ashore <br> Glad to Have a Friend Like You <br> Ciranda (A Ring of Roses) <br> Valentines | 4 <br> 18 <br> 228 <br> 272 <br> 398 | 1-1 <br> 1-24 <br> 8-16 <br> 10-1 <br> 14-42 |
| **Volume 2—My Time to Shine** | | | |
| **TIES THROUGH TIME** <br> (What things do we do together in the same special way?) | Time to Sing <br> It's a Celebration <br> Vamos a la fiesta (Let's Go to the Party) <br> Perot (Fruit) <br> Thanksgiving Is Near <br> Jingle Bells <br> A Kwanzaa Carol <br> Valentines <br> America | 8 <br> 372 <br> 374 <br> 378 <br> 380 <br> 388 <br> 392 <br> 398 <br> 403 | 1-5 <br> 13-30 <br> 14-1 <br> 14-9 <br> 14-13 <br> 14-30 <br> 14-36 <br> 14-42 <br> 15-11 |
| **ALL ABOARD!** <br> (What can we learn by traveling?) | Rocky Mountain <br> Banana <br> Same Train <br> All the Way Around the World <br> I'm Flying Home | 98 <br> 114 <br> 164 <br> 258 <br> 286 | 4-7 <br> 4-32 <br> 6-20 <br> 9-19 <br> 10-31 |
| **JUST IMAGINE!** <br> (How do we use our imaginations to do things?) | I See with My Hands <br> Dinosaur Dance <br> Who Has Seen the Wind? <br> Puff, the Magic Dragon <br> When I Grow Up (poem) | 148 <br> 168 <br> 324 <br> 350 <br> 397 | 5-47 <br> 6-24 <br> 11-33 <br> 12-28 <br> |

**Reading Correlations**

| Themes | Selections | Page | CD Track |
|---|---|---|---|
| **Grade 3** | | | |
| **Volume 1—Imagine That!** | | | |
| **FINDING MY PLACE** (How do friends and family help us grow?) | Hello to All the Children of the World | 4 | 1-1 |
| | *The Hippopotamus Song* | 33 | 1-55 |
| | Make New Friends | 36 | 2-1 |
| | Ahora voy a cantarles (Now Hear the Song) | 56 | 2-31 |
| | Family Tree | 72 | 2-53 |
| | Love Somebody | 94 | 3-31 |
| | Sing, America, Sing | 238 | 8-4 |
| | It's a Small World | 268 | 9-14 |
| | It's a Beautiful Day | 338 | 11-41 |
| | A Song of One | 344 | 12-3 |
| | We've Got Lots in Common | 366 | 12-25 |
| | Let's Celebrate | 374 | 13-7 |
| | Habari Gani | 404 | 14-24 |
| **THE WHOLE WIDE WORLD** (How can we learn about and care for the world?) | Never Smile at a Crocodile | 100 | 3-40 |
| | Kum bachur atzel (Hear the Rooster Crowing) | 138 | 5-1 |
| | Each of Us Is a Flower | 154 | 5-28 |
| | Erdö, erdö de magos (In the Silent Forest) | 182 | 6-27 |
| | Song of the Fishes | 244 | 8-11 |
| | Sarika keo (Bird Song) | 275 | 9-26 |
| | Shu ha mo (Frogs) | 276 | 9-30 |
| | Big Beautiful Planet | 326 | 11-23 |
| | El sapito (The Little Toad) | 336 | 11-37 |
| | It's a Beautiful Day | 338 | 11-41 |
| | Look Out for Mother Earth | 341 | 11-43 |
| | The World We Love | 342 | 12-1 |
| **GETTING THE JOB DONE** (How can we learn from everything we do?) | The Loco-Motion | 64 | 2-40 |
| | Together (poem) | 147 | |
| | Good Morning | 192 | 7-1 |
| | Sweet Potatoes | 228 | 7-53 |
| | Bling Blang | 240 | 8-6 |
| **Volume 2—Picture This!** | | | |
| **FROM PAST TO PRESENT** (How traditions affect our lives today) | Great Day | 58 | 2-35 |
| | The Groundhog Blues | 122 | 4-29 |
| | Do, Lord | 164 | 6-1 |
| | Hashkediya (Tu b'Shvat Is Here) | 206 | 7-17 |
| | You're a Grand Old Flag | 264 | 9-8 |
| | A Song of Greatness (poem) | 335 | |
| | Sing Your Story | 350 | 12-6 |
| | Chanukah Games | 389 | 13-24 |
| **ARE WE THERE YET?** (How can visits to other times and places make our lives better?) | Family Tree | 72 | 2-53 |
| | Walk Together, Children | 146 | 5-17 |
| | Mübarak (Happy Birthday) | 282 | 9-40 |
| | Artsa alina (Come to the Land) | 285 | 10-1 |

Reading Correlations

| Themes | Selections | Page | CD Track |
|---|---|---|---|
| **IMAGINATION.KIDS** (How many ways can we use our imaginations?) | Black Snake | 53 | 2-21 |
| | Let's Get the Rhythm of the Band | 84 | 3-16 |
| | Never Smile at a Crocodile | 100 | 3-40 |
| | ¡Qué gusto! (What Pleasure) | 132 | 4-45 |
| | Waltzing with Bears | 170 | 6-14 |
| | He's Got the Whole World in His Hands | 230 | 7-56 |
| | Don Gato | 352 | 12-8 |
| | If a Tiger Calls | 354 | 12-12 |

# Grade 4

## Volume 1—Seeing Is Believing

| Themes | Selections | Page | CD Track |
|---|---|---|---|
| **FOCUS ON FAMILY** (Who helps us find our talents, abilities, and dreams?) | T'hola, t'hola (Softly, Softly) | 132 | 6-7 |
| | Cumberland Gap | 138 | 6-22 |
| | Canción de Cuna (Song of the Cuna) | 144 | 6-31 |
| | Thula, thula, ngoana (Sleep, Sleep, Baby) | 227 | 9-27 |
| | Sailing Down My Golden River | 332 | 14-12 |
| **A WIDER VIEW** (What place do plants and animals have in the world around us?) | Gakavik (The Partridge) | 14 | 1-17 |
| | River | 58 | 3-18 |
| | Enjoy the Earth (poem) | 81 | |
| | Ochimbo | 134 | 6-11 |
| | Doraji (Blue Bells) | 174 | 7-36 |
| | Kookaburra | 186 | 8-19 |
| | Frog Music | 200 | 8-45 |
| | Pastures of Plenty | 280 | 11-25 |
| | The Birch Tree | 294 | 12-20 |
| | Sakura | 308 | 13-13 |
| | Prayer for Earth (poem) | 350 | |
| | This Pretty Planet | 355 | 15-16 |
| | For the Beauty of the Earth | 356 | 15-18 |
| | The Earth Is Our Mother | 358 | 15-22 |
| **KEYS TO SUCCESS** (How do learning and working lead to success?) | See the Children Playin' | 107 | 5-22 |
| | Yibane Amenu | 316 | 13-29 |
| | We Shall Overcome | 326 | 14-5 |
| | Love Will Guide Us | 328 | 14-8 |
| | Shake the Papaya Down | 378 | 16-18 |
| | La copa de la vida (The Cup of Life) | 414 | 17-20 |
| | Shir L'Shalom (Hand In Hand—A Song for Peace) | 419 | 17-23 |

## Volume 2—Seeing Is Believing

| Themes | Selections | Page | CD Track |
|---|---|---|---|
| **TIMELESS STORIES** (How do stories from the past help us live in the present?) | Soldier, Soldier | 11 | 1-7 |
| | Haul Away, Joe | 13 | 1-15 |
| | Oh, Danny Boy | 48 | 2-30 |
| | Rock Island Line | 54 | 3-9 |
| | Sweet Betsy from Pike | 244 | 10-16 |
| | The Glendy Burke | 262 | 11-1 |
| | Streets of Laredo | 272 | 11-14 |
| | Clementine | 341 | 15-1 |
| | Little David, Play on Your Harp | 394 | 17-4 |
| | Dayenu (It Would Have Been Enough) | 439 | 19-1 |

| Themes | Selections | Page | CD Track |
|---|---|---|---|
| **OTHER TIMES, OTHER PLACES** (What can we learn from reading about times and places we've never been?) | Tsuki (The Moon)<br>Over the Rainbow<br>Blow, Ye Winds<br>Route 66<br>The Bard of Armagh<br>Love Can Build a Bridge | 25<br>140<br>255<br>276<br>296<br>324 | 1-36<br>6-27<br>10-25<br>11-21<br>12-24<br>14-3 |
| **EXPRESS YOURSELF!** (How many forms can creativity take?) | Cantando mentiras (Singing Tall Tales)<br>Big Rock Candy Mountain<br>Sailboat in the Sky | 146<br>330<br>374 | 6-38<br>14-10<br>16-11 |

# Grade 5

## Volume 1—Fantastic Voyage

| Themes | Selections | Page | CD Track |
|---|---|---|---|
| **RELATING TO OTHERS** (What are the important things in life?) | Funwa Alafia (Welcome, My Friends)<br>Stand By Me<br>One Small Step<br>If I Had a Hammer<br>Love Is on Our Side<br>You've Got a Friend<br>Somewhere Out There<br>Children Learn What They Live (poem)<br>A World of Difference | 32<br>46<br>126<br>287<br>324<br>366<br>368<br>381<br>386 | 2-19<br>3-1<br>6-18<br>13-13<br>15-9<br>17-2<br>17-4<br>17-18<br>18-2 |
| **MY WORLD AND YOURS** (How do we show that we care about our surroundings?) | I Love the Mountains<br>Home on the Range<br>Live in the City<br>De colores<br>The Ash Grove<br>Roll On, Columbia<br>This Land Is Your Land<br>Autumn Canon<br>Oh, Watch the Stars<br>Garden of the Earth | 34<br>69<br>71<br>90<br>114<br>116<br>118<br>148<br>216<br>399 | 2-26<br>4-11<br>4-13<br>5-1<br>6-6<br>6-8<br>6-10<br>7-25<br>10-29<br>18-12 |
| **A JOB WELL DONE** (What do we learn from our experiences?) | Drill, Ye Tarriers<br>When Johnny Comes Marching Home<br>Pat Works on the Railway<br>Erie Canal<br>A World of Difference<br>Zum Gali Gali<br>For Children Safe and Strong | 54<br>180<br>182<br>262<br>386<br>401<br>484 | 3-16<br>9-13<br>9-15<br>12-18<br>18-2<br>18-13<br>21-12 |

Reading Correlations

| Themes | Selections | Page | CD Track |
|---|---|---|---|
| **Volume 2—Fantastic Voyage** | | | |
| **TIME AND TIME AGAIN** (What things are worth repeating over time?) | America, the Beautiful | 76 | 4-19 |
| | Scotland the Brave | 138 | 7-6 |
| | Come, Ye Thankful People, Come | 459 | 19-25 |
| | Green Corn Song | 462 | 20-5 |
| | Oy, Hanuka | 464 | 20-7 |
| | Deck the Hall | 474 | 20-29 |
| | Heri Za Kwanzaa | 476 | 20-32 |
| | Hitotsu toya (Temple Bells) | 478 | 21-1 |
| | Los reyes de Oriente (The Kings from the East) | 480 | 21-5 |
| | America | 486 | 21-15 |
| **TRAVELING ON** (Where do people's journeys take them?) | Bound for South Australia | 22 | 2-1 |
| | Arirang | 25 | 2-6 |
| | Oklahoma | 36 | 2-29 |
| | California | 52 | 3-9 |
| | Away to America | 57 | 3-23 |
| | La ciudad de Juaja (The City of Juaja) | 58 | 3-24 |
| | Wabash Cannon Ball | 136 | 7-1 |
| | Loch Lomond | 140 | 7-13 |
| | The Greenland Whale Fishery | 230 | 11-16 |
| | Shenandoah | 264 | 12-21 |
| | Orange Blossom Special | 266 | 12-24 |
| | Rocky Top | 348 | 16-6 |
| | Sail Away | 404 | 18-20 |
| **THINK OF IT!** (How do we find a new way?) | Play a Simple Melody | 72 | 4-17 |
| | Music (poem) | 95 | |
| | Under the Sea | 372 | 17-12 |
| | You and I (poem) | 388 | |

# Grade 6

| Themes | Selections | Page | CD Track |
|---|---|---|---|
| **Volume 1—Great Expectations** | | | |
| **DISCOVERING OURSELVES** (How do our relationships help us learn about ourselves?) | Lean on Me | 14 | 1-20 |
| | My Dear Companion | 23 | 2-11 |
| | El condor pasa | 46 | 3-16 |
| | Greensleeves | 49 | 3-20 |
| | Adios, Amigos | 57 | 4-1 |
| | Yü Guang Guang | 60 | 4-15 |
| | Your Friends Shall Be the Tall Wind | 201 | 11-1 |
| | Green, Green Grass of Home | 248 | 13-7 |
| | Water Come a Me Eye | 300 | 15-10 |
| | A Gift to Share | 393 | 19-24 |
| | The Joy of Kwanzaa | 462 | 22-1 |

| Themes | Selections | Page | CD Track |
|---|---|---|---|
| **THE LIVING EARTH** (What can we learn from observing the world around us?) | Magnolia | 16 | 1-22 |
| | What a Wonderful World | 62 | 4-20 |
| | I Walk the Unfrequented Road | 79 | 5-6 |
| | Like a Bird | 167 | 9-21 |
| | *Autumn (poem)* | 193 | |
| | New Hungarian Folk Song | 196 | 10-35 |
| | Alumot (Sheaves of Grain) | 306 | 15-26 |
| | Las mañanitas | 481 | 22-16 |
| **GOALS GREAT AND SMALL** (How do people accomplish their ambitions?) | Gonna Build a Mountain | 21 | 2-6 |
| | Bridges | 86 | 5-28 |
| | Give a Little Love | 140 | 8-5 |
| | Go, My Son | 188 | 10-24 |
| | One Moment in Time | 352 | 18-2 |
| | Cantaré, cantarás | 413 | 20-11 |
| | Under the Same Sun | 440 | 21-2 |
| | The United Nations | 443 | 21-4 |
| | I Am But a Small Voice | 446 | 21-7 |
| | I Wish I Knew How It Would Feel to Be Free | 470 | 22-8 |
| **Volume 2—Great Expectations** | | | |
| **THE WAY WE WERE—THE WAY WE ARE** (How can understanding the past help us live in the present?) | Red River Valley | 11 | 1-6 |
| | Bury Me Not on the Lone Prairie | 19 | 2-1 |
| | Blue Mountain Lake | 205 | 11-4 |
| | The Water Is Wide | 228 | 12-1 |
| | By the Waters of Babylon | 311 | 16-1 |
| | Run! Run! Hide! | 340 | 17-11 |
| | Good King Wenceslas | 460 | 21-27 |
| | Abraham, Martin, and John | 466 | 22-3 |
| | America | 484 | 23-1 |
| | America, the Beautiful | 485 | 23-4 |
| | The Star-Spangled Banner | 486 | 23-6 |
| **INTO THE UNKNOWN** (What can we learn from visiting real and imaginary times and places?) | Give My Regards to Broadway | 39 | 2-34 |
| | Farewell to Tarwathie | 43 | 3-1 |
| | Harrison Town | 97 | 6-9 |
| | Swanee | 118 | 7-3 |
| | Four Strong Winds | 170 | 9-28 |
| | Paths of Victory | 195 | 10-30 |
| | I've Been Everywhere | 226 | 11-38 |
| | The Water Is Wide | 228 | 12-1 |
| | Key to the Highway | 243 | 12-22 |
| | By the Waters of Babylon | 311 | 16-1 |
| | On My Way | 313 | 16-4 |
| | Cuando pa' Chile me voy (Leavin' for Chile) | 376 | 19-11 |
| | Goin' to Boston | 433 | 20-24 |
| | Eres tú | 473 | 22-10 |
| **I'VE GOT IT!** (How many ways can people be creative? | Bat kim Thang | 13 | 1-13 |
| | Surfin' U.S.A. | 260 | 13-21 |
| | The Purple People Eater | 448 | 21-9 |

Reading Correlations

# Teacher Notes

# Teacher Notes

# Teacher Notes